LIVING BY
GOD'S
GRACE

ROGER MATTSON

ISBN 978-1-959450-17-7 (softcover)
ISBN 978-1-959450-16-0 (ebook)
Library of Congress Control Number: 2022918802

Printed in the United States of America.

Book Vine Press
2516 Highland Dr.
Palatine, IL 60067

PART 2

CHAPTER 7

This will be a new chapter going into 2012, what will it hold in it's grasps? Will they start another War? Or will the fighting stop? Every year there has been more War and fighting and it's gotten them no where, they sure don't learn from them and that tells me that ignorance plays a big part of their lives. As for the President I don't see him making it another term, as he has proved to be just as ignorant as the last and we cant have that and survive. Enough of that! I wont make any plans because only God knows how things will turn out my self I will take it one day at a time and see what He brings to the table, things can change in an instant and it is something that just happens with no rime or reason things God does doesn't have to make since in our world as he doesn't work in this world , He works in the unknown and owns it along with everything else. I know my time is only the time He gives me and when He wants to take it back then He will but I pray that it's pleasant when it comes, maybe just go to sleep and be with Him. The miles I have traveled amount to not many in His realm for He is everywhere and I often wonder how He does it, in church today a friend said I was an angel for cleaning up her mess after she was called away while planting flowers. It was a good feeling in church and I enjoyed it a lot, when I see some people I can tell when they are having a bad day and that lets me know not to get too close. Randy seams to feel like he has to tell stories to feel important and I find that to be sad but he has always been that way and I think it has something to do with his not being able to read or write Stacy called him so they are talking in some ways it's good for him but in others it's not, he keeps telling her that he loves her and I know that's kind of sick but hey! What ever floats his boat.

He has no concept of what the word means and either does she, here self she just wants to get a hold of his money and he is too foolish to see it. I thank God for my life and I would never want her to be around my home as misery loves company, in church we shared the peace by shaking each others hands and giving hugs. I asked Randy when he was going to start to go to church with me and he said I don't know about that so I take it as never' but you can never tell what the future holds as it's not in his hands only God's, and no one knows what He has in mind. It's Monday and yesterday was a fine day we passed the peace in church and the pastor had to tell us to sit down as everyone wanted to keep doing it, kind of funny really! And then the day was filled with watching television. We didn't play any games, but we did go to Scandia after turning down the heat in the church Randy had to get some soda pop and I got a couple cross words but only won a free one. Then we drove back home, there are a lot of old people that drive on the roads and at times they seam to drive as an intoxicated people do wondering all over the road which is dangerous the other day it was a husband and wife going to the store. That will be hard when I get that old and they take mine at least I have 30 or so years before that happens, my nieces husband is on the road hauling cattle as a guy he knows bought a lot of them to bring back home his hauling brings in a lot of money during winter and it allows them to survive in this day and age. Stan is like me in many ways in the quiet department and we have always gotten along with each other, today it's clean up time at church and I look forward to it as the week progresses 'WOW' I didn't realize the month is already a quarter over with' or should I say a third? This month is flying by. Things are pretty good these days and will continue to be my days are going well and I'm now looking forward to what the future holds in store for us the brightness that God brings with him each day as we travel through it. My out look on life is getting better with each passing day and I kid around a lot more then I used to He said to bring happiness to others and I did that this last week by helping out a couple of people who had a lot on their plate just the slightest thing can help others, I also brought some food to the church for those who need it the ones that would otherwise not have anything to nourish their bodies this in it's self brings joy to my heart, if I had the means none of them would do without. And to me that would be a good thing all the things in which I take are packaged or are in cans so they will never go bad, I know can goods will last up to a year or so and Lord knows I had plenty. Even though Randy seams to get up early he doesn't last the day and probably never will, I cant tell what's going on in that mind of his so I wont even ask I recall being at that stage but then learned to adjust to my surroundings at least he knows not to talk to me this early in the day and that really helps people in general I don't like to talk to especially when I'm not awake and that's why I'm not sure that a mate would work at this stage in my life maybe down the road or in another life Ha! As the hands of time tick by. New things will come to pass will they be remembered by people or will they fall by the way side and rot like the paper they are written on, these are questions only time can tell as we grow older and wiser. For out time is not God's and he works in something much bigger, I can hear Randy coughing in the other room so he will be up for the day, it's 36 degrees outside so we could be in for a warm day unless it drops fast, this time of year you cant tell how the day will be as the weather flip flops sometimes one minute it's warm and then it changes without warning as for the weather people they too cant always tell what's going to happen. I still haven't gotten a card from Rod and his family yet but when I do then I will send them one don't know their address up at the lake, also Rosa-lee hasn't written me lately but I should get a card from her sometime. The friends in which I have I like to keep them close even though distance keeps us from seeing each other, sometimes that can be a good thing as people can get on your nerves and that can cause bad things to happen. Today the Journal here in Courtland is having sort of an open house for Christmas and I could go down and see how everything works you know get the feel of things in which make a news paper work. I have never seen the workings of one in action it's a smaller one and would be easier for me to understand, my days have brought many new things and they seam to get better as time goes on. My sleeping habits are the same and at my age I don't think they will change but they do give me a better out look on the day as the Sun rises in the east, I haven't heard the hoot owl lately so I suspect it went back home where ever that might be in some dark barn somewhere near here maybe at one of the farmers that live close by.

As the day progresses it will get warmer yesterday it was in the 40's and who knows how warm it might get today but I see snow coming somewhere in the near future. Christmas Eve should be fun as we pay tribute to the birth of Christ, I have never been to church that late at night and it should be something different then we will have service the next morning at the usual time. For some they think I'm a night owl and it really doesn't matter, in my travels I have come across many people some that are nice and others that pretend the part and the ones that pretend will take you for all you have if you let them. Back in the day I never trusted anyone not even the good people and I believe this takes away from life because when they could of helped you your self stopped them always being on the offensive takes something from life and stops you from understanding some things, but I'm glad that those days are gone now and another world has opened up. With me the Christmas season' is about giving to those who have a hard time making it and we try to bring joy to those who are in christen homes. As I travel this new path of life my world is not the same as it once was today it has more love in it and I share that with others who might be living that life I once lead, there are many different kinds of alcoholics and some hide it when others flaunt it. It's been a dreary day with dew falling the whole time and I believe we could get some snow to night if it continues so I will see if we get any by morning, my land half the week will be gone tomorrow and the weekend will be upon us before you know it.

It's been pretty darn warm the last day or so in the 40's and 50's and we haven't gotten any snow it's sure different from last year but we will take it. I sometimes think of mom during this time of year wondering if she can see me down here, and in a way I think she can for I too visited that place where she must have been one of those souls on that ride to judgment in life if you have one out of say 5 children find God then you did ok but also my sis found Him and that's even better. Did I do the things in which God would be proud ? For the answer to that question is with Him, I do know that what I learn is put to use in my everyday life and that makes me proud of my self I cant quote the bible yet but then there are those who can and don't understand it, in time those things will come and I will learn to live them I think that's just the way I am. Being able to live with a clear cogence is a great thing and I love God so much.

These are two different kinds of people one who is ashamed and the other that just doesn't care one way or the other, the difference is that one can be helped and the other doesn't want it and for them well they will go through life wondering what the world is really like. This one I live in today is less confusing once you wake up from that sleep you have been in all your life, you your self have to change your surroundings in hope to bring the real world into reality and this takes time. A lot of time and if you're lucky enough to find someone who has lived the life then you can have someone to talk with because they wont be judgmental but just getting on the right path takes time and the longer you wait the longer it will take. When I first came out with writing about it, I was the first to do so and then after time it became an obsession one that I hoped would change the world and even though it hasn't my efforts has paid off in warning others about it. My land' it's Wednesday and it raining like heck, as I put on coffee I looked out the window and it's really coming down this is unexpected. Yesterday they brought some food for Christmas and the pretty lady from church brought it, it was a delight to see her and her daughter and I felt in awe as we said Merry Christmas's to each other. I sort of felt like a kid that has met a girl that he likes I know strange but it happened I guess I'm still that shy guy in many ways Ha! My story still hasn't been published yet but then again you never know what God has in his plans, they are giving an award to someone this month or the next for writing talent and I want to see who wins and I will do that by watching the Kearney hub. I have been writing for a few years now and you never know what will come out of it just the thought of winning something no matter how slight is a good thing. They say as you write you grow and it allows you to become a part of what you're writing and my writing is a part of me, before in my early years I had to drink to get up the courage to ask someone out but today it's not that way and for that I'm glad when your young you cant see what is right in front of you but then when you drink to find courage it seams to go away as fast as sobering up. In my days of youth most of the women were older then I' and they would stay for a while and then leave and I think it had to do with maturity, inside I was still a child trying to get out I remember always wanting to go with the adults or who I thought was an adult. I would learn later that they got into trouble and I never saw them again, even back then God was watching over me and made it to where I didn't follow them it was like He was keeping me just out of reach of trouble. On many occasions I could have gotten what the others got but God said no, he is my child' as the years passed I learned from what happened to them and never did want to travel that path in which they took because it was a dark path and it left it's damage on them so much damage that it will take a life time to over come if even then. My life was spared by God to one day find my way in this life it's like I'm a part of something good in this world that needs to be in place somewhere down the line. Some say great change will come in 2012 and maybe I'm a part of that but it isn't a bad change that will take place like some think it will be something good, my changes will be of happy things and others say destruction will happen but science isn't always right and they fall short on proof when things come to be, will we be here for Christmas in 2012 yes and it will just be another year.

With the money they waste on predicting the future they could have already changed it many cultures have become instinct because they did something wrong and today we may go the same way unless things change, when I look at that pretty women it's like she goes into a trance and gazes at me. What does this mean? for there has to be an answer to all things in life as I pray in the mornings I ask for things that others can use like better health and a brighter day, and of course for the spirit to inter me as I go through this and each day many say that He knows what you want before you ask it, but you have to ask other wise you wont get it one day I wish my life would be easier but for now it will remain in it's state. I can hear the rain really coming down now and it's bouncing off my window strange how it's winter and the rain is falling you would think it would be snow but it's not. For some reason He thinks we need it at this point and it should help the crops, I learned a long time ago that things can change in a heart beat without you even seeing it then someone may point it out later. Life is full of wonders and we never know what's around the corner my life is one of those wonders as I still look for things that are lacking in my life. Many people around here are in the Christmas spirit and have their lights on their homes one day I wish to have the same thing but I cant get up there to hang them one of the prices we pay for not doing things right but maybe next year as things unfold.

In my childhood we put them up and never took them down this kept us in the Christmas spirit all year long as time allows it these things will be done. There is so much I have to do next year and I pray that I'm able to do it but only God knows the future not me or anyone else, Courtland is the place of dreams if you allow your self to dream and Randy does it each night this will allow for change in a persons life. The atheist are giving some people a hard time by complaining about nativity things that are up all through the country they seam to be a thorn in the side of those who believe as one man said in will be a cold day in hell before he takes his down, who ever came up with that crap is something else and it has hurt more then helped in our world today that's the Devil at work as he doesn't want anyone to get close to the other side an angel that fell from grace I guess he couldn't handle the goodness that God once gave him, but he needs to stay where he belongs far from grace. I lived in his world and it's not a nice place as it destroys the soul, many have yet to discover that He forgives all sin to those who repent and my little brother is one of them for he still condom's those who have done wrong to others he hasn't quite looked at him self yet and that will come in time the process takes a long time and he hasn't started yet so we will see. I have to clean the church today after bible school yesterday and that should be fun as I sing to the lord time seams to heal all things as we go through this life and in mine it has healed a lot from the slightest to the greatest. It's been warm this afternoon and I got the church cleaned but it played havoc with my back, Randy is sleeping this afternoon and has been off and on through the morning I call this the transition phase of moving here and I also went through it, in time this will pass and then he will feel at home. Through the years I have gone through many phases some hard and some not so hard but they had to be gone through I think it's a part of life, the phases are like it is when you move from one place to another the adjustment period where you get used to new surrounding's and that can take months but in time it does pass. It felt good to get things done at work they must have had some kind of party and I even found some candy the program there is good for the kids and it lets them explore new way's to learn about God and Jesus, half the month is over and we are headed into the home stretch only 9 days until Christmas and things are going fine I have been able to put something away and that will help in the months to come I wish for things to stay on track the way they are and with God's help they will remain on track. The insolation people called to let me know that they will be here next Tuesday to start the work on the house so that made me happy.

Now if they get the work done on time we will be set and the bills will go down starting at that time this will allow me to put even more away if things go right, we have a neighbor that is moving she is the forth person to move out of that corner house in the last few years and it makes me wonder if it might be haunted or else the bills are so high that a person couldn't afford to keep it up. I was in it once and the ceilings are 12 feet high which could account for a high gas bill, they have all been women anywhere from 30 some years to in their 60's even though I have never seen a haunted house they do say they exist but that might be in their minds. I wrote my sister today to see if she has seen my brother Rick some roomers are going around and I need to see if they are true, if there not then I will have to evaluate my little brothers sanity I could never figure out why others have to talk about others that are not around them. My land' my life isn't exciting but no need to talk about those who are not around me, live and let live is my motto in life and it has worked all my life you don't talk about those who cant defend them selves in your present's as for the source of the gossip she has been doing that since I have known her over 30 some years that is a world in which I wouldn't want to live because it makes people hate you. Just the knowing of your words not being privet and false thing added to them can destroy in the same way addiction can destroy the human spirit and soul, putting false words into other peoples mouths is a bad thing to do.

As for my self I weigh my words before they come out to make sure that they do no harm as I wouldn't want that to happen in my life either. As we traveled to town you notice things which you cant see during spring or in the Fall, like a house that was put on a foundation to keep a farm going that has been there for 100 years the farmers around here have been here for like ever! and then they pass it down to their children or grandchildren I don't think the people in the big cities know how lucky they have it as if things weren't grown here food would be higher then gas and it comes in a high second right now even though it's grown right here at home. I remember meat was 98 cents a pound and now some of it is as high as six dollars and they raise them wright here in Kansas and surrounding areas, no wonder old folks used to eat dog food to survive on Social Security when their other half passed away. If old folks didn't work then their spouces would kick in and support them this was the reason they paid into it, I couldn't imagine how it would be if this program was stopped the United States would have another War on their hands but this time the government would be fighting the disabled and elderly and also the veterens who get the short end of the shafty when it comes to taking care of them. The government sends them to War and then throws them away like a piece of dirt on their shoes, some give some and some give all and if you don't give all then you come home to a country that ignores you as a person and turns it's back on you. It's just been recently that they have been doing better as before they didn't care one way or another, some are used to bust the armed forces image but it falls short in some areas. For some that louse a leg or arm they build them a house to match their handycap but this is only done for one out of a million because they want other young people to join them and die even though their minds are not fully developed I remember wanting to join in my teens or early 20's and I made it through the testing but they desided not to take me because of my education or the lack of so I went back home and put it out of my mind, if I would have gotten in I would have been in the wars they fought in these last years.

But that never happened and I'm here today because of it back then I took it as a sign that I wasn't supposed to fight and I never have, my battles would come later in fighting addiction and that was a battle I wasn't going to louse. I had a couple of friends in my early years that I fought with and one of the times I was put into the hospital to have my head sowed up and the other one made me feel bad because I knocked him out with a can of pork and beans, he still talks about it to this day he was a bully and thought he could wip me. I remember the day nice and clear but I was drinking at the time me and his sister were fighting the way young people do and I went to see her at her mom's house which was across the street from my mom's this is where I lived when I lost my son Roger Maattson Jr. and although it had been a few years the wounds were still present, I loved him but the lord took him from me and I didn't understand why. While visiting his sister they were out in the back yard and had a tent pitched Bob and Dan, I remember it was about 100 or so out side and vodka was being drank he was a prson that flew off the handly when he drank and boy he did it that day. As he started to throw punches I backed away and ended up in the kitchen as the blows kept coming I tried to stop him but that didn't work.

The alcohol had blinded him to any reasoning and I knew that he would have put me in the hospital if I let him keep punching me. So I saw a can of pork and beans and picked it up and struck him in the head and he was out like a light, I never brought it up again but he did quite oftend I was talking with him as we stayed friends and he asked if I remembered it many times and I told him yes. But I didn't like to think about it, he said it was the hardest he had ever been hit and he saw stars for a few days afterwards. We still talk when I visit my grandchildren in Kearney but he is still fighting his demons, I thought he would have passed away many years ago when I took care of him at our home there but he is still going and I don't know how he makes it. Afterwards I vowed to not fight again and to this day I haven't had to his sister is still alive but in bad health with C.O,P.D. It seams to run in the family as her brother has it also my best friend Mark.As the years passed we all grew apart and they live in the projects in Kearney' and he still owes me four dollars from my last visit for he tells me it's in the mail Ha! That's a laugh' we used to go fishing together but those days are long gone as we got old and I moved away thank God. I never knew what to expect from him as he drank it was like Dr. Jeckel and Mr. Hide you were always on the defencive being there so I haven't went back to this day, many times I went out of my way to be nice but it never let me feel at ease. After my son's death we had a couple more kids and I learned to love them very much, but the up bringing was one sided with them as she spoiled them. And they didn't carry my last name.

And that hurt' but over time I excepted it and life went on. Then when we broke up over a guy that got out of prison and I left to Oklahoma where I started a carear in farming it wasn't what I expected but I learned fast and got along with my boss, we had many good times in the fields as he taught me and then I moved my mom and Oliver out there where we lived for a couple of years. The house I rented had a smoke house in the back and I would go out there to cook sometimes it was a blast at first but then became very board, my drinking problem got worse as time passed and it did this quite oftend with stress, then after two years mom wanted to go back to Nebraska and they moved her back. And I stayed on at my brothers house and that was a night mare, I didn't get along with his wife because she bitched about everything and I couldn't wait to get to work to find peace for there was none in the house hold. I remember coming home because I was in town and all I had to do is use the bathroom and she yelled because the tractor was too loude and then decided that I had to leave, I never looked back and never went back until 2 years ago and then I didn't stay all that long their world hadn't changed but I had and I didn't like being around alcohol and seeing the effects it had on those who drank which was almost everyone. Knowing only sober people had made it's mark or change on me and it was for the better, my life before was bit's and pieces never a full picture of what was to come or what would be and today I'm a happy person without the destruction that was once in my life change is possible for those who want it and then you have those who will never change but that's Ok' my life is much better today and I'm proud of what I have accomplished. I never thought I would be a proud owned of a home but I am today and I have many people who are behind me in this. As my friend said to me we all love you Roger and we are grateful for you being here,as time goes on I will build my palace my home in which I will spend my last years. Here in Courtland I have the things I need to keep writing and in time all will turn out good in my world that I created. My self' I never knew a place like this existed and it just goes to show that you never know what God has in store for your life as you travel through it, just a few years ago it was all I could do to survive and now it's much different then back then.. People here see the person not a number in which they judge you, and that's the way it should be getting to know someone can and will change things. This is my town and I will live here proudly, as for the rest of the world it will go on as it has been but I know I'm safe here in my new home town. When people ask where I'm from I proudly tell them Courtland Kansas' the place where dreams come true, as for the future of the town I see it surviving for at least another 100 years. So many generations here and new ones are starting all the time my time is delightful and I look to each new day, I was happy when she brought the Christmas meal and she kind of stared at me like she was in a trance. I had seen that look before with someone long ago and it was one of infatuation or I could have been miss reading the signs which I do from time to time it's funny how one person can be thinking one way and the other is thinking another. Her children are beautiful as most kids are in my younger days if I felt a connection I would act on it but it was usually the booze which did the talking and none of those relationships worked out, the longer I live here the more I change but it's for the better the other day Randy was telling me that this heavy women at the dollar store liked me but that is something which would never appeal to me.

Not even in my younger years, as I watch the hands of time go by it gives me insight to the new world that is coming my way and it's full of wonder. I didn't see the things which are unfolding until I reached my 50 year mark could it be that we do travel down the road we left behind to see what could have been in the other universe this universe instead of bobing back and forth from one to the other.

For sure this is the one I was meant to live in not the other, in some preaching it talks about how good deeds are passed down from generation in other words my grandmothers good deeds were passed down to those deserving of them. I wonder if my uncle was satisfied with his life and how it turned out I do know he had many things but did they really help him in his last hours of life here. My self' I want to be remembered for the things I did that made a difference nothing else, how long will I remain in this new place I have adapted to for each day brings with it a new ideal or thought to write about as for the people I cant say enough good things about them they don't pry into my business and I don't pry into theirs it's like things are in balance here and you have to have that for any good to come from your life. The world in which I came from was used up and I couldn't go any further there so He had me move on to better things, and I have found that here as others travel to find that place I don't have to look any more as all I need is right here except for a little travel every now and then. My years have been good to me since I moved to Courtland and it will continue to be that way as I have many friends which would do just about anything for me, these are things in which others don't see as they travel the road of life.

I watched a movie about a guy that left his home town and then returned, to find his old love which was waiting for him after 11 years, but this time he stayed as in the big city all he saw was people hurring to go somewhere and it was sad because they didn't show any joy in their faces. It was like they were running a foot race with life and they were louseing the race, O sure they were making a living but at what price the price of peace from within it seamed that even their thoughts weren't their own but I guess that's the price of the big city. As for me I'm a simple man and enjoy what I have and that is peace of mind, the road Randy has taken to be here was also long but I know it could be destroyed by a women. He was never one to be alone not like me but he has nothing to do as his education knowledge isn't any. But I do read to him from time to time in hope that he will learn in some way. I have many questions to ask God but he isn't here to answer them maybe one day things will be made clear but for now I will continue to learn many things. Although my life was side tracked for a short time things are getting back to normal and I love that as for the lady I think about. She will stay in my mind until I'm sure it's the right thing to ask my living alone has hurt in some ways but I got to know my self a little better and that's always a good thing, my keeping the guys perscriptions filled is a chore but after years of doing it things become like a part of life like it's natural for me to do these things. I know how nurses feel when they get a new person they have to learn everything about them and at first that is hard, back in the day when mom was ill she would take hers because she could read but with these guys they cant do that they have to depend on me for their med's. Randy must be resless I can hear him coughing in the other room must be having a smoke my land' you would think he would want to go back to sleep so he could breath but that's the habbit it just attacks you and makes you want it. The old man in the hospital was 90 something and had been smoking for 75 years with no ill efects wow' that's a long time, the nurce there was kind and I find her in my thoughts from time to time she said I should write a book and I told her I was doing just that. I think God talks through people sometimes to let us know that we are on track but I find that it's hard to let part of your life go to strangers will I remember what I wrote and if so can I start once again after the first one is out there? So many doubts about things and what will happen afterwards will I retain what I have learned or will it go away once I let go? For surely I can get a copy and keep in touch with what I wrote, so the cycle can go on. The guys are moving around and I hope they are not getting up this early, except to maybe use the bathroom. Harley hasn't bothered me yet so that's a good thing but he will in a little while to let him out, I find that at times I feel real good and then I have the times when it isn't so great but in those times when things are good it makes me want them more oftend and it makes me grateful for those moments when things are good.

When I find my self feeling pitiful it reminds me that things could be a lot worse, many people go through life always in agony which is something I wouldn't want at this time. I don't talk about death very oftend but I want people to celebrate mine when it comes, no tears as my life has been petty good later in life through God I have been able to help other people and that's my perpose while I'm here. I was sad today to see the condition of my brother Rick he seam's to have fallen back into Methamphetamine and looks twice his age it made me cringe as I looked at his picture and I thank God for my second chance. I don't see him making it through another curse as it destroys everything he almost looked like he was in a coma sitting in the chair and the bad thing besides his health is that his daughter had to see him that way for the first time they had met, he never knew he had a daughter and if he had it might have changed him but now it may be too late for him. He cant weigh over 110 pounds and I have seen him at 300 at one point it's like his body is eating it's self alive and that's when you know someone is in the last stages of the destruction it causes. That could have been me many years ago but God spaired me and let me start life over once again, Randy has a second chance also and I hope he grabs onto it with both hands because he will never get another one. Through life some get that chance to turn things around and for some reason others don't it's just the way it is O Lord help him with your power love and strength if it's your will this I ask in Jesus name Amen.

From childhood he was always a rebel and went his own way and spent many years in prison when I talked with him a few years ago he said he was doing find but a picture tells a thousand words he has had two hip replacements and that might be what helped to destroy him. My brother's have paid a big price for not taking his life back from the curse, and I feel blessed that I was given the chance. It's Sunday and Christmas is just a week away I went to church to pray for him yesterday and then got things ready for today growing up Randy and Rick would get into trouble together they were like dynamite and all it would take is a little spark to set them off and then they were in trouble and when you throw Methamphetamine into the mix it's always destruction. If he goes back to prison it's for life as he is a return person of many times and the law wont stand for it anymore, I just hope God will help him in this time. Even after the accident he was a good kid but something was always wrong, he wasn't the same child he was before. When dad died the State of California had the Red Cross bring him back to Nebraska they put him on a plane but then it didn't take long for trouble to follow him soon they were getting into trouble again and you can see the pattern alcohol was a constent in our lives and lead to many destructive things. My self I tried to stay out of trouble and I did for the most part except for drinking and driving and that got me in my trouble but later that would become a thing of the past as I destroyed the curse that almost destroyed me. I'm at a loss for words right now as him helth really bothers me, they say there are two kids of siblings one bad and one that is supposed to be good but you cant help but to feel helpless when something like that takes place and there is nothing you can do to turn back the clock, in hope that hings would have been different for truly I was blessed by the Lord' every state has brought it's troubles for him and Nebraska has put him away many times and it made me feel bad for him. I guess I'm the fixer in the family always trying to fix what has been broken but there are things that only God can fix and I have to learn to except that, going to Omaha to live was one of his wrong moves but he was in love and needed a person around him and why this is I don't know' through the years I try to be true to God and my self and I think that's who I survived through it all. He is still alive so there is hope that he could change but would he do it if he had the chance? Only he knows the answer to that question. In the day that they were last arrested he got out after a few years and Randy was facing 18 years because he ran and thought he would be safe at Rod's house which didn't work, going from one State to another only makes things worse on a person running from what they call justice. And it didn't take long for them to go and get him and then he faced a lot more charges. I don't like to go into that world because it isn't a place in which I have lived or I would want to live, we never know what God has instore for us until that time when he allows us to change or not change. When I saw him last he was pretty thin but we laughed and things and of course he coned me out of a few things before he returned to Omaha it seamed he wanted something to remember me by as for them both Rick and Randy they looked up to me for some reason and maybe that was because I didn't get into trouble. But that didn't stop them from bringing their stuff to my house as the one officer said Roger they are using you and trying to get you in trouble but we wont let it happen, I guess they were watching over me also.

One said that I was the only one who didn't destroy me life and for that I was rewarded by God to have what I have today. As for his everyday life I know nothing about it and probably never will his life that is as for mine I will continue to love the lord in hope that one day the world will get better, my journey will be a long one into my older years and who knows where that will take me. As the spurts of joy continue in my life I like it more and more and who knows maybe in time it will always be a joy, Shannon got the Christmas gift I sent her and Leroy but he had a hard time cashing the money order something to do with the check cashing place but he must have gotten it done. It's 26 degrees out side and that's warm for this time of year I'm excited about Tuesday afternoon and I hope they get it all done in a couple of days I think God is keeping it warm until the work is done and then we can have the snow as I wont have any worries about the cold after that the house will be sealed from the cold and the heat and they will put insolation in the attict that will help in many ways, living the dream isn't an easy thing to do but it's possible with the help of people that care and God Him self. Dealing with things has become more plesent since I moved to Courtland and I try to deal with them my self but if there is something I cant handle Kathy is just down the road to help me see things in a different light, so much to be grateful for. The love of God and friends and even those who are far away, it's getting about that time to heat up the church so later. My land' I was supprised when I recived two gifts while in church this morning and it was strange to get anything during this time of year.

For most of my life it's always been about what I could give never about me and this is the first year in which anyone got me anything. I recived a card from my brothers and sisters in christ and they said that they loved me and I also love them. Practice starts today at 10:00 this morning Judy is playing the piano and of course I will sing, we will try and get the song (The Cross) down pat. It's Monday and another week is started the early nights leave me wondering about things and at times I wish they would go away it's not like I don't have enough but things seam to always work out for the best, tomorrow they will begin work on the house to make it better then it was before when they had the program in Nebraska it was a good program that helped people like me who are living in poverty. Even here in Kansas there is a two year waiting period and mine has come to a close and now the work starts, I will be forever grateful once everything is set in place and it can only help in my home being better then before. All things take time and now my time has come to try and rise above what I am, listening to Joel yesterday my past life was a season that has come to pass so he could move me on to better things and that's what has happened. From the one bedroom dump in Kearney to this home which will be mine from now on, when you find you're self always in a hurry that's when it's time to slow down and let things catch up with you for God may bring somethings into your life for a season and others are there for ever. Although this is my home and always will be I don't know what He has in store for my future but the deck of cards will play out the hand, it's like all the things I dreamed about when I was young is coming to pass in my later years. I wanted them then but it wasn't the right time and he wont allow things to unfold until the season gets here, I guess in a way it's like the crops for every crop there is a season and it will not come to pass until it's ready. I have seen many changes in this life of mine and now I know that the changes were things that had to pass before the goodness could come to pass maybe in this life it's the experiences that bring on change. Lord knows in the early years my chances for success was slim but there is no limit to what can unfold, half a deck aid' is gone and after that we don't know what God will do but He brought me here for a reason. And it could have been to see that stream and mear image of the lake I will one day see in my back yard, He has never made things perfectly clear to me but He does show me signs that things are on track maybe my dream was stronger then I once imagined and it has to come full cicle when He takes on something He doesn't stop until it's completed that's the great thing about God He doesn't only tackle the problem we cant handle He makes it a thing of the past and then moves on. Like the people back in the day it was like they disappeared to never be seen by me again even my little friend I once knew lost his way in the world of addiction for surly his parents told him that alcohol was Ok but it wasn't as it lead him down a path of destruction. When he got out of rehab he thought it was Ok to go back to drinking and then it started again, trading one for another doesn't work because that's the one that lead you there in the first place from alcohol to Methamphetamine and then on to other drugs it doesn't happen fast but in time it takes everything from you. If more people could see how my life turned out they too would try and make theirs better, as things come slow they do come and even though time it's self seams to speed up it wont over run you.

My family was supprised when I recived the card from church but when you do good works you are rewarded for your services. You cant do nothing and expect something in return it just doesn't work that way, in this life nothing has a guarantee but with God all things are made possible as He watches over us in this life my land' family members get jellous when He shows some of us favor and that's just a part of nature I guess and it should show them that they too could have the same thing. As time passes my old life is becoming vage and will soon be gone as my new life is taking hold of things. I feel like I'm in a reansition period at this time and time will tell if things move forward when God moves you look out because it's going to be one heck of a ride He will bring you to where you need to be. In my days I have never experienced the things I'm going through today and it can only get better as time passes, my retention of things isn't where I would like it to be but that will only improve in time as I learn more and more. But I do find that my love for God never wavers even when I don't feel good as I know he will take care of such things, I find that fear is a good thing when you over come it but if it holds you back then it's just a pain in the butt, fear controlling fear is no good but when you move past that point then He will hold out his hand for you. Can a person fall and not know it? I think it happens all the time, as I grew up I didn't know I was on the path of destruction . Then later I felt the need for change it was like the spirit was telling me that if I didn't change the end would be near, but it also told me that God was right beside me to help me in this transition and that helped a lot especially when you have that feeling of death from destroying the human body.

God can repair what He created, but if you throw it away then you cant blame anyone but you're self. You see we are made in the image of God and he resides in us which allows us to call on Him when we are in our hour of need and He wants us to use him, as He uses us when He wants to get a message to others who don't know him. It says we are the light and He lets it shine through us it's like a glow that a lot of people want to possess but it doesn't show all the time for some reason just when He allows it to become bright. Satin once had God's favor until he fell from grace and then he thought he could do God's job which he never will be able to do, he thinks that Evil could rule the world and that's something the Father wouldn't allow to happen. In the final battle Jesus will rule the world for 1000 years and Satin will be in the pit during this time could it be that He is giving him another chance to change? This is something that could take place but the bible says he will rise again and then it will be over. This just proves to me that God loves second chances and He will wait for time to prove Him right, I can just about see the lady at the well who had been with so many men and she offered Jesus a drink. In many of the stories he used even questionable peoples to bring good to others and you never know who they are. It could be a person that is rich but with a not so religious past or life this is one of the steeping stones that can bring someone favor it's Tuesday now and practice went pretty good yesterday we are goinbg to do it again Thursday so it will be closer to the time and maybe that will help in some way as for the songs they are good (Thy Cross) it was the first time I sang it with music and it was great for the first time but we have to get more together on it (The light of the world) was also inspired by God and it's going to be a great song so I might end with part of that.how great thou are to be able to create in someone elses mind or give them the ability to create when something has been damaged at one time, for this proves that He is all powerfull to be able to mold a mind and repair the passage ways is remarkable but to also let it create is something else looking at the future many things could happen and I will let the cards fall where they lay. Do we live in a life where anything is possible? I think anything is possible with God but with out him nothing can come to be, He allows new things into our lives for how ever long He sees fit but it can be taken away just as quick. All those who had it all so they thought lost it very fast and it goes to show that He the father can humble a person at the drop of a hat as He did me so long ago but He can also show you favor afterwards if He feels you have earned it. As time passes there will be many new things that will come to pass here in Courtland from the births of new children to the deaths of those who we came to love so much. For any of us are here for just a short time but you don't see it until you grow later in years, I'm in hope that He lets me knock it out of the park you might say when Christmas Eve gets here and I can practice in the mean time. The guys are supposed to be here today so we will see how that goes and if they get the windows in then that's another plus for me and my two patients.

Back when I first got here my emotions were scattered and mixed up and I notice that it's that way with any person, but in time we learn to adjust and make a place our home. Many things have changed since that time and my home has become just that my home that no one can take away, for this was God's will and me helping the church was also His will. Something about me brings me to say yes to things like taking the job but also I enjoy my time there because I can be me no one ele, in the years prior I didn't know who I was and now I know I'm the child of the most high God that will bring things into my life that I need. My journey has been long and like some in the bible I have come to rest here in Courtland but the future holds many things maybe love but also it holds my spirit as it wizes through the cosmos wondering where it might land, I find that Randy needs to talk with people who are not from here and it has to do with gossip he never could get away from that crap and he relies on it for his moods wither he is happy or sad and that's sad in it's self. As for me I live my life away from such things because they are not good for you never have been and never will be, the confusion it brings with it can stop you from learning about your self and who you are he doesn't realize that it's a circle of misery and misery likes company as I travel my path I cant let anyone into where I am because they would destroy it by the negative forces that come from within O he can visit those places to try and find what he needs but in reality he wont find it.

You might say he is the link to the out side world the one I don't want any part of, to me the Omish have the right idea to live away from the evil that is out there but they also know that they cant hold back the young ones from seeing what it's all about and then thy them selves will make the decision wither their community is where they want to be. They had blizzard warnings in the western part of the State but we must have gotten lucky as there is no snow on the ground here thank God' but that doesn't mean it wont come later I just hope it holds off until the work is done here, then itcan snow all it wants. My land' I have been waiting for two years and it's about time for this project to end, all good things come to those who wait but we can be very impatient as people wanting things done right now. But not everyone is that way just people like me learning a new way of life, my grandchildrens birthday is next month so I will have to send them something because I wont be able to go making insurance payments that month. All the years before I was able to try and make it but this year is the first in which I have to pay out over a thousand dollars and that stops me from going anywhere. Maybe this next spring I can pop out there and see them that way Randy might be able to travel by then, as I watch them each day I am amazed at how they can sleep so much but I know back in the day I did the same thing and Oliver has always been that way since he stopped working so many years ago. When he used to work you couldn't stop him as he was like a die hard battery always on the go and never stopping, why my little bro is that way I don't quite understand you would thing he would like to love life but I know he cant do that being in a coma half the time. It's like he doesn't care and that will get the best of him one day he makes me want to get the best I can out of life and not waste any of it, I went to take the garbage out and they are building a quilt in the dining room. I guess they had to move it seeing they are going to have a show of some kind as I went to the bank my friend invited me to a Christmas lunch which is today Wednesday, my land I didn't think that I was a very important person but I guess I am. As with other home owners our taxes pay for a lot of improvements which take place here and I love that idea of being a part of a community, Mark is my friend and always will be when I first met him I felt it a connection between us and maybe it's the blood of being sweedish Herbs parents were full blooded sweed and that is something in which is special. I never felt at home anywhere else in my life like I do here in Courtland and I know that for them to show kindness they have to see something in me as a person, my temperment is high as I don't get angry very oftend and for that I'm glad this morning the guys are coming over to do the windows and that's a good thing the boss of the company called yesterday and said they would start this morning if not last night and I told him that I understood. The State got 4 to 8 foot snow drifts in some part's and I'm glad that God put it off from coming here like I asked him, my life is personal to a certain extent but I don't mind talking about my early life when I went through so much it's that part which lets you grow from what you have learned and that in it's self can allow you to help in areas which other might not know anything about. I think this lunch is going to be fun as I will be around friends and who knows I might meet more of them, when I was young my friends were counted on one hand as I didn't get out much among others and that has allowed me to be able to love my self and project that love which I feel inside. I call it God's light as my love for him and his for me allows this to shine through, back in the day this light wasn't allowed to shine because of the problems that I had and didn't know how to handle.

The people that live here are not of the disorder which comes from living in the out side world and for that I am glad we know each other by name and that can bring a brighter day. As for the weather it has gone from the State for a time anyway to return later in the month a head which will be in 2012, a year which will bring many changes from the slightest to the gratest and they will be for the better. The community is like my back yard and I can go anywhere in it and this · is brought on by the kindness of others that also share it even when I see things out of order like paper laying in the streets I pick it up and this is just a habbit because I don't like a messy yard Ha!. The guys are supposed to be here at 8:00 this morning so we will see what takes place then, as my life moves forward each day brings something new from a smile of someone I haven't known before to a hello from a strnger as I drive down the country road not dirt roads but the highway that leads to other towns. Randy sometimes asks who was that and I reply with just a friend as we are all friends in christ, many years ago I dreamed about a town like this and now I'm living in it and I believe it's God's will that this has happened so I can learn at a smaller scale. In the big cities there was nothing but confusion and this stoped me from moving forward there was to much corruption in those places and I couldn't grow the way I was supposed to, here I have all that I need back as a child I was taught not to take things which are not your's and it stuck with me through my life.

These things I don't do to others so I don't want them done to me, it says the meek will inhearit the earth and this is my little part of it. Something I can say is mine, will it grow in time who knows but it's possible somewhere down the road like the flower planted by a seed at first glance you wouldn't think it could become something so beautiful but later it does and it's God that allows this to take place and when it dies there is a carbon foot print of it being there just like there is something left behind of us as people mine will be my writing so others can see that even back in the day someone had the same problems and over came them. We as people can overcome almost anything but it has to have the approval of the father as He knows what will become of us just like when He sent Jesus, He knew that Jesus would die but would also for ever be saved to sit at the right hand of the father in heaven. My self I have epiphnys that I don't understand but I also know in time that He will make it clear and explain it to me if not in this life then the next, if you want to make God laugh tell him your plan. And I believe he knows the future not us and that's why he would laugh, our lives are written in stone wither others think that way or not just like Jesus we have a purpose for being here and when it's done then we move on to the next world where we will know why things turned out the way they did, people know me' even people I don't know and they know me by what I write and they can see that life can be made good all my stories are experiences that have happened in my life and through it all God has stood by me all the way. And brought nice and understanding people into my life, bad times are just that a bad moment I time and you cant judge the rest of you're life because of them for they are just a moment in which things didn't happen the way you would of liked them to. In my journey I had many of them but they somehow seamed to fade like with a head ache to be gone for a short time anyway and then return when you least expect it. Traveling through the road of life many things will happen some good and some bad but exceptence is the key to making it in this world, how do some measure welth many by money and that is the wrong way to messure it. I do it by friends and my spirit, it's the spirit that makes you welthy and the love of others have for you, money will and can destroy a person if not used properly as for my self there is a balance that should never be messed with. With me I give to help others even though I'm not rich I am in spirit, as I can feel what others are going through but then you have those who will take advantage of how you care and that isn't right. Learning to see these things can be a great lesson but it will cost you somewhere in time and that can also destroy you as you go through life, learning to know people is an experience in it's self how they are and if the spirits distort their judgement meaning alcohol or drugs or both. Through the years I can tell if a person has a problem with these things and it can stop them from full filling their oblagation to others because those two things come first in their life when life it's self should come first, not just anyone can see the things I can see and this makes me unique in many ways a one of a kind you might say. The sun will be coming up in an hour or so and the boys will be up for the day and I hope it's a good day for them, the things we watch on television make me glad that I'm not out there as something is happening in that world.

I think a president is just a pawn in a game of chess and they use him to lay the blame on, it's people higher up that really control this world or the United States. We had an exciting day as they came and done the work now today the inspector comes to sign off on the job, my land they were nice people and I don't feel the cold as I once did and that's a good thing. He told me that the heat bill should decrease by 25 to 30 percent it's calm in here now without the ind blowing through the glass and the insolation should really help there was some damage where the water ran down the old glass trunamite he said but he couldn't tell if it was old damage or new if he had to guess it was old, and I pray that it was old but now he said we arefixed up and good to go I'm supposed to meet Judy at the church at 10:00 this morning to go over my songs so we are ready for Saturday night now things should stay warm. Even the furnice runs less since they did the work and now winter can come it's been a good old house and I hope it last for a long time as many family members will come and visit in the future, my self' I liked the work they did but it all comes down to the inspectot when he comes today. My getting my own house has been a long time coming and now there should be less worry on my hands my self I thought it was the rain which caused the damage always running on the window seal but I could be wrong. He was telling me that they test for them differently these days by drining a steak into the ground and then if they attack it they put pait sticks in to destroy them but it also cost two thousand dollars and that's a lot of money for me.

As we move forward things will look up for this I know and I will pray for God to take the little buggers away now it's Thursday and it's a new day and I will soing my songs to the lord I thank God that the weather held off for this time but now it can return to normal, my bedding has to be washed bcause of the insolation but that's just a little thing at this part of the game and we have to vacuum also, for the day brings good things to us in this hour of need and who knows what tomorrow will bring. I got a text from Valerie and she said she loved me but I know it's not a close love not the kind between to lovers as two much water has gone under that bridge but I do wish her happieness in her life as I have always felt that way, she is the kind of person who needs to have someone live where she lives and that is not me for my home here is my home and I will be here until the end of time. Randy even came out of his shell for a short time and talked with the workers, I tried to get him to go to the bank brunch but he was too shy so I brought him and Oliver something home it was a nice thing that the bank did and Mark the president was there to great everyone as they came through the door, I was shy when I first came here and now I'm getting better as time passes the love they show makes it worth it and I don't feel that lonelyness here any more. Even though I didn't know many of the people, there was those who I know who said hi not going out much I haven't met them all but that could also be a good thing in this day and age. There were the old and the new lives born here to Courtland that will allow it to grow far into the future, I said hi to some people I didn't know but they didn't say hi back and maybe they didn't hear me or was just stuck up don't know which but that's ok it didn't hurt my feelings, I learned that there are many kinds of people and some just stick to them selves and I guess I'm the same way. At first we all put up that defence one of protection and it's hard to let anyone in to that privet place and I respect that, maybe one day when time has allowed for people to be more open then change will come but that might take a long time in the day when the lord comes those things will be a thing of the past as brothers and sisters join together in love and all the hang up will be gone. The large pain of glass was the hardest to get out as things were rotten beneath it but they fixed that thank goodness and now we will see what 2012 holds for us in this part of the country. I noticed that people don't really look at you when you eat as they are bussy doing it them selves so I shouldn't be so shy in this area, my church family loves me very much and I love them also. This morning I have to go to work to clean up what the children did yesterday and it gives me time to reflect on things that are happening in my world today as I am a mirror reflection of things to come. My wall of hardness has crumbled in my later years and it will stay there for now, but I supprised my self that I wasn't more nervice then I was and to me that was a good signe that things will come together later on down the road. Valerie said I was a dreamer of things to come and I guess that is ok' because my dreams have come true there is nothing worng with dreams, if you believe. And that I do as many of my dreams have come true here, in my days before nothing came true and that was because I was traveling down the wrong path, not the one which God had set into motion it was lie I took a deture in life and got lost along the way.

But on that day so long ago He found me and put everything back on track even today I think I understand my mom more then I ever did when she was alive and I love her more then ever. It wasn't her fault that things went the way they did as we all get lost at one point or another, for my dreams will continue as I go through this life and my home will be made solid once again if you don't have dreams then you have nothing to build on. Everything created was once a dream in someones mind at one point or another to be brought alive by doing as the mind is a powerful thing. Watching others they flunt their well offness but I cant see things like that with me it's giving to help others that matters in this life and if the lord wants to give something for that then so be it. I saw my little friend this morning out in her car and she is a night owel like I am strange to fine someone the same way as I am especially in a town the size of Courtland but she is here she once told me a story about how she came to be here but I don't know how true it is as she was laughing when she told me it, she said a women picked her up and gave her a place to stay but she had to volinteer to serve at a church function so she did it and has been here ever since serving God can come in many ways and this just shows one of them, when I started to go to church here I wanted to do more and then the job of janitor came up in a conversation. The lady who was doing it wanted to retire and they thought they might have to go out side of he church I heard this and without thinking said I would do it, it was lie God gave me that opportunity to do more and even though it caused some rifts at firt it all worked out in the end and I'm still doing it today a year later.

This was my first Christmas there and they gave me a gift which helped in more ways then one, I have a giving heart and I guess it's always been that way. Never been one to ask for much help but if it's offered and I need it then I will recive it, there arre many things in life that can take you to another level and I let it come when he thinks it's right. It doesn't do much good to try and rush the lord as He wont hear you if it's not the time for it to happen all good thing in time His time not ours. My land' I have tried to rush Him with no success on my part when I ask for something it usually takes a few montths befor anything happens and then even then I might not reconise it until later way later but it's still there waiting for me like it's written in stone. Singing went fine at practice and we got to know each other a little more, I told Judy about my parents and how they passed I felt comfortable talking with her and she was telling me about a guy that made it singing who used to sing at the church it was a nice conversation on my part and she listened we are going to go through the songs one more time right before the people get there at 10:00 tomorrow night she said I was good and Mark my friend said the same thing long ago so we will see what God has in store for the future it would take a while to get used to doing it where it wouldn't bother me to be in front of people but it's something that can be done. She also went on to tell me that I was God sent and I told her that it was him without a doubt, my songs reflect a part of me things that have happened in my life and I enjoy singing them there are some that are not finished yet but they are in my mind and they will always be there as they don't leave until they are finished, and I do know this is a gift that God has given me. My voice is unique and no one else has my sound as it s gospal with some blues thrown into the mix, I told her about being born out of the merrage and she understood that back then you didn't do that my singing is a treat for them and it's up to me to bring it to life. Through life my addictions had stopped me from persueing my dreams of singing and now there isn't anything in my way except for my taking care of those who need me, it made me feel good when she said Courtland needed me as much as I needed it and that's why God had brought us together, the Lord is good' and He doesn't make mistakes when he brings something together my heart will be in it tomorrow night and I hope it brings them joy because it brings it to me when I do it. (The light on the water) is a reflection of God and his wonderoious works in the world while he was here so long ago and (The Cross) well it's about a lost soul trying to find his place in this world which he has now found in a little own called Courtland the town of dreamd where my songs come together to create something beautiful it's like we were meant to be together and brought to gether in a time when dispair was knocking on the door the way she talked it was like new life was brought here and I'm part of that new life. She also said they will have to keep the coffee coming to keep me awake so funny' I see many things hat could take place in the future and I will hold on to them with both hands. Even though it was hard at first now that time has passed and the goodness will rise to a level like never before, singing only takes a little time and I have that to give in this place that I now call home.

Creating my own songs allows me to be able to sing then with my mind the way it is, for they are short and sweet like me Ha! Once everything comes together then I can find my place or my true voice and then watch out because I will be great. In my life I had always held back not to destroy what He had given me but it's time to let it come full circle I used to dream about being a star but He didn't want it to be there with the fighting of addiction on top of it. I have seen many fall from grace just because of addiction and now that it's over that is something I don't have to worry about, what really matters in a song? Not the music but the words the words that touch peoples hearts if they can relate to it then it's meant to be. It's Friday and the end of another week is about here but it brings me closer to the end of another year, to start a new one full of joy I hope 2 more days until Christmas then we have new years the beginning of 2012 and things will start poping the hard time is over for now and I hope this next year is much brighter. The kids want to see me but the expence is too great at this time, but will taper off later in the year. I have to messure things to where they don't put my home in jeaperty as it comes first in my world a secure home is a happy home and I do have some happy times here. When I watch movies on the homeless and starving it brings tears to my eyes as they try to survive in this country that's supposed to be so great, the thought of it being me is something that could scare anyone especially during the winter months. Couldn't imaging living in a box with nothing to keep you warm, even Veterans find them selves out there after coming back from war what's wrong with this picture when you fight for freedom and end up in another world you don't understand.

It's nice this morning and I hope for a warm day, but either way it doesn't matter anymore as the out side stays out there, we cant even tell when the wind is blowing because the windows are sound proof and they will be easy to keep clean as they fold inside to reach the out side. I am very blessed I my later years and all my battles have come to an end, and even though the fights have left scars they too will one day be gone from this soul so it can continue it's journey through life one of which peace will follow me the rest of my days. Back in the day my world was bleak with no sight of what would come from it and today I'm very blessed by what God has given me, even though it's hard to explain sometimes the answers come to me and He assures me that all is well in my existence where will this lead me I don't know at this time. It has been a nice day and it's supposed to be 48 degrees Christmas day which also falls on a Sunday and a weekend in which we have communion tomorrow I will go and clean a little before tomorrow nights service this will be the first time I went to a night service so it should be different from the normal things we do. As I grow in my faith I will also grow in spirit to except things that I never knew existed before to experience new things which the Lord has instore for me, we went to town this afternoon and got some things we would need over the holiday so we should be set for a while the church has become my second home and I love going there every chance I get. I feel it lets me connect with the holey goast and God, my love for Him has grown more then I ever thought was possible and it keeps growing the older I get strange how that happens and it was something I didn't see coming as a youngster, the difference has grown when I was young I didn't fit in with the normal things that kids did, it was like I was different in some way. For the things they were learning didn't intrest me and even though I was around them I felt alone as alone as I did in my mid age times it was like I was from somewhere different then they were and I couldn't explain it to others or to my self. I was from another world where my learning would be taught to me by God him self, I know this sounds far fetched but it was the way I felt and why I felt this way eludes me even today. A bigger picture if you will and I'm a part of that an important part, as for explanations I have none and as for trying to figure it all out I cant at this time in my life. Maybe everyone feels this way but I cant be sure of something Idon't know anything about, it's like a puzzle and someone took pieces of it and hid them and that's the first part of my life. All I know is whats happening right now and things are good for me, Saturday and my it's cold out went out for just a minute and it was like a deep freeze in my younger years it didn't bother me but now it doesn't let me stay out in it too long the boys are still sleeping and I'm glad of that Harley greated me when I open my door to turn on the coffee he is such a delight sometimes as he twerles around wanting to go out side I guess hegets excited, I remember when I got him I didn't think we would become close but we did and now I cant see the world without him he has helped me hrough many things and has always been there like Oliver in some ways but Oliver kept me strong by him needing me.

That in it's self brought me through many trying times as it let me focus on him instead of some of my own selfishness, it allowed me to see what the elderly go through and what they need to be happy and that extended into where I am able to help Randy also. A lot of times when we travel I put on that song brotherly love to remind Randy that it's the reason I brought him here even he helps me in many ways to see my self and to see where I need to change or better my self, I thrive on prefection but I also know that I will never be perfect none of us are in this world but it doesn't stop me from trying. I hink back to Walter when I took care of him and I know that was a test to see how things would go, but him and Oliver being in two different places wasn't a good thing because Oliver has needed me more then Walt was sick but I managed it for a while just long enough for it to do him some good and then he went to be with family in another state the last I heard he was doing well and I hope it continues I should send him a Christmas card and I will see if I have his address somewhere, he also helped me to grow in some ways but he too was very lonely when he was here. His friends did their best to take careof him but he needed more then they could give with living their own lives my land' it was him that helped to get my credit going as I had none when I first arrived he told Mark that I had never missed a payment and I was his best renter it seams many people have lived in this house but no more will live here because this is my domaine my home for ever my little part of the world that is mine.

Many things have come to pass since my coming here and they seam to only get better with age I'm going to see if Norman can move that pile of crap which resides in the back yard that way I can get it cleaned up so it looks nice next years, as for the mowing we will get another lawn mower and Randy can do some of that because it shouldn't all fall on my shoulders. In the beginning it was just me but now there is two of us and as they say share and share alike, the other day I told my daughter I was going to sing in church tonight and I wished she could be here but I know the miles separate us from things like this and I'm ok with that. One day she will hear her father and be proud of what I have accomplished as this is a big step for me in finding my self they say better late then never and I believe this with all my heart. It's never too late to start something new and I will sing when ever I am asked many people have heard that I sing well but they have never heard me and to night that will change for some of them as I hold there hearts in my hands only God can give you courage to do things that you never thought possible and He has done a good job here. The fight for freedon comes from within and you have to free your self of the things that hold you back in life and this is one of those things which held me back always being afraid of the unknown and what it brings with it failure is supposed to be good for a person it builds character they say, but you couldn't prove it by me in my life it's like God is fine tuning me for success and boy it takes a long time for that too take place Ha! My daughter sent me a picture of my son's family on my phone and I told her to have Leroy send me one of them and she said she would but I know it might take a year to get it, who would of thought I would be singing at my age surely not me and that also proves that God has different plans for our lives then we do and if you want him to laugh just tell him your's. this life of mine isn't mine it's His and He can do with it what He wants as I don't make things happen He does, and if I'm good at it then it just goes to show that he is right for some reason I don't hear my self but others do and that can make you if the right person hears you then you get that big break. But I'm not looking for that and that's when things start to show up when you least expect it. Singing for the church is an honor and I will do them proud not maybe but will do them proud they know this is only my second time singing imn front of people but I have a weapon and that is God standing by my side and I cant louse, before I didn't know he was there but now I do and he wiill always be there practice makes perfect and I don't seam to need too much of that. For He is my rock and my salvation as I walk through this life, I have my poem somewhere and maybe one day I will read it to them but for now I have to get through to night. The love of God is within us all but I don't understand why so many don't see it well I think I do as I didn't see it for a lot of my life, but once it was apparen then my life took on a new meaning all the things I believed before were wiped away and replace with the love for God now some might say someone else had to be involved for this to happen and I would say they would be wrong as it was only God who I communicated with in my time of despaired. And the change came from within not something that would happen if a person or person's were involved. I call it a transition of spirit becoming one with my creator.

Through the years my spirit was not allowed to grow as the addictions stopped it, it was like the light of life was shut off and the mind couldn't move past the stage it was at. Then came my demise and what happened after that for some reason everything changed even the spirits I saw were smiling in the other place of existence and I knew I had left my body it was a great feeling not to feel the pain I once felt and all the sorrow was a thing of the past for the time being anyway, it was like my mind was shut off and then restarted once again with some things missing and I sermise that it was at that time when somethings were added like the words epiphany and Melchisedek and this only drew me closer to things pertaining to Christ in the beginning I studied about Melchisedek and have much of his life momorised it was like I was supposed to know about him as he was ever present before Jesus and was made a priest continualy even Jesus was made a priest after the order of Melchisedek which leads me to believe Jesus was Melchisedek before he came to this place we call earth, it's Christmas day and there wasn't very many of us at church as last nights service went until after twelve midnight. My land' there was a lot of people there over 70 of them and 20 from just one family but it was nice to see them all, today it's like any other day except I'm writing this right now they have had a few good movies on and I enjoyed watching them as they break the bordom I know complain! Complain!. But I truly love my life here it's not like the life I had before I can complain now and it's fun you know take it in stride and joke about things that were once a tragity.

As they seam to not matter as much as they did back them, today I'm more of a free spirit and don't let things get to me as there are many things I cant change or would even want to if I could. Life is just that and I have learned to except it the way it is, I see others complain and say they wish they were somewhere else but I have learned that no matter where you go there you are. In other words you cant run away from your self so you have to learn to deal with what comes your way, life is so good at times but then you also have the things you really don't want to deal with but they come and they go to leave you in that place you want to be Monday morning and I slept in a little staying up doesn't agree with me at this point but it something I could do my getting up early has become a way of life for me, and it allows me my peace that I need nothing to do on this day except to get sugar the others that used to be in my life have all had something go wrong with them like dibeatas so they cant use sugar. My little brother was talking with his daughter and she told him about it, they seam to be mending that broken fencce that was once destroyed so long ago and it's working in time I hope thay will see each other and see what they have been missing. Randy told her about the lake that is around here so maybe one day they will go and have some fun I don't know what really happened between him and his children but it's apparent what once kept them apart is no longer there they seam to laugh when they talk and that's a good sign. Routh used to be a daddys girl and now maybe that can be once again, the only difference now is their ages as they are all grown up and ave kids of their own even Randle if my memory serves me right. He was telling me that they livce in a small town also just off of Lincoln or out side of it, that long night on Christmas Eve allowed me to see that others are up quite late at night they have been having this service at night for a long time and most of the people looked pretty chipper except for me of course like they say the early bird catches the worm, but I'm up long before the birds. These are great times in my life even with all that I do it seams to be fun to me I suppose it wouldn't be to others that stay up half the night, in my younger years it seamed I always ran late when it came to going to work but today that couldn't happen in the mornings I pray and get everyones med's ready for the day and my system works great the boys are usually up by 7:00 Am. And their day goes as well as you could expect Oliver has been doing really well these days as the cathider seams to be apart of him now with no infections to speak of. Life is just good at this point and I hope it will stay that way, social security has given a raise but it isn't much but I'm not complaining as every little bit helps in this economy. The storms have missed us and dumped 4 to 8 foot snow drifts in other parts of the state and this allowed me to get my well needed windows and the insolation in the attic. It's now as warm as toast in here and you don't hear the wind blow when it comes these windows are great and they have screens on them to open them up without the fear of bugs getting in during spring. I now know what my parents must have felt owning their own home but I wouldn't want to feel what it's like to louse it as they did. For this gife is from God and good works and it will continue to be that way until long into the future my land' life is great. Maybe one day I can expand but for now I am happy I'm hoping in the future that the children will come and go swimming in the pool down town but we will see when the time comes.

For the things which were fresh in my mind has somehow left and now I can focus on these days in which I live even the little trips to Belleville are exciting when we go and it gives us a change of scenery as everything changes with the seasons like life it dies off and then comes back anew to start the cycle all over again people with addiction can do the same thing, it's Tuesday now and I have some work to do this morning like the lilly bulb that is planted in fall it has to go througha freeze before it can come up to be a beautiful flower. As with people going through getting their lives back they too have to go through a process before they can start life over once again, with me it took getting rid of the addiction before I could come back and I had to destroy the one that was causing the addiction and that was a hard thing to do. It was like my body was controlled by two people or spirits one created by addiction and the other that was created by God and the one created by God laid in waiting until the others had almost destroyed him self and then the other showed him self but now that other was still a child and attained only some of what the other one learned the goodness of the child stayed and was very important it allowed the child to see the goodness that was not seen by the other as there was a wall put up so the other couldn't feel. By this time the person was way in maturity but the child was just that still a child in so many ways with no education but for what God had taught him.

Even though my learning was taught by the teacher of teachers it allowed the good things to stay and I would have to figure them out later in life. I didn't know that this world existed but I know there had to be something different then what I had lived all those years other wise what would be the perpose for me to come back here? The little boy was frightened of what would happen to be brought into a world that he didn't understand but he made it after years of learning. Later God would send him to a place where he could learn more about people and he learned that good and Evil is everywhere and you had to watch out for the bad things that could happen and he was able to avoid them for the most part, then after a few years in the new place he saw that there were many nice people there and they welcomed him this was the first step to anew life one where he didn't have to worry about others and he could focus on him self to make him self better then ever before he also learned that when God tells you to go somewhere He lets you know without a doubt because all things are not what they seam for most people are good and if you do what He tells you to do then in time you will see these things. Many times I have tried to figure out things about God but He doesn't seam to work in this realm of existence He has the ability to change us where we need to be changed and make us stronger then ever before this is His devine intervention and it can make us whole again. Each morning I can hear the train as it brings cars in from the out side world to be filled with our product's and I think that's a big part of Courtlands existence, new life is born in this town all the time and it also helps to keep it alive. I cant even amagine the stories that could be told here but I know there are many and mine is just one of them. The life spand here is a lot longer then out in the world where all the confusion is most people live to be in their 70's and higher and I hope to see that one day but for now Iwill enjoy these years and see where they lead, I pray each day now as it's new to me in this different life I give thanks for yesterday and today. In my other life it really didn't matter or so I thought but today it makes things go better and they do just that go better, the time of being in a wheel chair have seamed to fade like it has been wiped away from my mind and the only time it comes back is when I watch a movie on people going through what I had gone through, my memorie's are take away so I wont dwell on such things and that let me move forward into the life I have today for things that happen to us through life is supposed to teach us something how to grow past the things that could have once destroyed us. When I first taught my self to walk it was hard and the pain was out of this world but through it all I became stronger mentally and physically to grow in all that I do. I believe crolling was the hardest but before then I scooted across the floor which built up my arms to later pull me up when I started to stand even that has become vage today it's like life lets you move beyond what once held you back in life and then you are renewed with a new focus to move forward to better things. Christmas is gone now and New Years is this weekend and everyone will be celebrating to bring in the new year, people will be making resoulations; that they will not keep but I guess that's fun to some as for me I will take everyday as it presents it's self no fooling my self about things that cant come true.

I live in reality not a world that doesn't exist we went to town and got Randy a lamp so he could see his way to the bathroom at night Tuxies had a nice small one that will work just right for what he needs, tuxies is a thrift store in Belleville and we have become good friends with the people who run it or own it. We visit it when ever we go into town in hopes to find something we might need and it's a lot cheaper then buying something from the regular store, I bought most of my shades from there and they were very little in price compaired to the regular store which they would have cost 30 or so dollars I guess I'm a miser in some ways always trying to get the best deal I can for my dollar and it helps me to survive in this world and have nice things which will later go to someone else Ha! Even mom would visit these places to save a buck it's just the way we were raised, not being people of means and all maybe one day that will be a thing of the past but for now things will continue that way. It's Wednesday and it's a little colder this morning my land' I was just thinking about how we haven't gotten much snow yet we have had the freezing temps but not much snow and it's almost January this might hurt the crops for the farmers I'm really not sure but we did get a bunch of rain in the last couple of months, the ground hog is supposed to show him self in Febuary I believe and that will tell if we get six more weeks of winter my hopes for not getting snow until my house was done has come to pass but still no snow O well maybe later as I sure don't want a really hot Summer, I'm a little conserned about the ternamites but I hope they were old ones that have long died off. In the days and weeks to come I hope to get out and cut some of the shrubs in the yard so they wont grow into bushes and make the yard look like crap there are many things that need to be done but I'm too old to do them like climb on a ladder to paint the house.maybe II can hire someone to do it, you hear of people looking for work all the time so we will see what happens.

In my younger years I could do those things but now days my body is just too wore out except for the things I can do like write and mow the yard and work at the church which is my pashion or should I say one of them, in a way I'm afraid to let go of my writings as they are a piece of me but I also know that I would always have a copy of what happened in my life. And this is something I never thought on much but do I want things to be known yes and it would help others along the way, my life here in Courtland has been good but is the end of the trail or will something else happen in the future that will change things. It seams my account of things is in the now for the most part with reflections into the past where things were very different. Like in other novels it takes time as each day passes and no two days are the same change takes place all the time and I try to make each day the best it can be. My burdens have been many but I seam to come through them all as the days turn into weeks and weeks turn into months, I'm a simple man and love what I do although my time is not my own I make it the best way I know how and God is right beside me for the life I once lead is fading and new things will surely pop up better things in which I can share with others as the years pass. Some days go by fast but then I have the others that just go by normaly before they all wised by and now it's not so much just sketchey from time to time, Randy's birthday is next Saturday and so is the grandchildrens so I will have to send them something as for the big boy he can get what ever he want on his own then comes my birthday on April 12th and it will be like any other birthday no one will remember except for us who live here and maybe we might do a little something not sure yet but it will not make me feel older as that comes gradually with each passing day. how much time are we allowed on this earth and that question can only be answered by God, in the days of my youth I was a pretty good looking kid and I didn't realize it until now then I'm older and I can see that I could have been so much more then what had become but then again hind sight is always 20/20 and full of what if's and what could have beens when I look at a picture of me with my 107 year old grandmother I can travel back to that time but for the most part it was sketchy, I remember working on her old stereo and television as that's what I liked to do at 17 years of age always trying to figure out what made things work but I couldn't figure out my life strange how that works. It was a family trip that we had taken back to Minnesota because grandma was getting ready to go and be with the lord, I remember her voice as it quivered and she shook as old people do. She said that she loved me and that made me feel good at that time in my life what my mom had told me about my father didn't even come into sight as I had forgotten about it. It was many years before that she had told me and you just didn't retain things like that at that age my excitement was messing with the bad spirits, as they had consumed me long ago.

There wasn't much time that I didn't spend indulging in them but of course I couldn't do it around grandma as she forbid it in her home. Like I do today, it's just not a part of my life anymore and never will be. I know she must have had the same out look on it back then as I do today, I remember going to see her one more time after that but our time there was a little vage she had been put into a nurceing home for putting pot holders in the toaster and the family didn't want anything to happen to her so they took over her house the precher my uncle who had so much had lost it all somehow but he didn't live too long after that my aunt bunny was a funny person and I remember her but it's not so clear as grandma I guess she wasn't as important as grandma not to me anyway. The times of my youth seams to elude me in some areas and I was probably to intoxicated to remember them and maybe that's a good thigs at this time in life anyway, maybe too much pain in those times. When I couldn't walk scooting was my past time when I wasn't too intoxicated to get out of the chair, those were some bad times and even then I knew the end was near and I didn't care. But then later God would help me to care again it was the struggle of living that made me strong everyone around me thought and said I wouldn't last long but through that time in the light I was given hope that I would survive when it was said that it wasn't my time yet I knew there was a greater perpose for me to start living once again.

Even though later I would want to give up again He showed me that all things were possible through Him the father. The souls I saw were real but I also knew that it wasn't heaven and that's when I knew He was trying to show me that there was nothing to be frightened of, there were many sould as I like to call them waiting to go somewhere maybe to that final destanation which will be heaven or hell but it was strange because I wasn't in my body I just floated around until I felt that power which sent me back saying your journey hasn't started yet it was the same voice which told me to come to Courtland and it left no room for doubt I learned long ago not to ignore that voice because it was my keeper. Thursday morning and Harley would be up usually he stays a sleep until 5:00 or so but not this morning for some reason so I took him out side, he is my friend since I got him so long ago I guess he loves me also it's warm this morning warmer then usual and I think we will have a hot summer this year with no moisture to think of and you cant really tell what going to happen at this stage of the game. I hope we get some snow before too long it's only the end of December and snow can fall into April but not too oftend by this time last year we had snow of a foot and yesterday they said it's supposed to be in the 60's today, and then in the 50's the rest of the week Kansas is like Nebraska in some ways as they say you cant predict the weather in either State. Back in the1800's they called it the dust bowle because it could be so dry but I haven't heard that term in many years I do know that we had a better crop then most people last year some said our worst was better then most's best and this was God showing favor to this part of the country, the silage from the plant across the way wont be able to get through the windows this year as they are sealed tight with the new ones, I can hear the machines running this morning to bring the grain into or out of the bin's as for the hills of milo they are gone into storage for the year to be sold or used for next years crop, I saw one of my friends at church on Christmas eve and it was good to see him as he doesn't come that oftend, he owns a ranch and is very busy through the year some say he used to go all the time but something happened long ago I just pray that God will show him the way back. These things cant be rushed and people have to come to it on their own when they are ready just like with me it took years, but it did happen. I have never been one to push God on anyone as their spirit will tell them when it's time, I believe he is much younger then I or I could be mistaken and he just takes care of his self if I had to guess I would say mid 40's and he is one of the nicest people I have met. They say there was over 70 people at church that night and that's just about a full house but it could of held more if I had to guess I would say it could hold 125 people and that would be a third of the town, I have never been happier then I am here and the emotions become mixed from time to time but the good out wighs the bad and that's what counts in life for me anyway, today I will go and clean and get things ready for this Sunday Valerie text me a few time and said she loved me I think she is getting past the pain of louseing some people close to her. I gave her a pet name long ago calling her funny face' and I called her that theother day and she said it made her cry she said I hadn't called her that in a long time and I hadn't but I think it helps sometimes when they realize you haven't forgotten them.

She has had a lot of miss fortune in the last year and I hope it gets better for her in this new year may the sands of time wipe the bad memories away, we always laughed together and it was fun when she visited back in Kearney but now I have moved away and haven't seen her in over a year. She must live on a farm because she said her goat died and that's the only place where you can have one, she must be experiencing the farm life and that's good for her in many ways the fresh air and there is no one around to distort that reality except for maybe her self and the pot but that has been a big part of her life since child hood and she wouldn't give it up for nothing. It's her way of dealing with the world and for her it seaams to work or so she thinks, back in my child hood when I did it the stuff was an addictive to the alcohol because the alcohol hade lost it's punch if you will and I needed something more. But that was a phaze which would only last a few years and then it went away as fast as it came this in it's self told me that alcohol wasn't strong enough and then the other drugs came into the picture which were even stronger yet, we as kids experimented with all kinds of drugs but it was lead on by alcohol and that was my down fall alcohol and Methamphetamine that one did a lot of damage but God took care of that and I was able to start to live once again. With it brings sorrow and pain and a detachment from other people even though it lets you be sociable while in use but once it wares off look out because you need it to keep up that appearance or macho image that is just that an image.

Traveling was a big part of my life in the younger years but then even that wore off as the years set in and I couldn't drive any longer, 15 years I didn't drive and I don't know how I survived good thing Oliver walked back them. He has helped me through a lot and listened to my pain and sorrow but he also hung in there like God did and never gave up on me back when mom died my brothers came to live with us and that was a mistake as they got us kicked out of the home we lived in for 11 years and I had to live in my car for a short time Olivers dog even had to live in the car with me and that wasn't much fun, when all this happened I swore that nothing like this would happen again and it hasn't since that time. My other brother got a motel and he and his girlfriend stayed there for a time but for me it was th car as Oliver was in the hospital with his valve replacement being done Tom didn't much care for my brothers with good reason they destroyed all that they touched even our home, later we moved to a place that Mark had and that was another mistake as the land lord was a thief and stold from Oliver many times to line his pockets and it took 8 years to catch on to him. That's how he became rich steeling from people living inn poverty I had always wondered why we weren't getting a head and then we found out, some people! It's been a nice day and I got some yard work done then cleaned some of the wood work in the kitchen getting it ready to paint so it looks better. I find that doing a little at a time works best for me as my attention spand isn't very long Ha! Kind of funny if you ask me, tomorrow I will pay the bills so they are out of the way for the month and then catch the others as they trickle in. it's fun in a way and I like the responsibility as these are things I didn't get to do as a young man the women always took care of them, it's the little things that I like to do and at times it brings me joy to know that they are all taken care of and I'm the one that did it. Tomorrow is Friday and the end to another week they seam to still go by fast but not as fast as they used to in the early days of being here in Courtland, in many ways I'm still setteling in you might say but at least now it's fun and not full of confusion. At first I didn't know if I would always have a home but in time that situation was made clear as Walter helped me, I think others see something in me that I am still unable to see but I know when the time is right it will become clear. My mom would of loved it here back in her early days I can vagely remember her in her 30's and 40's when I was just a little one, and I did have some fun when she was a nurse it was at that time when I broke my leg playing in a tree and had to be rushed to the hospital where she worked things must have been bad back then also as the accident with the boys had already taken place and now that happened hospitals cost so much but you would of thought insurance would of covered it. I remember a nurce trying to take my tempature in a place other then my mouth so I slaped her hand and it flew across the room she didn't try that again, we used to have squirt gun fights with serenges that mom brought home for us to play with we were so poor that it was the only fun we had during summer, that and climbing trees and I never did that again I recall buying my friends Ice cream when I got out of the hospital and then mom kept the rest of the money to pay bills it had to of been very hard on them but they did the best they could with raising us at least there was love there.

I wish I could remember it all clear but it only comes to me in sections a piece one morning and then another later on down the line but it doesn't hurt any more like it used to, my land' my head would pound like a jack hammer was going off and then I would cry and ask God to take it away and he would in time. Many times it would keep me up at night and that didn't feel so hot, the publisher has been trying to get a hold of me and I egnore their calls maybe I'm not ready yet to publish my work not quite sure if I want to, as I don't know these people from Adam I do know it's time to move forward but I'm not sure about somethings to humble ones self in front of God is a gift that a lot of people don't see and with many of them they are trying to run a foot race with others. Like what you see in the big cities and that wouldn't be the life for me, everyone living on top of each other and the rent is out of this world twelve hundred a month for a apartment my land' that's ridiculous no wonder so many live on the streets. And in their cars then you have the ticket system and they can take your car if you get too many of them, here they don't have such things I have never gotten a ticket in my middle years not in the last 20 years. And I'm proud of that, it's a live and let live system here in Kansas O sure you hear about others getting them but you your self seam to stay away from that crap I drive very cautiously as I know I have others lives in my hands. The next month or two will tell if we will get any more snow but it looks like the western part of the state got most of it and they really needed it as they were very dry last year.

This next year will be very warm I think but at least we have air conditioning to keep us cool during the hot months it's something you have to have so you can survive Kansas was once called the dust bowl but I think it has improved since the 1800's my I could see my self riding a horse in 102 degree heat you would have to be very strong to survive back then but I would have done it. Homesteading was the way to go back then but I don't know if it exist today in the modern world, when we drive to Belleville there is a house on the south side of the road which has been vacant for over three years and it makes me wonder what will become of it also the house next to us is vacant but was sold at auction a month or so back wonder who bought it, have never been in it but hear told that it's a three bedroom with a deck that might be the one that I saw in the paper last week and I took it to be the one on the North side of pershing I will check on it today now that I think on it that house must be the one not the other one. Walt owned two houses but either one was paid off until I moved here to buy this one I'm in today and I'm glad that I got it. After a taste of living here I could never go back to Kearney, with all the drugs and disorder and the homeless is becoming more apparent in that part of the country before too long many will be living in the shelterd the new one they built is already over crowded it just goes to show that domestic violence is there also but our town hasn't been ravished by this plage and I hope it never is we do have the starving here and we try and take care of them so many need our help and we do our best. I give every chance I get and if I had the means I would give more but I'm only one person, Saturday New Years Eve' and there will be a lot of people out tonight this in the night that some people go out and get hammered so they can ring in the new year, these are things I used to do back in my early years but it never got me anywheres some will be killed in the highway and others well they will get into fights and be thrown in jail. I had a plesent day at church and I might get some new tools to keep it cleaner a floor scrubber to help get the deep dirt and then I can wax it to make it bright, I sure love my job and it allows me to do things the way I want them done. I have to face the fact that I cant bend over like I used to so I have to do it with an electric one but even then it should be fun, the boys are getting board but I don't know what to tell them as for me I am fine in this world I have to live in bordom doesn't bother me as I can always go to the church to get over it. Sunday the 1st of January. It's now 2012 and very early I might add some people have just gotten home from the bars in the big cities and will wake with a hang over but not me or any one elase that lives here, that part of life is long gone from the peace we find here or I have found here in Courtland as for some friends they went out to celebrate like Valerie. And those that still drink, getting this far has taken a lot but I'm still hanging in there my journey has been long and I hope otherss will follow my lead I'm not ignorant and understand what some go through trying to beat the curse but it's possible for them to get through it. As for Randy I don't think he remembers the times when he used to fight with me and that's ok for now but in time it will have to be made clear so he can move on, the remembering takes time as for forgiveness I have forgave him but even that he doesn't see at this time.

Many years ago before I traveled here I had forgiven them all the ones that done me wrong and now I'm at peace with my self , many people don't drink all year long until New Years gets here and then they let loose but they are the ones that don't really have a problem with alcohol it's the others that drink on a daily bases that destroy other peoples lives. It's already turning warm for this time of season and we might have a hot summer but there is still a couple of months left for it to snow if that's whats going to happen, soon I wont have to turn on the heat and we will get by with just the spring type weather it will be different not to have to keep the windows closed as now they have screens to keep out the bugs before you couldn't open them and now you can do it with one finger what a difference. Even the air conditioning will stay cooler in here as the house is sealed pretty tight to not let it escape, I know it wont go through the roof as there is plenty of insolation there to hold in the coolness. My home savings program is getting better as the months pass I seam to be able to save a little here and there and it will help in the months and years to come as you never know what might come up, in my early years I couldn't save a dime but today it doesn't seam to be a very big problem when Randy first got out it was hard but the lord taught me how to deal with it in a positive way and now things are good once again.

We went to Tuxies yesterday and got a few things and I got this awesome clock for my bedroom which matches my paneling the numbers are big so I can see them better and it doesn't strain my eyes which is a good thing today I have to do laundry and wash my bedding so it smells good once again, I would also like to get some new drapes for the house now that I have the new windows in and that would make it look really nice. I like my home to look good and homey I have a look I'm looking for but not quite sure how to get it that way maybe in time it will come to me, a different look for each room like going from one season to another maybe brown for my room and a tan for the living room and dining room then a white or yellow for the kitchen to make you feel alive. This home can be what ever I want it to be because it's mine and without God's help I wouldn't of ever had this gift. Since my move here everything is right on target and my love for the people has grown even more over the last few years, but it's still hard for me to except that others truly love me, my friends have taken me in and made me one of their own and for that I'm grateful and will always be. Who would of thought that things could come together at this stage of life but it did and all I have to do is keep doing what comes naturaly being me! What a great life he has given me and the only limits I have is what I put on my self, He doesn't look back like we do He just moves forward and we are supposed to also but for some reason it's hard for me in some areas. We make life hard not Him' and for that we have to figure out the things that make it hard for us as a child my father taught me to ride a bike even though it was hard for me it wasn't for him because he had already been taught by his father, to me life is learning new things and then being able to accomplish the task at hand and you don't give up then scoon you're a pro at it and the learning process fades away. Much like in life but boy I had to learn a lot of things and not the easy way either from one addiction to another and then being able to over come them and a nother would pop up but God gave me the tools to work through them even when I was at deaths door He brought me back to try and figure out what life was all about I know love fits in there somewhere but except for the love I have for Him I haven't found it yet Ha!. It's been a good day but I messed up by not reading schedule at church. We had communion and I didn't even see it but it was my first mistake and I'm allowed at least one, also I told them about buying a floor striper and they will see what they can do. This will allow me to strip the floors in the church and keep them cleaner then they are now, we also went to town and got some coffee and creamer for the rest of the month cant do without that as it starts my day each morning a friend said she noticed that I got new windows and I told her yes that I did. I really enjoy talking with my friends as it gives me a break from family members they seam to talk about the same thing all the time and it can get on my nerves, I don't like to show that part of me that part which blows up from time to time and sometimes I have to walk away. There isn't much that goes on at the last day of the week so it can be boring my excitement seams to come from cooking and at times I don't like to do that either, I think maybe I need a hobby, to take my mind off of the things which make me board but what would that be? Maybe get a car to work on or a piece of furniture to restore that would be fun, I used to refinish rocking chairs long ago when I lived in Oklahoma and it was fun. But cars would be funner as you can do a little at a time and then take a break for a while until you get more money, everything seams to cost so much these days and we live so far from anything that travel would be something we would have to do.

Maybe sometime in the future I can buy a car that needs very little work, but if there is one out there I haven't found it yet. Randy seams to sleep a lot and that's because he doesn't do anything but sit on his ass he will have to change other wise it will drive me nuts. Ya right' it's Monday the second and I was up a little early this morning today we will stay homeas we have went to town three times already since the new year and that's out of the normal for me but we needed things that were important, I try to limit the trips to once a week that way I can save a little on gas. That dam gas I wish it wasn't so high but I don't see it changing any timee soon . A long while back I wrote something that was published and it was called AVOID DRUG CURSE. And it went like this' Now that I see the destruction of Methamphetamine through sober eyes. I can see that alcohol and drug addicts really don't know what they are doing, unless they have a death wish. Sadly, some are addicted through o fault of their own because parents put the curse on them at birth.

We are all God's children. If he wanted our bodies to be that way he would have set those things into motion. I have seen some who are cursed go until their early teens before becoming addicts, but sadly enough, some become addicted at age 10 or 11. They cant help them selves and their parents cant help them either because child addicts have learned from their parents to hide it. I consider it a miracle I survived my life of destruction and got a second chance. Many others whither away and die without hope or faith. I was cursed at age 11. I didn't worry about buying drugs because they always were in the house. Children are curious. Some will sneak drugs right under your nose and you won't know until it's too late. A lot of parents think it could never happen to their child. Think again. It could be happening right now. Now that summer is here, more youths will be busted for MIP and DUI. A while back I was with a 16-year-old. Meth had destroyed his heart. Before he knew he was dying he talked about going to treatment, but the damage was done. He cried because he didn't want to die. That was another soul lost to the destruction of drugs. When things like this happen it really makes you grateful when it wasn't you. Cherish the life you have and if your child has a problem, help them. Looking back on these writings I was trying to help others going through what I had gone through and in many ways it worked for them to know that others have been through what has happened to them.

They need to know that they are notthe only ones that go through this thing called addiction as for those who have never gone through it, they cant understand it. And that's just the way it is. Even though a shrink can tell a persons state of mind they cant tell what's going on in there not really the demons you fight to take back your life is hard, and I have found out that they can be defeated by you and a higher power meaning God. Here in Courtland they are all gone and don't bother me here, and I believe it's because there is such a great strength of God here and the people are dedicated to Christ. This day will be a good one as we move forward into 2012 some say this is when the world will end and I don't believe such crap as no one but God knows the day in which it will come to an end . Not even Jesus knows the day and he is a lot closer to God then any of us and sits ar the right hand of God, science has tried to prove that we come from apes and this can and never will be proven because it's not true. I read the bible more as time moves forward and in time it will be the book that I finish if it's God's will but for now I will read a little at a time, it seams to draw you towards it even with reading a virse at a time. Our town is a place where the people run things like today the bank isn't open but it will be tomorrow, there is something special here but I cant quite put my finger on it as for my dreams they seam attainable here but not in other places and I believe it's God that makes this possible. I have a variedy of good samiratin awards from places I have helped and I keep them on my wall as a reminder of what is important, to help those in need that would other wise not get it when you share it does something to you a good feeling that cant come from anywhere else and it brings them hope to know others care about them. Frougely living that way has become a way of life for me and even though I save it doesn't seam to grow much except at certain times of the year, I don't messure my welth by how much money I have and I think that helps. Friends are very important to me and I have many but I don't use that to attain favor on anything even with my brother I make him save so one day he will be able to get the things he will need in life like a car and insurance so he can travel to where ever he wants life is supposed to be a happy time but with most it isn't because of things that were put into their path, when we fall from grace God allows us to attain it once again to live the life we were meant to live the one we were born into this world to follow.

Many of us take a road that wasn't designated for us as we go through life but in time we can find our way back to it. No matter how long it takes it's always there, God had our lives mapped out before we were born he had to of as he knows every hair on our head. Even the ones we have lost over time Ha! He seams to see the whole picture while we only see a fragment of it, if only we could see the whole picture we could help in making it happen or maybe we would destroy it as humans seam to do that sometimes leaving things in God's hands seams to be the best thing because I really wouldn't want to know what happens in the future just imagine knowing what would happen if you went to the store and had an accident it would make you not to want to leave the house. Could this be what mom saw and that's why she stayed home all the time when she met Oliver she seamed to not want to go out anymore except to move from time to time or she was just a privet person and didn't like what the world had become it was like she separated her self from it and didn't want anything to do with it. When the two of them first moved to Nebraska he had a 1957 car which later blew up then he had to walk many of the places he went even to work, he had always been a hard worker and would even hitch hike many miles to work and then back home. I didn't know all the problems my parents had but alcohol was one of them after the boys accident when we were little Rick must have been about 5 years old and Rod about 7, what would of happened if that wouldn't of happened could they have become a doctor or lawyer? We will never know' but it's a good thing they survived.

It's strange how some see things, as one persons blessing can be seen through their eyes as a curse and can destroy a whole life or family as it did mine. Blessings come in many forms and a lot of people don't see them until they have passed as with me many of them appeared at one time and then became clear later in the month or months ahead. And this makes me believe that I might be a little slow in some areas. As I watch some movies I cant understand how people destroy others lives and not give a shit about doing it, in most cases it's over GREED' stupid money as it too can become an addiction like drugs and alcohol what good is something that destroys lives? We need money to live but other then that it's a burden but I cant help but to want to see how it feels to be without worry in that department a life of plenty you might say, but just for a little while to get that feel of it. Mom didn't worry very much as she had Oliver with her and he took good care of her, all those years they were together and she must have loved him as for him today he can hardly remember her, it's like her memory has faided from his mind and there hasn't been anyone else since her death. I have taken care of him for many years and have done a dam good job seeing he wasn't supposed to live past 60 years this too is a miracle on many levels. For God has been good to us all and will continue to do so long into my later years. I cant wait to see the floor scrubber and try it out to see how good it works it will sure help me out in many ways and keep the church clean, some parts I will have to do by hand but not much just the corners and along the sides this will help in many ways and it isn't very big not like the big buffers which you can ride and they use at the school those ones are very big. I have used them before in restarunts to clean the floors but that was long ago when I was young and full of energy, not so much anymore as things change with age, this is a blessed day as I feel good and chipper and I wish that could happen all the time but it doesn't. Each morning I pray and give thanks to God for the day and for the day before, He is so great' in my time, I will accomplish many thing and I don't even know what they are yet funny how that will happen but I know it's coming and I hope it will be good things as I'm sure they will be my life is one of honor and I cherish it others know that I'm honest and that is something I will never change in all my time on earth honesty has always been the best policy and it has done me right. Watching a show it showed a guy killing three kids just for nothing except he was having a flash back on drugs, these things happen all the time in the big cities and it makes me sick that they couldn't even walk down the road without someone trying to rob them and then they ended up dead. Things like that doesn't happen here in the heart land and I hope it never does but you cant tell what the future holds if this is happening today imagine what could happen when the country gets worse people starving today will be long gone and new ones will rise up to take their places in this movie the girl made it but will never be the same and it was done because of hate.

It almost brought tears to my eyes because I know there are people out there like that, people who don't care about human life like they should and they are so full of hate what is wrong with the world? And some will rob you at the drop of a hat. O I know those things shouldn't bother me but they do and I don't know why being from a small town where things like that doesn't happen, in my town the kids can walk down the street and go swimming without any worry because the town people watch out for them as if they were their own. And that's why I love my town even though I have no kids here of my own security is a great thing to have, as the children grow and learn the ways of life. It's Tuesday and it feels like it's going to be a nice day again through my travels I have met many people but the people who owned the store in Flag Staff Arizona were by far different as we made it our home we would exchange different things for things like beer there were many in our party the motheer and two daughters and we were all alcoholics so we make many trips to the Indian store none of us except the mom had a License to drive but we did it any way. The mom bought two motor homes which me and Randy drove so we would have a place to sleep as we traveled through Arizona. K Bob National Forest was where we settled for a short time and that's how we met the store owner he was a nice man and liked our busness as we were in there each day after a while it got boring so I knew it was time to move on as I was just a youngster and no where near ready to settle down. By this time Diane was my wife and I knew it wouldn't work, then a few weeks later my brother Rod found me and told me that mom was dieing so I hopped on a bus and back to Nebraska. I went but the other two brothers couldn't come because they were still wanted by the law for breaking into a store. That was why mom left Nebraska in the first place to protect them or get them out of the state, when I got back to Nebraska it was three in the morning so I walked to my brothers house and beat on the door when he answered he said to come in and I asked how mom way and he said not good.

He proceeded to tell me that they pumped her stomic to releave the pressure from the fluid backing up in her lungs and that she was living in a motel when I asked why she was there they said they did all they could do for her but it became too much on Mary' they were going too put her in an old folks home so her and Oliver moved out on their own to the motel I told him that I wanted to see her and he agreed to take me the next day, at first she didn't quite know me but then it kicked in and she gave me a big Hug' She had always been a little thing but now she was real little and yellow, my showing up gave her what she needed and that was hope. Later my brother told me if she asked me to stay to say no because she would depend on me and not try harder to get well, when she asked I told her what the doctor said and she assured me that it wouldn't happen . The next day the manager of the motel brought a role away bed into the room for me to sleep on and then my mind was set to help her recover on many different times she told me that I saved her life because she was about ready to give up, but she never did and in time she got stronger the doctors said she would have to have her stomic pumped for the rest of her life but that to diminished over time as she got better they said she was the first person they had done that too and they didn't know if it was going to work but it did and she went on to lead a somewhat normal life, in time the yellow left her body and she gained weight my land' she was down to 89 pounds because of the alcohol destroying her body. As the years passed she got depressed and started to drink again after being on darvaset for many years when we were in the motel we played board games to pass the time and it was fun, we would take darvaset and play board games later we moved from there to a big old house and me and mom fixed it up. All her homes looked great that's just the way she was, she continued to get well and we had a great life at that time but things seam to change when you least expect it. All my friends wanted to come over all the time because mom was a funny person always laughing and having fun , she just had a way about her that drew people to her sort of like I am today then things would get bad my X wife came to visit and we got back togather for a short time I was working for a company and enjoyed my work and she wanted to be with me so we gave it a shot me knowing it wouldn't work but why not take the chance something might have changed but after a short time it was apparent that it wasn't going anywhere so we had her mother pick her up and she was gone. A few weeks later I met my childrens mother and we hit it off we were both alcoholics and comforted each other well in the end we split after 8 years and I went my way and she went her's right in the arms of a convict who later treated her like crap, they tried to brain wash my children into hating me but weren't able to do it because my babys loved me when things fell apart.

Later they would get to know me and love me even more while all the time her husband was trying to destroy that love but again it didn't work, she would later tell me that she wished she could do things over again and I told her that I had enough of it. I have always been a survivor in this world and will continue to be even after everyone is gone out of my life for this is just the way it is, I have been knocked down many times to bounce right back even stronger then before I think in many ways I'm like my mom a fighter of survivla and survive I will until the Lord takes me home. Even though she bought those motor homes we didn't stay in them much we would get a motel instead and leave them in the parking lot, strange how that worked later she would sell them at a big loss but by then money became tight and little did she know a check was waiting for her at home which would of allowed her to keep them, but by the time we got home they were gone. One was a Dodge and had enormous power it was nothing for it to lift the front end off the ground and drag the back bumper that was mine to drive and I had a lot of fun in it but that ended as all things do in life we drank and drove all the time but were never caught, and never hurt anyone after years of driving like that doing it becomes a normal thing. She then bought a station wagon in California and had the motor over hauled and boy that thing ran like a raped ape it had a 390 motor with about 400 horse power more then she would ever need.

And she raced it from time to time and people couldn't believe how fast it was for a station wagon, later she would sell it but that was after I had left Flag Staff many years have passed since those times and I'm glad that they are gone, along with the addictions that almost destroyed me. God surely has better plans for me in this time of my life and I will embrace them to the fullest, it's January thire and it's that time of the month to get stocked up on things we will need during the next 30 days. Next month there is only 28 or 29 days and that makes for a short month thank God' and then spring will arrive the time of year when everything comes back to life the flowers will bloom and the grass will grow. Very high if my mower isn't fixed but I will have Leroy work on it or one of his croneys for this will be truly a good year, Oliver has been around since the beginning since I was 14 years of age and he has grown on me, he is a great guy and is very loved by me as for others well they don't really matter at this stage of the game not even family matters when it comes to him I will always take care of him.my buddy. I got some news from the Kearney-hub that my letter will be published today and that inspired me once again by taking this on long ago I promised not to give up, no not to people but to God. And even though it's been months since my last publacation I have to stay true to my word as that's the only thing you really own in this world a word is powerful in some cases it brings healing and in others not so much if they are not ready for change, with drunk drivers they are sorry always after the fact and then they are not really sorry for the action. They are sorry they got caught andd things continue once they are out once again, it's a pitty cycle that will go on as long as the law allows it to happen. All the wasted money could of helped many people but instead it goes to lawyers and the court system, there needs to be something put into place that helps the ones that suffer because of their stupid repeat of the same mistake, my journey has taken me to different places in my mind from the thought of being washed up to the joy of being put back into print, but I think those are things you have to go through to see if you are still going to make it in this fight for life. Nothing has come easy for me never has, and probably never will. But that's what makes me different from others many go to a news paper to hone their craft of writing as for me I do it at home where I'm comfutable, but adjusting to having others arounnd me lets me be around them and still write and do a good job. Example Randy with him here it brings feelings that I havent felt in many years anywhere from joy to getting mad and resolving problems that arise. He is he helping hand that I talk about from time to time as God said we were not meant to be alone there is a joy with him here just the knowing that I can help to change his ways where they need to be changed really helps me in many ways and laugh my land' we laugh all the time but also there aree those dark moments when things don't go quite right and that's going to happen in anyones life. My little brother not so little anymore but he is still my brother with the same heart sencative in many ways and sometimes cries for no apparent reason except to cry and I have done the same thing many years back it's a release of emotions that get built up from not crying, and hey! They have to go somewhere right? He seams to have his best days when it's towards the end of the month and monbey has a lot to do with it, by that time your running low and the well has to be filled up once again no matter how I look at it money is a tool to survive. In the days and months a head I will write more and see what happens when I first started it brought me great joy and even today it does but not quite so intence as it did back then.

And that comes from doing it so long it's called growing in the writing world the one thing about teaching your self is that you do it at your own speed and correct your own mistakes, it's Wednesday hump day for some and for other just the middle of the week through the elections and everything else that goes on I haven't seen anyone I would vote for to run this country. Obama didn't do any good while in office so in my books he is out it seams they are all in it for the money and that's no way to run a country, they fill their bank accounts with money that should go to the people but they don't care about the people for this has become apparent in the last four years that he has run things it's time for change and it will happen. It's going to be a nice day and I willl check on things at the church my doing this job lets them come into the church without worry of it being a mess and my job is important not to only them but to me and God a clean church is a happy church my motto of course and I like to make them up from time to time in the years to come my bills will lesson as I get the house and car paid off that will be a great thing as I get on with age, my palace my piece of the world to where I don't have to wonder any more. A steadfast foundation which will grow with me in the years to come many wonder why I don't get paid for my writings but with me it isn't the money it's helping others that's important, the knowing that you made a difference in a world of millions and your mark will be left behind for others to follow. GREED' is something that destroys many things and causes many to think selling drugs can make them rich but it wont never has and never will.

In my early years I to thought I could get rich that way but in the end it's all hipe that they use to get you hooked and selling for them, many promas the world but all you end up with is the addiction that takes a lot of money to over come. Alcohol destroys many lives and if they had their way they would push it even harder then they do today, making kids think it's cool to drink and do drugs just to attain the main element MONEY' my land' they ship it out of the country by the boat fulls to other places and it's tanted by the blood of our children and young adults. To go to a foren country and be tanted again by their children and young adults. Second world countries allow the selling of these drugs and that's why they are second worlds but if drug addicts here have their way we will become one of them, going from a super power to a second class country that has been striped of it's dignity imagine this the United States used to be number one of the places to live and now we have droped to number 8 a far cry from being number one what happened? I know! The government shipped all the jobs over seas so they can be made cheaper and the people here cant afford to live so many go on welfare to survive and that drains the economy of what it has left. Where is these things that are being made? Surely they are not here, and what cost a dime to make cost you over a dollar so where is the savings' we are being drained and the presidents are doing it they no more care for the person then the man in the moon, addiction is on the rise and they don't even care they just want to keep destroying the country. My land' someone has to care but it's none of them that run for office GREED' runs those people and always will there is a set payment for presidents but with the kick backs from drug companys and others their pay goes from $150.000.00 a year to over a million and they pay many millions to get the job just for that purpose to drain the country the structure of the country is falling a apart roads are washing away and bridges are falling down but enough of that. Today was a great day as of now all the bills are paid and we went to Scandia to get some things for Randy, also my letter was published and that built up my spirit as for the weather it was nice and warm. I don't think we will get any snow the rest of the year so that makes this a very mild winter I just hope the summer isn't really bad and they get plenty of rain so the crops grow nice. This is my time of year when I get excited even over small things like good weather and seeing the animals play in the yard, most times these things wouldn't even register as good feelings but they do now and for that I am grateful. Mark at the paper is going to send me a copy of my letter and I will put it with the rest of them so the grandchildren can have it when I am gone from this world but that won't be for quite a while yet still have to find a mate before that happens, it's now Thursday and it's work time for a while this morning. I know many people will read my message in the Kearney-hub and I will see how they reply back in the day I used to get people that replyed quite oftend but I didn't know how to answer them on the computer as my skills were limited by not having taken any classes on operation of them. Many people need to help them selves when it comes to addiction but most are scared to take that first step and that's the important one to rid your self of the things that hold you back in life, my writing this early in the morning is the way my mind can focus it's goes back to the early days when I didn't know what I would do with the rest of my life a therapy if you will to make the mind strong again and it has worked, while everyone else is in bed yet I'm becoming wide awake, and then they wonder how I can be so happy at the time when they wake up as they have to deal with wakeing up and getting motivated.

I can be grumpy sometimes ans if I get that out then my day goes pretty well many say don't talk too me when they first wake up and that's something I understand, because I don't want to talk to others either it's a peaceful time when my spirit can be at peace as I hear the beginning of the day the birds singing and the other animals as they play in the yard this time is precious and not to many people get to hear these things. It's supposed to be in the 60's today very warm for this time of year but we will take it, in Febuary the ground hog will show him self and I don't think he will see his shadow this year as it's been a mild winter and that usually means a hot summer a time when you don't want to leave the house except to go to the store to get viddles and other things for the month. It's says my people will be separated from the rest of the world meaning we will live apart for the ways of others that are still wondering in the world, Courtland is apart from the rest of the world it's like it has it's own survival system and it works here. There are many religious people here that love God so I know He has to feel it. It's Friday and the out side seams so peaceful I slept pretty good last night and today we will do the shopping for the month, what I like about this place is that even daycare takes their kids for a walk once or twice a day. I remember on mothers day one year that they brought us a basket that was made by the children and that made things special, even though there wasn't a women here.

It was the thought that counted knowing the little ones made them with their own two hands was awesome it's the little things that I think He wants me to see, more isn't always better we have to adjust to things before we can go to things that are bigger. Today I will get some more things done and I'm ok with that because if you take on more then you can handle then you take that chance of messing thingss up and I don't want that, all things in moderation as they say then it gets done right. Sortof like taking care of the two of them at first you see a mountain but later it turns into a mole hill once you fully understand it many things in life are that way even if we cant see them at the time, my time here will be long but to Him it's just a short time as His is different then ours time that is I still recall looking down on the world and I can't quite figure out why I saw that except to maybe make me see some of the foolish things that goes on down here. Mark's I cant figure out why there are so many of them in my life some have gone to be with the lord but the other ones stay there must have been about 8 of them in my life and they all had something to do with me being here today. Could this be a message of sourt for surely they come and they go but they are there just the same the one that is close and helped me through my triles was strong and did more for me and mom then most folks ever would and now he is ill I pray that he gets well in the lords time, he is a good person and deserves respect my friend Mark O'Brien' we had many good times together I remember one time we were out in the country drinking beer and his wife was making supper, we didn't want to go back yet so he called her and told her that I hit a bagger and his teeth went through the raditor she believed it and we went home later that night. Many people do foolish things when they drink and we were no exception there was many times when we went out into the country to drink I guess we thought it was safer there not being in the city, I remember it was always hot out side and us being poor we never did have Air-conditioning the closes we ever got to it was window Air and that usually didn't work worth a darn so we would drink to stay cool that's a joke' looking back if we would have saved that beer money we could of gotten the Air-conditioning and would have been very cool. Many lessons learned through life what to do and not to do but in the end we become a better person if we learn from them, my daughter text me to say thanks for the childrens cash to get them something I have never known what to get them so I put that on their mothers sholders and she can take care of it, the house next door went down in price from twenty five to twenty and to me that's still too much as I'm sure the back taxes weren't very much maybe a few hundred or so. It's the lot right next to mine and it would give me a bigger piece of land but not much biggeras for the inside of the house I havent a clue of what it looks like but it does have a deck on it and the garage is out back seperate from the house. The trees cover a big part of the land and even my yard also the thought of having someone move in there doesn't bother me but I hope they will be christan folks and not drug addicts they seam to tear everything up. There was one guy that didn't want anyone living near him so he bought a piece of property and put a couple of shed's on it and a big garden, that one way to keep people away from you.

In time I hope to get another piece of property but for now I need to get this home paid off everything in moderation and things will come true for you. This is something I believe and who knows what the future holds for any of us, many of us go through life with regrets but we seam to deal with them the best we can every time a regreat happened we either solve it or we let it follow us through life to destroy us later as for me those things are of the past and don't exist anymore there are still many places around here that I haven't seen yet towns even smaller the Courtland a bump in the road you might say but they have activities for the community that draws others from around the country or neighboring towns some of the towns are only 12 or so miles away, they are a little piece of what was once a bigger place that got run down after people moved on. Although bordom is common around these parts I at least find something to do to occupy my time it's Saturday and the morning's have been wonderful so quiet that you could hear a mouse if it was running in he field, just a peaceful sound of not hearing the machinary that's usually running through the night when they are putting the crops in the bin's across the way. The town is usually very busy even through the night but every now and then the sounds are gone to bring a kind of peace and that's what I like about living here it's so still out and everyone is still a sleep, many of the folks work at night to keep the companys here going and there must be two shifts at least. I remember loading train cars back in the day and it was very hard pulling that down spout from hole to hole faving to ware a mask so the dust wouldn't get into your lungs my job back then was for Kansas and Nebraska gas company which owned the Alfalfa company where we made Alfalfa pellets an meal to be loaded into hopper bottom train cars and trucks we also bagged them and loaded them on closed in trucks 1000 bags a truck each bag weighing 50 pounds and we would catch them coming down a shoot some times they would travel very fast.

And that would be a day when your back would get a work out, I got many people a job there but none lasted very long except for thhe strong which was me. And I complained from time to time when they would push us too hard I spent many years doing that job and that's why my back isn't so good anymore if you weren't strong you wouldn't last long and many didn't last the day back then it was kind of funny but now not so much with all the pain I go through spending your life trying to messure up is hard on a person doing the job's of 4 people takes it's toal on you later in life. All you hear is them complaining the bosses that is while they drive around in their trucks getting hammered on booze, this happened every day and finely I had to call it quits after he got drunk and fired me not once but three times and he didn't remember one of the times because he was so drunk later we took him to court and we won but I missed my job it doesn't do any good to be drunk on the job they had a lot of fires from the pellets getting so hot and it burned up the bins and they even has us go into the hot bins without resprators and that made many of us sick, Western Alfalfa doesn't exist any longer as they had to close the plant because of the fires so today many of those people are probable out of work, give all those years to something and get nothing in return in the court battle they paid us $1000.00 in back wages which they didn't want to give but it was their fault that we lost our jobs osha had closed them after the fourth fire saying it wasn't safe any longer. The things some would do for money many years before I worked at the plant I drove a cutter which cut the Alfalfa and put it into roles so it could be picked up by a swather, that job was fun except for the heat as they didn't have Air conditioning and boy it got hot out there in the middle of no where. Fun times for someone young, I always tried to hard to please other folks but today that doesn't really matter anymore as long as I take pride in what I do that shows me that I'm not washed up yet. It's another beautiful morning and you can see that there is a full moon out to the west so peaceful here in Courtland and if there is anyone awake they are at home, this time of morning has always been precious to me it could be that it takes me three hours to get awake or it's just that I like the alone time which I don't get during the day. But at times it makes me think about my life and how it turned out, my little brother has to have contact out side of here but for me that isn't that important you have to let others go on with their lives and not interfear with it, as I don't like mine interrupted for God has a plan for each day and I let things unfold the way they are ment to it's Sunday and while at work yesterday one of our members came in to build a quilt for a family member who is going to graduate from school this is also something you don't see in the big cities. She runs the library and rides a bike most of the time her and her husband both work for the county and they are nice people, I have met many nice people since I have come to live here.

And as far as I know they love it here also it's a place where things stand still or should I say move at a persons own pace and for me that is a good thing, no one to make you hurry when you are working and that's important to a person like me after living a life of being told what to do by others that run a company my later years will be good as good as I can make them. As for my little brothers future only God knows where that will lead but I wish him the best in what ever he desides to do, other people I know didn't make it into my future so that shows me that they weren't meant to and I have to learn to let them go. It was strange how I came to be here but God left no room for doubt it was like I was being pullled here by a force which I didn't understand but once here I fell in love with it or I fell more in love with God as he made things happen that wouldn't of happened other wise, many things are hard to explain as I haven't explored that part of me yet but I will in the coming years. Some search their whole lives and not find what I have found here like my sister she is more like a Gypsy moving from one place to another not finding where she wants to be, as for me I'm home and will stay for the rest of my time. They say God is working even when we are a sleep to make things happen in our lives and I believe this' as He has already made things happen, I think winter is over and it was very mild this year so I will try and get the house painter if the weather permits but still undecided which color would look good, maybe it will come too me sometime.

As the days go by things will start to change as the trees start to bloom once again and the neighbors flowers start to pop up once again we have no out side water source so maybe we might dig a place to put one in the middle of the yard who knows' I do have to get someone to clean out the gutters so the water flows freely down the spouts, that in it's self would be a blessing not to have it rott away the wood under the windows they did a patch job but don't know how long it will last. There is a lot of responsibility to keeping up a house and I know I will be able to do it as long as I keep saving for that rainey day, you would think the trees would keep then away but it doesn't seam to do it, when they cut down that tree by the road the whole inside was eaten away and it was like only a few inches was holding up the tree strange how that can happen there was like a grub worm that was eating it away. We also have many volinteer trees that come up each year even from the ones that were cut down strange how they still try to grow it's like they are saying were not dead yet, last summer we went by the lake and it looks like a nice one but we didn't go into it as we were pressed for time and had to get back, it would be a nice place to go for a family outing or to do some fishing but I haven't been into that in my later years. When I was young I loved it but now not so much as my writing keeps me pretty busy, my writing to me is like a job but one that I enjoy and they say if you enjoy your work you never work a day in your life. The publishers hasn't tried to get a hold of me lately as I didn't return their call, but that's ok I'm not quite ready yet and the story goes on I also find humor in some of the things I do without even knowing it until I read it later so funny. Through the years I didn't think I would be able to be a writer as a matter of fact it never entered my mind, back when my mother inlaw lived in the lodge in Colorado it was very cold and we all had to bunch up in one room to stay warm, the kitchen was the only place which had a stove which took wood to operate it. And none of us were country fied we got our water from a stream and froze our butt off each time we had to go there, the town was Allen's Park just up the road from Estes Park about 30 miles. Her aunt left it to her or she had to take care of it either one but it was an experience, just across the road was a gas station which was only open during the hunting season and that's where I had to take my truck to be worked on when we almost went over the cliff. We had left Kearney to take my brother Rick and his wife Diane to Estes Park to work at a lodge, me and Diane had been divorced for many years when she got together with Rick and they found a job up in the high country where they were going to live. So' they didn't have a way to get there and I felt sorry for them and me and Mark packed up their things and off we went. I had just bought the 1958 truck I had and it needed to take a road trip to see how it would do on gas and some how we ended up on Vale pass in Colorado which took us in the back way to Estes park Allen's park was first on this trip and we stopped by the lodge as it had been vacant for a while and we went and talked to the gas station owner we had a few beers and he was going to follow us to Estes, before we knew it darkness had fallen and the roads were very dangerous so we set out and some how we got seprater. I was going about 50 miles an hour when my back wheel passed me up bouncing off the hood of my truck, it was a miracle that it didn't end up in my face going that fast with sparks flying behind me. Mark was in the pasenger seat and pantic set in I thought he was going to crap him self and later he told me that he thought we were going to go over the cliff, on one side it was 300 feet to the bottom and the other one heck of a ditch.

I kept the wheel strate and we skided to a stop just inches from going over when it happened I felt a calmness come over me like God was telling me not to worry, for truly God was watching over us that night then the guys pulled up and asked what happened and we told them. We put out flairs so no one would hit the truck and went to look for the axel with no luck during the night, the station owner went and got his wrecker and towed my truck back to the station and I started to tear it down so I could fix it. The nearest place to get an axel was in Long Mont some miles away but money was tight and I had to have some wired to us Mark did that while I stayed working on the truck, then come to find out the guy had an old 1958 Ford truck in the back that had the parts we needed and I bought them from him later that next morning we went to look for the axel and found it but boy it was toast bent all to hell. You tell it got very hot by the blueing on it and there was no bearing it was gone like donkey Kong! It took two days to get it going again then we headed home saying a prayer that we would make it the body damage wasn't too bad and I fixed it later but first we had to drop off my brothers stuff in Estes that trip was one I wouldn't forget for a while but then as time went by it faded like all things that happened back in those days. The things we choose to forget are usually bad things but then later in life they return to tell the story the whole story of our lives which for some is interesting, in many ways it lets us see how God works in our lives even when we our selves don't see it how He watches over us as we walk a path that wasn't our original one.

I am strong' and the things that happened are but a bump in the road of life even though they didn't seam like it at the time, I have always been strong and the problems that happened were just that a problem that was over come with the help of God. My way of thinking is changing as time moves forward more confidence in my self has made things better then ever, today I talked with Dennis and his wife and they told me that Walter is doing good and has gained weight he now is at 136 pounds hich is good. He has always been a fighter and doesn't give up on life when he left he weighed 106 pounds I am so happy for him, Dennis has moved from his house to his fathers just south of the tracks as he passed away a while back I'm glad that they have found a place where they can be happy and they have a seven car garage my that's big his wife said that she would have Walter call one day so look for a 606 area code and answer it he told them that he could live with them and she said no, she doesn't want a dog in their new house and you cant blame them Doctors said Walt wouldn't make his 70th birthday but he did there mustba a lot of love there for him to keep going. It's Monday and boy it's cold the frost is thick on my windows and I bet it's not over the teens out side Thursday there will be a funeral so that will give me more work but I don't mind because I do it for the children really Wednesday the parents are supposed tocome to the church so they can figure out what to do about a teacher for the children. And if they don't show up then that will say it all, many times He seams to test us about different things and maybe he is testing them now for only God knows what he is doing this is another day in which we don't know the out come until it's over but He has a plan He always does and always will I have studied on many topics but not so much on teaching others about God I have always let them see His work through me, it's easy to write about such things but to teach I really couldn't say never been there or done that. Through my years I try to show a good example as when I learn something out of the bible I try to live it and that's how I think it's meant to be, not just read but to be lived and sometimesI fall short when I least expect it. Melchisedek was a great man but I don't know if my thery is right as no one has told me that it isn't, it's another full moon this morning that's two in one month very unusual I think but I guess it's what it is. The months are getting better and in time things will turn around for there is stil many things I don't understand or I think I don't understand it's like things should be figured out the teachings I mean going to school to be able to teach children about God, every religion has their own way of doing things and I have never learned any of their ways the bickering I mean and I still don't understand why they do that but it's there in black and white for all to see, I know my mind is full of knowledge a lot of it and maybe it can be taught to others just by reading about God's Grace I know I could teach children to know about the lord.

For if I can read and understand it then it can be taught my teaching has been from God not human means for he is the teacher of all teachers, many times if you can put your self at a childs level then they can learn a lot easier and grasp what is being taught the church is like a fire in a fire place if you take out one of the coals it will cool and not produce the heat until it's put back into the fire and then it gets hotter then ever when people don't go to church they are like that ember and the fire fades and that's something we don't want in my years I have never taught others but being I have age on my side they just might listen and I will try something if they let me, I sometimes find my self getting signs that make since at the moment but then later fade away these are things I can't expain and why they happen I'm not sure. It's like an epiphany something good from God but it's so out of the norm and it happens fast, when I first got a glimps of why He brought me here it was strange because nothing had happened like that before. There are many things that I haven't experienced befor but I have come to realize that dreams can come true if you believe in them enough, as for me mine have been made possible through Christ. It's warming up out side to be a nice day and I got some things done at work, I feel at home in the Church as I talk with God about many things and He listens to me. I went and talked with my friend about getting my riding lawn mower going before spring and he said he would get it taken care of, it's nice to have friends like that in your life so life can be made a little easier.

They have been there for me and for that I am grateful we make our own way in this life and friends are important, I didn't think I needed any before but I now realize how big a part they play in our lives not only to help us when we need a helping hand but to also have fun with in the good times. It's pretty warm out this afternoon you can even go out with just a shirt on, Tuesday and I just got up yesterday seamed to go by pretty quick and I played with Harley for some time.. My land' he is spoiled but I cant blame and one but my self they have all kinds of political crap on television so I didn't watch it much and today I have to work for a short time, my days are pretty routeen and I am used to that but my day doesn't start until I have my coffee it's my wake me up for the day and I like the taste of it. The quietness lets a person think about how the day will go yesterday morning I went and got paper towels for the church and got them stocked in the bathroom so we shouldn't need anymore for a year or so buying in bulk is the best way and I just had to pick them up from the station across the street it seams the town works together and that's a good thing when people come together. The guy at the station asked how I had been and I told him fine, I haven't been in there for quite some time for what happened a while back with my car in life we have to take the good with the other things that happens but we also have our own way of dealing with things. It was Randys birthday last Sunday andd even he forgot about it until yesterday and then he slept a part of the day, which was cool until the snoring started but I noticed that it didn't bother me as much as it once did and in time it wont bother me at all I hope! The morning is a time to pray for me and give thanks for what He has given me in this life. There was a lady that said there was a nice thing written in the paper about Courtland and the writer signed it by not putting their name, could this of been the stranger that came through a few months back? I believe it could have been he said he was on his way back to where he came from to help his daughter and I hope he was able to do so' for her addiction is a hard one to over come if you don't have support from loved ones. But I know her father loves her very much and wants to help in anyway possible, it was strange how he had been sober for 20 years for his journey started in 1992 the same year that mine started and we are from the same state Minnesota what would the odds be that we would meet on that cold day a few months ago for his journey took him here if only for a short time. We talked about addiction and how it can destroy everything you hold dear to you but we also talked about how God brought us through it by His grace and love for it never changes even in the bad times of our lives. It's his love that keeps me going in this world as I know it's always there, I consider the stranger my friend in Christ and I wish him the best in all that he does if you look at it we are all on a journey in this life and if we make the right choices then we will make it just fine. I love how you can read a virse from the bible and it will grow in your mind, reading is important even if it's just a small amount at first then later you won't be able to put it away this is something I have tried and it works but I'm not quite up to many virces yet that will take time, in my days on this earth I over think things that shouldn't be and that may hold me back at times. But in the end it's all made right it's Wednesday and not very cold out this morning so the day should be a nice one as we go to Concorida for a few hours to visit Wal-Mart.

Somethings you can't help but do and we have to go atleast once a month, it's a change from the stores in Belleville plus I want to get some paint to do the kitchen and make it nice. These are things that come over me sometimes the earge to paint when things get too boring, as time moves forward there are many things that I need to have done like the guttters cleaned out. And I can have someone from here do that for me one of the younger people that can climb a ladder, which I am unable to do these days. Reflection ALCOHOL'S CURSE! It saddens me that a place like Walgreens would carry a chemical that causes six times as many deaths as all other drugs combined. But then. I must have been wrong, as I thought they were out to save lives. They know the destruction that alcohol causes in lives, and yet they want to sell it. The decision shows me that the mighty buck is more important then human life. I can imagine the concern of our father in heaven as more of his children die from the curse. When will people wake up? Probably not until they lose someone close to them. It saddens me that it takes death before people can open their eyes, and then they blame everyone but themselves. Our bodies weren't meant to be destroyed by this curse. I wish I had the power to convince people that no good will come out of this. I have been as close to death as the human spirit and soul can be, and I'm telling you it's hard to learn how to live again. Most don't come back from where I was. I consider Kearney as my home town and I hate the thought of the cemeteries being filled just because of the mighty dollar. I will pray that the council will think twice on this matter but I'm not optimistic because it will help fill he jails with people who hurts others and that's why they built it.

In the days a head there will be many changes as I improve things here in my home and later I will get someone to wash the walls so I can put a coat of paint on them there is something about the smell of fresh paint and the lord knows it needs it at this time, maybe I can borrow a step ladder from a friend to get the job done. Older people are funny to me as they are set in their ways in life with many of them they have a routine like I do, and they don't like to change it, I guess it's a mind set like with the older people who have come to church all their lives. As for the future it will take care of it's self like it has done since the beginning of time, we went to Concorida and I messed up by leaving some of my food there at Wal-Mart kind of funny really but had to call them and have them send a gift care for the amount of the meat. how could this of happened? Not paying close enough attention I guess, it's too far to drive fifty miles to pick it up here I thought I was getting a deal on hamburger and ended up with nothing. We only go there once a month so we have to get the things we need when we are there, I had made a list but forgot it here at the house so I didn't know what to get. The car ran good going there and now it's about time for a tune-up, I have never put one on it so I think it's about time as my car is very important when you live out here it's the only way to get around. The wind has been strong today with gusts up to fifty miles an hour and at times I thought it was going to blow me off the road not much excitement for other folks but it is for me, fighting the wheel to keep it on the road is exciting to me. We don't go many places except for Belleville to the store or to the doctor when needed the dollar store is my favorite place as they are reasonable on their prices compaired to the other stores. We will be going there tomorrow and I want to stop by Tuxes it's a thrift store and we find many thing there to bring home and use plus the people there are real nice they remind me of a family run business sort of like a mom and pops place. Thursday and it got very cold through the night yesterday was getting very cold towards the end of thee day, and they were calling for sub zero weather this morning haven't been out yet' but I will find out later each day consist of what He brings and it's always different no two days are the same. Last Sunday they were talking about a funereal today but I haven't heard anything else about it and I haven't seen it on the croll line on television not even this morning, many times when I write for the paper people get a hold of me to tell me how proud they are of me and that helps Valerie text me the other day and said how true it is what I wrote. Sometimes when I see how a person treats their mate it makes me not to want to go there, and it make me think I'm not ready for a relationship at this time in my life, the way they yell at each other is what makes me think I am not ready for such a thing. Just that is something I never did like even in my past ones' where the world was distorted before it's not now but that kind friendship can be damaging to a person. Maybe I need to work on my self a little longer Ha! Many times we can say things we don't mean but that doesn't stop the hurt that the other persson feels and I don't like to do that. It's thirteen degrees out side my land' that is cold and it's not going to get much warmer through the day maybe in the twentys this might be our last blast of winter for the year or at least I hope it is then we will have the warm weather and that's alright with me.

It doesn't seam like we had much of a winter but I believe God will help out the farmers with rain and such for the crops and I pray that the year is better then last year, although we were not meant to be alone I sometimes wonder if he leaves us that way until we are ready for a relationship? I know for the longest I didn't think about my brother coming here and then one day it came to me as I listened to a song called brotherly love it was like God had planted a seed and it grew until I got him here strange how that happened but it happened just the same. With me I never know when He will plant that seed for something to happen but when He does it does grow and the thing comes to pass, I learned long ago not to question why he does something because He doesn't have to answer to me if He so chooses; So many things will happen this year and I will except them as they come my way, as for my brother he will be here for a short time and I'm alright with that as long as he is taken care of but I don't care for his choice of women as they have been there before. And they didn't get along back then but it's his life and he has to make his own mistakes and I will sit back and laugh, we all need people in different ways and he has his reasons for what he wants to do so I will support him as long as she isn't coming here. That is something I wont do that women drives me nut's.

And I don't need that crap in my life my peace of mind is important to me and no one is going to destroy it, I told him that he should get a place in

Belleville where they are near a store she is doing this for Gorge not my brother he is just a pon in her game. Through the windows of time he will learn the hard way as that's the only way he knows, may God help him! The movies we watch for entertainment slowely warps the mind and some say it's a world order trying to take over ha! We know satin runs things here and he does everything he can to turn us away from God and he does it in many ways. Even though it's colder today like everything else it will pass as the temp starts to rise and tomorrow will bring a new day and a new warmth that will increase as we move closer to spring then we will deal with the rain and tornados; there is only one good channel on television and that's the Hall-Mark channel which shows movies of values love and caring of family and the struggels they go through, but most of them have a happy ending as with other channels it's nothing but violence and kids don't really need to see such things. Many things that are important to one person isn't always or at all important to anyone else and for some reason they think it should be what's with that? The things I do in life are only important to me and I don't care about what others think but you have those who do some even build their lives around what other people think, and that's something I couldn't do the only one I have to answer to is God and forget the rest of the world. For His love is steadfast and never changes like humans, they change at the drop of a hat and it's seldom for the better some even go through life blaming other for their own problems because they don't know how to face them. When a problem arises it should be dealt with and then move on but some get stuck in that rut and their life goes down the toilet just because of one problem and that's a shame, when life brings you down just look up and see the wonders that God has created and it can brighten your day at least it does mine. I can solve most of my problems my self but others are not so blessed they fight with them and end up louseing the fight, this is a constent with people fighting addiction they lack self confidence and give up on what they are trying to do, what is strange to one person may not be that way to others as for me I am one of a kind and for that I am glad. I hink keeping family away is my way of dealing with things that they do, I couldn't live with any of them as we are too differen't my drive keeps me who I am apart from the destruction that is going on in the world my new home town is awesome watching the animals in my yard as they play and chase each other around. This is something you don't see in other towns for the animals are a fraid of them and they don't want to get hurt any more then any of us do but you have those who are ignorant and would kill them in a heart beat in big familys there are many that have different talents like maybe one can paint and the other isa machanic then you have the other professions I was a late bloomer and I didn't even know what my profession would be until later in life, way later' beyond the normal years and in a way it may have helped me being new to things which others learn in their teens. It gives me a child like quality along with the adult attitude in which I need to make it in the world, we went to town and got groceries and saw the doctor and everything is going fine I also made some chicken and rice which the guys just love so I wont have to cook for a few days.

I really like a break from time to time they said today was the coldest; day this year and I believe it. Gowing out in it just about froze my butt off and the wind made it twice as bad but we got the things done that we needed toand that's what mattered. It was enough of the cold for a while and I'm going to spent the next couple of day's inside where it's nice and toasty, they can have the outside for a while. Another cold morning on this Friday but there isn't any Ice on my car windows so it must not of gotten to darn cold, it's strange how somedays there will be ice and other days not so much. But I take all the good with the bad and I'm glad that the good out weighs the other, they tried my brother on some new meds and the first day went well and I hope it stays that way. Meds can be trick and it takes time for them to work properly with me it was a hit and miss as they tried different ones but finely after a year they got it right and things are going fine the mornings are so beautiful as it lets me connect with the father as I pray, for the time passed has allowed me to grow in many ways as I make plans for my seasons which are going to come there is a season for everything a time to sprout your wings and fly above the heavens as your spirit takes off. Somedays are really great and we laugh about everyday not at each other but with each other and that brings on an excitement that can't be measured, I finely got Oliver over publishers clearing house and not that's another thing he wont be wasting money on. It took some convincing that it was a scam but finely he caught on and is now over it, this summer I want to paint but I will hire someone from around here to keep the money here in Courtland that seams to work for us living here. I got some new car mat's for the car and got a bargen on them so now I will throw the old ones away I like for my things to look nice.

It's only four in the morning and little brother is up and I cant be around anyone at this time of the day it throws off my sanity or my day of having some kind of peace, I know a women that might proof read my book but Iwill have to ask her before hand she is a nice person who works for the paper and has her own golf cart to drive in the summer time. We always wave at each other and say hi' there are many that have these things to drive around and they save on gas, when I first got here I had never seen anyone drive one but they are a fad around here and some have a canopy on them incase of rain one day I might get one when I am older. Even kids drive them around youths I mean, not children as they are too young and those things go pretty good. My little brother what can I say he makes me laugh with his unique ways and I make him laugh the days seam more plesent when we laugh and it makes for a good day as we go through this life even Oliver get's in on the laughter from time to time and that's good for him. It's things like this that make each day special and with each day there is something new for argueing there isn't much of that and when we get mad we voice it and then we are quiet for a time to process it and see what caused it or what went wrong and then work on it. Every problem can be worked out as we go through this life and then things get better with time, today I have to work for a short time but then it's back to the house to do what ever. We like to play games as they seam to pass the time pretty well and we don't get so board with the routeen of everyday things, I feel things starting to happen but I cant quite put my finger on it much like all the other times I couldn't figure out what was going on but in time these things will unfold as they have done in the past some really strange things go on in my life and they cant all be explained away so I just let them happen and watch as some wonderful things happen. The things I think hard on sam to come to pass in time but I never know when that will happen, while cooking yesterday my brother came into the kitchen and he went to touch me and got the shock of his life my body seams to build up an electrical shock or stores electricity for some reason and it has done that for quite some time, and when I touch something it's like I get grounded and the shock is born. I know that we have an electrical current going through us but I don't think it was meant to extend to the out side of us, Tiny died one time and I touched him and he came back could this be healing power? Or is it just a freak occurrence and if it is how come so many times I know He works in the supernatural and maybe I do to sometimes, there are many things I cant explain away so I will just let them happen I do know when we as a church put hands on Normans wife she seamed to get better and it took a lot out of me as my legs wabbled from the power leaving my body it was like a transference of power to her and this is the way God works through us. Many believers are stronger then one and that's the way it's been since the beginning of time, even Walt seamed to get better after an encounter with me these things are strange but to me it's no surprise as God uses us for good things not bad mind you but good and he never gives us more then we can handle as He knows our limits.

My emotions were many back in the day when I arrived here but now they are of peace and tranquility as the years move forward, many search their whole lives and never find what I have found here a life around friends that will help if you need it. Even if it's from a simple lawnmower getting fixed to a warm heart from a careing person you just don't see that anymore not in this day and time, we cant choose our family but we can choose our frinds and we have to be careful when it comes to them. Some can put on an act to get you to like them and then they can change at the drop of a hat, to reveal something you would never want to see a monster that could destroy you. Addiction is like that with some it doesn't change the good but with others it turns them down right mean like Dr. Jackal and Mr. Hide two people living in the same body and this happens all the time there are recorded records of thousands of people who goes through this, it was nice today with no wind and I finely got my paint for the dining room now all I have to do is get the job done and I think little brother will help me. We went to the thrift store and they had some paintings of Stephen Kaye and the price of them was in the hundreds mine would make nine of the ones they had so I would guess that my painting is worth five to ten thousand dollars it's the biggest one I have ever seen of any painting. If my memory serves me right he passed away in 1989 so I know the price will only go up, they seam to do that when they die. I couldn't help but feel joy when I saw the price of those ones and they had the price guide to prove there worth,

I got mine many years ago from a place called Sally's I remember the day well as it was very cold I didn't pay very much for it at the time of course I don't think he was as well known back then, my opinion of him is that he was very talented and you cant mistake his signuture mine has the 1950's look to it by the frame and all theirs is but a fragment of mine in size, I could show them mine but I have to do it by pitcher because it's too big to move. Today we are going to paint some so the house will look better I tried it out last night and it looked wonderful even though it took a couple of coats but that was on bare metal where they put in the new vents my land' it looked so clean and smelt good semi gloss is easy to clean and that's why mom used to use it for some reason back then I wanted something that might be of value in the future and who knows I might have found such a thing it looks beautiful on my wall and will look even better when the painting is done such a lot of work but worth it. I have to vacuum the cealing before I paint as I don't want dust flying around and sticking to it, but first off I have to clean the church not much to do there but it will take some time to clean the toilets and mop the floors a janitors job is never done but I like the title janitor as I do work for God, I told the church about the buffer and stripped that I want but I don't know if they approved it as of yet we will see in the next few week's if it happened. But if all else fails I will get it on my own doesn't cost that much, little brother got excited about painting yesterday and we were making all kind's of plans to get it done. Even the paneling would look good with that paint on it being it's just about the same color a long time ago before I moved in, someone threw some soda with booze in it on the paneling and stained it pretty bad so that has too be cleaned before hand. And we will get it done I am a very clean person and like things to reflect that I still remember my sisters granddaughter saying grandma their house is so clean as it was like she expected it to be a mess with single men living here and ny sis told her that just the way uncle Roger is heis always clean. This next summer everyone should be in Awe when they see it and my work into the house, I noticed that Stephen only painted flowers for some reason but he was good at what he did in the art world as for the painting I don't think I would ever sell it as it's a part of me now I have had it so long everyone that sees it like's it and ask's if I painted it but I tell them no, that I'm not the painter many years ago mom had a painting about that size but I cant recall what the subject matter was. She too liked nice things in her home I guess I get my personality from her so if you think about it she does still live on in me. As I look at the happy picture of her and Oliver that resides just above my hear right now it brings back times when things were happy she was only about five foot two but was a very warm person and would help a stranger in need as I sometimes do with people I don't know this is God's way of doing things as He helps us his children' for we! Are not strangers to God as He knows each and everyone of us and knows what we are able to do, He has brought me so far but I had a lot to do with it also as I am strong and I am his creation these bodies are made strong to help us last to learn the lessons of life. My land' the people in the old days went through many troubles to make it to the promas land and even though it took 40 years they survived and clamed what was their's to live for many generations and some are still here today their ansesters anyway, in the year a head I will do manythings that will change me and God will also do some changing in me and this I welcome.

No one is up at this time of morning except me of course and I can hear everything, it's so quiet you could hear a pin drop. But that's the way I like it no one messing with my mind just peace, how do people do it? With having big families. Very young I guess, I cant amagine kids running around screaming and raising hell that in it's self would drive me nuts. But maybe not! I seam pretty calm around them when I go to see the grandchildren but then I don't have to be around them every minute of every day, if I had to my patients wouldn't last long but I love them so much. In my younger days all I would do is work and sleep except for the times when the booze was more important it's strange how you grow past those stages and grow up if they don't destroy you first, there are many valleys and peacks in life and I have made it through them all at this time in my life I'm on a peack looking into the valley and seeing all the people. Will they make the right choices or will the valley fill up with water and drown them out? This is a question that only God knows the answer to I'm just a watcher watching over them in this great big world watching with questionss will they or wont they you decide! In my travels I have been to many cities and didn't really care for any of them from sun up to sun down people hurring to get to a place they cant seam to find.

My self peace is where you can be you, the one that the lord created you to be the influences of this world can and will destroy you without you getting to know your self, and many end up that way they think they have plenty of time to get rich and then find them selves and it just doesn't work that way. My journey has taken half a life time and things are just starting to come together, the Lord works in mysterious ways and what was back then might not be today change is what I'm talking about and we all have the ability to do it. The day went great as we traveled into town for supplies to get the dining room started and now it's half done, just the look of it is great with the semi gloss paint which later will be easy to clean. I also got a thank you card from the church and they would like me to stay for coffee after service on Sundays I haven't been doing it lately and they seam to miss me so tomorrow I will stay, they said they really enjoy my company as I do theirs they treat me more like family then my own and that is something special in it's self. And I don't want them to be disappointed by my not staying, I believe I have sparked something here and it's a good thing with each passing day things get brighter. After getting done for the day my back hurts but it will pass as day turns to night and I get some sleep, for tomorrow comes early for me each day as I am up before the chickens. I didn't get much help today but that's ok I'm used to doing things on my own and when I do it! I know it's done right the walls shine like a new penny and they will be easy to keep up as we go into this year, as for the weather it was warm and we didn't have to run the heat that much which is a good thing less cost less money Ha! I'm not sure how warn it's going to be in the next day or so I guess we will just have to wait and see. I hope the cold weather is done for this season but that's also something we will have to see about, I showed a pitcher of my painting to the guy at the thrift store so he could see how big it is and his is smaller in size. Oliver has been doing good lately but I had to give him some antibiotics to take for a couple of days and then he will really be good, the Sun is starting to go down so it will start to get a little colder but I don't think it will get too cold I hope. Early in the morning I will open the church and turn on the heat so it's toasty for the elderly people, I enjoyed today dispite how my back hurts and I know that He will take care of it by morning good night and God bless. Through the noise of little scampering paws I could hear Tobey coming as I threw out the peanuts in the back yard, he always seams to come when I do this and I'm sure other animals that enjoy them also his girlfriend must of got hit on the road the week passed as I had never seen them not together. There are many of these squirrles and sometimes they are in groups just playing around chaseing each other, I haven't seen the rabbits very much this year but they will come when the clover and grass is green. When Harley tries to chase them they just look at him like he is no bother and go on with their eating but let him get too close and they take off like a jet, with most people they pay no never mind to the animals but with me I like to watch them as they are His creation also. I'm always amazed at how squirrels can fly from one tree to the other like they have wings, the doves are something special a simble of he goodness which resides here in Courtland they were even good when they mentioned them in the bible. My arm was sore this morning from laying on it so I had to get it back in it's place and now it doesn't hurt so much, it's Sunday and I will go to service this morning as I always do and have coffee the things which have been happening are great but I have to take a break from the painting for a couple of days so my bones can get back to normal.

I was amazed to get the card from the church and it always makes me happy that they too are happy I try to fill the church with the joy of singing and it brings me joy also to not have to worry about being resized about my singing, my self I feel my voice is very special one that the lord created for all people to hear and in time they will hear it, getting nervious with 70 people just imaging with twenty thousand that would be a sight but with the lord by my side all things are possible. It's quiet out side nothing moving and I mean nothing not even air Ha! The pictures came out good of our gathering last year when my sis came to see us and I will keep them for ever I miss her and her granddaughter we had fun. Many years ago we had a falling out but I believe the fence is mended now you cant go through life with anger in your heart it's just not meant to be that way only joy. And then the excitement of seeing one another again after a year has passed, even if she moves I hope she will come to visit because other wise I would miss that time together. We live just far enough apart that it's comfortable and we don't get into each other's hair, my sister inlaw Mary texts once in a while and says that she loves me and that's good enough from them they are a people who stay to them selves like I do in many ways too much family can spoil the whole basket of Apples too many thing going on at once, I can solve one problem at a time but not many at once that's just not me with me I have to focus on what I'm doing in life to make me better.

It's going to be a nice day and I will enjoy it you cant tell what's going to happen from one day to the next you just have to have faith that He will take care of things, but Ido know even in the worst of days we seam to get through them God's goodness is everywhere and when we are weak He can make us strong even stronger then ever. He knows when we hurt and he will heal all things in time for He is the Alpha and the Omega the first and the last, I should of bought that couch and love seat from the hrift store but I didn't know he had a trailor to haul them O well next time' I will know this when I need to buy something from him it's a nice trailor and even says the name of the thrift store on it, he said he doesn't like to use it because of the price of gas and you cant blame him there it's almost four dollars a gallon. It's strange how some countries have it at under a dollar and others they bleed dry because they know they can get away with it. I believe the president has a lot to do with that and he lines his pockets, there is plenty of fuel here in the United States but they use the excuse that we would run out. What a crock of shit' sometimes when I write it's like there is a wall that I cant penatrate so my mind can explore other avenues the ones which are hidden in the back corners of my mind, then other times it's wide open and I can type just as fast as I can think Ha! I have to open the church at five thirty but that wont be for a little while I like to say good things about people as it brings out a special something that inside of us all a kind word has a lot of power but also it's a two edge sward and can cut like a knife and hurting people is not in my person, but there are times when I wish there was something more I could do I sort of feel like the care taker of damaged people sometimes but I know there is no way I can help everyone so I do the best I can in this world. Today I stayed for coffee after church and we sang happy birthday to John Blackburn he is a friend and I didn't know he was 83 years young if I had to guess I would of said he was only in his mid 70's , but I would have been wrong a long life time seams common around here with people living into their 80's and 90's. I told him that I hope I look that good at his age but only time will tell that I would have to live another 30 years to be even close to that I also thanked pastor Kathy for the thank you card and she asked if I was staying for coffee, from now on I think I will stay for a cup or two and have a couple of cookies tomorrow is Martin louther King's day so everything is closed. An extra day for the working people to relax before they have to return back to work. Change is enevidable I remember back when they didn't have a holiday for a person that was black but this person made such a difference in the movement that it was just a matter of time Martin was a good man. My thoughts on out present president was that he might do a better job but I was wrong along with over half of those that voted, we make mistakes in life so later we can correct them but I haven't seen one person I would want to run the country. I have to admit that I think a poor person would do a better job but that will never happen when the rich run the country, Bush did a crappy job as he was a puppey on a string enough about that never did like politics! It's another nice morning and it's Monday so I have some work to do today after service I went and locked up the church and did a few thingss around there but today I have to vacuum and that will take an hour or two depending on what I have gto do.

The love of God follows us no matter where we go and it doesn't matter if it's down the street or around the world for I know that He is forever in my heart, John was excited because his wife make him a German cake for his birthday everyone sing to him and he was like a kid and I think that's awesome I think some are still trying to figure me out but that's ok' I have the hand of God by my side ans he blows in my direction. I don't think any of them have ever seen me angry and that's because I don't get that way too oftend but when I do it's short lived as I ash for God to take it away, and even today I'm still learning, many times it's over foolish things that others cant help sometimes. Many of the old don't look their age but that's because they seam to live right, in the next month or so the grass will be turning green and it will be time to mow the lawn but not before I get my painting done yesterday I just relaxed so my back would get better and I can start painting again the shower I took really helped yesterday morning all that hot water beating down on my back relaxed the mussels. What a morning' it's awesome and everyone is a sleep, I am brought back in time to relive my friend Michal he was a young pup just in his 20's but he has lived a life of addiction his mom died because of it and then later his father, being brought up in a dysfunctional family took it's toal on them all after his fathers death he didn't want to live any longer and he went out and bought a case of wisky and that ended his life.

We just about grew up together and my family lived with his for a while in their garage that they fixed up for my parents, and the alcohol caused many problems between the two familys. Victor Dole was an Indian and a big man who didn't like anyone touching his stuff, I remember him because he always had money sitting on his head board and little Michal would sneek into his room and take it. Victor talked with a deep voice and when he was mad he let you know it he lived with Jerry and Leda for years and they seamed to get along but my family being there made things different, life was hard back then and we didn't have a home funny how that works no money for a house but plenty for alcohol that's part of the curse as it makes a person it's best friend to later destroy them. Many good people fall into that addiction but seldom do they recover from it there seams to be a link between the curse and them that fall into it and with some it gives them what they want like one might need courage and another strangth, but what they don't know is that this only last for a short time while they are under the influence. And then it's gone until the next time that they become high false courage isn't any good as it comes and goes like the wind never being stable some people say they found God which is wrong God finds you not the other way around. Some even kill and say that they heard God tell them to do so, this is a deranged mind with no direction I have never understood how a person can knowingly take anothers life these people are really messed up. The day started by doing some work at the church then followed by coming home and watching television and then by making Oliver some lunch, he is really into sweet potatoes; lately and things like this trend will go on until he gets sick of them in a few months down the road I get the earge to start to paint again but I don't want me back go give me more crap so I'm putting it off until tomorrow to give it time to heal, my spirit's have been up today and at time's I feel real good I wish it could be that way all the time but as we know that isn't possible. I haven't heard from family back in Kearney for quite some time and even Randy hasn't been talking to any of them which is a shock because usually he is on the phone every night. Tuesday we finely got some snow I was shocked when I opened the door for Harley to go out this is really a blessing for the farmer but boy it's going to be cold taking out the garbage but hey that's life, back when it should of snowed He held it off to get the windows in so now is a good time for it, but I didn't expect it not this morning I will have to make sure I put my long johns on because the cold goes right through my jeans. My land' just like Nebraska you cant tell what the weather is going to be like, life in the bible belt is like life in the heart land not much difference except for here you find peace but you have to feel at peace before you can have any of it and most are not that way many years ago I think I was looking for it but didn't really find it until I came here. Many of the preachers that televise all over the world say that God will bring the right people into your life that will bless you and He sure has done that in my life, there is something people like about me as it said in the thank you card that I recived last week they like my presents and that really makes you feel good inside even though I didn't expect the snow I'm glad that it is now here.

Through the sands of time we will all become better and for that I am glad and as I pray each morning I pray for them all especially the people here in my new home town. When life get's me down sometimes I talk with God about my problems but I should do it more oftend, when He finds favor in you it doesn't leave it just gets better and stronger as we go through life for He is surely my father. In the day's before I moved here He was trying to tell me that my time in that place was over and I think that's why I had so much dead time on my hands times when things weren't productive so I had to go and ccome here. I talked with Kathy about it and she said He does that with certain people, for the blessings have been many in my life and I never know when they will come again it could even be today. The doctor is going to see us both next month so we wont have to travel so many times to his office and that will save gas during the month, I don't seam to hear the wind blow during the night or even during the day since the windows have been put in and that is great it shows that replacing them did halp a lot. Before it was like the wind just blew through them and it was cold in here but not now, as I have said many times before things are great. I didn't see any snow falling so maybe it's done for the time being it didn't even get on my windows on the car so that's good now I don't have to scrape them. THE READING ROOM' an awesome movie about helping others through the hardship of life the process of learning, and how God will come through even in the worst of times. Giving chances to those that would other wise not get them, and then there are those who want to destroy everything because they are full of hate.

For some reason they don't have any goodness in them or it hasn't been brought to the surface they seam to want everyone to be like them and if this was to happen then the world would not be a good place. Some were brought up in gangs and this is reflected by their behavior here there was one man that cared and it lead to many unfortunate people going to collage or school, sometimes one person can make a difference my reading skills are pretty good but not where I would like it to be. The pastor of a church helped when the darkness came over the reading room after the fire but they pulled together and got it up and running again in time the person was caught and sent to prison, he changed many lives young and old and brought happiness to the reading room. I don't see enough of these movies and I wish there were more of them like it but other channnels only show destruction and violence, the Hall-Mark channel is the greatest channel I have seen on the tube as they run movies that touch the heart. It wasn't too bad out as I did my work but it makes you grateful for the warmth of a home a place that becomes a part of you, with our little animals like Harley for they too need love as we do, and he always wants too be around me as I play with him he can make me happy when Iam sad and he understands me when I'm blue just being around him can give you mixed feelings in the same way you get them with others that are around you. I didn't know that I was missed until I got the card and that shows the warmth that is in their hearts, a warmth of a family that doesn't get felt very oftend but when it happens it's so good and I can live with that kind of caring. The loneliness seams to fade with time and what was once a lonely existence has now become a life of purpose shoveling snow was fun this morning and it didn't bother my back so I'm good to finish painting and when I'm done with the dininng-room then I will start else where the inside of my home is my castle and I will make it beautiful so it will match the out side , work' it seams to take on a new meaning these days and I like that. It even makes me feel better at times I just got Oliver up this morning he slept in a few minutes and I always watch over him he has been my buddy and friend for so long that I cant count the years, the world wouldn't be the same without him and boy I would be beside my self. My world exist with him in it and the adjustment would be hard if something ever happened it seams like yesterday when things weren't so good but today I have learned to love life especially with people who care. Wednesday we spent the day getting the dinning room finished and boy it looks nice, just like new and then we got my paintings up after cleaning them. While at the church yesterday I recived a note saying that Karhy turned on the heat and opened the doors for Wednesday school so I left things the way they were, when you come into my home the first thing you notice is the frest paint and the smell of flowers which the plug-ins provide I change them once a month so the smell is constent and who doesn't like the smell of flowers, this month is going fast as today is already the 18th of January my efforts are paying off as the months click by and even my home is looking better God has had a hand in my making it here and I will give praise to Him for it was He that brought me here. They say and it says in the bible that He uses others to bring some favor and this has to be the case with me I haven't had many good things happen but theones that did happen are pretty great.

And today is a reflection of that the card is something I will always cherish as I move forward into the future for my friends will be friends for ever, even though I don't know some of their names yet I seam to stand out and they seam to like the person I have become. The one that the father created the one who stayed hid for so many years, his coming out is like a flower which has taken on new life and it grows slowely to see the things he has missed not being born before. Some might not understand that part, but I do. And that's what counts at this stage I am diferent from most as I feel with my heart it's not always with the mind and if I think someone needs a hug then I give it, it's just a part of who I am and I think maybe I have always been that way it just stopped when the addiction started strange thing addiction it stop's things from coming full circle and you are left in limbo not knowing what will happen so many things could have gone wrong while I was under the curse but it didn't and that shows me that God was there to bring me back when He found me that day. Some people wont ever understand what happened to me but I know and that changed this life that is writing this today, I never told the whole story to family because they too couldn't understand it but what I did reveal to them changed some of their lives too and that's a good thing. I think Tonya was impacted the most and then her mother my sister who also found her way back it's a long hard croll getting your life back but in time it can be done.

The walls look like glass in a way and then later I will move forward to the kitchen the arch way is finished but I have to do the cabnets and such, my land' how time flies it's already five in the morning and the boys will be up in an hour or two so they can start another day here in our lovely town as each day brings something new nothing is repeated in this world so you have to grab on with both hands and hope for the best, I wrote a letter to the paper so we will see what comes of it but they don't seam to like to publish about addiction and I don't understand why that is when so many could be saved. ADDICTION'S LIFETIME CURSE. Growing up and becoming addicted by the age of 11 is hard to overcome, especially when you never experienced life like other children. Anyone who allows a child to go through that will destroy their child's life. Maybe they don't realize at the time what they are doing, or maybe they do and just don't give a crap about their child. Imagine not knowing what the real world is about because someone fed you booze as a child. Some think it's cute. I believe that is because it doesn't affect them because they usually are already alcoholics or drug addicts. You can ask an alcoholic or drug addict and they will tell you that those two things come first. One day I saw a little boy in the store with his parents. He asked them for an ice cream.they replied. "We can't afford it right now." It made me sad, because the parents had their cart loaded with four cases of beer. Buying the beer was more important then to see a smile on their childs face. The child walked away looking disappointed. I couldn't help myself. I gave him a dollar. The look he gave me was priceless, and I will always remember it because happiness should come before sorrow. It's little things like this that children remember. Maybe it was the disappointments I experienced when I was young that made me give the boy money. And if it made his day a little brighter then why not, in a way I think it made me reflect to when I was a little boy and the other kids got ice-cream. Some of the things we learn as a child stay with us but then with the bad things not so much. Thursday' that memory of playing in the gravel at the church as a child must have been the connection that I held on to that kept the connection with God because I always knew He existed but through that part of my life we or I was disconnected. I would have to say I was the lost soul searching for something bigger then my self in this world of confusion then when those two things came into my life they seamed to fill the void that was there, here I took addiction or thought addiction was that part which was bigger then me and He let me find out different on my own. I cant blame anyone for my life at least from the time I became of age and even then I didn't have to follow others but that time is gone and now He is my life. I think in a way it was like He went fishing and I was the bait and the devil was the fish, he almost got me but then just at the right time the lord reeled me back in to be with Him, I didn't find God He found me on that day in the light when He said it was time to travel a new path a path that I would later learn was one of love and understanding. He had always loved me it was just that I couldn't see it through those blind eyes, in a way we are all blind until He opens our eyes a lot of people are born with God in their lives and I was too until I was taken away from it. They grew up to love the lord because it was in the blood of their parents and their parents and addiction can be the same way because we have to be taught and what we are taught comes from our parents, if we grow up with addiction it will carry on to the child there is something about it that kids cling to in the same way they cling to God if they are taught the way.

I remember through the years not thinking about God because the addiction came first that fight to stay some what normal, or what I thought was normal. I could do like a lot of people and blame God for what happened but He had nothing to do with it freedom of choice comess in here and that is a wright He gave us all. The power I felt was strong and it let me know that I was not alone even though at the time I felt like I was at the time, a guy I know is going to be with the lord and he had lost his sister a while back from the same thing cancer' it's a disease that destroys many lives every year and it's bad. That will be two friends that have gone from this earth and there will be many more. You don't really know what to say to them as you loose the words to comfort them, they would like me to go down there but I'm not sure what I would say in this case. As the years pass my love for God gets stronger but when it comes to a chrises I'm at a loss for words, when I let Harley out this morning it felt warm out side compaired to the last few days and today I will go and clean up after the kids bible school from yesterday. I'm still waiting on the buffer for the church and it will probable take a couple of weeks to get here, many times when we don't know what to do in certain situations we can ask God for guidance and He will tell us the right thing to do. The snow is still on the ground but it's leaving a little bit at a time soon to be gone and nourish the ground for the crops, I pray they have a good year in 2012 and make the years to come even better for the light of the lord is on this place and He has done some great things.

When life gets me down I look up to the lord and my day seams to get better, this is His goodness that is in us all when bad things happen we have to focus on the good things to take our minds away from that dark place and bring us peace. My land' all is good here in my new home town but there is movement for which I don't understand, as sometimes I see a couple have a loving moment it makes me want to have that also but through the years it hasn't happened for me. That time when they are the only ones in existence that moment of true love, I have to feel something before I can write about it and to this day that part of life has Stacyded me. The wakeing up to someone you cant live without seams so far away and yet I want it, but not the mistakes that comes with it I know you cant have one without the other so my search continues until I find her, someone who is happy with life and happy to be here could she be in this town? I guess He knows the answer to that one in the mean time I will work and keep doing what I do best. Most women want a home and that I have I will never have to wonder from my home as it's a place that God picked out for me and it's becoming better and better as time passes, sometimes that lack of love is missed or the human connection is but I have to find it. Many writers refer to my writings when they write something and include my name this in it's self tells me that I am on the right track but I have some doubts at times and that isn't good you should never doubt your self because of a lack of something for if you are truly in God's favor you lack nothing. The steps to being pulished is uncertain for trust is a hard thing to give someone and you don't want to get burnt; I will take steps to see what comes of this two thirds of the month is about over and next month is leap year for those who have a birthday once every four years, could you amagine getting four years older at a time not me. The rich seam to do away with their children if they are an embarrassment to their family name, and this is no joke money can make people do some stupid things you see it with people who have billions of dollars mostly though it happens with old money and they are the ones who think they are above the law of the land. That the law doesn't pertain to them as they are a society in them selves and they look upon us as burdens, people kill others everyday and it's not for a large amount of money in the drug world dealers will take a life if you owe them and cant pay, or they turn you into a mule to transport the drugs for them I have seen many people put in this situation and they always paid a big price for it. Even today they find travelers transporting drugs across state lines and they do many years in prison for it after the lawyers drain them dry before they go, sad existence and it follows you through your life the best advice I could give someone is too stay away from it because it will destroy you're life as you know it. I remember traveling across part of the United States as a teenager hitch hiking and boy it was a trip me and two women going from L. A. back to Nebraska in the last stage of it we road in the back of a truck with a trailor it was a very cold time of year but we made it when we left Ventura it was raining and when we got to Wyoming the snow was falling. I remember it was freezing out and we had to stand in it too get a ride but once we got one they brought us right too my door in Kearney, it took two and a half days too get twelve hundred miles but it was an experience that I would never forget.

I was in love with a girl whose brother tried his best to keep us apart, I was about seventeen at the time and she was the love of my life so I thought. We never did get to be together because of her brother as he followed us around everywhere we went, when we went to Arizona she wanted to come with us and he said no he acted like a child in many ways like he needed all of out attentrion and in time I got to hate some of the things he did. A very jellous man when he didn't get his own way with a women they seamed to not find him attractive or they just didn't like him, he tried to turn our friends against us but it didn't work and then in time he was gone like a wind that blew for a few minutes. The day has been a nice one except for the cold it seams to cut through you like a knife and you cant stay out in it for very long, Just walking to the mail box froze my butt off the weather has been strange how it can go from in the sixtys down to teen's I sure will be glad when spring get's here but then we will deal with the rain as it becaome the raining season, we went into town for some things and then back if you're car was to break down you wouldn't last long out in the cold. Tomorrow I will do a little more work at the church and then it will be set for service on Sunday, many times my mood changes and oftend it's better then it was earlier I would love nothing better then to be in that good mood all the time but it cant be that way in this life for every experience brings something new wither it's good or bad.

I have been thinking about me friend lately and miss not seeing her in the early mornings when she goes out side for a smoke in her car, I wish I knew if she was single so I could get to know her better. As it is she makes me laugh when ever I see her and that's something that doesn't happen very oftend O sure me and my brother laugh but it's not the same as with her. I think she moved from here but I'm not sure she might have moved across town, the winter or atleast today is cold very cold yesterday it was in the teens and this morning it must be in the singel digits. The cause and effects of addiction are not feeling equal to or less then others around you and sometimes you draw a false image of someone when they are high, and you try to be just like them at the time your mind doesn't know that they are high and they are just like you but usually by then it's too late when you're a child you cant see the person for who they are, all you know is that they have more fun then you don't as a child all you really notice is that they are happy and you want to be the same way. When my parents had a party they seamed to have fun but it was hiding the real problem that their lives had become out of control, many times I stayed up with mom to sing on her lap while my sister had a slumber party mom drank and sang to try and hide the pain she was feeling but being a little boy I couldn't see the pain just the having fun part because we would laugh and sing together Herb would buy her any thing to make her happy even a car one time because she liked the color and the radio worked it was a green color but he told her that he would have to do a lot of work to it, but she wanted it anyway and then on the way home it blew up so they had to have it towed after getting it towed he started to work on it and in 24 hours he had it running he tweeked the motor and boy was it fast, after putting in everything new and over sizing the pistons the car ran like new even better. When he was done he told her to take it for a spin around the block and that spin was the last time she drive it, she came back and said it was too fast for her so they ended up giving it to my brother Rod who was just turning sixteen and he put it to good use. He raced it many times beating newer cars but then the transmission coughed out fluid because it was only a two speed power glide and he caught the motor on fire and a milk man came by and put out the fire with milk. That was the last time he drove it and dad sold it, the tipical teenager. Later after dad lost his job we moved to different places and they drank more as the years passed and us kids started to drink or I did the numeness seamed to make everything that was painful go away, when I would try to go to school I was so far behind that the other kids would laugh and then it was back home where I drank to take that pain away and I more or less stayed at home and drank so I wouldn't have to face them. In the years to come we lived many places and in many towns but we lacked something a sturdy foundation to grow up in, we weren't the only ones living like this there was others but they had that place they could call home and they went camping for fun. As with us it was a way of life when we would stay our two weeks they would have us leave for a week or so and then come back mom said it let us see the country but I never did want that, the friends would come and go like the wind to never be seen again even though they said they would come back hey never did the houses we did live in were substandard so we could afford the rent and then mom would fix them up and the land lord would raise the rent.

And we would have to move again or go camping, even though we saw a lot of California' we didn't get the schooling we needed, the young people would race through the camp grounds with their cars and have no respect for the people staying there and this lead to many arrests for drunk driving for them even back then that was a problem. I remember running away once because our baby sitter was so mean and I made it across the field and came back because I was hungry, it was shortly after that when my parents lost control of their car and ran into a tree on a winding corner and it almost killed them. The story was that they went to their favorite bar and desided not to stay and headed back home when they both blacked out at the same time, they had one drink and someone spiked it there was nothing left of the car and it was only by the grace of God that they lived looking back this was the second blessing God gave them the first being with my brothrs getting hit but when your life is tangled up with addiction you don't see these miracles that are preformed you only see the disaster part which shuts out all other things like the miracle which took place. Why is it so easy to see the bad then the good? Must just be the way life is with most people. My land' it's only four degrees out side freezing cold, on this Friday' another week is about gone but the up side is that a new one is about to start and many new things will take place, if all goes well maybe my mower will get fixed by the middle of Febuary I cant mow the lawn with the push mower this year as it's too hard on this body.

Many people will have a nice summer going to the lake and camping and that brings back a memory about the people living in tents in California where they lost their homes to the government great place right! I wouldn't go back there for anything I like it here and will stay here. My thoughts on what others think about me I have none I am just who I am and that's just the way it is, I go through life not bothering others and they don't bother me it's a thing that works out fine. In my years to come I cant say what will transspire in my life but I know it will be good things, for the goodness that you do is always a thing that will follow you I was surprised by how they excepted me here as the old women had been here for many years and said they looked upon her as an out sider. I haven't gotten that feeling here but I suppose it could be something some feel, to me I'm just a christen in the search of love and understanding of other christens and isn't this the way it's supposed to be our fathers children loving each other until it's our time to join Him in that place He has made for us? Through this life many get lost but with God's love and understanding He finds us and brings us back to the path we were meant to be on. The path we were born to follow I don't know why my days start so early but in a way it lets me deal with things better, they used to have a saying early to bed and early to rise but I think they created that one back in the 1800's. Even though I'm an early riser it doesn't seam to take long for my mind to become clear and that's what it took back in the days when I took my life back the drugs back then kept me awake all night and iut needed to heal to the lord would wake me up. If this wouldn't of happened then I might of stayed damaged with no hope of recovery I knew I would have to do this on my own because at that time there wasn't much help out there for someone like me and Oliver would have died a long time ago, he needs a special kind of love and the job has been mine from the day my mom died. Through the mistakes I have made I found out a good thing and that is a person is only as good as his word because really that is the only things we really own, what we have in life is given by the father in one form or another it is He that makes all things possible and He uses others to get it for us. I never understood this before but now I have come to reaalize this fact in life, for surely he doesn't let the animals go with out so why wouldn't he make sure we don't go without and things come to us in many different ways like food being sent when we need it and friends which help us in our time of need O sure the favor has to be given back but it allows us to become closer to others that want to be our friends. When I quit going to coffee and treats there was a void left and they felt it so they sent me that card saying it this tells me that I am important to them and I have never felt that anywhere else, not in Kearney or any other place I have gone. The careing of people has seamed to be important to me for some reason and it's because I need to be a part of something like the church. The thing that stays with me is the lonelyness that I once felt so long ago going through addiction that is something which haunts me to this day, where was the people who said they cared for surely they never came around but to get something for their own needs and then it was back to their own world, as I fought for my life so alone and yet not so much when Oliver was there I guess I needed him as much as he needed me.

Through the years we made it and he is still going after they said he wouldn't make it eighty two years he has been on this earth, he was blessed by not having any addictions except to work my buddy' we have laughed and we have cried but most of all we stayed buddies through it all. The greatest friend I have ever had my buddy, I have seen him fight from the doors of death back to this world and I know his healtth when he is getting sick so I take care of that also. He has some debts but they can be taken care of it's so much to do for one person but I have done it well over the years, a partnership that will go on for many years to come only the lord knows when things will change so I don't worry about that too much. My dreams have come true in the last twenty years but it didn't happen until I moved here and God spoke to me again this will be your home and it is, through the tears and fears I made it no one else has much in my family but I have a home with friends who could ask for more? Life has been a roller coaster with it's up's and downs but I believe we all have to go through that in life from the tears to the happy times which life brings I have become closer to God then ever and will grow in spirit until it's my time what will the future hold no one can say but I wish the war's would stop they say they fight for peace but that's a crock they are trying to change the world and they cant even feed all of their own people.

I cant know what God's plan is but I know it will be for the better only when you can find peace in your self can you hope to find peace in the world. Most of television is destruction except for the Hall-Mark channel and they show good movies ones that can make your day go very well, a sight of hope in a world that is destroying it's self is a great thing and they bring it to the table. It's Saturday and the weekend has started some may even be up now having to get ready for work for with most people they have a six day week and with some even seven but my work is never done going through my mind and discovering new things that I didn't even know was there. Each morning brings something new to discover. In the beginning of alcohol and drug addiction people do it because it's fun but if they only knew the price they would pay later when they needed it to be normal or they thought, without it I never did feel normal because it had been a part of my life since childhood and when I didn't have it then the withdraws were too hard to go through when all it took was the tip of your hand to get over it. All people going through this shake in the first stage of recovery but then in time that subsides if the nerve damage isn't too offely bad, my self I thought I would always shake but after a while it went away like the addiction. In the beginning with just the alcohol many times I found my self in places and didn't know how I got there and this scared me but not enough to quit, I would then go home and stay there for weeks on end but even then I still drank. I was able to maintain enough to go to work each day but I took a very big chance when I had to have a drink before work using mouth wash to kill the smell and breath mints to keep it covered up, my life was out of control but being addicted I didn't see it and looking back my life had been out of control since childhood I started driving at the age of ten years little did I know that within four years I would see my brother go to facility for criminals a detention center and there he would stay until he escaped and tried to come with me and my dad to Nebraska, the detention center was up in the mountains of California in the middle of no where but he found his way to Ventura where we were getting ready to leave. He tried to hide under the seat which was folded down in the station wagon butt the law found him and returned him to the center, later after we left dad got sick and we got lost on our way there so I had to get him a pint of wine so he wouldn't shake so bad, it was an experience driving across country at age fourteen but I hadno idea of where I was headed and we ended up in New Mexico a hundred hiles out of our way. Dad had to sell some things for gas so we could make it and we did, my addiction wasn't as bad as dad's was and I could go days without it but then when things got too hard and I got confused I would drink. My parents got married out of high school and started their life together but then they had their troubles and mom fell in love with my real father resulting in my birth, although I was born in Duluth right after I was born my parents were convinced to move to California' where we stayed until the boys were hit that Sunday morning, mom had a chance to leave but didn't take it when my father offered she thought it would do too much damage little did she know that the damage was coming anyway. And she ended up leaving anyway years later, Herb couldn't seam to live without her and he followed her where ever she went a kind of stalking really and when she met Oliver in a bar she found someone she wanted to be with.

They snuck; around to see each other because Herb was still staying with her. It was strange really them meeting in a bar because Oliver never drank, later he caught them and threatened to kill them both so they packed up and headed to Nebraska in his big old car. Come to find out later Herb put out a contract on their lives so the story was told and they had to leave, even through that he followed them because of love, man that's some strange crap to happen. But she had been the only one since his teens and he couldn't let go. I have felt that before but it only brought destruction with it and maybe that's why I'm afraid of it who knows, is there a happily ever after? I guess you would have to experience it before you would know but it would be nice if there was. The alcohol among other things that happened destroyed their marrige and it is still destroying them today, they say for the goodness of God will follow you all the day's of your life even if you don't see it He is there to catch you if you fall. Herb was the quiet type and didn't show mouch emotion and what he held in might have caused some of his bad problems which took his life very early they said alcohol was like poison to his system and every time he drank it his life was shortened; the Mattson's were Sweeds and I remember grandma and how she talked very funny to us kids, I only remember seeing them once and never again as they must have passed on. The day has been cold but nice I painted some of the shelfs in the kitchen so that is less that I have to do later, it's fun when you can do it in your own time and not be rushed like they used to do when I had to work. Those people didn't look at you as a person they just went by the amount of money that was brought in by the company and I hated that but here in Courtland they go by the person.

The church where I work doesn't interfere with my work and I do the job at my own speed so it's done right I was asked about another job as a janitor but couldn't take it because it would have messed up my medical on socal security and that is something in which if you louse it you never get it back. Today we had pizza for supper from pizza-hut little brothers treat, and man it was good. It's now Sunday morning and not so cold on this day and I hope it warms up but they are calling for snow in some places this next week and I didn't quite catch if it was going to be this part of the country, I went to work yesterday and got things done for this mornings service it seams I enjoy working for the lord and I have the place all to my self and I can let my spirit run free while I sing when ever I do sing for the church it seams they bring it up and it's better that way. For my voice is a gift that should be shared when they want to hear it I was up right at three this morning and maybe this is an exercise so my mind can focus and that's why he had me start it so long ago funny how it's still with me today but I seam to get the rest I need during the night, I figured it out and I get about eight hours which is enough for me. I remember one time when I was sixteen it was on my birthday and mom bought me a car it was the nicest car I ever had a Thunderbird and boy was it nice a nineteen sixty and it had all the bells and whisels a new paint job with lacing around it light brown with a rootbeer brown lace job, and it sat about eight inches off the ground with baby moons and crome wheels. The thing I really liked was the way the steering wheel moved to one side when you were ready to get out of it, this was my dream car but it didn't last long when my brother stold it and ran down some chainlink fence that broke my heart but by the car being so solid it didn't hurt the body just something underneath and later the transmission went out and like a fool I sold it to the junk yard where they fixed it and sold it to someone else the car today would be worth $30.000.00 but that was one of my dreams that went bad I had a lot of fun in that car but it wasn't meant to be, then my dad bought a Ford from the junk yard and boy did it run it had a three speed in it and boy the girls loved it when I drove by their ouse and spun the wheels over later he sold it because we got into trouble with it. Then in Nebraska I would drive to work each day and off in the distence I saw a G.T.O. Judge it had to of been a nineteen seventy and boy it was nice it had out of state plates and I went to the office of the motel and inquired about it, the guy said a service man was going through to California and it started to knock so he left it there to pay for his room. I asked if he wanted to sell it and he asked what I had in mind? And I told him that I would trade my Ford for it and he agreed then I got it runing and drove it home another great car, the hood would open up like a regular one but it had something special the front clip would also open up and tilt forward, even though it didn't have a title it would have been a great car for show the motor was all cromed out and it has a special four speed in it a borg warner one of the best. Well to make a long story short I parted it out for a few hundred dollars another dream car gone because of addiction.

It seamed addiction has taken many things which I could of held on to but that's the was the disease is it only takes it never gives anything, and so many are fooled by thinking it does give things they feel it will make them rich and it never will in a million years. I saw one of those G.T.O. Go for $60.000.00 on Barret Jackson a while back and it made me wat to cry Ha! Just a walk down memory lane, although those things are gone I have much more these days with my home and the love of family and friends as that is something you cant put a price on. The other day I noticed that bad words were rubbing off on me so I told my little brother to stop using them I'm supposed to be teaching him good manners, but for some reason it was working the opiset and I'm glad that I caught it to correct the problem. It hadn't in in my vocabulary for years and now he had me using it strange how if you don't look out the bad things can sneek into your life and that's the devil at work, each day I ask God for guidance and forgiveness for my sins. Even when I feel uneasy I like to go to the church there is something there that I need and when I leave I feel fulfilled could it be that I belong in the church? For I know one day my story will be told and that would be a good place to start with a small crowd and then work up to other places. Where kids can hear the message of hope there are many that needto hear the message before they get caught up in it because once they have fallen into it then for many it will be too late.

Through the years I fought it everyday and it takes up a lot of time just going through the fight and they shouldn't have to go through it, study time is what they need and a preventing plan to stop it before it starts a ray of hope that they don't have to fall into it by pure pressure, soul-mates two people meant to be together by devine intervention to where they live out their lives together and when one is killed the other feels it even if it's miles away. So well connected that they know each others thoughts, does this really exist? Still I watch the Hallmake channel sometimes with tears in my eyes by the beautiful endings which follow and I don't watch to much of the other ones with there violence a beautiful story with a happy ending is a great thing and it could influence kids to do good things. There are many young people who don't know what they are doing when they become addicted to drugs and alcohol, in the beginning it's all fun and games but when they grow up a little more they will be fighting the fight of their lives. As it destroys their families and friends they cant see it comeing because it doesn't give any warning it's just like getting hit in the head with a bat and the damage is just as bad except the damage is inside not on the surface. The drugs destroy the brain and the body and leaves little left, I remember eating one time at a fast food drive-in joint and when I ate my food I fell out of the door of my car this was caused by not eating for a week and then trying to when I got hungry. The drugs let you feel like your full all the time and in reality your body has been eating it's self for that week, and this happens with everyone that does Methamphetamine some even see things that are not there this is caused by this certain drug as it destroys the mind. Many times I have seen people on their hands and knees chaseing little people around their own yard another bad thing that happens when this drug is used. When using it the mind runs a hundred times as fast as the normal persons does so the normal person could never keep up with the one doing Meth, my land' I have seen children killed by using the drug and it's a sad sight when they say they don't want to die but once started you cant stop the destruction when it damages the heart. One boy said he would do anything but theend was on it's way and it couldn't be stopped, there has been so many that I have choose to close off my mind to them if I could give advice to young people it would be to never start, a cold front came in last night just as it was getting dark and you could see the snow falling just a few hours earlier it was in the 40's so that was a supprise. Monday and the snow is on the ground it's funny how you can see it come in from the North I'm learning to be able to tell the difference from rain clouds and the ones holding snow the amount wasn't that much just enough to cover the ground. And make a mess of course, even the weather is teaching me something the plastic on my wheel well is falling off so I have to have that replaced sometime in the future to make it whole again I never could understand why they made things out of plastic just cheap I guess. Yesterday was spent going to church and then having coffee afterwards and coming home to watch television the cold plays havick with things made out of plastic and they freeze then get bent out of shape, the weather changing like this makes many people sick with the temp's going up and down especially the elderly as their bodies get worn out as for the young ones they seam to be as strong as a bull. Only ten more days in this month and it will be over then leap year is here for those born in Febuary, the year is off to a good start and it can only get better as time passes. Most folks look forward to the holidays when family will come to visit such a great time for them as when they come the church fills up, during Christmas one family had twenty family members come to service and man that a lot of kinfolk a strong family withChristen valuse and they seamed too be close to each other.

Many things goes on out in the world if the television is any indacation of it but with me I'm content just where I am, the only thing which would make it better would be to have a mate someone like me in many ways so there wouldn't be any fighting but I don't know if that exist. Here in the real world my lonelyness seams to creap up on me sometimes from out of the blue and that's something I can live without, each time my friends say hi it makes me feel good inside but then it leaves a short time later. To return again when the next person says it it's hard living here and not just anyone is able to do it but it lets you get in touch with your self and that's an important thing to survive in the wilderness, many people live on farms and that would be even lonelier when you louse a loved one and then your all alone except for when you go to church. But some women prefer that life after one has gone and the children are raised. The farms are the back bone of this Nation and they will stay until there is no one to run them anymore, some would think the children wouldn't return but there has been many that do return to run the farm and the numbers have increased over the years from twenty years ago. Courtland is growing slowely but it's growing just the same and I like it here for one day the numbers will increase even more, it's the people who are so kind that draws people here and once they feel the warmth of the people they want to stay or atleast I did. My friends are many here and no one has treated me badly here in the heart land, God seams to know where we belong and he will have us go there to move forward in life and He wont let you get stagnet in the things you do.

I talked with the pastor and she said yes that her daughter had moved, I don't understand why she is on my mind more these days then before but she is. Loss makes things more clear as we go through this life or does it? Maybe it's the not seeing her early in the morning that brings her to mind who knows for sure. Little brother is doing better at saving and in time he will be able to get a car in maybe a year or so, you can tell the wind blew hard last night as snow is plastered against the trunk of the tree in the front yard but it's calm now with no wind at all. I'm hoping the car will be a quick fix but we will have to see when they look at it, driving down the road you can tell when it's windy as it blows the plastic piece back and forth it's a nuisance when your driving and I don't like that, the day will beginn in a little while and the boys will be up ready to take on the day as for me I have some work to do this morning and then back home to maybe paint some more. I think we will have a good day as each one brings something different and you never know what! It will bring with it, the paper person is delivering the paper and it's five twenty six in the morning they are always delivering them early in the morning most of the people are a sleep at the time but it's nice to wake up and read it. Start the day with reading about all the garbage that is going on in the world and then give your opinion on it when it's allowed, Oliver should have gotten enough sleep during the last two days he has been very tired but in good spirits I had tests done on him today and everything is fine. The dark side as some call it when officers go undercover to stop a drug rings they sometimes find them selves doing some of the drugs so the gang or wont be suspicious, but most good ones can get by doing this by some kind of trick. And wither they catch it is anyones guess many of them found them selfs in a situation where doing it couldn't be helped or else they would be taken care of. THE DARK SIDE is when you enter that world of hell and not return, you see dramatized situations all the time about it on television but once in it most don't return it's like there is two different worlds out there three really the one with alcohol. And the one with drugs, then you have this one I live in today, when you get addicted to alcohol at a young age being in that world seams normal and you can maintain at first but then later the drinking seams to make you feel normal as it reshapes your mind to not be able to go on without it. Many people can go through life this way but problems will arise along the way like black outs and other things like forgetting where you are from time to time and some people even louse years of their lives because of it. And when the mind doesn't have this to function a person will try other things to take it's placee like Valum or Methamphetamine this stimulates the mind for a while but then usually tragedy happens like an over dose which happened to me as a child, I didn't see it coming but it came anyway and I lost five days because of it and ended up on a farm in Missouri close to death. When people go into this world for the first time they think it's fun and it is at first but later it destroys the life it has taken, a lot of kids do it during collage and find them selves hooked for life even if they don't want to admit it.

Later it will become an outlet to escapt from the real world a place where they can forget and it does that job well and then everything falls apart, and with some they never return, they seam toget lost in that world and cant find their way back. And this is when they loose touch with families because they don't want them to know what has happened, then as the addiction progresses they build their own world with out families and form new ones that their families wouldn't approve of, so they iceolate them selves from their familys and fall deeper into that world they have created even today you can notice people who are in a family of alcoholics they stick together and they have but one leader that runs everything and if they don't like a person then they are gone. Within my family my mom was in charge and if she didn't like someone they went out the door to not return but she could see a bad seed as some called it, everyone protected each other and especially mom' so she wouldn't have any worries she was the sweetest women I knew until you made her mad then look out you were invited to leave on your own but if you wouldn't do it then you were removed by someone in the house. Everyone loved her because she took in people who didn't have a home and needed a helping hand up, not a hand out and the ones that she helped were glad to keep the house clean for her. We didn't raise much cane as she was a quiet person and didn't like noise except for her music western music, and that part stuck with me even today after the addiction has long gone from my life the difference now is that I like to sing my own songs and do it in church.

After she left this world I still liked singing and it helps me when I feel beside my self sometimes it brings me comfort, in trying times like when I'm confused the darkness has gone away and the light is there to assure me that there are brighter tomorrows a head. It's Tuesday and the trash man will be here later so I have to do my part and make sure it's ready, I still have painting to do but not much when I got up little brother was up he seamed to not be able to sleep that happens sometimes with others and he even took out the trash good guy' later I will do it at the church and then they are set for the week. It's a little chilly this morning but the snow is about gone into mother earth to make things green again for this new year I like to watch the trees bloom each year as new life is brought back from a long winters sleep and my friends across the street grow pretty flowers each year which is a sight to see, there is someone that plants flowers at the church and they or her does a marvelous job it's so pretty each year. When I was young I couldn't see past a day and now a day is but a memory a split second in time almost so I have to catch it when I can other wise it's gone like the wind with just fragments of memory which some of it I forget. Little brother has come a long way since his arrival and I hope it continues so things will turn out for him the dark side isn't any place that I would want to see anyone but it will continue until addiction is destroyed. And I know from personal experience that it can be done if a person wants it bad enough finding your peace is hard to do but it also can be done with me it took God to find me that day and even then it took time, nothing worth doing comes easy in this world but it can be done with hard work. As for those that judge they will keep judging as it seams to be their way, my self I feel that if you live and let live everything will be ok' in your world. I look at it like this each family builds there own world and that's what keeps them proected, wither addiction is included depends on each individual if they are raised without it then they might not have anything to worry about but if not then they too might fall into it and that will leave them to deal with it. I'm grateful for the second chance I have and I wont mess it up this is like a dream come true to be here even after all the pain I went through but through my addiction times I knew someone was watching over me because things that happened to other people didn't happpen to me, it was like God had me in his hands and no one could grab me and this leades me to believe that I am a part of a devine something. Like I'm protected by God for some reason and for that I'm also grateful, I have many questions but only God could answer them so I keep them to my self in hope that one day I will find the answer. This world is full of mysteries and I would like to find some of them out one day when He thinks I'm ready for He knows all things, they say none of us are a mistake that God knew us before we were conceived and like when He careted the world He said it was good so I know there is a reason why he brought me here not once but twice am I a part of a bigger plan? I would have to be for Him to bring me back to get it right this time. Everything before it was created was once in someones mind and brought to reality by the mind for we are made in His image.

The road has been long and it still has a way to go, will my purpose be revealed in this life? It has to if things are the way they seam to be. God doesn't make mistakes never has and never will, maybe I'm a drop of paint on the picture which will reveal something beautiful the greatest art that He creates. Was I meant to be part of His master piece? Enough questions for now' in the years to come great things will take place maybe the start of His new order when He comes and that would be great a world without war starvation and poverty for the world would surely be better when He comes. Many years back some people gathered on a hill because they said that He was coming but this was a vision of one man and it never came to pass as many of them died on that hill to not see the father, it says that only the father knows when the time will be and no one else so that means no one knows and you shouldn't listen to anyone about it even the pope doesn't know the arrival of out father. Many times I get like an epiphany when things seam to be perfect but then rational thinking comes in and it goes away but while I'm in that zone all seams perfect lke it's meant to be that way whats with that? Am I visiting the supernatural where things are different they say science does away with magic but does it or have we just blocked that out of our minds the supernatural does exist because that's where God is He works in the supernatural as He says I am not of this world. The day went well but we got some bad news Jerry Gant isn't expected to make it until morning.

It seams the cancer got the best of him and now it's in God's hands that's two in the same familie brother and sister that the cancer has ravished their bodies. Maybe that's why I was supposed to move away there has been almost a handfull of people who I knew that have died so sad! I feel my life was spared once again to move here so I could start over one more time, I learned long ago that God wont take me before my time and it isn't up yet Ha! There are things that I will do in the future and when the time is right he will let me know what that something is. Jerry and Debby were only in their thirties when they got the disease and within a year Debby was gone so many broken hearts left behind but they seam to go on and survive the loss of loved ones. It's a new day here in the heart-land and there isn't much to do today the end of the month is upon us and another is about to start, the thought of Jerry is on my mind but all I can do is pray for him we seam to feel the loss really strong at first but then by the strength that God gives us the pain subsidess after a while it never goes away but it becomes like a bad memory or one that can be put into the back of your mind. My nephew is getting married in June and they would like for us to come but we will have to see how things are going by then if Oliver can travel or not! I realize it's only three hundred miles but we will see, the last time there was too many people drinking and it wasn't good as I had to leave because it reminded me of a bad time in life, through the years I have learned how to live without it but it seams my other brother hasn't his wife was telling me that he broke his ankle one time when he was drunk and is just now getting thecast off after three months boy that must have hurt. I believe it's going to be another nice day hump-day as they call it but bible school here in Courtland, there has never been a place like Courtland in my life and now I'm the first to settle here from my side of the family. When others want to come here I rather not have them live in the same town I look at Courtland as my place of peace and there wouldn't be any piece if family was to move here, we are too different and their lives well are their way of life I like the piece and they get into drama which is not for me. This is a special place one built for me and maybe others like me haven't dug that far into the history of the town as of yet, like was it here during th depression well it had to of been to be here today. Way back there was a dust storm and they called it the dust bowl the wind had tore up the top soil of the land and blew it everywhere, this was before they had a way to fix it but then a smart man told them how to stop it from happening again and it worked. I don't know all the particulars but it saved the day and it hasn't happened again, the ground here sucks up he rain like a spunge but usually they get by and don't have to irragate if they have a good year I have seen gusts up to sixty miles an hour and they can destroy a lot of things in there path Walt was telling me that they blew a building down andjust left the toilet sitting there in the open tragic for the building but funny to me the toilet that is. They said Jerry stopped taking the drugs for hiis cancer so that would mean they were making him sick I have heard of that doing it too a lot of patients they just don't like what it does to them so they stop it and then they pass away to go and be with the lord. Through the watching of television you can see the messed up minds of people police officers taking things to the limit and then louseing everything some even end up on the streets that they once protected to find them selves eating out of garbage cans like the others, a while before this happened she said she could never end up like those people and here she is one of them.

The only difference between them and others is two pay checks and many don't see this until it happens when they too end up on the streets, it can happen to anyone even me if I'm not careful things can fall apart at the drop of a hat for those who cant see past the day their in as for me I see a little further down the line from where they are and plan accordingly so things don't fall apart, my perfect women would be someone who is nice and loving with a spark for romance a little wild with convictions to the one she loves no drama for that I don't like. A clean person who takes care of her self someone who can share their dreams with you' and you share yours with them, finding this person would be hard here in the heart land because I don't get out much but maybe through the church I can find her new people hear about the church and some come to visit and maybe one day she will appear like an angel out of a fairy tail that kind of relationship would be awesome but you don't hear about those things happening in real life or maybe they do happen and we just don't hear about them. They say love isn't rational but either is jealously and those things can cause a lot of damage in a relationship for these are things that I have felt in the past and I don't like them the hurt that is caused by them is outrageous and it will destroy what's supposed to be love. Thursday and I have to go to the court house to find out about the taxes and then back home again to clean the church. When I got the home I was told that the taxes wouldn't run any higher then they did then and they have changed and I want to know why, for that is my right as I'm the owner when can a state do that for that is something I would have to look up.

This being my first home I have no insight to these things but I think Mark might have some idea about that kind of thing, it's not the money it's the principal of the thing. My friend Val' had a birthday and just turned 42 years old my it doesn't seam like it's been that many years but they do fly by so fast I told her happy birthday and she said she missed me not being around. I used to take her to lunch on her birthday and we would talk for hours she once told me that I was a dreamer of things to come and I believe that is true because back them I dreamed of having my own home and here I am it's came true, it seams all your dreams can come true if you want it bad enough and I wanted it bad the stranger' for some reason he knew I owned my own home I wonder if he was sent to check on me an angel of some sort could have been. Should I have invited him to stay here I didn't get if he needed a place to stay it wasn't brought up. He sure was a nice person the dreams I once had have gone now but I could never figure them out O well whats meant to be will be it seams like it might be another nice day here in the heart land' and things will start to come back to life once again yesterday it was in the fifty's and nice and warm it's already twenty three out side so it could be another warm day this Sunday the church is having a casual unch with worship my land' that is early for lunch but we have fun, maybe sometime in the next couple of months I will sing for them we have a few holidays coming up like Valentines day and a nother my spirit has been good lately and I like it that way no one bothers me when I sing and that's good because I would not like it if they did. I'm growing closer to God with each passing day and I enjoy doing his work at the church as oine day I might be a preacher just a thought at this time but you never know what the future holds for any of us I thought I would spend my life working for others and look at what has become of my life for this isn't the picture I saw as a kid or young adult it's like God knows what you will be way before you have a clue my taking care of these two will one day be done and then I will have to move on to something else and what better place to work then for God. Each day I pray in the morning and it seams to make the day go better, I didn't get into praying until the end of this last year but it seams to have become a part of my everyday life now and I enjoy it to humble my self in front of God and tell him what I want. It's a connection like no other and it lets me ask for forgivness for the things I have done like swear words which I had thought had gone from my mind, but have somehow returned this is the devil trying to get in and he has no power here only God can enter my world. It hasn't gotten to bad yet but if I didn't catch it then it would have and that wouldn't be good. It seams time has everything to do with all things pertaining to things here on earth and yet His is not the same as ours and that might be why we want everything done now and not later. But He doesn't listen to us on such small matters tell God your plan and watch him laugh this comes from him knowing what we will be and us guessing at it, we may amuse our selves for a time but in the end he knows where we will be called.

All through life I never knew of this concept and especially in my younger years, well I didn't know anything back then about God and how He worked in our lives but today He works in mine and I'm glad that he is my friend, you get to know God when you are alone and I think that's what he wanted when He moved me here he wanted me to take the time to get to know him as you can only do that when your alone with him. Not in the physical since' but in the spirit for my alone time is when He can inspire me to do things for Him I don't have all the answers but then no one does not in this world, you would have to come from the supernatural His words says it all. It has been a great day with warn temps in the fiftys also went to my appointment to find out that I wasn't the only one who's taxes went up, it seams all the houses that sold in my price range got their taxes bumped up but still that isn't bad compaired to others I know they pay eleven hundred a year. Courtland is growing and I find that to be so cool, the tax guy even said things are changing around here I believe God is blessing Courtland. The world in which I once lived is gone now faded from these eyes to not return, a new way of life is in my future one free from all the distractions which once filled my world, Harley is sitting by my feet basking in the sun as the rays come through the window and he is content being next to me this is something he doesn't do with the other boys, only me. And I think he loves me more then anyone has ever loved their master, but through the years I have spoiled him and I can't blame anyone but my self even though I try to sometimes.

It's strange how a place or change in people can effect a persons well being and can also make things better like I have said before some have lived here all their lives and wouldn't change anything even the kids which grew up here are starting to return, and maybe with them looking at the outside world wasn't what they thought it would be. Courtland has gotten some good things wrote about it and that's what draws people they don't want to raise their kids in a alcohol and drug infested community and Courtland doesn't have much of that from what I have seen but then again you would have to enter that world to see it usually as they stay to them selves, Methamphetamine users are usually up at night where they cant be seen my the everyday person they travel at night under the protection of the dark and usually if they get caught it's because of something stupid they did like no taillight or head light these things are very simple to fix but their minds are running to fast to acknowledge that things are happening I know about these things as I have went through them while I was with other people I had many close calls but was never arrested for drugs it was like God was watching over me for some reason and that also helped me with getting straight not having a record for drugs is a good thing but there was many times when they followed me at night to the phone and that was scary. During my time alone I worked on my self to make my self better this was even after my death experience and in time things seamed to get better the Meth addiction was the hardest but in time I over came it also and today I'm still here and a better person, we are brought here to teach others about the experiences in our lives so that they can avoid them and not fall into the same trap. And with God's help we can do that as he can heal us in more ways then one and make us strong once again if today is anything like yesterday it should be pretty warm out, and the ground hog comes up on the second of next month to see if he sees his shadow which I hope he doesn't otherwise it's six more weeks of winter and I really don't want that, just nice and warm not hot. Then the rains will come with the tornado season tornado alley is what they call it here in the heart land and it happens between here and Nebraska, storm chasers follow them through the season to try and get a better understanding of how they can warn people more quickly. Saturday and it's a little nippy out side yesterday was nice but not as warm as the day before this iss the time of year when the weather fluctuates from one extream to another and that isn't good on the elderly when it comes to colds and things they seam more exceptable to colds and such. Here in courtland many of the older folks at church seam to like me and I think that's a great thing, my I wonder what the day holds for us on this day getting the bills together is very important so they cn be paid on time so not to have them breathing down my neck. Saturday at the westerns should be on and many western movies come on early in the morning, like Rifel man among others back in the day we used to watch them with dad and boy that was fun, the boys are still sleeping and they shouldn't be up until seven or so. Then their day begins of watching television if it wasn't for television they would go nuts, It would be nice to have a teen center around here where the kids could go to stay out of trouble like a prevention place where they could have fun and learn about what drugs can and will do to you. It would be a good starting point in prevention and the kids would feel like they were a part of something, they would be responsible to keep the place clean and it would serve snacks at certain times of the day here in Courtland prevention would be the key. Having the ability to say No when it arises and knowing what to look for when people are trying to sell the crap even to others.

Every thing will start to grow now the buds will popup out of the trees while the flowers will come later only a few people grow flowers, I guess it's too hard to weed them with the soil they have around here but my lady friend across the street has a green thumb my land' it seams she can grow anything and have it look beautiful I want to have an out side spicket put in but it would cost a arm and a leg maybe if I dug the trench or had a friend do it that wouldn't cost so much, I have friends but I don't know what they all do for a living someone might have a ditch witch that would cut right through that ground. Today I have to clean the bathrooms and the kitchen at the church so it's ready for tomorrow I don't know what they have going on but it should be fun it's the fifth Sunday of the month and that's something special I will have to ask what the day represents they call it casual Sunday. I never had a place like the church that I could go too just to get away from all the crap that bothers me and that is a relief, there are even times when I feel the spirit inter me while I sing and that feels really good. When the darkness falls I'm usually in bed so I can get up to start another day this gives me enough rest to make it through the next day, some will say that it isn't normal for someone to get up so early but I say it's a way of life for me. I have done this for twenty some years and haven't had a problem with it, in the beginning it was to heal my mind and I didn't have a clue why it was that way but it was, in the morning your mind is foggy and if you can stop that from happening them you can cure some things that is wrong with the mind. Now it was God who started this healing process and in the beginning it was hard because I never did like getting up early in the morning but he made it clear that it had to be done that way, He let me know in the same way he told me to come here and there was no room for doubt when He talks I have to listen.

Through the years He has only told me to a few things and I do them, as I watch westerns it's like I am a part of that time so long ago like I might have lived back then I have a memory that's trying to come through of me looking for something I left here long ago. This is the first time I have had it except for the time before I was in the 1800 and amassed a great fortune but something happened and it was hid away for the future like I knew I would come back for it, why would this come to mind now? I don't recall it happening before through the years there has been something I have been searching for and now it's just starting to come to me but where would it be? If this came to me now then the rest should follow in time, I believe I was once famous back in the day of my demise strange. When the hands of time bring us through difficult times things change and we may not feel the change, why do things come to us out of the blue out of the middle of nowhere and plant a seed is this the way it is or is the mind exploring things that once was mighty peculiar if you ask me none of these things came to be until I moved here maybe that's part of the reason why I was sent. This world is full of things I don't understand and maybe I should let go of that part of my life always trying to figure out things, and take it as it comes. Let each day bring what it may and just look at that instead of everything else, Oliver didn't feel so well today or so he said as for the day it was awesome as my spirits were up and down. It's strange how that happens from time to time but I welcome it with open arms so many times it verys and some days are better then the others. Many times there has been times when I felt like going to sleep and sleep the day away but it never happens unless I'm real sick, I'm a bit lonely today even thought they are here it's like their not they seam to be in their own worlds sometimes but it's always been that way, even Oliver seams a little distent at times but he does talk more then before with things that are not important like television commercials Ha! He can be funny though when he laughes and mocks them people.. It's Sunday and I get the privlage of opening up the church and getting things ready for service they got some directorys yesterday and I'm not sure what they are for when I hear that word I think of phone books as we got one just last week so that might be what they are, as they sure were heavy. It's strange how when you first wake up your droggy but then in a little time things seam to come into focus I cant stay in bed once I awaken because if I do the day doesn't go very well I get lazy and I don't like that, I remember dad getting up early to get ready for work it was like an everyday thing where we lived and you would of seen others doing the same thing in the sixtys it was like it is with me today early to bed and early to rise.

I don't remember going with dad very oftend to work but when I did I was in awe the way he tore those transmissions down and put then back together like a puzzle he had put together a million times and didn't make one mistake. I guess it's that way with every prefession if you stay with it long enough it would be like tieing your shoes you never forget,or riding a bike. It's another quiet morning as I ponder what will happen with the day I do know the church should be open at five so it's warm nothing worse then a cold church and angry peoploe having to freeze through service but I dont let that happen on my watch responsibility is a great thing. And it should be treated as such, as time passes the things I should have learned as a child are being learned today a little late but just the same they are being learned, it's like I was caught up in a time warp with no memory of that part of things only the darkness that occurred and it was not a good thing a lot of what I went through has faded now and that's why I wrote this book back in that time when things were fresh it spands over many years as I knew those things would fade away when God thought the time was right and then life would go on like it should have as a child a fresh start with a loging of things which will happen if you fall into the dark side that side of life isn't good for anyone and those who wonder into it will find them selves close to death, and many won't come back from that placce. A world of confusion that will make you feel glad that you made it through another day to only start the process over again this will go on for years if not stopped.

And then one day you find your self all alone with no one to help you because you burnt all those bridges so long ago, as with me I never asked for help because it was my problem and no one else could fix it but me taking responsibility for what happened was a big step and then changing it was next. Going through withdraws was the hardest things because you always wanted to go back to it even if it was for a short time then guilt would set in and it made you stronger even though this sets you back you never quit trying, then one day God helps you with that and you never go back. It was like a baby step forward dealing with the loss of something on top of that wasn't easy either, getting discouraged because you cant walk weighs heavy on you and it seams at the time mind you that you lost all hope of recovering from such a thing scooting across the floor was something I had to do to get around and I know it must have been a sight but for some reason I knew I had to survive. The people laughing was a great heartache and all I could do is say forgive them Lord for they know not what they do, I guess some people were just like that mean and cruel there are many mean people that I don't understand and I really wouldn't want to. I got the church opened and the heat on so everything is ready. Back when I couldn't walk there was a hopelessness that I felt in the beginning like I was all alone and I was really except for Oliver he has always been there but fighting that fight I was alone within my self and O how my mind was messed up, trying to put something like that into words is hard so I won't try but I'm sure you could imaging what it was like if you ever went through it the giving up was a constent but shome how I made it through and I know God had something to do with it. Monday the beinning of a new week the church activitys are gearing up yesterday we had snacks with coffee while learning about the lord and it was nice. I kinda sat by my self until a nice women sat next to me and then we sang almost all through the service, and even though I didn't know all the songs things went well I was atleast able to sing the words. The shakiness I felt inside seamed to vanish as the service went on and then I was calm I remember that feeling from when I went to school when even we stayed in one place long enough and it takes time for it too pass but it does pass, sort of like when you meet new people but I have known these people going on three years now. But not each one personaly like when we get together like yesterday I really liked that kind of church service as people are more together in a tight bunch and it feels more personal. We laughed quite a bit and some even played with their grandchildren you could see that their spirits were high for the lord, it seams I am getting closer to them as time goes by and I love that feeling when we all learn and laugh.. My life is so much different then before and the books are teaching me things I didn't know about the church, so I will continue to read them, my land' this is going to be fun as summer get here and the kids will go to bible camp to learn more about the lord while having fun fishing and swimming if they end up at a lake. If this is the life mom lead before us kids I wonder why she left it love I guess can do strange things to a person especially if your young, in families it seamd that the boyfriend or girlfriend never messure up to what the parents want for their child and I expect it's been that way since the beginning of time. Love always finds a way so they say and if they are meant for each other then it's a good combination and they could live together for ever in that place where they become one, I was told a story one time about a couple that had been together for seventy years and when he passed at the age of one hundred and two she followed him four hours later my land' that had to be true love.

But how many do you think end that way? It's hard to say but there are millions of old folks out there and they all have a story to tell. I find it awesome how all churches are connected in one form or another and this must be why they all gather around Christmas time at one church they are like a big family extended across the community and the domanation doesn't matter Methodis churches have been around since the 18th and 19th century when times were a lot different then today, some even met in their homes and small groups even cell groups and the churches would come together as one big family it's like we are building an army for the lord to resist satan as he can get to those who don't believe or don't know how to come to christ but in the same since it's God that finds the person like He found me that dark night so long ago. In arriving here I didn't know what to expect after not being with the person I came here to be with. I believe God used her to get me here as He does with so many others, I remember walking into the church with my Methodist shirt on and I wore it proudly and they excepted me as being a brother in Christ even then I didn't have any idea of what would unfold because I didn't know them it was like I was a stranger in a far away land and boy was I nerves like I was the other day but different in some ways Kathy welcomed me and so did some others and then I knew I was home. And I wouldn't have to wonder any more slowely things started to change for the better and I became an usher and then the janitor.

And the things which put limitations on me didn't seam to matter, when I first started I couldn't stand very long and then with time I got stronger and the problem seamed to go away. This was the work of God to strenghten me and I welcomed it gladly, as time went on I got stronger and stronger and started to read the bible more which helped in many ways. I am amazed at how people are still driving under the influence of Methamphetamine even though they know where it will lead, it's like they are lost in the dark and they cant find their way out the ending of another soul as they slip deeper into the world where they wont know what to do. Tuesday garbage day, I can hear the trains running down the tracks it's a constent rooling of the wheels and now the noise is gone as it speeds off in the morning. This is the first time I heard it so clear and now you can hear the horn off in the distence they travel through pretty much all the time and I think it's too pick up grain from the elStacytors, many years ago I used to load them and boy was it a job back then I suppect today they do it by machine now as I used to have to hold the spout in the train car and tie it off on the railing or cat walk. That was on the train so many things change over the years I have been reading a lot in the last week or so about the church biblical foundation searies and it's awesome how we are the church and we are God's army.

There are many things I have yet to read and I like it so far I can tell that God has been busy not only in my life but many others even before my birth, so that gives me hope that even though I fall short sometimes he doesn't give up on me. For every church there is elders and they are the ones that have been around for quite some time. In the years that I have been a Christen I didn't know that the people are he church this is something I had to learn by studing and it's marvelous, with learning comes knowledge even after the fact that the addiction was gone in some ways I was still in the dark not knowing what I needed to know about Christ. But the good thing is that my learning will continue, I find pleasure in reding about God and the things that will come in my life with knowing more I can learn more but for some reason it has to be done at my speed once you can read even a little you have the ability to teach your self as God impowers you with His knowledge things that usually take a lifetime seam to be coming to me very quickly these days so slowing down would be wise you cant rush the teachings of God and that could be why they started me out with the job I have been doing all things is moderation. It's Wednesday the first of the month and today I wil get most of the bills paid all things pertaining to God take time and that's why they have study groups so they can talk about what they learned and you don't get confused about what you learn, the people who have been doing it for years understand each lesson and even then it takes a while for them to go through each chapter. The weather has been pretty good lately and even in the sixty on one day I just hope it stays that way for a while, back in the day when I studyed Melchisedek one person told me that my mind couldn't handle that kind of knowledge but if that was so then why was that put into my mind on that day so long ago? Maybe I try to rush things and if so that might hurt me in the long run questions they are to be asked and there is nothing wrong with that according to my studies, for we are supposed to only study for a short time and let it sink in the knowledge that is.

When I first moved here there was an old women, in her eightys and she must of understood what was meant by pouring new wine into an old wine skin for many people who have been in the church for a long time live by the word of God. But also I understand that my church isn't that old really, pastor Kathy should be able to shed some light on if I'm moving too fast. I have never read anything except the news paper or the word of God' and everything else I have no knowledge of I never read huck fin or any other stories of travel it's like that gap in time was lost in learning how to understand things. I don't find anything that is related to the destruction of the world of any intrest it's like I keep my self in a bubble away from those things that corrupt the mind, but one thing I do understand is that we are supposed to keep our selves pure from evil. Many times I wish I could return to being three once again and have the mind to travel that path He put me on back then but it could never happen sometimes I feel like I was left behind for some reason to maybe learn how evil can influence your life if you're not careful. I know even though I was in the dark my father watched over me and that was apparent many times when I could of parished in those accidents, but for some reason he pulled me out of them and I understand that it was because he loved me. As I take this walk with Jesus I want to understand and I know that in God's time he will make it so, almost everyday I am drawn to where we have the gathering of people on Sunday it's sometimes like a magnet so I know my job is being done right for the people I know want me there to maybe observe the way my life is changing.

Even in my studing they say it takes time for God to mold us and in a way it's like that tea-pot which started out as a piece of clay and then ended up a beautiful tea-pot that was priceless, our lives are that way in the thick of things He brings us to were we need to be in this world too much knowledge too fast doesn't let it's self build and ferment, and I remember it being that way in childhood I always wanted the answers right now but the mind has to process it. And I never gave it time to do that O well live and learn as you go through life and then in time you will get it right. It said He wont give us more then we can handle but we must sometime push our selves too hard and that can do more harm then good, I have it in mind to stop smoking so I will see what I can do to stop it maybe get some patches or something. I know it will be a challenge but I'm sure it would make me feel better in the long run and improve my health, also I will pray on it for God's help being short winded isn't a good thing around here when harvest comes around. This will be a test to see if it can be done lord knows I'm not the first nor will I be the last to try it, many people beat it and I want my health to last as long as possible. Thursday and Oliver was up early because he had an accident with his cathider andd it leacked, although it happens from time to time it's not something that happens all the time the monthly bills are paid and today I have to take little brother to the doctor. Oliver desided to sleep in his chair and he seams to rest there better then any where else, I was supprised to find him on the john this morning because his bed got wet so today is laundry day. He seams chipper on this mornine and that's a good thing for him it being so early I hope he stays in his chair when he feel's good he talks a lot and that's when I feel that things are getting better for him. Each morning for the last week I had to help him out of bed but today he got up on his own the elderly are fragual when they reach his age and you have to treat them with kid gloves as they go through the day but not letting them depend on you for everything except for things like getting them breakfast and their meals that part I don't mind and giving him a shower he can act like a kid at that time because he doesn't like water, through the thirty some years he never did like taking a shower and mom even had to yell at him a few times. Some people are just that way, as for his stories I have heard them all about fifty times but it's his way of keeping in touch with his youth. Or young adult hood when he was strong, it's funny how there are many kinds of love and it seams to form over the years I look at him like a father who took care of me in my teens and it's only right that I do the same in his second child hood as long as possible he is my friend and the bond we have built will last for ever. And now little brother not so little anymore but his mind is somewhat sketchy and he can remember somethings from the past but they are not very plesent most of what he talks about is race and how he doesn't like Mexicans and colored people as the gave him hell when he was locked up, and in time I hope he change's that. As we are all made equile in God's eyes, my life with Oliver has been a challenge but then everything in life is that way in one form or another.

The Lord stands by me in most everything I do and it makes it easier when it comes to helping them for without God I don't think I would have been able to last this long. At imes when I feel weak He makes me strong so I can go on, the day should be a nice one some say in the sixtys and that's a nice day. Today has been good so far and I have been up for an hour or so and then Oliver wants to come in my room where he wont be quiet and that is hard. At least I prayed before he came in and that gave me peace to let him come in Ha! He is a cantankerous old fart but we seam to get through things, his eyes are closeing right now maybe he wil fall back a sleep in a while I have to wash his bedding so he can sleep in it tonight cant let him go to bed with it wet. Too bad those bags are not leak proof but nothing is perfect in life when the pluming starts to go down hill you got to do what you got to do, he likes to be close to me for some reason and maybe it's because of the years we have been together that bond which seams to get stronger with each passing day and I notice that it's the same way with little brother. One morning when he got up he made a remark that he wished he could feel as good as I do each day and I told him that it was God working in my life and what he doesn't realize is that he could have the same thing if he would get closer to Him but that is something I cant push on him maybe by seeing so much he to may want to change. Pop's has fell back a sleep and he looks funny with one hand covering his chest but he seeams at peace, and it's always been that way when he is around me he feels secure and can let everything go to fall into that realm od sleep.

Many times when we travel he will sleep and then I have to wake him up because I get lonely funny how that works, but it's funny. When he was young he liked to travel but not so much since he was in his sixtys today he reminnds me of a puppy dog content being by the person he loves, even though he can be a cantankerous old fart I love him dearly we have fought many a battles together and still came out on top and that is good. I hope I live as long as he does boy he is a fighter and never gives up, at first I didn't know if I could handle it but God showed me that there isn't anything I can't do when there is love involved imagine all the years over thirty of them and I have been taking care of him for the last twenty. Praise God from who all blessing flow, John Westly was one of the first to start the Methodist church back in the day and what a great job he did for the lord. House groups cell groups and church groups all coming to the lord to spread the word of the gosple it must of really been hard back then with no cars like we have today, and even harder in Jesus time when they had to walk for miles and miles. Many times the people had self doubt but God somehow helped them over come it by telling them to do their job, it's our human faults which stop us from doing things because of the self doubt which is in all of us. My little Harley' the pain in my butt he is so cute. The memory of first getting him was priceless but I wish he would have been trained not to potty in the house and I can't catch him to rub his nose in it so he will stop, I wish I knew more about animals how to train them that is so I wouldn't have to clean up after him. Back in the day you rubbed their nose in it and then threw them out side but today that would be dog abuse Ha! Like with other things that have changed so much everything is abuse, I remember when a whippen was a part of keeping children from doing wrong but today they say it's better to give them a time out what a crock! It's been a nice day in the sixtys but the ground hog saw it's shadow so we have six more weeks of winter and the storm is on it's way here, they are saying eight to ten inches and if they are right it will be the most snow for the year. But a great start for the spring this warm weather never lasts long though and I don't expect it will this time either, in the days coming I hope we do get some snow that way my car can get a wash job without me paying for it. The day is coming to a close and the sun is going down to bring a better day tomorrow, the better day is here nut the rain seamed to have come with it so the beginning of the storm front is coming in and the rain is falling like all get out. I can see the storm heade this way and it's just thr beginning, the rain will be here for a while and that;s ok because we need it. It seamd that most things depend on God;s plan and he has always known what's best for his children what they need to survive in thid world. In my years on this earth I didn't know He took care of us, but after many years of addiction I leared to trust his wasy, when it first started my faith was weak because I didn't trust any one including Him. But throughh time He showed me that he was my keeper and would do anything that a parent would do for their child. a parent that cared anyway. In the days too come the storm will blow over and leave things for us too clean up but that;s ok we are human and strong to me it's a time when people pull together to help one another and that;s one thing this community does in a chrises, As the rain falls the grass will start to turn green and it will have to be mowed but that wont be for a couple of months.

But when it starts my yard will look beautiful once I get Norman to move the shrubs from the back yard, there is much painting to be done but that will take time. It's just getting started that is the biggest step because the house needs to be power washed so the paint sticks, a brown with light brown trim would really look nice and it wouldn't show the dirt as bad as white and the grass needs to have ferdalizer on it so it will grow better then last year, my family thinks I got a good deal on the home and so do I my land' it's been here since 1919 which is a long time so it needs care from the elements . And one day I would like to get the trees out of here and I have someone in mind Norman would do it for the wood and that would save me some money. In this part of the country you have to save for that raining day when your caught between a rock and a hard place this will allow you to still survive and go on with life. I surely wouldn't want to have the other peole do the job because they leave a mess when they are done, and it takes almost a year to get it cleaned up as it did last time, pick your friends wisely and they will usually do what they say they will do honesty is the best policy between friends and that way they remain your friends. As for the others well I can live without them when they did work last time there was alcohol involved and nothing gets done right when spirits are involved., but I have to give them credit for getting the wood out of there.

After the problem with my car I don't trust them and if I wouldn't of gotten my car that day it could have ended up in worst shape then it was. At least I can live without cruse control and a horn until it's fixed one of these days but that will cost me more money, the other day I got the church really clean the floor any way it's not quite the end of paying bills but that will be taken care of today hile I'm full of piss and vinegar the house payments are the first to be paid so our home is not in jearpety, God is sure good to me in this economy and I can afford to keep everything on track. When I write sometimes my back hurts and it has to do with this chair sometimes but it also has a shock on it if I was to use it, choices that's what He gives us the choice to think and understand things that we might not understand it's like I'm searching for something but what could that something be maybe love, or maybe just who I am. That is smething I never understood when people ask me if I know who I am. Like it's a trick question or something and I think they want to know if I am a child of God which I am, even though I wondered in this world all alone in the dark for so long even today I find my mind going to places where it has no business but I cant underssstand why it goes there why it wants to confuse me and when I try to shut it off it's no use it's like it has a mind of it's own separate from the body who knows maybe it's supposed to be that way to wake uo the body to get to work strange way to do it but it does it just the same pressure can cause it sometimes but I'm not under much these days. The Mayor is a laid back kind of person and it seams nothing bothers him that's the way I would like to be, Tom is a great guy from what I know about him and has accomplished many things and from what I felt he seams to like me as many do. Party line has some carpet for sale which would probably fit in my home but I have no idea who I would get to install it, that in it's self would help it stay warmer in here that and the new paint would really work good in here with somenew curtins, Randy is up and that is unusual for him as he usually sleeps until six or so. He must be excited about payday which is today he doesn't have many bills just help with utilitys and his phone bill, at first he couldn't get one a phone that is until I steped in for him. The phone complan knows me and knows I'm always on time so wegot it under my name and he has been good about paying it so far. I let him know that it would be his first start to establish his own credit and then later he can have it put into his own name, I have been on the ball for a few years and it paid off by them knowing I am honest plus I work at the church next door to them my church sold them the property and it was a good deal for them. The rain is still coming down and I know the snow is just around the corner it's supposed to hit after midnight to night and boy it will be icy, with my studies I'm taking it slow because my mind can only absorb so much at a time and if I over do it the learning turns into confusion Ha! The rain is still coming down pretty good this afternoon and you can tell that it's going to snow sometime to night being Friday my friend text me to say it's raining like the dickens in Oklahoma and the ponds are filling up that's a good thing because last year they about ran out of water there, and they lost a lot of cattle. Saturday when I got up this morning the power was out and it made me think to the old days when they didn't have any and how they must have gotten around, although I have a couple of flashlights and oil lamps it was awesome in a way. Reliving times when things were harder then they are today we were like a couple of blind mise walking around here, I could tell that they did a good job with insolating the house because it stayed pretty warm even after an hour. When before we would have gotten pretty cold the snow must have been heavy on the lines to causse it to go out.

I believe the town has a generator that turns on when such things happen and it's a good thig as all our heat is run by electricity the blower part anyway, little brother got up when I was walking around with the flashlight he had never seen that happen in the time he has been here and I think he thought it was neat. Harley wanted to go out but that wasn't happening at the time because we didn't know how long it would be out and I'm not freezing my butt off for a dog, fun times in Courtland. We did get some snow but not as much as they thought thank God' our town may be small but the people are close and that's a good thing here in the heart land. As for those who live in the big cities they can have it I'm happy right here where friends are not too far away, as I talked to one women the other day she said she was stocking up on food just in case it got too bad but she was conserned that her internet didn't work because she pay's her bills that way, O well some day they will get it right. Funny really all those billions of dollars and they cant stay on line. It goes to show that money can't always buy anything, there are some towns around here that only have fourty or fifty houses in them and they have many activitys to draw people there for this is the Christen way of life here in the heart land. Later I have to go out and sweep off my car so I can see to get to the church and get communion ready for tomorrow it's such fun doing that for the people, I have given my life to the lord' and it's not because I feel like I owe Him something, it's just that this way of life is better then the one I lived in before all alone lost in the dark.

Randy is watching television I guess he couldn't go back to sleep after the excitement and it was exciting to me anyway, the sun should be coming up before too long and then the day will start by shoveling snow not a good start to the day. Oliver even woke up for a short time butt now he is back to sleep off in his own little world, he is doing better now then the other day so that makes me feel a lot better it's like we have this connection and I can tell when he doesn't feel very well, this might be part of why he has lived so long I catch things before he get's too sick. Back in the old days people hardly went to see a doctor and they seamed to live quite a while but then there were those who passed because of simple things that can be taken care of today by medication. They say people are living longer these days because of medication the average living to seventy years compaired to the eighteen hundreds, the wind is blowing like the dickens coming in from the south it feels like so I will have to bundle up to stay warm. I don't like it when it takes my breath away so cold on this day, so many things are taken for granted like the warmth of our homes and the light to see with these are things we need to survive in this world of His' back in the big city I never thought of such things only that I paid my bill and it shouldn't be turned off for any reason, but there was a lesson to be learned there also never take things for granted because your life could change in a heart beat. For all we have is given by the one who gave us life and that is God the father, things change all the time and we have to change with them otherwise we will be left behind. My friend Jerry Gant died last night after fighting cancer his sister and him now are with God, strange how the same cancer took them both within a year and their mother is beside her self with grief. These are things I will have to get used to because it will happen more times then not, even I will go and be with him one of these days and you never know when that time will be but I do know I have a home when I get there death to them came so fast that I barely had time to process it but death is hard to process anyway even with faraway friends. I wasn't very close to them just knew them through people like my X she was their aunt and stayed close to the family there in Kearney, I went to church this morning and got things done for tomorrow I just hope it doesn't snow anymore today or tonight. Sunday and the snow they said we would get didn't make it through those vast skys and for that I am glad but they say six more weeks and anything can happen by then, I couldn't sleep so why noy get up and have my coffee it's a peaceful morning and at least the power isn't out on this fine morning. It was sad to hear the news of Jerry and my daughter text me last night to tell me that she loved me, she said she was nume from the news and I comforted her by saying I know honey. Many things we don't have control of and when that happens we have to leave things in the lords hands, I get the feeling that I could have been one of my friends that passed if I would have stayed there in Kearney not that drugs or alcohol would have had anything to do with it because those things have been out of my life for so long that they have no place in my life. Even today there is a peacefulness in my life that I wouldn't trade for anything else because it's mine, something that is inside.

As time moves into the future my brother is getting along pretty well and he has a big heart when he heard the news back in Kearney he said I'm sure glad that I don't live there, I keep in touch by reading the Kearney-hub on the computer and just last week they arrested twelve people for drugs, the numbers don't seam to decline as when one is arrested there are others to take over and those numbers are usually five to one depending on how far up the ladder they were. If they only knew where they are headed they might think twice before walking into the darkness of addiction, through the light back then I saw a brightness for those not tangled up in the darkness and although I couldn't read what was in their minds I knew they had found peace and the love of God' within their lives this is where they difference is not having to worry about such things makes life more enjoyable. Although I find my self writing about such things it's apparent that it was a life lived long ago, my land' funny when I say that because that's where I'm sitting on my land something I wouldn't of had if I would of followed that dark path so long ago redemption is sweet for me and my life is a constently changing, yesterday I opened the door to the church so the guy could come in and warm up if he needed too he is the one that takes care of the outside and keeps the snow off the walk so people can come to service without falling. There is a material on the walk which at one time heated the walkway and I guess it hasn't worked in some time, they have it on the back like porch or step for those who are handy capped maybe one day they will get it going again.

This new life is one of wonder for each day is new and the search for new things is always on my mind some people know my name and for me that has been a challenge, to remember each persons name because in my younger years I chose; to not remember them so it wouldn't get me killed. Besides you don't want to remember people that travel in the dark, they can come back to haunt you later in life. I find that what the bible says is true you don't have to worry when God' is watching over you in many places they will have a hard time finding peace, because there is always a reminder an old friend or what you thought was a friend that wont let you change. I found that when the time is right God' will move you and he wont leave any room for doubt about you getting out of there it's just that plain and simple, through the darkness there arose a man crippled from his past life but through it all he walked once again. Only this time he walked with God' who showed him the way to a better life, although it was hard God' showed him favor and made the impossible possible. He moved to start life over and he found his place in a little town called Courtland, in the beginning he was scared but through time that was all taken away by the one that brought him. He went proudly to church wareing his shirt of honor which a christen women bought for him when he turned his life around just wareing it showed that he too was a child of God' and they excepted him. He had always been a honest man even in the dark part of his life and they saw this, when he got to the town he had a house waiting for him and he moved into it in hopes that it would one day be his.

CHAPTER 8

When he moved to the new town he made friends with his land lord who was ill at the time and he helped to take care of him, the cancer had a hold of him and wouldn't let go Walt is a nice man and helped him out with getting the home. His first home, by what some consider a risk wasn't important to Walt for he could see the goodness that resided in him. And one day I heard Walt say that He sent the perfect person talking with God from what I understood, one day when he went to see Walt it was like he was in a coma and he rushed to where Walt used to work so they could do something. Not being in the town too long he didn't know what to do, later they would tell him that he made the right call and they called the emergency unit which they determined he didn't need to go to the hospital too much of something caused him to sleep hard. Later his daughter came to visit him and they made plans for him to go to Wisconsin where she could care for him a lot better and today he is still doing fine considering he has lung cancer, one day I saw a friend of Walt's and asked how he was doing and Dennis said he was gaining weight that he weighed more then I do. On that day him and his wife were cleaning out the garage of their old house and I asked where they moved to and he informed me that his father had passed away and they were moving to his house with a seven car garage just across the tracks here in Courtland, I was glad that they didn't move too far away even though we don't see each other very much. On that day so long ago I didn't only get to know Walt but also Dennis and his wife among other people.

When we had the storm long ago, maybe a year or so about four people came over to clean up the tree limbs in my yard and as I tried to keep Oliver out of their way I heard one guy say they are nice people. It took another years before the yard was clean enough to mow the grass, I would clean it when I didn't have anything else to do and I had many of pulled shoulders during that summer. The system here from what I can gather is run on honesty being a farming community most of them get paid each month, but trust has to be earned by the people here so I have no problem in that department. When your life isn't clouded by other things you can see more of what's going on and usually it's good thing's the church later hired me too be the janitor and I have enjoyed it after the getting used to it, that in it's self took some time but today I look forward to going to the church and do my part. I don't really look at it as a job it's more like giving back for the kindness I have been shown and through the years I will continue to do it, with all the writing I have been doing over the years besides my helping others my arms give me trouble in the joints. But I'm grateful that it's not all the time, back in the day my older brother told us to come to Nebraska I must had been about thirteen at the time but we didn't make it until I was fourteen. He called it the good life and it was.

But I like it better here in Kansas not complicated just the simple life of a small town the people here have lived this life for a long time some even from the early nineteen hundreds and beyond, but there is long Gevity here as most live to be well in their eighties and some even longer. It's like this place was blessed at one time with long life and it continues even today. Church was good today and then we went into town and forgot the milk, I keep telling them that I forget things but they must not pay any mind because they for get to remind me O well it must run in the family. I remember mother being that way so she wrote everything down as I do most of the time. I think others make you for get sometimes when they interrupt you such a bad thing to do. It's now Monday and I got a little more sleep it's almost five in the morning and the full moon is still out off to the west, I found out that there is no single women in the church that are my age and the ones who spiked my interest are married so that is out of the question. Maybe I will meet someone from another town but who knows, I guess the lord wants me to be alone for now. It's like they say there are a lot of fish in the sea but they are just not here in my church, so sometimes you have to look else where but also you have to be careful, I talk to one women at the dollar store and I always look for the signs of them being with someone else as that's another place I wont go. You never want to break up someone who is in love or thinks they are that just isn't a good thing, tomorrow is the time to take little brother to his appointment and then off to Wall-mart to check things out and get some of the things we will need for the month, it's a time when you can take your time and not be in a hurry. The store isn't as big as the others I have been to but it has what we need I just wish it was closer to my home so I could save on gas and who knows maybe in the future they will build one in a town like Belleville' but the rides are nice when we go there as the country is beautiful this time of year. They said we were supposed to get more snow then what we got and I'm glad that we didn't get it because I don't like to shovel snow, I bet Kearney had a mess to dig out of with there thirteen inches of snow. Many times while living there I had to do that to make money but that was back in my youth when this body was strong and we had to do it by hand no snow blower because we couldn't come up with the money to get one, it kept us strong during the winter months but the waste of money was great back them. I spent most of my younger years more alone then with someone as the confusion was great with a house full of people that drank and boy did we drink, it was a way of life in the same way church is a part of others lives we to was separated from the rest of the world, not wanting to hear all the carp that the government was doing with this country. I think the day will be a warm one and we will get rid of the rest of the snow and they said in church that the rain helped in a lot of ways, as we passed some of the fields they were saturated with water and I don't think the farmers can get into their fields to put on the chemicals. There were many anhydrous tanks out in the fields to fertilize the ground but getting in there is impossible at this time anyway, maybe in a week or two things will look better. My daughter has passed most of her tests to get her G.E,D. And graduate from high school, I told her that I was proud of her and that made her feel happy and she said thanks dad. As for taking care of things I do the best I can but some make it very hard on me maybe one day they too will wake up and smell the roses but for now I will have to deal with it until that time.

We will see how the day goes and it went nicely. Tuesday the trip to what we call the big city, around here anyway. Concordia although I'm sure it isn't over the size of what Kearney was thirty years some years ago when I first moved there, the way the three towns are laid out it's like a triangle and it was the same with Kearney, Gibbon, Elm creek, it's triangle but towns that are in that alignment seam to grow well and no' I don't have any idea of why it's that way but it is. They say forty percent chance of snow today but I'm in hope that they are wrong, as for the boys they are still a sleep and I hope they stay that way for a while the old fart' didn't want to get up yesterday until I sweet talked him to get up but then he was ok, I have to use love and common since before he will see things and sometimes I have to bribe him just like an old person to want something while they go through their second childhood. Today he wants a malt so I will get him one but not sure if it will stay frozen until we get back but. I will try, if it melts then he can drink it instead of sucking it through a straw, my friend Stan has been ill lately in Oklahoma and I hope he gets well soon my nieces husband he is no bigger then I am just a small guy but such a hard worker for his family branding cattle and doing farm work to survive in this economy he also drives truck and hauls cattle across the country. They are waiting on test results to see if it's cancer, my land' how that is going around.

I just pray that I never get it or others in my family, it's another quiet morning here in Courtland and I like that. Me being here with just my thoughts random thoughts that cant sometimes be controlled the mind such a complexes thing and yet it helps us to make it through the beautiful days that God brings before us. As we travel today I might pick up some new tires for the back of the car my land' they are getting wore out I have had them since I bought the car. I replaced the two on the front last year there are some places in Concordia where you can get a good deal from what I hear, last Sunday there was an older women that sits down from me in Church and she looked very down in spirit so I went up to her and said you look like you need a hug and she replied I do so I gave her a hug. In hope that it might brighten her day older people need that sometimes to lift them up, I don't share my spirit very often but when it's needed I am glad to share they say it rubs off like when you ware after shave and hug someone the scent rubs off and our spiritual feelings does the same sharing the peace and grace of God. Yesterday I worked for a while and it made my heart feel good to get things set for Wednesday school now it can go on without a hitch, and the children can learn more about God. They have been having a hard time trying to get things going steady but with the help of some mothers and the lord things are worked out and they see no problems in the near future, as I go through the chapters each one different from things that are happening in my life at the time. It's like time is stopped for that period. In the coming year I hope to see many new things that will bring my world full circle, but I know the search for the answers will be as long as my life span, like those who came before me. Many will never find the answers but it's the search that keeps us going. I find that I am not like anyone else and that's the way Jesus wants it he isn't impressed by how much you can recite the bible because some can read it and not learn what he is talking about. With me each piece or paragraph is meant to teach us something and in the search we may or may not find what we are looking for, it's like a communication with someone. It's Wednesday and I text Stan to let him know that I am there for him. And he said I was an inspration to him and in faith he has been my friend for a few years, at times I am closer to him then he realises, there is something in me that can since when a person is in despair and I don't know why that is. A cencor of when a person needs a hug and I give it gladly, like the women in church. Even Oliver and Randy need it once in a while a boost of spirit you could say and there are times when I need it also and there is nothing wrong with shareing this with others that are apart of you, I have seen many things in life and some you can change and there are others that just need a little work' it's only three in the morning but O so peaceful except for someone moving around in the other room but he will fall back a sleep. When I read something it seams to stay with me even if it takes a while, I have never read anything but religious writings by people who teach the word of God but still none of them are in agreement about the lerning and teaching of God's word it's always about who is right and who is wrong. As for me I follow and live by what I sometimes feel inside like the hug with the old women it just was an impaulse and I get them sometimes, it isn't something you can explain you just know it's there. Shannon will graduate in the near future so she can go on to a better field of work which she has wanted to do for sometime now, and the sky will be the limit for her.

We got our church directory and I look the same as I did three years ago and that's a good thing Phyllis is the women I was refering to, I wasn't ever much good with names but I'm getting better in my years. Yesterday was just a road trip as Randy's parole officer wasn't in they said it would be next month on the sixth, it was fun driving home in the snow we stopped and got some fast food because they closed the other restaurant that we used to go to either they are going to rebuild it or put something else in it's place. This time I didn't forget the food that we bought but I wish we would of forgot the salid my land' don't they tast that stuff before they put it out? It was so bad tasting that the dog wouldn't eat it. I remember as a child mom would make mine special because I didn't like the other kind that was made with spuds and boy that was good nothing like the garbage they sell today, she could have made millions' I sometimes wonder what happened to Gordy my uncle we never did see him again after he left back in the sixtys my land' he was funny and loved us kids even when he got my arm caught in the car door. He would take us places like to the park so we could play and have fun he was an inspration to me, he was in the service like Greg was but a different branch Marines I believe and Greg was a swab. They built things like Air strips so the other forces could land in other countries he died at a very young age, while he was still in the service he was on leave when he went for a drive in the mountains to a bar and then on his way home he went over a cliff and fell to his death. The police said they wouldn't of found him except his tail light was blinking three hundred feet down in the canyon it was a mess my mom had to identify him Greg had a twin sister who also died in a car wreck.

I can't even imagine what Dale went through with all that tragity in his life it must of really been hard he was a great uncle Dale Roberts and Gordy Roberts are long gone now and have been gone for many a years, they seamed to fall like the Apples off a tree, one an iron worker and the other a priest. Then later Grandma would follow but she lived to be over a hundred years old, I don't recall Grandpa's age but it was no where near Grandma's she lived by the good book and that brought her long life. I vaguely remember her, a little women like my mom just reaching five foot tall with a calming spirit. I don't recall her yelling at me as a kid just her kindness and she let me fix her television when I was there I was still in the detention center back then so I couldn't of been over sixteen years of age, then later we would go for another visit when they put her in the old folks home for trying to cook her pot holders in the toaster. I remember before we left to go there, I had a 1968 Olds and the pan gasket was letting oil past it so I changed it but being a foolish kid still I left out the front and rear seal and my land' I went through twelve courts of oil on the way there and back a great lesson learned. Being young you always try and take the easy way out and that doesn't always work, I loved the car and had it jacked up in the back and my uncle would give me crap about it saying it looked like a grass hopper in heat. Boy those were the days' today I have no idea of where the ones still living are they could be anywhere in the United States. But I'm sure the young ones now have familys and lot's of children, they never did keep in touch except for the few times they stopped over in Kearney while on their way to California' they must have been well off to have a place in California and in Duluth so long ago, Dale took Herbal Life a natural supplement for his heart. I looked up to him as he was my friend and he bought me things when I was in the hospital with my broken leg Ha! He would even come and get me sometimes and bring to his house and I remember playing in his boat a cabin cruiser and boy I had fun. They had an old telephone from the eighteen hundreds that hung on the wall and I would want to play with it but that wasn't allowed. He did have a wife and her name as Penny I cant quite picture her though for that part has long faided but I do know they cared for me and would bring me to their house sometimes and me and my cousin would play out back Aunt penny had to of been beautiful because her kids were but like a lot of people back then they stayed to them selves, it's strange how the priests wife was named Bunny and Dales was named Penny. But that's just the way they did things back then for those two brothers anyway we lost touch when I was very young and I don't recall seeing them again until it was close to their end of time, Dale came by and stayed a couple of days once when we lived in Kearney but that was back in the eighties I remember his big Thunderbird it was a pretty red color and I washed it for him if my memory serves me correctly, it's Thursday and I want to get my glasses fixed these ones may be what is causing my headaches and my land' I hate that. When my Cousin was in her twentys they also came to see us and I remember her because I had just gotten off the hill' as they called it back then Y.D.C. Youth Development Center where I spent eighteen months.

I wasn't proud of that time but it taught me something and I carried it through life, after I was there for a time they let me go and see my grandma in Minnesota, we thought she was dieing or I did and I needed to get away from the place. It's strange but the alcohol problem stayed with me even through my time there and it was right there when we returned from the trip and I got drunk before I had to go back they gave me four days to make the trip and we were back in just three days leaving me with an extra day to tie one on I got into trouble coming back hung over so they put me in lock up' then in a few months I was free. I went on the town with my cousin and we went to a street dance and had an awesome time, we ended up talking about her life and I asked where her Husband was? She replied in kind that they had an open relationship and he did his thing while she did hers. Strange thing even back then but I guess they were happy we later went swimming and she was beautiful, trying to recall your past lifeis hard sometimes but that's just the way things were back them the life we lead can be strange sometimes but it's life just the same, I didn't see my self being alone at this age but it happened.

And I didn't see my self living the life I lead today, through the sands of time many things change and I wonder what she is doing today funny cant remember her name. Dale had another daughter Connie and she came to visit after her car accident, it was a miracle that she lived and she was nice don't know what happened to her either but I hope life was better in her later years I can recall things better then the average person who lived a life of addiction because my mind was allowed to heal. It was a miracle that I can tell my story, while complaining about my taxes I found out that my home was built in 1919 so now I know it survived the depression and for it being so old it's really not in bad shape. It amazes me that the home was here before cars became very popular, I have always been amazed about the history of things and I don't now why just amagine the people who lived here and there has been so many. But that stopped with me for the time being but who knows what the future holds for this place, it's been a nice day and I got my glasses fixed finely now maybe I won't get so many headache's the day has ended so it's off to bed. It's morning and I can tell it's cold out, cold and quiet except for the dog scratching at my door so I told him to go back to bed. Little brother wants to get a car but he doesn't have the money and it's once again hard to convince him to wait until he saves it, very inpatient' but he doesn't have a choice. All things take time so patients is something he will have to learn, up a little early' but once I'm awake that's it I'm up for the day. Stan is doing better and I hope it continues, he is such a good friend and we keep in touch by texting on our phones poor guy went through some pain with what is making him ill, also my daughter got a new used vehical but this one suits her needs more then a car with all the children she takes care of. From the picture she sent me in a text it's a S.U.V. And that will give her more room, little brother my land' he thinks he is in love with Stacy and that's just something that's in his mind. I hate to see him get hurt but that's what will happen to him if he persures this, they never did get along the last time and she is the same as she was back then eight years ago but that's his problem and he will have to deal with it when the time comes, I can tell he is thinking about going to see her by the way he is asking me directions and wanting a car he doesn't even have a license to drive any car and the only place he can get one is in Salina which is eighty miles away they don't give oral driving test in Belleville because they are not set up for that knd of thing. I try my best with him but he seams to not want to do much and he is getting bigger in his weight. I know he doesn't understand many things but I have to keep trying in hope that he will make it here on the out side he is a little hard headed but in time that should change or will it? I have tried to get him to go to church but the only time he went was to impress my sister nd that's no reason to go. Maybe one day God will reach him for this I hope, when my time came for a move I listened and it brought me here as I knew He was sending me a message to start over and even through the hard times I survived and brought my self to this time and space my space which I needed to move into the future. It says that you can get stagnate and your works wont mean anything if you don't listen to the lord, our church is growing and that's what it takes for a church the bible school is doing the growing and that because parents want their children to learn about Jesus and what he gave up so we could go on. Before coming here I could get into movies that were full of not so good things happening, but In my time here that has changed it's like I can't stand to watch that kind of thing any longer. A change that resides inside of me which won't let me watch it like I used to, I felt it coming on for quite some time and then it happened. It was like I was being changed from the inside and what a change it was, strange how that can happen.

Then other times I don't want to be alone, could He be changing things? I knew early on in life that I wasn't like others but I didn't how different I really was. Could others see these things happening and if so what will that change bring? I sometimes feel like I'm not from here and that I'm a visitor from somewhere else but how could this be did I fly here or was I brought and droped off strange feelings to have even for me. For each day seams to go by so fast it's like I cant catch up with my self or maybe I'm not seeing things the way they should be, am I living a life of illusion or are things the way they seam? Even today I get up way before others do and my world is different from theirs in many ways. The freedom to be different or a curse that keeps us there, I have known people who have gone through their whole lives being a liar and I could never see what it got them, some do it to feel important because their lives are not what they would like it to be and some have done it so long that they believe it them selves, my land' what a pitiful life that would be to deceive people just to make your self something your not. During childhood there were many but I have only met a few in my adult hood and they have mental problems, it's been a cold day here in Courtland but I am hoping it will warm up so it doesn't chill me to the bone. As I have started to read the word's in the biblical foundation searies they seam to be an easy read and I will continue on with them and get the rest of the searies when I have the pastor get in contact with the publishing company I believe I'm missing about three of them but I do have the rest, of the twelve. They shed light on things that I didn't know about and if you are going to learn about Jesus' this is something you need.

I stopped reading them because I thought we can only take in so much but I can read a book a day and that is fast for me anyway, it almost lets you go back to that time and want to know more about what He did for us two thousand years ago. The bible is the word and in the beginning was the word and the word was God He created the bible for His people to live and it's supposed to be the right way. Do no harm to others is plainly written in this text all the worldly goods will not matter in our second life for we will have no need for them, from what I read the laying on of hands gives us great gifts really all the gifts we will need when he comes for us on that fine day and it helps us help other meaning healing the sick. That time when we did lay hands on Mrs. Hoard I felt as if something had left me and went to her as my legs shaked in the years when he was here so many followed him they say when these bodys are used up our eternal soul will live on for ever we were created to live for ever and He has our names written in the book of life, each time we ask for forgiveness our slate is wiped clean and this gives us a new start and a chnce to come to Jesus. I was surprised when I read about how much power is in these hands of our's for He works in the supernatural and if we become molded to this world of things then we may not make it to where he wants us to be. The Lords prayer is given to us by him so we can pray right another gift from the father, even today I don't know how to pray with all my being so when I pray the Lords prayer it helps me, He created the prayer for us and it is said every Sunday in church but we need to say it each day to make us strong in our faith, even the writer of the biblical foundation searies explains many things that we need to know to make our lives better, it's Saturday morning' and I was awaken a little early by my dog scratching on my door he can be a pain sometimes but still you have to love him. Yes he is daddys little boy and he wouldn't let any harm come to me, strange in a way how he looks out for me as if I am number one in his life and that the way we should look at our father in heaven. As it is He that takes care of us all this reading has to be absorbed and then processed but that is Jesus's job to take what is put into the mind and then have it make since. I don't know why our loved ones fade when they pass on, maybe it's so we can handle going on with the lives He has given us. I do know that at times of being depressed, we can conjer up their memory to help us through difficult times and that is a good thing. In the days right after she left the memories were strong but then as time passed they faded away like falling of the sun after a long day, I see things which intrest me sometime on television they seam to spark a memorie which was once long gone from my life and it's brought back if only for a moment. Harley spent most of the morning in my room with me and that was very unusual for him, maybe dog's get lonely also being the only dog in the house Ha! I have been working on another song that should sound pretty good when it's done, but it takes a lot of time to create them as you have to reach deep inside of your self and touch that love which I have for Him.

In some of the shows like rifle-man' it tells about how raising up a son back then was quite a job and how they taught them the values of life and the rights and wrongs of life, the world didn't move as fast as it does today and things took time. As for people they haven't changed much you still have the many different occupations; those who work hard for what they have and even ladies of the night, I never could see my self with one of them and that's because I'm a one women man. In the year prior to these fifteen or so I recall many time calling out to my father confused and not knowing what to do, and many times if it wasn't for my love for Him I wold of tried to leave this place in the fashion that I tried before. There was always something that stopped me and I believe it was that love that grew through the years, and it will follow me unitl the end of time here. For how does one get born into a country where a lot of folks would say he is not from here he cant even speak the language properly, talking about the rich that were once in he same situation as for them I really wouldn't want to be in there shoes. The life I have is better then I ever expected so they can keep their glass houses but they should remember not to throw any stones at those glass houses, in my world God is the only King. And as for my heritage' well it is what it is now and I am a child born of God that fought and scratched his way to where I reside and live on this Sunday morning. Through time He has brought me from death it's self to this place I call home, take your riches and take that false pride for they have no place in my life for I have seen the curse that takes so many lives in this world and I have destroyed it with me the one most likely to fall, I get my strength from God and in the beginning I didn't even know where it came from until He found me that day so long ago.

How many trears does it take to fill an Ocean? For surely I have caried enough to fill a river for it is only by His will that I am still in this body of mine for one day He will come and clame what is his and those things that were important here will no longer have any value. O Lord in heaven hear what I say to you today for I love you more then life it's self. As I read some of the things I need to know it will be His will that puts it into action, in the day that it's needed for at times I am drawn to the word like a magnet but first I need to be given instructions by someone that has been through the teachings of my Father. It's another cold morning but it should warm up a little this afternoon, I notice that the warmest part of the day is around three in the afternoon but it takes a while for that warmth to inter me for each day is a gift that the lord gives us. As with each morning I leave my bedroom light on with the door open just enough for me to fine my way back from the kitchen and then I feel safe it kind of reminds me of the light I had seen so long ago and I feel safe in it, no I cant see the floor because I am focused on just the light where I once felt warm and safe, in that day who would of thought I would make it to here I needed to be as for others they didn't have a clue. Sometime He speaks to me when my mnd is receptive to his call and He ashures me that all will be well in time, I say more by not speaking as we communicate through the gift of telepathy. I remember being able to do this with mom before she passed and even at times she would ask me to bring her something through using it and then she would ask how did you know and I told her that I felt it. During that time I thought we were both going to be with the Father, but His plans were different from ours. I like the notion that one day we will be together again but there will be no memory of what took place here except on the day that He reads from the book of life. Still have to learn more about that part, Whitney Houston is dead' she had been struggling with drug and alcohol addiction for years and it finely won. As it does with many people who are famous that's two of them singers which have passed in the last year. I wonder who will be blamed for this one? With Michale Jackson, it was his doctor. I wrote a little letter about it what most people don't undrstand is that for each Star or Whitney' that passes there are thousands of people who are not known who leave this world also. But to the world they are what is called insignificant because they didn't make aname for them selves and they are of what the rich call lower class of people, imagine that a thousand to one for each soul is equil to the other the way I look at people. Monday and we got a small amount of snow last night just enough to cover the ground, it was pretty when I looked out the window and the street was covered with fresh snow that had fallen during the night. Just glad that I didn't have to be out in it, planting time is just around the corner as the farmers have their tanks out in the fields ready to go when weather permits it seams they are always on the ball. Courtland will one day be well known as this is something I have seen in my mind but I'm not quite sure what it will be for as of yet, the lord has been speaking to me lately and reading is part of His plan it's like He is getting me ready for something that will happen in the future and only He knows what that will be. I have had the books sitting in plain sight for over two years and it has been just lately that He has drawn me to them, food for the mind.

A way too get me to understand without confusion like a food stick that you put into a plant to make them strong, the bible is His way of talking to us and the books give reference to where we should read or confirm if what we are reading is true. Many things or words I don't understand and that is something that will take care of it's self in due time, the books have given me a lot of information that I didn't know and I am drawn to them like a cow to water when it needs a drink. You can hear the equipment across the way running and it has been running all night in preperation for the season that is coming our way, they seam to know when to get ready for things to come. I was telling the pastor about studing the books and some of what I have learned and her face just shined she then said God is speaking to me, and this I knowis true. There will be some things that will try and stand in my way but I will hit the delete button and go on for the love of God is powerful. He talks with me when I feel alone mostly while I am alone it's His way of telling me things will be alright. As I saw Whitney on television this morning my land' she was beautiful and she talked about her addiction and how it had come into her life she even said she let it in and it was the devil she said she became the devil, and this is true. He waits for that moment when he can get into your mind and destroy it but God has greater power and so do we for He gives us the power to cast out the devil, but some don't know how to do or use it.

In scripture it says that a curse can be passed down through four generations and it talks about how a son didn't want to be like his father, then later he lost his way and ended up just like him. My thoughts on the matter is that if God's isn't there to help a person then they have no way to over come it, only He can give us the power we need to live a righteous life. Everything has to be in accordance with God to live this life without fear, for we are only here for a little while to learn what we need to know. As for generations before my birth father I have no clue of what happened back then, but it was apparent that there was some kind of trouble going on. We as individuals have the power to stop a curse if we are strong enough but if we are not so strong then He can help us, many don't know this and it's a shame to wonder around in a world that you don't understand bring me peace in this world because without it the world is confusing this peace I talk about is given by Jesus and He paid the price on the cross two thousand years ago so we wouldn't have to suffer so much. Tuesday morning' the number which had called me theother night had no answer when Icalled it, strange howe that happens sometimes. We didn't get any snow last night so that's a plus and I already took out the trash last night here at home and at the church because I knew it would be slick out side this morning and me and ice don't mix legs are still unstable on that crap even today, you have to know your weaknesses and avoid things that can do you harm. The determination of Whitney's death isn't in yet it seams they found her in the bath tub and she was dead the cause not determined as of yet but if they can they will cover it up by saying she hit her head or something, as with all stars they don't want people to know the real reason. When they showed films on Michal Jackson while he was growing up you could see the pain in his eyes but that's just my opinion, later in years they would blame his doctor and he would go to prison so much scandal. Many people turn to the drugs and alcohol because it makes them feel good but like with him and her it only works for a little while and then you fall from the top of that place you were, all the things that were important befor in life are not that important any longer the only thing which I find to be relStacynt today is getting to know Jesus and that path will lead you to where you need to be. With age comes wisdom and knowledge and the ability to use both, but use it wisely because it could hurt others just like with writing it's a two edge device which can cut both ways stronger then the strongest person. I have a feeling it's going to be a wonderful day' and my spirit is great. I find that when He does something great in my life I have to tell someone because I'm so happy and this isn't always a good thing to do because they seam to get jealous, I guess it's always been that way a part of human nature that isn't productive jealousy can doestroy some things when your in a relationship and that's something I have been through not very enjoyable because it causes more problems like anger and hate. Could those things be gone from my life or would they have to be tested at a later date? when I get one Ha! Date that is. Wednesday morning it's a little warmer out this morning, they say it should get into the fifty's which will be nice even if it does rain. Later we are going to town for some things and I want to stop at the thrift store to see what they have I like the people there especially the ones that run the place.

My land' the days are going fast for sure time don't stand still around here and each day brings something new from a smile to a frown from laughter to sorrow but at the end of the day we seam to go to bed with no anger or regreats. Thursday and Oliver is doing find he must have been depressed for a few days because he wouldn't eat tht much and I found out that he gets mad sometimes because he cant go out during winter. what he doesn't realize is that he is prone to getting sick if he goes out in the cold, I told him that I will take him out all he wants during spring and the summer months and he said ok' now he has started to eat better. He is a great person and I love him dearly and after praying I know he will get better. He likes the trips to Grand Island to see the doctor as it gets him out of the house and we talk boy do we talk about everything under the sun It's like he is a part of me and I would never want to loses; him such a great friend or should I say father. As for making it through winter we have, and now the hot months are in the future with temps in the hundreds but that wont effect him with having central air we will all stay cool during that time Febuary is half over with and March is just around the corner, in past years I have seen it snow into April but that doesn't happen very oftend maybe once every few years or so. Oliver is like a part of me we have been together through the good times and the bad and we have made it this far, as for others he is more important to me then anyone else I have held him when he has cried and he has been there when things weren't so good for me but love always prStacyiled through it all. Moving here was hard on him but we also came out on top.

Many years ago I thought about putting him in an old folks home and I couldn't do it, not when I was alone also we developed a good relationship and we have been together ever since over twenty some years and he had been doing good. I want to get him a new chair to sit in a recliner of some sorts that will make him comfortable that way he will be able to watch television in style, it's strange how I write my life down but these times will be gone and I want to be able to look back on them and smile about the good times we have had. Nothing last for ever but we can catch time and freeze it for a time in what we write and that can last for ever, just like the letters on addiction they froze that day in which they were written and made there way to the internt for the world to see. For me this was a great acomplishment because in my old life I never seen it coming and it was out of cherictor, it was only through His love that I was able to do those things it was He that taught me these things, the ability to be able to focus on what life should really be like and it's been a long ride to where I am today. Through the love and understanding here at home and out of the home there is a peace which I never thought I would find, it's not nice to go through life in a fog because you miss so much but then when you find that peace and your mind is clear then you know everything will be alright. And the little things don't bother you like they used to, for it is God that can give you peace in the mind in the days a head we will see an improvement in my buddy and then I will be happy once again. Friday I had a dream last night about Diane my ex wife. I don't know why she came to me but she did an boy it was confusing yesterday went pretty well I even took Oliver for a ride bcause it was so nice and he seamed to enjoy him self I also got him a slush puppy that he likes so well. A friend brought over some boost for old folks and I gave him one and he liked it, so that should help with his weight gain plus she brought over some other stuff which does the same thing that can go in his cerial, while in town yesterday I saw the women which used to work at the dollsr store and said hi which she returned in kind by saying hi back don't know why she isn't working there any more but I miss seeing her there. My land' it's hard to wake up this morning as I was up a few times last night and didn't get all the sleep I needed but I will be ok' in an hour or so, as for yesterday it was fun going to get little brothers perscription and then back home it's fun making these trips when it's nessary or at times when we have to have something different when we go on them it seams to change things from sad to happy. As children it doesn't take much to amuse us like with the squirt guns mom used to bring home from the hospital so we could have water fights it was a cheap way to have fun because we couldn't afford regular squirt guns. They did the best they could for us and even with the addictions I turned out alright, getting lost in this world takes a lot of time to over come but now that I look at it there was just a bump in the road of life. One that threw me off my feet but I got up again with the help of my Father' the computer age is changing so I will have to change with it what was once new is now old.

So I will have to get a new one that will last hopefuly until I'm done on this earth the things seam to be touch screen but with a key board so you can use them either way, all I have written will be transferred from one to the other. Then it will be like starting over again, there is a program on television about free money which the government holds they don't tell people about it and keep it a secret. This is so wrong but someone is blowing the lid off of it if you have money coming from a person who dies they keep it a secret and hold on to it. Imagine the homeless which might have money out there that could be the difference between living on the street and having a home, yet they don't get a notice from th government and it sits there. It would be awesome to find something like that and have your world turned around, the guy says that the government don't want you to find it because they use it for self gain what a crock! But it doesn't supprise me that they would do that, my father could of left me something and I wouldn't even know about it. Many times in life not knowing is better then knowing if it will cause problems but then problem solving is a part of life and it can bring you closer to Jesus, when you need help solving it He works in the supernatural not in our realm of existence so everything is different there. What we think is a solution to something may not be right in His eyes, we as people seam to do things half way like the time I asked for His help with people comeing over all the time they were selling drugs and wouldn't stay away so I asked Him to help me with the problem and low and behold everyone of them vanished.

And they were never seen again by these eyes, it's hard to change your life when others wont let you they try and stop you by bringing the drugs or alcohol to your home. And that's when you have to say no more and if need be throw them out of your home, one time I went with a women who was a drinker and that didn't work out very well and it showed how dependent she was on it. Each night after work she had to go to the bar' to unwind she said and I found out something about my self and that was that I am a very jelous person and the devil would enter my mind making me think she was cheating on me, now wither she was or not didn't really matter because the seed was planted. Those feelings in them selves made me not to want to be in a relationship because if you don't have trust then it will never work, those things can make you turn away from feelings because they are not plesent ones to have. Saturday morning and all is well I wasn't surprised when my daughter told me that she felt numb from her cousins passing as that is something your never ready for in this life, and for them to both go so quick was tragic. You just don't know what to say to someone when that time comes. When mom passed most of them had the bottle to jump into but then as time passed and I get my life straightened out I didn't feel anything no pain or sorrow just numb like Shannon felt by the time mom passed I had been straight on the alcohol part but the others were still drinking my life was an up and down ride so full of confusion about the world and how it really was. But in the end I think things turned out alright, the falling from those things really made me stronger in this part of life anyway and it's great how it's turned out. I could never say in words how I feel about my new life and friends this is something that comes around once in a life time, the responsibility with the church is one that I really love and I look forward to going there every few days it's like that special place where you can think away from the confusion of others thoughts, sometimes it's like I can pick up on other peoples thoughts and I don't care for that. But I guess it could help in some ways like in communicating with someone who has a problem, so many would talk about their problem if just someone would listen and I find that some parents don't want to hear about them, and this is caused by them their selves fighting with addiction and that reminds me of the guy whos family went to church every Sunday he brought up his kids to think it was alright to have a beer or booze but not the drugs this in it's self is an oxymoron because one is the other they both distort reality and let a person inter that place which doesn't exist except when your high or drunk which ever the case may be. Some will even go as far as to say they cant start the day without a drink and I have been there close to the end, and when you think that way the end isn't far off for most of them they will fall and fall hard. Sunday morning and it's calm out side and O so quiet that the birds are not even up yet I remember being up at this time in the morning in Kearney but it wasn't the same quiet as it is here as even the fog moves in sometimes. For there is truly something differen"t about this place and the other towns, it's like they are all in a vallley and some more so then others, every now and then we stop in Scandia to go through the museum but we haven't been through all the buildings yet but they have some wonderful things there. As we drove through the town we saw a house with pillers on the front porch and it looked like it was built in the old days like the 1800's it was all stucco and had been boarded up for quite some time.

It looked like it was made during the revival period or when the south was fighting the north, but that's just my opinion. Who ever built it had to of been very well off back in the day, I love the sight of things from time passed as most of the homes were built by hand and not by modern ways. Imagine a bunch of people getting together and building that home it looked like it was once the grandest home in Scandia now wore down by the elements but with some work who knows it might be liveable once again, I would love to see the inside of it. And it's grand wood work if it still exist with many of them they go in and gut them but I have a feeling that might have not happened there. But I do know that the roof would leake after so many years, with my home I was lucky that he had replaced it not too long ago because that would of cost a lot of money. Off to open the church here in a few minutes so It's ready for service. Sunday mornings are so peaceful and I really like going there it's like I'm a care taker and that is awesome the church has been around since before I was thought of and now I take care of it, I wonder who the other people were maybe one day I will find out. I hear people talk about the world out there but for some reason I don't want to be a part of it even Jesus said we are not to be a part of the world of things that the devil has made, living here I don't have that temtation and it doesn't enter the picture of things in my world. The peace here is soothing and as of yet no one has tried to ruin that so each day is welcomed.

Harley is such a wonderful pet and he loves me dearly, yesterday the pastor was walking her dog and harley was barking at them she turned to look at me and I said he is going to get ya and she said ya right. She knows harley and I very well and wekid and joke around from time to time, getting to know people in a small town is hard at first but once you make the first contact then it can be fun O I'm sure people gossip but I don't get that close to where I hear what's going on and it will remain that way. My self I don't want to hear such things in my life if you can't say anything good, then don't say anything at all. In my younger years my X would start all kinds of fights over stupid things like gossip and it hurt a lot of people because usually it wasn't true, someone says something and then as it goes down the road a little more is added and before you know it none of it is true even in the bible it talks about gossip and how it shouldn't be started in the first place. I do know it's usually started by someone who doesn't have a life to live of heir own and that kind of thing doesn't stop it just goes on and on until there is a fight of some kind. Monday shock of the century I recived a call from margreat and she said she loved me pretty messed up if you ask me, seeing we broke it off as her not wantng to be my friend and now she does. I was shocked to hear from her as I had put that in the past like all bad memories when we split it was like she stuck a knife in me and I don't want to ever go through that again. It's going to be a nice day as far as I can tell and I hope it's like yesterday with the temps being in the high 40's, I don't have room in my life for her at this time and I'm not sure if I ever will. But it is funny that I had just asked a women if she was married at the dollar store and then I get a call from Margaret so strange, it's like day ja voo all over again but this time I have control of what will become of it my sanity is more important then a women at this point in my life, plus I have enough to take care of with my boys. Yesterday Randy was joking around and told me to tell her that he is single and I told him I couldn't do that to him, why after all this time? The question is, I surely could of went the rest of my life not hearing from her. Here in the country friends are hard to find and maybe she lost hers who knows! She also said she has a druggie accountent that wanted to meet me but I don't know about that she didn't make it clear about what for, life changes us all and who knows she may have changed in some ways but that would have to be seam. Church went well but I didn't stay for coffee and we went to town. The asking if the women was married had been weighing on my mind for some time so I just had to ask, this is something out of my comfort zone and it was kind of scary at first. She said it depended on which day of the week it was but legaly she was kind of in a joking way and I think that is what drew me towards her she is kind. Things are going pretty good these days as Oliver is doing good and so is little brother, Oliver really likes that boost drink which has all the vitamins he needs for a balanced day, plus it's supposed to make him gain weight I was worried when they said he weighed 167 pounds but his weight goes up and down in his old age but now he is on track I sometimes like to hear little brother talk in his sleep, and I try to figure out what he is talking about. I haven't been able to figure it out yet but maybe some day he told me the other day that he is getting used to having a good nights sleep and that he feels so much better this is from finely getting a balance to his med's that he can live with, all good things in time I will talk to Leroy about getting my mower going within the next few weeks that way it's ready for the summer months.

I said a while back that I felt change coming and maybe this is the start of it. The not knowing whats going to happen is a mystery and I will sit back and watch it unfold, Presidents day and why they have this day is beyond me but it get's some out of work for the day. Coffee something that makes your day or at least the beginning of it and I'm running low so back to the store I will go, it starts off your day with a nice aroma and brings everything into focus for that wonderful day you will have. I can hear Oliver sturring in the next room getting ready to start his day in a couple of hours he is yawning to get the sleep out of him it's always a good day when he feels good. Watching the news a guy jumped off the Gorge Washington bridge because a guy posted that he was gay on twitter and other social networks, they are tying him in a court of law with fifteen counts what is the world coming to? My land' it seams everything you hear is bad nothing good and that's why I don't live around that crap, you couldn't buy what I have here the peace and quiet and such good friends' you just couldn't put a price on it Courtland is the place to live if you want serenity and not the hussel and bussel of the big cities. My story "life in a small town" will stand the test of time and those who read it will try to find a place here but it's limited by the amount of space which opens up and this living isn't for the faint of heart because it's hard and you have to travel to stock up on the things you need for the month. It's like living in a protected commune and that's a good thing these days, no worries about people robbing you.

Courtland the place of dreams where your dreams can come true if you believe in them strong enough, I do know my dreams have come true here. And in a way so has my little brothers, for it was here that he got his freedom from the ties that binded him and even though he can be impatient they will unfold in time. I learned a long time ago that He works in His own time and space if we can make it happen He can bring about the supernatural and make it a reality, for this is what he does for us His children. God works in my life even when I don't know it as He never sleeps like we have to imagine that never having to sleep but that's why He is who he is. We are starting to get some rain and I hope we get a lot of it so the crops can grow like never before, we were blessed last year by plenty of rain and our worst was better then the rest of the countrys best this shows that the lord is watching over us even in times of doubt. I have plenty to do this summer with the lawn and such but before anything the mower has to be fixed, so I can do the work and I trust in Leroy to get it done, he is funny sometimes as he doesn't want me to start cutting my lawn too early because around here once it starts it not done until the end of the year, it's like keeping up with the Jones and I can relate to that but don't except it. The day has been nice for a Monday but the over cast sky's makes it a sleepy day also as we sleep off and on through the day, I could go to the church but then I wouldn't have anything to do tomorrow so that's on hold for another day. Randy tries to sneak some sack time in but he cant do it because he snores and that gives him away big time, I have to laugh when he tries because it's so funny then I tell him to quit snoreing and he says he is not snoring. Little things like that is what makes things intresting around here and a laugh or smile is worth a million bucks, come to find out Margret just wanted to apologize for the way she treated me when I first moved here so I text her back and told her tht I except her apology. Things like that have to be set right and now she has done it, I was quick to think she was up to no good but that wasn't the case it seams through time she has changed, and that's a good thing. Maybe in the future we could be friends but only time will tell that she also mentioned an accountant that wanted to meet me so I will wait and see what happens, Tuesday and I had a wicked dream about having a lung desease and it was like my brother Rick was trying to kill me for some reason kind of scary really and then I woke back up to go back into the same dream wird crap if you ask me. Through the days until summer I will get my house fixed up with different little things I get from the thrift store and that will make it nice, I still cant get over how my sister thinks my home is nice and that means so much to me for some reason maybe because she is more like mom then she lets on with her short stature so many things are different now days as most of us are strung around the country but we have never been to far from one another maybe a state or two away. With whats been going on inside of me I'm not sure how long things will last but I'm happy that I came here to Courtland where my dreams have come true, it's strange really even Margret calling me to say she was sorry for past things she has done, I really thought she would start something but she didn't and that's good let bygones be bygones and forgive those who haave done anything to you.

For that's what it says in the bible as the days of addiction are behind me I cant help but wonder what would of happened if I wouldn't of changed. but that's not something to be brought up now when my world has, I don't know why things are this way, to live the first half in the dark maybe it was so I would recognize between the two. For this side of life is more productive then the one of living in the dark where you wake up in a different zone each day where others are the same way, in this life it's the same each day except you have different things you do on certain days and this world moves at a much slower pace so I can stay up with times the traveling I did in my younger years helped to lead me here and that was a good thing in my books the serenity of knowing your neighbors. There is another side here but I havn't met it yet the younger people with their hipper ways, I would like to get one of them to clean my gutters and maybe I will sometime this summer things here are or should be kept here pertaining to money and such. It would be awesome to have a christen youth center here in Courtland that way the kids could have something to do so they would stay out of trouble, I'm not sure the people would go for it but it wouldn't hurt to ask and who knows some of them might stay here after school to work on the farms and in the elStacytors. My self I don't see any draw backs to it but then I wouldn't be paying for it the bank will, I would have to get up the nerve to ask Mark and then see what he says. Have a pool table and some games a soda pop machine and pin ball, as for taking care of the place the kids can do that.

· Would it fly? Yes I believe so and it would bring many of them together the ones from the country and here in town and other towns would even come to check it out. Let it be a christen enviorment where they can get to gather to study the word of God that would be so awesome if that could be brought to light, I wish I could be blessed with plenty that way I could build it with what God would give me a sort of share the welth things that would last for ever. There are many young people that think there isn't a place they can go other then to like partys to have fun and that's when they fall into the world of darkness and it's not a nice place to even visit because the getting hooked factor is high, and no child should have to go through that I still think of the stranger from time to time and I wonder how his daughter is doing and I hope he was able to get her help as the drug she was or is on is one of the worst to overcome. I wonder if the dream has something to do with my past life? But I guess I may never know the answer to that question as it hasn't returned since that time or maybe it was trying to show me that part in which it could have gone wrong, yesterday was a nice day in the fiftys and I think it will be the same today if it's his will. The weather changes so much around here that from cold to warm then back to cold again, this morning Harley had me take him out and then scratched on my door to let him in. He is such a good friend and the good thing is that he doesn't talk back just gives a hundred percent love, a long time ago I used to let him sleep with me but the shedding thing stoped that having to wash the bedding every few days wasa night mare. He just sits in my room and sometimes watched television when he isn't resting under the bed, I can feel the spring fever coming on and it's strange because I never noticed it before in life but when it hits it makes you do some strange things and at times I feel goofy for some reason like I'm on the prowl for something that is created by nature. When I moved here I had a few goals and one was to own this house which I do and the other was to have safe transportation which I also have, these things are attainable if you believe in your self and God and when he tells you to do something you should do it. Writing about the town has made me an asset and owning property has also made me a big part of the community, and it's a great feeling knowing there will always be a home for me here a place where I can call it my own. Prayse be to God for making this possible and of course Mark my friend to who with out him seeing something in me it could have gone the wrong way but he believed in me and for that I'm grateful. When things happen that we don't expect sometime we have to adjust to the situation wither it's life cut short or you are thrown into something unexpected, life it's self is just a loan, that will be picked up somewhere down the road and as for us knowing when that will be we wont know until it's that time. My self I hope to live a long time but I also know that it can be taken away at anytime and a person should be grateful for the time they have here, the life we lead can bring good things into our lives but also it can bring bad things if we don't watch out.

I believe He brought Randy here so I could learn to be around people once again and learn how to deal with some of the things that comes with it. But a lot of it is confusing and has to be separated in the mind and dealt with so when the time is right I will be exceptable to change, change is always comeing in one form or the other from the slightest to the worse and for me the worst has long gone with the addictiions that once plaged me. When you become part of a community they become a part of you and in a way you are both linked together, and if you are lucky maybe you can give something to them with a smile or a hug that will last until the end of time memories last for ever they seam to be a part of our lives that we can take with us on that long journey through life. Happy times and also bad times can follow us through our lives but we usually hope for the happy times' then the other which can hurt us more then help us, in the days which are in front of me there will be many more changes and I'm in hope that I will adjust accordingly there are many new things which will come my way and my two boys will be a part of that, even Harley will share in the things to come because they are good things. The control factor with parents can go either way but some parents can destroy a child by having too much control, a lot of them don't realize that the child looks up to them unless they feel threatened" then it turns to a mess with anger and they get lost, and feel all alone then they turn to others like people you wouldn't usually let them hang around.

Drug delers use this time to get them hooked on the drugs that they will later sell and then it's all down hill from there as their world spins out of control, by the time parents see the changes taking place it's usually too late for the child because the parent is in denial. They wont believe that it could be their child these are the parents that never have been addicted to alcohol or drugs, as for the ones that have been they tend to feed the addiction for some reason and it could be for many reasons they are lonely or just need someone to get high with. Tipical addicted parent my land' most of them didn't want to have a child in the first place and having to bring them up just throws them into a depression, as they sulk about their bad breaks in life they will say why me! Well why not you as it was you that created the problem in the first place many of them say that. And never get over it, they replay it over and over in their mind to only lock them selves into a cage like the bear in the bible even though he was let go he would wonder five by seven foot back and forth then finely they had to put him down. Thursday and my day is starting out pretty good so far this morning I have to clean the church and then it's easy sailing until Saturday my new computer came in and boy it's bigger then the one I have been using I hink this one will be used as my writing computer because I cant take I out of the house and the other one can be used anywhere where they have wireless internet this will allow me to even be out side and it has a web cam on it for taking pictures. I never thought I would be able to get one but now I have and it will help with what I have to do, the things it can do are miraculous and in time I will get to know everything about it but it will take time. In April it's my birthday so I got it for a present because lord knows I wont get any other, a treat you might say' yesterday it was nice and warm out and we got some rain last night that will help the farmers in the fields they say It's going to be a stormy season this year with tornados and a lot of rain I just hope the house holds up during this time. For each year is different and you never know how bad things will get until it's right on top of you strange how that works but that's mother nature, last year we had to put a bucket on top of the stove to catch the water before it got into the stove but now they have that fixed. I hope' today I'm going to talk to Leroy about finding someone to dig out my gutters that way the water will drain off easly and not cause any more damage around the molding to the windows you really have to watch hese things so nothing get's out of hand my house is my home and it reflects a part of me as a person, a lot of people can see part of you when they walk into your home it reflects a image of who you are. Everyone one loved my moms house so clean and she had great taste in the little things and I'm the same way buy something beautiful for a little of nothing and make it look great, shut-ins are usually that way because they don't want to deal with the world and as crazy as it is I cant really blame them. Mom never went anywhere and it wasn't because she wasn't sociable she just didn't like going out, but those who came to her home always felt welcomed but she decided who could hang around there and who couldn't with many of them she would throw them out the door because sshe could see that they were no good. In a way it reminded me of the people who lived in the desert with their tents not many were allowed in those tents but many gathered out side of them to go in meant you were someone special and that's how she was. And she didn't let just anyone in because if she did then no one would be special.

Memories good memories when things weren't really bad but good, her palace her domain and she was the queen just a loving soul that wanted to be left alone for what reasons it really didn't matter. My mom' one of the most careing people I knew and she helped many people get back on their feet in times of hardship but cross her or steel from her and you were gone right out on your ass she didn't believe in steeling and would not stand for it. When I was very young singing on her lap was the funest thing we did together even the sad songs were given a smile from her as she looked at me, who knows maybe I was trying to get into her world to see where she was in thought and time passed but I never could except towards the end then it was like we thought the same thoughts very strange but also a gift of some sort. I remember when they told me she was gone and I lost it, it took six cops to get me off her bed as I wanted to go and be with her it was the most deepest hurt feeling I ever felt but He seams to heal us in some way so we can go on with life and explore new worlds that we create of our own. Courtland is now my world to create what ever I want and I have opened my doors to Randy to see if he will change and be able to one day go out in the world by him self this is a part of giving back for the life the Lord spaired on that day so long ago, a gift to little brother from someone who loves him very much. Friday and the wind has died down from last night boy it was kicking hard and even a time or two I thought it would blow Harley off the porch.

He can be so funny sometimes with his short little legs, many years ago I had a little dog called refear and boy was he a card when I first got him he would hide under things like the bed or a chair, and the first time I reached for him he bit me but I didn't show any fear an pulled him out from under the chair. After that time he was always close to me and if anyone would approach me he would growl at them and they would leave especially if I was sleeping, we became good friends like me and Harley are today and even he will growl at someone if they get too close and act like they are going to hit me so funny, even kidding around he will growl at the boys. The love of a pet is very different then the love for a person as a pet doesn't talk back but people do in the days a head things will change and I hope for the better five more days in this month or six then it off to March towards a new month filled with many new ventures. I hope we get to go to GRAND ISLAND, IN Nebraska instead of waiting until April but we will see what happens then, it's a nice ride and Oliver loves it to see the country side. And who knows maybe they fixed the roads by now you can tell when you hit Nebraska, their roads are bad. Compairied to the ones in Kansas, Harley is sitting on my bed and he should feel lucky because usually I wont let him on it but he is being good and he looked so lonely wineing at the door. Sometimes I think he sleeps with his eyes open as he looks so relaxed with his eyes going every which way and it's so cute when he does it, the boys are still sawing logs I can hear Randy snoring in the other room but he doesn't do it as much these days, as it seams to come in spurts then he breathes normal and then it kicks in again. During the day he tries to hide that he is falling a sleep butt then th snoreing kicks in and I kid with him by saying you cant fool anyone! Your snoing gives you away. Each morning I pray and it seams to help in many ways by giving me peace of mind, I find that I let to many things bother me these day and Jesus brings me peace with that. As time passes I will learn more about the understanding of Jesus, and in doing so grow closer to him even in the bible it says that peope will become jelous of us as we go through this life and they are the ones you don't want in your life. As they can robb you of your peace and make life harder then it really is, and you don't want that especially if you have gone through some of what I have through the years. Many times gossip will spread and that's not a good things because it hurts people and living here it would hurt even more one day everything is alright and then boom, I just don't pay much mind to it because it is what it is gossip they can talk about other things. My world is different then theirs I don't need to make up things to be able to talk to people, in the days a head we will see what happens in GRAND ISLAND. The car has been running fine these days and I'm in hope that it will last another few years it's a good older car and even though I have had to have some repairs it's gotten me around just fine, it gets serviced every two thousand miles and I have kept everything up to date a few months ago I had it serviced because the transmission hadn't had it done since I bought it and I had put over ten thousand miles on it, they say to service it every six thousand that way you wont run into any problems I still miss my cruse control but it's something I can live without for the time being. I still remember the Ford that I moved here with but it was wore out and needed so much work, living here has brought me closer to knowing my self better and it's letting me get closer to Jesus to try and understand things about him and his life.

The way of the lord can puzzle us sometimes but through the years He brings us more understanding why we should turn the other cheek you might say. When things bother me I try to talk to him and find out why those things happen and usually He has an answer for others doing what they do, but me understanding it is sometimes hard in a way it's like tralking to someone on a telephone you know they are there but the lack of not seeing them brings many things with it. It's like I know Jesus is there and I have seen many things he has done in my life and for some reason it's easier for me to love him then it is a person as with people they change in many different ways and it's not always for the better. Love can change in a heart beat and that insecurity can make you do some foolish things that you normaly wouldn't do, my self I don't know if I could love a person like I love God or if it's even possible. The day was another fine day and I took the boys to town with me then we came home and watched television until bed time, it's now Saturday and I have some work to do at the church the weeks seam to go by without a hitch and my job gets me out of the house when I need to, each morning I have to get their Med's ready for them with Oliver it's became a part of life and with little brother it has became no bother to do the same if he would have learned to read he could take his own but that's not the case with him and when you love someone like I do them then it's all worth it just a laugh or a smile brings it all together, and that's what brotherly love must mean. in the middle of life taking the time to care for those who other wise would be in an old folks home Randy told me that he was grateful for me being who I am.

And if he didn't have me to care then they would have put him in some place and through away the key and I couldn't let that happen the ties that bind us is our mother. She was a great lady and would of done the same if she was here, way before he came to live with us I made sure that it was ok' with Oliver because he is the first priority in this life I have taken on and he agreed that little brother should come here.I talked with God on many occashions and He put it in my heart to take him in, after he got here I had second thought but they were wiped away when we got his Med's straightened out brotherly love is somethings special and even though he had done some things in the past it doesn't change that he paid the price and should now be able to move forward. Maybe one day he will go back to church but for now it's too big of a bite for him and that I understand, it was hard for me at first but then I saw the love of the people and it made me want to go more often. In the future when things change he will also change so we will see what happens my joy is something I treasure and when you share that with someone it makes it even better then going it alone just a smile from them makes it all worth it. And in the end I'm glad that I brought him home to where he belongs, a lot of people should try this thing in which I have done because there is great rewards in it not monetary rewards but rewards that are given to the heart, I believe this is what I was made to do careing about those that I love and help them in their way in life. When they put him in prison it didn't help because he was locked up in a place with nothing to do and they have no addiction program there, to help them with their problem I'm in hope that Randy will be able to take what he has learned here with him where ever he goes. When I arrived here in a way I was still lost but not as bad as I was before, then Courtland opened it's heart to me and I have been changed. Just the peacefulness is something to treasure without all the noise from the trafic only a car or truck goes by every now and then too let you know that the day is beginning and they are off to work to keep the town going like they have for so many years, a couple of years ago they built a new fire station and it's nice then they put in a cable place where I go each month to pay my bills and I like going out and meeting people, the people there are nice and they know me by name as they do Randy as he pays his phone bill there. It's the little things that I like a person going by and saying hello and a smile from someone you don't quite know yet, in other towns it's not so personal and people don't really care one way or another about you. Strange how that works in different places, the end of the day is here and tomorrow they have the M & M Auction at church afterwards, last year I didn't stay for it but today I believe I will community things are what they are into and it brings people together from all around to say hi or just have a good ole time in the days a head they will have many different things for the kids to do like bible camp during the summer. The time has been good to us and we look forward to seeing people when we venture out during the beginning of a new month, Mark always says hi when we go to the bank and I enjoy the people there they are so nice not only to us but other people that are a part of the community. Some will even stand out side and visit with each other just the closeness grings joy to my heart.

It's only three thirty and my day has already began it takes time for me to get used to the day then everything goes fine, little brother tried to get up at four thirty yesterday and his day didn't go to good as he would fall a sleep and his snoreing gives him away. I told that he should force him self back to sleep that way his day would go better, spring is just around the corner and the storm season will start each year brings it's own challenges when it comes to weather but the lord seams to carry us through it although the thunder and lightening; can crack like a whip sometimes some say we are in tornado alley but none of them have hit our home yet thank God' but many of them touch down around here like year before last when it broke the branches off of some of my trees and then they had to take out a couple of them. Walt let some people clean it up but they didn't do too good of a job at that time I didn't own the house but now I do and others will have my business Mr. Hoard wanted to do it last time and didn't get the chance but this time he will get it if he still wants too do it, the days are warmer now and the nights are just a little chilly soon everything will start to come to life the grass and the trees will begin to turn green one again, and my neighbors will start to plant their flowers wish I could do that.

After storm season it will get mighty hot out and the farmers will be out in the fields trying to beat the weather so they will have a good season, this is a process that is repeated each year as the grow the food for the people here and in other countries. If it wasn't for the farmer many more people would starve then there is today, that always puzzled me how so much can be grown and still there are kids eating out of garbage cans in the big cities this is the lords day be glad in it. The end of the week starts on Sunday then Monday brings a new one with it, to see what He has instore foe us. The morning is beautiful and it's another page of my life as time goes on here in Courtland, most people don't get up early on Sunday but to me it's another day to explore as I pray each morning it's nice to talk with the father and He likes talking to me it gives me time to just talk and not be interrupted that time of peace when all the world is shut out and it's just him and I "just me and Jesus" a great title to a song, don't you think? I will have to create one for him awesome. Later I will go and open the church and get things ready for the Auction I love getting the church ready to be opened so people can come together and enjoy them selves and worship God' many times I just go there to sing because it brings me peace from the everyday hussel and bussel of life it's self. O what a friend I have in Jesus' always loved that song, mom used to sing it every now and then and boy would I listen some good memories from time long gone. One day we will meet again in the great by and by but only the lord will know when that time will come I hope I have many more years here as I enjoy writing so and I have to take care of my boys for they wouldn't be happy anywhere else. God has brought me a long ways and I hope it last for a long time through the sands of time many will rise and many will fall but I my self have concored them all, those things that almost destroyed me. Are gone like the wind, to never come back again. There are many people who can do the same thing I did but it's taking that leap of faith which frightens them, it's like jumping off a clif knowing that He will catch you before anything bad could happen, now I'm not trying to say you should try this it's just an expression for his love is greater then all our understanding and it's different then the love we feel for people, it's much deeper. Had a dream last night but could only remember parts of it and boy was it silly, the making of something which wasn't worth what they were asking for it. My dreams come more frequient lately and I don't know why but with some of them I get really upset and that is something I don't like it's like I have been detached from these feelings for many years and now they want to be noticed, strange if you ask me. But many things are strange in life and why should this be any different, just like when Margret called that was out of the blue and with no reason but she said she loved me. Maybe I don't understand love but when I asked for someone to be brought into my life why would it be her? We are so different from one another and not a good match, or He could have been using her to bring the other person into my life cant figure it out! Time will reveal what's going on before my time is up I wouldn't mind getting married again if I could only find the right person. But finding her is the problem maybe she will just walk into my life not! You have to look for them nothing comes to you out of the blue or at least that doesn't happen in my world. It's getting close to opening the church so I have to get ready, the auction was great and we had a lott of fun all the people there had a good time and I got a few things for my living room it was nice to see everyone so happy and laughing as the Auction guy made some funny jokes.

It was the first time I had went to one of them in a church that is, we talked a little to each other and I couldn't get the smile off my face it was a happy time for me on that day, at first I wasn't going to go but something inside told me that it would be fun. They do this each year to raise money for the church and what was exciting is that money didn't seam to really matter it was a bunch of loving people just there to have a good time and they bid on anything that would help the church to keep moving forward into the future. This was all new to me as we all seamed to be connected in one way or another, we also had bisckets and gravy and I wasn't nerve's at all knowing most of the people there only if it was from a distence for some, truly this was the high light of the year for me anyway I got an old coffee set that had some damage through the years but that just gave it cherictor to know someone used it way back in the old days when they had a buggy and wagon history is a great thing and it's up to the people to keep it going. As Margret loves me from a far I cant go back in time for that is something that's not meant to be, I my self have loved from a far and it will pass as time moves forward. For the chances we don't get to take teaches us something even if it's not to make the same mistake again these people taught me to love them and that I have done, for my years here have been great ones and I look forward to many more.

Through the years things will get better then they are even today and that will bring me even more joy as I live to be an old man here in Courtland, no one looked at me like an out sider and that was a warm feeling. In the time I have left on this earth I hope to make my home a part of what's inside of me and who know maybe it will be historical many years down the road. There was one young women sitting next to me and she was so kind, her and her mother was keeping record of what was sold the book keepers you might say and they were having a good time along with the rest of us. My shyness seams to have faided and it's making me feel more at home here not having that worry any longer really helps and it will make me a better person during this time I have here. Many of the people live out in the country where they farm to feed the people here in America and abroad but I still don't understand why so many starve to death in a country as big as our's my land' how time flies when you write about things that are close to you and this town is one of them I would of liked if Randy would of went but he is still in that shy place which I hope will leave him in time. The antiques I bought could be polished but they say it takes away from their value if there is any and I don't want to do that, everything that was in the auction went to someone and I know they will treasure it or put it away in their closet to bring it back next year when the auction starts all over again. Getting involved with the community really makes you feel a part of it and it's a feeling like no other, as for what will take place in the future only God knows but there are many things that they do to stay together. It reminds me of when they would create a settlement back in the old days and it has lasted all this time what a great place too live. My daughter has gotten a new car so maybe she will come down this year but I don't get my hopes up too high because you never know what tomorrow brings, we have to take things one day at a time for so long I didn't know why they used that word but now I know, we can do only whats in the day and the lord takes care of the rest, through time it's self we are allowed to only take care of whats in front of us what pertains to this day and not tomorrow. As tomorrow will take care of it's self as it has done for so many years even during Jesus time when He came to die on the cross, it's Monday again the last Monday of the month and on Thursday the new month will be here leaving only fourty two days until my birthday, my land' time is going by fast "but hey" That's life right? None of us know what will become of our lives as for the jobs we hold they are just that jobs something we have to do to survive in this world created by the father, only He knows what our true calling is and He will bring it to light when the time is right. This journey I am on is one of wonder and only He knows where it will lead in the end, as for my heritage on the Hanks side it will remain lost as if it never existed, but why it had to be that way only my birth father knows. For me life will go on but that part of me will remain lost and that hole will finely be filled at least I tried to find him in this vast world, we went too town and got little brothers med's so they would last the rest of the month it's been a nice day but I see rain off in the distence as the clouds roll in from the northwest all and all it's been a good day. But that is coming to a close as night is falling and it's about my time for bed three in the morning comes pretty quick but then I will write some more, as for the church it's clean but not quite ready for next Sunday. Tuesday morning and we got the rain that I saw coming, it's strange how when you have been here for a while you can just about see what the night is going to bring weather wise and he streets are wet with moisture.

    I get anxiety attacks sometimes and it's not a feeling that I like but then it goes away but it's something I wouldn't wish on anyone. I don'tt have a clue what starts them but they cant be good for you, the years from before might have started them but I thought that part of life was gone not to return again. I hear that many people go through that and they live everyday of their lives that way my that would be a night mare' the last time when I had one they had to adjust the med's, because they were messing with my mind.the price you pay for a destructive life in childhood but you have your good days also and I thank Jesus for that, these pages of my life show that you really want to stay away from those destructive forces that will destroy your life. To all children please say "No" to drugs and alcohol in my travels there have been many times when He could of taken me home but for some reason he didn't, and it could be because he wanted you to know that your life can be better without it. None of us know how long we will be here so make the best of it and care and love your parents because most of them do their best in trying to love you, to all the little ones don't even give into pure presssure don't let anyone try and tell you how to run your little lives for each one of you are special and unique, one of a kind you might say and none of you are the same. The rain was needed here in Courtland and it gives a good start to a new year one with good crops for this I pray in the years to come I will talk about many things my life' and how it could have been a lot shorter if I wouldn't have changed, for this life how ever long or short is the better one to choose even with the bad days it's much better for He loves us all and wants us to be close to him no matter how far we wonder He will be there to help pick up the pieces.

No this doesn't mean to go and screw up on perpose and then come back to him, it means to stay on the right path and if you fall he will pick you up as He did for me so many times before. There are many roads we end up taking but only one leads to Him, with His love so powerful and true. When I was a child I didn't see what the destruction would bring but then later in life it hits you and your never the same, my life today is a blessed life and I have the things I need to go on. And I hope to make it a few more years long enough to tell my story to people in person that would be a great accomplishment in my life time and then I wold be happy to be able to take a tragity and turn it into something positive. To make a mark on this world that would make people think twice before they experiment with the dark forces which come with alcohol and drugs I wish I knew the out come before I let them in my life "for sure" they would of never made it into it. Children were given to us to love just like God loves Jesus but so many don't care for some reason wither it was an unexpected birth or they just didn't want them in the first place, but if that's the case then they will not get the up bringing they so badly need. We all have a testimony to tell but for some it's very hard to get it out as with me it's been over twenty years and I'm just now thinking about doing it, He brought me here for a reason to start where my first miracle happened. I hope this will be a good day as I have asked God for it, when you write you go through many different transitions and it allows you to bring more of your self out those feelings you were too scared of in the beginning, for some reason they get locked away in the back of your mind to only come out when He thinks you can handle them and that sometimes bring out that anxiety which isn't present. Today is the twenty eight the end to another month in the long line of months too come I will see what I have to do to get an audience of kids so they will hear the message. It's still raining this morning as I watch the puddles in the streets fill up with water, you cant see because it's still dark out but the puddles throw off a reflection of the house across the road, they seam to get up about this time to go to work. Listening to the news in the car they talked about someone getting hurt driving down the back country roads and she was from here in Courtland. It seams she swirved to miss a deer and lost control and the unit had to be called because she got hurt, this is common around here and it seams the deer run into the car not so much in front of it but into the side of it weird' back in the day I remember a horse jumping through the windshield of a car and my land' the girl was hurt bad. It was on our way to work and if we would have been five minutes earlier it would have been us sitting in that ditch with blood all over us another near miss by the protection of the one and only God, it's night now and a storms came through here like all get-out and knocked out the power, so I made sure my flashlight was fully charged with new batteries. The lights out thing doesn't happen very oftend but when it does you have to be prepaired so you don't fall and trip.

Before bed I could hear the thunder just raddle the sky and it sounded like a train, they said in Nebraska there was a tornado but they were waiting on conformation and if they got it that would have been the first in history to happen in February. As for us the rain it fell in buckets and saturated the ground as for the winds they hit fifty miles an hour and they are still blowing this morning it's the twenty ninth the last day of the month for this leap year. Yesterday was Marks bithday as for his age I don't have a clue and I told the girls at the bank to wish him a happy bithday for me, I would of done it my self but he is a busy man these days and his door was shut meaning he was with someone conducting business. I cant amagine how things are out side during the night but I hope the wind didn't do any damage in our small town. Not sure what the day will bring but I'm hoping for the bast as I do everyday, when the lights went out last night Randy said he better get him a pickle and I just laughed and went to bed. Tomorrow I will go and get my computer finished so I can start to use it didn't want to use it without it being protected so that way I don't have to worry about people steeling things out of it this world is full of thief's. But also good people, not sure if bad weather is called for today but we will see what happens, the night reminded me of when our parents would take us camping and it would rain with the thunder and light flashing across the sky us kids would get scared but not our parents they conforted us saying it would pass in a little while.

The memories of time passed seam to make their way into my mind and even some things I thought I had forgotten, what a ride this has been since my life has changed as things I would never think twice about come back to me. Randy said he killed a spider on the counter yesterday and I think they make their way in because of the rain but I have yet to see any of them, and I sprayed for them so if they try once again they shouldn't make it in. I woke up a few times during the night but then fell back a sleep and was up by four this morning my sleep habbits change but not very oftend as my body seams to only need a few hours to regenerate and then I am off again to face another day. A great day which is given by the father. As I watched mysteries; they seam full of things that grab the mind it's like opening a door that had been shut for so long very different from the real world but peoples minds go there to create different things for movies and such but also some get caught up in that world and never find their way back, which is also strange in this world of ours. This afternoon I have an appointment to get a hair cut so this hair will stay where it belonge and not on my neck, now that this task has been done I look forward to tomorrow morning so I can have full use of my computer through the days I was edgy and I think it has something to do with the other things I go through and I hate that feeling. Tomorrow I will see if they can change things again because they are not working, sometimes the pain is so bad that I can hardly stand it, I wish I could find away to not have to take them but that's out of the question at this point and surgery is out of the question, maybe in the future something will come up to take the place of it. The day has been nice and the night is upon us but not able to sleep do to the pain in my legs and back sometimes I wish I didn't have these things but it's something that cant be changed without surgery and I don't want anyone cutting on me as I have seen what others went through and it wasn't a pretty sight I asked them many years ago to do surgery but they told me it would do more harm then good so why go through it. The hair dresser was new and she did as good a job as she could but it was nothing like my regular women that cuts it, she is in the hosptal having something done to her and wont be back for two weeks. So neeedless to say I will have to have it cut again in the near future, as for the day we went to Scandia and got smokes and pop for the boys and saw that beautiful women again it's funny how she makes my heart jump when I see her so beautiful. Things seam to be fine this morning and I'm looking forward to another day. March first and there are many things to do going to Belleville a couple of times it would have been nice if I knew friends over there then we could just go for the day but that isn't the case so we travel back and forth. The country is the place to live if you want to get closer to your self and those around you but it can be lonely sometimes, there is a house across the way that must be haunted because many people have lived in it and none of them have stayed long only a month or two then they pack their things and they are gone. Strange I have been in the house once before a few years back and talked with the women that lived there and she seamed nice enough but she said she didn't like it there because it was too lonely and she was a people person so she moved out.

There has been at least five people or familys that have left from there it's an old house and the heat bill must really be high without central air or heat. There isn't many houses left here as they are all being sold or are sold when I first came here there was about eight houses and now only one or two, the kids are moving back so that's a good thing I talked to one of them that went to collage and she said the city life wasn't something she wanted so she came back. She also said she was born and raised here and wanted to come home, the world out there wasn't something I wanted either so here is where I will live, no storms last night and it looks like it will be a nice day they are calling for temps into the seventys; and boy that's going to feel hot compaired to the cold temps we have had in the last few weeks, then they talk about snow this weekend from extream to another and so on and so fourth. This will be a beautiful day if we get the temps up there. It's strange how you can get used to some people and when they are gone you really miss them even if it's on a vacation, but usually they return and things go back to normal. The guys are a sleep and they wont be up for a couple of hours, back when they told me I wouldn't walk again my days were full of anxiety but the doctor helped me through it somehow and it became a thing of the past for many years then with my mind on other things like learning to walk again it was gone. In those days I had cried an ocean of tears but I never gave up, and made it after a few years.

Even today I don't quit on things even though sometimes I want to and I have felt that my suffering was somehow to teach me something, my mind takes off on it's own sometimes and that is something that I don't like it's like I don't control it but then later it comes back for sure I wasn't expecting this to happen in life. Most people keep such things to them selves but for some reason I have to write about it and maybe because I want kids to know that alcohol and drug addiction can destroy them, it isn't plesent to go through this on your own but I have been doing it for as long as I care to remember. My land' it's been many years since I stoped the curse but does that carry one with it? I sure hope not, or I could just be getting old. I can hear people going by on their way to work and it's getting to be that time of the morning to get the others up the day was great as the weather was warm and we even drove with the windows down. It's still taking me time to get used to how this world functions but I'm getting it slowly, today is going to be a great day it's now Tuesday and I'm sending something back that I thought I wanted. Good thing I have time to do it, we can be rambunctious some times and make mistakes but we are allowed to correct them. Like the guy said things are not always as they seam for some thing are made out to be better then they really are. A lession learned from the facts of life, it's Tuesday and I don't think the weather will be as nice as yesterday some say snow and others say rain so we will see what happens later. My friends look out for me even when I make a mistake they don't say it but the feeling is there, it's funny how you think you want something and then later you find that things are fine just the way they are. I am sure that I'm not the first to make mistakes and I wont be the last, in the future I will be happy with what I have. The days seam to go a little slower or at least yesterday did and now things are going the way they should, I wasn't watching what could happen if you want to much too fast and that can hurt you. In the years to come a word of caution if you think you want something ask before you get it, I know I can do what I want but that isn't always the case in this world and the pioneers new this back in the old days. For they just survived to cross the country I'm that way only in a newer age of things I crossed from Nebraska to here and from Minnesota to Los Angeles to five other States many miles to find where I needed to be even today I find my self feeling guilty when I get something for my self but that's always how it's been all through my life. I don't need much when it comes to me but I have to be careful when I get some things. The day has been pretty nice except for a few things and they will work them selves out in time, not many days a head before things will turn really nice and I look forward to the spring time. Saturday and as usual the government has messed up my checks, this happens at least once every two years or so and one branch blames the other, it takes two seconds to mess it up but three or four months to get it right again. And the person hasto suffer until it's corrected, many times we find our selves getting angry but that never helps when you have to communicate over the phone and you live so far away from a main office three hundred dollars is a lot of money to someone that has a house payment each month and then utilitys, but they don't have any sympathy for their fellow man. They just take and not even send you a notice before they do something, the Social Security blames the State and the State blames them and the blame game goes on, in all my years things like this happens and they wonder why people have to live on the street. I moved away from the cities so I wouldn't have to be a part of that system and it seams they follow you every where you go. In all my years they never messed with things with out sending a notice first but they must have changed something just grab and run and the sad thing is that I have to bare the burden, this all happened on a Friday so the people were eager to get off work for the weekend.

I let Harley out this morning and it looks like it's going to be another nice day here in Courtland but you cant really tell until the sun comes up and you can see the sky. I can feel when the weather is going to change either by sight or feel as my joints tell their story to me, yesterday I went to the church and one of my friends there was taking down some Christmas things and this morning I have to go and clean up a bit but that's no biggie to me. It's the joy of being able to help in any way that keeps me going, my anxiety has let up for the time being and I hope it doesn't return for ever as far as I'm concerned. As for the questions they asked on the phone I didn't quite understand them but I did my best to answer them and time will tell if everything is alright, my property taxes have went up and doubled in the last year and that hurts when you are poor but there is nothing you can do about it at this stage of the game. Just reflecting back to my childhood I can see how hard my parents must have had it and then the accident happened which must have sent them over the edge with the bills and being taken to court for the hospital bills wiped them out it would be too much on any family trying their best to make it. And like most folks that louse their homes they ended up living in a tent, in California still today many familys have ended up living in fields like we did back in the sixtys.

And they have to be strong to survive, today my faith is being tested to see how strong it is and I know as long as I stay strong in my faith I will also survive, they might break me material wise but not in faith for the lord is my shepherd and I am one of his flock. Each day I pray in the morning for things to get better not only for me but for those suffering the sick and the weak and even for those who who are strong, and I know that one day things will be alright many time worry over takes me but I try to put it out of my mind in hope that things will change for I am the son of the one true God. My father in heaven, He must have known this time would come and He believes in me. They say He knows everything before it happens and He had to of seen this comeing, maybe that uneasy feeling I got a while back was a message but those feelings scare me sometimes as I am not used to them. Many people don't show whats inside they hold it in this is what causes mental problems with some and I can see why, the managing of things can get to a person if they don't have a routeen to go by but mine workd well for me. Even though I can get caught up in the moment bad moments they seam to pass and I become stronger because of it, and life goes on to bring more of them I wonder why He brought me back. Was it to prove that the human spirit can over come anything if it wants it bad enough? I know I'm still here so it must be able to. Even the fast days are becoming of less concern as we go into spring, my body is strong for what it's been through but boy do I get stiff at times is this to let me know that the future will hold more of this? Or is this to show me that this is as bad as it gets for this is truly something He knows because I don't. Scooter funny name really but it was given to me at a bad time in my life maybe to not make fun of me but to kind of soffen the blow that I wasn't going to recover, I have talked to a few people that knew me back then and they said they never thought that I would recover and if I could do it then they felt they had a chance, I always felt that inspration is the key if you can inspire someone then they can make that transition from addiction to living the life that He planed for them. He knew us before we were born and continues to know every step we take before we even take it and even though we wonder off the path sometimes he watches over us. And in many cases stops destruction before it starts, like when I was in the accidents. On the mountain when it happened I felt a calmness come over me like everything was going to be alright but my friend didn't feel it all he felt was fear, we could of went to the right which was a three hundred foot clif or to the left which would of also killed us but instead I held onto the steering wheel and prayed and we came to a stop skiding to a stop just five feet from that clif I didn't know it at the time but He was sending me a message, saying I have your life in my hands now He could of let go but then I wouldn't of gotten the message and in a way that helped me to see that my life needed changing. He had given me that same message before here in Kansas when I survived the crash here all those pounds of steel didn't make it but I did, and the two brothers who was to survive getting hit at an early age stood by the car and watched as they got me out. I find that He talks, but so many don't listen as they chalk it up to luck. It was like He was letting them see what I saw as a child but without the blood trying to show them that miracles do exist and they were one of them and now so was I. We had some things in common we were all miracles of the father.

Years would pass before I could see this and more miracles would take place, just me surviving; the addiction was a miracle as it destroyed my body, nothing was going right when I tried to end it with alcohol but I think He was saying if I saved you all those times surely it wont end this way. As time passed this man that wasn't supposed to make it until morning knew that He had a greater purpose for his life and even then he was slow to respond but in the light he was given a gift of only two words epiphany and Melchisedek and later in years it would lead his to searching for these words. In the mean time he would have to over come more things that would inter his life Methamphetamine would give him a high like no other and it came and went at first but like the other it put him on a path of destruction self destruction. The alcohol and Meth had all but destroyed him and then he was awaken, and turned his life around this would be his last chance of getting it right and he did finely. Now his mind was messed up but he put his faith in God and went on that search for the gift that he recived in that place where there was no pain or sorrow. Yesterday went fairly well except for the news I got in the mail, but that will be taken care of in the near future, things that happen are far fetched and I don't see the purpose in it happening, but I talked with one of my sisters in church and things will come out ok still today I get up set over things that I have no control of but I'm learning still. She said no one really understands the government or their ways and of course they are never wrong she helped me out a lot to understand things.

And for that I am grateful, my sisster in christ how nice of a person she is. I have to except that sometimes I need help with some things and I shouldn't feel bad about asking for help, before my pride wouldn't let me do that but now that my years are beyond fifty' I realize I need all the help I can get. Strange how pride seams to mellow out when you get older in the future I will try to except the things which I don't understand and get help with it, it's Sunday and it's going to be a fine day as my sleep made things a little better funny how that does that and this is a new day that He has given me thank you father. The grass is starting too turn green as we near spring and it will be nice to mow the lawn every now and then, just doing that seams to give me peace as I think about things in deep thought about how He saved me on that day so long ago.when things seam at their worst for me there is always someone to lend a hand to try and help me understand and this is His way to let me know that some people really do care, (friends) how great it is to have them. During the bad years He stayed by me and He is there even today. Mark Konz told me one time that I was special person to share my life with others in hope to change the things I can help change and I have never given up nor will I. Slowly I'm finding that peace which I know is inside of me but I wish the government wouldn't interfear with my peace, in many ways I try to be a part of my community and slowly I am getting there my church family is the greatest and I love them so family is important and a church family is even better. My understanding of things are different from those who never dealt with what I went through for if you haven't lived it you surely couldn't understand it. In the future I hope to get things back on track and go on loving my life here in Courtland' for I have never seen so many care about me the way they do, surely this is the place for which he sent me to write about this life of a lost soul, as sure as I know there is a God I will learn things in this life also. Not having a sturdy foundation to grow up in has made it hard but I will keep learning, I cant stop what has happened but I have come a long ways and it was His will that brought me this far yesterday we went to town but couldn't open the windows like we did the other day it felt good to let the breeze blow through my hair or what I have left of it ha! Kind of funny really but it was nice. My job is what helps me to stay strong through time of uncertainty, and my faith has brought me so far. My church is where I go when I need a stronger understanding of things and He usually sends me there when there is someone that can help in some way, things that make me happy is the church and now I'm starting to fit in even more wow who would of thought that the father could bring so much with out being here O wait He is here' and you can see it in everything, for this is His creation even we are a part of the system of things he has brought to be this is the first Sunday of the month so communion is today and I have everything ready for a great day. When things get you down just look up and watch the wonders of God unfold for he is in control of all things that have to do with life, from the breath you breath to the legs you walk on. As I am sarounded by my accomplishments of the gift that was given to me, I see many things and one of them is hope. Hope for those that really want it and a knowing that He can bring you through anything in life but never be afraid to ask for help, this path I am traveling was set when He came to me and told me what to do and through the years I like to think that my message will get out.

In the past there were many what if's what if it isn't good enough, or what if I make a mistake so I try and do my best with what I have in hope that it will get published, all the other times my stories have inspired many to change from the curse and live life the best way they can. And He will not let them down or leave them when they fall Lord knows I have fallen and He has always picked me up to go on, as for my life it isn't mine it is his as He is the one who said it is good before I was born and let it happen he knows everything about us and He knew it would happen before it even started. A learning process you might say to make us stronger in many ways a way to make us the best we can be. This Sunday was a nice day except for the wind blowing really hard, it looked like it was going to rain earlier but we didn't get any the wind is coming from the north so I'm not sure if bad weather is on it's way or not. Today I stayed for coffee after service and then picked up a little and came home to make chicken and rice, and boy was it good the guys have been eating on it all day as they get hungry and I made enough to last for a few days. I like it when one meal makes three or four others as they love it so much, tomorrow is the beginning of another week and new things are coming with it. I have to make a few phone calls tomorrow to get things straightened out with the agencies then we should have another nice day, the day is coming to an end so it will be off to bed before too long.

For with each day He seams to bring something new even if it's just a wave or a smile from someone you know for things are going really well and we are still surviving. Monday and there is a three quarter moon out in the western skies a picture perfect moment while I let Harley out this morning, and then I heard the old owl hooting out side and pulled my little friend to the door and got him in the house. I have heard many a stories about owls swooping down and taking off with their pray, and my little buddy isn't very big just a meal for one of those big guys they say some get to be as big as a hundred pounds and they have excellent night vision and can see as good as we can during the day. For at night I am blind and have not mush sight except for about twenty feet with a light. I haven't heard the owl out there for quite some time but he or she has returned and now I will have to keep a closer eye on Harley' when I let him out, Walt told me a story about a racoon that attacked Gismo one time and he wouldn't go out for the longest time poor little guy. I have a tree that looks like a Christmas tree right next to the house and I think he is making a home in it, it has to be fourty or fifty feet high and it would give it real good cover to not be seen the only way I knew he was there was by it's hooting. The days are starting to get warmer so spring isn't that far off and I hate to think about the bad weather which is going to come our way some small towns have already been hit by Tornados and the damage was great as it destroyed the Methodist church there in Henry-Ville. So many hurt by just the wind of a tornado and left homeless, we were able to have been spaireed from the storm this time' but there will always be another during this season. As I pray' I pray for those people in that town even though I don't know them they are brothers and sisters in Christ and you try to do the right thing, as of now they are accessing the damage and don't want any interferance from the out side, this will let them see what kind of disaster relief they will need to recover from this natural disaster. Many things happen that we don't expect, and all we can do is our best to try and make things whole for them once again. As the sands of time runs through the hour glass many things will happen that we will have no control of, and all we can do is pick up the pieces and move forward in hope that it wont happen again. They say there has never been a tornado in Febuary in Nebraska but yet this is the first year of it happening, some say real bad weather is coming but that's just one farmers opinion and there could be more of them saying that but I haven't heard of it. As we move forward into March the year is just beginning and there is so much to look forward to all the flowers and trees coming into a new year, for life it's self reborn to start another season many times a lot of people don't look at these things but I do. As it reminds me of my rebirth back in the day I wasn't able to see these things being in that fog of life long gone, the things in my life have to be recorded it's like my learning should help other not to have to go through the same thing. Why should they have to travel that wrong path if I can somehow help them to divert away from it, no one should have to go through that. And the great thing is that if they so choose He is there to help them even if they have already fallen. If it's caught in the early stages then they can recover faster then those who have lived a lifetime in it.

Some don't even know about the Lord and what He can do, but I feel if they can learn about Him before they live in that dark place. Then they wont ever enter it and it doesn't matter if it scares them out of it better to be scared for a short time then to have your life ruined by the curse of addiction, far too long people have been turning a blind eye to the destruction and now maybe it's time for the world to wake up. Let them see that the party life is going to ruin them in the end, the Media never shows the afterwards of a life destroyed only the so called good times they have while they are in that other world so many hav died and many more will follow unless they see where they are going especially children for they are our greatest resource and our future. They are the ones that will out live us old farts and bring us into a new beginning of things to come, my friend asked how I was doing on Sunday and I told her good for it was a brand new day and I was glad to be in it. It's always nice to have someone for whom you can talk to when life gets you down, before I didn't have anyone and now I have a new friend. Her husband is a great man and I really like him, I like all the people at my church for they are my family also. The family in which I'm glad to be a part of my spark of divinity is ignited when I write well! Most of the time then other times I cant get the pilot-light lighten but that's on a bad day.

As I walk through this life I give thanks for everyday I am allowed to be here and I know it's His doing. He loved me so much that He gave me a second chance and not everyone gets that. But I do know if your time isn't up then he wont take you, without experiencing the fullness of life. Do some get this gift very oftend? I really cant say because I have only met one other that has gone through some of what I have and is still here today he is the stranger who destroyed his addiction in the same year that I did, could it of been done without God's help? I my self' don't think so, for it is Him that gives me my strength. And my beautiful voice or I think it's beautiful and I will use it in the coming months if it's his will. Through life we meet many people but seldom do we make many of them friends, for one reason or another but with me I don't look down on any person because at one time or another I have probable been in their shoes. It seams like it might be another beautiful day, I just hope the wind is done doing it's job my land' it blew; like a dickens yesterday but it was warm out and that made for a somewhat nice day. As I read some of my letters from long ago tears were brought to my eyes but there was something different they weren't tears of sadness they were tears of joy because I know if something makes me cry then others would also and that reaches deeper then anything, emotions can bring change and also let you know that someone else has felt the same pain that you once felt many times emotions can bring change but it's up to the person to follow it through. Yes emotions last but a minute or two but touching the heart can make a person want the change if their life is out of control, for many years my emotions were what I would say shut off but then one day my heart was softend once again and I cried like a baby taking it's first breath. Jesus somehow took something that was num of emotions and make it cry like the first swat of a baby's behind, my land' I must have cried for days but then it stopped and I was full of joy all those years of holding it in was released; and my life started a new journey with many tears. Being an emotional person can help a person in some ways to reach deep inside of you and bring out those feelings that can bring change but the heart has to be brought back to normal for that too happen, we are meant to love and go through those emotions and maybe one day the right women will enter my life. I dearm about the happy ever after when two souls become one and they even sometimes think a like that would be awesome, to help each other instead of argueing and fighting not to condem or judge because you think you are right because usually your wrong and the false pride steps in and then look out. I was brought up and told that men don't cry 'what a crock' we all do sometime and just wont admit it, it's part of what makes us human and helps us sometimes when things get hard. As for me when it hit's the flood gates open and only the sea can hold them all. It was another nice day and it's coming to a close, the people I called didn't return my calls so I'm hoping that they will get to me tomorrow. The anger has come to the surface but I cant let it get the best of me so I hold it in and hope that it will pass no good has ever came out of anger but if it isn't expressed it will destroy some things inside of you, I think I will go and get a lawyer to get things settled once and for all then I can go on with my life. It's Tuesday and I have to take out the weekly garbage for them to pick it up, I look forward to each day as each one has some kind of excitement in it even if I don't like it sometimes but that is life.

For some reason I can see some things that are going to unfold before they happen, but it isn't little thing just the future of what will or can happen to me. The people of the church understand me even with my secrets they seam to care about me as a person, I was created to be a writer but other things take from that as you would think the past would let go it only lets me know that it still controls my life in many ways. For I will ask for help and see what happen, my life should be my own in the human since but other let me know that they can destroy it in the punch of a button on a computer. In a heart beat they can destroy what addiction couldn't and do more harm, I love my life here in Courtland and nothing is going to destroy my freedom but wait a minute they can! Through the years they have been paid back twice over and yet they want more to bleed me of what I have accomplished and leave another person to parish with no thought of life at all. When things like this arise it ages me faster then life should but I am a child of God and there is noting that will interfear with the life I have here, I have never reached out for help in that since but I am going to have to. I don't understand all the garbage that the world goes through as I am a simple person with an understanding of things in a different way, through they years the amount gets bigger and bigger even though I pay it each month it's a never ending well and they will milk it for everything it has and then some unless it's stopped.

Today my mind is clear for the time being, but later it will maybe get a reprieve that's what I am living a reprieve it's like I'm a fish on a hook and in time they will reel me in. I give thanks to Jesus for each day that I can stay alive for this story is all but over, life is strange to me it's like they want to keep you in a cage like the bear and always have you in reach if you get out of place. Harley' had me let him in this morning so he could lay on my bed and he looks so cute sleeping there, but at times I think he sleeps with his eyes open as he turns one eyeball to look at me. So funny my little buddy many times I would have gone nuts if I didn't have him around but he can also be a pain sometimes dogs are very loving and they don't hold anything against you when you get angry that in it's self is awesome, today I have to take Randy to see his guy in Concorida then we will be back home at about two in the afternoon so that will shoot another day in the butt. Then we are off to hump day so at that time I can read the news papers they send. And see whats going on in the out side world but many times I don't want to hear about it the destruction of things when they could be saving more lives is a waste, my mind it very bright as far as I'm concerned and at times wow! Never had a loss for things before except for the loss of thought. It's like I need knowledge and sometimes others can block it from coming but it doesn't stop me from searching for the answers, when I was told that I was loved I felt a warmness that I had never felt before and it stays with me everyday that I live and it help me to go on' my church family is strong in places that I am weak but strength comes over time to those who truly want it. The seeds of addiction that is planted early will one day cause havoc in a persons life growing up with it in a childs life will surely cause big problems later as they will remember how their parents were in their childhood. It's strange but as the mind develops it takes on some of the parents habbits as curiosity brings them to try what their parents do, for instence if doing good works is in their lives then they will probable follow that. But if they get a mixture of that with alcohol or drug abuse they can and more likely follow that also, I have learned that a childs mind is like a piece of clay and a lot of times it's shaped by what they see or learn and they can become confused and not know which to follow. At this time you better hope that they choose the right way because if they choose to follow the road of destruction then there is a bigger problem and the good works didn't get molded into the mind. Not as much as the other and when they get a tast of addiction the real world becomes less important, I have tried to help others see that the path of least resistence isn't always the better one when it comes to addiction. And many listen but then again there are many that don't know how to get out of it, it's like you are all alone as you work or wonder around and ponder what to do next. And the addiction always has what seams like an easy solution to only put off what you should have done in the first place and then that becomes a cycle, and you cant seam to ever break it. A cycle like the seasons of a year, one ends and another begins and before you know it twenty five percent of your life is gone and no matter how hard you try you cant get away from it, this is what some think. But I know that the curse can be broken I did it my self so long ago but it took Jesus to bring it about many times there was times when confusion traveled the pathways in my mind and it was very confusing, even today I find my self not being able to handle very much stress it's like my mind cant handle it and instead of letting it explode I try to reason it out, then in time it goes away like a thought but sometimes it's not that easy and I cry. It's Wednessday morning and I can hear the plant across the way running and usually I don't hear it but today I do. It had to of been in the high sixtys just yesterday and it was nice to have the windows open for the first time.

Not only in the car but also in the house, you can lift them with one finger not like the others which were too heavy. Even in the living room they open and that is something that will help as spring is just around the corner, I give a little about my life in hope that others would see that the curse can be broken my life has been an open book and I'm in hope that one day those who read it will be able to over come the addictions that will destroy their lives if they don't destroy it first. Through the night it was in the fifty's just a short time back that would be considered a heat wave. Time has not let me connect with my father so things will go on as before my days are full of joy most of the time but then when things change for the worst I find my self not knowing what to do in that situation as it's a drastic change, I have somethings that were brought back to mind which I had forgotten and now I will go on another journey to take care of it before a certain person passes away. He has a way of bringing certain things back to mind if we haven't taken care of them so they can be corrected and then I will be able to move forward with out worring about things that disstract us from life it's self, in time I will make that trip in hope that all will betaken care of. Church family' they are great and it seams to help in a lot of ways, to have someone you can talk with when things seam to be out of control. And they seam to understand things in which I didn't think they would be able to, as I travel down this new path most all things are new to me. Where fear wasn't afactor in the other world it is part of this life but in time that will pass.

As I started on this journey I had a hard time with spelling things but through the years that has gotten better as He taught me new ways, and it has taken a lot of time to get it right. My scrap book is coming along just fine as I put the memories in it, my daughter wanted me to do it for many years but I never seamed to find the time and now it's coming to pass. The things I have accomplished are many but they will go on after I am gone He said to leave something to help others and that's what this will do, for the news papers only run the story for a day but this will last for ever if it's done right. My song 'the light on the water' was liked by my Church family and now sometime in the future 'The Cross' will be heard. I was supprised when people told me walking by my house that my family thought it was good, there is something that is in me that wants prefection and as we all know that doesn't always happen but I try and that's what counts. The guys are still a sleep and I am glad that he isn't up this early but he helps me more these days then before and that is a good sign, living out loud I think that's what I do. Not so much in the talking department but through my writings and if it offends someone it's not meant to, my life experiences have brought me through many things that others cant connect with. Although my love for God is but a grain of sand in the Ocean compaired to his love for me, I find peace' when I need it knowing that one day that grain of sand will live for eternity and that love will continue to grow. Thursday, morning I had a resless night dreaming about things at one point there was a bear chaseing me and it seamed that no matter how hard I tried I couldn't louse him. For some reason I was hiding some food and he could find it with his keen smell and then I woke up and it was time to get up, never had a dream that close to wake up time before usually it is earlier in my sleep but this time not so much. There is many beautiful things where I live and I like that. The grass is natural for around here and they call it water grass, maybe because it stores it's own water but when you cut it it's hard on the mower so they say. The day is a little colder then yesterday we woke up with it being about fifty five and then the temp changed and you could tell that it was going to be cold as my bones that were once broken let me know about the weather change, strange how that works' when your young they don't seam to bother you but once your bones get old they let you know things. In the future I will travel to make things secure for my future and my grandchildrens this way they and my children will always have a place they can come if they want to get away from the rat race, I don't like them being in that place when they could find happiness here where I live. Mostly I wanted to secure a place for the future so they can come here when they get tired of being locked up in the projects of the cities, they would have a chance here with all the loving people and there are many kids their age, it would be like an adventure as they would have to stock up for the winters.

It would take some getting used to but in the long run I believe they would be happy, what's not to love kids need other kids and although it would take time the friends they would make here would last a life time. My life has changed so much here that I would love for them to get to know the beautiful people, in hope that one day they could build on and make this place what they would like it to be. I had a vision about my home and it lead me here to where I have found peace, and I have never wanted to go anywhere else except for the short road trips to the other place when in the beginning. I was very lonely but in making those trips I realized that the closer I got to coming back I couldn't wait to get here, in a way it was like going on vacation but nothing could give you that feeling as you got closer to home. As time goes on, there will be many changes and if I do things right my children will always have a home a place they can call their own one day and all they would have too do is pay is the property tax and insurance for the year and even a child could do that. Shannon and Leroy are pretty smart and would know how to survive in this beautiful place. They would even have a thrift store to go to, if they need anything. I have noticed that at times my mind is as sharp as a whip but then other times not so much. But I think that's natural for people to be that way just like happiness is something that comes and goes, we experience it for a time and then it's gone to return again later part of the cycle of life many different emotions that come and go like the wind blowing in a storm.

I love it when it rains, especially the thunder as it cracks across the sky letting us know that it's in charge of what will accure in the next few hours or moments,

I have a few things to do today but later I will be back home taking care of the guys making them meals and making sure things are the way they should be. Being a care taker is something I was meant to do, I have been doing it most of my life with mom when she was ill and then later when Oliver got sick so long ago. Most people get paid by others but for me it's something in the heart that makes me want to do it, a love for those who loved me back and most of the time it's enjoyable as we laugh together and cry together but the good times always seam to out way the bad as we go through this life. Oliver loves it here and also do I it's my dream unfolding slowly and I am not in a hurry because I know Jesus is in control. When my existence is threatened; I do what I have to do to get things back on track and then go on with life. When I have a problem I don't understand people are there to help if they can and I never had that before, everyone always wanted something from me in that life I had before and here that isn't the case. They seam to just want to help, and for that I'm so grateful. I find it strange how when you move to a new place or town you can get the wrong impression if you don't meet the right people but in the end things seam to work out, as you feel the love from those who care about you. Friday and again Harley had to wake me by scratching on my door so I would let him in, another day has passed and it was warm once again warm enough to open the windows one of them anyway, and you could feel the breeze blowing in the house a time to enjoy and have conversation with the guys. As we went to town people waved; and I waved back in kind even when things feel like they are not going right just a wave; can change that some how' and make things better. I have a feeling this weekend is going to be the first one where warm weather might dominate and make it awesome but that is just a feelng of someone that isn't quite awake yet, even though yesterday morning was cold the warm weather seamed to take over around noon and make it nice as heck. In the coming months I will make a few road trips, and I know they will find Oliver in good health his weight depends on how he feels and unlike a baby you cant brest feed him. My land' eighty three years is a long time and he will turn that this June, I can tell that he is starting to forget things but it isn't that bad yet something said every now and then repeated later in the day. But I'm only in my fiftys and that happens to me, a lot of things I have to write down so I don't forget them at the store but that is normal as age comes on us all. As for the things I have to take care of it sliped my mind and then He reminded me that it has to be done, then I can plan on doing things in the future but right now that has me at a stand still. The guys seam to love to go for rides as you can see different things at different times of the year, when the winter months come along you can see for miles then everything starts to grow and covers up what was once visible by the necked eye then the green starts to show it's self to make everything beautiful once again. It's like He is saying here is the start of a new year be glad in it, the squirrels; havent been out much this last winter or at least I haven't seen much of them. When I first arrived they were everywhere and I felt sad when I would see one in the street, when mom was on this earth we had a pet one that we named tobby and the littler bugger would store his nuts in the flower pots after the flowers would die off for the winter.

In the years that I have taken care of Oliver he has kept me company and I him, I wish sometimes that he would always be here but age seams to get the bigger hand of things when we get old and all I can do is care for him. As time moves on I will stay busy by taking care of things as I have done through the years and hope for the best in all things that come our way, as for change it's something that cant be stopped for each day is different and brings new things with it. Later I will talk with someone and see if they have the right equipment to get some jobs done, when I started to write. I figured you need three or four things to be successful and they are to make some of what you write funny and other parts to not louse sight of the conversation and the other to touch deep into their souls and then make them cry, not all things are as they seam as you reach people with words none of us are the same but yet some cry at the drop of a hat and others are not as in touch with them selves. For some reason He wanted my life to be an open book and that I have done but still we have the things which we wont share, I find that when I get mad it's usually at my self but I also have to realize that life isn't perfect. And we wil never be, all we can do is our best and hope that it's good enough. My friends have been good to me here and I think that's what Ihave been missing all my life, through the years we moved so much that friendship was something that wasn't there you would make one and then you had to move for one reason or another.

And now my friends will be for ever because I found a home. My travels are over except for he occasional road trip which only takes a day, or three at the most. My little buddy is still sleeping on the bed and he is at peace just knowing I'm right here. The hoot owl hasn't been making any noise lately so maybe it went home not sure how big it is but it lets me know when it's around. I always thought they stayed in barns but that must be a misconception on my part, in the wild they don't have barns out in the wilderness so they must stay in the trees and fly around the town to catch the critters; and maybe that's why the squirrels are not around here as much as they used to be. Or they got hit by cars anyway the numbers dwindle as time moves forward. I remember when I was 14 years of age, boy I was in trouble alcohol seams to do that to people especially to children. As far as I can remember I didn't get to live that childs life I had to grow up too quick and take on things a child shouldn't have to take on, but there are many kids today that have to do the same thing and that can lead to the wrong path. Saturday I don't think He would of used children as examples if there wasn't something to it as some say back during that time children didn't have any value to the every day person they were disgarded if they weren't what the parents expected. And to me that was sad I didn't even know this before, and the learning process continues. Children today cant be thrown away like garbage and I believe they are our greatest gift from God. It's hard to imaging that they would throw a human life away but it says they did, my land' that would be like throwing away our future and if it would of continued we wouldn't have any children today. It says come to me like a child and it could mean being eager to learn but don't quote me on that,children want to learn and that's why they ask so many questions to store information for later in life. The weekend is here a time for the workers to relax and then they are off back to work on Monday and the process continues as each day brings something new, yesterday was a real good day and I felt better then I have felt in a long time it was like all my worries were gone and I could enjoy the day. A blessed day you might say with a clear mind to take in new things, I have made up my mind to only go to town on Wednesday. That will be four times a month and that is plenty as the price of gas is going to be too high in the coming months, I made a prediction back in 2005 that the price would hit six dollars a gallon and even though it took some time that will come to pass. My land' it's already getting close to five, the oil companys are making a killig off of the gas as they raise and lower the price at will and of course the government doesn't do anything about it they just keep taxing them and when the price goes up they get more money. Many people say less government the better and that is something I wont go into you might say it's not my cup of tea, my memories come back to me from time to time and for the most part they are brought back to teach me something and I learn then it goes away for a time to let me move on and maybe one day I will catch up with the world and live in the now. I know there is a reason for things coming to light, this late in life. And it could be that we travel back down the path we leave behind to start a new. My scrapbook is full of information that would work just as good today as it did in the past as it will never change, people can look it up even fifty years down the road and bring those things into the present as they are stored on micro tape. Which will last for at least that long, we had a power outage right before bed time and then it came back on later and my little buddy had to get me up so he could go out side.

In the bigger cities they don't have them unless a bad storm hits and then look out because all of it usually goes out, when I lived in Kearney a tornado hit just three houses away from mine or it was a bad wind which took off the roof of a truck drivers garage. I lived on Ave B at the time and I was glad that it didn't hit us I think this will be another good day as we move forward into 2012 some say bad things will happen but I don't see or feel it at this stage of the year and maybe what they are talking about is the hike in gas and they just don't know it, everything bad that happens is open to interpretation as everyone has their own view of things that will occure in this year. Some say it was predicted thousands of years ago and I don't know if that is possible if we have advanced as much as they say, science uses those opportunities to try and explain things they cant explain. And usually they are wrong, I have noticed something in my life and that is each day I sing to Jesus and I never know what will be created but I do know the songs are for Him. And also they bring a kind of peace within my soul. This is something that has taken place within the last two years and it's not a hard thing to do just a joy that makes me feel good as the feel good is a gift for singing to Him. I never felt it before and it's awesome, many people agree with me on the effects that addiction causes what it destroys and what it can lead to in the future. "THE CURSE" As I call it is sometimes passed down through generations and it can go back as far as four, not knowing much about the history of my birth father leaves me in the dark. But it cant be as bad as the darkness of the addiction that I had to destroy, in my life I have been searching for something but even today I am bewildered; in the dark you might say.

In the years to come many things will shed some light on my life and I will embrace it like an old friend to try and understand it, the world isn't as it seams and a lot of people will do anything for the mighty dollar even destroy the life of a person they can take advantage of the meek you might say, the ones trying to do right but they wont leave them alone. They take until the person fights back and then try to take more these are bad people, but on another note a friend had a heart attack and was taken to Lincoln Nebraska where he can get the help that he will need. I met him when I moved here and he is a friend of Walt's, I never thought this would happen but it just goes to show that you never know what can be around the corner. Later I will have to check on his wife but first I will find out more from my other friend at Church, life is very short so we should embrace every minute we can. The weather is nice except for the wind but you can tell that spring is just around the corner, tonight we set the clocks forward and it gives us another hour. But that will take some getting used to, but it's ok' we do it every year at this. Later in months to come it will be warm until nine or ten at night so the air-conditioning will be running twenty four hours a day, I am sure glad that we are on the budget plan when it comes to the electric during summer. Otherwise it would eat us alive and we would be broke all the time. My daughter got her deploma for completing high school at the age of thirty two years, but now she can go into any field she wants to and I am so proud of her. Just me telling her those words made her feel so good and she told me so, I was surprised when they told me about my friend this morning and it came as a big shock. As I didn't know he had anything wrong with him he is a hard worker and has lived most of his life right here in Courtland working for the same company for over fourty years, his dad went not too long ago to be with the lord and he got his fathers house. I can see why people live longer here as no one is in a hurry, and they are not up tight' like other I have met in other towns like Kearney. It's Sunday now. And the night went pretty good but it will take like I said some time to get used to this time change, I cant help but think of my friend and wonder if he will be alright. I do know that I prayed for him when I heard about his heart attack and I hope that the lord will bring him back home, so many things happen at times when He wants to get your attention now it will be up to him to listen and take to heart what is being said. In my life it took a while for me to come around and sometimes this is because as a person who has never heard Him before it's hard to make things out, but in time He will make things clear to those He is trying to reach. It's a lot to do with tuneing Him in so you can talk and that can be hard sometimes, when my time came for change it wasn't easy but I made the desigion in the hospital to never mess with those spirits again and I havent to this day. My life force was determined to find the answers another way and I pray that he can do the same, this morning I will pray for him on bended knees and ask God to bring him back to his loved ones. He is like a fixture here in courtland the same as the old buildings that still stand a part of history that will live on. I know his wife has to be worried and I hope she finds the comfort she needs, as He says there is a season for everything and everything has a season but it is God himself that will deturmen if he comes home.

At this point many prayers will be needed and I know many people care for him in this tight community of loving people, the news came to quite a shock because I didn't see it coming but my prayers are with him. I didn't realize it before but I will need permission from those people I used in my story and if they don't want tobe in it then their names will have to be replaced by characters and then it will continue this is the second part of my life and most everyone knows you travel back down the road you leave behind. It's just that some do it in their minds and others like me do it writing, and that's how there becomes a record of a lost soul "the life of a lost soul" will be a good thing to leave for many to learn and if they take it to heart then change is possible. I heard that the old will dream dreams and that has started in my life not too oftend but still it has started, in the years to come my story will be of many different things but then again like it says if you want to make God laugh tell him your plans' with life comes many different things before birth and then birth into a big new world that is different from the world of being in your mother. But with guidance from her we seam to make a mark on this world also, no matter how slight, some are done to teach and others to learn from our experiences so they too may not have to go through things we went through. Prevention is the key for children as God gives the gift of change and no matter how slight change comes almost everyday even if we as people don't see it. Through the years I have seen many who don't want it and that's their choice freedom to choose is another gift but many don't see it that way, and loose their way in life like I did at a young age.

I find that with some it's takes knocking on deaths door before He will come and find you but when He does change will come in a matter of time. But how much time is really up to the person, if they are like many they throw away the thought that it was God and chalk it up to luck. But that couldn't be farther from the truth there is no luck only Him giving you a message, and they might not get it right away' but in time, it becomes clear as clear as day when the sun shines and you are able to start to hear Him when he talks to you. It's beginning to get warmer out these days and many will go and have fun at the lake on the weekends, and maybe I might throw in apole if we ever get down there. Before we went down the back roads so going that way isout of the question because I would get lost Ha! Many people' like even me, don't like hospitals I never have cared to stay in one longer then I have to and then I was out the door to recover at home where I would prefer to be just in case I left this world, the wanting seams to come out when someone leaves us as I remember wanting to be with mom on that portable bed when she passed. At that moment' the feeling of loss was the only thing I could think of and I didnt want to go on without her because we had always been together, through the hard time and those which were really good I guess I thought we would always be together but as we all know that isn't always possible and life goes on. I remember the police trying to get me away from laying next to her and boy they had a hard time doing that, it took six of them to pull me away and I cried like a baby wanting to go with her. Then through the years things changed and I was able to except that she had left me and it changed me in some way because I never did want to get close to anyone again. And then the one time that I tried it didn't work out, but you would of thought I would of wanted it more since she left and that wasn't the case. In many relationships they agrue fuss and fight and that wasn't something I wanted, maybe I was looking for that happy ever after which has still avoided me to this day except for my relationship with Jesus. He never changes for His love is for ever even if you mess up and Lord knows I have had my share of that, but I always seam to bounce back better then ever and stronger then before. When I cry He holds me not like we would, but in words' letting me know that things will be alright and that helps me through the hard times. Later I will see the sun come up and then the birds will be singing it's a beautiful time of the morning as many times I can see the moon going down in the west, all I have to do is look out my front door to see the beautiful sight. And it lets me know if the day will be nice or not during Spring' it reminds me of movie clips from other countries when the fog sets in and then burns off as the morning goes by like those old movies back in the eighteen hundreds when the castle sits on a mountain and they have a mote of water sarrounding it. I know someday soon I will have to put away my letters into my scrap book to save then from falling apart so my children and grandchildren can read them one day, it will be my gift to them so they might not forget what addiction can do to a life. Avoiding it is the best way but if they fall they can see that it can be over come with them, and not be passed down.

It's been a nice day and we even went and got a pizza in Scandia, the rain has been also falling for most of the day but all in all it's been a plesent day. Monday and in two days we will venture into Belleville I'm curious to see if we can go that long without getting on each others nerve's but I think we will make it, I missed the pastor not being around for a few days but I know she is back now as I saw her on the road on our way back from getting pizza. My land' she is a very busy person. I hope she doesn't mind being put into this journey as she and others are a part of it, who ever enters; my life' becomes a part of the story and that's a good thing atleast to me, I saw the women at the store who hadn't been there for quite sometime and she made us laugh. The rain must have been falling most of the night but that is a good thing for the farmers as the crops are growing right now, looking at the winter wheat it looks healthy and should give a good crop this year if nothing goes wrong like bad weather or other unforeseen natural desasters. I like the rain but mostly for the free car washes and of course it makes my grass green, one of these times I will be able to put in an outside water spicket so one day I can plant some flowers tulips; would be nice as you plant them in the fall and they come up the following spring so beautiful, I had some in Kearney and just loved them Rosa-lee helped me with them and she has a green thumb what a lady she is and that reminds me I have to write her sometime. In the days when I was growing up we had many good times camping and such and it seamed like I was always trying to impress the other kids by being able to do things they couldn't like drink.

And then later it would lead to other bad things I remember running away one time and hitch hiking back to where I once lived in Los angeles, and they found me sleeping in the back of the store we once managed Stop an Go market. Still today I don't know why I went there maybe to find a part of me that was missing. But I was brought to the police station and they called my parents, I know they had to of been angry because they had to drive over a hundred miles to pick me up. It was like I lost my childhood there and wanted too find it, by this time my parents were fighting and I must of not been happy so I was looking for a saloution to the problem. Which I never found not there anyway, many times in life we try to fix things but we usually end up making things worse then before. This is the human side and when you have no direction you wonder in a world that you don't understand and then one day you try something different like alcohol or drugs and it seams to help in some way, but the price you pay is very high and that problem never gets fixed it is only made worse as it puts things off. Until later in life when the problem gets worse and sometimes your mind even forgets about it, until it comes back later to haunt you. No child should have to go through that in life as it makes life really hard later in years, with some things what we seam to think is a saloution is just another problem stacked onto the others and they have to be solved before we can find the main cause of what brought things on in the first place but later I was able to fix what went wrong. "A picture of me without you" was a song that my mom would sing to me, and she would tell me that I was the reason she kept fighting to stay a live it was like I was everything to her in the days or years leading to her leaving this world. I could see the sadness in her eyes, but then I would make her laugh and then she would say it's a good day. I guess I saw what she had to give up for us and that made me want to make her happy, we laughed and we cried but all and all we had become happy in that world she created a protected world where we tried to bring joy to others. Many of the adults that came to live with us had no home and I guess they had burnt all the bridges within their families, you might say our place was the last stop for them to get it right before they ended up on the streets. And many went on to get married; it was like the last stop before you loose everything which most had already done. Through the years we knew what hard times were and if we could help then it must have been His will, she never talked about God but I knew she had to believe as I could see it sometime when her spirit would light up. Maybe if I would have been forthwith about it she would of opened up but I wasn't because I didn't know anything about God at that time, all I knew was that something had taken place in my life for which I didn't understand. Many times things happen and we don't know why until later in life but I sure loved my mother, the seeds of addiction were planted early and even though I didn't understand they took root and grew like nothing I have ever seen. That is something that shouldn't be done in a childs life as they will grab onto anything for hope, I remember being so lost that I grabed onto anything that showed a glimer of giving me hope. But then after a few years I came to find out that hope comes from Jesus, and I was looking in the wrong places. You cant find hope in a psychic as they will try to give you that to only make it worse after they take your money.

This was a great lesson learned and I learned it many years ago when I was trying to find my way and then God spoke to me again. And I put my faith and trust in him, I was like a blind dog trying to find my way except I didn't have the since of smell like they do. After all those things happened there, I moved here, to start fresh and have a new beginning of what I should have had before but starting over was very hard for me not knowing anyone. And never having any trust in people had damaged me in some way but through time I never gave up and they became my friends my trusted friends and I wouldn't change things for the world, He knew what would take place and He thought this is where I belonged and I do. They only know what I tell them so I am in charge of that at this point of my life and when the time comes my life story will be told not only to them but to the world. Today is going to be nice as the rain quit and the fog has lifted the blue sky is beautiful, and I'm in hope that they will pick up my mower this week to get it going again' then I can get the yard done. I also gave Oliver a hair cut this morning he has needed one for sometime now but wouldn't let me cut it until today, the day is coming to a close so peace be with you. Tuesday and I'm not awake yet the morning will be filled with things to do as each day is, yesterday I went for a ride by my self to get away from things just a plesent ride to clear my mind of things. And it made for a better day, my little buddy is looking at me while sitting on my bed and before too long he will be fast a sleep like the rest of the household. Harley dreams sometimes and I know they have to be happy dreamd because nothing bad has ever happened to him.

I still remember Gismo and how happy he used to be to see me when I used to take care of Walt, things you do for friends is usually paid back by good feelings and those feelings are what makes it all worth while. Walt told me that when he first moved here he didn't have anything and in sixteen years he had a house plus another to rent out for extra income when people would pay their rent, that's something that's hard to judge wither they are people of purpose or their just people struggling to make it too the next month of their lives. When he met me he must have seen that I was a good person and I was never late on a payment, this showed that I was responsible and had others that depended on me for their survival. When addiction inters your life at a young age you your self have no control over it as it starts out as being fun or it makes you fit in with others, and when the people you know are all alcoholics it's a part of everyday life from morning to night and as time passes there are times when you can do without it but they are not very plesent times when you shake like a dog crapping razor blades. When I was fourteen I swore I would never get that way but the curse had a different plan as it became worse over the years, the alcohol and drugs had destroyed most of my body inside and out and the ageing process started it was like it jumped into high gear, and everything started to fall apart and it wasn't plesent especially the shaking. My legs couldn't stand on their own and according to the doctors that life in the wheel chair was as good as it would get, and that's when I knew He wouldn't of brought me back to survive that way. I had so many things wrong that the doctors must of thought it would be easier to tell me the thngs they did, but like in the coma I knew there was a greater plan otherwise what would be the purpose? At this time the brain damage was done and it was hard to remember things that happened. The shrink they brought to my house told Mark that my eyes didn't correspond with my brain and that I would never get better. At that time I was still drinking and had to scoot across the flood to get around and it took all I had to do this, I felt alone so alone and thought why even try this was what I call a pitty pot. And many people go through this when the recovery process starts and I felt like giving up once again to go and be with mom but that wasn't in the cards you might say, later after asking for help God told me that He would help me and brought me through it. But then later my world would fall apart once again and He never did leave my side even through those times, and I am still here today but with a better life then before. I looked out this morning to see the stars off in the distence so the day is going to be warm day and I'm grateful for that, they were talking about it being in the eightys very warm for this time of year but it can change in a heart beat' as everyone knows here in the bible belt I never found out why they call it that. In Nebraska they call it the heart land' and say it's the good life which I have to admit the good life it was, for it was there that I over came all my addictions to alcohol and drugs and started over again if people knew me back then they wouldn't expect that I would be here today. In many ways my friends were paying their last respects to me back then and later they would tell me so because they had no idea of where they would be when I left this world.

But I had other things in mind' If I could somehow reach them and show them that fighting was worth it then maybe they too would fight to over come the curse that tried to take me. Even today I have many followers that look up to me because they know I never gave up the fight it's self will take you to places that you never knew existed, who would of thought that He would show me the place for which I didn't have to be afraid and all my sorrow and pain would leave this soul. The message He gave me back then still sticks with me today and I believe that's how my mind was healed, getting the typewriter was just a step in the changing of thngs but the learning of how to use it really stretched my mind. I cant keep track of the early mornings and late nights that He would wake me up, at first I thought I was going nuts but when He would talk to me I knew that wasn't the case. The mnd is a mussel and like all other mussels they have to be exercised to stay strong this allows it to create and if there is any damage then that can be healed in time, but nothing good happens over night as I know all so well. Then He started to teach me like a student His student and His child you might say I was home schooled by the teacher of teachers and when confusion enters that place it throws everything off and I have to ask for help from others that have been in and seen that big out side world that I am not supposed to be a part of.

My understanding of things is different from others that live in that place where I don't belong or travel to it, I think the people here are supposed to help me in some way and in time I will find out where they are supposed to help me. It could be with getting things straight and on track but only time will tell that story. I have a dream' that one day the things I want to do will come to pass, and my dreams seam to come ture with a lot of work one day there will be a place where kids can go so they wont be influenced by the thing that can destroy their world. It only takes once for them to fall into that world of darkness that can and will take them out of the light and into that place where they will be lost, I have been there and it's not a good place to be and then you spend the rest of your life trying to get out of it. It's noon and the temperature is rising I have been out side and it sure is nice. The warmness is really great and some are riding their motorcycles what a great day for it, I'm wanting to get my mower going but they havent picked it up yet and this is very weighting on my thoughts but all things in good time. I want to get some backing for my book so I will have to check around but in the mean time I'm going to show my work to others and maybe that will help in some way. It's night and I was awaken by Oliver because he couldn't sleep and then he went back to bed. The trains are going throught with there whisselss blowing full force and it's awesome sometimes, it reminds me of morning when I'm not quite awake you know that time right before coffee when the mind is clouded and you cant think very well. The heat of the day is staying around even after the sun went downand it makes it had to get to sleep, with the tossing and turning because the pillows seam to be not conferrable. And t keeps me awake, later I could hear a truck racing down the road and it makes me a little angry because of the kids that play out in the streets or near it, this was the warmest day of the year so far and I hope for many more as long as things are safe for the future of the town it only takes one person to mess things up and I wouldn't like for any kids to hurt. The world of addiction is a hard one to understand for those who have never been in it, and it would be hard for them to grasp the situation it would be like an addicted person trying to understand a christen life not ever knowing it or having ever been in anothers shoes, the foundation wouldn't be there. In that world nothing exist and it lets you excape the reality of the real world allowing you to create your own place where you can feel safe, although I recall things from that time in life that's not a place that I take lighty because at one time it was my home. People who excape into that world don't really want to come out of it and many will stay in it until it's their time to go, the learning process stops when you go into that world it stops from the time you start using the spirits' and the mind is stuck in that place where he wants you. I fought hard to over come my handy cap and I climbed; those mountains that He the Father put in front of me, my spirit wanted to live but something was telling me to go to give up and we know who that was. The fight for life has been a give and take thing but when a person is addicted to alcohol and drugs all they do is take. And this is caused by the addiction having so much control, people who say they control the addiction are out of their minds. And this is something that will never take place as it has always controlled them who think that way, yes I also thought I had control of it but when it puts you on your knees it lets you know that isn't the case. I cant count the times when I prayed to God over the toilet saying if 'He' help me I will never do it again and that lasted but a few hours until I drank my self back to that place where I felt normal or what I thought was normal.

Just me reliving these things takes it's toal on me but if it would save lives then it's worth it many have heard about the path I am on and they are waiting to see what will take place in the coming years. The addiction cycle that starts in a childs life is sometimes brought on by sight meaning they see it everyday of their lives and like most children they mock what they see in their parents and in others that are close to them, a childs life is supposed to be a christen life that is shaped by the parents and God and if this isn't present in their lives they will look else where for it so watch what they are taught because it can go either way the lack of love is something they will look for and if the parent doesn't give it then they will look else where for that connection. And the other person isn't always what they seam they can and usualy are people trying to get something, they too may be lacking something from family and friends because they have burnt every bridge within that circle. And find them selves also all alone, my self' I was always a giver and maybe in a way I was trying to ease the pain I saw in a person but that doesn't excuse the fact that they needed help a different help, that I couldn't give when I was in the same boat as they were. When addicted people get together they enable each other and call it a party, and even though it's fun at the time later they will wonder why they cant get past it. Children are more exceptable to alcohol and drug abuse because they think it's the grown up thing to do and that kills more of them then any thing, they get their licens and think it's ok to drive and drink.

I have lost count of the teenagers who lost their lives to alcohol related deaths and each year the numbers go up, "WHY" does this happen? Most are not educated about what will and can happen when the two are mixed. This is something I know O so well, and even though I have been in a few car accidents it was always someone else driving but I survived and I am here to tell about it today. If a person takes a good look at their lives they would see Jesus at work but they seam to turn away from the thought that there is a God who watches over his children. The road we travel is the road we leave behind and later in years when things change they will be the memorys which could help other people to not travel that same road of destruction, how many will do this? Well not many' because with most the brain damage is so far advanced that they will be lucky if they can remember their own name. there are many stages of memory loss and depending on the person they may not recall any of that life to record it, I have seen children so far gone that they never did recover and it took their lives at a very young age. Like my friend Michal he was the funniest person I knew but the curse took him at only twenty four years, I knew his parents and they drank most everyday like mine did and the confusion of life took it's revenge and the next thin I knew he wanted to go and be with them. And later in years I wanted to do the same thing, when your brought up around it and the ones you love die that leaves it like you are lost. Because you weren't prepaired for the real world in other words they didn't get you ready for the future, and you become all alone it's especially hard if you didn't make friends because you have no one to go to. You feel traped in a bunch of confusion and cant figure it out, now your facing the world and don't know anything about it so you are put between a rock and a hard place and if you are not strong then you take the easy way out and that too some is death' I would of liked to stay where the light lead me but you cant argue with your maker. I sometimes wonder about what would of happened if I would of just refused but I dont think it would have been my decision, I look at it like this He loved me so much that He wanted me to learn what I needed to know before I go to that place of peace. It's a beautiful day on this Wednesday and the birds are singing just out side of the door, such a beautiful sound as I watch them play and chase each other. Today my mind is working overtime and I feel change coming not bad change but good as my world is being formed and I know He had me do this job because everyone suffering needs to know that others have suffered right along with them. I cant put into words what this new life means to me only God knows how much I love things since that day so long ago, but it wasn't always this way. His love is there for all of us who choose to follow the path He set in motion for us before our birth, I find it awesome how he looked at us and said it's good and then we were put into our mothers womb to grow and become what we end up being. In the end we have been given many chances to live a godly life and if things go right then in the end all things should balance out, as for what people think that doesn't really matter because we or I don't live for them only God matters in my life right now.

As I move forward in life I seam to never go back to people that have had a bad influence on me and as far as girls once we part it has to stay that way for me anyway, I wont go back and repeat problems of the past as that wouldn't make any since to me. I see people going back into a bad relationship and they end up not being together once again and that is a waste of time and of life, as they are both so short. The day has been nice and I got lucky they picked up my lawn mower so they can fix it, now it's just a matter of how long it will take. Thursday morning' and I just got some coffee I hurt bad last night but then it let up during the night I wish I knew what was going on but I don't and you have to travel so far to see a good doctor and it's something I cant do at this time. Maybe when I go to Nebraska my old doctor can check it out as he knows me better then anyone, it's going to be another nice day but I have a feeling the hot weather is coming. Yesterday we had to open the windows because it was so warm then towards the end of the day it was really hot until the sun went down, a friend I know said Courtland was in like a jet stream and that why we get unusual weather here. This I think it true, as there is not any other explanation for how sometimes we are blessed and others are not. But on the other hand we can get some crappy weather also and others don't, this town is very blessed in many ways with good people and things seam to come together when a need is created.

In my time here they have excepted me and even my family even though we all have disibilitys from life past and I havent seen anyone put down or even look down on any of us, they seam to want to help when we need it in some way praise God for through who all blessings flow. My writing career is one that is taught by the father and it lets me express my self in many ways, so others can see that what seamed to be the end doesn't have to be that way. The addiction part of life was just that, a part of life that I had to go through so that many other people may avoid it at all cost so they don't have to experience it. As that leaves it's scars deep scars that you will carry for the rest of your life if you so choose to take that path of destruction, the good news is that the curse can be destroyed with the addicted one even if it has been in the family for generations but the person has to be strong. Mentally strong that is, for the other helps but it's not as important as the mind. The mind allows you too over come things that would usually destroy the everyday person, and it's a good friend to have in this battle because in the end only Jesus knows if you will make it or not. But I like to think that everything will be alright in the end, as you do the best you can do. Helping people is really important because it allows you to give a little of your self to those who wouldn't get help other wise and that can lift some of the burdon off of them, the getting used to doing things for others isn't a burdon but it's like helping a family member and we are all brothrs and sisters in Christ and as for God. Well He is the father of the family and He teaches us how to live with good values, my birthay is next month around Easter Sunday and I think I want to sing on that day to let them see how God has helped me. Each day I sing something to Him and I'm experimenting with things that I make up as I go which is fun because I don't offend Him in any way if I get the words wrong, I just correct them and go on to make beautiful songs. I had a recording contract with a recording company a few years back and it's strange howw I forgot the song but I do have a tape of the song somewhere and one of these days I will dig it out, I remember writing it about someone that I loved but she didn't get it some how, and I think the singer had something to do with it as he couldn't sing worth a darn. I remember laughing about it a few times and then I put it away. I had talent back then and I know it has improved since then, what cost me back then was way too much and today I get it done by a friend in my last church he is such a great guy. Slowly those thigs are coming to pass and I want to get them out there also if that is His will. When I sing' I feel compleat it's like a part of me and that might have something to do with mom, a memory which has seamed to fade some' and I don't want it to leave. Not quite yet, Rosa-lee said some people like that kind of music but it wasn't my taste at the time I was looking for something different. And maybe that's why I started to sing them my self, that way I couldn't blame any other if I got it wrong. I guess I am funny that way if you want something done right then do it you're self that way you can change what ever has to be changed. in life I have always had to do things on my own because others sometimes confuse the facts and they will have you running around in circles and when that would happen I usually didn't get anywhere. Harley has gone back to bed after sitting on my bed for a few hours, I guess he thought that there was nothing happening that he could uderstand Ha! My scrap book is coming around but I have many things to do yet and I am hoping that things will come full circle within the next few months, my land I am already a known writer and Author so my writings should get some attention from those who want to read about my life.

I have found that what ever He sets into motion cant be stopped by man and I know this is the case with my life experiences for they are real and not fiction, everyone in my family wants a copy of my work so that will be exciting to see what they think when it's done. As we go through this life we will fall many times and like a child we will need the help of others to pick us up once again, this is nothing to be ashamed of it's just a part of life. And with Jesus He does the same thing for us brings out the goodness of others too help us in our time when we don't know what to do, in the beginning of everything we do there are complications for one reason or another but as we move forward things seam to come together like learning a trade. You might think it's what you want to do but then later change your mind, even though this hasn't happened with me I know that others have gone through it in school. Not knowing if they want to be a teacher or a machanic it's just something you have to feel out, through the years I have found that a lot of people are stereo types when it comes to people who have had a problem with drug addiction. When some get mad or upset they will call a person a junkey or drug addict and this just causes anger between them, what they don't understand is that a lot of people becomne addicted at no fault of their own it was just a way of life that they had no idea that there was another way. With many of them they are searching to something that they cant find and the drugs become a part of that search, which later they realize that the drugs are not part of the bigger picture.

It's easy for the ones who never went through it to lash out because of anger and that in it's self can cause more damage, then if you were to punch them in the head. The cause and effects of alcohol or drug abuse very in each person. And many of them are lost way before they get hooked on such things, judgement should be left to God on that fine day but there are those who just don't care and like destroying others lives these people should be put into prison where they cant hurt others. But for the ones who look at their lives and know change is needed then they should be given that chance to turn things around, and with many they have never known any other way to live so they have to be taught all over again. As with me it was like being reborn again from crolling even scooting and then like a baby learning to pull you're self up, the mental trials really took it's tole on this man having to do the things a child would do but with a grown up body and mind. This in it's self made him feel like less of a man and this was another problem that he had to deal with, as for people can be cruel when they laugh at someone who is going through such a thing. The people who get addicted and sent to prison are not treated for the addiction they are just sent away so society can get a break from them and then they get out to repeat the process, to me they don't want the problem to be cured, if they did so many wouldn't return. It's like they don't care about the people on the inside or the people of the communitys, many times I wanted to stop writing about the problem but something always stop's me and I have to go on. In hope that one day they will take it seriously, I was told one time that I care too much but how is that possible? To care to much. He gave us a heart for a reason remembering why my sister fell so hard it was in my neghews 18th dirthday and he had been out with friends and on his way home a truck driver fell a sleep or he did and the truck hit them head on' killing him. It was much like what made our parents go over the edge except he didn't survive lie the boys did, there was much grief and it became easier to find comfort in the bottle it seamed it was that way for most of the family. As the curse was always there with all of us hiding hust under the surface, I remember her being dadys little girl and he would take her each week with mom to buy records of her favorite bands. Very jelous was us boys because it seamed like she got everything she wanted, back then our parents where already drinking so something must have been wrong later in years my sister said she would never end up like mom did, but louseing her oldest boy made her the same as mom trying to find the answer where it didn't exist after years of doing this she asked God for help and like with me she got it but just enough to worry about what others think and that weighed heavy on her so she quit going to church. Then she came for a visit here in Courtland and I brought her to my church and let everyone that was there meet her, after service she told me that she had been struggling with what others thought and I told her to return to church and that was satin trying to keep her from God. We had a nice visit that year in 2011 and we kept in touch for sometime after that and then she said they planed on moving to where they used to live in the big city.

I hope she got past that part of worring about what others think so she can find the answers she needs to find, through time I had been angry with her for things she did but when she came to visit we were able to put that all behind us as we mended that fence that had been broken for so long. I notice when we get older those things seam to fade away but we have to make out peace so we can go on, we laughed many times in those two days and I sent her home with some of my pickeled eggs which she loved by the way.Harley has gotten up with me this fine Friday morning and he sits by me feet under my desk maybe to protect me from something not quite sure, they found out that my mower needs a starter so I told them to order it my land' a hundred dollars is a lot of money but when you have to have something done you have to do it then I shouldn't have any more trouble with it, as for the push mower Randy said it started right off so I wont have to worry about it this year thank God. I was hoping my sister would come down this summer but it looks doubtful at this point maybe one day we will meet again when she can get away, the day looks to be another warm one as we move into spring, which is next week. And then it will really get hot as summer approches in the next year we will do many things but keeping the lawn cut is real important, I slept pretty well last night so to day should go very good each day the fog rolls in and then out again by noon this is caused by a air flow which goes through Courtland according to some, and from what Igathered some think bad weather is coming our way.

For each day I look forward to and I am glad in it just to be here, it could have been the other way around but it's not at this point. I recall many time when my brother wanted me to go with them to do things and I always declined because I could since that he was going to get into trouble, it was a gift to be able since these things a gift from God and it kept me out of trouble through the years but you have to be able to see it coming and know how to use it as for those who got into trouble well lets just say they became a product of their own destruction and many of them have repeated trips to prison. Such a waste of life when they could of just said No to the drugs and their children follow in their foot steps because they knew how much money dad had when he would sell it. No one has ever gotten rich by getting people hooked on drugs on the contrary they have fallen and fallen hard, by the time they pay lawyers all they have gathered is gone and they are left with just time spent in a place that doesn't give a rats ass about them. The problem will take years but people can be cured if they try hard enough but it always comes back to the mighty dollar, communitys don't want to bother with it so they throw the problem somewhere else. But what they don't realize is that the people with the problem are people from there communities and they will be back because they feel safe there. It's like throwing away human life and some don't think twice about it O you have some that care but for the most part many don't, and until that out look is changed then we will continue to have the problem. I talked with my daughter last night and she is going to talk to her mom about going to the lawyer with me in May so things can get better. It seams I have been fighting this battle for over 30 years and now it's time to put a stop to it, and wipe thigs clean. Many of my friends don't understand it either so I am not alone in this realm of not understanding, as we grow things from our childhood are taken with us and it can cause many problems in our lives. For the lack of self worth to having doubts about our selves even today I struggle with some of those things as time seams to not wipe that away, but that is something that you have to work out for your self as time goes by. Through life I was always a loner trying to take care of those who were sick and although I helped them it hurt me in some ways not getting to know people like I should have. Trust is something that should be easy but with me it's always been a hard thing to do, as for living I didn't get to travel the world like some but that was ok' I would of loved to have done it and write about the things I saw in other countries. As a writer I have to live it to before I can write about it, many years of my life were lost because of addiction months would go by and I wouldn't remember any of it because of the destruction the alcohol caused. One day I would wake up and someone would tell me that it was May, when I would remember it being March. So much time lost from the time I was a child I even fell many times and didn't know it until I woke up the following day or so, not living in the real world let you forget all the bad things that made there way into your life and after time it became a normal way of life. God must really love us to take care of us like He does we can louse track of time but He brings us through it just the same a constent love for His children even when they cant take care of them selves.

We louse so much when we don't know Him and we louse contact with family when we don't even know we exist. On many occashions he knew that God was right there with him because he could feel it deep inside and through the love that God showed for him he was able to open that heart that was closed to others and let them in. does miracles happen? Well in my life they do, as He brought me from death it's self back into this world that I thought was so cruel, you see he didn't get to know the world the first time aroung and He gave him a second chance to see the way the world is supposed to be. But in even doing that, feeling something like love is still new so he is learning as he goes through life this second time around. In many ways he is still like that child who got lost so long ago trying to find his way in this big ole world, God knew he would need help from time to time so He took him and placed him in a place where people could show him the way. Show him that he was worthy of the love he deserved, and in time these things will come to pass. As he went to this new place he would write about the place and the miracles that happened there and this was good in the eyes of the lord. Today we had some guys working across the street and Randy asked if they could pick up the pile of limbs out in the back yard and they agreed to do it, I had been trying to get rid of it for sometime and now it will be gone. It might take sometime to get things done but in the end it gets done to make room for the grass to grow once again, I had been looking at the pile for oer a year and it will be nice to finely get it gone.

There are other things that I want to do around here but you can only take one step at a time, Oliver is trying to give order's like he has always want to do but like back then no one listens. The things he wants doesn't make since today any more then they did back twenty years ago, but he tries it's like he wants to be the man that gives order's. By the end of the day it will all be picked up and then the yard will look nice, the way it did before the storm hit two years ago. I just hope we don't get any bad storms this year because it takes so long to get things back to where they once were, it's like all things that are bad. Time seams to be the only thing that can fix it that and hard work by those who are affected by the disaster. It's great that there are people who will help in some cases when you cant do it because you don't have the equipment, but hey! I would do it for others if the shoe was on the other foot. Harley cant help but to look out the window and want to be out there with them so he can have someone to bark at we didn't realize there was so much crap and I can see why others wouldn't of wanted to do the clean-up but this person was true to his word and cleaned it up Randy went out and gave another ten to him. It's hard living here as compaired to the city where you have everything more or less handed to you, it's Saturday and it's ass still as it can be ut side with just a car going by every now and then not much trafic around here as the day will start for others in anout two hours or so. As for the heat of the day it allows us to not have to turn on the heat in the house good insolation I guess, the guy that done the job said it was very warm for this time of year as he was sweating from hard work and little brother replyed that he thought it was beautiful. We sat on the back porch for a time just looking around and realizing that we have it better then the homeless or others that don't have a place they can call home, having disabilitys really limit's what you can do in this world but if you have a strong will then you can create many thing even if it's only in the mind. Each day I try to think of new things we can do without it costing much and this year I would like to paint if that's possible the pillers need a coat to last another winter as they are cracking from the paint being so old, so a little at a time we will accomplish that but as for the high places we will need a ladder. Every year people make resolutions which are seldom kept but my resolution is to survive in this world and become stronger then ever if it's God's will to keep pushing forward in this world and let people know that a good life is possible if you want it bad enough you cant let things like addiction destroy you in this world. We as people were ment to live the good life once we figure out what it is and you cant do that with the mind all screwed up, the reason alcohol and drugs make life easier is because you don't have to feel anything or worry about things which are happening but it's up to us if we choose to egnore others who might need our experiences to help them out of a jam like with addiction it will destroy your very soul and make you sub human in other words just a shell existing in a world that doesn't care one way or another if you are alive or not. I was told by a women one time when I was messed up that I stood up for her when it came to her old man, this was something that stuck with her even though I told him off it somehow gave her the strength to over come the addiction that had been destroying her life, that in it's self let me know that she cared about my opinion and we stay in touch from time to time on the internet where she voices her opinion very clearly to those who run over others.

Many times people don't want to hear about what is happening in their lives, but what they don't realize is that someone standing on the out side can see where they can make things better. A lot of my time is spent trying to figure out how to help without hurting people because some are very fragial in the beginning as I know O so well, you see I was that way I would even cry at the drop of a hat until I got stronger in my life. Many people today think I am a kind person and for the most part I am, but as with us all I also have a flaw as most of us do and that is that I am not perfect. And sometimes I wish I was, or do I? would being that way allow you to help more or would it cause more problems being full of you're self and thinking you are above others this wouldn't be something I would want to go through. As it hurts other peoples feelings as my little brother pointed out one day when I got mad, and that brings out another feeling guilt. Which is another thing I don't like I yell sometimes so I must not have over come that yet, at times I wish I could go through a week without worry or those other feelings but for somne reason it's not in the cards. Where is that peace I try so hard to find? Is it in that place where I went for a short time, no worries or pain that seam to have come back on me. I like working in the yard but a few times last year I over did it and I payed a big price being sick for a wheek really gets to you as you feel like your going to shut down, but then the kindness of others comes around and it makes you feel better because you know someone cares, this town is truly blessed by the people and by the father' and it makes me strong in many ways.

I feel like I'm living my dream in a since but not all the miracles have happened yet. So far time is on my side if it even last for a year, He said there is a season for all things and in reality we don't know which season is ours for it could be tomorrow or next year there is just no way of knowing. From the life of long ago to today is miraculous just the changes boggles the mind as I still feel change coming, it's an enlightenment that a lot of people don't feel. Or maybe they do and it's just new to me the one who's life keeps changing, joy is my great gift as I love that feeling like the joy of bringing a brother home after many years and trying to help him to adjust to the world he left behind so long ago. Although he has been away the love is still there after so many years, the brotherly love you felt as a child while you played by the lake or ran around the front yard yelling things at each other (na na boo boo) all these things were lost to me for so many years and now for some reason they are coming out again. His time away has hurt him in many ways and the place they sent him didn't help, it only hurt him deep inside. But still he ismy brother even though he has changed on the out side his heart is still there and he is another one who can cry at the drop of a hat. Many things he doesn't understand and that is because he cant read or write but I try to teach him when I can by reading out of the bible sometimes or the upper room, I know what a struggle it can be because I went through it many years ago when I had the brain damage. But through it all He seams to teach us no matter what condition our human form is, when I brought him home I cried because he was over weight and he had black rings around his eyes. It wasn't what I expected but still he is blood of my blood and today sometimes we laugh and sometimes we cry but life is good for the most part, I remember taking him and sis to church and I introduced them and they were greated by many, and when I told them that he was my little brother the pastor said she couldn't see me being anyones big brother, meaning I'm just a little guy my self and that's ok' I like being who I am and in many ways I'm like my mom just a short guy. Now my sister she is really tiny, no bigger then a minute. And I can see mom in her as they were both small with a big heart, looking back I have to say that challenges were always around each corner but we seamed to make it to this stage in life, and if God willing. It would be another miracle if I live to see my golden years of sixty or seventy years. Now that would be a story, to over come through so much and then live so long for that would be awesome. I havent seen the family in sometime so maybe a trip in the future might come this way but first things first our life here has to be secure with no problems before that can take place so we will see what becomes of the future, It's Sunday and the morning is warm much warmer then in previous weeks and it isn't even officially spring yet. Such warm weather so early in the year makes me think that the real hot days of summer are going to be just that, I do know now that if we didn't have air-conditioning it would be really miserable but the lord provided a way as he always does when it comes to life. As I think back on the days when we didn't have any it makes me wonder how we made it in the sweltering heat, I don't recall it ever being this hot in Nebraska but with each state they have there own weather conditions. We don't have the cool breezes that you would expect with spring just the hottness even in the early mornings but who knows it might change.

He seams to make everything possible as we move into 2012, I know the trips to Nebraska will be hot ones so are lucky to have air in the car also. To people who have lived here all their lives this is probably a tipical hot year that they are used to but to my self it's still new to me and my guys, little brother' has never had to be out side except for the times when they let him out in the yard for exercise. You would of thought they would of let him work but now I know he wouldn't of been able to with all the med's he is on, the other day we were sitting on the back porch and talking about how we can fix things up and getting rid of that pile of crap was the first step. Just doing that made things look so much better and it keeps the varments away it looks so nice now as the soil is blck from being rich to grow things, thing which used to take a week to do somehow takes longer but I think it's the body slowing down as we reach middle age. Ha! The days are good and you can see the farmers go by as they head for the fields even the grass hoppers as we call them head out to the fields to spray some kind of chimical on it, No they are not the little bugs but a big machine with tires as big or bigger then a man and boy can they move. Going down the road they reach up to fifty miles an hour and you could just about drive your car under them, what a sight' as they have long sprayers which come out of the back that sprays the fields. It has to be some kind of ferderlizer that helps the crops grow and maybe it holds down the soil.

Not sure about that but it has to do something, back in the 1800 they had a tragedy which they called the dust bole, and the top soil blew away from the strong winds but over time they fixed that problem or so they say and then they never had it happen again the problem was fixed by a man that headed the agracoulture program. It's so still this morning and the only noise you hear is the augers running across the way they seam to never stop except for a few times when winter is here, so I'm assuming they have break downs like with all things relater to the growing things and getting them to market. Yesterday was nice until later in the day when it got so hot that I had to turn on the central air, my land' that is very nice to have making it 70 degrees in here was like heaven. At first I opened the windows but as the day wore on it became too hot so we kicked it on, being we are different in nature some thought it was too cold like pops he has one arm that gets cold on him but he covers it up with his sweater and then he is fine. I wonder sometimes if things will get to a normal keel as it's hard sometime with little brother, his meds seam to make him sleep even during the day and I know going to bed at such a early time of the day will cause a person to wake up early and of course his snoreing lets you know when that time is. He is funny in a way because he will try to sneak some sleep and I cant help but laugh because the snoring just doesn't let him get away with it, this summer some want to see us but I told them that I cant make any promises; as pops is really old and I never know how he will be feeling when the time comes. Oliver and Randy need the care I give them and if I wasn't here then they would be in a place where no one would care and that would estroy them, I have seen long turm care and the old folks sit around like they are in a coma and it made me sad to see it. As the years go by I know things will change and I have to be ready for it but will I be ? As it's never easy to louse someone you love or even if something happens to me what would happen to them? I like to think that other family members would take them but I know as well as I am sitting here they wouldn't. It's like everything is money driven no money no compation but that is what it takes to survive and that's just what we do survive no one wants for anything but I don't know. I would like to try the life without worry for a while and not have to worry about things that could take everything away, at times it's like I pop up my head to breath and then the wind is kicked out of me saying you are not going anywhere but then He tells me that I'm doing ok' to assure me that better times are coming. And my day becomes one of delight just to know He is listening to this soul, my life is much better these days as I continue to move forward into that world which is so different from the one before. And He walks beside me as I make this trip I think life is supposed to be full of up's and downs and good and bad so we can tell the difference between good and evil, do people hide how their lives really are? You know the seans behind closed doors when others cant see or hear. Do they fight and argue and think it's normal? My self I know these things exist but are they needed to have a relationship? I try to avoid such things because I don't like what they have done to me in the past and I don't think anyone would want to be called names. Maybe what I want doesn't exist and if it doesn't then I might find my self all alone in this world trying to find it, the day was beautiful as the wind blew gently and I got to even talk with my friend at church to share some of my life.

She knows people and sometimes knowing others is a great thing, I gave her part of my book in hope that she can have it run off and this way I can move forward a little. Each step in this process brings me closer to getting published, as I watched her read my article you could see that it touched her. I'm not quite sure of what I am looking for maybe that connection that will bring everything together, I felt sorry for pastor Kathy today as she was ill so I said a prayer for her too get well. I think it has to do with the weather changing as you cant really tell from one day to the next how it will be, but the cold is gone for the year. For Spring and Summer and then Fall, we didn't get much snow this year not inch wise anyway but boy we had our share of cold days let me tell you. I find it strange how the mind can turn letters around when you first get up and then you don't catch them until later when you read through what you wrote, it's like the mind isn't strong when first awaken but then when you catch the mistakes it's easy to correct them. It's Monday and the weather is warm too warm really this morning there isn't even a breeze just the calmness and the quiet except for the augers running, sometimes there is a train that comes through bu other then that just the quietness that a small town has. As for hearing about other and their everyday lives I don't want to bring some things to light that have happened as the past is better left where it belongs, some days I want to just sit on the porch and look at the town to see the wonders that have occurred here.

How many other miracles have taken place here and how many other stroies are here that I havent heard yet? The list could go on and on but what I focus on is the lessining of pain as others go through life. I know my story has reached many lives but I feel the need to tell more so they will know that they are not alone in this world many people fighting addiction feel all alone and it doesn't have to be that way, I asked permission to use friends names in my book and they said it would be fine as long as it's the truth. As the time moves forward there will be many new things which will take place and it will be nice to see these things, my home is going to be fun to fix up and Randy will help in some ways two brother trying to make a home the best it can be but it will really look nice once it's done. My mower should be done today and I will give it a spin around the yard, as for the other mower Randy said it still run's fine. My land' it's been the best mower I have bought, only fifty dollars, and it's still going five years later. With life comes caution and you have to be careful not to hurt other people now some writers look for mysteries or hidden things which would sell books as for me when that can bring pain it's not an option especially with older people, some have great stories but others have hidden secrets which should stay where they are other wise it would destroy them. The greatest gift you can give a child is a part of your self time is importand when they are young, I was supprised when Mrs. Balckburn gave me some treats on Sunday morning well John gave them to me for her and in a kidding way he said he hoped I chocked on them he is funny when the mood hits him, beck in the day when he was young I bet he was the class clown always making people laugh. What a great quality that is, to make people laugh and brighten up their day. Many of the other people are the same way but none are quite as funny as John, just the other day he said if his wife and kids were trained like his dog then he would have it made. And another person replied that his wife and kids were smarter then his dog! I don't see much sadness here but it does exist for those who struggle to get by, I have known that sadness but it doesn't exist much these days. Like the wind it's gone from this life and was replaced by peace which comes my way from time to time, the peace isn't a constent but it comes more these days then before and still today there isn't a day that goes by in which we don't laugh about something. A joy which we share between brothers, we thought we were having a tornado this morning as the wind blew like hell and the thunder was really loud, we didn't expect that kind of weather this morning but I bet the farmers are glad. And still the rain continues through the morning, I love to watch the birds as they play and take a bath in the puddles in the street. The trees are starting to bloom and there is one down the road that is awesome as the green is on the out side and the white blooms are in the center, it's like the cycle continues the cycle of life, which shows it's self each Spring. For all that happened to them last year is gone and they have no mind to have any memory of the destruction that changed them, they just continue to grow as God put them there to do and they become more beautiful with each passing year.

Through life we also continue to grow but being so different we bare the scars from life past and our memorys contain that which caused the the destruction or growth. Like the trees we continue to grow stronger and with most the scars become something of the past, if we were more like the trees we could go to sleep for the winter and wake up fresh. And start all over with no memory of the past year a clean slate if you will, in time we will grow past those years that almost destroyed us and with hope God him self will renew our lives and give us a brighter out look on things. Sort of like starting life all over again to learn to love and understand things that we once didn't understand, even today I look for answers but they seam to avoid me so the search continues. Tuesday morning' it's very early and I was awaken by Randy to take him to the hospital he has been having trouble with his stomic and was bent over in pain they are checking him out now but I had to come home, havent cared much for hospitals so I had to leave. He has my number so they will call when they find out something, if I read blood preshure right it's 180 over 110 and that scaes me. And the worring continues as I take care of them, even today they don't really know whats wrong with him and that doesn't make things any easier. Taking care of both of them has it's hard times and also the good as you cant replace a smile or laughter, this is going to be a long night as I cant get back to sleep over this situation I was told that it's better to leave things in His hands and that's what I will do.

My friend got my first part ofmy book ran off onto paper so things are moving forward but at a slow pace. Harley is bugging me to take him out so I better do it, he can be a pain sometimes but he is my buddy my little guy who helped me through so much. As I pray for my brother I know that He will bring him through this time of anguish, and make him well again so he can continue with the friendship we have started to build. We all go through life with many different problems and his is his health, like mine it isn't what it should be but we push on to try to make the best of what we have no matter how you try sometimes things don't always go our way. But in saying that I know He will take care of Randy it's His job you might say and He loves us so much, driving at night isn't something I like to do but when it comes to people you love you will do anything to make sure they get better. You might say that he has now also became a part of my life here. I called him to make sure that he is ok' and he said that he was. I don't like the feeling of helplessness but when it happens then that's when He takes over and you cant have a better doctor then Him, it was midnight when I took him and now it's two in the morning so later I will have to take a nap so I'm not so tired come the middle of the day. Love for a brother is special because the closeness you had as a child can be reignited even though it's not an easy thing to do for some I have been able to do it. Love is funny because it can sometimes bring you through many things like anger or jealousy, those are things I don't like not even for a moment. And when they make there way into my life I shut them down, this morning is nice with just a touch of cold but it wont last long as the day goes on and the heat replaces it. Yesterday was also nice with a warm breeze and we left the door open for the day. It's strange but when I pass by where Randy sleeps it's like I can hear him breathing, as I read the pages she brought back it's like going back in time to a place that I'm glad to have left. New things happen all the time and more new things are just around the corner, new memories and new good times as we go through this new life we have started it's now four in the morning and I am wide awake ready to take on the day as I do each day the porognoses for Randy is unclear but they lost his blood pressure when they took him into the operating room. Then they stablised him to move him to Salina where he got scared because he didn't know where he was, now today I will go and see him he said he wanted to come home but it would be nice to know what's wrong with him so they can fix it, when they said e needed surgery I was scared but through prayer I was calmed inside to go on too deal with the day. You would think I would be used to this kind of thing but I'm not I just hope all turns out alright today Oliver wants to go with us me to Salina and Icant see it hurting anything except if I get a ride from someone else. I think the not being on his med's caused art of the problem but I know there is something deeper an uneasyness that resides in him but what is it, my land' if this is what the drugs has done to him when he was messed up then I am blessed more then I thought. When I called Salina they had no record of his med's so I had to give them the information and the male nurce said that really would help, the health care system is not what it should be and I can see why people take loved ones to Nebraska either today or tomorrow I will bring him home once they get everything figured out. It's Wednesday and yesterday seamed like a year with all the confusion, it rained all day yesterday and now the farmers should be happy with all the water it also brought in some little cridders and I had to kill one in the bath tub darn spiters are a pain.

In the coming year I hope he doesn't get sick again but we will see what happens you don't think much about good health until you come close to louseing it. Harley is watching me as he sits on my bed the little shit he keeps poping up his head for some reason so I took him out and I noticed that it had been raining over night, so I hope it stop's before the day begins. The family was worried about him so later I will have to touch bases with them and let them know what's going on, as nformation permits. Sometimes we are put into situations where it test us annd the out come is based on how we handle it, I cried yesterday but them I was made calm by the spirit. The only thing was that I had never done that before not in front of other people but a pastor is a different story they seam to bring peace when it's needed and this is their job. I know many people care about us as they called to see how things were going, in the future I will take him to another doctor at a different place. It brought me to a different understanding of how life is so fragual as we go through it, one wrong move and that's it. As for things here they are fine and Oliver doesn't have any concept of what has happened and in a way that's a good thing he needs to stay in his world where he feels safe, in the days a head I hope that things will get back to normal and it should just the three of us going on with the lives that have been given to us. Randy needs the love that he recives from us just as we need his love, I went to see him and they took out his gallbladder and he is ready to come home.

I will pick him up tomorrow morning sometime, Thursday and in a while I will go and get Randy it will be so nice to get this behind us and him back home. My land' he scared me for a while but with prayer he will be returning God is awesome and He takes care of us even in thew worst of times, Kathy was very helpful in this time and I'm so glad that she went and saw Randy. And now we will be back together again you don't really realize how much you love someone until you almost louse them and it has been the same with Oliver when he became sick on many occasshions, it seams the triles is what bring you close to people and God has surley done that brought us closer to one another. I'm hoping that little brother might start to attend church more now and I think he would find that many people would also care for him, he is a good soul and has always has been. Like me he got lost in this world but God has a way of bringing things to where they need to be, I can see us compairing scars in the years to come and joking about it but for now I am just glad that he will be home in Salina they took good care of him and changed how I felt about doctors. The good Lord is everywhere watching over His flock in this time I have gotten closer to my pastor and shared some of my life with her at many times we need to talk about things to others and I know talking with her doesn't leave her lips it's a two hour drive to Salina and I think I will enjoy the ride there and back, yesterday I was so tired but I slept in this morning so I would be rested for the trip. The rain fell most of the day yesterday and the planting surely is getting plenty of water to grow I hope we have a better year then last even though ours crops were better then average they could always improve. Through the years they seam to get better then the year before and I hope that continues through out my time here, Mark called and I told him the good news that Randy will be coming home and he said awesome many people prayed for him and I thanked them who prayed on Facebook you never know when tragity will strike so it's good that God is close and answers our prayers. Pastors are in charge of our souls and mine is the best as I went through that time, it was like a calmness came over me saying everything was going to be alright. This I have no doubt was God gringing peace to my soul, it was a feeling like I felt when I moved here no room for doubt that it was God who spoke to me. I picked Randy up and he couldn't wait to get home now he is resting so he can recover fully and that will take time. Also my mower is back at the house and it rruns like a top it was fun mowing the lawn and now we are getting rain again. Friday morning and It feels good to see my little brother in his bed for some reason it brings me peace to see him there, O wait' that's brotherly lee love. As our time together moves forward we will have some good times and I thank God that he is with me, one nurse took the time to explain things that happened while he was in the hospital but I know inside something happened that shouldn't have and it scared the hell out of them. In future cases they should check things out more before they put someone under, but that aside God brought him back to us and for that I am grateful, Leroy drove the mower over yesterday and boy was he in a good mood. I consider him one of my closess friends that I have made here besides my church family which I feel very close to, my experience with this ordeal brought me even closer to Jesus as I felt the calming effect when He let me know things would be ok' the balance between life and death is like a teter tauter one move towards the worng side and the out come can be very different.

The things we learn as we go through life is to never go to a hospital that isn't equipped to handle emergencies. Because death can be just around the corner if they make the wrong call, as for me I will hope that He will always watch over me as his child. The rain is a constent this morning and I think it has to do with me mowing my lawn, I do know when I wash my car thaat it rains most of the time. All the folks back in Kearney were praying for Randy and many people who don't even know him prayed also along with me but it was the prayer that I and pastor Kathy prayed that brought me peace. It's nice that people care and love others this creates a bond between them and as time goes on they get closer I never had a family this big before and it's nice Randy was just telling me that he feels great this morning and for that I am glad he likes to talk about what happened and how good he feels prayes God who brought him home. He said his system seams to be working fine now so he knows that what he had done will make him better, mother nature seams to bring us rain when we need it so far anyways this year and I hope it continues through out this season so the farmers can have good crops. It's only four thirty so I hope he can go back to sleep for a few hours to get his rest, the temp is getting back to normal with cool nights and mornings I even had to turn up the heat some to take the chill off. My lawn looks good when it's cut but when it isn't it looks bad by me cutting it yesterday that took off the top layer so the moisture could absorb into the ground better making it more green.

As this day goes on I will do my chores and that conceits of getting their med's ready for morning and then feeding them I am a care giver to my family and now I know that God was getting me ready to take care of them, Mark O'Brien was telling me that it was God that brought me to Kansas and this I agree with other wise Randy wouldn't of had a good place to come to and he wouldn't of made it back in Kearney with all the bad influences there are in that place. It says I will prepair a place for you and that is what He has done for little brother, made him a place right here in Courtland' KS. The road we lead will determine how life will be wither it's good or bad but through it all He will watch over us because we are his children. It's a long and rocky road but in the end I think we find our way. Through the sands of time we all have a chance to come to know the father, and if we don't then who can we blame no one but our selves sending the computer back was a good move so now I can make happen what should of happened so long ago to wipe the slate clean and have a fresh start of things which will come in the future. It was strange how just those few days seamed so long but everyday life goes so fast 'What is with that' I think when you live the good life it goes faster and when things get messed up time seams to slow down for a while anyway, the heavenly father has a reason for doing what He does and we as humans may not see the reason for a short time until later when time has passed. Just like the young man that pointed out something to me as we were having a converstion some months later about how everyone disappeared, even though he was brought up in the church he seamed to see what God had done. As to me not seeing it at the time, he was a good kid but got lost somehow in the world of alcohol and drugs Leroy was a nice young man but being taught it was ok to drink but not to do drugs messed with his mind also. I believe he was in his twentys at the time so many years ago, he went to rehab but still had that mind set which was wrong. After getting out he seamed to be alright and I never seen him again, Saturday morning' it seams to be nice out side and I can see a star shining off in the distence, the train is also going through blowing it's whistle. I hear it more during this time of year then in winter the rolling of the wheels as they connect with the track and there always seams to be a strange sound as the wheels roll, my little friend must be visiting family as I see her car down the road with her lights on it's been a long time since I have seen her and I hope she is doing well she is a hard worker and helps the elderly in a nurseing home from what I have gathered little brother is still a sleep and I hope he stays that way for a while, also Tonya taxt me to say her mom lift her husband and is now living with her and Stan in her words she is free to come and go when ever she wants, and I'm hoping for a visit next summer if she can come. Randy was telling me that Mark told him that they filled his stomic with a gas so they could take out his gallbladder and little brother seamed so amazed at how they did that, he is doing fine for now and I hope it continues that way he will be strong once again and we can have some fun this summer if it's not too hot out, I have noticed that people who go camping these days have campers with Air-conditioning on the top of them to keep them cool and to me that's the only way to go.

It's not like the old days when all you had was a tent, it seams that's just for kids these days as they can take the heat better then us old folks. Maybe one day we might go camping but for now the hot weather would cause more problems then do any good, I'm satisfied with the memorys of time passed when I was a child camping and walking miles to just get to know a girl. Even though those days are gone the memories are still there as a reminder of what once was a child playing around and having fun, I remember mom with her glass of wine saying it was good for you and we never had a second thought about it. All we knew is that it was our mom and we loved her no matter what, in the years to come she would switch from one kind to another saying change was the spice of life. And it was when we would switch from one camp to another taking in all the scenery, such beauty that I havent seen since that time, and will probably never see again. It seams we are moving into another episode of change the grass is getting greener; and my mower is running once again Randy seams to sleep a lot since is surgery and the snoreing is bad it can almost wake the dead but that will pass as time goes by. Sometimes I have to go into my room to get some peace or out side Sunday morning' and it's going to be a nice day, the birds are not up yet so that should tell you how early it is I wish I could sleep in but that isn't possible at this time. In the beginning this was my house of peace and now it's like a buffalo storage unit with all the snoring so I am going to get him an apartment down the way.

That way I will get my house back and I believe he will make new friends in the process, as I cant take care of him all his life. But he will be near if he wants to visit, the place is only two blocks away and they are nice apartments. There for a while it wasn't bothering me much but with his pain med's it put's him to sleep straange how that happens, for each med seams to have knock out power and he has to fight to stay awake to me this isn't normal but in the prison system all they want to do it keep them catatonic sort of llike the people in nurseing homes, they sit in a chair and wait for their time to come I am always looking for better ways to make things better but at times it's like I am fighting a louseing battle as peace is hard to find in this world anyway. Many of my neighbors were out mowing their lawns yesterday and you could hear them all up and down the street getting things ready for summer when the grass will grow like wild fire and the temp will be in the triple digit's a good time to stay inside, I will keep doing my job at the church and one women brought in a buffer so I can strip the floors. This I will do in the coming months so things look better I seam to have some time on my hands and I enjoy my time away from home working in the church for that is truly where I find peace away from everyone just me and God someone I can talk my heart out to. It's strange how I thought I would have been further by now in so many ways, but things happen in His time not ours. This morning I will open the church but as for heat there is no need but before too long we will have to turn on the Air-conditioning when that temp gets up there just like in winter the temp cant be above 70 degrees at least for most of us and many of the people are older then the average person. O we have some young people but they don't come very oftend as they take care of the farms along with their parents, I was supprised to see that so many young folks are returning to where they grew up. This in it's self shows the condition of things in the outside world and many don't want that kind of life. In the big cities there are people getting killed all the time, and you hear about it on the news each day kids going to school and getting killed for what I consider no good reason and then you have your gangs which kill for fun sometimes but it's usually over drugs and space who owns what space or blocks in a community. So much has changed and it hasn't been for the better as we approach the end of days, during this summer I will probable go nuts if I have to spend much time in this house but I will find other things to do that will give me some time away from here. Next month our road trip will be fun if everything goes right then it will be back home to start doing some planing, life is so precious and we hope to live out a long life but only God knows how long that will be. I wouldn't mind living into my 70's but we will see what the lord has in store for me my strength even comes from Him and I pray that He keeps me in good health for that time, this year they have open mic night but my songs wouldn't fit in with their so called image as they are of God and my life. Some tell me that I have that hard life look to me and I can live with that as it hasn't been a picnic the rouged look of the out doors men. Margret said she didn't like that pretty boy look and I find that not many care for that look because around here most are farmers and the other wouldn't fit just right, I took a nap yesterday and it helped to make things better I get moody sometimes and even I don't like that. Getting snappy with folks isn't me and it makes me feel bad. So I have to step back and take asecond look at what I'm doing, the folks here are real and they care for their familys not just blood family but also the christen family they adopt, if they say they love you, you can bet that they do.

No phony crap just caring people who believe in you as a person this in it's self is a delight when you have gone through life with a lack of it, and it's hard to imagine that they would have enough room in their hearts for you but they do. Mrs. Blackburn is a person that really cares, her and John are very kind and John can make me laugh as he tells me someof the stories that have happened in the past but with most of those stories I keep to my self because they are the past. A part of the history which will be told by someone else because I know some of the people who it pertains to and I like them also, my friend that I let read about my life story said I would do good in a corporation that deals with addiction and I told her that I didn't know how to find them places so that planted a seed and only He knows where it will lead. March 25th and most of the month is gone and then another will start, April my birthday on the 12th and Easter Sunday is the 8th that means my day will be on a Thursday in the middle of the week. Another year older and less in debt Ha! As I watch the price of what I owe on the house drop it gives me joy to know that one day in the future it will be mine forever and that no one can take it, my little piece of heaven right here on earth where I will live out my life. Not too many people can say that today with the way the world is but it's nice to know that I can, I pray that I will see the day it happens and who know how many of my family will live here after that it could be here another fifty years but the property will be here for ever. It's strange how they can tax you for fixing up your home, it's almost like cheaper to let it fall down but most wont let that happen I couldn't even imagine what the taxes are on newer houses but if mine were any higher I wouldn't be able to live here.

Thank God that He gave me something I can afford He seams to know the things we need to get through life and He is a great provider, it seams our situations are taken care of as we take care of our obligations to full fill our part of the deals we set in motion. I have always believed that we shouldn't take on more then we can handle because if you do then you loose it all, and the years and time are wasted. It would be like throwing away years of your life to end up where you didn't want to be in the first place. It was a beautiful day here in Courtland with temp's in the 70's just a great day all together, I talked with little brother about getting an apartment and he agreed that it would be best for all concerned. I'm glad that he understood because I need my life to be my own and with others around it just isn't, my peace of mind is important to me and if someone loves you then they will understand. I told him that I still love him but I need to be by my self for sometime, caring for people is important but you cant let it destroy your life just like you cant let addiction destroy what God has given us. Monday morning' it's an awesome day and I can tell that it will be warm this afternoon. The short days of winter are now as if they faded away like the snow which once covered the ground and now the long days of summer will be upon us before we know it, instead of the darkness being only a few short hours the hours of the day will be longer with it not getting dark until late. For each year the seasons change in some summers it's very nice but with others it's so hot that most couldn't sleep without some kind of Air-conditioning, we have come a long ways since our arival here and things are moving forward in a good way. Yesterday at church John said he knew he wouldn't be around in ten years so he got his wife a new car that would last her when he goes to be with God it's like he see's whats coming and has excepted it being 83 years old his life has been a ver long one like most people who live here. We all have something we have to do in life and his passion is cattle as he goes out to the farm each day around eight in the morning, having a purpose is important in life and I have come to realize that writing about my life is my purpose, the people here are not all like John he is one of a kind like me unique and I think we all are that way in one fashion or another. He was telling me about how his brother kept a few cattle for him when he went into the service and then he built them up from there to make a good life for his family, I have seen some of his kids when they visited him and they sing in church what an awesome family. He seams so close to his wife and I know that when the time comes they will be like the yellow ribbon that was broken two parts making a whole severed by making that journey to the promise land where they will see one another again. Life is precious and the body can be hurt very easly but we go on and live out our lives with understanding that one day we all will go to that place He has made for us, I oftend wondered how people see us as I know we don't see our selves the way they do.

Last week a friend in church said he was sorry he didn't get the lims out of my back yard but the strange things is that I had forgotten about it and it didn't really matter to me we all have things to do to survive in this world and we forget some thigs along the way it's just part of life. Through the sands of time change is always coming and we never know when that change is going to affect us, but when it does we pick up our selves and move on to another day week or month depending on where we are at the time. I never thought or saw that I would be here but yet here I am, the wonders of the Father is something I may never understand and yet as each day passes I'm glad that I am here, to experience change as it makes it's way into our lives like it says we are the clay and He is the potter. Our lives are being changed even though we don't see it at the time that piece of clay is being shaped into something beautiful, maybe even into a beautiful tea-pot with rhinestones that others cant put a price on. It is the Father who see's what will become of us or what we will be made into as for us we see nothing of whats going on while He works in our lives, there are many examples of what he can do and some are told in stories about the bible. So even children can understand that God the fatther loves them very much, he can reach into the simplest; of minds and help them understand his love.

As none of us are the same, some travel a long and hard road and then others learn about His goodness very young in life and still stray away from the path. To find them selves in trouble later down the road so He picks them up and leads them back to the path they should be on, and He can do this many times in a persons life until one day when it sticks. As many would call it luck when they survive but luck has nothing to do with it, that is our Father reaching out to us to let us know that he is watching over us. There are many thing's to do here and I like to do my part they are having a brick signing for building something here in Courtland not quite sure what it's all about but you pay to have your name or what ever on a brick and they use those bricks to make something very neat and people can read your name or message years after you are gone I guess it's a way to say that you were a part of history, imagine all those left behind who might be looking for you and couldn't find you until that day when they read your name on a brick that should last forever they have many things here that would be unusual to others, that don't live in this part of the country. It's a community thing that people likeand in some way I believe it brings people closer then in a city setting, in the city people don't get to close to others like neighbors and here it's a lot different. The sun should start to come up before too long as people are getting ready for work, I have also found that writing about your life can open memories that were once lost to you and they can be some good ones. Like a love that once was and how it came to be, we all go through a learning process where we grow up and fall in live with someone but with most of them they are forgotten. Like the women who had three children when I was in my teens a very beautiful women who had left her husband because of abuse, we got along really good and I met her in my 17th year of life even then they had low income apartments where she lived and I cared for her kid's very much as we took them camping and fishing. I met her at a gas station on Ventura ave in California where she had car trouble and we hit it off, I couldn't see how someone could hurt such a women but that just goes to show how a spirit can be broken if you don't treat a person right. We both smoked pot at the time as it was a phase I went through during my teens, our family was going camping and I invited her to go she was reluctant to go at first but then a friend of hers said she would watch the kids so she went with me. It was the best camping trip I took in my youth and wouldn't you know it I didn't remember it until just today. We had a beautiful day and my mood was very good with no problems to think of I'm still getting Randy used to the idea of getting his own place and it would help him feel independent which is something we all need, Tuesday and the wind is blowing pretty hard this morning it feels like it could blow in a storm because it has that dry feeling to it, like in the winter when you know something is brewing off in the distance. When you live somewhere for a time you can feel and see the change in the weather, but if I'm wrong then it's going to be one hot day. March 27th and the month is about over things are changing but I cant quite put my finger on whats going on, it's getting to where I don't like to watch television much any more with the things that are on it violence' seams to be at every broad cast. In the big cities and it confirms that it's nice not to live there many time when things seam to get to me I go out side and work in the yard, yesterday I did some weed-eating and my right arm shook for the rest of the day and even into this morning but I got the job done and out by the mail boxes looks better with the weeds gone also it gave me a charge of energy that lasted until bed time.

The weather is strange around here but we learn to adapt to it and go on with life my personal feelings on Randy getting his own place will give him dignity and help him to grow, the women that I met so long ago finely had to go back to her husband and I never heard from her again I sure loved her with her beautiful ways, it was like one of those romance novels. I wonder what ever happened to her? I sure hope that life was good to her, I didn't have much experience with women back then but we did have fun. As we drove to the camp grounds she sat next to me and no one could keep us apart, then when it was time to go to bed we had a sleeping bag and by the next morning we ended up at the steps of a trailor and some guy about triped over us it was so funny but we had a good time. We spent a week there and then we had to go home back to the big city Ventura' we all lived on the Avenue where most people who were struggling lived and the gang there called the Avenue Rats adopted Oliver and my mom as members they called her big momma because she loved some of them and took them in sometimes when they didn't have a place to stay, it was like she was trying to save them from going down that road of no return. She was truly loved by them and they would do anything for her, Jerry my adopted uncle was an iron worker that had plenty of money but he had a hobby many of them really but he would go behind the stored and get his produce out of the trash cans and he would take us with him.

The food supply was endless and we would fill up his pick-up almost every time and what we couldn't use he took to other people who were starving from a lack of food. We all did our part and reaped the rewards as we never ran out of food when he was around, then when he had to go to work his women would take over and we kept going almost every night or early morning. Sure parts of the produce has little marks on them but they could be cut out, and the rest was good. He had been doing this for years before we came along so I think at one point in his life he had to live that way and there is no shame in that, even though he made a lot of money he would only spend it on what he needed and that was usualy alcohol. Being an alcoholic my self I understood the need for it aand he shared when he had enough, strange how that has just came back to me after all these years Jerry Allen was a great person and he treated me good when I would come to visit my friend and my buddy. I remember when his girl friend accused my mom of being with him and even though it never happened they played her game, and we had many a nights laughing about it. He seamed to like to make her jealous but she didn't like it much, all these memories comeing back is a sign that the mind is coming back to normal or I'm reliving my past as it comes to me it wasn't until later when he married the mother of his child who was 14 years of age, and he didn't like the idea of my little brother being with her as he was 16 years old at this time. Like two kids in love nature took it's corse and they had a child and then later married, neither of them got to grow up as teenagers do they had to go right into parenthood so they struggled to make it through life the best way they knew how to end up divorced later in years. It was like they were kept in a bubble by her mother and Randy didn't develop mentaly like he should have with the alcohol always coming in the door, later I married her sister. She was older then I was and already hada baby well a son who was five at the time I thought I was ready for a relationship but apparently I wasn't and it didn't last long about three years. And then my mom got sick and I had to return to Nebraska to take care of her, so many true stories and the ones I forgot about seam to make there way back into my life at this time. After I got married we went up into the mountains to a hot springs to celebrate and that was when everything changed for the worst, she thought I needed changing and she tried hard to do it but that didn't work. It made me resent her and I didn't want to be around her so I would wonder off in search of something, maybe that perfect person that would like me for who I am. Other thought I was a good person but she found fault in most things that I did never happy but maybe that's the way life is supposed to be, not in my world.I was rebellious in my youth for some reason but I worked hard and that didn't seam to be enough either. As fast as I made it she spent it and it was that way with all of them, but with her I thik she thought that she was older and knew more about life what a crock! Over the next few years we went back and forth but in the end it was over like the house of cards that fell. Many times they would always want to move to a better place even within a year or so what's with that? Stay at one place for a year and then get a wild hair to move down the block, confrontation isn't something I like but it seamed they kept an argument going between family and like any parent her side would believe her lies. Alcohol and a relationship doesn't work not for me anyhow the arguments would lead to fights and then the next morning no one would remember what happened.

The best thing to do is get a pet! As they wont argue. So many foolish mistakes and yet we live to write about them, I bet He had many laughs about what people do. Which brings me to the time I remember looking down from somewhere up above and shakeing my head at what some argue about, I was with someone but I don't know if it was a dream or if it was at the time when I went through the tunnel so many pieces still missing' and yet they are still coming in at different times. Is it the search that keeps us going? The search to find the purpose of our lives. And why are memories so important? That's one I will have to see about in the furtur, even today the times seam to get mixed up of when things took place at what time but what we know for sure is that it did happen sometime in our life. I remember hitch-hiking from Nebraska to California when I was young and then coming back with two sisters it was at a very cold time of year and we road in the back of a truch an 18 wheeler, at first he wasn't going to give us a ride but he later told us that he was quiting the company so he thought why not. He never knew it but he probably saved our lives that day as we were freezing in the snow on the side of the road, we had been there for hours and no one would stop for us imagine that! I wouldn't want to try that these days as people are too scared to take the chance any more. One time I was taking Oliver to Grand Island and a guy was hitch-hiking out on highway 36, we went on and when we returned he was still sitting there eight hours later.

But if someone knows you and knows you are from around here they would pick you up a neighbor or someone who has seen you around, this is a tight nit community and they look out for their own. I guess you could say that it's like a locked community with out the locks, and if you don't belong here they will also let it be known. Such a great place to be a writer, it's Wednesday morning and it's early the 28th of March just three days left of this month. During winter we accumulated a ton of food and I took some to the church so some of the needy can put it to good use, this is something I like to do because it's the right thing to do and we have people here that need to eat also. I wish I had more to give but later the boy-scouts will also be coming around and I have to save some for them when the food drive makes it's way through Courtland, to me giving is a part of life and it has been done for more years then I can count. Doing it gives you a feeling like no other and it stays with you for quite some time that feeling which shows that you have a heart, in the early days it was something I wasn't able to do but now I even collect certain things to bring to the people who are in need. Randy is healing and in time he will be him self again, but it scared the hell out of me just seeing him brought tears to my eyes because I knew how close I came to louseing him once again. I have a feeling it's going to be another hot day as I let Hraley out this morning to wonder around, Walt once told me that wild animals walk around here and at one time Gismo got into it with a raccoon and he wouldn't go out for quite some time afterwards. My self I think the wild animals must feel safe to wonder around town, I do know many of them have visited us here at my house when I had the pile of limbs out in the back the trees are good cover for the squirrels and they play each summer and I cant help but to wonder what they are talking about when they talk to each other, do they abide by what we call being connected or do they just run from one mate to another. Strange things to think of but it's there from time to time, for the most part they seam happy and can fly or jump pretty dam far when trees are so far apart. I still get the burning in the back of my skull from time to time and when I'm having a bad day it feels like gravel in there but I give thanks that I am still here, I can hear Oliver in the other room but he wont be up for a while the ladies came yesterday and I told them that I was a little angry about what was told to the people in Grand Island and she apologized so now that is behind us. I was talking with mmy pastor and I told her that I felt like a caregiver for a hospital and I'm the only worker and she laughed and said you are a care giver, I guess I'm more then that really but I do it for love in which others do it for pay. Not sure how long it will go on as that is something only the lord knows for sure but I will try, the situation with Randy is one that I went through so many years ago after getting out of the hospital the med's they had me on could stop a horse an with time my new doctor got me off of them and in the end I turned out ok' I remember our first visit he told me that one of the pills could make a runner not make it down the block, so he put me on something else that would allow me to have a better quality of life. The trees are starting to bloom and some are so pretty with their purple flowers and others with white, the grass is also growing and I have cut it once but I am now waiting for it to get thicker so it will be even when it's cut.

Maybe one day I can plant some seed and have a much greener lawn without the water grass. But for now things will stay the same until that day comes, I have to do a little at a time as things develop and we go into the new year as time passes things will get better and I wish some would see that as for my pop's I will take care of him until I cant do it any longer but he is my best friend and we have been through a lot together through tears and laughter we have made it a long ways. Being a fairly calm person, when I get upset it takes me to a place that I don't like to go, to another place which is full of confusion and it turns my mind into a battle field it's like I'm fighting a war and it's not a nice place to be. I have fought this war before to stay alive but I don't recall winning the battle that has brought to where I am today, who knows how many times this will take place but as long as I am alive I know there has been some progress. Is this the soul surviving or is it the spirit that will one day take me to that place where I will live out eternity?. So many things which will come clear one day, I sometimes feel like I was thrown into a place to see if I would survive and many are watching to see the out come. Off in the distence, is a great palace which sit's on a hill that was once a flame. What are these things in which I see a figment of the mind or something I saw so far back that I didn't remember it until now, and why now? The day is turning out to be nice so no rain in sight not for today anyway.

Lately I have been experiencing; things, new things and I can feel change in the air but this happens every year at this time. Could it be spring? Earlier in life these things never happened but now I feel them which are strange to me. Thursdy morning' as I looked out the kitchen window I could see that it had rained some with some people they use a rain gage to tell how much they got, but with me I look at the puddle in the street and if they have water in them then it has just recently raining. I have noticed that many people can be brought into your life for many different reasons and if their not around tomorrow then they were never meant to be there, He has a reason for everything and it just that some weren't supposed to be a big part of your life and be with you later in life. Valerie was one such person and I learned a lesson from being around her back then she was to show me that I am strongin many ways and that I can resist temptation when it came knocking on my door, she was always the girl that liked the bad boy's with motorcycles and that kind of person is one that I wouldn't want to be. In many ways she was a risk taker always looking for excitement wanting to be noticed for her wild ways and maybe that's what drew me close to her, through the years I saw her with her boy friends and mostly they had addiction problems. Maybe in her own way she thought she could fix them but that would never happen, her most recent being a guy that died on a bike. The risk takers is just that they play with life in hope to beat the odds but in the end they usually louse, I text her from time to time so we can stay in touch but the feelings I once had are long gone like the days of winter, not to be repeated again. I am learning that each day is renewed so we can start the day fresh and hopefully renew our way of thinking. For the past is better left where it was, writers can seam to bring things to light that have happened in their lives but once written they should be left in the book that they write. I think when life is half over we are allowed to travel back for a while because it's a part of moving on, they say we travel back down the road we leave behind and with a writer they can do that on paper. But what about those who have to go through life not being able to record what happened? Are their memories lost or do they carry them to that eternal place we call eternity?. Feelings they are strange one minute you feel happy and look forward to the day and then change comes and sometimes messes things up, but you go on and hope that things get good again and usually they do. Many people feel the search in life is the answer to us being here and some avoid answering a question by using that terminology, one lady said it's all in the search but for the life of me I didn't understand her. I think we all look for answers in our own way and hope that we will find them but with us being only human it's probably simpler then what we expect it to be, I know my self that I must comfuse things more then they are, it's just my nature to try and find the answers and then in the end there wasn't an answer or if there was I missed it all together. This morning is pretty peaceful as Randy is resting well, him and Oliver have become like two kids but different in many ways and sometimes it's like having Peat and repeat as one will ask a question and then the other the same thing two seconds later and when that happens I have to throw up my hands and say well as I look up to the heavens, and hope for an answer. It reminds me of something I read called what do I do lord. Friday morning' and the day yesterday was nice at noon or so I received a call fron the managing editor of the Kearney-Hub news paper Mark and he wanted to know if I was talking about my brother in my last letter which I was. We have been friends for years now ever since I started to write and he commended me on it being a good writing, as we talked I told him a little about my brother and how prison didn't do him any good when addiction comes into the picture it shouldn't be an option to not get the person help.

And only when they realize this will things change, to them a person becomes a number and are no longer a person and this strips them of their dignity. Will Randy recover? That will be left in God's hands only he can preform miracles but I know if he tries he can still become a better person then before. For with God anything is possible, in time I will try to reach into his world the one where understanding is limited because of his lack of being able to read or write. Not being able to do these things leaves a narrow path in which he sees the world and for right now he is used to that path and comfortable in it, when I wrote the letter I have to say I was angry as people who visited loved ones in the prison said he was close to death. What was I to do? I took out my mighty pen and wrote letters to bring him home. My love for my brother is not limited by any narrow window for it is love it's self, and the world needs to know that life is stronger then death if love is in the equation. It was God that brought this about first by my hearing about his condition and then by a song, who would of known that a song could bring someone out of such a thing but it did. That and a whole lot of love, as the day came when I went to pick him up I was scared of what I would see but what I saw was a soul reaching out and as He would do I took him home. I wanted to cry but I held back the tears and showed him the love that was inside of me, the letter could be out today but in writing it I hope people will listen and understand that human life is more importand and get people who need help the help they need.

I try my best to show him that he is loved and in his own way he sees this and tells me quite oftend that he loves me, my other brother had been in trouble many times and yet he got lesser time then Randy. Go figure what happened there, maybe I have always been a fixit person trying to fix what others broke but I try and I do a pretty good job at it. For on this day, I hope my words of hope will be heard and an other will speak up about what needs to change. The people who see my little brother want to cry because of what they see as for me I look past the damage and see the soul reaching out for help, as the lord allows I hope to have many more years with the closeness we share. Mark has been following my writing since the beginning and he sees that's inside of me a soul reaching out to othes who have gone through the same thing, and who knows my coming here to Courtland could have been the setting for bringng my brother home. As we talk some days he said he loves it here and for that I am glad it's important to be comfortable where you are going to get better, and I know he will grow on people as time goes by as he has grown on me. In some ways he is still afraid that they will try to harm him, and to me that isn't an option. The pen is stronger then the sword and I will use it to the best of my ability to keep them away from him, Mark him self was editing my letter so I know my message will be heard by those who can bring change. In 2012 I will write about my brother in many letters to somehow change things that are going on, but with it there will be people who say well why did he get into trouble and then the addiction will be addressed once they open that door. It seams I have been fighting the addiction problem for like ever! But as long as it exist there will always be a story to tell. For it has to be stoped, his struggles goes on but like time it also passes to bring hope and understanding to those afflicted by the curse. In my years I have seen many who have fallen but not too many that would get back up, with my brother it's like the damage has erased the memory of his addiction and at this point that can be a good thing it would be like God wiped the slate clean and now there is room for a new start. A start without the burden of what destroyed a good part of his life, now the question is, can he learn. In time we will see, I like to read to him every now and then in hope that he will retain some of what I read to him and if this is possible then he can learn all over again. And who knows in time he could regain the knowledge of a whole new world, one without the addictions that caused him so much pain. The mind is like a computer and it retains a lot of information so teaching him might be a task, but I will try and show him that the world is beautiful if you learn to live in it the right way. When the mind is damaged time is important no matter how much time it takes I will try and teach him, but I also know that he will need to learn more then I can teach him so I will call on my church family for help at some point. Can we be taught all over again? Yes' I am living proof of that fact as my mind was once destroyed by the curse, that tried to destroy me. For each person is different and they have to be approached in different ways so they are acceptable to learning, and God makes that possible.

If I wouldn't of had Him, then I wouldn't know where I am today. But we have to put forth the effort to learn because nothing done wrong ever comes out right, Randy being here is a miracle in it's self and it was brought on by the father. It's like things happen in stages and once they start no man can stop them they have no power where God dwells, just the journey to making it this far was a long one and I know the journey is far from over. But in the days following the publication of the letter I will see what others think and weigh it to my beliefs, the mega millions lottery is 540 million dollars my land' that would help a lot of people from starving to death. So many play it but what would be the odds of winning? I wonder if they sell tickets here in Kansas, so many people die each year from not having enough food and yet they say we are the richest nation in the world, and when you ask why they don't help the starving and homeless they say it wouldn't be politicaly correct to help your own people. What a crock of shit' they just want to keep people in poverty so they can have someone to look down on, it's been that way since the beginning of time and will probably stay that way until someone changes it as for the people today they wont do a thing other wise it would have been changed already. That's one thing about history it's like a book of things that have changed over the centuries and you don't hear about the ending of poverty, or even a big dent put into it so many could of done something but chose not too. If I could things would change in a big way maybe I couldn't stop it but I sure would help with getting food to those who need it.

The weekend is coming and tomorrow I hope will be another good day, I am going to mow the lawn this afternoon and ride my lawn mower. It's fun too drive, and it's something I didn't have in my younger years it's like a toy to me and it's exciting. I have to have some fun in life so why not, I feel closer to God when I'm out in the yard. Just Him and I, as I go into deep thought about life and what will become of it in the future. Will the good things I feel come too pass? We will see! Saturday morning' through the day on Friday we worked in the yard and the mower ran very well, it's a time of year when some things become fun when you have someone that helps in the best way they can. Tomorrow is the first so we have communion and I will get mort of that ready today, it's a pleasure doing these thing and it's fun I would like to get many things going but my boys come first before all else, life is so precious and I know we will have a good one here in town away from those who think the world revolves around them. I find my self careing for my family above all else and I think that's the way it's supposed to be. When things get tough we seam to manage through it all when people say things about you we need to shrug it off and go on with our lives in hope that all things will be made better by and through Him the one who created us, we went to the thrift store yesterday and they didn't have anything we couldn't do without so we came home. It's a nice and cool morning but you can tell that later it will get hot, yesterday it was in the high 70's and maybe even in the low 80's and that was hot to me anyway as I tried to use the air-conditioning in the car it didn't seam to get very cool so I will have that checked before our trip to Nebraska and they can do that right here in town, there are many things which can be done here in Courtland as they have serviced for over 100 years I like that my home has been here since 1919 boy I would of liked to hear some of the storys that have come from inside these walls, or not. Depending on what they were. As they years pass things will imporove and I will become closer to those who are important to me, yesterday pop's went out on the porch for a while and enjoyed him self just looking around at the different things. I don't hear the augers going this morning so the plant must not be running at this time, my house has withstood many storms and I hope that it withstands many more. In my time I havent seen such a closeness that the people here share when tragedy strikes they are there for each other to lend a helping hand and then life goes on, all the things that I thought was important seam to not matter here it's like the rest of the world is just that. A place far away and it hasn't got any thing to do with life here some of my friends have been missionaries back in the day that is something which a lot of people close to christ do help other so they will have a better life. The feeling of uneasyness has passed and I wonder who won the lottery last night they had the drawing at 10:45 so we weren't up but they do give a number where you can call to check the numbers. The biggest lottery in history and if no one win's it will go up to almost a billion dollars, my land' that's a lot of green stuff I don't play it very oftend maybe a few times in my life but that excitement gives you a charge and it makes you excited for a short time anyway. Not something I would like to feel very oftend.

Last I heard it was seven hundred and some million dollars, boy would that be a lot of suit cases full. Enough about that in the future there will be many more lotteries and some will top this one, in just a few hours it jumped from six hundred and some million to seven hundred and some about close to a hundred million jump. As people were going to other states to play because their state didn't have the lottery. On the news it showed people in lines as they made their way to buy a ticket that many people you would of thought they won a super bowl pass for life. Here in Kansas you just o to the store and get one no lines and no hassels, I couldn't imagine waiting four hours to buy one when the odds are so low but people do it and it has to be for that charge I was talking about it's four thirty in the morning and still the birds havent awaken yet, they usually start singing around five or five thirty and it makes for the beginning of a nice day Oliver is moving around in the other room must be restless. Well they said the winning lottery numbers but none of mine matched but one so no riches for me right now the winning ticet was sold in another state but they said there could be other winners out there somewhere, I wonder if you can replay the numbers you bought if so then I will play these again in a few weeks. It's not something you really want to get into because I hear it can become an addiction and many have lost everything because of it, their homes and their families.

When something becomes an addiction it consumes you and nothing else seams to matter in your life not even your children. Through the years I have almost fallen for things which could be destructive like psychics during my journey I felt that all hope was lost but instead of reaching for God I reached out to them and that was a big mistake they took my money and what they said never came to be, nd it didn't take long before that became a thing of the past. And I know there are others who have fallen for the same thing, they feed off of hopefulness and that can destroy a person if they are at their weakest point. Watching a news segment about Whitney there was a guy that would of helped her but the family told him to quit gossiping in other words leave her alone. Sunday April fools day' the man went on to say that her family was enabling her and you see this all the time, it's like they don't want them to suffer so by some oxymoron way they feed the addiction. She had a 15 year old daughter and she went up to this person and asked him to help her momma and then she was pulled away from him, at times like these it's important to get away from the enabling people because more then likely the person will die in which she did. This guy could see what was going on and only wanted to help but the people around her didn't want to see it. Manipulation is something that addicts learn so well as they have to survive and yes their families will feed the habbit so they can get back to what some call normal, manipulation is something that can and will destroy a person and you see it with a lot of alcoholics also.

This is when the family becomes addicted to the person and their addiction, the addicted one will even cry to get what they need and it's usually others that will secure the product for the addict espcially with the people who are rich as for the people of the lower class they have to secure it on their own because they don't have people bottle feeding them. When someone dies that is rich or should I say a preformer there are thousands of others that are unknown who die in the same fashion, with family there is something inside that doesn't want to see the suffering so they think or feel they are helping and all they are doing is helping them to die, the man that I speek of was on top until his own addiction destroyed a lot of his life, but now old and gray he is making a come back in hope that it will be the right way this time and I wish him well. Family choose to not see what they are going through they to be able to block it out of their mind even though it's still there. I choose to not interfear in others lives because of this same problem, I took my self away from the world that helped to almost destroy me. As for those who choose to let loved ones destroy them selves they can live with the grief and keep fooling them selves about what really took place in that loved one's life, as time moves on there will be many more celebrities that will parish because of the curse of addiction and no one can help them unless they want it. Wanting it is the key but even family can hold you back if they are anything like that one. Some will even say it's a phase and that couldn't be further from the truth, she did an interview a while back and she said that it had taken over but she thought she had it under control. But when you use nothing is under control and before you know it that life is gone.

With the many who died in the last five years you would think it would of opened some eyes but it hasn't they keep falling like flies. Then the family wants to blame the world for what happened when they had a big hand in it, this Sunday was great and thr pastor asked if I would sing the song I wrote called the Cross and I agreed. I was going to do it on Christmas but my throat was giving me some trouble at the time so I was unable to do it, it will be this Thursday when we have a special thing happening. I was delighted to say yes. So things should go well, it's

Monday morning' and it's humid out the humidity must really be up there as I feel clammy little brother awakened when I went to the kitchen so I told im tht it's only two thirty in the morning for him to go back to sleep. I felt special when she asked me to sing but I'm sure there are going to be others as we go into lint season, the news paper people already came by as I saw the neighbors light on across the street . They are an older couple and she loves to have her plants during this time of year there house always looks nice, and they must have a lot of friends or children that come to see them from time to time he still works from what I have seen maybe at his farm where he has cattle and raises crops for the worlds consumption. My land' if it wasn't for people like them a lot of people wouldn't be able to eat, they are all farmers in one fashion or another. Some raise sheep, and others raise cattle, but it's not like it was back in the old days when one was against the other.

Today they get along and you see them both when you travel down the highway, some say that sheep are stupid as they have to be lead almost by the hand to water and food. In many ways we are that way when it comes to the father as we learn new things concerning his love. This is another day which I am glad to be here, as I watch Harley he reminds me of how I was when He found me on that day being bewildered; and not knowing what to do next. But as time passes we learn to adjust to things in this different world. The mornings are quiet except for the noise off in the distance, it almost sounds like trafic on a highway but it's not it's the machines at the pland just down the road and of course the sound of the trains as they bring box cars in to be filled. The railroad is a big part of the surival of the town but it's the people who make it what it is a great place to live. As the year marches on there are going to be so many changes not only in life but in the way of life, as more people need to open up about things as for me I open up a little at a time so one day it will be like walking into my home and family will be there to say hi. This might not sound like much to others but it would be a great thing for me to accomplish, just the easyness of being that way would be great to me, the longer I live here the closer I get to the people and it brings me joy to be able to sing to them. If they didn't think it was good then they wouldn't listen but my voice is created by God and it's supposed to bring joy to others, the day will bring new things and I hope it's full of joy. As I look at the elStacytors off down the road they must be a hundred feet high and fourty feel around my land' that can hold the hole harvest from one season and more, Hannson and Muller trans ports the grain from the field and then back to the field during planting season. And I know they help the farmers in many ways, it reminds me of a buddy systen and I believe they too have been here a long time, they supply jobs for those who are out of work and I think they haul other things also as they have a fleet of trucks always on the road, if I was younger that would be something I would of liked to get into. But now days my writing has become a big part of my life. Although I am a care taker it's nice to write about our everyday lives here in the heart land so much goes on and the people here are great, I could be having a bad day and just the wave of a hand can change all that as the person seams to know me from somewhere and it's usually from church. Many of them only come once in a while because of their jobs but hey! Better once in a while then not at all. My song the

(Cross) was written out side of my church during one frosty morning and it stuck as the months let me put it all together, with me things come a little slow because I have to hear the music in my head and it has to go with the words to bring them both together , what a great delight He has given me the ability to compromise and create the music in my head how many can really create with out instruments is it all of them or just a few my self if it doesn't sound right then it's no good, but different people have different taste in music as for me I don't like opera as I could never get into it but there are those who would spend thousands of dollars to hear it. I guess I'm just a country boy, only writing songs that touch the heart. You can never tell where He will take you just like with writing I would of never guessed in 100 years that I would take this path, only God knows where we are going and if you think you know just tell him and make him laugh his plans for our lives is way different then ours. O we might take on a career but in the end He craetes us to be what we were born to be.

And you or I don't have a clue of what that is only He knows what lies at the end of the road. Just like with Jesus God knew he would die before he was even born, and yet that didn't stop him from bringing him here to die on the Cross for us. For He knows all before it happens and he even knows when our time is coming, yes he knew I would say yes to the pastor. It's amazing how He has such insight I had to turn on the air this morning it was like I was being smothered and that's from the smoking who knows maybe one day I will be able to quit, I am happy in this day as Randy is healing just fine his wounds are coming along and he seams to feel better with each passing day.. I have to take him in for a check up on Thursday a follow up to make sure everything is fine, the feeling I got as pastor Kathy prayed for him and held my hand as I prayed was out of this world. I went from being distraught to being calm as God assured me that he would be alright, I had never felt this before but it was a nice feeling like an assurence that He would bring him through the ordeal when the doctor said that Randys blood pressure droped it scared the hell out of me. And then he said they were going to transport him to Salina because he was too unstable to go on with what ever they were going to do there. The doctor messed up and almost lost him, and it makes me wonder what they were trying to do. Now that this has happened I will never go to this hospital in fear that I might not come out, you have to have an expert in that field you cant just let any Tom Dick or Harry try to do surgery on someone, does he even have a licens to cut on someone? Or is it a hands on thing by some idiot that wishes he could be a sergent.

In the time when I had mine done my doctor got an expert and things were fine. Could he have a law suite we will see, you don't go into one hospital and end up in another one 90 miles away. Just that fighteen experience would make you not to want to go to another doctor around here. Tuesday morning, it's early and I couldn't sleep today we have o go to Concorida to take care of some business and then it's back home once I get my oil changed if they have time. Through the year last year many things changed and I have become closer to the people who go to my church Harley is laying on my bed once again like he likes to do each morning and he looks at me with one eye open, he is so dam cute. Back when we first got him he was just a little thing but now he has grown into a pretty big dog for his size fat wise that is my land' it's another day here in Kansas and I look forward to this day every day really when things will get to be nice out side, the worries which once bothered me are gone and I have put them in His the fathers hands as He will do my fighting for me in the days coming we are supposed to get some rain but we haven't seen it yet the trees are blowing like hell this morning so something is up in the weather department they say were supposed to have a bad year but we will see I sure hope we don't. I had a dream about someone and he came down here for some reason it was someone that I don't care that much for as he gives me bad vibes but it was only a dream or was it? A prediction of something that will happen down the line I'm in hope that it's not. I find it strange how people adjust to things and it's awesome when it happens, my sister is doing fine after her brake-up with her husband but I wonder how long it will last she is a person that has to have someone in her life altogether different from me. As long as I am left alone to do my thing I am fine no complacations with drama or any other stuff that comes with it. We have become a unite that functions normaly in our own surroundings by being left alone we grow and survive in this world that is somewhat new to a couple of us but all in all we make it through each and every day with out a hitch. Yes we have family problems but they are taken care of within the family the way it should be. O Harley' my friend. He shows love when others show just the opiset and I can talk to him just like if he was a person, and he gives me unconditional love sometimes I think he understands when I pray in the morning as he watches me when I am on my knees or maybe I hope that he does. Someone who can give feelings with a hug and he loves me so, he wont let anyone else take him out side unless I am not there. And then he will, it's a mixed up morning as the sun will show it's self later in the day but my thoughts are also not what they should be as in the mornings it's hard to wake up, for me anyway. in the years to come I will be a part of the helpful not the helpless a part of a community that cares for it's people. And who knows where that might lead, our place here is solid and it will be a part of my life that I will never forget just the people have excepted us and you know they have a heart of gold. When I see someone who needs a hug I am glad to give it, it's like it belongs there at the moment just that hug shows that you care when someone is having a bad day or is confused about something.

We all have those days and need a hug , the women that I asked if she was married seams to have a lot of kids. And her husband is about our age a quiet kind of man from what I saw, but then looks can be deceiving sometimes when you don't know someone. Meeting people over the internet isn't a good thing to do as I found out so lond ago, they can seam to be a nice person but once you really get to know them in person things change they can go from a careing person to a deranged; nut case. As she made me feel like I was in love that soon changed in just a month or so to where I didn't even want to see or be around her anymore. I guess it was my last try to find love and it didn't work out, part of it was my fault because I was in a state of self doubt. Then she gets a hold of me almost three years later and said she loved me very strange after so much time, it's raining his morning and the wind is blowing the trees like all get out I knew when I saw the wind earlier that something was headed our way. It's that time of year when the heat will play havic on weather conditions, this will bring a lot of tornados later in the year. They say we are in tornado alley which gets the worst of them then Nebraska is second as you can never tell when they will hit. It's been an awesome day as the problems which were bothering me have come to an ending, gone to not come back for ever I hope. I asked for help from my father and he made things possible, as what my mind cant handle he takes and fights for me, such a strong love He has for me and I Him.

I still have something to do but this time I wont let it slip by my grasp, Harley has been acting strange eating the grass outside but I have seen it before and he will be alright. We also went to town for some chicken but this time we bought it already cooked so I don't have to do it, my spirit is running very high today with spurts of joy but soon after they come they are gone like the wind that takes the leaf up into the air and drops it. To slowely float to the ground, God has shown me that He will always fight for me if I let Him many times we don't ask for his help and that's when we louse. There isn't anything God cant do and He can do things that we cant understand, as we are limited by our own understanding what seams rational to us doesn't limit His ability to do things out of our realm. We cant phantom the things he can do as He created all things even the universe, just try to picture that in your mind I don't believe you can. When I was afraid once I got here, in time He took that away and now I am living the good life in which he told me I would O I have my problems but when I cant handle them I give them to Him. I went and paid some on my bill at the station and it made me feel good, maybe oweing someone some money isn't so bad as long as you be honest and pay on it honestly. They are my friends and always will be and I look forward to talking with them each time we visit, it's strange how things seam to fall apart and you get confused to only have God the father to help make them right again. Even through the darkest hours He seams to bring forth the light which will shine on you for that time, when you feel alone. Wednesday morning' and we got some more rain last night. It wasn't expected but still it came, and now the grass will grow even taller before I cut it. It's like the dandy lions' are takeing over as there are patches of them in the yard. If you were a wine maker then it would be great but I'm not so they are a pain, my neighbor has some guy do hers so I will see what he would charge to get rid of them. As they are not pretty to me, as I look at the picture of mom it seams she stay's in my mind for a short time anyway and I'm glad that I kept her picture, it seams like a life from long ago and I have excepted that she is gone. Before my recovery I hadn't excepted it yet and I had to do that all over again sure I cried but that wasn't the same as saying good by' the way it should have been done. Yesterday Randy got permission to go to Grand Island with us to take Oliver in for his check up, it will be the first trip he has taken out of state he said his now friend said hhe was doing well. At first he didn't care for him but as you follow the routeen set up for him then things got better more freedom for Randy and I hope he can handle it. I know he wants to see people in Nebraska but I just go there for Olivers sake to make sure he is doing fine, little brother also got a lead on a car really cheap so he can have something to fiddle with to occupy his time during the summer and spring months, he will have to get it going on his own. The rain will now let everything come into full bloom the trees that don't all bloom at the same time and the flowers which come up at different times also, I was thinking we would have a hard month but God fixed that by getting everything going they can mess things up with just the push of a button but for them to fix it can take months and I was blessed by it not taking so long. They replaced what was taken and now I am whole once again, through all the trials I seam to have persevered and came out of it alright 'blessed be the most high' the one who takes care of me in these trials.

The day is going to be a rainy one, but I thought it would be a hit and miss thing which it isn't as it comes down in buckets, security is important in life to have something put away for that day when things get messed up and if it wasn't for that thing could have been worse then what they were. The rain brings out the rabbits to eat the clover and I like to watch them as they sit there without a care in the world, even Harley doesn't scare them when he barks at them, they just go on eating as if he isn't there until he gets too close then they are off to another patch just at the other side of the yard. These are things people in the cities don't get to see the beauty of God's creation at work in the country, back in the 1800 things weren't as fast as they are today and for some reason I liked that just a normal pace for walking and not this speedy crap the world has speeded up since that time and some get lost in it. As the month moves on things will start to get better my mower will run ok and I will be able to cut it when I please, usually in the morning when it's cool out side there is something fun about riding my mower and maybe it because I can get it done so fast just a few jonts across the yard and it's done. All the bills are paid so no worrys about that thank God' I love paying bills as it makes me feel importand and it darn well should as I never miss a lick unless a tragedy comes up or they short me on my check. As for the good things coming this was one of them and I know there are many more which will make it's way into my life this summer.

There is so much I want to do and they are good things if I only had the means, but you never know what He will put into you're path. Today is the 4th of April just eight more days until my birthday and I will be 53 years old it's a great day to be alive as I love it here in Courtland' my new home. When I met Margret something moved me to move here and it wasn't her so much as it was God giving me an out of the life which had become mundane at the time. It even said in scripture that God would use anyone to bring good things into the life of one of his children and that means even people you wouldn't want to be around not that she was but it never turned out the way someone would of thought it would. For the thing they call love was just for a short time and then it faided like the sun going down in the west, compairing things to nature is something I have always liked to do. Having a connection with something other then my self, my little buddy is sleeping on the bed and it seams he has gotten over what ever made him ill yesterday and I can tell this by his perkeyness such a great friend my little buddy. When the trees bend in the wind it's like life you have to bend with it or it will break you a little give and take you might say, and over the years the trees have leaned towards the direction in which the wind blew the most just leaning to welcome another one of the winds later down the road. As sometimes when joy inters my heart I feel so happy and wonder why it cant be that way all the time. Is this something we will feel when we go to that eternal life some say messure that times a thousand and that's how it will be in the end of this life as we know it. Some say the world was created for us to live on and we will return one day when He awakens us we will all be given a piece of land to grow things in, as the world was created to handle us all those who believe in the once risen; christ our lord Jesus, and who knows this might be my piece of land in which I am supposed to live on I just got it early. Thursday morning' and it rained most of the night, the streets were flooded as the water ran down the gutters of the street like the river in my dream so long ago. I still remember asking him to show me a sign that this is where I belong and then the lake in my back yard appeared, not a big one but enough to show me that this is my home, then on another occashion he showed me the creek which ran down my walk and out to the gutter these are somehow connected with my journey I this life. Even though to some it wouldn't be practial to assume these things it hits right on the button with me. Some like Mark O'Brien said it was his will that I came here to prepair a place for my brother, and I have done that. It was scary almost having lost him but now he is better as time seams to go on. He is back to him self and now we can go on a trip or two during this next month, it's like we are the three musketeers and it's fun to be together I have went from the quite one to be the talkative one go figure! Or at least I think I have. The moods change from time to time but all in all we get along better then the average family, Randys temperment is like mine but I sometimes get mad at things and they think I'm going to blow a gasket so they tell me to not get so up set. I believe they know how hard it is to take care of them so they help in any way they can and I'm grateful for that, living with others takes patients and it a give and take thing as we go through this life. When the time comes for him to venture out from Courtland he will see that out there nothing has changed it's still a dog eat dog world and everybody is out to get something from you.

Here it's so nice compared to out there were they will take instead of give like a true christen would they have that attitude of what you can do for them. And that isn't any way to live since I moved here I try to do my best with what I have to help others and it's the greatest feeling on earth, to help is the key to a good life and the feeling cant be matched not by anything. This place has shaped me in many ways to be a better person and welcome those who would other wise not feel welcome and it can be by only a hug or a smile for life is something to be cherished and we are supposed to be glad in each day that He brings to us. It's four thirty and Randy said good morning as I went out to get some coffee, he isn't usually up at this time but today might be an exception he is mostly chipper when he gets up and I think it has something to do with what happened to him, he called it the scare of his life and I can understand that, so many things to do like cleaning the church for tonights service but I sure hope the rain stops so the day will be a nice one. It hasent rained in a couple of hours so maybe it's behind us, with hope that it is. The day will bring good things as it's a special day the dayof the last supper

I believe but don't quote me on that' this whole week is full of different things happpening with the church and I am glad to be a part of that, other churches have came around and wanted me to go to them but I cant see it at this time. It's like they have followed me from Kearney strange or it's my imagination they have been by a few times and I just shrrug them off because I'm happy where I am.

Today I take little brother to the doctor and make sure that he is healing ok' don't want anything to happen while he goes through this process, in the weeks and months ahead we will do different things but he has to take it easy for atleast another month or two. I know so well what he is going through as I have been there but also it's hard to just sit around because it wares on your nerves, all things in good time as the lord says from the montains to the sea we all live in harmony hey that's good O if it was true with everyone that would be awesome. As I watch movies on television you can see the destruction alcohol causes in young peoples lives and what is strange is that they cant see where their lives will be in a year. Mostly with collage kids they get lost and they have to depend on it to get through the day, you can see that dark road where they are headed and yet your helpless to warn them of whats going to happen. The media uses these encounters too make money but what happens further down the road when they are so addicted that they cant go an hour without it. It was a joy to sing tonight at the church and they said they loved it. Some of the people shook my hand while others gave me a hug, pastor Kathy said it made her almost tear up and that's what a song is supposed to do. Bring tears of joy. (The Cross) is one of those songs which talks about life and Jesus how He died on the Cross and how kids are today, and when they get up-set. Even though there was only a handful of us there we celebrated and passed the challis around at communion. Just this night will stay for ever in my mind as we move forward into this new year, and the lord willing I will sing again sometime in 2012. I have been working on another song which I hope to have done sometime in the middle of the year, my songs talk about struggles through life and how He can bring you through anything for He is the greatest the one and only true king. Although things come to me in a song form they bring with it hope that everything willl turn out ok' (The Cross) was originated here in Courtland one time when I was sitting in front of the church on a cold and frosty morning when I didn't know how things would turn out but with it came faith that I was where I needed to be, for surely it was God talking to me. Strange how things work out when you put your trust in God there I was not knowing what would happen and then sometime latrer it would bring not only joy to me but to others. Now here today three years later life is good and my songs continue to be inspiring by those who love to hear about the father I give all praise to Him, the one that gave me this voice and the ability to write whats in my heart. It's Friday morning' and it looks like it's going to be a good day until the rain comes later this afternoon they are saying a fifty percent chance so we will see, my closeness to the Father is something I cant explain in words because it's too deep to bring to the surface and I have excepted that fact. But the songs bring out part of what I feel and that seams to be enough to draw some closer to Him in some way, the heart is a funny thing as it speaks to us and intertwines with the soul for this is a great thing in this life.

As time goes on Randy is starting to change his way of thinking he said he is trying to do like I would do in the same situation when it comes to people who were in his life long ago. I guess I influence him also because you cant move forward until you let the past go and that means those who had a bad influence in your life. As for me I don't need that and I march forward into a new world where good people reside, for God brings good things to those who are faithful. Dear father I repent of my sin's make me be the person you want me to be in Jesus name amen. For this life is still full of wonders and I want to experience it, when the mountains bring down the snow it goes to the sea and I look at my relatrionship with God that way for I am a vessel of His that He uses and I am glad to be one of those shown how to reach people, even people I never thought would give me a hug came forward to show the lovce they feel, how awesome is that? All I want people to know is that He is there for them even when the hard times are upon us, my land' He will never forsake you for He is our father the one who said it was good before we were put into our mother to be born. Friendship is important in life but the love for God is stronger then anything, we as human beings make things tuff in life when it's supposed to be fairly easy and I am learning that as each day goes by even at fifty some years of age. How great is that? Still learning after all I went through my God is good, when you give a part of your self to Him then He gives a part of Him self to you in knowing it will help you through life.

Sometimes I have a hard time when I talk to people unless I know them fairly well and I'm still getting to know my friends, in the years to come I hope to put on a show that will bring my talents to the surface but first I have to get the songs written and sent off to my friend. Who will help in anyway he can, for a song tells a story and can sometimes heal a person and that's! a good thing. My songs are mine and no one can do them like I can and that's what's so awesome, they are mine a gift from God who so loved the world that He gave his only begotten son Jesus Christ. Who would of thought that He would give me this gift also but I think He knew that I would have to be able to write before this could come to pass. My He is always thinking, only he could bring a mind back and equip it with this great gift and this makes me happy, for my songs are a living part of me my gift from someone who loves me. Could this be the beginning of something wonderful? For only He knows the answer to that question, as for the songs they are always in my mind it's like I create each day with new words bringing them together to show that He is still working in my life. And He will always be, my spirit creates them and I sing them what a partner ship! Randy want's me to wake him this morning so he can check on a car, but I hope he thinks it through before he makes that final step because it can cost him in the long run and he doesn't want that, patients is a great tool if used right but use it wrong and it can cost you dearly. It was a great day and I got the lawn mowed so we will see what tomorrow brings, they are calling for rain tonight and in a way I hope we don't get it because what we got the last few days is enough until the ground takes it in. The night is falling upon us and soon it will be dark and everyone will be out to play, going to the bars isn't something I would like to do so I stay home not wanting the headache that comes with that kind of behavior. As I remember them so well, Saturday and we didn't get anymore rain last night so that's a good thing. This morning is so calm as we move into another day , this month I'm going to try and finish some of my music so that next time they will have something different besides the ones I have already done something new that talks about my day and how He brought me to be here. In the mornings I listen to the birds sing' and that's a good beginning to the song. There are very few that can do what I can do and it's an ability that I will keep alive here as God has kept me alive to write them, a gift that will live on after my time is no more on this earth I still have the first song I ever write but for the life of me I don't remember the words, good thing I kept the tape. My songs today are different from that one as it pertained to the love I had for someone and there was many mistakes which they caused by me not being into it. I have found that if they are simple and direct then people understand them better my new song is one of spirit and how God can lift you up and show you the way this is something Hehas done in my life. But I also notice that I would of never been heard if I wouldn't of traveled here to Courtland, that voice and music would have been lost for ever and no one would of ever heard the words of love that I have to Jesus. He is the foundation for my songs and there is nothing more solid then Christ for He will be here long after I am gone, and they will play my music when the time is right. Even in the bible it talks about music and how we should show our love for God through it, I have so many songs and yet they come to me in peaces to be put together like a fine puzzle that will show others the power of the father. I cant count the tears hat I have cried the tears that flowed from these eyes and yetif it wasn't for them I wouldn't be able to touch peoples hearts like I do, praise God for who all blessings flow. Back in the day things weren't going my way so I had to come to a place where I could put my talents to work.

And today I am here, who would of thought that it would bring me to a little town so far away God that's who as with everything else in my life he knew that I needed to be where I can work on my writing and music, a two for the price of one you might say 'Phyllis' said to never give up on my songs of Christ they seam to touch the hearts of Christens here and they would touch the hearts of others, when they get out. People need to know that the father is there for them as He was for me , you might say that this is my stage Courtland and the church is my audience. As for the women who came up to me and shook my hand that in it's self was awesome and it gave me a new friend, 'Nancy' came up and said she just had to give me a hug and that felt great. I talk about my writing songs to pastor Kathy and I tell her how I find my self singing in the kitchen at times exploring new way's to write about God and what He has done in my life, I think He gave me something back that I never knew I had as the addiction all but destroyed my mind. Even today I am still getting to know my self the one that got lost so long ago, for I believe this is my calling the place I need to be in life but I cant help but feel there was a reason for me going through those trials early in life. And it could have been so I could have something to write about, you have to feel something before you can write about it. That's the way my life has been and I am able to turn that into something beautiful for a tear of joy is priceless and nothing can come close to it, as it brings healing into someones life.

As the song goes God only cries for the living because it's the living that's left to carry on. Awesome so many different things that goes through the mind, in time I will be able to write about all the pathes I have traveled and who know where that will lead only God knows. So much to do, I have to work today for a while so the church is ready for service tomorrow this is where I get some of my inspration as I look at the 'Cross' that He died on. it's not the one which is in the church but it's a symbol of how much He loves us. The days are filled with joy and consern but all in all things are good Randy started yesterday by getting his days mixed up and this lead to going places which we shouldn't have gone until this morning so we will have to start over. But this time' we will call the guy and have him meet us at the bank because we got lost yesterday and wasn't able to find is house, strange being the town is only three hundred people. I don't know why he wants a car he cant drive it with no licens, but he seams to always put the cart in front of the horse. Not a good way to start out, in a perfect world he would get his licens then get a car but this isn't a perfect world never has been and never will be. I have a feeling it's going to be a hot day so I will turn on the air later today so we will stay cool, I guess the years have made me soft but that's ok' I will spend most of my time creating my music and having my friend help me. My friend is a mystery to others but I know him from church another church which is far away, each time I have asked him to help he has always said yes and never asked anything in return. It's not always about money' with some folks and then with others that's what it's all about strange how that works sort of like good and evil in a way.

CHAPTER 9

April 7th' only five days until my birthday and with each year that passes things seam to get better then the year before, the closeness between my church family has far passed my expectations and we are becoming closer with each passing year. It's strange how close you can become to other people and let them into your life, there is a brightness that I have never experienced before and maybe that's because I never let anyone get that close. Until now, it lets you share parts of your life with others and this can open doors that were once shut. There is a place where we are supposed to be in life and He will guide you to that place if you listen. In some of the bible He talks about a place that He will prepare for you and I have a feeling He brought me here because it's where He wanted me. And we shouldn't ask why He did it but except that He knows what's best for us, I went and did some work today and now I'm staying home for the rest of it and watching television great thrill of this day any how. Tomorrow it will be back to church in the morning and then lord only knows what I will be doing for the rest of the day, maybe working on my new song to see how far I will bring it into reality. Sunday morning' and Harley came in a little while ago to wake me up so he could lay on my bed, the little shit does that from time to time and I still don't know why but I think he gets lonely. I always wondered why my eyes swell up and now I think it's from elegies, in the future I'm going to try and get another opinion on why they do that because it's not normal.

I love Sundays the going to church and the day that follows, as for our so called rain there wasn't any. When I go to the church to work, often I will see the rabbits eating in the yard and then they takeoff when I pull in but they don't go far just out of reach so they feel safe then they start to eat again. This is natural with the rabbit as they to feel safe, in my own yard they don't run off as I can almost walk up to them and the squirrels they are neat, I like to watch them as they talk to each other and chase each other through the trees it might just be me but they remind me of a couple arguing and then they are on their way jumping from limb to limb. During the winter I don't see them quite as much as they must have a place in a tree in which they go to weight out the winter, sort of like we have a house to stay warm in. They also have a home that God provides for them, many times I wonder how they must live in that world they have created. My theory is that we all create our own world in which we live and we decide who is allowed to enter that home this gives each family control of their own place on this earth where they raise their children. And if they mess it up then they cant blame others for the job they didn't do, as we go through life we are the ones who shapes their world and that will determine the path they will take through this world. My mistakes were many and now I can see the things which I did wrong, but at the time of making them I couldn't see none of them.

Strange how you are allowed to, go back down the path you leave behind. As the time moves forward there will be a different change in thought through out the world. But I don't know how or when it will take place just a feeling I get when change is coming, it's supernatural this feeling I get and I have seen it many times like when I was sent back, trying to explain it isn't my specialty but there is someone who could explain it better. And that is Jesus' when I sing my heart is filled with joy and I believe it's because a window is opened that was once shut. The song is my creation of what I see in the world and how I let others see what's in my world the way things might be the sorrow and the good of things which people see all the time but choose to ignore it, in the bible it say's they will sing praise to God for what He has done and I try to do that with my music as He is in each song. In one form or another, to me it's just a way of saying thank you for the love you have shown in my life. A record for those who might be fighting that fight I once had to fight, did I come out of it untouched no the scars will be there as a reminder of what not to do when things get ruff animosity will always be there from those who want that kind of life to continue like with the people who sell it to others and that is a problem they will have to work out. There is no quick fix to these kind of problems only hope that one day they will be a thing of the past, in the next year there will be many songs which will go through my mind but only a few that will be brought to light the message of hope is alive and will continue through the ages. We are but a speck in the existence of the creator that made us and I cant imagine that power being let loose in anger as he loves us all, I was moved by the kindness that was shown through the people at church on that day. And in a way, they too could relate to what I wrote but I think the message is received better when it's in a song, for some reason it opens the mind to reacceptance and is taken to heart. For the love of a child is precious even in the eyes of God the Father, as I listened to how they used to throw children away in a pile like a garbage dump it made me sad to think that some life was thought of as worthless and this has changed over centuries, this never should have been but it was. Maybe that's why I don't like to learn about such things, knowing that life was a pick and choose thing if you wanted a boy and got a girl you would just throw them away like they never existed. In the bible He talked about how we were known before conception and to me that meant we had His approval before mom had us, the birds are singing now, so they finely woke up from their nightly sleep. I love to hear them each morning as each one sings a different tune, music is such a great things and it opens the mind to acceptance so we can hear the words which are related to the song, but birds don't have words and we as people need them to complete the song without words we don't have a song it's just a lot of musical interments. Church was good today as they sang happy birthday to me and Judy made me a cherry pie, it's a great day. Monday morning' the beginning of a new day they changed Oliver's appointment in Grand Island I wish they would make up their minds but hey! That's veterans right? And it's something that happens only once every six months. I find that I am receptive when people talk about things and I take most of it in like a tape recorder in some ways and I didn't know I had that ability. It's something that has developed since that time so long ago and I know I didn't have it before especially when I was a child, because I never listened to much as a child.

It's going to be another nice day and I'm glad to be in it. So many things have changed and I feel glad that I am making strides to over come things even today, as for my friends they seam to be many in the church and one day I will sing for them all but for now my song's are important and they have to be completed the one about me falling is good. And in time, it will bring tears to others eyes as it does mine sometimes but on the up note it also talks about How He showed me the way. The way from the darkness and into a new life where people care about your well being, last night you could hear people out mowing their lawns and you could hear those powerful mowers going like a bat out of hell. This year will come with a gift from the Lord but I cant quite put my finger on it of what it's going to be, but for some reason I can feel it coming change is in the air for some reason. Our time here is short compaired to God's time and it would probable be but a blink of an eye to him but He seams to manage to take care of things we need. In my memory' there are many things stored like the words to a song when it comes on the radio, as I know most of them it's like a joke box in many ways, the song starts and then the words become apparent. Like I have known them all my life but I don't know how to tap into that storage place, like the juke box the songs come at random and maybe that's why they say our minds are like a computer. Funny really to have so much memory and not know how to tap into it, my songs are making space in my mind for my memory banks and I just hope they are compleat before they are down loaded into that space where they will remain for ever. I believe writers tap into something which others don't even know is there, a place where others cant go as they go on with everyday life for they live in the now the day even though they are wiser from experience.

As time approaches we will see if the end of the earth comes this year but I have my doubts, I think I would feel it if something like that was coming . I feel change but nothing drastic like they are talking about, in this world money seams to rule most things, and people will say or do anything to attain it. As for me not so much it's a tool just like what a machanic uses to fix a car, this morning I can feel the moon as it's off in the south west this time of morning is so beautiful as with the Sun when it beates down on you when it's hot out side. The universe has a balance and it has to be kept balanced other wise many things could happen like hurricane's and tornados which trash the world. Some natives say it's God washing the world clean from the filth but in society these things are not correct, does society brain wash some people? This could be something that could happen in this world today with the people who are sent away. Many things I don't understand still, but in time they will be made some what clear, more clear then they are right now anyway through time we are allowed to grow and make our selves strong in what we do. As for the things that follow us they too become a things of the past. Kathy said I was bashful and it's true as I feel that way at times but looking it up means awake self aware and this I know O so well, the day has been nice with temp's in the seventy's and there isn't any rain in sight. This morning we went to town to get some food for a couple of days and now I'm baking stake for supper, this is my first attempt at making it this way so we will see how it turns out. If it's good then I will do it more oftend so I don't have to stand and cook for such a long time I still remember mom sweating over the stove for hours making bread, but she liked doing it that and her cinnamon rolls being a prep cook really brought her around after she was ill and when she got the job of prep cook of the chain che would go and teach the other cooks to make what she made but not all of them could cut it. I remember when she made the first giant cinnamon roll, it brought the country kitchen out of loosiing their place to thriving. If she could see it now how her big cinnamon roll's are all around the untied states. Being the inventer of them she never did get her just due as the others took credit for it, they had backing and she didn't just like Herb they could of made a good life but it wasn't in the cards after not getting his loan for a shop he struggled to get by, and the rest is history. It was odd how they wanted him to workfor them after his passing back then in the seventy's I guess it took time to check out other places he worked but by then he had gone away to be in heaven, he gave up was the way I looked at it because he had lost his one true love mom. They were kids together and out of high school they married and had three kids this was in the fifty's so things were still strict and her family being religious well something must of happened as they separated and then I came along. What would of happened if she wouldn't of met that service man? I guess I wouldn't be writing this today and you wouldn't be reading this, we travel many pathes in life and hopefuly in the end we come to the right one. It's kind of like the creeks that branch out but in the end they all lead to that greater body of water the ocean where they can flourish even the salmon go back up the stream they were born in to start the cycle of life all over again and then the cycle starts over once more as the little ones make their way to the ocean.

As the numbers increase they are used and cought for everything from feeding us to the animals we keep for pets even some other animals get a taste of that great fish called the salmon. They are born in fresh waters but over time adapt to the salt water of the ocean, for life it's self is something special and we adapt to many different situations. isn't it strange how we could go from Minnesota to California and then to Nebraska like the fist finding our way home, this is remarkable born in one of the coldest states to end up in the sunny one and then back to the cold even where I live today is cold in the winter for Courtland is my home now. Will I ever venture out again? Not likely, but you cant tell what God will do in your life... for things are ever changing and we cant tell what will happen in the supernatural, I found my poem today that I wrote a long time ago and it was good to read it once again. I will see if I can read it in church sometime in the future or put it on the bulletin board so others can, I believe it can touch a lot of people's hearts if they choose to let the words in, it allows healing when a person feels down and it can help for others to understand the writer. Along with them selves if it pertains to them, many years ago when I wrote it those feelings came to the surface and I believe many people go through the same thing when they go through a break-up it's like your world is lost from you and you have to start over again. Not knowing if you want to take that chance again, that in it's self an make you weary of others as you go through life. But through time and understanding things seam to change and a lot of times it's for the better once you get past the boo hoe! Why me part.

Later in time I will break out of this bashfulness but I also know that others have the same problem like me and it's just something that happens in life. Why do we aquire such things? Maybe it's something we are born into or a flaw, but the good thing is that you can over come it in time and it helps if you have friends that understand it. As for us we are only here for a short time but God helps us through so many things in life with his patients, in the time when things seam the hardest we are allowed to somehow survive and over come what was holding us back. Thursday morning' as the the day begins I notice that things arer different the once felt peace is not there any more and I have to find it again, my love for my brother will never leave me but I am the kind of person who only finds peace when I am alone or taking care of Oliver. I will have to explain to him that I need my space and he should have his, I did what I set out to do and that's to get him out and now it's time to part. It's not like he will be far away just down the street and I can help him with some of the things he needs help with, peace and fulfillment or the lack of, can make life harder then it's supposed to be and I find that it's something that I need really bad in my life. He has a hard time with being alone but I know in my heart that he will make some friends there, should a person ask another to give up their life or life style for another? I my self don't believe so' the life I have is a good one but it lacks the peace it once had so I will try to correct that otherr then those things all is well here on the home front, there was a letter about the death about a youth that died in Kearney and it seams alcohol was at the center of attention causing the death in an automobile accident, it's a shame that more will die because of it only when they open their eyes will the killing stop. Each day many young people die from one addiction or another and it keeps increasing, it's supposed to be in the sixtys this afternoon with a chance for rain going into the weekend but the chances decreas getting towards the weekend down to 20 percent. The weather in other parts of the world is disturbing but at least it isn't for our town so no worrys' here in Courtland where we are safe, when the day starts to come to an end I look forward to the next day a new beginning to a different time when you don't have a clue of what the day will bring. As for the summer it's going to be very hot but at least we are getting our cool mornings now and even a frost or two from time to time, the other day I had some ice on my window of the car and that supprised me for this time of year. This morning I watched Antique Road Show and boy they had some good stuff onn there, I have always been interested in things from the past and how they become worth more today then they were when they were new. But as time passes the price of things go up and the dollar is worth less and that's why some invest in Gold because it can only go up and not decline, in the morning's I find more on the bible then during the day as some teach on television Pastor Murry' is a good one as he shows proof of what has happened and what will become of things in the future, Randy is upset about what happened to him and I can't blame him. What happened shouldn't of happened so we will see what takes place on Friday, I have noticed that he is forgetful from time to time but then he has gone through a lot. Thursday April 12th I would have been born at 5:04 this morning although it's only 2:30 I wasn't here yet Ha! It was shortly after this that my parents moved to California.

182 | *Roger Mattson*

In 1958 so this would be the closes time line to when they left given a week or maybe two I would of gave anything to be that fly on the wall listening to why they left so fast. In those days many people moved around maybe searching for that place where they belonged, I recall my parents saying that the car broke down somewhere and dad had to fix it by using old parts from another car. And that same thing happened to me once in the hills of Colorado, when doing my brother a favor on that part history repeated it's self but I survived and that's all that mattered. Mark on the other hand got the scare of his life but I brought him home safely to go on and have a good life, he like me had always been a giving soul and I learned a lot from him. Yesterday he called to see how things are and I told him about Randy wanting to sue the hospital and he said to go for it. Because it should of never happened the way it did, in life many of us make mistakes but Randy doesn't seam to want to let this pass. What happened so long ago couldn't be helped and the main thing is that I am still here after so much happened, Yesterday I thought it was going to rain as cool as it was but the clouds passed during the night and nothing came of it. The future what will it hold for us? for sure we don't have a clue about time that hasn't gotten here yet so we live in the day in hope that the next will bring something new, something that might make things better then they were before. They had a tornado that hit an air-port and the damage was great but no one got killed thank God' it showed the parts where everything was flying around the air-port and the damage it caused what a sight of mother nature as she unleashed her force on humanity. Even with all their technology they did not of seen it coming if it wasn't for the camaras, I lived in a shell for so long during those times of addiction and it's a place that I wouldn't want to go again.

As time allows I will keep moving forward in hope to over come those things that have somehow made it's way into my life and with His help I will over come them once again. During life we all have set backs but we also have the strength to over come them given time and the right circomstance, through the years things seam to get better and yes I have some regrets but He gave me the strrength to move past those things and start with a new beginning. I know I will need help to over come some of the things I cant do on my own and at that time I will ask for the help of my church family. Helping someone out is supposed to be just that but then for some reason in time they take advantage, and then you have to stop it. My works over the years had shaped me but now I feel that is being threatened by a force that cant be seen or heard, will I over come it? I believe He doesn't put a mountain in front of you that you cant climb so on that note I will survive and keep pushing forward to that place where He wants me. Struggles are what builds us as human beings and the ability to over come them is what makes us strong not only mentaly but in the physical since also, this day will be like all the rest no one or a few will remember my birthday and that is something I have learned to except a long time ago as it's only special to me and no one else, I havent written Rosa-lee lately so I will drop her a letter to see how she and the family is. I hope they are fine, but I'm sure they are I cant remember her daughters name Christa I think but I'm not sure. In the memory of my mom I write as she is the one who said I would make something out of my self, and I have. Riches don't matter to me as I have always been a survivor in this life, as for the ones who didn't stay around they weren't meant to be here today they weren't part of the bigger plan that God has set for me in the future and I am ok' with that. During this next summer things will come together like the puzzle I saw when I go to that special place where I am all alone with God His understanding of things is much more then the understanding of people and He knows our handycaps if we have them and He deals wwith us accordingly, even the simplest mind is allowed to be able to understand him as he works His love into our lives. The struggles come each day but with faith I seam to get through it, but it's like an existence of a soul not a growing thing which I felt when I first got here when things were easier, having others around is very distracting and I fight with it each day and in a way I get tired of having people around me. It's like I want to be alone so I have to do something about it, and in time that will be a thing of the past. He needs to grow as he is still in that box that life created for him so long ago, it would have been better if he would have been out in the wilderness so he could grow and learn. But that wasn't the case and now he is afraid to go out into the world, when I bring it up he goes to the negative things which could happen and that will keep him in that box.

Like the bear that was put in a cage at a young age in life, even though he was now free he walked those fifteen steps back and fourth with the cage gone. This is a mind set and if not reversed then it's whole life will not let him go, he will continue to walk that area for the rest of his life. How can a person help pray comes to mind asking God to take that away so you can help, I my self have went through that time in my life but with His help I was able to over come it or did I? still trying to help the stray dog because I feel sorry for them. A quality that can get you in trouble sometimes but with some it's part of their character and makes them want to do other good things for people is it a flaw? or is it a blessing to care that much only help family so far and then you have to let them make it on their own. Otherwise they can make life really messy, they will take advantage of you and that's something you don't want. My job with my little brother will end sometime in the future and he will survive on his own and I hope he meets someone who can help him maybe someone he can love because he needs that in his life, as for me I seam to be content with my life the way it is and I could go the rest of it alone except for sometimes when I need someone to talk with and my pastor is a good listener when it comes to that. She has been doing her assigment for many years and loves thee lord deeply she is in charge of our souls you might say feeding us the word of God. In faith that we may one day go out and spread the word of God. We are all disciples and back during Jesus time He sent His disciples out in different directions.

To spread the word of God to the four corners of the earth, I find that I need to learn the history behind the one true God and how things came to be. I have went to bible school when I lived in Kearney but when I would talk with others they didn't understand the long and drawn out words that they used either, when a writer they quoted would use them. This to me makes it hard to know where the writer was coming from in many cases, there was one who had total recall of everything and he used words that meant nothing in my world and this to me was mind boggling. One day after bible school I asked Rosa-lee if she understood what had taken place and she said she didn't have a clue, who knows maybe that's what learning is all about trying to find the answers to thing's or words you dont understand. And then in the end you become a better pupil or student, many when they get older they forget more then they learned but during the learning they take in bits and pieces of something which sticks with them for life a piece here and a piece there making the person who they will become later in life. Does schooling really fill a void that might stay void if schooling isn't applied? With many they can't learn, for one reason or another. What causes that? Could it be that the mind doesn't want to be filled with what society wants to put into it. There are tribes that have never seen society, does that make them less intelligent? No' they don't need to fit in with something they don't have any use for, and yet they know that there is a God' the one creator of the universe and all things in it. Some societys never know how to read or write but yet some become the elders of their tribes and are looked upon as people of wisdom, their lives are not complacted with things they don't understand or have any use for and yet they seam to live longer then people who are living in society. This should tell some about something they are doing right, take a person from the U.S. And they couldn't survive where these people live. And to them they couldn't survive here, this would be like being locked up in a bear cage for they know what true freedom means. Friday morning' and there is a warm breeze outside after the rain that fell during the night, you can tell a storm isn't far off in the distance. It's strange how you can feel it when the weather is going too change there is a clammieness in the air that will turn to a storm within the next day or so, many people wished me a happy birthday yesterday and even Mark called to wish me a good one. I was about a sleep when he called and then it took an hour or two to get back to sleep, it seams my days are different from those I used to know because by 5:00 in the afternoon my day has ended and they stay up another few hours. As my niece wrote something special on my face book page it felt good that she cares so much, my sister also called to wish me a happy birthday which supprised me in many ways as she is having her own struggles right now but she took the time to do it and that's all that matters such a big heart. The day will be filled with new things that we cant imagine as of yet, because they havent happened yet, only the day will unfold them to see what they will be. My life is good for the most part and I am adjusting still today to new things, dealing with my own problems and those of my loving brothers and pop's makes it like a group thing.

I still have songs going through my mind and it's His way of letting me deal with things nothing like a good song to keep your mind off of things which are happening, as for my life when I look back to when I wrote all the time those days seam to fade. And I have to believe that it's making room for new memories good memories that will last until that day when I go home. Making preperations is a hard thing to do but my time will be quite a while yet I hope, long enough to say good morning to those who I love. April 13th and a cell is building up one that plays havoc on this part of the country they say it's supposed to hit tomorrow but I'm in hope that it will move off and go somewhere else maybe another state. They say a chance for tornado's and that's something we don't need att this point, I told Tonya to come down and we could go fishing in the ditch by my house and they laughed she asked if they should bring the minnows; and I said yes because that's all we would catch. Maybe one of these times they could really come and go to the lake for some good fishing they have the vehical for it, and it would be a blast to get together one more time all we would need is a camper so I wouldn't have to sleep on the ground. It would bring back so many memories and make new ones for her to share with her and Stans kids. They are great kids and I love them dearly, when we visited them a couple of years ago the kids got along with my grand children and they had a ball riding horses even I got to ride and for the first time it was great, I felt like I was in the old west back in the 1800's when the cowboys did their round up. Such a great feeling to be able to feel some of what they were feeling back then, riding around the farm even though I had to walk the horse slowely it was still fun sitting in the saddle and pretending that I was a cowboy' now Stan, he is a real cowboy out there on his horse each day checking on the stock and seeing how the weat is growing these are things a real cowboy does each day of his life. Plus he drives truck to take the cattle to market, all the works of a cowboy.

I never did ask how old he was but that really doesn't matter, it seams we all have a job to do in this life and we do it to the best of our ability to go on to better things later in life. But family is important and you should stay in touch with them as we make this journey to that place where everything will be made right, a place where worry doesn't inter the picture and there is just the goodness of our father. The boys are still a sleep and they wont get up until until six or so and that makes me happy, to have my time to my self and share some of it with God in the morning. For each day brings me closer to the one that I have love for and that is Jesus Chist' when I watch movies about some of the miracles that he creates little brother ask's me if I think that God could do that and I reply yes, as all things are possible with God and blowing out a fire would be nothing to one so great. I have never loved anyone or anything as much as I love God and when you try to make that connection with a person it doesn't happen for earthly love cant compare to spiritual love for God. Each day is filled with His love for us and we are but a speck in the sand compaired to His love for us, when I watch Joel Osteen each Sunday his message gives me hope for the days a head and I can relate to his teachings as his message is always good for those dealing with despair and confusion. It seams to let you focus on the good things and not the bad, to bring some light into our lives where there might have been darkness for a time,as I watch movies about Jesus it shows that he could tell what would happen before it came to be, thus giving Him sight of time to come which makes me believe that he knew of his death way before it took place. Such a great love He has for us even today as yesterday for Him His self never changes, but by watching I would say that He looked upon us as children and their actions showed the same. Not yet grown up children don't know what the outcomne of their actions will be until later in life when they grow, the floggings were more then the normal human could take but He took them so we could live and our sin's be taken away. No person today would do that as He did but He took it and went on to have ever lasting life with the father sitting at

His right hand on the throne in heaven, now this made me feel good that He loved us so much that He would die for us. Not just a few but all of us and we livce today because of him, the knowing of me even before I was conceived; let's me know that there is a purpose for my being here. as it say's God doesn't make mistakes and none of us are mistakes in the eye's of God. Is there anyway to tell before hand what He meant for us to be? I don't think so as He is the only one who knows why we were born. And only He knows what the outcome will be in the end , maybe that's why some say if you want to make God laugh tell him your plan. Because if it's different from His then He would laugh, I know He has a since of humor because He gave me a little of it and we laugh together sometimes. He want us to talk with him and we can hear Him if we listen close enough, it's going on 6:00 in the morning so it's time to get things ready for the boys and the day..

I have a feeling this is going to be a good day so I will keep that out look on it, the weeks seam to go by quickly and a year is hardly any time at all. When I was young things didn't go anywhere near as fast but today it's hard to except that our time is shortened; by time it's self, what has changed we are only bigger then we were before. But even with that what brings so drastic of a change, I guess it's just life. I talked with a lawyer today about Randy's case and he thinks we might have a melpractiece suit against the doctor so we will pursue it and get the papers of what happened in the operating room. This thing which happened shouldn't of happened and it has to be made right, I couldn't even imagine what he went through and either could anyone else unless they went through it them selves. The lawyer said if he could be any further assitence just call and I will hire him when the time comes to move further, I know they have to keep records of what happened so I will get them and call. Saturday morning' and the train is blowing it's whistel you can hear the wheels as they roll matal to matal it makes a constent who-who sound and then it fades off as it gets further out of town, it's the 14th of the month and a sheriff truch just went by patroling the Nebo hood it nice to kow that they watch out for us as we sleep or some of us anyway. The night was resless as my arm was hurting from laying on it and then I would have to switch side's which didn't help any, they are calling for thunder storms today so we will see what becomes of it. I'm hoping they are wrong but there is still that chance how ever so slight, and the only cover we have is in the closet, there used to be a celler here but over time it started to cave in so they filled it up with dirt.

Back in 1919 this would have been a nice house but time has got the better of it and now it's just an old house with stories like everything else from the past back in the day it would have been modern with it's floor furnace. The people before me have made up dates meaning Walt and I was glad that he did it because all I had to do is put in the central Air to even things out, for summer and now all is well with things in the house. I believe many new things will happen in this next year and they will bring change in our lives, while I let Harley out the air seamed to be calm but also strange in some way and this happens when a storm is off headed this way, as for the morning it's going well so far but I have only been up an hour so really that an assumption but I have high hopes that it will be a good day. Tomorrow I will go to church and see my friends will what happens in the future affect how our friendship is? For surely I hope not but we will see how things go. Will that love that they say they have tower over those things to come only time will tell that story, when I moved here things were alright but change is a things that is constent, and with each day it comes without us even knowing it sometimes. It could be a change in someone else or just a slight change in us as we go through life, it took some time for things to become clear about what happened at the time it was like everything speeded up. Yesterday I mowed the lawn and then it really looked nice I love how even it looks afterwards everything is done and it leaves just a few spots which has to be done by the push mower which is fine with me it lets me get some exercise. The dandy lions were blown all over the place like little seed carrieing umbrellas and many of them were in my hair, kind of funny really how they carry the seeds to other places. There is other plants which carry seeds to other places but I cant remember which ones they are it's a way to make sure that the plant survives through another season, they call my lawn water grass as it stores water in it to survive through the summer as for others grass theirs seams to be prettier as they have no weeds in it. Through life many things are brought into our lives and without them then change isn't possible but He seams to make a way for us to make it, you can never tell what will come of something until it's done and then the change can bring many things with it. From good to bad things depending the circumstances in this life I don't judge other as I know He will do that in his time, all that is left up to him but if something happens here and we let things slide then then we are not doing our job. Fear is good for a person and rising above it helps us to grow Lord knows that I was a fraid to move out of my comfort zone and go to a place where I had never been before, this took a lot of faith and He gae me that faith I needed to move on with my life. If I would of not listened to Him it's hard to tell what would of become of my life, back then it was hard to move on but today I am glad that I did' just the change in people helped me with so many thngs and I'm glad that I live in a town that say's they love me. Tonya and sue were nice when I talked to them and I hope to see them this summer if they come to visit, but only time will tell that story. As the years pass I hope to get closer to those who have been absent from my life and maybe start a thing to where we can visit once a year.

The lawyer seamed to think we have a case so we will wait to see what will take place later in the year but there might also be some friction and I never did like that kind of thing. Being in a small community they might not like the attention which could come from this kind of thing, and my self I know I wont like it but when something is done wrong to someone then it shouldn't happen to someone else. How many before him have had this happen? Only He knows the answer. Him and the one who took the chance when is chance exceptable it's not in medicine, when you took an oath to not do any harm you took an oath to protect the sick and help them. In the 1800's they had to take chances to find new ways in medicine but today not so much. They have warnings out for Kansass & Nebraska about thunder storms that will produce tornados and damaging winds but I hope they will pass by us not destroying anything, they said we have ample notice so no one should be caught with their pants down. And be safe, this is the first time we have gotten such a warning that I know of and I believe it's because of a new system they put into place as we get weekly test on the television. Who knows this might save some lives in the future the house is without a basement so maybe in the future I will have one built so we are protected by the elements, tornados are common around here and it would be nothing for one to take peoples lives if they are not protected. Even when we liked in Nebraska we didn't have a basement but we survived even when the storms hit just down the block I know it was devine intervention that kept us from harm.

Back when we first moved to Nebraska I was 14 at the time and the drive from California was an adventure it somehow made me feel grown up taking dad across country, and I think in his own way he enjoyed it also not having to drive. My self I had no clue of where we were going and it showed as I got lost, if you could picture it back before they had cars it would of taken me a month to get there. Looking at the country for the first time was invigorating and I loved it until we got lost of course, but then dad got us back on course and away we went. The storms are supposed to hit both sides of us this weekend and us being in the middle I hope for a miss by a loing ways, it's been cloudy all morning and you can tell that it's just a matter of time befor we get slammed by them. As for the house I pray that it stays where it is and doesn't end up miles from Courtland. These storms are supposed to be real bad the worst in years, we had to go and get some smokes and the women at the store said we should sell tickets to watch the tornados. She has always been a funny women and can make you laugh some people can do that and others don't have that gift, Sunday morning' and as I took Harley out I could see a flicker of light off in the distance which light up the sky so it must have some rain with it. I haven't heard the weather for today but I hope that if it's a cell it will pass, it's a little windy and the air is dry, last night my back yard looked like a lake as did most of my neighbors the ditches seam to of filled up mighty fast, as the storm was right over us and you could see people flocking over to the neighbors when the sirean went off, they have a basement and the tornados couldn't touch them there. For their family must be pretty big as I saw three vehicals fill the drive-way preservation of life is important around here and their families go to where they feel safe. My home has been here since the early 1900's and it has surviver for nearly 120 years if my math is right, during the storm we noticed that the floor is weak in some spots so in time that will have to be fixed and find out why it's doing that I know' old house. And repairs is something that has to be done on all old houses they call it renovation and it might be fun to do it. There are many weak spots in the floor but I chalked it up to age, as I watch segments on past country singers some met with their death after being addicted for many years but Jonny Cash comes to mind as he dealt with the addiction to Methamphetamine. But in his later years he lived to be pretty old in his late 70's or early 80's for someone to go through that and be able to write about it is a great thing, others like Michel Jackson and Whitney Huston were taken before their time or maybe they just didn't want to fight anymore. That's just my opinion' you hear how people tried to help them but it didn't work out that way they found Whitney in the bathtub and drugs near by on a table, the person which looks at the cause of death said she had bad scaring in her nose from using cocaine for many years. With people of fame the family likes to cover up the cause of death, when it comes to this kind of thing thinking the people are stupid but they know as everything they do is in the press. Other have also went because of alcohol like Keath Whitley another taken by the curse of addiction, so many' and for each one known thousands of others fall by the wayside. The ones that no one cares about, some could have been saved but that just wasn't in the cards for them.

Being one of those not famous I wish I could of saved them but my life goes on and in time I hope to live to be in my double digit of 7 or 8 mark. The only one that I know of in my family that lived long was grandma at the age of over 107, the others not so mush in their 60's and 70's aunt bunny is still around and I should try to contact her sometime if I can find her email address. She was married to mom's brother the preacher I believe of one of the others, but it would still be a link to understanding why things happened the way they did. As I'm sure stories went around in the family about my father, cant tell what the day will be like but I saw the stream as it flowed down the side walk when the ditches were full. It all seams to flow towards the south when things fill up but where it goes from there is beyond me, this morning I will watch Joel Osteen on the television he seams to touch on subjects which helps others to rise above their own problems and help others. One day I may find my self doing the same thing but for now I am a student trying to learn the ways of christ, God seams to give me a little at a time and then time to process it which brings me to believe that he does know our limations and wont give us more then we can handle. This brings to mind the mountain in which He has us climb from time to time, if He didn't think we could make it up that hill He wouldn't of gave us the notion to go up it. My alone time is just that and I like it because I can talk to Him without others around, and it gives me peace for a time anyway.

Being Sunday I don't know what the day will bring, for each day has something different in it and it could be many things. But I look for the positive things like a smile or a hello just these two things can make your day bright or dark depending on you and how you feel at that time, even though the time is faster at this age it's do able the days seam to go by like a whirle wind to balance out later by the week. Strange how I try to figure out things but at times it's fun it's like I'm searching for the answers to life and I don't know if I will find them here in this one, the journey of 20 years has been long even with the speeding up of time it seams long. I cant remember if it was like this in the beginning of this journey because that certain time eludes me these days, I can hear the wind getting stronger out side, and I hope that it's just that only the wind. Monday morning and the wind is still blowing not quite as bad but still blowing enough to bend the trees. Early in time when John the baptis went to prison he spent many years there, but then he was forgiven and went on to do great things even baptizing Jesus him self im water. As time passes I'm in hope that my brother will find his way to christ, but it will take time. Jonh got religion in prison as for little brother there was no one to help teach him. So I will have to try and do that in this community as for those who don't understand him well in time they will have to grow and learn also, skeptics some say that change isn't possible but I know different take a person away from one thing and teach them another. The adjustment process is long, and the trust factor can take even longer, in the day's so long ago satin had his influence in his life but he doesn't exist in my world ' shouldn't we forgive as Jesus did so long ago? When I moved here I was talking with Mark and I told him that people don't forgive as easly as God does and it's a fact. Some people let fear run their lives and this shouldn't be but it happens all the time. After a time the thought of John being a person that went to prison wasn't there any longer, and he preached the gospel until his time was up here on earth for his crime was paid by Jesus dieing on the cross. I can hear the train off in the distence as it comes into town and you cann hear the wheels as they are metal on metal, steam used to run the engine of the train but now it's powered by a great big engine called a diesel. Just the size of the fuel tanks are as big as the train compartment where the driver sits, it's going to be a nice day even if the wind is blowing. Many times I have wondered about things but with some things you don't ask questions you just wait and see if things turn out different somewhere down the road, as for judging people I learned to leave that in the fathers hands because we as people let our emotions get too involved. And maybe it's better some times not to let people know about what has happened in our past lives. In the old days He was here but now we are waiting for his return,, the power to help someone is something not everyone can take on, but even with my doubts sometimes the father assures me that I have done the right thing... some seam distent like they are fraid but there challenges can sometimes get the best of them, will this be something that will pass with time I really cant say. For that is something which is inside of them and not me. Something which God will help them with, as for what will occure in the future I have no control of but I do have today and I can make it the best it can be.

During my time here some seam to get distant but for the life of me I don't know why, as I am the same person they grew to love. What has changed could they have let fear into their lives I sure hope not, for I am the same spirit, many times when we don't understand something we can go to God and ask him for a signe which He will give. I have done this many times and always got an answer to the question that was on my mind, how great thou are! The days are quiet during the mornings, and it brings joy when I can have that time to my self in hope that I can figure out things which otherwise wouldn't get answered. My thoughts are of the church and my friends and I cant figure them out right now, maybe in time they will see that they worried about nothing. But for now they have to make up their own minds on many levels do we live like christens or not that is the question? So many questions and in the end what will become of things for only God kows what will take place in the future not us His children. As to Him we are just that His children and we will make many mistakes in this life and learn from them, my daughter and grand son was sick last week and it's because she cares. Taking care of all those children lets sickness into the picture, day care is expensive so she does it for friends so they can work. The morning is about to beginn for the boys as little brother is starting to get up, I want to try the scrubber at the church to see if it will take off the wax build up on the floor if successful it should shine like a new penny.

Mondays are not as good for some as it is for others but it's just another day in our lives, a day to adjust from the weekend to the work force. And get back on track to deal with things again. With me my job never ends as one day is just like the one before getting things ready for the day, and pray that it will be a good one. For change is constent in a constent changing world and even though we are apart from the bigger part change doesn't Stacyde us, today little brother didn't listen to me and requisted his records from the hospitla I told him to wait but he has no patients when it comes to thing. I think it has to do with his condition and what is wrong with him, his premature actions can cause problems which isn't needed at this time but in many ways he is like a child and gets excited. I don't know what will happen in the future about what happened to him but something needs to be done to make sure it doesn't happen to someone else. I try to figure out why the doctor asked if he was disabled as it shouldn't have had any bearing on treatment, and why he tried to preform the surgery is beyond me or my understanding. There was plenty of time to get him to the other hospital, during this time I had my pastor with me and we prayed for him then while praying the doctor came out and said that his blood pressure bottomed out. Then he said they got him stable so they could transport to Salina, why wasn't this done in the first place? Then his life wouldn't of been in danger the pain that he had caused him to have the nurse call me crying was uncalled for. Then I was moved to call them back and ask if they had his med's chart and of course they didn't and I had to read off each med that he was on, and the male nurse told me thank you that will help. It's like if one mesases up then the other steps in to fix things, only time will tell what will come next. Why that question bothers me I cant really say about his disability, would he of tied it if he wasn't disabled? That question only he knows the answer to but I have a feeling it may get answered sometime down the road if this is taken before the board. Many things in life change our prespective of things and the lord is right there to help us figure out things, if my pastor wouldn't of been there I don't know what I would of done. She helped to comfort my soul during that time and I'm grateful, when we prayed at her home I felt that all would turn out alright it was like Jesus was talking to me and I went from being distraut to calm in just a few minutes. This is something that He does for the soul and spirit, it's Tuesday morning' and it's going to be a good day the birds are not up yet but they will soon be and then the music will start… Such a good beginning to the day as I listen to them with their different sounds. I wont let this interfere with my life and my learning of the father a lot of what happened seamed to go fast but I felt that God knew I couldn't handle looseing him at this time, my brother has been through a lot and no I don't condone what he did so long ago but it was just that so long ago and he paid the price for his crime. A new beginning is what's taken place here and I hope to get him to go to church, for the lord can and will reach all his people and wipe the slate clean. Yesterday we went and mowed the lawn together and it was fun he felt useful and that's something which will help him in the future, on that day I prayed hard and the lord heard our prayers. Pastor Kathy asked what was happening when I went into like a trance. And I told her that things would be alright, and that now I could drive. I was scared to before we prayed.

In this life I try to undersand all things but what happened that day was a signe that this is where I belong for the lord can take care of anything with a power so great. When you feel alone just look up and He will be there as He promised, when the doctor said his blood pressure bottomed out pastor Kathy said it was a good thing because he would be sent to a better place that could take better care of him. And they corrected the mess up which had occurred, when someone takes on something they should know for sure that they can complete the surgery before hand and in this case they couldn't. so many try and fail but that's how things are done with some. As for Randy' I'm glad that he is still here. Through the frost I see a cross that shines for the lost. Such a great song' today I have many things to do and I will try and fullfil them as the day goes on. For each day brings something new to do wither it's the lawn to mow or other things we choose to do but at the end of the day we usually get things done, today is trash day here in Courtland and then we will be set for another week the lawn looked beautiful when I got done yesterday everything so even and the weeds cant be seen from thee road Ha! Just a great day' all around. I can hear the train off in the distance it sounds so far away but then within a couple of minutes it sounds like it's right down the street which it is, they move fast and are going 24/7 to pick up things which have to get to there destination. My land' they have been doing that for over 100 years and still going strong.

Will they ever loose there worth? Not likely plains havent even been around as long as they have and look at what they can do these days, shorten trips by days or even hours. Wednesday morning' and it's cold my mind has been dreaming again and it's strange how that happens sometimes, yesterday I painted some on the windows and trim of the house and I have to say that now it looks better with my touch, many times I wanted to do it but just haven't had the chance until now. While I text some people I notice that some of them don't keep the same phone or they just don't get the message for some reason, but that's ok in time they will see things the way they really are, I have to live my life the best way I know how and that's by my self without the rest of the world. The painting is just one step in the right direction of getting things together for the day when it comes. The opticals that I face will come one day and it will be a time when things come together like the wind when a storm comes from out of nowhere, yesterday I met Marks son and he seamed like a nice young man. I asked if he was going to take over for dad and he said one day after he learns the roaps, so he has plenty of time to learn the banking part of things, you can tell he is his fathers son and he will be a good banker. The things to come we cant always see until they get here but they give us sings and that's when the storm hits, I'm going to try to cut back on some thing and see if the mind changes this is something which I'm not sure of what will happen but it will leave a record for others of what not to do if they suffer from such a thing. My insides have been giving me heck but that soon passes and then my day goes pretty good, we laughed quite a bit yesterday and that always makes for a good day. I ask God to bless others each day and to conbtinue to heal what ever is wrong in their lives especially those fighting to stay well, my guts haven't bothered me much this morning so I'm hoping that will make for a god day. One of my friends made the wrong change and I cought it to return it to her as that would of made things short for her but we fixed it so that's that. I want to see another doctor so that will be making a trip back to where I used to live as for the ones here they seam to not care as much for the person, I don't know what it is but there is something missing and I cant quite put my finger on it maybe it's the friendship that I felt with my other doctor. Hey it happens' Dr. Nelson was always a good friend it was like we had a connection of some sort and I miss that these days the bond of caring can help in many ways and it encourages us to get better. Yesterday I saw a guy driving a four wheeler and he had his dog sitting on his lap with his paws on the handle bars it was awesome to see and it must have taken some time to train him to do that. It's just the simple things like people driving a four wheeler up and down the road, which makes these things awesome it's like living in the back country where you can have fun if you so choose. I got an angel yesterday and took it down to the church little did I know that it matched the one of Jesus in color so I stood it to the right of him, awesome to see how well they looked together, sort of like a match made in heaven. I like to do things out of the ordinary because other don't expect it an even I don't sometimes, it's a thing in the moment and it has brought joy to some I believe. How do people preceive me this is something I my self cant see but also I know it doesn't matter really it's only what God sees that really counts, back in my younger years I couldn't see my self or who I was to become and today I am a person who learned to love God. I also know that who I was isn't the same as who Iam today, we travel many paths.

And on our way we go through many changes, in the mornings I like to watch the Antique Road Show as it comes on at 4:00 in the morning such a delight to see such old things and how the value has increased over the years one chair was estimated at $300.000.000 dollars my land what a great buy for something the man bought in a bundle package. I have always wanted to go and be a picker or bid on storage units where things are sold because people couldn't pay their storage bill, it's like treasure hunting and the finds can be miraculous. When I was a child I found a two dollar bill dated back in the 1800's but instead of holding on to it I sold it for a fifty cent profit the mind of a child looking for that extra change, I don't know what the day holds but I hope it's something good maybe a smile or a hellow from a friend to brighten the day. Randy went to pay for copies of his medical reports from the hospital so now all we have to do is wait for them to send them by Tuesday of next week, then we can get things going with the lawyer. Thursday morning' it gt a little nippy last night but the days have been nice since the storm. Yesterday a guy came by because he needed to get in the church after he fixed the gas meter because someone hit it, so it had to of been done at night I suppose when the young people are out. Just like the time when someone hit a pole a while back at two in the morning, night owl's I guess or someone coming back from a party, this morning starts my work time the gas pereson came and asked if I could let him into the church and I told him I could when he was ready to light the hot water heater.

And other things that ran off of gas someone had to of hit the meter pretty hard because it broke the steel box frame that was built around it, and that was made if two inch pipe. My night was a good one as I slept pretty good with nothing bothering me but Harley this morning my little buddy has to be close for some reason when something bothers him, or he just likes that safe feeling of being next to me. As for the days they still seam to fly by but I have adjusted to them and have learned to just enjoy them as much as possible, we got our food from neighbors yesterday so that lets us stock up once again to help others when they need it. Back in my first couple of years I was too proud to ask for help but that changed when I learned that there is a circle of helping people and if we need food then it's there and if others need it, it's also there for them also. It's a great feeling to give and I have always like to do that. Back in the day I had to always be the reciver but now I am able to give back and help in a small way, yesterday I did some scraping on the trim of the house so I can get the rest of the windows painted. Which makes the house look nicer one day I will get the floors replaced and then I will be happy, the test they did with the fan after the windows were put in revealed that there are some weak spots in the floor so they have to be addressed and taken care of. don't want to fall through them, we also did a little work in the yard to spiff it up a little so it would look better and we got some holes filled. So many plans if everything works out the way it should. I would like to bring this house back to it's original glory when it was first built but with some improvments like another bedroom or maybe even two and a safer bath for Oliver where he can hang onto a bar and not be afraid to fall while taking a shower, I have given my life you might say to taking care of my family and it has it's rewards even if it's just a smile or a laugh for the day, my days are being filled by good feelings and doing little things like cleaning the light's in the living room an dinning room. Thank God that Randy is able to balance him self better then I can, it seams what I lack in ability to do he has it. So we take on many things that I wouldn't be able to do on my own, it's great' and he helps with other things. I would like to doa lot of things but only time will tell when things will come together, we are blessed with good things from God and the ability to help others is a great thing although I can see the face of a child as they recive food I know they are smiling because their bellies; are getting full. For these things I don't need to see because I know the food is getting to them, taking care of our community is a great thing and in time I hope to do more. I really want to build a teen center where kids can go to not be tempted by alcohol and drugs, a christen teen center in the middle of town or off on a lot somewhere close to town. And a place where they can have a bible camp, for the summer months a place where they can go fishing and camping. The counslors would need a cabin and the kids also when time permits it to take place, I can just about see it now as they learn about Jesus and how to live a christen life away from the destruction of alcohol annd drugs. A place where their full potential can come alive an they can be the best they can be.

Right now it's a dream but in time it will be a reality and they will learn the love of God. I wish I could have had such a thing but maybe it's not too late to make others dreams come true, isn't that what life is all about? Us as parents leaving a positive mark on this world for the kids to enjoy and learn what it's like to be close to God the father. Accomplishing this could change things in a big way and I would love to be a part of it, Jesus has a way of reaching everyone especially children. It says come to me as children and I think that's what He meant with the mentality of a child but don't quote me on that it's just my opinion, little brother is like that in some ways but we uunderstand each other so maybe I have it also. I do know that I love God and I have a special place for Him in my life as He walks with me each day that I live, as for the confusion it's gone for now but He can also take that from us when it get too hard to bear. Even the things which bothered me only a few months ago are not there any longer, and it opened a door to except other things and for that I'm grateful. It would be nice to be the first to stop hunger in small town america doing it one small town at a time starting here where my home is, imaging a child never having to worry about getting something to eat at school. Awesome and they would look forward to going and learning each day. Many people would pitch in and make that a thing of the past, for we all have something to give no matter how slight.

Kid's getting up each morning at camp and listening to the birds sing as they have breakfast and then read a small passage from the bible, to start the day. But thank God for the food they recive by prayer, is this something He would let me bring forward only He knows the answer. But it would be a lot of hard work and I think there are plenty of young men to do it, the beginning of something new and helpful for these are things which I would do first off given the chance. Changing lives in a positive way' the giving of something is more powerful when it changes lives for the better, time will reviel it's self to allow good things too happen if you have it set in your mind but the Father has to allow it to happen or take pace. The change from bad situations to good the other side of the coin you might say, when things first started to happen I didn't know how they would turn out but I put my faith in God and He brought it forth. For what was in my mind was brought into reality by the great one the one on high Jehovah our lord and savior. For stories of God have been written in stone in some places hid from the world until they were found, this is something that happened long ago before we were even thought of. Even before our parents were thought of, what made the search start? A thought in someones mind a searcher wanting to find the truth of the past. People traveled the world to search for what they didn't understand so they could try to understand it did they find what they were looking for? Or did they just like the hunt for answers. My dreams are starting to come into the present could this mean that my dream will come to pass for the mind is awesome, if things are brought into reality then it means that my efforts are going to come true. My little buddy is laying on the floor looking up at me and I think he wants to go out, Friday and I started on the mens room yesterdaay to see how that little stripper would work and I have to say that it worked pretty good so far. Very supprised and it only having one wheel to it lets me get close to the walls, but still I cant go whole hog with it just a little at a time but it's getting clean then I will start on the other rooms when I can do it. I just thank God that it will only have to be done once a year, and then it's over. As for the te rest of my job I enjoy it and I think it shows even though sometimes I forget to do something they politely write it on the note pad in the kitchen, through the years since my time here I always wanted to get it better. You know make things nice for my brothers and sisters in christ and they have been patient with me and all I have on my plate, many of them have to wonder how I do it with my loved ones but through faith and undersstanding I seam to make it even though at times I become agitated with things and then have to talk with my father so he can show me the way. I have grown in spirit since I came here and that helps with a lot of things like understanding things which would of drove me nut's before life to me is like taking steps and each one is painful at first but then the longer you walk the less you feel the pain. I can remember walking the rail road tracks in Grand Island it was after I had taught my self to walk the car had broke down and we were going to hitch hike but first we had to make it to the edge of town the calfs on my legs hurt like hell and I was out of breath, but I set it in my mind that I would make it and I did we were picked up by someone who I cant remember and then it was homeward bound and got home in a short time. Needdless to say I didn' leave home for quite some time after that, through time I learned to not travel with others who cant drive very well. For many things are coming in this year and with some hope all will turn out alright my equity in my place should allow for me to fix some things up, so things can get better my time here should prove that things always get better.

When you try your hardest to be a good person this allows you to excell in things you do and bring good things about. Things you never knew could happen in ones life for whats happeneing now wasn't something I saw coming and I don't know what will come next will it be good or will it be bad? I like to think that the goodness will concur and rise above all other things. I would of never guessed that my time would be taking care of other people but that's the way it played out and I am still learning even today, learning the things that I should of learned long ago maybe as a child. With each passing day something new is learned no matter how slight and it will make things easier for later in life, my daughter text me and said she got the pictures I have been asking for and she will send them off today. So I should get them by Monday at the latest, its hard to not have pictures of your grandchildren because you cant see them grow other wise. When miles separate you, I love them very much and sometime I will have to go and see them if they don't come here this summer. They are like a flower which grows taller and taller as time passes but the picture lets you see how far they have come since you seen them last, I like to cover the walls with my family tree you might say, but it makes me sad that my garnd sons wont carry the Mattson name it will be O'Brien but I know they are a part of me and whats in a name they still know grandpa and that he loves them. Even though miles separate us we are together in spirit and that makes all the difference in the world, if they come down I will let them ride on the riding mower so they can have some fun while they are here.

But wether thay will come is another thing I like to think they will, today I will try to finish painting around the windows so they will be protected from the elements, that way the house will withstand the winter. And I will be able to do more next spring. It's like baby steps and each step lets you imporve something, the wonders of this world are ever changing and we change with it to bring good things about not only for our selves but for others also. I like the thought of the smile that reached all around the world in started in a small town but was carried from one place to another, finely ending up in another country where the people were sad by a desaster which had happened. That smile gave them hope that help had gotten there and now everything would be alright, in the village they pulled together with the christen people who came to help and the village was rebuilt as if the disaster never happened. This brought around joy to the people and they celebrated a new beginning one of faith which had eluded some because of what happened, their faith was restored as they saw a bunny hop across the road they had built and went to eat in the clover. Many of the animals returned to their village where they had felt safe before the destruction. Then the christens; went to the next village to bring them joy also as the fire had destroyed many villages, they rebuilt the huts and then planted trees so God could help them to grow once again. And the pastor told them about not lousing faith because God was watching over them and that made them very happy. Tomorrow there is a flea market in Scandia so I'm going to go and have some fun, it's not too far just eight miles and they have a lot of exciting things to look at. Also we have a bake sale at the thrift store here in Courtland so I will go to that also, a lot of things going on this weekend and it gets us out for some fresh air. I like to keep our money here in town or close by to help the community thrive more then it already is,and it helps others which is a good thing I didn't realize how hard some people have it in this day and age but they do and if I can help in anyway then bring it on. People helping people is what it's all about and it's nice when you are allowed to pitch in, I have some gloves that I can ware when I do the floor and that way it wont get on my hands like yesterday as that stuff can make you sticky where it gets on your hands. I feel this is going to be an awesome day and my job should be done by noon or so if I get there early enough, this will leave the rest of the day for getting things done here at home. I can accomplish many things in a twelve hour day and for the most part it's fun especially when I can get help with some of it. Randy helps and he gets excited when he accomplishes; something and that to me is a joy in it's self. It's like he is growing and learning new things but this time learning it the right way not like before when things were hard and when he needs help I gladly give it to him, the bagger compartment came off the lawn mower and I helped him get it back on. When I first had to do it my land' it took me hours but then those hours paid off by being able to do it in ten seconds what a difference in time. It seams I had to learn things the hard way but the good thing is that I learned them and then it became easier to show others how not too have to do it the hard way, and in time my confusion turned out to be a blessing to others not to have to go through it. I could of yelled because it happened but instead I felt like a teacher.

Just like when I do other things new if someone knows a better way of doing it then I welcome it, Saturday and we had some people that looked at the house next door they are a growing family as the couple had three or four kids. Since my arrival here most of the houses are gone sold off a long time ago, I remnember a couple of them being built in the 70's and they went for around thirty thousand which was too high for me not knowing anyone here. But as time went by and you got to know people they allowed me to get this one a starter home if you will to see how you handle things and I do just fine with what I have been blessed with. At first I didn't know how to ask for the loan but then Walt opened that door for me by talking with Mark and it was on like donky kong, I got the house and they backed me for the first year so I could get on my feet then it was up to me, and as of yet I havent missed a payment. On anything it shows you are a stable person when it comes to bills and I get mine out as soon as they come, it's a far cry from where I was all those years ago but I made it by the grace of God. Still even today I give many thanks to my friends because without them I wouldn't of been able to do any of the things that I do today, people helping people is the key to making a community that will thrive in the future what a great thing as we move into the next five years and by then my home will be mine all bought and paid for. But five years is a long time from now, not really to me because the days go so fast but to younger people it would seam like eternity. They say with some their lives flash before them when they are in a dieing situation, but with me it's in the passing of days so fast like time was slowed down compaired to that flash in sixty seconds that some experience.

When I go to bed it's like I cant wait until the next morning so I can arise and start the next day in hope that my wishes will come to pass, I don't ask for much just a longer time of being here in hope that I will learn more and be here to see my grandchildren and children grow. My son is working now at Wal-Mart super center as a machanic and that is something he has always loved, in time he will grow in his job if he stays with it and who knows one day he might run the shop. He is such a great young man and I am proud of him making his way through life and it hasn't been easy for him either my little boy' but not so little anymore being in this late twenties. Like his father did he takes his kids fishing and they do a lot together as a family, and I know his women loves him even though she gets crap from his side of the family that lives there were he does. It's like a play back for his mother because she was the same way as his wife not wanting him to have anything to do with family funny how that worked out as she has to see a little of her self in that aspect of the equation. When your young you cant see a week down the road but when your old it's like you can see years into the future in some things like here you want to be. And there isn't anywhere else I would want to be at this time in my life, this place allows me to become better then I once was not only in writing but in other things as well. It's like my privet class room where I learn things which Stacyded me in my younger years, many go through life not being able to type and it's a hard thing to do but I managed to learn as God guides me in this life. The finger thing is eye and hand coordination wich helps to heal my mind and get everything in sink, through the years it has helped to heal what was once broken as in the beginning my eyes didn't correspond with my brain. What the hell does that mean anyway? My mind says one thing and my eyes say another it must have been one hell of a conflict they were having very strange, maybe that has something to do with my walking not quite sure. Yesterday I got a device to use on the windows at the church so they wont streak this is a great thing because it will stop the confusion in my mind about getting the streks out, nothing worse then smeared windows on Sunday morning when they should be pretty. I find my self wanting to do more and in time I will do it but I need the right equipment and it's hard to get it for some reason. But in time they will see that my idea is the best, and who knows maybe I might have to get it on my own. The price is right and what they have now doesn't quite cut it, the machine is so old that it started to smell like it was going to burn up and you don't mix water with electricity unless you have a death wish. They are having many events today like the bake sale at the thrift store and a flea market in Scandia where you can get a good deal on things, I like to go to them and look around it's quite fun but I haven't yet bought anything when going to them. Who knows maybe this will be the day. It's supposed to be in the 70's today nice but not too warn, as we get ready for the day to see if we can find any treasure in the ruff. Funny really' but it would be nice I would like the hunt to find that something which no one else has like the thing I gave Mark for his birthday. Now that was fun' and I know he will keep it for years too come like me wondering what it is.

I find it strange how we hold onto things and even forget we have them until we dig through things. Sort of like the people at th flea market but it's fun to go to them and see the things, we even went to the thrift store and got some brownies and peanut butter cookies. Sunday morning' and I slept pretty good last night the people had some fun selling at the bake sale and I bet they got some funds for the cause,, all these things I missed as a child but now I am making up for lost time. One day I will do many things which had slipped away so long ago I feel like I have been giving a second chance to experience the things I needed to. In the other world it was a narrow path without communication with others and today it's just the opposite but that path was exciting In your younger years because everyone did it. But then through time that seamed to fade as the people starter to leave, and I'm not talking about moving away either they would die off and then you were left to greave if you did at all and that exciting place became like a a prison until someone else came along to fill that void that had been taken away. Loss is hard even when you can cover it up, my years really don't let me get too close to others because good by' is hard, as for the funerals I don't even want to go to my own. But I know someday it will come about if I could leave any advice for kid's and young adults it would be to never go into that other world where things seam to be easier, because taking back your life isn't an easy thing to do. As with me if it wasn't for God helping me I wouldn't be writing this today, I have had good times and bad but the good things seam to stand out now more then the other.

Time will let you get caught up in that world until your world starts to fall like the deck of cards and then you have to pick your self up and go on with life even if you have to learn how to live in it all over again. Through the sands of time everything has to stay in balance, and if it's not then you have to get it back in balance. One thing that is not allowed and that's to go back in time we can only move forward in hope that things can get better and for the most part the do, with a few bumps and bruises; along the way. Moving to Courtland was the best thing I have ever done and it really changed my life, it put me in a place where I could make a difference and I think I was meant to live in this kind of community. Where in the other I didn't even have a name it was like I was someone who took up space, in many ways I am still that child that didn't get to grow up and it comes out sometimes when I least expect it, so that's something others will have to except because it's a part of me the joking side of me that likes to have some fun. My mom and I used to laugh all the time and maybe that's part of why I liked to be in her world it wasn't complicated like when I would go home and have to listen to all the yelling. I remember many times getting up early in the morning and taking off because I wanted too have a good day' and if I would of stayed home it just wouldn't happen. The negging was something else and it made every day hell, I still don't know why I picked that kind of women but it seamed I always did. In that other world a good looking body seamed to take priority above all else and it usually would end up biting you in the ass, I can remember her getting out of bed and saying God another screwed up day. This in it's self would set the day, and it would go bad so I would leave before she got up because I didn't want to hear it, at moms it was peaceful and hardly anyone argued even friends would come over there to getaway from their own situations. When I moved to Oklahoma she wanted to come and start over mom that is and she came later when I got a house set up, I remember the smoke house in back and we had a pare tree. I used to refinish old rocking chairs for a hobby and that was fun but I really liked to fish when we got the chance, but I didn't like the snakes' water moccasins, and they would eat my catch one second they were there then the next only the heads were there. Still don't know why they didn't catch their own, but it was fun. I spent a few years learning the farming business, and loved chaseing the baggers around the field they would attack the tires and then I would drop the disk on them cutting them in many pieces and then there would be more. They couldn't of been very smart because they couldn't of bit through those tires in a 100 years of trying very bad attitude sort of like my X when she got up in the morning, Yesterday I painted and got the windows done for the most part and boy they look good I love that color of white and it's very bright, before I started it really liked like crap but that changed very fast as I got it on and it took on that new look. It's oil paint so it should last for a few years I'm hoping, and in time I would like to do the rest of the house if my health allows it. It's strange how most people wont change unless self preservation is threatened; life it's self usually has to be at steak before change takes place in us as people.

As with me, it was a do or die situation. And I chose life over the alternative, church went very well today but I missed John and his wife not being there. I sure hope he isn't ill that seams to be about the only time that they miss church, or if they go to see their children. Monday morning' and it's my first time overflowing the coffee pot but at least I got some, the night was chilly so I had to close the window during the night and then turn the heat on low so it would be warm for the boys this morning. Yesterday was pretty cool as I went and did some yard work as for here in the house it was muggy so I think I will get one of those machines which takes out the humity, the lady who runs the Antique place has one and maybe I can get it at a reasonable price I asked about it the other day and the one person said she wanted $80.00 for it but I know there is wiggle room there to barder, Walt had one and it really helped with his breathing as it would us being smokers. It takes the water out of the house and puts it in a bucket which is right in front of it Walt's house was a littlee smaller then this one but I think it would do the trick in the living room and dining room, the day is starting out fine as they are still a sleep and wont be up until later in the morning as I sometimes reflect to life in my younger years what was fun back then isn't so fun today but I know there must have been a reason for things to turn out the way they did, but for the life of me I cant understand why maybe one day it will come to me.

As a child you cant see past the day you are in if even that far but as we grow those times seam to fade and they are forgotten to only come back later in life, they say things happen for a reason and when you can recall them then it's good to write them down to see what kind of life you lead so that's what I am doing here trying to see the picture you might say and see if it was fulfilling to see if your life was full. And mine was very full just with some of the wrong stuff in it, like the curse. As for living here I have many friends and some even come to help when I get ill. Never had anyone do that before and it shows that he cares, being a writer I'm sure that many have read my writings but they don't give feed back and maybe that's because they may have traveled the same path them selves at one point or another. But it seaams we all end up in different places and maybe that's why the stories are intresting to see where a person came from and where they end up, do most find their way to the father or do some end up staying lost? Quite the delima don't you think ? But I do know that most don't talk about it as it becomes a secret in their lives and maybe even forgot as time allows you to do that. And I have a feeling that things are coming to an end for me to write about it the things a young child and needs to get out sometimes. In my younger years I only talked with my mother and dad and they seamed to think that no other was good enough for me, I have found out that when a parent believes that way a child louses in the long run. Because they seam to stay to them selves as I did for so many years, and when I tried to get into a relationship it didn't work out so well' Tuesday morning and it's already the 24th of April. The days still seam to fly by but I now know that it's normal, no wonder older folks say life is too short enjoy it while you can. Although the days seam to go by fast the years seam to stay the same from what I can tell about them. At this stage of life we go from counting days and weeks to countig years and it can be hard to do, as at times three years seam like three months but I can tell the difference when the house is about to get paid off. When things seam to get out of hand I talk with God about the things that bother me the most, and He brings me peace. Are we searching for that enlightenment that I felt so long ago? In a way I think we are. That feeling of no pain or worry just the feeling that we know that it will come one day. Today it's supposed to be hot very hot in the 90's so I will get my work done early and and then come home where the air-conditioning can keep me cool, I thank Him for that gift as it allows us to survive in this day and age. All things are connected to God and His children as we move forwarde in life the believers here out weigh the non believers I think' many can find His word just by picking up the bible but a lot of them might be afraid, of what they will find. I know that praying helps to change somethings in the mind according to science. And it can also bring you peace in hard times when confusion is right out side your door, I find that I listen to people more these days as being a writer seams to do that to you after years. When things seam of intrest to me I find my self using parts of their stories, just a few months ago I was worried about things which were happening but in time it worked it's self out this was something that God helped me with and a beautiful women from my church family which I consider my friend, and I hope I am hers and her husbands also. This next Sunday we are having a fifth week lunch at the church where everyone meets in the eating room for service, we do this sometimes and it's a lot of fun. I believe this brings us closer to each other in many ways shareing a meal does that sometimes and if they need any help I will be glad to do it.

Us being the church is brought together so we can talk and get to know each other a little better and it's fun, the one women hasn't been at the church lately but I guess each person has many things to deal with in their own lives. I will try to get the floor cleaned a little more this week for the celebration it will be fun, in the younger years my parents always had a car and a station wagon but the station wagon was used for camping and it was used for us kids to sleep in when we had other friends come with us on our ventures. Then one time it broke down, and they had taken it away when the accident happened with the boys. Dad always liked station wagons for some reason and maybe it was because you could sleep in them, you know being one with nature and yet still having a mattress for the comforts of home. I remember shakeing it when I would get up for the day and the other kids would get mad because I wwoke them up so funny back when you're a child, mom would get up each morning and make breakfast and boy she had to cook for a lot of us, just the smell of bacon would get you out of bed and start a great day. As we would go fishing early in the morning when th fog was just lifting off the water, here in Kansas we could do the same thing but we would have to get a cabin on the lake. It's something that has come to mind since Randy came to live with us, as children it was fun and I believe it would be fun today sitting out in front of the cabin having a cup of coffee, with a fishing pole resting in the water waiting for that big one to hit you're pole. It's only 10 miles by the short cut but about 30 or so by the ash fault road.

It's something we will have to try and do maybe this year if we get the chance, I know pop's would like it as long as we have plenty of food for the weekend. He has been doing better and eating like a horse which is a good thing he really likes cinnamon rolls which they make in Scandia at the store and I guess it reminds him of when mom made them so many years ago, she would be supprised to see that they became so popular after her death. The other day I heard a song about the devil still being a challenge to someone but he knows he is getting better, and it reminded me of how we all fight him some times but with the strength that God gives us we seam to get better, it's takeing me many years but still there are some things that will change in time but the more you get away from those thigs the stronger you get and He never leaves you no matter what because He knows out struggles and our limitations. It's Wednesday morning' and I mowed again last night it was dreadful hot but I did it anyway, and then had to wash my hair because of the things flying around out side. I find that it's better to do it in the morning while the grass is still a little damp that way you avoid the heat which can make some of us sick, it was kept cool inside by the air and it's one of the greatest investments I have made to this day. Also we had a barbecue and made hamburgers which I lost one while cooking them clumsy me, but boy were they good. Even Harley liked them, it seams we are doing many things I never thought we would do but it goes to show that change is possible even when you don't think about it. They are calling for another hot day in the 90's again so working in the yard is out of the question but we are supposed to get a repreave sometime in the week with temp's in the 70's. I have noticed something different this year butterflies…. Are coming out all over the place and some are really beautiful especially the big ones which are black and yellow, I have never seen so many of them. But I think their coming has something to do with the crops but I'm not sure' this is going to be a good year as we move forward into it and I pray that things keep going well. This morning I can feel the temp going up as it's going to get muggy but at least the mornings are somewhat cool, I find my self at a loss for words sometimes so that shows me that there is a break in my future. A break from searching my mind to do other things which is always a good things, while at the Bank yesterday they gave me a pamplet on identity theft and I was amazed at how they can steel your money. What a bunch of pigs when they can steel from others and I didn't realize how easy it can be for them to do it, protection is the key to this not happening. They can even steel you credit card number without it being taken out of your wallet, good thing I am cautious about such things. They even call you on the phone and try to deceive you into different things as for me when they do that I hang up to never talk with them. One time' I got a call annd there was a pause so I hung up on them, this shows that they are calling thousands of people at a time and trying to rip them off, old people fall for such things more then young people but the threat is still there for us all as we also move into our later years my self I only trust the Bank.

Maybe because I know each one that works there and I'm sure they look out after my intrest to protect me from such scum. The morning is about to start as the boys are sturing in the other rooms so later' got to go and get things ready for the day later in the day I got the pitchures from my daughter and thanked her. The kids have grown so much in the last year that I didn't reconise them, my land the one is 12 already and the other is 9 being the oldest one is Jaden then Jacy. Eric is 8 and he is growing up to be a big boy when we got the pictures pop's thought he was Shannons old man in one picture but then his eye sight isn't as good as it used to be, also I got the lawn mowed again the dandy lions are getting bigger each day and they give off a seed which makes more of them so I do it when the wind isn't blowing because it get's in your hair and makes you have to get it out, I seam to find peace when I mow the lawn as it's like I go into a trance where I can talk and sing in another place which isn't here. It's very fun to do but I can only go there when I'm on the mower, strange how that comes about. It's now Thursday morning' and I slept pretty good last night when I got up I got the coffee going and that always helps to make my day then Harley wanted to go out so that I had to do and now he is sleeping once again. The little guy seams to know when I wake up and he wines at my door until I let him out, for the years he has been with me has been good ones and I don't know what I would of done with out him to talk with. He seams to understand me more then people if that's possible and I think it is, my little buddy' my friend.

I had a dog once before but for the life of me I cant remember what happened to him his name was reefer and it was fitting at the time because I was 17 years old and smoked pot, when we first met he bit me and went under the table so I reached for him and then the friendship was on. No one could come in my room if I was a sleep because he laid on my bed at the foot of it and would bite anyone that bothered me even the girls, it was at a time in my life when I thought I could handle two girlfriends. But that didn't last very long, as they ran into each other in my yard.and then I had to make a choice which ended up being the worng one, the company I worked for would fly us to other states to erect steel buildings and grain bin's and I was gone a week at a time. Very good money but it never did last long being young it left your pocket as fast as it went into it, still cant recall some things from that time period but I was a reserved person and quite baskfull with he girls until I got a few drinks under my belt then it went away, and I guess I never got to grow out of that because I'm still the same way except now it's women and not girls. It's very early but I'm up at this time most mornings less confusion you could say as I don't have to listen to the guys and how they raddle on about things, I call it my time with God as each morning I pray for others in hope that they have a good day also I listen to the weather each day so I can see how the day is going to be but it's usually a good day when the temp's not in the 90's but we have to take the good with the bad no matter what. A person reflecting on their lives can bring back many things which they thought was gone or didn't have any importance but those little things make up the persons character, and can trigger other things which occurred in their lives which was thought to be gone. In my search for things which happened back then I found many things which was shut out of my mind, long forgotten because of what I'm not sure. Do we open a door by remembering things which we thought we forgot or is it just that a glimps into the past that will go away again in time? When things come back sometimes I don't want to remember so I put them off until they can be excepted, by the age of 17 years I was content in my life thinking it was a normal life but it was far from it, I had achieved my importance at that stage in life and others wanted to be around me. But it wasn't because of me as a person it was because of the alcohol and drugs we did together a whole different thing from today, those people didn't make it into my future and there was a reason for that change was coming and they didn't belong where I was going. At each stage of life people are brought into our lives, some for just a short time and then others who will spend years being close to you. What is this connection? For surely if He didn't want them there they would be gone, like they others that wouldn't go away so many years earlier and He made them be gone, many things have been taken away from people to thought and memories. But I believe He had a reason for this, it's like when you give something of your self if it isn't good then no one wants it so if they are not good then He takes it away. For your own good, so you can go on with life many changes will come in ones life time and many will be from bad to good and also it can be just the opiset in some cases but I like to think in the end all things are balanced out.

So we can move on to better things which will happen sometime in life out triles are what makes us as people the good times and the bad shape us for things to come. Get's us ready for what we cant see at that time and place, I don't know if I would like to see the future because nothing would be fantastic when it arrived it would just be another thing you saw. Will I be here in ten years? If I am many things will have changed by then, the day went very well and the temp was nice not exceeding in the 70's. before I turned in for the night the rain started to fall but that's also a good thing as they are planting at this time, we made two trips to town and got a few things so we can barbecue tomorrow. It seams we are getting into that kind of cooking during these warm days. During the summer before I never really wanted to go out but something has changed this year and it might just be Randy coming here. When he arrived I didn't eat much but since then my appitite has returned and it could be because I was so lonely I don't think anyone should be alone when you can bring family closer to you. It's been a win situation for both of us even with the triles we went through, adjusting is hard but it can be done our miss understandings in the beginning were just that and it gave us something to work on. As with most things many times I wanted to throw in the towel but I stuck it out and here it is a year later, and we still make too many trips to town. When I thought I was going to louse him my heart broke. And for the life of me I couldn't understand how such a thing could happen and why it would happen, here this big man looked so helpless and could have been taken but He told me that things would be alright.

It was like I went into a trance and felt the goodness of His love, and I'm sure pastor Kathy saw what was happening as for me I love with all my heart and I believe the lord knows this as He has to feel the love I have for His. By sight no one would guess that he is my little brother him being much bigger then I but that doesn't change the fact that he is, I have a connection with him that I don't feel with other family members and that makes things special between us. I can feel when he is sad and I can feel when he is happy or confused and if you pile that on top of my own feelings then at times it can be a mess, I also feel this connection between me and Oliver so I'm dealing with the feeling of three people and it can be hard to please them all at the same time. But I do my best, just the other day we went into the bank and someone said here comes the Mattson brothers in a joking way but it felt kind of neat in a way. I can talk for Randy but I will live out my life right here in Courtland where my friends are, I had an Idea about getting a tractor and hireing on to do some fields around here which would bring in some money.... This would allow retired farmers to relax and enjoy their golden years, plus it's something I like to do as long as it has air-conditioning because without that I couldn't do the job. It seams what I was taught by Jack has stayed with me even after all these years sot of like riding a bike you never forget, the rain which started last night has gone for the time being but I know it will be back to bring more moisture to this part of the country. Looking at the wheat it's nice and green and about a foot tall and I'm hoping the good lord will bless this harvest with an abundance. last year was fairly good as our worst was better them most peoples best in other parts of the country. Friday morning and it's a warm breezy day, kind of muggy out because of the little rain we got last night but still it should be a nice day, I have some work to do at the church but that shouldn't take very long. I'm becoming a pro at this kind of thing and I enjoy my time there in God's house where I can be alone with Him and talk about my day sometimes, the enlightment is very real there and I take it all in with enjoyment and even sing from time to time when my spirit feels up to it. Now that tractor will be on my mind for quite some time but I will try to put it in the back of it for now. Could someone make a living hireing out to other farmers? I believe so but it would take some doing on the part of a few people not just one person as for the operator I have done it with the best of them and was pretty good too. My home will stand the test of time as it is blessed by the lord, my feelings are very real for my brother and even though I tried to ignore them at first it wasn't meant to be that way and I'm glad that he is here with us today. When he first got here I could see the brokeness inside of him as being locked up wasn't a good thing for him and being unable to get the help he needed only left more work for me but that's ok he is the blood of my blood. We do most things together and everyone that knows us knows that if one of us is there the other isn't far off. We have created a bond that was once lost by miles and time but even that couldn't keep us apart, God talks a lot about brothers in the bible and how if you cant forgive your brother then you wont be forgiven and that's just the way it is. For all the things they have done to me I have forgiven them and hold no anger and I feel the love which is there between me and little brother, as time moves forward so will we and who knows we might still be together in the future.

For the things which brought us together was love for family, would I have done this for others who would of wanted to come here No' because if everyone is treated the same then no one is special. Even to bring him here it took a lot of soul searching and then I even had my doubts that it would work, but God played a big part in my decision as I asked Him what I should do. I knew I wouldn't of been much of a person to let him die in that place so I brought him home, in the beginning he had night mares but they have seamed to fade as he adjusted to his new surroundings. I heard some of his night mares and they must have been brought on by pressure negative pressure from bad people who don't care about anyone, and it had to be bad to reach that far into hiis mind but through the help of God today they are not so bad. At times it's just like he sleeps like a normal person who snores' they cant damage him any more so now he will be healed with the help of God the father. When we walk together it's like mutt and Gorge one skinny and one large and it shows how life can change a person in different surroundings. As we went for a ride yesterday the wind was blowing in my hair or what I have of it, and it felt good not having the temps in the 90's just a cool breeze blowing through the car as we went down the road. I thought he would fall a sleep because he took his night med's before we went but he didn't and we had fun, it's these little things which we will remember later down the road when we are old and gray and we will laugh about it.

During this year we will make many plans to do things and what will come of it only time will tell but still the making of them will be fun, the other day he asked if I wanted to go to the lake but I didn't really want to. So we have put it off for a while, the wind is getting strong outside blowing in a storm from what I saw on television last night and the weather could get bad. But we hope for the best in all situations and leave it in mother natures hands as she has the final say on things of that sort, in some states they are seeing temp's in the below 0 mark wouldn't want to be there right now. We take each day as it comes and pray for the best and I believe it helps when you talk to God about your problems. He seams to put most things into prospective so in some way we can understand them and why they happen, the storm passed but we got plenty of rain as the road ditches were full of water. And running down the road, they don't stay full too long just for a few hours but yesterdays rains should of dampened the ground plenty so the corn could take hold. Farmers have been out in the fields for days planting corn which is stored not too far from here like Jack did, they stroe it for the following year to replant so they can have another great crop and if all goes well they will have a good crop this year. The crops are moved to many different locations once they have matured and been harvested and the cycle continues as that's God's plan and man's to keep us fed, Courtland is a great part of the cycle to help people not starve to death but it's the government that distributes it. And we all know what a cracked up job they do to feed the homeless and starving, many of my neighbors are farmers and boy they work hard to get everything in the ground on time, after a while it becomes like a cycle and they know just when to get everything started so God can bring plenty. In a good year they can see their crops multiply by 100 fold but it can also be by 60 fold sometimes,, it's Saturday morning and the drains have receded from the ditches. The ground here is like concrete when it's dry but give it a lot of water and it becomes soft so the seeds can be planted to grow into something to help man kind, how there can be a shortage of food is beyound me but they say there is. They have a plant which processes the seed and put's chimicals on it to keep the bugs from eating it the process is down to a science with corn but it has yet to be done with wheat, which I'm sure they will do it to that also in time just plant and water it and not have to worry about it being destroyed by other little buggers. I have seen a lot of butterflys this year more then in other years and some are beautiful but others not so much, maybe it's the way things are kept in balance who knows. As for my lake and river they still show up when the rains come in but they go away just as fast it gives me a glimps of my dream to let me know it's still possible for them to come true. It's a calm morning and most of the water has gone into the earth to be sucked up so things can grow, what beauty it is to see things as they pop up through the ground and sprout like the arms of a child reaching for it's mother I like to write about many things in my life even the seasons which seam too change every few months the growing of thing which I see all the time here. My writings are not only about fighting addiction it's about life in general, things some take for granted like the birds and other animals just the way they were created is a wonder for each have something special about them.

My way of thinking may be different but in many ways it's the same as your's you just don't see the things that I do. My little town' is a place where people pull together sort of like Dodge city when it was started many years ago and it grew into a great place which is now one of the most talked about placed around, it started with just a few people that had a dream and they made that dream come ture over time. Sure it was hard but they did it, many places like Courtland were almost instinct but with a good writer and the words they can help in some way. Who knows maybe somewhere in time my writing of things will bare fuit, just the other day I saw a editorial I had written in 2011 which I never thought got published in the Salina Journal it seams some wait for the right moment to publish some things when they fit the situation and that gives them leaverage in some things, my neighbors seam to like what I write and that is a good thing when you live among them. I havent met anyone who I haven't liked and that is rare in this world today, a kind word or a wave from a friend you haven't met yet can make my day. It's like someone is being brought into your life for the first time and in many ways your not sure how to act but in time it becomes clear, just be you're self. For so long the emotions had taken over and I didn't know who I was but when the smoke cleared I found this kind and careing person except this time the addiction wasn't there, growing up that person existed but that addiction had blocked a lot of the kindness from showing it's self and you don't want that to happen in your life.

Going on three years now I have been excepted and people have learned that I'm as honest as the day is long this in it's self is a quality which many lack for different reasons but it's a good thing to have in this life. My journey continues and change is inevitable, it will be coming even when we are gone from this world so we have to change with it or parish in not doing so. At the end of the mile which leads to highway 36 it says (Welcome to Courtland) and on that sign many frogs have made it there home, after a good rain you can hear them as they say ribit' they must be little green frogs, as they don't sound like a bull frog. I like hearing them when I drive by the sign because it lets me know that home isn't far away. It's the only place where you will hear them as they have made that certain place their home also like I have made Courtland mine, it's funny how we pick our own place to call home but once we do it seams to become a place where we will live out our lives. Will they change that place? I don't think so, your home becomes a part of you the person or frog seams to put down roots so they wont have to travel any longer. And although most of them are born there it's called home for them from birth, it's strange how many seam to return to where they are born even the children that are now grown have come back to Courtland where their lives began to maybe take over the farm or they just didn't like the out side world. That is full of destruction, here in Courtland it's the simple life where you can wave to your neighbor and get a wave back in kindness, and you don't have to worry about getting robbed when you leave your door unlocked because your neighbors know who belongs there and who doesn't. people looking out for each other so they can live without the stress of worry, there are many things offered here like a park and swimming pool that the children can walk to without worry of them being abducted it is a cold morning and I even had to turn on the heat to take the chill off the rain brought with is a cold snap which brought the temp's down, but it will get warmer as the day moves on. I'm just glad that we didn't get that really cold weather that hit up by Canada they can have it. The weekend came mighty fast as the day's flew by and next week will be the same, it's like time is moving in fast forward and I don't know why but it's doing it just the same. Although the days and week's are doing this, the year seams to be normal or I just cant grasp that far into time, at this time. I would do almost anything to have the days like they were when I was a kid, for the mind couldn't focus past a moment at that time and our parents didn't let in the outside world which could corrupt the mind. Tomorrow will be a good day as we the church have a gathering for the fifth weekend where we have brunch in the morning, not sure what they will have but I will stay for coffee anyway and maybe a little longer if I have a mind to. Many or should I say one person hasn't came to church in quite some time and I miss her smile, things are set for morning and I had fun. When I got home we had a barbecue and I mowed the lawn such great fun with the three of us sitting on the back porch and laughing it had been only the third time we have cooked out side in three years, but there was only me and Oliver before. My little brother is such a delight sometimes and our connection runs deep it's like I can tell how he is feeling without him saying anything and when he gets up set because of something I can feel that also, it's like the connection I had with mom all those years ago before her passing. This connection is hard to explain but when he got some bad news on Saturday, I told him not to worry because it's something I can take care of.

He is a loving soul and though still confused about how things work on the out side world many things I can help him through. Yesterday we were talking about having a tree removed because it's dead and he suggested that we leave the trunk of the tree about three feet high so we could build a table on top of it. good thought and we might do it, by getting one of those spools that they roll wire on and cutting off the top and varnishing it so the weather wont destroy the wood. Harley met me at my door this morning to take him out but as I did he must of smelled danger because he wouldn't leave the porch so I had to bring him back in there has been lion's reported somewhere in the country and even one guy had a picture of one last year taken by a night camera which goes off by movement. No reports of any being around town though but you never know something frightened him but then it could have been something small like a skunk or another cridder running around, I was talking with Walt when he was here and he told me a story about how Gismo got into a fight with something when he let him out and for months Gismo wouldn't go out side because it tore him up a bit. The mowing was fun, because th rain had dampened the ground and the crap wasn't flowing through the air just a nice breeze to keep me cool. In the beginning many things had to be worked out with little brother coming and I asked God for his assistence in making the transition because I didn't know if I could do it but then one night he answered me and said it would be alright. For the things I went through to adjust he had to do also and with me already being through them it was just a matter of helping him, like a teacher teaching their students as they learned to teach a certain subject that will help the kids to learn and grow.

When things get confusing Randy has a hard time with dealing with it and this I can understand because it through me for a loupe when it happened to me. All the confusion seams to hit all at once and at least my mind couldn't deal with it, so I reached out to others in hope that they can help in some way being they went to school maybe they have something I lack. It's Sunday morning' and all is set for church now I just have to open the doors this morning I seam to get everything ready during the week and that leaves little to do on the actual day it's just now 4:00 in the morning and the others are still a sleep, if either of them get up too early then they sleep a lot during the day especially Randy and his snoring is too much for me and at times put's me in a bad mood. Lately he is trying to find things to do so he doesn't sleep and that is a good thing, my day starts at 3:00 in the morning and ends at five in the afternoon which by that time I am tired, yesterday we had barbecue pork steaks and brocks which were really great. We tried some potato salid that they make at the store and it tasted like crap same with the macaroni salis so no side dish but it's good to know not to buy that crap next time we get chicken. Yes chicken they have the best fried chichen I have tasted in a long time and we get it from time to time, it's a lot easier then cooking it my self. But one day when the price of chicken goes down I will stock up so we can barbecue some of it and I make that great' so many things we used to not do. We do today, and it's because Randy has come to live with us, life was getting boreing before I picked him up and I think God could see this and didn't want it too happen so he put little brother in my heart. I think they knew he was giving up after being away for so long and he needed the love of a brother to bring him back I could see the distence in his eyes when I first got him out it was like he was far away in a distant land that wasn't here and he couldn't believe I had come to get him. The years had been hard on him and I knew I had to bring him back to that place where he would feel safe and loved. These feelings I don't have with my other brothers just Randy, could it be because we are just 18 months apart? Or is there something more to it a deeper connection that binds us together. My experiences with the church and God seams to influence him but still he knows by rights I could of left this world a long time ago, could this be one of the reasons why the good Lord kept me here or sent me back? I guess only Jesus knows the answer to that question. I still see the old man from time to time who read my name on my belt buckel and we talk as he ask's if I'm staying out of trouble, he reminds me of dad by the way he shakes but the shakeing doesn't seam to bother this man like it did dad. If things would have been different dad could of still been here, his memory doesn't visit me that oftend but when it does they are good memorys a kind and quiet man with a lot of love. I hope to see the old gentleman again when I go to Belleville he is such a delight, there is something about him but I don't quite know what it is yet next time I will ask his name.

Many things have changed during my time here and I am sure I will see many more changes before my time is up to be with the Lord' for each day is a gift brought on by change and we as people have to change with it not very complicated if you just go with the flow, and except the change that will come. If you couldn't do this then God wouldn't of put it in front of you so you have it inside of you to bring this about, when they messed up my check I was beside my self because I had not a clue of what too do but He told me to go to the church and low and behold a church member was there, my friend in christ explained what it said and it calmed my spirit so I could take action on my own behalf. Confusion isn't your friend it's a way to try and mess things up and the devil has a hand in that, for he doesn't want you to get a head unless you sure come to his ways and that will never take place. My love for God cant be measured, not by human standards. For no one can feel what's inside of me a bond that He is my father period, He stood by me when I didn't have anyone else not that I would of wanted a human to stand beside me because with humans there is usually confusion and that would of just added to the problems I already had. His ways are different and He is patient with us His children. He allows our minds to try and figure out things and if we need help then He will help if so asked, no interference when you try to get it. And if you get it wrong then he will set you straight in His own way which is different from ours, the supernatural what is it? A distant plain between two places where things happen which cant be explained in the terms of this world that we live in today.

The place where the impossible becomes possible only by the will of God' His world different from ours and we couldn't exist in it, but things that happen there can be brought here but only through thought and prayer. What really happened to those people who disappeared? When they wouldn't leave me alone. Did the supernatural remove them and take them to another place where they couldn't hurt anyone else? Only He knows the answer to that one for the love of God is with me even after I started to find my way still lost He guided me to a better place where I was removed from their destruction. At times I visit other places which isn't of this world but at times it frightens me and I find my self pulling away from it, what would happen if I just let my self be pulled into it? Would I have a better understannding of what He is trying to do for me or would it drive me further away from the fear that lies inside of me as a human. Quite a delima don't you think? It says he will not take you to where God's grace wont protect you could this be true? It has to be, for all things in the bible tell of the truth. Church was fun today as we sang songs and had brunch the closeness I feel when we are close makes it feel more like a family surroundings it was just good ole fun and we got some new members, they are children and I hope they will be with us for a long time to come. Monday morning' and I'm looking forward to the day, good news it didn't rain last night but it did off and on during the day yesterday. my mind is a little slow during the wake up process but in a bit it will be going once I get my coffee. Harley was wineing so I had to take him out to do his business the morning is calm with no wind so we shouldn't have any storms coming, I started to put some of our activitys on face book so my friends can know what's going on instead of them worring about things with us, this gives me more of a fan base for when my book will come out. Writing after a while becomes your life except for the things you have to do to keep going like work and other things, my life is good right now but I know with my family things will and can change. The things which drew me here is still here, and I love the peace of mind that I find in this place one women sa next to me yesterday as I sang and I believe she liked what she heard. The songs I had never heard before but I cought on mighty fast, ass my eye and mouth cordnation were in sink but sometimes they are not. That's from the damage which occurred from the addiction so long ago God seams to be healing that part of me, my songs are written by my ability to understand the meaning of the song which tells a story. When I wrote (the Cross) it was played millions of times in my mind to make it just right so I and others would be touched by the little story that unfolds, my gift to the Lord for things He has done in my life they say He knew I would be writing before I was born into this world. Just as He knew Jesus would die before He came to live upon us as people, such a wide range of knowledge. Knowing things way before they happen I wish He could give me some of that insight about what's going to happen with me but He must know that I will find out later when the time is right. That was the first time I put anything like that on face book but it will peek peoples interest to read about what happened in my life, and maybe in a way when they read it they too can be helped . As time allows it my writings are getting read all over the world by people who need help and that to me is a great thing, but will they grasp the whole thing or just parts that fit their situation.

When I moved here I was broken in more ways then one physicaly and mentaly but through time that has been healed by the one I love so dear. For God has healed so much I didn't think I would ever sing but through my family in christ and God He made it possible, it really moved me when some say tears about came to their eyes and that's what a song is supposed to do. Open that door which is usually shut into the emotions of those who might have been hardened through hard times in life, but are now softened by those words many times people can be healed by just a few words said at the right time and only the father knows when that time is in someone's life as for me I go by the feel of things and usually things fall into place even when I take that chance it brings hope to those that might also be bashful to sing or talk in public. One guy told me long ago that he couldn't do that in 100 yeard but what he doesn't realise is that it's just fear which stop's him and that is something which can be over come. When you have support from people that love you, if I was back in Nebraska this step might have never took place and I think God saw this and that's part of why I am here in Courtland, so I canm find my self and be the best Ican be. . . . I was equipped with many talents as this was something God put in me many years ago before my birth, He knew what I would be doing on this day before I came to be and He must have a lot of patients to have stood by me all these years I look at it like this I am a work in progress and as many works in progress time plays a big part in it. And I have been given time to make better what was once almost destroyed, second chances do they really exist yes' by all means they do, and I am living proof that this can become a new start for those who have fallen from grace.

I can't tell what the future will hold but I have to believe God has good things instore for me, when I fall I pick my self up and go on. Like Joel O'Steen said we all have to go through disappointments of people saying no but there is a yes out there and my yes came when I bought my home, it was a yes and even when I needed central air that was another yes. For He has found favor in me and it has to be because of all the No's I went through before I got here, in my life there has only been one yes before by a bank and that was paid off. Who knows my life might be full of yes but you can never tell until you ask, take that leap of faith which will lead you to where you want to be. As some put it do your best and everything else will follow, have faith that God will take care of you in your time of need. And love Him with all your heart, I put that in there my saying. As I prayed a while ago I know it's going to be a fine day because the Lord is with me He resides inside of me and we share some of the same space which is within, my thoughts are of Him for the most part and I like the feeling He gives me when He cheers me up from a down day. We are like the children that come to church we learn new things all the time, but in a different way then they do as our minds have stopped growing not that they cant learn because they can ours is just a little corrupted by the crap we listen to that goes on in the world. When fear is allowed to enter our lives it can do one of two things it can make you grow past it or it can control you and you wont grow past that stage of life fear is a good thing as everyone has felt it. It ignites something inside but it isn't meant to be a constent feeling just something that visits for a short time to leave once it's done, many like scary movies because the fear gives you a rush. And some become addicted to that feeling and will watch movies over and over again until that excitement goes away. This is a new beginning of another week and I look forward to seeing what will unfold, many things will happpen and they will all be a supprise because they will be unexpected but in the tangled web we might see some gifts from the Father and who knows what supprise He might have instore for us it could be a visit or a stranger that comes by the church to recive some help in some way, I still think of the Indian which visited last year and wonder how him and his daughter is doing. I hope for the best within his family and pray that his little girl will get the help she needs along her journey, life is a journey and we never know how it will turn out but having faith and love for God seams to help us along the way. The knowing that He is there when we stumble or fall to pick us back up and continue on that path He chose for us. Even when we cant see He is our eyes and when we cant walk He is our feet as that's His promise to never forsake us when we need him to help in this life, He is our creator' the one that made us who we are and our past lives shape us as we venture down that path of life so we can reach the place where we will reside for eternity. As I see it, our bodies are just a vessel that can survive on this planet so we can get ready for the bigger picture the one where there will be no worry, war, or suffering, not even the pain we feel now will be there.

For this is His promise to us His children, a life free of the things which inslave us we will have no need for worldly things there as all things will be provided even land will be given to us so we can grow what we need to live that life promised. I couldn't imagine doing nothing in that life as it would get boring or maybe that concept doesn't exist there who knows, it would be a great place where all our brothers and sisters are friends like a big family that loves each other. Each day we are greeted; by our neighbors and go on our mary way to do what ever we will do here. Tuesday morning' we are headed to Grand Island this morning around 7:00 this will be Randy's first trip back to that state since he bgot out we will only be there for the day because Oliver has to see his doctor, his original doctor retired so he has to see a different one who we havent met yet. The trip usually takes a couple of hours one way but we get to see the wild life off in the fields of Nebraska, it will be a nice drive and we stop along the way to get something to drink and eat last night I thought we might get some rain but it must have missed us so we have that to be thankful for. It's early so the guys are still a sleep and I wont wake them until about 5:00 we still have to take out the trash so it get's picked up and then we will be set, everything has been checked on the car and it's good to go this will probably be the last trip we make this year to that part of the country so I will be glad when we get back home.

Funny how home is such a delight when you go on a trip at least for me when I get close to being back I feel an excitement and it's a good feeling because it's your's, the home that is' all my other friends can only dream to have what I have as most of them live in poverty also. But here in Courtlnd you can have something to build on and that is out of their reach back where I used to live, the slum lords take their money and it's never seen again but here you are allowed to have something to invest in like your home and property and community we are a small one but we are mighty in our numbers most christens who love the lord, for this is going to be a great day. Strange how you can remember some things from the past but when it comes to yesterday many things we forget, maybe it's because it's making room for things that are important. It's the 1st of May and usually I pay the bills on this day but they will have to wait until tomorrow only one day off in sending them but they will get there on time as I checkd when they are due and I still have a grace period I'm starting to wake up now that I have had some coffee and that is a good thing, for the day will be full of excitement in travel Randy will get to see some new things and meet some new people. Like I was he is shy in many ways but he has something I didn't have and that's the willingness to reach out and say hi to people he doesn't know, this would do him good when and if he attends church but these things cant be rushed like Jesus He has a lot of patients with us. God seams to let us figure it out as he waits for us to come to him and I believe that is a great quality of His, this year I will have to get new wipers on the car as I have to do each year I thought they should last longer but I guess not because the ones I bought at the parts store didn't last but a year. Matinence on a car is costly but we have to have them for things like these trips as we have to keep everyone is good health, and I do a good job with Oliver and little brother. Our friendship is growing stronger as the months pass between me and my little brother as there are many things he doesn't understand but then I fix them for him and we go on. Still today I am learning new things, how to care and take care of the one I almost lost it frightened me when I had to take him to the hospital and it made me realise how fast life could be taken away, but through faith in God he pulled through so we can live out our lives and be happy. If that never happens again I will be happy, the balance between life and death is very close but our love is stronger and I hope to look back one day and say hey! Do you remember that day when I had to take you to the hospital? By then it should only be a memory. The last time we went it was so hot that you could fry an egg on the concrete but I thank God that we had the air-conditioning, that in it's self let us stay cool until we got home and then I was a happy camper to be able to pull to the front of our home and then run into the house where we also had air-conditioning. Mark the banker knew that we would need central air so he let us put it in what a life saver he was on that day when I cought him at the gas station, the kindness that is shown here has never been something I have seen before and they joke and laugh with you not at you like the unkindly people did when I was recovering if that never happens again it will be too soon. My little buddy is laying on my bed and I hope he knows that he has to get off of it in just a little while, I think it's my smell that draws him to where I have been and he sleeps knowing he is protected.

I don't know what I would do without him as he is there when I need someone to talk to and he doesn't talk back like some people do. Our time is getting closer and I have some work to do before we leave. Wednesday morning' on Tuesday we left home around 6:30 in the morning and it was a lovely ride except for the fog we ran into in some spots but other then that it was an awesome trip. Oliver couldn't eat before hand so we took him out to the golden arches for some breakfast and then lunch before we left, the doctors said he was doing fine for a man of his age and I think he over stuffed him self on lunch because he felt sick on the way home. And I think it was the big malt that he had, but when I stopped for gas I had him get in the back seat and lay down for a while and then he felt better. The doctors said he was lucky that he had a family that loves him as we do and that mademe feel good, the nurce asked questions about if he is happy where he was living and he replied yes. They also asked him some more questions but they were personal, I believe they ask these questions because many old people are taken advantage of and that's not the case especially when he is loved. On the way home we stoped to see if he wanted something to eat again and he said no. it was a hot trip until I turned on the air and he rested most of the way home, the trips take a lot out of him and I so when we got here we rested for a while and then it was off to bed. When I first turned on the air it took a while to cool the inside of the car but once it started to cool off it got pretty cool a lot cooler then it was when I had the windows down.

Pop's cant take the heat like he used to and it takes a couple of days before things get back to normal what causes these things to take place? Even with me it takes a couple of days to get back in sink but of course I drive and that takes a lot out of me. On the way back the wind was blowing really hard so the car was being held back by it and it took more gas, yesterday was May day the first of the month and I didn't make it to the bank because we didn't get in until late. So this morning I will go and pay bills. It's the fun part of the month for me and I see my friends there, we laugh and make jokes and just shoot the shit for a little while then it's off to get things done. This morning I have to mow the lawn sometime, and I like to do it when it's cool out other wise I don't like doing it, spoiled I guess. When I got home I expected to have to get the trash can back in the church but a nice person did it for me and I didn't have to do it great to have people who will lend a hand sometimes, after a short rest from the day I was up and down most of the night but I was glad when it was time to get up, wakeing up at three thirty a little extra sleep there by half an hour. Some people how could they not want to help their elderly family members? But then some say they don't have the time and they are put into long turm care facilitys, my self I have seen them and I guess for some there is no alternative. But with Oliver it's a whole different story, my land' he never had any of his own children but he ended up with two that love him very much. A blessing from God to him and to me in many ways because I can talk to him about my problems sometimes, a childless man that ends up with children, is a real blessing and I really love him my pop's. he has been around almost since the beginning and the love has grown over the years this man took care of mom and us kids and it's just right that I do the same for him who knows he might live another ten years. Many things cant be explained but all that matters is that he is loved and he is safe here with me, as for the years I have done this I have lost count although it really doesn't matter the time that is. My travels have been many and I have taken him with me everywhere he loves to see the changes in the world meaning the seasons for with each change he sees something different, a car that was once buried; by the brush and equipment that was revealed once the cow's ate down the brush so many things to see, horray' it's been a awesome day as I got most of the bill's paid. To some of you that might not be anything to have joy about, but to me it secures that my foundation is solid to me anyway. The simple things to others hasn't always been that way for me over coming the things I have had to, when the mind is destroyed it takes time for it to heal and with me it took many years. Just the simplest of things were like pulling teeth when the mind cant focus and correct mistakes made while that time of your life was present, now today things are in forward and with each passing day things come together as a whole. Being hump day half week is gone but we look forward to the rest of it, and who knows we might have a barbecue tomorrow. Chicken sounds nice but if we have that I will have to cook because the others wouldn't O well I think it would be fun, today I also mowed the lawn and I have to say it looks great. I do these things in the morning when the coolness is upon the earth that way I don't get over heated and the day is real enjoyable. On this day of May 2nd the heat is muggy and I don't stay out in it long, as I don't like that sticky feeling on my body and 'no' I don't need a bath. Jokes such great things to make you feel good or happy, tomorrow I will have another great day.

There are things in Courtland which seam to make me very happy and I wouldn't trade that feeling for the world. Just a while ago we went to get some bread and a child at the school yelled out Hi Roger' this in it's self is something that would of never happened anywhere else in the country. For our community is small and people really do love each other as people, the closeness is that of a family like brothers and sisters. Thursday morning' and it's hot and muggy this morning and nothing is sturing out side I was only up twice during the night compaired to my three or four times I usually am so that's something different. I looked up the omen for butterflies and it said that it meant a good harvest, among other things it also said that shy or introverted people are like the butterfly keeping them selves in a protected cocoon. The butterfly is the only thing that can croll and also transform it's self to fly, they are believed to be a good omen to some tribes in other countries. The reason I looked it up was because when I opened my back door a whole bunch of them flew off, I had never seen so many in he years that I have lived here as a matter of fact this is the first year that I have seen them at all. The wonders of God doesn't seam to end they say the introverted person will soon come out of their shell, the morning is like one you would see in an old movie over in England hot foggy and just still very muggy in the house also but this should pass as the air sucks out the humid. When I was looking at the wheat crop the other day it seamed mighty full.

And beautiful just like a dark green lawn but you wouldn't want to lay in it with it's prickly seeds, Oliver is sick and I cant figure out why when they gave him a good bill of health. He says it will pass but it worries me anyway if he isn't better by this afternoon then we will have to do something. It's hard taking careof someone you love because feelings come into the picture and you only want what's best for them. I gave him acouple of flue pills and they should kick in by this afternoon when they get sick it makes me want to cry as I feel helpless at times but then again that's just me. The bond we have created is built over the years and I guess I'm just a centamental fool' it's the third and what a start to the day but things will get better as the day moves on, when he gets the flue there is nothing the doctors can do because it has to run it's course and his is doing that now. They say when love is entered into the equashion people are better taken care of and this I believe is so and when I pray I know that God hears my prayers to heal the ones I love. Period. For this is his promas to me in time's when I am afraid, God's love is for us all but so many ignore his promas and think they can make it on their own to only find out later that they failed. It says He had a plan for our lives before we were conceaved and in the end I believe that we will be on that path He set out for us, and it goes with that saying if you want to make God laugh tell Him your plan. His plan cant be changed but ours is always changing with our human minds, pop's is resting in his favorite chair it seams that he can rest better there then in his bed. I'm glad that I'm in somewhat good health other wise they wouldn't have a home and would be put somewhere else and I know from what I saw in care facilitys that they wouldn't last long without the love they need. The temps are unusual and I havent seen it like this in all the years I have been here but then again change is coming, the helping hand of another is comforting when you need to converse for my love for my brother is very helpful in some situations and I am glad for his company during these times. I got my work just about done at the church, the kids must have had a popcorn fight because it was all over the place. Such fun when I go to work and sing and boy was it hot in there, pop's is doing better as the day goes on and I expect he will be back to normal by tomorrow's end. The butterflies are getting thicker out side as each day passes and it is a sight to see there are many different ones from yellow and black to just moth's. Friday and they flew pop's to Salina on life flight, he has an infection in his heart and my sister hand a stroke blood clots formed on her frontal loab of her brain. This morning we have to go to salins and see how pop's is but he is a very sick man, we cant go until it's light out because I cant see very well at night or in the darkness. My land it came on all of a sudden like the last time this morning I prayed for them both and I know that God will take care of them, with pop's it was with his lungs last time and now the heart so I will have many miles to travel in the next week. Sometimes I think that he may be tired but he is a fighter as my Sister is, I have to believe that the good lord will watch over them both and give me peace of mind and spirit so I can handle what is taking place.

I prayed this morning for his help and guidance and strength as these next few days go by they say tragedy happens in threes first it was Randy, then Oliver, and my Sister. In the coming few weeks we will learn the outcome of these things and I pray for a happy ending, a new start you might say. I still don't understand how veterans' missed something like this with all the tests they had run but it's like the nurce said when people are old it can hit them in a second. Not showing any mercy until it's taken care of with God by his and her side who could be against them? In the time I have been here this is the second time and I pray that it will be the last of bad news for some time to come. As for explaining what has occurred I cant, for only He knows the answer to that one' but I have asked for people to pray for them both and with the power of more then one I know the situation will get better. For my feelings at this time cant be explained as I am in Aww with disbelief, and it reminds me that I am God's child and as His child you have to ask your father to take over sometimes and leave it in His hands. Earlier last month or so I said that I felt change coming but this wasn't expected, I thought good things were on there way and it still could be that way if all turns out ok for them. I will have pastor Kathy pray with me later this morning, and maybe she can help in some way from what I read the pastor is in charge of our souls to guide us to where we need to be and right now I could use her strength because mine is still growing, like the child learning new things all over again.

When things happen like this it in some way makes us stronger in our faith, and I will stand strong as God walks beside me. I didn't get a call from Salina so he must be holding his own at this time and that could be a good signe, the love for a sister cant be put into words as it's a deep feeling reaching deep down in your spirit. I pray that this day will be full of good news instead of the other it's strange how one can become beside them selves but with His help he can take that worry away and replace it with His love. For He gave his only begotten son so we could live, if the situation takes that other turn then they will be with the creator and be more happier then they were in a long time. Saturday morning and I am sad Oliver has passd away my buddy my friend, I will miss him I know he is in heaven with Jesus but still my sorrow is real as I learn to go on without him. My brother says that V.A. Will cover things when it comes to the funeral so I will find out today for sure the grief I feel makes me want to cry the lonelyness which is upon me on this day leaves a hole deep inside, I have never had to bury anyone especially my best friend and father. I find some comfort in my pastors words but it doesn't stop the hurt and my life will never be the same, through the years we have laughed and cried together but we had always been there for each other to comfort and to share the love we felt. I am very angry with he Veterins as they should of known how bad he was but they for some reason ignored it and shipped him back home in my book they didn't care about the person for which I had a grest love for and now he is gone to never make me smile again. For in life we live and we die that's just a part of life the cycle which takes us to eternal life with God, for now he will be made whole and walk straight. The things which made him special was his smile and him love for me, for without him in my life it could of turned out much different I coud of went the other way but he stood beside me every step of the way. My promas has been fulfilled that I made so long ago to my mother and now he will be with her safe in the arms of Jesus, each day I got him up so he could start a new day with a smile and now that smile isn't going to be there anymore it's like something was took from me and I will miss him more with each passing day. It says God doesn't shut one door without opening another so we will see what takes place. My family said they are there for me but I have to depend on my self to survive this tragic loss to me he wasn't only my friend and father but also my greatest inspration to how life can be. I need to grieve for a time and I am beside my self in this time, we did many things together and nothing can take his place in my heart. Dear God I ask you to help me through this time when I need you the most for my pain of loss is real and I don't know what to do don't leave me father as I feel so alone and want to louse it, shower me with your love and take care of pop's in Heaven as I know you will. Many feelings fill me right now and not all of them are good, when others close to me went away I could drink the pain away but that's not the case here as my life has been transformed from that one to this one you gave me hope and faith to only test it but why did he have to go? The house is so empty with out his smile and the getting him out of bed. By nature I want to blame someone so can I pick on you? For I don't like how I feel he was my sunshine my spark to get up each day and go on.

This new chapter brings sorrow deep inside help me with this father, help me to understand these feelings and why I hurt so much. I want to cry and it wont come out. Maybe because I know it's human nature to be sad, when something like this happens also lord bring Randy peace as he goes through this chapter also as we will need each other. Sunday morning' the habbit of getting things ready for Oliver will take time to change, we have the funerial set for next Saturday at 4:00 Pm. They were nice at the place which does the work on people who have passed and we will bring my family here from two states some will come and others well we will wait and see. The reality really hasn't hit yet or if it has then the worst is over, just getting the funeral thing taken care of is a blessing and as I expected Veterans wont help unless every bill he had is paid and there is no way I could ever do that. In the end he was very sick and had been for quite some time, I think in reality the V.A. Hospital knew he was dieing long ago and just wouldn't tell me which is not right, I am able to find peace in knowing he lived a full life and I did the best that I was able to do to fulfill the request my mom asked so long ago. Now he is with her in the sweet by and by and it's a place where they will find each other, old habbits are a thing which will take time to bring on change but I'm sure that it will happen. The lord has brought me this far and I know he is with me' this world in which I live now is scary because you don't know from one day to the next what's going to happen. My children have gone through many funerals in the last couple of years so if they cant make this one then it's ok' because I know they loved him.

Tonya and her family are coming up this next Friday and it will be nice to see them and tell their stories about the fun times they had with dad. I will bring him home as he loved this land and never wanted to leave and go back to Nebraska, his final words were I love you as he kicked at me. My world was shaddered by his passing but things will heal for my love for him will never change my buddy, my father, my friend. God doesn't colse one door without opening another and for thatI am glad, Pastor Kathy has been a god sent in all this and has helped a lot so now all we have to do is get past the funeral and go on with life. No matter how hard things seam to get God has been there for me like He said he would, through life we go through many changes people we love leave us but we as a people have to stand strong to carry on with what will become of our livs my land' who knows what He has in store for us, like someone said to me this life is scary and in some ways it is but also keep in mind that we were born to live and then go to a better place once we are done here. My life will never be the same without him but also I know he wont have to suffer any longer, I remember all of his stories especially the one about John Cash and how he helped to build his first house after he became a star. Then later it got burnt down by a truck back fireing in the field, such great stories. I find it intresting how true life occurances happen in my life as if they didn't then I wouldn't be able to write about them, the happy times and the sad, for you have to have both when you go through life and if your blessed then you can write about them and make a new chapter in your life. Father I love you so and I will miss your smile and big heart, I think deep inside he knew it was about time to go and be with God. As time got closer he watch Joel O'Steen and found comfort in his words I will truly miss you dad. I can hear Randy talking in his sleep but he is doing better these days as he is no longer in the place where something must of happened, I fine him enjoyable' at times and for the most part we get along just fine. Now he has his own bedroom where he can feel even more secure, it will be harder since dad is gone and I feel like a part of me has been taken away. For our love spaned over a thirty some years, from childhood into adult hood we stood by each other and did the best we could it's now time to move on and who know what tomorrow will bring a smile, a laugh, or even a tear may fall when least expected. Rod and Mary are coming also but my sis wont be able to come as her stroke has left her learning all over again, sort of like I had to, she will learn new things in life and be grateful for them all as she learns each new step. I pray that God will help her as He helped me, through life we go through many changes and even though we don't understand some of them later they become clear it's a part of life. The kindness from others I didn't expect but it's a good thing when they open their hearts and show you that kindness with a smile or just a wave, if I didn't have the support of the community I don't know what would of become of things now. But they are all there and I'm proud to call them my friends, in many ways dad inspired me to change my life and he even helped me in doing so with his patients and love. When the change was happening I couldn't see it but later it became clear that he loved me very much, my storie is one of over coming the odds and I have done that and learned may things through this path in life. And my journey continues Courtland is the best place for me and here I will remain, yesterday Randy was telling me that he could never live alone.

And he wont have too as long as I am around for the love of a brother is something special when we were children we fought like all kids do, but then in time we became strangers going our own way in life to later connect strange how that happens. God brought us together once again for many reasons but I believe it was to show that forgiveness is the best policy, in the coming days we will cry but we will also laugh about the good times with pop's and how just one day earlier he was driving a cart around Wal-Mart and scared the hell out of a guy. I never seen anyone just so fast and the Spanish girl just laughed with us as he took off for the other side of the store, I have learned many things in life and one is that we are all different and that's a good thing for He made us all different no two the same not even twins who are conceived at the same time or seconds apart. They have a connection like no other but they are not the same, now many more doors will open but what they have behind them only God knows. Going on without my buddy, my father, my friend will be scary but I will survive in this world of the unknown. The change from being young to being old scares the hell out of some people, as they watch friends go to the ever after. Shannon has a hard time with going to funerals and that's because she is sensitive like her father. My self I don't like them either for this is the first one since mom passed, but it has to be done when it's your mother or father you might say it took this long to get over her's so I will morn for pop's for quite some time. Then it will become easier as time moves on, the pastor said she would get communion ready for this morning and I told her that I took out the bread yesterday so it's ready, she has been a blessing and I am glad that she is my pastor she seams to make things a lot easier during this time when my heart is broken and she even bought me a mault yesterday on the way home from the funeral home. The Lord brought me to the right place when he sent me here as I learn more about him and his love, Kathy was telling me about how she goes to the old folks homes and visits with the elderly.

It takes a lot to show that kind of love towards others and her daughters are good with them also as they work for nursing homes. God gives us all gifts in different areas in life, and it's a joy to do them. Monday morning and the town is quiet, I don't know where everyone will sleep but we will make room for the short time they will be here. Just having that many people here will be hard but I'm grateful for them showing up I need to make room for my kids so they have a place to sleep. This will be very confusing but te lord will provide, I didn't invite too many people because my house isn't that big. As for many of them they might have to stay at a motel, the wind has been blowing for most of the morning and all of last night but we haven't gotten any rain as of yet. This is a hard time not knowing what to do about things which pertain to a funeral but maybe Tonya can help in some areas like getting hold of the people we need to contact, there is always bills after someone dies so we will see what happens there, I miss him so much his smile and his good morning. There is an emptyness here now like a part of me is missing but I know in time that those wounds will heal and there will be another thing to fill that void, death is final and there is no give and take but in life he really did live a long time 15 or so years longer then they thought I will miss you pop's as I know you are with God and mom. If you are able to see me tell mom much love, we live and we die to go to that eternal place where we will be made whole once again. He must of really loved us to put up with all the things he did when we were children and now it's his time to rest, God I know you will take care of him. In the days we will see each other again as the dove flies around here I will think of you being on it's wings and flying around Courtland. It's hard to sleep sometimes but my mind will except his passing as going to a better place which God has made for us all, yesterday I mowed the lawn so it would look nice and Randy pitched in like a trooper to help. This morning he is talking in his sleep and I think it has to do with the passing but I cant be sure, for this is a great day the lord has given us Jan Carolson brought over a smoked turkey and salid and a pie which was very nice of her. She has always had a good heart and she is wonderful to take the time to do this for me, you don't find people like them just anywhere and they along with Kathy have enriched my life greatly. Kathy is a bubbly person filled with the lord's goodness and you can see it most everyday, I don't know what I would of done without her help in this time. As we move forward change will come again as it does when time brings it on to make things better in some ways and help the passing of loved ones. On another note my Sister is doing pretty good so far and Tonya said she is a lot better and for that I thank God many prayed for her and I believe that helped, now my life will move forward into the unknown to see what He has instore for me.

My I'm glad that I moved here Kathy has helped make many things easier and the funeral home will notify Veterans and social security that in it's self is a great help, the guy I met was really nice to do these things for me.the weather is unusual for this time of year with the temps being so high but I also know that it will pass in time, Tonya and Stan is paying for Rod's gas to get here and others will need help with gas with the price of it these days, as we move into this year further along I will adjust to things being different and my life will continue on the path it's on one of loving God and trying to understand life as we know it. There has been many blessings during this time and I should focus on them instead of the other, for God has made a place for my dad in heaven. I think he knew what was happening but didn't let on spareing me he confusion, it's going to be a nice day here in Courtland and today I have to go to the bank to get things taken care of. Tuesday morning' and I let Jack out yesterday for pastor Kathy and when I let him in I couldn't find him, usually he is very hiper so I left and came back home I don't know when she got home but when she called it sounded like she was very far away. It's trash day so I will make my rounds and get things taken care of as I do every Tuesday also I know that Tonya is going to be here in two and a half days along with the others, my quiet time has been more lately and I wish things were easier but only time wil tell what will come down the road. It will take time for this to pass but I'm in hope that it wont take too long,

Such a change from before and I try not to dwell on things I cant change, did I go through this with mom and if I did I don't recall it. It's time for a new beginning but I'm beside my self on what to do. For things which had importance doesn't seam to be that important any longer now I have to take care of Randy he said he couldn't live alone. Am I my brothers keeper? When you think you are at your lowest point he somehow pick's you up. Shannon isn't coming because she has been through so many of them lately and I cant blame her as life is hard enough without depression following you around, you have to over come and adapt to things and thee way they are, Harley slept with me most of the night staying beside me I think he knows what I am going through at this time. And he loves me so many things I don't understand but I'm in hope that soon things will change and bring about good things, the fight for life continues and I know that once I get past this stage things will be prett good once again. I know my friend morned for a while after her husband passed and still you can see it in her but she has moved a little past it and comes to church on Sundays. Maybe one day I will cheer up but for now I am down with many worries on my mind this is what others must feel when life throws you a curve ball, but you have to stay strong and know that God will take care of things. Through the years many things have tested my faith but I have always bounced back to go on with life and that's what I will do now, go on with life and learn to be a happy camper. I feel that family might help, just them being around could change things. Could going to Oklahoma help in some way it's possible but I really don't want to hear all the noise of other people, it's going to be a nice day I noticed that the wind isn't blowing any longer and we didn't get any rain so that's good the temp was supposed to be in the fourtys but not sure if it made it. As time moves forward the day is getting closer Mrs, Hord stoped by and brought some cakes over which was really nice, I feel cold this morning but I'm hoping for a good day and part of my problem could be depression. I cantt even imaging how sis feels as she is coming home, she will have to learn some things over again but they expect a full recovery and I thank the lord for that. The house seams kind of empty without him and things are very different. Even this time which was once a time for peace has changed, and we dont know if we will take a trip or not to Oklahoma, taking it might bring change for a short time. I find it hard with just the two of us now as I pray that things will work out ok' once we get past this funeral. I also realize that this happening wont have the same impact on the others as it has had on me as it will take time to grieve the picture of him and mom is approbate for the service but then it comes back here to the house where it will remain. But it wont symbolize sadness it will remind me of the good times we had growing up as we learned the rights and wrongs of life. There has never been anyone that hasn't cried from loss in their own way when they louse a mom or father, but life goes on and we get stronger as time passes. When we feel pain it lets us know that we are alive and we should extend the time we have on this earth, running away from where you live wont change things because where ever you go there you are. Many times we think if we do go somewhere else that it will be better but it wont in reality so I will start a new and hope for the best.

Lord knows I have a lot of friends here and maybe it's time for me to focus on me. And then the rest will fall into place as each day passes, I can feel change taking place inside me and this day is a little better then yesterday and the day before. Wednesday the beginning of a new day and I will be glad in it from it's another day the lord has given us. Many people deal with grief in different ways one women walks a lot of the time around town, and it gets many jokes but we all know that it helps in some way for her to deal with things. I will try something new within the next few weeks to take the place of taking care of dad, they say it changes the brain when you have done something for so long and it will take time to adjust to a different way of life. Before I was shy or introverted bashful as the pastor put it but that might become a thing of the past as I get stronger, Randy is good company why this time is visiting me and he gives me encouragement when I feel lost. And for this I am grateful. I know things will get better as we have each other Thursday and things are looking better tomorrow Tonya will be here and the pastor is seeing about my song getting recorded it seams someone has a sound system and they are going to help if they can and that would be awesome. Many things are going to change and my journey will take another road I believe I have excepted the things I cant change so it's time too live once again, and who knows where that might lead for only God knows that at this moment in time. My whole life has been put on hold and now could be the time to break out and see many things I haven't seen before, and I could even have some fun which hasn't happened in a long time.

To a new beginning!! in the time a head I want to learn many new things and I will see if I can learn what it means to be happy, happy beyond belief, a purpose which will set my spirit free. I have thought of maybe going on a trip and seeing how other coultures live and maybe helping out if it's possible, for my friends are reaching out to me in some ways by telling me that they are thinking of me. Even my neighbor came over and said I was in her thoughts I haven't felt such warmth from other before and it's difficult, because no one has care that much before but I will learn new ways and except the change that is coming my way. The exceptence of loss and the new changes in life will bring about joy as I move forward, a christen community is the greatest place to live and although some go to other churches we are tied together by one thing and that Is God Him self the greatest power of all. Pastor Kathy is a trooper and I noticed something about her she is bubbly just full of life and love for others, she was able to help and for that I am glad. Next I will try to change my habbits of getting up so early but I tried this morning and it didn't work so well kind of funny in a way but none of us change over night if staying up later will help I will try that but we will see. For today is a new day and I'm glad to be here, when I go out side I listen more to the birds and look at the beez as they fly around and my since of smell is higher then usual I smell almost everything unlike before and maybe that's Him showing me that things can be different. Unlike before I want to tast the honey of the nector's and see how sweet it is, my friend is awesome. And she say's God blesses her each day I want some of that but it will take time to acquire it and put it to use, I thought I had found peace but it's not total peace not the kind which others have, or which

I think they have maybe in the years to come it will come with it as I study the word of God. Me being someone who wants things to happen now have to learn to be patient so He can open the doors which need to be open, for He has opened one door and that's working at the church but I cant help but feel there are other doors which need to be opened. For His grace will follow us all the days of our lives, change comes at it's own time and that time hasn't come fully yet. The mind has to be able to except certain things which in many ways mine hasn't yet but I'm optimistic that it will. With all my friends bringing over food I don't know where to put it all they are so giving at this time bless their hearts, many people don't know what to say but that is something I wouldn't find words for either…. Many people cant deal with funerals and I am one of them so I don't think I will go to any more not even my own, because I wont be here….. After my doctors visit I will get more involved in the church more then I am now, and see where He takes me you know go for the ride and try to embrace things in a different way a new out look on things, and learn to adapt to things in a different way. Friday May 11th Tonya is supposed to be here sometime today and we will let them have the room pop's used to sleep in Randy told them that they could usse it for the night. Rita a friend from church sent a card and said she was thinking of me at this time, I believe she iss the one who lost her husband not too long ago so she knows what I'm going through. I will just be glad when this is behind me so that new chapter can start. I'm hoping for a great day hell it will be a good day because I'm going to make it that way, one more day until things will get back to normal through the years I have changed in so many ways and change is still taking place. For He has things for me to do I just don't know what they are yet Rod is supposed to be here tomorrow and it will be good to see him he never stays long during these things but him just showing up shows that he and Mary have a heart.

A toast to new beginnings, and learning how to life once again there are a few role models around here not naming any right now but they have something I want and that is joy in their souls. To many introverted years taking care of others has left me in a position to start to learn once again and there is no telling where it will lead, for a weight has been lifted off of me I never knew any other life taking care of people first with mom and then pop's many years spent doing that and it has or was a routeen but now I can focus on me the one who the father created. It's now time to find my next path, the morning is a calm one and not even a lief was blowing. It's the peace here which draws me to conclude that this is where I need to be at this time, I have everything I need to survive here and who knows where I will be lead next. It's time to clean house you might say out with the old and in with the new to get rid of what I don't need and I don't need much. This will be a new journey towards the unknown and I will adjust as time goes by. Saturday morning' things are looking up, since my arrival here three or so years I found out that they love me more then I thought to days is the day and I don't know if anyone will come here it's the 21st centry and money is tight with others being able to drive a few hundred miles, many other didn't care much about our lives before so why should it be any different now. My new family on the other hand has helped in many ways by bringing over food and other things it's like the family

I once new is fading unless they supprise me which I doubt, but my new family is here with me. I my self couldn't afford a funerial so the Church took care of it and lifted that burden off of my sholders.

And in return I will volinteer at the thrift store during the week, as the pastor asked if I would do that my reply was sure it might be fun, a little time to give for the giving of so many of them is worth it to me and in time who knows what will come next. I realize others have their lives and they can go on living it apart from me as I learn to have a closer walk with God, the town will do all it can for me to stay so Courtland will remain my home. For the love they have shown is a gift in it's self. Many have said I am in their thoughts and that let's me know that I am making a difference not only in their lives but in my own for the power of God is here in this little town I have grown to love. It's windy out side so we might get a storm but it hasn't gotten here yet one women my barber said the farmers were out in the fields trying to get the corn planted before the rain hit's and then it can take root, the community is solid here and I am a part of it now as for my children I can see them once in a while but it will be quite some time before that happens. Pastor Kathy is a card and she can make me laugh which is awesome sometimes. She above all knows parts of my life that others don't and it's fun to chat sometimes as she her self has many stories about her life she said she has traveled to other countries but preferred small towns. And I think it has something to do with bonding getting close to the people, my self I still like to be by my self at times and so does she but instead of watching television she reads books. Maybe trying to fill those shelfs that someone said we have in our minds and if that the case mine must be mighty empty Ha! They have offered me things that others have never offered me before and you can tell they are true to their word when it comes to loving someone. So far I have gotten six cards from friends but one was from my daughter with her big heart, I cant predict what will take place in the future but I know that life will go on as it has for so long. And with life comes change for the better if that's your goal, in this life God comes to see us through the hard times and holds us close to his heart. Back many years ago I would of never thought this kind of life would be possible and it just shown that we as people don't know His plan for our lives for it is different from our's, He set it before our birth and in the end we will do what He has planed for us. After Rod said he would come, I never heard back from him so I doubt if he will come to the funeral before it was me and Oliver and we survived just fine now it's me and Randy and we will do just fine but it takes two in this world to survive because one cant do it alone not enough finances with what one gets. It just doesn't work, it looks like it's just us today but that's ok. The service will be short, my life has been so different from theirs a sepration that occurred long ago, although this new journey will be different it will bring new things with it but what those things will be is out of my sight at this time. Pastor Kathy said a nice sermen yesterday and it was short and sweet, through life many things change and we seam to change with it. As a rock can wound the wing of a dove we have to use caution when talking with others not to upset the balance which has occurred in some places.

Now my inter self will start to appear but I'm not sure of what it is yet the careing child trying to find it's way or just that bashful adult that didn't grow past that stage, either or both will be good. In the day's of wine and roses I didn't give much thought to others and maybe that's because I didn't give much thought to my self at that age, for the things that once stopped me from breaking out isn't there any longer for they are in heaven with God. I wondered one time when I talked to Dr. Nelson, how he was able to help at the church he goes to in Nebraska being so busy with patients and such but he told me that it just came to be that way over time it was like God showed him how to make time and eventualy it came to be a part of his life remodeling when needed and helping out with other things. There were many things I could have done in my life and it makes me wonder why it took so long to come to find what I have here, not that I'm complaining but the work would of been easier back in the day's of my young adult hood. Yes" I know, back then I wasn't ready through the sands of time our character in us changes…. and what's meant to be will be and we hope that otherss can get along with what's let loose, the time's of wine and roses is gone but many lessons were learned along the way, when it came to family I was there for them mom and Oliver but now they are gone and I have to get back to living. Finding that one person who might make the connection that has been absent from my life for so long, do I take a chance and find happiness once again.

My time is more flexable now then before so we will see what takes place, pastor Kathy said I'm a lot like John and I think that might be a good thing but I'm not sure yet. We move in different directions and as we get older sometimes it takes two to compleat something or bring about compleation and there is nothing wrong with that because everyone needs a helping hand sometimes. When we had the service she talked about how pop's wanted to eat everything because I starved him and he wanted to take home her pie it was funny to me so I laughed it couldn't be helped. He always thought he was starving even when mom was here so this was nothing new to me, it was like he would strike out so others would listen and he didn't care if he hurt someones feelings either. Sunday the 13th of May. And now things wiill change my Sister is doing better but there are many things which are not believeable with some family members so this I throw caution to the wind. Going through life and not excepting that rejection is out there is not realistic. And I have to say that my life has been different from those who have had to be in a relationship for that part has been long gone I want to try new things and I can catch on pretty fast with some things for the lessons learned while working for Jack has stayed with me over the years like it was embedded in he mind to remain until it's used again and who knows what the future holds. Kathy asked how old I was and although I wanted to keep it a secret I let it out so much for secrets, I wanty to believe I have 20 more years on me but the Father is the only one who really knows. We should take it a day at a time and if we have a good day then be grateful for that day and give thanks for that one, to the older people I'm like a youngster and to me they are not old just a little blessed, today is going to be a great day as we move forward into it and we should feel joy as He gives us each another one. I hope they have air at the thrift store because it can get mighty hot in there and I don't like the heat but if they don't, I have a solution and it will be cool anyway. In this life we take many chances and if it's for a good reason then I know He is there. For helping when you can can bring it's own rewards maybe not is monetary form but in other ways, lord knows that food is out of the question they have filled my fridge with way too much and it's not good to let it go to waste. But you cant eat it all either, some people talk to hear them selves as for me the less said the better unless it pertains to something, raddleing on isn't a good thing not to me anyway. Even in others I can see the childish disposition which occurs when the second childhood comes to be parent and I think it's awesome to be able to relive that childhood. We all go through it at a certain time in our lives but do we remember it in that place in the mind when our time comes to be? Or are we aware of it at all maybe it's just a phase like addiction was in my life to teach us something's. During this time my mind is adapting to something it's like it's making new pathways into somewhere that it has never been or it's been there and just left a long time ago, but anyway it's a new feeling one that hasn't been before. Jan got me a plant to put into the yard where we can place my friend, this will be a plant that blooms and grows into a bush I think it will look awesome. Sunday and church was fun and me and John talked for a bit before the others got there and I offered my help if he ever needs it, I thanked most of the people but still have to thank a couple more it will take time but I will get it done. So many cards and I think it might be better to do it as a groupe, as time goes by many things will change as for the thrift shop I will try it out and see who it goes. I got a hug from some of them as I told them thank you, they really care about me and that will take some getting used too but it feels good Harley went out this morning and I didn't have any trouble getting him back in.

The days here are filled with what ever you want to do so now I will have to find something occupie my time so the bordom doesn't get to me but my spirits are up, the thing which was making me ill has passed and now things are fine strange how some things can do that too a person. In the next year or so I will try to write some new songs and maybe get them published for there are two in my head but they still have to be worked out, the setting here is of an old town which survived through the depression and many other hard times and I believe it's the people who made it happen with their love and understanding of each other they seam to pull together when things happen not like in the cities where it would pulls them apart with me they helped the best way they knew how and I could feel the love which was needed at the passing of pop's. but now life must go on so things will change the way they should, the change of things will come and we never know what tomorrow will bring. It was mothers day yesterday but after a cup of coffe I left to come back home where I changed the fuel in the lawn mower so it wouldn't burn up and now it's running fine to last for a few more years.

I heard little brother the other night and his old friends were trying to get him to come to Kearney for a visit although I know it would be a disaster, if he desides to go, then he will have to make his own mistakes. As we all have to do in life his one friend is an alcoholic and I know he just wants his money as for the rest I would say it's the same with them. I like to think what I am doing for him is the best thing, right now anyway and if he gets to where he wants to leave later down the road then so be it but he will find that others are not so understanding as I am. They will bleed him dry and then disgard him like a piece of garbage, for that's the way they survive in the big old world out there, I would never let them get that close to me but he has a big heart and fall's for the women in distress like Stacy. Poor guy thinks he is in love, and he knows that it would never work but you cant stop the heart when it sends you signals funny about that even though you know it wouldn't work you for some reason have to try and see where it leades it's the same with addiction when you fall back into it for that short time to see if you are missing anything. It reminds me of a test rocket platform where you make the same mistakes until you get it right and then go on to the next project this happens so oftend in life when your addicted to things that destroy lives. A thought for the day do you feel blue because you lost a loved one if so just look up and know that their pain and sorrow is no more and they are in the hands of God the father, many times we all have to go through unexpected loss of someone but the good news is that He is there for us and can calm the things which make us louse it, for a few days the depression would come and go and then it was like it was lifted away by a force much greater then mine. In the times when depression hit me it's like a weight was lifted off of me by a stronger force and I realized that He was doing his job, the lord never seams to give us more then we can handle and this allows us to survive in this world. Where will my future take me in the realm of life? For that is something to yet be seen, and I will see it when the time is right no expectations at this time and we will see what unfolds later in life. Monday, we went to Concorida this morning and had my oil changed and then to Wal-Mart to get some things we needed and on the way home we stopped at Micky-D's for a hamburger and fries. This might not sound like much but it gave us some time on the road to change our prespective of things, and it made me realize that I have more friends here then I ever had before. Even today I got a card from a friend and it's nice to know that people are still thinking of me in their prayers, such a change from the life I once knew. Then we had to go to Belleville to get Randy's med's and some pop to last a few days, now we are set for a while and wont have to go back into town until we really need something today was a great day all around. Our barber came while I was trying to sleep but I was suddenly awaken by the bark of Harley she had brought over cookies that she made, such thoughtful people. I saw my little friends car parked at her mom's and wanted do something!!! But maybe that might happen later, getting to know her I mean. well you can never know what time will bring your way, as I try too sleep many things seam to happen that detures me from getting the job done but I will now try again until tomorrow then. Tuesday morning' and I feel like I'm not awake yet. As we went to Wal-Mart yesterday I met a lady at the cashier and come to find out through her, she is the one that owns the land that Margret lives on or she is married to him that does. Then she said enough said right, and she was right! In my time here I haven't seen Margret but once or twice at the store in Belleville, it seams He tells me when to get away from certain people and I do it when I get that alert. It's like a signal that trouble is coming and I don't want any part of that, through the wine and roses days it wouldn't of mattered but through the years I have become more sensitive to these things.

And it doesn't allow me to shut it off like before my mind catches everything and it cant be wiped out like before so it stay's for a time anyway, strange how the mind works to let somethings in and other things not so much. As it adjust to the new way of life, tomorrow I start work at the thrift shop so we will see how that goes I havent made any promases until I try it because it isn't for everyone very small in there but I'm hoping it will be fun what's two hours or four hours a week, and it get's me away from the house for a time. Some say some stopped coming to church because they didn't want to do it so if I take the time to do this they might return and I know God would want that to happen. These days my worry alarm has gone since pop's went to be with God because I know He is there with him and that lets me explore other things to do since the others know about pop's they also know that I am now free, and I'm sure that some will check me out. The thrift store is a place where I can meet people and tune my people skills so I can be around them more they say many people come in there so we will see what goes on, my little friend isn't around much anymore but I hope in time that maybe we will cross paths once again. She' like her mom, is bubbly and that is a great quality to have we both work in the elderly people care realm where it takes a special kind of personn to do that.

Many years ago my family had a chance to step in and help with pop's but none of them would do it as they like so many others had their own lives to live. But I couldn't see him not having a home so I stayed to take care of him, born into this world without a family or louseing it left him alone until they met that night in a bar my land' he didn't even drink alcohol he was there to find someone and he did, there are many years in which they were together and they loved one another until they were parted by death it's self, and now death has brought them together once again. Will he give her the crap he gave me? Only God knows that one, but I'm glad that they are together and dad for only harmony exist up there such a long time between deaths but I'm sure that time doesn't matter in the place where they have gone to be with the Father. Courtland is my sanctuary a place where I feel at home for others don't enter this place just off the streets it's a peaceful place where harmony exise, I have seen many addicts go back to their old ways but the ones that make it somehow find peace. Peace in which they have never felt before, life's journey is one of change and learning and what happened yesterday doesn't matter much today but for some reason we see things in hind sight and that's ok for some. In my life I get many bells and whistels that go off but through it all I survive and keep on going to maybe one day find that special someone. Through this journey I think I have always wanted to find love but I cant get over the argueing they go through, just the other day I saw a women yelling at her husband because of something at a gas station not washing the windows could have been it but still to embarrass him like that was truly uncalled for, and then again it might be four play!!! Who knows. The twisting and turning of the mind can be a turn on' with the right person. But if it isn't with the right person then all hell can break out. The day was a good one and now it's time to relax as the sun goes down, we pretty much stayed home and had a barbecue but that was the excitement of the day. Wednesday morning' I learned last night that Stacy was in the hospital again because of her lungs she visits there quite oftent any more each time she has a problem with them. The doctors tell her to stop smoking but she never does and that causes her problems, many people are being put on resprators these days in hope that it will help but with some it doesn't. When I go to start work today I will see how things go but I have always wanted to work at a thrift store and who knows I might like it, others have run it for quite some time but it interferes with some of them's lives which causes them to maybe want to stay away from the place. I have visited there many times and liked what they are doing to help with other things, and I will try and do my best to help I have seen other towns which have a clothes drive or open a little place in the church to sell them and help the people struggling to make it in this world at this time and it's good to be a part of that something bigger then I.

I don't know how but the man up stairs brought me here for a reason and maybe it was to help in this way, I needed to be a part of something and feel like I was a part of it and that wasn't happening in the bigger places for I felt like a dot on a map there. Since pop's passing I feel like I'm starting over but this time without the worry of things happining with his health, it's been many years since I haven't had to worry and with all things it will take sometime to get used to it. I am pleased that they are together again in a place where no harm can come to them safe in the arms of God and there is no better place to be, my learning of the christen ways is slow but in time I will open up and feel the joy some feel when they talk about the father my joy for you come's from within and I know you know that my lord. What will be will be in the future days a head and I hope all will go well,, the exceptence here has been more then I expected when I first arrives three or so years ago. For I have advanced while others have fallen to a lesser place in which they were at just at the same time those years ago. But I have learned so much about grace and how He seams to give it to us. We are limited by our own minds and it can scare the hell out of you if you loose control, today my mind is exceptive and alert in Jesus name Amen. I can feel that I might not write for a while to adjust to these new things which I feel is going to come into my life.

God will never take you to a place where His grace won't sustain you this is a good thing He does for us His children. As I look out side there is a peacefulness about the town, and I see it each morning as I check out what the weather is going to be like in my mind if it's windy then it will rain but with calmness the day will be a nice one through the years here that seams to be the way I preceave things. On another note a plain crashed near Elm Creek Nebraska it's the town where my doctor has his practice Dr Nelson' he inspired me in many ways and he will always be my friend, him and his wife are christens and they have a good life out in the country where they raise dog's for hunting. He also has a cabin in Estes park Colorado where they go once a year, my friend. Many years ago I got a signe that I was supposed to stop the medication that I was on and I put my faith in God that He would take care of me and He did it was almost five years since I saw the doctor and I went back to him. His wife said that I looked ten years younger and that was by my strength in God that became healthy once again, then I saw him and he was surprised. He asked what I had been up to as he thought I had went to a treatment center and I told him that it was God who delivered from my burden. Supprised he checked me out and I had a cold. I told him that my back was hurting so he put me on the medication I was once on and things were fine, when I needed him he was always there and he said that he was proud of me to over come such odds. It seams when I was at my worst God would step in and take over for me and make me strong. I have seen many followers in this world and there is only one bad thing about being that way and that's following the wrong person as some can guide you in the right direction others can guide you in the wrong way leading to their destruction. Like with little brother he was guided by another in the wrong direction and lost a big part of his life, then when I got him out I had to deal with the getting him on the right track and with God's help he has been doing pretty well we have to pull together to survive but we do it and have some fun in the mean time. Courtland' is a great place to let them get their lives together as for Randy he will have to stay with me for years to come if he wants too. He isn't world savvy and wouldn't know what to do in that place, so that's why I had him come here to get him ready in case he ever wants to try and make it out there. You might say that this is a shapeing place where he can learn about God and how He will help him if he want's it, but exceptence is totally up to him because it isn't something you can push on another person. Thursday morning and yesterday I heard that Walter has passed on Monday they must be sending a card so I will get one for him, the thrift store was kind of fun but boring also as we folded a few cloths and I got Randy a few shirts Beverly offered to give me a couch so she can gt it out f the ware house and I told her that I would let her know sometime today. My next scedual is Saturday at 2:00 so I will go and help again, the things are changing and I can feel it but I have to keep my peace of mind my alone time where no one can penetrate that balance I have achived here in other words my time for God for without that I am alone, Harley keeps getting into my bed while I sleep so I'm going to have to put a stop to that as I got a fle bite on my belly and it itches like hell. For it belling a hot day yesterday the inside of the building was pretty cool.

Although I don't like them, funerals that is. I will take the card to Dennis so he can send it off for me but that means another trip to town O well' it's a nice ride, he lived a good life as hee told me his stories about coming here to Courtland when his pick-up broke down and he loved to fish. He then ended up staying here and working at S.&W. For many years as a machanic then to buy his first home here and then another later down the road for rental property the only problem he had was having people pay their rent on time, which I understand as many have it hard these days. But in my opinion that comes first in this world because without a home then you rally don't have anything and lord knows it's harder to pay to move then to pay the rent, my constient payment on time is what got me this house and even today I am never late with the bank my history talks for it's self and I shouldn't have to say something one of the girls that works for the thrift store has lived here most of her life and you can tell that she had a tough life she talks a lot and I met another women and I liked her accent she is a southern girl and is nice. It seams I'm meeting more people these days and who knows maybe one day it will get even better, they can tell I'm not a talker except for when I have something to say and my words are thought through before I reply to something in the days of wine and roses I never thought much at all before I replyed to something but that was a lesson learned after the tragedy in my life.

And it still holds true today. While going through the ware house it was mighty dark in there with no light and I had to be careful not to fall, the thrift store helps a lot of people in need so my time is worth it to give two hours twice a week and it lets me meet new people that I other wise wouldn't meet. The southern girl is cute and she likes to drive around on her gulf cart with her grand children which must be such a delight for her in this small town which now is my home, through the tough times I have made it and I will survive in this world of uncertainty. When I first got here I didn't think there were any women but now I have noticed that the possibilitys are great for a get together it's just that some are spreaded around and not all go to church as I do, many things are different when you don't go to church and others have their reasons for not going. Could this be an opportunity to try and bring some into this place once they get to know me for I have no alturnative motive, the southern bell stays to her self as far as I know except for her grand baby's and she likes to talk about them which is a good out let I can tell she doesn't talk without knowing what she is saying and it leads me to believe that she is a grounded person. Sort of like me in a way, but I am more different then any other person my patients gives me great ground to get to know others and that is a gift from God Him self' who knows what will happen in the coming year? For my life is changing each day since pop's passing there has been a weight lifted and my time is my own now except for the little bit I do for Randy but he is no bother in this segment and he helps with the house work. As the time moves forward new things and opportunities will show them selves and only He knows where that might lead. If a person has the strength to survive here then they can make it almost anywhere, but my self I would never leave this place for which I fell in love with, it's my home after searching for so long in life my little piece of the world. I have met other women and they are trying to land a rich farmer and maybe it's because they think money is everything in life, which it isn't. it's just a tool like the tractor which plows the field the ground and the tractor can bring in much money but one without the other isn't much good, it's only when they are put together that they can bring in a great crop. But the tractor can have many uses and it can make life much easier when used right for hauling and other things. As I used to watch Jack he had it down to a science the time and everything for which to plant and he was great at it, for the things we learned in younger years can astain us through our older lives and make that part a little easier using the mind instead of brone can have it's advantages for the mind is a great tool if you don't destroy it. I see the unfolding of many things and it lets me open a door inside the one that was hardened over the years, after my last relationship I had all but given up on the opiset sex but when I look at some women it makes me think it might be possible once again to try and find that special someone and if she was here then all we would do is grow old together the fantasy or vision is to have everything go right and I know that would be asking for a lot but it's my goal two souls bound together by love a love that will stand the test of time. No drama ha! That in it's self would be a miracle as most women like to talk you know that right brain and left brain thing! But I'm not into that the new seams to ware off with some women and then it becomes boring, that's why I need a certain kind of women one that can hold on to me once they have me and I haven't found her yet but I'm optimistic'because you never know who He will bring she doesn't have to be a church going person just a fiery understanding person who would love me for who I am and not try to change what God has created here in me his son.

I have spent a better part of my life changing so now maybe it's time to get back on the horse once more to see what has taken place in this transformation the once was isn't there any longer and the could be is right in front of my face to shape into something for which others haven't seen yet. For temtation comes in many shapes and sizes and the good should out weigh thebad but does it? When we see all the destruction that goes on in this Nation of ours or is it even ours? Not ! When money takes presedent over human life then it's the money they value over everything else and I find that to be true in this day and age. As for the past before I came to be I can't say but I bet it was the same way the killing for a piece of paper my land' as for the world I live in you need it to survive and if that wasn't the case then I wouldn't have it but we all have to eat and drive our cars so we can stay in good health, living here in Courtland' it's like the 1800's to me in a since not being able to find a store just a block away. But there is a bigger picture here and He is teaching me how blessed I really am even though I don't always see it sometimes, I have notice that I pay more attention to others in the since of listening to them and that will help in the future to get to know them for who they are and not what they have or have been for it's only what you have become that makes you the person you have grown up to be. And this is learned through life experiences the addictions that caused you to fall from grace can help you not to do it any longer if the lesson is learned right, a few days ago I lost my music over what had transpired but I know that God wont keep it from me as that has become a part of my life.

And it brought me great joy to sing like never before it seamed to replace something and that could have been stress or just gave me an outlet to express my self in a different way. For God wont take you to a place where His grace wont keep you safe, for grace is given by God and it cant be bought like all else in this world. I didn't even know about how he saved me so many times until I got here. He wanted to show me that other miracles had happened more then even I thought, and when I got lost He was still there to pick me up in that fog of elusion. Friday morning' yesterday I sent a card to Walts family and Dennis is putting the address on it for me, he seams to be doing better since his hart valve replacement and he looked very good I caught him working out back of his home but I rang the bell first and then walked into the back yard. I tried to wonder where he would be if I was him and bingo there he was our town is small and I didn't have any problem finding his house since he moved. When I was taking care of Walt many found out about it and the other day I was invited to visit someone husband that is getting up in years as his health is failing, I don't know why but some seam to like to have me around and maybe it gives them hope for a while anyway. The old mans wife seams to think that it might bring him some joy if I play cards with him from time to time through my years I seam to have an effect on the older generation for some reason and maybe it's because I have seen where they could go not all the way but to that place where there is no pain or sorrow, yesterday we had a barbecue and it was pork chops mighy tasty and we didn't have to heat up the house the process was effortless and we enjoyed it very much, during the wine and roses days I slept most of the time thinking my world would end but He had different pland and now I'm up most of the time except for the few hours that I do sleep maybe trying to get back in balance once again who know? The chapters seam to go pretty easy once I get them started but still there is a long ways to go my life has been a quandary of different pathes and only He knows where they will lead, tomorrow I will volunteer again at the thrift store even though it get's boreing there is something to be learned there or maybe it's just being around people for it truly makes me feel like I am blessed hearing some stories. I feel my peace is something special as I listen to others raddle on about their lives as for me my quietness is a gift so I can catch little things which could make for a good story. As time moves on there will be many things which I wouldn't want to reveal to others because then my writing would be nothing the things I have learned can take me far in conforsation today I have to clean some more in the church so it will be ready for Sunday which isn't far off. Also I like to watch the elderly people as they ride their culf carts around in this day and age it's cheaper for them to do that then filling up their cars to do the same job for most of the bill paying is done here in town and I think that is awesome when a town is pretty thrifty in that fashion through the years many have noticed me and I don't really mingle much except at church but after living here for a time word gets around. My tribute to the thrift store will bring in some money for them and that will help others in need people struggling more then usual will be able to get the help they need and that too me is a good thing.

I can do more here then I could of done in a bigger town for those who help others can have a feeling of accomplishment a peace which is like no other just joy. As for the loss of pop's I know he doesn't suffer any longer and that makes me feel a lot better these days as I move forward, the promas I made' has been filled. and now he will be on his own wtching over me until it's my time to go a long time from now the sorrow is over and now the living has to start and it will be intresting to see where it takes me. I have notice that Randy has the same temperment as I do he even cries at the same shows that I do so we are connected in a different way then most. Our emotions are somehow connected as for the others in my family I have never felt this connection but with Randy, yesterday we also got some T. shirts that should last a couple of years as the others wore out in a year these are thick and can withstand a lot learning is why we were born here and as each day passes I learn more from kindness to careing from joy to sorrow which I hope is over for a while but in learning you have to be able to help others without making judgements on them and that's something I am able to do. Lord knows I have been where a lot of them are in this life, from the struggles of surviving to the good feelings when you can pay a bill with the help of others. My life is one of honor and honesty but that was taught at a young age, I have never wanted much in life just to be free of worry and now that is a blessing!!! Wouldn't you say? The helping of others is great when you can talk to them and hear their stories as everyone has a story to tell.

Will love find it's way to me probably if I'm not judgemental for we are all different in many ways when I know I can trust someone I open up but if that trust is broken then I clam up once again to not let anyone in what a delima do I or don't I? for trust is a great thing and I know I am trusted by most of the people I have met. Just to have someone ask you into their home is a sign and what you do with that sign is totally up to you, the one girl is a bragger about her kids and how big they were at birth kind of strange to some but it shows love for them after becoming a grandparent it's mostly all you can talk about personalitys are always different with some they will go on and on and with others they don't do that so much as their memories are locked in their minds like a treasure box not to be opened until it suits them. We all leave here with our treasure boxes of our past life and the things which brought us to where we are today, as for yesterday it's gone and we start a new day with the hope that it will be a good one the ladder of life can be really great as we learn to climb it but make a mistake and miss a step and you can fall on your ass, to start over once again. I must have fell many times because I'm still climbing the ladder. But that's ok' my ladder has many lessons on it and as you learn one you move on to the next step, I still don't know why I use that concept but it seams fitting for some things. What step am I on ? Well no one really knows for sure but I like to think I'm close to the top in my experiences the learning process which takes us through life the do's and donts which lets us come together with others. In Kearney Nebrasska, I didn't get out much really didn't want to because I thought the world didn't have anything to offer but here it's different for these people are real and have a heart for that life which has long passed has sprouted a seed one of kindness that had been in me for many years but couldn't come out, the trust factor wasn't there and it is here. Where some are kind and others well I haven't met those ones yet, for they are far off still in the distence maybe one day they will become closer but for now I'm just starting out and their trust factor isn't solid yet. We went to town earlier and got chicken for supper and the wind was blowing really hard. The dirt was all over the place blowing through the windows as we drove down the road, also we were going to get a motor home but changed our minds when we realized that a car is in the future so we can survive in this place of ours. Without a car you are lost and I know I will need one later down the road as this one has a lot of miles on it and you have to have Air-conditionig out here in the heat. I haven't talked to Tonya lately since she didn't come to the funeral I guess I was angry because she said she was coming and then had Stan call and give a line of crap but I wasn't angry with Stan as he was just the messanger, I tend to not reply to people that lie to me and really it hurts me not them. My life is going good right now but I also know that things can change in a heart beat to not being good, as I have said before I still have a lot to learn about people and why they act the way they do as some of them are full of shit and act like a person they are not. As for me I am me and no one else I don't change like the weather which I find to be a good thing, the pastor drove by and waved to me this morning and it felt good. The wind is blowing still and I am staying out of it expecially when it's 91 degrees out side and the hotter weather is coming, we will see temps into the tripple digits by next month and it will last for a month or two.

It was nice to know that I will be able to get a different car in the future one that I wont have to sink a lot of money into, and that way I will be able to save for something special in the future and who knows what that might be. I think things will work them selves out later this summer and who knows what might unfold the church has offered to help out if I need it, for those who know me have fallen in love with me and I never thought that would happen in my life time and it just goes to show that you never know God's plan and if you think you do just tell Him and make Him laugh. He has taken care of me through the tough times and even the good times as that's His job to take care of the ones He loves, change is right around the corner and I feel it just as I can feel the weather as it changes. during my time here things are getting better and I realize that you don't have to know it before it happens just go with it, Saturday morning' and it's nice in here as for getting the sleep I need it seams just a few hours does the trick because once three in the morning get's here I'm up. Things are different now there seams to be no arguing and that's good when little brother get's tired he goes into his room so I don't get mad from his snoring today I have too go and do the floods at work and then go to the thrift store later this afternoon to volinteer this breaks up the same old routeen and gives me a different look at things, and I like that for some reason. It was intresting that I can still get a car if I need one later down the road and that is always an option for the days here are very hot and I don't like to travel without air, just the other day we went to town and boy I got tired just from the heat blowing in my face and Randy dozed off for a few seconds.

The heat can be your worst enemy also and cause an accideent I cant count the times when others have traveled into my lane on the highway and I had to be quick in thinking, its going to be another hot one and we have to stay cool in this kind of weather as my blood pressure goes up sometimes and that's something I don't want. Through the time of wine and roses I never had to see a doctor because I wasn't aware of anything going on in my body until it was too late but now days it's caught before it can get too bad and that's a good thing, when me and Mark used too work for salvation army it was fun also and that's how he furnished his house with others want not"s. Mark is gracious at the bank as he would do just about and thing for me within reason and I will always have my house as a back up to move forward some think that if you have credit you should max it out and that isn't the case with me I weigh the prose and con's before jumping into something that way I can cover my ass because nothing good comes out of building debt and not being able to make the payments. Kathy is a fine pastor and she get's along with everyone for she is truely a great person, the other day her daughter was out sun bathing on the drive way like they do each year at this time it just goes to show that Courtland is very safe for all of us a community that would stick up for us all

I call her my little friend and that's because she also has a big heart like her mom. The people here are awesome and I love them more each year through the time's when it was hard they helped me and I am still becoming a part of this great town I have heard there are some horders that live here so that shows there everywhere not just in the big cities, my land' time is going slow today for some reason many things change when you pray and they say it can be seen as other parts of your mind starts to work it allows you to focus on things which you might not have been able to before using that special part of the mind which God intended you to use long ago, when you get caught up in the rat race of life you loose sight of prayer thus things fall by the weigh side but still even then He stays with you through it all. To bring that part of it back to you when you open your eyes, I have noticed that people get on the effencive when they feel threatened and they strike out at others to me this is wrong because it can cause other problems which wouldn't of happened other wise. But we learn and go on with life in hope that things will work them selves out over time, in this life we are all different and we all have special needs for none of us are the same. If you take away someone's dreams then you destroy a part of them and that's never any good, help them to bring their dreams to pass that way they will feel hole complete in the things they do. All through life I was told that I couldn't do this or that and it hindered my growth in many ways to stop me from growing in the right way only when I took my life back did I learn that what others have to say doesn't matter but by then time had moved on and many years had passed, time lost for learning and knowing that we are all a product of the lord. In the time I have spent here I have learned that we shape our own lives and if we are blessed then in some way we can shape some others also.

When you take care of other people we somehow let a part of us be transferred to them and weither that is good or bad depends on us as people for surely if you're a good person then they will pick up on the things they need to pick up on, my self I keep my self at a distence to observe the ways of others and learn from those I wish to learn from but there are many things I don't wish to learn which are not good to me anyway. Pride is a good thing but it can also wound a person if it's false pride, for that can lead you down a path of destruction. One where you cant see the forest from the trees and no one wants that in life. To be blinded by something false isn't a good thing. Sunday morning' they had a funeral yesterday so the thrift store was closed at noon, I didn't know the person but she must have had a lot of family and friends with the turn-out many people have lived here most of their lives and I have been here just a short time compaired to them. But I would of liked to of been raised here with the christen values, I am going to the church later this morning and see if everything got cleaned up if not I will vacuum and do other things that need to be done. I went to the church about 5:00 last night and some people were still there so this morning the early bird get's the worm and I will get things done. Most people are not even up when I am and that gives me an advantage to get a head start on matters that are important to me and others, when it comes to work I seam to enjoy it more then before and I believe it's because I'm not under pressure any longer. When I volunteer it brings me joy to learn the roapes and see how things are done.

Although I'm still new at being around people in time these things may come easier, as I get to know each one of them sort of like when I first started church here three years ago and I still don't know them all personaly but I'm more at ease around them. For the most part, my persona is different as when I write I let some see a part of my life and in person it's not so much, for when you write you can think and with people the time you spend together is quite shorter you don't have that thought process in gear for that short of a time. Randy wants a television in his room so we are going to see what it will take to accomplish that task in the coming week, they also have a television at the thrift store that they said I could have and if it works then he will be set, the thought of the motor home is still on my mind but I'm not sure if it would be a good investment should I take the chance or shouldn't I? if nothing else we would have a home on wheels to travel, people need some fun in their lives and this would give us some as we could do different things and even the thought of renting it out could generate income. Plus I could take some of the old folks to the lake on an outing so they could fish or what ever, but none of that wont happen if I don't make up my mind the taxes would be high but that would be taken care of when by renting it out for one week-end the possibilitys would be great even though the summer months are short but then you have spring and fall which can be a little chilly and it has heat to keep you warm, weighing all that it might be a good idea so I will think on it some more. And then make my final analyses I have the funds to get this thing off the ground but will it fly? I like to pray on things if I am not sure about them and hope that He will give me some advice because he has never steered me wrong yet. This opens a door to which things can move forward I could even sell my pickeled eggs and hot dog's in my motor home on the lake along with pickeled sausage hot and smoked. These are things that can rake in money once I go public, all through life I have been afraid to take that step oout of the box or comfort zone and maybe it's now time to do that…. To take a chance on something made in this world and see where it takes us, it would blow Randys mind to be able to make sure it's running good all the time and it's greased when needed it has it's own generator so it's self sufficient and can be drove anywhere even into the mountains. It's a little nippy this morning as we got some rain last night and the bush is planted where pop's is at, it looks nice by the front door and we can mowe around it with the push mower. Last night Randy came out of his room while it was raining and said God made it rain because we burried pop's and the plant needed water, what a lovely thought to have on the same day as we put him there and it goes to show that he has God on his mind this in it's self is a move forward in his learning that God loves him. For so long he has been torn between the two forces and it looks like he might make it to the other side for God loves us all and it's a shame that more people don't see it, at 5:00 this morning I'm going to go down to the church and open it as I want to be back to see Joel O'Steen at 7:00 for some reason he makes my day and gives me food for thought. Monday morning' the 21st of May I went back to church yesterday and got things taken care of and got my times when I go down to the thrift store, it's going to be a nice week and I have to mow the lawn sometime this morning. Yesterday it was too windy as I didn't want that dirt and crap blowing in my face, it seams to plug me up tighter then a drum on the other hand if I do it in the morning the wetness seams to keep that down a bit.

Monday's are a time to relax and just take it easy as for Tuesdays I get up and take out the garbage so the dog's don't scatter it around the neighborhood we really like to keep our town clean. The days seam a little shorter when I go to the thrift store and I haven't figured out why yet, maybe because there are people there but I will check it out. We never did get that couch so that's gone but I think we would be better off without it for the time being, yesterday the weather was pretty cool and I didn't have to turn on the air-conditioning that should save some on the electric bill next month. Even though it's been many years since my wine and roses days the things I learned still stay with me, but they weren't applicable in the early days of recovery because the mind was so distorted even after you get it cleared out and the healing process takes a long time even though at times you think your healed. When you go from that stage of life and take care of others you learn many things which will bring you to walk closer to God, because you cant learn it on your own patients that is for when the time is right He will give you or teach you the things you need to know. Time isn't always kind to us as people but through it all we seam to survive in this world that he put us on we are not a product of our parents although we hold some of their traits we were created in God's image like Jesus we were planted in our mother, except our mother wasn't a virgin we were conseaved through sex which lets us be what He intended us to be as we grow and learn the right's and wrongs of life. Many others besides my self believe if it isn't your time then He will not take you from this world and I have seen this many times with my own life.

For His plan is written in stone and our stories are written in the book of life, what does it say? Only the Father knows that story but one day we might be able to read it if it tickles our fancy. From what I understand our future was laid out before we were born and He will see that it follows that path even though we wonder from it sometimes, maybe we are headed for greatness and if that's the case He wont let aanyone get in the way of His plan for God holds all the power to bring things to a close when the time is right and who knows maybe this is where I will stay for the time being. They say nothing can interupt God's plan for us his children. As the days pass the changes are coming and I can feel them what will they be? My journey has taken me many places but never out of the country, why is this? Is my life blessed for surely it has to be for me to survive all the things I have survived. Taking care of mom and pop's kind of put my life on hold but why for so long could it be part of my training to get my mind set for things to come, for truly there was a reason for it that I don't understand. For He has ways that we cant even think of Him working in the super natural gives Him more. Will it bring about good things? For surely He wants what's best for us Valerie text me and boy she is getting heavy, she went from a little thing to a heavy one must be eating right or the other I wont go into but it's nice to know she is thinking about me. We had so much fun together in the time that has passed but she didn't make it into my future so she must not belong here with me. People come and they go but true friends are in your life forever if that's His plan, it's going on 5:00 Am and little brother will be up soon to start the day with a smile so much different then the years before, it's like all the negative forces are leaving and the good forces are on there way to bring joy and happiness into this place for which I live. The eyes of the lord are over the rightest, when you worry in life it takes away from your peace that He wants for you. And I had to learn that the hard way Tuesday and I feel it's going to be a hot one today as for sleep I didn't get much, now days it's still the adjusting period but most of my friends are still supportive there is three of us who lost family and two of them were husband and wife there is another Roger that lost his wife and of course the allen family that lost their dad, and I who lost pop's. The other family who lost someone I wasn't aquanted with but she had lot's of family, many of the ones who passed were up there in age like pop's being 82 years old. The time to celebrate their lives I when they are gone and you can do that by learnig to live once again and not let their passing be a stage of falling into a depression keep the mind busy so those thought don't come around and in time God will heal those things you cant deal with for the loss of a loved one is hard and for a time there will be an empty space in your heart. When others in my life have gone to heaven I used to drink those feelings away but now days that option isn't there as I travel this awesome path of life without it, I cant thank the people enough for their support in this time and their help has shown me that others do care for me here in Courtland. The community with a big heart that's what it should be called.

In all my years on this planet I have never seen such caring from others and it goes to show that when God is in your heart you learn to care for others, there is a reason why I am here and maybe it's to learn too trust others again as I kept my self from doing that for so long. As for my faith it will never falter in this lfe for I know God watches over me and gives me signals when things are not right, where will things take me in this new world for surely He has great plans for me. And I have to be able to see them when they come my way could he have opened a door when little brother came to be with me? As He truly knew that pop's time was coming way before I did and He didn't want me to be alone through this time. As I can feel the past closeing a new future is opening up, one of wonder and who knows where it might lead, many others have seen my weakest moments during this time but still stuck by me because they know what it's like to loose someone in this world. My life is full now days as I move forward into this new year and no matter how hard I try I still cant see what it will bring with it, but I know many things will change. The plant we planted is doing fine and it has new blooms on it and we put it in a place where it can be seen by all those who pass our house I look at it as a simble of strength and I know in years to come stories will be made up of how it came to be there. All small towns have quirky stories about something and my house will be one of them as we move into this coming year, I just hope it doesn't scare off the kids at Halloween. Not' they need a little excitement at that time of year as it's full of goblens and other scary things that move in the night.

My now pop's can hand out candy like he used to do except now he is in the yard and can see them coming the goast of Oliver lol mighty funny. During this time of year the weather has been different and they say it's going to be a strange year as they had a tornado in Nebraska in Feb' this is the first time ever this has happened and with it brings change but what change I don't have a clue or who knows maybe it may be no different then the years before just a freak incident that occurred by nature it's self, when I first learned to live in this life so different then the last one I was scared because all things were different from the life of elusion and in that world you shaped it to suit your needs even though you were always broke by keeping it going not being able to save for a raining day when things can fall apart. God showed me that all the worry in the world cant change things, it just adds to your misery and were not mean't to live that way. This place brings people together to some how bring common ground to everyone and that is a great thing in this life as we move forward one people that created this place so long ago and it's still growing today over 100 years later the people here come from all walks of life but most are just trying to survive in this world the southern bell has been here for 17 years and others just as long maybe trying to find that balance in life where you don't have to worry so much that peace which He can bring to us when we need it most in life. Through the years that I was in other places I never found that peace until I came here and even then it was hard to aquire until I found out where I needed to be, Walt was a great help in my making this my home and he opened some doors for me as he was in the same situation when he first came here all those years ago and now my home is just that my home, the beauty is everywhere around here from the birds singing to the squirrles playing in the yard and the rabbits eating the clover such a sight to see. There are other animals around here also just a few weeks ago I saw a lion cross the road on our way back from Belleville, I just got a climps of it out side Scandia when it ducked into the brush after crossing the road. I could tell it wasn't a domestic animal like a cat because it was too big and moved too fast, it seams they are getting closer to towns maybe to find food more easily as it has to be hard to find it out in the dust bowl. The privlage to live here is all mine in a way it reminds me of when mom and dad had their home they were buying a tight nit community who looked out for each other but the place they once had is gone now and others have takenover it as Los-Angles has grown so much, no more quiet communitys exist there anymore for the years have changed so much. A friend visited where we used to live, and while she was there a gang came over and took things out of her friends home and her fiend said it happens all the time what a way to live. And this was 15 or so years ago I couldn't imaging how it is today, Wednesday and I work for a couple of hours today but it's no big thing and I have some things I'm going to take down with me so they can make some money I don't want too be dependent on the caring of others as that's not me but I do like to help out when I get the chance. As time and space changes so will I and who knows what we will see in the future, many times I have been called a beyounder someone who draws this strength from the heavens and not the universe like others do you might say they said while others draw from the stars with their horoscope being in different places.

As I great each day with a prayer it's others that I pray for and not so much for my self for those who have showed kindness towards me, it's going to be a hot one today but not as hot as Saturday so that's something to be grateful for. During the day I don't write as much as I used to but that's because I find plesent times during the day when I just want too sit back and relax for this feeling is new to me and I enjoy it very much, there are man things you shouldn't do when your fighting addiction and one is to not let anyone have control of your feelings while your going through this tough fight because it can make you fall back into it others can destroy what you have created and it can start by just a few words when your self esteem is low others can try to rain on your paraide thus causing you to fall back into the drug or alcohol addiction I tried this once and she had somehow gotten control because I fell in love with her, she drank everyday and I didn't drink at all causing a conflect between us and it didn't last long before I had to get out of there. Somehow God let me know that the two worlds didn't belong together because they were made up of two different things and one of them had almost destroyed me before, this in it's self caused me to shut down when it came to people that dwell in the spirit world where I don't belong any longer. Through the years I could tell people that drank and did drugs so I kept to my self mostely trying to preserve the gift that God gave me and it worked knowing He was there for me companionship didn't seam to matter after a while and maybe that was because pop's was there to keep me company, someone to talk to when I had a bad day or a good one companionship is important and it allows us to vent to others besides our selves.

My land' when I moved here we had all kinds of trouble with Oliver's health and I was beside my self not knowing what to do in a emergency thank goodness I has friends who know what too do. When I started to care for Walt I think pop's got jelouys and made him self go down hill a bit but then he poped back an became strong once again to drive the nurces nuts at the hospital, I know they couldn't wait to get rid of him and then one nurse asked if I could handle him and I told them that they had seen him sick but this is the way he acts when he is well. And it was a delight to see him in that condition which meant he was ready to go home. His health lasted a while about a year before he became ill once more but I caught it early and med's took care of that and we went on to enjoy our lives here where we belong. He said he never wanted to leave Courtland so he rest's here where he belongs, now I have three guardien angles watching over me these days and as time allows it I will become stronger then ever. Does God look out for us? I truly believe He does and He wont leave us alone for He brought Randy here because he knew pop's was coming to be with him in heaven and I would have gone nut's without someone near, all of us are no further then 100 years from going to be with God and some even closer and there are many things that we have to learen before we get there but what they are eludes me at this time maybe it will come to me in the future, as I grow older in this life. The motor home sticks in my mind and also Randys so we will see if they still have it, it's something we could live in when they do the floors in the house and there are many other things we can do like fishing and camping and maybe even take some youths on a camping trip from time to time this would be a delight to them also it will have storage space to put in a tent and other things we might need. Something tells me that it would be a good investment with the lake just a few miles down the road and it would get us out of the house for some time to be with mother nature. Change is unavoidable and it's coming wither we change with it or not is up to us but it's coming just the same, I learned a long time ago that there is good change and there is not so good change but I like to change for the good to maybe bring in some money to pay bills and keep everything on track. There is nothing wrong with asking it in this world and I will make it one way or another, most of the people here have campers and not motor homes so they have to haul them to where they will sleep at the lake and I wont all I have to do is get into it and drive and if the car breaks down then I will have it fixed so many things I can do with a little freedom, to let my spirit sore beyond the heavens and come down for a landing. Sounds like a fairy tail but it would be exciting I find that it's hard to start a conversation not knowing what to say sometimes so I try my best and hope I get it right. With family it isn't hard but wih others it's quite a chore I had a guy check out the motor home and he is supposed to let me know if it's worth the money to get it other then that it's up in the air for right now, my friends don't want to see me get ripped off and either do I the adventages of livinng in a careing community is greater then lving anywhere else and the careing continue's the thrift store was boring but it's something to do.

And in time that might change I got a text from Valerie last night and she sent me a picture of her, my how things change in just a few years. Also we closed early yesterday because there wasn't any business and one of the workers had to go to the senior center for some get together, she has to walk where she goes and boy was it hot but I have a feeling she does it all the time. In the waiting chamber many things run through your mind but when you can focous on other things then it isn't so bad, one of the women has lived here most of her life and I know her husband Greg they are the farming people in which I talk about very humble. Getting to know how to communicate will be a task but in time it will come to be a thing that was once hard to do but not so much anymore the wind is blowing hard this morning like all get out, and you can tell a storm is coming from somewhere my friend said that they started to irragate the crops because it was so dry so they are hoping for rain to ease the burden of having to irrigate, I hope they get their rain and I hope they have a good crop this year also like last year. When everyone else had it bad not that I want them to have another bad one because they all need the crops to be good to survive in this economy my land' the one women has lived here for over 30 years and she likes it out on the farm. I can see her helping her husband when he needs a helping hand for they are great people, many of the farmers rent the land from others as Jack did so long ago. He is still in my mind from time to time and I really lked him and Louella such great people also, the last I heard his family was helping him with the farming and that was about 8 or so years ago.

The time has moved so fast over the years but that's ok we are only here for the time that God allows and then we go and be with him in that special place he has prepared for us. Although the motor home would be nice if it isn't meant to be then it isn't as we really don't need any other bills right now. But through it could bring great joy for us and others if they so choose to want to go to the lake for the weekend and not rent a cabbon, I know Marks concern and it's valid he wants to see how things will be infected with Oliver gone from this earth will we be able to pay ourr debts and this is something which will be taken care of. I should always listen to my reasoning because it guides me in this world and although it hasn't let me down yet it could if I'm not careful. I wonder how long my secret will take care of me will it bring me through these hard times or will I fall on my face not likely, but there is always that chance if we stray away from what is important survival has always been my goal in this life and I have done it just by getting by and I think God wants more for us, He would want us to grow as we get older and bloom like he flower to become something beautiful a sturdy rock for which we can stand on that wont crumble from the pressure in Belleville the telescope said they would publish my book but they want a lot of money is more better or is short better? That is the question, things are working out in many ways and if I have patients things will come around. But I cant jump the gun when it comes to decision making bad influences can make or break you and once your broke then it can take a long time to get fixed once again, and during that time you don't know what will take place. So maybe it's better to stay in the safe zone for a time many of my friends thought I would move away but that isn't the case here, as Courtland is my home many other have survived here and so will I. When I watch things I'm very observant and when a couple plays tricks on each other it's usualy the women that get's perturbed and I find that to be funny, but when the shoe is on the other foot then they fight what is wrong with this picture? He takes off and goes fishing while she stews and get's angry not wanting to admit that she played the same prank on him, my conclushion is not to play such games in life as it will bring conflict that doesn't want to be there my land' it sounds like a dear A.B. letter to her fans. Through the years many have come to the breaking point when it looked like there was no way out so they grab the thing which makes them forget and there is no better way to destroy the mind and body then to fall for that thing called alcohol and drug addiction. In a life long gone it was always easier to grab that forgetfullness and hide from the real world, it allows you to feel like your protecting your self when in reality your not. Through the many years I became lost and at first didn't know how to find my self, then God spoke to me saying all will become clear as you walk the path I have set in front of you. I have not ever been on this path it was new to me and the confusion was great trying to straighten out a life that had lived so long in that world. I couldn't talk to others about it because no person that has not lived in that world would understand so I did the best I could and went on with life, they say there is good and evil but even in that world I didn't seam to cross that line to evil. It was strange because others would come to me for refuge a place where they could feel safe it was like my courage came from the addiction and that's all I took out of it, that feeling of being strong beyond belief. And I never had any enemies they would come to me because I was different and wouldn't judge them for what they had done, but also I had to protect my self by turning some of them away because I never got in trouble while I was in that world.

There were many that wanted what I had but they weren't willing to go that extra mile to try to change their lives and them being around me brought with it trouble. So with my change came a new family of friends but they were different like me in many ways instead of the addiction having control I not took control of my own life and started down a new path but with it came fright as I had never felt fear before and it's something I don't care for. Around every corner I felt it but it wasn't something I couldn't over come and in time I did, many people who I thought were my friends weren't they used me to try to get a head in the other world and for that and other reasons they were taken away to not return. When I found out that little brother was so ill at first I thought he was one of them and then in time God showed me that he was to be brought here and it reminded me of a saying in the bible if you denie your brother I will also denie you and then it started the bringing of him to this place. The first time I saw him I had to hold back the tears because he didn't look too good he was twice as big as he used to be but not in a healthy way, just the trip took a lot out of me but we got him home to where he will be safe. I could see the scars that were inside as he talked in his sleep and yelled at people who weren't there, this went on for months until he grasped that he was no longer there behind those bars the things he went through must have been hard on him but now his worries are over as long as he sticks to the plan and sees his parole officer once a month. In the shaddows there is always someone watching over us and if you do good then things will happen in a good way, the summer is a strange one and you cant tell how it will turn out until it passes but I pray for a good crop this year for my friends and church family.

As this year is supposed to be the end of the world for which I don't believe many are building bom shelters such a fools game to make money from them that can afford it, anything to make money as it's the root to all evil if not used in a good way. Since the beginning of time when they first made money people have killed over it to posses it seams to bring them great power in their minds anyway, many of the rich run this country even still today and they deside who runs for office when the time comes and those who win are like a puppet on a string doing what the rich tell them to do. In centeries past they have ran the show staying in the shaddows just out of reach to bail out others who have become rich after ripping off the people for their rights all our forefathers would roll over in their graves if they could see how they have destroyed the constitution with reading things into it that were never there and the changing of things by a word that was never ment to be turned around. All gimics to trick the people as many of them are not strong in their own minds, as we move forward things will change but it will be up to us if that change is going to be good or bad in the twilight of the night I can see the stars glowing off in the distence and it lets me know that He is still at work making our lives better then they were before we being only people have a problem with reading too much into things of no significant meaning but it's all good in the end we just waste a lot of time which could be used for something else. Some say we travel back down the road we leave behind and I believe this is true but to what extent is it so we can look over what we have learned, or is it a glimps of what once was and how we changed. In this world we all make mistakes and He lets us learn by them in the beginning I was like a child being taught the christen way of life and it wasn't easy at first as things came to me like it would a child first crolling and then standing and finely walking to learn the next step. Little brother is still crolling but it wont be long before trust comes into the picture the trust of others as he makes his walk through life, when you move to a new place it's like life starts over once again and I don't want to do that anymore the picking up the pieces and starting over somewhere else is not in my life at this time or ever again. It's not oftend when you are excepted into a community and then life get's good for one more time, as for the motor home I have desided not to get it because it wasn't practical to pay out that much money for the use of it only a few times a year in the end I will have no regrets. The paying off the house is my first thing to do as I walk through this life then things will get easier as time passes this world is one in which you have to look out for your self to get a head other wise you will fall and louse everything, many fall from grace but the good thing is that you can get it back if you ask.

It's now Friday and it's the beginning of a holiday a three day holiday memorial day to be exact and many people will be going to the lake so they can camp and have a good time, they say the fishing is great but we will not be going until maybe later in the year. There will be many times when we can go but it get's mighty hot in this deselent place, Dennis is doing good since his heart problem has been taken care of but he has to take it easy for a time to fully recover. The birds are singng this morning and it started a while ago it brings the day to a good start just listening to them as they make their music such a delight to hear them as they go through the day even in the afternoon you can still hear the joy of them singing for they are God's creachers part of the bigger picture if you will. The car hasn't given us much of a problem lately so maybe it was from over filling the water tank on the side that caused it to over flow, Saturday being it's a holiday the thrift store wont be opened today so I have the day to my self. I mowed for a while yesterday and got the worst of it or did it get me with the wind blowing all the cuttings into my face, such a delima to cut it or not but it got done for the most part. The slight rain we got yesterday didn't amount to much as it was gone as fast as it got there sucked into the ground like a spunge and it didn't help at all, as we went to town you could see the center pivits running like hell and the wind carring it far from where they expected to go.

I think if they get some rain they will be ok the corn crop is in the ground and doing fine as it's already three or four inches high like a baby getting ready to come out of the womb at birth, it's strange how thing grown and pop their heads up through the earth like they are reaching for the stars for truly this is nature at it's finest and it feeds so many people as we go through this world. I never thought of such things in the other world because it was always there for us not wanting for food was in it's self a blessing but back then you couldn't see it the things we used to take for granted have somehow shown them selves and that's why I write about them, through life we take so much for granted and then later see it as we grow older the weather is humid this morning and you can feel the humity in the air not very good but atleast we have a machine that will take it out of the air in the house and that's a good thing. Harley had too go out this morning and he didn't stay out long so I realed him in like a fish on a pole and then he was happy, I cant count the times in which I have been so happy in one place but I am here and little brother helps with that as there isn't a day that goes by in which we don't laugh and that iss a blessing in it's self. He was telling me that he said something to his niece and I asked why he would want to plant a seed like that in someones mind because it wouldn't be something that I would plant. You should only plant good seeds not the others that will hurt someone but some people do it and maybe that's because they are not happy with the way things are going in their own life, it tells a story about them and how they really feels, when it comes to life. For this is something I couldn't do to others and I chalk it up to inexperience with communication between him and others, not being able to talk much with christen people has left him open to all kinds of things. But in time they will learn not to judge others if they too don't want to be judged as that's something only God should do. My life has been a private one even with what has happened in the younger years and the only reason I'm writing this is to bring others to believe that our triles can produce fruit, it's not so much what happened as to why it happened. And now days the lessons learned can help others to over come their addictions, in many ways I could be like others and only change my life but if I can help those who lost faith then it's my job to try and help in someway. This started by a gift a gift to be able to write and I didn't nderstand it at first but now I know it can bring comfort to some fighting the same fight, many say that alcohol and drugs have been here since the beginning of time and it has but also other things have been here just as long like murder but it doesn't make it right to go out and kill others some are self centered and only think of them selves they feel that if they over come something it shouldn't be shared and it's wrong but that's my opinion and not theirs. In other words change your self and let others fall and chalk it up to being blessed. This to me is narrow mindedness and will never help others that have fallen, it Says we should leave our mark on this world something to where others can learn and if you hord it all to you're self then it diies with you. In the beginning Jesus helped many people and he didn't pick out certain ones that didn't sin for we all sin in one way or another, and at the end of the day if we help just one person then it's good. What would of happened if I ignored the wanting of help from my little brother? Would he of ever got it, in my opinion no' he would still be in that place louseing the will to live as he had already done.

For the love of a brother runs deep and if you can help him in some way you better well do it. When children wonder off to try new things it's not always a certain thing that they will come in contact with the bad elements, I have seen fathers who drink and go to church but somewhere in the mix of things their child can get mixed signals and think it's alright to dabble in the spirits. Why' because dad did it and he was a good man, there isn't any difference between alcohol and drugs it's just that one is legal and the other isn't they have been fighting this debate for centuries and with many it gives them the excuse to go into one world and back again thinking it's ok, many children die each year from being run over because of drunk drivers and their excuse is that I didn't know what I was doing at the time. I havee seen judges that were busted and then let off because of who they were. This in it's self might not mean much to some but the familys suffer because of it, many times in the mountains I drove drinking as a young kid but the influences that were around me meaning a parent figure did the same so I thought it was all right but it wasn't and I'm grateful that no one was ever hurt because of me. It was like a way of life for those who were around me and their battle started many years before I was even born, it was like I was being shown something and I just didn't get it at the time. Those times over shadowed the times when I was a child of three years it was like the days of going to church were wiped out of my mind and they didn't return until my later years when that part of life was gone, it was only when I stopped destroying my life that I realized it was time to move on and get away from that curse that followed me for so long. You could call it the awakening of a souls that had been a sleep.

Through the years I tried to mend what had been broken through my writing's to find out why some follow the path of destruction, and with many. They have never lived any other kind of life except for that one it's bread into them by parents when they see it on a daily bases, and they figure out that if their parents use it when they become weak them more then likely they too will follow that path. Don't get me wrong' good parents become weak sometimes and they don't know what to do and the availability of alcohol gives them something to try, and in many cases it works but only for a short time then when it wares off the problem comes back and it starts all over once again. I don't have and probable never will have all the answers but I do know that you cant hide in a bottle, because one day you will have to croll out of it and I mean that literaly. I have had all that He gave me taken away to later be given back once I got on the right path but what a journey, no one knows the pain I have suffered to get where I am on thus day but life is getting better as I move forward and who knows in time those memories will one day be gone also and the only record of it will be this that I am writing today, I truly believe that our lives are recorded in the book of life which God has with him. The length of the writing isn't something that important it's the message that is brought out so others can learn from them, it's now Sunday and it's muggy out side making it a place you don't want to be as you sweat your keaster off in it. The time is coming when things will be brought to light about our lives and how we handeled things, for this journey has been a long one from where I was to this place of peace w all have a destanation and a time when we need to be there and He makes it possible for these things to come to be, but what are they? What is the secret to life to be happy and enjoy what He has given us or learn from our mistakes and move on to better things which will come later down the line for surely we cant see the future..As I watch some movies I find that some people are nut's and where they come up with the ideas for them is out of this world, being on the out side looking in it makes me want to stay away from such things. For truly the minds that think this stuff up is out there, but they are writers just reaching for something out of the ordinary to make movies to show the people how some of the world is. People destroying people just for power and fame their 15 minutes of fame which doesn't last long, when I talk to some people I find my self at a loss for words so I don't say anything just stare off in another direction pretending to look interested at what's happening out side, as it's hard to find things to talk about when the other person hasn't lived in your world. People skills is important and I think that's why they had me volinteer at the thrift store, but it may work in time as for now it doesn't and that's because I'm not a talker like some I know staying in my comfort zone has always been my way. And I don't let many people in that place which is mine, even as a child I weighed my thoughts before voicing my opinion and it hasn't let me down even through the tough years.

It's the beginning of a new week tomorrow and sometimes it get's boring sitting around and watching television but by the living of the day things become better, I need to find other things to do with my time maybe go and visit the guy down the block. From what I understaand he is in his 80's and his wife was going to ask me to come over but forgot to ask, the elderly need friends also as they take that walk into the other world where they will find happiness. I don't know why but they seam to like me for some reason and just a visit from time to time can change things for them like playing cards or just talking and listening to their stories about how they came to live in this fine town. Monday memorial day' and it like any other Monday hot and humid as the day progressed yesterday the wind blew really hard and I thought it would blow in some rain but it didn't some at church said they have never seen May this dry and last year it wasn't the lawns around here are very dry so smokers should watch where they are smoking as for me I always watch and make sure they are put out before disgarding them. We went to bed early so we could relax and watch some television before we went to sleep, and as usual I was up during the night. I will try and change my sleeping habbits but it's not going to be easy getting up at three in the morning has become a way of life for me over the years and it gives me my time to be alone away from conflect and other things. The ability to stop drinking took a lot out of me through the years but it has also made me strong in some way's like learning to write and have people hear my words, through the end I will never stop writing.

In this time when they say the world will end in December because of an old calander the Miens created and this I don't believe because only He knows the date of when that will take place. It's another attempt for science to prove them selves and they wont, just like they tried to say we evolved from apes what a crock of crap we are all created by God and that's just the way it is. And no matter how hard they try they will never prove any different it says give to caser what is his, and give to God what is His. Meaning this world belongs to the father but that's just my opinion on the matter. It's very nice in my home this morning as I don't have to deal with the heat and things are good for the most part, in church the pastor said only about half the people here in Courtland go to church which is fifty percent but the other half doesn't know God for some reason and I do know when tragiity happens some blame Him for their loss which isn't the case He gives them internal life if they choose it even after they have left this world, they get a chance here and then again when they leave this place we all seam to call home.

Our real home is in heaven this is just a place where we mature before going there and in time we will be brought back to live here for eternity, it say's He created this world for us for ever and I don't think he will destroy it. Wakeing up at this time of day let me find the things which I have questions too and I hope He will answer them in time, is time on our side well in some aspects yes. But in others no for it seams we never have enough time to do the things we need to do in this world in my time here I have missed only a couple of days at church because of illness and now I know what caused it to happen but just going was a challenge as the devil has me always questioning my self but those days are gone as I learned to shut him out, for only God is allowed to inter my domain as I don't like the other it's as if he is like the old addiction taken away to not return in this spirit it would be nice if we could connect with that spirit that dwells within us. To see it's ability it has to change on our level and not his, is this body truly a house that will return to the earth when it's done learning for I know our spirit can travel to other places because I have felt mine do it and that other place wasn't here. I floated around like a goast with no body on that day so long ago and I was ashured that others go to that place where I went by seeing them and they were souls from long ago. I usually don't talk about it because no one can connect with what I saw heck it's hardly something I can talk about so I know how they feel, but it doesn't change the fact that it happened and it changed my life in a lot of ways. Melchisedek and the search for epiphany changed many things and it showed me that the lesser is better then the great for Melchisedek wasn't even mentioned at the slater of the Kings in many of the stories but he recived one tenth of Abram's spoils what a great thing to happen. For someone who's mother or father wasn't even mentioned in the bible, the King of Salem which is the King of peace. Brought forth bread and wine to Abram and he was the priest of the most high God which many people don't know, even today it's not talked about because the scribes cant figure it out and it's up for debate. Usually these things get dissolved but I haven't heard of it yet, will it always be a question that lingers in the back of peoples minds or will it be brought to light somewhere down the road? I have heard that someone clames to be Melchisedek somewhere here in the United States but this I cant believe as He wouldn't of waited this long to bring it to peoples attention.

And what would be the point for him to show up at this time to secure that what we believe is something that's true. I have only told of this storie but once or twice to people who have been in the other world and surely they couldn't get it out there, I have learned that the mind only needs so much sleep and then it gets restless wakeing up for the day to start a new one. And it doesn't matter what the hours are as for me if I get up before most people and I cant seam to stop it going on 20 years it's become a fixture in my mind getting at least ten hours seams to be enough and then the search continues to find things that can help others with their addictions, but why so many years you have to see things unfold or at least I do. Tuesday morning and I'm barely awake. We had an argument yesterday about something's and I got very up set it seams he doesn't understand about bills and how they have to be paid, to meke it in this world. His lack of responsibility over the years has left him thinking the worng way, so that has to be fixed someway and

I will try to help him if I can. Being away and having everything paid for he never got to learn about paying bills as he had three hot's and a cot with no worries, my little brother welcome to the real world. In many ways he has never learned about paying bills as Rosemarry used to pay them all and he didn't learn how to do such things. Its going to be something he will have to learn, he thinks he cant make it on a few hundred dollars for a month because he smokes and that takes a big portune of it. If we put our minds together we could quit with the help of some of the things which are out there.

And the doctor could help with getting them underway my land he never smoked in the place he was in and he did just fine, but freedom brought the idea back once he got out. If I had eight years of not somking I would of never gone back to it, but that's just me. Our pastor smoked many years ago and now she is having trouble with her lungs after not doing it for so many years so does what they say stop what will happen in the future I don't think so. If the lungs are damaged then they will stay that way and maybe not bother you until later in life, Mark O'Brien's mom quit thirty years ago and is now in her 80's and the damage is just starting to bother her it seams to wait until you are in your later years to take hold if you quit. So it's like rolling the dice wither it will destroy you in the end, the old man at the hospital said he was 92 years old and he had smoked for 75 years with no problem and he wasn't about to stop. I think it has to do with your body tipe as if you are over weight or caring a big load, I have had trouble with my lungs for quite some time but the situation seams to pass with an inhailor once in a while. Even though quitting would be the best thing, I have yet the strength to stop the dirty habbit so I will ask God for help and then maybe He can give me a hand there are many things which He can help us with that we don't ask because they seam so trivel to us but we have to break down that guard and ske for help. Through the time of change he will guide us to where we need to be will I be able to not use the inhailer only He knows the answer to that question, my faith has brought me a long ways and if He would help me with this it would only make it stronger. I find my self missing pop's from time to time as the old habbits are hard to break getting up each day and getting things ready for the day as he slept, the mind has to be reprogrammed to except change and although I'm willing to except that fact it will take time for it to happen, we set our sights on many things but only accomplish a few of them as we go through life and there is no turning back the clock at this point we just do what we can do and hope it's enough. I have learned that change comes gradually and if your lucky then it will come full circle, to lift the burden that once hung over your head as for some things they will remain until it's time to let them loose so we can grow further in our christen life. I have learned many things here in Courtland' and one is to be true to your self as you go through this life, and other things will take care of them selves I'm in hope that I will see family members later this year but with the price of things I'm not sure if they will come here or I will go there for truly His love will let me do one or the other so I can have a change of pace to make my life not so garded, I cant get over how my friends protect me from making mistakes when it comes to motor vehicles. For Mark truly wants me to not make a mistake and get a lemon that will fall apart but little does he know that I can pick out my own car as I am mechanically inclined and have never made a bad deal on a car, I talked with Herb last week and he said he wass sorry for my loss of Oliver and I thanked him for his consern. I really like him as he reminds me of my dad the only one I ever knew and they even have the same name, my father has been gone for fourty some years and if he had lived he would be Herbs age now. But his memory is still there even after all these years, we had so much fun together when I was a child. But age has taken on something different and he is just a memory a spirit which looks over me during this time.

I wonder if we have more then one angel who watches over us and if we do then I should have many, a love lost' many years ago a women fell in love with me but there was a problem she was married to my brother who was in prison. We got along so well that we felt like we were a part of each other but still the problem remained she was my brothers wife, during the time she stayed with me we never crossed that line but I have to say that it did cross my mind. She was like that soul mate for whom you could live out your life with and there was never any argueing between us, so many times I wanted to make love to her but that problem stopped me dead in my tracks. My brother wasn't so gracious as he married my X wife after we split up and they never got along I couldn't figure out why he would find her so loving but he did or maybe it was an ego trip knowing he could have something I once had, but I couldn't do that to him why? Morals I think anyway the women I fell in love with would later die by a hit and run driver on a highway late at night walking to get a tire fixed she had a tear drop on the side of her eye and blond hair she was a loving soul and he never deserved her. She was full of life until it was cut short on that black night so long ago, she stayed high all the time and we did it together while he was locked up and then he got out and treated her like crap by beating her when he would run out of drugs. It didn't take long until she left him and moved away to try and get her life straightened out, and that's when it happened.

Could I have made a difference? probably but I didn't like conflect within the family and he could be a handfull, many times we fought because he thought I thought I was better then him which wasn't the case. I didn't like to be around him because he got people in trouble with the law and that curse followed him around for most of his life, to this day I havent seen him since I moved and he has fallen into his old ways he also found out that he had a daughter which wasn't expected and I hope she has some influence with him but when they met for the first time he didn't look so good. The years have not been good to him and it shows with his body falling apart two hip replacements and other medical problems which will end his life before it's time. He has two sons which one got hooked on drugs and life hasn't been good to him either as he has Aids or the H.I.V. Virus although medication can extend life it's not a good life having to be checked all the time to see if it has gotten worse, my land' he is so young but the up side is that his brother turned out to be quite a man going into the service and fighting for his country. He is the only one that ever went into the service and liked it, I saw my X wife many years later about 30 years later and she got big so big that she has to order her clothes from the tent and awning company. We were young when we married and didn't know any better but the years taught us that we didn't belong together, from the words I do' she tried to control me which didn't work when your only 18 years of age. I didn't know it then but I still had a lot of rambeling to do and she was in the way of me having a good time, which by the way didn't stop me from shopping around. Then I met Stacy and thought she was the one but later that would turn into a desaster because two alcoholics don't get along except for sex, and that wasn't enough to tie the tie that binds we spent 8 years together and she wanted me to merry her which wasn't going to happen through the loss of my son I went into a depression and really didn't come out of it until my daughter was born. And then she became the apple of my eye, we were going through a hard time then because it wasn't working I spent most of my time working but loved being around her when I was off work it was always nice to get her the things I never had and then within a couple year's or son was born their names were Shannon and Leroy still upset she didn't give them my last name so they were raise as O'Brien's. My first son was named after me and had my last name Roger Leroy Mattson Jr, and is in the cemetery in Kearney Nebraska. Wednesday morning' and yesterday morning was pretty cool during the morning hours but then it got hot once again our part of the State only got showers the other day not amounting to much but every little bit helps, it's very dry for this time of year it only being May but I'm optimistic that the rain will come when it's needed most. Today I go down to the thrift shop and I have some old things to bring down there they call them new old things but someone can use them, through the time I spend down there I see different people and I like that part of the work but I have yet to see the Spanish people who come through there to get clothes for loved ones in Texas. There are many different people here and I haven't met them all but only half the town go to church services and the rest well they do their own thing to stay busy, we are all contected in some way if not by church then by the life I once lead for many people are caught up in that world.

And don't know how to get out of it, that is a world for which I don't even like to visit because it's so easy to make the wrong assumption. Even the younger people can get caught up in the rat race of life and fall very hard to only pick them selves up later in life when most of it is gone, sure the aspects of life goes on as they have children and such but the odds of their children having kids that are addicted is great as the curse is passed down through generations. It can skip a whole generation and not show it's self until it's ready and this happens quite oftend with our children even presidents have had a hard time with alcohol addiction even president Bush, and he ran our country while going through this addictive stage in life but then he had too choose between his family and the booze and choose family. Any one who is honest with them selves and others will admit that it's easier to take the easy way out of something and addiction lets people do that so they don't have to face their problems, but what they don't realize is that the problem that caused it will be the first one to show it's self when they try to take their life back and it has to be solved before you can go on. Putting it off just causes more problems and when you bury your self in them then you don't know how to get out of them many piled on the other until they are so mixed up that you forgot which one caused the problem, lack of self worth is a strong one that get's people because it makes them depressed and instead of getting out of that they choose to go deeper into it by alcohol or drugs which lets them leave this world for a short time anyway.

In my early years I didn't have strength to ask out a girl unless I was boozed up and I would get that way for just that purpose then once it happened I would back off of the booze and see where it would lead, courage in a bottle as I called it and it worked so I never did change it as it made it easy to get the girl. But what a mess it caused when she found out that I wasn't the person she met just a ccouple of days ago, and they would ask where he went because they liked him. It was like living in two worlds and I spent most of my time in the one that let me escape reality, because this one I live in today is much different from the one of destruction in that one you didn't have too anwser to anyone so you could let your problems go but they never left you, they stayed in waiting until they were solved. How could a person live in both worlds? As time went on it became harder to stay out of this one of reality as the other took over and I became lost in it the reasons were clear I just couldn't deal with the real world until the other was destroyed and that's what I had to do. So the other world had to be destroyed and it would take an act of God to do it, I then became a disaster of my own demise and pushed it to the limit. Thus crippling my self by the curse, they gave me six months before I pushed it and after that until morning if that long but God had different plans for me when he came to me while I visited that place far from here, it was like nothing I had ever seen and I knew my body didn't matter while I was there. It was like He was showing me that I do have a place to go when my time is up here on earth and not to be afraid of death because God had me in his hand. Although I experienced these things I learned that if it isn't your time then He wont take you, you will be returned to learn the things you were supposed to learn. I liked it when He said your journey hasn't even started yet but you will know when it starts. For this gave me hope that there is a bigger picture of my life and what will become of it, only He the Father knows when things will unfold as everyone of us has a purpose in this life. The giving up became a thing of the past and He brought me to where I needed to be, the journey to this day has been a long one but I am known all around the world for my writings. And I believe this was his plan. As you give of your self He returns to you what is yours, although I have traveled many pathes this one seams to be the most important so far and it's one of giving and helping other through these hard times in life. I could have been like others and thought of only my self but that's not who I am, I'm the giver of things which I have control of. Knowledge is important but it's useless unless it's shared and in the mist of things if you help just one person then it's all worth it, as a child I was told that I would do great things but being a child I never did pay any mind to it. The human body is only a vessel to bring about life but it's God who says if it's good or not and believe me if it wasn't good then we wouldn't be here, we are spirits created by God and housed in these bodies so we can full-fill our journey on this place we call earth. In reality many don't make it to where they should be and this is caused by many factors which we as people bring on our selves. Thursday and things went well at the thrift store yesterday as we watched the storm come in and when we saw that we weren't going to have any business in that two hours we closed up early. The story dropped quite a bit of rain and the thunder cracked like a lion tamer poping his wipe although it didn't last but an hour or so I'm sure the fields got a little soaked at least near here to Courtland.

It was just yesterday that I ask Him for a sign that He hears me, and two things happened the rain and little brother wanting to quit smoking as I do. I ask for the sign's because I need assurence that He is with me and hears my prayers, and He came through with flying colors. The ground has been dry lately and they needed the rain the puddles in the streets were full so it took a little time to sink in, now thingss should go pretty good in that department. It was an isolated storm and I hope we get some more later down the road but just the rain not all the other crap. This will be our first month since pop's passed that we will see if we can make it and I'm optimistic that it will happen even though things will be tighter then before we as people have a survivls instinct that kicks in when we are backed against a wall and that is working now as we move forward. My home is a place where love is all the time my peace of mind does exist here and I enjoy it very much, through the times when things get hard the church has offered to help and in time I will have to take them up on their offer which is a good thing, the thrift store is getting better as I go when my time is scheduled and I even enjoy talking to others as they tell their stories about life, but they only give a little about it and that's ok. Being a writer I listen more then talk it's like I'm searching for that one story that I can write about, the one story which will bring another chapter to this journey in life. Each day brings something new and usually you don't know what it will be but so far it's been good and it makes me wonder how they survived back in the old days of 1858, well in many ways it was much simpler then no cars to drive or gas worries.

People where traveling from Courtland too Belleville in a wagon and it must have taken a day to get there and back and they would have had too stock up on food to make it through a month for I believe they didn't travel every week unless they were well off and had others do it for them. I can survive in my new home town even if I have too rent out a room but I don't think little brother would like that thought so I wont address it at this time we will see how it goes in the future. Having out siders come into my house would cause some problems and I don't like stinky feet which most people have as for us it doesn't exist in our family, I remember taking in a friend too help him out and boy his feet did stink bad and it was very unpleasant the thought of that happening again turns off the notion of having someone live here. For we are all different in many ways but being clean is a must in my domain, I oftend think about the days of the horse and buggy and how they made it through the ruff times for they were truly pioneers trying to tame the country that would later become Courtland Kansas' many of the old people lived during the depression and they made it to today and it makes me wonder if they had the curse of alcohol here back then seeing this was a place so far out of the way. We hear about how it was in New York with the gangsters but you never hear about small towns which were starting out at that time or just starting to grow. I have a feeling that Courtland has always been a peaceful place but I could be wrong only the old folks would know for sure how it grew to become the place it is today, it's like a time capsel preserved for the future and the people are the same way as they like things the way they are with just a little growth from time too time to stay up with things that are happening, my friend that owns the thrift store is very nice but I think she works to much being in her later years she is up at the break of dawn and works all day long but that might be what keeps her in good health running a business is a lot of work, and it's a big place with many employees taking care of your own is what it's all about. When I first got here she told a person that she thought I was a nice man which I am and it wa the first time I had a complament like that when I took care of Walt I had to go over there to find out what to do when he was ill, and they called the unit to check him out come to find out he took too much of his med's and was sleeping so they didn't take him to the hospital. Shortly afterwords he left to be with his daughter in his last days and dies after his 70th birthday, he lived longer then they thought he would and that was because he was a fighter a short man like me but he had a heart of gold may you rest in peace my friend. After he left I talked to him a few times but then my calls were never returned and I chalked it up to his illness but I know he must of thought about me from time to time as he looked at the Fosse-Troll that I sent with him to remind him of our good times when we had coffee together. He was my friend and will always be in my heart, he liked to take fishing trips to Canada with friends and I wish I could of known him back then and seen the excitement on his face when he caught one of those big fish I bet he was like a kid when he got some ice-cream.

Through life we all go to a better place once we leave this place but it's our choice if we except God as out saviour, many wont do this and for them well I say it's your loss for God is good and loves us all. The connection I had as a child somehow stuck with me even through the years as today I still remember the three year old child playing in the gravel out side the church before service, that was a connection which stuck with me even though it went away for a time because of the life I lead. I am living proof that the mind can be healed with time but it takes the love of God for it to happen, as He created everything we are. Many believe that we can heal our selves but I give credit to God for my miracles and He guides my life on this last part of my journey. How many stories will arise out of this life was I sent here to maybe change something in others that they have given up on? Or will this show them that hope is always near as close as exceptence if they have a mind to. If I could give some advice to those people it would be to never give up on taking your life back because one day it will happen if they don't die first, for the ones that give up loose everything and with most they never get it back. Imagine peeling an onion and with each layer a part of your life is gone starting first with your wife and then children, and soon to follow is your parents because they cant handle the mental illness which comes with it. You could compare it to War for they also come back damaged and soon they too are without the ones they loved, mental illness is brought on by many things and War burns out many people as the country they loved turns a blind eye to them.

Pop's didn't have to die they just quit caring about an old man of 82 years, they said he was doing fine but in reality he was dieing and they didn't want to fix what was wrong. And I blame them for his death because they lied about his health what a crock of crap when they can do that and get away with it but that's the government, use people and throw them away like garbage what I'm trying to say is that there should have been something they could of told me but they choose not too. Friday morning' and another week is about gone, some look at it like hey the weekend the day we get off work but as for me it's just time in the life of someone hurting at this moment. I have never been one to show sorrow but that doesn't mean it's not there lingering to show it's self from time to time but I will learn to deal with it through prayer and other means I spent 20 years taking care of him, and I always did a good job but I felt helpless when the time came because I knew there was nothing I could do to fix him once again. It was beyond my scope of understanding the body as it got too old, the good thing is that he had 18 more years then they gave him so long ago when his heart went haywire my pop's was a fighter and he fought till the end. It's June now and just a few more months of hot weather and it will be over, the rain we got really helped and now the grass will once again turn green it seamd God knows when we need his help and He gives it gladly so the crops can grow and produce a good crop, next week we are going to the doctor to try and quit smoking and this will save a lot of money so we can get a head. Iit seams you have to give something up to be able to make it but that's ok because its not good for you anyway. My intestinal problems seam to go away when I have a little snack so that on my list of things to have during the month, and it will help in so many ways. I don't know if it rained last night but if it did it will be welcomed by all in cleaning out the closet yesterday Randy found two mice and got rid of them to be thrown in the trash on trash day. My land' I didn't think we had any of them but we did, on the fifth we are going to get some things you plug into the wall that drives them away those and spiders they guarantee that they work so we will see. Don't need them around here as for insects there are not very many of them and that could be because I sprayed around the house before the hot weather got here. We have taken many things to the thrift store that were pop's and they should sell very well I didn't realize he had so many clothes as he would ware out the old ones before he would break out the new so the new ones didn't get used much at all. In his early years he walked all over town picking up cans and what ever else he could get and he brought many things home from televisions to stereos which we fixed up and sold for a profet to buy beer back in those days, then as the years passed he got older and couldn't do what he did before but still he tried. The years were good to him until his bladder went to heck and then he slowly declined I guess I could see it but didn't want to admit that he was leaving to go to a better place where he wouldn't have to suffer any longer, that place where he will meet up with mom and chase her around for a while. Later I will write a letter about pop's death because it's the right thing to do but I cant do it now the pain is too fresh, I know that if they had a medical center around here not as many people would die in that aspect they are behind having to fly or transport someone to a bigger city.

Maybe one day it will be better but for now it will remain the way it is and people will have to drive many miles for good help, like Dennis he had to go to Lincoln to have his heart valve done. In many ways it's like the pioneer days except you have cars today for emergencies to get you where you need to be, I was told that the only bad thing about living here was the health care if someone needed surgery and I thought I could handle that. Which I can but if something happens fast then there is no hope. For this is my dream home and I will not leave it not yet anyway, through life we have too make our place in which we feel at home and my home is here in the middle of no where and I find peace here. Many would say I am nuts for living so far out here but at least I don't have to worry about people bothering me everyday drug addicts coming to my door, it's a fine life for which I'm grateful for and even today I'm meeting new people and getting to know other more deeply the ones I already know through church. Out side of the church they are different it's like a whole new world and they go on with their everyday lives working and going to events which would help around here for me to go to some of them, but time will tell if that will happen there is more freedom here and I have only seen a speck of it as I stay home most of the time. Need to get out more' then I have, Randy found some programs for the computer in the boxes that were never unpacked so we will send them to the thrift store along with maybe a computer that doesn't work very well through the years I have collected a couple of computers which have part of my writings on so I kept them in hope that no one would get a hold of my work. For every page brings something to light about my life and I don't want to loose any of it by mistake, I have been writing so long that it feels like a part of me to get up each day and record my thought's and memories.

My land' I got carried away with all that has been going on and sometimes it's hard to focus but then later it will become what it should be our future depends on us surviving and I believe we will make it in this land called the dust bowl. It's also called tornado alley because of where we are it's like an ally where tornados form, I just hope they never hit my home. Saturday morning' and it's a little chilly it seams the weather we should have had in May is hitting us in june strange happenings but we can deal with it, my land' May was hot and the ground was turning brown but now it's green with the rain and cool weather. It's a blessing to not have to run the air conditioning because we will need it this next month and beyond the hotest months are July and August when it can get up to the tripple digits for at that time we wont travel unless it's in the morning while it's still cool out side. The heat kicked on so I know it's below sixty eight here in the house and it's no telling what it is out side maybe in the fiftys or so, I have a lot to do today with getting things ready for communion and making sure they have what they need for service tomorrow and then the thrift shop at noon until two these things I will try and get done before then and then the rest of the day is free time for me unless I have to mow the lawn. We got the main bills paid but there is still a couple that havent came in yet, I believe we can make it if we budget things right and life will go on like before things will be just a little tighter is all. This kind of budgeting will take time to get used to but we will take it as it comes and hope for the best. Here we worry about things like money when others are more worst off then we are and they make it just fine without worry they seam to be used to not having anything but just having your bills paid is a delight. Knowing you will have a place to rest your head is the most important and everything after that well you have to take it a day at a time, I still have some things which can be taken to the thrift store and they can do with it what they want. I heard a wwomen telling someone that they have racluse spiders around here and they are one spider which will make you sick if bitten by them but they stay in the dark where they cant be seen, horders have a lot of them when they pile up crap in their houses those and mice which I also don't care for. Tuesday we have to go to Concorida to see Randys parole officer and then we will get one of those plug-ins that chase them little varments away maybe into the neighbors house where no one lived, the weekend's come quick around here and then they are gone like the wind which blows in the storms that last for a short time. Here in Courtland you can tell when a storm is coming by the wind that blows, sometimes it will be for two days and others it can be for just an afternoon but it lets you know that it's coming. It's strange how the past doesn't seam as important as it did so long ago for years it stayed with me to write about and now not so much, for it's what you do with the time you have remaining which is impotand not all the other stuff you went through which brought waves into your life. Waves like the Ocean to come a shore and then back out to sea even the sea washes it's self from debris that comes upon shore to decay away sort of like our life passed. All that garbage has to be washed away so we can fill our shelf with something different like the start of a christen life.

Through my walk with God He has shown me many things love and understanding and above all he stands by me in my time of need. Although there are still many things I don't understand in time He will help me with those things as there is still a lot that I don't see, the growth of this place is going slow but that's the best way for it too happen I am now counted as one of it's residents and I believe Randy is also that makes it two more people which will live out their life here and watch Courtland grow in the coming years. How much will it grow well only time will tell that story and I hope it's a good story as we grow closer to the people, my friends reach out to me in hope that I will stay and I will as long as possible. But God has something He wants me to do and although I'm not sure what it is yet He will let me know in due time I wonder what it would be like to be a pastor it's something that has been in the back of my mind for quite sometime the taking care of souls which will one day be headed to eternal life, the bringing together of people with one purpose or cause to help others. When you give He gives back to you and it's like a circle sort of like a ring with a constent band of gold brought together to keep things in sink with the universe living a christen life is importand and others see what unfolds through the years, they see the goodness which is brought to those who have very little in this life but that little seamd to be enough for some and they are grateful for what they get no matter how slight it is. I have seen movies about such things and many here in the United States suffer because they lack in something wither it's mental illness or just suffering from the curse which had brought many of us to a cross roads.

When you're addicted to something like drugs or alcohol it destroys many of our natural instincts; and causes us to follow that wrong path which we soon get lost in and then we wonder for years in a world that we don't understand. Until we learn to understand it and by then the real world couldn't be further from our minds, just focusing on that dark place takes all we have to try and understannd why we were brought to that place in our lives. Could it be so we can learn what others go through everyday of their lives and maybe help to try and bring them back from that dark place which they have created? The freedom of choice something He gave us all' even kids, we meaning parents' have the responsibility to shape a childs life but if the parent is messed up then they cant do their job and others have too step in and do it for them. And with it brings anger because they feel like they have been doing a good job, then when others are brought in it becomes a mess because you end up going through court and they don't do the job any better. They put them in foster homes where the people only want the check and if the child has too many problems then they ship them off to another foster home, these kids become more damaged then before as they feel no one wants them. And what started out as good intentions becomes a tangeled mess and they end up living on the streets with no one but them selves unless they are picked up by a pimp and sold into slavery. This happens all the time in this nation and there is nothing many can do about it, slave sex trade is out of this world and even children are destroyed because these people and they need to be stopped. They are even sold to other countries to rich basterds and end up with no freedom at all. This isn't what He had planed for us His children Courtland is small enough to where people care for each other and it's a true careing like a parent should care for their kids it's the only place where your kids can walk down the road and not have to worry about if they will make it home or not, in the bigger cities you don't see this and it's like you have to keep your loved ones close even the elderly as some cults will recruit them because their minds are weak and take them off to some camps far away just to get their money. Most of the illegal things that go on are because of greed and they want that all mighty dollar by not working, these people are the lowest and they destroy lives without thinking twice I couldn't imagine going through such a thing in this world but it happens every hour of every day and the so called law cant keep up with it. Even over the internet you can buy a bride, they don't call it that but just the same that's what it is. Dealing with those things have never came up in my life and for that I am glad, yesterday we went to panther paw's and I saw this old women trying to get gas and helped her to get things going she was a sweet old women and I enjoyed helping her and she said while I was leaving you did your good deed for the day. Just little things like that makes the day worth while and the people who wave because they know you are a good person seams to lift your spirits and make the day all that much better.

It's always been the little things which mean the most and has the most value, not the big things in my life. When a child says hi it shows respect and when they say they liked your song it brings out an inter peace that comes to the surface and makes you glow for some reason, to see the world through a childs eyes that would be a hard thing to do but in many ways I am like a child and sometimes it comes out to play. I guess it needs a break from the adult which influences it, we all have a child inside of us but for some they don't see it until they become old and go through their second childhood and maybe that's what I like about older people as they too can act as a child and I get along with that part of me and them. Through my adulthood my child has shown it's self many times and even had to destroy the old part of me the one which tried to destroy me all those years ago, this gave way to being reborn in the christen faith and still today I travel that path one of goodness and trust, which makes life much easier. Since I moved here there isn't much swearing words except for a time or so and of course little brother that will take some time to break him of that but it will happen in the future. Harley is looking at me laying on my bed kind of hinting that he wants to go out side so I better let him out, he is funny sometimes but he can also be a pain when he doesn't get his own way so I oblige him at times because he is my buddy my little friend and I wouldn't know what to do without him.

He has been with me going on four years so he must be about five years old by now that's thirty five by dog years seven to one from what I heard. My little guy is always there for me even in the worst of times and he doesn't hold grudges like people do, or talk back like women do just a calm little shit that likes to play one of these times I'm going to take him for a walk but boy can he get into trouble not having has a girl dog yet he is mighty feisty. In the time when I brought him here he was very good in the vehical and we take him on trips when we are going to be gone for a time, as I know he doesn't like to be alone none of us do really not even me Randy has been a big help in many ways and just the companionship has helped a lot talking about the years when we were kids and how we went fishing and such, some of the best years were back then when alcohol wasn't involved. My parents were great and they did the best they could considering the burden they carried after the boys accident, it's strange how you wish you could of understood what was going on back then but it wasn't possible at our age. Sunday morning' I got the things done that I had to do yesterday and my friend brought the couch over that Randy wanted so now we have two of them one for each of us, but it's a good couch and should last quite a while even though the colors are so different but hey no two personalitys are the same right? Yesterday got pretty warm about 81 degrees so we didn't go to Concorida too hot for me, the plant we planted is doing fine but we have to water it every two days with a bucket which isn't any problems seeing we do it early in the morning when it's still cool out side. This morning I have to finish communion which is fun to do for me anyway getting things ready so our day will go well and to me it's a way of giving thanks to Jesus for what He did for us so long ago. I helped Beverly put up some baby clothes while I was helping out and that is a joy when I help over there, through this time it was fun.

CHAPTER 10

To create new things to do is also fun from time to time as my life is unfolding but in the midst of things I have to be able to do other things. Our journey in two days will produce something but weather it will bare fruit is another thing completely, I like to travel but not too far because of things I have to do. My life has taken on a whole new meaning being a part of something bigger then my self and people depend on me for things even though my part isn't very big it will grow with time, taking down the railing wasn't as hard as I thought it would be but we got it done and now it's back up where it belongs so our porch looks cute. As for far away friends they don't seam to text very much anymore getting on with their lives it just goes to show that the world will keep spinning even when were not there anymore my kids are doing fine and Leroy seams to be getting along as well with his new job if he stays with this one he will be set for many years to come learning the inn's and out's of the mechanic business and working for a good company like Wal-Mart they will never go under like many of the other big companies. Through the times when he couldn't handle a job I thought he would never make it but it's nice that he has proved me wrong in that aspect and I wish him the best in all that he does, my son will carry on the mechanic tradition and make him self and me proud. But it's not about me it's about him, when I was taught to write I never thought I

would make it but through faith in God and my self I have made it to this place that I never saw coming.

What brings us to places that we never seen before if it's not by some Devine intervention then something else is at work here, maybe a look at the past to see things we may have forgotten like the accident so long ago that had become a bluer because of what had happened with that part of my life. A reminder that He looks over us even when we cant see feel or touch Him, for sure I'm supposed to know about this thing which could have taken my life and didn't. When God is for you who can be against you? The ones who don't have a good out look on life or the others that want what you have but don't want to do the work to get it. In a crowed I don't like to be and that's just because I am me, for they don't have anything I need for all I need is me. When the storm comes in those others I don't need, why because I have me. When I fought the devil it was just me as everyone ran away and left me, and that just left me. Fighting for life I was set free but no one was around but just me, it's always been just me. Traveling in that world which used to be with all the demons after me who was there to help me see? Only God and He is all I need. Through the dark corners of life who set me free? Only God who brought me to be. Through this life when I thought I had friends who showed me the way to be, only God who came to save me. When I lost the will to live who came to me only God to set my spirit free. All these things come to me by God who set me free, the journey has been long but through it all I had God to help me along.

People come and people go but God is there for ever although we cant see him He stands by us through the darkest hours of our lives, and if we finely come to see this then things get better. All the bad things seam to go away to shed a light on something new a smile from an old friend or just a hi from someone you haven't met yet can turn your world up side down. People reaching out to you because they need a helping hand can bring you joy beyond belief, the heart breaking because it's afraid to reach-out and hold the one you have feelings for when these things are not met it stop's growth in this world of ours it stop's you from growing in a positive way, as rejection is a part of life. Some deal with it better then others but for the one who is bashful it's like slamming a door on their face and they retreat back into them selves like the turtle does when it's threatened by it's enemy's, to not come back out until the coast is clear. These things I don't like to happen to me and I wouldn't do them to others to hurt them in anyway, no one looks at life the way I do but there are people who have feelings for others and never voice them because it isn't the christen thing to do. But what is the christen thing to do? Go through life not having what you want because others think it's wrong or should you ask God for his advice? The world is ever changing and we have to change with it or get left behind for change is sometimes good for us but a word of caution never change in a bad way because it will bite you in the ass when all is said and done, even people who are afraid of life sometimes miss opportunities which could of made them happy like with me when the addiction had control. You seam to function but that kind of life isn't for most people and the ones who have never experienced that world wouldn't want to visit it, in the world of christen faith they don't dabble in the spirits or shouldn't go into it because if you don't have experience in that world those others will eat you alive. They would be like newbie's it takes an art of knowing that world and even when you leave it you louse that edge that you once had by being brought up in it. A life of destruction can make you wise if you can get out of it as for me I never felt that I belonged there or anywhere for that matter as the curse makes me num I was able to do things that I would of not been able to do on my own without the thing I had grown up on it gave a way of life that I could function in but then later I had to destroy that to see what He had planed for me. Just yesterday the pastor told me that they are going to help me so I would stay for the love they have shown is really deep, my acceptance into this world was excepted by many and this new way of life is really interesting and my stories bare fruit with others as they too change the way their life is. A life once lost has somehow found it's way back to the life God had attended for me, I cant say what will unfold in the future but I know if this is any indication then things will be alright. From destruction to finding my way home after so long so no one can tell me that it cant be done the demons are gone and now the angels will come to guide me the rest of the way home. Doing two things isn't as hard as I thought it would be taking time to go to each one is exciting really and it's different, through time the other people will get to know me the ones living without Christ in their lives and maybe they too will see that their lives can be better as mine has become. There are many steps to getting back your life but as you take each step it gets easier as long as you don't have people messing you up in your walk with Christ, today is Monday and it's a new start to the week when many make mistakes at work as for me I don't have that pressure because I do what comes naturally just be my self in this world. Many say if you like your job then you never work a day in your life and that must be what I am doing because I enjoy working for the lord, baby step's is what it takes to get things going then when you have everything down pack you move on to more things I figure that I could make it here alone if it came to that but Randy is a big part of this equation now.

When thing get even better then we might go on a trip to break the monotony and get a new prospective on this situation of our lives. If you see how old friends are doing it can give you a glimpse of what could of happened if you would of stayed and usually you wouldn't of liked it, because people can stop you from growing in the lord and usually it's because they have become jealous of your good fortune Joel had a segment on how some can hold you back because they want to keep you in a box more or less shape you to fit their image of what you should be and when you let them do that you take away from God's plan for you. God knew what you would be before you were born and His plan never changes but a persons does because we are only human and with our minds being the way they are change comes quite offend and it's not always good. For my life is one that turned out good and in the mix of things many good things have taken place, as for my home it will remain my home for ever and one day people will know that I lived in this place we call Courtland, KS. My life will be a respectable one of honor and true grit with a little wideness to make room for improvement.

This place is everything I need to survive and I see the happiness in others as I leave church and they say good by Roger, and I reply by flickering my fingers in gesture and they giggle every day I learn something new as my church family becomes closer to me it's like they are excepting me with my faults because they can see the change as I go through this life. But the only one who matters is the father Him self and when I talk about Him it's also Jesus for which I talk about, because they are three in one like the water that we drink. It's water but also it's steam, and Ice which returns back to water this is the understanding I got from a sermon trying to explain the trinity. And how it can transform within it's self to bring us peace and love many years ago I would of never understood this concept but through my learning it became clear as the father doesn't work in the natural just the supernatural and that's how he can make things happen for which we cant understand as our scope is narrow by our understanding of things. The birds are singing this morning and it sounds beautiful as they communicate with each other, I only hear this in the mornings and I like to think they are saying hello to each other as the day begins. They will fly around until they get tired and then fly around some more building nest's for their young, when I first got here my nerve's were very nervice and after time they turned into a strength and I know this should of happened while I was young but it didn't and I think I'm better for it. I guess I'm what they would call a late bloomer but I'm ok' with that because I know there is plenty of time to learn and it doesn't really matter how long it takes because we are only here for a short time, I still want to get to know my little friend and see what she is all about as I cant stop her from coming to mind from time to time. It's like I'm drawn to her spirit for some reason and I know I like her she is like her mom in some ways but not so disciplined more free spirited and bubbly with a zest for life, she comes around sometimes at her mothers and lay's out to get a Suntan but something stop's me from engaging and going over there to say hi' or how are you doing. Never have been good at words with the opiset sex but that will have to change as time goes on if I'm going to find someone to grow old with that special person that compleets me on this earth, I know she is out there but where? Could she be right in front of my eyes or an I trying to hard? These are the questions for only God can answer. My world changes everyday as He brings new things into it and for the most part they have been good things but nothing compairs to the smile or the wave from someone, you would think bigger is better but it's not to me just a kind word is much better then all the gold in the world and people are more important then any of it. We were brought here to learn to love and maybe feel some of what God feels for us but His love cant be measured because it's so vast like us with children when the day doesn't go so good we give them a kiss on the head and say a better day tomorrow, even with getting upset' nothing can take away from that love that we feel for our children and that's the way it is with God but on a bigger scale. As He has millions of children that He say's that too tomorrow will be a better day, and then when tomorrow comes those problems are not so important. We even forget about some of them because they didn't stick in that important part of the mind, traveling between two worlds is a hard thing to do but with God on your side you can do it. Pop in and out of the old one to check things out and seprate what could help others and what wouldn't be of any use to them, this is an art which not many can do but He gives us the strength to do it.

As for coming back that part is easy but it wasn't always that way, in the beginning it was hard to not want to come back because you knew in that world you could hide from what was bothering; you and in this world you have to face the everyday problems which inters your life. Tuesday morning and it's going to be a busy day but I will have everything done this morning at least by noon, and then it's back home and we will see what happens after that. I got up early because I couldn't sleep which happens every now and then as for my writing the paper I haven't been doing it lately because really I haven't wanted to but I'm sure that will pass once I can concentrate again, talking with my daughter I told her that I think of Oliver every now and then and she said it would be that way for a while but for me to remember the good times like our trip to Oklahoma when we had so much fun. I would like to ride a horse once again as that was the highlight of my vacation when we went to visit although it was very hot during that time of year, it's hard to believe it was two summers ago but time seams to go so fast. Little brother has been here for a year now and he is doing good although the time moves so fast each day is pretty much plesent as I greet it with an open mind of exceptence and take things as they come, when I get used to things being the way they are I will try to find some not so hot work to do so I can make some more money to put away for a rainy day when I will need it as things go now I pretty well set as far as bills are concerned but I seam to need more.

The getting up early hasn't let off any but in time I hope to sleep longer and that way my days might change and I wont be so tired when it comes to the middle of the day, once I eat something I get really tired like I did when I used to be in Kearney but I know that will pass in time it's like all my energy flows out word and then returns to sort of charge my batterie kind of funny really but then not so much when I fall a sleep. Randy wants me to get him up by 6:00 this morning so he is ready for his appointment and then we will head home as we are not going to shop this time. Thursday we see the doctor to try and stop smoking and I hope it works so much money wasted by lighting up and there are other things we can do with that money like pay bills and get a head so we can take a vacation one of these years. By now Tonya should be moved to her new house it's on a ground level so no climbling the stairs will be in the picture for anyone my sister is doing fine as far as I know and I hope she gets well soon. For a while I thought she wasn't going to make it but God has bigger plans for her in this life and He is keeping her around to finish her journey that He set in place for her before birth, strange how that works if your time is not up then you will stay on that path laid out for you by the father. Her life hasn't been an easy one either but through it all she has come to love God and that's what matters. The starting to get to know other people is slow and that's the way I like it because it gives me control of how far I will want to take it, my steps are baby steps as I move forward into these new sarroundings of being around non christens or if they are christens then I just don't see them in church many people that I know who are of the christen faith don't come to church very oftend as they have different reasons for not coming. Although they believe they don't practice it but at home or where ever and this is something we don't judge when a seed is planted then it's up to God to make it grow. In hope that it will take root to make the flower blossom into something beautiful, no one believes the same and that's what makes us unique with our minds going in different directions. But somehow we seam to connect with each other in the belief that we all have the same God, the one who created everything including us His children. Through the frost I see a cross that shines for the lost the lost souls trying to find their way. Open your heart and you will see that Jesus loves thee, the same as he did yesterday. This I believe has been the way it's been since the beginning of time and us as people have a hard time seeing it because of all the garbage that's in the world today, but what about not seeing it back in the old days when this garbage wasn't there? For surely the path was the same back then trying to understand and unlock the mysteris which was laid out in front of us, many older people believe it's in the search and in searching the answers will come but if by some reason you don't find the answer then lay it aside and if God wants you to understand it then it will be made clear. When I grieve I find the answers by getting on my knees and praying to God for understanding and that's all I need as He opens up my understanding to why this had to happen, we are born into this world to die and this is a fact although it's a beautiful thing we as people don't see it that way because something is taken away from us. A child or loved one who we have cared about is one day gone and it leaves a void that has to be filled by something else wither it's another person or just finding our selves praying for answers, which will come when the time is right.

The loss is usually great especially if it's someone you have taken care of for many years, like pop's he was my companion for better then 20 years and it was just the two of us. When things changed then our lives had to change with it and that included him leaving this world to be with the father, for I can take comfort in knowing he is in a better place then this world. A place where he is whole once more without the burdens that made him weak on this planet, through God's love and understanding he is strong once again like when he was young and he will never grow old any longer. For he is free from the body that was wore out here and now his spirit lives on for ever in that place we call eternal life, although he wasn't a church person the spirit of God was in him through those final hours as I could see it in his eyes. It was like he was saying not to worry because I go to a better place, I liked it when he kicked at me in his bed as I drew a heart on my chest and said that I loved him. It would be the last thing I said to him so I like to believe he went in peace knowing that I loved him, my whole world was built around taking care of him and then it was taken away just like a flick of a light. But I will recover in time to have those great momories of our time together, I believe mom knew that the others wouldn't watch over him and that's why she made me promis her that I would as she loved him so.

We all need someone in this world and in time I will find my best friend and love but I have no idea how long it will take, months or years it doesn't really matter because we are only here for a short time. When my father died I wasn't sad for some reason but then when it came to mom I felt the loss and it was great, maybe because I took care of her also fighting that battle of what we call life. She would get well and then fall back into it again and it was like she was being drawn by the curse especially when the med's didn't do their job any longer, as for dad the shaking didn't stop because the alcohol was the only thing which could control it and I knew it was hard on him parkens seamed to control him and doctors said alcohol was like pouring poisen into his systen because his body couldn't handle it. I didn't know much about that part of the family the Mattson's side or the Roberts for that matter they seamed so far out of our lives and their lives were much different from ours, although they were religious they seamed seprate from the life we had become accustom to and they left this world before us or I if things would have been different then I wouldn't be here writing this today. So I have to think that what was meant to be has become, and I will move forward into the world of the unknown as I cant tell what will be in the future. Who knows maybe there is someone here in Courtland which will be the one I can't really say as the days turn to weeks and months into years things change. There will be new people moving into Courtland within the next year for this is something I can feel and maybe there will be someone for me, patients is something I have learned long ago by the grace of God and if it takes longer then that's the way it will be. And who knows maybe Randy will find someone also if the lord is willing, does writing let you get in touch with your inter self? I believe it does and it can give you a picture of how close you are to your beliefs wither it's close to God or other things which have no purpose. To me things like material things are of no importance in my world as they are just things that people like to attach them selves to so they can fill a void and I guess mine isn't that deep. The day has been hot so I'm glad that we can be inside where it's cool, after that hot ride to Concordia. We didn't stay there but to see Randy parole officer and then we headed home as the wind made it much nicer going down the road, it's strange how I don't like the heat but then again I don't like the cold during winter either there doesn't seam to be a middle ground in that department because of what my body has went through during my younger years. Who knows maybe it will change in the coming years but for now it will stay the same very uneven lol, while the years pass I see many changes coming our way and it will be nice to see them for they will be all different and better then years passed. Wednesday morning and I slept good except for the dreams not quite sure why they were there but it was like I was fighting resistence and I don't like those kind of dreams, many times in the past I have had them but was able to fight them off it was like something was trying to enter my space and no one does that without my permition or the ok from the father. Things and change takes time and I'm not ready for that step yet, I have a hard time focusing on things and that's another thing for which I don't care for. Going back to when it all happened there were many things for which I'm glad and one is the ability to over come the life that I left behind. But does this world have magic in it the kind of magic which can change things in a persons mind without them knowing it for truly this cant be because we are our own person each one of us.

If you listen to a person that reads the stars they will claim that they can see into the future and that's something only God should be able to do, but that doesn't stop them from trying and they make millions of dollars from it. Today the thrift store is open and I still have a few things to take down there before I go and help out, the church councel gathered yesterday I think to discuss my job here and it will be approved with them the bills are paid for this month but it doesn't leave much for fuel and other things which I will need later in the month but I will survive and go on to something important in the coming months. I have heard about people turning their lives around and I believe other like to feel they had a hand in it for the path to a christen life should be a happy one free from the ties that once binded them this life I take on will be better then the one before because the feelings will be apparent as they change, as for the ones that didn't make it into my future they were not meant to be here and that's a good thing to know so I put them out of my mind the best I can but some still connect with me from time to time and I think it's because they still have feelings for me. This change wasn't easy in the beginning it was like all the life was drawn out of me and then put back in a little at a time, Walt is going to be burried here I guess he wanted to come back home and rest he lived a big part of his life here and I guess that was his last wish. I wonder what happened with Gismo and I hope he is doing good where ever he is they were like two peas in a pod always together riding down the street on Walts gulf cart, through the years he had many friends and I'm sure they will be at his funeral.

Enough about death we the living are going to make a difference in the future and who knows what that might be but the lord, I have seen many things come to pass and I know many more will find their way into my life for each day is a gift and when we have some faults the struggles make it better, others would rather hear the struggles and know you have had them, that way they don't feel out of place. My fight for life lead me here to a place that I didn't know anything about but in time the adjustment was possible to make me a part of this gracious town' I still cant figure out why they like me unless it's my love for God, because I don't talk much in the realm of being a jabber jaw I'm a person that takes everything in and annualizes it I guess and then if I find something interesting I will write about it if it pertains to me life there are many things which pertains to my life here in Courtland and there isn't a day that goes by which I don't have something to write about. Today I have to mow the lawn as the weeds are getting high and have to be knocked down, my yars is always cut nice but this weather has stopped it from growing right much too dry for this time of year but I will keep it cut to keep up appearance. Sitting on the corner lot many go by my house everyday and I haven't been ashamed of the yard yet, nor will I ever bee. Even in the heat of the day I have mowed it with a push mower but really that's too hard on me so I spend a little more to keep the riding mower going and it only takes an hour or so, and I can sit down and do it. The church is a wonderful place to meet people and if they like you they will open their hearts to you, but this takes time it's been going on almost three and a half years since my coming here and they have always been nice to me except for a person being in a bad mood or something and when that happens then you pay no mind to it because you know it isn't about you. The being an out sider has me puzzled although I wasn't born here it feels like I have been here all my life, and the people open up to me unlike in Nebraska where they don't take the time to get to know the person. As for us ever getting a loan in Kearney it wasn't possible because you are not a person just a number on a piece of paper, with no value even if you paid your bills on time. Enough for this is a great day and we should be glad in it, this morning I'm watching Antique Road Show and I love looking at things from the past and how they made it to this time in history. Some of the things were created back in the 17th and 18th centery I have always been interested in such things it's like I'm a part of that time and got lost along the way, strange I know but there is something that draws me to such things. All things relating to that time in history, some of the things they show intrigue me and where they are found sometimes is out of this world, under old buildings and in attics such a delight to see such things. In the future I would like to go and find treasures to bring them back to life so they can be seen by the world. I have many plans that I would like to do in the future but things stop that from happening, but I know in the future that my wiseness will be needed in the experience to help some others. The process is slow to get people to trust someone with such a thing like addiction.

I have said it before overcoming addiction can be the start of a new life it doesn't have to be the end, Thursday and yesterday we got a pizza for supper but it wasn't what I wanted. Also Tonya called and talked to little brother and said her mom went back home to be with her man, and she was not going to interfear with her mom's life any more which is a good thing because she has to live her own life. And I believe that's why I moved here to get away from all the drama which comes with family, the idleness of such thingss not being in your life can sometimes bring you a peace and that's what I like about my life the peace of mind to do what ever moves you and not having others interfear with that, we all make our own worlds and mine is peaceful for the most part I can be by my self or be around friends if I so choose that action. They are tearing down an old house which a friend bought because it's right next door to her this will give her a bigger lot a real big one about two or three lots together this is something that needed to be done because the house was destroyed by cat's going in and out of it, old people like their animals and this women had a many cats that she fed but now she is gone and the thing has to be tore down. Others have bought lots next to theirs and made them into gardens for growing food but I'm sure not all of them do that, the house next door to me has went down in price from twenty thousand to sixteen and I see it even going lower in the months to come. Although I haven't seen inside of it just the property should be worth a couple of thousand as the house is in bad shape, when I came upon my home I was blessed because it was still in fairly good shape and I do a little here and a little there to keep it up.

And it will improve in the years to come as I take on other projects to make it an even better home carpet would be nice but it's not in the budget yet. In time it will be but until then we will keep this one clean so not to have any little bugs come in like fleas and such, harley was up earlier but then went back to bed and I hope he sleeps a while. He was so cute yesterday when he ran around the house like a jet and then started to hack I told him to slow down but that didn't stop him he just went on and finely I told him to get some water and he ran to it knowing I would fill his bowl, I saw Margret yesterday when we went to get pizza and she just looked at me I could tell that she had calmed down since the last time we met and I didn't say anything to her in hope that nothing would start. It had been three years since we were together and I didn't miss it a bit, some are just not meant to be together so they should except that and move on with their lives lord knows I have. Today I have to check on things at the church and make sure that everything is clean this is the part of the job that I like making sure others can come to a clean church and enjoy them selves while they are there. In a small community people know about you weather you are someone who is trying to change your life or if your just a burden to the place for which you live and they will treat you aaccordingly as for me I stay to my self most of the time except for when I help out when I can. On this day I'm going to try and quit smoking with the help of my doctor so we will see how that goes even a decreas would be nice and it would save a lot of money in the long run. To maybe buy something special somewhere down the line that I might need. In my move here I didn't just come blind God showed me that it was the place I needed to be and He gave me many signs starting with the lake and the stream, it's important to pray on things you don't understand and ask for His guidance and if you find out that it isn't for you then you can always move on. I felt like a kid being turned out into the wilderness to find his way and my way lead me to here He uses others to get us to where we need to be, weather it's in a big town or a small one like Courtland when people louse a part of them selves it's hard to except that they will never be whole again and it doesn't matter if it's within the mind or the loss of a limb. I have learned that it's better to give then recive the feeling that is! that you get when you help others through the years many have come to feel this feeling and I am one of them. As for the mountain He had me climb it is behind me now and I made it to the top now there is just a gradual slope for which I will walk down and learn along the way and if I need help then He is there to lend me a helping hand. My land' this world is better then I ever expected and I live in this great place there isn't really more that I could ask for except for more understanding, our day went pretty good and I got some stuff to stop smokeing but I know it will take prayer along with it to beat the beast which has had it's hands in me for the last fourth some years, although the stuff could of cost a hundred dollars it didn't cost me that and I take it as a sign that it's time to quit.

So we will see what happens in the future. Friday morning and the weekend starts to night after work is over but for those who are harvesting wheat, it continues through the weekend or until they get it all in weather permiting in the years before some people have gotten hurt by machinery and one man almost lost his life by getting rear ended when he was transporting a tractor and a tank of anhydrous ammonia which ended up in a field full of mud thank God he wasn't hurt very bad. Things like tractors and big Mac trucks travel the highway all the time and they have has some horrific accidents once in a great while, I was told about a family from Colorado that got hit by a train and it cut their heads off and they blamed it on not having cross arms on the tracks never did hear what happened with that case. But it was long ago, although I worked for farmers before I never did have an accident that could of put others in harms way and it was fun to do the work with air-conditioning in the tractor not getting above 60 degrees in the tractor except for when I had to go out and fix the disk or repair it. Farming life is hard work and they should be respected for what they do in this world, we have to go to town today so we can get some things and Randy's med's to keep him on track as I looked in on him this morning he was like a little baby rolled up in a ball just sleeping and he looked so peaceful there in his bed.

The doctor said I will have to train my self in a different way when I stop smoking by doing something with my hands so I will try to take up something else as the brain changes when you take the copret out of the picture. But I will try anything to see if this will work for me as smoking has been a big part of my life since the age of 8 years, if I can stop the others then why not this for nothing has ever come easy for me when it comes to being addicted to things that are bad for you but I'm willing to give it a try. As we traveled yesterday you could see the people out in the fields getting the harvest in and the wheat looked better this year then last so I pray that they have a bumper crop, as for my days I don't have to mow much because of the lack of rain and the grass stays short for a longer period of time. When you change from being addicted to something the brain changes in many ways and you have to compensate for the change like with the addiction to alcohol and drugs you have to change to something positive and with me it took God to help me and He didn't let me down. We are all stronger then we think we are it's just that we don't realize it until the change takes place and sometimes we think hey why didn't I do this long ago, as we go through life we are searching for something and sometimes we think we find it in bad behavior and then later learn that isn't the case we just got stuck at that place or got addicted because it felt good at the time and then over time it took on a part in our lives, a lot of times I smoke when I write and in my mind it must bring something to me like a thought or it helps me concentrate better I cant tell at this time. Chantex has a 60 percent success rate so this is my best shot they say weird dreams occure with it but I'm sure that verys with each person as the mind and body go through changes, as the days and months go by I will record what happens and see if the benefits out weigh the burden. Sometimes I feel like people are praying for me as I can feel it and it's beinging on change, but what change is it bringing on will I except this change? If it's good then yes because I like change lord knows that my change has been happening for quite some time now and it will continue until I get my self to a normal state without any addictions, I feel that would be awesome not to have any of them any more. But time will tell, many things come to mind when you try to change your make-up but I will put that off for another day. This morning is different for some reason and it's hard to concentrate on things so maybe I should try to bring other thoughts to mind, it's the end to another day and I thank God for it as each day is given by God so we can go on with life. No matter what happens through the day He is there for us even when things don't go right, but at the end of that day I know everyone can count their blessings and they out weigh the other thing that might not go right. In my life I always looked at the bad side of things and now that my life has changed I try to look at the good and give thanks for His love. Saturday morning and I slept until four this morning very odd for me but seeing that usualy I'm up at two or so the Chantex did give me dreams but it wasn't anything I couldn't handle and now I'm on day two it was plesent in here during the night as the air-conditioning did it's job of not letting me sweat I cant even imagine not having it my land' it would be like a sweat box. In my time I have only had two places which had central air and I have always been grateful for them both living in this part of the country, we got a call from Mark O'Brien and Randy talked with him while I was driving home it seamed to lift his spirits talking to him and then afterwords he was quiet for a time they talked about how he was doing and such and how Kearney's crime is getting worse but all in all they had a good talk.

Although I think little brothers misses his friend it's not wise to travel there this summer anyway after his blow up with someone he has to learn to be grateful for what he has and although he doesn't realize this yet he will in time. He was told that he needs to change his attitude and never come in like that again, it must have been like hehad a flash back to where he was before and that is common with some people. I do know he sometimes makes up things so he can feel important and he doesn't have to do that because he is important, he seams to get up earlier in the last couple of days and I don't know why but he has been up later at night talking to

Stacy and finding out what's going on in the city, he seams to laugh a lot when they talk so that's good for him but I hope she isn't trying to plant any bad seeds in his mind. People don't see the things I see in the same fashion so we are all different in that since. This morning I have plenty to do and then back down to the thrift shop at noon to help out for a while, my friend said someone got the other speakers which were down at the store and took them home for us they were too big as I have a hard time placeing the ones we got Randy but he will have fun with them when he gets everything he needs for them and I will try to help him get them for him, in a way he is still like a kid which can be a good thing and he is protected in the place which he lives he has now went back to bed so he should sleep until 7:00 or so in the place that he feels like is his. The birds are singing out side my window and I love it to hear them each morning, as they too welcome the day.

Life today is better and it keeps getting better as He brings us through each of these days, as for the world out side I don't have much to say about it as they do what ever they do but I hope they are wise in the decisions that they make in bringing strength to our country, as time goes on the wars have stopped but I'm sure they will get us into another one in the future trying to show up other countries which is stupid. Always having to show that we are the strongest by inflecting brute force upon others, Sunday morning and it's just three O clock the dreams are getting to become more frequent and they are a pain in the butt because I wake up and cant go back to sleep fore some time but I will try to stick it out and see if it does it's job, yesterday I wrote a letter to my friend Mark at the Kearney-hub to be published so we will see what happens there. It's been some time since I wrote one but if it's like any other thing I write then it will be in the paper, having a hard time wakeing up but it will pass once I get my coffee. Yesterday I met Mark's wife as she came into the thrift store to find some silverware she seams like a nice women so in the future I will know who she is, it seams that I'm meeting more people as time moves forward or they are wanting to get to know me and that can be a good thing as you go through life I think I peack their curiosity as I am different from most folks and I'm learning their ways. I text my daughter and asked if she would want to come down and she said she would after Erick's doctor appointments in Omaha I told her to just let me know when she wanted to come and we would send her the gas money to make the trip, it would be nice to see the kids for a couple of days so I can give them loven's I miss their smiles. My land' it seams like many things are taking place from the change in things here to the wanting of her to come and see me it's been two years since we have seen each other and it shouldn't take that long but I know she has her own life to live with the kids, I haven't seen any of the grandbabys for that matter as I have three grandson's and two grand daughters. Through time we forget sometimes what it's like to be close to the ones you love and that's something that needs to change also that bond which happens when family is close to each other, through the years I have stayed to my self except for people who don't do the addiction things to me they are the bomb and represent the good part of life and that inspires me everyday to do things different. None of this coming over at all hours of the night to see if you are awake even when the lights are off, they seamed to be night owels as they traveled from town to town selling the stuff and when they would get busted it was for stupid crap like no tail light or driving too fast opening them selves up for a long stretch in the prison system like so many of the people I used to know. When Randy came to live with me he talked about the people and how they talked about me and how I was the only smart one out of all of them to take back my life and in many ways that in it's self helped many of them to try and do the same thing, as each of us leave a mark or impression on the lives we touch, but weather that mark is good or bad is up to us as people. Through the sands of time change is coming and as with all good things that change should be good, but if it's not then we have the power to change it again and that is given to us by God. Many go through life lost or experiencing the bad things in life so when the good things come we will know the difference, hard times hit's everyone but it's how we make it through them that's important.

If you let the devil take over then more hard times will reveal them selves and you will never know the goodness of God, only when you except change can you hope to make a difference in your life and others and that's what it's all about isn't it? Bringing goodness in to other peoples lives and it doesn't have to cost a thing because some change can come from just a smile or a wave to someone you might or might not know there is something about a gestuer like the wave of a hand that passes something to others or that smile which brings one back to you. It's a sign of your feelings and how you are doing, many times you just lift a finger and wave it back and forth while your hands are on the steering wheel this lets them know you acknowledge that they waved at you and your doing it back in kind. So many different ways to pass good power to others as you go on with your day, a lot of people don't want to stop and talk so they do that in kind and maybe in time it will open a channel to getting to know them later down the road. Taking to kindness is easy for me but I didn't see much of it when I was in the other world, as many of them were not nice when they wanted your money and they just wanted to get in and out again to get more money for the operation so it would continue far into the future. These people never did care for anyone and one time a guy was going to kill someone and I talked him out of it, it seamed he understood that the person didn't understand the values of life and common knowledge in other words he was slow.

This guy had plenty of money and knew that if he hurt this person there would be nothing to gain out of it so the victum apologized to him and he went on his way. Stupid people fall all the time in that world and the ones who do the bad deed well they are not very bright either that's why they use them for that kind of job no morals I guess, exploitation of the weak has been going on for centuries and usually they use the weak at mind starting with kids and if parents are not careful about bringing them up they may loose them to some one that will destroy them in the end. Even the weak at heart can be manipulated; by an expert just look at the hookers on the streets and the kids running dope for someone they all lacked something which the person gave them. Wither it's love or a sturn hand it's something they didn't get when they were growing up and this is a shame because it could of all been avoided if the parent did their job in raising them, as for the alcohol and drug infested homes they will loose one or more of their children to the curse and with some they wont even know it as they will move away so they cant see it. This is another way to loose a child or young adult, and they can bury them selves to where they can never be found again. Some don't want to be around their familys because they opened a door which should of never been opened, the exceptence to alcohol and drugs and then their world falls apart and they ask what they did to deserve this. Tipical of someone who cant deal with life on a normal bases when they have a problem and cant solve it they seam to run and hide in the same thing that caused the problem, in the first place. When they could of gotten over it many years before, the weakness is passed on and now their children have to figure it out if they can. With many parents they will say not my child and they are so wrong why not your child. We went to town when I got out of church and spent some money we didn't have but hey you only go around once right? As long as you don't go over board then your ok' in the future I want to get my book published so I will make strides in doing that in the next few months. We have been praying for rain and now the clouds are setting in and I hope it comes full force for a while, I didn't stay for coffee this morning so we could get to town while it was somewhat cool out but it had been muggy all morning Randy put some food into the trash and maggits appeared within just two days so we had to empty it into a big bag in hope to get it out of here on Tuesday morning he wont do that again. As for this afternoon it's been boreing so we took a nap before closeing up the church, I need to find more things to do during the day so I don't get too board and if I stop smoking then I will be really hipper and have to find something. I do know that there has to be more that I can do and maybe I can find it with the church, the thought of becoming a priest has entered my mind but some things will have to change before that can happen and they have to change within me. The thought of serving God has always appealed to me, and if I took at it I'm doing that. But I see a bigger picture somewhere down the road of life once I learn more or maybe I have already learned some of it and it will come to me when His plan becomes reality, we as people have a narrow mind and can only see what's in front of us in some ways we are like the horse that has side blinders on and only God can see what we cant see. I along with others try to figure out what God's plan is and if I could learn how to just let things happen then it wouldn't be so hard on my mind.

For idle time is not good for you when you have a lot of it and I realize that it's that time when you sometimes grow in understanding. God get me ready for what you have in mind for me, and give me sight of this occurrence when it's going to take place as you know I need to be ready before it happens so help me in this situation before it comes upon me. Give me the wisdom I need and the understanding it takes to work and talk openly with others as I move forward in this life, tomorrow we are going to get the carpet cleaned because Randy doesn't have enough to do so he can stay awake during the day. I clean it twice a year because of Harley and his accidents right now he is under the bed playing around and then he comes out and looks out the window trying to see if other animals are around, it never fails when we go to town I forget something that's important and it has to stop. In he past I always made a list but that hasn't been working lately because I still for get to write it down, space case' I guess. Monday morning and we got the situation taken care of with the garbage so now we wait until tomorrow morning when the trash man comes ifthe box is still here with the wild animals around we took it ans sealed it in a box so we will see. The mornings are tipical as I look forward to the day but I have today off and most of tomorrow, through the night I dreamed some more but I don't worry about it any longer because they are just that a dream. If I could sleep longer then I might have felt better but I'm told that the body only needs eight hours and that what I get even longer at times, it's strange how when your young you tend to sleep until ten or so in the morning but now that option isn't there what is with the mind when it functions on less then it used when you were young.

As the years go by and you get closer to old age so many things speed up but the body slowes down and I think some of us are afraid of this happening, with me if I don't get up when I do then I think it will throw off my day and I'm comfortable in the way my day goes. As it's not fast or slow but just right for this middle aged man, it's going to be another hot day as the muggyness is still around but my flower is blooming once again so I think it will Be all right it strange how they seam to die a little and then grab back on to life and start growing once again. Yesterday I watched Joel Osteen and he talked about closed doors which is a part of God's plan for us if we feel something feels right it might not be part of his plan for us so he will sometimes close the door and later open up a new one, which will make things much better in our lives. I remember when I was going to get a new computer I had thought I deserved it because I never got my self anything but I was wrong. He let me know by the guilty feeling I had aquired and then I sent it back He was trying to show me that the time wasn't right and I respect His decision and it didn't take long before the funds were back into my account, although I lost a few dollars I gained a lesson and that's not to be hasty when you try something new. There will be something coming up in which I will be able to get a head but I don't know what it is as of yet, as the times come upon us you can never know what He has in store for you as the goodness of people is great in this little town. Courtland, KS. The place where dreams can come true it's not like any other place as it has magic, and the wonder of the mind can advance you in to a beautiful place where most of the time nature takes presidence over most things and God helps to bring the rain which we could use right now, O mighty God bring about the rain we need so everything can turn green as this is something only you can do. Jesus wave your hand and bring about your power to bring the rain, Holy Spirit, like the water which takes on three forms join forces and bring about the moisture we need in asking these things I call on one God creater of heaven and earth to bring this to us on this or the next day in Jesus name Amen. Some ask if I'm going on vacation this summer and although I could it's not wise at this time adjusting to new things takes time for me so time is what I will give it there will be plenty of time for the other when things come to be where they should be. I was supprised when Mark's wife noticed me at work and I shook her hand she seams very nice as a matter of fact all of his family is nice Mark is a sweed like me but I'm sure he has more of it then me as I'm five nationalities all from the old country. I don't know how they deturman it but that's what I'm told by my mother Irish, French, German, sweed, Finish. What a combonation I guess it means that I get along with everyone which I do, for the most part that meand my children have the same blood line and their children so that part will carry on through the ages. I never did ask what Shannons husbands was but I'm sure there is some other ones in there with my grandchildren, and then with theirs when they have them it will grow even further, yesterday it was some friends anniversary and they have been married for 41 years my land' that is a long time.

When people marry and get their kids raised I wonder if the spark is still there to carry them on? For truly love does last for even with some, and with others it dies and they go their seprate ways to try and find it again. As for my loves I can only remember one and she got away but it was by my doing and being foolish I wonder where she is now, last I heard she had moved to Texas I do recall she had twins two girls which would be about Shannon's age my land' how they grow. Her name was Linda Weston and she lived in a little town calles Shelton Nebraska, she seamed like the perfect girl for me until her brother through a wrench into the mix being jelous and not wanting her around. We were very young and I was heavy into pot at the time traveling across country working although I was addicted to these things she held a piece of my heart, one day she and another girl came by when I got a weekend off and one didn't know that I was two timing them and I got caught and then had to choose. Sex was a big thing back then and Linda wanted to wait so I choose the other girl which later turned out to be a big mistake, being young I thought I needed it and it cost me big as she left crying. We remained friends but that's as far as it went until one time when we found our selves together having a party in my basement, and then we moved to Phoenix to get away from my brothers going to prison. It was a bad move as we didn't have anything when we got there and had to live in a crappy hotel, but mom loved her kids and would do anything to not see them in prison. That was a waste because they ended up there anyway.

And at their age they would of only done a couple of years Randy anyways but Rick he had been in and out of there many times so he would of probably gotten more time, as it was they had to stay away for seven years and then they could of went back but Rick blew; that by comeing back befor that time and they got him and he went to prison anyway I guess he thought it was like a delayed sentence of 6 years. Randy came back after the seven years and they didn't do anything to him, but the other blamed him for his stupidly. My self I have never been and maybe it's because I have morals and wouldn't do what they did to others because it's not right. Through life it was like they were seprate from me you know not made out of the same cloth and I stayed at a distence not wanting to share in that kind of life, so I had some good inside and I tried to keep it alive which I did. Even with the addictions I didn't get into trouble like they did because I knew I was different something special that God created but I didn't know why or how things would come to be I just knew that what they did was wrong, it's strange how you can be brought up in the same family and be so different and see things so different. But I guess they didn't think before they acted I remember trying to figure them out when we were young but it wasn't possible because we were so different and my mind wouldn't go where theirs went in the realm of taking instead of giving, the world is strange because if I wasn't like I am then little brother wouldn't be here today he would of served his time if he lived that long and then he would have been thrown back into the pit where he would have been eaten alive by the people who would of used him and thrown him away, the people he wants to see are those people and he just doesn't want to see it so big brother has to look out for him so he doesn't make the same mistakes. Are we truly our brothers keeper? Yes as it says iin the bible. But I can only handle one at a time otherwise I would go nut's. It's like I'm a care taker for others and it can get you annoyed sometimes, but what's a person to do? When the world is so messed up hope for it to change in the coming years and pray a lot lol. I cant imagine Rick's life right now and I wouldn't want any part of it, as he is still going through the addictions that got him sent away for over half his life only when he realizes that his life has to change can he hope for a better one free from the ties that bind him. I haven't heard from him since Randy came here but I hear he isn't doing too good so I pray that he will find his way one day, out of that darkness which has a hold on him. Tuesday morning, yesterday went pretty good as we trimed some branches from the trees anf threw them in the road ditch, then we trimed some bushes to make things look good. I told Norm about the tree which is dead in the yard and he said he would mention it to Leroy as he is the one that burns it during winter, there was a guy at the house next door cutting the grass and we asked to look inside so I left my number and we will see what happens, my self I think the house is shot but it could be fixed up if you had the resources.which would take a lot it needs a new roof plus windows just to make it liveable but that's the way a lot of houses are any more, the train is coming through this morning and I can hear the whistel as it blows mighty early but they have a job to do also. I remember loading the cars back in the day and it was fun sometimes getting them ready to be shipped out to other parts of the country, so the product could be made into food of all kinds and then they charge high prices for the product which many couldn't afford.

I try to help others as oftend as I can but my recources are limited and I can only do so much but what I do makes me feel good inside. As for my life' it's simple now with the work I do and most of that is helping others I'm in hope that my latest letter gets published and when and if it does then I will put it on my sights like face book and twitter O ya myspace also, which reaches around the world. They all seam to do that anymore and they are in many languages only knowing English is enough for me and if they want to translate it then that's fine also, sometimes only words seprates us but in other countries they have to deal with the curse of addiction also. And in my journey I sure some of them have read my work as they too have to deal with it plaguing their land also, it seams the fight continues even after the addiction is gone but it becomes some what of a thing of the past. Buried in the back of your mind as a reminder of what not to do, and I compare it to loosing a loved one as their memory is always there but it's put in it's own room for learning perposes, as for temptation it leaves to not return again unless under pressure and then you have too use the skills you learned to stop it in it's tracks so it doesn't fester into something worse like falling back into old habbbits as with everything you take out of your life which is negative you have to replace it with something good and positive other wise it wont work. Like when I beat the addiction there was a void that had to be filled so I started to go to church and God filled that void and in time it wasn't there any longer sort of like when you quit smoking you have to find something to do with your hands.

And this could lead to a better job or you can just work in your yard more the call is yours, with all addictions in your mind there is a reason for it a nervice condition or something worse maybe you are trying to destroy your self. But what it all means is that change has to take place your body is sending you a message, so learn to listen to it. Yes I know how do I do that? There is a spirit inside of all of us and that spirit is the host of the body and it will point out the changess which needs to take place and all you have to do is listen and obey, my spirit talked to me many times and I didn't listen until I was at deaths door why does it take that for some well they are heard headed and have never listened to tha voice which God puts inside of us and I mean all of us. This world takes from us the importand things that can keep us alive like the spirit of God which is in all of us, people who don't believe will try to make you the same way and this is because they are bitter because of something that happened in their lives and they don't want peace they would rather try to disprove the existence of God and in doing that they become further away from what they are searching for and this makes them even madder anger isn't a cure to anything it only drives a person further away from the grace of God. Grace is given you cant buy it but it has to be given by God and if your against Him then you only hurt your self, this I learned in the early days when I wanted to die and have it over with but through a miracle He showed me that I really didn't want to die I was just crying out for help because I didn't understand how to live in this world, my life had always been in the dark and I never saw any kind of light in life but through it all I survived to go on trying to help others that are or was going through the same things, even though I didn't think I would make it here I am twenty some years later still doing my best to help. Now if that isn't commitment to the cause what is? And I do it from the heart not the pocket book because there is nothing there, I made a promas to God and I entend to keep it even if my arms fall off. Through the years I have helped many see that their lives needed to change and that's all I can do is show them for they have to want it before it could ever work, it's like a horse you can lead it to water but you cant make it drink just the suggestion should be enough. This women I know has tried to beat the curse since I met her and she hasn't had any success except to change from one drug to another and she has convinced her self that she is better but that's only in her mind as she lives out a fantasy in that other world, she text me yesterday saying she went back to the guy that married and dumped her many years ago she is taking steps backwards in time because she lost her daughter and someone else she was going to marry. And now she is back on the things which screwed her up in the first place, although I feel her pain I glad that we never got together back in the day because her destruction could of caused me a lot of damage falling in love you think with the heart and not with the mind and that can bring on something you don't want. Through the years I have found peace with Christ and the other things well they play second fiddle to my love for God, for each week I learn something different while attending church and also looking up the scriptures for the next week this gives me some insight into what the next week serman will be and I can follow along better because I'm not a speed reader. Slow and easy is my way of learning, those who don't make it into your future were never supposed to.

A wise saying, as people come and they go but true friends will be for ever in your thoughts and I only have a few that are that way and they stay in my heart. I notice that I have friends with the same names and three or so of them is named Mark for surely this is some kind of sign could it be that they watch over me possible but others would excuse that thought but not me. I have two of them in Nebraska and one here and they are all connected to my life in some way what a gift to have this kind of thing in your life, it's like He is making sure I am taken care of. And we have another Roger that has started to attend our church after louseing his wife a while back, it doesn't matter what brings you to church as it in it's self can bring change and heal things that other wise couldn't heal from a broken heart to a spirit wounded. Wednesday other wise known as hump day the middle of the week, it got pretty warm yesterday and I have come to realize that many are a lot worse off then me and little brother but as long as we make out payments we will go on. Randy was telling me that he talked to Mark in Nebraska and he doesn't even have cable because he cant afford it which a lot of people don't have such things. Living here in Courtland it's our only intertainment except for church and such and of course what work I do to get away and try to keep things at an even keel I have talked with some people and and they have done without for many years and don't know what it would be like to have such luxurys, as for us these things have been in our lives for like ever because there was always someone to pick up the slack. At times I want to venture out but I wont do it when things are going so good right now lord knows things can change in no time at all, I have been surviving for over 40 some years and I have always made it and will continue to do so through the next four or so years. I haven't heard from my sister and I pray that she is doing fine during this time of recovery, my days are going good these days and I look forward to each one as it brings something new.

Just the drives we take calms down the spirit when the natives get ressless, and iit's a good thing to do as we move forward in this life. I saw the girl at the store and we shot the shit for a few moments she asked what we had planed for the day and I told her cleaning carpets, she is a nice person and I wouldn't mind getting to know her better but she is married and to me that's a no. so I will move on to check out some other ladys which there isn't many around a place this small, strange how life is when your young even you pick and choose when you could have played the field but I guess that wasn't in me being a one women man most of the time with a little slip up from time too time trying to compare their differences. But in the end there wasn't any difference just different minds that were set to their way of doing things, I remember one girl and her name was Dixie Web. She was just a little older then I and we had a good time together I believe she was 19 and I was 12 the difference in age didn't really matter to us because we were in love and at my age it was puppy love, we drank and did rugs together and I thought I was on top of the world well that lasted about a few month and then like a child with no values I traded her for a car. I know stupid but I was a child with the mind of a 12 year old I never could figure out why the older girls liked me but I guess I was cute back then and they couldn't keep their hands off me. O don't get me wrong I liked the attention and I had a lot of fun until later in life when I shot a squirrel sitting on a sign I had moved to Nebraska in hope to find the good life but hunting for the first time got me in trouble and my whole world went to hell in a hand basket after the state got my records from California when I went to court for hitting the sign the judge told me that I had to go to the youth development center so I could straighten out my life and I thought my life was going good. During my time there I lost my wife to be and she went out with my older brother which wasn't nice so I hated him for a long time and then when I would come home for visits we would get back into our sexual things but it wasn't the same as she fell out of love for me. Then I heard she slept with another guy I knew which was old enough to be her father, and they got caught in a corn field my land' she was 16 years old but iin the end I put her on a bus backto California. I guess we all have to find that special someone in our lives and it was apparent that I wasn't the one for her any longer, maybe I bloomed to early in life who knows. I never did see her again but she comes to mind sometimes while I'm thinking of other things young life is vibrant and everything seams so fresh at that age strange how that changes over the years when you find out that you destroyed that vibrant life and then you spent the rest of your life trying to straighten it out which happed but by then your old and the excitement is gone. Denneta Pirkle what a girl, she came to Nebraska so we could be together as we thought our love would last for ever, and then her parents came to get her but she wouldn't leave with them and they asked why? She then told them that we would marry and they said we were too young but if that's what she wanted then she had their blessing. She was to let them know when it would take place, but the time never came.

My land' I was so in love with her but through trouble we were separated and her needs weren't being met so she explored, to me this was a tragity because being in the same town and not being able to see each other tore at my heart. The courts gaave me time and I did it but with reluctence and that made it harder. I had never had anyone tell me what to do so my anger would come out and that got me in trouble but I had to find a way to see Denneta, then I found out that you could go on visits if you were obedient and then I was good so I could go home for a day or two. Things seam to slip out when you come home after being gone and mom wouldn't keep any secrets from me she told me about her nights out on the town and how she was sleeping with other guys and boy I lost it and told her she should leave and go back to California, it hurt like hell but after her bar hopping it could never work out to me she was damaged and it couldn't be fixed by any means that I knew of at that age. I then went back and got my time done with and I was an angry person hating the world because I lost my love, at

16 years old it's like you lost everything but later you would learn that life goes on. After my release my two brother got into trouble and we moved away from Nebraska for a little while but then the love bug hit me again and I fell for an older women she had three or four kids but boy was she hot she lived on Ventura Ave, in Ventura California. I was still very young but loved to work on cars, we met at a gas station when her car wasn't running right and I told her if she brought it over to my house I would fix it and she said she had no way of paying me and I told her not to worry about it.

She had moved there from L.A. where her husband lived but she was getting a divorce and this started a beautiful friend ship, we would take walks together and talk about life and she shared some of her experiences with me saying she married at a young age and it didn't work out because her husband was controlling and never let her do anything but take care of the kids. My land' she was beautiful but also tall about 6 foot tall but to me that didn't matter, we made love quite offtend and she was good at it for being only in her 20's maybe 26 not quite sure but as time went on she ended up going back because her husband found her and threatened to take the kids. I saw her a week later and we said good by another broken heart being mine, there wasn't anything I could do because her kids came first and that I understood. Then I met my wife which I wish I never had, it was a love and hate relationship and those never work within the time we married it was fairly good but that changed when she got the piece of paper and that made me mad she tried everything to change me to what she thought I should be and that didn't work in the long run I hated the way she had changed and I let her know about it even on my wedding day she was trying to make me change so I got together with her friend in the mountains such a bad start doomed from the start. We didn't stay together long because I felt smothered and she was chokeing the life out of me, within 18 months we split and I got a call saying that my mom was dieing so I headed back to Nebraska to care for her, this gave me the break I needed to try and find some balance in my life. I ended up careing for mom while she was ill and then I met someone I thougt I might be happy with which I never did find happiness. As she too wanted to control the situation and it made me wonder why they were that way, and after that I just stayed singel much better off not having to answer to the opiset sex for my actions. And in a way I had to find that balance or what would work for me. I knew there was something I needed to do even in those days but I didn't have a clue of what it was, I had always felt separated from others like I didn't belong there for some reason, and then after drinking my self to death and going into the light I knew something was going to happen a devine intervention spoke and said that it wasn't my time yet, that my journey hadn't even started yet and that I would know when it would start. That was the end of my drinking, O but what damage it caused to this body and I would have to figure out what the message was that was given to me. There is a bigger picture to our lives and with some comes greatness but we as people don't see the big picture because we go through life with blinders on and have a narrow view of things, the blinders don't let us see what's beside us or in our scope of seeing that beautiful painting, only God can see what will become of our lives and if it's a shot down the tubes then I don't think he would of brought me back just for that He could of let it be over way back when.

Many changes have come into my life and even at times I have thought the door was going to close but there was one miss conception it wasn't my door it was other peoples, why would I feel their doors closeing do I have something which isn't developed yet? A gift which hasn't come to light or am I grasping for something that belongs to me? I do know that there is something special about me but I can't figure it out yet. Many times I would like to know but then other times not so much, the birds are singing this morning so I will take it as it's going to be a nice day. Also the train is coming in to pick up it's loads and the sound is not bothering kind of plesent really, it lets me know that the world is still turning and if I wasn't here it would still be. Life goes on and we are just a part of it for a short time and then the kids take over the old die and the new is born to bring about new things, what will become of things when I take the place of the old and a new child is born? One thing I do know is that the world will go on and God will continue to influence those who are lost in this world of ours, although He doesn't talk like we do He speaks to us through the mind and each time we pray a channel is opened to a new part of the mind. Will this unlock the message He has for me I feel only He knows that one, but He will let me know. It's thrift shop day and I will go down and do my part it's kind of fun really. The people there are opening up and I feel like they are checking me out in some way but a good way trying to see where I'm coming from or how intelegent I am, which I am very smart in my own mind get it? Many people like drama in their lives but for this guy no' I would rather be locked in a box then to carry on with drama because most of it has no meaning in my books just griping and bitching because of something not done right or you do it right and they just need something to bitch about, it must be that right brain left brain thing, which they talk about.

They say a womens mind runs even when they sleep trying to find ways to confuse us men and I believe that if they are that board but I don't think so, Thrursday and things went fine at the thrift store yesterday as I sourted out pance for the pastor to take to another town that needs them. I was kidding with Janet and I think she got confused about how old I am and I gained another pair of jeans along with my faith shirt that somehow made it's was down there from my home. Today is the last day I can smoke so we will see how that goes, can I start a day out without a smoke well it may be possible but timtation will be there stareing me in the face. If I can pull this off then it will go down in the news paper about my beating this addiction also, many people have tried to stop smoking and many have failed I also got some C.D.'S Yesterday of country music and my collection grows without it costing me an arm and a leg yesterday I tried my C.D. Player in my car and it still works it's a miracle! But I do have to clean it so none of the crap gets into it. It's nice that others listen to the same music because I can still keep my collection and add to it for pennys on the dollar, and I have some great songs. All the artist that I like and then some in many ways they influence me in my writing of songs, and the talent grows beyond belief. I come to realize that God gives us all talents and it's what we do with that talent that shows Him that we are on the right track for in the future I will write more of them. I really like to write songs which tells a story about the world and how I see it through these eyes of mine, but it all takes time as with everything we do the mind has to create in it's time. None of this rushing crap which would take away from the essents of the song. In my world I am the creator of my own songs and they have to come from deep within where the soul is. My song' (Don't cry for me) has been in my mind for a long time and it gets longer as time moves forward and only I will know when it's ready to give others a chance to listen to it, because if it doesn't work for me then others wont understand it either it's all about the story and without it then there is no song. Who knows maybe one day one of mine will make it big and be used for something like bringing people to Christ' could that be part of the plan I cant say at this time, many things can come into play during a life time. Just like with writing it can be a supprise out of the blue. I never knew His plan for me to become something different then what I was when I was younger, I thought I would be forever working for someone else and them telling me what to do but through it all He brought me to a different level of existence one above where I was as a young man. Using the mind is a great thing when you can create instead of destroy and everyone has a voice even the little old lady who sit's in her chair lonely' through the years I have been published more times then I can count as I lost track a long time ago. I am known in Kearney and here but I feel the need to go further into the world into that place where many don't want you to go because in that place the government is in it, can a person reach that far without leaving their place where they feel safe we will see in the future as for now I will ponder the idea and try to find an angel of approach.

This morning feels humid and I know it's going to be another hot day in Courtland' my land Summer hasn't even gotten here yet, but I can see the temps in the tripple digits in the next few months. I took a sleeping pill last night and the dreams didn't come like all the other nights before, and I slept pretty well as for my tummy problem it seams to have gone away since I started eating prunes every now and then and I hope it's something that wont come back. Yesterday I was excited to go and do my little part at the thrift store and boy did I laugh and it was because I was happy, I cant hang around this house all the time because I would go nut's watching little brother sleep most of the time. I think he might be getting depressed for some reason but for the life of me I cant figure out why, there was many donations yesterday and I met a few more people ones that I haven't seen before. But in time I will get to know many of them and who knows where it will go from there, when we go to town Randy seams excited but then when we get back home he looses it for some reason maybe he needs a hobby or something so I will see if I can do something maybe find a classic car for him to work on. I know what it means to be sturr crazy, with nothing to do with your time but sit around and then you get lazy as that seams to be the problem. I feel sorry for those who have no vision of the future even if it's only into the next day at least that's something. My writing is a blessing for me as I can express my self without others trying to interfear with my thought, the gift that keeps giving is what I call it. And many hear your thoughts and words but you don't want to destroy just help in anyway possible.

The one women I work with must of went to Hastings Nebraska' to see her daughter for a while because she didn't work yesterday, last week she said she might go and I hope she has a good time. With me going from solitude to a noisey place makes me want to come back home, and the closer I get to home the more excited I get because I know what to expect here where my world is. Every day you hear on the news where someone is killed or raped and it makes me glad that I'm not a part of that destructive world, this recession they say is the worst in many deckaids which causes people to robb and steel from other and they say they do it because money is tight Boo Hood! Everyone is in that shape but you don't have to break the law to survive and hurt others. Many do it because they are Evil and it's in their nature just like the ones that get sent to prison, you would think the government would want to help change them in some way but they don't, it's like the money is in keeping them locked up because they can use them for slaves which was supposed to be out lawed in the 19th century or 18th not quite sure. Working a day for two dollars is stupid but on paper they see bigger numbers which they put in their pockets the wardens get most of it and build for the time when they don't have to work any longer, and I bet if they did a an honest check on them they also get a kick back from the drugs sold in there. Many States cant afford to build a prison so they have investers put up the money and then the state gives them 30 or so thousand dollars to keep each person in there which is a bunch of crap because most people out here live on less then ten thousand, that's three times what it takes to live in the out side world the prisoners; should be living like kings with that much capital floating around. They used to care about rehabilitation and now they don't as they just sit there and do their time and a lot of them sleep their lives away doing nothing. What a shame' that life is thought of as a piece of meat to be disgarded after it's eaten, and even then it's thrown back into the place which didn't help them in the first place. The success rate for prisoners to come out and make it is very low with those who are addicted to drugs and alcohol, and when they are some how put into a treatment center even then the rate is only one percent one out of 100 people will over come their addiction why! a lack of self worth. Friday morning' the rain I prayed for came last night, and early this morning. You could hear the thunder crack across the sky as it lit up the night it was very noisey but at least we got our rain. Someone was supposed to have ayard sale but I don't know if the rain will stop it hopefully not they can always have it in the garage or the house it's my first day of not smoking and I already want to pick one up but we will see what happens as the day goes on, when I write I always smoke as it has helped in concentrating in the past so now things will change. Little brother slept until after eight yesterday morning which was something different with him and he didn't go back to sleep for the whole day thank God. There is plenty of room here for someone too open up a carpet cleaning service starting with your own home being cleaned by the rug doctor, ordering one could lead somewhere and they will ship it for free. Could love over come anything? It's a place which I haven't been in a long while and really it's a place that maybe I don't want to be at this time in my life, but

I know somewhere down the road I will have to embrace it or live out a lonely life. The day is starting out ok' but I have a feeling that if it wouldn't of rained then we might have found some things from the past at the garage sale.

The beginning of the weekend to night and everyone will celebrate not having to work there is a thing about Courtland and it reminds me of a quakers community where everyone lives their lives and if someone needs a helping hand then it's given by those who love this fantastic place, I seam to get by with just a couple puffs off a smoke and I hope it will decreases even more as time goes by as for my will power it's pretty good but it could be stronger. The thought of saving money really helps in this fight and who knows in time this just might work, 'my thought for the day care for others as you care for your self' this in it's self can bring joy to others that might also be a lone. My thoughts are not on writing as I seam to draw a blank writers block I guess, we had a good day as we got the rain we needed a little over 2 and a half inches which should make a difference in the growth of the fields. Also we went to a garage sale and I got an old guitar which had to of been made in the 1800's if I had to guess, I have seen some go for big money being that old and I hope this in one of those. It would be nice to finely find something that wasn't a piece of crap and make me some money it's unlike any other guitar I have ever seen with it's wood grain showing through so proudly. There was one time when I saw one go for $4000.00 dollard and that was on pawn stars, so many don't know what they have until they get it checked out and that's something I will do in the future. It's Saturday and they will bury Walt at two this afternoon and then have aparty for him at Dennis's house but I wont go unless I'm invited. You have to be cautious around some especially when your not sure of things that Guitar is sitting proudly in my closet but I wish I had a case for itto keep it safe.

Although I'm on this stop smoking regement it hasn't worked completely as I take a puff from time to time, but it does bring to my attention how oftend I take a hit. Maybe within a week or so it might become a thing of the past my doctor said it could take up to three months to stop completely so I will hang in there and see what happens as for now I am unable to stop completely but even a cut down is good, it's going to be a nice day as the air is keeping us cool then later at noon I will go to the thrift store and see what's happening it's a bake sale today and I hope they have some goodies for me to bring home afterwards, the weather is strange around here with the humidity so high but the pump hasn't been having to work as much as it used to with that dehumidifier going in the house. You can really tell a difference in the quality of being able to breath especially if you're a smoker, it seams to take that heavyness out of the air allowing you to breath with ease in my journey I have seen many that have had to struggle to take a breath and in reality I don't want to go through that if I can aviod it. It's strange to look up at mom and Olivers picture, and know they are together once again in heaven. My land' if I have angels watching over me then they are two of them along with dad Herb, these bodies produch children but we are given the stamp of approval by God before we are born and it's great to know that He has a plan for each of us. I take the knowledge that I recive and put it on a shelf so later I can recall it if and when needed, I hear that we all have shelf's that is loaded with knowledge and this is something I just found out a while back, so my shelf's must be a mess with much of the knowledge being about the things I went through at a young age. when is a good time to restock them maybe in the near future I will do this I hear many say they got excitement out of reading a good novel as for me I have never found excitement in reading something and maybe that's something I should explore because those things I have missed out on as a kid. I know the pastor reads certain books but she doesn't let her mind get into just anything, all things we have learned along the way should be used to help others in some way and if you cant relate to them then it's a no win situation. But if you can grab their attention then help could be on it's way, it's a mixed up world and most people with addictions don't read I know I never did but then one day He woke me up and for that I am grateful through the years I have gained more knowledge but I know there is much more to be learned and I will learn as my mind is exceptive to it. Some read all the time and I can't see what's going on in their world and maybe that's a good thing, not knowing the worken parts of their mind. In life I have traveled many roads but I never expected that I would find a peaceful place like where I live, in all my time here no one has botherd me and I mean no one which is nice but when I need something all I have to do is ask. The people here are loving and they know about the life I once lead and they felt I was worth a second chance also, the grass should be turning green once again with the rain that we got and it shows me that my prayers for rain has come to pass. The river is up from what it was and this should allow them to irragate when they need to, for the rain doesn't only plemish the ground but it allows them to store up the water not used at the time for future use.

God seams to come through for us even in the worst of times and makes things good once again, this will be my first bake sale so we will see how things work. I do know it's by donation and they put it in a big jar so it can be used for things of importance, I'm working in the back of the store and trying to get things situated so they are not hard to find, and so far it's working. Time seams to go by fast when I'm back there and no one is telling me what to do which is a plus because I don't care for that, show me what needs to be done and I will do it gladly but no talking down to me. Which by the way no one has, we all seam to get along just fine as we work and it lets us open up and get to know each other a little better you might say it lets us pick each others brain to see things which we might have not been able to see if we didn't work together. As for me I think I'm average but others say I'm above and maybe that's something to do with me finding the answers to things I'm interested in. I seam to always have an answer to the questions which are asked and maybe that's how they tell how smart you are I don't really know, little brother will be getting up before too long and I hope he has a good day also. This afternoon I went to Walt's funeral after working at the thrift shop and boy there was a lot of friends that he had there, only about six of us said something about our friendship with him and me being the one who knew him for the less time. He was a special friend and will be missed by all who knew him and I like to think our friendship was special, I also saw Dennis and Walts daughter and shook their hands.

There will never be another Walter and peace be with you my friend. I got a ride from Beverly and her family to the funeral as my car doesn't do good on the back roads, maybe in time another will come my way lord knows I will need a new one in time. Dennis invited me over to the party they are having for him but I don't think I will make it, but it was sure nice for them to invite me, I have yet to mop the floors at the church so maybe I will go later and get it done for tomorrows service or in the morning when I'm bright and awake. Norman was also there to pay his respects and we chatted for a few minutes, all in all the day went very well. I could see Dennisses wife crying as the sadness set in but that's too be expected when you loose a close friend, in the future life will go on but there will be one less table setting because he is gone. My friend let me see that goodness comes in many forms and in this life you have to do what makes you happy and no one else should be able to stand in your way, with me I had to change and I did it because it was the right thing to do for me my self. Each of us has a destiny and we do what ever it takes to bring that to light, my self change has been there for the taking and I embraced it when it needed to inter my life too make me a better person or try to help me in understanding things I otherwise wouldn't. as for this day it's been very hot and humid more humid then most days because of the rain, and I hope for more rain in the next day or so. Having a house gives you confidence and builds up your self esteem to where you feel good about things not only certain things but things in general, I don't know if the rain will come tonight and it didn't. Sunday morning yesterday at the flea market we ran into a guy that knows about Guitars and he said I should be able to get $50.00 or $75.00 dollars for it, but something tells me that it's worth more. He went on to say that it was home made that someone crafted it and they did a good job, it's going to be a busy day as I have to mop the floors and fold the introductions for the service. Then tomorrow it will be the start of a new week filled with many different things, in the days a head I want to try some new things if they come my way so we will see what will happen or take place, we still have our Spanish people living across the street and I think they are migret workers to work in the fields and keep the weeds down. I used to do it a long time ago and it was back breaking work but they seamed to get a field done in a day or so depending on how big it was an 80 acher section could be done in a day if it wasn't in to bad of shape. In my day there were many jobs anywhere from building earth stoves to working in the forest up in K'Bob national forest up by Falg Staff Arizona, even then the jobs were tight as we traveled to many places from King-man to Phoenix Arizona and beyond Colorado to Venture California, even then we spent most of the time camping trying to stay away from the rat race in the cities where all the people were. With the two motor homes we could of stayed in them but as the driving got to us we would stop at a motel for a swim and a shower which cost a lot even back then, I have seen the grand canyon and many other places but for some reason I always returned back home to Nebraska where it all started. When we went to Minnesota in my teens it was nice to see grandma but their lives were a lot different from ours it was like we were born on different planets, grandma talked to me but it was like she was holding something back from me and I have now come to think it was something about my father.

For the years are gone now and still today nothing about him so that will be something I will have to except as there are many that don't know who their father is, and I'm just one of them. But I will keep the memories the good ones that I made in my mind, which is that he was a good person and got lost somewhere in time. Although he was my father I now have another and that is God as I go through this life, I have always had God as a father but just didn't know it until I woke up a little. And maybe that's what we are doing here we are being awaken to travel to that place we call ever lasting life, where everything will be good like it was supposed to be in the beginning before they ate from the tree. All our sins washed away by the only one who could do it Jesus Christ, god has been around before all of us and He will continue to be long after we are gone and He leaves His mark on many of us as we go through this life. The words of the bible are to teach us and help us understand what it is like to live that Christen life without all the destruction that can occure in that time period which we live, and maybe in the end we can take some of that knowledge with us. Lord knows nothing else will follow us when we leave this place, will there be memories? I guess when you go all the way to heaven you will find out. It's muggy this morning at least in here, but it will subside as the day goes on I know the church is very muggy as the air hasn't been on in a few days but that will all change once I get over there and turn it on. Many of the people that went to the funeral I had never seen before and I'm sure they were farmers which Walt worked on their equipment I didn't know he was a diesel machanic another thing I learned and they say he was good at it.

I guess sort of like dad but he worked on motors of less compression, I bet they could have had a lot in common if they both would of lived. The morning is coming upon us as it's getting to be about 5:00 Am. A good time to go and clean up what hasn't been done, as for little brother he will sleep until later and then get up to met the day. Like the pastor was saying yesterday many don't know why God sent them here but he did just the same and in time they become part of a bigger picture, a bigger plan of things to come and no matter how you look at it He does have a plan for the people here in Courtland KS. And maybe in time some will see what unfolds but for those who have passed their years they will be with the father in that place which is grander then the grandest palace. Monday June 18th there wasn't many people at church because of all the different things they have going on like vacation bible school in Scandia, through the grape vine they had nearly 28 kids attending which is about the number of kids they have here during school time. It's a great things for them to learn while they are young and in time it might bring them back here once they get done with collage it would be like in the movies that I watch, when they come back to the nest and carry on the tradition that their parents started when they were young which with most it's farming the getting up early wouldn't be a problem with most of them because they have done it most of their young lives feeding the chickens and watering the goats and who knows maybe milking ole Betsey. All the wonders of home, I recall wanting to be like dad as he would come home all full of grease from work and mom would chase him into the shower. I loved to hear them as they bickered back and forth in a kidding way and then finely dad would give in and get the job done, I recall hearing did you wash behind your ears and sometimes he would go back in. Rodney the oldest boy would also be chased into the shower after a day of helping dad on the weekend, I think it gave him a feeling of self pride to be able to help at his age. I recall Rod being skinny and long legged as a kid but now he is short and big I guess we perceive things differently when we are small and we look up to others bigger then us, Randy and Rod look somewhat a like with their big gut's and short legs but they are brothers so that part must run in the jeans. Even sis is short like me, it's strange how sis said she wouldn't be like a certain person and and then it came to be as she ended up just like her each time I see my sister I see the resemblance from the one who gave birth to us as they were both short. Mom was a fighter when it came to surviving and she fought for many years until she couldn't fight any longer and then she went home to be with the Lord. Like with Oliver' it was their time to go away and not have to fight any longer in this world, at times I get sad but then it goes away to let me go on with things in my life like everyday things which allows us to live on even after our friends are gone. The everyday things in life seam to fall into place when things need to be done and life goes on, Harley has been acting strange for the last couple of days so I will have him go to the doctor if I can get him in it's like he is unsure of him self and he hides sometimes under the bed, I have been that way in the past and it's not a good feeling.

Today it's supposed to be 100 degrees out side and I don't have to tell anyone that I will stay inside away from the heat. During this time I will write and search my mind for things I might have forgot, it's strange how things come back to you after the mind is healed and then it lets you move on with new things that will fill your life in the future. For what was important back then isn't so much any more, how long will it take to collect that many memories once again another half a life time? O I don't think so as the hard part has been done the learning and the doing of things which you never thought you could do, my land this life wasn't in the cards not in the ones I saw in my younger years. But like others in this life I fight to survive and in time this life will become more easier as I get older, I think my parents wanted us to have a good time when we were young because they knew that our lives would be hard later on. And fun we did have but now things are different and sometimes I feel like I want to break out and go wild, the humidity is high this morning as I can feel it in the air but at least it isn't as bad as out side. I find it strange how much people got paid for doing things back in the 18.00's as today that wouldn't amount to much at all a few cents wouldn't buy you anything in this day and age. So they must have saved a lot back then when I see antiques from that time I'm just amazed at the quality of how they were created, if I could have a house of old furniture then I would be thrilled to hold on to the past and make it possible for it too reach into the furtur. I have seen strange chairs go for $125.000.00 which to me is out of this world I guess it depends on the maker and how famous they were in their day. Tuesday morning and it's nice and calm for some reason the power went out last night and I don't have a clue why except maybe a storm went through, the feelings I get living here is like no other and as time moves forward it will only get better. Through the sands of time many things change and hopefully in my time thing will get to where they are on an even keel meaning each day as for now my emotions run ramped and I cant figure out why this happens. When I write it's like I'm in a box and the rest of the world is shut out except for what you hear on the news or read in the news paper in the time when I moved here things were exciting but also kind of frightening, and if I would of stayed with a certain person then my world would of fallen from where it is today, there is a bigger picture but He isn't showing it to me at this time.

My picture of what life shoule be doesn't necessarily correspond with what it is, as I see living out my life here as for the things I need they are met the eating and things for I have more food then two people could take in and some I donate to the church and other deserving placed like the boy scouts and even the post office sometimes. My life here is a simple life sheltered from most destruction that happens in the out side world for they are there and well we live in this great place, later down the road my duties will increase and I will take on more work of writing maybe find something that will help others in some ways. My thought are always with my kids and I hope they are doing fine in their lives as they grow and become stronger my scrap book will only be used when my grand children are in trouble, because it's not a proper thing to let them read unless they start down that path. This way they will know that grandpa had once went down that path and pulled him self out of it, my whole reason for recording these things is to show others that it can be done going from deaths door to living a pretty good life with just a few hitches to it. In a way I hope it rained and knocked out the power that way it will help the crops and stop my grass from turning brown once again, my quiet nature lets me see things in others which isn't in me and that can help in some ways to make me a little more open as for some which don't open up at all. They have to find their own way to find that privet place in their heart where things are good, I still find my self worring about things but I also realize that doing that worring doesn't do any good. Funny always searching for the answer, but never finding what I think it should be. A small town lets you get in touch with your self and my advice to anyone searching for that answer is to go there or at least visit that place where you might find that peace you have been looking for, the world is full of confusion and the further you get away from it the quicker you will find out who you are. Not what others want you to be but who God created you to be as these are two things all together different from each other, what we do in life is just a pass time it's not our real journey for that knowledge is in God's hands and only He knows our true path to enlightenment. We can search our whole lives and never find what He already knows so think twice before you think you have it all figured out, because in the end you really don't.

Will we ever know the answers to the questions of life probably not but it's fun to try to find them sometimes, at times this place brings flash backs and it's like I had been here but in a different time when things were different the old western times come to mind but how could that be we are not brought back to life to live it over as I would think once is enough for anyone, none of us will sail through life knowing all the answers because that just isn't possible. It's a really hot day and the winds are 40 plus so I will spend most of the day in side except for the trip to town that we took when it was cooler out, at times I get the inkling to do something and then it fades like it was never there, to only come back again later in the day. What brings on these things bordom comes to mind or maybe it's something that's coming up in the near future a change that I don't fully understand, or something that will change things. Every now and then when something is going to happen I will get these feelings and even when they happened things are never clear, just like working for the church I felt it then and one day it happened within a month or so, most things that have happened was unexpected but that's the way things happen around here leaving no mark that they were even there and I adjusted to them just fine. In time I want to be known for my character the guy that could make others laugh and feel good when they are down, this in it's self can make me feel good also. My letter to the Salina Journal was a hit and I got many replies from friends on Facebook and Twitter by me taking it there it will get read by many people all around the world and if they want to reply then it will happen in their time not anyone elses.

Tomorrow is hump day so half the week will be gone. I like that day because I get to go to the thrift store and check things out to see if I want any of it, before I put it away. I also know that others in town have read my letter as they get the new's paper each day, it seams they like to read things about their town when it's something good and my writings are always good when I am moved by something. Wednesday morning and I can never tell which day will be an inspirational one as each is different in many ways sometimes I have one full of the holy spirit which lets me reach deep inside to find that place where I like to be and then there are others which only let you get a glimps and then you loose it for some reason. It was fun yesterday as we spent most of the day inside Randy didn't get up until 8:00 Am and he seamed in a better mood then most day's, it had to of been in the seventys in the house and a wopping 97 out side. Man was it hot' I'm not sure what temps this day will bring but I hope it's lower then yesterday, when the addictionn cycle starts it doesn't just let you know that your hooked you can go years before you even think you have a probem with it as for me even when I got put in the youth development center I still didn't think I had a problem with it not until years later when I had to have it. When your young and strong you can fight it off somewhat but then when you get into your late 20's it will show you whos boss, my self I never had a problem with not making to the restroom but many of my family and friends did and sometimes their mates would find them in the closet and really get mad at them this is caused by the alcohol destroying their kidneys and in a stooper they would head to the closes place that resembled the pot, and when they were confronted by family members they had no recollection of what had taken place and it was like they never did it to them anyway. But in the real world it did happen and the loved ones are hurt because of it, this is just some of what a family goes through dealing with someone who is an alcoholic. And the alcoholic goes on with his or her day like nothing happened, my writings are true accounts of what a family has to endure even with the blackouts that some go through. When I was much younger I fould my self in jail and for the life of me I didn't know why I was there then come to find out that they picked me up for drunk driving a blackout that I didn't see coming but of course no one sees them coming that's why they are called blackouts, although you function in that world you don't ever get a head because the money is spent on the alcohol which the government loves as they get their taxes out of it. Right now they are taxing cigarettes making them cost so much that no one would be able to afford them and the government gets richer off of them with each passing day they use the ploy that they don't want kids to smoke which they could care less about the kids it's all about money and how they can rake in more of it, they don't want to raise taxes on alcohol because that's the last front and without those taxes they would run out of money they are trying to turn peoples focus away from the destroyer of life. So they will keep using it they are conglomerates a body of the rich who really run this country like the mason's but only bigger, the ones who destroy lives like they were nothing and they are allaround the United States and other parts of the world. Imagine a society of the privileged never wanting for anything and they could get what they needed at the drop of a hat.

And it was built by old money form boot legging and other things which were once against the law of the people, then in time what was illegal became legal by them changing things to fit their agenda. Although we never see them doesn't mean that they don't exist out there somewhere, they would be the ones with the advanced capabilitys to never get sick while other drop like flies even from the slightest cold or the flue. Through time and science we have been able to extend life from what was about sixty years to almost a hundred, and although I wouldn't want to live that long it's nice to know that it's possible and. Science is great in some things but still it doesn't explain our being here as that's something only God could do create a race of people who in time will over come anything that comes their way. Going from the grave to living a life of goodness, we are all people in a world that could be the best but also it can become evil a very delicate balance those two things. Thursday and it rained like the dickens last night as the stream in my dream came back to life for a while and ran down the side walk, I didn't see the lake as it hadn't rained enough before I fell a sleep but it was a possibility that it came later, during the night. It was fun working at the thrift store yesterday as I and Jan talked about different things shelves in the mind where things are stored and what's in some of them, in a kidding way I told her that mine was empty and she said no their not. The strength we have inside is really strong as we go through this life and it seams to get stronger the longer we are here or that's the way I preceive things in my world.

My world' what a thing to be able to create and separate the bad from the good and keep what is best in the realm of goodness, as for the other well I have no use for it. It's strange how even in that other world my strength brought me through for surely the good out weighed the bad that was in that place. Even when others got mad at me they couldn't act on it for some reason, it was a world that I really didn't belong in and even then I could feel my self trying to find my way out away from the darkness but it took death before He came and got me or close to death, His strength out weighs ours by a mile and I felt it that day so long ago when He sent me back how great is that? I went from falling to floating in a place where I had never been before and my body didn't matter there. Just like it wont matter when we leave this place when it's time but that's the key time if it isn't your time then you will be sent back to finish or start your journey through this life, our visitors must be hard workers and it will take time before trust can be established as for me I keep my car locked until trust can become pertinent but it will happen in time many have come here and stayed for a while but some have also left and Ibelieve it takes a certain kind of person to be able to live here. Someone who wants to learn about them selves because if your not at peace with your self then you wont be at peace here, many struggle with things in life and I went through some of those things but through time it becomes easy to see the person who is inside of you, when I talk with people and run out of conversation I look else where like out side with a smile on my face looking at other things until they talk once again in many situations we don't talk at all and that's when I glad that others come in and ask how things are going. As for others opinion of me I really don't pay any mind to it, because people think what they think! My self I like to look at the goodness that I KNOW IS IN EACH AND EVERYONE OF US' and if some change that then it's up to them. If my world can be of goodness then why cant theirs? But I have seen some that don't look at the world the way I do, and that's their loss for surely goodness will rain upon the earth when everything is in balance through this life I have come to understand many things. AND ONE OF THEM IS THAT IF YOUR GOOD TO OTHERS THEN THEY WILL DO THE SAME IN RETURN if they are not full of hate, by the time you meet them. HATE IS A STRONG WORD' But in life with some it does exist and it destroys many things, my day starts with my peace of mind and that I get by prayer and talking to my Father. GIVING THANKS FOR THE THINGS HE HAS BROUGHT INTO MY LIFE, FOR WITHOUT HIM THERE WOULDN'T BE ANY ME. The train is coming through and it's getting ready to blow it's horn, you could just about set your clock by it's arrival each day especially during the week. ALSO I CAN HEAR THE DOVES OUT SIDE AND I BELIEVE THEY ARE SENT HERE TO WATCH OVER THE TOWN' IT'S LIKE THEY HAVE LIVED HERE FOR EVER. I have some scripture to read this week and it will give me some insight to the serman for this next Sunday, pastor KATHY' does this every week so peoploe will read GOD'S word more then they do now. Some will throw it away and others will read the message that is being sent to us with each passage it OPENS THE MIND TO EXCEPTENCE AND THAT'S WHAT A LOT OF PEOPLE NEED EVEN IF THEY DON'T WANT TO ADMIT IT. For the love of God is in all places even in places we least expect it.

To me true love comes from God for there is no stronger love out there anywhere, my heart was filled with joy as I got published by both of my news papers the Kearney-hub, and the Salina Journal both in the same month which is a fist. The managing editor of the Kearney-hub told me hat clarity is perfectly clear because my stories come from experience and not book learning, in book learning they have no experience of the real life experiences only what they read out of books and that doesn't cut it in true life they don't experience the destruction that comes with addiction. And that makes their guessing very tricky because if they are wrong then someone dies, my triles have been an open book and I can see the distrotness in others that might not be seen by those who think they can learn about it in a second hand vision if you will. MY WRITNGS TELL THE STORY OF HOW IT CAN BE OVER CAME BUT IT ISN'T OUT IN THE PUBLIC AS OF YET MAYBE IN TIME THIS TOO WILL BE A THING OF THE PAST, and then some will follow my lead and over come their own addiction by hearing from someone who really knows what they are going through. It's Friday morning' and I'm barely awake the force which brings me to write each day has been with me for quite some time, and I come to the realization that it has to be my spirit a strong spirit that holds the knowledge from the past. During my letter yesterday I brought up the legalization of pot and how hey are so gun hoe on getting it legal, for this substence too has to be smoked and many will end up with cancer because of it. Sometimes I feel like the kid that took on the giant in the bible and before too long they wont like it, before I was like a pincel prick in anoyance but now I have taken it to a different level to try and stop the destruction.

As time moves forward thousands of people have read my stories and maybe even millions and I hope I have changed things because in the end if you don't leave a good mark on this earth then you have left nothing to be remembered by, as I great this day I will be glad in it and pray that my spirit will shine through and give gladness to others who might be down in spirit. Strange how the spirit can do that but at the end of the day it stays with you through thick and thin, it seams to sleep when you do and awaken at the same time each day in hope to put more knowledge out there so others will understand that the road to destruction is a lonely one traveled by the spirits which don't want them to be free. It's like a society that wants to keep you within it's walls because the goodness is just out side of them. Many people have made millions off of the destruction of life and they see no value in people getting their lives back, so they keep them traped in hope for them to spend millions on the poison that will one day take their lives. MY VISION LET'S ME SEE WHAT IT HAS DONE IN MY LIFE AND THE DESTRUCTION WAS GREAT, BUT ALSO IT HAS GAVE ME THE WILL TO TRY AND GET PEOPLE TO LISTEN TO ME. Don't destroy the spirit which has brought you into this world because at one time it was one of God, but through the years it has become one of confusion lost in a world that it doesn't understand. And they don't want you to understand it, many don't know their spiirit because it has been corrupted by many things in this world from politicians to the government in general for they are like the clan and will destroy anything that gets in their way. Although the people are stronger they choose not to show their strength and why this is I really cant say at this point maybe afraid that they will destroy the lives of the poor who knows the real reason for this kind of thing. T.G.I.F. And many things will happen on this day in history, although you wont hear about them until later in life a child will die and so will many others but only the rich people will be made public to the world why is this? Because the others don't matter and their ashes will be thrown to the wind like they were never here in all this regime and roll there is a message but only a few will be able to understand it's meaning and they are not one of them. The harvest is being done just one of many this year and everything is going smoothly God brought forth the rain that I prayed for and others, when I ask Him for something I also ask for a sign and He gives it gladly. Yesterday I mowed the lawn as it greened; up nicely, to make things look very nice compaired to last week when the ground was brown. I sometimes find my self deep in thought or I think it's thought but draw a blank strange how that happens sometimes, through the window of time many will fall and those who do wrong to our people will also fall at their own hand. Only good will prStacyil in this life and only the person will know if they are good or the other, in this mind there is a life time of knowledge but like with all things it's hard sometimes to bring it to the surface.

So with patients and persistence it lets a little come to the surface and then I have to write it down, for me to figure it out I have to let the mind rest for a time and then move forward. The heat was gone for a while but I think it will be back today, the life of addiction has destroyed many in the last 100 years and I don't see them trying too put an end to it anytime soon. With some they have excepted it because it's been around since time it's self and they believe it couldn't ever change because of the time frame, but they would be wrong for everything there is a season and for every season there is a change people just don't know what the change will be. I have dreams that one day these things will take on a new apperience and go from addiction to a cure, the cure exists now and it's in everyone of us but it has to be ignited before it can bring change take the passion for getting high and transform it into a passion to take a persons life back. And this will give hope and where there is hope faith isn't far behind, how I was able to destroy the curse was brought on by the need to live. The need to show others that the addiction is like a problem that can be solved, but there has to be a a separation from those who don't give a shit about the ones trying to change. My self' I took my life to another level not nessarly above others but in a different direction and fed my mind with things it missed while I was away in the darkness of the other world, this might sound vage or even boring but it's not for the light will show it's self in time. And I saw a place that I never knew existed, a place of goodness that supersedes everything that I lived through.

My world today doesn't have or soon wont have the negitive forces that lead me towards the darkness that almost destroyed my life. Saturday morning and the rain was coming down pretty good you can srtill hear the thunder as the storm moves off, my land' I asked for some rain but I didn't think we would get this much. Looking at the television the storm reaches into Nebraska down to Belleville, and I know we got our share for a few days. It's the 23th of the month and the day is going to be humid but no fear because it's nice in here and the house is well insolated to keep the elements out, it's these kind of rains that make for a good crop but also it can be gone and dried upin a matter of days. Our last rain a few days ago weren't quite dried up yet as the ground was still wet and this on top of that should set us up for sometime, I don't hear the thunder any more but that doesn't mean it stopped raining just the noise is gone. My land' you can hear the wind blowing like heck as it whissels through the trees, off in the distance you can still hear the thunder but at least it isn't right above us. We fired up the grill yesterday and my stomic gave me hell all night as it's not used to that kind of food very oftend so it will be a while before we do that again maybe a month or so, I wanted to get a carpet cleaner but with the mud I think tomorrow would be a good day we will see as the night turns to light very dark out yet. It's strange how when it's dry we pray for rain and usually we will get it butother parts of the state needs it also, as I got up this morning I saw lights across the way and the first thing I thought of was my little friend I'm still in hope that I will get to meet her and maybe get to know her if she isn't taken. I like the things I have seen in her and I think she is very nice, I guess you could say I'm an admirer of her by far this bashfullness lets me stay away until I find out if she is single and then if she is willing I will talk to her. You might say I'm finding out if there is some kind of chance to become friends, so far two inches of rain has fallen so that should really help my grass should grow once again and I will have to mow more oftend I started to do the floors in the womens bathroom and today I will do some more to try and finish it up. A guy wrote me on my letter and I wrote him back it seams he is trying to change my mind about pot and it wont work, because that's just the way it is for I see no good in making pot legal they are just after the mighty dollar and it's that plain and simple their goal is to become rich and I wont change my mind about my decision. Just look at California even with the millions of achers they have growing the stuff they are so far in debt that they will never get out, I just don't see any good coming out of it and I know it will lead to other destructive things happening. Once you give a child the ok' to start doing drugs you have lost the battle. On another note it's going to be a beautiful day before I heard the weather out side I could tell that it had rained by the reflection off the street it seams to shine like glass after it get's wet sort of like it does during winter when it turns to ice. No reflection no rain and it doesn't take much just a soft falling of rain, since my arrival here my connection with friends has grown and they care so much that they don't want me to leave and with this in mind I have become part of a bigger family the family of God and others. No other place have I felt such warmth and I have lived in many placess during my life some small and some big.

But none can compare to Courtland, a town just off the beaton path where the people live in peace and if excepted then you have a place for life. Not just a stop to spend some time but a true home where people will let you know if they like you and you will find out if you like them also, they become a part of you a circle of love that extends into the future. As for negitive things entering your life there is non unless you let or invite it in and this can make you stronger as you move forward, little brother has his quirks as we all do but they seam to come together and make something strong as he grows in comfort of living here. And in time he will grow strong to over come what had taken part of his life also. I wish his learning skills could be broadened and who knows maybe in time it can be, he is smart in many ways but I need to find that opening that I know is there. Could I find love in this place that has become my home? Shurly the possibility is there but time plays a big part in it, finding that special someone who would and could love me for who I am my soul is pure and so is my spirit. When the feeling comes when

I need to be loved I have nothing to hold on to and that leaves an empty space the inter twineing of two bodies is something that I have missed for some time now and it would fill that void that has been empty, the sitting down and having coffee in the morning when we awake to the going to work and getting a kiss before we leave each other and start the day. As for little ones those day are given by God if the timing is right, but I don't know if the temperment is there for that any longer.

Just the getting up and starting the day with someone would be a good start refireing that connection between a man and women that has been out could bring on many new things into someones life a closeness that could never be severed. Then to go on to be together for many years until our time is up, someone to sit on the porch with and swing back and forth while the dog plays in the yard. That family connection that has been missing for so long, and the travel to go to places where you have never been before and then coming back to that place we would call home Courtland KS, in my vision I see it all but right now it's just a vision with missing pieces. The women, the dog, the family, but in time it could be a beautiful picture. My land' Sunday morning and I slept late, now this is different for me anyway but it happens. Yesterday I learned that a farmer bought a couple of houses so he can have a place for his hired help to live, and I think that's awesome. This morning I going to turn on the air a lot earlier because it's supposed to hit 100 degrees and it seams that the humidty really gets to people like my self. I noticed long ago that Spanish people are hardly bothered by it and I think it has to do with where they are born, because Mexico can be really hot during summer months especially deep Mexico away from the Ocean. In the small towns some come from towns smaller then Courtland where they take care of their loved ones, so having a home to stay in here must be a blessing I remember my friend Lidea that is originally from Mexico she made it pretty good being a translater over here and raised her children here to become high officals in the Government like cop's that protect Government officals, and she is one proud lady her husband is also nice and man can he work on car's I hade him do some work for me a couple of times. It's strange how we meet people in this life and they come from many parts of the country and do many different things as they learn to survive in this world but we all have our parts to do when the lord calls on us as people, in my existence I'm a warier trying to change things so the world might be a better place for the next generation. Can I accomplish this task I believe so with the help of others, but I realize that it takes more then just my self and many are catching on as I survive and move forward. Here in my town I am left alone to carry on my fight without people bothering me and then I send the message off to other states and such so if they choose to help then they can. By the reply I recived many pay attention to what I write, where as to before they just shrugged it off and no reply was received. A writer seams to get noticed when the subject is carried on with strength and they don't back down, as that is me as I take this too the boundrys and see where it goes in time if my hunch is right those who want to have these things made legal will try something somewhere down the road but at this time they just write like I do. Trying to open that Box that should never be opened they also try to convince me that the money would be good to help those fighting addiction that would be like an addiction trying to cure an addiction. This person said that he was an avid user of the stuff meaning he wasn't addicted to it but the truth would lay in the time he could spend without it and not go through withdraws, the word productive person came up but the truth would also lay in what he considers a productive persoon could it be that he is one of the people who sells it? And if so what productive job does he have besides that one. It's 4:30 Am and I'm going to the church to turn on the air-conditioning so the day goes better for my family, as lord knows it grows all the time. During this time of year you never know how many people will attent the service.

So I go on the assumption that a hand full will come, but next week is the start of a new time we go from 9:15 to 10:45 in which I hope more people will be up at that time. I have had others say that they will come when the time changes and I hope to see them when that takes place, for each person is different and they should feel good about coming to church because if they don't then something isn't right. My presents is shown each Sunday as I learn more about God and how he takes care of His own it was cool this morning in church but it didn't take long for it to get hot as there was more people then I expected. Next Sunday I will turn on the air the night before and see how that goes over, after church we went to town to get a carpet cleaner and got it all the way home and had to take it back the dam thing didn't work! The temp has to be 100 plus out side and it makes it hard to breath especially for older folks even the ones that don't smoke. As for in my home it's very nice and we give thanks to God for having such a gift during this time in life, although I'm fighting some things in life I'm confadent that they will become a thing of the past sometime in the future. We all have struggles in life but with a positive attitude there is nothing we cant over come, most of the day is gone now going on 4:00 in the afternoon so things should start to cool off in a couple of hours but it wont be noticed until later around 10:00 to night. I saw the women that works at the dollar store and she still makes my heart jump, funny how that workd. I remember one time me and a friend went four wheeling with his truck and we got it stuck, it was a bad time in my life for two reasons one by this time I was off the alcohol that about done me in, but by most means I was still crippled barely being able to walk he had to leave me behind.

I had been introduced to another drug and it was a killer but it made you feel like you could do anything. We were in the hills and I felt like I couldn't go on, sort of like the kids that got caught in the snow storm that years in Nebraska and they passed away. We had no water and the truck was up to the floor boards in it but it couldn't be drank, being at least 5 miles from the highway by going over the country hills. This tested my ability to survive. Then as I was walking I saw a house with the brush so high that I had to wade through it and finely came to the house where a women gave me a drink. My companion left me there knowing he could make better time on his own and he would come back for me which he never did because the drug made him spooked like those kids, finely the women called the law and they brought me home safely. And I never went out four wheeling again. My body was in survival mode and I survived, I remember later when he came by he said they impounded his vehical and by that time I really didn't give a crap. Later in years he got arrested and was sent to prison and I don't know what happened after that, for many years we wrote back and forth sending Christmas cards and then we lost touch. He treated me more like a brother then my own and we even called each other a brother from another mother, he was the bad boy tipe that women loved to be around and I was just the oppiset the meek person that got along with everyone. I believe I didn't want to remember this story in my past because something happened I got a glimps of God's love for me because I know that could have been the end for me, yet He gave me the strength to go on and find my way home. It seams He has always been there to help me through the bad times and yet I couldn't see it at the time it's only by hind sight that I see it now' so many times He brought me back to try and awaken me from the sleep I was in and He never gave up even when I gave up he used someone else to make sure I was safe. Just like in some of my journeys when I thought I couldn't go on He brought me through them. I recall Him doing that many times now but back in the day it couldn't be seen, it's like my life is supposed to be recorded so other might avoid the same mistakes. Methanphetamine is the destroyer of life and now I know why and how Hitler failed in creating a destructive race of people, I give thanks to God for bringing me through those times and no one would want to go through them! As for today the days let me write about such things so kids might stay away from it. Monday morning and I know it's going to be another day of being hot and in the tripple digits so what work has to be done has to be done in the morning while the weather is cool, as for the people I used to know they are all gone now except for the ones that made it past their addiction. And I hope they continue to grow in life without it, as the days seam to go pretty fast it lets you know that age is upon us all.

There is a song that is called don't blink' and it gives you sight into how fast life really goes so it shouldn't be wasted. As for the girl I wanted back then I havent heard from her in many years, but I'm sure she is out there somewhere she married my friend and then we lost track she had a child but that also I don't know about my land' she would have to be in her teens by now. It seams I have many friends that are named Mark for my brother from another mother name was also Mark' it's been many years since we set eyes on each other but who knows maybe one day we will meet again under different circumstances, they moved him around a lot and we lost track of each other. It's strange how things come back to me at different times but in that happening I have no control, the day went very well but it's coming to the end we had to get some things from the store and now I realize that things are going to be harder then once thought. As little brother is already out of money he seamd to not control his spending and that is something I cant help him with even though I could. It's strange how some people can spend and expect it to refill it's self without their help, I learned long ago that if you don't keep a safty net then one day you will fall and not get back up. But other don't see life that way and I believe that's why they never get a head in life, well it's about time for bed so I will write some more tomorrow. Tuesday morning, yesterday was full of emotions and the day was very hot as we went out a few times with no plan but we got what had to be done taken care of, things get confusing to me as I have to pick up the slace when Raandy can't pull his own weight but I guess that's what brothers are for. In the future he will have to learn to conserve what he has to last the month because it's too hard on me running the whole show.

While he was away, he didn't get to learn to survive so now it's time for him to go to school for it and I have a feeling it's going to be the school of hard knocks' and that's my school the one I learned in by pinching every cent so that it will last, he gives me the sad story that he cant make it on the money he has and that is an excuse so he will have to put a spening budget into effect. And if things have to be cut then that's what will happen, as I can't keep digging into my publishing funds. It's taken years to save something and he can't break that part of my life, my future goal is to get the word out there to those who know who I am but can't put a face to me. A while back when I had my gullbladder taken out a nurce asked if I was the one who wrote about the stories on addiction and I told her that I was, she then said it was nice to put a face to the one who helped others see the light you might say. Although many know my name they cant connect my face and that's something I will take care of, because not many people have a computer and I guess it would be like trying to picture a ghoast. I never did see the women again but it was nice that she read my life stories about the destruction of addiction, that in it's self showed me that there are people out there who are hungry for answers of how and why they became addicted. Although everyone knows the answer most can't dig that deep to find the real cause to their addiction because it's buried beneath the other problems they have, the process is like peeling an onion and once you start you don't want to stop because you want to find the destructive force buried beneath the layers. And it could take years before you feel like your getting close, to start I need a small audience so they can help in this coming out process they would be the ones to let me see if my message is clear because you don't want to go and confuse them more then they are. This message would be from me to them and it would bring some light to the person I am today, in my life God played a big part in me being able to over come what I went through and for that I will be always grateful. I have kept to my self so not to have any excuses to fail in this fight for life and I have succeeded in the reality of things other don't want you or anyone else to be able to over come this addiction because it makes them very rich, taking from the meek who have already fallen on short comings and driving them deeper into the realm of not feeling those feelings which makes us human. This separates those fighting from the rest of the world and then they are labeled, but this can be something that is short lived once you take those first step's and in doing that you have to learn to egnore those who have quit fighting because they said it was too hard these people are the ones who are on the brink of destruction with God on one sholder and the devil on the other, and if you don't know God then you will follow what you have known most of your life leaning towards the devil. As you have survived in his realm in the past but in doing that you loose the closeness between you getting to know God, and that's a shame.

The fight will start when you are tested beyond your knowledge and as you grow you will learn that God has always been there for you, you just choose not to see it. Until you travel back down that path you left behind I would start by a prayer and then go into my views on life and what started the addiction in the first place, my addiction anyway. I see me doing this within the next couple of years so I can spread the word that He is there for us all, as many think He isn't. Many think' they are not worthy of his love which would be a mistake because we are all worthy and they would give up on them selves before He would ever do so. My life has become a simble of what can be done if you want something bad enough and life can't hold you back only you can hold back the goodness that God has put in front of you, we sometimes find out selves without words to express our selves but when it comes right down to it only God can give us what we need to help others, when I first started to sing my songs my human instinct said I couldn't do it but God said I could and He won out over my thoughts. All through life I didn't think my singing would go anywhere but I found out different later in life as God's love embraced me. When I was on stage it was like He brought out the best in me and everyone said they loved it, even the pastor said it brought tears to her eyes as I know she had to of pictured me in my struggles. But then later those struggles become a strength that con't be measured on this planet anyway, my life is a testament of what the human spirit can do when given the right opportunity.

In this fight you never want to forget where you came from because when the time presents it's self it will be a place that you will want to return to, the beginning' God wont ever have you do something and then leave you hanging and if you have doubts then He can clear them up also in the progression of your life and bring about a new you the one you were born to be, not the one that life through you into in the beginning of it or in the end. Wednesday the middle of the week I didn' hear much last night as Randy slept, for some reason he didn't snore that much as I can recall, it's almost the end of the month so for that I am glad independence day is just around the corner and the kids will be fireing off fire works usually it goes from the 21st of the month until the 4th but I haven't heard any this year going off yet. Maybe because of the dryness and the lack of rain, I do know that fire season is here also, we went to the market yesterday the farmers market just down the road and they have all kinds of things to buy as they grow all the stuff their selves every kind of vegie you would want among other things like organic stuff. It's just a mile north of our lovely town so people don't have far to travel to get to it, the closer to home the better as far as I'm concerned. In the coming month I will try to limit our trips to the big town of Belleville and try so save on Gas because we can really go through it as I always put in five bucks to keep the top half full. When I was growing up we were lucky to have a quorter of a tank at a time unless we were traveling from one place to another or camp ground looking back we must have really been poor because gas was 25 cents a gallon nothing like today where that wouldn't give you a drop. Ido know that saving for that rainy could be a life saver if you could manage it, I have so much to be thankful for as my bills are always paid on time and sometimes even before they are do that way if something comes up I can catch a break but that time hasn't hit me as of yet, the bank always comes first because they are my first stop on the third of the month and they have been so kind in the past especially Mark my friend. According to the history channel a native calender will run out on December of this year and they believe it will or could be the end of things as we know it. Which I think is just something to get the scientist more recognition there is a reason those people went by the way side over a 1000 years ago and their kingdom fell, as for my thoughts on it, no one knows the end of times but God him self and even then this world wont be destroyed. He didn't create this place to destroy it and it will continue on even after we are all gone. There is a purpose for my writing an although things don't seam clear right now they will in time, in His time not mine or yours. The hot months are here to stay and I'm glad that they only last for three or so months and then fall will be here, when things get baren and the trees louse their leaves such pretty colors when that happens the reds and gold colors as everything goes into hibernation for the winter, like the bear which gets it's self fat for his long sleep. As for my self' it's a nice time of year when the heat is gone and the winter moves in to nourish things for the next coming year, I can hear the birds start to sing out side my window and it lets me know that sun rise is just an hour or so away such a beautiful sound. And the rabbits will be eating the clover in the yard as the squirrels play and run from tree to tree, it seams they talk to each other while the chase goes on and then they are gone. Courtland is like their big play ground and boy they have fun.

One of my church family members was walking by and she said hi as I was sweeping off the side of the house to get the cobwebs off and today I'm going to trim around the house so the weeds will be gone for a while anyway. This transition to being around people will take some time because I find my self not having much to say to others, my world is quite different from theirs and I'm not used to saying much and that is the quiet side of me. I guess I'm an observer and put down my thought in my writings as for being a people person that could take some time but for now I'm content with my life, little brother talks less then I do and maybe that's why we get along as good as we do. Pastor Kathy asked if I liked working at the thrift store and I told her that it was ok' anything to help and it's only a couple of hours but I don't know if I would want a full time job at doing it because I would get too board, my travels have taken me many places but I have yet to see some of what I would like to see. Maybe in the future I will try to go with the pastor and visit the old folks who cant get out, many of them have to stay home because of the heat and they are just too old or ill to be able to come out. I know she has to see many of the people out on the farms because they cant get in, just her smile I bet lights up their day and brings them hope in difficult situations; as for the ones that are house bound she brings the word of the lord so they know things are still ok' in the world that they once lived in. I couldn't imagine being stuch out there on a farm, but some do it even until it's their time to go, it must be the place where they feel the most comfortable. That place of peace for which they cant find anywhere else, the place they were born on and the place they will die one day.

Finding that place of peace is hard to do sometimes but in this place I have found my nitch, the one women wants me too go and visit her husband but I'm not sure if that would be a good idea. Or maybe it would as he is very old and has problems with his health, the watching of someone degenerating isn't a pick nick but I have seen it many times and it hasn't hurt me any. The getting ready to go isn't an easy thing to do but they have people who make it easier and maybe give them an understanding that we will all go one day to see each other in the by and by, it's getting light out side so my day will begin in just a little while, they are calling for the day to be in the 100's around 107 on the low end, and 110 on the high side. Also they had a fire out west caused by a hot exhaust on a car so they gave a warning about the chances being high, it took firemen from neighboring countys to help with the fire. Even people from Nebraska came to help and I know that had to be a big help to them fighting the fire, we sit almost on the border of Nebraska and Kansas which you could throw a dime either way and be in a different state. One town is just 30 miles from here and that's almost where the lake is, about half way. I went and cleaned at the church getting the windows clean so they are ready for Sunday service on the first' which is also communion the first week of the month, already the temp is in the high 90's and it's not even noon yet. I wanted to do some work out side but it's just too dam hot and when it's that hot it seams to drain the life out of ya, and that's not for me during this time of year. Except for those working the town is very quiet as most people stay inside away from the heat, it's strange how during the summer they tell you to stay inside and it also goes for winter as the cold will freeze you in your tracks. Thursday morning' yesterday while at work I picked up a book called the guide post and it has some inspirational stories in it about peoples lives and how God brought them through tragedies after they had just lost faith, many things happen in life and a tragetie is one thing which will open your eyes. I especially liked the one about the farmer and how he got so angry after looseing his son at age 23 I can relate to that but with me he wasn't that old yet, my story is one of finding my way back after being gone for 30 some years, my life had always been out of control but in the end my journey lead me back to my children, after my and their mom's break-up I was lost and thought moving away would help. But in reality it didn't, before my move I got them both something to remember me by. But now I realize that nothing can compare to the love of a father, running was the one thing I was good at but I didn't realize that no matter where you go there you are" my mind was never compleat because of the problems I had so I took the easy way out and tried to run from them, only to end up worse then before. I always had my mom to lean on but this time I took a job out of state" a nice man needed a worker to help him on the farm, because his son had gotten married and was starting a family of his own. And this didn't leave much time for any thing else, I spent a few years learning the trade but I had a monkey on my back hitching a ride. Later I would bring mom and Oliver out to live with me which seamed like a good idea at the time" we lived in garber Oklahoma where the town was very small, but we survived and we had everything we needed including the monkey on my back. Mom was the same was with her carrying her monkey, which she had done most of the years that I can remember, she was a nice person and everyone loved her even the guys that moved them out there. And got everything set up in the house.

I think in my own way I was trying to give her the better life she deserved. It was a nice house with a smoke house in the back, and we even had a pair tree in the back yard that we could eat from. The monkey I'm talking about was one that carried great weight with it and in reality everyone I knew had one of these guys hitching a ride. Oliver was the only one who didn't have one so he did his own thing trying to help out with bills, as for saving money it wasn't in the cards at that time because most of the money left after the bills fed the monkey" and boy could he eat. Every cent almost went to the monkey's habbit and then we were left with nothing but a big head ache and the shakes for a few days, carrying a monkey on your back can ware a person down and when they get mad look out" mom would do her thing and try to make sure that the monkey didn't get angry but the more you feed one the worse they seam to get. This had been a big part of my life even from childhood, and I couldn't get it off my back no matter how hard I tried the more I tried not to feed it the worst things got so I found my self feeding it so life would be normal. Or what I thought was normal, he went with me everywhere and I had to have him even go to work with me which wasn't safe because all he wanted to do was play, and that wasn't exceptable in that line of work. The day would start around five in the morning and go until mid day and them back to work until it was time to go home, at that time the days were very hot sometimes reaching 120 degrees. But that didn't bother me being in a tractor where it was cool, in all my time there the heat never got to me until I had to go out side to fix something which broke.

My teacher taught me how to fix the things that might break but that monkey was always holding on to my back. Later we lost the house and mom wanted to move back to Nebraska, so she did and I traveled back and forth to work for my boss. Jack could tell that my little friend was causing problems' but he never said anything and maybe that was because he had a little friend at one time on his back until it caused an accident that almost took his life"he was a quiet man of few words and would do just about anything for me but he stood quietly and and kept his opinion to his self. Finely things got to where I had to leave Oklahoma for good' as I was staying with my brother. And me and his wife didn't get along, it seamed no matter how hard I tried nothing I did was good enough for her, and I could do nothing right. On the day that I left they wouldn't give me any of the money that I had given them and I had no way to get gas for the trip, it was like they wanted me to leave but they wanted me to walk over 300 miles" by then our mother was back in Nebraska' and I made a phone call asking her advice on how to get home. And she said to put your brother on the phone, and the yelling started, by the end of the phone call my brother gave me the money which I knew his wife didn't want to do. And then I started back home, my car was an older one made in the 60's but it was a good car and made the trip. On my way home' that monkey started to play tricks on me and I had to calm him down, so we stopped at a store and fed him. This left me tired and others must have noticed it because a state trooper pulled me over, and asked where I was coming from. I told him that I was coming from Garber Oklahoma and drove right through to get home in Kearney Nebraska' he then advised me to pull over at the next rest stop and rest. Which I did pull over, but then I went back out on the interstate because home was only 90 miles away. I remember the high I felt as I pulled into town, and I should of taken the state troopers advice but the monkey wouldn't leave me alone. I then called my boss and told him what had happened, and he said he wished I would of let him know what was happening before I left because he could of done something. And I took it as he would of found me a place to stay, this was another opportunity that I missed. But it must not of been in the cards because now it was too late, and for years after that I felt bad because I felt that I let him down. Even after coming home that little trouble maker was still there and he would hitch a ride until my demise, but after that I destroyed him. And he never returned' he was persistent while he was in my life always taking and never giving anything back, and at first I missed him for a time but my life was going to take a turn for the better, I later had to teach my self how to walk once again. And when they say you have to croll before you can walk this I found to be true, at this time my little friend was gone. But another one would hitch a ride later after I could stand, and boy was he a pain in the butt.

For many years' I cried as this journey was going to be very hard. First I lost the use of my legs after they discused my not making it until morning, but before that I traveled down a tunnel and I saw a light at the end of it. A light so bright that I knew I had passed over, the abuse had destroyed my body and now I wasn't in it it was a strange feeling but then I heard a voice and it explained that it wasn't my time to go. That my journey hadn't even started yet, and that I would know when it would start. Then there was a power like nothing I had encountered before and I saw souls from time passed, but where they were was something I could hardly believe. It was like a train waiting at a station and they were looking at me, some in old clothes worn in centurys passed confederate solger's and even some wore robes; like they did in Jesus time. Was there a message there? I believe so' then the words came Melchisedek & Epiphany I had never heard those words befor and I had no idea of what they meant. But in time I would find my self reading the bible trying to find the message and their meaning, then one night I prayed and asked God what would become of my life? Not having any knowledge about life other then working with my hands and feet, what would become of me? This lost soul. He then told me to get a typewriter which was a strange request because I knew nothing about writing. Then after I got it' I asked Him what for was I to do this that you asked of me? And He said not to worry that He would teach me the things I need to know. My grandson Eric has been going through some health issues and I know God will take care of him and heal what is wrong, he is my littly buddy and I love him dearly.

As this time will tell what's wrong and find some way to fix the problem, his mother is scared right now but I have asked God to calm the worry that resides in her heart. I know there is no problem too small for God and He has promised to help in time of need but also we need to give thanks to the father, even when things don't turn out the way we expect them too. Friday morning' yesterday was another hot day and I think we will see them into next week. As July is one of the hottest months in these here parts, Sunday is the 1st and I'm starting to understand why some farmers don't make it to church. After reading a story from the giude post some have to run everything on their own after the kids leave for collage and that keeps them busy as they have to take up the slack which the kids used to do. But I guess it's different with each farmer depending on the load they have to carry, my mentor on farming who taught me all I know made me the replacement for the work his son used to do. So that gave him time for church and he went. Maybe not every Sunday but atleast more then if I wasn't there, I remember him and his wife getting in the car to go on Sunday mornings while I fueled up the tractor. And I believe his connection with God is what made him the way he was, looking back' I don't recall him getting mad very oftend or if he did, he didn't show it on the outside. But his patients is what helped me to learn, I used to do many things for him even clean out the grain ben's after planting was done, his son was more or less like his father mild tempered and helped when he got his own fields done. Things were kept in the family and he is still farming today, Louella his wife did many things for the church like the ladys here in Courtland getting things to look pretty for when service came to be on Sunday morning. Even when she planted her garden, I helped' by turning up the ground to except the plants which grew very well in the Oklahoma clay. A dark red clay that was like snot when you drove on it, many times Jack had to pull me out of the ditch because my car wasn't a four wheel drive and it would just slide off in it. And sometimes if it rained too much he would pick me up in town to avoid the time lost by having to pull me out, the monkey was still with me back then but I believe Jack has something to do with me getting my life back. It's the experiences we go through that lets us learn from our mistakes and if we didn't go through them then what would be the point of life, as each day is different for a reason to sometimes bring change so we can grow in our faith. I wrote Luella a couple of times and she wrote back but then cut it off by not replying, it was after my close call and my mind was still trying to learn and figure out why things happened the way they did. And to her it might have been to confusing because she was strong in her faith and at that time I wasn't, it had been almost 15 years after my leaving and she still remembered me. And said there was no hard feelings, I remember the gas wells' and how I had to maneuver around them not to hit the pipes and it was fun after a time. Strange how those times come back to me now twenty some years later, but until now most things had gone away from my mind. Our triles in life are what makes us who we are, and if we learn then that's a plus.

As time moves on I hope to see them one more time, to thank them for their help in my growing up. Plowing the fields gave me much time to reflect on things. And make me wish for things that finely came to pass later in life, my land' Jack has to be about 80 years old by now so I hope he is sitting on his porch and enjoying his time. I havent been to Garber since my leaving so long ago and I believe I could still fine my way to their house where I used to work, mom played a big part when it came to me being a good person she taught me how to be a person of honor and not to do anything that I wouldn't want done to me. Even though my problems were self inflected I also solved them with the help of God. And I like to think that I turned out better then I thought I would, although I sometimes forget to pray in the morning something I do so when I'm working in the church and it happens in different way's but mostly by singing. The words seam to come out of no where and then I put them together in hope that a song comes out of them, a song that will touch the hearts of others and let them know how much God truly loves them. It's the beginning of the weekend to night, so many will party and let their hair down you might say I just hope no tragedy happens during this time. In my years I have been in that place where some will go and that's something I don't wish on anyone as they travel that dark road, that could take them from this world. And no one sees it when it's coming no more then you can see a car hit you ten miles down the road, it's unexpected and if you survive then you have a long road a head of you trying to bring your self back to where you should have been in the first place.

During the wine and roses days' the mornings were the hardest as you tried to remember what had taken place the night before. Even then the mind couldn't remember what it remembers today, and I believe that's what they call a black out. Traveling the country roads of Arizona was fun when your young but there was no goal no purpose for what we were doing. Except to have fun and get drunk, maybe that was my free time in life with no worries but to fish and travel. And get kicked out of some parks because of the alcohol, we started each day at camp by having breakfast and then doing dishes and if we stayed more then one night we would fish for supper. The partys were something we did each day as that's what alcoholics do it let you escape from the problems of the day, and when you have five or six people around the problems could be many. I believe they call that drama which impacts everyone who is around you, even people that are not in your party the alcohol brought out the loudness in a person and I don't understand why that was maybe the fear of not being heard. Then the repeats of people saying the same thing over and over again and again which could drive a person nut's, in this world the less said the better as you don't want everyone to know your business. But if you have something you don't understand then your family in Christ" can help you if you want the help needed. I had always been a quiet person and never asked for help even on the long stretch of road when I found my self lost so long ago, my land" I was in the middle of no where and had no water or money just wondering around and not knowing how I came to be at that place. And still I don't recall how I found my way back to where ever I was going, for sure apart of that picture is lost somewhere in my mind and who knows maybe one day it too will show it's self, the morning will start by mowing the lawn and then other things will take place as they present then selves. With each given day something new happens and I never know what it might be a smile from someone new that you haven't met yet or just the wave from someone passing by, these things are what I call a spirit booster and some days it can make your day. Especially if your down, and then you have your self who determines how the next 24 hours are going to be and I like to be happy during this time when I'm awake. Dreams are something which God allows us to have and they can be a road map leading you to a place where things are possible, my journey has taken me to some of these places and good things have happened. But also if you don't follow through with it then it just lays there until you awaken, my idea for a business has been with me for many years and until I act on it nothing will become of it. So I think' maybe it's time to give it another shot, before I think the timing wasn't right and now maybe it is, so I will do it on the side and see what will happen. Many of the materials are given meaning the cost is almost none, leaving me with no over head just my time to do it. The town is small so word will get around and those who drink beer on the weekends would really like my product as they go good together. In the realm of the sausage, many different kinds can be made. From hot to mild and it would even work with the other things I can create, God has given me this idea so it shouldn't fail or at least He has put it in my mind. And hey what have I got to loose? Could I make this happen if the idea is there then why not!!. Saturday and the month is gone, I have a few things to do this morning but other then that I will spend the day in the house. Yesterday was the hottest day so far reaching 108 degrees and they say the next week is supposed to be more of the same, the rain we got really helped but even that doesn't last and they are irrigating once again.

It's strange how things take place just going out in the heat for an hour or two was enough as the heat bellered through the windows of the car, it was like a blast furnace bith the blower on high. As for other things like the crops, they seam to grow taller with each passing day. My time is devided by the church and the thrift store butt I have noticed that I get more done by doing both things, and I like it. With each trip to the church I do something new and just last week I finished a job that I was going to do for months. Accomplishing things gives you a good feeling especially when you don't get interrupted and you can sing while you work, all the things that stopped me from moving forward before are gone now and the sky is the limit. As I pray most mornings many things that I ask for come to pass and it shows me that He listens to our prayers, Eric will go for his finel test on the third and I ask that God bring good results so he can go on with his life of growing up and bring some peace to Shannon. My little girl which isn't so little any more has made me proud going back to school so she can help the sick, she is like me in many ways that way giving a little of her self to help others who have become ill and I know she can accomplish anything she put's her mind to. The giving of ones self is such a small thing to us, but to others it helps in a much bigger way I'm going to later see if my pastor might need some help when she takes the cloths to other towns I knoe her breathing bothers her some times and this heat must really be hard on her, the other day I read the guide post all the way through and it opened my eyes to a lot of thing. For me it was easy to read with it's bold print and I understood the storys without confusion, this is how I would like my writing to be.

No confusion in reading it, I slept in a little this morning and it could have been because I didn't go to bed until eight last night this is something I'm going to try more oftend in hope to change my sleeping habits. Many of the towns people don't go to bed until late but they also don't get up as early as I do, and that will always be a part of me. God's way of reminding me how far I have come, I guess writing about life comes natural to me but it wasn't always that way. Before my demise I never knew I could do what I do today and it goes to show that we all have talents that are unknown to us in this life until it's tapped into them, the hidden secrets that are in the mind. I don't talk as much as I write, and maybe that's a good thing. Otherwise you wouldn't be reading this and learning about my life, although there are very few people here I have learned that my talents are many. And most of the people who have heard me sing think I do it pretty well but my voice is for very few at this time, there is no other man that sings around here and I think it's because they are also bashful and have a fear of not being good enough. One guy said he couldn't do it in 100 years but I know better, he just needs a little encouragement. I didn't know this but people wanted to congradulate me when I sang last time but being bashful had me running out the door afterwords and not staying around, I guess the thought of any rejection scares the hell out of me so I do the song and head for the hills and probably miss some good feelings which I could of used. My friend Phyllis told me to keep it up and never give up on it. And that is something I will never do, she is a mother figure and when I see her down I have to give her a hug. She is so nice and so are the other women at the church as they help in anyway they can, the guys talk about the football games and farming and not knowing the teams here in Kansas I pay no mind to it which maybe I should learn more about their teams. John gets a little up set when Nebraska beats his home team but I guess it's been that way for years, I would of never guessed he was in his 80's but he is and boy he is a card making someone laugh each Sunday. I can see that he is getting prepaired for the day when he wont be here any more and I will miss my new found friend but I hope he remains for many more years to come. No one likes to see a loved one go but it happens and there is nothing we can do to stop the cycle of life, it's like we are born into a life that will end in death. But the great thing is that we will go to that pace where we will live on in spirit for eternity and see loved ones once again, nothing will be taken with us except memories none of the problems will exist that we have here for they are burdens of the flesh. And we will have no flesh where we are headed we will float around like casper the friendly ghost a soul no body, we will have no burdens of addiction or if we are crippled that also will be gone just a perfect soul. Some say that we will be given land to grow our food in the earth, but they are also the ones that say we never leave earth.

We don't assend to a higher plain of existence and that's hard to swallow for me anyway, as I have went to a place that wasn't of this earth and I know there was a reason for it. Many are scard of death and I was one of them but after my demise that didn't seam to matter any longer, when the time comes will I be frightened that could very well be? But I also know that it isn't the end but the beginning of things to come a place that He has prepaired for us maybe that perfect place that was supposed to be in the beginning. Sunday morning' it's the first of July and yesterday I heard fire works for the first time here in town starting off the celebration for the kids anyway. I haven't gotten involved with blasting the fire works off before as I have no children here and my little buddy doesn't care for the loud noise, on the 4th we celebrate indapendence day the time when our country became free from England. I believe that's how it goes, then wewill have fun day which falls at the end of the month. I was excited when the rain came late yesterday and it must have gone on through a great part of the night unless I'm mistaken, now the yard will grow some more and look nice during this hard time of the year we seam to get some rain but then it's gone as fast a the ground sucks it up leaving the big cracks in the ground as if we had fishers. I did some triming yesterday out in the yard and one friend from church commented on how nice it looked and then went on to say that it wasn't always that nice with the other people who lived here, I did get a bite on my ankle and I hope it doesn't take a long time to heal but it itches like hell. And trying not to scratch it takes all my will power, today is communion so I will go early and get things ready.

That was my first gift to the people taking care of that, and then came being the janitor. I remember being uneasy when I first started trying to get everything just right and then as time passed it became second nature to me, Janet had done it for 20 years and now it's my time to carry it on as they like to keep things within the church. It's strange how something are brought up in the news letter trying to get others to attend church more oftend during this time of year, as for me it didn't pertain to me as I'm always there on Sunday not missing a beat except for a couple of times in this last three years.. It seams the heat draws them away from the church for some reason or it's just that some like to indulge during this time of year, but attendence isn't what it should be and I can see how Kathy might become depressed from time to time. As for my self I need the closeness that is between me and God' but I also know that that He resides in us and not in a building for what God gives shouldn't be squandered; with the way things are in my life it might be too much to become a pastor at this time so I will let God deside when the time will be right. My life is a testament to God's work and how He can bring someone back from the brink of demise to live a somewhat normal life, I have picked up on doing more reading these days and I like the Guide Post. That is full of inspirational stories about how He interceads in some peoples lives bringing them from a world of destruction to one of peace. Many people haven't seen that world which is just around the next block but little do they know it could strike at any moment and they too could fall into that dark place which is hell to croll out of, the kids of today are exceptable to the curse and many don't even know it yet as it can hit a person like a ton of bricks leaving them helpless. Angels' could they be watching over us and coming to our rescue when death could be trying to take over our lives. From things that have happened in my life I do believe they are there like the cop which stopped me on that dark road that morning going to Kearney. For surely he wasn't from around here because I asked him for directions and he couldn't give me any saying he wasn't from around here I believe he was sent to stop a disaster from happening, and that disaster was mine. We went back the same way we came and ended up taking highway 281 the same highway that the accident was on back in the 80's when they got me out of the car. God was watching over me back then even though I didn't know it at the time and He still watches over me to this day, although it's the end of the week tomorrow will be the beginning of another one filled with many new things. Although the 4th of July is a day to celebrate it's also a time to reflect on the things we do in life the good and the not so good, what will be more apparent the things you do to help others? Or the selfish things that you think you have to have like material things which make you seam more then you really are. Some people think riches are by the things you have like cars, trucks, and money, but I don't see life that way' I don't messure wealth by the mighty dollar it's by the friends you know and help. Looking back on the child of 12 years that died because of drugs he would of saw being rich as being given more time to live and growing up but that wasn't the case with him because his body got destroyed by the curse that takes so many young people today.

As a child you don't see these things comminng and they can hit you in a second leaving the parents dStacystated and asking why me' when it wasn't about them. Parents can see much better then a child for their sight is atleast into the next day to where a child can't see past the moment, it's strange how when your young your caught up in the moment, and then the older you get that moment can be extended into a little longer time but never over a day until you're in your later years and I think it starts when you're about 25 when the mind is fully developed, lord knows it doesn't happen in your teens as that's when I used to get into most of my mischief. Not being able to see what my actions would bring about although I could see more then most, because getting into their kind of trouble was not an option in my mind dowing the things they did like taking from others things that weren't theirs. Thinking they would get rich off of steeling things that others worked their whole lives for' not an option in my world. I remember thinking when they would get home with their spoils at what a wast it was to take something that wasn't theirs and it made me want to stay away from them even more because I knew they would also steel from me given the chance. It's still dark out side so I can't see how the day is going to be, but I bet it will be humid with the rain we got so I will turn on the air-conditioning pretty early this morning. Everything I have done in life has been by my own doing with no help from others because no one can help you until you are able to help your self, even in the dawn of things I have found it to be struggling at times. No one to lean on' because you are afraid that they couldn't understand your situation.

As I continue on this path, I'm in hope that I will be shown a way to communicate better with other folks and maybe make a friend along the way one who would understand me as a person. For this is something I haven't found yet in this life of up's and downs, do we ever get a clear understanding of how life is supposed to be or do we just sometimes guess at it? As for the joys of life' they are not yet a constent but I'm hoping they will be in the years to come. So many things I still don't understand but I'm in hope that the picture will reveal a bright sun light full of the good things in life, at times I feel like there should be more to life more then what I'm seeing now. Will it come to pass? Will I ever find the true meaning to life or will it be a search that goes on for ever, I uess only God knows that answer at this time but I do try to always look at the bright side of things. Just being able to pay my bills gives me a delight a good feeling inside that can't be replaced because I know so many others can't do that in this depression it's like it was in the thirtys except you don't have the elegal sale of alcohol, Courtland made it through those times and I know it will continue to make it as the people pull together and make it the way they did back then. So many things are better this time around we have the ability to stay cool during the hot months which wasn't around back then I think!! And the cars are able to also keep us cool if they are running right, many people couldn't do their jobs if it wasn't for the air-conditioning; traveling back and forth to other towns for work as for the town it's self, there could never be enough jobs to keep everyone working so they have to travel I'm going to try my hobby again and see how it pans out, who knows this time might be a charm there has to be a way to start a business of some kind but you need to try it on a smaller scale to see if the cards fall into place. Will the chance be now? We will see. Monday, the church service was good yesterday and we had quite a few people come, then I cleaned up for someone to have a shower of some kind. It's been a nice weekend all and all as we got the rain we needed but we ccould of used more, not too many people sit where I do but Kathy's grand-daughter sat next to me this Sunday. In my time there many have come to say hi each morning and that's a delight but still I'm not as free spirited as some but that's just the way things are because none of us are the same, as we have built our own worlds where things are different from one family to the next. People don't seam to loose their Christen values when they don't come to church because of the farm or the work they have to do, for it is the goodness of christ that is inplanted in us all. I recall going out to eat with Rosa-lee and a friend and they said grace before the meal I had never done this before and at first it felt strange but then after a few times it felt good, like when you first start a job that feeling of uncertainty that passes once become solid in the job. Kathy goes on vacation this month and I hope she enjoys her self as she visits with friends and her youngest child in Denver Colorado, I believe his name is David and he has had some health problems in this last year. I pray for her save trip as she goes away for a while a short while because we need her here she takes care of our souls, and guides us in the direction we need to be guided. I was very supprised when she told me that I was important and they didn't want me to leave.

That in it's self gave my spirit a boost as I travel this path, she answers most of my questions when I have a difficult time trying to figure out some things in my life. But she and others are there to give me support, I still think of pop's from time to time and how he used to make me laugh but the greaving process is about over with as I move forward into this place which is new to me, the town has made it easier for me to adjust and let go of what used to be. This month I'm going to clean the carpet if they have the machine fixed or have gotten a new one which I hope they have, I put out the flags yesterday for my friend that usually does it and she thanked me. Just little things like that makes me feel good because I know they appreciate it and if they are still standing today I will take them down. My job is a good one and I will probably be doing it in another five or ten years as I grow old here in my new home town, what is a home town? Is it where you were raised or is it where you settle down as you learn the rights and wrongs of life? Courtland will be the place that I will travel to eternal life and I believe this is the place that God wants me to be, as He has given me all the answers to why I'm here with the lake and the stream that grows and flows down around my house and each time I ask His to confirm my thoughts He shows me gladly but is this what it's all about? Becoming a part of a community that is full of love and maybe finding your self in the process. Yesterday was a lot cooler then the days before as the rain brought down the tempature and the church was cool also as we had communion, there was another couple that attended church and I had never met them before so I hope to see them there again in the future.

The meeting of new people is fun at times and even though we didn't have any children yesterday one of the adults went up so Kathy could have childrens time. We all laughed and thought it was cool that she would go up like that, she is another free spirit and you can see it in her smile and laughter. She retired from the bank a while back and is now doing what ever on the farm, as I start to read more these day's I find my self learning new things but I have a blockage somewhere in there and I have to stop for a time so the headaches go away but in time I will break through it and be able to read longer, could this of been what caused me not to excell in school? I do know that at times it comes in spurts my reading goes real fast and then slows down making it hard to sound out the words. It's like a good day and a bad one, one day the words come easy and then they come hard and confusing. But in time maybe this will pass like most things which come my way, nothing has ever come easy to me and I think that's why I never give up. The thriving to become perfect leades me on a trip and I never know when or where it will lead, in all that I do in the end it becomes a wize with experience. Like tieing your shoe or putting on a pair of pance it becomes second nature like life' I was informed that my friend Leroy Hord was in an accident and got banged up, I pray now that he get's well and has a full recovery. He told pastor Kathy that he may come to church and I pray that he does sometimes it takes a tragic thing to open someones eyes and maybe this opened his as the cards are in play now to see what will happen. It was an accident which brought me here so I would know that miracles still happen, it's strange how God works sometimes but all in all we know that we are loved by the one on high. The creater of the universe the one true God, as too why it takes such a drastic move sometimes only God knows. I will get him a get well card so he knows I'm thinking of him during this time, as he is my friend and as far as I'm concerned he will always be. Him and his whole family, such a scary was to change but sometimes it happens that way, we went to town to get something for lunch and supper but before I left I went and told Leroy that he is in my prayers each morning. Tuesday morning' and I slept pretty good. I would of swore I got the coffee ready yesterday for this morning but I guess I didn't because I had to do it, it's trash day so I have a few things I have to take care of. Leroy looked pretty good but I could tell he was hurting so I left him with his coustomer and away I went. The morning is quiet and everyone is still a sleep except for me of course, I can recall back when my addiction started I couldn't of been over 8 years of age although I have said 11 years. It was at that time when it started to get me in trouble having the mind of a child I thought it was cool to try and drive and impress my friends telling them that my parents said it was ok' when in reality it wasn't ok with them, I remember my dad buying a car from the junk yard and it was very fast I took it to go and impress a girl because if you had a car back then you were something so I thought. Later I would get pulled over and they called my parents to pick me up and I got an ass chewing not to do it again, but for some reason I felt free when I was alone in the car not having to hear any of what was going on between my parents. I can't quite connect with what I was thinking back then but I know it was to get attention, being so young I even went as far as to run away and hitch hike 90 some miles away to where we used to live.

From Ventura, to Los-Angeles, and the cop's found me in the back of the stop and go market that we used to manage. Maybe I was trying to find something or someone but they took me to the police station and called my parents, and they came and got me. Later they would split up and dad moved with his brother Ray in Los Angeles' Ray was older then dad but it didn't take long before I wanted to go and be with him, I had taken a car that mom had and did some work to the motor putting on a pan gasket so I would make it but it still used oil like heck a case of it in just 90 miles, a lot of what was going on is still foggy because I was so young but I knew I wanted to be with dad. When I arrived he told me that I had to go back home and then he put me on a bus I recall being heart broken because I thought he didn't want me, but then he said it's not that I don't lover you. My life is messed up right now and I have to get it straightened out back then they had twelve step houses and he went to many of them with no results. His parkens couldn't be controlled by medication and alcohol was the only thing that would stop the shaking and a machanic had to have steady hands when working on transmissions, as the years progressed he got worse and the worse he got the deeper he went into his own world. Like most addicts do when the chimicals in the body are thrown out of balance but once he drank he seamed to be ok' for a time, so he tried to limit his drinking until the shakes went away.

He was in the Navy but after a short time they gave him a medical discharge because of his parkens and then he came home. This was before my birth, many times I tried to figure out how and why he felt the way he did but I was unable to do that, then he tried to get a shop in Los Angeles but that didn't work either so he went a little more over the edge and finely gave up on him self, all through this time he must of thought that God had given up on him but the truth is that he gave up on him self. God was there for him but he couldn't see it with all that was going on even when the car accidents happened which there was three of them. God protected him and mom when the vehicals were totaled and they somehow survived, one time smacking into a tree and being thrown out, mom carried a piece of glass in her leg for over 30 some years until it worked it's self out. I recall pulling it out when she got so ill, many bad things happened but also many miracles took place that they couldn't see at the time the survival of my two brothers when they were hit by the car, and dad going over a cliff on his way to work even the ambulance driver said it was a miracle that he survived and the car hitting the tree. My parents said they had just been in the bar a few minutes when something told them to go home so they finished their first drink and left and the next thing they knew they were in the hospital, they said someone sliped them a micky which caused the accident I remember seeing the car afterwords and I don't know how they made it out alive but God knew and I believe He was sending them a message trying to get their attention. But as with so many a wall was put up and it never got torn down even through the miracles that had taken place, my self I was awakened by a force stronger then my own showing these things in my own life. I thought the first was my death but it wasn't, it was the last. But only by that happening was I able to see the others the three hundred foot cliff when I lost my axcel and the accident which happened here in Kansas' but why did He bring me back to the first? So I could see where it took place and assure me that He has always been there for me. All through life the struggles have been hard but standing strong in my faith I survived, as I believe I'm a vessel of the most high God the one who created me in His image. And when I say I'm going to do something I usually do it, as for material things they have no meaning to me because they just last a short time. I get all my strength from God and only He made it possible for me to be here today, I would of given up long ago if He wouldn't of been by my side in this thing we call life. They say He shows favor to those who believe in Him and lord knows my beliefs are strong as I go through this life, as for the tragitys they are behind me now as far as I know but I will also be tested sometime in the future. Wednwsday morning' the 4th of July. Yesterday my little man Eric got his tests back and they are normals for someone having neurofibromatosis so he should be ok the spots on his body are from having that disease. Thank you Lord for answering my prayers on him! Many things will happen today but I pray that the fire works don't do any harm to the children as they play with them, although we got some rain it wasn't enough to stop the threat of fires in this area so people have to be really careful.

In the realm of my job this afternoon it's been canceled because of the holiday and will resume next Saturday. It seams we all have many things that we do and it creates a balance here in Courtland, my helping others has lead to others helping me and that's something I'm not used to because I have always been a giver and not a reciver so that will take some time to get used too but in all reality it's something new something brand new, our income has become a lot less then when pop's was here but we are making do with that we have by less trips to town. This will cut things a lot as we move further into 2012 and get readt for 2013, if all goes well' my property will be mine in a couple of years but the savings has to become a new way of getting everything paid. And I have to find a way to make everything work, as for the credit cards I'm going to have to find a way to pay a few of them off and keep one of them. That way there will always be atleast one to fall back on, in an emergency when things become tight. I have many things to be thankful for and the women of the church is one as they help in making it possible for me to go on and survive here, it's strange how I always was a giver and now maybe I can see how it feels to be on the other end, how those people feel when a kind heart brings them something. As I sit here and write I'm brought back to the time when childhood friends would say that I had the coolest parents but where are they now? The things which made my friends think they were cool has taken them from this earth far before their time, and I really wonder sometimes if they can see what I have done with my life that mom' helped to bring into this world born like the son of God through a womens womb but not created by the one on high not given the spirit that Jesus had, other wise we would have been born without the sin that He died for. He died so we could live and so many don't see that these days. My learning of Him is slow but I'm sure before my time is up my full understanding will be better then it is today.

It seams when I learn something it somehow stayes with me and with some things I even live it, like in many stories of the past. I try and do good things which I have learned as for the rest it's somehow thrown away because I have no use for it, as the day goes on my heart will be filled with joy as the little ones have their fun. I can recall those days so long ago when we were excited about the forth of July the fireing off of fire works as they celebrated the independence of the United States. Many years ago we were the number one place that others wanted to live but since those times we have fallen to 25th place what has happened since those times why did the United States fall so far down the line? I believe it's the government wanting to bleed people of what they work so hard for. The medical system has fallen apart and in other countries the medical is run by the government who pays the bills when people get hurt, but in this country they bleed the people when things like accidents happen that draws them into poverty. California has really got problems with people louseing their homes and I think karma has something to do with it but this is just my opinion on the matter as the state lets people grow drugs to be used by even children which is a not exceptable at least not in my world. When I write an article it seams the only ones that reply is those who want to see the drugs made legal as they are in a fight to get rich off of others addictions, the pain which addiction causes can and does cause people to take their own lives because they don't see any other way out. For they can't see past the addiction as it closes the mind to looking into the future, there are many ways to get past the destruction but first you have to reclaim what was taken from you and that's control. Many will say that the addiction doesn't control them but those words show that it is, just like some say that can never happen to my child and they are also wrong especially if they have had the same problem. All children want to be examples of their parents and if that example is cursed then they too will be cursed because usually they see it everyday with the mom who can't get off the couch or the dad who goes to work and then comes home in a bad mood because the alcohol or drugs have worn off, but once they get the level of what ever back into their system then they seam to be fine. But' their not fine the substence is just letting them act that way until later when it gets down again, the highs and lows very from person to person depending on how bad the addiction is, as a child of addiction I didn't think there was a problem and I never did think there was one because it was a part of everyday life. I thought everyone woke up and went to bed that way and that was the cycle of life for surely my parents wouldn't steer me in the wrong direction they were supposed to love me and want only the best for me to be able to go on after they had left this place we call earth, if the time could be reversed I would of never touched the stuff but it can't be reversed and I had to learn the hard way by taking it too deaths door.

And today it's worse then back then or I just think it is, I don't recall hearing about the drugs you hear about today the Methanphetamines and other things which cause people to loose their homes and other things including their own blood. People are powerless over these drugs and the drug runs their lives not the other way aroud like some would have you think, those people are foolish in even thinking that way. Even when they did surgery to take my gullbladder I didn't want any drugs but the pain was great and they said it wouldn't hurt me, I spent only hours in the hospital and left because I knew God would watch over me and then in a few days I was well to not go to a hospital again unless I was dieing and that hasn't happened yet. The day has been a warm one but there hasn't been any fire works going off as of yet I think the kids are waiting until to night when it gets dark. As for my car it's leaking antifreeze somewhere but I can't track it down so I will get another one, I'm also getting board staying around the house listening to Randy snore because lord knows he does that a lot. Thursday morning' and last night you could tell the kids must have been having fun, as you could hear the fire works going off. O how I remember that time as a kid when mom and dad stood out side with you and helped so no ones house got burned down we were living in the suburbs where all the nabors were buying their own houses and everyone looked out for each other, even the german imagrents that made their way here to find the good life. I don't know what my parents were paying for their home but it couldn't of been too offely much for that time, our home was like what they call a ranch style and it had a two car garage connected to it. And we also had a chain link fence that went around the property, it was strange that the boys got hit because our parents taught us to be careful when we crossed the street and always use the cross walk.

But that morning after church the boys were in a hurry, writing about what happened has helped me in many ways as I never was able to talk about it before it was just a memory locked away in the back of my mind. Many things that were locked away have surfaced since my finding my way out of the dark and being able to talk about it, it seams to give you the power to release the bad things that had happened and it makes room for new things. Good things which replaces those bad times, like my love for God and others who I would of never met if those things didn't happen. As each day starts I pray for my family and friends in hope that they too will have a blessed day, in the realm of addiction you never get the chance for prayer because your time is filled with trying to figure out how you will survive through a day let along a year. And now with that gone each day is a gift without carring that burden around, although I had friends they weren't real friends not the kind you would want in your life every day. Not like the people I have found here in Courtland for they are true friends the ones that will brighten up your day if you were feeling down because of things that are out of your control, why do we worry about such things? Why don't we turn it over to God. With some they have never done it before and it's hard too relinquish that part of admiting we are powerless to handle it our selves. Change doesn't come over night because it wasn't over night that it happened, this is when it's good to have time on your side as it can also help in some ways, getting lost in the wilderness can bring some things into prespective like the will we have to push on, and then by some miracle we move forward to find our way home. Even though little brother is here with me in many ways I would still be alone if not for my church the smile from them when I go to church and the wave from some of them as they drive by, as things change my home will stay here and I will grow old like the rest of my friends, to exsprience new things which will come into my life.but through it all I have found that place where I belong, even kids say hi as I drive by the school yelling out my name because they know me from church. And strangers do the same when they read my belt buckel as I'm walking through the store, it's like a message of who I am and it brings me pride when I think about it. It's almost Friday and everyone will be getting off for the weekend to do their own thing, and I hope some will find their way to church to help us celebrate God. The one who made it possible for us to be here today, through my trials I have seen many changes and for me they have been good changes from coming out of the dark where I couldn't see to the light that has made my life bright and filled it with hope. It was strange when my daughter told me about Eric but in the past I had prayed for him and I knew God was still on the thrown where He had heard my prayers before, to me when our prayers are heard they are not just forgotten they are carried through time and made new each time we bring them up. And God's help or words carry for ever, when things get tough I look towards the heavens because I know where He is and always will be.

The Alpha and the Omega the first and the last. I can hear people going to work out side and it's early but we all have to make our way through this world He created for us, to make it better for the children as they grow and learn new things. So many of them could be and thing they want to be in this world and who knows maybe one day a president could come from such a town as ours, the possibilitys are endless for a mind not destroyed by the curse. A clear mind not tempted by the very thing that can destroy them, why do children think it's cool to be a part of a family that is infected by addiction? In many cases the parents seam to be less strict and let the kids do what they want and to a child or young adult or kid that seams to be cool and everyone wants to be around them. I noticed at a young age that if your parents owned a business then kids in school all wanted to hang around you, like when we owned the store so long ago. The girl friends found their way to your door wanting to be a part of your group so superficial but being a young person it made an impact on me not seeing the real reason why they were there, or maybe I did see it and just wanted friends because I never had them before. In school I never could keep up and I think that brought on some of the reasons for the addiction's and little brother was the same way as he got kicked out of school by going drunk which brought him to the youth development center also. But he was different not stubern like I was back in those days and he got out in six months, with me it took 18 months over twice as long but there was one difference I stayed out of trouble and regrettably he would not. And it caused him many problems that he couldn't solve, and that lead to other things.

When we left to go to Phoenix the two boys were on the run but the law couldn't touch them because they hadn't gone to court to be formaly charged yet, it was a struggle to survive in that place living on the streets in an old beat up truck and a car. But soon we found a place where other homeless people stayed and we fit right in, it was like an old apartment complex and many were in the same situation we were but we got to know each other and had many barbecues.

I remember one guy sticking me with a fork and the barbecue sauce stayed in my arm for God knows how long boy that poker was hot as it singed into my arm, I don't know why he did it but he apologized and that was that. The place was like a whole different world and it reminded me of one of those concentrate camps that you now see in history books, some of the people would get up early and go to their jobs but for the alcoholics most of them stuck together trying to figure out how to get their next drink and us kids were right along with them seeing we had the same problem, drinking made us younger people feel like we were a part of the grown up's inter circle. Oliver would go around and collect cans out of the garbage so we would have something to eat that night and mom would have her toddy for her body as she called it, it wasn't an easy life but later we found a house in the projects on west Madison street and we stayed for a while until mom got deathly ill and almost died. We had a lot of partys there and Rick stayed in the back house with his girl friend and kids and boy did they fight when they didn't have their booze or drugs, my older brother was very sociable when he was high but a very angry person when he didn't have what he needed many times people suggested that he should go to anger management classes but it never took place and as the years went by he got worse until his girlfriend left and went back to Nebraska, the one place he couldn't go because they would of arrested him. During our time there in Phoenix us boys traveled back and forth to California' trying to find our place in the world and that's when I met my first wife Diane, she was still young and had a five year old child but was going out with an older man from Los Angeles a man twice her age. She lived in her mothers back house where I would visit while the older man was back in Los Angeles, to me he reminded me of a pimp only using her so I took it upon my self to take her away from him like I had done before with another girl sometime before. We hit it off and became good friends and did many things together after about six or so months she decided she wanted to merry me and I thought it was a good idea at the time but later learned that my age difference would be a problem. It was a good day as I did some work at the church and got one of the floors done, next it will be the other one and then just one more to do. It's nice to be able to go there when I'm down but also when I feel the need to get away for a time and be by my self, my marriage didn't last very long and I never got married again and maybe it was because I didn't like the feeling of being bossed around by a women or I was afraid of failure. There were many times when we tried it again not marriage but living together but that also didn't work, then later she married my brother which didn't last long either. So maybe it was her and not me like I thought. I do know that two people with addictions shouldn't be together because one enables the other and that's never a good thing, when I took my life back I tried to be with someone who drank and that almost destroyed the relationship.

As for finding someone who didn't drink that never happened, because by that time I was more or less set in my ways, and I don't know even to this day if that kind of situation would work. Always looking for that perfect relationship which never came, it's now Friday morning and it seams the time goes by real fast. I want to do more things these days because I can't quite sit around, when pop's was here I was always busy doing something but now that part is gone so I have too occupy my time with something else and I will find something. I would like too spend sometime with the pastor and see what her day is like because I know she never gets board living the christen life is something I would like too check out. Besides what I do today my car is still holding up and I hope in time to get a different one but we will see maybe it will last another year, in my younger years no one ever bought a new car because it wasn't in the cards and even today if I did have one regertering it could cost too much so the that in it's self would make it impossible. Back as a kid my friendshipes with women or girls didn't last long and it was because I was not grown up enough even though we would find our selves tangeled in love the excitement went away and I would loose intrest very fast and that was because I was still that child that didn't get to grow up properly or that's what I like to think. My kids are the best part of me and even though I and their mother didn't get married they still carry part of me inside of them, with Shannon it's her patients with others kids and she does a great job with them. And Leroy he has a little of my everything but still he turned out pretty good.

It's a guy thing with him and I have watched him grow from a far to see if he can over come what has been put into his path, and so far he is on the right track s far as I know. Life throws us many curves and we as people have to be strong so we can take it on and become better then we are at any certain time, but it's what happens in the end of life that makes us who we are. Will I expand and grow into that person God wants me to be yes!! I have no doubt. And life will go on to where only He knows what the finished product will become. Everyone will be excited today because it's T.G.I.F. And they have the weekend off but I wonder how many will come to church this Sunday? For surely they have time for God if they want to take it and come for an hour, since my return to life I have stayed close to the church once I found it so long ago and it brings me peace to do things for those involved…. We the people are the church a body of people brought together by the Lord to learn and understand what we are capable of learning, and although each of us has a different view they seam to come together and make the church strong so it will be ready for the next generation of our people. From the ones that are little today to the ones who will come after them, many people who know me understand that God is a big part of my life and always will be. My persona reflects my being and I have never asked what others see but one time I was told that I looked like a professr with my glasses on so funny!! I have a feeling that I will go and get another car from Tom and Lenny in Kearney, all my vehicals have come from them and they have lasted a long time, they should give me a discount because I do advertising for them in the great state of Kansas' Tom is a christen man and is honest he has never done me wrong and for that I am glad. My land he even sends me a Christmas card each year to keep in touch and he doesn't really have too but he does, we are going into town this morning to get some things to last the month because we all need to eat. I also brought some food to the church yesterday so they can give it to the food bank and help the little ones who wont get a lunch, because I believe school is out for the summer. I would of never guessed that poverty would be this bad in the United States but it seams to have happened, at least now they recognize it and can make changes if it isn't politicaly incorrect. Why they use that word is beyond me, I guess the big hucky bucks came up with that one. Before they had to project an image and not help their own people just other countrys, I call it a show of power but it's not just a bunch of ass holes tring to get them selves to look important. Here in Courtland people care about each other and they project that in the things they do, not so much my the strong men but through their caring that they try to hide because a man is supposed to be strong and not show emotion. This is a misconception because even Jesus showed His emotions and cried sometimes especially when he talked to God although they were one, sometimes I wonder if my journey will end here and have a happy ending as for now I know my place is here and no one knows what the future holds for any of us. Being in this town at this time is something He wanted for me, to learn on a smaller scale what life is all about.

In the day when Jesus arrived, many wise people knew of his coming and by the spirit He was protected but I can't help but wonder what happened in those days and years that He was growing up as there are only guesses of where He was. Was he taught by the bible or was He taught by a school which I don't think they had back then not like today, my mind runs deep and I can only take in so much at a time and then it get's processed in time but what I learn seams to be put away and I can't recall it at the drop of aa hat like some can. Do we really keep what we learn deep inside for it to show it's self later when it's needed? Or does it go in one ear and out the other like school back in the day I think not' it's getting light out so now the days starts. It was a nce day and I got a new car, well new to me but it should last quite a while although the car is a little newer then I'm used to. It had a bad winow control so the guy is going to fix it on Monday it's strange how when you get older you want something simple and you end up with a Grand-prix, I remember a friend having one years ago but it was the old style not like this one I got now I just pray that it will become a part of my life now and last ten or so years. Because it will take five of those to pay it off, I have always had a nice car but this has a little more. Saturday morning and I slept in a little longer then usual but that's ok, today I have some things to do which will be done this morning while it's cool out side and then off to the thrift store to do my part. In my life all things have come hard to me but here with friends they seam to love me as I move forward, I could of never asked for a better place to live then Courtland when I came up with getting a different car my friend backed me and that's something I'm not used to happening.

Although the car is equipped with a super charger it's something I wont use very oftend because I seldom go over the speed limit, don't like those tickets because they can drain your pocket and that's something I don't need at my age. I asked God to bless my car as it will become an extended part of my life through the years I never expected to be loved so much but here in courtland I am as for family I don't have the ones who taught me well but I know somewhere up there they are watchiing over me and I hope they are smiling. Next Tuesday I have to take Randy to parole so he can get that behind him for another month he has been doing really well since his arrival over a year ago and I see no problems with him in the future. My self I will find something to do with my extra time and I will make it in this great place we call home, the stories of my life is ever lasting as each day brings something new to the table and I never know what's coming next Randy was more excited about the car then I was and he thinks it's a good buy. But to me only time will tell if that is the case if it makes it through the winters then I will be happy, with me it takes two years before I become comfortable with a vehicle. And that will be in 2014 which isn't a long ways off as the months go by so fast, I feel a spiritual connection here one that I have never felt before. And I know it's a good thing because God is behind it in many ways, as it was Him that brought me to this beautiful place the place where the doves fly around and walk the streets like they have been here since birth. I had always heard that doves are a simble of God in many ways and they are mentioned in the bible, as the dove flies it's very graceful and they will sit in the road which I make sure I don't hit one. These things are important to me and I look for spititual things that others don't, really there are many things that I do which others couldn't care less about but they are important to me the person I have become. It's going to be a great day and next week they are calling for cooler weather which is something I will be grateful for but I know it won't be the last of the hot weather we still have the indian summer once the weather changes. although the summers are hot we are allowed to move forward into nicer weather and then you have to hope that your car is working right to make it through winter. Having a front wheel drive car allows you to get around in the snow better because the weight is all up front to allow for better traction, my journey has been very good so far and I hope in time that I will advace to maybe be a teacher of some sort a teacher of life experiences and what addiction can do to your life if you let it get out of hand. Things people need to know so they don't take that step into the darkness of life, addiction makes life much harder then it would be if you didn't fall into it. Because you loose all the little things that a child should learn when they are young, and I don't advise anyone to have to go through that. Because at my age it's a lot harder learning those things, the value of friends are important but also the value of life is something very important. As I go through the next two years we will see how things become, and I will learn more with my closer walk with God' trying to learn His ways. In the world today more and more kids are falling vicTom to the worthless people who see their weaknesses and exploit them to become rich , and although they never become rich they have it in their minds that they will.

Only death follows them but most end up in prison looseing everything including their families such a wast in a world where family is so important, from the child that cries because his parents would rather buy drugs or booze to the person who has to live on the street because the addiction has taken it all away even their spirit is wounded by this curse and many don't even know it. This place I talk about, is a place. I have been, and it's like walking in the dark in the pitch black of the unknown. People on Methamphetamine don't know where reality was left and the unknown began wondering around in a world that they don't recognize because the drugs have taken over, and the only excitement is when the person comes to sell them more and boy do they get excited. Not knowing what they cut it with, which could kill you in the drop of a hat. It was a great day and I got my work done and had fun folding cloths at the thrift store just simple things like that make me happy. I don't have to go out and spend money to be happy my car is working fine except for a couple of things which will get fixed when I talk to the guy again, I believe and hope that my wheels will last for ever well not for ever but a long time. Driving it is a lot different from my old car as for some reason it seams bigger but that could just be me, in my younger years this would of been the car to die for but like they say better late then never so funny. I know when I see my son again he is going to fall in love with it, and want to drive it, but that will never happen as I don't let anyone drive my wheels.

This morning we checked everything out and everything seams to be kosher so now when I get the window fixed and the on and off switch for the air-conditioning I should be set to go, well night is falling so I will write some more later. Sunday morning' and it's raining out side when the rain started I was a sleep but this morning I could hear the thunder and see the lightening it was very bright, I and Beverly were the ones that worked the last shift yesterday and I enjoy her company. If it wasn't for the thrift shop and my other work I would probably be very bord but I'm not, when I can work a couple of hours now and then and do other things at the church, it seams I'm building my life around doing things here and I like that the helping out when some need it. The thrift store is growing and we get many things in that others can use and it doesn't cost an arm and a leg like it does in the big cities, I have been to other thrift stores where they charge almost half of what it would cost at a regular store and that's just not right. Our thrift store caters to those who don't have the money to go to bigger towns and pay those ridicules prices for used things which can still be used for things like work, and also for dress when need be I get most of my clothes there as somee are like brand new and even have the tags on then. Amazing what some people pay for some things and then not even ware it to later give it away, in the future I see the thrift store growing into a good business that will help many people here in the heart land. The heart land and it extends into Nebraska and Kansas but in Kansas it's also called the bible belt and tornado alley, many nick names for the States which helped to tame the west. And many out-laws came through this great State trying to hide from the law back in the 1800's quite a history for Kansas and I'm sure if the history books were searched they would find out little town in there somewhere I don't know how long it's been raining but we sure needed the moisture as the ground was cracking from being so dry, I saw Leroy yesterday and he is doing better it's the first time I saw the bruses on him and boy he must have been in pain. But the good news is that he is recovering and that's what matters people drive their four wheelers around once in a while, to have fun and I think that's awesome our own little paradise out in the middle of the heart land a protected place where everyone is safe. The pool has been full for the last month or so everyone getting wet to stay cool through the summer months the little kids as well as adults, such a great sight to see them so happy. The day will be clamy from the rain and the humidity will be high except for in here where it's always nice and you can breath without any problems it's better to get the humidity out of the house so everyone can enjoy the things we do at home. Pastor Kathy should get her self a humidifier for the time when her lungs give her a fit that way it would be easier for her to breath. Little things like this a lot of people don't know about even Beverly tried it and she can tell a difference, she was amazed at how much water it sucked out in just one day and it will keep doing it until it's all sucked out and then you only have to empty it once every few days. With me being a smoker it makes a world of a difference and it's so much easier on the lungs, funny how just suggesting something can catch on and then they will let others know about it so they too can breath easier. The end of the week and now another one begins the cycle of life goes on, not like when you were a child as in those days one day was like a week to us today.

The little tikes live in the moment and we adults live in the week or at least I do and maybe it's because of the life I lead who really knows, the air-conditioning takes the humidity out of the house some what but the other makes it work less by taking it out also. Causing the air-conditioning not to have to work as hard to do that job there by bringing down the electric bill. A great change and life is more comfortable after being out side in the sweltering; sweat, when you think others don't listen to you. You might just be supprised as they try suggestions you might make, here in Courtland all is well as we move forward into the next half of the year and then 2013 will be here before you know it. I am glad that Randy came to live here, but also I'm glad that he didn't have to live out another three years in that hell hole which had already done enough damage to him. In the next three years he could be out into the light if he so chooses I know he also get's bord but it beats the alternative of being in that place, he hasn't been out to see his so called friends back in Nebraska and in a way I don't want him to because I know how mean they will be laughing about his weight and making fun of him behind his back. It's a not so nice world out there and right now he needs to be protected until he can become strong once again, not that I can do that for him but God can help.

I haven't heard the rain in a while so maybe it quit for now to come back later when it's needed, it seams He knows when that time is. As for mowing the lawn, it will have to wait for it too get dry and that won't happen until tomorrow. Sunday is His day of rest but for me I have to do a little work like straightening up after service, so if they have something going on tomorrow the church will be clean. I like to keep things up to par and I'm proud of what I do, the womens bathroom is very clean and I have a little more to do in the men's just my way of saying thank you to all who is involved in my transformation and yes I believe that's what it is out with the old and in with the new. Trying to reconstruct a life from what it once was to where it will be sometime in the future, such a blessing and we all have the power to do this in our lives no matter how bad the old life was at one time. God finds a way to help us heal and start a new as we move forward into a world where things are different, I can't count the years spent in the house back in the dark times maybe to many to want to remember plus the times weren't that grand back then. The high time of the day was getting up and cleaning the house and then getting high or drunk and this was a normal thing, so I thought. The growing up in that situation became my life also not just my parents so the curse was handed down and I carried it for so long, I remember thinking it had to end with me but by then the curse had already affected my child and he carried it. Not a good legacy to leave someone, but he also has the strength to destroy it and I pray that he does. As for it staying with me it hasn't and that is a good thing a thing of the past to never come back again, like turning a page in a book and moving forward to read what happens in the end and hoping the ending is a good one. I know my life has a happy ending because what once was is no more and who knows where it will lead, God that's who and He isn't telling me anything O I believe He could tell me the ending but what would be the point of ruining the life of a lost soul? Many times during that time I wanted to give up but something inside told me not to. It was God letting me know that the next step was just a step away and giving me courage to take it, I have always been the kind of person that makes the impossible possible just because someone said I couldn't do it. I think it made me stronger in many ways knowing they couldn't do it and I could, but it was God who brought me through it all because in many cases I wasn't as strong as I needed to be. And that's when He showed me that all is possible through Him the Father' it is said that He works in the supernatural and I believe this is the case other wise He couldn't of saved me so many times, all things belong to Him and we just borrow it for our time here. I know when I leave this place I will take nothing with me and it will remain maybe in my memory but who knows for sure, I would like to think that maybe I made a difference in this little part of the world anyway. From a life of destruction to finding peace in a world I grew to love, but not the whole world just this little part of it where I will grow old and die one day. As for death it's self it's not so scary any longer because I know that I will be with my Father and your's in that place he has created for us, and on my stone it will say don't cry for me. Monday morning and it looked like it rained once again Icant tel how much we got but any is better then nothing, after church we went to town and got some teash bags and other things we needed and then I cosed up the church funny thing was that someone left some cup cakes and they read for you Roger and your brother Randy, such thoughtful people and I think it was Judy Blackburn John's beautiful wife. Today they are supposed to fix my window so there wont be any rain getting in you have to have secure windows on a car if not for the rain not getting in, but also to keep the thiefs out. If things go right then this will be the newest car I have ever had, driving it is different from my other one but going down the road feels like I'm in one of those really expansive cars.

I also mowed yesterday and even with the rain we got night before last the ground was still dry so maybe last night changed that, as I could still see the puddles in the street this morning. This car will only be worked on by the people I know I can trust which is Hord oil or the other machanic who has his own shop, the cruse control was something I have missed since the guy messed it up a coulple of years back and now I have it once again such a delight not to have to have your foot on the gas peddel all the time. As for sounds, the stereo is the best and it works good to make those trips more enjoyable as you go down the road. Tomorrow we will take it to Concorida for Randys appoitment and then back home, Randy knows a guy that will paint the hood for a reasonable price but we will have to go to Kearney for a couple of days and that would be ok because I could see my grandchildren and my son and daughter. The worry of making it somewhere is behind me now as this should be a dependable vehical, and I pray that I can make a few trips with it. My friend at the bank said it was a good thing that I didn't get the motor home and I agreed with him telling him that God told me that I would be getting a car or needing one, it's not strange to me that things happen the way they do it's like a voice that tells me when things are going to change. And I take it as His voice letting me know that change is coming, back in the days of wine and roses I didn't hear this voice very oftend but I did hear it when trouble was coming and that lead me to stay away from it and it kept me out of trouble many a times' I can recall when my two brothers were going to get into trouble on that night which sent them to prison they wanted me to go with them but that voice said to stay home and I did. To only hear later that they had been arrested, my voice as I call it has guided me in the right direction over my life and it has been the voice of God.

Even when I thought I was alone in the world that voice has been there every step of the way to guide me in times of trouble. To show me that I wasn't alone but back then I couldn't see it because I was blind in that darkness, when your blind by sight another sight that you can't see kicks in and it takes you to where you need to be. Like with my moving here it wasn't by natural things but by the spirit that dwells inside of this body of mine, it is much stronger then this body and it guides me in many things that I do which is a God sent. Thinking back it has guided me through this life even when I couldn't see right in the dark, a gift from the one that loves me to help me get through this life and not make the mistakes that my brothers have made. I am set apart from them in that fashion a seprate souls that is guided by the one who created me, even the words to my songs are given or approved by the Father and that lets them become mine my own creation made by me. As many songs play in my mind there is but two who can bring them into reality and that's God and my self, something made from love and not destruction. In my mind there are a few more songs which is coming together and in time they too will become my songs, very beautiful songs which will touch the hearts of many. I have never heard a song wrote for the passing of someone that can comfort the ones that are left behind and that is a bridge I'm trying to cross, as the words come slowely not to offend anyone but then not everyone is going to like my choice of things that will come. All my creation comes to me in spurts and I have too connect the dot's when the right one's come along and if they are right then it all falls together, but I also know that the songs are created for my situation and the things I have gone through in life. From the heartache and pain lived in this life, but also the joy and happiness that is brought into my world by others. One of the songs has to do with my time in the mornings, and it brings great joy when it becomes closer to a finished product. And sometimes it can take up to a year depending on the song, I seam to enjoy the creating of it, bringing the right words together so others can feel what I feel when I hear it. Something new that has to do with the human spirit and how free the human spirit can be as it leads us on an adventure, through the world as we become more of what He careted us to be. A free spirit can and will go far if it's nurtured; right and allowed to soar beyond the heavens like Peter Pan Ha! Through the years my spirit hasn't been able to do that until just recently but the mind has to let it do it. Allow it to take off and become what ever it wants to become, and this is something that can't be achived if addiction to drugs and alcohol is in your life for those two things limits; the mind from becoming what it wants to be. And that is a great lesson learned so take it to heart my down fall can be your flight to fame if you let it, don't let those things into your life go for the brass ring and be the best you can be. Many people who rise too fast to fame fall real hard because they think the drugs give them something and I'm here to tell you drugs have never given anyone anything they only take from people. What do they take? you name it. Your whole world, no one has ever came out on the up side when they allow drugs into their lives.

And you can just ask them, children taken away, family not wanting to be around you because they can't stand to see you that way. What's important to them isn't important to you because you don't live in the same world, your's isn't real illusion isn't no where near reality your lost in a fog and can't find your way out which makes you not so bright, as for the high it's only in you're mind no where else it's in a capsul just running around until it run's out of steam. To only make your body crave it more then before you think you can take on the world but usually you can't take care of your self as the world you once knew is crumbling around you and then you burn all the bridges you once had, and no one wants anything to do with you at all this is hitting rock bottom and your love of your life finds someone else that can live in the real world. From having it all to taking the big fall and you my friend might not get up, the world will still go around weather you're here or not as when your gone you go back to dust. Just ashes that God once breathed life into, did He make the mistake? No you did, when you thought the world was something you could or should alter I have lived this life and no one knows better then an expert that it's the wrong path to take. The rain is falling again and we have gotten quite a bit as the stream is running down the road, little brother is sleeping quite a bit lately and I don't know why but maybe he should get a job as the sitting around isn't doing him any good.

When he first came here I didn't expect this' but I may have to make the decision that he won't like in the end but I can't deal with his not doing anything all the time and that's that. With Oliver it was old age but that's an excuse he can't use, to night I'm going to an art class it will be the first for me since like for ever and who knows maybe I can be taught to be an artist we will see, Mark's wife is teaching the class I believe and I have just gotten to know her. Many new people are coming forward and I'm slowely getting to know them, the rain quit. After falling most of the day, but that doesn't mean it isn't going to rain again to night lord knows we can use a lot more. Art class was different but at least I'm trying something new and after words I slept like a baby, it's been a long time since I stayed up that last and I'm going to class all this week to see what it will bring will let my draw and paint. I haven't painted since I can't remember when except for houses back in the day and that was fun, I think it lets you bring some things out that might be inside the house I drew long ago is still in my mind and maybe to night I will draw it. For some reason there is a kind of peace when I'm in class and

I really like that as it lets you clear your mind of all things, our teacher is very young maybe in her 20's and she sees things in a different way then most folks. This is another step in getting to know more people, my mind doesn't seam to wonder when I'm in class and when I left I told them that it was a pleasure and that it was very therapeutic meaning to me anyway that it was fun. During this life we all find something we are comfortable at doing even if it doesn't make any since but who knows what it will bring to the surface. Tuesday morning' and we have to travel today to Concorida and then back to Belleville so the window can be fixed, that in it's self will stop some of the worrying about the inside of my car getting wet. And bring me' some kind of peace. The car I bought is a chick magnet and they seam to like it even from a far, things like painting should be part of therapy to calm what's inside. When I got home it didn't take long before I fell a sleep and I have to say that I slept through the night for the first time in years such a delight not to wake up. I'm going to make today a good day and pray that all goes well as I move into the late hours. When I went to school as a child I didn't have art class but if I had maybe I could of brought out some of what was inside, and that the point of doing things to bring about a change even if it's something small. I bet that the world is seen in many different ways by each person and I don't have a clue of how it's supposed to look because my sught of hings is black and white with a tint of color. In my life there has been many walls put up on the inside so in time I hope to break them down, and see the beauty that I write about like the birds and the other animals which exist here around my home. My little buddies as I call them for they too share this piece of land and we all get along just fine, through the years of being here Courtland has been good to me and I couldn't think of a better place that I would want to be.

As I heard my sister went back to her old man I wasn't supprised, but then I heard she went back to Tonya's sis has had a hart time finding the place she wanted to settle, and until she finds it. She will keep looking, I hope one day she will be happy in her decision when she comes to that place which will grab her heart like Courtland has grabed mine, for me this is the place for which I belong and I will remain until I get old and gray. Maybe in the future I will find someone here but for now it's just me and Randy two batchlors living the life we want or at least I'm living my life the way I want, I don't need all the drama which comes with being around a lot of people for my world has been created for me and if I'm lucky then someone will share it with me someone that is like me in some ways but with their own personality, I guess in many ways I'm starting to wake up as a lot of people are becoming part of my family. And I feel comfortable around a lot of them I'm building a family here, to maybe replace the ones I lost so long ago as we all need friends as we take that journey through life. Someone we can laugh with and not at, someone who can make you smile and look forward to the next day when the birds sing in the morning, just that human touch when you get up in the mornings can set the tone of how your day will go. My journey is going to be a long one and truly you have to have a careing person to take that journey with, the making of love come's to mind as two bodies intertwine and you collaps from taking each other to going to the stars.

Haven't been there in a while so I will see what the future holds, in this life I have only wanted to be happy and now that is a possibility, but not at this time. I'm still trying to figure out things in this world, and who knows God could bring things to my understanding. My car is armed with a security system so I shouldn't have to worry about someone breaking in to it, as they would have to see the flickering light on the dash saying that they will get caught. Just peace is all I need so I can write and bring out what is holding me back maybe going to that place that frightens me sometimes would ease some things only God knows where that is. As for my kids coming here they said they would try so we will see what takes place, I never infringe on my kid's to do something they are not able to do, or want to do. And they seam to come around on their own it's been over a year since they stoped by and I still hope to see them at the end of this month on fun day' but I wont push just let things happenon their own. I am learning now that the things you learn as a child stays with you even the bad things which children see, and of course the good. Without a foundation it's hard to grow the right way as with me there wasn't one until I moved here and now the church is my foundation and God is my parent. As I look back He has always been there in my darkest times and He brought me through a lot of misfortune, as I was being guided to where I am today. I had a great day as we went on a road trip and also got my car window fixed, now no worries about people breaking into my car not that it would happen here but other places. Like when I go and see my daughter and son in Kearney, the people there will be jelous because they never moved forward and I keep moving in that direction. I never see my self going in the other direction because that's not who I am, and even if things get harder I have advanced and not fallen back. Many people have life a lot harder then I but I also realize that I do what I can to help them also. To night I have art class again and it seams to bring me peace but also I don't know what I'm doing there not having any education, but hey' you have to try new things in life to find out what fit's you so I will keep going and see what takes place. Doing art is something that every talented person should try last night we had more people show up and who knows maybe there will be more to night, it last for a few more days and who knows maybe I will get something out of this. I have noticed that I sleep later then I used to and that throws off my getting things done, I was kidding with Mark's wife and told her that he should come to class and she snickered a little bit. One of the women work at the bank Betty I believe, and she is funny at times everyone there seams to have fun joking and laughing just a good old time as we learn new things. I seam to slowly come out of my box that I have been in for so long and the people are so friendly even the ones I haven't met before, Courtland should be noticed for it's kindness and how people old and young come together to have some fun and learn new things. The teacher is mighty young but she has no problem with teaching the younger and the elders as they have fun together, when I'm there it's like I'm in my own world but then I realize it's a time to have fun also so I will joke with some or any of them they have known each other for some time but I'm the newest person there having only been here for a few years. The being a part of something greater then my self bring me to believe that there is life after addiction the Courtland fine arts building set everything up and I would like to thank them. I wish little brother would come but like I used to be his shyness stops him, but I'm hopeful that he will come around. Wednesday morning' today I have to do some work at the church and then it's down to the thrift store for a couple of hours, my days and part of my night are used to learn to communicate with others.

Do I really want to mingle with other people I believe so but with great caution as I know all people are not like the other I once knew. Little brother is hinting that he wants to visit Kearney but I don't know he seams to like those drives when we go somewhere and as for my self I don't mind it either now that I have a vehical that is dependable and has a stereo. With my other car it was like I didn't want to take it on long distences sweating all the time and not having a good air-conditioner, when the temp's get into the 100's it's just not plesent. I can hear the bird's this morning as they seam to flock to my house and sing like all get out, although I'm doing new things I cant let it take me away from my other things that I do. My attention gets distracted very easly and I can loose track of the things I have to do, learning is a great thing even at my age and like they say your never too old to learn. I spend some of my time reading the owners manual on my car so I will get to know it better as time moves on. Thursday morning' on this fine day I got up on time my usual time that is' but I could have slept another hour or so, the doing different things has brought on opportunities which I can use or not. The ability to sleep in longer if I so choose and get used to adjusting to the different hours, I was talking with the teacher at art class and she comes from a family of gifted people and she teaches at a school in Scandia just a few miles down the road. I saw a painting that her mother had done and it was awesome, a tree with a hole in the center of it where an owl could of once made it their home or still did. Who knows what's in an artists mind but it's a great gift, we have all been given gifts to bring to this world as it says we are God's gift to the world sent here to do a job that no one else can do only us the chosen have this gift.

Before I came here I really didn't know who I was but now I feel I'm that gift that can break down the wall when it comes to addiction. And no one else can do what I do when it comes to writing about such things, the gift of insight lets me travel back in time and bring out those things I lived through. My lack there of education has allowed me to be taught by the best teacher of all and that is God, Him self' I don't have all the confusion that others have or may carry around in them. And I'm able to stay on the path for which I was born to be on, all the other things for which I lived through was to see if maybe in time change could take place and I could bring out the secrets that were' or still are inside of me. Each day brings something new and I except it as I travel through this life, I can see a change in the weather somewhat as the mornings are cooler for a short time anyway but then next week it's supposed to be hot once again but only in the 90's the season is beginning to change as we move forward into fall but Indian summer has to hit before that season get's here then the crops should grow a lot better, our moisture is doing better then other parts of the country as the drout has hit them more then it has hit us here in Courtland. A gift from God is all I can say what will happen with my life? I do know that my writing has to continue and I enjoy it most in life it's sort of like the painting classes when you can go inside of your self and be alone without anyone bothering you and create things from the mind using the gifts that God has given you, to be able to separate you're self from others is something that can bring you peace of mind. To go to that place where you feel safe and not have to worry about someone envading your space, it's like two worlds exist and you own them both or God does and He lets you travel in both of them. Today is my day off so I will find something else to do after doing something at church, but I do have art class again tonight and I look forward to it. Our teacher is named Destiny which means that which will happen in the future, how true what a great name and it says it all. Even her name was a gift for her family to give such a name she is surely loved by them it's our future which holds the key to many things, the union between two boundries brought together by fate is fate what will become of us and if so does God bring such things into this world of ours. Just thinking about such things brings a kind of peace for which I don't understand but the future will unfold what it's supposed to and bring things into existence that are supposed to be. The mysteries of the unknown what will it hold for many a bringing of another world one of peace for which others have never seen, how does someone put their head around that just learn to except that which will happen in the time to come. We are all here for a reason one that we don't fully understand but God him self knows what will become of things we only guess at, does he reveal such things to us? I believe he does when the time presents it's self.

I have traveled through this land in hope that one day I would find that other half, or part of me. That part for which I will one day be complete. The sands of time can't stand between what God has in store for your life as His power is above all else and nothing exist that matters when He has made things to be a part of this world, our dreamd allow us to see a little of what will take place but like in most dreams we forget them after seeing just a glimps of them. I have had dreams which I could go back into but those are far and few in-between it was like traveling between two different places and it felt great when I could revisit the place if it wasn't too scary, like falling into a pool not being able to swim but then having the ability to breath under water what a trip' I get a thought to travel and see my daughter and grand babys I haven't seen my kids in two years and that's too long. I really want to see Leroy also and see how he is doing, time seams to change most things and living here has surely changed me. I'm not the same person any more it's like a spiritual transformation has taken place and now I'm a part of that transformation growing in spirit to become something I was born to be. It's like everything that I had dreame of having is now coming to pass but a lot later in years like the clock was reset and now I get that second chance, that chance to get it right this time around. And only He can allow that to happen, will my dreams unfold or were they the thing that kept me going? I believe only He knows that answer at this time. I have to take little brother to see his doctor today so we will travel a little bit today not far though just a few miles, and I'm glad that the doctor isn't far away. The car like drives it's self so it's no effort to take him just the sitting is all and I have good music to listen too, there and back. The month is about half over and then it will be August and hopefully it will bring with it cooler temperatures but I won't hold my breath just yet so funny.

I hope we have another mild winter or maybe we do need more snow to balance things out the moisture would be nice if the snow was a lot heaver though, but I do know that this winter will be spent along and try to figure out new things for reaching people. In the darkness of their mind they see no way out as I went through the same thing, the times when you have to face that your life is out of control. And even though many will stay on the path to destruction they are given a chance for change, a chance to turn everything around and with inspration they can take that chance and use it to bring out that person they were meant to be. I believe we are God's gift to the world and even though some get lost along the way He opens certain doors to give us opportunities to find our way back to the original path we were set out to follow, and accomplish the things we were ment to do when we were born. Even in getting lost we are taught things that become a part of our lives in later years as for instence my becoming a writer, all through life I never seen it coming' but He knew it from the beginning and He knew I would be where I am today. The struggles through life is a part of our growing and no matter how you slice it, in the end we will become what He set out for us to do if destruction doesn't happen first. That my friend is free will, we choose wither we make it or not and if we do make it them that's where we will be. Through the younger years living in that fog was a part of me becoming the person I am today, and He knew what would happen to me so He gave me the gift to write and He gave me the people who influenced my writing so I would stay on this path that I'm on. I can't say what will take placce further down the line but I know He walks beside me and guides me when troubled times show them selves. Friday morning and art class went well as I finished up my project and to night is the last night so I will go and pick up my painting, it was an experience. A good experience as it let me be my self and go into that place that I call my own, things like this helps and you get to know some intresting people Destiny is a good teacher and very talented and I can see why she became a teacher to teach the children and broden their minds. Some schools have done away with art just like they took prayer out of the schools and that should never be because it takes away from the building of the mind of a youngster, although I didn't get much schooling I'm still learning today even if it's just by doing things which our town does together. Courtland is awesome, because it brings things into my life that otherwise would of never happened, sure it might not sound like much to others or they might be too proud to take something new on but to me it opens a new world for which I never got to explore before. Letting the mind go to where ever it wants for a short time anyway, and there were many people who stopped in and did an art project age doesn't matter it's just a time when people can get together and have some fun, at first I was shy but them they made me feel right at home allowing that door to open that had been shut all these years. My writing allows me to say what's on my mind and this is it, all communitys should have such an opportunity for people to mingle to get to know others that live around them.

As many people know God brought us together for a reason but what that reason is has to be figured out by us. Funday is coming up and many will have family come home to camp in the front yard and have a good time the homes they once lived in have gotten smaller since they started their own families but there is still room for prayer before each meal and that's what matters, the christen values that still exist here will never leave it's like a home base for what made many the way they are and shaped their lives before leaving. Life experiences is what makes us who we are and if you can help someone along the way then that's what you should do. Today is going to be an awesome day as we move into the weekend and I get to look at my painting, it might just be a glimps of what could have been but at least it was fun doing it. Things like this doesn't exist in many places and it should. Mrs. Johnson was very kind to have opened the doors to the fine arts center and I learned a little about the history of Courtland and some of the surrounding areas. How things came to be from time passed, mostly a farming community where they feed a big part of the world if those people only knew what it takes for them to eat then maybe there wouldn't be any starvation in the United states, my life here is a plus as far as I'm concerned learning new things as I go along and meeting new people. I came here to be able to write the way I see things and that's what I do you see many years ago I was stricken by a curse which took my ability to walk and they said I never would be able to do it but they didn't know the power of God when He set's His mind to something and with his help today that curse is gone to never return also my mind was damaged but then again who better to heal that then the one who created it.

Many people think that alcohol or drugs can inhance their ability to thrive in life but in the end they find them selves trying to destroy the thing that they thought would work and that takes a lot of time from a persons life. My advice is to never try and alted what God has created because in the end you loose so much time with those you love, an ability is a gift from God but what you do with it is either a gift to him or can be a curse. Don't live out your life experimenting with things that will one day destroy you, live the life for which God put you here for and embrace each day as a gift. Little brother might have to have back surgery and if this is the case then we will get it done, it's only by getting the car that it will be possible to make the trip where it will have to be done for truly the lord is watching over things in our lives and bringing about change so things will get better, yesterday I washed the car by hand and it didn't take too long just some vinegar and water and a good dry towel and boy what a difference as it brightened up like a new penny. The day went pretty well but boy it was hot, I also brought my new friend a thank you card for her kindness during art class she is a great person. The connection between people has never been easy for me but she made it easy because of maybe her age as I was brought up in a different time, through the years my being alone has become second nature and I don't know if my world could bring in someone half my age. Time seams to somehow always leave me by my self like before, maybe one day the other person could or would make the next move. Such a delima in my life to know when the time is right as I get no signals to move forward, one of these days it will come to pass when women ask men out on a date. Through the sands of time I hope someone will see things the way I do, like a person said one time maybe the women will be strong enough for both the man and her self letting her make the first move. I want someone in my life but so many things come into play and I havent learned to get past that as of yet. Saturday morning' today I will go and put the last touches on the church before tomorrows service, Randy is doing good these days and in September on the 11th he will go and have his back surgery done. I haven't yet told my daughter and son that I'm coming down because I want it to be a supprise, supprises is something that doesn't happen very oftend and they might enjoy it but it wont happen for a couple of months. They are going to have a display of our art on fun day' and for some reason that doesn't bother me like it might have so long ago, so many things have changed since my coming here and I'm not just another face in the crowd. Like I once was back when the world was black and full of mysteries of the unknown, we seam to find our way in this life and it's great when things work out for the greater good of things. Once again I feel change coming but like all the other times I can't put my finger on it so we will see what happens later down the road, for on this day many things are moving around in the universe can a connection be made when things are so different the falling in love of two souls that are seprated by many years. In my days things happen like clockwork the getting up and starting the day so early finely I'm at a loss for words. But what brings that loss? Not being able to connect with a thought or bringing things into existence so they can be made a reality.

The fine arts were very generous by letting us use the building for our learning of how to let the mind go and create something new this is the first step in my getting to know more about the people here and I'm glad that I got to know them over this week of creating, I felt a connection with one of them but I don't know if she felt it also. Does age separate us from going forward or is that something which is created and seprated by the mind brought on by our not understanding some things in life, many people at that age want children and my days of having them is long gone. Not' as many people have had kids until their late 70's I think only God knows when it isn't possible any longer, in the bible one women had a child at 80 years old I believe and man I bet that was hard. But it was made possible by God and no one could undo what He sets into motion, my journey has brought me to try a new thing and that's painting but it also opened my heart to a certain someone. Will I get the chance to explore the possibility of moving forward or is this something I should keep inside? Fun day is just around the corner so we will see what will take place. The exploring might be good for me, to let the mind travel to places it didn't want to before. in the world that I have known it wouldn't be proper to advance but when there is a connection then shouldn't you follow it? The day is going to be a good one as I do the things which bring me joy. Being scared of the unknown can bring many fears into play I haven't had any feelings for anyone in a long time and maybe I'm scared of them especially when the other person is so young but 27 years isn't young to her probably.

Can love find it's way if it's real? That is something I have never seen but it could if it's strong enough, with many people today age doesn't make much of a difference as some who are young to me may feel old to them selves and want someone who has been a little salt and pepper to their age so funny. Many don't want the adolesent child who has yet to grow up so they find someone who is beyond that. Someone who has gown through the mistakes of addiction and are now comfortable in their own skin you might say, Destiny what a beautiful name given to a beautiful women and it's very fitting of her, a free spirit that knows how to have fun. But also calm in all situations, she would have to be being a teacher and her classes well they are very fortunate the kid's that is. Will I see her again I sure hope so and maybe then I can find out more about her, the thought of rejection can sometimes stop you out of fear especially when you have lived the life I have. Nothing in the other life has survived except for the lessons learned while going through the gates of hell so maybe now it's time to live that life I heard so much about, it can't hurt to try something new and find out more about someone who stays in your mind. The travels through life brings certain situations which can help you move forward should we be afraid of age? Not so much in this day and age if you try something and it works then you could be happy, but if you try it and it fails then you might pull back into that shell like the turtle does when it's threatened; how many chances do we get to find happiness that I don't know but I will try and find out. I could see my self being with her and maybe she sees the same thing but you never know until you try, it's getting to be about that time when I go and face the world for the day so later. Sunday and yesterday was a nice day although all there was to do is read a good book, they had something at the church afterwords and I don't recall what it was. But I went in and made sure that it was ready for this morning and now in a little bit I will turn on the air-conditioning, because it's going to be a muggy day. The things I like to do for my friends and it's always nice to be comfortable while church is going on, pastor Kathy is in Denver visiting her son as he has been ill lately and well she just needed to see him and then she will travel to see old friends that she has known for about 60 years, she is a blessing to this community and I hope she stays for years to come because she can teach us all a lot with it comes to God. Is the being a person of God made for everyone I believe so it's just that so many don't know their full abilitys when it comes to loving him, I believe many people are there on the brink of finding that connection but can't quite make it and I have been there. For God's love supersedes all of our understanding back in the day of Christ there were many doubters; and although they seen the miracles take place they still didn't believe, why is this? The human mind believes what it wants and if your brought up in not believing then it's hard to break away from that mind set. In my life' there has been to many miracles to ignore the many times when I could of surely been taken like the accident here in Kansas and then in Colorado when the axel shot out from the back of my truck, they were all sign's that God had control but me being only human I wasn't able to see the miracles until later in life.

As they say hind sight is 20/20 and we surely can't see into the future in each instence there were people around to lend a helping hand to dig me out of the car here in Kansas but in Colorado there was just God to show he was still in control. Even today I don't know how the wheel didn't go through the windshield when it bounced off the hood of the truck, I must off had an angel looking after me it was so dark that you couldn't see your hand in front of your face. As I listened to our preacher preach there are many things that touched my thoughts and they say when it doesn't touch something inside of you then that message isn't meant for you, but someone else. He seams to bring enlightenment into my life through Kathy and the others who say they love me and that is a delight does not having to worry bring more peace the not having to worry about bills and other things which can take away from the peace were supposed to feel. I remember when there was nothing but struggles and that brought discomfort to me, but also it might be a learning tool to make us manage our funds more thriftily. Back in Nebraska it was hard all the time with no end in sight but then He guided me to this place where things are very different, the friends I used to have back in the old days weren't friends and they didn't make it into my future for a reason. The reason being that God has different plans that doesn't include them, Randy was telling me that as he talked to some people in prison they admited that or said I was the only smart one because I didn't get into the trouble they had gotten them selves into.

As for my thoughts on that subject I just couldn't do the things they did because it wasn't right, when I was a little boy and took hat ice-cream was enough to last a life time the fear made me not want to feel it again and I don't recall that feeling coming back. My parents had plenty back then but me tryng to show off to a girl caused me much unwanted pain, I'm amazed at how I turned out nothing like it could have been if I would of traveled down that road. With my kids they haven't ever been in trouble for taking something that wasn't theirs and for that I'm glad a good lesson learned or it just could be in the jeans, do others see and live some of what's in my life or do they ignore the what is put in fromt of them. Only they know the answer to the question. Monday morning' as each day brings new things to my mind I can't help but wonder that if I could get published I would have my pick of the women I wanted, if things went right I do know that the older farmers are always looking for a young bride. The ones that have been here for most of their lives, in the cities everyone is open to getting a head but as with many women they want a life of being taken care of when pop's was in the hospital he seamed to like this one nurce and she said if he is rich then maybe something could be done as she was looking for a rich husband. My self if that's what they are looking for then it leaves me out because money hasn't been my fortes all I know is that if you're good at something then that will follow later down the line especially if that's God's will no one can become something good unless God is behind it, since that time when I made Him that promise I have kept my word and still today I'm moving forward trying to ignite that flame that will one day burn for ever. Knocking out the need for people to hide from the real world as we know it, I had a dream that the end of it was the best thing that ever happened and it changed so many things in the world but it also took some science to accomplish this to happen. Right now the world is out of control with so many homeless and the starving and that contributes to the addiction cycle I have never seen any good come out of someone who sit's in a park and shoves a needle in their arm just so they can shut out the world. Methamphetamine's is really taking over as it gives you false hope and makes you think you are someone but that feeling is only in the mind and it plays many tricks on a person. The two collage kids had never used it before and when it's first introduced into the body it gives false reading of what's really going on, they were late for an exam and were very tired from partying and someone suggested it to them and when they used it they flew through the exam and aced it so they thought it was a good thing. Another false reading then they were headed back home for a school break and it was snowing, Meth is something that cooks the brain as the body hit's a temp of 108 degrees and causes confusion I feel sorry for the two collage kids because they didn't know what could happen and street drugs don't come with directions. When I heard they lost their lives I knew the pusher had done another couple in, they said they were talking to cow's and thought they were people but they couldn't understand why they wouldn't help them, they had lost their way in more then one direction as they ran out of gas on that dark and lonely road. What seamed to be their saving ended up being their down fall and I have seen this with more then one person, they were lost souls that never got found until the cold of the night took them from this world.

Much of the Methamphetamine comes from Mexico and it's the strongest of this drug, and as time moved forward they gave it other names like Ice which is even stronger then the regular Meth. I remember when it first came to Kearney or the first time I tried it, my brother was in the basement living and him and a buddy asked if I wanted to try it. I then askd what it does for a person and they said it gives you energy so I tried it and then there was no turning back the euphoria it's self was a trip but then after coming out of that you were wired like your body was going a 100 miles an hour and in your mind you thought you could keep up with it but in reality it was the only thing moving that fast. In time you could feel your body degenerate and then regenerate, it was like turning on and off a light switch and over time it was destroying the body first you experienced the loss of your teeth but this took years and then the loss of weight which really messed you up. Many of the people picked at them selves and caused sores on their face and bodys, such a waste even the rich didn't stay rich too long because of the price which took all most of them had. It was the only drug that you could make in your kitchen but the smell alerted their nabors so they would take it out in the country to empty farm houses and cook it. In all the years that I knew people doing this they all thought they would become rich but none of them did, they all ended up in prison and it cost them so much for a lawyer that they lost everything. And today the hospitals are full of people who have fallen under this spell or curse, during this time alcohol didn't come back into the picture there was something about it that didn't agree with Meth use the combination of the two would collide and it didn't make for a good high.

All the people I used to know are gone now and have never intered my life again and this was God' way of telling me that it's time for the change, it was the hardest things I had ever done but I knew it was either that or live a life in agony as the destruction was great. O many of them came around for a time but then one day I asked for God's help again and like before he brought me to the understanding that change is the only way, I didn't see that He would relocate me later but he did and in doing that my life changed and those things became a thing of the past. Trying to juggle my life with taking care of pop's was a chore but in many ways it helped with over coming those addictions, pop's never had any addictions to over come so he helped me in many ways especially when I wanted to give up. I knew no one else would care for him and that I had to do it so that got me on a schedual trying to balance things out and it made me one of the greatest care givers there has ever been. And it still goes on today with my little brother, he say's he couldn't make it without my help but he under estamates him self as he could do these things on his own. We underestimate our selves when we have always been just a step away from the bottle or the high that will take us to that place we have grown up in, not knowing or tasting the real world leaves us venerable to those who are stronger in the real world but in time we also become strong in this world when we take it seriously. Many wont even try to bring them selves into reality sort of like giving God a chance, if you have only known the devil then the scale is balanced towards him, but once you get a taste of what God can do then the weight is shifted and it makes you curious to learn about the one who is so great. It's like sometimes I wonder if all people will be able to understand what I'm writing about? And although I know that people who haven't dealt with addiction would have a hard time knowing where I come from, their family members that are fighting this curse will fully understand. And then they could teach the others and they too might be able to understand what family members are going through. A mother who lives her life without addiction is truly blessed and that blessing can be passed down if the child hasn't already tried the curse, what most don't understand is that it starts with a lacking of something in the childs character and it can be as small as the lack of love or a child feeling like an out cast, compairing one child to another is seldom a good thing because the other child does better at something this develops a guilt complex because they feel like they will never messure up to that other child or older sibling. And when they fall they usually fall hard because they are the one that is bashful or shy, and alcohol or drugs take that away as it does something in the brain. Maybe blocks those feelings that makes rejection just a thought, rejection is something that I can't stand because it sends a signal that your not wanted. And we all want to be wanted in this world, it's the beginning of another week and what a week it will be so full of different things that we haven't seen or heard before. This morning I'm going to water my little plant by the porch and then maybe wash my car in the back yard, Mark asked if I was going to clean the paint off of it cleaning it so much and I just had to laugh but I like a clean car. Tuesday morning' and the train is going by I can hear steel on steel as the wheels rub together with the tracks, it's funny how I haven't heard it in quite a while I used to think it went by each day but I guess not or else the different times in which I got up it had already passed.

I'm thinking of getting my car transferred sometime this week or I could wait and do it in the beginning of the month, things are going good lately and the days are very hot all the other countys around us are having it worse off then we are but still we need more rain. Each time I have prayed for rain it's come but it seams to be just enough to tease the crops and land, as for the corn this year they say it's not going to be very good and some farmers are going to make it into feed so they don't loose the crop completely. This in it's self will probably drive the price of corn up and those who do get some kind of crop will do good, last year our bounty was better then most as the rest of the country was. As their ground was dryer then a pop-corn fart' and even the grass was burned up, this caused some to sell their cattle a lot earlier then usual because they didn't have enough feed to keep them until the regular time that they usually sell them. Many farmers are hurting, so they say. But I have to believe that we in Courtland are doing better then most it can be seen in the country side as you drive from either direction from Nebraska even into Oklahoma you can see just a little green and it's here in and around Courtland' to others having a car with air-conditioning is just a normal thing but to me it's a gift because we never had such a thing being poor and all, going into this next year I will try and save for the things we will need to get by. And hopefuly we will make it another year I know looking that far into the future isn't a very optimistic thing but that will change in the time which is about to come, my greatest thing is surviving now that everyone is gone and I have to do this on my own.

In the years of wine and roses I didn't care much either way but now I want to try and make a name for my self and maybe that will help, or I have already done it and I just don't know it. Little brother wont go out much except to the store and I hope that will change in the future but only God can make that seed grow as I planted the seed long ago when he got here, the Spanish people waved to me yesterday as they headed back to the fields this is a sign that they are friendly and are open to getting to know the people around here. Yesterday I vacuumed; the church and it's ready for the events that they might have I like to keep it clean so they can be proud to bring family and friends there and it makes me feel good, it's trash day so I will take it out also. I would like to find someone who could help me get my deploma and Destiny comes to mind maybe she could help if she wanted to but I would have to ask before that could happen, now that I have moved forward there is no going back so I want to accomplish as many things as I can before I get too old the elders here think I'm still a youngster; meaning I have many years left to do things I didn't get to do while I was a child and young adult. Taking it as far as it will go, learning all the things I didn't get to learn when I was a youngster, could the mind be more exceptable at my age then it would have been back then? For surely time has given me more experience then I had as a child and it has grown a lot more, my patients are more then they were back then but is it enough to retain the things I need to know? I guess I will never know until I try, I remember back in the day when mom went back to work after being off for almost a life time she seamed to thrive in what she did and I think age had a lot to do with it. As we get older we seam to slow down and are able to focus on what's at hand, and she went far but they stold her creation the big rools she created. It seams each time something good was going to happen something messed it us and then she passed away to them getting everything, but I realize that we cant dwell on things which didn't happen and we have to go on to maybe make something new in a different direction. My being able to write about my life and all that happened just goes to show that God is in charge, we can make any plans we want but if it doesn't fit into the full picture then it wont become part of it your life. I can remember when I was 27 years old and my world revolved around the darkness even in thinking I found love that too destroyed the only chance I had to make it in the construction business, or He had another plan and wouldn't let anything stand in it's way. If things would of happened back then I surely wouldn't be doing what I'm doing today, so maybe it was His plan that I didn't get to take over that part of the company. Another time that I could have been well off but back then I would of blown it and who knows where that would of lead, being honest in a relationship is important because it can make you or break you. I remember Stacy telling me that she was having trouble with the baby, and although it wasn't true. I did what any good man would do and came home to only find out that she lied and said that because she was lonely, this made me angry and I lost the job that could of taken me to the top.

Did He not want me to make it back then so I could be writing this today, I guess only He know the answer to that question. As for that life it's long been gone, but it would have been nice to see that side of the coin the side that let you not worry about the material things like bill's and other things. Me making it this far shows that those things weren't nessary for me to survive but the things that got me here were very important, Courtland has all the things I need for spiritual growth and I embrace them each day as another door opens up to let me grow. Destiny still goes through my mind from time to time and I asked God to give me a sign if it's meant to be but I havent gotten a signal yet, there is only a certain kind of person that draws me towards them and I havent figured out why it's that way I guess with some I can see the kindness that resides inside of them and how we might get along, I do know that she would have to be a patient person and I would try to be the same. Through my grown up years there was much that I missed but now I think I'm making up for that in my life, I noticed that I cant sit around very long any more and have to find something to do. During the day my mind is mixed up and I cant concentrate on things especially with Randy around but I also know that in time that too will pass, my life goes through stages but in the end it always comes back to where I am today. Even the traveling that comes while I'm a sleep is short lived when I'm awaken and shaken back into reality, as for my visitors that came too see me in the beginning when I first moved in they havent been around since that time. I believe they were just showing me that they mean no harm.

Finding my way through this life has been a trip, and I'm glad for the friends along the way they brighten up my day and I see them a lot. In passing mostly' but also at some of the places I venture into, lately my mind is running faster then it usually does and I think it's because I have let more people in not quite used to that but in time it should balance it's self out. My take on things have changed since my arrival here and I see how the other side of the coin lives without the shadows being a big part of what my life was each day is unique and different bringing new things to discover, some days people are more friendly then others and I guess it has to do with their mood as even mine changes from time to time. I like the good days, the ones that allow you to smile and feel that way inside I wish everyday could be that way but it just doesn't happen although I ware a smile most of the time. Not in trying to hide what's inside but to bring others joy because to me that's important, also I can since when someone needs a hug and I give it gladly to maybe brighten up their day or make things not seam so bad. I wish I could get hugs but I only get them from people far away and it isn't physical like it should be, I'm bound and determined to find me someone who can be a part of my life and I will find her if not today then sometime in the future. Just the feeling of being close to her would brighten up me life and days, even in the bible it says man wasn't meant to be alone and I have had my share of alone time. Now it's time to get back into the world and have that special someone that I can wake up to each morning and hold tight. My celibate days are going to be a thing of the past but I wont just jump into it, she would have to be special before I would take it to that level you see I'm old fashion when it comes to that part of life. This morning isn't bad and I saw a couple taking a walk a morning walk before it get's too hot out side. They waved hi to me and I returned the wave in kind also I saw a neighbor that lives by the church and waved to her, and she waved back what a great start to a day. The women by the church works a lot because she is always gone they were saying that it's the worst drought since the 50's and it's very wide spread spanding over many States, and some are getting disaster relief from the government because of the crops failing. My thoughts on the subject is' that we will have a better situation then most and I pray that all crops do as good as possible, as for the outer States around us they are very dry and even the pastures don't have any green in them because of being burnt up from the lack of water. Wednesday and the rain I asked for arrived last night but the only way I could tell is by the puddles in the street, through the night I had heard some strange noises but I had chalked it up to the augers running down the road, and it was probably the wind. Also I got the car registered and now that behind me until 2013 which will be another year of driving without worry, through my time here many things like the new car have happened so I don't have to worry about making it to work. All I have wished for has become reality here in Courtland from my home to the car and many other blessings by the people I have gotten to know, even the guy at reliable auto for which I met him and his wife they seam like down to earth people sort of like we are. They said they went to Sturges on a bike run and the weather was really hot, as for me I don't care for hot just the cool breeze blowing is fine for me.

My car reminds me of one of those cars from the fast and the furious, with it's tinted windows. But I did find out something and that's when the sun beates on the windows the tint reflects the heat away from the inside of the car which is a good thing. So far nothing has gone wrong and I hope nothing does for a few years anyway, at first I thought it was the last year that they made the car but I was wrong they made them up until 2008 or nine so getting parts for them will never be a problem. I have never had a car that is this fast and when I pass someone it kind of scares me with all that power, but in time I will get used to it, I have had an itch to take it on a trip but for right now money is tight so I will save for a while and see what happens by next spring. I find my self resless these days because we have to stay in because of the heat but I also know that it wont last for ever. By the time I go to work this afternoon it will be in the heat of the day and I'm glad that there is air in the thrift store other wise it would be 150 degrees in the shop, we take turns in two hour shifts that way no one gets too board and for the most part if can be fun. I text my daughter yesterday and she said it was also hot there in Kearney that she took the kids to the water park and could only stay for a couple of hours, and had to come back home. As the addiction cycle keeps some going in and out of prison there is still hope for them if they dont go back to it, but with many they do even after years many years without it and that shows that the addiction can hide for the time that they are there. It reminds me of a rodent going through a maze and if they can hide they will, so no one sees them then in an instent they pop up and start running again trying to get to that piece of what ever is at the finish line' which with addicts it's the Meth.

What does it do for some? Well with many it makes sex great so great even that the women will trade that for more of it and that's how many of them attract Aids and other venereal diseases. I had a friend that had the H.I.V. Germ, and along with that and his drug use it finely killed him just last month. I had known him most of our lives and I knew he wasn't going to last long after he contracted cancer, the damage from addiction is wide spread and it destroys many things in a persons life. And all in all it's not worth the loss to those who have to bury them. I am blessed not to of had any kind of that curse, beck in the beginning it seamed like so much fun and it was until it takes a solid hold on you and starts to control you're life many people will tell you that it doesn't control their lives and they would be lieing to you. Always the drug or alcohol controls the person and that's just the way it is. I'm watching Antique road show and I love it but it only comes on at 4:00 in the morning which makes it impossible for most people to watch because they are still in bed they are not like me, well no one is like me really! We are all different. My friend Mark O'Brien said Donnie was in the hospital for a couple of month before his passing the strain on his body was too much with the drug and alcohol abuse. These days I find it harder and harder to recall things that have happened in that life and maybe it's time to move forward, as each day passes I find more delight in going out on the town and just saying hi to someone. When the day gets me down usually someone else can bring me joy and it doesn't take much just a wave or hellow, from a friend can set the day. When I first went to get the car registered I felt a weight being lifted off of me getting it done, the guy I bought it from said it's not unusual for those kind of motors to laast 300.000 miles such a delight to hear seeing it only has 93.000 giving me many years of joy out of it. I like to have a car last at least 5 years but this one should go way beyond that as I don't put that many miles on a car, worry free driving for the next few years anyway and by then my house will be paid for. And that is a great accomplishment for me owning my own home has always been a dream one that I didn't realize could come true but it goes to show that when your able to over come addiction you can have those dreams the ones that were out of reach before. Little by little I'm making improvments and in a few years it just might be like new once again, the way it looked when it was first built in 1919. Knowing when it was built helps to keep records of how time has been pretty good to this old place and when it's just about paid for I will refinance it to make repairs where they are needed meaning this house will be here for a long time. Most of the homes around here are still standing from that period and it was before the great depression, Courtland survived back then and it will survive this time in history which they compare it to that time. Maybe in time things will get better but as with everything only time will tell what the future holds, I'm glad for the rain because now I don't have to water my plant by the front door and in a day or two I will have to mow the lawn once again making my yard look nice once again.

During the night you can't tell if the rain has come unless the thunder makes it's presents known but all in all we need what the Lord brings us. It's only by His goodness that we are doing better then the rest of the country and although I wish them the best we are somehow getting the better end of the stick, is it through prayer that God is being good to us? Is He hearing the words we send to Him? Always! God hears our prayers and it even says it in the good book. Thursday I found out that my grandson stop's breathing when he is a sleep and that' not good my daughter said they might have to do surgery, I told her tokeep me posted. Many new things are coming about, this week has been a good one so far and Mark asked if I would sit at the art's building for an hour or two on fun day it seams they want me to get more involved in community activitys which I don't mind, if my little man needs me I will go and see him for a day or two and help in anyway I can. My little man Eric means the world to me and he loves papa' I pray that all will turn out alright when things are said and done, these days I'm not afraid to ask for God's help because I know he can cure what's wrong like He did with me so long ago. The ladies will do some deep cleaning at the church as they do it once a year to get into the places that I don't get into for they are places that I don't know about and it's no reflection on me as a janitor. Our church is big and I do a good job as to keep it up for services, in the days a head I will do many things but I will have to go and see my little man his neurofibromatosis causes him not to breath right and it showed up in his sleeping test they did in Omaha. He has always been a hiper child but with a big heart and sometimes I can help but wonder if the chemicals might have played a big part in this situation his father using.

I don't know what the situation is between them these days but I do know they got a divorce a few years back, as for how their life was going back then I thought they lloved each other but then the control matter came into play which caused them to break up. It's hard enough making it without the use of drugs but when you throw that in the mix then everything goes to hell, one time she told me about finding a needel in their home and that's never a good thing even though he said it wasn't his, his friends had to of put it there people using Methamphetamine don't think period when it comes to leaving dangerous things laying around all that's in their mind is the next high, I can still recall when I got pulled over many years ago and they checked my car to only find nothing. Then when they let me go I drove down the street and did the drug I had under the seat, just this experience frightened me and well I never did it again. The company you keep can destroy you also even though we never had the drugs on us many of them were taken away because of what they carried in their pockets. For some reason it made them feel important to have something others needed it was a charge like no other or a high in it's self, knowing that everyone needed what you had and they could tell you no' the addiction made you feel powerless when you didn't have it but like a king when it was inside your body. The mind thinks it's invincible and you can run like the wind, a persons behavior isn't normal under those circumstances and even after years of being off of it the mind has to rebuild it's self or God has to reconstruct it. For every bad thing you take away it has to be replaced with something good like with me it was the one who helped me through those dark times, and He has been with me ever since my rock, my foundation, the solid one who created me before I was even in my mother for He is my true father. And today He lets me grow at my own speed knowing the limations that I have, it's strange how He knew I would be writing this book before I was even born, as He sees all things the whole picture of what my life was going to be all about has there been any supprises to Him I don't think so. If you look at your life and ask your self if you did all the things you thought you should have done and the answer is no then you should take another look and try to correct it. As for the way my life started out I would have to say no I didn't like it, but for the other half I would have to say I'm trying my best to make what was wrong right. In the real world we all make mistakes and that's just the way it is. But to have the power to correct those things which almost destroyed you well! That's a gift only given by the father, my new life is far from perfect but I'm able to live in this real world that is changeable. In the old life I was nothing but in this life I'm something, something new a born again christen who wants to learn the ways of this world but not to get so caught up in it that I fall once again, some say I'm a vessel from God and that might very well be but I have to stay on track so I can grow in the right direction.

Not letting any of the old ways back into my life for they are a thing from the past, I hope to be able to live by taking one day at a time. That way I won't be able to see so far a head, that too could be a bad thing as it says live for today and the rest will take care of it's self, pastor Kathy has been away for sometime now and I will be glad when she get's back, I miss her sermans and it's not the same without her she is the light to our little town and she shines bright. I thought I saw a little mouse in the kitchen so I will have toget one of those things you plug in to chase them away and I think they might have one in Belleville at the true value store, if not then we will go to Concorida to Wal-Mart and I know they have them. It's the first one I have seen this year and I don't want them making a nest in the house because it can take a long time to get them out of here, as for everything else all is good these days. I believe there are many women here it's just that they are cautious when it comes to men for their own reasons of course, I kind of feel like I would like to get to know a couple of them one being about my age and the other a bit younger but who knows where it might lead. The younger one I felt a connection with although I can say if she felt the same thing, and the other she is funny at times and would be fun to be around. I don't know much about their situations except one is a teacher and the other works very hard trying to survive in this world of ours, but also I'm not rich like many of them are looking for not a farmer that has lived here for many years. Just a guy trying to create a new place I can call home for ever sounds so final but it's what I'm looking for, and in many ways I have found that place here in Courtland no destruction of the things that almost destroyed me so long ago. Just a quiet place where I can live in peace, the eyes are the window to the soul and mine must show a lot from years passed. I'm going to try and set a mouse trap and catch that little bugger and throw it out side I don't like rodents in my home.

Through this next winter they will try to make their way inside and no one likes their company, I don't like the thought of them crolling around on me while I sleep if they do get that close to humans which I'm not sure of. Through the years I have become a strong person and I think it shows to many people always taking care of business when I need to and not falling short when the bills need to be paid, this shows responsibility in the areas where it needs to be. Living the life I wished I had many years ago but then I wouldn't have made the trip here to courtland, for some reason God wanted me to move here at this time in life could it be to learn the goodness of the people here? You know" getting to know people on a smaller scale and then enlarging it as time allows it. Gaining a trust and getting to know how things work as for the things I do, money doesn't seam to matter as long as my bills are paid. And time well it's given as I have never been one to be stingy with anything I have been here almost three and a half years and trust is just starting to show it's self honesty is the best policy nothing can take it's place. In the future I will make many new friends and maybe one day start a group for those fighting addiction what better place then right here where we live, there are many towns around here that I haven't been to yet and want to see as addiction is everywhere even in the small towns where it can be hid from the rest of the world. Alcoholics are like the gay people were many years ago always hiding it in the closet and it doesn't have to be that way people that want help need to open up and for the others well they will come around in their own time. It's something that can't be rushed but sadly many will die before they bring them selves to admiting that the problem exist, like it took with me. If He didn't find me that day I surely wouldn't be here today, and even back then I didn't recall the other miracles that had taken place. Why is that? Why didn't I see these things for surely they were right in front of my face, all I can think of is that we as people only see in hind sight and that allows us to adjust accordingly as for even seing to the end of a day is beyond me and I find that strange. It's like our past can be seen but not our future, so make the adjustments to better your life and with hope and understanding things will come to be the way they should be. As for the fear that once had a hold on me it's gone and I pray that it wont return, I have many things that I want to do in the cominng months so I hope all goes well when I do them. I have been working almost two years at the church and I have enjoyed it even the people are getting to know me better and miss me when I don't come for coffee, it reminds me of a puzzel in a way when a piece is missing you cant see the whole picture but when they are together it's such a beautiful sight I know strange way to put it but it's my way just the same. I'm different from you or anyone else for that matter and that's what makes the world so beautiful, like the birds with their differences they are all beautiful but separated by each others voice making them unique in their own way. For each child born is unique separated by their own little quirks and we learn to live with and deal with each one making them into the person they will one day be.

I never want to be like any other person because no one can love like I do and no one has a heart like mine it's the simple things which makes me who I am and it's a gift from God to be able to let others see it. Even though I don't see what they see I know it can't be bad other wise it wouldn't be, He doesn't give His approval of something or someone who is bad and if He does then that just means that change is possible to turn things around. God's love and understanding out weighs anything and He teaches us like we teach our children and if a mistake is made then He understands and we move on, we as people torture our selfs much more then He would when He forgives us we are the ones that don't forgive our selves and that is something we all need to learn to do. Friday the 20th of July there will be many people coming to town next weekend as funday arrives; and it gave me an idea for making things, but the selling of them would have to wait until next year at the same time we can make a sticker that says fun day and what the product is and that it came from me here in Courtland, although they will be made during the year they will last because they will be sealed in canning jars and the longer they sit the better they will be. The people will only be able to get them here in courtland which will draw more business to the town during that time, it's hard to create them so I will have plenty of time to do it through out the year. It will be a great idea if I can get everyone on board, there will bebany different kinds and they should sell pretty good. This could start my dream off and who knows where it will lead, I sort of started it in Kearney but then let it go and this could give it a new start. Could it be my way out of poverty I think so but I will have to take it one step at a time.

It will be like a fairy tale the lost soul that found his way to a small town ande careted a living from hard work, by doing this each year things will slowely come to pass and I could mass quite a bit within two or so years and Randy could help also making him feel good once again if he doesn't eat them all. I dreamed about it many years ago and now with commitment it can be a reality, lord knows my car will let me deliver them to near by towns but they will get their start here in Courtland' the town of dreams where my deams have come true and when they make it to full production then people from all around will come and want to know where they originated. This morning I'm going to go and clean the corners of the church one corner anyway and then see if I missed anything afterwards, T.G.I.F Thank God it's Friday. A quant saying as I first heard it back in Nebraska many years ago, the capital wont cost much to make my idea and it could be a great thing so we will see what happens later down the line. My little man is on my mind so I will pray for him this morning that he will get well, although our situation is better then the rest of the countries we still need more rain as the corn isn't doing as good as it should but even in a good year they have to irragate and I saw the center pivits going full bore just down the road, I text my niece yesterday and sent a picture of my car and she liked it. She also said she was glad for me which made me feel good, my house should be paid for in three years if I don't borrow against it and that will make my home mine. A place that will be here for another many years my place of peace where it will all start there has been many things happening since my arrival here in Courtland and the good things can and will keep coming if I do things right. Many live their whole lives and try to make dreams come true and now at the age of 53 it's time to see if my dream is feasible could I create a company here in this small town of dreams? We will see in the next year' even the kids could get in on it as there would be plenty for all those who would want to help. But first it has to be put into motion, many small companys started in small communitys where the product could be fine tuned and then they branched out into factories. But I could want to keep it here with the towns name on it quite quaint I think, in my life I have always had to do things on my own to make something happen and now maybe it's time to move forward and create what I have put off for some time. In my younger years the thought was put on hold because of the trile I had to go through and now I will see what happens thirty some billion people out there and I know some of them would pich up on my idea to make money. It's only through God's help that this will come to be and if He shows me favor then it will become a reality just idea makes me feel good inside but it will take time for it to become something to be proud of. As of now many things have unfolded in my favor and if it stays that way then the dreams will start to develop by what my little brother says you cant eat just one of the pickeled sausage so they should go over good, when he ate the first one it had been sitting for about a year' and that's when they are at their best giving them time to fermint in their own juces.

It's quiet this morning except I can hear the auger running across th road O how I remember those days when I worked at a plant similar to that one in Nebraska, Western Alfalfa owned by Kansas and Nebraska gas company it was one of the best jobs until they closed from too many fires. And lost a lot of money but it stayed a float for a few years getting the bin's emptied, the plant had been there in Odessa Nebraska for over 30 years. Many things come to mind when I think about those times, the girl who had a horse run out in front of her car and it ended up almost on her lap that day was a bloody mess but she survived, we were running late to work and if we would have been on time it would have been us instead of her. Thinking back there was a reason for us running late and the man up stairs was watching over us, strange how you don't see these things until later in life, a reflection of what could have gone wrong but didn't. for truly God watches over us in times that we need Him, even in the dark times I knew there was a god but somehow from childhood I had lost that connection. A distraction brought me away from Him but surely the distraction had to of been a constant thing to keep me from thinking about him, maybe it was the things that were happening in our lives at the time when I was very young. For our God is great to have brought me back even after 30 some years, and even then it took time to fully come back and embrace the goodness He showed me. What was a dark life had been brought to see life differently, it was like I was locked in a box for all those years in nothing but blackness. Our triles bring us far in life if we are allowed to see past the workds of the devil as he wants us to stay in that place where we cant see the goodness of God.

Many times he has tried to destroy God's work and he hasn't succeeded; for God had the power to bring me back and then He put his mark on me so the devil couldn't touch this soul given to him. Being in the dark he was given a chance to destroy me but in the end God stepped in. could it of been that I changed something it's possible, did the dark one loose this battle with God also like he had done so many times before even by tempting Jesus saying he would give him control of the world or part of it. As for me these things have no value for they were and always will be God's domain, His creation and what is His can never be the devils. Dark I know but fact, what would of become of the world if satin wouldn't have fallen and Adem hadent of sinned? We would of known the goodness from the start and people would of lived longer, Nowa lived 140 years I believe, that was a lot longer then we live today. The life spand of people today is almost 70 some years and they give credit to science but is that true? Or have we had the knowledge all the time and didn't know how to use it. God can make life long or short and I believe it's His will wither we go on or are stopped in our tracks, for surely He didn't have to spare my life all those times but He did and I think it's because He could and He wants others to know that miracles still do happen. From the birth of a child to the love He has for us his children we are just a little bigger.

CHAPTER 11

Yesterday we went to town and it was such a nice ride when you don't have to fight the heat, the heat seams to take all the fun out of doing something but when you have it then things go just fine. Saturday morning' and yesterday I wrote an letter to the Kearney-hub well to Mark Konz the managing editor of the paper. And he wrote me back and said he would get it published in his own way of course, it's like sometimes we can talk in code and I like that. Through many years we have remained friends and he does most of my editing for me and get's my messages out. Now I will write some more when the mood hit's me again, it's a funny thing about news papers the message you sent has to do with things in that community and drug and alcohol abuse has to do with every community in every State' so my getting published usually isn't a problem. I haven't written anything for the paper here but in time it will show it's self many things have to be right before I can trend on new territory and that's just the way it is with me and it's that way with many papers. Today I go to the thrift store at noon, and work until two. Then next week is Fun-day and I will help out with that also it's their celebration for the year, and many people come from all around in a way it's like Sturgis but on a lot smaller scale. I'm hoping that it isn't to hot but I know that wont happen it's always hot at that time of year, but the celebration will go on as it does every year. I can stand about an hour out in the heat and then it's back into the coolness for me.

I was never asked before to participate so I don't know if this is an honor or what, but I do know I have been excepted into my town of dreams. In the coming years I will learn to have fun once again as it has been absent from my life for quite some time, and I will write about my experience so the world can read about it once it get's published it doesn't take long before it gets on the Web and then all my friends can read what I have to say about things. Who would of ever thought I would be read so much in the coming years since I started almost eight years ago? Not me! But you never know what turn of events will happen even my thoughts on opening more treatment centers has caught on and they are popping up all over the place. The twelve step program is fading as they are a constant reminder that people don't get cured and that's not so. The programs like A.A. Is good for the beginner to direct them in the right direction but then as they grow past that stage they need to know that they can be free from that curse. And a constant reminder that they cant drink, by this time their spirit needs to be set free and put that part behind them. Home is where most alcoholics stay except for the time they work or are driving which isn't a good thing because it does more damage then good. I have visited these A.A. meetings and they let you admit you have the problem which is good but also you have to learn to deal with what caused you to have the problem in the first place. And with many it's many different things from the loss of a child or significant other' or maybe just that they couldn't deal with a certain situation, in human nature many are weak and look for something that will help deal with the situation and alcohol has been around for like ever. Since the time when the government got weak and gave into greed not caring what could happen if that Box was left open and yes you know what Box I'm talking about, through the ages they bleed something for all it's worth and then say it's bad for you but that doesn't stop them from going further to bleed it some more until there is nothing left.

When I was a kid smoking was ok' but now 40 some years later they want to stop it and they use unheard of gimmicks to try and stop it. All kinds of things come out of the wood work to detoured some from smoking but if the truth was known it was a by product of alcohol and drug abuse, they always try to cover up the fact they were wrong by making alcohol legal. And now that they want to stop the smoking part they want to legalize pot that causes cancer O what a tangled web we weave when we first practice to deceive. In this life we are all given what we need inside of us to be happy, even though some think they will find it in the alcohol or drug addiction and that couldn't be further from the truth. The peace I have been looking my whole life has been found right here in Courtland' and I have never found more likeable people anywhere that I have traveled over the 40 some years now, but trust isn't just given it's earned and the person you are born to be can shine here like in no other place I have found on this planet. Mind you no one gives anything but if you are true to you're word then it can be earned, when I arrived here I felt like a fish out of water being left alone after a relationship failed, but it didn't take long before I was on my feet again and doing many things although my ability is limited I do my best and that's all God asks of us and even though we cant see into the future somehow we know everything is going to be alright. For it's God's love that carries us through, my life is better then it's been since my early years and I know that God is right there watching over me. As the world of addiction continues I'm in hope that one day all those who need help will find it in their own way, as for my world' I'm glad in it, and I will continue to live my life here where I have found peace. No one has ever said any bad things to me in the time I have been here and I'm sure if they had something to say they would have because they are not bashful, not like I am at times but it's funny how those things seam to pass with time like a baby bird breaking out of it's shell to breath in new life looking at the world for the first time and not knowing what to make of it. Those who over come their addiction will also feel that way in one fashion or another and if they find it too hard to deal with then they too might go back into their shell like the turtle does when it's threatened by it's enemies because they feel safe in that place that they call home. Not everyone can break away from the cycle of addiction because it takes strength and I'm not talking about physical strength although that helps in some ways but mostly it's mental and if brain damage has accrued then the fight will be even harder, they said my brain damage couldn't be undone as the eyes and mind were out of sink not sending the right messages to where they needed to be, and yet you are reading this today. What happened? My thoughts on the matter as you exercise the mind it becomes stronger and that's what God did for me my attention span wasn't at all any length of time. And it had to be built up and He did this by waking me up at all hours of the night and morning and it didn't matter what time it was as I don't think He sleeps. I recall being awaken at one in the morning all the way until four or five and it wasn't by a gentle shake either it was more like a boom and my eyes were open and then not being awake I would stumble over to the typewriter and start the day.

On many mornings I would ask him why he was putting me through this and He would reply that He was teaching me as promised. Many times I tried to ignore Him but that was no use because He was much stronger then I was, so I would drag my butt out of bed and away I would go. For a person that couldn't hardly grasp what was happening I did alright for the most part, and as time went by I learned it was like going to school 24 hours a day and he did it with kindness. Even though I wanted to quit many times that wasn't an option, having lost the ability to comprehend some of what was happening I just road it out and hoped for the best, and later the best showed it's self. When I got published this was unheard of, here I was writing with some great minds and mine had been damaged. But I had an advantage the things I write about are not things you learn in a book like with the others they are life experiences and that gave me an edge, because I'm not book taught I'm taught by God the teacher of all teachers. The one who gave them the ability to learn by reading through a book, my mind creates by what I live and it's my understanding of things the way I see them. Not a person that has lived 100 years ago my writing is about today and what I have learned with the help of God, through the darkness came a light and I saw the light which brought me back here to this world even though I didn't want to at first. My spirit and body were tested beyond belief and even though I was crippled somehow my spirit survived and what a strong spirit it is, many times I thought I was at deaths door but that didn't stop me from moving forward my heart sometimes felt like it was going to beat out of my chest but that made me move further.

In testing my strength' would I survive was going through my mind and I kept pushing the envelope for surely if my time was coming then it would surely happen, but it didn't and I made it too my destination on that day I walked more then three miles after the car broke down and even further when it happene again. All I can think of is that it was a test I was afraid to do it on my own so He made something happen that would engage that survivla mode and I did survive to become a little stronger, even though these things happened my legs shake even today as I stand up for any length of time. My God is my buddy and my friend and we will be together until the end, Sunday and I missed the thrift store yesterday which was a first.a word of advice don't thrive for prefection because there will be a time when it let's you down and then you feel bad much worse then others can make you feel. This morning is going to be a good day no matter what and this mistake will pass, we all make mistakes and it's up to us to correct them and that I will do by apologizing; to those who had to cover for me. In life' a mistake is what makes us strong. When I can make good for a mistake' this thing with meeting more people has thrown off my routeen of what I do each day thinking about things I shouldn't have but that too will pass as time allows it. My loving daughter called yesterday and we talked for a while it was good to hear her voice after almost a year, she is back to taking care of kids and you have to be a saint to do that kind of work, kind of like us who take care of the elderly as the patients it takes a lot of them, more patients then most have. I'm going to turn on the air early this morning as yesterday it didn't seam to get cool enough in the church when I turned it on for a half hour or so, my mornings are still early but it takes at least an hour to wake up and then things are fine. I knew something was wrong when my day didn't go right and I was telling Randy that something wasn't right it was like a sick since and I was right I missed an important thing but it didn't dawn on me until around five last night and by that time I was ready for bed. Next weekend I have to work for an hour or so but other then that only on Wednesday from 4:00 to 6:00. When I was talking with Shannon she was yelling because the kids were raising hell but she seams to get it under control pretty easly as they are good kids and don't give her much trouble so she says. I told her that I would go nut's with that many kids around but then maybe not, as she has told me many times that I have changed from the way I used to be. Next month I'm going to try and go see her for a day or two and then head back home, it's been so long since we held each other and said I love you and that needs to be done once and a while so we keep that connection. Most of the elderly people here have their grand children who comes over once in a while and I know that really helps especially when old age is with them, just the knowing makes a big difference the knowing that they are loved.

I have yet to go and see the older gentelman who is ill but I saw him out mowing his lawn just the other day and that shows that he must be feeling better these days, for some each day above ground is a blessing as bad health seams to affect us all at one stage or another. But then we get well and life goes on, the kids really like fun-day and they are young enough to with stand the heat and enjoy the day. But with me it's not so much as it does some not so nice things to me like my breathing. But in my home it's always nice as the days and months of summer go by, I cant wait until fall' when the temp drops and it becomes cool once again before winter set's in, and it's at that time of year when I will be able to see how the car does in the snow. It rides high enough to where I shouldn't have any trouble getting around but our trips will be fewer to town as the snow will be beating down and covering the ground, sometimes I even like to play in it as my neighbors like Mark tell me to get back in the house before I catch cold. People here really care for their neighbors it's not like in the city and they talk to you when the mood hits them, I have met people I didn't know but for some reason they seam to know me and they are kind as they wave or say hello in passing one guy noticed that I got a different car and he was the first one to say anything as for my friends it's just another car that get's me around and really that's what it is to me just something better so I don't end up walking because that's something that isn't good in this heat, it will knock you down on the side of the road and leave you walking. Although I think my neighbors would pick me up if that happened, next week the town will be full of people.

So many will have to walk to the different sights but most of the fun will be in the park with the talent show and such and the kids can have water fights, they will have sing longs', and just a lot of things to do for the little ones I'm not sure what I will be doing yet but they will let me know before the day get's here. Will Randy come? Probably not as he likes to stay where it's cool and it will be everything but cool out side, if I like doing it then I will continue to go each year but I have to get my product ready for next year that in it's self could bring in some change to put away for a rainy day, a day when things get hard and you have to help your self out of something, which you never know when something might come up. I haven't heard anything from Leroy lately so I should give him a call sometime next week and see how he is doing, hopefully he is still doing good. I do know that God is watching over him so he should be doing ok' the last time we talked he loved his job and that's what makes a person want to go to work enjoyment if you like your job then you will never work a day in your life so they say. This morning I will watch Joel O'lsteen at 7:00 and then the day will start he seams to give the day a better out look and I love that, his stories brings great joy and he doesn't leave anyone out even the addicted ones that are fighting for a new beginning in this world of ours for they too have a purpose in God's house. And in this world over coming addiction is a battle that so many loose because they give up and they need to know that God is there for them, some have no idea that He is right beside them in this fight and they think they are doing it alone like I did so long ago and were not alone as He walks beside us every step of the way and if we fall then he is there to pick us up and help us go on I cant count my tears over the years but I do know they could of filled a river. In those times I didn't see any way out of the situation I was in, and today they are gone except for the little time they visit me to recall them and share them with you the ones fighting the same fight I fought so long ago, the learning process is priceless but we seam to get past those times that we think we will never get through and that has to be God making a way for us too go on. Would I want to go through it again? No because it does something to you the change is out of this world, although you think you won't survive some how you do and you go on to better things the things you missed in life because of what happened. Growing up too fast takes something from you the innocents that a child is supposed to grow through, and then you have to somehow find it later in life not the innocents but the things you missed like the learning process in the first years of school. The fun things like art and just playing like a child does, although many things I cant recall at this time I know that later they will come to me before my time is up my time of writing that is. Not death' when you live through something like I did you want to know that all is ok' that you changed that part of life which was destroying you. And if you are blessed then you might help save a few other lives as well, the road I walk is only by the grace of God. He made it possible for me to be around this long and who knows the length of time that will be given to me? only He does. I know in my mind there is a key to the answers I seek but like with the bible if I don't understand something then I will put it aside until He wants me to understand it. You can never rush Him because he knows best and He knows the time when things will become clear, our understanding of things is much different then His as He can make the impossible possible there have been many times when I didn't know the answer to something and when I slept on it then it became clear.

This I figure is His way of helping us when we need it, no confusion just a way to get the message to us and low and behold when I would try it the next day it worked. Church went fine today and I thought some would be up set, but no one was. And they understood we work in shift's of two people and the lady that I was to work with handeled it for two hours, Pastor Kathy had a nice vacation as she saw her friends of 60 years and visited Mark in Denver. She asked for prayers for Mark and I will pray for him that he will gain some weight so they can start his treatment they had a very bad shooting in Aurora Colorado at a threaded where 12 people were killed and about 50 were hurt as a gun man opened fire on them at midnight when a new movie of bat-man started. This to me shows there is evil in the world but also there is the good and she was releaved when Mark called to say he was alright, I could never pretend to know what was on that persons mind but he must have been in a dark place to take other peoples lives. It's like it's the young people who do these things and it makes me wonder if he might have seen some action in the service as many that have gone to war have done something like this but usually they only take their own lives such a waste, but they come home to loose everything. It's now Monday the beginning of another week so there will be many new things going on as they get ready for fun-day here in Courtland, as I listened to the guys talk at church it used to be bigger but over the years it has shrunk to where it is today. But who knows maybe it will start up again, they talked about the old days and they are in their 70's and 80's so it must have been about 20 or so years ago when it was at it's peak.

My time here has just been a few years so maybe it might grow once again who knows, I did find out that I beat my self up more about missing work then anyone else ever could. And I was glad that they forgave me about that day of missing work but I also know it will never happen again unless I'm real ill, this town is wonderful and so are the people in my younger years all people wanted was to push me to see how much they could get out of me, and today it's not like that. Just people helping each other and working in harmony makes for a peaceful life, each morning I go and trim around the yard so the weeds don't get out of hand and it's great as my yard looks nice. As for hobbies mine has been writing about my experiences and how they might let others see that addiction doesn't have to be the end but the beginning of something wonderful, even changing when half you're life has passed can bring you happiness salvage that part which is important and know you have made a difference somewhere in the world. I look forward to reading my letter in the paper next week sending a glimmer of hope to those fighting the good fight and taking back what was taken from them. Their lives' which is very important. Adults can understand where I'm coming from but as for the younger generation all I can do is have hope that I reach them also before they throw away many years of their lives, nip it in the bud, you might say. Before they fall to hard into that dark place where it's harder to get out of, in my early years it would have been easier to over come it. But even at 32 years old it was possible when the lord found me that day, and even then it took many years before I completed the transference of taking back my life. People need to know that having an addiction to alcohol or drugs doesn't make them a bad person because I have never had a bad bone in my body, I just got lost in life and had to find my way back to what I was missing. Before it was a dark place but with God's help He lead me to the light and showed me that my perpose wasn't the life I was living, I punished my self living in that dark place no one else. But also I didn't think I deserved God's love, but I was wrong and there are many out there that think the same way. Forgive your self because God has already forgiven you, you are the one keeping your self in that place break free and let the spirit of God into your life and the rest will fall into place as you work hard to correct that misguided life, what you were brought up to believe is false and what was programmed into you was also false the saying you were no good is false because God looked at you before you were planted in your mother and he said it was good and no one gets a false approval from God.even the people with disabilitys are approved by God because they have a purpose in this life and we don't know what that purpose is until it unfolds in front of us, it could be something that brings out the kindness in others you just don't know at the time of birth. I'm sure He didn't mean for many to go through life with heartache and pain but it does happen and we have to adjust accordingly over come the things that make life so hard.

Being brought up in an alcoholic home your parents try to do their best, but sometimes in life the unexpected happens and it throws them into a state of destruction and when children see that on a daily bases they too grab on to it, that thing which gives false hope. The destroyer of life, in my years of addction I have seen many cases of the kids going the wrong way but instead of the parent correcting this problem they somehow feed it and that is never any good. The drinking started with me at about the age of 8 or so years it wan't until the age of 11 years that it started to show it's self by my wanting to drive all the time and that's how I learned to drive at a very young age when other kids were in school I was having my own party and driving around trying to pick up girls not a good life for a child but I seamed to have survived but that life had made me not to want to be around girls very much as they always caused problemd or I thought they did and they were just handy to blame everything on. It's always easy to blame someone else for what you have created but still sometime in life you have to be the one who changes, after the age of making your own decisions you are responsible for how your life turns out. But if you have never lived a life without addiction then to make a change is very hard, because you have never known any other way to live I'm not using this for an excuse. But there is nothing to compare the two and that's part of why children should never be introduced; to the curse, when it starts before grammer school then their recovery is slim to none and the none is usually what happens.

Which bring on the life of a lost soul, a human spirit that wonders through life knowing there is something out there different but they don't know how to find it. And when that happens only an act of God can bring them to where they can see a glimps of hope and hope is what starts a chain reaction. That hope can give them faith and the two together can bring change, to a life that was once lost for surely God wouldn't let someone pass who hasn't known these things. The right to choose comes into play here because if you have never known the two parts then you can't choose and we can't leave this world without making that choice to follow or egnore the gifts that God offers, in the bible it says we as humans are above all things on this earth all the animals and the fowl and yet the Father takes care of them so He really must take care of us also with what we need to survive in this life. Since my change I have known the goodness of God in many ways but I also know this' you have to do your part to make the circle complete and He will help you do this as He teaches you. The mind has to be stronger then I have even began to dream of, and I'm sure if we could use it's full power we wouldn't be able to understand it. It would be like the tree of life which He told Adam not to eat from and we all know what happened when he did, it cursed us all but then Jesus came and took the curse upon Him self and died on the cross which set us free to live, now that is love. Would we give our lives for him as he did for us? Human nature says no' but we really couldn't tell unless it was tested. The love that took is out of this world, and how or why it took place I have yet to learn as I am the rock that is thrown into the pond that causes the ripples in the water. Tuesday morning and I couldn't sleep it's 1:00 Am. I could of tried to sleep more but it would have no avail I remember these kind of times when He was teaching me and there was always reason for it, Mark's wife called yesterday and asked if I would sit at the art gallery on Saturday from 7:00 to 9:00 so the people could see the art and I told her I would. At least it will be cool in the building and not be hot as hell, honesty plays a big part in this life and I'm glad that I have always had that built into my character. It's trash day so I will get it out a little later I can remember when this was the only time when I was awake back in the bad days but now it's different the birds are not even up yet as they too need their sleep, in this world of ours. Yesterday I tried to find my old friend Tom Clifton from Ventura California' it seams a young man with his name is on face book and I asked if his fathers name was the same so I will see later if he replied. It's been over almost 40 years since we have seen each other but even time hasn't erased that memory of him he was the first friend that had hair like a black man or close to it but he was as white as they come. We lost touch after we moved away and he comes to mind every now and then, I remember almost dieing when we went on vacation in Missouri with his mom and Max but my demise didn't happen so here I am today trying to connect once again, he was a little older then I was but boy we had fun during that time. Going to corner market to get beef jerky and his mom was a frugal person not giving him money for candy when he wanted it, looking back lets you see things that you would of not remembered if my time would have been cut short but here I am all these years later and the memories are still there, childhood memories of a life long gone. The young man must be in his 20's or so and that would make him young enough to be Tim's son, the last I heard he was in a motor cycle accident but that was so long ago.

He has lived in Ventura all his life so I will see if we can connect sometime in the future and maybe renew that friendship, there is some equipment moving this morning it's the first time I have heard it this time of the morning, but then usually I'm not awake at this time. My quiet time is very important to me some look forward to their vacations but with me my time comes every day while others are a sleep, and maybe that why I see the world differently then most. By the time they get up I'm fully charged and they are just opening their eyes, a great setting for a person like my self and my people skills are getting better as I learn to grow and except other into my life. But I take it slow to not off throw the balance which has become apart of my being, I remember when Tom and I was walking down the street in the river bottom where we lived two girls came up to us and did something mean I guess we were making too much noise while one of them were making out with their boy friend and their mother came out and caught them. Just flashes of memories at this time but I'm sure the whole picture will come in time, he was a funny guy always cracking jokes to make people laugh just good old memories from a life long gone. His mom got caught when she brought a guy home from a bar and they were in her bedroom, back in those days our mothers did that from time to time going to the bars that is. But that's where mom found Oliver and they stayed together until the end even with their argueing they seamed to love each other that one part that makes a hole, my memories of them will stay for ever as all good things do.

I remember there being a hit on Oliver so that's why they moved to Nebraska they were scared that the hit person was going to get them. But as time passed that also passed but they never did get their own home buying one that is and they did ok' us kids were very young at the time and some were stupid and got into a lot of trouble but I seamed to learn from their mistakes for some reason. So I stayed out of trouble most of the time but I did have my moments when I drank, many things come back to me now that were once lost in the dark corners of my mind and looking back some of the times were fun. My parent's were good people but for some reason life beat them down and they did what they had to do to make it in this world, I like to think that they did ok with me even with what happened in the early years. I don't play the blame game because life is just that life and we get by the best way we know how, no one can say what will happen tomorrow wither it will be a good day or a bad one but we face it and we see how things go. The grace of God is there for us and you cant buy it as He gives it freely to us all, when I write I go to a different place then where I am. A place that I feel safe in, and can write what's inside they say writing lets you explore those things which would never come out otherwise the things which build up and can cause damage later in life. Although my journey into the light was a glimps of what's to come. now days. I'm not afraid of the things I didn't understand our greatest journey will be in this life so make sure you help those who need help because one day we will have to answer some important questions, the machine or grass hoppers as I like to call them have been going all morning and I think some of the men work through the night putting on chimicals in the fields. As for the corn crop they say it isn't very good this year as many are using it for feed for the cattle, the drought has hit us pretty hard this year even with the rain we got it doesn't seam to be quite enough but I'm hoping for the best. Many places wont get any corn from their crop's as they have burned up from the heat, please lord give us some more rain! Although it might be too late maybe the next crop will be better and make up for this one, although the rest of the country was hit bad last year we seamed to fair better then they did and people could see it from miles around. People traveling could see the difference in just a few miles of how green our little part of the country was, compared to the other counties just next to us. Being people of God' we pray a lot for His goodness to shine on us and usually He brings what we need, not too much but just enough and things usually turn out alright. Our town sit's off the main highway just a mile so we are a safe community where life is good, it doesn't seam to have the bad elements because we sit in a kind of front or where the weather seams to be like a jet stream and I think that helps a lot. While other places get the bad weather we seam to fair pretty well considering they are just a few miles away but also when we get a short burst of rain some of them can get as much as 2 inches, very strange. And then other times we will get the better part of it, just the way it is around here, before I moved here they had a tornado that destroyed a building just down the road from me and the only thing standing was the toilet.

Never could understand the weather and probably never will as it has a mind of it's own, Omaha Nebraska is just a little over 100 miles from here and I have yet to go there. Never did like the big cities, just going to get Randy I got lost a few times and that's not a good feeling, when you're from a small town you learn to love the smaller things in life and family is important to those who live here with some they feel the closeness and it binds people together. Even our pastor say's she prefers a small town because it grows a closeness that you cant find anywhere else, and it's like we are all brother and sisters. To me it isn't hard to give someone a hug that you know and I enjoy doing that with friends, it's sort of like giving your brother or sister a hug. Except it's more personal with them then it is with your blood family we have never been real close it's like something has always been differen a sepration maybe by my father being different then theirs but we are nothing a like, sometimes I wish I could of known my father to see what that side of my family was like and would I have the traits of him more then what's on this side as I am way different. I like to think I have a meek soul that is always looking for the good in things and that's something I don't see in many people it's unique and it's only found in very few, even through all that I have been through I have never lost that part of my self that part which wants to be love by the right person a yearning for that connection that will make life full.

But even today I haven't found it, could it be that connection that has been lost between my father and me? They say a person cant be complete until they see the whole picture and a big part of my master piece is missing. I would of given all that I had to know him but then I could of ended up with nothing and today would have been a lot different then it is now, for all I am and what I will become is created by God is there something I have yet to see? A piece of my life that I don't quite remember at this time could a person know they have a child and not want it yes' but they would still know that they have it and that it exists. And you would know that they would have questions, although these things pop into my mind from time to time I cant let them stop me from growing in my walk with God' you can never guess what's in someone elses mind but I do know by my mom's words that he was a good man. So I will leave it at that, and move on without knowing why he gave me up. Could the addiction been caused by trying to hide the pain of not knowing him or will I ever be able to dig that deep into my mind only time will tell what's buried in there. Do we live in the real world or is it an illusion of what it should be? Or what we think it should be living in the other world was real to me at the time but then when I took away the drugs and alcohol it became plain at first with no excitement except for what I created. Wednesday morning' or hump day as they call it today I have some work to do and then it's off to the thrift store for a couple of hours yesterday I cleaned the carpets the best I could and it looks nice after getting the stains out of it. Randy did a good job of fixing the carpet machine and it works wonders thank God, as I went to take the trash out I could tell someone was working in the church so I didn't bother them and left. On Fun-day I will sit and watch the art gallery for a couple of hours at night and then it's back home, Beverly will be taking care of the thrift store on fun day so that gives me plany of time to do the other things I need to do. Over the years I have created my own style of writing and every one can tell it's me by how I write my words, even people from places far away know my writing and that's something I never expected not from a person that sees things differenty then those who read my work with time comes good things and with good things come change a chance to leave thing behind so you can become the person you were meant to be in God's world. Everyone has baggage and in time you grow to where you can leave that baggage where it belongs and that's in the past, yesterday it was 102 degrees out side and we spent our time doing things inside to make things better and get things ready for winter. Because we will spend a lot of time inside when it gets here I love to watch the snow fall during those months and how the squirrels play in the trees as the snow falls, it's like God is renewing the earth for the next season and I hope next summer is better then this one. Here I am talking about next year when this one still has a long way's to go, when a person becomes someone different they need to make sure that the change is for the better and although this takes time it will happen with the help of the father because with Him all good things take place. It's like slowly things are changing and my mind is also changing for all the bad thoughts that were once there are gone and they are replaced by the good that I can do around here where my new home is, also yesterday I mowed the lawn but there wasn't much to mow because it's so dry it's like the earth has sucked up the water and now we need more rain. But my flower is doing fine out by the front porch as I water it each day or should I say morning, I have yet to see my editorial in the news paper but I know it's coming out sometime in the future hopefuly before Fun-day but we will see.

    I like writing about my life both the good and the bad and I know that later it will be all good as I make the transition from the other life, and fully become what I was meant to become the one that God created me to be not the one I was, so long ago. When addiction enters your life you also take on another person inside of you and this one is created by the addiction, an alternet you the one that does things that the other wouldn't do and they call this a split personality. Some people will like just one of these personalitys while others will like them both, but when you take your life back one has to be destroyed and this is done by getting rid of the one that the drugs and alcohol created, as this one is destructive. And when it's out of your life then you can make the other strong, with me I had a child inside that was locked away in the dark corner of my mind and he wanted to get out real bad but couldn't. Until it destroyed the one who had become weak, all those years of abuse had made the addicted one very weak and the time was right to wipe him out of existence still today I don't know how I did it but it was done and the child was let loose. He was curious about life you see' he stayed a child all the years that he was held in that dark place, it was like he was being held against his will in his own body. But now he was free the first thing he wanted to do was to learn all the things he missed in those almost 30 years, and God helped him do that by teaching him to write about his life. In that time he was helpless but he even learned by the others mistakes. He was very bashfull because he didn't get to grow and learn the important things which would help him later, these things he would have to learn on his own and he started by remembering how loving God really was.

Although he didn't fully understand why God gave him a second chance he knew that he would teach him the rights and wrongs of life but he would have to find the right place, the right place to learn. And he looked but couldn't find it until someone connected with him through a device called the computer, while teaching him self to use this device he noticed that he could write words that would melt the heart of someone and this lead to change, good change because of his bashfullness and they later met to try and ignight a light that had been brought on by his witty ways. Anyway it was a failure but not before he moved to this quaint little town, at first he didn't know if he would be excepted by the town because the women changed when he moved there and he felt all alone in a place that was new to him. Imagine leaving your home of 30 some years to a place that was out in the middle of no where so he thought at the time, so different from where he came from and he felt out of place but there was a church and he attended it each Sunday in hope that he would connect with the people of God. A women that he considered like his mother bought him a shirt that said the name of the church he once attended in his home town, and he wore it one Sunday letting them know that he was a man of God. And this opened a door to exceptence and as time passed he grew in his faith to love all those who were a part of his now congregation, it didn't take long for them to notice that he was truly a man of God' and that he was changing his life. As time passed they offered him a job taking care of the church which he gladly excepted, the people took him in as if he was one of their own, into their family and when he didn't stay for coffee they missed him and let him know it by sending him a card. This is the miracles for which God preformed to bring him into another demention one so different then before, he didn't know it but his new life was unfolding. All the things which happened in his old life was being peeled away like an onion to reveal something new and as time moved forward the once distant family was now becoming part of him, and it was then that he realized God had brought him there for a reason and as time moved on their hearts opened even more. He had heard about people changing from one life to another and now he was living that change, through the kindness of one man he bought his first home 'ever' and loved it. But sadly to say his friend passed away from the curse of cancer but not before he returned the kindness by taking care of him, Walt had come to the town many years before with nothing like he did, and he wanted for him to have the chance that he was once given. As their friendship grew he had to go and live with his daughter in Wisconsin' so she could watch him closer and two years later he passed away and was buried here in the little town that he called his home Walter rest in the cemetery just out side of town and he is here in this loving town that grew to love him.

As for me I still live here in the town of dreams as I call it and one day I too will rest by my old friend and maybe go fishing with him, one day in the sweet by and by. By moving here I don't want for much as I have a good car to get me where I'm going and a nice home for which I live, my dad has passed also here and he rests on my land where he wanted to be they are both safe in the arms of Jesus. I still have my little dog Harley and he is my buddy, also I have brought my little brother here to the town of dreams which I hope all of his come true also one day. As for my land it cant be taken but with it comes great responsibilities and I hold fast to them taking care of what has to be taken care of, for truly love does exist here in Courtland and I will be here for many years to come. Getting to know the people is something that's good and I get to know more of them with each passing day, as for the world out side it only exist when I'm out in it and then it vanishes when I come home. Thursday and we got some rain last night I could tell when I saw the coffee pot light blinking which means that the power went out while I was a sleep, that and the street is wet. My letter came out yesterday and it lacked passion but that's a news paper foy you. I guess they take that out because it sells papers well at least it got published, the rain was greatly needed and maybe now the grass will turn green if we got enough I was reading something yesterday about how when they took prayer out of schools it was replaced by guns.

Not a good swap at all but they did it, and now there are people paying the price for that swap when will people open their eyes? And see what's taking place. In my time that I have been on this earth I have seen the word of God traded for guns, and peace traded for war and the word God taken out of many things even Christmas has suffered because of God hater's for they must surely be the work of the devil. When I was growing up we said a prayer in school to start the day and usually the day went pretty well but now you have kids bringing guns to school to plan an attact against other children. And it's expanded into public places like the theater just this month at midnight for surely we are in the last days. The killing where will it stop? The social network is going to hell and many will see it fall, I have the day off today so there isn't much going on but fun-day is just three day's away and people will be out having fun. It's the high time of the year like with many places they have a carnival once a year. Well Courtland has fun-day but through the years it had been dwindling down but there are still those who come, I find it strange that in these times when God found me the world is going down hill and kids are killing kids is there hope for the world? Yes always' but things need to change and people also need to change. Here we go to war and say it's in the name of peace but it's not, just a bunch of politicans trying to change things to fit their agenda next you will see people carring guns into stores I'm just glad that I don't have to see it. In this place where I live there hasn't been any violence to mention except for the fights between family and that has been happening for hundreds of years the squabbles between husband and wife or between siblings, my life doesn't have that drama in it and for that I am glad, O little brother and I get mad sometimes but it never leads to any violence just harsh words that couldn't hurt anyone. But for the most part I try to live a loving life free from the hurting words that others use, in our lives many things are not there like anger or just being nasty and we have a great day by saying good morning. For the other things in life take away from it but I guess in a relationship the tension is supposed to be healthy because of the differences between people, I find it strange how little brother is a lot like me, hard to anger but when it comes it leaves just as fast. I have always been that way even in the other life but I spoke what's on my mind if I saw someone doing someone wrong and in many cases they listened to me and changed in that fashion, I believe the volinteers are curious about me and come to the thrift store to see who I am. To see the new person who has come to live here, everyone knows I'm here but many don't know me, and I see people bringing in things just to get a look at this person which I don't mind. Some are even pretty and they catch my eye as I sit there and read, not much to do until we unpack things for the store, Beverly usually has a smile when she comes in and is in a good mood which makes for a better time when I'm working I always like people to smile it's the way it's meant to be. You never saw Jesus in a bad mood and if he ever was he discussed it with God, why cant the world live in peace? It seams they always have to be at war if not in another country then right here at home. Always there is a war somewhere and now I can see why parents want to protect their children and not let the out side world into their lives, for this job isn't for meek at heart. I could go on about why people kill people but to no avail would a good answer come to light, with many it's mental illness and it's brought on by the situations that the government throws our troops in when they fight for something that isn't there. Well my car got washed last night so that's something else that I wont have to do on this day, and I hope we got a lot of rain last night at least enough to keep the dust down for a while.

I have taken up reading to broden the mind but I don't read just any thing, the Guide-post is a book full of inspirational reading about God and situations that connect with Him, and I find that I can read it for hours or until my eyes hurt. The book has brought me much joy seeing I wasn't much of a reader until I moved here to Courtland, since that time God has brought many new things into my life from new friends to just the reading of a book. You see I hadn't always been able to read not until God came and saved me so long ago, my triles have been many through this life and education wasn't in the picture as we moved too much not staying in one place very long stoped what chances I had for an education. By the time I was three years old we were always on the move from one camp ground to the next until we could find a cheap enough house to live in and even then we didn't stay long because of the alcohol problem that existed in the family, but they tried the best way they knew how to see that we had a home for a short time anway and then it was off to the camp ground until they could save enough to get into another home. Our stints didn't last but a few months after the boys were in the accident one Sunday after church and it was that which broke the camels back. Not having insurance for their hospital stay and surgery the bills piled up and my parents lost everything including their faith, they had moved to Norwalk California' from Duluth Minnesota where I was born. But the reason they moved was because I was born out of wedlock, when that kind of thing was not looked upon as something good.

And my mothers family was very religious. Although they remained married I wasn't of the father that the three other kids were and this made things not so good, Herb the only father I knew at the time and my mother were looking for a new start. Because living in Duluth wasn't an option when you have a brother that's a priest, and I'm sure they didn't want my birth to get out knowing I had a father that was in the service. So off they traveled to California for the new start this was in the year of my birth, in the year of our lord 1958. I didn't know I had a different father until I was in grammer school and by then they had settled down and had a home to call their own, but they found a place and started to buy it. Back then we were an average family and I remember going to church and loving it, us kids would play in the gravel at the church until service started and then one Sunday after church the two boys got hit by a car out side of our home and everything went down hill, although times were hard my parents seamed to love each other so I thought and then everything fell apart after looseing their home and car's. I can only imagine what they went through as the bill collectors followed them across the country trying to collect for what the women had done by hitting the boys. It must of felt like they were being chased by a demon and they turned to alcohol who knows to maybe shut out the feeling of being chased, but in the end the alcohol took both of their lives. Herb was only 42 years old when he died, way too young but his medical condition couldn't be controlled by medication alone. And alcohol was the only thing that would stop the shaking of his hands, parkens disease got him a medical discharge from the service and he was never the same after that. Friday and I checked on the title to my old car and they will be getting it to me, I visited with my friend Mark and he got to learn more about me but I still don't say much about my past even though I don't mind doing it. Today you might say is the start of "Fun-day" and tomorrow I will sit at the gallery for a couple of hours, they are having a tattoo artist showing his work and who knows maybe I might get one you can never tell. Through the years I have lived here things like the mornings have been very precious to me and many things come to mind as each day passes which allows me to get rid of some of the old memories and make room for new ones the good ones that will take their place in this life. My creating this things which I do today will help many later down the line, and maybe stop many people from making that mistake of falling into that dark place which is hard to get out of. As for my part God had to of blessed me by healing what was wrong all the things which were wrong in the mind were healed over time and make whole once again through his healing and love. A lot of times it's been hard to understand why He picked me but that should be apparent because He knew me even before I was conceived and that which God says is good is defently good, it was hot again yesterday and it made you not to want to venture out but I did it anyway the humidity was very high. Harley seams to never see the squirrels in the yard any more or maybe he just knows I wont let him chase them and figures what the hell it's not worth the effort. My training him hasn't done much good about going to the potty during the night but in time it will take, I don't like yelling at him but it has to be done at times and it's like he understands because he heads to his cage when I scold him.

My life is changing the longer I live here and it's a good change somehow He is bringing things into perspective, my reading has improved a lot as the words are nice and big in the books that I read but I don't like to read garbage that would take away from learning and maybe that's why I only read stories that are inspireing and have a good ending the stories of other peoples lives intrigue's me and can open some ideas for my self, in the early days during our first year many things took place and now days I'm like part of this grown family that doesn't seam to judge or if they do they keep it to them selves not wanting to throw off the balance of things here. My father' was born in Shaw Minnesota the only father I knew anyway but I believe his parents came from the old country and came here in the late 1800's I wish I would of known more about them but we never went to see them except for maybe one time, so much of our history is missing but who knows maybe I can find out something somewhere in time as my learning improves. Mom was born in Duluth Minnesota where she went to school and was a bible school teacher, she would tell me stories about how strict her mother was and she allowed no cussing in her home. It was a strict up bringing but all in all things were good for her and her other siblings, grandma really loved us kids when we came to visit and she was a great women in my books. As for grandpa I didn't get to know him as much as grandma but I heard he wasn't as strict, I guess it's that way in every family one being stricter then the other sort of creating a balance that would make good children.

As for my uncles they were a little wild except for Gordy of course him being a preacher and all but they lived the way they wanted to and it was nice when we got too see them from time to time. In the end of their lives they came to see mom and when they traveled they would also drop by, maybe to mend those fences that got broke early in life. Gordy was the oldest and he got gray that all I can remember about him ageing before his time, but he did live to be in his late 60's or early 70's which to me would be about ¾ of their life. People around here live to be pretty old as I have heard about some living into their 90's, my friend John Blackburn' is 83 years young and he doesn't look but in his 60's that! Must be good living. He served his country and then came back here to live out his life taking care of cattle, he was telling me how his brother kept a few head for him when he went in to the service and when he got out and he built up his heard and he has been doing it ever since. Courtland is a great place where life is hard but also it's what you create of it, in the future I hope that there will be a mark for me here something to remember me by as being a writer and helping those who have gotten lost as I to got lost in the life of illusion where things weren't what they seamed. Here I went through life with the understanding that everyone drank their problems away when in reality it couldn't of been further from the truth. Saturday morning' I slept pretty well last night and today the town should be full of people, I never did find out how fun-day started but it has been around for at least 50 years meaning John and Judy must have been in their 30's when it started. And it must have been at a time when people would gather from near by towns and farms to just have a good time, but I will find out the story later so I will know some of Couurtlands history and see the many things that brought the celebration into this great town. There is something that makes this town different from others but to me it's the town of dreams or second chances, for what I gathered a lot of people don't know my whole story so I will keep it that way for now anyway. Back in the day, I was told that people would want to hear my stories because they are many and I tell them very well but it wasn't always that way, there was a time when I wouldn't even go out of my home, not here of course. But back in Nebraska because I felt like I didn't fit in to the new world I had to create, in my life I had to create a few worlds to protect my self as I grew in faith and made my self strong. Although they were lonely places I had my kids that would come over and visit which helped more then they will ever know, just their love helped to make it all work and as I grew stronger I was able to move on and find something new. Not to replace them, but to make my world stronger so I could go out in the world and learn about it. But I had to take baby steps to build confidence in my self and in time it worked but it also took an act of God to bring it about, to me it takes God to help you through those times when you don't understand what's going on the times when you think there is no way out He seams to make a way. Replacing bad habbits isn't the end but the start of something new and we have to adjust to that new way of thinking as it's nothing like the old world you used to live in.

In those days or years nothing made since and it brought a disconnection from reality and now you were living in a world you didn't understand when you were straight. At this time you couldn't phantom living out side of the world of addiction and it was too hard to change, like many others that tried and failed what they didn't realize is that everything is hard at first but in time things gets easier as He makes them strong and the bad thoughts go away in time. Many of the bad thoughts were erased from my mind because if we had to live with them then that wouldn't be a good thing, but they teach us something. To cherish the good days and hope for more of them and as life goes on they do return and you can separate them making life as good a you dare to. We were born with the spirit of God in us, and this allows us to create but if that connection with God is severed then we grow up with the wrong idea of what the world is supposed to be like. Today I can almost see what would of happened if things would have been different but that doesn't change the fact that there is still time to bring it into play even at my age. I am following the path that He put me on but I'm just a little late in getting there, from the gates of hell to my father finding me my life has changed showing that it's never too late even with the bumps in the road and looking back that's what they were bumps, not the canyons; I once thought they were. Many times I thought I was falling like the time in the pool and then He caught me and helped me to see that life wasn't over not for me anyway and I would go on to live many years after that.

Finding your place in this world is hard if you have no guidance or certain path to follow, when I was young I was told that I was special and it's something I have always believed maybe that's because I always felt different from other folks, like I wasn't from their world and I had a greater purpose. In the light I was told that my journey hadn't started yet and that I would know when it started, although these things I believe it hasn't been apparent yet or made clear what my journey is all about. Except that no matter what this world does to you God has the final say of how things will turn out, meaning there is a purpose why you were born and he will see it to the end. What will the future hold? Only He knows that. This morning we went to a yard sale and bought a couple pairs of jeans for me and a blanket for Randy the women there was nice and then we moved on to see if there were any more but didn't have any luck, while driving around we saw Dennis walking and offered him a ride but he declined saying he needed his walk for his heart. I sometimes try to think about others who have taught them selves instead of going to school and the only one I can think about it one of our presidents being brought up in the woods where there wasn't any schools so he taught him self to read to then later become president and freeing the slaves. Sunday morning and fun-day was exciting as they played music even through the rain, I got home at 9:00 and went to bed but then got up a few times to still hear the music off in the distence I really couldn't tell what time it let up but it must hve been late, many people came into the art gallery to have a seat or just cool off trying to beat the heat and some even ate the dinner there. I spent some of my time cleaning up and then text my daughter and chatted for a time, there is something about the building which brings me peace and maybe it's the history or because it's just big who really knows. The peoples spirits were up as they also danced in the rain and had a good ole time, as I releaved John and his wife they stayed for a little while and I talked to other folks that I had never met before and it was fun. There were over a few hundred people and they came from every walk of life some even riding motor cycles from places far away to enjoy the time they had here, I cant say how long it rained but I do know it was raininng when I left last night and hopefully it washed my car to save me from doing it this morning. Little brother was a sleep when I got home and then I let harley out before retireing hoping he wouldn't go potty in the house, now this morning I will open the church and get it ready for services this morning because I know it's going to be hot in there. As many drank beer the kids were excitred to just squirt each other with squirt guns trying to stay cool, I'm always amazed at how kids are so full of energy and running around like chickens with their heads cut off just playing and having a good ole time not knowing anything about the world out side of Courtland. Courtland is like a cocoon protecting them from that place they know nothing about, and I find this to be a good thing for them because they will see it one day and not like what they see. They need to be protected as long as possible so they can learn at a simpler pace, enjot this time my little friends for one day you will become apart of it. The bigger picture where life will change and you will have to take on responsibility for your future one guy asked if he knew me and I replyed I don't know but my name is Roger Mattson for which he said he had hard the name.

And we shook hands it's always nice to meet new people as you go through life and sometimes it can lead to a good friendship. Mark was there when I showed up talking to the tattoo artist and then they left to go somewhere there are many more things to do here then I first thought and places for which I have never seen before but in time I will come to know some of them, while I enjoyed the party it's the first one that I have went to since those days so long and it was exciting. Before we closed up there was a women using the toilet but I only saw her off in the distence and boy was she cute from what I saw of her, but I had a feeling she was trying to get away from someone because right after she came in a man was right behind herand then he left and she stayed there while I left. I pray each morning as my alone time is allows me to in hope that Jesus will bless my friends and family and heal those fighting addiction and other life altering things in their lives and I say a little prayer for my little man Eric in hope that God will heal him during this time in his young life. Many believe as I do' that prayer helps those who need it and it's a privilege to do this for them, as it says in the bible if two agree then it will be made possible, I went and got the church ready for this morning so everything is perfect. This is the day God has given us so be glad in it' in the world of addiction many things come into play the wanting and needing of it can be daunting as it lets a person hide from the world they once knew. And what I can say to them is go back' yes go back and face that which has made you want to hide, for in this world of darkness you wont find anything which will bring you peace for very long. As a quick fix never works but only for a short time be strong and God will bring all the bad things to pass.

And in doing this you can take back your life and be stronger then ever, for each time you grab for that quick fix you are throwing your self further away from living the truth. And the further you wonder the further you will have to make the trip back to taking control. My friends that world isn't for you so full of darkness and not feeling those things that He meant you to feel, I love you all other wise I wouldn't be doing what He sent me too do for His light will shine for ever and it's up to you to follow it. Many would give all they have to be able to over come their addictions but with some it's just not in the cards, and I believe those people are the ones that are stricken at an early age. Not the ones that are only just recently addicted but those who have spent their whole lives trying to find that thing they have been looking for to only find out that they had it all the time, for everything you need to be happy is inside of you and they just didn't know how to connect with it. Me or I was meant to be the way I am an understanding person that wasn't meant to go fast in life, and there are many like me they just get caught up in all the confusion and trying to keep-up with others isn't a good thing to do. Today I like the life I have found and yes in many ways I'm laid back as that's just my nature, some go to addiction because of lonelyness and others because they cant seam to find the answer they are looking for and being inpatient doesn't help in anyway for all things take time and if your patient then it will come. My little buddy is looking out the window hoping to see something and he will see it but it might take all day what is the difference? He will give up and go into the other room because he didn't see anything when he wanted to, and we as people are the same way "no patients" as everyone is in a hurry. Look at older people they know the answer because they have lived it and know it doesn't do any good to try to run a foot race with life. Monday morning and my eyes are not adjusted yet not am I awake, but here we ar at the beginning of another week. Yesterday I could tell that one of the older men in the congregation was feeling poorly but the good news is that he will have an opration to correct what's wrong and I hink his wife has to have surgery on her knee afterwards. They have been married for many years and I believe it's around 50 or so but I pray that he will get well, so they can be happy once more. I have been around people who have been sick and I can tell when these things are teally beat a person down, yesterday being the 5th Sunday we gathered in the overflow room and had coffee while we had service and it was a great O time with everyone laughing and shareing stories. Miss Allen wanted to thank everyone for their support after her husbands death, it's now been a year since he went to be with the Lord and her kids really helped her during this time. Especially her daughter that comes to church with her from time to time children can give hope to a parent during these times and her's stepped up to he plate. When someone passes a church family can give you hope where you might of thought there was none and this is something I'm still getting used to but boy it's great.

Even during the dark times a light seams to shine on us to help us make it through the difficult times to some how bring hope to us "the grieving, some of the things I have seen have helped me in many ways the coming and going of the old and the young. The young as they are born into this world and the old that makes room for them for there is always a balance in the universe just like good and eveil but the good usually comes out a head at least in my thoughts anyway. The days are hot while the mornings are cool sometimes just in this last month, I remember many a mornings when the humidity laid like a blanket over me when I stepped out side and that something I don't care for. But all I all we seam to survive and move on to the next day in hope that it might be cooler, and usually it is. July has only another day and then August is here another month that can be hot but we will see what happens as we move further into it, my other grandson has found his way to face-book on the computer and he wrote me so I wrote back but havent gotten a reply as of yet. If he gets the hang of it he will write and we will stay in touch by that means anyway my land' they grow so fast. In church it was like a big family and I got to meet a friends daughter and her kids, she is a little women and her kids look just like her you can tell that apple doesn't fall far from the tree she lives in Omaha where my brother lives but I didn't bring him up. The chances of her knowing him is slim to none as I don't believe they would travel in the same circles, I can see change coming but like with all the other times I cant tell what it will be. All I can do is pray that it will be a good change to enrich the lives of my friends and close family.

Bringing them joy and happiness through out the year, my plant has been thriving since the rain came a couple of days ago and it has many flowers on it blooming more each day. My mind seams to be changing as I move forward into an older part of life, a part my dad didn't get too see because of his passing also I wonder if he would of ever got that shop if he would of still been around in his

50's probably but time didn't allow that to take place. The days are starting to feel like days once again as I train my mind to except each one as it comes, the cleaning of the church starts this week and they will get every nook and cranny so it stays clean through out the next few years. They say it's done once in a great while and then the rest is up to me but I feel like I will lend a helping hand during this time to get to know things better God's house is His temple, many people had family over during fun-day and some even came to church which I thought was great. The gift of you is a precious and it's more important then anything else you could give a child, the shareing of your soul so a child could see what you are made of. The kindness and the giving side of you that part which doesn't get to show it's self very often, as children grow they need to see that you are willing to help others when they are in need that way they too might do the same one day. Although we don't do it enough just that glimps can bring a child in a different direction, one that will help them later in life.. Tuesdsay and it's the last day of July, I slept in this morning and didn't get up until almost 5:00 I also had a dream but for the life of me I cant recall what it was about strange how that happens. I was thinking about visiting Mark Konz when I make that trip to Nebrasa to see my daughter, it's been years since I have visited with Mark and he always inspires me when we meet as for the subject of addictioon it will be around for many years to come and I might not ever run out of things to write about because the numbers keep growing even though people are getting more help. The day that they get things under control will be the day I can let go of the curse that is driving everyone to that dark place, some even say that they feel like nothing unless they are high and this is a bad depression when they feel that was, people on many other drugs besides the usual illegal ones have a need to fall in and out of this world to deal with the things that are going on. Wednesday or hump day as they call it, I slept in again and it feels different then getting up at the usual time for some reason my eternal clock is busted or out of wack, I mowed the lawn yesterday so I don't have to worry about that for a few days. Starting on the 11th I will have to put more time in watching Randy because he is gooing to have surgery on his back it's an out patient thing and should only take a few hours. As they make an inch cut and cure the problem then he should be like new once again but working is still out of the question for a while anyway, the years have left it's mark on him but still it's better then the addiction he once had. They will do the surgery in Salina for which I'm glad as it's only about an hour or so drive from home and if I have too I can make sure he is ok before taking him home, it's times like these which tests your faith and I pray for the best. I like taking care of him as he is usually a good patient plus I love him so' when he sees me changing he feels he can do the same things and it works for the most part. My jobs gives him hope that he too may one day do the same, when the television shows disabled people making it on their own I point out that he can do he same in hope that one day he will be able too.

In the big city he wouldn't make it with all the people that would take advantage of him but here in Courtland he has a greater chance because people know him, and care about him. In story books you read about the wonderers things some people do in a small community and those things happen here. The town has taken me in and make sure that I have what I need so I can go on and be a part of this great place I call home, I still have a few friends far away but most of them are family and as for the others that didn't make it into my future well hey never belonged here. Even Valerie didn't make it but a great lesson was learned with her and that's to never try and go back in time because it doesn't work, I find it strange that God knew where I would be on this great day even before I wass born, so my life here should be set in stone or written in that book of His if only I could read it' but I don't think that will happen not at this time anyway. As I watch the kids it reminds me of a little village in a fairy tale book where they grow up and venture out in the world to only come back to the place that they grew up in, to carry on where their parents leave off so the world can survive to me this part of the country is very important to people being able to eat and without the people many more would starve to death. Then those that already do, what happens with the crops after they are harvested it's like they get caught up in red tape and are sold to the highest bidder so that would mean others make the decision of who gets to eat or not. The price of beef is out of this world as some of it hits as high as $ 6.00 a pound just for a steak so the poor have to eat other things except for that and buy things within their budget hamburger reaches almost three dollars a pound making it hard to get also, it's like if they are not getting you at the gas pumps they will get you eating.

My land' you can hardly afford to travel 100 miles any more to see your family and that's getting bad well have to go a storm is passing through our town and we might loose power so later, the storm has passed and we didn't loose power. Thursay and the rain hit again last night, I was supprised when I seen the light flicker across the sky and then the thunder hit. At the thrift shop it was a good day and I got to meet another nice person, it's like I meet someone new each week and that can be exciting. It's now August 2nd and the new month is going to be a good one. As for washing my car the rain has taken care of that but I wish the carwash would get finished so I would have that option also, I don't know what I was thinking when I thought Randy went in for surgery this month but it's in September on the 11th and he will have to tell his parole officer even though it's in the same town that he is from. Things are getting a little tighter as the months move on and reality is setting in but still I feel we will make it ok' by not making to many trips to town, the thunder is still sounding off but in the distence meaning the storm is moving somewhere cant really tell as the night is still upon us and it's dark out still. It's getting louder now and it seams like it's right above my house so maybe I was wrong it's like addiction can be sometimes you think it's gone but then it hit's you to let you know it's still in charge as I have felt those feelings before especially in the early stages. If you can make it at least two years then you have a great chance but anything below that there is still that chance that you might relaps even if it's for a short time but it will go away, to allow you to stay on that path of freedom. When your body has been used to it for a long time the mussels have to be retrained because they will tence up and ache like hell then you have to put it in God's hands and pray for the best, I have noticed that at times it seams the whole world is coming apart but in reality it isn't that's the change from the drugs to not having them when things get tough. It takes years before the mind can become straight again but if it's an childhood addiction then that's all together different because even the choldhood years were not spent being straight and it's a hard thing to do. With me I had no education except for life experiences so I taught my self to read and that really helped except for the headache that would come from the mind not being trained when you were young but in time that too also passed like the day that has only 24 hours in it. Many say what doesn't kill you makes you stronger, and this I find to be true. But that little time in that hell makes you not to want to visit it again and then you move on, it's the things you experience while your straight that makes you want to keep it in your life, to never want to go through that again and live that lifeGod has given back to you. Even today while things are good it's like that part of my life didn't exist as it gets further and further away in my mind. Not all people go through the same thing because none of us were created the same way we are all unique and different in many ways, it's God who allows us to heal in our own way and bring about a new you, never should anyone compare them selves toany other person because you are not them and their path might be different then your's as they might be heading in a different direction.

I have noticed' that when others see the lord shine in your life then they too want to be a part of that or have that in their lives and why this happens is God's secret because he hasn't told me why it's this way but it feels good when it happens. The change from living in the dark to finding God's favor is an experience that only comes into your life once and it's called that second chance, which He gives us all that opportunity to make right what was wrong. In the world of addiction you survive and that's all you do, no light that shines when people see you just that dark hole and it's up to you to pull your self out of it. Friday and things are back to normal in getting up, I believe today is clean day at the church when they do some painting and such and then it's up too me to keep it that way for a few years which wont be a problem its sort of like a spring cleaning I think but it gets everything ready for the next few years. Also I have to pay bills today and get them behind me to make the month go smoothly, I know the rest of the year will go smoothly as things become more in tune with my situation. And as long as I can keep my bills paid then things will go great in many ways I worry too much because as long as the bills are paid then really I have it made, but it doesn't stop the wanting of having a little money in my pocket. Many years ago I asked to see the other side of the coin but that is something I haven't seen yet, who knows maybe one day it will come to pass but for now I'm content the way things are. We wanted to see my daughter but that is out of the question for now maybe some time in the future it will become reality the seeing my grandchildren would be great but they also know that grandpa has responcibilitys to the church.

The living here is grand as we take one day at a time or a week at a time as the days still seam to fly by so fast, many years ago I worked for the store mom and dad had but those practices don't seam to exist any longer with the new cash registers and such but I bet I could learn them if given the right training and it would be something I would like to do maybe one day. I cant tell if it rained last night but they are calling for it through the weekend and in to the early part of next week if this happens then we should be set for a while anyway, the street cleaner came down our street day before yesterday and they do such a good job keeping things clean I have only seen them a few times since I moved here and Randy didn't even know we had one. Getting back to the addiction problem many can over come it when the right situation presents it's self and they take advantage of it, but letting it go on can and will destroy the users family. Many think only the addict is effected but it goes much further then that, I recall many times waking up screaming because of the addiction and you can never tell when it's going to leave your body. It can be in the middle of the night or during the day if it happens during the day you can just use and it passes but during the night the demons come out and play games with your mind causing you to go right back into it. I cant really say why it happens sometimes at night but it does and it frightens the hell out of you, as for feeling better that will only come when the addiction is destroyed and you find a balance in your life a balance that is constent so you can learn to love your self as God loves you. And when you find your self sober then this process can start I can still remember asking Him to help me through the tough times to not follow through with what I promised like making love to the toilet the body rejecting the things you put into it. Such a bad time but it passed and then it was back to the same ole things, not learning anything. What brings people to that point? To take it as far as it would go. With me many times I didn't want to be here and wanted to get it over with but that wasn't His plan for my life, in the early years my thinking was off by believing every family lived that way which I found out later that it wasn't the case and our family was just lost and they made the best out of a bad situation. Mom was a beautiful spirit and so was dad but life beat them down it was like every time they tried to get up something would happen to knock them down again, did they see the miracles that God had put in their paths or did they just see the bad part of the situation? The loss of material things, for surely those things can be replaced but their bodys couldn't be. Why do some think in only material things and not the spiritual things for surely the curse didn't let them see these things and made them blind to the fact that God always has and always will love them. The cries of the human spirit are heard by God' but there seams tobe a blockage in the mind that doesn't let them see what should be seen, with me in my writing it was like sometimes I was up against a brick wall and nothing would enter or let me break through it. Like a wall of nothing that I couldn't break through, what would happen if one day I found the key to that room is it a place that I wouldn't want to go or would it be something beautiful? At this time I really cant say but there is resistance there holding the door shut. Saturday morning and they got the over-flow room painted so now I will go and put things away being my days start earlier then the other folks do, I'm glad that this only takes place once every few years. Last-night I went and checked on what they had gotten done and the piano and pictures have to be pushed back and made right but it has wheels so it shouldn't be hard to move, once that is done then everything should be in place. Also there is comunion tomorrow so that has to be done also, when I get there I'm going to turn on the air because it was hot yesterday and today will be the same. As for the bigger things someone else will have to put that away because I just cant move it.

This will give me the morning to get things done as much as possible and I like to do my part in the church then today I have the thrift store at 12:00 to 2:00 and I'm off for the day so my busyiest part of the day will be this morning or until I'm done with things. As for the main part of the church I vacuumed, and it should be clean enough to eat off of. It was another morning of getting up a little late but that's ok' still I beat everyone else up by about six hours or so just the habbits of being a writer I guess early to bed and early to rise. The people of the church has been so kind to me that for some reason I'm guided to go and do this job to make sure the church looks good. Being a part of something so grand is what I have always wanted and this is my helping hand you might say, being I'm coming up blank for things to write maybe I should stop for now. Sunday morning and we saw some old friends yesterday in Belleville as I was getting gas, it kind of blew our minds in a good way as we hadent seen Denny and Bob Eggie in years. Even when we lived in Kearney we never got too see them so this was kind of a top off to a good day, we then shook hands and they left to go back home from working on some race car down here. Denny is married to my kids mothers sister which would make him their uncle, time seams to have been good to them both as they looked great and Bob said he reads my articals all the time in the paper which also made me feel good. Even time didn't seams to wipe our faces from their memories and they said we were looking good, I asked Denny if he saw Randy in the store and he said yes over by the food not that he needed any. Joking about his size' but we had always joked around even when we were young.

Then on the way home Randy started to cry because he was so happy to see them again, behind the truck was a race car trailor that he does work out of or else he was hauling a car in it. Couldn't really tell for sure because it was closed in, I remember Denny racing stock cars many years ago but then he retired to spend time with his wife Cinda who had battled with kidney disease for a long time. But after a transplant she got better and I believe she is doing well these days, I recall long ago as we sat in a bar and me and Stacy told the family we were thinking of marriage and Denny said good we need another fool in this family. Well we never did get married but me and Denny stayed friends all thee years, strange how things work out. Those were the dark days of my life but friendship seamed to stay between us and that might have been because we didn't see each other very oftend like yesterday the chance meeting of old friends, I was amaze that Bob remembered me but he did and it's my writing that brought that about. The gift from God that keeps giving and it's still doing it today, if I hadn't become a writer I wonder if the memory would have been the same probably not. In Kearney they look at me like the one who changed his life through the power of God which is a good thing for me and them if you really look at it, well the church is clean and all I have to do is get communion ready for later this morning and clean windows. Each time I will clean a different room that way it will stay that way, my life long job will be to continue working at the church as many others have before me and I look at it as if it's meant to be, He brings us to the place we need to be at a certain time in life and my place is here where I have many friends. During just that brief moment of seeing them again brightened up our day and what a great day it was, who knows the next time we go to Kearney maybe we can stop in and see Denny again friends passing through this world at a cerain time to bring joy to someone. Randy hadn't seen anyone from Kearney since he got out but Denny is one of them he should of seen if the time was present just a good ole boy from the past. In the future you never know who you might run into being just on the border of Nebraska and Kansas, time seams to catch up with us all and it's nice to see friends once again. As for ever moving; it will not happen here with me just the saroundings brings my writing to a new level. Yesterday was fun as we put things up to sell in the thrift store it was just me and Beverly that worked and I also got to read a little to pass the time but it was fun as always to work with her, she is the owner and knows where everything goes so that's no problem.

At first I didn't know if I wanted to meet new people but now I'm glad that I did because they are all kind in their own way, some hardened by the life here but kind anyway. The one southern girl doesn't wave when waved to but I will keep on trying as you never give up on people, and only God knows what the futue holds for any of us. Maybe one day she might bring down that wall which seams to be in her life but for now life goes on and who knows when it might change, the ladies that were working was glad when I came to releave them after their shift Judy is a sweetheart and I love it when she plays my music. Just the melody keeps me on track when I'm singing and trying to not mess up, this morning I need to mow the lawn as we got enough rain for the grass to grow and boy it looks good nice and green. Not like the other parts of the country where they havent gotten any rain, we are truly blessed here in Courtland' and I believe we might even have a crop to bring to market. The migrate workers were bringing in mellons down to the market which is only a mile down the road and I think they ship them all across the United States to places which can't grow them, they live right across the street from us in a corner house and there has to be six living in the house, they get up each morning and head to work rain or shine. Many of them come to the thrift store and buy clothes to send to family that live in Texas where the price is much higher. You might say we are the bargen center of the central plains just people trying to get by the best way they know how, some compare these days to the time of the depression but I really cant say seeing I wasn't born back then not until 28 years later, glad that I missed that one.

My grand parents would of seen those days though, when crime ran rampet and the outlaws were running a lot of things at least that part has changed or I think it has. Little brother is still sleeping and I think he will rest until 6:00 Am. After the long day we had, things here still have me puzzled but with many of the people you can see the goodness and how much they love God. The adventures in life brings us to many places and we don't always see where we are going why is this? We might start out at one place and then end up clear across the country does He know where we will end up and if so doesn't that give Him the power to change or stop the bad things from happening I believe He does have that power but if He changed things then we wouldn't have freedom of choice which is important in our growth. Which gives us the power of change the power to know the difference between right and wrong and what we need to do to bring our selfs to that place we need to be in life, we can go through life wishing things were different but do we really wish that to take place? For it's our travels that makes us who we are the journeys that gives us things to talk about later in life. I see it as there is one thing we take with us when we go, and that's memories nothing else goes with us into that eternal life and that helps us know our loved ones when we get there so they say. Nothing that happens here seams to matter when we reach the other place even the life we lead is like a faded memory only too be kept alive to notice certain things. Monday morning and I'm awake yesterday in church we were kidding about how heavy the piano was and I told john that I almost came and got him to help me at 5:00 in the morning and he replied that he might have told me where to go. I like it when I can kid with people that way but it took a long time before I had the nerve to just be like family, no being afraid of being out of place this morning I have some clean-up to do and then I will be done with the hard things that have to be done. Randy got the weed eating done also yesterday and now I have to mow the lawn sometime this morning while it's cool out side never did like the darn heat, after church Randy told me that he talked to Denny and he side he was in shock after seeing us that he didn't know what to say. And that's something I understand been there and done that many times, but he did tell Randy that I looked good and he wants him to find him some cars as that's what they do these days to make a living. Time seams to have been good to some of us and for others well maybe not so good but we survive and go on with life hoping to live a lot longer then we have so far, Donnie passed at a very young age but the years before had taken it's toal on him with all thee drug use no more suffering for him in this life. Seeing Dennie brought back memories of times when the drugs had a hold on me but there was moments when good times where in the picture, Dennie never did drugs but he liked his beer and I believe even those days are over for him as the drugs are over for me and now the good life begins the days of not destroying what God has given us and trying to figure it out seeing all the goodness that is right in front of me. Being a born again christen is the life to live not having all the crap which was at one time in my life, as that world doesn't exist any longer. At the art building they are having zomba classes but they are something I will have to miss all the jumping around would probably kill this ole man Ha! It's the simple life that I look forward to these days and getting by the best way I know how.

Me and little brother just kicking back and doing things for those who need our help as long as the bills are paid then we can make it in this great place we call home. The bashfulness has gone when it comes to my church family but not so much with others, in the church I feel a kind of peace a serenity that you should have, but in the world you always have to be careful of others. We went and checked out a stock car for Dennie and when we went into the guys house I just wanted to leave and I didn't understand how someone could live that way unless they had a lack of self worth, just the smell about knocked me out. Maybe that the difference in how some people are raised not quite sure,, mom always had a clean house and I believe it rubbed off on me as I didn't fall far from the tree some say apple but that's their usage of words not mine, it's going to be a good day because I'm going to make it that way and before long the birds will be singing to bring in the new day I can tell it's going to be another hot day and they are saying that it could even reach into the triple digits again as high as 107 degrees. Not the coolest day but it's here just the same my car needs to be washed also so we will see what happens there, sure with the car wash was fixed. Doing it by hand is hard but also it gives me pride when I see it afterwards, and that's a good feeling.

Before mom passed I was pertty out of it getting my life back in order all the confusion that was going through my mind had done it's own damage, but over time it became a part of what I like to call growing up without anyone to help in anyway I guess that's what made me as strong as I am. I notice many things that have taken place since the bible and prayer has been taken out of schools and none of it is good, the killing of those who saw things differently then others has cost them their lives all because of athiest and this shows me that they never did believe in God just the devil and it's daunting that they would want to push their beliefs onto others. Christen beliefs are something that is given and we choose weather we want to believe or not but these people try to push theirs onto others by saying there is no God. For surely this is the devil at work in a weak mind one that cant choose for them selves, there is more going on in this world that this mind wouldn't even want to grasp or think about and it's nothing to hear about others killing others for foolish things like money, wanting that grasp of power some think it gives you. I don't like and never have cared about such things knowing someone would want it more then life it's self even if it's just for a short time. The things it can give you only lasts for a short time never over 100 years and then it's gone, and you fall into that realm of greed during that time. With wealth comes a big burden and that's everyone wanting it, when a person hit's the lottery you have relatives that you never heard of coming out of the wood work to clame their little piece of the pie. Which later you learn that they don't exist greed hits most people and it's because of the mighty dollar, if one day I should win it I would help and protect the kids and the young adults that live here in my now new home town using that kind of money to make things better then they are today. Not just one person getting help but your community to help build and make it stronger then it's ever been before, making sure the kids have what they need to make them selves better and stronger then ever before a community that stands by their residents. Like the guardian that looks after us Jesus Him self, many times you can see how a child is raised by the way they answer questions on some subjects and it reflect their parents beliefs although life was hard for my mom she never let anyone see the bad things which were taking place in her life. Each day she greeted it with a smile and I think that's why I liked to be around her so much, she would do everything in her power to help others because she knew what it was like to struggle through life not having anyone who cared wither you lived or died. Her struggles made me stronger in my character making me want to be like her in many ways, the giving heart that never took anything in return except to maybe have them help around the house when it needed cleaning because to her your house is a reflection of your character and her house was always spotless even in the last days of her life. My taking care of her was a gift to her for being who she was, as for the others in the family they never came around unless they wanted something a baby sitter or just to borrow money when they were broke and it was nothing to them to use the kindness until it was gone. Why does children turn out different when they are raised by the same parents? It has to be the way they preceive things in life the child that is, as for my self I saw the goodness but with the others they saw something else. Rick would talk about dad tieing him up in the back yard like you would a dog but this never took place not in mmy memory.

And my sister Susie saw mom in a different setting making her out to be the bad person which also wasn't true but that could have been from her being spoiled because dad got her anything she wanted when payday rolled around and in the few times she didn't get what she wanted she through a fit. Making everyones life a hell because she was neglected or so she thought, I find that you have to use caution when you spoil a child because like addiction later in life they can and will destroy others to get what they want and that is just nature taking care of things that others created. Although I tried to correct my children when they did wrong the other half would jump on me saying their not my kids they are hers and I should leave them alone. I asked her one day why she does those things and she replied that if she was to do that they would hate her later in life and she didn't want that, but she couldn't see that later our son told her that quite oftend and I think if she would of allowed me to take that role this wouldn't of happened but also the alcohol addiction she had didn't help either, being a hateful person was intensified when alcohol was thrown into the mix making it impossible to be around her. I cant count the times when the law was called and that didn't help matters any except for almost causing her to go to jail. Tuesday morning and there is a storm brewing as I can hear it out-side it woke harley up and he was barking because the screen door flew open this is a first for that to happen especially this time of year. When I opened the door the whole sky light up and the clouds looked awesome.

I don't know why it happens that way but every time I wash my car it does that so maybe I should do it more oftend, now harley wont go back to bed but that wont bother me any. Usually the storms hit at night when the temp is cooler the thunder is cracking off in the distance meaning more rain is coming so we will see what happens hopefuly it will pass before we have to go to Concordia. Little brother woke up also when the door flew open but I told him to go back to bed, even though we are getting the rain we needed there are puddles that stand in the streets making it hard to drive on the roads from all the big trucks driving on them. Tuesday is trash day and I hope the trash cans don't blow away with the wind the way it is, I did Randy's paper work for the year and I hope it's good enough it was the first time I have done this being a payee so if it isn't right I'm sure they will let me know. But other then that things are still going fine here, and our days are filled with joy as we move forward towards 2013, through the year many things have changed with pop's passing last night I had a dream about him but I cant quite remember what it was about it was the first one since that day and I hope it's a good sign, the thunder keeps cracking and I hope the storm moves on after droping what we need. I cant recall when we got a storm during this time of year but then usually I'm not up when they come, only seeing what was left behind after the fact. Yesterday was nice as I cleaned the church and got things ready for next Sunday, but now there is some other things that has to be done like painting the back room and they should paint the childrens room as they are a little ruff on things being kids and all. I'm not sure how far I will take things in my writing but it's apparent that this venture has to stop somewhere will it lead to where I want it to go? The helping of others can be a great thing if it's in the right setting connecting all the dot's where they need to be connected, making and hoping they might see that life after addiction can be great. It's been a life long battle but in the end this life is much better then the one I had befor, the feelings of love that returns within a person makes it all worth the journey. And the return of the things that got lost back when you did, for truly my life is good and so is that of Randy's as he learns to adjust to his new way of life. I hadn't seen him cry in quite some time like he did when we saw Denny and Bob but the release of those emotions helped him in many ways and in the future it will make him stronger in more ways then one. Still havent gotten him back in church but maybe sometime next year it will happen being around all those people for so long made him not want to mingle with others so I figured he just need some alone time,, and maybe he will come out of his shell. As for him taking care of his own money I don't see a problem with it his only problem is reading and writing the lack of education plages us all in this family some worse then others but still we survive and go on with life, as best we can. I don't hear the storm any more so it must have passed at least for today but I know my car will be dirty again so cleaning it will be another job that will have to be done. In the realm of surviving we barly get by but with us together we make it and I can see the kids talking about us later in life saying remember the Mattson brothers that lived on the corner.

My name will be remembered; even after my time is up here bringing me a comfort that I can rest easy at knowing they remember the one who changed his life in a town called Courtland, KS. It's funny how Bob remembered me by my writings and not just my personality Ha! Well we are all remembered by something we do wither it something good or bad but I prefer the good deeds we do to be remembered by not what once was but what we turned out to be. The change of things can make a big difference in this world taking a destroyed life and turning it around to let it shine, Wednesday morning and it's thrift store day when I get to spend some time doing things that are fun. For the most part anyway some mornings I graced by Harleys presents as he can't seam to, not be by me when I get up. And his wineing drives me nuts other wise he is a good dog, as I get up each morning my mind is foggy until I get that coffee in me the rain yesterday was very short as we drove home and I saw Mrs. Hord at the station in Belleville where I saw Dennie and Bob I'm just guessing but she must have went to the doctor, it seams I run into many people I know from near and far at that station but it's always a delight to see them. I shook her hand and asked how she was doing and she asked the same for which I told her that I was fine, she is a genteel women and she went on her way. I pray for her each morning in hope that God will take her cancer away and she has been doing fine so far also we went to Randys parole officer so he could check in, and then we went to Wal-Mart too get a few things that will last the month.

In this world we sometimes need to see old friends if for nothing else but to see that they are ok and Dennie seams to be doing fine along with Bob, yesterday or should I say last night Randy got a call from Mark O'Brien saying his brothers friend was found dead in his apartment and that Bob his brother has a bad liver and colon cancer. I remember Bob and I thought the booze would of killed him long ago but now I guess it's just a matter of time before it happens, there is nothing worse then being ill and knowing you time isn't as long as you thought it would be it gives you a respective on life and how fragual it can be. But we all have the power to change those things which destroys many lives if he would have changed he might not be in that situation now but he didn't and so life goes on only without him in it. But the good news is that he will get his second chance it just wont be in this life but the next, in some religions they believe that we remain here on earth because it was created for us and in others they believe we go to heaven where He has made a place for us. God is great and what ever he does is fine with me the Alpha and the Omega the first and the last the creator of all things including heaven and earth and all that's around it. For it's going to be another good day I and Judy worked to day together and although we didn't have but a couple of customers I learned more about the town, she had played the piano at the church for 52 years and I told her that's a long time. She also said the church used to have more members but the way I took it that was 30 some years ago when she and the others were young John had two older brothers which have died only leaving him at this time and Judy says he doesn't get around like he used too but their trips to the farm is something they have done for a long time. I can imagine how they were in their younger days, Thursday morninng and I got up at the regular time yesterday one of the cusstomers was dressed like she was back in the 60's with the bettles glasses and such and come to find out she lives just down the block from me it seams judy knows everyone in the town including the people who don't come to church and she has their stories of how long and how many kids they have along with some of the things they like to do, the women couldn't of been any older then I was back in my early or late 40's there seams to be many people from many walks of life and they must like the simple life here in Courtland. It's going on a few years since I moved here and by the end of next year my home will be about paid for then we can move on to buying something else we might want, just to own a piece of property is huge in my life not ever having anything before and if I ever venture out into the world I will always have a place to come back to. A place that God set-up for me. Just hearing about the others that are living out in the world it seams my life here is far better then they have it, many of the people I used to know have passed on and they were very young compared to those who died of old age some even in their 30's and 40's and even a few in their 20's as for my self I hope to live until my 70's or so God willing, and then I would consider that a long life for me anyway. The lord works in mysterious ways and we can never tell what his plan is until He reveals it to us, if it wasn't for my faith things would have turned out a lot different then they did and I'm grateful for that knowing that He has my back even when I get sick. As for my job at the church it's mine until the end of time or until I get forgetful but I don't see that happening at this time.

Judy said I should take Randy to see the people in Kearney for a weekend and that might let him know how good he has it here so maybe sometime in the future I will do that curiosity is something we all have and he just might need to check things out for him self, I find that in a small town you get to know who you are and when you're out in the big world you never seam to find the time to do that and there is no better place to do that then here in Courtland it helps you to become who you are and in years I will become better then I am today it's like this place becomes a part of you and you it. Our town looks like the green pastures you see in a book where everything around it is dieing and that's the only piece of heaven there is, you can go 20 miles in any direction and everything is dried up even cattle are dieing because of the drought. Last year our worst was better then their best when it comes to crops and I believe it will be the same this year and I see it as a sign from God that things will get better, the drought is what makes it hard on people but we have been blessed to be able to survive in this place I now call home. Many make their millions while I just write about the things which happen here but their millions cant messure up to my life for all the money in the world couldn't bring what I have and that's piece of mind and soul, I wanted to be rich at one time but hey you cant take that crap with you for it will be left here for someone else to pay taxes on, as for my body it will be given as a organ doner.

So maybe another person could live longer, isn't that what it's all about the prolonging of life to those who might not of been given that chance otherwise? A child given a liver for today just a piece of one can grow into a full one as it's the only part of the body that can heal it's self, so they say. But I also believe the mind can heal it's self if given the right conditions with His help. In my experience all that is destroyed from addiction can be healed but even today it comes with a price, my enzymes in my liver is still off but you have to take into account that it was almost destroyed.by all the drinking so I'm very lucky but I do ok' and stay away from things that would hurt it. I asked Judy if she knew Destiny and she did but just by her work at the high school and Jr. High being an art teacher she still crosses my mind from time to time and I think she is awesome who knows maybe one day she might read these words and if she does you go girl! you are the bomb sorry I didn't get to tell you that in the short time we met but I'm a bashful person and carry that curse. In the future things might change but if they don't keep being your self I really liked your red look with your hair, should a person persue someone half their age? And try to make a connection it all depends on the ability to take care of such person, but nothing is written in stone with me when I paint it brings me into a different place a place of peace sort of like the place where I talk to God and maybe that's where I need to be there are only three places where this happens and that's when I mow the lawn or paint and when I pray it's like an alternative reality a place deep inside where no one can touch you and it lets your mind become a part of that place with no real thought but to create and communicate with Him the father. I had never visited that place through painting before but maybe it's a sign that I should do that only time will tell, what could of happened if I would of taken it up as a child? That's a picture I will never see because it didn't happen. Painting lets you bring something out that inner talent that might have been hidden all these years and from what I understand they say it's never to late to grow more in what you are or could be, we will see what happens in the future months. Friday morning' and the days have cooled off yesterday was omly in the 80's and they are calling for more of the same for next week. This is the cooling down period for a while anyway, I have been awake since after 1:00 but fell a sleep a couple of times Randy is getting more sleep during the day nd that's not good for either of us because it drives me nuts with his snoreing and I told him so. So we will see if there is any change, this cooler weather will bring us into fall my most liked season of the year when things change, as for summer I'm not quite sure if it's over but I do know that indian summer comes once a year here when it gets hot again. I still think of pop's but I also know that he is in a better place, in the future I cant say what will happen in our lives but I do know Randy should be better after his surgery and I pray that God will give them wisdom when they do it. My little brother is important to me and I only want what's best for him so we will venture into this winter in hope that he over comes the things that are wrong with him. It's going to be a beautiful morning as the temp's should be in the 60's my new car is doing fine and I wash it by hand in the mornings when it's cool out side this way I save on money and who knows maybe some others might have me wash theirs seeing the car wash is broke down. I always use vinegar that way it cuts the dirt and it gives it that pickeled smell Ha!. Little brother says he cant tell when I'm up but it's very different with me because I can tell when he is up by just the movement in his room.

I don't know how someone could want to sleep all night and then all day also, but he is getting into hat cycle which will have to change, but I have to admit that there was a time when I did it many years ago when I spent the first year sleeping on the couch because I had no bed. Those were the tough times but I made it through it and today it isn't that way for little brother he inherited Oliver's room which was well equipped wanting for nothing and I even got him his own television for his room making it easy for him. The other day we went to panther paws and there was a lot of people that are working some kind of construction they stood out by their tattoos; and everyone of them had them all over their arms and this lead me to believe they are not from around here just some guys out to make a living in the heart land. If I had to guess I would say they were working on the pipe line that is going through Kansas, there is a lot of that these days here in Kansas, Nebraska, and Oklahoma. And I believe it's natural gas but I wouldn't sware to it, I remember when I was that age and lived in Nebraska and they flew us to other states to work and set up a charge account so we could eat at a certain place like they did at panther paw's and then when we got our checks we went in and paid them always honest and they didn't mind helping us out because it brought them in a lot of money. There had to have been ten guys so I took it that they were a crew of hard workers, I do know that we visited the bars each night after work and tied one on, but that wasn't a good thing.

Going to work in the mornings with a hang over messed up things because the mind wasn't clear but we got the buildings put up and moved on to the next job, it's strange when your young the alcohol makes you think you can take on the world if you had too but that was something I avoided at all cost. Most of them were in their 20's and that's when your at your best in physical health or so you think but alcohol makes you take chances that you wouldn't do if you were sober and that's what gets you in trouble, I bet they have a tab at tags also to relax after work. O what I would do if I had that part of my youth back it would be so different, not making the same mistakes again and with the knowledge of my older years and the youth of yester years. I coud tell that they drove to the job as we did when we arrived at out destination there was always some who traveled by truck to the job even if we flew because we had to have our tools to complete the job. With my brothers we never worked together because that wasn't a good thing to do, but then later I got them a job with me at Western Alfalfa which worked for a while loading and unloading trucks catching 50 pound pags of pellets and meal made us stronger then ever before. Then after the years had passed that strength dwindled as illness from drinking set in the curse had hit me full force and it wasn't going to let up until one had lost the fight, I cant count the doctors that said I wouldn't make it and I was pretty young then in my late 20's but it took a great deal to kill me and when it happened even then I didn't give up. It was the light, that and the knowing there was a God who cared for me that brought me back and even though it took years the fights were good ones, for the place I visited wasn't ready for me or I it. So with what ever power He sent me back until it's my time, was I supposed to come here in the original plan and if so what is my purpose? To do what I do today, and show others that it's never to late to find the one that created us. This journey has been a long one and it's no where near over until the fat lady sings, I do know that Courtland is a special place because I have never met any others like the people here. They seam to bring out the best in me as a person and maybe I do the same for them in a way the goodness that is here is beyond anything I have ever seen before and it out weighs the bad by far, face it they help others in many ways giving to those who hurt and bringing comfort to those who suffer through lifes tragedies. It's a little piece of heaven right here on earth, although there is evil everywhere it seams to be at a very low rate here in Courtland. When we had a bad storm a few years back there were many that came to help when the trees fell in my yard and even those who drank thought we are good people, they must have as they said we were nice people I guess they expected the other. As many people can be mean, I learned a long time ago that if you show kindness it's usually returned but show the other and things can be that way also. In a way I'm like those who show me kindness as I return it to them as it's given, but do me wrong and I wont have anything to do with you that's just the way I am. It's a part of me to be kind to others and that's because I want the same as many others want the same thing from me, it's like I wash your back and you wash mine and that's just how I look at life sometimes.

Many' think it's a weakness to cry or show emotions, but to me if you don't show these things then there is something wrong. Even Jesus' cried when he talked to His father which is or was normal between them and the father always came through. As I pray or try to remember to pray each morning I always ask for healing for those who are ill and old in hope that they will have a good day because to me one good day can make up for a few bad ones, and I have faith that my prayers help. Our trip to Salina should bring more healing to little brother and I hope it's all down hill from there I can see change in him but it's very slow so I will be patient and see what unfolds, he has slept in this morning and for that I am glad maybe he will stay awake on this day of August the 10th change is still taking place at the church but it's slow and that's a good thing you never want to rush through things because if you do' then mistakes are made. Each time I go to the church it looks better and one of these days I will volunteer to paint the kids room where they play just an act of kindness that I feel inside. Saturday morning' and I don't pay much attention to the out side world except catching the news once and a while and even then there is so much violence that I usually shut it off, but also I know there has to be some good things happening it's just that the news would rather report on the bad things because it seams to sell more and money is their big goal. There is someone going to a rehab here but I didn't catch who it was but I have a feeling who ever it is they might need help afterwards and I will be here for them should the opportunity arise, in the beginning is the hardest as some places attack the addiction I aproch it with the mind set that it can be over came as a problem by finding out what caused it.

As with me and alcohol it was a lack of self worth being brought up without getting to live a child hood as we are children we always want to be like our parents. But if they are alcoholics then we can end up the same way and when we get older we take on that curse because it worked for our parents, or so we thought. As children in the learning stages of life we learn from our parents mostly (Why) because that's where we spend most of our time is with them, school is just a small part of a childs life and if they are confused when going then learning is harder as with me I never did feel like I fitted in. It was like I took all the problems from home with me and if you cant figure them out then your confused so learning takes a back seat to the problems and the mind wont let you go there, I remember that I couldn't wait to get out of school because the other took president to my learning. One time a teacher came to the house and toold my mom that she thought I was an exceptional student except for my concentration and she wanted to help me but by then I had lost my intrest in learning because of the alcohol and girls that had come into my life they seamed more important to me with the mind of a child you can't focus anyway because you live in the now but now that I'm older those things done seam to cause the problems they did back then. Now I have the time to strengthen that part of the mind that became so weak as a youth living in the now is a lot different then today when a week is like a day and my youth is gone, but if I could of learned back then. Then things would have been different, not saying the addiction wouldn't of still happened but I would have been a little smarter and maybe I could of used longer words to say the same things

I'm saying today, which to me would be pointless because most addicts only have a limited education. Simple words seam to work the best for simple situations, even in bible school the long words couldn't be understood by many that went to high school or collage and to me that just causes more problems because you spent a lot of time trying to figure out what the long words mean. My life is a true testament that addiction can be over come by the wanting of the human spirit and the searching for the answers of why they wanted that life in the first place wither it's by choice or just being a product of their up bringing. No one sets out to be an alcoholic but it can bring relief to troubled times or so a person thinks, many times the curse is not carried by the parents but it was let in by a generation before them and it can lay in waiting for that weak person that comes down the line. Also medical conditions can cause it to show it's self and as we all know they have meds that can stop pain of all kind, my friend Mark takes intrest in my life as I talk about how I over came many of the addictions that intered my life. Addiction is something that will break through a wall if we have built it in our lives but the sad things is that when you get straight that wall goes back up, so what do we do? With a straight mind we need to tear that wall down brick by brick so it cant be put up again. And by doing this it frees you from that excuse that you can't do this or that, in this fight for life you have to have God in your corner there is no if or but's about it, for atheists. It can be a tree or something they can see until they become stronger but in the end it's God who helps you through this fight for life and denial doesn't help it just confuses you, some are brought up to not believe in God but that is also a product of teaching by parents or significant other with a grudge or quirrel against God.

In my learning there was only God who pulled me through no human had anything to do with my surviving the fall of my world, as a matter of fact people said I would die long ago but as usual they were wrong and I'm writing this here today. But learning everything over again was hard especially rebuilding your life as with me learning to walk again was hard because everything was destroyed, one thing they say is true you have to use your knees before you can walk and even your butt from time to time. In the early days they called me scooter because I had to scoot across the floor as I had no use of my legs and even then they said I would never walk as a matter of fact I didn't think I would either, but He had bigger plans for me and what He sets into motion no man can stop. It was hard getting out of bed and ploping down on the floor thank goodness for floors or I would have been scooting around in the dirt and it was at this time that I started to learn patients, which helped in many ways especially later when I started to take care of other people I guess it was my way of thanking Him for his help during this trying time in my life. I never asked for anything in return and I think that was also my way of saying thanks and it gave me many years to try and get it right this time. As for tears there were an ocean of them but they subsided as most tears do and I moved on to fight more battles that were a head of me, and that's when I learned that God wont put a mountain in front of you that you can't climb. And each time I climbed it I became stronger in faith and in love for God, as for people they came and they went as the wind that blows a storm in during the winter, as fast as they showed up they were gone to never return leaving beind my strenght even stronger then before driving me to not want to be like them.

I believe my success was in doing something they couldn't do as they left with their world falling apart, they even asked if I would help them out by doing drugs just once more and I replied not on your life. That's when I asked God to step in and make them go away because I wasn't strong enough to do it at that time and He did. But I didn't see it until a friend pointed it out to me I hadn't seen him in a while, but I had went to church with him a time or two his name was Leroy the same as my son's name. We had done drugs together but I was trying to change and I still don't know why he stopped by that day, earlier in the year I had been so broke that I had to borrow some pants from him and he went to get a pair of his little brothers so I could go to church for the first time with him and we had a good time then it stoped when he didn't return. Come to find out he had gotten deeper into the drugs and ended up in a treatment center for alcohol and boy he looked not so good, he told me about meeting a girl and then things started to fall apart as they fought about things like money and such and of course the drugs and alcohol. He had a good job but I think he messed that up also he was a welder and traveled to other states to fix things in grain bins, my land' he made good money but spent it just as fast on the curse. I don't know what became of Leroy but I hope he found his way out of the darkness and who knows maybe one day we might see each other again if he is still alive and made it into the light, I remember making a will a long time ago but it got lost. Which it isn't any good any longer as at that time I didn't know which way my life was going to go, that's how scared I was back then the not knowing was really hard because everything was so messed up inside my thinking among other things wasn't right but still God brought me through and healed what needed to be healed. It took almost a deck aid before I could become rational and try to figure out things but the experience really helped in many ways. It was like trying to fit pieces of a puzle together that had somehow got lost by children and I had to find the pieces before I could start, but I believe there was a reason for this to take place and it made me who I am today a person who loves God more then I could love a human being. Although it would be nice to have a companion to go through life with so I can feel human love once more, bring the right person into my life Lord a person I can love and grow old with that one who complements me as a person and I complement them. I know there has to be such a person here somewhere lord, help me find her. Sunday morning' yesterday afternoon was different as I felt like talking for once and I talked about how taking prayer out of schools has hurt us in some ways that and the people who burnt churches back in 2005. I don't know why that came up but it did and I got it off my chest, so much change but some in the wrong direction. We put away some things that came in and I got Randy some hangers for his clothes, she said she couldn't understand how one women had enough power to stop such a thing and then I came off with her being an atheist.

Still I don't understand how one person could do so much damage it had never been a thing that I my self would get into but it intreaged me for some reason. Politicts has never been something I have gotten into but still some things make me wonder, these are things my family tried to protect us kids from when we were young and I'm glad that they did. For they are people I will never understand trying to fit in with the rich as my beliefs are that they really run this country and not presidents, they are the ones that do the dirty work for those who really run the country. Enough of that crap. I feel something is going to happen in the near future while listening to others I picked up on that someone might be needing help after treatment and I hope it comes my way, if it's who I think it is I will be glad to try and help them alcohol and drug addiction is the same in many ways but what others have to realize it that they are both drugs. Just because the federal government made one legal by loosing faith doesn't change things, when they should have been at their strongest point they droped the ball you might say and gave into making alcohol legal because the rich wanted it done. Yesterday was nice out side and I expect today will be the same with the lower tempatures but still I have to make sure that the church is cool for my brothers and sisters and get things folded for service, I cant see out side yet but I think we might have gotten a sprinkel or two which will be good for the grass.

Poor little brother got up to early yesterday and you could tell it by his sleepyness through the day he doesn't seam quite there when he doesn't sleep right, but all in all he was fun to be around. We made hamburgers for supper as they are easy to fix and they are fast to make. It's the simple things that bring us together and loving this town really helps, I haven't heard anything from Leroy yet about the tree in my yard but I'm sure he will get to me when he gets a chance if not then I will have to hire someone to cut it down which I really don't want to do because they make such a mess out of things. And it takes months to clean it up when they leave things laying on the ground, around here there is no where to take things to burn unless you know someone that has some land that you can burn trash on. And that's a hard thing to get done, as I glanced out the kitchen window I could tell that we got some rain and it might even be raining now as the puddles fill up in the street this lets me know that I will have to wash my car again in the next couple of days this winter might be a cold one compaired to last year in 2011 we didn't hardly get any snow but this year might make up for it and then next year might be even better then this year harvest wise, this community depends on the crops to make it better each year and I hope for a good year this coming year one that super seeds what we have gotten so far this year. But I also know that He takes care of our needs and we don't need to worry like we do, but I guess that's a part of being human the worry that is. Through my time here things have become a part of me and my friends become closer with each passing week and month they seam to trust me and that's a good thing because a lot of what they tell me I keep to my self, I can still remember some of my mom's friends when I was young and they would come over for coffee and go shopping together, but one person that stands out is Owna and they would go out for drinks. It seamed that pop's was always in the picture even in the younger years when we were very young but by the end of his life he couldn't hardly remember mom, or else he just didn't want to talk about it. He was a great man and did his best to provide for mom and us kids and in a way it must have been hard on him because we were troublesome kids with not much direction and we always had to have the alcohol in the house but mostly to impress our friends, for us to get a beer was like other kids getting a pop except we never ran out of it and we never lived far from a place we could get it. If we woke in the morning and had a hang over it was always there in the frig so we wouldn't get angry like most alcoholics do when they don't have what they need, this was everyday life to us from as far back as eight years old but it wasn't that easy to get at that age we had to sneek it but still not a normal up bringing. I recall always having gum to kill the smell of beer when I would go somewhere but surely they could tell the normal people that is, it was like we had our own little circle of friends and most of the parents were alcoholics so we didn't have to hide it from them because they too smelled of it. And they couldn't tell unless they got right in front of your face which never happened, could they see what was unfoling and if so why didn't they try to change it? Maybe they thought it wasn't their place but only the parents, sitting up with mom on certain nighs she would sing to me and the records and I believe this is how she let her sorrow go so she could go on with life as she knew it.

Back then looking back it was in the early stages of the curse and she could of stopped it but why didn't she? I would of like to of been able to understand her sorrows but I was too young, she could of shared what was going on but she must have know it would be too big a burden for a child to handle. But still we remained close while I was around her and even when she got sick it didn't take long for me to come to her, I felt it was the least I could do for the person that gave birth to me. O she could of done like other mothers do today and aborted me but she didn't and to me that is a great gift, because she knew she would have to leave her home town of Duluth and go somewhere else. That and if she had gave me up then my little brother might not have been born because getting an abortion back then was dangerous they didn't have it perfected like they do these days. I wish I had more pictures of her when she taught bible school before everything happened I know that had to of been a better life then she ended up with or was it? A lot of young people rebel when they are brought up in a strict home I cant imagine trying to messure up to her brother the priest and if she did try! it would have messed her up. None of us have the answers to why things happen the way they do but I do know that God brought me into this world for great things, if nothing else but to show people that change is possible. I am a product of the one any only true creator of the world and universe and nothing can change that part of my life.

Always when I talk it's about something I'm interested in and I'm a good listener but mostly I observe and that's something I didn't always do, or I did. And just didn't notice it until I was reborn, never was much of a talker but the taking in of things has made me wiser then my years. Giving hope to others is a great feeling because before it starts you can see the blankness in their eyes, and when they get the message then you can also see the change that glimmer of hope that can change everything. Especially in children as their world lights up, that wanting to learn more like they are getting fed for the first time. I still recall the old women that I made pot holders with around the age of seven years and how her eyes lit up when I made the first sale you would of thought I gave her the world, but it was just an act of kindness to help her in her time of need did He send me there that day or was it curiosity of a child? Either way it did a great thing for her the little ole lady that made a difference in my life. And although I had forgotten it for most of my life it returned to show that it was an important act on my part of life, doing good for others seams to have always been an important tool and in time it"s usually returned even if the other person has left this world and this can only be done by the super natural because this is reality and God is the super natural. It says He is not of this world and if this is true then we can only be with His in the super natural which means we too will join Him in that place He chooses for us. By no means do I have the answers but the search is interesting as we go through this life He created for us as people, my life has been by no means easy but I have persevered and came out on top and through it all I have stayed a pretty good person. It's afternoon and things were intresting in church as some people came to preach the word of God along with pastor Kathy, as for the rain it wasn't much but it did a little good for the grass. And by tomorrow the grass will be greener the rest of the day will be a kick back day as most Sundays are, taking it easy as that's what we are told to do on this day. Then tomorrow will start a new week and we will find other things to do. But we wont know what that will be until it gets here no two days are the same in this life and we make the best out of each one, through the years of addiction there were many times that I lost a year and didn't know where it went theist loosing many things but the loosing of things that got me in into that world was the greatest loss because most of my life was forgotten until I took that life back, it was like all or most of my memories were forgotten trying to survive in that place I now call hell. Monday morning' I slept pretty well during the night until earlier when a dream woke me and for the life of me I cant remember what it was all about. Like I have said before the wanting to be like your parents isn't always a good thing , but there is exceptions to that rule. Kids minds live for today or think for today not going past the day they are in unless a parent promises to take them somewhere and then it can extend into the next day but never further then that. When my parents would take us to the lake we were always excited and invited friends if their parents would let them go, and my sister always got her way along with Rod being they were older. We had some exciting times as we camped in those tents and mom and dad were right there with us except when dad had to go to work, I never knew how much money he made but at that time he must have done very well driving 200 miles a day for the summer back and forth from big bear mountain to Los Angeles.

This was before the accident with the boys and then it ended after that and we knew a bad turn had happened, mom being who she was, was a person who made sure we always had food to eat and she survived in her own way without us knowing the particulars. But we were always taken care of, my sisters days of being spoiled were about over then and that good life wasn't there any longer. I do recall mom going back to work in the emergency room at the hospital trying to save the home but even with that it didn't seam to work and I remember the bank coming and getting things like one of our cars and the furniture but as fast as they hauled it out more came in the back door as they tried their best too hold on. Other then that my memories are a blank because I don't reall the time when we moved, the hospitals must have gotten rich back then taking peoples homes but I guess they had to do what they did to survive. From then on we rented the places we lived in but for some reason dad couldn't hold a job and it wasn't long before we ended up out in the cold. Maybe that's why they took us camping most of our lives when we were young, my self I didn't care for it but Rod must have because even today he lives on the lake in a camper with his wife and his kids are not far away. When I went to visit a few years ago they asked if I wanted to move there and of course I told them that I didn't, by this time I had my house and I wouldn't leave it for nothing especially to go and live in the heat there. I would have had to give up all that I had worked for and there is nothing worth that, I believe Courtland could grow but they need to put in more houses and not fancy houses either just ones that people could afford to either rent or buy, I see more people wanting to get away from the big cities and live the country life which Courtland would be a great place for that especially if they can get more jobs here.

As for my self I don't know what the job situation is but I do know mine is solid and the schools are out of this world here, it's something you wont find anywhere else in the heart land the teachers really care about the students and want them to excell in all that they do. In our church we have a few retired teachers and they taught here for many years getting the kids ready for life, and some leave while others come back to live out their lives here. I guess there are not too many people like me that prefer this life to the other but then again I'm not like other people, I have seen many of the children that have left and then come back during celebrations and if you didn't know their parents you might not put the two together one women has three girls and everyone of them looked like their mother meaning the father didn't dominate when it came to looks but boy are they beautiful like their mother. Do we really go back to where we were conceived to maybe find something that might not be in our lives that question I can't answer, but I do know we travel to try and find the right place for us. Just look where I ended up in a place that is really giving and full of love my life will remain here and I know my friends will support my final destanation of setteling here in Courtland. For me I can't see living in low income housing where you throw your money away each month but if they had some here the money would be used to build the town stronger and better then ever, and they wouldn't be places that are 50 and 60 years old. They have low income apartments here but even with that they are small and there are so many living there I almost moved into them but if I had I would have had nothing and lets face it I wanted my own home, and it doesn't matter how many years it takes to pay it off because in the end I know it's going to be. or is mine, my little piece of heaven right here on earth. There is a kid that races around here and his dad owns the shop down the road you can tell he is spoiled because he always has his car or truck in his dad's shop for one thing or another and the cops are at his house from time to time. He works at true value so I know he doesn't make much and those hot vehicles have to cost a lot to keep up, good thing his father sells tires because he burns them off quite a bit. The other machanic built his shop from the ground up and he does great business working on everything from farm equipment to cars and trucks. He used to or still does work for Womack Ford and he sells cars for them, the older people trust him and he gets cars for them making sure they are in good shape so they will last a long time this is a great thing he does to help his fellow neighbor. It seams we all depend on someone for our safety when it comes to a vehical because it a part of life here in the heart land without one you are stranded and that's not a good place to be. When I moved here I was frightened all the time but then after a year or so I seamed to calm down but it must have been the newness of the place, and even traveling I was scared for some reason but that part I never figured out. O well we all go through change and it can be that way sometimes especially changing after addiction when new feelings come into the picture.

Going through life not feeling the full force of something can frighten anyone, but with time it all passes and you become a new person, brand new. To start things over again even seeing old friends can bring you joy when you haven't seen them in many years, like with Dennie and Bob people will hear about them running into us for sometime until they excitement wares off, and then things will return back to normal or until we see them again either here or in Kearney. In the future I would like to invite them down for a barbecue just them and I think we might have a good ole time talking about years passed and how we turned out in these later years as no one expected me to still be alive after the destruction. It just goes to show that we don't know what the out come of our lives will be that's something better left up to God, because we can feel death and it doesn't happen until He feels it's time. Misconceptions are always happening with us as people, we think one thing and it's just the opiset but good seams to follow all that God does in our lives there I was frightened like a little kid at my age scard of my own shaddow and He brought me through it to become stronger and better then ever. (How great thou are) the one that hold us when it's dark and becomes our light when we need to see, even the times I couldn't walk during the night have seemed to fade from my life like the addiction that once controlled me. Tuesday morning' in the days when I was fighting the addiction and people who didn't want me to stop it became really hard to do both so I didn't have any choice but to ask God for help and behold He was there. Scoon as I focused on the addiction and destroying it it was like the other problem was gone and for some reason even today I cant remember their names not that I would want to.

In that world you are better not to remember names I recall one time when a guy came over and he was mad at one of my brothers because they did something to him and he was out for blood, the guy tried to show him how he did him wrong but he couldn't see it from the brain damage that the drugs caused so I reasoned with him and then he went away it's strange how you have to save someone when your in that dark place not knowing if the other person will turn on you too but he didn't and that was that. If you cant communicate with someone when their hight then in that world you don't last long, I could tell that the guy came from money because of his car but later he would loose that also it was a Jag-Wire which cost a lot of money in the little time that we talked he said he liked me but didn't want anything to do with my brother as they couldn't really tell between right and wrong it was like his mind became unwired, and it was later that they both went to prison. I recall a cop coming over one time because my brother wanted me and pop's to bail him out of jail and the officer told me to leave him in there, his words were you have tried to help them both and it hasn't done any good so let him sit. Roger you have come a long ways don't let them destroy what you have left, but being blood I felt obligated to help if I could but I put a stipulation on the bond that I could pull it if trouble started and later it did so back to jail he went. And God took them out of my life also so I could have time to recover because if it was up to them I never would of, they seamed to like that place they could take control of when ever they wanted to. And being crippled at the time didn't help matters any because I was no match for them in that condition, then eight years later I was moved by the spirit to help little brother and God brought him back into my life once more, it was a great battle in my mind wanting to and then not wanting to but God is persistent and then the song came on brotherly love. I had listened to the recording many times but never heard that song being it was number 5 on the C.D. And it brought tears to my eyes and I had to get him out if it was possible. And low and behold within a year he came to live with me but this time things would be different I wouldn't have both of them around just the one, my little brother. My other brother was a manipulator and took advantage of people which isn't a good thing to do but I guess that's how he survived being locked up most of his life and he never did come to turms with that he did it to him self. It's garbage day so I have to get the trash taken out this morning, it's already the 14th of the month and half of it is gone tomorrow Antique road show is on at 4:00 in the morning so I will watch that as I get excited when I see the old things and there value. The years have taught me many things but the most valued was to always be your self, be true to your self and then everything else will fall into place many may even want some of what you have when they see change. The people whoo used to come over at two or three in the mornings faded off as things started to change but there was always Valerie that still stoped by and that also had to change, we met one night long ago and I had always cared for her but I also seen how she treated her boy friends and that wasn't good as she preached about their addictions and not her own.

I once thought we might get together but I later learned that He was showing me something that I shouldn't be with someone like her even if my horemoans were telling me different so I walked away. She has been with many men and they have either left her or passed away two have passed in the last few years and she went back to the one who dumped her, thinking she can save him. Wednesday morning' and I read a little last night from the foundation searies learning the new things which will help in my walk with Him the father. And I absorb it a little at a time trying to live by the word of God, my understanding of things has always been different then others and maybe that's what has set me apart from other people but still I have my own way of doing things. I believe I'm an aquired taste by others but then I am happier then most but what they see I don't have a clue, trying to understand what's in the bible is sometimes hard but like I said I take it a little at a time not to destroy what I will learn. For the taking in of a grain of salt will do more good then trying to swallow the whole cube, the thrift store will be open today so I will go to work at 4:00 this afternoon and do my part to help. Also I went to take in the trash at the church and they have it set up for a funerial or some kind of gathering but I didn't see any cars there during the day, it must be within the next few days or so is all I can think. As money runs short we will have to cut back on going to town and then maybe thins will pick up as for my next pay day it's a ways down the road so I have to make do with what little I have left.

In a way it's like a challenge to see if I can make it but I know somehow it will all come to pass, as I learn to budget once again. They are saying it's supposed to get to 100 degrees today and I sure hope they are wrong because it's been so nice these last few days, not having pop's to take care of really hurts but I have faith that we will survive I have to maybe get another job but just a small one to help in things. As for the bills they haven't been a problem yet but I worry to much about those things I do know that other bills are coming and I pray that I can get them paid but you cant cross that bridge until it gets here. Going from having enough to just getting by is really different and if it wasn't for others then things would be a lot harder they seam to look after me in many ways. It says God will provide for us His people and I find that to be true as my friends help in any way they can, I learned that the people are the church a body of souls watching out for each other and they came through when pop's died taking care of everything and helping me out which none of my family did, I guess they have always been the ones that wanted to see if anything was left to them which nothing was so they didn't bother to show up. My family now is the church because they have shown me more love then my family has in 20 years the sepration of church and state is a body of people who do good things to help those in distress. What is today going to be like not even I can see three hours a head but I do know this day will be what I make it a day of peace and smiles, my land' it's only three in the morning and I have been up for a while now time for coffee. I know the harvest of the corn will be here shortly and then my eyes will swell shut during the night, as they bring it in. This is just part of living here and I seam to always make it through it no worse then before in life you have to give something to recive something and my home is what I recive by living here, that and good friends is all you really need to live in this world I thought my family would be closer by this time and I find that they are just as far apart today as back then but that's just my opinion on family matters, my days are still filled wih joy and I will survive no matter what as surely things could be a lot different then they are but Hey! Life has to be exciting right? My Antique road show will be on in a few minutes so I will watch it for an hour and see all the brilliant things they bring onto the show. It has become part of my week to see it when it comes on and it makes for a better day, I know there are many places that have antiques around here even houses down the road off the highway with their big sign's preserving the past as we move into a new age. Thursday morning' I started to read a new book and it was number one on the best sellers list, and reading it is a delight. It will be the first book I enjoyed reading I found it at the thrift store and brought it home to broaden my understanding of ligature and if I finish it, this will be the first book I have ever read that's a hard cover. Or any book except for the guide post and the bible but what I'm trying to do is see if it influences my life in any way" not many things have caught my attention like this book has. It's almost like I can speed read it and it opens channels that I didn't know where there, I even read a little to my friend that was working with me. And it was so different then anything I have taken into my mind before so I will keep reading it. In just two hours I read almost 50 pages which to me is a lot. The wind is blowing this morning and we are hoping for rainso we will see what happens, my neighbor came into the thrift store and they are going to start to work on building their home just down the alley this will bring our population up by two more people and a dog, not counting the dog of course. They seam like nice people and it will be nice to get to know them, my world is shaped by where I live and I'm glad that I'm here.

Jan at the church said they are havinng a wedding on Saturday so I will have to clean up before Sunday morning that's my job, to make sure everything is done just right and cleaned so we can have service on my favorite day of the week. Church seamd to be my life now and in time you never know what will happen only God knows all the answers not us as humans. Little brother has been dreaming lately and he yells out but he never remembers his dreams, except that they are there" and they are strange. I cant tell about my dreams any more as if I have them they are not leaving any memories of them, going through life trying to recall thing that have happened is hard sometimes because it isn't all cut and dry, a memory here and one there when He allows them to come to light. Bringing about change in some areas, not bad change but good and then I go on with my day. In my world there is many things I don't understand but then we all have that in our lives some more then others we weren't meant to live here for ever this is a testing place or a place that gets us ready for the longer life we will live in heaven, some people think they have all the answers but not me all I have is what He gives me and that's good enough for me and who knows what the future holds for any of us? I do know that material things is something given by God as a loan because really you cant take it with you when you die. Even the ground I call my home is a gift from the father and one day someone else will reside here long after I am gone for in our spiritual bodies we will have no use for what is here, many believe we will reside here for ever and if that was so then these bodys would be needed but that isn't the case.

It says we were created for God's joy as everything else was here on earth, even the birds and ant's. he wants us to enjoy things like having fun and even sex that what we were created for to enjoy life and so he can enjoy us we are all good in the eyes of the lord. He made me to be me,, and you to be your self all things were created for his pleasure even Jesus but you cant get to God without loving Jesus Christ his only begotten son who died for our sins. I also find it exciting that He takes pleasure in every aspect of our lives we were created to please God and this book is teaching me that by explaining things I can understand , I have never gotten joy out of reading before but I am on this day and hopefully many more. When something is made so I can understand it I take it as a sign that I'm supposed to read it,, as I don't find any confusion in it and it brings joy to my unnderstanding…. Friday morning and I slept pretty good except for the times I had to get up, the mornings have been cool and they started building just down the road. My land' they have hills 10 feet high, from diging the basement so you know they will have to haul a lot of dirt away. The people are in their golden years so I believe this will be their home from now on, and I guess they have also traveled to get here but from where I don't really know, right now they live in a stream line camper which I know must have been expensive but at their age just putting down roots is a great thing or at least it would be for me. Yes Courtland is growing and there are nice people moving in, the lot they bought is a good one and it will exist for many years to come. Little brother is having trouble with some papers and I don't understand them so we will have to see if we can take another rought of taking care of this problem paper work I hate it and will never understand it because my mind wasn't programmed to mess with such things I guess that's why they have beek keepers for just that. But I cant let it get me down I had to turn on the air-conditioning during the night to stop from sweating as it's getting to be that time of year when the weather is changing. Good ole seasons that come each year, bringing change to the world many times things come full circle but for the times that it doesn't there is left an opening to let things in and there not always good like this paper work just a mess and I don't know why they waited 10 years to bring these things onto me. It should be them that do this mind blowing crap, but again I wont let it get me down. Tomorrow is the wedding and the two love birds will be joined in marriage to spend their lives together and make new children for this world, from what I gathered they have been together for some time now and they will go to another country to live for a while he works for N.C.I.S. A branch of the service.

I have never met the people but their families have lived in these parts for quite some time, many of the families around here have children in the service and they are proud of that. I still remember wanting to be in the service back when I was young but things didn't work out and I just wondered for many years lack of education is what stopped me but that didn't get me down I went on to have two great children that now have children of their own I just hope they never have to fight. It's the end to another week and the beginning of another weekend, the birds will be siinging here in a little bit and I will enjoy the music. It says God knows our mind so He must know that I writing this here today and I find it intresting that he lets us make the mistakes we do but I also know when I watch a good movie it trigers something inside a wanting or needing to live for ever, why are we wired to live for ever? They say it's in our D.N.A. The wanting to go on and survive at all cost's deep inside the mind that place we don't visit very oftend in that sleep realm where the mind isn't awake or working that we know of. Saturday morning' the day will be one of relaxation and what ever else comes along, I finished the day yesterday by washing my car and now it looks as good as ever. It's hard to keep a car clean when the car wash is still broke but maybe in this that will be fixed many people see me washing my car but it onlt takes a gallon of water or less and boy dies it shine viniger is the best thing to use because it cuts the dirt, that and a couple of rags. It gets to my arms though and later I can hardly move them but like they say no pain no gain.

Little brother needs to do something during the day so he doesn't get so board but he uses his back for an excuse, as for my self I can only be idle for so long and then I have to get up and do something. I heard him on the phone talking to Stacy and then saying 2003 so I took it as they were talking about my car as she might be curious about it, when we lived together she had to always know everything and she is still the same today. Yesterday I showed Randy a picture of her on face-book because he hadn't seen her in many years and I have to say that for her age she looks much older then she is the cancer has broken her down that and not eating, she cant weigh over 90 pounds but still she loves her grand babys and is close by Shannon. Will I ever find love again yes I think I will but it will take time as all good things do the picture of my grand bably was very nice with their grandma on face book. The social network where people stay in touch by placing pictures and notes to loved ones but mostly I use it for getting the message out by putting my published letters on there letting people know that help is always just a click away. My journey is still going to be a long one as each year passes, they say we are here for a short time to somehow get it right to be prepaired for the next life the one that we will spend eternity in. today is the 18th and the month is winding down, what makes some of us want to talk about our lives through writing? To me it tells a story and there is nothing better then a good story, it lets a person see that their life isn't so bad and that adversity is everywhere even in the small parts of the country. And with some who loose hope it can egnite that within them and give them the drive to go on or move forward, my self I like my story because many haven't gone through a lot of what I have. And it lets them know that it's alright to struggle when that time presents it's self it's a part of life and we all go through it, when I feel a tear about to fall I never try to stop it because it's a thing that helps with our emotions. Is it a good thing or bad? In my books it really doesn't matter but I like tears of joy. Those feelings which can bring people together and hold them tight, Sunday mornig' and I will go early to get things ready for service, they cleaned up most of it after the wedding but it needs my touches. I don't know what they threw for rice but we will see weddings unlike funerals are a time when the family unit starts out so really it's the beginning instead of the end of life. next will come the children and with great teaching they will become a part of the community sometime in their lives, but we will see as some don't come back and live out their lives here in Courtland but in those big cities or other countries. If they all came back then Courtland would be really big Imagine knowing three hundred people that rairly happens in a persons life where I came from and we started out as a family of five, the only one who had the same amount of kids was Rod and I'm not sure what the number of grand kids there is in his family. With me and Randy we only had two kids but I have five grand babys through my children so that should leave Rod with over ten, as for Rick he also had two but then another poped up after 20 years of fooling around with some women and she seams nice. When I first heard of her I thought she might give him the courage to over come his addiction but apparently not, as I hear things through the grape vine. I wish him the best in his endeavors and hope that he can too one day find his way out of the darkness. The church is my life now days and I do my best when it comes to taking care of the things I need to, for my life is so different now and I pray that goodness followes me all the days of my life.

The day is going to be a day as we pary and give thanks to god for what we have and I ask him for the knowledge to do the things I have never done before, for this should open a door to knowledge I'm trying to get little brother a waver on something and I pray that it comes through without a hitch so we can move forward and stop this mess of things that took place ten years ago. If others were around then they would know what to do but this is my first time so we will see, the doing of things which are new to us gives us more of an education in the learning department and then they leave and things go to another stage. I will go to church early this morning so maybe I can get back and watch Joel Olsteen on television at 7:00 I seam to really enjoy him but also I have missed his sermans for the last few weeks by just not being around the television you have to do what you have to do and pray for things to turn out ok' I got the church cleaned this morning by going in at five and working until 8:00 Am. I love getting up early so I can get things done and then have the rest of the day to my self, I was talking to John and told him about going in at that hour and he said now I know your nuts so funny. We then traveled to the dollar store for some things we needed in Belleville and then back home to watch Armageddon which is a good movie, although things happen slow around here it's just fast enough for me at my age. It's awesome to live where I do in a place where people really love their neighbor and it's not a bunch of hype. Monday morning' and it nice to hear the train as it brings in rail cars this morning this is the first timei have heard them in quite some time, yesterday the lady's has more of them then us men but that's normal seeing they are women. One told me that it was cold in the church so I shut off the fan in the over flow room and then everything was ok' it can be hard to please everyone but I try.

During the time I was in church Randy checked the mail and title to my old car was there so today I will take it to the car dealer and get that behind me so I can move on. As I don't like to leave things undone plus that way he wont call me again I know he has to of been worried by it taking so long but the computers are going through a change over and finely they got it right. During my reading period I read 80 pages and then had to take a break until my mind absorbs what I have read, it's strange how that happens it's like a flood of learning and then my mind needs a rest. Now I will see things differently by reading that book and going on that adventure. Is what it says true well it was written by a man so it's open to interpretation now the bible was written by God so we know it's true, but I still struggle with it sometimes and when that happens you need to put your understanding a side and wait for Him to help, the celebrations are behind us now like fun-day and the wedding but we made it through them both.... And I'm sure there will be more weddings here in the future or at least they are talking about them happening this year, I believe there are three more of them as the young people become one in that union. Marriage takes a lot of work and probably to much work for this ole bachelor living in my own created world where I don't have any one telling me what to do, the train is leaving now as it takes the loaded cars out to the big ole world and other companys make different things with the crops. As for the farmers, they will replant and go on with their lives it's like a chain the planting and then harvest to see where they stand at the end of things and if things are good they go on to repeat the season. Agriculture is the back bone of this state and it makes it what it is today and the farmers hope to have their children carrie it on when they get too old to do it. Some will return and others well it's up to them but more of our young people are coming back to pick up where their parents leave off, for what I gathered Courtland is a retirement town but they do have younger people here to take care of it and make sure things are running right, as for me I guess you could say I'm retired and my writing is my hobby to one day help others fighting the good fight of addiction but still life goes on and we do the best we can. I read about the man that made the movie of top-gun and he threw him self off a bridge and has now died what would make a person take their own life like that? Not happy I guess, even with all he had money doesn't seam to fill the the heart. He also done other movies like Beverly Hills cop two, even in the out side world with a lot of money happiness cant be bought. And with it' you can't find that thing you need, I don't think money buys happiness but it can make life a little easier so you can live longer but the real thing you need is to be close to God my walk with Him has has brought me further then I expected and the road isn't over yet for with each year comes change a better understanding of things in this world and even though we slow down our mind is still alert. It's about time for little brother to get up and face the day and we will travel to town and see my friend at reliable auto, Mark at the bank knows him as they went to school together back in the day.

It's always good to have friends even if you have only known them for a short time it can later lead to a life long friendship. Tuesday morning' and yesterday I got the title to the guy from Belleville so now he should be happy and he asked how my car was running and I told him fine. But the test will come this winter and once that's over then I will really know, Randy took out the trash last night so it's ready for them to pick it up and all I have to do is get it out at the church. On Monday they were pouring the floor of the basement in the new house that will go up just kiddy corner from us and next will be the walls, this house will be the newest one built here in Courtland as all the others were done long ago. I still can't get over how big the electric bill was at O.B's house being only built maybe ten years ago by Hud, the struggles we go through are not much compaired to his back in K town' just the other day I wrote an old friend that still lives in K town and he is doing fine his name is Rick and we used to hang out together back in the dark days when addiction had a hold on my life. But now it seams he has changed his life also he had always's been a good person it was just at that time when the addictions seamed more important then anything else. It's like we all go through that stage but with love and hope we seam to come through it and then make our selves stronger as we heal, he seamed excited to hear from me when I wrote him and he wrote back maybe in time we will see each other again if that's God's will'" there are many that have followed my lead and took their lives back and it will be intresting to see if they make it all the way home. To that place where the addiction doesn't live any longer, it wasn't hard to find him on face book as many of my friends are on there maybe hoping for me to write them once again.

He asked if I was still in Kansas and I wrote and told him yes, and that little brother was with me here in the sunflower state. I have to check my mail on face book later to see if he wrote back but I'm sure he did it's just that I don't get on there very oftend, I feel another chapter coming or change as I call it but it's good change and not the bad. I will be glad when these papers get filled out and they are sent back to where they belong closeing but another pain in my side so we can move on. The day is going to be another good one as we move closer to fall and the temp's cool down, things are simple here in the heart land but every now and then my peace gets messed up by the government so I hope in time that it will all get straightened out so the worring can go somewhere else. Wednesday morning' or hump day as many say it's hard to wake up on this day but in time it will pass, like all other days. I know each day is different because sometimes the words come easy and then on other days not so much, but things are still good as we get closer to little brothers operation on the 11th of next month I'm hoping that he will get better after this is taken care of and then there will be no excuses for him not to do some work, it's been over a year since he came to live with me and even though we have had our up's and downs we get along pretty good, I'm amazed to how antiques seam to stand the test of time and many look as good today as they did when they were created. They seam to be a part of our history and will live on for many more years to come. Just the price of the things has increased 100 fold and sometimes even more, things here in Courtland have given me hope that one day a circle will be completed the circle of life and how things change when each day is different I go to help out at the thrift store this afternoon and each day of working there is also different while people bring in things to help others that might have it a little harder then they do. Thursday mrning' the 23rd and progress is coming with the home down the street, there were a few people working over there as they poured more of the basement to get it ready for building also the thrift store was fun as I got some more reading in but it seams I'm drawn to religious books and not so much of the others, it's like my mind is learing the things it couldn't just a few years back but I find delight in the stories. Still it says te greatest learning would come from God's word meaning the bible but I can only take in so much before I have to stop and give my self a break I have asked for many things but know it will take time before it gets here and then maybe some change will accure in the past I have always gotten what I have asked for but I use caution when I ask for such things not wanting things to get worse or further in debt. I still can't tell what others see, when they see me but I'm sure in time it will be brought to light. I worked with another person from my church that I hadn't worked with before and we laughed and had a good ole time but most of the time was spent reading and then Beverly came over and we had a few more laughs before closeing and then I came home and ate before going to bed. The chicken I made before going to work must have been good because Randy ate most of it so I had a couple of pieces now wanting to get my guts up set while I slept.

Thinking back I know now that mom teaching me to cook has helped in many ways not having to go out to eat all the time has brought me closer to my family and friends that are here and the ones that have passed away. I guess it built a bond between us, yesterday I went and finished at the church and now some other things have come up like getting the stains out of the floor where something was drug across it this is where the scrubber will come in handy so I can get a big area at a time and get it over with. I waiting on the 3rd to get carpet cleaner so I can finish my carpet for the winter but all things in good time as the lord put's it. My friend asked one day if I had always been close to God and I told him not at first but maybe I was closer then I thought as He watched over me and brought me to where I needed to be. In the city I was never my self because others invaided my space and getting to know who you are is important but I still feel there is something bigger in my future something inside is trying to emerge and I don't know what it is yet, but I'm sure when it comes out there will be a change in things as I know it and I'm not afraid of it because it has to be something good. There is a power in the name of Jesus, there is a strength in the name of Jesus, there is forgiveness in the name of Jesus. And that's why we are forgiven in the name of Jesus, he has loved us before we even realized it and He blessed us before we even knew it. Over two thousand years ago the father sent him here so we could be saved knowing that his son would have to die to correct the things we done wrong for one mans curse was passed down and it took a pure soul to take back the curse, it couldn't be done by a human because we are not pure but He did send his son.

I take delight in knowing that he would die for us his children as a lot of us would die for their's, and many hope that they too will have their children out live them. As I hope mine out live me, in this world there are dreamers and there are dream breakers the ones that destroy the dreams of others and although this happens it should be stopped. The mind of a child is not corrupted by this world until they start to grow but while in their little world they dream of all kinds of things and if given the chance they can make those dreams come true, but addiction will try to stop them in their walk of life clouding the mind with things that shouldn't be there. But for those who fall into that world they become lost, through my experience there is one way to find your way back to the real world. And that is threw God finding you and He will do that when the time is right, through our travels we don't know how things will turn out but God knows it all even in our darkest hours He sees a way to bring us to where we need to be as He gets us ready for our journey to eternal life. What I write about is my beliefs and my opinion of how He influenced my life by taking me by the hand and guiding me even when walking was out of the question but with all that He does in time everything is possible through Him our lord and savior. Our rationalizing; doesn't always work in His world of mystery in the supernatural where He makes the impossible possible, when we see no way out of something it's easy for Him to make things clear for us. And if we trust and love him then there isn't anything we can't do given some of His power, it is written that He wants us too be close to Him and have a personal connection better then what we have with a very close friend. But we have to find the connecion through our faith and belief in the supernatural and being through what I have been through I find that He is my bestest of friends, always there when I needed him even in that dark place He never left me even though I could never see it at the time. For now days the tears that I once shed are gone and replaced by joy and understanding not full understanding but in part enough to know that He will always be there for me to help me when I need it, and even when I don't need it He is walking beside me in this world. Many times we laugh together as He also likes that to, as for talking to him I do talk more to him then I do people sometimes and that's ok' because He is my creator and my best friend. I wish more people knew Him better then they do but some shut them selves off and maybe because it's hard for them to grasp the reality that God does exist, well the day is about to start and my little buddy harley wants out to go potty. Yesterday I cleaned the floor at the church and gave part of it a good waxing to brighten it up some and really I had fun doing it and then it was back home, it strange how some things are a delight to do while others are not so much. Friday morning and we got some rain last night it had to of been quite a bit as I heard it coming down in buckets and the power must have gone off because the coffee pot was blinking. Maybe by tomorrow I can mow the lawn once again as my volinteer trees are starting to get a little taller, as for the rain it has stopped for the time being but they are calling for more to night according to the weather guy on the television. I read another 30 some pages in my book and it seams what it says makes since the wanting of God to be my friend, by this view point it seams He wants us all to be close to him and that's a good thing.

He must have adopted us before we were born it's just that I seamed to have gotten lost along the way in my journey and that when I fell into the darkness. I find that He has always been there it's just that when we get lost we louse that connection with him, but once again we can find it and move on with getting to know him it's sort of like when a child louses his or her way after leaving home if the parent did a good job they will stay in touch but if they get lost then the parent might not ever see them again. I have read about people who have left home to never be heard from again but this is usually by choice because something happened that made them want to be separated from what ever happened and then you hear about them 40 or 50 years later after the parents have gone from this earth, there was one women who lost touch with her family and then they found her after fifty or so years but it was only by death that they found out who she was because in her life she had stuck away almost a million dollard in her house and they didn't know who to give it to. And then there was a man that went through the same situation he lived like a hermet and dug out of trash cans to eat, but in the end he also didn't trust others and put him money in his house and they found checks that he never cashed from social security amounting up to thousands of dollars hundreds of thousands and they never found his family either. What made things so bad for them? Did war destroy the guys mind and he got lost also there are many reasons for people getting lost and not all of them have to do with addiction but usually in part there is some kind of mental illness and the drugs they have them on takes it's part in making them forget.

Even our dry period's have left us better off then a lot of people and I cant believe the people who have died because of mosquito bites in Texas but I sure hope they never come this way, my land' they would kill a lot more because my people here are old. As far as I know they have never found out how they attracted this disease but it is transferred when they bite you and boy it can make any person sick young or old, but I'm sure it hit's the old harder because their bodies are not as strong as they once were. Stagnet water brings them around so I make sure that there is no containers laying around that will gather the water, as for the house down the street progress is coming around and they opened up the house next door and started to do repairs on it. It has been empty for a couple of years now so the stinch has to be gotten out of it then with some work it could be liStacyble once again. Little brother was in a pretty good nood yesterday when I came back from working and his spirits were up, so much to be thankful for here in my town of dreams my mind is also clear today with nothing holding it back like on other mornings when it seams it's in a fog as I read the book (What on earth am I here for) I'm learning how to be a better part of the body of christ and as it points out we are all a part of each other as believers. Being a christen is being a part of something bigger then your self and I know now that's why I was sent here to learn these things. Just reading a few pages this morning has given me more understanding of what I should have learned in my younger years, but even so it's not to late to start learning even at my age. This will be the beginning of a new experience for me sort of like another chapter in my life as I learn more about the christen ways, the valuse or closeness is something you would of expected in your birth family but in many cases it's not there so this will be that learning experience that will make me better then I once was. The rain is falling once again and it's a delight to be getting it after the drought maybe now things will start to take off as God brings this to us in hope for the crops to get better, I do know that the next crop will be better as fall is on it's way and the fear of drought will diminish like the days of summer that have passed. Saturday and it's early like the many other mornings the rain fell a little more yesterday so not the ground should stay wet for a couple of days anyway. They got the car wash fixed or at least I think they did but still I will wash my car by hand for a while or until it's solid enough to drive on. I know Norman had to also be glad that it got fixed because it brings in money for him and his family, I havent seen him lately now like I used too as I think he is taking care of his wife being sick and all. I learned that my son lost his job because his girlfriend broke his ear durm and he couldn't go to work, their relationship sounds like the one I had with his mother it seams when he tries to get a head the women knocks them down so they can keep control. Control has always been an issue with his women.

Also Mark O'Brien called and the news is never much good' and it makes me glad that I moved away from K town, Kearney for short. As my life has changed so has my understanding of things that will never be again I feel my spirit growing the part that will last for ever in that place we will go later in life, as for my book I keep reading it in hope that I will come to find out things that I didn't know back in the early days of my life and I'm finding it very intresting the was God wants us to live and such we were created to help others in many ways and not shy away from the battels we will go through during this training period, but I do know that with a lot of what it says I do today so something good has come out of my life and I'm a vessel of the most high God, thought of way before I was born. I know none of us will ever be God but his likeness is in all of us it's just that a lot of people don't see this in them selves, live like you would like others to treat you and bring happiness to those you can. Obeying God lets you be transformed it's the holy spirit that brings change when you except God into your life, you are allowing change to take place and sometimes you don't even know it but God sees it. This is the mysteries that we sometimes don't understand, at the times when I feel change coming this is the spirit that moves in me as God brings chance to my life it's the fireing of suffering that brings in the gold of goodness.

My reading lets me understand some things for which I didn't know before, it's God who brings on change in our lives but we have to do our part as in taking that step forward. Even those who cant read can be brought to God by the supernatural, I have seen many people with disabilities in reading that have somehow became close to God and it's brought on by the holy spirit as God can see our limitations and knows how to work past them as nothing is impossible when He works through the supernatural. We as humans cant see how this is done but the spirit of God can do anything, even the things we cant comprehend. We are created to be like christ and according to the word we can do this but with it comes much commitment to learn these ways, through His love we as human beings can become a part of His family. Sunday morning' and I believe the rain has stopped for the time being, we did well yesterday at work and I met a few more people including the Spanish people and some others and they were all polite. You meet many people here and business was great these people I have never seen before and it's always nice to see a fresh face, one of the girls that came in was with child and she wasn't much more then a child her self but they were kind and then left. I used to get nervous being around people I didn't know but now that all has passed like the problems I once had in that dark place so long ago, it's funny in a way how some young people are in a hurry while others take their time and go on as if it doesn't bother them. I was asked to leave the church doors open so one women could get some coffee on before 10:00 this morning so I said I would, many years ago I used to watch movies about the people who lived out in the middle of no where like the Waltons and that's what these people remind me of, those hill people. Where you get to town only once a month and do your best to get all the things you need, with the many small towns around here it's hard to tell which one they came from. Maybe today I will get the lawn mowed so it looks better as it gets greener, it says that He knows the battles I have fought so I take it that He knows the ones that are here now and the ones coming as they build character and make us who we are according to it character is our strongest part as it teaches us patients and lord knows we need a lot of that in this life. My character is what people see in me and for the most part it's the best part of me it even goes on to say that others may see something different on the out side then I do and maybe one day I will ask what they see as sight is in the eye of the beholder, as for others I see many different walks of life and each one has their own story. I could tell that the family came from being poor but still you could see the love that they feel for each other two sisters and their mother, the baby was of Spanish decent and the mother white. I made the little guy smile, as he sat there quietly I like to do that sometimes and my smile seams to make them smile. The girl wasn't any bigger then a minute so she had to use our stroller to hall him around the store she said he weighed more then she did and I thought that was kind of funny, I really didn't understand the reason for the store but now I do as it's hard to make it in this world and you need every break you can get and the store provides that for the people who don't have a lot of money. I remember my mom going too the thrift stores, as we were growing up. And it was always good to go and see the things they had but mostly we got clothes and they were nice clothes, living in a tent back then we didn't need new clothes as they would of gotten destroyed by all the ruff housing we did. I really liked going fishing and finding my own hiding place where I could catch them, I recall one time catching a big bass' just under the boat dock and boy I got excited hauling that big fish up the bank and down the road as everyone asked where I caught it. But I never did tell them because it was my fishing place where I could be alone and then be excited when I caught one. We didn't have a boat like many of the other people but we made do with fishing off the shore, and then when I needed a change I would go to the streem and catch crawdads and later eat them or use them for bait to catch those big bass.

I recall meeting Mary' she lived Los Angeles and had come to lake catices with her parents she was a beautiful girl and we did a lot together, but holding hands was our past time as we would walk around the lake she was there for a couple of weeks and the moretime we spent together the closer we became. And it broke my heart when she had to leave but before our time was up together we had kissed and just cuddled in her parents camper it was puppy love back then and I knew when she left that I would never see her again and on that day we went swimming and played by the fill canal where the water came into the lake. I remember that time because mom drank wine and we snuck some to take with us, everyone thought my mother was cool because she wasn't as strict as their parents and she didn't mind if we had a sip of wine or a glass but that wine didn't tast very good but she was on a budget and it was the cheapest thing to drink.back then, today my mind is clear as I move forward into the day. It says that He knew how my life was going to turn out before I was born so now I know that He knew that I would have struggles and He knew that I would be here in Courtland at this time in my life. But why the secrets? All I can come up with is that this is just the beginning of what's to come, it says He wants us to be closer to people and learn to love as we were created for that purpose so we can become a part of His family. And it's always better to help others and that's why little brother is here among others that come into my life, giving and helping is one of the greatest things you can accomplish along with learning to be like Jesus. As for what we leaarn here will take a life time in these bodys but then we will shed them like the caterpillar does and our spirit will take over.

From the moth to a butterfly what a beautiful analogy sort of like going from a baby to an adult except with out all the heartache. If I'm perceiving this right' before I was born He knew that I would have to fight the addictions that I went through so that must mean he also knew that I would remember the accidents that accured which helped to bring me here and the not working out of Margret after my getting to this place, for God is love and He wants us to also love and make mistakes along the way. Living alone isn't what He wants so now I will find someone to spend time with and live happily ever after, I guess I got it wrong in that prospective but change is always possible there is someone! but I never got up the nerve to ask her so maybe I will work on that. The worst thing that can happen is that she would be married and then I would have to look else where, these things take time with me because I don't just give my heart to anyone they have to be compatible with me other wise I will shy off again or maybe not' only God knows that answer, and He can give me the guts to stumbel and then pick me up for that is His promas to us… Does it matter their religion? I don't think so. We laugh together and kid with each other so who knows mayby there could be something there' and she asked me to wash her car which I don't think she would ask just anyone, I did notice that she gets butterflies when she is around me and maybe that's a good sign I know it is when I get them. He says we are not meant to go through life alone and that's why He created the beautiful women. So we can have a partner in this life, the day is about to start and the birds will be singing in a little while to start their day also with a song, I have seen one or two of her kids and I believe they don't live far from here it's always good to be close to your friends and family it shows love and that it does exist. All I can do at this time is try and reach out and see if there are any ties that bind her to someone else, don't let me make a fool out of my self. Monday and it was warm last night I had a dream but for the likes of me I cant recall all of it and what I remember I won't say, probably because I don't care for the person. It's my day off and I should have slept in but I didn't breaking the chain that has been with me for like ever, I would need an alarm clock. My days are usually filled with doing something so we will have to see what happens after the sun comes up. I should clean up the church and get things back in order so they can have their meetings and things like that, it's their life also taking care of things that need to be taken care of. As for being in a hurry I'm not' at this present time because there is a lot of time in the day, it's strange how things that used to be important are not any more and we go on with the day or week to only find out that things could and should have been different. But I only take things one day at a time now because looking down the road only confuses you or me, as for my thoughts for the day they havent gotten here yet because I never know for sure what the day is going to bring and some days are better then others and that can be just by a smile or someone saying hello' we all change from day to day.

But when it happens sometimes we don't even realize it, it's said that our change will take a life time so don't be in a hurry, that our completion will be finished when Jesus returns so enjoy life and be happy and learn to love because God is love. Tuesday morning and I'm invited to a luthern church on Sunday five miles out of town Mark my friend at the bank said they were having a band so we will see what happens, many times other dominations invite other to their church to hear music and worship with them. I feel close to music so now I can see how their band sounds, my self I would really like to get my music heard but I have never had a chance and maybe this might open a door who knows only He the father does. If nothing else I will get to see how they worship God but I'm sure it's in the same way that we all show out love to Him, the father as I think back my uncle was an Stacyngelist if my memory is right and in doing that he brought a lot of people to God through the years, as for me it was before my time as I walked on the other side of the room you might say but never got to see him preach. I do remember his home with it's big pillers all white and the porch for which they must have spent many hours with him talking to his kids about the bible. For that time has long passed and so has he but his wife still lives and I havent seen her in many years, I recall her being kind just being aunt bunny but I also don't know what became of their children one was hurt in a car accident and remained crippled but she was funny even with her disadvantages as a matter of fact we saw her more then any of them and the last I heard she lived in Duluth still today.

Through my life I will meet many other religions and the thing that brings us together is God the creator of all things, my land it feels hot in here so I had to turn on the air to bring it down to the level I'm comfortable at. He seams to bring different things into my life when He thinks I'm ready and according to the scripture the father is never wrong which I believe with all my heart, in my life' I was meant to go through the things I did and He knew this from before my birth so I take it as a sign that things will get better from here on in. the struggles and the heartache were a test to maybe see if I would come back to Him and if that's the case then it worked. Just the glimps of things as a child stuck with me going to church at a very young age stuck in this mind, but for a time it was wiped out while I went through the dark times the times of addiction almost wiped out my memories of my childhood. It must have been the playing out side of the church that triggered those memories and brought them back to life, dad I believe loved to go but then on that day which almost took my brothers lives it became too much and then the devil took over and made them a part of this worlds curse. As I was for so long from the time I can remember until the lord woke me up, there is nothing that comes close to living the life I live today and I'm grateful for what He has given me. My new found friends and a brother that had become lost to me so long ago and these things cant be bought for my brothers love is given freely and he is always amazed at how things come to me through my love for God we all need that second chance and that's just the way it is, I have to take out the trash this morning but it isn't very full so maybe I will leave it in this week. O wait' it will be full once I empty the smaller trash cans. My time here has taught me much as I move forward in my learning and I learn at my own speed which is a good thing because a rushed mind can wonder like the lion in search of it's pray, becoming close to God has brought me a long ways a very long ways as I am being made into a solger for the lord. A vessel that will grow and become what he was meant to become in the beginning, will my destiny bring me to that place where

He wants me for this I believe will happen, but only in his time and no one else's. He is patient with those he loves and gives them every chance to become what He creeated them to be, but we don't know what that is not until we become that part of life that he has set aside for us. My town of dreams lets me focus on the here and now as for the other world everything was scattered brained and I couldn't focus but I tried and that in it's self brought change, enough change to get me here in Courtland where I should of belonged a long time ago when the accident happened. At that time I was being shown that miracles happen and that maybe here is where I belonged but with a young mind full of distractions I couldn't see it, as at that time I just wanted to get home where I felt safe. In that other world where nothing made since, I still don't know how I survived but I do know that the father was watching over me and He could fix what was wrong with me. Why wouldn't he? He created me. And I know He saw something good inside of me, the not being corrupted by the world or something else which He felt love for.

My life will be one of learning now and even though my time is half over I still have the other half to become closer to the father, even when we take walks or I go somewhere He seams to be right there to protect me in my battle of life and to help me if I need it to brighten up another persons life. You would be amazed at how just a smile can bring joy to others and I ware one even if I feel sad, when you take your self out from family it gives you a prespective of the love you feel for them and them for you. Wednesday morning' hump day as we used to like to say I'm amazed at how Randy seams joyest each morning when he awaken and it adds luster to the day, as for things they have been going very well and I told pastor Kathy about the other church wanting me too come for a visit. And she was happy for me but asked if I was going to get comunion ready for service there at our church and I assured her that I would because that's my job and I love doing it. She was sure that I would have fun so we will see when the day gets here, l always wanted to see another church and see how they give thanks to the father. My church has always been the same and I'm happy where I am, through my years of finding the right church the church I go to has been my favorit because I get to be my self and learn at my own pace. If I was to be rushed then things would be not so nice, as it says it will take this life time to grow in maturity so I will be ready for the next important thing which will take place in eternity. It's the first time I have heard the crickets out side of my window in a long time but they are sounding off this morning churping away.

I always look forward to getting to know other people and I thought it was awesome that Mark's son played in a band that is of christen faith, maybe one day we can play together and see how my music fits in with theirs, as all praise goes to God' for giving us the ability to create such things as songs and they talk about a part of our lives and some of what has come out of it. The good and the bad but also the sorrow times when I thought things wouldn't turn out the way I thought but in the end all parise goes to the one who created us His people, my songs are created from within and then the music is set to them not the other way around like some do it. When you start something new it takes practice to get good at it and then in time it becomes a part of you, a good part of you that lets others know how much you love the Father and we all do it in our own way through deep feelings and love. In the realm of finding your self He lets you know where you need to be and my church is just down the road, I have went to other churches but I never got into being a person who hip hops from one to another even though I have seen the teachings of other religions my church is where I belong. Many times I wondered what religion grandma was but what ever it was she lived to be quite old knowing the closeness of God in her life, I recall mom saying she didn't cuss and she didn't allow it in her home but I'm sure grandpa sliped once and a while being a man and all. I can picture her in my minds eye reading the bible every day sitting in her rocking chair, she must have had the patients of a saint with five kids as mom must have had with us through all she went through. Even though Herb was slow to anger he could get that way but not very oftend from what I remember, and I know we had to of made him mad from time to time like when Rick got locked up for the first time. And he became out of parental control, from then on it was all down hill for my brother and the accident had a lot to do with it. Now days I don't know where he is but I do hope he is ok' with his life. It's strange how God knows where we should be at a certain time in our lives and he brings us to that place weather it's through someone good for us or bad He seams to use any means possible to bring us to that place and then He lets them fall away like the peeling of an orange so we can grow in our faith and learn to understand it, it's going to be a nice day as I go and pay my bills so the pile gets smaller I don't like having them so I get rid of them as soon as possible giving me that feeling of relief that they are gone, to only come back later next month and the cycle starts over once again. Thursday and I feel like a zomby as I taussed and turned during the nightt but I'm still here feeling like I didn't get any sleep. It's strange how that happens sometimes but I'm sure it will pass as all things do as I start to wake up, my legs felt like a touth ache and there is no worse feeling when you try to sleep but He took pitty on me and make it go away for a time, it seams my battels are with my self when I run a patterned life and then it catches up with you on a certain level. Trying to meke your self strong once again is hard work especially when your mind isn't awake but later the coffee brings you around and you can start he day. Today is better the the day before if I can just shake this sleepiness, still with the demon on my back in time I will shake him off and be free form what holds on tight to my spirit so I cann move forward my self I don't see how some make it by taking all kinds of medications but I guess it had become a way of life for them.

So you cant really knock it, in life things get thrown off chimicals that bring things back into alignment and it has to be brought back into balance by the drugs they give them as for me I don't like that feeling of not being awake and so many drugs do that to people who are not used to them, and then the mind takes awhile to wake up. Many years ago my other brother had them and he ate then like candy couldn't amagine what his world wass like but it couldn't of been good walking around like he was in a trance and then some prefere that life so they don't have to mess with this one of reality, my morning usually starts at 3:00 Am but today it was at four wanting to go back to sleep to make the feeling go away but only being awake can change that feeling in hope that it wont appear again. This is my day off so I'm going to relax for the day. Friday morning and I'm really sick today but I don't know why my legs are shakey and my eyes will hardly stay open along with other things that are wrong got to go back to bed. The illness has passed somewhat but still feel like crap, it seams to hit me around this time of year as the weather changes. I try to chalk it up to old age but really I'm not that old compaired to the elders of my town, I wish the pain would go away that's in my back and legs and it does for a while but only to return later. If I would of known the work I used to do would of caused such destruction I would of never did it but I had to feed my family, and then the disaster that took place afterwards didn't help any either. Being in a wheel chair for so long destroyed the rest, all I can do is write about it today and even that takes a lot out of me but there is a message here don't destroy what God gave you because in the end you will loose later in life.

It's labor day weekend and I have to do with my other jobs because church doesn't take a holiday and things have to be in their place, all the time I pray that the pain will be taken away but to date it hasn't so I will be patient and pray that He will hear me. Are some supposed to suffer through life and cry because it hurts so much or will He find mercy on me and take it away so I can move forward? I do know that when I first moved here things were worse and I was job and homeless but through christ those things were brought into my life and I am so grateful, I am going to visit another church and I'm not sure why they invited me but there must be a reason for it as God works in mysterious ways that we as people don't uunderstand and why we don't understand it, is beyond me. Or maybe he just doesn't want us to understand it and that's why He is who he is the Alpha and the Omega the first and the last. In the last two days I didn't sleep rolling around in the bed just crying that He would take the pain away but He didn't it was like every tendent in my legs ached and I wanted to cut them off because if they weren't there then they wouldn't hurt. The pain is like it was when I first learned to walk again everything stretching again for the first time after many years. I know that it was my fault for the things that happened with my body but I also know that He knew it would happen long before I was conceived in my mother, it says He loves us so did He let this happen so I could write about it so others don't do the same? Or if that's the case then He knows others that will fall under the same curse and He will let it happen to them also if they are not warned. Alcohol addiction the curse can be handed down through 4 generations and even 3 of them might not experience it but then out of the blue the 4th one will be pleged by it to effect 4 more generations of them so when will it stop? I do know it has to be stopped by the person and even then that might just free the one person, and not the others so it's a trial to see how strong some are. As with me it took death before He opened my eyes but even then it's a long battle and it doesn't stop once you stop, there seams to be a place in your mind where the information is stored and when you think about starting it up again that place lets you know what will happen all the pain and sorrow and regreat that will kick in once again if you deside to travel that path. It's been overr 20 years and I wouldn't want to go there again, it's just too much for one life time to go back there. If I didn't have the pain or reminder of that life I might not of been here today but the memories keep me on the straight and narrow and helps me to enjoy most of life. I do know that when I leave this world all that this world took from me will be given back and all the pain and sorrow will be gone, in a way it makes you want to go there but I know it's not right to take or destroy something God has given you for one day He will finish the job He started on me but weather it's in this life of the next I don't know. I noticed in many familys all looks fine on the outside but the root to the problem lays inside the person and when they don't know how to deal with the problem they choose a destructive pattern like alcohol or drugs. This gives them some kind of relief to make things easier in their mind anyway but not in reality, mother always hid her problem and never got the help she needed either which lead later to her death.

The world is full of people who can't deal with the rage that dwells within so some hide it while others just leave it out in the open, alcohol and drugs has been around since the beginning of time and maybe it will be until the end only God knows the answer to that hard question. But as for me it has stopped here within this body not to come back. Tanner is my friends child or should I say son in his 20's and he will be playing the drums on Sunday and I really want to see if maybe he could play my song so I could see how it sounds with a band behind it or a key board. Saturday morning and I slept good last night and my back didn't hurt at all finely some relief, today I have to wash my car and then go down to the church to get things ready for Sunday in the mean time this afternoon I will work at the thrift store and hopefully make a lot of money for the cause which is always a good thing many things are taking place which will make a difference here in Courtland and maybe I can be a big part of it. Getting my song noticed would be a good thing and then I could go on with the rest of them that are still in my mind the great gift that He has given me shouldn't be squandered could this be a door that is opening or is it a time to hear what my mind had created with more then a piano behind it, it's funny how things can work out sometime but you never know what will come next in your life. Music is the gift that keeps giving and everyone likes music, it's been around since the beginning of time also and will be here long after we are gone.

It's too be enjoyed by all who love the lord in my book as for the rest of the other some I cant understand it's an expression of who we are and our triles in life, what brought us to where we are today and where we are going. Tanner is like his dad even his voice I cant tell them apart if they are off in the distance. My time here was made possible in part by Mark his father he saw something in me when others didn't and took that chance on this soul what a great feeling to have someone who cares that much, yesterday was warm but not as warm as as the days before and I can feel the change in the season as the temps stay below 100 just a great time of year, through the next year we will see if anything changes in my music but if not I will continue to write the songs and make many more of them at least they can be something that can be passed down to my grand babys so maybe they can get them published but I will try to get it done on my own the Lord willing. (The Cross) was written right here in Courtland so this place is it's home it was written when I felt lost sitting in my car just looking at the frost and ice hanging off the trees and the Cross in front of the church what inspration God can give us at times of trouble. Then after that things started to look up and I made Courtland my home for ever more. Now' I don't know if they can play my song but we will give it a shot God says not to hold back the gifts he gives us so I will try and get it going, children like the song so that should be a good sign and you never know where something can go unless you try to bring it to life as God brought us to life and look at what He has done for us his children. (The light on the water) was also done here in Courtland so it's fitting that it's played here first before anywhere else this will give it it's birth place and as we all know everything has to have a birth place like we all have had. My hopes are somewhat good that it will get played if I take it to Tanner and I know that we cant always see what will become of something until we put it to the test, but through hope can come many things that we cant see until they are tried and if you don't try then it's your loss. Who knows this might be the birth of something new in my world and others and if one day it's played in K town many will come to hear the one who learned to create music after the destruction of addiction, for it was those years that brought this on the feelings and other things. But mostly it was the spirit of God that gave me the words and I breathed life into them by writing them words of hope and faith, all things are made possible through the eyes of the Lord' what a great thought, and He gives us the courage to see things through just getting the song to him will open a door and you can never tell where things will go from there. Courtland is a small town, and it can be one where a new kind of music came from if all works out ok' but with everything there is a season and the season has to be just right. In the book I'm reading it says that He gives us gifts and we will know these gifts when they present them selves and we are passionate about them. The owel is hooting out side this morning it sounds like a hoot owel or it could be a dove I really cant tell as they sound the same to me. But what ever it is it's up early even before the other birds that sing in the morning and it's beautiful to my ears anyways, so many things I hear that others don't and it can start off the day just right courage is something that is built and it will take time to be able to sing in front of a lot of people but it is attainable with practice and good people behind you.

As I listen to the birds sing each morning I give thanks for the day do you remember when I fell so long ago you picked me up and showed me the way. It's how I start my day and the birds let me know that we all have a purpose in this life and we don't always know what that purpose is until that time comes to show it, and you never know how old you will be when it comes your turn, I always thought a band started when you were young but that's not always the case. And age doesn't matter when it comes to doing what you love, the day went fine as I got all my work done and had a good time at the thrift store then came home to make supper and kicked back and watched television until bed time. Sunday morning and some people have bought the house next door, they have been doing work on it for a few days and got the north foundation in where it was all rotted away. It's a lot of work but in the end it will probably pay off for them, I met one of the guys and he seamed nice so if he does move in at least we will know each other. Which is always a good thing no one has showed much intrest in the home in quite some time so now maybe we will have neighbors. As I and little brother went over to look at what they have done after they left the wood borers had ate some of the wood underneath the house but I think they caught it in time to stop the damage, as for my home it's solid and will last for many more years as we continue to grow and learn about the town more, today is the band at the other church so I will be going there for this Sunday but I still have to set uup communion at my church before hand which is a delight for me to do.

They say God has a plan for us all and I believe this job that I do is His plan for me, to bring others together in His name and take care of His church and the joy it brings me is great. Just the thought of belonging makes me happy and my friends are so kind in this town of dreams and that's what it is to me a little town of dreams. Beverly and I laughed a lot yesterday while we put things away and there is much more to put away next Wednesday when I return to work once again, although it's hot outside during the day the air-conditioning keeps us pretty cool inside the thrift shop and we talk about people and the things they bring in to help others who have it harder then they do. It seamd to make others feel good to help in the giving of things and that feeling cant be replaced by anything it builds up your pride in a good way, and like others we all have to much that we can get rid of some of it. I can hear little brother coughing so he must be having a smoke I just hope he isn't up for the day at 4:00 Am. Which I found out that he is, so that may or may not be a good thing depending on if he sleeps most of the day he can be funny sometimes through the time he has been here he has had to adjust to many things and he has done very well considering his life has changed so much, the love for a brother is great especially when in some ways we are a like especially in the emotional department as we can cay at the drop of a hat when we watch a good or sad movie. But for the violent movies we don't watch them as that kind of crap isn't in us it seams, but we are all different and some like those movies the ones that are deranged and get into it. Before I moved here I didn't mind watching them but something has changed inside of me and us since those days so long ago, the miracle of modern age has let me keep up with things on the computer and it seams I know just enough to stay up with it, but I like writing more then anything. The writing about my town and the good people who live here, as some move away others move in allowing the town to grow a little at a time slow growth is better then a fast influx as when that happens some things get destroyed. It's early but it's going to be a good day as we hear new music and see the celebration of God in His house for He too will be listening to the voices that He gave some people and He will be proud in listening. He gave us all that we need to minister and some do it in music while others stand at a pulpet and teach the word of God' to Him we are all brothers and sisters and should help each other in that fashion. Even my little buddy has a job to do, and that's to keep me company during those lonely times and the exciting ones. To play together in the good times and the bad but be thankful for all the good times we have in life, the picture I too of little brother has come out good and my daughter put it on face book it also shows my home where I proudly live and that also looks nice compaired to the other places

I have lived long ago in the past. My friends can now see where I reside and they have to see that things are good for now with us brothers together living my life the way I always wanted and who knows what the future holds for us in the town of dreams. Sunday afternoon and the invite was canceled but Mark will let me know when it's on again, my learning about my purpose in life continues as each day passes and I'm almost sure that it has to do with singing. My ability to create songs is still strong and I practice all the time to fine tune my ability to maybe one day be the best at what I do or atleast bring fullness to what He has given me.

I do know that my church has shown it's love for me by telling me it will always be my home and that's the greatest feeling in the world, as for learning more about what I should do I'm sure in time it will become clear. As clear as the sky is blue when the storm has passed, I'm not used to writing during the day so this is different for me at this time. All the things I'm not used to writing about because in the morning my thoughts are not as wide as they are during the day, I got my car dusted off and cleaned the door jams so they wont build up crap on them. Tomorrow is the beginning of another week and I will learn more as the week goes by and who knows what the end of the week will be like, as the world is changing fast. I wish I could of gone to the other church to see what it was like but now it will have to wait until they invite me once again, I told Mark' that I wrote music and that I would like to get another propective and he told mee to talk to Tanner the next time I go to the Bank. I cant help but think that something could happen if we got our two talents together so we will see what happens in the next couple of weeks. As for this day it's about over and something different will show it's self by tomorrow, honesty is one of the biggest pluses in life that and doing things for others and finding our own ministry. The one that was meant for us as a person, like with me addiction gave me the tools to help others who have gone through the same thing and it's my responsibility to develop that ability so I can show them that they too can over come the curse that almost took my life and it would have if it wasn't for God. I need to develop a way to show them that He wont let them down because I know for a fact that He stood by me every step of the way bringing me to where I am today.

Through the darkness He showed me the light and reached out His hand so I wouldn't be scared and fall to the ground that would have sucked me up. Instead He brought me from the gates of hell to show me how beautiful life could really be, and that I need not be afraid of what this world could of done to me because with Him by my side nothing in this world could hurt me. I went and locked up my car but I'm hoping I wont have to do that for long seeing winter will be here and no one would break in to it being we live in this great place . We don't have a police force but a couple of cops live here in Courtland so the crime is minim but you do hear of demistic violence with some young familys but other then that it's little to nothing, when it comes to crime. The temp is about 90 something out side so it's nice to be blessed with a place that you can stay cool in the heat, Monday and I woke up to it being pretty coolin here so I shut of the air. According to the things I have read many of us will find what we are good at and then do it for a time my delight is doing what I do today taking care of the church and also the thrift store, but also I like my singing if it's not in a crowd for now but that to can change in a heart beat. In the beginning it was just a thought but then it turned into one of my dreams but being I had went through that life of addiction my train of thought wasn't right until He made things better and then it was all wheels forward. How could a person not want to show God what He had given me and it was in respect for Him that I couldn't ever say no when I was asked to sing because it was by his power that I was able to show my love for Him the Alpha and the Omega. All I do is for Him because He made me who I am this person that feels now and loves with all that he is worth it's like it says our time is but short here and it takes me a little longer to check and feel things out to see if it fits me this one person who has been shown the love of God, as for the church it's my home and always will be and it was the people who made me feel most at home. I didn't realize that a church could help you find your way especially out here in the heart land, but it has even though I have a ways to go yet I will keep learning from my friends in christ, I synced a consern in pastor Kathy's voice on Sunday but she need not worry because I will be there for them just as they are there for me and my joy will also be theirs. This morning I have to cut the lawn on the other side of the side walk to make the grass even so it will grow in harmony but I wasn't able to get to some of it because of the work next door so I will keep trying until it's done with grace' we all grow and mine was stopped by the addiction but now it's growing again and I can't tell where it will lead, maybe to that other side of the coin I have talked about in the past but one thing will always stay with me and that the love others have shown me through the years. Never and I mean never forget where you came from because usually that's where you get your start even through the hard time we seam to rise above our mistakes and make things better for it is God who brings us through it all in the end. I can hear the crickets out side this morning right by my window and the noise lets me know that it's safe out there, for if other animals were around they would stop churping.

My good fortune and blessings have been many even though I couldn't always see them but through time and hind sight I can see them clearly, we as God's children only see in hind sight clearly that is and only if we look for it. As for learning that to takes time and in some cases we don't see the resoults for many years and that's because the mind takes time to process the things we have learned but don't let that be a problem because in the end we may all be a little slow. That's just the way we were made, for those who have total recall of things I feel sorry for them because it would be hard to live the same things over and over again, some leave a small town to find fortune and fame but what they don't realize is that it isn't where you go it's what you learn that matters, and if it's meant to be then it will happen no matter where you are. I have found more peace here in my town of dreams then I have ever felt anywhere else and I have been and seen many places that can't compare to Courtland, the universe turns and goes around and no matter where you go there you are. Some think changing the place you live will bring more into your life and I say it's so in some respects but no matter where you land you still have to deal with the everyday problems of life and they wont be lessoned by the space you have. We all create our own world and then we have to adjust to that world and if it's all messed up then we will have to make changes, and mine needed many changes but I also know that He the father knew I would go through the things I did just like He knew Jesus would die for our sins.

In my beginning He knew my life. And how it would play out, and for the longest time I wondered why people said if you want to make God laugh tell him your pans. Because usually His is a lot different from what we perceive, ours visions are not like His because He sees things clearly and we well don't. with all the things that go on in life we get lost in the fog or at least I do. How long is a life spand to me living to be in your 70's or 80's is a good long time but in the bible it has been said that the one who built the arch lived 140 years and that's how long it took to build it. Everybody thought he was nuts but that didn't stop him from filling his promas and then the world started over again with just his blood line, but I don't know if that was before Jesus came or not. Many of the deciples had many problems depression among other things which meant they weren't made perfect none of us are made that way we have to have our quirks so we can find our way and we don't find them in the same way, one person might know from birth what their mission is while others go a whole life time before they know or get a glimps of what's to come. The people who wondered for 40 years were lost for a while as it was only 11 miles to the destanation so there had to be something they had to learn and it just took that long sort of like me I guess it took almost that long to find my self but He gives us that time to complete our journeys, in the bible it says he doesn't let you start something without giving you the time you need to finish it. In other words He won't set you our in the wilderness and not give you the ability to return as He leaves nothing unfinished everything is brought to completion because He is complete the maker and creater of all things. My land I'm still amazed at how on some days I can write a lot and others not so much for this is Him working in me, the day was nice but also hot as the clouds covered the skys and the rain came for just a short time, but then left again we also went to town and back to fetch some things and now the day is over bringing a new day tomorrow where something different will come up. This morning I got the lawn mowed so now everything is done. Tuesday morning' and I donthear the crickets that odd, when I went to town yesterday Mark asked me to pit up something for him and I did then I had to get coffee and creamer because my day doesn't start without it. Coming this winter we will get everything ready for the few months that we will more then likely stay inside so we better get some games or something to occupy our time, it's strange how we as people change with the seasons our moods and our out look on things but' we seam to adjust to the different things around us. The crickets have started in and they give you some kind of peace in reading that book I have found out many things that will help me later down the road like my purpose for this life among other things. I'm supposed to use what was given to help other people and I believe I do that but it only comes out when I write, little brother remembers when they called me scooter and I couldn't walk I asked him how he remembers it and he told me that I used to hit the end tables when I would go somewhere and that was something didn't remember. I had been around people that were bad in the curse before it happened to me and I recall saying to my self that it would never happen to me, but it did' those who I recall being that way never did recover as for me I'm writing this so there had to of been something different about me a stronger spirit or a drive to survive that brought me here.

In my or others youth they or we think we can take on the world but that is short lived once you start going down that hill we thought we had climbed, it was like being a bomb but the only destroying effects was that our lives would be destroyed. And the bomb, well it would survive leaving little pieces of me on the ground that would have to be picked up and put back together again but boy what a process, it was like starting from scratch building this life all over but this time there was something different and it had to be done just right and only God could help you accomplish this. Although I have never seen the father I always knew He was there, to help where I didn't understand things. It might of only been by a suggestion but things were put into my mind that I followed a thought or some advice that would make me better then I was at that time. Through the years of addiction reading was never in the cards because it was too hard and my mind hadn't been developed like it should when I was a child, so like everything else I took the easy way out and didn't read. In my mind there is a block that only lets me read so much before my head would hurt but through the years it seamss to have gotten better, they say the mind has to be worked like the mussels in your body or else it will get weak so now days I work it as oftend as possible and that block seams to be less letting me read more to correct the problem, and I believe many people have this same problem in their lives and they don't know what they are missing. Randy has the same problem but I read things to him on the television and that helps us both.

My sister was the smartest when it came to knowing how to read and do other things which pertain to learning but even with that she never finished school getting married at 16 years of age from personal experience I believe our mind has pathways and sometimes one or more get clogged and then we loose intrest in learning which I know was one of my problems. Just being able to write this book to me is a miracle as I never knew I had that ability. It was God that brought it on after He saved me and sent me back here to do my part in this world, my friend Mark Konz the manageing editor of the paper told me that my life experiences is what makes me different from those who learned by reading books as books can only talk about what they read. Those who have never lived through it cant possibly know what happens inside the body as everything breaks down and builds it's self up again, and the emotional side of it could kill you in it's self. All the years, of feeling useless and all alone drived you to a very dark places and at times you don't know who to get out of that dark corner that exists in the mind. But then one day you talk to God and ask Him to take it away and He does by opening a door that lets a little light into your world, did He feel obligated to help or did He know from the beginning that the day would come when this would be needed? For truly He saw my path before I was born and knew I would need Him to bring me through it. He wants us all to need Him and if He has to He will bring you to that place where you will ask like He did with me He wants us to be close to Him like a father should be close to his children. The understanding of life is not for me to guess at but it does make you curious about the eternity and what it will be like, my glimps of the light was just a fraction and I think it was to show me that there is another place and that I shouldn't be afraid of death here on earth. I do know that my body didn't go with me when I went into the light it was like I became something else and there was no pain like I have had to deal with here on earth, it would have been easy for me if I had stayed there. But that wasn't His plan and now it's been over 20 years since my visit and still I haven't been able to talk to anyone about it except for God and maybe a few that would listen like pastor Kathy and Beverly, I always feel like I'm alone in this world seprated by my experiences that no other has gone through. It's like a bridge I cant cross because part of it is missing and you ache to reach the other side because you know there is beauty in the full development of the picture, that master piece of beauty that you somehow fit into. Maybe the life ever after where you can shed all the pain and finely find that peace you felt in that visit so long ago, at that time I didn't need this body as it remained here while I went there and that feeling was like no other a sepration that felt like it was meant to be. Most don't get to feel that feeling but they are better off because there is no one here you could talk about it too no one who has gone and came back and then struggled to make life the way it should have been in the first place or maybe I'm trying too hard to have things the way I think they should be only God knows that answer but it's Tuesday and I have work to do so I will close for now. Wednesday morning and last night we had a bad strom I only heard it for a short time Randy said he had to go out and pull some branches off the power line to the house and they weighed more then he does and I'm just glad thathe didn't get hurt. It was like the storm brought on a dream about an old friend that passed a long time ago from cancer.

He has been gone for over twenty years so it's hard to guess at why he tried to kill me and all I caan remember saying is no God no. then I woke up and Randy told me about how bad the storm was does the universe bring on dreams if a tornado is close by maybe but then matbe not, but I have never had a dream so violent and in the end he said this is a mercy killing but for some reason when I talked to God he went away. Violence has never been in my life but in that dream it felt so real, I just pray that I don't have another one like that again. It's still dark out so I cant see th damage for the storm but surely I will see it later this morning it happened on Sept 4th of this year. Randy also said the neighbor was chaseing his trash can down the road trying to catch it, I wonder if he caught it? I remember hearing something like a train out side and I looked out my window and the trees were bending like in a hurracane what a night. Now that the damage is done we will check everything out I sure wish I had a camra that worked that way I could take pictures but I don't so there wontbe any pictures. Strange time of year for this to take place but we did get a lot of rain as the streets were flooded with water, our town of dreams could have been damaged but we were protected by the hand of God but that's just my opinion. The last time a storm hit like this it took out two and a half trees in my yard and it took almost two years to clean it up, but everything passed and no one was hurt so I thank Him for that, it felt like the roof was going to blow off the house or lift off of it but it didn't and for that I amreal glad. It's strange how when nature hits all you can do is ride it out but there is a hopelessness because there is nothing you can do.

So today we might have some of those branches to try and cut up and if needed we will see what else we can do. So far things have been pretty good but it goes to show that desasters can happen anywhere and that no one is beyond the destrucction nature can cause. I wonder how the house next door faired in the storm when light comes we will see, little brother was kind of pumped by the storm as it got him excited for some reason but now that has passed and he is fast a sleep. Mother nature can show her ugly side sometimes but then she bows her head to the father if He so chooses her to, like a friend in church said one time we live in a jet stream of some sort and that gives unstable weather at times. One person who lives just a few miles from here may get an inch of rain and we might get two or visa virsa you just never know, the tree that lost it's lims has been dead for quite some time so I not supprised that the lims came from that, but it could have been worse and the whole tree could of fallen. So we are very lucky, Ha! I don't really like that word but it fits for now. I checked around and found cheaper insurance for my car so I an going with it when they send me the papers this willl save me some money that can be used else where so I can stay on top of things, they must have did a good job on building this home because it's still here after almost 100 years it has even out lasted the concrete on the steps that lead to the home, but later I will have to replace it with wood or pour more concrete to make it stable once again. The house on the corner is still on schedule, and they are putting in a ward craft home. There are 4 new homes being built around here some out in the country and others like the house on the corner here in Courtland, my self' I believe people are wanting to get away from the big cities where crime is at almost every corner and settle down in rural areas where it isn't so bad. This will allow them to have that piece of mind that they wouldn't get in those big cities, I work at the thrift store today and it will be fun I believe we have quite a few things to put away but you can't really tell until I get there and see what's going on. I like my job and will do it for ever or as long as I'm living here it gives me purpose and it's serving Him by helping others. I saw trees bend like they did last night but only in violent storms and the train noise I heard it when the trees broke a few years back, and I was hoping not to hear them again but that wasn't the case in this life all we can do is our best and hope for goodness to follow us so we can teach others how to help them selves when it comes to living in the darkness of addiction. My hope is that teaching and goodness can transcend to others so they can over come some things in their lives as I have had to do on many time and something changes with each time you change. I don't have all the answers and probable never will but I do know if you do your best then usually things will turn out ok' things are changing with each passing day and this will probably happen for many years to come.

At times it scares me but then soon that passes to reveal something new to us and that's what makes me think we all as people can make a difference, and it doesn't matter how slight as long as it's in a good way. My self' I think I'm a deep thinker maybe to deep and that can scare the hell out of you sometimes and I don't like that because it shouldn't be that way. Listening to the news in a city near here only about 100 miles or so away a child was killed while sleeping in her bed and another women was shot in the head at the same time in a trailor park. So much violence and I don't like that, it almost makes you not to want to watch the news because here where I live you don't hear about such things a stray bullet hit the little girl and I pray that God is with both her parents and the women who got shot in the head, it almost makes you want to cry. As I learn more about the father I also learn that my life is a testimony of his love and greatness and the things He has done in my life is supposed to be shared with those who haven't heard of his wisdom and power, when you haven't been a teacher of the gospel people seam to believe and take in more because they know you havent been taught to preach by a school your accounts are new and they are of things that have happened in your life our whole life is written by God from before birth but with us or at least with me what I write or say has to be lived before I can bring it out in the open as that's just the way my life has to be.

There are things which have happened that I cant even recall them because they are somewhere in my mind and in time they will be brought to light, something to be shared with my brothers and sisters but for now they havent showed them selves. And it reminds me of something He said there is a season for all things and all things for the season, I think that's how it goes! The afternoon went well and I got the branches put on the garage slab so now all I have to do is pick up the little branches and then the yard will be ready to mow again, according to neighbore we didn't get much rain but the wind was bad as at one place a trailor hit a gas meter and there was vehicals everywhere to stop the leak. Well the day is about over so I will close until morning. Thursday morning' and they are calling for some rain to night or tomorrow but we will see, also they are calling for it to get to 45 degrees during the night and in the 70's in the day, a far cry from the 100 degrees we have gotten used to but Hey! We will take it, I can remember the frosty mornings as a child while we were camping and boy the fire felt good when everyone got up and mom cooked bacon and then eggs in all that lard. It's strange how we lived but others have it far more hard these days then we really had it back then but it shows that the housing in California must not have changed much as people are still being put out of their homes like they were back in the 60's.

Yesterday I remembered a guy that was brought up on being taught to steel by his parents and it still happens today, they would travel from town to town robbing people and taking their children but in doing this they couldn't leave any witnesses. This kind of thing is still happening today by people who come from other countrys and feel their nationality is dwindling in this country I couldn't imagine breaking in and steeling from people and then living like nothinng happened no congence I guess, as for my life I have been very fortunate to have had loving people that care for me and others like they do. the crickets are churping this morning and it's a sign that better things are coming our way. It's strange how you can go through the months and not notice such things but then later all of a sudden hear them it's the little things that He brings to our attention when we are feeling down and it seams to brighten up the day, in time I want to go and see things I havent seen before and maybe that will give me something to write about. A different culture or just the way some others live, as I watched the news I saw how some live and it's not to far from here but I my self wouldn't want to have to go through that. As I have had a slum lord before the ones that get rich off the misery of the less fortunate, they rent houses or trailors to them knowing that they don't have the money to take them to court for them not fixing things that need to be fixed. And then they bleed them dry of their dignity and make them keep paying, with pops he had Jerry for a time and that guy paid him for working with his own money from his social security checks making him think he was getting a head when in reality he was buying lawn mowers and saying he paid for them and then taking them away from him when he would get mad. This man clamed to be a christen and if the truth was known he gave offerings by using tendents money. Over the years many people died in his subsidized homes that he wouldn't fix and it made me wonder how he could look in a mirrow each day to shave knowing this had happened over and over again" we tried to sue him but it takes money and some of the lawyers wouldn't do it because they knew him and went to church with him.

They would say that they had heard about it happening before but they didn't want to believe it, it goes to show that some don't care about right and wrong. Not even if it's hurting or robbing; someone, their morals are all wrong but hey!!! That the way it goes in the world today, all through my life I have always been a person who stays to them selves except for a few friends and it's no different today then it was back then except today I don't live in that dark place where I once lived. Granted the two worlds are different in the one you live from memory to memory with nothing in between leaving a void that is empty but then when life is almost taken away it's like you awaken and want to know the things you missed those blank spaces seam to become important but you don't know how to fill them in and then as time passes you start to remember the things you somehow forgot but it's hard because the darkness started as a child. At a very young age, it's like somehow you were programmed to think and do things different. Were they the right things? Well yes and no, the values are important the ones that kept you honest but the struggle was hard living sometimes in that dark place and then getting a glimps of the light you might say but getting that glimps some how stuck with you for a time and gave you hope that maybe there is a better life then the one you had been living in. then as years pass you fall deeper into that dark place untill He brings you out of it, the words that my journey hadn't started yet gave me hope that change was on it's way. But what change? As more years passed things changed for the better but it was a battle all it's own, the learning to walk again took it's toal.

But I couldn't give up and I didn't except for a few more time that I fell back into the pit. It had been the only life I had ever known and I felt at home in the dark place, then He showed me how life could be different if I would just trust Him. It was like He was trying to convert me from the darkness to show me that the light would be better and over time I saw that His love was bringing me somewhere, a bridge had to be built from the darkness to the light and it would be me that would have to test the strength of that bridge and this was done by a step at a time. For each step forward I would take one step back and this went on for a time not knowing how long' but in time my forward moves didn't have any moves back and then I realized that He was taking me somewhere but trust was an issue because I had trusted the darkness most of my life except for that little light that shined in me, that light that showed me right from wrong that goodness that I knew was inside. We all have good and bad in us and this world is corrupted by the bad but with some if they are kept away from that dark side and taught that life can be beautiful then there is hope that they will stay away from the unpleasant things like trying to find the answer to problems in a bottle or even courage in that place which has no good qualitys. I guess or I know it was my security blanket to not have to face the world and all it's destructive ways, strange avoid destruction by destroying ones self not a good concept' but as time went by I did find that the one step forward did lead to walking over that bridge but that was the beginning and without my knowing it people would play a big part of my walking forward in this new life I had discovered it was like getting rid of the old and building with the new. Replacing people from the dark side with people that had faith in Christ, and although I sometimes found their way strange to me it didn't stop me from embracing this new life. Then with time they became like family real family people you could kid with and laugh with and do things for like getting someone a cup of coffee and then later they would do the same building for eternity in hope that you will see them later down the road in that place which was gotten ready for us by Jesus. For He said I prepaire a place for you in my fathers house and it has many rooms, our life is a testament to Christ of how He helped to bring us where we are, and how we got there. The struggles and the over coming the darkness to get to where we are today, this is something we cant do on our own because He has to find you first. Some say they found the lord but it's the other way around and He lets you know this by his love and understanding, He want you to have a relationship with Him and He wants to bring you into his family. I used to think that the church was a building but to my supprise it's the people all working for the good of the world to try their best to help those who are fighting to survive, my story can bring people to God and it's my job to do so. As my situation can reach into others who have gone through the same thing I have and give them hope for a brighter tomorrow, for in life there is no easy fix only that walk in the darkness until you are brought to see that there is hope for those who want freedom from the dark place in life. As for my past it will stay there until I'm ready to share it with others who want freedom from the curse that will in time destroy them, I like to think that my knowledge in writing his will help many.

And let them know that life can change for the better my land' there is enough suffering in the world but they can over come it. If it wasn't possible for change then I wouldn't be here right now and the dark forces would have won the battle, but with God all things are possible even the things we can't see because we sometimes try to walk in the dark. With the father you don't need sight because He sees for us all, through the ocean of tears that these eyes have cried many thing have happened from the rebirth of this lost soul has brought a person joy even after the dark days of addiction. A word of advice" never let a child drink Booze because in the end if they don't find their way they loose and no good comes from an empty vessel, as for my mind it's healed today by the power and teaching of God" as for the rest it's open to interpretation and everyone has their own point of view of things'" we went to town for groceries and got quite a bit so food shouldn't be a problem, as the day went on I got some more of the yard cleaned up and now I can run the mower to cut up the little twigs that remain. Tomorrow I will do some things and hope that all will turn out ok making sure that all is well at the church, next week we have a garage sale at the highway 36 state garage sale it reaches clean across Kansas and people come from all around to sell the things they don't need any longer and boy can you buy stuff if you have the money which leaves me out this year. Maybe next year I will have saved some to buy something I want, but I'm used to doing without as I don't need much in this life as long as I have my health and good friends. The church should make some money and I will take a few things down there to sell to help the cause, I have things I don't need so why not put them to good use for the church.

Well the day is coming to an end and the sun will be going down in a few hours so this will end this for now, and maybe later I will come back to it. If not, then tomorrow will be another day that the lord has made. Friday morning and we got our rain last night. don't really know how much but the thunder was loud I also had another dream but this one I couldn't remember and maybe it was because it wasn't violent or something was different, they say children dream but to the best of my recollection I never had any so maybe it's just now starting in. it's like everything has been delayed in taking place maybe until this time in my life who really knows the answer but the creator. As for sleeping I slept most of the night or until 1:00 this morning but that isn't far off of my original time, such a delight to hear the rain as I know we needed it pretty bad or should I say the farmers did while they plant their new crops. Our neighbor got home last night or early yesterday afternoon and you can always tell when he makes his presents by the sound of his semi this last time he was gone for almost two weeks, and now he will spend some time with his family. In my time here I have seen many people come and go but I never got close to any of them and maybe it was because they didn't stay very long but as for me I like the old light fixture that keeps on working no matter what doing just the opiset of what others do. It seams when I'm put to a test I beat the odds and out do what others think I can do bringing me to a new place which is alright with me. Th book I'm reading has had my attention for over two or so weeks and I'm about done with it, to only start on another in the coming weeks. It's like my mind is growing in a direction that it's never been before a new adventure that can take you to different place and time, not reading as a child left me grounded to this earth to only wake up and go to bed each day without the adventure that most kids get to live through reading books. What I find nice about reading is that you pick and choose what you put into your mind and by being able to do that you shape whats inside on your shelfs as I call them, it lets your mind wonder through space and time to places that you have never been. This should have been open to you when your young but the addiction took that away leaving things blank for the most part except for what I learned with the hands on method but the experiences remained but without much of a wanting or yearning for it. After my demise things started to change and my mind went a different direction it went from machanics to the working and learning of things that weren't in my life in my younger years, and except for the learning I enjoyed it well by real truth I liked it too but only when progress was apparent. Writing became my passion once I got the kinks out of it and what I mean by that is the learning how to read and write, it was like the mind for learning was there but never taught so God taught me" with different ways He" even taught me how to spell during this time and boy that was a chore, but in the end He taught me pretty well with what I needed to make it writing and the Dictionary helped a lot also. As I can put it in the palm of my hand and take it everywhere, I can spellout most of the words when I'm reading and it doesn't take long by sounding them out beinging a story together that makes since to me.

The Father has taught me all that I know when it comes to getting along with others and how I would like to be treated is how I treat other people. With respect and kindness and this has brought me many friends but also hindered it with some and maybe that's because they don't do the same, some walk away because I'm different and hey!!! So what' at least I try and reach for that brass ring which is showing kindness towards others. The southern bell' is one that would be hard to reach because she lives in her own world away from other and her family is the only thing she shows intrest in, I have tried to wave at her going down the street but with no reply so I quit waving. But maybe in time things will change you can never tell, time changes all things as it did with me. I know she has grandchildren and they seam to be her life so that's a good thing it shows she has a heart in there somewhere, everyones life is changed by different things that have happened in their lives and sadly some of those things are not good. Many could know the goodness of God if they just gave it a chance but most are scared like I once was, my land'" it isn't something that happens over night it's a learning process and trust has to be built. Even after I came back it took years before I could grasp that I was supposed to learn something from the two words I was sent back with and the message could have been simple just the less was blessed by the greater; meaning all can come to God and be blessed Melchisedek had no record of birth or death and yet he was God's priest. And the king of peace, why wouldn't they talk more or keep records of this great man? For truly he was loved by God as we all are.

Even Jesus was made a priest after the order of Melchisedek and this leads me to think that he had God's favor before Jesus came to live with us here on earth. After Jesus you never heard about Melchisedek it was like he vanished; but he was around in the beginning in the first book of 'GENESIS' Chapter 14 virse 18 where he met Abram and gave him bread and wine. Abram was a patriarch and even gave him a tenth of all this lead me to believe that he was real great in the eyes of God who sent Abram to war. Just a few thoughts of mine or my opinion which could of caught my attention and brought me to study further about this person or spirit. Epiphany the first word relates to a church festival but I didn't find it in the bible just in the Dictionary and I asked people what it meant and they said something good with God, T.G.I.F. Is the beginning of the weekend a time when workers take a break from a long weeks work to rest to begin a new after two days of rest. As I look at mom and pop's I feel a piece come over me and that is a good feeling knowing their worries are over, mom has been gone a long time but my mind has become ok' with her being gone the wondering if I did the right thing by taking her to the hospital has faded but the good memories still remain in the back of my mind so I can go on and still learn the things I didn't get to learn when I was young. The bibly is my teaching tool but sometimes it hurts if I study it too long, and that lets me know when to stop for a timebut then I go back to it. Saturday morning' and Randy got a call from the nurce on Friday to get some information, they way he talked it shouldn't take long for the surgery and for that I'm glad then we can come home so he can recover. As the days go by he will have to take care of his self while I work but he wont be left alone for to long as I only work a couple of hours twice a week, when he had the shots it didn't take long for him to get back on his feet and then things were back to normal. The gas is going to cost a lot and I hope we can still survive but I'm optimistic that things will show them selves as the time gets near. I might have to ask to help so we can make the trip but I don't see a problem unless the church can't afford it. I will talk to Kathy, and see what she says everyone has medical emergencies and this isn't any different because it has to be done. My land' it's like I'm his care taker also but that's ok' this is something God expects us to do for others, and I can make it up someway I like the jobs I have and it lets me bring my abilitys and put them to work in a greate place meaning the church' my home away from home. I'm on day 39 of the 40 day journey in that book and it's great reading also it opened a path-way in my mind to things I have never experienced before, who would of thought you could take journeys in your mind but they have been talking about that for quite some time, and all writers take that journey sometimes when they need to refreshion new things to write about it's like research and the ideas form to bring you to another level. I'm sure huck finn would have been a good read but I missed that one by not knowing how to read while I was a child, who knows maybe it's not too late. Your never to old to learn and the books can still bring a person joy, as for confusion" that is something I wont read about because I don't like to be confused when I read in reading you can experience things that others don't as you can keep the book a secret from others especially if you don't find anything good in the story.

I guess for now I don't like violence in a book but there are those who find it intresting to read about such things. I will pick what goes into my mind and that way it will be all good, I can hear the owel out side and it comes around once in a while but then the crickets stop and you cant hear then so I guess it's a trade off of which sound you hear. Some say the owel sounds like the dove in a way and if that's the case then they both sound beautiful, there are many doves around here and I'm carefull not to hit them when driving down the road here in town. To me a dove is a symble that God is watching over the town but I'm sure not all people here feel that way but that is what makes us different as we are all unique in our own way, you read about them in the bible and in other books "like as the wedding started they let go twelve doves to symbolize the purity of their love" awesome thought. For the little things that others don't see,, with me I see them like that smile which can make a persons day" or the wave which lets you know that someone knows you these are little things with much meaning no matter how small others see them, I remember seeing a friend that is now my insurance girl and she was doing some shopping in Belleville at the market and we both wanted some pork roast but didn't want the whole package so we both chipped in and bought half each. And this let us get our roast and we were both happy' I didn't know her name at the time but she knew mine and I told her to have a nice day and we went home and had that roast. It just goes to show that with two some things are possible.

Small things can lead to bigger ones later down the road, it seams many know me but I don't know them yet "at least not yet" people notice the things you do and if they are bad then your known for that attribute but it's always good to do your best to be kind and not put on a phony façade. I have found that most people are kind even if they don't want to show that side as some feel it shows weakness "but not me" God has given us all a good heart and it's up to us to keep it that way even though some turn from it depending on how they perceive things we are not all made the same and the differences is what brings us together. And usually if one can't do something another can by what they have learned through life, life experiences is what makes up the picture when it comes to your life and you create if it's beautiful or eugly. I see how people change from one day to the next and it's not always plesent but we except it and move on hoping they will connect with that more plesent side again. Our lives are full of mixed feelings and they change all the time from one minute to the next but there is a balance that we can achieve if we walk close to God for it's Him that brings peace to us his children. We are to become like Jesus according to the things I read and although I try, I fall short by many things like the things that make us human the different emotions that can fly off the handle sometimes. And although I don't mean to hurt anyone this can take place if your not careful, I try to think before I act or answer a question because offending someone isn't a good thing, and it can hurt those you care about. My natural aspect of things is to see good in everything then if they show different well then that is the way they are, I recall being told to always look and give a positive thought to people then if they show different well go on your way. Many people are not meant to be in your life as you grow some come into it and then they leave this means that they are only there for a short time to maybe help you with something and He uses many people even the bad ones to bring you too where you need to be, He gives us a since to detect things that will or will not last like a relationship. Showing insecurity in things can bring doubt to others and this can drive them away leaving a big hole inside you that you don't want to happen again, but being human we seam to make those mistakes again. "Why is that"? why do we travel back to that place? Is it a habbit from failed relationships before and if so why repeat them again with me it's wanting to know if the future will repeat it's self and in wanting to find that out you loose. Because there is no room for trust and if you cant trust then you loose, take one day at a time and if you can do that then things can become strong. Learn from each other the likes and dislikes of each other but most importently give things time to develop and let your self's grow on each other so you can become a part of each other two halfs make a hole, I like the happy ending the thought of people living together for 50 or so years but that isn't always the case in this day and age. Many are only together for a short time to maybe learn a lesson about them selves, and I guess that's ok for some but my thought are old school" the wanting of a happy ending which only comes with God. And maybe that's because He isn't around to nag on you but avoiding that aspect can cause you some harm if you don't learn to get along.

My adjustment to this new life has taken a long time but I'm optimistic that all will become apparent in this time I have taken, I have never been one to make a move on a women unless I feel secure about them being single and finding that out takes me a long time as I check everything out not wanting to ruffel the fethers of anyone. I know some say you have to fight for what you want but conflect isn't in my D.N.A. And that's why I don't like to fight I believe that God will fight my battles by changing their hearts, even the cultures in the 1800 didn't believe in violence some that is. Religious colonies traveled across the nation to find that place where they could live in peace and live in harmony without the use of guns, just wanting to work the land to build a place for their people being God's people. Separated by the belief that He would deliver them to their destination the land for which familys could grow and God's word would spread to others wanting the same thing. Sunday morning' and the coffee is great. I have somethings to do early this morning and then it's back home to get ready for church, yesterday we didn't have to turn on the air at the thrift store because it was nice out and we put away a lot of things that were brought in by others one women brought in some games and I bought one so we would have something to play this coming winter, winters are boring in this part of the country well boring everywhere really. As more people have to stay in because of the snow and cold but we will have our coffee and games to play and just maybe it will go by fast, last year we didn't have much snow so I think this year might make up for it but we can hope for the best.

During spring and summer the temps are up and down but still we make it, the southern bell was in yesterday and she was the one who brought in the games, doing some house cleaning and she said she has a lot more stuff that she will bring down later. We talked about the big city's and how they are overran with drugs and violence and how the little girl died in her bed just the other day, she then went on to say that she lived in that kind of inviorment when she lived in the city and relly didn't want to go back. And you cant blame her for wanting to keep her family safe from that kind of thing, to me there is no safer place then the small towns that look after their own and keep them safe. As for my self I wont go back to that big town living because it isn't safe not for people like me or really anyone for that matter, the noise in it's self would stop me from being able to write so my plan is to liveout my life in this town of dreams that I have found. There are many that wouldn't want to go backwards in time and I'm one of them, my life is what I make it and it's good for now in this little place which drew me here three years ago four years really and I have been doing my thing and surviving. Along with little brother who makes some of my time very plesent as we are a like in those certain ways, the train in pulling in as I can hear it off in the distence beinging in train cars to be filled for the outside world. I havent heard the report on the corn crop but no bad news is good news as far as I'm concerned, next year I will see if I can get a job maybe helping a farmer a couple of days a week and then maybe I can get enough to get my hobby published the life of a lost soul will be a hgood book and it will shed some light on the addiction problem that exists even in rural areas as for my living in that world it's like a life that has passed, but still the memories are there the ones that keep you from making the same mistake again in this world that is so short on time. At the most we have 100 years to get things right and if we don't then many will fall to satins rule, from what my niece told me I helped to change her life but only the father can see if she really did change but I have no reason to doubt her and she talks about God in many of her messages bringing me to believe there has been a change and in that happening her children have also changed wanting what God can give them which is love. I don't know what would of taken place if He hadn't found me that day and showed me the light which will carry me to the other place where I will live for ever, the thought of leaving without learning what I needed cant be comprehended in this mind of mine but I have a feeling that the dark side would of won that battle if God wouldn't of found me on that day. And then my new found friends wouldn't know me as I believe they too have learned something from my being here in Courtland' the beauty is in the eye of the beholder and I hope that they see the beauty that God has given us even in this little town which I call my home, many have lived all their lives here and know there are places where you wouldn't be able to hold on to the dreams that are visible here. As for trying to figure out why I'm here I will embrace the things that are all around me and do my best to make it better in anyway I can. God's love is all around and I can feel it when it presents it's self but it's not a constent it's something you just know is there and it makes it hard sometimes to explain it sometimes like my journey.

That I took if it was me I would say that the person was nuts to talk about this thing but that's what He wants, as for me it's a work in progress and in time there will be a conclusion to my life story. Our lives are a testament to what He can do with us even bring us back to finish our journey on this planet. Will we complete our mission? For this I have no doubt,, otherwise he wouldn't of given a second chance to wast time here. This world gets us ready for what's to come, but I also believe people blow things out of proportion and make things worse then they really are because he said not to worry and they do it anyway by scareing the hell out of people. I noticed something and it says when all God's people are saved then He will come so that makes our jobs more important then ever if we want to see JESUS Then we have to help the others that are still lost and we can do that by guiding them to the father. Our life stories can bring many. How, when and where. He changed our lives were we ever lost? And what brought us to that place we became close to Him? During my 32 years I had fallen as deep into drugs and alcohol and I had no clue what life was without it even when I couldn't sleep all I had to do is take a drink and then morning would come it was that simple. Those two things I thought cured everything that was wrong, the quick fix would later contribute to the quick fall. And when I landed it was hard everything I believed was false, everyone being like we were and now I can see that they weren't, as a matter of fact people who drank drew the same people just like drug sellers drew users and as long as there is a market for it they will not stop. I could of gone through my whole life and not known any different if the father didn't find me that day so long ago.

As for questions, I have many but they will have to wait for that time when He can answer them. Monday morning' and I was talking with some ladies at the church yesterday and for some reason through them talking about an elderly many my friends came into the picture, and I told them about them needing a liver transplane and how they have cancer of the lungs. In saying that I thanked God for gtting me away from there K town that is. And then I said how He will use others to ful fill one of His blessed children destiny and they said that's for sure, a minute later John came in and asked if I was preaching and then we laughed and went and got coffee. The church helps in many ways when something medical comes up to get us there and I have never had anyone help me or us like that before what a blessing, I started to read that book again but this time I read that your only supposed to read a chapter a day and this will help better in uderstanding the book giving you time to absorbe what you have read. In other words I read it to fast but now it should be easier from me to read it and get something out of it this time, in a way I felt like a preacher and it felt good sharing what had happened in my life and how the Father brought me here. For a few minutes it was like I was giving a serman and then I came back down to reality, I'm teaching my self as I have done so many things in my life and it's Him that opens my mind to understanding . If we can read it then if it belongs He will make it understandable to us as individuals as none of oflearn the same way, I'm taking a few things down to the church on the day of the sidewalk sale you might say. People will be coming from miles around to get good buys on things they think they might need and I have a computer that I will donate to the cause for helping others it's a pretty thing all nice and black but I will have to get it clean before I take it. It was something I bought long ago from a friend and I just don't use it as it's to slow but someone else can have it speeded up, for their purpose. I can hear the augers running down the road so they must be bringing in the corn from the fields not that there is much to bring in but a little is better then none and He will multiply it by a 100 if it's His will' this day starts a new week and as I was working at the thrift store I thought a women came in that is a friend of destiny's. And she was nice it was like it was her first time in the thrift store and she shopped for quite some time getting some things that she needed, I wish destiny would come in. And then I would talk to her, I have had a feeling that she is special and I really liked her with her individual ways. There are still many people which I havent met yet and getting to know her might be fun if we clicked well together, sometimes if a person interested in another they will sent a friend to check them out not wanting them to know that they feel something for them. And as many people do this some of the fun in seeing what the other thinks about the situation, if you have your close friend do the spying then you can sit in the back ground but in the translation something is missed a heart beat can make the difference and the spy isn't going to feel that. Only the one interested in the other can feel what's innside as for me I would rather have her come her self and do the checking and if the two hearts meet then it can go from there, my bashfulness has stoped me many times when ity comes to approaching a nice women and a chance missed is just that.

I remember her being quiet but always there when I needed a helping hand and that attracted me to her, her individuality being one of a kind and the niceness helped a lot. Does 20 some years hurt things well it depends on the two people. But if they get along then it could be a match made in heaven, her being 27 shouldn't matter but I know at that age they are wanting children because before to long that time period will pass and then some miss the boat, but through christ it's never to late as some had kids at the age of 70 or so. I couldn't imagine giving birth at that age but it does happen when He sets it in action one women was in her 80's and He brought it to pass, the day went well and now we are ready for our road trip in the morning. It was nice to see that the car is ready to go and nothing had to be added to the fluids meaning it isn't using any, the trip will take most of the day because I don't know how long Randy will be in surgery but I pray that all goes well and that he gets through it without a hitch. The church helped with fuel so we shouldn't have any problems with getting back, they seam to always be there for us even though I don't like to ask for help they encourage me to move past that and I'm working on that part trying not to feel so self absorbed. Well the day is coming to an end and the sun will be going down before too long, it seams when I go to bed early I'm still up until tiredness sets in well chow for now. Tuesday morning' and we will be off in a little while to Sallina to get Randy's back fixed, I'm in hope that his back pain will be gone shortly after he heals and it cangive him a better quality of life.

When I let others know that I get up at 3:00 Am. They say they could never do that and they ask what I do in that time and I tell them that I write, you can never know the things you do can help others when they travel the same road that you traveled. I learned that my mother and father were choosen to be my parents even thought Wess wasn't in the picture for my growing us. God knew the D.N.A. It would take for me to to make me and they had the perfect match, I used to think it was about him leaving me when I was a child but it wasn't it was about me living for God. He knew before I was born that my birth father wouldn't be in the picture and He must have been ok' with that, the things I have learnd has brought me to where I am today and He even knew I would end up here in Courtland after my survival of the dark place I was in. it's said that He knows every move and thought that we go through and the strides we over come to get to where we are going, when I talked to the ladies the other morning I felt comfortable as if they were a real part of my family. So I take that as a closeness which is forming and it's an awesome feeling just knowing I can talk to them about how God uses others to bless His own, in a way the life in K town seams to be fading as many of the old people I once knew are leaving this world but the ones which stand strong in the faith are living on. Rosa-lee is still hanging in there but I havent heard from her for a while, so I will try to write her later in the month but for now I have to make sure Randy is taken care of and gotten back into good health. The prison system didn't help in him getting better as I almost lost him once and now we are moving further to get him back to where he needs to be, on this day I know that he was meant to come here so he could build his life back up and I have to say he is doing a fine job. My being his teacher is easier because he also learn's at his own pace and nothing shoved down his throat causing resentment, and he is a good student. Our journey will take a couple of hours but that isn't very long he seams to want to get this taken care of and it will help to make him feel whole once again. The crickets are churping again out side my window and I know they would love to get into the house as they seam to like to get in the church sometimes but they don't last long in there as they get eatened up by their enemies, this will be the first road trip for the car except for when we go to Concorida but I'm talking about one of a distence of over 100 miles. I like to take baby steps when it comes to breaking in a different car that way if things go well a longer trip could be possible but not until maybe next year, I know the kids want to see me and they tell me that they miss me but I can't just up and take off when I have responcibilitys to my jobs. And others that need me in my town of dreams, I like doing what I do and as far as I know it's doing that which allows me to be able to live the life that He has chosen for me and sometimes it's not always what you do but how you do it. And that can make a big difference, things don't happen very fast here and for that I'm glad as we get older we seam to not be able to do the things we used to do, but if you take pride in what you do. Then you should feel good about those things age gets to us all and we slow down so we have to take a wiser job and maybe teach others what we once did in our younger years.

As for me I do the best I can with what I have, and that's all the father askes of us but we must not loose sight of our mission and spread the good word to those who may not of heard it before. God wont take you to a place where his grace wont protect you and I find comfort in knowing that, Randy took out the trash yesterday so we wouldn't have to do it this morning but I still have to get it out at the church. And they know I have to go to Salina this morning so they will bring it in "such good friends" last time I missed my turn in salina but I hope to find it with no problem this morning, there is a big difference when you go between seasons as sometimes the trees are going into hibernation and the hospital is easy to see and then other times you can't see it for anything as the trees are full and hide the place. But we always make it, the trip we nice but I used a little tranny fluid so that's something which will have to be fixed. Wednesday morning' and it got hot yesterday but by leaveing in the morning it was cool until we got there and then the heat set in the guyi got the car from isgoing to fix the problem and that makes me feel better, still till this day driving takes a lot out of me and I don't know why but it passes with some sleep and then I'm ready to go. Little brother didn't have to have surgery so they gave him some meds that should help for a time, it seams like that's all they do anymore in this world of getting people taken care of. I have to take the car down there on Friday at 1:00 after lunch but that's the only time he has open for this week so I had to take it. Today I work at the thrift store and that should be fun to see some of the things which others have brought in, my work with Beverly has become quite plesent as I like doing what I do the looking at things some seam to be tired of and then you have the horders and they just keep their stuff hoping one day that they will be worth something.

Which in reality they are worthless and have no value, through the years we have been in many garage sales and what we bring usually sells so we will see what takes place on Saturday. In the time I have been here we have always made it but the bad word of worry is coming by to visit and I don't like it, as I went to take the trash can in yesterday I and Kathy scared the heck out of each other. And at least it wasn't just me, it was both of us. I hope I didn't scare her too bad, the train of thought was interrupted but that's ok' in the night I ran into Randy twice which is different because he usually sleeps as sound as a log, such a strange thing to happen in the dark of the night but then it was back to bed and morning arrived on time as usual. I havent heard from my kids lately but I will see them soon as time is only relStacynt to us and it doesn't exist to the father. It says if you get confused or flustered you are trying too hard to please which isn't a good thing O man' they took off Antique road show what a bummer. I like watching it each Wednesday morning but not today O well maybe next week, I used to think that things were high on price here but after going on that road trip I find that there not. As a matter of fact, in the city it cost a lot more then here so be thankful for what you have, the struggles in life can sometimes bring you down but if that happens just look up because He is there for you no matter what. Sometimes we can see our writing in other things that people do but that should be a testament that others are reading what you put out there and to me that's a good thing. Money seams to be a big part of things and if you don't have it then life can be hard very hard' as for doing more then I'm able to do right now it would be the death of me but I know in time I will have to try and move forward in my learning to bring about something special. I do want to be a priest someday but don't know how to attain it and maybe in time Kathy could teach me only God knows for sure, was I meant to be a man of God according to the book yes we all are meant to have a mission in life. A mission to spread the word to those who don't know it or have fallen away from it, I yearn to feel things that only God can give that closeness which will one day bring us together like father and son the boundry that is between us has to be taken away and I don't know how to do that as yet. Thursday morning' yesterday went well but not too many customers just about three of them, but we hope to have a lot more on Saturday with the state wide garage sale there even putting up a stop sign in front of the thrift store. They said it drew customers last year so we will see what happens, people from all around come here to spend money and that's awesome. As for the rain we needed we got some last night and now the grass will turn green once again, harley is up this morning and I don't kow why because usually he sleeps until around the time Randy gets up which is a lot later then this. Some days he acts strange and I still havent found out why it's like he hides from me for some reason but it could just be his way of dealing with things, and that's ok too.

I can tell that the weather is getting colder and before to long the heat will have to be turned on to stay warn but indian summer should be on it's way once we get our first freeze. And then the temps will rise again for a short time, and then plunder for the winter, the house was sealed good when they put in the windows so it's nice and tight for the snowy times which are coming and we can never tell how cold it will get until that time gets here. Or the amount of snow we will recive during that season if it rains real good before the freeze then the winter weat will be good and that I think is there most important crop, but survivla really depends on all the crops here in the heart land which the corn wasn't very good at this time. Maybe next year will be different if things go right, God has brought us a long ways since we came here and I'm hoping that we can handle things since pop's went to be with Him' according to some our earthly tents are just that. Sort of like camping before you go home to that greater place which He has built for us a testing sight to see if we have come to love Jesus like God does, my journey has brought me closer to him in many ways but still I have a ways to go to be ready. I feel in my heart that there is more to do an when the time is right then He will bring things to pass, I have read that no one knows when He will come but the time wont be until all His people are saved so we need to get into gear. And then He will bring his people home to dwell in the house of the Lord, will I see this in my life time here on earth I cant say for sure but I hope I at least make a stride towards it. The girl in Scandia is getting ready to have her child and she isn't very big I just hope it's strong and healthy for her and brings her much joy as she goes through life raising it, many people are having babies and Courtland has it's share of them each year.

Last night the thunder hit hard as the rain began but then I fell a sleep and it didn't wake me up, but I could see the water on the streets this morning looking out the kitchen window. And it was very wet I hope it was enough to record that way we will know how much we got, this weekend will be exciting for some as they spend some of thrie hard earned money here in Courtland to build our economy I think it's awesome to give to the church as they do so much for others who need it during tough times and it's nice to be a part of that in this day and age just being a part of the bigger plan makes you feel good inside knowing you helped people who other wise wouldn't have a chance. During the time when I really didn't think we would make it we somehow pulled through, and that's what counts during these later years in life the belonging to a community that cares for other is a great thing and it's good to be a part of that even if it's a little part it makes a difference. My friend had to go and get some mellons to put out side the thrift shop this will also draw customers as people are curious about things and want to know what's there, I believe it's all in the drawing of people that makes things sell and then once they are there nature kicks in and they find the things they need or want. There is also a few garage sales in the community hall and I'm sure they will do good also bringing in money to help some make it through winter, that' a tough time when you cant go out much and have to stay in playing games and other things so the month flies by. When you feel traped in a corner or I feel that way I pray for things to get better and usually it does. My love for God is stronger then it's ever been and I hope for better days as we go through this time in my life, for some reason I have no doubt that I will survive but I know there is more for me to learn if I can just figure it out. I could be making things harder then they are or reading more into the picture then what's there but I ask for His help in making things more clear, we as people sometimes try to hard and that's when you know something isn't right and it even says it in the word' the scars of being pushed have left a mark and it needs to be undone so I can find my purpose in this world some say it's all in the search. And there has been many that go their whole lives searching for the answer, I met an old lady that believed it was all in the search so that left her with her own journey to figure out. I saw Peggy yesterday and I noticed she didn't have a wedding ring on her finger, could this be a sign that she isn't married? I will have to find out down the road. She is funny sometimes and we laugh from time to time but I do that with most of the people in the bank as we are like brothers and sisters and we are if you really look at it, we are all brothers and sisters in christ but I don't know if there is someone special in her life so now the asking part comes into play. Friday morning and the garage sale starts today, I have been working on a stragidy for a story about marijuana and the reasons it shouldn't be made legal. Science says that it causes cancer in a guys privets along with Emphyzema of the lungs which my uncle had when he died although he never smoked cigarettes. So the things that are trying to stop by having people quit smoking will appear with the marijuana use. As I just got done sending a letter to the editor I'm in hope that the message gets out about the destruction that pot being made legal will cause and I know some others will not see things my way. But that's ok' as it's just my opinion and that's what the page is for. Thought the years I have kept my part on trying to open peoples eyes but will it be enough?

Will they see the destruction that it will cause? Only time will answer that question but there is hope and where hope exist then there is a chance in that shallow window that some see out of. My hole life has been against the things that almost destroyed me, am I wrong from trying to stop it? I don't think so, but people can rationalize anything so all I can do is give a little food for thought and maybe they will pick up on it. Saturdays morning' and they are saying the corn crop was better then expected but then as much as we prayed for it no less was excepted. The day is full of things to do as thhe garage sale is still going starting at 9:00 this morning when I go and do my part and sit at the church while customers come in I can tell it's going to be another cold morning but hey we will get used to it, the getting to know others has become easy after just a short time so that part is behind me now. One women Jan called yesterday to see if what I wanted for the printer and I told her $25.00 but they could have the whole thing for $ 75.00 which is a good deal for someone. Especially around here I like to give good deals because it brings people round to check out other things. I think from now on the mornings will be cold and you can tell it's going to be that way by the way the squirrels are out gathering their nuts for the winter and the way the leaves are falling from the trees so fall is here even though it seamd early, not much time to get the house next door fixed and the other built on the corner as they both will need insolation to keep them warm for the cold winter other wise they could freeze without it like I did for a couple of years.

But hey! We survived and that's what mattered, I hoping that in this next year I can find a program that does roofs for the government that way I can qualify for the low income part and get a new one. That would really set things off, as time goes on we try and do our best to stay alive in this town of dreamd where we feel at home. Yesterday my car was fixed and now I don't have to worry and longer about traveling the guy said that it will take a while for the trans fluid to burn off but that's something I can live with, we have these garage sales once a year to raise money for worthy causes and you never know when your time of need will set in but I hope for the best in that department and go on with life, you could see people coming in town as we left yesterday and I know they all must have bought something even if it was just a trinket to remind them of the state wide sale. If I had the room, I would stock pile things until next year. But I have only so much room in this house of mine, many do it anyway as they have many things they don't need any longer it's a way to get rid of the things no longer in use like my things that just sit around in the closet with no purpose. I want to take my guitar down but I'm afraid I wouldn't find another one so nice and I want to take lessons so I can further my writing career with music my songe would become more clear if I could connect with the tunes but for now they will remain in my head until they are ready to come to light that is the beauty of writing songs creating them in your mind before the music is put to them and then write the music to fit the song what a way to go! In doing it this way you own the song and no one else because they don't have a clue of what's in your mind. The creating is great especially when the church hears it for the first time and they enjoy it, they are the first to hear the finished product and that makes them special our talents are meant to be heard for God's enjoyment not so much ours but His and that's why I write them. If it wasn't for that day when He came to find me my songs would of never been heard by my friends and I like the input when they like it, as for being told that it's bad I have done that many times so I don't need that. We are our own worst judge of our selves, because no one sees us the way we do and the words to a song tells a story a little about your self and how things happen in your life. Many times I have beat my self up because I couldn't get something right but then in time it's made clear but getting mad just makes me more determined to find the right thing to fit the situation, when I write a song sometime it takes a year to get it situated in this mind of mine but once it's there it doesn't come out until I'm ready for it to show it's face. I have yet to talk to Tanner about my song's but we will see what happens next week maybe the time will present it's self, I do know there are many songs left inside of me but it's me that has to bring them to the surface and then if need be they can be built on to make them longer but I like my songs the way they are because they give just enough to make the people want more and to hear more of the story. All that I do comes from inside and all that I am is created by God, He had His sights on me way before I was born and He knew that I would do this one day and maybe it was the struggles that brought these songs into existence the struggles of life that brought me from the pit to where I am today. For as well as He knew His son would die here He also knew I would live after all that I went through and in time this could work to my advantage singing a song and then talking about dream makers and dream breakers bringing in the curse of addiction could set the stage to draw people to listen to the message that He wants them to hear and me of course.

I would be the tool that he created so many would understand that life could be beautiful without the use of drugs and alcohol. If this is the way it's meant to be, then I pray that He will make it happen and bring the people to hear the message. Hope is a main stay in over coming such a destructive thing in life but with God by your side no one can destroy what He starts, no man can stop the power of God not even on his best day so people should bring forth their problems and bring them to God' He brought me a long ways and now I have to figure out a few things but I'm positive that He will help me in this endeavor and not forsake me. We are all His children and boy does He love us, from before birth until eternity for this is His word and He is the same today as He was yesterday. Never changing. Sunday morning' and I pretty much got most f the cleaning done last night so church can open on time this morning also I worked with Jan and there are a lot of them in this part of the country also. I got lucky and can now pay all my bills for the month anyway no it isn't luck it was His doing. I met still more people as the garage sale took off for the weekend and all of them were nice, even the kids had fun going from one sale to another to see what they could get from them in the realm of toys and other things to play with in a way it reminded me of a holiday where the kids were happy because they could just run around and enjoy them selves. Still I have to mop the floors nd that can be done later this morning, we have a new custermor at the thrift store and she has been there twice now and I expect that we will see her again this next week also. Like many people she must be looking for a bargen in these hard times also trying to survive in this economy is really hard if you don't have anything and it seams we are all that way, just getting by as we go through life and hoping for the best out of things.

As we now move into winter the farmers can slow down and kind of kick back once the crops are in the fields wheat is what they will now plant so it can take root and become a good crop for next spring when the rains come and winter will keep the crop safe as the ground freezes and put's the seed into a dormet stage you might call it limbo until it can become really good because everything the wheat needs is right in the seed when it's sprayed with a certain chemical no bugs can get to it and it has a better chance, I saw Mark the other morning during the garage sale and he looked really good I think he might have been out at the garage sales seeing what some people had. As for anyone else they has some people coming from all around coming from Colorado and they had a U haul behind their vehical picking up on the bargans that were out there to have. I believe they might have had a shop of their own back home and were filling it up with things they got from around here in Kansas, I like to use my mind to think that they are also making a living in their own way and it's a good way being honest and making a living enjoying the thing they do and that's important in this life making sure you have enough to survive but never looseing sight of God in the process a balancing act you might say and it would take some getting used to because temptation is everywhere and it isn't always a good thing, but we try our best and move on with life in hope that we will stay on the right path of life. My look on life is that if you got all the devilish things out of you then the good will surely follow, tomorrow is the beginning of a new week so we will see what happens there but I know He has something good in my forcast a helping hand from a friend or giving that helping hand to others that need it. You can never tell what's on His mind and you never know what He will put into your heart to bring change into the world. As I said the weather is changing and fall is just down the road but we never know what gifts he or she will bring with them in the changing of seasons, I was told that the neighbors house has arrived but I have yet to see it. I talked with her last week and she said she would be glad when it gets here so she can get everything set up and I know she has a lot of work a head of her in doing that with winter coming on it will be like running a foot race with the seasons to get everything ready before the snow falls. They have some things in storage so that will be their first step to get them, and get it set up. The work next door is still going on and they had to do some pluming because the old is worn out, so the new will come in making it a good and sturdy home for someone. It seams many are wanting to move here to my town of dreams and maybe they are hoping for the same thing just a quiet place where you can gather your thoughts and not have to deal with the violence in the other parts of the country.

My regrets are few as I move forward into the coming year maybe my life has changed for the better and I pray that it keeps going, in the direction that it's in. The augers are running this morning across the way and the crickets are not churping but then it might be too early for them also, it's like the town never sleeps just going all the time to sustain it's self. My friend Phillis was ill so she had to stay home and recover my prayers are with her so she will get well soon, many believe prayer doesn't do anything and they could never be so wrong. Humbling your self before God is something that changes the mind eturnally and they say you can see the change in the mind even on exray, for some reason it wakes up a sleeping part of the mind to give some more of an understanding of things. Being we only use 10% of our mind I wonder how it would feel to have the whole thing wake up? Could that be part of what happens when your spirit leaves this world to go where He will one day send us? As the things which botherd us here become of non importance our mind can grow in a different direction the class room is what they are callling this life here, and we are the students to learn new things and old things that we might have forgotten which could help us understand things better as we age. For in the beginning I couldn't recall the things which took place in my life but with time He brought them to light so I could see that He had been there all along, just because we don't see it doesn't mean that it didn't happen for some reason certain things get pushed to the back of our minds and are forgotten. Like the three miracles that happened when the mind is filled with the dark side of life you can't see the good things which have taken place because they happen so seldom that you loose track of His goodness.

I remember the tears that I cried but they have faided and to put a mark on when, why, and how come they occurred I can't but I know they happened and there are many rivers that are full from them. Like right now how come this comes to mind? Today I'm a very happy man' but it seams I always look towards the future when maybe I should just be looking at today. Wondering if things will stay ok with financial things if the money thing was something I didn't have to worry about then I could focus on other things more but for some reason that takes up a lot of the time and if I'm doing this wrong I wish He would tell me I would give anything to not have to worry about such things. I do know the rich have no money worries but many of them are not happy, but money just makes life a little easier. The time you could have helping others would be a better way to spend that time, feeding the poor and giving them a start in life that you never had but I also know if you didn't go through the struggles in your life then you can't grow past those and learn from them. For some reason He knew that my life would end up the way it is today and He also knew that I had to go through the pain I went through to learn and grow, for some reason it wasn't in the cards for me to live a blessed life from birth like so many others did He not want me to know my birth father? And if so why!! Because as far as I'm concerned that piece will always be missing.

CHAPTER 12

A new chapter of the future is right here but I can't write it until it comes into play, that why it takes so long to write a book. My land' Monday morning, and another day that He has given us I can tell that it's cold out but according to the weather man, it's supposed to be nice as the day wares on. The stuff at the church will be taken to the thrift store and this morning I'm going to go and clean, it's that time of year when we will start bible school and the pastor said 24 kids so far are ready to learn. Such a great thing the leaves are already falling when they shouldn't be but hey mother nature knows her job, even the grass is being dragged in to the church as it starts to die for the year so that leaves more work for me but no complaints here. It's expected at this time of year, they are starting bible classes for the older people also but they are being held in Scandia to start things off and then they will decide which place will be better here or there. If they were having it here I would go but travel cost gas, and it's about $ 4.00 a gallon. Which to me is out of this world, just like food the price has gone so high you can hardly afford to eat but we get by and that's what matters. I wonder how it was in the dirty thirty's some say that people couldn't afford to by things so they made them and they were just as happy, sharing a meal wasn't uncommon when you went to visit people and I think that time might repeat it's self once again. All our brothers and sisters pitching in to make things a little better as we move into 2013, in John the story in the bible it talks about the anti Christ and it says his name but I will have to study it to find out where it is and with that I will need help, it also says that God's people shouldn't worry about such things so I wont but others need to know what's going to take place. When you learn we are like a child or a babe but then as we get older we learn to do things for our selves and God's gifts seam to slow down as we grow into maturity and learn to do things for our selves.

In my learning it takes time to learn the things I need to know and understand but in the end I believe I will make it, other wise He wouldn't of put me on this path of discovery to find out the things I need to know although my journey is a long one I know He will be there to help me through it and help me to understand the things I need to learn. My journey started late but your never too old to learn as some say and I'm living proof that God can teach anyone no matter how this world has destroyed some of the things they could of learned as a child, the only difference is that now my mind is that of an adult with just a little bit of a child in there somewhere willing to learn new things as they are presented to me in this new kind of life. In a way I can see why He didn't take me because I had no knowledge of the world and what my mission was but now that I'm learning I will be accountable for my learning, lack of knowledge is something that can hold you back until you learn about the creator and why He made us His children. Our problems are our own created by us but with His love He will step in and help, for us to understand why He is who He is even though we may have gone through life not knowing him. He gives us that second chance to learn and live the life that was meant for us I have never seen a person who's mind is always set on study because there are other things in life that take up time and maybe that's why He gives us the time we need. I have many things to do today but they don't take up much time really unless things are really dirty, my job lets me do things at my own pace and this in it's self lets me do a good job and bring honor to God' everything I do is for Him and I'm just a vessel to carry out what He isn't able to do here, and maybe these things might be something He needs help with in other words I'm His helper as many other folks are. For surely He doesn't run things like a thrift store as He is too busy in the cosmos or that other die mention where the impossible becomes possible.

It's humid this morning as the season is changing and we will get a lot of that these next few months but you learn to put up with it and go on through the winter. I should get a bunch of books to read while winter is here and broaden this mind that the lord has given me, for this is a chance to make it wiser and stronger then ever like the mussels in your arms and back. If not used them they shrivel up and fade away. Tuesday morning and it's another cold one but no frost of freezing as of yet, I talked to Robert at church and he said thee corn crop was fair so it did some good to plant, from time to time I get a strange feeling and It's one that cant be explained like many others I have had in the past could it be a test? It says He test us from time to time and I believe this to be true, to maybe test our faith and see if it's still strong. In the beginning I didn't think this would be a diary but through time it has taken on that shape, as for the old it is gone the old ways of addiction but new things have shown them selves and I stay busy most of the time. I can only imagine how Greg does it getting out there every morning and taking care of his farm and then getting the fields planted for each crop. But like with writing after a while it becomes second nature to you just like the jobs I do for others as the days and weeks pass Tuesday's are different here then in K town we never knew when the trash was picked up but in our small town it's every Tuesday letting us get everything ready for them to haul it away. Randy found his little machine in the garbage and has yet to get it going, but with his determination I can see him getting it going maybe this winter, in the book I'm reading the chapters are only about three or four pages one for each day on a 40 day journey. The Author says it gives time for God to make things take root and of course I'm very impatient but I think that stems from childhood thinking the answer should be answered right away when it cant be because all things take time, some people asked if I went on any trips this year? And I had to reply that I didn't with the funeral and other things that have gone on. Little brother is still a work in progress and once that is finished then maybe a trip will be in the cards but for now money is too tight just trying to survive, but if I have to have struggles then this is the place to have them . A place where people care about you and would miss you if you up and took off, my life here' is better then it's been most of my life and I think my friends see that and God for that matter my home is stable and I love working in the yard also I look forward to meeting someone further down the line as people get to know I am single.

During the next year or so I will get to know more people as they come from all around even the smaller towns, if you can believe there is one smaller then this one. But there is and some only have under a 100 people which would make it like the smallest community there is, I can remember when Kearney wasn't so big and the smaller community's had to go there and then as time went on they grew and became their own little piece of the world with city offices and other things that helped them grow. Gibbon Nebraska was the first place we lived coming to this part of the country and Rod more or less grew up there, and then he met Mary and it was love at first sight. It's hard to imagine him being 16 years old but he wanted to live on his own and he did, moving from Los Angeles with a friend to Nebraska was his great move and he never went back because of hard times. The stories he used to tell about sleeping in cars and such would make you think twice about stopping what you were doing when you love something so much as he did Mary, through their fights and all else they made a life and became a family and are still together today 40 years later. I remember they were just so different like water and oil but through it all they found a mixture that worked for them, I always thought of Rod as the tame one and Mary the bitchy one that if she didn't get her own way she could make life misurable and she did a good job at it. But also I can see her part of the picture because she wanted what she wanted and no one would stand in her way of getting it.

We never did see eye to eye but that's ok' that's just the way life is sometimes. My life here in Courtland is my shot at having something and I do things my own way which seams to agree with my life style but I have become closer to God here or understanding what He wants from His family and in time I will grow and understand more. The one thing I have learned is that all things take time and nothing is instent not in this world we cant be programmed like a computer because time is what it takes for understanding things, my mind anyway has to process things and that in it's self takes a lot of time for me anyway but as I grow in faith and hope I know that our world has more good in it then bad. The quiet time is when I'm alone and it doesn't matter what I'm doing, that time when you can separate you're self from the rest of the world and feel like your in a seprate place where no one can touch you but the spirit of God and I talk to him like I did in the light when my body was seprated from my soul. It was at that time when I realized there was more to life, more then what I had experienced in the years before that happened. Being a lost soul is lonely especially when you don't have a clue of what life is all about the things I learn today should have been learned in childhood but they weren't for some reason. Does going to school get you ready for a carer and if so then maybe it was meant to be this way, as my learning today is more about God and Jesus' not science and math for I don't believe those things are relivent to God. He wants us to know that our lives in eternity will be for ever and those things only pertain to life here on earth, what will become of us when we reach this other place? For the riches there out weigh the riches here and those here only pertain to here, nothing we have will ever leave this place it's only borrowed from God as He owns it all. Then when our time comes we will or He will pass it on to others who might need it in this life. When I visited a church a long time ago I was told that even after death we would remain here because the world was created for us, I find this consept hard to swallow because the world couldn't hold all that have died and all that will die in the future but heaven is much bigger then this place we now live. The bible says my father has a house and in that house many rooms which is being prepared for you. And when it talks about our homes here they are called a tent and a tent doesn't have a sturdy foundation, everything pertaining to God should have a sturdy foundation it is written and it's so. And that leads me to believe that the fathers house is real and not fictional, will our minds ever let us grasp the things we need to know or will it play tricks on us from time to time? Testing us to see if we grasp what He wants us to know, in my journey' many things have brought me to believe that miracles do happen. Some call them luck which I don't believe and others well freak accidents, but the truth of the matter is that he works in many different things and I don't have a clue how he helps us all. Even from the child crying He can bring comfort and wipe away the tears, to the person fighting addiction who has given up on life because they see no way out. I have been there and He brought me back even better then before but still learning. How is He able to wipe away the tears from a fallen soul and let them go on as if it didn't happen, and not let them return. They say everything is recorded in our minds like a computer, our hurts and sorrows and the happiness faids like it was never there but those emotions come back when we need them, to bring those feelings alive once again. They are something which is in our D.N.A. Wired into us before our birth, we all want to live for ever and that too is wired into us to help us to get ready for what's to come.

I don't understand the love between Him and I but I know it's there, more so" then the love I have ever felt for a person. And maybe it could be because He has shown love to me without all the crap that we humans put attached to it, many times I thought my time might be up but in the end He brought me through it and I was better for it. The day hasn't been a good one and I don't know how we will make it if I have to pulll all the weight, it seams that little brother just likes to sleep instead of doing anything and it really pisses me off is this another test to see how much I can take? And if it is my fuse is getting short I want to show my anger but with it comes ignorance dam I'm mad and that is a feeling I don't like. Although I'm angry I will bare the cross that weighs heavy on my back, I don't know of anyone who would let someone live with them for such a small amount that wouldn't get them a shoe box to live in. But with careing comes pain and it makes me wonder why I even do it for others. Wednesday morning' and I know summer is over by the feel of the coldness, it's been getting down into the 40's and then in the 60's and 70's during the day. If this is any indication of what's coming then we should have one heck of a cold winter. So I will have to turn on the heat within the next couple of weeks, it seams the older people get sick at this time of year and so do I from time to time but with taking care of my self better maybe this year will be different. It's strange how the seasons change and the weather with it, going from hot to cold and then sometimes hot once again with Indian summer. But it's that first freeze which determines if the winter wheat will be a good crop or not.

My writing was never meant to talk about crops but it's part of my community and I'm a part of that so it has to be brought up. I'm going to talk with Tanner sometime this week to see if my songs would be able to be played by his band, I would like to hear it in a different setting one by different insterments instead of just the piano I do know a keyboard would make it sound good and the others as well. Many find them selves in drugs during their break out but with me those days are long gone and the memories bring on my songs to God the father and Jesus. I felt that this might be a sign but with those feelings they come and they go just as fast as they get here and it's hard for me to determine if they are a sign from the father. I call it an epiphany something good because at the time it feels right in every way, but then it fades on the same day as if it was never there and then like a dream it's gone to not return. What are these things that happen? For surely they feel right at the time so good even that you feel as if they are a part of me. Like something you want but don't deserve I have had those feelings before but never acted on them because they felt so surreal and they say if it feels too good to be true then it probably is. Yes' the Antique road show is on this morning and I love it and it's history as each piece of history tells a story of families and what they did back then in a way giving some the history of those who came before them. My heritage is unknown on my fathers side but it's well knows on the creator who created me, in my finding out things. God is the one who said I was to be what I became and I wonder if it's turning out the way He planed? I guess Him being God He could change or wipe out any disappointments but I can't see him doing that with the love He has in His heart, patients is something He is known for and of course he created them so it has to be something we are taught as we grow in faith and love. It's going on 6:00 Am. And the day is about to start little brother is coughing and he isn't even up yet O well that doesn't mark out how the day is going to go, as I look inside my closet I can see that there used to be a door which is right by Randys head. The house was built in a strange fashion but then it was built a 100 years ago so what do you expect! During a time when things were built by hand even the molding is wide and very ornate at least it is to me not having anything to compare it too. I can almost picture my home back in the day all brand new with it's cellar just out the back door I almost wish I was there having a new garage out back which deteriorated from the elements over those 80 or so years. I wonder what it cost to build back then? A home in a place that seams to of stood still over time except for what's gone now like the garage and the shed which used to be out back, the trees have to be as old or older then the home giving it shade during the times when Air-conditioning wasn't even thought of yet. I believe it had to of been very hot here and farmers had to of had a hot time out in the fields with just an umbrella to give them shade, even today some old timers do the same thing and I have seen it when they are in the field. Here you have someone almost 80 doing the same thing they did most of their lives awesome how they can still go on without the modern tractors of today where you control the temp inside of it and can go on for a day at a time.

It's Sept 19th and most of the month is gone but we will make it through this one as we have so many before, it's not plesent wondering all the time if you will make it to the next month but it keeps you busy trying to find ways to maybe cut corners so you will survive. Thursday morning' yesterday I learned that a women I have known is going to be living across from us in Chesters house that they sold it's just across the alley from us. She goes to my church but hasn't been in as much as she used to, but when problems arise then you have to take care of them and that can cause emotional things to happen which is hard to deal with. I have seen her husband come to church but with jobs being what they are it's hard to make it each week I believe they had a farm out in the country which must have been sold to make the move to town it's going to be another cold morning but it will soon warm up as the day goes on. I worked with a different women yesterday, and she is so different from me kind of a talker but I would rather read when things are slow not knowing really what to say to out going people. She talked about her husband who has died and how he used to like to check on the crops when they were driving down thee road complaining about the weeds and things just a past time for the old fella I guess, my self I have never been a talker but that goes to show the different personalities we all have and that there has to be someone for everyone even for a talker. Owna was a talker back in the day and I think she did it just to hear her self talk complaining about everything her kids did.

As for me I don't see change in that department with my soul, for I talk to the father when things get me down and it seams like a main stay to me. I may not be rich but in a way I am, with the people who care about me the women I was talking about has went on a weight watchers thing and has lost 80 pounds maybe trying to change her self in some way. We all try to change in hope to make us better in some way and maybe that was her way of bringing her self back, I really can't say but she is a good person and I like her she is also quiet in her own way like a lot of people. As for the women I worked with she is the only one I have found that is out spoken the way she is, but I'm sure there are others that I haven't met yet for surely she isn't the only one. I seen one women that has started to come in the thrift store and she is young but also a talker but you can tell she knows when to talk and when not to she seams so full of life and doesn't know where to put the energy, but she is nice and polite and will grow into a beautiful women if I had to guess she would be about in her mid to late 20's at that age to start a family. I see so many different kinds of people and they all have their own stories from divorce to making it on their own in a little town they call Courtland, Kansas. If you can make it here you can have a pretty good life once you get past the bills and such then it's smooth sailing when all are happy, I used to see her walking to try and loose weight and even offered her a ride once but she didn't except and then I understood. In this life we all have baggage and some get rid of it when others carry it round with them through life, as for mine I don't know if it's gone away but I have been working on it trying to fix some of what's wrong like the life of addiction I like to think of it as a problem that's gone now. To not return but you can never tell what's beyond the hill on the other side of the mountain, although He wont give you a mountain you can't climb that doesn't mean you won't fall off the other side and roll to the bottom. Is there a perfect life this I can't really say but the bible says there is, as for the apostles like Paul and the others they all suffered from one thing or another like depression, and some wouldn't do what He asked causig him to be eaten by a big fish. Do we understand when He talks to us I don't think so, not at first. Because it's so fast the visions appear and then they are gone in just a matter of hours not letting us grasp them fully, but then if they reaper you can get a glimps of what's going on. Friday and the water bill is late but no charge or that happening and they don't know when it will be out something wrong with the computers in the city offices. The change in the weaher has many feeling it, as the body changes to meet the needs for winter coming on and we haven't had to run th air-conditioning. Change seams to always be in he air the plant next door has been running night and day trying to keep up with things, getting the corn in from the fields and transporting it other places. The plant is summular to Western Alfalfa the plant I worked at for many years filling and unfilling the grain bins as they make there trips to other countrys and where ever to be sold for the farmers. The dust is what gets to you and only being just a jont down the road we get the dust over here and washing the car doesn't do much good during this time but you have to keep it off other wise it looks like hell, Randy didn't feel to good yesterday but I chalk that up to the change in things. The body getting ready for winter and I think we all feel it at one point or another, but in time it will pass and things will get back to normal.

Tomorrow it's off to the thrift store but soon they will be closeing for the year as they are not open during winter only through spring summer and fall but the things they do really helps the community. Like with one person who wants to move back here she is disabled but want to be around family and friends so she found a place in Scandia but she needs a frig, and a stove. And the church will help with that, from what I understand she was in a car wreck and now has seizures which means she will need a lot of help if she should deside to make the trip but medical where she lives is good and takes care of everything and she has to find out if they would do the same here. It might be an opportunity to try and help in some way but we will see only time will tell in that situation, bad things can happen to good people and it isn't an easy thing to deal with. The travel it takes to get everything set up, but if it's meant to be then He seams to find a way to bring things together, it's strange how things just happen with no rime or reason to it and that God bringing things together for some purpose. How I got to this time and age is beyond me but I'm here and things are still holding together like a fine glue which can stand the test of time, for the days are nice especially during the late hours of the day when it gets the warmest, my journey will last for many more years as time sets in and allows us to grow in the spirit of God and you never know what will happen from one month to the next for change is always happening and all we can do it pray that things will come full circle in this life He has created for us.

I'm finding out that there is more to do here then I once thought but with all things it takes time like learning about God and how one day he will take us home to be with Him in that big house on the hill. I do know that you can get wrapped up in things in this world, and that can throw you off track trying to do earthly things tryiing to get a head. My opinion on things was wrong but then many of ours, are that way. The beginning of a new life takes many turns and some can confuse you as you move forward, even today the world is a lot different then the one I grew up in and in that one I didn't know day from night being in the dark place which once rulled my world. The light shines much brighter these days as I pull my self up out of bed to start the new day, and some days are harder then others if the night hasn't been a good one but as the day wares on things seam to brighten up giving me that glimmer of hope. It's late in the afternoon and the day is coming to an end but not before we went to town for a few things to tide us over until next week, I tried to catch Tannner at the bank but he wasn't in today so I will have to wait until next week to catch him and see if we can make things happen with my music, and although I don't know what will happen it's a start all he can say is that it's a no go. Saturday and I slept pretty well except for the dreams that tried to explain them selves, isn't that a hoot? The days are winding down until the end of the month and then it will be payday again. But this next month will be tighter then ever and we will have to budget more then ever in hope that we can make it better then last month because if it wasn't for the sale of something we wouldn't have made it, and even then. I don't know if I can stretch it until the end of the month but I pray that I can. Back when mom was alive she knew how to stretch money an now being her son I have to figure out how to do the same in hope that I can keep the things I have and not loose them. My songs are coming back to me but in a different way giving me a glimps of christ hanging from the cross and the pain He must have felt a He died for our sins, but also the joy. As He had to know that He saved us from sin' I can't imagine what He went through trying to explain things to his followers, and how one day they would be in heaven along with him. Noha was a delight to God and it took him 120 years for him to build the ark and he did it precisely as God instructed, for He didn't just say to build an old boat. And then the flood came and our heritage started wih Noha because the rest of the world was wiped out not leaving a soul except for the animals and Noha's family, thinking about that time people must have been really out of control more then today which is hard to swallow with what's happening in the world today, I talked with Mark in Kearney O'Brien that is and he seams to be doing ok' he let me know that April is getting married in the second month of 2013 and they are getting ready for it. Not sure if I will go but I wish her the best as she takes that walk down the ile into a marriage that will bring her the kids she wants, to me she is still a child but then I don't see her very oftend anymore with the miles that separate me from going there. This will be the first good news I have heard out of Kearney in a while but still time stands in the way until that day come's and you never know what will happen in that time.

I'm making strides towards finding someone but even with the wanting too comes the timing factor and that's always off for me. But I never give up hope that she will find her way into my life, I cant help but feel that she is here in Courtland or close by. And why this feeling exist I havent a clue, maybe it's hope that keeps the wanting alive that and faith that He will bring the right person into my life. Mark also said he had a dream about me and that someone well off left me being taken care of when they passed on but this is something I havent see or heard of, maybe it's something that's in his mind that he wishes would happen during this time in my life he has always been a dreamer also like my self dreams are what helps to keep us alive and in a way they too can bring hope for survival. Although my life will go on there will be many things which will stand in my way so I have to find someway around those troubles and build on what I have right now, the bills are getting paid and that's the most important thing at this time. What I would give for the not having to worry about bills getting paid it would give me more time for study and focus but I don't see that happening right now so we will get by the best we can and hope for a miracle in the future. And if God willing it will come to pass, you can never tell what He has up his sleave because He never lets us know what's in His mind. If it was possible I would talk to Him and find out what He wants of me but I don't see that happening any time soon or ever for that matter, so we go on with life and hope for the best that it will turn out ok' and we can survive. My chores get done so no one has to worry about things in the church and I do a good job, just the other day while driving down the side road I saw a piece of plastic bag in the street and had to pick it up.

I had done this before with a news paper but why did I do it? It was like an impulse something that was right and I couldn't just leave it there, I find my self doing things like that and it seams natural. One day I found a bracelet in the road and still have it today not knowing who or why it was there but it was pretty and maybe I kept it as a reminder to let me know that I see things that are out of place who knows? I missed work today dam it' it doesn't happen very oftend but when it does I can kick my self in the ass. Now I have to apologize to the others that had to cover for me, I don't kno why this happens but it does. And I'm going to have to make sure it doesn't happen again, I can't figure this out! Other then that the day went pretty well but little brother has been sleeping most of the day O well. Also I got the car washed and now it looks beautiful for another week I just hope they are not too mad because of my missing I do know if it was a normal job I would be put on probation, so I better mark it on the calendar. Sunday and after washing my car yesterday it didn't take long for it to be full of dust once again from the factory down the road, it's a fine dust and I know it has to get in your lungs but as of yet no problems in breathing but I bet it's what makes my eyes swell shut and once they are done for the season that too will stop. I know it gets to Randy's eyes also as he wipes them quite often, I put my thoughts on my network yesterday about how God is our father and our parents were the ones with the right D.N.A. To bring about our birth and one of my realitives agreed with me, the network reaches around the world so it's written in many languages it's my part in bringing God's people together and I will continue to do it for some time to bring joy to him. We are all given the power to bring about change good change that is and it's expected of us to help in anyway we can, through the years I have been given a gift and I'm trying to put it to use but in the right way not wanting to step on the foundation that is an has been solid through the centuries. My love for the father grows with each passing day and it gets stronger all the time wanting to know more about our learning experiences and how to apply them to everyday life, the guy next door is going to move the lims from my concret slab and haul them off and for that I'm grateful now it will be clean once again. The missing of work at the thrift shop bothers me and now I will try my hardest to not miss another day, and I will make it up somehow in the future the window of opportunity willl open somewhere down the road and allow me to correct what has taken place and then the balance will be set right once again. This morning I got mad at harley because he pissed on the floor by the bathroom, and I stepped in it but dogs will be dogs and when you have to go well you have to go it's the price you pay for having a pet. The laps of time is something that happens from time to time and it's like I'm not here for that time, bringing about missed opportunities durning that time. As for the day it was nice and things still get done even on the weekend as the building of the corner house continues they poured the step's and the porch to the house getting it ready for the next step of the construction which will be the building of the very top of the house so the rain wont get in, then the back porch will be built.

On the house next door they are doing the foundation on the front of the house but I cant tell exactly what's going on there, they bring in equipment and then haul it away after the day is done good thing Scandia isn't far away or it would cost them more then it is, the people who bought it are nice and they do the work when they have time off from their regular jobs it seams Courtland is growing wither it wants to or not. A little at a time is good growth and those who move here will be happy if they want to get away from the drug infested cities where you find it on every street corner a way to an end, in my time here going on 4 years I haven't seen the drug part of our town yet and I find that to be a good thing but if it does exist they should know that they can find help with getting off of it. I have started to try and reach people over the internet spreading God's word and I pray that it will accomplish something with helping others, but right now it's a test to see what happens. The planting of a seed to see if it will take root and grow. Monday and you can hear the machines still down the road at the plant, I can't remember how long they will run but I do know until the corn is all in. And that will take some time, maybe a month or two as for funds they are running short and I can't figure out why they don't last the whole month but I'm sure something will come up even if we have to cut something somewhere. It's not like when pop's was here, during that time savings wasn't a hard thing to do but now with less, you just barly make it although the bills get paid I used to not having to worry about such things.

Christmas is coming and I wont be able to get anything for others like I did in the past but I believe we all fall on hard times from time to time and people just have to understand those times along with the good it's a part of life here in the real world and we have to bend with the times good and bad. There wasn't many at church yesterday but many went to wedding out of state I believe and in doing that maybe it was to hard for them to make it, in the past I always had enough money but with little brother here the food goes fast and then we struggle through the rest of the month when it comes to smoking there is never enough and that's what breaks us with smokes being $ 6:00 a pack just $ 2:00 over the price of gas so I think we will have to cut down in that department, and stopping on your own will give you a since of pride if God chooses to help me like I have asked of Him

Monday's are slow and it's the time when we go to town to pick up things like the little things that we miss buying when we were there before like room fresheners and such and although I woul like to have a good memory about things they seam to slip my mind from time to time. But that happens with us all, the family of God' is supposed to love each other and that is very important to him because he is love, all powerful and mighty although His love runs deeper then ours He still sees the strides we make working towards that goal. And if everyone could love like Jesus does the world would be a better place, I do find comfort in knowing that when we go home everyone will love each other and the things that were important here won't be of importance any longer. Our trials are trials that we need to over come in this place we call the world, a training place to get us ready for our long journey to eternity and although we can't understand it with our minds we can find comfort in knowing that He has built us a home where we will go on for ever. It says He notices it even when we do little things that have no significance to us as with us it might be a scond nature to do something with no thought that will leave a lasting impression on Him the father. I find that if you read something over and over again it has to finely stick in you're mind and in doing so it can bring change in a good way, but it can also be the same if the message is wrong so we have to be careful about what we put into our minds. Time is the most important thing you can give someone that and love so that's something I have to figure out, I show my love to others by giving of my time but a relationship builds a stronger and greater love for others. to wake up next to someone would be great if you can find that person who you can grow old with. I believe that feeling is wired into our brains like the way living for ever is, it's something we want and it will always be there. Truesday and it's pure silence you can't hear the augers running at the pland that means they are done, or they have broke down. Either way the dust has stopped floating in the air and that's always a good thing. Yesterday was the last trip to town for a while so we will spend the week around here, I had to turn on the heat the other morning to check out the system and make sure everything was working right plus it as cold in here. And the chill had to be taken out of the air, my songs are not for our pleasure but for God's and you have to have a certain audience that can feel what you are trying to say so maybe sometime in the future things will come full circle but for now they will remain with me and stay in my mind where they were created.

The love I feel for God runs deep and I express it through my songs that I create every day in my mind, maybe one day I can bring them out and share them with the world but for now they will remain safe in the place they were made. My learning continues as I study a little each day in hope that the message will become clear in my mind so I can teach others the wonderful news but with me I have to understand it first otherwise I can't teach it, the other afternoon I took Jack out so he could do his business and it made me feel good that I was the one pastor Kathy asked the trust factor is there as it should be in a small town. Jack was so excited to see me and I think he remembers me, even though we only bump into each other from time to time he Is hipper when he gets excited but he also seams to know why I'm there. And if he could he would thank me, Phillis has been on my mind lately with her being sick and all and I pray that she will get well very soon, as the days change so do we as our bodys adjust to things like the weather it brings a change in our thinking as well as the things we do. During his time of year writing becomes a past time and looking on the internet becomes a bigger part of my day trying always checking to see what others have to say and seeing how family is. This has become important to us even though we can't touch each other we can communicte with words and that seams to be enough for the time being, but I do miss seeing my grandchildren and maybe sometime in the future I will be able to see them but for now it's not in the cards. The train is coming through to drop off more box cars to be filled up and then they too will head down the road, making here way to God knows where.

The whistles lets us know where they are as they make there way through town, I can amagine how it must have been back in the 1800 when they ran on steam. The weather has been warm today in the 80's but I know it won't last for long, and I'm hoping for snow by Halloween when the bring the kids around on the hey bales. It's something you don't see in the bigger cities but here in Courtland we keep the kids safe from harm, it's a delight to see their faces light up as you let them take as much candy as they want but you can tell the ones that were raised with discipline, because they are the ones that only take a couple of pieces and leaves. I love that part of the season when your heart feels good about giving, well it's coming to the end of another day and tomorrow I won't miss work again marking the time on a piece of paper and putting it out in the open where it can't be missed even by me!!!. Wednesday and I talked with my daughter on Tuesday afternoon and she proceded to tell me about how she and my son in law went out for a couple of drinks and the next thing she knew she was in the hospital. It seams someone spiked her drink and she thought she was going to die, this is something that should keep a person out of a bar as there are many people who do this kind of thing. And she isn't a drinker, just one every now and then to be sociable. It brought back a time when my parents hit a tree after their drinks were spiked, today they should have the resoults of the drug test so they can see what happened. She also said she was full of bruses and her eyes were black my land' what is the world coming to? She also said she couldn't move anything on her body and that is a sign that she was sliped a micky, I told her that I'm glad that she is alright and that they would find the answer in the drug test. I don't know what I would do if I lost her, I'm wanting to see them in this next coming year so I must save up for a road trip to Kearney. It's a nother quiet morning but yesterday they were stockpiling corn on the ground for next years crop, I'm not quite sure why they do it that way but they do and it stays with the big heated tarp covering it up and keeping it warm and dry through the winter. It's Antique road show this morning so I will watch it at 4:00 and it lasts until 5:00 an hour show of all the things from the past and how they survived over the last 100 or so years my land' they canceled it so that's not going to be seen, I have felt that something is going on but I don't know what it is it's a feeling I get from time to time and it has no explanation just something changing and maybe it's just that time of season who knows. The coffee is good this morning and it didn't take long for it to wake me up as it's the same each morning, my neighbors are still working on the house next door and they have come a long ways since they started. Now working on the face of the house and building up the front so the foundation doesn't sink any more, it's still hard to believe it's a three bedroom because it looks smaller then the home I live in. watching them work it's like a work of art as they do one section at a time and then move on to the next, as for the porch it's gone and I don't think they will put another one in it's place at least not as big as the last. Maybe just a small one with a cover above it. Many have looked at the house but none of them ever boought it until these guys did and they are going to flip it.

It's become a very popular thing to do these days with homes becoming so high but I have a feeling it still might sit for a time, as I looked out the window I saw that it has been raining so I got the lawn mowed just in time and now maybe it will turn greener. In reading my section today it talked about how we are not perfect as we all have our own faults and the church is supposed to help us with that, and I didn't know that our pastor has to give account for us to God. My land' she has a big job with all of us sinners and if conflect happens in the church she is supposed to bring peace or a balance to setteling things, we are all different and with our differences many problems happen. But He also says he doesn't like gossip one person talking about another and that's something I stay away from, I was told in my youth that if you didn't have anything good to say then don't say anything at all. Because it will cause hurt between your friends and no one likes to be hurt, I can't tell if the rain is going to fall all day but that doesn't stop my work from having to be done and I take pride in what I do in hope that my best is good enough . As for people bitching about my work there is none or they hide it so I can't see it. But my job is very important to building my life even today trying to change my ways isn't for the faint at heart and it takes hard work taking care of everything like little brother and the many other things I do.

It says that He notices everything we do from the smallest to the greatest meaning even picking up a piece of paper that someone through on the ground, do others watch the way you're life changes this is something I have no doubt about. But they are not as important as the way God sees you because it's Him that we have to be accountable to, not humans. As I think about the kids that will have to endure the life I once had to it brings tears to my eyes, all the tears that will be shed because you feel so lost in a world that you don't understand. The gift of an education is greatly needed if you are going to survive in this place he made for us and ever though I can do things I could never do before there is still something missing, but putting my finger on that something is not in the cards right now. Thursday morning' and it's quiet, nothing is moving and I don't hear the crickets as they haven't been churping for quite some time. I talked with my daughter again yesterday and she is still feeling ill from the night before and I hope nothing happens to her, as for the kids they are fine and doing well in school so there is no worring there. Many things come to mind when I hear about such things happening to my loved ones, but I know God will watch over them even though they are far away and protect them in that place where so many are on drugs. The day is going to be a good one as I go and get some things to last the month, also I was able to secure the taxes payment when they come up but it's going to cost in the long run maybe more then I expected. Trying to take care of things is harder then I thought first everything is going fine and then it's like there is never enough but why these things happen is beyond me, but in time things will turn around and I have to believe that at this time in my life as long as the bills are paid then things should go by pretty good until next year bringing about many new things like getting a handle on all that's brothering me at this time, letting go of Randy's phone has caused another problem and that's paying back the early hook up fee of too much money. It seams to be when I let others handle their own things then things fall apart, and I'm supposed to be handeling things not him but I cant blame anyone but my self. It's morning again and it's a little chilly but the night went pretty good yesterday I went and paid off my bill at the station so that makes one less bill and I hope that things are going to be good for the rest of the month. It's nice to wake up to the quietness with nothing bothering me, yesterday I saw Kathy walking her dog and she waved to me it was after I washed the car and was headed home. Being Friday' everyone will be looking forward to the weekend when they can relax from a hard weeks work, I feel change coming as the month is about over only 30 days to this one and then October will be delivered which is Hallowen the 10th month of the year when all the gobblens and ghosts come out to play, so funny' but the kids like it. During the next year I plan on studing the bible more to see what appears in the realm of me being taught new things, and from what I understand He will bring new things into my life it's the holy spirit that moves you during these times. And it isn't always a great feeling as sometimes it can be just a nuge, some don't understand the trinity and as near as I can place it it's like water one substence but with other qualitys like steam and ice but always returning back to water meaning the main force is the water. This is how I can relate to the father, son, and the holy spirit, three things coming from one substence one power that is greater then any other power on earth.

And God controls them all, I found it interesting how we are suppose to be like christ but it wont take place until we leave this world to take that finel step or adjustment. But to me it seams love is a big part of us being here that and helping others, for when we are called upon to give account of what we have done here He wont be interested in what job we had only wanting to know if we loved his son the way he did. If we were able to change the dead works from dead to living. The how long we have here doesn't really matter but it's all in what you did with your life were you able to love your neighbor as you love your self, I still struggle with some things but as the holy spirit moves me I believe things will change as the works of God starts on the inside and works there way out. It says if you read the bible for a half hour a day you canb read it in only a year, and if for an hour twice a year. But many still don't understand it's full meaning even after reading through it, it's the spirit which gives you understanding when the time is right and when that time presents it's self then it will be made clear. A pastors job must take a lot of time studing in the word and I hear that some know the bible from one end to the other and have it memorized virse by virse this would really take a love for God, and I think I would be good at it so I look forward to Him teaching me when He thinks the time is right. I do know that I control nothing when it comes to the full understanding of God but I'm confidant, that in the day I will be taught by Jesus.

Learning the scripture shouldn't be rushed because when you learn one thing it takes time for that to set in and make it understandable, but if rushed. Then you have all kinds of things tryiing to make them selves known at one time and that doesn't work so good. I pray for God to show me the way to being a good christen so I can have and find what some of them have, or maybe I have found it and just don't know it but I don't see that being the case. With many things we don't know what's going on until it happens because He doesn't let us in on his secrets, it's hard trying to figure out things but that's just who we are. Only human and our minds wonder in different directions in search of the answer or at least mine does so maybe a rest is needed so things can come full circle. But we will see in time if I'm on the right path of becoming closer to God. They are having a gathering at the park on the first and Tanner and his group is preforming, they will be having chilly and some other things like S'mores and hotdogs it's a nice thing for them to do that. Seeing it's all free to the public even parents could get a break by taking the kids there or not' because it will probably be the last out side gathering for the year and I wish them the best of luck. As for hearing there music I have never heard it before and should go to see it, if it rains then it will be in the fire house so it's on no matter what. This will let them show their gift to the town and being new here I don't really know if they have played before, the town is separated by the people who has lived here all their lives and the out siders as some call them. They are people who have moved here from the out side world and found that they like this kind of life away from the out side world, I have only heard the word out sider used twice and that was by older people even though they lived here for 60 or so years they still looked at it that way and only they know why those words are used. One women was in her 80's and came here from New York' and lived on a farm until she had to sell it to make room for a lake so they could store water for the farms during the drought season, she told me that she lived right in the middle of it. Her children were born here so they weren't considered out siders but she was, as for any other people they too must feel like out siders but I put no value on such words that make some feel they are not a part of things because none of us are really as it all belongs to the father just on loan to us while we are here for this short time. Saturday and it's early but the coffee is on to wake me up, yesterday the service engine soon light flickered so I have to have it checked but the good thing is that it didn't stay on long before the computer corrected the problem so I believe it will be ok until I get it serviced, other then that it's been running fine. These newer cars have so much going for them but when something happens" the gas milage goes to hell I have been running ethional in it sometimes and maybe that's not a good thing to do but we willl see as time goes by. In the old days you didn't have computers to mess with but they changed them because they thought the computer could do a better job What were they thinking" but usually they never go out expecially when the car only has 95000 miles on them in the realm of getting something newer you take a chance as with all things in life and hope for the best and hope that the seller told you everything about the vehical my main use for the car is to use it for work so I can serve God and make trips to the store when need be.

Without a car you are stranded in the wilderness and I cant let that happen so everything has to be checked the motor oil is due for a changing so that will get done here in a few days to keep everything up to par. This morning I have to go and clean the church and then it's off to the thrift store at noon to maybe make some money for the church but it's not all about money it's the helping out that's fun to me. Lately I have been feeling something and I cant tell if it's good or bad, an uncertainty it's like I'm unsure of my feelings but inside know I havent done anything wrong and this happens from time to time. I know my life is for doing good and that's just the way Jahova made me, different from other that run a muck and live for the things I used to live for. It's going to be a nice day and tomorrow will be even better when we go to church, but with me it's different I praise God each day in one form or another, before I started praying each morning I used to never do it. But now something has come over me and I try to pray each day in hope for change not only in my life but in others also. They say faith can move mountains but prayer can do something I haven't experienced as of yet, but I know He looks after my needs as I go through this, it's what I call a transition period where you go from one stage of life to another. In hope for a better out come then you got in the beginning of life, one set apart by changing who you are. It says you have to be born again before you can become a part of God's family and lord knows that has happened in my life anyway, and it will continue.

Until everything has been made right but focusing on change can be hard if you don't take a break from it and that too can make you nuts. You cant please everyone in this life for that's something that can never happen so I go on with life the best I can and hope for the better good of things, I was asked what kind of ice-cream I liked so I have a feeling someone will bring me some in the future. I have also found out that there are some things which should be left a secret, but that's something I'm just now learning to much talk can hurt you also even if you don't mean for it to and maybe that's why I have always been a quiet person not wanting to ruffel anyones fethers by saying the wrong thing. Little brother is feeling better these days and we still laugh from time to time breaking the bordom. I got my ice-cream also this afternoon after I got off work pastor Kathy brought it over such a delightful person and she told me it was for dog sitting. Sunday morning and it's quiet, as I took Harley out before bed the guy from next door said hi as he was checking out the work the power company did in restoring the power to the house next door he is a nice person and I like him even though I have only met him once or twice. Some say he built the apartments in Scandia and he does good work whick I agree with,as the house is looking better all the time. On another note the house down the way has a garage floor built on it and room for a patio they are sure making them selves a nice home and with luck it will last them for the rest of their lives. Winter is coming there is no doubt as the trees are changing color as we went for a drive you could see the reds and yellows in the trees as their leaves fall to the ground meaning that this season is about over and I hope winter wont be too bad but like every winter before I will go out and play in it letting the child loose that's inside of me. Wednesday I will go and pay the bills so they are behind me and then hope that we will make it the rest of the month something always seams to bring us through it and that's a delight for me any ways, Randy was telling me that Lonny was driving my old car after he put awater pump in it so I know that car will last him for a while, it never gave me a problem until it started to use water and then it was down hill not being able to fix it. As long as you have a good car living here is nice but loose that car and it's like your traped in the wilderness not being able to go anywhere and the solitude is very real, many things are changing and when the storms move it it's like something happens and the dreams set in so strange. This morning I will go and open the church and get things ready for the day as I went to the thrift store yesterday it was me and Beverly working getting things put away and she gave me a vibrating coushion which relaxed the mussels in your back so I took it because it was free it looks like it would be for a car but it's not only for the home with a big plug in that operates it, and who knows maybe one day I will use it. When I'm older, I saw many of my friends on face-book yesterday and my daughter text me to say it's ok' and she has been craming for a test to get her degree in being a nurce I'm so proud of her, being able to do that. She has always been a smart women and I know the kids will be the same way hidden talent as God calls it and we all have it without knowing it, little things and big things that don't surface until need or tragity hit us and then somehow it's awaken to bring change. I would of never guessed that I would study to become what I am today but through persistence life has brought me a long ways. God tells us that it's our life experiences which become the most important and how we treat others along with other things but to live for Him is really important, I recall my mom saying one time to someone one of my brothers I believe that she brought him into this world and she can take him out. It was in a joking gesture but she said it just the same and I thought it was funny, as the years go by many things will start to change.

And us being where we are can also change, you just don know what He has instore for us it's 5:00 Am. And little brother is still sleeping except for when he got up earlier he seams to live for the next day which there isn't anything wrong with that but he forgets about the day he is in. I believe he is looking for something and he hopes to find it in that next day, but what could it be? A change of things. We were talking the other day and he said he was glad that he didn't live around the others in Kearney because he knows they would bleed him dry, I don't know what it is but others are more focused on what they can get from others and maybe that's how they survive but that isn't the case here in my town we share the bills and hope for things to get better as we go along. The way it was done when we were kids everyone pitched in to make life more comfortable more bareable to move on to other things which would take place if everything was shared by the unit a family unit that seamed to love each other, living in solitude lets you reflect on what life was and how it will be in the future and I always hope for the best. It's like the town has abopted me since I moved here and if one of them are upset or angry because of something there are many others that are not, it's like a balance and I'm glad that it's that way. Although I'm far away from my kids I still know that they love me and it shows in my daughters texts. Monday and I'm barley awake but I can hear the augers running at the plant so grinding isn't over with yet, they have started to stock pile the corn on the ground just down the road from me and then it will be covered with a tarp to keep it fresh through the winter I haven't figured out why they do that yet but I will find out.

This morning I have to go and clean the church after yesterdays service so things will be ready for Wednesday school, and Kathy said they had 32 children making it bigger then a lot of services on Sunday when it's just us old farts me being the youngeast or maybe a couple others. My television wasn't working right so I unplugged the converter box and let it rebut it's self and then everything was fine, thought I wasn't going to get to watch it last night but that changed and I fell a sleep with it on. The mornings are boreing any more and I cant figure out why it used to be my time of day but the thinking has changed and that could be because I to have changed. Harley keeps scratching on my door to get in but he should know that it isn't going to happen this early in the day, as we drove to town the other day we saw caterpillers crossing back and forth across the highway, something I have never seen before not like they were just like they were on a mission to hit the fields. My self I wouldn't have noticed it but little brother did see them first going from one field to the other, if that's what they were then the cold should get them before anything can get damaged by watching them they were on a mission and cars didn't even bother them. They say we are like them but some compare us to tea pots being molded by the father into something beautiful our lives are not ours we were created for His pleasure and that's our mission in life to become what He wants us to be, and in the process we become better people without the burden of the addictions and other things that can destroy us while we are learning the new things children learn at a young age if they are permitted by their parents to do so but like with everything else parents can destroy instead of helping them find their way through life. And alcohol and drugs can deture them from the path leading them into the world of the unknown. The world created by alcohol and drug addiction can blind a person to what God is really doing and once you're in it then you loose sight of this part of the real world, the one you were created for. And in that world it's dark and you cant see, it throws off your focus and puts you in a different reality then the one I live in today. When Randy was ill I called the pastor because she seamed to have a closer connection with the father and she could get my prayers heard and it worked they stopped the operation and sent him to another hospital that was equipped to handle what was wrong. If you could of seen that doctors face he knew what he was trying to do was wrong and he sent him on his way as for little brother he was scared to death that he was going to die. And it was on that day when I knew that God had heard my prayers, it was out of the ordinary to have a priest there before anything happened but she was there to a sure me that God had control of things, I always thought it was strange how the doctor asked if he was disabled before he moved forward like his life might not be as important as someone who didn't have a disability. And I think it's a shame when a doctor thinks in those turms, like he is looking at a piece of defected meat. God says all life is sacret and we should use every precaution to preserve it, as for me I treat everyone the same and it doesn't matter what disability they might have. I thank God that my little brother wasn't taken from me on that day because I love him so much, could you imagine being given your brother back to loose him within a year of his coming back into your life?.

As with all things which God gives he won't build up your faith and then pull it out from under you, this would be a cruel thing to do. Today my faith is stronger because of what God did on that day and as for little brother he is doing fine by the grace of God even though his eyes are still not open yet I will leave that in God's hands, the longer I live here the more people treat me like family and I have grown in many ways with John he is like me in many ways and he is easier to talk to then some of the others. Although I would like for it to be that way with them all that in it's self will take time, as they don't attend church every Sunday. With the Blackburns they are there every Sunday except when something comes up that they have to be out of town but other then that they are there, it's strange how you can grow close to some and others they stay just out of arms reach for some reason maybe not wanting to get hurt or get close because of something that might have happened in their lives long ago. Robert's tests have come back good so I know God is working in his life, I feel for those going through things like cancer and I pray for them all Phillis is on oxygen so she cant go far from home and I pray for her also in hope that she will be able to return to church one of these days. As for Michel he is doing pretty well out in Colorado and getting better as time moves forward in time I hope he will make a full recovery and be able to go on with life and enjoy it he is so young, as for Kathys grand daughter she is attending school in another town and we don't get to see her very much but when she comes home she attends church and she is a delight to be around.

The kids are back in school learning new things and they seam to really like bible school when they can have fun and learn at the same time. And maybe in the future I will try my hand at being there for them Wednesday school would be a good starting point to learn to teach, could that really happen with this life of mine. Bringing about something I dreamed of doing for some time now, I wrote an article on it long ago could it be brought into reality? I guess only God knows the answer to that one. But it's something to think about, Tuesday and yesterday we stayed home but I got the church vacuumed so it's ready for Wednesday school this morning is mighty cold so I had to turn on the heat to take the chill off. My land' now I know winter is here, today is trash day so I have to go back to the church later and get it ready for the garbage man I sure wouldn't want his job doing that during winter months. But it takes us all to make things work in this world, tomorrow we will go and pay bills and then on Saturday go grocerie shopping to get enough food to last the month. It seams when we get it all at once it gets eatened up mighty fast so maybe we will get half at a time making it stretch a little longer, the storm came in yesterday but was gone by mid afternoon but the leaves from the trees filled the ground and they were beautiful all the reds and yellows it was like He is telling us to get ready because winter is coming, so I have to get another jacket being mine got sold by accident. I have a flannel shirt but it isn't quite warm enough with the temps going down so next time we go to

Concordia I will try to pick one up, dam I wish I wouldn't of lost that coat it was so warm. During the winter not many people go out except to work and then they stay home where it's warm trying to break the boredom that winter causes but we seam to make it through it ok' my self I will have my days of working at the thrift store and the church to keep me busy but little brother will have to stay in so maybe the walls might get a cleaning this winter who knows for sure. The winter months of solitude can and will make you stronger mentaly I do know that Randy is used to this kind of thing and well as for me I have grown accustom to it also, in my taking care of the sick and mentaly challenged but I feel good about what I do because I know if it wasn't for me they would be in a place where they wouldn't like it very much. I feel that my world isn't as bad as those who have to live with the notion of taking from people as with me it's a give thing giving of my time to make sure they are taken care of and trying to make sure that their lives are as good as it can be, can I give more of my time to help more? That could be something to ponder over the next few weeks so we will see what happens. The time when I moved here still visits me but it isn't as bad as it once way being scared and all, but I hope in time that it will go away and bring something new to the table that fitting in is importand but then others expect more and more out of me lord give me strength to do the things I can and do them well, once I was told by my doctor in Nebraska that he didn't think he had the time to help at his church but once he started then it somehow worked out he said it was like God had made time by some miraculous move ment in time. And then things got easier as he helped more and more, it seams He will make the time if there isn't any..

Yesterday I saw a few church people going from door to door and Jahova witnesses do that kind of thing along with ladder day saints, but they were gone within a few minutes and I didn't see them the rest of the day. It's strange how each religion believes that their way is the only way, and some even mess with snakes testing their faith by weither they get bit or not to scary for me. Through the winter we will try new things and we do this every winter to try and break the boredom and bring about some excitement into the day, Phillis has been on my mind and I hope she is doing well' she is like a mother figure and encourages me when I sing telling me to never give up on your ability to do something special you like. Such an inspration she is to me, with her being ill and winter coming. I don't think she will be at the thrift store any more this year, she has to be in her late 70's or even early 80's and I believe she has lived here most of her life and she loves the lord very much. Many people who love God live a long time and then they go and be with him in the end, they go to the place He made for them as it says in the bible my father has a house and in that house there are many rooms and he has one of them for you. That would be a great feeling just knowing that you are thought of by the one so powerful, and His son Jesus Christ' the morning is the coldest so far as the temp this morning was 38 degrees and that tells me that the big freeze isn't far off. But it's goingto be a nice day.

I went for a ride this morning and saw a deer almost hit a pick-up and the guy slowed way down not to hit it, in this part of the country it's not uncommon to see this especially at this time of year when the seasons are changing from being hot to cold. When I first moved here I didn't like the heat but with the air-conditioning it makes it bareable so you don't have to roast in that wiltering heat, but I think all people are the same way. Especially the elderly as we get older our bodies don't work as good as they used to, I would almost give anything to be in my youth and know what I know today so much could have been different and I could of found out the things I needed to know when they would of helped the most or could I' it says that He knew everything before it happened and had the power to change things. So I take that as a sign that my life was supposed to be a struggle, and the addictions were permitted to happen by Him. Today I believe there was something to be learned and only by going through the triles could they be brought to light, could it be that he wanted me to experience all the bad before the good so I would know the difference but surely that didn't have to take place but then He sees things way different then I' once in a while I think back to when I made a pact not to have something in my life but since that time it expired, I havent found a women that I could love as much as God' I tried having one relationship in that 20 years but it didn't work out. And maybe the reason was that I was trying to have it messure to God's love for me, when I went in to the relationship things were fine but then it started to decay like a cancer eating away at it. And the new wore off and we had to go our seprate ways, if it would of happened in the old life it would of lasted longer using chemicals to hide the real truth. Darting in and out of reality to try and make things seam in balance, but in that life I didn't know the father or His love so I would of compaired it to the old relationshipe and they were held together by false hope, strange how you see things differently today but could that be age? For I don't feel the need like before to be with someone and maybe that just part of who I am but I do know we weren't meant to go through life alone, and if I really look at it I'm not alone because I have the family that God has brought into my life along with Randy. I was supprised when I missed church one day because they missed me so much that they sent me a card telling me so, and there is no better feeling then when other say you are missed and loved. This is something I had never felt before a closeness and love that stays in my heart, my family never said these things to me in all the years that we were together. And as for their mother well that was a wreck waiting to happen and it did, although I tried to get her back she found lust in someone elses arms which if I looked at it honestly the relationship should have ended many years before it did. I can still remember the games she used to play just trying to make me jealous and it worked on the inside but I never let her see it turning and walking away as if it didn't feel like a knife being turned in my guts. Having children is the worst reason for staying together especially when the love is gone because the bitterness is felt by them and they shouldn't have to feel that in their young lives.

My life could be a testament to what not to do in the name of love, Wednesday and I hear the dryers running in the plant down the road so the moisture percentage in the corn must be too high. It's time to go back to work at the thrift shop and see what goodies they got in, the guys from Scandia came down and worked on the house next door for a while last night and they were kind enough to haul off the branches that were in my drive way. And that's a good thing for me anyway, they have been nothing but kind to me and of course I to them the way it's supposed to be. My dealings with others is to be kind and they will be so in return. The night got chilly as morning came but all in all I slept pretty good then the heat kicked on and took the chill off but for the day it's going to be another nice one not too hot or cold but I can tell that the big freeze is just around the corner. My understanding of the life here is that everyone helps each other and that way a balance is kept and things go fine, if someone gets up set then you let them get over it. Not trying to change their mind or opinion of what they feel because they have to live with what ever they deside to do, it's that way in life and I let nature take care of it's self. It's early and Randy is moving around in the other room he said he didn't get to sleep until around midnight night before last making for a resless night as his med's had run out but getting them filled today so he should sleep fine tonight. The balance has been thrown off and now it will be put back right, it's strange how the body can get out of sink and they find a way through med's to bring the balance back to normal or close to it leaving them with having to have them to be some what normal.

Through the years I have had to fight the things that have happened in my life long gone as the body is thrown out of sink by the things that have happened, the bodys thermostat has been thrown off by the way I lived in the first 32 years of my life and that's something I wont get back but through time I have learned how to live with it that way changing many things and how I do them. But it's doable if you adjust too it in the right way, many things have changed in my life from the things that have happened and in a way it has made me a better person more loving and not having that hate life attitude. I have seen others that have over came alcohol but they seamed to have picked up a hate you attitude, like life wasn't fair to them that and they are usually the ones who were a mean drunk in their past life. Such a bad way to live but they survive for a time anyway and they reflect what they are, as with my life I was just grateful and live with that attitude trying to help others if they so choose to want it. Not putting them in a vice you might say to change that has to come from them, my whole life has been fighting back and I think it gives me a better prespective of how to approach them without condemning them for something that was might not have been their fault. Childhood addiction isn't the childs fault it's no different then if you want too be like your parent and she or he has a respectable job, it's something that is taught we all want to be like our parents it's just natural mom being a nurse who would of thought I would be more or less doing the same thing? Taking care of her and then Oliver and now Randy it just goes to show that God can change things without us even realizing it, making one adjustment after another. He created what I do today and now I want to be more like Him if that's possible. Slowly he changes the things in our lives and many times we are not even aware of it a tweek here and a tweek there until 'Boom' something has been changed. my life has been created by many different miracles and I call them miracles because with most of them I cant explain why they have happened and He uses some shaddy people to bring them about but as long as it gets the job done then He will use them. Like if you are a person with no means He will use a person with means to get you a head or where you need to be, my journey here to Courtland' was brought on by meeting someone that He knew was different from me but He used that person anyway to get me here. Why would he do this? There was or is something here that I needed to help me grow in a spiritual way, but instead of just giving me what I needed he used that person to bring about a change in my life and to also maybe show me that human love cant compare to the love He has for me. Needless to say He was right' as that infatuation grew old and died but His love is still with me even today, it's spiritual and not of this world as anything of this world dies in time and His love endures for ever as does His foundation for life it's self. I had fun talking with Mrs Allen yesterday while working at the store and then before we knew it, it was time to close. As for Wednesday school I was pastor Kathy at home when I got home so things must have went well there also, the weekend is about here and the folks will be getting off of work for the two days as we talkes she told me a little about her life and her likes and dislikes about doing things making it a good conforsation to kill time. Her husband was one who passed away just a couple of years ago from cancer, she told me that her kids still work the land and I took it that they kept the acrage but sold the farm so she could be closer to town.

And I can understand why, it would get pretty lonely out there by your self plus moving to town lets her walk when ever she gets the notion and she doesn't have to worry about any one bothering her in this little town. The freedom to wonder is here and the neighbors watch over our people making it a great place, for the longest time the loss didn't let her talk much but as we all know in time all wounds are healed by the grace of God. Even with my loss of pop's she helped me to over come the loss so I could be strong once again and in a way it's like we all help each other when those times are brought into our lives. I could hear thunder a few minutes ago so I know there is a storm in the area and who knows what it will bring rain or snow either one we could use at this time, we also talked about the quietness that is here the serenity that you won't find anywhere else that I know of, it seams the whole town knows that I'm writing a novel but like me they have no idea of when it will be done will it ever come to a close? That is something only He knows, when I came here I didn't think there would be much to write about but as the time and space moves off into the distance things change and you become closer to the things you write about like church and other things that have an impact on your life. From the smile on a childs face to them being ornery because they cant sit still so full of life and they will have many years to work it off, some will stay on the farm and others will move on to things they feel they need in their lives.

But many will come back because the out side world isn't for them, they will be drawn back by a power stronger then what's out there in the world of drugs and alcohol. And finely rest here where they were born or brought here from generations before them. The thunder is loud right now as the storm passes and the trees are blowing back and forth, maybe to remind us that it's in charge and not us humans for with a swift blow a tree could fall and destroy what we as people built. The rain is falling but I cant see out side being so dark but I can hear the trees as they whip in the wind, it almost sounds like a train when they hit real bad but I don't since that at this time just the giving of the strength of the trees as there branches bend to mother nature, as for the crickets I don't hear them this morning and havent heard them in quite some time but that thunder is shakeing the ground and the lights are flickering from time to time meaning a power outage might happen, but we will see. They had the first president debate last night and we will see what happened late today but I know it was full of lies. Just two fools trying to get elected to drain the country of it's resources, enough of that crap. The art center is having dance lessons for couples and singles so that's a thought for the future maybe learn how to dance. I turned on the raido station to see what the weather is going to be and havent heard anything as of yet so this storm must not be on the radar for them to check it and this happens sometimes just a short burst of rain that only hits here but I did just see a streak of light through the curtains and I can hear the rain or hail falling, such a sound only created by the one on high letting us know that he is in charge, although summer is over the grass and other things need to be watered and the only way it gets this is by the rain because our water faucet out side has been cut off from it freezing during winter. And no one wants to croll under this house for some reason maybe the spiders or the moisture that accumulates in dark places, water grass is a grass that needs no water very oftend each morning it waters it's self somehow and then sucks it back into it during the day so strange' I'm' thinking about trying to fix my computer I got from walt so that will include tearing it apart and making some changes to the hard drive in hope to speed it up. And if it works then I can start to use it for other things back in the old days I had torn many of them apart and had even made one out of two so we will see what takes place later this month who knows luck might be on my side, harley has been wanting to go out but I know he doesn't like the rain and thunder as it sends him under the bed so be patient my little friend' Randy has slept through the night so I know his med's are working. He spend three days without them and he hardly got any sleep so he might make up for the hours that he missed by sleeping in for the next few mornings. There was nothing about the storm on the radio so that's a good thing, now later this morning I will go and clean the church I like for it to be clean at all times just because that's the way it should be, the rain is still falling and harley didn't stay out in it very long little curd. It's the end of the day and it's been cold all day long but I kept my self busy by singing different melodies for my love for the lord. Friday morning'and I haven't had my coffee yet, my it's cold people who are alcoholic's are not usually fully awake because of many things and some of it is that they couldn't deal with certain things that have happened in their life.

Like tragedy, Valerie had many things go bad in her life and she was searching for a way out and thought she found it in marrages that didn't work. And then when looseing her daughter she got lost even furthers and reverted back to failed relationships hoping that she can make them work, I have seen her in many of them but she had to have control of the situation even though she was as messed up as they were. Looking back I can see that a relationship with her would of never worked although I thought I was in love with her and it would of ended up destroying us both, two people with the same problem cant fix each other and it doesn't matter if one is on one drug and the others is on another. When I isolated my self it was to get away from such things, to try and fix my self and over come what had happened so long ago I have been told that I have psychic abilitys that haven't fully came to power and I can see this sometimes in the things I do or preceive and it can be scary at times' when you bounce from one thing to another trying to find that balance that you know is there, I know there was a connection between me and mom the ability to tell what was on each others mind and answer each others questions before they were asked, with us it was kind of neat but we didn't understand it at the time and then she went to be with the lord. These days are a lot different as I find my way through life in hope that I will one day find the answer to why some things exist and others don't an even keel to all things and what they can become sometime in life.

I find that my songs bring me closer to feeling whole but there is still something missing maybe that connection to my father and the wondering what it would have been like to get to know him in this life. That part of my being which has eluded me in finding him and why he didn't try and find me in all these years, just the thought of knowing him makes me wonder if my life would have been fuller with his presents or if it would have been worse then it was? I guess the answer lies in him. Through life many things have shaped it but in the first part of it I was a sleep you might say not wanting to wake up from the dream and then one day you take it too far and get to know that life isn't as bad as you thought. In my wakeing up it took a little at a time before I knew that He had bigger plans for my life, and He showed me a little at a time that life is supposed to be beautiful. Then the little things came into view like the animals and how they played and sang songs my prospective of the birds and the squirrels in my yard, although you have the strength to over come something it can take years before you start to see things the way they are meant to be in life. It's strange how back then I couldn't see past making it until morning not knowing if you would live or die, and it took years before I realized that He was looking after me and even then I didn't have any faith just courosity and the will and hope that there was something different in this life I was created for. Change is a hard thing to accomplish with it's twists and turns but when you aquire hope and faith it's then that you have a chance to live for the first time. For some reason I find peace in the church so much peace that I can sing and feel at home and that's something I never felt before, I always have to feel like I'm a part of something and I believe I find that with helping others and that's why I do things like being a care giver, it's strange how it started with family but then went on to helping others even some I didn't know but that bridge was completed by the time they moved on. And they knew I cared for them even with Walt' one day I heard him talking and there was no one around and his words were you brought me the perfect person. There is many rewards in taking care of people not physical rewards but the kind that come from inside the knowing you helped someone in their last days, will I have someone who cares enough to help me this I still have a problem with because most people get paid for it. And my self I do it for pleasure to try and make them feel better not me, who knows what the future holds when it comes to careing but with me that is something that will never change. Pop's was my inspration for careing and now that he is gone it will live on a gift that keeps giving, as I look at his picture with mom I know they are at peace, I have noticed that the neighbor is home across the street he is a trucker and is gone most of the time hauling different things across the country. My land' he has to make good money, being able to have all the toys he has motorcycles and four wheelers along with having them painted to match each other, I remember going on the truck with my brother and it wasn't plesent bouncing around like you were on a wash board road. But I'm sure things have changed since those days back in the 70's and early 80's hauling corn cobs for heat stoves boy his boss made a killing at that business the contracted out of grain elStacytors to haul the stuff across the United States.

But he wasn't home much, like the guy that lives across the way. Just poping in for a weekend and then heading back out so his family could have a better life. In my 20's I worked mostly for construction companys that rebuilt the highways in Nebraska and other States although it paid pretty well the money didn't last but a weekend, my women could spend it as fast as I got it but I didn't care at the time because I was in love or so I thought. Never could put my finger on that one but it must have been to stay with her for so long, I think my first marriage being a flop made me not want to take that plunge again as I liked the thought of being free if something better came along. But you learn after a life of being alone that things could have been different. But my spening the last 25 or so years alone had been a quandary, when I first started this journey of finding out if I would live or die I told Him that I would stay celibate for 5 years to show that I really wanted to live and then when that time passed I had learned about how much God really loved me. And things couldn't quite messure up to that love He showed me trying to find the same thing with a women didn't work but it brought me to a place different then where I was at a place miles away and then I learned that I had been there before. The beginning of finding out where the first miracle happened in my life, this new thing had Stacyded me through the years and my mind had forgot all about it. Well the relationship didn't work but I was brought to where I needed to be so I could remember, this was God's doing to make things right in my mind because without all the pieces to the puzzeel you cant put it together.

God will bring things to pass in a good persons life even if He has to use others to accomplish it and I believe that's what He did in my case, through the computer I was able to connect with the first women since I was celibate and things were going along fine but my not having much experience with women brought on a lot of problems and self doubt, and looking for answers it scared this one away but I was fine with that because I was used to being alone and after being together she somehow didn't full fill the thought I had in my mind of love. For the only love I had felt in the last 25 years was the love of God and I believe I thought I would find the same thing in this women which didn't happen, so we went our separate ways and I grew stronger in my faith we all have our own beliefs in God. But through the years" one thing has been constent He molds us into who we are supposed to be, like the tea cup that started out as a piece of clay He seams to mold us from the inside out not the other way around with some they might look ragged on the out side but have the inside's of what the lord created. Even with the women that it didn't work with, she didn't want a pretty boy' because she didn't want to have to worry about him cheating on her. O well I guess to each their own my self I'm looking for a friend and then if something happens well then so be it but I have to feel something or love before I will even move forward. And maybe that's part of why I'm still alone today trying to feel a love that doesn't exist, I don't think a women could give the love that God gives or anyone for that matter but if it's possible to even come close then it would be a match made on earth. Someone who can bring joy into a already happy person, to bring things to a new level. To share in each others love instead of trying to destroy the others already fragual state in the beginning. Insecurity isn't a good thing but it's something that happens and if two people love each other then there shouldn't be anything they couldn't help each other with love is supposed to be able to withstand all the problems that might arise in a relationship. We went to town and seen a home coming march up and down main street and there were many different companies; in the paurade, the day is coming to an end and now it's time for bed good night. Saturday' and yesterday we cleaned the carpet in the living room, it didn't take much effort being we did a little at a time. It's needed it for some time now and now it's ready for winter, my land I don't like a dirty house and I know I could never be a horder how do they do that? My little guy harley is a sleep on the couch and he looks so peaceful there but once he knows I'm up for the day then he will come and bug me as he does everyday wanting this and that so spoiled for an animal but I do love him. It's work day getting everything ready for tomorrow at church and then it's off to the thrift store for a couple of hours, I can hear the augers at the mill going 90 miles an hour and they have been running all night and will continue until all the work is done getting in all the corn for the year. During the next year many things will change and my new family will get closer to each other, I don't know if I will sing this year but we will see it's only by invatation that I do these things and if they ask me to pray on it then I know they are serious. Each year I try and sing at least one song although I sing to my self and God each day other's like to hear it also for each song I write tells a story.

And I notice that they have something to do with what I have seen or written in the past wither something like the birds or the animals of sorts, for some reason kids like my songs and I'm glad for that because usually they are about them in some way. And the world which is changing all the time if a child can be inspired then they will go far in what they do. My land' it's going to be a good day and I believe I get up so early just to see how the day goes because usually by the time most are thinking about getting out of bed I can tell if the day is going to be good or bad. That's me trying to get a jump on things,, we also have to get groceries and boy we need a lot this month as we are about out of everything a restock you might say, and then we will be set. Most of the can goods go to the people who are starving around here and it's part of our job to help them, I have been in the same situation and although afraid to ask for help it was given anyway to make sure I didn't starve to death. In life there are many curves and if we do the right thing then we can avoid going over the clif you might say, many people are going through hard times but I notice that even the wealthy are pretty thrifty during this time and maybe that's how they survived and became the way they are Beverly gives of her time and such to help others as does all the women of the church. I hope Phillis is doing ok'.

Someone took her to the doctor a while back and she is still on oxygen. I didn't know she had lung problems but I guess she does, I miss her sitting in front of me during service. I recall her telling me not to give up on my song writing and singing so I have taken that to heart, this is something that God has put inside of me and it's supposed to be given birth too and then it's supposed to be shared with others and Him the father. Although He has an advantage because He hears it before anyone else as I sing it in the church such a great way to connect with Him as I go through this life He has given back to me, as for needing others to sing I don't as the parts come together in my mind before music is ever set to it. In my mind the music is already there and it allows me to bring the melody out in the real world so others can enjoy what I hear, my perception of things are different from other because I see it in a different dimension. A place where no one else can go my serenity room you might say and I can go back to it at any time and pick up where I left off, my songs start off with bits and pieces and then over time they are brought together connected by my music which plays inside my mind, the one they said was destroyed so long ago. I believe we all have a drive to survive and if it's possible we will survive but the adjustments can take many years but when your done then life takes on a new meaning, one far from the life you lead before. Many times I saw my self close to death but I still fought to stay here maybe in hope that something good will come out of this life, I can hear the train coming and it's bringing in new cars to be filled with the crops that were grown around here and then they will be shipped to other countries for consumption. As for a food shortage I don't see one it's just others driving up the prices to get rich, and in doing that the the hardest working people suffer because of it not being able to afford gas to get to work or go any where to see family which could be far away. The government will never change and until they do we will continue to bite the bullet, and pray that it wont explode. When people read things about you they can use that against you later in life claming they can see something when there's nothing there to see, people trying to connect with the cosmose oftend tell you things that have already been made public in hope to make money off of you this is something that happened to me in the early stages fo taking my life back and it almost drove me further into a depression. But once that contact was broken then I was able to move on, a word of advice don't go there!! It only breeds trouble. And you have enough to handle at that stage of life, there are many that will use you and you cant let that happen. I went through many years not knowing weather I was up or down but when I landed on my feet I started to peace life together, as for the beginning of my life wasn't to hot but the second part slowely changed and I became who I am a loving person that would move heaven and earth if it was needed to help someone. It's the end to another day and now I'm bringing it to a close. Sunday morning and my land it's cold' yesterday didn't warm up either so maybe were in for a cold snap, now I wish summer was back so funny how we or I get that way' but it's something we cant change. We went and got grocries yesterday and although it looked like a lot in the basket and having to carry it, when it's put away' it doesn't really amount to much but it should get us bye for a while. If it was just me here it would last the month but no matter what we seam to survive, I have a feeling it's going to be a long winter so we better get settled in.. this will be a time to reflect on what has taken place in this last year because the next year is going to be different the two people running for president I don't trust but that's just my opinion and I'm intitled to that I see many things happening in the next year and they are not good always putting in their two cent's and enciting war it seams to be one thing there not good at but still take it to that table. When will they learn? Surely not by history it's supposed to teach them something but all it teaches them is to try it again.

No one' ever wins in war and many suffer because of it the land of the free is it? During my time here I have noticed that these people are as free as it gets staying away from the corruption that occurs in the bigger cities and making their own world inside of a world and we all tend to do that with our lives just look at raising kids. They are protected by the parents and it's their responsibility to not let any of the out side world into their's, as it was when I was a child we as children don't hear of the wars or even see them until later in life when we become an adult but through things that happen many are made to grow up to fast having to take care of their parents and siblings then that child becomes an adult while the parent goes through Rehab because the pressure became to much and they broke or got lost in their self inflected worlds. Even though my parents got lost they tried their best to do what they thought was right. My mom's world became mine until I broke away but then later I was brought back into it when she got sick preserving life seamed to be my thing if I could help in anyway and in the long run it hurt me more then them but the thing is that I didn't realize it at the time. Would if I could, do things different? Yes but that's neither here or there it's something that's gone now and all I can do is pick up the pieces, and go on in hope that things will become more then they were then. We are happy here in Courtland' and it's a place that I thought I would never find, some have to have the big city but then there is those who only need a little to survive like my self.

For every season brings something new and we don't always know what that something is going to be but it comes anyway, and in many forms. Each of us preceives the world in a different way and if you fall into addiction that in it's self can make you think it's the end but it's not. It could be a way of seeing the world in a different light, He knew everything that was going to happen in your life before it happened so that means while you were going through your triles you were protected. Just look at the tragies that occurred while in that state can you remember that accident where you could of died but didn't? That was His love protecting you and He knew this would happen it was planed that way to bring you to a different place you needed to be later in life. The search seams to bring us to places we never knew existed like me coming here Courtland is out in the middle of no where but He guided me here for some unseen reason, maybe it was to find out who I really am. It's going to be a nice day even though it's cold and I will go down and heat up the church so it's ready and get communion ready also, this is my job that helps to keep me going and in time it might grow to something bigger who knows. Kathy is the best and I like her very much she seams to give us food for thought but we are the ones that have to eat that food of knowledge and let it grow inside of us bringing us to another state of being that place where we will grow in spirit. I can hear the augers again this morning my land. They must run 24/7 until the corn is done and then it will be shut down for a while during winter and that's when everything will get rebuilt like the bearings and other things I recall those days so long ago and it was a hoot when things were going right everything working like clock work. The groupe will preform next Saturday and they are even selling pies, love pie! So maybe I will get one if it's in the budget. Randy also loves pie, cherry pie is the best I think and they go for about $10.00 when I first came here it was a free will donation but after a couple of years they figured out that some were only giving a couple of bucks and the ladies weren't too happy with that. For each one is a labor of love and they shouldn't be short changed, just like with quilts the ladies have been making them for 100's of years it has been something the churches have done since forever. If you talk with some of the ladies their mothers and grand mothers did it before them and it's a tradition, never have found out what they talk about during that time but it's cool that they do that for other people and have a reffel to see who gets it. Kind of reminds me of the old days when their parents did it back then times were also hard like in the depression I wonder what it was like back then, many say that food was hard to get and you could go and visit a neighbor and share a meal and it wouldn't cost you anything. Just a community that loved each other kind of how it is today except times have changed the years that is maybe not so much the people. Phillis has people who care for her and take her to the doctor, this is something I never have seen in the bigger cities even family my family anyway usually couldn't or wouldn't have the time for such things.

But here it's different, there is a kind of love between these brothers and sisters and maybe it's been here all along caring wither they get the help they need when it comes to being ill or just having a good time being together. In the beginning I was stand offish but then later came to realize that others could love me for who I am this had never taken place before and it was new to me so I took baby steps in getting to know them. I remember going to my first M&M Auction they were shocked to say the least that I had came and to be honest I was shocked also but I had fun and it was exciting for me, it was like the new member breaking out of his or her shell to experience something new in this new world that I had become a part of. And I got a few cool things, which I will cherish for ever. A part of my new being is taking place a new me that will grow in spirit and in faith. At times I feel like I'm a son that left long ago and has finely came home but I cant explain these feelings there random like, and sometimes I think there is an off balance in my feelings and I don't know why. Some days go by with out a hitch and others I feel like I might have done something that wasn't right but I cant put my finger on it, through the years I was isolated from the out side world except for things like going to the store. And that might have hurt in some ways but here I mingel with others and that can bring change good change mind you but it would make me slow in response to some things that others find easy to respond to.

Like the child who got lost in the wilderness when he found his way home many things had changed and what was easy for the others wasn't for him, he somehow changed and the others didn't know how to take that change. And the boy felt lost just by being gone during that time, sepration can throw things off balance and sometimes even the parent don't know what do do so they get him a shrink in hope that things will return back to normal but they never do because the experience was out of the normal realm of things. And I feel like that child sometimes, hoping to find what I had missed during that time of sepration I guess' in time things will come full circle but until that time I will continue to wonder what I had missed. Writing can bring you into a different world one where many cant go,, but as long as you can separate the two I believe you will be fine. Monday and it's another cold one I didn't sleep too good last night because I was miserable such a thing happening I wont repeat it, but I will never eat beef and bean wraps again. As they really gave me a fit take my advice if something iss ten for ten dollar it's probably no good. My land I never had such a problem before but it hit me full force, being Monday I have to check on getting the car looked at and make sure it's ready for winter. The church is clean and now I can relax for a day or two except for getting the car looked at, I can feel things changing again but not quite sure what the out come will be my whole insides have been giving me heck but in time it should pass as everything does in this life and then it will be Katey get your gun once again' once again. And then I will be fine, I can hear the mill going full bore once again so the harvest isn't done yet but it shouldn't take much longer the way they are going around the clock, the smaller things must be done down here at this plant and then the others down the tracks a bit at Hanson & Muller, they bring in the crops and transport them to where they need to go having a fleet of trucks. I also ate some cookies and that might have made me that way also but they never have before, I told Kathy that I would like to check out bible study next week when they meet here in courtland it's just a thought at this point but I need to see how they study in hope that I might learn something that I don't already know. Which could be a lot, or who knows maybe I can study on my own and see what I get out of it. My reading is better then it used to be but there are still words that I don't understand in the bible or in the reading books and maybe that because of the lack of schooling I really cant say for sure, but I also know that my prespective of things might help them also giving my view on things maybe different from theirs seeing I was taught by God. When you tell someone that they don't really know how to take it because they were taught by a teacher, will our differences clash or will they coincide with each other only He knows the answer to that question. Many years ago I wrote a letter about how if the addiction didn't take place I might have been a teacher but it never did because of what happened, in the bible God is all about giving second chances to all the people He loves but it's up to us to relearn things in the right way. Although I'm curious about bible study it doesn't mean that I shouldn't give it a chance and who knows what!! You can learn when you get others opinion on matters. A new week and it will go by pretty fast as all the weeks do and hopefully things will be ok with the car just needing a oil change or a tune up. I like to watch old westerns and how the good guys prStacyiled when all was said and done.

Even in a movie there is hope for better things later in life. "Lonesome dove" was a good one. And it's awesome to watch, it seams they don't have as many westerns today as they did back in the day but when they show one it's usually pretty good. The women looking for her love in times of great distress and fining her man that comes back to her after the cattle drive, and they live very happy together. Morning is about here and everyone will be getting up to face the day, going to work and making a living it was said one time that each day is a gift and should be treated as such. Tuesday and I feel better today or this morning my land eating that bad food really made us sick and it's an experience I wouldn't want to have repeated, yesterday was a holiday so we couldn't go to the clinic but through the night and yesterday it passed or al least I hope it did. I usually don't buy that kind of food and now I know why, such a scary thing to go through as even little brother was making love to the toilet. So we through them out in the garbage so not to make the mistake of eating them again, who would of thought you could get so sick. Living out in the country some places must cut corners putting out the things which should have been thrown away in hope to make a dollar, I can tell it's cold out again so I will bundel up to go down to the church and get the trash taken out before they get here later thisw morning other then that I'm still waiting on my car getting fixed but I'm sure it will happen once they get time yesterday they had a big truck down there putting on new tires so that took them quite a while.

All things in time and time makes all things come to be, strange how that works sometimes. My days that are spent feeling like crap make me grateful for the days that are good, there is no compairson in the differences one day your asking for relief and the next your asking for Him to bless those who are ill because you know who it feels. Phillis was at church on Sunday and it was nice to see her as I shook her hand, such a great lady. I'm taking Randy down to get his med's this morning and I hope the car doesn't give us any trouble it's been doing fine here in town but on the highway it chugs a little and then stops doing it. I didn't see Leroy yesterday but I'm sure he is around, also I didn't know he had a brother but he does an older brother it was the first time I met him in the store that day, after living here for four years but I guess there are many things that I don't know about other family members. Even with my own I don't really know all that happens, this winter could really be a bad one being we missed the bullet for the last couple of them but we can hope for the best and see what happens. When I get ill I usually ride it out knowing that He will take care of me should I fall really hard it says that he will always take care of his own and bring them through the tragitys like illness an other things that might happen while we are here. Faith that He will do this can bring you through almost anything, I remember laying on the couch many times and asking him to take the pain away and then waking up the next morning and having it gone, showed me that He is really there could the pain of gotten really bad and knocked me out? It could have but that part I didn't remember just when it was gone and I woke up to the feeling of goodness by the absence of the pain that was once there. In my time here I have always paid my bills so being that is very important to me all else comes second even personal things like getting to go to other town's or a ride, everything was closed yesterday being it was the discovery of america Columbus day" I think that's why they celebrate it or I could be wrong but a holiday just the same. As my mind travels back in time I recall me and my dad going fishing in the mountains, we sat by a stream and caught trout I remember it because it was a brisk morning and we had a fire going to cook the fish it was a strange morning because the saroundings were familiar like I had been there before and I had once or twice but until now many of my memorie had Stacyded me being lost somewhere in the back of my mind, it's strange how some of them come back to let you relive those moments that were once forgotten. In life many things Stacyde us and are forgotten but through the sands of time they are brought back for one reason or another to maybe show us that they weren't forgotten just missed placed through the sands of time. This would allow us to bring them into the future sort of like up date them so they are not gone for ever but we do have some things that are better forgotten. Like accidents why would He let you bring those things back? For truly they have no use except to remind you of things like the miracles which took place so long ago, and in doing that helping to build your faith stronger then it once was. Do people sleep less when they get older? It seams that way to me, it's after noon and the day is going fine as I feel much better then yesterday.

It's starting to get windy out and I can feel a storm coming in. Wednesday and I still don't feel my best yet but I'm hoping for that to change, although the morning is another cold one it's nice in here but my eyes still swell shut from the dust that's in the air. But that shouldn't last but a few more weeks, hump day and they still havent gotten to my car so maybe I will take it else where and get it done. Waiting has never been my strong suite especially when they should of gotten it done on Monday, like they said they would. I havent heard anything about Mrs Hord and how she is doing lately but I do know she is a fighter strong by the things she has had to over come like cancer among other things and boy Norman loves her so. It's a love that was built over many years here in courtland and they are still going strong today God bless them, as for the kids meaning Leroy I havent seen him in quite some time but he does go on vacation every now and then to get away from the every day rattle and roll of working his butt off. It's thrift store day when we all pitch in and work a couple of hours also it's bag day all this month when you can fill a bag with anything for three dollars, it's a good way to clear out the place for new stock which seams to come in almost every day by other people. A great way to help others get some of the things they might want without it costing them an arm and a leg, I didn't like giving out my credit card when I paid my bill but in tough times you have to use them to get by and then pay them later, I called to check my balance and it was less then I thought it would be and I'm hoping no one is using it because if they are then shit will hit the fan. Later I will check on my balance again and I shoud get a copy of where I used it.

It's hard enough to make it without someone steeling your card without you knowing it. And young people might do it to try to survive also but it wouldn't be right, I just checked on it and everything is fine so no more worries there. Now back to my life in doing this I'm hoping to build my credit score even higher then it is now but I know that will take about a year as all things take time but I'm on the right track and who knows maybe I can take that trip next year to see my grand babys God willing' it feels like it's been a very long time and it has almost two yesrs and I don't want them to forget grandpa as kids do that sometimes. I will be paying on Randys bill for the next two years so that's something I wont do again because I cant afford extra bills when it's hard enough to pay the ones I have now, but through life we live and learn and sometimes it's the hard way but we learn just the same and those lessons should make a difference in our lives. My job has been going good for about two years and I haven't had a vacation yet but one of these days I will, and I know it will happen. To be able to see loved ones is a gift in it's self and I know they will be excited but I never stay very long only a couple of days and then it's back home to my beautiful place where I find peace and serenity far away from the hussel and bussel of the city life that has it's hooks into everyone. I usually know what's happening by staying in touch with them on face book and they can stay in touch with me the same way modern communication makes many things possible even in the back woods of Kansas. We are so close to Nebraska that they call this place the hart land also and the bible belt because of the religious colonys that settled here so long ago, and not all of them were big either just people trying to find their way and that connection with God and His son' my understanding of thr trinity is that all come from one being and you can compare them to things here on earth like water although it's water it can take on other forms like steam and ice but when they all go back to their original form it's water being God him self. I guess that explanation is the closes that the human mind could understand or at least mine anyway, as for life it's self I'm still trying to figure out why it has to be a challenge each day as it seams we are all fighting one thing or another. And the many challenges brings many other things into play many times I wish for my days to be good without all the crap that's attached to it and health problems seam to be a constent, a constent reminder that the past doesn't leave you alone and at some point those things can haunt you and it makes you wonder if you will ever get past that point. The point of no return, I try to move forward but there always seams to be something in the way and even things like thoughts can throw you off your game. Thursday morning and it's another cold one out side. Yesterday I took my car to the machanic and he is going to tune it up for me this morning, according to him it hasn't been tuned up since it was new and he said I will get better gas milage once it's done and I wont have to worry about break downs. With these new cars you have to keep everything just right so they will preform the way they should, the car liked to cut out when it was put under a load and with taking Randy to Concorida it's better to meke sure that it's running right. From what I understand he is good at what he does so no worries there, things like this come up sometimes and it's something you have to have done.

Yesterday I had a ball working and we laughed to break the bordom such a fun time at work. I understand the people here a little more since my arrival, and to be able to laugh is exciting to me any way. We took the car for a road test and he could tell what was going on in the first mile, the younger men have went to school for these things and can do the work faster and better then the old farts. Like with my dad this young man is teaching his kids how to be a machainc and there is no better teacher then your own father, and they can take over when he retires when he is old like I am Ha! We never know when or how the future will turn out because that's in God's hands even if you don't go to church He has a way of making His way known. The mill is running once again and they should be done in a month or so a head of schedual, also the train is running to bring in hopper bottom cars to be filled. So much work going on and the world keeps turning even when we are at a stand still. Once I get the car back, it will feel good to drive it with it's full power they weren't meant to be driven like a grandma like ii do sometimes. My friends are still my friends even when I think there not, for some reason my mind plays tricks on me from time to time making me think some are against me and maybe that my doing when I feel ill or sick. Little brother is moving around and he isn't quite up yet being only 3:30 in the Am. I was glad that the bank backed me in getting my car Sweedish American state bank, is my backer in most of the things I do.

And for that I'm grateful. They believe in me and that makes me feel good about my self, in the other world I wouldn't approach them but here they take care of their own. I have a great feeling about my home even more then I had before when in doubt bring it to those who care for you and something will be worked out in some fashion, my home is my security and as long as you have that then you are ok' I believe I only owe about ten grand left on it and once that's paid down then I can have a morage burning and secure my home for life. It feels good when little brother tells me that he has slep good during the night just that lets me know that I'm doing a good job of taking care of him. It's hard to believe that just a year a go I almost lost him but I'm sure glad that I didn't, his spirit is strong and he will be around for a long time building hope and in time faith I hope. Enough to believe that God is taking care of him, for this is something I think he knows after what happened and we prayed for him. When faith is strong it can be seen by many even unbelievers that don't have the connection, to many things have happened for me to not believe in the one who saved me on that day so long ago. As I draw on His strength for each day that passes and He lets me know that He is there for me when ever I need him such a great father, as when others didn't believe in me He did to bring me to where I am today the one true God Jahova the Alpha and the Omega for my problems seam to be nothing different or surprising to Him the one who holds a room for me in His house in the sweet by and by. Through this life I have learned that if your honest and help others then things can fall into place but it's by his doing not our's for we are only his children put on this earth for His pleasure and if things get too tough he is there to lend us a helping hand in this battle we are fighting to get his people back to where they need to be. Many go through life not knowing him and to me it's their loss because they miss out on many things, even I. At this stage of the game, as I still have a lot to learn and I will stay learning until my day comes many years down the road. It would be foolish to think that we only go when we are ready because many have gone not knowing

Him, and I don't know where they are kept until His return but I like to think they are a sleep until Jesus awakens them to give them that final chance to follow Him the son of the one on high. He is like the tea pot maker and we are like the unfinished pot that has sat on the shelf for many years until He decorates us into what He wants us to be. At first we look plain until he puts His final touches on us and then we shine like no tomorrow, I like the way He molds us to be better then before and it's done without us knowing it as it's done from the inside out. This lets us go on with life as He does His thing with our spirits and in the end we shine like a new penny, better then we ever thought we could be like that beacon in the night that guides the ships to safety when they approach land in a storm. No one knows how he does it but it's done just the same to make us better then anything we could of ever done on our own and in time when it's done right we take on another form in a godly apperience made in His image to reflect Him in our lives, like with our parents that want children" they yearn for the closeness and desire it but they can also do without it. Meaning they can find some other way to find that connection wither it's through adoption or taking care of those who need it, but God desires an intimate relationship with us all it is written and it is so, this day has been a good one as I got the car fixed and now it's ready for winter no more worring about that crap any more.

It got pretty warm today and we got in some walking, boy it made me feel a lot better just to get out in the fresh air was a delight. The sun is going down so morning should come pretty quick, also I had to use my wits to get some things going and now tomorrow I will have to work again, I might have another job if things go right and then it can be applied to my account to pay off my house faster. Well it's getting about that time chow' my land it's only 12:06 and I couldn't sleep so I thought I would write some. Although it's Friday morning it's just barly and I know later I will get tired and probly fall back a sleep about the time I usually get up. It's strange how things like this hit you sometimes but you have to do what you have to do, and hope for the best yesterday Herb gave me a ride on his gulf cart so I wouldn't have to walk home and we talked for a bit. When I look at my faith it's made stronger by seeing him in good health because I pray for him in all my prayers, it's become a part of my life. And it shows that they are being heard, he told me that I have a good beard and I told him that I was going to braid it later and he said that he might also do the same he asked if I was still the janitor at the church and I told him yes and that I liked it very much. Then we drove around and looked at the new garage that was built onto the new house just down the block, it's going to be a good addition to the town having new people and especially because they are ver nice people.

In the time I have been here I have gained the trust of the people I have met and they have gained mine which isn't an easy thing to do, but still their kindness has out weighed any dought I might have had of them. Learning to trust people again has been hard but so far it's been worth it and God seams to show me who I can trust. My priorities are with the church and then other things come second but still you have to make room so you can help out others, the things that drive others doesn't seam to matter to me as long as I get my bills paid and I can stay alive. To have no worries would be a God sent and if this takes place then I will be alright spreading my self through the town doing a little here and a little there to sort of help out my brothers and sisters, in the coffee shop they are needing help but others cant seam to make a living if they have to travel here from other towns so we will see what happens later down the road but if I help them then I wont have to travel either making it just a hop skip and a jump to down town. My math skills are very good most of the time and there is a way to survive in my way of thinking, it would be nice to be able to have everything paid and make my mark here where I live although our town is small it belongs to the people and they decide what happens. I saw the girl at the dollar store and I noticed that she doesn't have a butt' mighty skinny but also nice, with a great personality. When she came to work she looked mighty tired but that's to be expected if she works all the time. I asked her once if she was married; hoping she would notice that I was singel and want to date me but that didn't happen. But you cant stop trying to find that special someone that might be just around the corner. Only He knows where she is. That little flower that stands out in the rain all alone waiting to be watered, life here can be hard but also when your honest you can be offered opportunities that might help you out later in life and build your character more then what it is now God seams to change us from the inside out and I find that to be awesome. In many ways I'm a dreamer but I believe in time that my dreams can come true even at my age, it's our dreams that keep us alive and if He want me to live then He brings things into our lives that can bring change and it doesn't matter how slight it is He uses us to show others that there is hope for everyone and not just certain people as we all have the ability to let others see How he is working in our lives. It's hard to believe that I once laid in a bed unable to move, such a dark time for me. But then one day I slowely got out of that bed and started to come back to life, not knowing if I would be able to do it. I remember the pain because when I ascended it was gone and then when I returned it came back with me, maybe a brand to let me know that what happened was real. It not being my time yet. and maybe the journey I'm supposed to starts here there couldn't be a better place for it to start, I was supposed to have been here earlier in life but my bus missed the mark, and it took a little longer. Like the christens that wondered in the wilderness for 40 years although it was only 11 miles it took some a life time, many things are not always what they seam and our perception isn't always what He sees. He has an advantage over us we as people only see a piece of the puzzle and He is vesting in looking at the whole picture. We cant see the way things are going to turn out but He can, and He knows every move we will make correcting our every move if it puts us in danger, even going as far as saving our lives if it takes that for things to happen.

Our lives are His design and He will do what ever is nessary to bing things to pass, but nothing He does is bad only good and it's for the bettering of man kind. If things turn out the way I see them then my life here will be set spreading my time between some people and making sure I have enough left to rest and enjoy my self not wanting to destroy this gift the good lord has given back to me. I seam to know my limitations and I wont over do it, meeting new people might be fun but I have to watch out for the lost souls that could make things harder.

This could get intresting in the future if the picture is beautiful but if it's not then nothing ventured nothing gained, He never gives us a mountain we cant climb and that is something which is great about Him. It's now the time I'm usually up and I tried to go back to bed but it didn't work, so needless to say I will be taking a nap later today. T.G.I.F. The beginning of another weekend and church is just two days away then afterwards I will check out bible study at 5:00 in the afternoon, through time I will keep learning how to be around people, and it's not the same as it once was back in the day of the dark times. Everything is different no drugged out people who don't understand you just people trying to make it through life the best way they know how, and in doing that everyone can help each other in this thing we call life. My little harley is up but I'm not going to pay attention to him at this hour. It seams he knows when I'm up and I guess he also gets lonely being the only dog in the house, I cant hear the mill running this morning so they must be taking a break.

As I put the things I read into my mind I know that He will do the rest and bring about the good things I need to learn on this journey. My self I don't think I was ever meant to be in the big city not to live and learn anyway, it's like my whole life is about learning and I need my piecce to absorbe it all in and make the changes that need to be made within me the one He chose to give life to once again. My out look on yesterday was good as I laughed with Mark & Herb it's like we are family not by blood but adopted in the since of brothers, and Herb is old enough to have been my father so I treat him in that respect. It's going to be another cold morning so I will bundel up when I go to pay my bill, no bill is a good bill and if they are kept up then no worries but get behind and then look out everyone and their brother is calling you wanting this and wanting that so I try to avoid them like the plage that took over Rome, my land I'm getting writers block so I will close for now. Saturday morning' and I slept through the night to only wake up to a storm passing through, the lighten struck and the power went out for a short time but came back on just minutes later. It seams it has passed but that's just my thought at this time you can still hear it off in the distence and the rain came down pretty hard, we get these storms from time to time but usually they don't amount to much. Harley had to come in with dad because the storm scared him and he is now laying quietly on the bed 'big baby' afraid of the noise. These storms seam to bring change for some reason like with me I thought it was about 1:00 Am. And it was already three marking my time to get out of bed I usually don't sleep peacefully but last night was different, and boy it felt good. The repairs were more then I expected and I'm glad that I wont have to have it done again at least for a while anyway. It's almost Sunday and then church will be here it seams to be my best part of the week, and I'm glad when it arrives brothers and sisters coming together to worship the lord and we have to have a good clean place to do that, as for working at the coffee shop that's something I will have to think on. And who knows' my little buddy seams content at the moment feeling safe by his master and he looks over at me from time to time maybe wondering what I'm thinking also got to love my buddy the little shit has been with me since the beginning and I hope that will never change. As for the day I feel it will be a good one inspite of the storm but I can tell winter is on it's way, just yesterday it was cold most of the day trying to warn us of whats to come and for us to get ready for it, the primitive life is a good one even with the power going out from time to time but I kind of like that. The mill isn't running this morning and it's nice not to hear it when you first get up just the peacefulness of the morning and the rain hitting the window lightly making that noise to let you know that the yard might be getting enough water to turn the grass green once again befor the snow falls in the realm of trying to bring things together it will take some time but I believe it could happen if that's the way it's supposed to work the train is coming in as it's whissel is blowing off in the distance. As for the love I feel for my family it's stronger then ever and who knows maybe I will get to see them by next spring and then maybe we can go out on a pic-nick or something to reagnite the closeness we have always had.

In small towns the people run things like the coffee shop and other businesses; and in doing that costs are kept down so things can keep going. Such a great community when people pull together to help one another, I noticed that my hair is falling out more these days but I chalk it up to old age or maybe middle age because I'm not that old. When I take on something new I usually have to think about it so I don't make a mistake, the rain is starting to fall once again but the lighten and thunder has passed I hope. My little buddy is awake now and he is licking him self cleam giving him self a bath and chewing on his toenails, getting ready for the day you might say. Many things are happening here and although they might not amount to much now in the future they could lead to something wonderful in life everything starts out as something a thought a wish a hope but it all starts somewhere like in someones mind, a coffee shope is as good a place to start as anywhere else and who knows where it will lead. I know that the people in the businesses go there for their morning coffee and it gives them a good start to the day when they have a long one a head my love for the town makes me want to volinteer to help them through this tough time. In the time I have been here many have opened their hearts to me, and for some reason they feel comfortable around me maybe because of what I went through or it's just because I'm a great person which I am, I get along with older people better then the ones that are insecure about them selves meaning the ones that are in their 20's or 30's. As with me at that age I was very insecure but through time that seamed to take a back seat to life it's self.

I remember mom was very ok with who she was or that's the impression I got from her and if she didn't like someone then they weren't allowed into her world. It was reserved for her family and closes; friends even in her darkest hours she was strong, probably stronger then even I thought holding on to life with both hands and making it through the hard times. When they said she would also not make it, and if she did. Then she would have to have her stomic pumped for the rest of her life, which she survived and went on to live for many years after that. What my story talks about is survival and how strong the human spirit really is even in sepration from the body the spirit can come back to go on for a long time. When I was in that bed I couldn't see past the pain but through time it came to pass that I would go on and be here today, to maybe show others that giving up isn't an option and that we have to go on until our work is done here. What is our job? Does anyone really know? For surely it isn't a career because mine didn't last, what I thought was way different then what God had in mind. Before we were born He knew what would become of our mission and He knows the out come of my life, what I will accomplish and what I wont the bringing together of something that we cant see I guess that is 'for His eyes only'. And He isn't shareing these things with me I will have to learn about them in the future. Sunday and we got more rain last night and this morning also I went to work a little late but made it just the same they had a lot of business with the spanish people coming in and others. Yesterday it got pretty warm for a while but now the temp is back to being cold as I looked off in the distence you could see the clouds gathering and at bed time you could hear the thunder letting us know that rain was on it's way, through time and space things always seam to work out for us Im going to try and paint some this winter with the colors that Mark's wife gave me to see if maybe something could come out of my talent if there is one, measure what ability I have in that department. I must have slept pretty good because I don't remember getting up during the night like usual. Such a way of life that is here and you are able to do what ever you want, and no one bothers you not even the ones that could, as I walk through this life I find my self wanting to take more of a change in getting to know more people it's like you could never get to know them all but with some it's a delight, shareing stories about our lives and just trying to make that connection which will in time bring us together more closely then before. I find that some people can be wrong at times but we are all that way sometimes, making the wrong asumptions about things and certain situations. My mind sometimes goes to the bad things instead of the good and maybe that's because of my up bringing you know' growing up to fast, and never having that time to be a kid. Through time much of that has changed and today I try hard to look at the positive side of things, even with some of the things I do grace is right there to carry me through. My songs take on a life of their own sometimes showing things that I have lived through and how God has carried me through those times with His love and understanding letting us know that all is possible through Him the father.

Looking back many things have come to pass from my trip here to my living here so I can learn what I need to know. Tonight is bible study and I will see what it's like for the first time here, and maybe make more of a connection to reading the bible more. Finding that part which is causing me to not make that connection, as for the father I know he is what they say he is but I want to get closer to that connection. In this world I have been disconnected from what I should have learned long ago when a childs mind is more receptive to the taking in and learning but I know or I hope that connection can be made even at my age. I do know that in my earlier years I was too high strung to sit and learn things like with school it seamed insignificant at the time like my mind was way to advanced for such learning, but today now that everything has slowed down reading is much better and at times I feel my mind still going faster then the words on the page. It's sort of like speed reading. Reading faster then my mind can grasp things, it's like I had done this in an earlier life a life I might have lived long ago, could there be such a thing as reincarnation someone brought back to life after their life was cut short by something they couldn't see coming or is it a myth? I do know that some of what comes to me is like it's been there all along a ruminants of something long ago and it could be something I learned as a child but I don't recall it ever being taught my mind is strange sometimes but in time it will all get figured out. I do know that music was a big part of my life at one point but at what point I can't really say as a lot of things still Stacyde me, on some days my mind is like a whipe coming back with answers as fast as I can think of them. Then on other days it's like my mind was shut off and nothing comes to mind, what causes this? Trying to hard I guess.

Through the years they have said I wouldn't live but I did, then they said my mind was shot destroyed but it wasn't. only damaged not destroyed and I believe it was wiped clean to make room for more learning like a hard drive of a computer it can be deleted so more can be put on it. But the old stuff never really goes away it's just kind of covered up. All that helps me learn is given by the father or atleast the idea is put there by him and it makes me want to search for that answwer no matter what it is, if I could have had the ambition I have today back then I would of excelled much further then I did. But even if it would of happened I would have come to this place because it was part of His plan and I would have been writing this if that was also His plan just a different subject would of occurred or would it? It says that our lives were marked out before our birth so this tells me that He knew the path I would lead. The closeness to death that I would take and the bringing back of that life which was almost lost, or was it? Maybe I was always safe and just didn't know it or understand it, sort of like He did with others in the stories of the bible. Showing that He had control all along and that I wasn't in danger but only in my mind, if that's the case then He sure can scare the hell out of us. But that can pass as time moves forward, I remember when I drove the u-haul here when I moved. The thought of a new life was scary not knowing at the time that Margret wouldn't work out it was the first time I tried to love someone other then God and it didn't work. What was that saying? And then I didn't try again in all the years that I have been here, I don't give of my love but once in a while and even then I have to feel that love which can hurt you if it's broken. And my ability to deal with others wasn't that fine tuned back then, to me nothing compairs to the love of the father human love can change in a heart beat but His endures for ever not being taken away so you have to go through the heartache. To me that's worse then anything, all those years of being alone had left it's mark on me but my love for God never did fail. You cant expect human love to last and I think that's a part of growing, the wanting it to last can bring you closer to the person but the fights can also drive you further apart. I guess I was looking for that ever after where you give and take but it didn't happen, it's all fresh in the beginning but then if it's not right quickly it falls apart the newness went by the weigh side and it got old fast. But I guess that's life in the human since O what a great life we could have if we found that connection and it doesn't hurt to try again once the healing is over, but living here there would be a lot of talk if things didn't work out between two people or would there? Many have problems' and I never hear about them but then again

I don't like gossip and stay away from it, even God says gossip isn't a good thing breaking a connection between people isn't something that is good. With me I like learning and who knows in a relationship you can learn a lot their likes and dislikes and what they feel in their hearts. I think there are a few widows liviing here and they have to be lonely also like me but I have an advantage my solitude has been going on for almost half my life and I can live that way where others cant they seam to need that that part and who knows maybe I do also and just don't know it, the lack of love in the human form has been absent for so long I have become num to the feeling of love and maybe it's time to bring that back into my life once again.

It's going on 6:00 Am. And in a little while I will have to open up the church, I don't know how cold it is out side but I'm sure I will find out as I warm up the car and get it ready for the day. We still havent had the indian's summer yet and there is no guarantee that it will come this year but a good sign is that we havent had any snow yet only rain and that means it's still to warm for it to snow. Beverly was excited and I thought it was neat how she was playing with the little kids that were in the thrift store yesterday, one of the members from the church had her grand daughter and kids there. It's always a delight to see new people and it also showed me that not all people from the same tree or family have the same traits, we are all unique and special one of a kind with no one having the same quirks. I could see the identy of each of her children one quiet, one out spoken, and one inbetween, just the combination you want to see in three boys. We have a visitor in the kitchen a little mouse so I put out some traps to get the little bugger, Monday and half the month is gone, yesterday after church I went back and cleaned some things and then came home to rest being I was tired. They had the celebration at the tent by pinkies and there was music but we didn't get down there and others said it was much fun, this is something I didn't know they did. For the first years of living here I stayed in my home most of the time, but now I will slowely break out into going to such things.

As for the night I was only up a few times but then it was back to bed trying to get the rest I need to make it through another day. Time seams to still go by so fast but I think it has slowed down just a taste and I think that the body goes through changes from the old life trying to adjust even after all these years, strange how things work sometimes. A coupple of people I know lost their mates and now they are trying to go on and I hope they find what they are looking for some seam to be able to pick up the pieces and others are very cautious like my self, in a way I think they are the strong one's because it's hard being alone. But change can also be in my future as I get the nerve to ask someone out for coffee and who knows where that might lead, I do know that I like her and I think she also likes me so now the only thing to do is make the connection and see if it's the right one. My land' I don't want to spend my years alone not my older years but I know it will take a lot of adjustment on my part, we all start out slow and then take it one step at a time and coffee would be a great step so we could get to know each other. I noticed when we had art class she seamed nervous around me and that can sometimes be a sign that someone likes you, or at least I hope it does. My greatest element is having Mark as a friend that way I can find out if she is married or not and then she doesn't have to know that I'm checking her status, I have done this in other relationships and it worked out fine she knows my situation and that I am single. One of the things I like about living here is that you can take your time in getting to know someone and it doesn't hurt anything, like with the people here they get to know you slowely and then they open up letting you in to make that connection of being your friend. She seams to have been alone for sometime except for her grand children and children, maybe something could come of us being friends she is quiet to a certain extent and I would like to get to know her even more then I do now. Monday a great day to start something new Ha! What should it be? I didn't see the little guy running around the kitchen so maybe he got caught, we will see a little later when it gets light out side. It's like something is going to change but then again I cant put my finger on it, maybe a friendship will emerge out of this little town lord knows it's been a while since my arrival and I havent met that certain someone. Not yet anyway but the lord has a way of bringing two people together if it's meant to be, the intertwining of two souls brought together by a common thread loneliness. It would be great to grow old with someone other then your brother and maybe in time he could find someone also that could adjust to him and his funny ways, he has many qualitys that are good and now he is on the right track to maybe move forward. In our younger years we seamed to find sisters but I don't see that happening here in Courtland but we would be close to each other if he would need me for help or other things he couldn't handle, am I my brothers keeper? It says in the bible that we are, and it also says to forgive them 7x7x7x7 but what that means is that you should always forgive them. The love that binds brothers together should always be kept open because they all do something stupid sometimes, it's strange how you can be close to one and not so much the others distance seams to break the ties that bind in some cases. But then when you see each other it's very exciting for a few days anyways, and then it's back home to go on with your life separated by the miles that have kept you apart. Randy is the only one I have been close to, but I think that because we are so much alike separated by only 18 months in birth I think he got my temperment passed down from mom.

And that's a good thing, she was a great women with her own ways of doing things. I remember her making bread in the wee hours of the morning and having it ready for the meals, her rolls were really great and I think that is something she taught her self or she learned it from her mother in the hard times in life. Being able to stretch every cent to make a difference and feed her children, when they first move to California the car broke down and dad had to repair it behind a gas station replacing a Rod and then they were on their way again making it without a hitch, and coming to rest in Norwalk where we lived until that day when the boys got hit by that car. Strange how something like that can destroy things in a persons life and then they have to survive the best way they know how no matter what it takes, but being a child we didn't understand the hardships they had to endure during that time in life all we saw is the fun that we had going fishing and camping, to a child they don't see the cost or anything else that is aquired in doing these things only the fun. Parents are supposed to protect their children from such things at such a young age and in that happening some had to grow up too fast and that's not good. Be a child as long as you can, because when you get older your children will reflect what they were taught the good and the bad. We all see things in a different light even if we are raised in the same family, Sue was names after grandma and she was also spoiled getting her own way by dad having the newest records on the market because the other kids had them, as for the boys they had to endure without because there was so many of us and just one sister.

Mom was spoiled also as they took their weekly trips on Saturdays when dad got his pay check and us boys stayed home, but the car was always full of food in the early days that I can remember and we would carry them into the house. Memories are blotchy, but as time moves on they seam to come back a glimps here and a glimps there. Maybe so we can record what life was like back then, harley had to come in and sit on my bed to check out what I was doing poor guy doesn't like to be alone either just a natural thing in this life. Not wanting to be alone that is, it's like he know when to bother me and he usually gets his own way being spoiled like Sue was as a child. He looks at me and wags his tail in hope that I will let him out but it's not going to work, the day has come to an end and now it's time for bed so later and God bless. Tuesday and I had a dream about Bob and this was the first in many years, when we were young he used to like to fight and many times he tried to fight with me but usually nothing happened until one day when I went to see his sister. We had spent 8 years together, but he was the kind that liked to put his nose where it didn't belong so that didn't help matters any he was living in a tent in his mothers back yard along with Donnie and they fought all the time. Bob like playing the bully and when he got drunk it was hard to get away from him because of the names he would call others. On that day he came after me and got me cornered in the kitchen and no matter how hard itried I couldn't get away from him and then it happened after he his me a few times I picked up a can of beans and smacked him with them and then I left later he would tell me that it was the hardest he had ever been hit, and for some reason he liked to juke about it. My self I don't like such things to happen and that probably because I had a peaceful persona violence had never been in my life and that was because of choice and when threatened; it was like another side would come to the surface and calm the situation people always found me untouchable and some would go as far as to attempt to hit me and then something told them to back off. It was like my spirit was talking to them and then in many cases they would become friends with me, this dream about him might mean something or he could of left the world I really cant say right now. We interpret things in many ways but I don't have an answer to the dream right now, it's trash day so everything has to be put out side for the garbage man it seams we all have our jobs to do in this world of his no matter how small it is. It's something that has to be done like cleaning your house or making sure that your yard looks good these are things that show what kind of person you are a reflection of your self in many ways. I got up early because of the dream but only by an half hour which isn't much, I heard a few weeks ago that Bob is dieing and needs a liver transplant because of all the drinking. Really I thought this would happen many years ago when I also took care of him in his hour of need but he pulled through and then we parted ways, I heard that he was on his back because of the pain he is going through but that's just something I heard. And we all know how things get when it goe from one person to another, he is disabled because of the disease and there he will stay until he come to know him self, through the years I could of ended up on skid roll sleeping in a box like all the other homeless people but I don't like the big cities and all the congestion.

During the next few years we will see what goes on as we try and make it, things could of turned out worse then they have and I have many to thank for my home. It's only by the grace of God that I landed here in Courtland and I do what I can to help others for the help that was shown me, the indian summer is here as yesterday it got pretty warm in the 70's I believe and they are calling for hotter days just a head and then winter will set in making it cold for the rest of the season, such a strange season we seam to have through the years most of the people I used to know have passed away and even some I would of never guessed like Debbie and her brother they seamed to go so fast when the cancer hit them they were both gone within a year of each other, and my daughter still morns them today. Even Donnie passed after fighting cancer and a few others which names I don't recall, that's the sad thing about them but people should know that they are in a better placce and have no pain any longer for the lord has taken that away. I truly believe that I was brought here to get me away from the place I called home for so long, a fresh start to try and figure out things in my own life some say that I have supernatural abilitys that havent been taped into yet, and this I believe but what good is something if you don't know how to use it. One women said the forces are with me it's just that I don't know how to channel the power but good news is on it's way on October 31st when they come to help me.

Such strange things are happening and other supernatural people can see it's on it's way but why cant I see it? The one it's supposed to effect, for truly I feel things changing and they change at least once a year but why cant I grasp hold of that ring? Could this come from my father was he this way and if so was it important for him to stay away so I could grow and learn things on my own? There are times when I feel the forces at work a flash from time long gone that I had never remembered before, the flickering of a light that no one else sees and then a vision like no other. When I first came here I didn't remember about the accident but then it was revealed to me sitting at the dinning room table one day, so many unexplained things and yet I still havent figured them out. Some say the spirits see what's happening in my life and things are about to change they have seen my suffering and that also is about to change so I will wait and see what happens in the future, I have always believed that it's God who stands by me and He is the one directing my steps as for those who say I'm gifted I will have to see it before I believe it. It's going to be a nice day and I thank God for each one of them as I awaken each day I give thanks for that day and the one before that, no matter how hard it is to go on I like to thank God for the things He has done in my life as if it wasn't for Him I surely wouldn't be here. Wednesday morning' it was a quiet night last night and I slept pretty good yesterday I mowed the lawn so I could get the leaves on the south side of the yard and into a pile later so they can be used as moulch for later some even burn their leaves in small piles to get rid of them, the thrift store will be open today and I hope a lot of people come to buy up the left overs from this summer. Making room for the winter things people are going to need to get through the coldness of this winter, many of the people are from Mexico I believe and come down here to work the seasons and then returning back to their homes when the harvest's aree done. It's strange how some of the people that live in the United States wont do the work they come here to do, and with many of them they don't want them to do the work either so selfish but it has to be done. And they do a good job at what they do, I was in the same boat once except I live in this country and traveled from one state to another and had some fun at times. I had my brothers kids thinking I was cool back then when I was messed up and although it wasn't intentional they told me later that I was the coolest uncle they had. It must have been my personality, in the years that followed I went down hill with the alcohol destroying many parts of my body and it was only by His grace that I made it to where I am today. Having a good out look on life is important and it brings others a spark of hope that there will be a better tomorrow, I have seen many that go through life not happy and that must be hard 'as for me' I will always be grateful for that second chance that was given to me over 20 years ago by the one who lovs me the most. I seam to be aware of the unknown, the forces that work in this world and I feel them especially during a storm when dreams seam to appear for no reason. In my younger years I was told that I was special but as with most who have a mother that loves them I thought it was just her being kind, but too many things have come to pass that makes me believe she was right about some points things happening that I cant explain. I had what I thought was a dream when I was a child about falling into a swimming pool and being able to breath, even though the addictions destroyed a lot of memory that certain one had always stayed and was never wiped away.

To maybe remind me that there was something special about me, who knows what the real meaning of that is? And then the accident that took place on the mountain although Mark just about craped his pance I stayed calm it was like another force was watching over me making sure that nothing happened. And before that the accident that happened here in Kansas, another time when I was saved by that same force many don't remember such things and either did I until I moved here to Courtland almost 4 years ago and even then it didn't show it's self for a long time but when it appeared it was within a few hours not enough time to really put it all together until later when I tried to search the news papers. And even then I didn't get anywhere with what had happened it was like it wasn't important only that I survived and remembered it, there are many forces in the world and I think we don't understand them all or really any of them unless we are equipped and taught about them who knows maybe someone might teach me about it one day. But until then I will wonder why things turned out the way they did, it's a beautiful morning and the quietness is really great as I watch the Antique road show and see the things from the past even dresses made out of paper that are now woth thousands of dollars worth almost nothing back then. The price of things increase through the years and although some cars were worth twenty five hundred dollars back then it would be much more today, some of the old cars today go from twenty thousand dollars to $150.000 which leaves only the rich able to buy them.

Maybe one day things will come my way but for now I will contine on the path I'm on. I can hear the wind blowing out side, so I'm thinking we might have a storm coming in. but that's ok' with me, during this time of year you can never really tell what the weather is going to be like living in a place where there is a jet stream and maybe that's why I can feel things change, you surely can feel things move and hear them a gust of wind as it passes through and then it's quiet for a short time. Randy must be dreaming this morning as I can hear him talking to someone who isn't here, could he also feel the things I feel cant really say for sure. But it's possible being we came from the same place. Small towns are the greatest places to live and even pastor Kathy like them and chooses them over other places that are crouded, she once told me that it's the family inviorment which she likes and I can now see why. Although things move slower here there is no need for a faster pace like in the big cities where everyone run's over each other to get to where they are going, I guess I wasn't meant for that world because even in my younger years it was mostly small towns none of them over 30.000 people. It seams I only need a few friends in this life He has created for me and with that I'm fine, last night Valerie called and wanted to talk it seams she has gotten her self into some trouble with the drugs but picked her self up and is moving forward. I'm sure Glad that I don't live in Kearney any longer, with the drug problem they have there it seams to never end in that part of the country and as time goes by it will increase. I think about her from time to time, but still gald that we didn't get together. That in it's self would have been a mistake and it would of never lasted, my time here has mellowed me out and now I'm at peace not that I wasn't before it's just more so today then it was back then so many years ago. The living here is good compaired to any other place I have lived according to my memory and change comes slowely here like with me it's just a good fit, I'm hoping our winter wont be too bad but I do like the snow when it falls getting out there and moving it the best way I know how brings life to this body of mine. I can remember living in Flag Staff Arizona, and the winters there were hard we slept in a camper and it was all we could do to stay warm, but we survived and made it until spring to only move afterwards to Kingmen where it didn't snow as much. A little town not much bigger then Courtland but the stay there didn't last long either so far out of the way but they did have good fishing during spring and summer and we camped for most of that. Always moving not setteling down in one place but the curse followed us around and no one had a drivers licens except for Irean, not a good life looking back and it caused a lot of problems having siblings living together. Fights all the time between mates, today Irean lives in Lincoln Nebraska, and all the kids live with her still even my X wife has taken up refuge back in her mothers home it's cheaper to live as a unit I guess then to live alone. That way they can break up the bills and only have to pay a little each, it was done that way back then and it will continue until the unit is broken up by death or just getting tired of each other.

Diane remarried and had a daughter after the two boys but the marriage only lasted ten or so years, I recall her telling me I was her first love but I guess

I didn't feel the same way. When we went together everything was fine but then when we tied the not' it all fell apart. It was like I was a piece of meat and she owned me which didn't go over very good because I resented her and did all I could do to get away. I was looking for something and it wasn't found with her so I ventured out to find what I was looking for, while in Arizona I got my big break and had to come home to Kearney, for some reason I couldn't live with mom being ill so I took care of her until she went to be with the lord in 1995 I my self was recovering in 92 but I seamed to be able to care for her and at that moment in time that's all that mattered. Thursday morning' and I will clean the church again after Wednesday schools things will be good for Sunday, yesterday as I worked with another women I found out that her husband passed in 1995 the same year my mom did and he was a earth mover running heavy equipment. She seams like a nice women about in her 70's but in real good health or at least she looks like she is, a very calm person and we talked for a time and then read books. My self I'm interested in devotional books trying to see how some looked at life, and how they dealt with problems and with most of them they took it to God when they didn't have the answer. There is suppose to be a connection between them so He can help them in making desigions about certain things that pertain to his kingdom each book gives that persons opinion about things and how they are brought together. Valerie hasn't called so she must be alright, she seams to only call when trouble has set it's sights on her maybe to feel safe by talking to me she used to do that when I lived there so long ago and would even come over at all hours of the night.

Just to talk, I seamed to have a way with some people of calming them when they are distraught by their alcohol and drug addictions. She said she has no one who could do what I did back then and I had helped many in their hour of need when it seamed that the world was falling in around them, I believe she might end up doing some time this time unless her X husband can bail her out of this one like he has before many times I'm sure, she has a way about her that makes others feel sorry for her and that leads to deeper problems but I'm not her judge just her friend of many years. When you get tangled up in the court system it's hard to get out of it because they seam to be able to track you for as long as you are on probation or what ever other stipulation they put on you, and if they don't want to deal with you at all they ship you to another state hoping that might help. Which it doesn't when your whole life has been connected to drugs and alcohol, the change has to be wanted and if it's not then they will go on putting a bandaid on it in hope that things might change later down the road. When you have a drug in your system for a life time then it's hard to get it out especially pot with all the T.H.C. That comes with it, which can lead to cancer later down the road. It's another cold morning and I could feel it when the heater went onat 68 degrees, cant sleep when it's hot never have been able to. The weather man said it's supposed to be windy today also but we will see I still don't hear it this morning like yesterday, but that can change in a heart beat as it has done so many times before. I believe harvest must be over as the mill hasn't been running for the last few days just peace and quiet with nothing sturring but the animals, the wind yesterday blew the leaves out of the pile I had built and now they are gone leaving just a few on the ground for mulch during the winter. Last week the kids didn't make much of a mess after bible school so I'm hoping that's the case this week but we will see every week is different and it's fun to work by my self and sing when the mood hits me just m and God so he can hear the songs I have created for his pleasure. It's like all that we do is supposed to please Him and that a part I don't fully understand yet but in time I will, I was told that my world will change so I have asked God to show me if this is really true on the 31st and through 12 months things are supposed to change and my whole world is supposed to open up. Bringing in all the things I havent had in my life I could do great things with this blessing if it's true so we will see what the future holds for me. In the realm of miracles, I would like to start a car business and some other things to help others besides my self. As I have searched the internet for ways to make money I find that many of them are scams just people trying to get your money and I haven't found one yet that would do me any good or anyone else for that matter. They seam to give you just enough information to keep you sinking your money into them giving nothing in return, my land' how can there be so many thiefs out there but I guess that's the way the world works in this day and age the under achiver doesn't have a chance with all the crooks out there.

If it takes being a crook to get a head then I guess I'm out of it because I couldn't break someones heart that is probably already down on their faith or luck as some call it, I was taught to help those who are down not beat them up even more then they have been already. I can hear something out side but I cant tell if it's the wind or the mill across the way but I'm sure I will be able to tell, when it gets light out side. The people down the road are getting things ready to move into their new house and the women seamed very happy when she came into the thrift store to get material for her windows. And the house next door is coming along just fine, I can see them gtting it done in a few months so they can flip it for some quick cash I'm going to talk to the guy the next time he is in town working on the house. So maybe they can get that old tree out of my yard, because at this point it could fall either way on my power lines or his and cause a black out. If it fell on either one of our houses it would cause a lot of damage and that's something neither of us want, prevention is worth a pound of cure in this part of the country. I think it's the wind that I'm hearing because it isn't constent like the mill would be unless they are testing something like an auger bearing, when the wind blows you can hear it through the trees and lord knows I have a few I really like the pine that sits in my front yard. The doves sit in it and cue, letting you know they are there sitting on the branch and they never leave here like other birds do.

They stay year around not wanting to fly south for the winter like all the others do making this their home for ever I think' for some reason I try to miss them when I'm driving not wanting to hurt God's creatures. You hear about them in the bible and how they stand for purity or at least that's my take on it, I think they are beautiful being all white like the driven snow that falls in the winter. I recall the first time I heard themi thought they were owls but then I was corrected by one of my brothrs or sisters in church, it's like they are a simble of this town a good place where God shows favor to many things. I also noticed that they are going to build a new deck on the house next door and I think that will set it off making it look really nice for the next person that buys it, I hope some girls move into it so I can meet some more people. Or a family doesn't really matter but I pray that no drug addictss move in don't need that kind of thing around us because with that comes trouble it's unavoidable when that stuff is around. As I like my peace and that will be taken away if they move in, God protect me as you have been doing and never let trouble move in next door. My arm hurts today sleeping on it wrong makes the joints hurt, but I know it will pass in time it seams to always do that as the day goes by. Maybe today I will work on that computer and see if I can get it going by using parts from the other one to speed it up a little faster, the wind is blowing like hell so I will close before we get a power outage and I loose my connection. Friday morning' yesterday the wind blew like hell all day long even enough to make you think it could tear off the roof of the house but it didn't. and now this morning it's blowing again as you can hear it through the trees, I saw Herb yesterday as he was driving home and passed my house when I was locking up the car. He said he was headed home so he could get warm, he sure loves that gulf cart and I'm sure it saves him a lot by driving it instead of his truck, the wind made things strange again it's like we are connected in some way strange I know but things happen when it blows like that. The good thing is that only a few branches fell out of the tree and they are small enough to where I can just pick them up by hand, I went and vacuumed the church yesterday so now I only have a few things to do before Sunday. People are sometimes odd when their personality changes but I bet they say the same about me also having good and bad days during each week, some days they are happy and others sad but maybe that's life. I try to be the same all the time. But there are those times when being happy doesn't fit into the day, just a normal day brings a mulitude of feelings and I think it would be nice to always have a smile on your face when ever possible. Through the years I have seen many changes in people but with the older people they seam to be set in their ways wither it's happy or sad, I sometimes think about what they have had to live through but in the end they have survived to be here today. What would be their opinion on the world today compaired to say back in the 30's would they prefer then to now? Or vice a versa. Other then the wind it's a quiet morning and I think the wind is going to leave us for a time, but it's nothing like yesterday when it was blowing from 35 to 65 miles an hour. I told Randy it would be a shame if lighten hit the opening on the house next door, as it would of burnt to the ground. In the years that I have lived here I always thought that our other neighbor was using the garage next door but come to find out he doesn't, it's been empty all these years and I believe the guys will do some repairs to it and maybe make it like new once more.

I look at them buying it as a mercy saving because without them rebuilding it surely it would have fallen apart beyond repair and now it will have a new out look on life, so some couple can have a fresh start. Like with my home it's a grest starter home for someone just starting out in life. Their first home and I know it must be bigger on the inside then the out, my home doesn't look very big just looking at it from the road but when people come into it for the first time they seam to think it's nice. And as you all know that gives you a good feeling, there has been about 8 people who have come in since I took it over people helping me and Walt when I bought some of his furniture they had to deliiver it for us like the bedroom set that is in Randy's room. There are many things I would like to do still to make my home a better one and there are some things I would like to do at the church like painting the bell tower and the shed so they might last longer especially last through the winter months because the fiber board is looseing it's paint. And the bell tower is all steel so some oil paint would stick to it just brightening it up a little could make a world of difference, my little guy has come in to visit me this morning sitting on the bed and giving him self a bath. He has been with me from the start of this new journey and I hope he will be around for a long time to come my buddy, and my friend. Even though he has been with me all this time he is learning new things still today and I tease him from time to time, I taught him to let me know when he wants out to go potty butt that might have been a mistake because he barks when he wants out.

But it could be worse, at least I didn't teach him how to jump on me. I sometimes wonder what he is thinking when he lays there on my bed so quiet, I guess he feel secure when he is near me because he will scratch on the door until I open it. The years have changed me in many way as I don't get over excited as I used to anxiety I believe is what they call it, and it can scare the hell out of you. The wind is blowing only once in a while and it's too dark to see if we got any rain or snow but during the end of the day, it was getting cold and I didn't hear what the weather was going to be like for today so we will have to see as the day wares on. I haven't worked on the computer yet to see if I can get it to work better so that will be something I will do in the future maybe during winter when it's so boring. Take it apart and clean it and maybe try to fix the speed of the unit, back in the dark days I used to work on them all the time trying to fix what was wrong with them sort of like I do with some people trying to make it better then it once was. It seamd I have always been a fixer of things if it's in my power and maybe that's just the way I am a part of me trying to find what's wrong with something Ha! So strange. When he bugs me harley that is' I try and tell him to be quiet but he seldom listens to me the little shit. The wind seams to blow in spurts and then subsides; for a short time to only start up again so maybe it's not over yet. They said it was to only last through yesterday but here we are three days later and it's still blowing, I looked on the internet and they showed a star that was trailing through the sky last night it almost looked like a ship. And then they showed a planet that has changes some strange things are going on in the universe and I feel connected in some way, but why? Through life many changes take place and I wish I knew what was happening. Are some of us connected to other things that we don't know about like the stars? Or maybe we have a connection to something and don't know how to use the power we were given long ago. For truly if we have something special inside and don't know what it is or how to use it then surely it could be lost, you would think that what ever it is would be watched over through the years until the time is right. And then the help would come to make it be the best it can be, can others see the things we cant see for some reason? And if so shouldn't they come to help bring it full circle? So we might enjoy that gift which probably isn't given to just anyone. I have felt a sepration all through my life like I'm a part of something bigger then what's on this earth, and I don't know why' this has been this way. A part of a bigger plan that will one day show it's self, no wonder I get confused sometimes. The vision of looking down from above is still there and I don't know why could I have been shown something that' supposed to help me in some way and if so then why havent I put it to use yet. Is there something inside that I havent been able to tap into yet? I guess only God knows the answer to that question. Saturday morning' it's going to be another cold one so it's good that I'm an early riser so I can turn on the heat before Randy gets up because he gets colder then I do, the mill is running this morning but there doing most of the work by trator and using an auger. So they can pile it on the slabs which are on the ground. I think they are about done but I cant tell how long they still have to go, almost ¾ of the month has passed or should I say 11 days left until Halloween when the kids come around for their candy. That part of the year brings back some fun memories as dad wouldn't go out with us but he loved going through our bags.

So he could pick out his favorite pieces and make his own stash to last him for a while, as we all know many fathers probably did the same thing and it made us kids happy to see him doing that. I wonder now if that's where the candy came from when we had candy fights in the tents while camping such a good time. I recall many things that were lost by the addiction taken away for a time by the darkness and then given back when I could handle them or sort hem out, things that were forgotten so long ago but then brought back to life by the one true father. It's like I get a picture of certain things and then they seam to leave again not letting me dwell on them for a long time, so they cant cause other problems like depression. Just a glimps of a time that once was and then it's back to this time where things are good, I have learned that when you write a lot in time your writing becomes better and It's like they say a mind not used gets lazy like the mussels in your body. I like to write about happy things but also with that comes some sad, that's just the way life is but in our travels hopefully other can see those things which have happened also in their lives. I try to relate to others so they can see that others go through the same thing they do and hopefully they can relate to my story of finding my way out of the dark and into this now beautiful world in which we all try to survive in. Many live without worry, and I do also at times but for some reason it always returns to see if we have made any progress trying to understand why things happen the way they do. My look on things is that we are like pebbles in the sand and the tide comes in and then back out again, bringing out the best in us the love we might have not felt or we did and it has to be refined to teach us that God does exist.

There is always time to make the connection with the father but by the time some do many tragitys have happened in their life and maybe that's what brings them to Him. I know my lessons have taught me a lot in the realm of getting along with others and opening up to get to know them, just a handfull of years ago I thought I would always be alone but He brought me to a great place where I could step out in faith and get to know some great people, for the life of solitude is fading and a different world is letting others in. my caution sign that dwells inside of me still works and it tells me when trouble is headed my way but the good thing is that it hasn't gone off in quite some time here. Also letting me know that this is my safe harbor, I learn from the older generation and for some reason it brings me a peacefulness because some of them don't see the things I have seen or lived through it's all new to them like they didn't have to deal with such thing because they were protected by this place where dreams come true. If I asked them about such things they would have no clue of what I was talking about, I still remember the old women that wanted to help her grand son because he was fighting the addictions I once fought. When she askd how I beat it I just told her that God brought me through it and He will do the same for her now 40 some year old grand son, it's never too late because He wont let you go through it alone He is always right there to pick you up if you fall and put you back on your feet. Even when I thought I wouldn't make it He shook me and woke me up, putting His arms around me and telling me that He loved me. Through the hard times He will give you the strength to go on even if you don't think you can go any further, the things doctors and others said didn't amount to much only His words brought me through those times. Many times I get panic attacks but he somehow brings peace to my heart letting me know that his love is right there, and that I shouldn't worry. My it must be cold as the heater keeps warming things up in here bringing things to where they need to be, Randy is still a sleep and he must of slept well as I didn't hear him through the night yelling at someone who isn't there. The more time passes the less he has those night mares, which used to wake him an I up for surely his spirit is becoming at peace with God standing by him. No worries little brother nothing bad can happen to you when your protected by the father. Many years ago he used to roll back and forth and sing o sweet pea, and we all thought it was funny but even that has passed through the years he doesn't sing that song any longer, maybe it brought him peace no one knows for sure. Sunday mornig, and it's chilly once again Randy wantss to visit Kearney this next month an I would like to see my children and grand babys so if things go right then were off for a day, it will be nice to see them and how they are doing after a year or so it might be the last time we see them or a while at least until next spring. So we need to visit and give our hugs and kisses enough to last for a time when maybe they can come down here and visit for a couple of days. It seams I or someone else here has to make the incentive to bring things together or else it wont get done, but it would be nice to see them again.

During this time I will have to have someone work at the thrift store forr me and I don't see a problem with that, my land' it is cold so the heat had to be turned on so the chill would go away later I will go and open the church and take the chill off there also. My body is going through some changes right now to get it's self ready for winter and my joints ache from the change. That and sleeping on them wrong, it's strange how when you come to middle age you can tell how you abused your body by the aches and pains that accompany them, working hard to make a living has really left a mark but that's something you have to deal with as we get older and hope that relief is somewhere out there. I don't know just how long it's been since my last trip to Kearney but I do know my children need to see me as my daughter said she missed me a lot and she doesn't use those words very oftend, off in the distence I can hear either the augers or a train coming in to bring more cars to be filled but that's something you hear quite oftend in this town of dreams why do I call it that? Maybe because it's my place where I can dream and I'm treated with respect which is something I had missed growing up, having to be an adult at a very young age does that to a person. Always trying to keep loved ones out of trouble which didn't work most of the time because they would end up in jail anyway. Even now I'm doing the same thing trying to take care of Randy without the worry of him going to his old ways and so far he is doing good in that department and I don't see anything bad in his future unless he falls for someone in Kearney, which would turn the tide of events that are headed our way.

I do know if he left that things would have to be changed and to be honest I don't know that I could carry the whole load of all the bills, but I will only think of that if the condition should arise. His life wouldn't be as good as it is right now if he left and if he left then that would be the straw that broke the camels back because I'm a person that only will give one chance to him after all the other chances I have taken with him. In life you have to be able to see when good things are taking place and he would not find any other that would do the things I have done for him, the world is full of users and he would be taken advantage of. Money is the greatest reason some take advantage and once it's gone then they will throw him out on the streets like all the others before him, my home has given me a solid foundation that and the church and I will never move from here and loose all my friends. My journey has taken me to a place where I get one shot at stability and it's here where I will stay no matter what!!!. I feel that my book will be published and then it's up from there being able to help others in any way I can. Just doing the right thing brings joy to my heart like it must have done for Him, making things bareable for those who have to struggle through life and hope to bring them joy in their time of need or rest. Like the things that were done for those who struggled in the old days and having their lives changed by a stranger that poped into their lives out of no where I want to be that person if the lord will allow it to take place, church was fun as I ate some rolls that one friend made and then brought some back for Randy other then that it's been a hot one this afternoon. And the guys are working on the house next door getting it ready to be sold one again, today they are putting on the deck so you can get into the house and it really looks nice. Monday and the thought is seeing my daughter and son excites me and I also know we will have to come back the next day, but still seeing each other will last the winter and that's a good thing. It's another quiet morning and I don't hear anything running from the mill or and other place, it's the 22nd and a lot of the month is gone bringing us closer to the day when we will go but yet on that week I have to make sure everything is ready for church and Wednesday school. While I'm there maybe I might see a few friends but in reality they are people from a time passed when things weren't going so good but still it was them that helped me get away and start over. I'm curious to what they are doing these days and if they ever over came their addictions, it will be like a glimps into the past. When I first moved here I traveled back and forth a few times to maybe see if I was missing something and I found that I wasn't when it came to the drug people and when I left' I couldn't wait to get back home and the closer I got to Courtland the more happier I was and maybe it was because I knew it's my home. Travel lets you see things and how things might have changed if you would of stayed. We all have to find our way in this life and mine lead me to this place, my town of dreams. where I have many brothers and sisters that really care for each other. Kathy was excited when I told her about the trip and I know that she is with me when I travel on that highway which will lead me back here, nothing can change my life now and how it will take shape in the future, here is where I came and here is where I will stay.

Until that fine day when things will come together for the better good, one of our members did the reading out of the scripture yesterday and they need more to also do it so maybe in time I will pick it up and try my hand at something new , I like new things and you can do them at your own speed making way to new teaching . Getting past the bashfulness is a great accomplishment and it lets you move forward in your walk with Jesus reading the words that are created by the pastor, for surley life is good when you can over come those things that held you back for so long 'making strides' is my thoughts on the situation being able to move forward in life and feeling good about what you are doing and what you have accomplished. For things that were hard before seam to come together so we can grow in the word of God, my travels are a part of life and we have to do that if for nothing else but to grow. In the spirit of the one who created us, sometimes we seam to find our selves lost but the good news is that He will find us in this big ole world and help us to find our way back to where we need to be. As a child I got a glimps of what the christen life was and although I didn't follow it because of things out of my control, that glimps was enough to keep it's memory in my mind. And then later after 20 some years I was brought back to it by the father after living the life in the dark, it seams we all lived there, the whole family. Until He found me on that great day and brought me back to that place where I was as a child. And now my education into the christen life has started, I notice many changes in my self from getting closer to him to being in love with Him but still I cant explain how it all took place it had to of been through the supernatural because it started from the inside out.

When change comes from within you don't see it because that's where He does his greatest work and it can be very slight at first not noticeable to other only you, as you grow in spirit. If He wouldn't of found me then I would of died and nothing would have been gained. But for some reason He saw something in me that was worth saving maybe so I could help those who will have to fight the good fight in life, yes I call it the good fight because when you win that fight it opens doors' many doors, that would other wise be shut slowely I'm finding my way through this life but it takes friends and I'm not talking about just any friends but good christen friends. That will help you as you mature in the christen life of being with them and God the father, I cant tell how the day is going to be but I hope it's not hot like yesterday I really like the coolness because you can always go in the house to warm up, as for turing on the air that I don't want to do because it will raise the electric bill again and it's high enough from the summer. Reading is a great past time and it truly allows time to move more quickly, the day is a cold one compaired to yesterday and the night will be even colder. I notice that with each passing day my love for God grows stronger and even though sometimes I forget to pray in the morning, I somehow get it done before the day is over sort of like catching your self when you forget something at the store. I always hope that my prayes from the day before will carry on to the next day, I do know that many have asked for them, not to get them until the timing is right now here I'm not talking about ours because only he knows when everything is in line forit to take place. Harley is buging me to let him in my room and I hope he goes back to sleep I got my ticket for the paper and sent it off to me this paper doesn't have as much as the Hub back in Nebraska, but then again they must not be as big as the Kearney-hub still in their growing stages it will take a long time for them to get to where the Hub is. I would like to keep getting it but the trial period is about over and I know the price will increase by two fold and times are tight right now so I will have to let it go not to get deeper in debt. But it was nice to read while I had it, usually I buy the paper from the stand and that's not very oftend but maybe once every two or three months. As for the night I didn't sleep very well and now it's Tuesday, my how time seams to fly by and before you know it we will be on the road by next Friday to make that last visit for the year if our finances allows it. My little buddy is sticking like glue to me this morning and he has been wineing for the last couple of days, Randy told me that when I left the little guy started to cry the other day and that's something I havent seen him do before maybe he is getting closer to me as I play with him a lot more these days. And I think he really likes it, this time I don't think we will take him and maybe Kathy can let him out while we are gone. My letter didn't make the cut to come out in the paper so maybe next time they seam to not get me as excited as before when I was first starting out and some call that growing as a writer, when the mind opens up to create new things. And then leaves the old things behind, in writing it allows you to let others see how a life can change and how it can grow from one of destruction to one of learning about the wonders of God and His son Jesus Christ. We as people are ever changing and at times those changes stay with us the good ones that is, I wouldn't want the bad side of life to last forever only the good things that help us grow in the right direction.

I know that things will be the same back in Kearney because you cant see into each persons life but the good thing is that some of them could have changed. it's holding on to that change that is hard because most havent known the love of God the father, even with me it took many years before it set in and became a reality. Flip flopping back and forth trying to change for the better and then holding on to it so life can be better, just ten years ago I never saw what was going to take place but little by little change came to be and the change was good. He opened some doors that would later lead to me having this place where I live today and my little buddy harley is the apple of my eye as far as pets are concerned, it seams He is there for me when I need Him, the father that is and for the most part I'm pretty happy even with the triles I go through today. I wanted to supprise them when I showed up but Randy had to let them know we are coming, I hope he can deal with the things that will surface when we get there because people like Leroy and the others will probably cry because of his size. My self' I don't look at that part only the inside of a person because that's where God does His best work, the molding and shapeing that takes place usually takes place from within but people just see what's on the out side and many judge from what they see. In a while I will take out the trash down at the church and then it will be ready for Wednesday school' so many learning new things that pertain to Christ and in the long run their worlds will be shaped by what they learn, I love reading the things they have learned as they hang them on the wall for all the church to see. It shows their growth in learning the bible and how things came to be.

I learn in a new way, much different then I used to. And what I learn I try to put into use in my everyday life hoping to become what I was created to be, we were all created to be like Christ and I believe if we accomplish this then the world would be a better place no anger towards one another just a kind of love that would last for ever. When Randy gets up each morning he is usually a happy person but then there is those days when things are a little out of wack, and I find that this happens to each of us not by wanting it too' but it just happens through what has happened in days before or just a bad night. Wednesday' and they just about got the fence up across the alley, by looking at it plastic comes to mind as I believe that what it might be made of. I went into the church and sang for a while just vacuuming the day after service, for some reason I find a peace there and I know it has to do with being by my self. And knowing that the father is there with me well He is with me everywhere I go but my connection seams stronger there, I had a dream last night about some people chasing me for some reason and then I woke up. Such strange dreams but I get them every now and then and then things are back to normal or what I consider normal, it's another nice morning and I look forward to the day. I had to text my daughter to let her know that we might not be able to make it on the 2nd because it would cost too much a trip is something you should plan for and save for so it doesn't take from being able to pay the bills, because once that starts there is no turning back and life becomes hard but we will see what happens down the road. Secureing the bill money is the most importand thing at this time of year and others are not going to help you with that, so you have to do it your self' and pray that you get the job done, and that there is enough left to eat to make it through the month. Funny I always wondered how mom felt when it came to these things and now I know, the being in charge of survival and making sure that everything was paid on time because really after that it's all down hill as long as you can hold on to what you have like your home. Some of the tree are still shedding there leaves so it really doesn't make much since to rake them up, not yet anyway. I saw Mark the other day and he asked what I was doing and I replyed in kind that I'm paying billls, it always starts at this time of the month and ends no the 3rd or shortly after. With each passing year I become closer to the one who created me and life is becoming more clearer but I know sometime in the future I will have to make some more change to get a head, so we can maybe take that trip and not have to worry about things. I'm working today down at the thrift shop but before that I have to check the church for Wednesday school to make sure everything is ready for the children, but this morning I'm going to watch Antique' road show at 4:00 Am. Which will be in ten minutes when it's on it kind of makes my day and changes my perspective of the morning or the day, it opens a window into the past to a time when I wasn't even thought of. And it's nice to know that some things survived even from 200 years ago, although the value was less back then today it's gone through roof. Pottery is a big seller these days ranging from $10.000.00 for a piece of fire place art.

I always wanted to go to an estate sale and pick up some things which no one knew the value of and then finding out that they had made me rich. I know pipe dreamd come to us all at one point in our lives Ha!! But everything I have found has been less then perfect, one lamp was valued at $30.000.00 and I'm sure it didn't cost anywhere near that back in it's day. It's getting closer to Halloween and the kids will be out gathering their treats at the end of the month. Thursday morning' and I have a lot to do, it's the first morning I slept in since I cant remember when. It must of been th getting up so many times that left me tired and this morning we have gotten some rain so the wind must have blown it in during the night, and it's still blowing as I can hear it through the branches of the trees. Sometimes it's like your one with mother nature the unseen forces that exist but it's never meant for our harm, it just does it's own thing through the wind. The white fence is about up across the alley and although it looks nice I believe it's not too sturdy being plastic and all they have been working on it for about a week and should have it done once the weather permits maybe by this weekend who really knows, we went to town yesterday to get Randy's med's and then it was back home so I could go to work and we had fun but not too many people showed up making it the least amount of money we have made in quite a while. Business verys with each week some days are good while others are Not' but we do good things when it comes to helping others, with my self' giving is always better then getting and I like to do that because the feeling last longer when you give.

God expects us to help those who have a harder time then we do and it gives me a connection with them in some way, maybe because I have been there before in the world with nothing butt the clothes on my back wondering what was going to happen next. I'm reading a book at the thrift shop and it tells how our needs are met by the father and no one should have to go through a day without a meal or some place to sleep, I can see these needs being met here in a small town because they have Christen values but what about in the places where there are few people and they don't really care for others? Atheists wouldn't care one way or the other as long as their needs are met and then those asking for help would be turned away. That's something I could never do, but I use caution when I invite someone into my home. Is that right? I think so in this world we live in today and with some crimes it happens in the small towns off the beaten track of the rest of the world. But I always try my best to do the right thing and let Jesus's image come through me when ever it shows it's self, helping people with things they cant control seams to be something I like to do from time to time accomplishment is a great thing weather is small or big depends on the person, the women at the dollar store is getting skinny and you can tell she wasn't always that way. I saw her mother I believe and she is a big women really into her beliefs of christ, I could see it in her face as the two of them were shopping and I waved to the daughter in a polite way. She replyed by waveing back' I do know she has a few kids maybe three or four no wonder she works so much, the wind is picking up now and it's blowing very hard maybe blowing in a storm, that will bring some rain. Friday morning it got cold last night so I turned on the heat, yesterday it was cold all day and you couldn't shake off the chill as it cut to the bone. It's the twenty sixth and only five more days in this month I don't recall it being this cold this early last year as a matter of face it was still mighty hot back then because the kids didn't have on coats last Halloween. I hear different stories about how things have changed like with the farmers taking the kids around on the hay wagons for Halloween. The older people miss talking with the kids, because they all come at once and it's not as exciting for the older people they just pile up to the door and then they are gone just as fast. Although it's for safety and they get home faster it still takes the joy out of it for the adults, I can remember Halloween when I was a child we were only allowed to go to certain places for safety sake but still our bags got filled to last for quite some time and dad didn't have to buy any candy for a long time. I havent heard from my sister in quite sometime and I hope she is doing well these days after her stroke, it's like communication was cut off by her family and that isn't normal with her being so head strong later today I will see if I can find her on face-book and write to her if they havent cut that out also. She was just starting to communicate again after so many years and I miss writing to her, I have a feeling it's going to be a very cold winter compaired to last year but we will survive and I will get to go out side and play from time to time once it makes up it's mind on what it's going to do. I love to watch the animals as they run around in the snow and leave their tracks in it, the snow is so beautiful during that time of year and I'm glad that we don't get really deep snow here just enough to show that the seasons are changing.

On the 4th of next month we go back to standard time when the clocks are turned back or fall back being it's fall, then in spring they will be set up an hour again keeping it light out until ten O clock. Although the seasons change my time of getting up doesn't as it remains the same no matter what, it's like it's a part of me being up before anything or anyone else T.G.I.F. The beginning of another weekend but to me it isn't any diferent then any other day but there is change as each day brings that. The change in the weather or a change in our perspective of how things will go during this different time, my little buddy hasn't bothered me this morning so he must be really tired on this day. His wineing has gotten worse but I think that will change in time maybe he is adjusting to the season also. Each month brings me closer to having my house paid off and then it will be mine. Such a good thing to look forward to then maybe I can save to go somewhere like on a real trip to a place I have never been before, but if that doesn't happen then I'm content just fixing up my house so it will last for many years to come. Security is a great thing to have and a lot of people don't have that these days as home owners are louseing their homes to the fat cats, it's really bad in California and I'm glad that I don't reside there any more. I have notices that kids are really impressionable and they can follow the wrong path just as easy as the right one, last week I saw a kid being followed by a cop car, because he was riding a motor cycle through town at a high rate of speed and when I looked at him it was like a walk of shame because he knew he did wrong.

I recognized him as being Margrets son a kid I met before I moved here, he is a big young man for his age. There were a few kids following them and I have a feeling he got into trouble. But I guess we all were young once also, Saturday and I got my check yesterday and now it's put away for bills on Monday trying to still figure it all out. I went to town to get a couple of things done and found a good deal on a pork roast' it seams when assistence comes around they hike us the price of food and then at the end of the month they lower it. So being a good shopper is a must around here trying to get the best deal for your buck, most people don't look at the prices but I have to so I can survive in this day and age. My journey has brought me to not being afraid to ask for help if I need it and I have never been turned down praise God but our trips to town will still have to be cut in half if we are going to be able to save for a rainey day. I would like to find another job but with that comes a risk and I'm not willing to go into that at this time maybe sometime in the future things will change but for now things are at a stand still, this morning I'm going to work and then go down to the thrift store to volinteer my time so others can be helped as for the morning it's cold but not as cold as yesterday for that cold didn't seam to go away hanging in there all through the day but I hope it will warm up later this afternoon but I wont hold my breath. I got the song put together that I will sing later this year now I have to get it all put together in my mind like it was meant for me, which I think it was in a way bringing two things together that out linees my life or a part of it. Such a great thing to do when you know others will hear the words, the song I had recorded long ago was the first step in my doing things for my self because God knows no one can copy what's in a persons heart. Back then it was the love for a women but it didn't come out right so it never registered in her heart, then I found the love I have for God and that made my songs come to life. It seamed I had just enough love for the people and God to create what's in my heart and it felt good to sing this at certain times, many years ago I couldn't do the things I do today but as life changes so do I. Learning new things' along the way and, I hope things will change for the better in the coming years allowing me to move forward and to also grow in the spirit of God. Maybe in time I might be able to sing in public and that would bring great things to be but for now I will do what I do now and sing to my friends, I wish there were others that weren't afraid because it would sound great to have my self and another to be able to sing praise to God the father, every one knows how much I love the lord and that's the way it should be but I cant see doing it for places like a bar or anywhere else just for God. That would be a good title 'Just for God' and it would go over big in christen society, I still recall the young women that said she would buy my C.D. If I ever put one out, just those few words helped me to realize that I sing pretty good for someone who was taught by God and of course my mom a I sat on her lap so long ago. Such a beautiful voice she had when in her 30's, always singing in the kitchen while baking bread and making other things so the family was fed good. Little brother used to eat worms out of the garden and dirt clods which gave mom concern so she took him to the doctor and he said it was nothing to worry about his body was lacking iron and many kids do the same thing.

After that he could eat all he wanted but the phase didn't last long and then he stopped doing it as he grew, we do things sometimes that we are not aware of, like with the dirt. Really he probably didn't even realize that he was doing it, but it was something his body needed so it reached for it, as we grow some of the changes we go through we are not aware of but others see it. Sunday morning' like when a hard man becoms gentle many people who are addicted are gentle souls but the alcohol or drugs make them something there not giving them that courage that they have lacked in their lives. At the time they don't realize that they were made that way for a reason, there are enough angry people and they weren't meant to be like thouse others. In the day when I was young I couldn't do a lot of things so the alcohol and drugs gave me courage to attempt to do them, that first time you ask a girl out if the alcohol wasn't there I probable would still of been alone but it gave me courage like the lion in the fairy tale' then once it starts it's always easy to reach for it for a back up. But now those days are gone and I try to look for the signs of a single women like no wedding ring or if they might flirt with me, but even today I miss a lot of chances my life has been one of fixing my self and not so much of looking for the perfect women that I can go through life with. Most of my joy comes from God as over the years I have come to love Him, it seams to be enough for the time being but who knows maybe one day she might find her way into my life. My letter came out in the Salina Journal yesterday and I have to say it sent a message to those who are still in the hands of the devil, maybe it will shine a light on their addictions so they can over come them in their life time.

I realize that no one sees the world like I do especially the ones that have a hard time with getting off of drugs and alcohol at first it's a mighty force but then in time it fades to become less of a problem. Many times they will want to give up but they must push on to get to that place where it wont matter any longer and they can move forward, into a world that they will grow to love over time some times we make the wrong mistakes but if that happens He is there for us and His love shouldn't ever be doubted. My land' He created us for God's sake, it's another cold morning and our fall is about over bringing us into winter where the town will close up for the most part. The elders will stay in during these few months so thy will stay healthy but come next spring they will be out planting their gardens so their homes look nice during the next 6 months. Summer isn't all that bad as I get used to it with each passing year, but staying out in the heat can get to anyone if they don't use good judgment. Yesterday we had fun at the thrift store putting things up for winter, and taking down the things for summer it has to be done each year because it's not a big place but all in all we seam to get the job done, Beverly is a fun person and she laughs a lot when funny things come up making for a good day. I cant sleep when it's hot in here so I have to keep the heat down at night, that too was something my mom couldn't do she had to have a fan or a window open for fresh air just the way some of us are made I guess. It should be a nice day if the temp desides to go up but in the last few days it's been cold reaching down into the 20's a sure sign that winter is coming. Just last month the squirrels were getting ready for the winter gathering nuts an wal-nuts for the winter, does anyone really know where they live during winter? Surely they don't live in a nest! Maybbe in the trunk of a tree just down the road but they do know there way to my yard. I love watching them as they run around in the yard and fly from tree to tree, such a sight when the snow is falling. And I like to play sometimes when I shuvel snow it seams to be enough to keep me in shape during those times, in winter you don't see as much activety because the older people cant get out on their gulf carts. And some love those things, Phillis drives hers around quite a bit in the paraide and to work at the thrift store during summer it seams to give them a freedom from being cooped up and they really save on gas here in our little town, one day I will get me one if I can save enough to afford it. It's a quiet morning and I will go out in a bit to heat up the church it's like I'm doing work for the father helping in my little way so I can feel good about what I have learned over the last years since my rebirth, in my eyes this means given a second chance like starting life over except this time you only have so many years to get it right this time. And maybe that's why He sent me here because I see more christens; in my line of work then not, it's like out of sight out of mind. In my former life I was all alone except for Rosa-lee and a few others in K town, I needed something that is attainable here in Courtland' and I have found many people here willing to give a person a second chance.

Many are willing so they can see the change them selves and it gives them also the notion that hope is still alive, a transformation that can be seen by the necked eye can renew a persons faith if they have doubted it in the past. Some christens can loose their faith for many reasons and one could be the loss of someone dear to them, but as it says He never changes He is the same today as He was two thousand years ago it's us as people who change and you can never tell when it will take place. Because we are a changing people just 20 years ago society was not as fast paced as they are today and yet they feel the need to go faster even though nothing has changed on the earth not time anyway for every day still has 24 hours the same as it was in the beginning, some things have come out of the years. People are living longer and we can see this in the elders living to be in their 90's. My land' back in the 50's they could expect to live into theit 70's but that was about it science has come a long ways, or is it science? For surely Moses lived to be 140 years or was that the one who built the arch? No matter he lived a long time. Christens know what I'm talking about just last year they were talking about a man or women who died after 120 years oldest; person on record to our standards; I don't know if I would want to live that long but it's possible could you amagine if I was reading this in 100 years that would be a world record for someone like my self.

It says that God wont let you start something you cant finish meaning you have all the time you need to find you're way in this life. What a great thought knowing you will be able to make that difference you started out to make, and that He will always be right by your side to help you accomplish this task. Darn good thing He doesn't age like we do' in my time here there is a person who looks after a lot of things and does his best he's like a guardian and there are many things that he and his family does to bring people together like with the art center having art classes, and now a supper where everyone is invited. It's a great thing this man does him and his wife, just this last summer I got to meet her and she is very likeable they bring on activities so some can get to know their neighbore, and if it wasn't for them I wouldn't know many of the people I do today, I was once a wonder traveling through this world not knowing to many people but then I was welcomed by a people that opened their hearts to me and in return I learned to love them also. This was something I didn't expect but over time excepted, I couldn't see how someone could love me until I realized that I too was a great person. In my former life I wasn't able to see who I was, blinded by the addictions that ruled my life for almost 30 years. Monday morning' and I was watching a guy on television who was on intervention and I have to say his life was really out of control, he would start his day by doing Methamphetamine and then follow that by 42 pain pills through out the day followed by 15 more hits of Meth. Although he smoked it I would hate to see what would happen if he shot the meth it would probable kill him. This is what a lot of people go through when they give up on life and know no other way to handle it, I have been where he is and it's not pretty just living to exist in a world you don't really want to be in. with him it will take a lot of love to get him on the right track if he makes it at all. The body gets used to the drug and with some just getting off of it can kill you, I bet like my self he has thought the end was near on many lonely nights. What causes this kind of behavior? With most it starts out with a problem they couldn't face and then after doing the drug for a while to cover it up the drug takes over and you forget what the problem was leaving the drug to be the problem now. It's can be a great loss to loose someone this way but it happens when they loose touch with reality, I could tell he was a big man but now was about down to nothing as the drugs eat at his body. It will be interesting to see if he makes it, bipolar people are very exceptable to Meth addiction as it seams to do something to them to make them feel normal. Or what they think is normal which isn't by far, even other drugs can make you feel like you have everything under control but you don't. Last night I took Jack out to go potty while Kathy was gone to see her granddaughter away at school, I believe she has won some kind of award but don't quote me on that. She lift after church and had to pick up her daughter so she could go with her and they were going to drive together. This next Sunday they are having biscutes and gravey at the school to raise money for the church which is a good thing and it helps to keep the church going, although they havent asked me yet I'm sure they will sometime this week to help out as the people pile in. I did it last year and enjoyed my self very much just filling the water juge and serving in the line, it's a community thing and everyone eats all they can for a low price. I wish Randy would go to improve his people skills but he is like I was when I first moved here very bashfull maybe in time he might come around who knows.

My land' I was so shy but that seamed to pass after I made it to one of the suppers and saw Kathy's daughter there she made me feel at home, and then everything fell into place. It was like I was a part of something bigger then I was and I was a part of the community, many people live out in the country so they don't get in but once a year to eat a great meal made by their christen broothers and sisters. I wonder if her daughter will be there this year she is such a delight to be around and she is bubbly like her mother in many ways, she tells a story about how she was picked up on the highway and a llady took her in andonly asked one thing of her to help out with the supper and she has done it ever since. What a great story, I have always liked her but was too shy to ask her out and now I think I lost my chance but who knows maybe it will happen again sometime in the future. But for now I will remain alone with my little brother and hope that he may one day find someone in this world the Lord has made for us, I know he wont live with me for ever and then it will be back to just being me in this world. What separates us from others? Is it the that part of wanting to be alone so we don't have to deal with the everyday things others have to go through or is it that we feel we are so different that we don't want to walk on that slippery slope and maybe affend other people I have never been able to put my finger on it. But I feel there is something that keeps us separated and who knows maybe I'm dealing with something I don't understand my self, a sepration of the mind from others that have here heads filled with things that make no since to me I really cant say at this point.

One day it will all be made clear but for now I will have to deal with the shadows when they appear the unseen forces visit from time to time and if I understood them more then I could embrace them to find their meaning. Tuesday and we have to take a trip later this morning to Concorida for Randy's visit to parole so that's behind us, I also noticed that our neighbor has motion lights out in her back yard since she put up the fence but I don't think they are supposed to stay on all nigh long. Just supposed to go off when people enter her yard, the fence looks nice but you can tell that it's fake being only plastic. The morning is quiet and I know Randy will be up early getting him self ready for the trip, he sleeps a lot these days and I cant figure out why but that too will reveal it's self in time. I still have my guitar the little one that is and when we go to Kearney next time I'm going to have it strung with new strings' I can't tell how old it is but it was made from a kit and a guitar guy said it's worth is about fifty dollars. So many things come into our lives and then they are just put away for that rainy day when we might learn to play them, always going to learn new things which allows us to keep dreaming as least it's that way with me. It's dark out still' and I cant tell how the weather is going to be but they say in the 70's today making it nice for a short time anyway and then it will return back to the cold. Mighty cold' during winter with winds up to fifty or so miles an hour, those are the days when your glad that you have a home and pray that it cant be taken away. That piece of ground that becomes your's while your living, then once your gone it doesn't really matter who get's it because your not there to enjoy it any longer. I thought about leaving it to my kids but I don't know if they would move here and if they wouldn't then maybe they could sell it to help them through life but I'm in hope that they would move to get them away from the drugs and alcohol that plages this nation' many that have lived here and left have come back when they ralized that the people were only looking our for them, but with some it took a life time before they realized this was the case. And then they found their way back later in life to settle where they could be close to the ones that cared. Some call it nit picking but with others they just want to do something, I heard someone say that they would rather not help someone who smokes and it's a good thing that not everyone feels the same. You cant condem someone who has an addiction just help them when they need it and hopfully they will come around in time, it's all about timing and as we all know you cant stop time. I always look for the good in people and as my mother said always look for the good that way if it turns out different then you can say you tried. Addiction is brought up from time to time in the sermans and sometimes it relates to me in another life, but it can also relate to this life with many people but you can only put it out there to see which fish swim around the bate. And if they are hungry then they might bite, never and I mean never' direct anything at one person because it may shine a light where it isn't wanted only exceptence can bring someone out of that dark place when they are ready and not before. I struggled for many years and no matter what others said I wasn't going to budge as a matter of fact I pushed away and went deeper into the depression and drank like a fish as the alcohol let me block out all the stuff they were saying.

A person who thinks they are holyer then thou can destroy a persons self worth and they have no business going to a place that they have never been. Taking any person that hasn't been addicted can destroy instead of help for they havent lived through the dark times when your soul feels like it's being tore in two directions. For they have only known the dark side of life, and not the part in which God can help them many people think they can help but they cant. Not the ones who havent lived the life' and best intentions doesn't work in that world, most of the people who are fighting this fight havent found what they are looking for in that bottle or in that high, so sometime they will be willing to try the other path but it's hard just getting off of it tears at your soul and spirit. And this is when they are at their weakest point broke down by all the destruction that has taken place in their lives. With me I have never had anyone so most of my focus has been on how to break free and in time breaking free was made possible with the help of the father, anyone who thinks they can do it on their own without a higher power is only fooling them selves it takes more then that' and when you think there is no way out that's when He steps in to bring you to a new day. Still today I cant explain how I'm still here but I do know that when He sets his eyes on your life change is coming and you don't know which way it's coming in, but it will be known to you later when the pain subsides little by little. Cry all you want my children for relief is coming your way' once you except that you cant do it on your own. The strongest person on earth can be brought to their knees by this monster and it lives in a bottle, doesn't take much effort to lift it to your lips but when you put it down the sun will start to shine once again.

And the day will be a new day, some say that I might have traded one addiction for another being God' but this is not the case for my love for God is by choice. And I live in His love not being stopped to take up the old ways but being taught that there is another way, a chance to see life through sober eyes and then make the choice weather it's good or not. A rebirth of a soul' so it can choose for it's self, I never seen life through sober eyes before being only 11 years old when the curse hit me. But once the layers were pealed back I found that life could be quite beautiful, even with the struggles that I still go through today. Sometimes I wish I had someone who has gone through what I went through that way I would have someone to talk to. My memories are very sharp when they show them selves and as for my little brother he isn't on the same page as I am, but I can respect that as he fights his own demons. In the light at first I didn't know where I was just that it wasn't here because no one floats without a body here. I believe He was trying to show me something, and that could have been that there is nothing to be afraid of in that realm of existence when it comes later in life but first I had to finish my journey before I could go there. We all have a journey or a job but what that is only He knows and at times He isn't telling not us anyway but he did shed a light on that I havent accomplished it yet, and that is a start. It could be something simple or it could be of importance a change in the direction of things to come could be a focial point. Many have left their mark being only one person like many that have been in books the creation of light by the bulb and many other things which have encompassed life to advance to where it is today. The creation of the computer was a great step in making it possible to bring the world into your home, for what could of taken many years to accomplish can be done in seconds like connecting with places like face-book and myspace' although many people of today may be illiterate they can seam to find a way to connect with others even though education wasn't in their lives. Wednesday' and it's cold again I found out that the car gets 29 miles a gallon on fuel better then before I got it tuned up this may allow us to go and see the kids for a day any way being it will only take about 8 gallons of gas, there and back. I'm hoping for a great ride when we go, none of them have seen Randy and I hope he enjoys him self without others making fun of him while we are there I need to see my son and see how heis doing and I pray that he is fine. I do know that he likes fast cars but I wont let anyone drive mine as it's my life line to other places when we have to go, one thing I like about a car with a computer is that the car makes the adjustments so it stays running right such a great thing in the world today. it's the 31st today the last day of the month Halloween for the kids and they will be coming around at about 5:30 tonight on the hay ride to get their candy, and then they will have a chilly supper afterwards in the art center. Given by the nice people who own the building Mark and his wife they seam to do a lot for the town and they help many people trying to make it. I know Mark likes to hear my stories of life and how I was able to turn things around, talking about it to him is easy not like with a lot of others he seams very interested in the triles that has brought me here.

Our first stop when we go to Kearney will be Mark's house and then we will go and see the others as time permits. When pop's was here we would go and visit everyone and it will be the same this time but we will be pushed for time, as Randy has to be back on Saturday some time' the time we spend there will have to last for the winter because it will be next spring before we get back there again or next summer. In my life here I'm able to make it by doing my best at what I do, and I know that I will survive no matter what. I had a dream last night about Destiny but I cant quite remember it all, maybe it will come to me as time permits

I sure hope so, my life has come a long ways since I left Kearney and I also notice that the paper here is willing to help with my messages to those fighting their own addictions maybe by reaching them I can improve some of the things inside of me. It's like I was meant to write the things I write and maybe that's why I was sent back, to bridge that gap between the normal and not so normal as the normal would put it. For they should never look down on others with problems because in reality they have their own that they hide. It's going to be a busy week for many around here as they have the day for the kids today an then the supper this Sunday after church many will come from miles around I do know there are a few towns of just a few people but they live there for a reason. Many being born there and don't want to leave their homes such commitment to carry on where their family started, many that live here stay for the same reason.

Living here is a great joy and you have your life to your self no one bothering you when you want to be alone, except for the ones that live with you' they can be a pain sometimes but we seam to get over it as we do with most problems and work through them. Antrique road show is supposed to be on this morning so I will watch it at 4:00 this morning love the things they gring to the show' and I get to see them. I would love to venture out and see what I could find on the dusty roads of Kansas, many millionairs have made their fotune in Kansas but for the life of me I couldn't see in what, but they have made it just the same. And have collected many things like the guy in Dodge city' my land he had a lot of stuff race cars and anything that went fast just sitting in a building, these people were visionaries seeing the value of things when time changes for surely most of the stuff wasn't worth much back in it's day but now has become very valueable some things like rings and stuff, but there is one draw back about the show they show the same thing over and over again as they don't get enough funding to bring in more shows. To support for them to bring in new shows would be worth the investment, many people could broadcast their antiques and sell a lot of it like the guy in Dodge city' my land I never saw so much stuff like hot rod's. I first saw it on pickers as they travel the back roads of the United States finding things that are still out there. Do people get mixed messages from others or false hope that something might materialize into something, I think so but being new to this kind of feelings I believe I get a lot of things mixed up like with a women I met. One day she is not wearing a ring, an then the next time she has one on so hard to tell if she is married without asking her. I have never met a women so mysterious or she could be playing with me, trying to see things that are not there could also be the problem. Through the years I have become detached from the ladys and get my messages mixed up but maybe that's a good thing I cant really tell at this point, but in time I hope to find her the one that's meant for me that little spit fire with a good heart Ha! The pickings are slim here in the back woods of Kansas but also many ladies come into the thrift store and maybe I will connect with one of them in the furure I know there has to be someone. In the dark days I just put my sights on them and went for it trying to impress them but I have grown out of that in my new life, what they see is what they get and I'm a good catch as far as I'm concerned. On Friday our trip will be as early as I can make it but we have a few things to take care of before we leave and I don't want to forget anything like I do most of the time. I don't know why it is but I don't remember like I used to forgetting things when I go to the store altimers I guess. Jaden and Jacy will be glad to see grandpa after two years, my' how they must have grown in that time. Not so little any longer growing into beautiful little women with their lives just starting, and my little men all three of them two toe heads and a brunet it's going to be a delight to see them again. Will they remember Randy? I think so, but not his size for he too has grown in more ways then one. Well the day is about to start for the rest of the world so I better get ready for the day. Thursday morning' and the children came last night and about got all the candy I love Halloween but only in the since of giving and seeing the kids faces when I tell them they can have more, one little boy reminded me of me when I was at that age shy and bashful so I took a hand full and gave it to him. It's strange how you can see your self in the looks of others but I know he will grow up to be a good man one day, for the shyness should only last a few years if he stays on the right path.

At first I didn't think anyone was going to come but then I heard the tractor coming down the road in front of my house you cant miss that noise of the diesel engine, when I first moved here they didn't have the hey ride but it caught on once they started and I think the kids like not having to walk all across town. Now today I will go and clean the church so it's ready for this Sunday, no one sees me when I work because I do it so early and in the hours that people are gone. That way no one is in my way or I in theirs when they have something going on it's just a good fit in the hours that I work, this must have been something God had seen before hand and said it was good. So that's the way it will be, like I said when I first came here there was no hay ride and I was very shy you might say I was broken but then through the years I started to rebuild my self trying to learn to be open and get along with others but in the beginning my shyness was very overwelming and now it's not by the help of a friend John Blackburn he too showed me that there was nothing to be afraid of as we would sit in the foyer and greet people as they came in the door. To me he is a great man and our friendship will last for quite some time, I wish I would of known him in his earlier years I bet he would be a good friend to anyone he liked. For the month of November we will be the ushers and it's the first time we will do it together, I think this is a good thing, the morning is cold as I had to turn on the heat to take the chill off. Although John and the others are a lot older then I' they must look upon me as a kid compaired to their 30 some years difference for they truly could have been in my fathers years, as for the trip to Kearney we wont be takeing it! just too much to see through in my work and maybe in spring things will be looking up more then they are today and by then, the house will be paid down even more and maybe I can get some things going in the realm of business for the house can be used for collateral to maybe start a small business.

A car business would be nice one that builds old cars, even a picker business, where we go to different places and buy at auctions the things that have become out of date by time and then set up a place here in Courtland' and have the towns name along side ours Mattsons' maybe make dads dream come true that he didn't get to finish while he was here. So many possibilitys in this world now I have to find the right one to make me better off then I am today, as for the property I have that and I could put a few cars in the yard but just for a short time while they get rebuilt by the brothers yea I like that. As for things coming my way I can still see them, just don't have direction at the moment. But I know it will come in time if I work things right, many kids need some direction to stop the falling into addiction so maybe I will start to give seminaries on how to avoid this curse lord knows I have lived the life so I know what I'm talking about. If you can save one life in this world then you have made your positive mark on the world and that's why we are here right? If you can bridge that gap between young people and let them know that you see what they are going through then maybe just maybe that wall will come crumbling down, fear is no way to control a child that just makes them not want to ask for help but becoming their friend that is something special and they wont be afraid to bring what's bothering them to the table. I guess what I'm saying is we need to help them bring their dreams into reality, my fears should subside here in the next year or so and then maybe I can go out there with confidence and bring some of them home. My church would be a great place to start once I build the tools I need and grow a back bone to just get out there and help these kid's yes I said back bone. Some of us think about our own problems then those of the ones who will proceed us later in life, but at some point we have to speak up to let them know that the world hasn't forgotten them. They say with age comes wisdom and that's how it should be, as parents we have lived through some of what they are going to go through. I tried to make a difference by the news papers and now maybe it's time to take it a step further by getting out there and letting them know that we are here for them no matter what's bothering them. I could talk my self in and out of doing this but in reality it wouldn't get me anywhere because I would be still standing still, so in the future I will break the ties that bind this souls and see where it takes me. Friday' I remember when they told me that walking was something I wouldn't be able to do any longer and just the force from those words broke me down, and at that time I took them at their word. I asked about physical therapy and they said to be honest it wouldn't do any good at that time. To go home and try to recover from the other things I was going through, so I did and eventualy things started to look up.

Taking things a day at a time was my only recourse but still that dident stopt the tears from flowing I was so lonely and had no one or so I thought, the lord would vist from time to time but what he was saying was hard to understand at the time. Telling me to get a typewriter and things to start a new life as if recovery wasn't enough he gave me more, then in time I found that this was a time to change things. And all that I learned in the former years was washed away like it never existed, maybe pushed into the back of my mind like the addiction was to stand as a reminder that I would never want to walk that path again. It only took a few years or so before I would be published by the news paper, and that's when I knew that my messages had to get out to try and change things for other going through the same thing. Hope is a main stay when you are going through such a thing, here I was' this broken man trying to give others hope to pull through this destructive force and I think it's what kept me strong. A force so powerful that it let me share my life with others and it would go on for many years to come, most people couldn't share such things but something inside told me that I had to do this. And in my writings many found hope to go on so they could save what was left of their families, and still today my message goes on but not like it was at first. Back then my body ached as it does now but the ache is different in some ways. For with everything comes change and when you take on new things your focus changes for many different reasons. After finding the words that was put into my mind I started to learn about the life of Melchisedek which brought me a little closer to the bible.

My mind had been damaged by the abuse but I felt it was on it's way to recovery like my body was and in time it would become strong once again. But during this time the tears still fell like the water going over a fall' and it made me wonder why I wasn't allowed to parish in the light. No one should have to go through so much pain but I endured it and came out better then before, pain no matter what kind can pass if given enough time but it leaves a mark to let you know that it visited you. I had a helper at one time and his name was Juan, he came from Mexico and stayed with me for some time when I went into a place so I could go back home after my demise and he was a good friend helping me when I couldn't walk and taking me to the stores so I could ride the carts around kind of like pop's liked to do. But then he had too leave and I never heard from him again. As a matter of fact this is the first time he has come to mind since that time, it's like He lets a little in at a time to remind me of what once took place. Very strange how these things happen but they do happen, that life seamd like a life time ago but still it sneaks in on me from time to time. As in the beginning so it was in the end, alcohol went first to be over came and the lord helped with that but it wasn't easy just as getting addicted takes time so does over coming the strong force. They told me that I couldn't go back into the same inviroment but yet I knew I had to take care of mom so with the strength I had I proved them wrong, and returned home after a court battle. And I never did drink again, trying to keep my self busy by scooting out to my car and working on it in the drive way, we lived on 2nd Ave' in Kearney and I'm sure many went by and saw me out there wondering why I scooted around the car. I tried to keep it a secret but they had to know as even when they busted me brother they could see that major damage had happened to me and mom wasn't any better as she couldn't get off the couch at that time. It was like my brother was always in trouble and we got the blunt force of him stupidness, bringing people round that were less reputable then any one we ever known. Later he would spend many of his years in prison and blame the world for him being so stupid. He later rented the basement of the house and brought his so called friends there which his friends drew the attention of the police, as they followed them to where they would go it seamed they had been investigating those other guys for years to build a case so they could put them away for many years. With us being unable to get around we stayed in the top half of the house and that was our world nice and quiet for the most part and life went on, it was like we were devided the good from the bad and the bad stayed in the basement closer to hell you might say. Many people that are put in prison for Methamphetamine cant wait to get out and start over again, thinking they have it all figured out where they went wrong the first time around . But in reality it's the same old song except this time they are being watched from the get go, and none of them last over two years afterwards and they are right back in the prison system crying because they don't know where they went wrong. It's a fools game and only fools play the game, they all think they will become rich and none of them do I have never seen anyone get rich off of destroying others lives not counting their own but they try and fall many times and they system fails then when they have no treatment centers for them.

This part of that life I really don't like to recall because it's not a part of the growing process when you take your life back. But it's things that happen in life, Saturday and I believe communion is this weekend I will take my part in being an usher for the month which is something we do one month a year. And it's fun' before coming here I had never done it before but it's something all the men do for their part in the church, yesterday Mark O'Brien called and was wondering why we didn't make it down so I told him that money was low and we were barely getting by. Which he understood, it's going to be a nice day and I'm hoping it will warm up later today but we will have to see as the day wares on. I'm coming down with a cold so that wont be nice but still there are things that have to be done, and I have to do them. It's like my place in this community and everyne has something they do no matter how slight it is one women takes care of the flowers while some one else takes care of the lawn, breaking things up really helps to not make it too hard on any one person and they usually like what they do like with me. I would like to try and preach one of these days if the courage stays with me when I attempt it something new takes some getting used to and it will take more then once to gt used to bringing the word of God to my friends for every pastor starts somewhere and this would be a great place to start but it always takes time before some will trust you into their church that has been with them for so many of the years that they have lived. Memorizing things is hard for me but yet I'm able to do it with time on my side.

Trying new things can really wake up some people and I have has some ask if I was going to preach but it's usually laughed off by me, I know one day I will trake my place in learning how to bring them the word of God but it's Him that tells a person when they are ready. And if they don't get the ok' from Him then the time isn't right, for change takes time even with someone just starting out I know they see something in me which they don't see in anyone else, maybe a spark of what He can do in a persons life by turning their life around and giving them hope for a brighter tomorrow. Lord knows my life was nothing but a shell until I came to know Him and Jesus Christ, the pit in psalms 3: 1-3 talks about God saving a life and that is something He has done in my life. Even though I didn't understand it at first, He somehow reaches us through our limations and brings us closer to Him in ways you would never expect maybe by making something make since that you didn't understand before like when I learned that we the people are the church. For this is something many already knew but to me it's something new and it changed things for me in so many ways, being reborn in the name of Christ gives us all a new start and hope for others that have fallen short of His glory. Was His plan for me known from the start? By Him it may have been but it wasn't known by me the student He seams to draw me to certain things and then I read and learn what it is by my understanding for we all see things differently and no two people are the same when it comes to perception. My self I know that life long christens see things differently then my self because they have never been to the other side or visited the place that steels your soul, but the good thing is that they can relate by their own understanding of things and learn about that place where they never want to go some feel you have to be perfect to preach the word of God but if that was so then we wouldn't have anyone preaching. My life is a testament to what God can do with a lost soul shapeing it so it can live once again in his realm of existence although we don't leave this world He gives us a little part of His. To help us build His kingdom and bring people to Him it says that He will return when all His' people are saved so if we want the return to be soon they many should get busy bringing his people to where they need to be right? The morning is dragging although it feels like I have been up for hours it's only been one and a half this is false perception like I talked about earlier, but that's ok' it will just take a little longer to great the day. Yes I can be funny! At times of tiredness, I have wondered how someone could teach two churches but I know it takes a love for God that is far beyond what regular people feel. And pastor Kathy has that love even though conflict can arise sometimes. Patients is the key and lord knows Kathy has plenty of them as she deals with so much, she is a women of God and her travels takes her to many places, she has worked on missionary travels going to different countries and found that she liked small towns because it was more of a family atmosphere. And I believe that's why I came here to get the family feeling, which is awesome. When your young and in you're 20's it seams to be all about the good times even if it destroys the family unit. When the women wants stability the man only wants the partys and even today in my older years I cant figure out why that is, maybe they feel like they are going to loose something.

Then as the years pass they seam to loose more then they ever thought, which makes life hard in the second half. I believe we are given two parts of life one where we make our mistakes and the other half where we spend the rest of our lives trying to fix what's wrong not a good way to go but it shows that change is always possible Sunday morning and the time changed so I'm up early yesterday I got a call from pastor Kathy and she was nice offering to pay the way so I can go and see my daughter and grandchildren and of course my loving son Leroy. Although it's been two years since we have gotten together I feel the need to connect before winter hits, my loving daughter is now 32 years old and Leroy is 30 it's hard to believe so many years have passed since their birth's but as with everything else time catches up with all of us and we make the best out of what we have. It seams like yesterday when they were young and now they are beyond grown up raising their own families, the grandchildren are also getting up there and before long one of my daughters girls will be hitting the double digits I just pray that they never fall into the dark forces of addiction like I did' and have great families to help carry them through maybe this will be the generation that the curse skips it's been known to happen. On this day of November 4th time has slipped back one hour and it really throws off my days, but I will adjust in the next few days and then things will be where they need to be with me getting up at three in the morning again. I was plesently supprised whe Pastor Kathy offered to sent me on that trip and I know it will do me and Randy some good to get away for a couple of days or just even over night will help.

When I lost that connection with my kids so long ago it hurt us all so I don't ever want that to happen again because a childs love is very important even if they are grown up now and my grand babys are also very important in this life of existence thaat is changing all the time. Yesterday I got a pair of new boots from the thrift store and I mean new it's like they have hardly been worn but it will take some time to break them in, sort of like my life it changes for the better all the time. By thegrace of God' there are so many people that havent seen or heard from me in many years and who knows maybe we might connect while I'm there maybe in a passing when we go to the store or just running into each other on the street to say hi! Most people remember me by my writings, the ones that know me anyway by face. As for the others they just know me by my name and what they read in the news papers when they are looking for that connection with their addictions I have always been in the paper to help in the time of need. I still remember the old women who called me on that day so long ago about her grand son, I hope she was able to help him but I have a feeling she couldn't connect with what was going on in his life at the time. If you don't understand the addiction then you can't grasp what's going on, she said he excelled in school but that could have been part of his problem being pushed to excell can cause many problems like not being good enough just the way you are and many parents do this. Not thinking twice before they act, my land' children have to be given a chance to be children other wise they feel out of place even in their own homes and that builds self doubt which can eat at them all through their older years starting in their 20's which is the time they try to experiment with alcohol and drugs to lesson the stress that has been put on them. We live in a society where a lot of people think others have to be perfect and that's just wrong, because none of us will ever be perfect that is something only God is and of course Jesus Christ. Our savior' we were born into an unperfect world and no one will accomplish being perfect so take some advice! do the best you can and be good to others and you will recive your reward when you earn it. Some think that they are not seen when they do wrong but they couldn't be further from the truth, as He sees everything before it even happens through the days and nights while you sleep He looks upon you and before we were even born he said it was good otherwise we wouldn't be here. For all our struggles are seen before hand and He has an answer to why things happen the way they do. I am a vessel of God learning new ways to live and understand this world in a new light, God's love is the strongest force in the universe and we will always be His children. Just as our children are our's and when we fall or stumble He will always pick us up, with some we fall more then others but still His love doesn't diminish, He just knows that we need more help. One day I heard of a boy that couldn't read or write but the Father found a way to reach him and show him that he is loved, and slowly he learned these things he had a blockage that didn't let him connect the dot's between the paper and his mind so he was healed and then went on to be a very rich person. Not only in his love for God, but also in the material world as well what gave him the drive to push forward? For surely the everyday teachers didn't know why this was happening but God did and healed what was wrong.

What I'm trying to say is that no one will ever love you as much as God does not even parents, for they were a means to bring something great into the world and were used like the rich man who helped the born again Christen to move forward. God will make good out of bad even by using them to help His people become better so they can learn what they have been missing, it's election time and a time to vote for the next president of the United States, I'm torn between two forces one being good and the other evil if what I had read long ago is true. In this world' we have to try our best to help others and a Christen might be just what we need in the white house. So now it comes down to the wire do we let things go on the way they are? Or do we grab this chance for change? Will it help to change or will it hurt? So many unanswered questions for surely we don't want the help for the disabled to stop because of a wrong choice. Things to messure before casting that vote giving our jobs to other countries isn't a good thing and if it continues then the United States will fall one of these days, I asked for guidance from God and in time He will answer me but still torn on how to vote. In a way I feel like a child that has been let loose into the world for the first time with no experience in how things are run, sort of like playing poker for the first time you don't know when to hold them or when to fold them. If I was running for president then I would know that things would be done to the best of my ability but politicians lie most of the time just trying to get a good job that will pay them for the rest of their lives.

I called on the president in one of my letters a long time ago but I know my words fall on deaf ears, here they send me emails wanting money but can't answer one question about the suffering in the United States by the addicted and afflicted. Even presidents fall into depression where they become addicted to things like alcohol, but they don't bring it out until they are out of office. I have wondered how a body can fall down for no reason that we know of at the time, and then get back up and go off to where they were headed although it was a moment lost it cant be recovered. Because there is no memory of the venture it took, strange but O so real. For this I have done in the past, the moment is recalled but what happened during that slight second is not. So many things happen in ones life and in many cases it could be Him just showing us how life can be gone if were not careful, and how we wouldn't be missed by our absents; for time is set by Him and how much of it we will have. Is anyone an asset to the father I mean really an asset? I see it this way we were created for his enjoyment so to me that means He wants to take delight in bringing us to Him. Although we live in a fallen world it's not by His doing but our own or should I say by one man's and that's something I'm still trying to figure out, but what I have come to understand is that's where being my brothers keeper comes from. Monday morning' church was good yesterday and I went and cleaned it after service while others went to the school and got that supper going. I have never been low on funds before and I don't like how it makes you feel not being able to give more then I used to really drags me down but there is other things I can do come next spring like painting the garage at the church and the bell tower which stands by the back door, small things can make a difference just as big ones can plus it would really look nice when it gets done, I see the bell being done in silver and then the tower in white matching the garage. Also the inside needs some paint and I will take that on also but I havent told anyone yet, just my way of giving that helping hand which God has given me through the years. It would be best to do it when Wednesday school is out for the year and I cant quite remember when that will be yet but I know it's after winter is over, many things can be done with just the use of my hands and they still work pretty darn good and who knows maybe Randy will lend a helping hand by that time, we will see how things go I my self think we need some animals on the wall in the nursery and I think the kids would love it. But again that's something the church will have the final say about, I look forward to many things changing in the future and who knows maybe I might become a teacher of the word, I will have to see what the father says about that. It will include a lot of study and many days and hours of finding my nitch in the church, as for being excepted I think that could be something that is foreseeable when the time comes. My land' the lord works in mysterious ways and we never know what He has in mind as he keeps that too Him self until the time is right, here in Courtland I'm closer to the forces that once eluded; me through my life and sometimes it's scary' but also it can be a blessing if and when others want to listen.

My shyness isn't as bad as it used to be but still that's a work in progress as I grow and learn, and nothing is pushed on me like it was when I was young. It's like nature is taking it's course and it's working on me trying to bring me to where I need to be in this battle of fighting for God, and what a delight I feel as I move forward into another year. Just two months left in this year and then it's Katy get your gun, for truly He knew that things are going to change and in that change so would I. Harley perked up his ears when I went to get coffee earlier letting me know that he is watching me on this morning such a great dog, my little buddy. I didn't go to the supper last night as I was tired from my work at the church but I know the supper was a great success as it is every year, all the brothers and sisters coming together for a great cause. I sometimes wonder how Kathy does it but travel is always in her schedule going from one town to another to see the sick and give them hope that tomorrow will be a great day, as I live from day to day each day bring something new to the table a thought an action. I know down inside that my heart is pure as I get up set when I see what's going on in the world all the violence and things to that nature, it's something I cant change but still I don't have to like it. All through life I was distracted from my main perpose and I have a feeling in the future I'm going to see what that perpose is, I was only married once and I learned that it wasn't for me maybe in a way He was trying to talk to me but I couldn't hear Him with all the blank days and months that I traveled through.

I guess you could call it dead space where most things didn't regester the mind being bland except for survival and I knew I had to survive for a greater perpose, to maybe come to this place at this time in my life where miracles do happen, you cant build your beliefs; if you don't trust and if you cant trust then you need to make an adjustment. In the beginning everything was hard to do but now it's easy meaning this is the right place for me. But it wasn't always those thoughts that settled in my mind for everything came in stages the stages for which He created, my starting point for learning has begun and I find that I don't like a lot of books unless they have a good story behind them stories of hope from those who go through horrific changes in their lives. But I do like the happy endings where they over come those hardening times, addiction can make a person very hard and even harden the heart to where it doesn't want to let others in but in time it can be softened up by others who care about you, my land' when Randy came to live with me he was a wreck but God knew I could help him, so He made it so' just like He knew pop's was going to be with Him now. And I would need a replacement or someone to fill that void which would soon form not letting another in for a long time, this was something He didn't want to see and He must of thought that I needed to find my way without interuption from the opiset sex. To me women can be very distracting and take away from the path your on, with all the drama they carry with them. And I always try to please a women and that to can take away from your focus in life. It seams my being only has room for one right now, but I'm optimistic that in time all things will come together like the plant which meets the ground each spring to produce the beautiful flower to only grow for a short time. But it's memory will last for a season, Monday is the start of another week of working and making a living for so many families, and the thrift store lets people like me buy almost new things for just a fraction of the price it would cost in a store like Wal-Mart or any other retail store. This gives the people more room to buy food so the little children don't have to starve in this life we lead today, there is a justice here in Courtland and I'm glad that most people don't break it so life can go on with no interruptions. The town seams to be tranquil from other places I have been over the years and I'm very proud to be a part of it, even though I'm considered an out sider my heart has found a home here and maybe that's because I'm like them in many ways. Taking care of my own life and helping others going through hard times, I wish the world was all like this. Tuesday morning' today we vote for a president also my friend Mark gave me a new bible called the power of life bible, and now I will read it through the years it was written by a great Stacyngilist and I have watched him off and on over the years on television such a great preacher and his son followed in his foot steps. I have been torn between the two running for office in the presidency so we will see what happens at the polls today for even I don't know who I'm going to vote for. At this moment in time, I do know change is needed but will we get it with either of these people such a delima. I don't want to see 'in God we trust' taken off our money but I'm afraid it might happen anyway as many don't believe we are a christen nation. These are just my views on things happening right now.

Although the time change has come my getting up hasn't changed as now instead of three in the morning it's two, something inside doesn't change with the times but that's ok' maybe later down the road, trash day today and we got ours out yesterday so Randy wouldn't have to get up so early. It's been a great year and I know next year will hopefully be better a turn of the tides you might say if they other guy gets in to run the country. Although change is good I'm wondering about what's going to happen will our christen lifes be threatened; or will we survive. And be free to believe what we are taught, my life before I didn't have to worry about such things and it was easier to just look away but now I vote and have to vote my congence and hope for the best as the two of them cut each others throat until the last minute. We will see what takes place later today, Kathy stopped by yesterday and gave me the money to go and see my kids so now it's just a matter of driving down and seeing them this week. I Know I will be happy when I get there and see their faces, my first stop is Mark's house and then we will go from there but harley will stay home for the day that we are gone. My mind is blotchy with thought not being able to focus on things but as the day passes that should clear up. Giving me great vision of the day. Some people who have been bitten by the addiction bug go their whole lives without knowing what's going to become of the world. But when your reborn you learn to trust that He will take care of things like he has promised, all the years of being in the dark seams to make you not aware of what's going on blocked out by that dark curtain that hangs over your life not letting you see what's coming.

When we are kids our parents protect us from the evil things that happen but then when you start to break out and live on your own it's hard to adjust from that to what's going on. Every year I live here I learn more about other people and what their habbits are, with some they read the bible each night before retireing to bed and I think and that would be a good thing to pick up on as it would help you sleep better something I have to try. In many ways I'm like the child learning this new way of life, as each day permits; something new is brought to my attention a good thought or deed that can change my life and the way I look at it is that it can only get better with age as our actions slow down to let the knowledge and wisdom of God into our lives there is little that can go wrong when we let the father into our lives, each day still brings something new into my life and I hope I will always survive. My land' it's going on 5:00 Am and it seams like I have been up for many hours instead of just three, but that's the way it goes sometimes as the day begins. It's dark when I get up and it's light when I go to bed just the opiset of how it should be but then again we all have different hours of work and play. It has been said that if a child is forced to grow up too fast it can make them insane foolish to what reality Is, and why parents would want to do that is beyond me and if the parent is also a little off then it can be transferred to the child. A curse of the mind, a lack of being able to focus on what's real and what's not. Wednesday and we will be off tomorrow for Kearney the tank in full so we will leave from here, I don't know yet who won the presidency but I hope the better man won and now change can take place. Many say that our nation has changed because we have so many different religions here and it's like a gathering of many religions in which usually each country has just one or two we have five or six. The land of the free they call it but I wont go into that being I'm new to how the world works and I don't care for politics, I do know that in the voting it could go either way as they were neck and neck just the other day. I seam to be getting up still at the same time the old time not the new and it makes for a longer day, while at the church yesterday I saw some beautiful flowers in the foyer which will make their way to the sanctuary in the next day or two. Very beautiful' Randy cant wait to see Mark after so many years and I called his wife last night to let her know we are coming on Thursday hoping to get there by noon. It's going to feel strange going but we will make it ok' and maybe have a little fun, breaking out of our comfort zone you might say. The connection between friends should be kept strong if they are good friends but for the fair weather friends the ties should be broke and you have to go on with your life. I know Valerie is staying in Kearney until she gets her stuff taken care of and then she will go back to her home town where she will live out her life hopefully staying out of trouble, I wont tell her I'm coming as I don't want to be around any kind of unlawfull acts and she can find that kind of thing. Then after seeing my family we will head back home and go back to work like it is most days, it's hump day as some call it and half the week is gone I'm hoping to be back before the snow falls on Sunday and I think we will make it to start the new week. I know harley will be ok' while we are gone I will just have to put out more water for him so he has enough and as for food he never wants.

My land' it's hard to believe that it's been two years since I have went down there but it will be nice to see everyone and just say hi, for my next trip I will try and stay a week but that wont happen for another year or so I don't like staying at other peoples houses there is that lack of freedom which I feel here in my own home. And I think everyone feels that way it's good to visit but I sure wouldn't want to live there, who knows maybe I can come back with more ideas for my writing, the adventure of going to Kearney very different from my new home town where I know most people by name. many years ago I couldn't see past K town, living there most of my life but with everything change comes and new people come into your life to help you grow in a positive way. If I would have been asked many years ago if I saw a religious person in the white house I would of said I don't know but now the possibility is there and we will see what happens. President Obama is reelected and now we will see how the next 4 years goes, I'm hoping for more change but we will see what happens and that's all I have to say at this point. In the realm of politics that's a job I wouldn't want to have so we pray that he does a good job and let it go from there, today I will work at the thrift store before going to Kearney tomorrow with the car getting such good gas milage it should only take a few gallons to get there and maybe we might have enough to make it back. It will be fun to see if it can go there and back on a tank, and if it does then we can make the trip at least once a year or even maybe two who really knows.

The gas prices have fallen in the last few months but I'm afraid it wont last long with OPEC getting rich off the people, they use many excuses of why they make so much money but the truth is that they bleed us for all we have maybe they can come up with an alternative and make fuel out of garbage that way we kill two birds with one stone they are doing it today with methane gas in some states but I havent heard anything lately about it. Who knows where tomorrow will lead they are making break throughs everyday just look at wind power! I see the trucks hauling them across the United States or at least here in Kansas putting up towers to make electricity for homes here in this state anyway. A great accomplishment for a thought that came into someones mind and made a reality, it's Antique road show day. And I just love it' with all the different things they show and what's neat is that a lot of things were passed down from generation to generation and in keeping the stuff in great shape. Through the years I have learned that family is very important, and it doesn't have to be family by blood because if you really look at it we are all brothers and sisters created by one creator and thrown into this world by the father. One father who wanted to make something to please Him self and He wants everyone to be a part of His family, not just a few but many. Abram went to rescue his nephew and they were very close Lot found his way in life as he was also given part of the land and became very wealthy. The stories in the bible talk about closeness the closeness between Abram, lot, and God the father. It seams no matter what version of the bible I read it talks about Melchisedek, not in length mind you but a glimps here and there about the good things he did. And he held many titles king of peace, to the king of righteousness, all out standing accomplishments to only be heard of a few times. But it starts in the beginning in GENESIS way before Jesus was mentioned, and later He was made a priest after the order of this man who was so great. To me I see that God does things in a big way not just in small things but big and great, for after the seed was planted in Mary without a husband He would later plant our seed using a husband and wife. In my trying to understand this I believe He wanted us to see that with Him' all things are possible. From my own experiences I have seen His work first hand when He brought me back here, but still today I'm sure He had His own reasons for doing so and with not understanding why or how I have learned to be patient and let Him change what needs to be changed from the inside. Out side change, can be done in many ways but only the father can bring about change that only he can do. It's something you you're self can't see happening but others can see many things we can't like your actions compaired to the same action just a year or so ago, the growth in your growing to be a better person and the things which become important to you, in you're walk in life. Never underestimate the things you can do for with God all things are possible, just imaging where you would be if He hadn't come into your life. From my personal experience I wouldn't of been abler to climb the mountain without His help, love, understanding, guidance. Thursday morning' and we will be on our way in a few hours yesterday was nice and I got the car washed so now all we have to do is hit the road. It should only take a couple of hours to get there, and then we can spend the day with the kids once they get out of school.

It will be nice to see Mark once again and who knows maybe some other friends, yesterday I got everything ready so I wont forget anything and now it's just a matter of time bfore we are under way I feel the kids will be the happiest not seeing grandpa in quite some time but I also know that they forget things fast and go on two other things but my time there will be short as I have to be back on saturday sometime to make sure the church is ready for Sunday. The thrift store didn't stay open but until 5:00 yesterday because we didn't have any customers, that and Marys leg was hurting her my she is a great women and she was married for 69 years that's a long time a love that lasted through the ages. I hope Randy does good with others while were there I know Mark will be glad to see him after almost nine and a half years, the night was a cold one again but if it's anything like yesterday then it will warm up and be a nice day. Relieable auto is now running adds for their cars and I have a feeling they will do well, my mind is at a blank right now so this should give it some good input to create some more and see how things are going. I know many people have given up the drugs there in Kearney because of my writing and understanding of why and how they got addicted a great day is in store for us when we get there Shannonn will probable make us dinner if she is up to it or if not Mark will so we shouldn't have to waste any money. And that will help for when we get back, I know harley will be ok' because he wont be out in the elements.

He has and will always be an inside dog my little buddy my friend, I tried smoking the same smokes Randy does and my land' they are bad almost not worthy of smoking very harsh on the throat in a little while I'm going to go and make sure the church is clean don't want to leave a mess for them to clean up plus it will leave less for me to do when I get back and that's always a good thing going through the motions of making the trip a good one. So many things run through your mind at this time getting everything just right and keeping my friends happy here at the same time, such a delima this is supposed to be all about fun and if I have anything to say about it that will come to pass. Being it's cold out I don't think fishing will be in the day but I can see my two children, and find out how their lives have been going. In a way I would like to see my old doctor and maybe I will while I'm there, my land it's been so long. And he makes me laugh we are old friends and he has helped me in so many ways with religion among other things, he told me once that if you make time for God he will make time for you. And that's what has happened through the years God has made time for me the one who loves Him so, Dr Nelson has always been there for me in the past and I know he would see me if I so choose to see him on this trip, maybe I could find out what my guts are doing. And why they growl like they do, as I read about the destruction of Sodom and Gomorrah they really had some evil people there and I can see why they destroyed the town such evil shouldn't exist and back then they didn't want it to spread. Like a wild fire of today, it was something that had to be done, through the years there has been the same thing going on but still He hasn't destroyed the world. Maybe the timeing isn't right or something or He made a promas like before not to do it again who really knows' all I know is that He is love and if we want to be like Him in any way then we must follow His teachings and do what the good book says. Friday and we got home this afternoon it was nice to see April and the others, I met her husband to be and it reminded me of when I was at that age. Saturday we had a good time in Kearney but it wasn't like it was before the town has grown so much but I saw a few people I knew from when I lived there before and they remembered me.but I couldn't place but one of them and that was a women that worked at a station, I was amazed at how they could place me after not going down for two years. As for my grandchildren they gave me a hug and said they loved me along with my kids, Leroy is doing great working for Wal-Mart and he has been there for 8 months making it the longes and best job he has had I'm so proud of him, working in a place where he can put his machanics to work and the sky is the limit with his future. We stayed at Mark's and played cards until 11:00 the other night but then I had to get my rest, needless to say I wasn't up at 2:00 in the morning that next morning but I did get up at 4:00 Am. And make coffee for my self and them and went and got breakfast for us adults after the kids went to work, they don't have cable or dish television so wee watched moving on Disk for the next day until we had to leave because I forgot Randy's med's for a second day. The kids work at Morris press putting together cook books, and they plan on getting married in Febuary they seam to make a good couple and I hope they have many years together April just graduated high school and will now take on the life of a wife.

My it was good to see them again but then that morning Randy wanted to come home as so did I leaving the big city behind yes it's big to my compared to my little town of Courtland' now life returns back to normal and we go on with our lives as we know it. Today I go back to work at the thrift store and get back into my own way of doing things, through the years I will travel back once in a while to visit again now that my car is ok' it only took four gallons of gas to get there and even less to get back. The first thing we did when we got home was to say hi to Harley and boy he was glad to see us waging his tail in excitement and wanting to know where we had gone Ha! My land' he didn't even mess in the house but a little bit but we took care of that. I flurted with the women at the station and she flurted back like we were old friends, Jan the neighbor of Mark's came and played cards with us and boy she can be funny just kidding around with Mark as they played, putting each other down but in a fun way. I gave the shose to Linda Mark's wife as they seamed to fit her better then anyone else, I have come to realize that Randy is very important to my life as my brother has now become my friend in this world of ours even this morning I didn't get up until 4:00 Am. So maybe this has changed my sleeping habit's a bit and now I will get up later then usual making for a better day who really knows what time is the best time it all depends on the peron I guess. Stacy and Randy was talking about her moving down here but we will see how high that eagle flies change is hard to most people and I don't know if she could do it, but miracles do happen in this world of ours.

God has seen to that and I have seen many of them through the sands of time many things change and with people there is no difference breaking the mold of what used to be and ending up in a different place then where we thought we would be. I have a duty to God and others to keep the church and things in order or cleaned for my time here is unknown how long it will last but I hope it's for many years to come. Sunday morning' and I slept pretty good, once my home is paid off I will try to get the money to have my book published but until then I will continue to write. I'm hoping that the structure will continue to grow as time passed and there will be many more trips to see my children, my oldest granddaughter is growing into a beautiful girl and she knows it. While we were there we saw my daughter twice and each time she gave me a hug making the trip worth it, also my son Leroy gave me a hug and they have learned the important thing I had taught them and that to say I love you when it's in your heart. Leroy was so proud of him self and he had every right to be for my son has come a long ways from the boy he used to be, following his dearms of being a machanic with the help of Wal-Mart. Who would of thought just a few years ago that he was struggling with the curse that I thought might take his life over, but like his father he over came it and can now move on to better things. This is another proven test that addiction can be over came if you have had the curse in your life and go on to better things, for my prayers have been answered when it comes to him as each morning I pray for God to protect him and my daughter and grandchildren. Although I'm a hundred miles away prayers seam to travel through space too where they are like a bubbel of protection that incases their lives so I don't have to worry so much and that in it's self is a relief to this spirit, the father seams to be able to do the things I cant do even through the distance of miles and time. It's been windy the last day or so but the winter storm isn't supposed to hit us today they are just saying we might get some rain which would be fine for us anyway it's too early for the snow right now so maybe it will hold off for another week or so. While in Kearney I thought we were going to get it, as the weather turned cold very cold in the morning but when we got back home it was warm as toast such a difference in just a hundred miles. I told Leroy how proud I was of him and gave him a big hug hoping my strength would transfer to him and help him in anyway he need it, the church taught me that when we hug someone it transfers part of us to them and I hope they both felt the love I was sending to them and the grand babies, for we will meet again in the spring when things are different and dry from the snow melting. What I thought might happen happened and that doesn't make me feel to good but I look over the disapointment of them trying to get him to move down here, and life will go on. They said they will come down this next summer and we will see what happens I sure hope they make it so I can give the kids a ride on the four wheeler, they would have a blast on it or even on a gulf cart just putting around the streets of Courtland, who knows maybe this will be the first step in bringing us closer you can never tell. My daughter has a puppy and it's so cute just Harley's size and they would get along good together, she is only a year old and my daughter puts pampers on her when she comes into heat so funny.

It's the first time I ever saw pampers on a dog but that's my daughter making due with what she has to save money, it was the best visit I have had yet and I really loved that little dog who knows maybe one day she might come home with me so Harley has a play mate. Leroy's little dog is also like harley they seam to like the little ones like I do the ones that fit in your hand but his is all brown with a pink nose no bigger then a minute could almost fit in the palm of your hand. When I tried to pet it it tried to bite me but that's natural for any dog when they don't know someone it reminded me of a little rat it was so small so Leroy put it back in the bedroom so it could have it's tantrum, he has all the tools he needs to start a shop almost and he does a lot of work out of his garage. The growing of a family is intresting to watch as our children make their way through life and it's great that change can come to those who need it most just 6 years ago he was fighting the demons and now he is on the path that will take him away from those things which plaged him so long ago I couldn't be prouder of him my son Leroy. My land where will things be in ten years I hope he will have his own shop maybe through him his grandpas dream can come true. In this world you never know where life is going to take you but there is hope for those who fight the good fight, and go on to make their lives better then it once was before. Then you have the other side of the coin you might say the ones who no matter what will continue to destroy their lives, even when they have been given bad news about their health they continue on.

The destructive path until death hit them, such a waste of a life. For with some change isn't possible but it's by choice not by what could have been. Monday morning' and yesterday was cold most of the day, I was supposed to see Dr. Nelson this morning but we came back early so I will have to see him later when I can get back up there. I shared my trip at church and thanked Kathy once again telling some about my daughter putting a diper on the little dog she had, tomorrow is a funeral so I will have to make sure everything is clean for the guests that will attend and then do so again when it's over for Wednesday school. This time of year many things are going on with the kids and other things in town and it will last until January after the new year is rang in, the one girl that I saw at Mickey Dees' is part of the Giger family my brothers wifes family it took a while for it to sink in but it did havent seen her in so long, she was vvery little when last I saw her maybe even a baby if my memory seves me right. We all grow up and learn new things that take us to different places in this life as for me it brought me here and well others stayed where they must belong, as for Kearney it has grown but the streest are still a mess making me wonder if they will ever get them done. The towns main street is still brick like it was beck in the 70's they have taken them up a few times but always put them back down for some eason maybe because they don't ware that much compaired to cement that breaks apart and crumbels iinto dust, most of the towns roads are bad over the years and the highways are not much better making it hard on a vehical suspension. Who knows maybe next trip they will have it all done right, Mark was telling me that the hospital has a vascular unit for people with bad hearts but they keep fireing doctors for some reason O well maybe one day they will get it right. It was nice to get back home after the visit and there has always been an excitement when I get close to my new home maybe because I know this is where I belong with my friends and God, I feel out of place when I go to other places and maybe that because I know where my home is here in Courtland. And even Randy said he got bored when we were there. They tried to get him to try and come there to live and he said no because I was the only one who got him out of the place he was in, and he couldn't do that to me. For he is one great brother to think that way plus he likes it here where he can be his self. No phoney put on, have to be put into place and he can be him self without being ridiculed by other folks just a bit ago he asked if the heat was on 70 and I told him that it was, but he was cold so I made it a little warmer in here he side it felt like he was sleeping in a tent such a funny guy!!. During the next few months it will get colder and the heat will have to be turned up some more even because the cold here chills you to the bone sometimes, cant really say what the winter will be like except that it will be a cold one as for snow it varies from year to year maybe one winter we wont get much and then the next it's very deep not allowing us to travel very far but we have been very blessed this last year with the roads staying clear for the most part. My knowledge has grown since I moved here getting to read the bible a little more and books that feed the spirit not the stuff I used to read so different in this place. Mark my friend said he reads this one book each night before he falls to sleep and it's a great book I know the preacher that wrote it and have seen him on television with his son many times.

If I would have stayed in Kearney my learning wouldn't of advanced as much as it has and I would have been stuck back in time. Moving here is my breakout time to learn new things as I move forward into my new world, but my world is so different from my old friends. I learned something about a person I was interested in and now I wont pursue it any further being she has had a few husbands, but that wont stop me from looking further and who really knows the person for me is out there somewhere but only time will reveal who she is. They got done with the house next door at least on the out side and a few people have looked at it but no takers as of yet for it still needs more work to be just right, I still call it a fixer upper because it needs better heat and at least central air, for this part of the country anyway the heat here is dry and it can get to 110 degrees during summer. Making almost unbearable, they took out the little air-conditioning unit that was in the side of the house and pluged the hole that was there but now there is no air at all, so they will have to do something before next summer. In the many memories of my childhood it seamed my parents always got a good deal on renting a house but they always had to fix them up and maybe that was some of their excitement until we would have to move again. don't quite remember if it was by choice or if the land lord like the work they did and wanted to rent it for more money and I know my parents wouldn't go for that seeing they had to do all the work.

One time we rented from a rich guy and he had an army duck as they called them back then, it was the vehical that landed the army guys fighting the battles on shore. Dad worked on it for him and got it running it was part of a collection he had of army stuff from the past, I believe it was from world war two and boy that stuff is collectable today. It seamed dad was always missing that break he wanted to have a machanic shop and if he would of gotten that break he would of gone far, in a way I think his pride was hurt because he knew he had the know how' to make a go of it he was a great machanic the best I had ever seen. I know if things would of worked out different he wouldn't of passed at such a young age, my land' he would still be going today, Courtland would have been the perfect place for him but now it's a little to late. Once my house is paid off I would like to open a shop even if it's just minor tune up's and oil changes, that in it's self could bring in some money so we could get going on an adventure that wouldn't end. People really like me here but I need to build something to last out my years, the day was good and it warmed up enough to wash the car and we went to town then again tomorrow we have to go to another town so the day will be busy. Tuesday' as I continue to read the power of life bible I find the stories very intresting it talks about Lot and others who I have read about some time before it's a great book. Many things to do today and some travel is in store so Randy can see his parole officer, it will be a great day when going down there is over for that reason anyway. I didn't get to see Valerie at all while I was there but then I didn't want to sture up old feelings I might have had for her. It's been almost three years since her daughter passed and when I talked to her last she didn't seam to bring her up which shows growth in healing, as we went to the dollar store yesterday we forgot some of the things we needed so maybe we can pick them up on our way home from Concorida as we go right by there. Again the morning is quiet as I write but I sometimes wonder why I write at such an early hour, even though some days are better then others for the most part the days are happy days or not filled with sorrow. I don't like the days' when things feel like they are falling apart but those days are far and few in between, as I try to keep my self busy with any thing I can do. Wednesday and things went fine going to Concorida' as we traveled there, the roads are in good shape compaired to Nebraskas roads being so full of pot holes. After getting back little brother found out that Bob had to go to the hospital it's like he is playing that game of live or die but I wish him thee best. As the day brings forth new life I pray that all is good here in our little town, as for sleeping I slep well last night giving me a new and better out look on the day but I have many things to do before Wednesday school this afternoon. The car had a frozen door yesterday so I gave it s shove and it came open, I just hope it doesn't do that all winter because that wouldn't be good, but I'm optimistic that it was from washing the car. I could see where others have pried open things on it before and I hope that doesn't happen this winter, through the years I have never had such a problem with cars but with each model things are different thank goodness for hot water if it does happen. It's another cold morning but they say it should get warmer as the day goes on and that's a good thing. The bible that I'm reading gives little parts of what happened so many years ago even before Christ time and it talks about brothers and how they were so different, one being good while the other took for granted what the one did for him. At times we read about dreams that are planted in our minds, these dreams are brought on by our life experiences and if we do things right then those experiences can be what we do to bring praise to God when he helps us through these times.

My life should be helping others and I do that with my writing but until it's published it helps no one.

But my writings in the paper's seam to help in Many ways, Thursday and it's another cold day I worked with John's wife yesterday and we talked about different things. I wish the words came as easy as they once did in the beginning but time seams to change everything, for what was once so importand has now becomne a memory that chooses to stay hidden. Although my thoughts were once fresh now they have become like stale bread, I'm still in the running you might say and my work gets pubished by the news papers but I have a goal to finish this thing I have started and it will take God's help in doing this. Like the memories of a child they seam to go away to only return later like that road you travel back down before you pass from this world, my short time memory has improved some but my long turm has been intacted for quite some time. For these things they said would never come back, 'has' by some miracle. It's Him that brings these things to light once again but still there are those who wont believe this is possible, I don't know why but others also get excited when they go on trips and get closer to home maybe it's thee knowing that everything will be ok' once we get back home, it's like a thrill that I feel knowing I have a sturdy foundation in this place so far away from my family. As the time moves forward I hope they will one day come here to live but with out the others that seam to be tangled in the web of deceit.

My self' I cant live anywhere that I'm not comfortable and in the clan down there I also run out of things to say it's like I'm from another world then theirs, for my love for my kids will never change and theirs for me and really that's all I need at this time in life. Knowing I fixed that fence that was once broken makes me strong, all addicts have to mend that fence and with many it will take years like it did for me but they have something special usually the love of a family member wither it's a son or a daughter. As for many they will have to loose it all before they finely admit defeat that the chemical is stronger then they are. In my days when I was using I couldn't walk down the road at night because they would think I had drugs on me and the strange thing was that I never did, it was their way of checking up on me to make sure I was ok' I never did put it into that prespective at the time because I was living in a panic it was like everyone was watching me and that was part of coming off of them, slowly going into a depression from the chimical inbalance not a good feeling when you think the world is after you. Many of the people I knew back then would run to my home for protection but still today I don't know who they thought would protect them as the police could go into anyones house if they thought drugs were there, in the days when I was crippled they thought I had robbed a gas station 'which I never did' but they wanted to check my house and they treated me like crap. I told them that they had the wrong person but still they didn't listen until they brought over a detective who knew me and then he set them right saying I couldn't of done it not being able to walk and all, on that day was the first time I was ever called a lier and it hurt because I had never been called that before not by anyone in my life. Before that they wanted to know where I put the gun which I never had and they were rude telling me that if a kid got the gun and killed him or her self I would go up for murder, I don't know how many times I told them that the real guy was getting away while they were wasting time but for some reason they had their sights on me. I guess that's the price you pay for having brothers in trouble all the time, but surely they knew I had never been in trouble before with that kind of thing, then in a couple of days following they caught the guy and he was someone who had done it before. I never got an apology and maybe they were too ashamed to admit they were wrong, all through my life I had never did any harm to another person except for a fight or two when I was drunk but other then that I didn't believe in it. As the bible says do on to others as you would have them do on to you or I think that's what it says, anyway it's a good saying to live by and it's served me well for over fifty years. The week is about gone, and then the weekend starts not sure what the weather will be like but I do know it will be different then last weeks. God's plan for our lives is bigger then we can amagine we are like the sheep not knowing what the next day will bring, He has a bigger plan and wants to see it unfold. Before we were born, He knew how our lives would turn out from the worst days of our lives to the best days He saw everything unfold before it happened. As with my life He saw that I would one day make a difference by living through the triles I have lived through, for our problems are but a speck of sand on a new way of life that we would one day follow.

And through the sands of time we would go through many such triles to find out where we belong in this world created by Him the father, as I read the bible I find that God spoke to Moses like He does to me sometimes and it doesn't really matter to me if others believe what I recive from Him, but back in Moses time he was doing something to bring God's people out of Egypt and what a task that was to convince someone with a hard head like the leader of the people. His people lived 430 years in bondage but it just goes to show that turning against brothers happened even back then, but it was through this that one became great and ended up doing God's work. The problems they faced was the same back then as it is today and I can relate to some of the thing that happened back then, my self I have never been like my brother different in everyway that I can think of and yet I have always still tried to help them when it was in my power, as for them I always stood alone the long wolf you might say' a separation between good and evil when the evil side tried to show it's self. And when this would take place I put my self away from the destruction that it could cause others, I always tried to only hurt my self and now I really don't know why I did that. Maybe not feeling worthy of feeling good I really cant say, but today it's different for some reason as I like to feel good and even though it only lasts for a short time I know that one day it could last for ever.

In the kingdom of God, but I hope it comes before then so I can enjoy it here on this planet where I was born. Friday and the weekend is about here, this story is about a little boy that traveled through life and although he faced many things that could of destroyed him God made those things the things he would one day teach about so others wouldn't have to go through them. In his life he was a bashful peron shy from not being able to live the life of a child. And going into adulthood at a very young age, what other kids lived he didn't because of the curse of alcohol and drugs. Then one day after many years of abuse the curse won out over him and they said he would only live another six months, but this was unexceptable in his eys and in God's. then after his demise he traveled into the light where he was told that it wasn't his time yet, that his journey hadn't even started yet, and he was to go back and he would know when it started. He loved being in the light where all the pain and sorrow was gone but now he had something to go back to a promas that things would be different, but at that time he didn't know he would come back crippled by the curse that almost took his life, at the time this was unexpected but there was no turning back. For the light had faded and he found him self in a hospital bed, he recalled the doctors saying they didn't know why they brought him back but little did they know that they had nothing to do with it. Because it was God that found him on that day so long ago and it would be God that would trasnform his life to a better one, in all his years he never seen the world through sober eyes becoming addicted at an early age, but he had heard stories of how beautiful the world could be if he would try and change the things which almost destroyed him. While in the light he was given two words epiphany and Melchisedek which was strange to him not knowing their meaning he searched the bibly for the answers and while searching for the first he found the last hich intreaged him so over the years he read about this Melchisedek being a great man and the priest to the most high God' maker of heaven and earth. While growing up in a dysfunctional family he never got to go to school very much leaving him with very little eduction, but while recovering and learning to walk all over again which took almost ten years he asked God' to help him as he had no purpose to his life not being able to work any more because of the damage that was caused and God told him to get a typewriter which didn't make any since to him but I did it anyway. And then getting discusted with the way his life was going he asked again Lord what do I do now and the Lord replied and said don't worry I will teach you, now he was dealing with many things at once the nerve endings in his legs were defused and he still wasn't able to walk to well plus my short turm memory was gone, not remembering one thing from the next but he did remember God's promas that he would help him. As time passed things started to improve I got my memory back but only after many years of getting up at all hours of the morning and night, but still depression had set in and I didn't want to go on then he gave me hope by having me write about my life and how destructive those two things can be in a persons life and then he told me to send it to the news paper where I lived. I never thought I would be good enough toever have anything published but it came true after many of them were sent to the editor, and hope was born still today this now older man lives in a place where God sent him and still he writes about the destruction these things cause in a persons life. Psalms 30 1-3 tells how He brought me out of the pit from death it's self and I'm here still alive, even today some things get mixed up but I'm a better person today and I have over come many things that others have died of. Brought to a place where things started to happen for me.

There was a triger that started the move but then He uses others to get his people where they need to be, much of what has happened in my life I don't understand but I know He has something special in store for me. I have over came the addictions that once plaged me and with His help I have learned to walk again although my walking isn't perfect it works for now, the life I once lead is a thing of the past and today I love my father the one who helped to bring me back to see how beautiful the world is. So much has changed since that time so long ago.

CHAPTER 13

Even though my life has taken a new approach many of the people I have know have passed away even pop's after taking care of him for over 20 years since moms passing. My out look has also changed as I still learn new things each day and Courtland has become my home. I live each day to the best of my ability and pray that my following years are good ones, my little brother lives with me as it was God's plan before pop's passed to go to heaven I guess He knew that it would be hard on me without someone around that I could care for. In the 8 years that Randy was away no one wanted to help him but God put it in my heart to bring him home as I made the preparations for his release I knew it would be a long shot if they would let him out but I knew I had God beside and who can refuse Him? Right! For no man can do what He can do. In the beginning I didn't know if I could deal with it but after a while I found that my love for my brother out weighed any problems that might arise from him being gone for so long. In our younger years I never did get to know him very well but since I brought him home I find that we are the same in many respects especially in the emotional part of our being, one day a tear came to my eye because of a movie and I looked over at him and he also was tearing up. Maybe we are more alike then we ever thought, lord knows we are 18 months apart in birth and maybe some of me was transferred to him, or it could have been through our mother one great lady with a heart of gold.

I had never been close to my other siblings for some reason, but there had to be a reason for that. And maybe it was that my life would later take a different path. With the ones that I cared for they wouldn't even consider it being they had their own lives to live, but I did too. It seams I cant say no when it comes to caring for loved ones I guess I'm just a softy because I could feel their pain and the feeling of being a banded was something I knew all so well. Many times I have seen Randy cry because he felt that no one wanted him and that's something that shouldn't be. I have felt that trying to learn to live, going from one world to another to me life is all about being around people that you love and who loves you. But we all have to have our own space our alone time so we can stay on the right path, Randy didn't think anyone cared wither he lived or died and I know that feeling all so well. But if we are blessed then someone you least expect will step up to the plate and lend a helping hand, like God did for me, I did for Randy. Showing him love any respect and it's something I expect in return and it isn't asking for that much, I remember things from the past which he did to me but we have to be better then that. Like Jesus did for us forgiving is the best policy, it allows you to start fresh and in doing that you will follow a new path which only God knows. Saturday' and it's a strange morning you can hear the dog's barking down the street like they are being bothered by something and then it quits, to only start up again in a few minutes. Maybe a wild animal is going through the town who really knows, the coffee is what wakes me up and I'm glad that I have it each day to give me that wake up if it really does, my self I like the taste and that's what keeps me drinking it. I can hear the dogs and they are right out front waking up Harley and now he is barking, I hope it isn't someone taking things because I didn't lock my car door.

This is another story about my life of today and boy how things have changed from the younger years. My taxes come due this next month on the house so I'm hoping that I can pick up some extra work to fill that void which comes every year we will see what happens in the next week or so, it's at this time when I feel helpless and I don't like that feeling but it's the first time that this has happened so maybe things will turn out ok' it's strange how I never had this problem until pop's died, we shared everything and always came out on top with no worries but as time passes we change and things change with us. I pray that things will continue to work them selves out so different to be getting poorer and not being able to save anything but I have to hold on and do the best that I can do with what I have. The noise has stopped now and the dogs are gone for now anyway, it's the first time I have heard them out in a pack in the time that I have been here but it's getting closer to winter so food might be hard to get, if I wouldn't of had to get the car fixed things would have been different and this wouldn't of been a problem but you can never tell when things are going to break down. I will ask for God's help during this time and see where that leads me, I was once told that I could get some help should it arise and now it looks like this might be the time. Through the years I haven't asked before but we all need a helping hand from time to time that's just the way it is in this world I spend my time helping others and now it's my time to need the help for surely it will be there for me. As God takes care of his own little children yes we are His own and he has known that this time would come before I was even born. What sight He must have' to see the whole picture before it is lived and who knows where this might take me! Maybe to another level where I can grow even further into the spirit for surely he sees everything before it happens and has made a way for things to turn out ok' I will leave it in God's hands and see what happens. After I pray I could hear the dogs off in the distance but they seam far off so maybe Harley can sleep a little longer he really gets riled up when they come close to the house, it's like that's his domain and they are not welcome there, not in his yard. As we go into winter many things change and you have to be really careful as the roads get slippery and so does the side walks, but each year we seam to make it through the bad storms and come out better then the year before. This town has become my home and I never want to loose it I was brought here by the father and I think He knows where I should be, later I will be asked to pray on me singing so I will ask him and see what he says. Before I used to just jump in and say yes because I felt it in my heart before they even asked, most of the time my heart is filled with joy but there is those times when I'm not sure about something and then I wrestle with my self about it trying to figure out what to do. But in the end things seam to come together and time moves on like the sand in the hour glass, I know that one day my writings will be published in my book and the stories I write in the news papers is like the catalysis that starts me on my way. Getting known is the biggest hurdle and that will lead to people wanting to know more like the fuse on a stick of dynamite, and if the story is good then there is no stopping what will take place next. From the child lost in the world to him walking up the hill that God put in front of him.

It's a life long struggle but on his way he found the love he had been looking for and that was the love of God. He never could find it with a person because he was looking for that special connection that can only be found in the father, he had always felt that he wasn't from here like he was from a distence place where he was once able to look down from above and see the mistakes other made, he cant seam to stand to see people hurting so he does his best to try and ease their pain if at all possible. And there is many ways to do this' some by talking and others by doing but he knows he is the only one person so he does the best that one person can do. God sees his love but he also sees what he struggles with, Sunday morning' for some reason he has always needed his along time, a time to get things together so he can go on with his day as for people he doesn't lik to be around them first thing because it causes confusion. And to him that isn't a way to start a day, this side of life he never expected the wakeing up in pain from sleeping wrong it seams what you do when your young comes back on you in later years. I wish I didn't load trucks as a young man but it was the only work to feed my family at the time, driving in the wee hours of the night to get to my destanation so I could put in a long day' as a young man I did more then I should have having 50 pound bags flying down a shoot into my arms and then stacking them in a truck 40 feet long. I remember working on the interstate running a ditch which to cut out the patches to be repaired in 110 degree heat and that was fun but also very hot.

Then when I moved to Arizona I built stoves earth stoves up in Flag-Staff and boy that was a pud job just welding the parts together. But that was also a place I didn't want to be, always having my brothers around it just didn't work for me trying to build a family with so much confusion going on, the alcoholic years did no good for me and if I would of stayed then things could of really gotten bad so mom getting sick was a blessing in the respect that it got me away from a life that was going no where. Now looking back I should have been a nurce because I spent many years taking care of loved ones that the others wouldn't take care of, like pop's and mom and now Randy. As the years go by I'm in hope that my time will come to where I can be with someone who will spend out their life with me, for the things I did for other has to have been seen and it makes me wonder if I get the kindness from mom as she did so many things for others also. Taking in the homeless and giving them a purpose and showing them that they are loved. These people were latterly living on the streets with no where to eat or sleep because at the time Kearney didn't have a shelter for the homeless. If they didn't have a job then they had two weeks to get one because she had very little money but she shared what she had and hoped the goodness would ware off on others, her world was full of kindness in the end and I think she needed them as much as they needed her. Like with us' her love extended through space and brought me home to her for I could feel when something was wrong like with my little brother there is a connection that I cant explain and maybe it's spiritual I could since that he was fading in that place so I was prompted to try and get him out and it was a good thing that I did because we almost lost him after he came home, most people call on a pastor after a person goes or dies I did it before and he lived. I had never seen a doctor so white when he flew out of the operating room that day saying that his blood presure droped and they had to send him to another town, we were praying just before the doctor came out and my pastor Kathy said it was a good thing that he would get better care there in Salina praise God for the miracle because He brought it to pass. Would he have made it if he would have been still locked up? That question will go unanswered, I had only known miracles to happen in my life and to see one that was apart from me was a life changing thing. As I sat at the pastors house I felt a spirit come over me and it put me in like a trance telling me that he would be ok' and I know Kathy saw what was happening with me as she said whats going on Roger and I replyed he will be ok' this was the lord letting me know that he had it all under control, I really don't know what would of happened if the lord hadn't steped in and that in it's self made my faith grow a little stronger and let me know that the lord watches over us even when we don't see it. Later I will open the church so it's ready for the day then I will see my friends and John will ask what know for sure, and I will reply that it's cold out. I hope that my friends are here for a long time because I don't like to see them leave me but some of them are up there in age meaning in their 80's or so, I seam to fall in love with people and when they leave this earth it hurts a lot to where if I only let my self like them it wouldn't hurt so much but I cant stop who I am it's just a part of my D.N.A To love others once they get close to me.

I guess I have loved many but the true feeling of love comes from God the father, Monday and a new beginning to another week. In three days it will be thanksgiving and pastor Kathy asked what we were going to do for that day and I told her that I was going to make a turkey with a couple of pies, it didn't dawn on me that I should of asked to make it over at her house just my way of thinking I guess plus I knew Randy wouldn't go any where to eat being so shy and such, in this day and age you should learn to mingle with people but he doesn't have that down yet and really never will until he breaks out of his shell that he had built around him self. O he will talk to some prople but not too many, yesterday I found my self getting up set and I had to bite my tongue to not explode, hiding my feelings or anger is something I do pretty well not wanting to show ignorance or is it ignorance? Maybe just a part of life that we all go through I do know that even with elderly people they say things they might not mean but they seam to over look it and go on with the day as nothing has happened. And some of the things said would of make me angry if they were pointed at me I guess no marriage is perfect and they learn to love and live through the things that love brings with it, I recall fighting with the ones I was with many years ago even with my childrens mother and she gave back as good as she got it. My land it's been so long since that time that I had forgotten about it, that could be something I'm missing in this life. When you're alone you don't feel those feelings that you feel in a marriage and going into one might be hard, then you have the prows the ones that cant live without another in their lives and they live to make things their way and if it doesn't happpen that way they leave to only marry someone else later in life.

And then it starts all over again, or they don't let anyone else in and go through life alone making them selves miserable. Through the years I have learned that you should always be kind to others and that will build a strong cherictor, even when things don't go your way sometimes you should suck it up and go on instead of becoming something your not. After I wake up the day seams to go well but I'm sure there is some things that others see in you that you don't see, the little things which makes you different from them a little smile or a grin that brings a little sunshine into their lives. Phillis is doing well after her illness and it's the prayers that brings the healing to those who are sick it seams God hears the prayers of others who care about each other, the bible says to love each other as you love your self and this is a fine thing we do from time to time but there are times that you are angry with your self and that shouldn't be reflected to other people, although I live in a loving place I still fight with my demons but the good thing is that I'm getting better with each passing day month and year. Headed in the right direction, to one day be free of the things that bother me like staying alive to live past the age that any others did in the same situation. For each day brings with it something new a different mood or just a time to be angry at things that don't always go your way. My family will see one day that I was meant to maybe be alone or not' He seams to bring people into our lives to help when we need it but he sure is taking his time on this one maybe wanting her to be perfect for this guy that has traveled along for so long, I do know He is teaching me something right now but I havent quite got a hold of what it is at this time. All those years ago he put writing into my heart and like most things He does it stayed, and with each passing year it seams to get better but only with His help. What is it that He is saying to me? For everything I write, is about me. So it's fact not like the others that search through stories to find what they need mine is all inside locked away like in a vault with only one combination. All things come to me in pieces it's not like a flood of things coming at once but bits that show them selves a little at a time, even the best of writers take years to try and get things right but my story is personal not like any other. From being a lost soul to being found by God, and then taking the rest of your life trying to figure out the things which should have come naturally. I have come to courtland to be at peace not only with my self but to learn some of the things I may have missed being in the dark, it's like I'm a child still trying to learn. Out here this is allowed to happen so maybe I can find what I'm looking for that piece of me that got lost so long ago. I seam to love children with their simple ways and it doesn't take much to bring them happiness not compaired to adults their lives are so simple with their loving parents there to take care of them, but my isolation seams to keep me away from seeing the simple things that makes their lives rich in love by so many. November 20th and thanksgiving is just two days away I will spend the day cooking so we will eat a meal and then the left overs will last for a couple more, The animals should get some good bones during this time.

Randy can help with the cooking so I will get some help and then we can watch the paraide on television or a good movie, it's that time of year when they have the old Christmas movies from the 50's and 60's that time seamed to be a great time without the destruction and other things that are happening today, but one thing did happen back then. Like the hippy movement, when the people were against going to war so many died in that war also but the one that came back were rally messed up from the chemicals that were used in that war. As for those who refused to go they found them selves being put down by the government because they didn't want to die for a hopeless cause, and in the end the United States didn't win that war either. No good comes out of war never has it been that they have ever won one because no one wins when it comes to takeing human life, I have never liked for people to die and when I hear about it something inside hurts bad. Maybe it's just the way I'm made, and now they want to stop Christmas along with taking in God we trust off our money. No matter what happens I cant except them doing what they are doing destroying our way of life. In that respect I wish I was still a child so I didn't have to hear about it, protected by our parents for those things to be filtered out of our lives. I have 30 days to come up with the payment and I hope my friends can help me, I don't know how these things work with property taxes but I'm sure they can be troublesome if it isn't taken care of. For the end of this year is upon us and then we start a new year one I hope is filled with joy and not bad news.

For time seams to bring new things with it and I hope our church will grow beyond what our hopes are, may the lord see fit to make us stronger then we have ever been. I always look forward for some reason when it comes to things that are going to happen to maybe stop some of the things from becoming problems, this can be a gift or a curse depending on what happens but I always hope for the best in these times. The children will all get a present from the church to help them through winter usually a pair of gloves and a beanie to keep them warm during winter. This is a great thing the church does for the kids that get put into a home because tragedy has intered their lives, but many of them come out stronger then ever and become a part of society. A good part that that will one day have children and families of their own, when I was young I also had to stay in a place like that to help me get on the right track after all the years of running wild you might say. Although it took me longer then most to get out some of what was taught stuck with me and later in years it helped to change my life but boy was I angry while I was in there because I didn't think I needed to change little did I know that change came anyway so it must have been something I needed. I remember on the day I was put up there and I cussed out the judge to only make him as angry as I was and that didn't work out very good. Wednesday and tomorrow is thanksgiving I seam to not be awake yet so coffee time' I kept my bird in the refrigerator completely froze that way it should be thawed by tomorrow morning and then I will cook it. I got the stuffing in a box like I did last year and will cook it all together with the giblets from the bird it should be a great meal, for the tow of us. It's nice to have Randy' here during the holidays because he can help with the cooking and help to keep me company I havent cared much for the seasons in a long time it's like they are not the same as they once were but that's ok' I will get through it. I still long for having a family here but I don't see it at the present time, as time passes maybe something will show up and make things whole. I really miss having kids for some reason the way they play and get up on Christmas morning and open presents or could that be me that I miss those things about? My opening presents and the excitment I used to get on that day so long ago. Life isn't as exciting as it was when I was a youngster but I do have the good days when things go right and there is some excitement in just the hellow of someone passing by or the wave of a hand from a friend that's going down he road. I do know that many times I miss read messages from friends but I think they should know me by now and know they have to spell it out or be more blunt in their message, a lot of people have family come by and spend those days with them but mine is just as broke as I am not having the money to travel to other places besides their homes so they do the best they can do with what they have. As for talking about being broke I couldn't be any broker then I am right now and the money just doesn't stretch as far as it did just a few months ago. But I'm holding on and one day this house will be mine if I make it, then I will have a place I can truly call my home. Randy said he was frightened that if something happened to me he wouldn't have a place to call home but what he doesn't realize is that I'm not going anywhere.

God has taken care of me so far and I don't think he will leave me now, I got upset when I saw some more smellers in the womens bathroom then there should be. It was like someone was sending a mssage that it stunk in there which it shouldn't of because they get cleaned each week, but I did try some whipes they got and maybe they have a bad oder I had never used them before so now I will do it the usual way. The women bought them and maybe they never smelled them before it's about time for Antique road show and I'm going to watch it in about 10 minutes. I really like that show with all the neat stuff, who knows what they will have on there today or should I say this morning? The president has traveled over sea's to a country that we havent had much contact with over the years so we will see what happens there, maybe he can open a path way' to sell some of our products. So much has changed in the last 25 years and I don't think it's for the better so maybe this might bring good change, to the county. I sometimes read more into things then there really is and that's my own fault, the road show isn't on today a detective show is on about how they imprisoned people from over seas people from Hong Kong and that area back in 1941 through 45 when the war started. It's hard to believe that the United States was able to take their freedom from them just because they were from china and other places, but with war comes panic. I find that history detectives is also a good show going back into history to find the answers to some stories.

So awesome to see their search and how they find answers, I would like to do the history of Courtland but I'm afraid not many would be interested in it. Has there always been an attraction to certain people here something that has drawn certain people to this town? Courtland originated the name that is in New York many miles from here and the old women who was in her 80's came from there. Could there be a connection for surely her father was a gangster but she choose to move here to Kansas to Courtland where she remained an out sider even after living a life time here but her children wasn't an out sider because of their birth being recorded here. My coming here was brought on by a fluke but as time went on I became apart of this place out sider and all, was it the accident that drew me to this place so long ago? For surely the father wanted me to see the first miracle that had taken place in my life, but the flashes from that time came after I was here for a few years probably meaning I wasn't ready to see them before. As fear was in my life at first at times I get a strange feeling that I don't understand and I'm in hope that one day these things will be made clear, for life is still a mistery to me and I want to find out why I feel so different here then in other places. Is there a force beyond my comprehension and if so will it one day show it's self so I can understand the story the story of a lost soul? In the world today many write on then selvess what they feel they are and the other day on television I saw a guy that had lost soul written on his fingers. This shows how he feels and for some reason he wants others to know how he feels, lost in a world where he cant seam to find him self which I know that feeling all so well trapped with no way of finding direction and when this happens only God can find you. My how I recall those days and at times I wish I didn't' even today I sometimes feel lost but noting compaired to back then when the world was falling in around me, in my early days here I was broken down even further then I was when I arrived and maybe that was so I could build this new world I live in today for it is so different from my youthfull years when all you thought about was the excitement in life. The drinking was the high light of a day but then you paid fo it for a couple of days, I recall telling God if He would help me through the sick part that I would never do it again to only go right back to it. What would cause a person of no faith to do such a thing? No faith' or little hope for a good outcome. It's only when something tragic happens that we seam to open our eyes but even then it's only for a short time until we find our selves in the same place we didn't want to be before, in my life I find that others can give you many things that can help and it doesn't take much the assurance of knowing that they are there for you can bring you to some great places.the day is about to start for the rest of the world so I should go out and see what it brings, I do know I have work to do at the church today so an early start would bring things to a close. And then it's back home to get things ready for tomorrow, what a great meal it will be if everything goes right and Randy will have his fill like no other day this year. Thanksgiving day' I was up earlier then usual but there is a lot to do with getting things ready for this afternoon as for the bird it's about 12 pounds just enough for two people living alone, and then the cooking of it should be fun to see if I still have the nack of doiing it. The pastor came by yesterday with some food from the food bank so that will help also to make it through the month, as for my problem I still have to talk to her about it but I thought it better to wait until the holiday is over but I cant wait too long as December 20th draws near.

And it would be a shame to loose what I have built up, through the years it's always been about other people but mostly I have enjoyed the task of helping others through different things that I do andin the future I will do more but right now money seams to be the problem. I wish I didn't need it but it helps to stay alive and there is no getting around it, my worries take away from my character or He is trying to teach me something maybe to be stronger in adversity and to have faith that things will be ok' we as people panic when we don't have enough to be comfortable but I believe it's a stage we go through as we grow in spirit, my self I don't need much but what I need is accentual for my survival, even the people set free from bondage were taken care of by God through the things He did in their lives. Parting the red sea allowed them to escape from the ones that held them in bondage for over 400 years, so I know my problems are something He can take care of. For surely He wouldn't bring me this far to dump me on my head it's like one part is saying things will be ok' and then there is the other part saying to worry, but the not to worry side seams stronger then the other so I will lean towards that side for surely it's a better feeling. In this part of my life I have the chance to do the things I havent been able to do in my younger years, like singing always afraid of what others thought and that stopped my growth by now I could have been a great singer. But that was put on hold and now I know it's still not too late, the giving of my voice to God could bring great things.

When I see others who have not done what they are capable of doing it makes me strong in some ways just the knowing I too could of missed singing to others and to God Him self, my songs are created for God's pleasure and he never gets tired of hearing them. As a matter of fact He wants to hear them every chance He can and I think that's why I sing so much at church using different songs to bring Him praise. In my life it's always been the lost moments when I could of done something, and now it's about weather I do it or not the choice to stay in that lost life or come out of it and spread my wings to another beat. I work for God and I enjoy it very much, there isn't many places where you can sing and do God's work at the same time for truly you are the light of the world shine on thee. I have put together a song and I used another to bring things to light in hope that others will see what He has done in my life, will they grasp the miracle which has taken place here? I guess only by singing it can they put the things together and see what has become of my life thus far, I want people to know that God is doing things today like he did before I was even born and I'm just a tool to bring things to light. If they so choose to hear, my daughter is taking test for school and I hope she passes them for with that education the world has no limits so proud of her. It's going to be a nice day the temp is already in the 50's and I know it will get warmer as the day progresses, I also notice that I'm drawn to religion more then before wither it's by the things that have happened in my life or the people but I do know that my life is taking a turn away from the one I lead so long ago, it's mysterious how He seams to work in my life, bringing new things into it, that weren't there before. Just my thoughts have changed and the cuss words that used to be there have long gone from my mind. But why and how does He do these things? Maybe by letting us see what it looks like when others use them like when I catch little brother using them and I try to correct them, trying to show him that it isn't pretty to hear. And then he watches what he says for a time but then it starts up again, like the lord says a little at a time because no one can change over night. The bible that Mark gave me has helped a lot and has given me a better understanding of how they lived back in the day even before Christ's coming, it says he was in his thirtys when he started to preach but it was like he came out of no where as there isn't a solid thing that says how he grew up at least not that I have read. Did he have a normal childhood? Or was he just not mentioned during those years? We do know of his birth but then it droped off for quite some time and I have many questions that will probably not get answered. With my self I didn't wake up until I was in my thirtys a sleep in the darkness until I was awaken by God to learn the things I missed. But now I know that God was there every minute watching over me when evil tried to take me from this world, my self I can count three times when this occurred and each time He stopped it from happening and a calmness would come over me a calmness that wiped out any fear of the disaster happening, a fulfillment at that moment that somehow made me feel not afraid like God was sitting on my lap or I was sitting on His. What brings these things to pass? Is it a connnection that we have with Him to show us that He is there for us? Surely I didn't have much faith back then but later it would grow like the flower which comes up each year.

Even people who are not close to God have a chance to change the direction of their lives if it's headed in the wrong direction, for this is a promas that He gives us all. So much to be thankful for from the wakeing up in the morning to going to bed at night. Even for the tears we cry when our hearts weigh heavey and we don't know what to do. Judy brought my pie yesterday and my land' it is good, Friday morning and I tossed and turned all night, as I think about things the weight of them weigh heavy but still change is coming but what fashion of change is beyond me at this time. I went and cleaned the womens bathroom the other day and now there is no reason for having so many smellers in there, I still couldn't tell why they were there in the first place. As for Christmas presents we don't have the funds to get them for the kids so maybe a little at a time I can send them one, and that will make up for them not being there on time. This will be my first year without pop's and everything is not as good as it used to be or that's the way my mind is thinking at this time, but I have to believe that things will get better in time. The day will bring new things but what they bring is beyond me maybe some cheer or maybe some good news from somewhere out there, my being alone is becoming a problem although I tried to find someone it hasn't worked yet but I don't know any other way of going about it. But something will come to me later this year when things pick up, why do we go through these things of self doubt? Is He trying to send a message to me to trust in Him more then I do know? And if so then I know things will work out.

My whole life has been taking care of things on my own and it's hard to admit defeat by my standards any way, it says trust in the lord and he will make all things possible. I thought for so long that I was doing that but I must have missed something, for my love Has not faltered for Him but it's now that I will need his help money was never the problem before and maybe I took advantage of that situation even though I tried to save it always seamed to not be enough and then later it ran out, could I be making a mountain out of a mole hill? This could very well be the case out of the man with little faith. But I always thought I had great faith strong faith for this is all new to me, I will talk to my spiritual adviser and see what she thinks God has always found a way even for the people who left the state of bondage and went to the promas land He gave them or promised them, out family tree can be tracked back to that time but that too would take time it seams all things take time weather it's good or bad but with hope we seam to make it through the ruff times and come out better then ever. I believe they said they would help with these things when they came due and I hope my memory serves me right because I need the help now more then ever. Things seam to change for the better when you keep in faith with God and this is probable a bump in the road that I'm making bigger so now I will tell my self to settle down and what will be will be, all the worring in the world wont help. It's the 23rd of the month and this one is about gone to only bring us into Christmas the time of still giving thanks to God for what He has done in our lives, so many things to be thankful for my life, and my faith, play a big part of this story. Surely He brought me here not to fail but to succeed in what I have taken on to do in my life. For sometimes we can make sorrow out of happiness and not even know we are doing it. What would bring these blinders in front of our eyes not sure at this time, but it will come to me in the coming month. Awesome' Antique road show came on this morning and I find that things are worth more if they have a connection to someone that was well known.like the person who killed president Lincoln' although it was a tragedy the cane of a guy called Mud went for thousands of dollars because he was sent to prison and then saved many lives when a sickness broke out in the prison. So much history that I wouldn't of know if I didn't watch it. This next year I will take on many new things to try and make it and this should help in someway, you can never tell what a new year will bring but we must have faith that things will turn out ok' as for the grand babys they will be another year older just coming into the double digits and I could see the change in them since the last time I saw them, so proud of how they turned out and the hug they gave me will last until I see them again. Change is animate for us all as each year bring that new thing into our lives the new things we havent seen or had in the past, a new found faith, or even a new found love could be just around the corner and we cant see it yet. Does our bad habbits or our past seam to follow us? Yes' for some reason it's always there learking in the shaddows to be brought up again, but is this what God wants for us to stay in one position and reflect on things that could have been. Or are we to change that and move forward to hopfuly grow in a new way' enough for today. Saturday and my it's cold, I could hear the train coming through earlier and it sounded like it had a bad wheel with the thump budy thump it was making on the tracks. It was the first time I have heard that noise in all the time I have been here and it almost sounded like it was closer then it usually is.

My senses have been heightened for some reason it's like everything is magnified by 100 times, at least my arm doesn't hurt this morning like it did yesterday. So much to be thankful for, the thrift shop is closed until the 28th and then it opens again so things should go back to normal. I miss going there twice a week as it has become apart of my life giving of my time and looking at the peoples faces when they get a good bargain and take their things home to create things. Many of the people that come in are from little unknown towns that still exist off in the country and farms that still exist off in the prairies. I asked one girl where she was from and she said out west not wanting to give to much information about where she lives, or where she is from. People more or less keep to them selves like they don't want to be apart of the out side world and you cant really blame them, grandmothers bring their grandchildren into the thrift shop so they can get new toys and play with the ones that are there while they shop. It's a different kind of life here far away from the drugs that plage this world, no gangs here and they wouldn't be welcomed in this society unless they changed their ways. Just the ascents of life here allows you to move forward away from the things which could of taken your life if you would have stayed in that old world, I have seen many people that have left Kearney because if they would have stayed they would have surely died or went to prison. Even moving to bigger cities where they could get lost and no one would know them, I had a friend that I used to get high with and boy he was out there but even he saw that he needed to change and Tyler' moved to Omaha Nebraska.

The last I heard he was doing well and had been straight for five or six years but we all have our own way of doing our sobriety and staying straight. I would of never thought that he would make it but he did the last I heard, after a few years he came to see me and he rode his motor cycle down to Kearney. Although life may never be perfect he found that living sober was way better then getting up each morning and maybe finding your self out in a field during winter wondering how you got there, I cant count the times when he was lost and showed up at my door step higher then three people should be and wanting gas because he ran out just down the block. But through it all we remained friends, I haven't seen or heard from him since I moved here so it's been going on five years but I always wish him the best and hope he is still out there somewhere. His family had a farm and they would use it to have a place to get high at but after a while I believe they lost it because of back taxes or something I cant count the times the law was out there to arrest him or his brothers for one thing or another peace be with you my friend. My land' the stories that come to mind are ones I would rather forget but they seam to come out maybe to wipe that slate clean so new things can be created new and better things. Mark another old friend, it seams I have known a few Mark's about six of them in my life, when I was falling for a girl she was very nice but also had a bad addiction to Methamphetamine I thought we would get together but then Mark poped into the picture and she went with him. Later they would marry and have a couple of kids, Mark treated me like a brother more hen my own family but the common thread was the drugs and then we went on a road trip to another county. He had a four wheel drive and wanted to check it out to see if it worked so we went down some roads we shouldn't have and got stuck and then ended up walking across country. I was in no shape to walk far so I had to stop at a farm house and they called the cops to give me a ride by this time he had taken off and they found the truck. And then they gave me a ride home thirty miles away, after that happened I didn't leave the house for a couple of years knowing it was only by the grace of God that I made it home. On that day I thought I would surley die but the lord brought me through it, to let me know that he was there for me. So many mistakes were made in my life but through it all God was right there to bring me through it and bring me home, my land' He must really love me. On many of my travel's I shouldn't have made it by my own power but He gave me what I needed to make it that extra mile to strive towards that goal of making it to where I would be safe home. The realization of time is strange in the world of darkness for an hour could be days and days an hour depending on how high you are, I cant count the time lossed by the world of darkness as one day might be what you call normal which isn't and the next could end up being a week and you think it's a day. This is what I call a lost soul when you can't connect with the real world or what others think the real world is, many don't want to be in the real world because it's so stressful to live in it to them.

But I find that living and living high is so much different and my land' it cost so much to pay for the drugs that wipe your mind clean or what you thought ws clean. In the years that things have changed most days are on an even keel but still you experience things you never thought would come up again, so you deal with them the best you can and move on. As my life continues there are many things that I never expected to materialize but even though they do it just makes me stronger to move forward, does my experiences shed some light on things for those still fighting the good fight? I sure hope so. In my life today I do the thing which I never got to do and it brings me joy to be a part of God's family, I am given encouragement by the ones who see how much I love God, and that makes me stronger. To move forward and become closer to the one who brought me through so much, two spirits brought me here to Courtland but one was unstable or not a good spirit this one brought fear and it was like I was fighting a battle. I drew a conclusion in the beginning that all things here were like that spirit, but then I went to church and found out that things weren't what they seamed. I made a mistake by judging everyone by what one person reflected and found out that this is the wrong thing to do, given a shirt by a friend showed that I was a person of God without me saying a word and people even came up to my car inviting me to mingle with them for coffee after church John is the one who made me feel the most welcome.

Like John in the bible he had a way of being friendly and that made me feel less out of place, later after a while we became good friends but in the beginning my shyness wouldn't let me get close to any of them. A safety shield was put around me until I got to know them better blinded by the first impression really took away some things but later I would get them back, with me it takes a long time to get close to someone or something and in time He brought us together. It was at a time when they needed someone to help at the church and for some reason I just jumped at the chance even though I was still feeling out of place that move brought me a little closer to being a part of something more then my self, this was God giving his approval to move forward. I had always been shy around others especially when sober but being drunk you don't feel anything, not having any feelings about what others felt and not really careing one way or another. I have come to the realization that people are important and we need each other to help us through life and God wants us to be together, to help each other. No gossip or the making up of things to put others down but to empower them so they become a part of us and our lives. Love your brother and neighbor like you love you're self although this is a hard thing to do it can be done. As I move forward in this day the things I will do will reflect some of my character and He builds our character from the inside out, Sunday morning'and yesterday I went and done some work at the church. It's a place where I can be my self and not have to worry about others coming in while I work, granted it's not a nine to five job but it's my home away from home where I can talk to God.. It's very early going on 2:30 but I couldn't sleep any longer with the change of seasons comes change in us as people the body getting ready for winter mankes many changes sort of like it did when I was taking my life back, I don't know why I notice these things but I do. And maybe in my younger years I noticed them, and was afraid of what was happening making it easy to wipe it from my mind by the use of the chemicals. They seam to let you forget what could be natural like if your connected to forces beyond your comprehenction, many times I have felt my body moving in another direstion away from this place we call our home, floating in a distent place that you have only heard about in a dream or seen in movie. A break between reality and the other place I may have come from, with me I have always been hard to anger not wanting to visit that place that many say is a part of being human. But then again just a relationship is hard for me when they seam to yell and fight all the time but they to say that's a part of being human, why don't I like these things that most take pleasure in? have I been away from it too long like the alcohol and drugs for surely that cant be the case. Even though I get mad sometimes I try to move away from that negative force thinking it isn't good for you, and it makes me feel like I'm a lamb just here for God's pleasure. Can you change what you are by avoiding natural things that the human life is supposed to go through? In the mornings I'm in a world all my own with nothing to interrupt me and my thoughts trying to go through the memory banks that are somehow stuck in my mind. If the mind is like a computer then why am I afraid of what's in it? For surely it cant hurt you because you have already lived through what it holds and it didn't hurt or kill you then.

The world is in a terrible state this is something you see every day and I don't know why I pay so much attention to it, here where I live it should be the furthest thing from my mind. But pleasure is a hard thing for me when you don't know how you will make it from one month to the next I must make a plan to survive but what should I do? They say we have the ability to create new things and there must be something I can create maybe tap into that place where there is a store of things we can bring into reality, or maybe I have created something right here and I just need to market it. How do I get these words out to the public? So they can understand that they are not the only ones fighting the dark forces of this world when it comes to addiction for truly God didn't teach me to write to just let my words sit around. But I also know that the timing has to be right before things can be brought into reality, everything God created has a way of coming to us if that's his will. The misfortunes of my life has created a thing like the connection a way to look into a lost soul's mind and see where he or she is coming from like the projector that shows the movies but I'm not like anyone else as others cant go to the places I have gone and talk about it. Why is this? I do know that I have never found anyone to talk to about my journey to the place very few go to and come back from is this supposed to be a secret? And if so it's not nice to have something happen and then have to live with it the rest of your life.

A sepration between my self and others and then try and tell me to get to know other people is like an oxymoron, everything strange and it makes it more complicated. But the good news is that it's going to be a good day, I have to step back from the serious things in life and enjoy the roses. Sometimes going to far in thought can make you leave this world we are supposed to live in and that can mess you up sometimes the not being able to bring you're self back when you want to, like that room where you can meditate and be by your self although it's supposed to be good for you I can sometime not get out. This winter is going to be a long one and I know bordom is going to set in, maybe I can take that time to advance further in completing this chapter of my life. They say that memory doesn't always serve us right or correct but the connections I have made are what I remember, or is it what I want to remember? Not' I don't like to recall many of the things which I write but for some reason He wants it to come to light. In all my years even in black out's I never did any harm in fighting with others and that brings me to believe that violence is not in me He didn't equip me with that for some reason maybe to show that it's something you don't need to make it in this world, my world doesn't have that but I'm sure if the situation came to be then I would defend my self from getting hurt like I did one time when I was drunk, but even that day I didn't like the out come had to have 27 stitches in my head but I guess that's the hardest part of the body. And boy what a head ache the guy was also drunk and boy he felt bad crying like he killed his best friend which I was at the time his only friend and I had to ask him to leave. The amblance had to come and haul me off, the stitches hurt more then the gash that was in my head but that too passed in time. I was a hellion in my youth and the only way I felt normal was to be taking in the spirits not a good thing' I started driving when I was about 10 years of age in the city but even then I was always drunk or close to it. But I was also very careful and never had a wreck until I took Indian Betty's car, I was maybe 10 at the time and they wanted to lock me up but she wouldn't have it. Good thing she had insurance because they fixed the car or she collected off of it and got another one, my' I loved that car, so big and the people in the projects liked it also. You see a girl was the one I wanted to impress but instead I made a fool out of my self. And she never talked to me again, why do kids like to be like their parents so bad? It's in the everyday things they see, mom getting up and cleaning the house every morning why dad gets up and goes to work. Making the family solid and seeing it run like a well oiled machine. Although this is a good thing when tragedy sets in the unit can take a turn for the worst and everything breaks up, then alcohol or drugs find their way into that unit and makes things better for a while. It seams to allow the parents to function for a while anyway and then when taken out it starts to fall apart again and separation comes into the picture, one not wanting that kind of life any longer goes to someone else but still the curse hasn't left. Because it's in them and doesn't like to loose, they can go their whole lives thinking it isn't them but it is the curse has taken them to that dark place where they will one day fall on their face. Weather it's by coming close to death or just hitting rock bottom for they are one in the same, being brought to that door where anything can happen. Survival is born into us and we all want to live for ever but we as people sometimes cut that short, even in fighting back we go on for a time to only what some call loose. But is it? For it says that He will give one last chance to become part of His family even after death as we know it a chance to be a part of something bigger then we can comprehend.

Monday church went well yesterday, there are many things that bring us to where we are today and now I know that not dowing something can be as bad as doing it. This morning I pray for strength to

Stop the bad habbits I have like smoking this is a waste and you have a hard time breaking this addiction so I asked for help. When I am able to do this then that will be a sign that I should stay, pop's never had any of those bad habbits and that's how we survived through the years when we were together and by my coming here I should be able to do it on my own with his help' I know it wont happen over night but slowly it should disapear if I buy less of the product. The strength I need is inside me and I need for Him to make it stronger so I can beat this curse also. The beginning of another week is a time to get ready for the things to come and now we have many things to do, I notice that when I work my mind isn't on smoking so maybe that can change things and it would really be great if there was no smoking in the house. When I stopped the other addiction it was still going on with others but I was able to over come that like I should be able to do with this one by maybe slowing down to two packs a week if I could do that then I would know that stopping is on it's way, we will see as time moves forward. So many things I want to do and saving would allow that to happen, breaking free from that would help a lot. Today I have to get the right mind set and carry on through it, the nights have been cold and the mornings even colder but we seam to survive at this time I'm still going to write my stories and carry them through to the end or until I'm not here any longer. What makes a person thrive towards something what gives them that drive to move towards to thing they want the most like saving for that rainy day when they just want to get away and breath for a while.

Surely like the drugs we can stop the bad things that are happening and imporve our health, they say you can be winged off of things that are bad and I know that's what it will take to over come this pelage. Our bodies get used to the chemicles that are in the cigarettes and with some they go through with draws like with dope so it has to slowely be tapered off of so the body doesn't go through the withdraws, my land' this will be another battle and if I can accomplish thiis then there isn't anything I cant do. While I was a kid I remember picking up cigarettes off the street and smoking them, one time it was when I was hitch hiking and out in the middle of no where. I don't know why I did this but it had something to do with being lost in the desert such a scary time all alone with no one to talk to and no one would pick me up except for the truckk driver that brought me home after a few days, he was such a great guy and he even fed me as he ate at a truck stop. I find that I have really been alone most of my life separated by a force that didn't like to mingel with others, like the shepard man taking his sheep to market.

Alone in a world where it's me that chooses weather I survive and go on to better things, but why do we have to bring our selves to that breaking point? Do we have a destruction mode? To see how far we can take it. Or are we just stupid and want what we want, I do know that there was less smoking beck in the 1800's because you couldn't get it anywhere but in the cities. So I think part of my journey is self discipline so I can become a stronger person, this would bring me to a better place in my mind if I could say I remember those days so well. Through history many have done this thing and doctors say it's brought on by not having anything to do with your hands a nervice condition but I don't see that. My land' I have been months without it back in the day but like alcohol it seams to find it's way around things like being locked up when I was young, just 15 years old and I had done many things that most people never see in their lives the traveling and not wanting to stay in one place became a habbit so I would move on hoping to find what I was looking for. The strange thing was that I never found it until I moved here, this is the first place I really wanted to call home. The mill down the road is always hireing so maybe I will check them out sometime in the future, the only thing I cant do anymore is load trucks by hand but I can run a scale and unload the graiin trucks, that used to be fun back in the day. Experiences are something you can fall back on like driving a tractor or just fixing a disk when it's broke down in the field, these things I have done before and really they are still in my heart but I don't know if anyone would hire me being broken up from the past yes they would if they could see me work for I am His master piece I am good at all the things I do. When you bring up negative things then you bring with it negative actions and that is never good, but praise what you are and do then with it brings positive actions and in the process you feel better and move towards that goal. I am finly made, I am a masterpiece, I am a child of God created in His image, their image.

This shows me that we all have the ability to change, my land' a women got 500 years in prison for selling her daughters for sex and money. What! Is the world coming to? It showed he in Buffalo County with her orange jump suit on and she looked like it didn't even bother her. They also arrested five men for having sex with the children. Kearney is where it happened and about four other counties in Nebraska' you could never write about all the bad things that happen but just this one was enough to make a person glad they they don't have to be around such things. Nebraska got snow this morning so it's just a matter of time before it reaches here in Kansas just being over the border, the snow wont last but a few hours because of the warmness but winter is knocking on our door. And change is coming, I would like to talk about dream makers and dream breakers! A dream maker is a person that lets things come to them naturely, and a dream breaker is one who tries to destroy those dreams. With many of the dream breakers they try to bring things like drugs and alcohol into your life, and this is never any good. As it destroys what God has given you the ability to create. A sober mind has many abilitys and when that is taken away you are left with nothing nothingness a blank slate that cant keep ot attain a goal. Through my younger years I was introduced to the curse of addiction at a young age, after seeing my brothers hit by a car after church my family fell apart and my parents started to drink to hide the pain of hurt and looseing all they had worked so hard for. This was the beginning of the last time we would go to church. My seeing this happen had a wounding effect on my spirit and later I would find my self following in my parents foot steps. After that we never did have another home to call our own because my parents also lost their faith, what was a miracle by the boys surviving had somehow made my paarents think it was a curse. And they wondered in the wilderness for many years like the people of moses did over two thousand years ago, although I was only three years of age at the time the scars stayed within me and the night mares continued until I was about eight to ten years old and then I started to drink because my parents did it every day. I could see the difference in them and they seamed happier when they had the spirits within them, which must of lead me to believe that life would be better in that state of mind. Little did I know that later it would destroy my life along with theirs, dad died at age 42 from alcohol and mom later at the age of 59. Way to young to pass from this world, by the time I was the age of Jesus I too would pass away but God had bigger pland for my life and when I went into the light he told me that it wasn't me time yet. That I had a journey to complete and He sent me back to this world, they pronounced D.O.A. Dead on arrival when I was transported by ambulance to the hospital it had been the 23rd time they had to pick me up because of seizures that destroyed many parts of my body including my liver, while I was in a coma I could hear the doctors saying I don't know why we brought him back he wont make it until morning. Little did they know they didn't have anything to do with my return, Machell Randal was the name of the women that sold her children in Kearney for sex shme on you, later when I came out of the coma I realized that my legs wouldn't work and this scared me very bad, not being able to move would change my whole life and I didn't know what to do later I would see the doctor and he gave me the news that I was crippled, and would never walk again. The brain damage was very sevear and my nerve endings had defused. This is hard to talk about sometimes because it's like living through it again, but I know it's my mission in this life to help kids stay away from the curse that almost took my life from me. My love for kids makes me want to just take it out of their sight to never come back into it again. Through the years I seam to feel others pain and I dint know if everyone feels tht but I do, the day has been a cold one so cold that I had to have the heat on all day not reallt what I expected but hey! You take what you get. Another day is here and tomorrow is the 28th the day the thrift store opens again. The ladies were talking about how they went down there over the holidays to do a few things surely they must have been board, which happens to us all some times. I would like to find some odd jobs to do and maybe that can bring in some extra cash to pay bills. I know many of the older women have things they would like to get done so that might be a starting point helping them, we will see what takes place. We have an editor at the paper and maybe he can give me some pointers on my writing how to improve things with it and such this would spark some kind of intrest within someone that is into writing the story is about Courtland not the first part but this part of almost a thousand pages of memories that are recorded here in this out look on the life of addiction. I have talked to many and most don't understand it especially the ones who have never gone through it, for they too are lost when it comes to understanding what a loved one might be going through it's like trying to mix oil and water.

Although impossible to do the two can be separated, my grand mother was one who never understood it but then she was a bible reading person and it's never talked about in there except for a few times. One of the disciples had gotten drunk one time and his three son's found him two covered him up when he was nude and the other brought shame he was cast out but the other two found favor by covering him don't remember the whole story so I will stop here not to talk about something I'm not sure of. As I travel through time sometimes when I get stressed and I feel a calmness that comes over my soul these two mixed feelings are intertwined one minute calm and the next not so much like they are trying to test each other, but usually the calm win's out. Bringing me to another state of mind that I'm not used to being in, it would be awesome to have that feeling all the time but it's not that way just pieces of it exist in my life giving me a glimps of what could be. Many of the people around here have a calmness about them like they don't have a worry in the world and I hope to one day attain that peace, many people go through life so out of it that they too have never known the goodness of God. And I believe it takes away from life for I my self have only tasted this goodness once in a while, but it seams to return from time to time making me feel good once again. Although my spirit is stronger then before it's ressless and sometimes it doesn't know what to do with it's self, and I'm trying still to figure out things. Trying to connect the dot's you might say and find the answer,, many older people say it's all in the search and we will be searching until the end of time as we know it. To only find the answer when we go to that house He had built for us with many rooms, I was told that some believe we never leave this place we just return back to dust to be awaken later and then given some land to grow what we need to eat. But we will see our loved ones again when they are brought back.

To me this is confusing as the earth would be over crowded, maybe I don't understand that part yet or my mind cant connect with that. I do know that the same believers told me that my mind cant comprehend the things about Melchisedek and yet he is still in my mind after all these years, like a fixture of a memory like mom and dad there for ever. Some things don't stick in my mind but he has, even though the bible doesn't talk much about him I have read what there is and he held many titles from the King of peace, to the king of salem, a priest continuly, the priest of the most high God. One day I will study in a group and try to find the answers I'm looking for to calm that reslessness that resides in me, for I want to know the answers to this puzzle. And who better to answer a question I might have then my pastor, right now I believe I'm growing spiritually and He has a plan for me to break the old saying that public speaking it the hardest thing to do. My pastor was the one why got me to sing, by just three words 'get over it' I don't know why but this triggered something inside and made me think I could do it, they say that fear is good sometimes maybe because it's something you can move past but it takes that step forward even if you fall on your face when your around friends it doesn't hurt as much, public speaking is something I know I would be good at as it brings out my passion about the things that have happened in this life of mine, the good and the bad which brings me to conclude that my journey will start at this point. When I take that fist step, Wednesday or hump day as some say it. My land where does the days go? In this side of life time seams important and I can relate to that song 'don't blink' that Kenny put out taking to the old man of 100 years, it's a good song and it lets you see how the old man felt as time flew by him. Through the years when I was in the other world time didn't exist for me just the days and even then they flew by pretty fast, I recall wakeing up on a Monday and before I knew it Friday was there. Not knowing what took place during those fourdays but the mind didn't have to deal with such things as time. In that life years would pass and before I knew it another year would be here, and I would be another year older. In this life each day has a purpose from getting up in the morning to going to work and then back home again, it doesn't really matter what the job is as long as you have one to help you pay your way through this life. And if one isn't enough then if you can you try to have two to have the American dream of having a house and a piece of land no matter where it is,, my self I picked my place and I'm still here today trying to make it through the bump and grind of everyday life my worries are still there but I am learning to deal with them trying to find that place where I can feel at ease about things it's a place that I have visited before back in another time that I recall. As long as you try your best then you can make it in this world but it's the getting the hang of it that's important, breaking thing up here and there just enough to make it through the tough times. Like a friend said no one can break out a lot of money if something should arise so you hope that the people are kind and give you credit or a payment plan that will help you through.

I know another person that knew how the system worked and she got by just fine in life the roaps as she called it, and it's something I will try. To make it through this tough time of winter paying down the debt of what you have is very importand and they know you will be around for many years to come but they add on a charge for this lesson of not paying the whole thing maybe a couple of dollars but that's ok' because in the end you are still surviving. Back in the addiction world you always let others take care of the finances that way they could get yelled at when something went wrong but by doing that you never learn anything on your own, when I fist started to take care of things it made me proud and believe it or not I looked forward to paying the bills it gave me a since of pride to know that I could do it and we all need that right! I see many things differently today then back then, and I'm glad that He found me that day to maybe let me see that I can make it in this world on my own. And one day who knows maybe I will rise above this state I'm in and not have to worry. Lessons is what we learn in this life or at least I do, and if you can take just a little bit out of each one then you are getting a piece of the puzzle even though you don't know what the full picture will look like. For only He knows how it's going to look afterwards. I go back to work at the thrift store today and I hope it's warmer then yesterday although the cold was dry and it didn't seam to chill you to the bone, like the cold of the days before. Thursday went to work yesterday and had fun laughing with Beverly while she put some things away but the time there only lasted an hour and the we closed for the day. I let out that I would like to find something more to do maybe drive a tractor or odd jobs to make it, it seams we all need extra change to get by in this life we all need to feel useful so we will see what takes place later down the road.

Although the mornings are still cold yesterday warmed up to 50 degrees by mid day, leaving it nice. I fought with going to sleep last night for some reason, but within a few hours I was where I needed to be. It's always hard to wake up in the mornings but hey! It's been that way since the beginning of my time on this earth fighting the sleep to open your eyes. But then after an hour I seam to be wide awake ready to take on the world I got my pay check yesterday but it seams to be gone as fast as I get it by the bills that have to be paid nothing savable there as each day takes money to survive. But the good news is that I'm still plucking away at getting the bills paid, it's like I'm going through a transition from having enough to not so maybe I will learn to cut back on things I do know that you can be happy with just getting by if you try your hardest and not let things take you over anxiety seams to play a big part in life and it can hit you sometimes when you least expect it, but it's nothing that can kill you that I know of just leave you like a shell all frightened and scared. It seams to happen when your body goes into over drive for some reason, like when pop's died it kicked in and made many days like hell. Through the time that I have been writing I have always hoped to have the ability to write long stroies like the one of my life. The boy that was frightened by what happened to his brothers at the age of only three years, you would think that I would have been to young to remember but it stayed there hidden until later in life. Around the same time Gordy caught my arm in the car door which left a scar but that's also something I remember from being so young, what traps those memories? Is there a place in the mind that we done see very often? A place where things hide from us so we can go on with life as we know it? And if so why do they pop up just now and then? Sophisticated so strange. Many years ago I was working for a grain elStacytor that had caught on fire and we had to go inside to remove what was left and that was fighting not knowing when it would start back up again, this happened three times when I was there during the eight years of loading and unloading trucks. The company gave us shares in the company or Kansas and Nebraska gas, later I would sell them and get $40.00 a share now I wish I would of kept them my land they would be worth a lot today as both companys are still going strong. Hind sight might be 20/20 but it does no good when it comes, but maybe it opens a door to look back and see part of the picture that will unfold in your life and if that's the case then mine has been full of hit's and misses or I could be looking at it wrong, they say we only use 10 percent of our mind maybe if we could use 20 percent then we wouldn't have any war's. Some say we learn from our past but I find that to not be true as history has a way of repeating it's self like with every war that was fought, no good comes out of killing but still it's done every day. The war we fight to stop people from killing goes on even after the service men come home to find them selves living on the streets. It's kind of like they search and destroy their own people, they pick them to fight in war's and if they make it home they still fight for their lives to survive in a country that they have no home in.

If they are with childen the women cant stand to be around the mental illness so they take to the streets in hope to find something a connection that will make them feel whole once again. People lost in their own country with no way of finding out who they were fighting to fight your own is scary. Today I will go to work after Wednesday school they leave a little of a mess but hey that's my job in this world and someone has to do it, there is a place for us all no matter how you look at it everything has to be done and I take pride in what I do although in my years I have been able to do less and less still pride is a big part of my doing things with age comes less movement but we find things to help other no matter how slight and we seam to survive and move on like a general he might be a general in his youth but later he might be a janitor like me with only the memories of the past. Should he write them down so not to forget them? Maybe but most cant sit down and write I find that many can't do this they talk about writing a book but it takes a special something to be able to accomplish this task. To go back and try to make since out of what's there learking in the four corners of the mind, trying to get a picture out of our lives for they say if you can do this the picture should be beautiful. Someone won the power ball last night, five hundred and fifty eight million dollars that's one lucky person. It's the most won in like for ever, half a billion they say. I bet the person will have people coming out of the wood work to say they are related, when you talk to people who have won some say it's a blessing while others say it's a curse because it controlled them instead of them controlling it.

I got one of the numbers but that nothing, it's going to be a nice day because that's what I choose for my self a great day to be here. I am a masterpiece, and I am blessed. Not by material things but with spirit for I have always been blessed and just didn't know it, as the days will be like before my life has purpose and I delight in it. From sleeping in a run down shack to owning my own home is a gift and I'm grateful to the lord and the church for all they do for me, even the bad days are blessed 'why' because I'm a man of God all that is good comes from Him, if you look at it we get our kindness from Him not counting our grace and many other things that make us good people. Even the church going women who says a little to much has her or their good side not meaning to cause havic but just being out spoken because of the way they have always been the negging women. But we all have a place, and someone who can put up with us, the one who bring some good out of that life and creates other life to make them different from who they are it happens in all familys as with mine, I'm very close to being like my mom as for my father well never knew him but he must have been the same way for them to connect the way they did. Two souls brought together to bring to life me, God must of felt that the other kids father wasn't the right D.N.A. To bring forth my being like some in the bible born of one but brought up by another, and he still loved me like his own that says volume of Herb well the day is about to start. Friday morning and it's cold out side we need to count our blessings and be thankful for good friends, through the years I recall not being able to sleep because of things which ran through my mind and the alcohol allowed that to stop along with the drugs O sure it was just for fun at first but then as time moved forward I or you came depended on it because we knew the dreams would stop with it's use. not knowing how to deal with dreams stopped them from coming. Many things don't make since to me even after all these years but I still search for the answer somewhere in my mind, when we dream we go to a different place a place not of this world like in some movies we are drawn to an different reality where a lot of times the dream isn't even remembered. But I know one day when I go there I will remain. You know in you're mind that you dreamed but it's like a place you cant just go to all the time. It's not like the room which I have visited to be one with my self so long ago, for that room closed and I haven't been able to go back there and maybe it's because this is that room now. Brought forth by my being here when we are kids we can sometimes have a make believe friend or a place where we feel safe this is something that was taken from me by growing up to quick and maybe it hurt things. Always being able to block things out by tiping a hand or just getting high. Today I welcome those things when they come my mind is my own at this stage of life, for all who left this world without knowing it I wonder if they stay lost or does He give them sight once again to make that choice of becoming a part of his family.

There are many things that give us the drive to survive like when they said I wouldn't make it, for surely they didn't know what He had in store for me and when I left the hospital I somehow knew I was blessed and forgiven for my transgressions. The journey has been long but through it all the ties that binded me have been broken but not without a fight. The breaking of the cures was slow for me first one and then the other but still learning as I went along, learning about God and how he can wipe away the life that almost took me from this world. The second chances are given and I believe He gives these chances to many but many don't connect the dots so they can move forward, somehow they get lost in limbo and remain there until the time is right for them. I am a masterpiece created by God to make a difference in my short time here on earth some say a beyounder a special person who draws his strength not from the stars but from heaven it's self by passing the stars for strength to move forward, my thinking isn't like any others as I know no one who writes like I do. Channeling his thoughts from a life that could of went the other way if it wasn't for the father, there is a arch angel called Mark who looks after people and it makes me wonder if he might be watching over me along with my parents keeping me from harm so I can move forward to discover my full potential and my mission. Do others see parts of whats inside of me? For surely they see the good as for the bad well it doesn't come to the surface very oftend, being kept in check by the goodness when things like anger arise. I just change it by good thoughts hoping the bad will go away and it brings me peace, He can seam to correct the bad things and change the course of our lives if we let Him into our lives. For we are like the tea pot that was left on the shelf and then made different to shine like the gem, when He is done with us.

We are so beautiful that everyone wants us, or want's to be a part of our lives. But there is a balance between good and evil and the good out weighs the bad it's been that way all through time. What would of happened if destruction didn't take the course it did? And I would of followed the path I was on. For surely I would of fallen to the depth of the pit, burning in that kelm that can make things beautiful or very ugly. But like the tea pot I made it to that place where I'm looked upon as a beautiful sight. The train is coming through this morning as I can hear it's horns off in the distence but this time I don't hear the broken wheel so they must have gotten it fixed, you hear so many things at this time of the morning that you wouldn't give a second thought to during the day. The big diecel motors puffing out smoke as they haul things to market all things have a purpose and a job to do, like each one of us although it may be small to us it's very important to the survival of man kind. For love is very important even if we don't think we need it for one day it will find it's way into your life and if it does hold on to it. I think loss is something that can scare you and not wanting to feel it again can make you vier away from it which can only hurt you, like the poem I wrote as I walk through this life I find my self wanting to keep my self sheltered from pain not physical pain but the pain that comes from the heart, for this pain to me is unbearable and it can wound the heart like a rock that can wound the wing of a dove. So many different things travel through my mind poping in when least expected, letting me know that there are still things to do and just seeing things through these eyes brings me hope for a better day tomorrow. Saturday December 1 the day is cold again but it could get warmer by noon,we are expecting temps in the 50's or 60's which will make for a nice day. At the church I only have a couple of things to do like get communion ready for tomorrow and a little cleaning, I find it mighty nice to be only working a few days a week during winter and although I find my self getting board maybe it's supposed to be that way. My it's hard to wake up this morning, I can remember during my younger years I couldn't wait until the weekend so I could celebrate making it through another week of work so I would get drunk and have a good ole time. Me and my wife from long ago you see although I wasn't old enough to drink that didn't stop me because others would procure it for me so it was as easy as falling off a log and friends that were old enough always had their frig loaded with booze. Back then you didn't hear about it being against the law like you hear today and I like to think I had a hand in passing that law as my letters went through out the State of Nebraska, later I would hear about a law passed that if someone got hurt while someone bought the minor alcohol they too would face stiff pentaltys and up to a year in prison. Lord knows someones mother wouldn't want to sit in jail because she bought the stuff for their child and they ended up killing someone, but many times when the starting of drinking starts at home the parent tries to deny that they ever gave it to them putting the problem onto others so they can make them selves feel good but that doesn't work too good because they know inside what has taken place, they had dodged a bullet by blaming a place that sold it to their child.

A few years back a 18 year old went and bought alcohol from a liquor store in Kearney and then later was killed while driving around with friends I believe and the parents sued the liquor store, although it was not right to sell the liquor to the child the probmen started way before that in the home. Parents think in many cases that they are helping their child and their not, and slowly the children are being killed by their own parents. And they use every excuse under the sun from at least he isn't drinking on the streets and I know where he is, but they don't look at that at some point they have to go to bed and they cant watch them then and they sneak out and get killed or worse they kill someone else. I don't remember quite why my drinking started except for my insecuritys which was a big part of not feeling excepted, being that one who never quite fit into the mold of being cool or smart that piece of the puzzle that didn't fit into the picture so I was thrown away or at least that's how I felt, then when I was under the influence I seamed to fit like a glove as the insecurities faded away to not come back again until I sobered up. Which was usually after the weekend was over. Although being insecure was normal at that age to me it was not a thing you wanted to go through and the alcohol took that away. Like an eraser to a black board and it wouldn't return until the alcohol was gone or I sobered up, only when parents take responsibility will there ever be a declind in kids being killed by alcohol or drugs. In my youth I never had to buy the alcohol as it was there for the taking and mind you this doesn't mean that our parents are bad it's just when a person gets lonely they don't want to drink along I know I never did.

When you take on a role of growing up you should take the responsibilitys of being responsible but that's a hard thing to do when you're a kid, just the act shows your not responsible enough for your own actions. When I wrecked that car of Bettys I could of killed someone but now looking back He must have been with me even back then, keeping me safe from harm. What a loving God we have in Jesus, today I can look back and see these things which could of ended up in a desaster but back then I couldn't see anything a life headed down a dark road and then finely coming to see the light. For this path He knew I would take and I like to think He knew I would end up on this side of the road, and if that isn't love then I don't know what is. He saw me through all the troubled times and still gave me that second chance ' how great thou are' through the years I have traveled a few paths but they all lead to here Courtland' I know I have been close to this place before and then later something brought me back, maybe the first miracle but more important the love of a town' with me there has always been conditions to me receiving love but here I don't see that. I remember Judy saying that they love me and at first it was a hard thing to grasp, did He let them know that I was coming here? I think he could have. But I will never quite know for sure unless they tell me, through the years and tears we seam to find our way to where we need to be and we pray that all things will turn out ok' and even with doubt comes that ray of sunshine that will brighten up our lives so we can go on to find better things. For He seams to watch over us even in our darkest hour when we are full of doubt and fear, but the good thing is that there is always a rainbo after each rain to show His promas to us. my daughter was in an accident this morning and I'm glad that they didn't get hurt. God seams to protect them for me as I pray that each morning, the car is gone but it can be replaced. The safety of family is more important then anything and I thank God that they are ok' shaken up but ok. You don't know how important things are until you hear the bad or good news of the situation, and then you have to know that you're prayers have been herd by our father to bring them to safety. The day is about gone and the sun is going down so now I will rest until morning when I get up and open the church, Sunday morning' I could never figure it out why I cant write during the day for some reason it has to be in the morning. I used to think it was because my mind was fresh but thinking now it's not really awake yet until I have my coffee, while talking with my daughter she told me that her X husband wanted to control things with her accident and of course me being dad I told her to tell him to take a hike. I never understood why some have to have control over their mate but he has always been that way, and on many days he has made her feel real bad when she didn't do what he wanted different strokes for different folks but she should take control back. I told her about houses around here and she could buy one and have a good life with no worries about having a place to live for the rest of her life also, but I also told her that I would never interfear with her life unless she asked for the help. And through the years I haven't has to do so she and Leroy are the light of my life and always will be, I knew long ago if I started to pray that He would hear my words and take them to heart protecting those who I love family and friends. Shannon told me that it was like the truck was lifted up and moved over keeping them from more harm, this to me was the father watching over them as I ask him to do when I pray.

Some might chalk it up to luck but I give credit to God for keeping them safe for he knows my love for my children. And it flashed me back to when my brothers got hurt although it was God that saved them the message got messed up somehow and my parents ended up taking another path and maybe it was that path that brought me to where I am today closer to God and Jesus. After that bad time we traveled through life and then another accident involving alcohol took place two accidents really almost killing both of my parents another sign that He was near them but still they couldn't see this, they recoverd but the blinders were still on them not letting them see what a gift He had given them. Their world fell apart slowly but even then He watched over them mom recovering from alcoholisum and then going back to it destroyed all that she had done I was proud of her when she finely said she had enough but the transition was to hard on her and she only knew one way out so she took it, like Michel but he gave up early in life being only 24 years of age his life force seamed to dwendel and go out only wanting to be with his parents in heaven. And boy do I know that feeling of not wanting to be here, I had felt it many times. But God won out and I still here today making my way through this life he has given me, I have no regreat that I have come so far but the road has been hard. No one said life would be easy but I'm grateful that my days still go on. I laugh and cry and am happy that I'm here in my little town. For my first miracle happened here or not far from here and it brought me back to see the wonders of God, my mission is to tell my story to maybe break the curse here that exists so other wont have to go through it. I'm a master piece, created by God to bring a message of hope to those who may have none.

To maybe let them know that he is there for the asking and He wont forsake them in their hour of need, through the years I have grabbed on to Him with both hands in hope that He can change the things I cant change the thing which are on the inside. Being free from the alcohol and drug addiction has left me with some tools to get started on a new journey, in this life we don't know what tomorrow will bring but through hope and faith we seam to be brought to a better tomorrow where we can laugh and cry if need be. But I always look for the good things a smile or a wave or just a hello from a friend can set the stage for a good day, my self I don't know what the cards hold in store for me but I do know that my mission will be done before I leave to go home. In my younger years I would always get up set, but instead of taking it out on others I would walk away and deal with it within my self letting it pass so maybe it wouldn't come back again and usually it didn't for quite some time, letting it disappear from my mind would help to control it when it came back later. A gift of control in the mind of a lost soul, in the beginning I had to learn to say No' and then have the strength to follow it through which took control. But then aftter a while I had to give it over to God because I found that I was still weak and He did something to make me who I am today, only once did I try a drink afterwards and really I didn't liike it. Not even the taste' and it made me wonder why I had ever messed with it in the first place, it's something you can use when you want to try new things that way if you don't like that new thing then you can blame it on the booze. And many people I believe do this from the frying pan into the fire you might say and it will give you away out or a piss poor excuse not to do something again. Many times I used the excuse that I was drunk and didn't know what I was doing this gave you a pass you might say but you don't want to ever try the patients of someone when using it especially if they are sober. You can go through life making excuses when your not in you're right mind like the guy that went to jail for drunk driving and lies to the judge that he will never do it again, to only get out and go right back to it. In this story he went about three days and then had to have that drink to only find him self drunk again but this time he was trapped in his car with no way out and a child laid dead on the street, although he made the promise to the judge he found him self going through remorse because of the child that was lost to his parents. Why did he not listen? Chemicals had control of his life and no matter how hard he tried he couldn't over come the curse that was put on him. In the bible it says the curse can last four generations skipping one or two but four just the same, no different then having one child not stricken by it and another knee deep into it with a life out of control. What sets them apart? Maybe one being weak mentaly while the other is strong, no different then one child being shy and another being out spoken character flaws maybe or just God's designee as none of us are the same.

It's almost Christmas only 22 days to the birth of Christ, but some say he wasn't born on the 25 th of December. Does anyone know his birthday? God does but He isnt telling you or me. In a bit I will go and get things ready for the service today it's advent and we will learn many new things about Christ and God I try to absorb as much as possible but still there is a lot I could learn and you never know enough. My travels brought me to this place of learning and with others help I will go far to understand what He wants me to learn, Ha! Public speeking that can be taught in church by reading scripture so maybe that's a step I will take, I'm confidant that they wont mind listening to this guy and who knows it might lead to something great. To me public speeking is changing lives weather it's by telling your own story about how you came up from a life of desaster or if you speak the words of the bible they both inspire people to do better and if your blessed then you can really make a change in many peoples lives. I faced long ago that some inspire and others well they seam to get their stories out to bring big change, could you imagine going from a life of destruction to a life of being changed by God that in it's self could rocket you to another level of existence and many would follow you just to see if they could do the same thing. Being a priest would be a great thing because you have seen the other side of the coin you might say, the dark side of things in this world that others havent seen. My journey has taken me to both sides of that coin on one hand you don't know if you are going to live or die and then by a miracle you are brought out of that darkness to start over, to see if you are favored by the one who brought you back.

This is a tricky thing because sometimes you feel blessed then other times you feel cursed, but in the standing of you're faith you seam to survive to move forward into that place you have come to know as home. Christ was ridiculed but in His standing strong God guided him in every move for they are one in the same, like the water which can take on many forms still it remains water one substence that can take and make different things frozen it becomes ice, heated it becomes steam, but in it all it still remains water one substence that can take on different forms. My self' I can't think of any other thing that can explain God except that he is our father and through Him, He brought Jesus to this world giving a part of Him self so we could live. Now I'm new to this understanding of things as for everything created He created it for His pleasure, my land' since the beginning of time we were supposed to have a good life but through that time something went wrong. But people seam to find their way through the tuff times a broken hart can be mended just by asking God, we all seam to struggle through life but it's better to have Jesus by your side because He lived through what we struggle with sin. My journey is far from over and I know there are many things I have yet to learn like controlling my temper when I have to do things over again and I do that by taking a step back and looking at the situation. The first day of advent was yesterday and it will continue through the Christmnas season of 25 days, bringing about the birth of Christ' our savior. People' some of them say they don't celebrate Christmas and this is something brought on by athiests after that women changed a law such a waste that one person could destroy such a great time of the year. But it's people who chose to follow her lead so it must of never been in their hearts anyway. As life changes I too have changed from the inside out trying to live by what I'm learning not to sware when it comes to mind has made it possible to avoid these things to change my way of thinking and put those bad habbits where they belong no where as they wonder out in space with no foundation to cling to. This gives me the ability to bring new things into my life the goodness that He wants us all to have for now the tears don't come as they once did so long ago except for watching a sad movie from time to time to keep the tear ducks open for the future when things happen. It's Monday and another week is here boy the time goes fast they will have many different displays at the church one complamenting the other and with that comes the open hearts of others the ones who love God to do His bidding for the goodness in the world. Do we as people need to cling to something bigger then our selves? To maybe help explain the bigger picture and how we can't possible be here without Him the father. I was amazed when I remembered the time when the government anounced that I had died, through the years it had gotten lost in my mind to only show it's self today. But why today after all these years? Another glimps of the life long gone but still things come up from time to time I guess it was the living in my car that had made me upset knowing it took so much time for them to recant that I didn't die, they even went as far to send my children checks to close my account through Social Security very unfair that I had to loose my home and live in my car with Tiny for a few months. But through it all I survived and maybe that's part of what also made me strong.

Only God really knows for sure, but anger wasn't in me just sadness that I had no one around to help in some way, all through my life it's been like I was the only bowling pin standing at the end of the lane. As the years pass I know I'm safe with God standing next to me to take the things I cant handle and make them to where I can. As for the answers my search goes on and by the time I find them I will be where I'm supposed to be, Tuesday' I was supprised when I got up and Randy was already up before me washing clothes, I'm so used to him sleeping in until later in the morning but this new medication has him awake. I'm not sure if that's good or bad we will see as the day goes on, it's another cold morning but I still have a little to do at the church later this morning and the trash has to be taken out it's my job to take care of the things which the others cant do and I enjoy it very much. I got the tax payment for this month but I'm going to have too try and save for the other half putting away a little here and there squeezing my budget even more then before in hope too make it by next May, many things come into play when you own a home and you have to stay up on the payments owed, hoping to make it until the end like the horse running it's race and if it wins then you get that prize which is the final papers saying you really own it. Many years ago this wouldn't of been possible but through a person with a good heart it has now become reality, we all have to have someone who believes in us and my church and friends are those people and I'm glad that they are in my life to help to keep me strong in my faith and church and in my self.

When I first moved here I had nothing but a dream to having a piece of land where I could grow old and a person saw something in me and helped, although he is gone now he will always be remembered in my heart and mind the one who took a chance on a stranger that was trying to find his way. Frightened by the unknown but would later find him self being a part of a great community the community of Courtland, KS. Will the town be here after I'm gone yes' I believe so for many more years after. And little brother will have a home when I leave this earth I will make sure of it, he is frightened that he wont be able to survive when and if I'm gone buthave no worries my little brother you will be taken care of if I have anything to do with it this will be written and no one can dispute it. My way of saying thanks for your friendship, harley is bothering me but I try to egnore him hoping he will go back to sleep probably no such luck. In the future we will see many more things that will shape our lives and help to make us better then before the sounds of the trains have a calming effect off in the distance, and it lets us know that we are safe in our little town with no one who can break our piece. For this is important in the life of sobriety, as for the things I do little brother doesn't think he can do them like pay bills because of his unability to read and write but there are people around who can help in a pinch. All it takes is to ask one of the children of God and they will lend a helping hand, I know the pastor wont be here for ever as she will venture out and want to see what the world holds for her. As for me my journey is over and I will live here for all time in my home, but' the possibilitys are endless here and you never know where the lord is going to put you in his house we can only wait and see what unfolds in this place of God's. as for my emotions they seam to run deep which I don't know if everyones does, but mine is like I'm in another place a place of peace that I take to heart. My daughter text me yesterday and said the insurance company wanted to settle with giving her money for pain and suffering and then paying off her car and getting her another one, she asked if that amount sounded good and I told her it depended on if she could wait or not. A lawyer could get her more but that takes time and I think she want to give the kids a good Christmas, so the ball is in her court you might say in this life you have to do what you think is right and I know she has a good mind to make up her own. I'm just glad that they are ok' that's all that matters to me, in this life we get only a few times when things could come together and you have to grab them in hope to make a better life out of the one you have but always do things with honesty if not it can come back to bite you in the butt and no one needs that. Even in the dark side I was honest almost to a fault but it helped to make me who I am today a person that has no regrets about being honest for surely it's the best policy' in my later years I hope to be able to get around like I do today but I also know they said it might happen, the looseing use of my legs again but I try to put that in that back corner of my mind where I don't think about it. Like the people who have left me so long ago and even some of them never come to mind forgotten by the things which have happened.

You or anyone cant tell what the days or months can bring until they are upon us as people, catching that moment in time when you hope for the best and pray that your life will be complete. In my travels I have been to many places like Allens park Colorado, that my friends was a tough time being out in the middle of no where trying to survive with just the littlest of supplies and hoping the wood wouldn't run out. Maybe it was a test to see if it was possible for us to come through it, we spent a winter there but no one connected with the people because there was very few that stayed during winter. Only coming up there during hunting season and in the summer, I don't know what happened to the lodge but I'm sure Irean sold it. She seamed to have many properities left to her by family that had passed away and let me tell you it was a test to be able to survive in the cold of winter with just wood for heat, later we would leave and go back to Kearney, Nebraska. To only have to bring Irean another car after hitting black ice on the road, when we got there the car was toast so we had our work cut out for us changing motors and transmissions we were young and it took about 12 hours. Back in those days we were fast and good machanice so good that the guy wanted to hire us to do work for him. But we had a life back in Kearney so we didn't take it and within two days we were back on the road headed for home to the place that I grew up, I guess it was my home because so much happened there I was only 14 when we moved there but I had stints away so it wouldn't get so boring I guess traveling was in my blood maybe a way to break away from things and get a different prespective on life but still I always returned.

When mom was young her brother came out to Kearney and he brought his daughter she was a beautiful young women much older then I but she took to me and boy we had fun. I asked her if she was married and she said yes but that they had an open marriage, I didn't know what she ment me being so young and all and then we went swimming and she had a good time with me. Then we went to a street dance because she had never been before. They didn't have them in Duluth Minnesota, I like to think she had a good time and then she left and we never saw them again until her dad came back out to see us in his last days of his life. He also worked and played hard and it ended his life much sooner then it could have lasted, it seamed their generation was faiding out as each one went in their own time to never be seen again. Grandma lived to be over 107 years and I believe it was because she was close to God in everything she did and she stood strong in her faith. No foul language was to be spoken in front of her and she wouldn't tolarate it from anyone, for she loved God and many could of learne a lot from her one of the sweetest women I had ever known, by her 107 birthday she put pot holders in the toaster and almost burned everything up according to others so they put her in a home where she later died. How long she lived is beyond me as they never got a hold of us for the funeral, I wish I could of known her more then I did. But it wasn't in the cards you might say as the miles kept us apart, I fixed her television once and boy was she happy so many holes in the memories and I cant connect the dot's. I do remember the bugs floating in the stream by her house water bugs and they scared this little boy at the time a memory still embedded in this mind of an innocent child at the time I couldn't of been very old but I have no idea of my age. Wednesday morning and I'm up along this morning, by little brother getting up so early yesterday it wore him out and he slept by noon time. I knew it would get to him not being used to it and all, as with me it took over 20 years to be able to get up that early and even then it has it's draw backs. It started many a years ago when mom was ill when I first came back to Nebraska she would wake up around that time because she couldn't sleep the alcohol had done that to her and she had to find a new way to break that cycle, and in time she did but then I was the one dowing it as I almost lost her one night while sleeping. She was a beautiful soul but I couldn't take the chance of looseing her and in time she went from 89 pounds to 100, her doctor said she was a miracle to have come that far and this I believe was the case. She was the first person to have her stomic pumped in history to realave the fluid from her belly but it was something I couldn't watch, and I would stay in the waiting room while it was being done and then we would go home. The memories are still there about her thanking me for saving her life and although they don't come to the surface very oftend they do visit once in a great while, but through time a lot of memories leave to never come back making me stronger in some since. It was always hard to see anyone in your family when they are close to death but I stuck it out and she was strong once more, stronger then before and then after 12 years she fell once again but this time there was no coming back from it and she died on December 28 st 1995 by this time I didn't drink any longer because in part of what I saw and the second chance I was given, I quit in 1992 when I passed and only fell one time because of the strain I was in but then God found me once again and helped me. Through time I got strong and made my own way but the weakness I once had was gone and I really became strong. Not body wise as that would take time.

Throught the years I had excepted what had happened and I kept my promas to her about Oliver but now he has also passed so nothing is holding me back from living once again except for taking care of Randy with his mental problems it's like he is also lost not knowing what will become of him if I was to leave this world but don't freat my friend this will always be your home in a place where people care about their brothers and sisters, the closeness here is like nothing I have ever seen and like my friend said the people here wont judge you by past problems. As long as they stay in the past, whn we went to Kearney I could tell that he didn't feel at home nothing like he does here and I find that to be a good thing. When people pull together there is a bond of some kind that develops and I see it when I'm in church for the shyness I once felt has all but faided and we talk like we have known each others for at least 10 years, each of us having our own quirks but looked over. Being a writer I see things which others might not but I keep them to my self not to offend my friends the quickness of words that are not always throught through but forgiven because they have been together for so many years, most of my friends have been together from anywhere of 40 years to 70 making them like that well oiled machine that goes through life just as smooth as silk. They seam to have that love which will carry them to the end of their days here and above, they have made it through the hard times of the dirty thirtys and then went to war, to come back and take up where they had left off. I havent seen war except for what it does to people and I didn't like what I saw.

But the cause through time has kept some of them together some solgers still meeting once a year even after all this time has passed. But the numbers are dwindling as some go to the sweet by and by, I wonder if they will meet again up there? I find that many of us go through life alone maybe to write about their stories and in some since show others that they shouldn't do the same. Writing is good' but what you sacrifice is that connection you long for that person you could grow old with love it's self is something you might have to give up might. People become writers for different reasons some say they are shallow while others say they are just board, but my reason is that I have made a promas to try and stomp out a curse that has plaged many over the years. My stories are lived and not just some random mind making things up if I havent lived it then I can't write about it my mind isn't that complacted, and it cant be measured by random thoughts of how to love your wife or husband. It's quiet this morning but I do hear something off in the distence maybe a train going across the flat lands I like to listen for things, but it hasn't always been that way only after I started this journey was I allowed to catch different sounds and things. When I first learned to walk I didn't like to go anywhere because people can be crule to someone that is different what may be a miracle to one can be a joke to others with full use of their bodies. The kids I met one night didn't know my situation and they thought it was funny to make fun of me, and it almost caused me to never go out again but instead of jumping on them I asked God to foregive them because they didn't know what they were doing. And on that night something changed in me, and it was a change for the better. And I grew stronger in more ways then one my faith grew along with my understanding that some say things to just fit in. and I was glad that I wasn't one of them, then I went home and cries to releave the sadness but the next day I was back at it scooting around the house trying to make my self stronger, and days seamed to fly by sort of like they do today then the years went by. I had to use a cane for quite sometime and when some would laugh I gave them a poke and the eye that it's not nice, but they seamed to get my point and said they were sorry, like the alcoholic to only have it go away until the next time when it's done again. They don't seam to care about your feelings until you point situation to them, many times I thought this could be you. And then how would you feel, Thursday morning' and work went fine yesterday but I forgot my jacket at the thrift store so today I have to go and get it back before it's sold. I visited with John and his wife for a while' and they told me stories about a cantankerous old man that used to live near by, John got along with him but very few people did as he lived in his own world. Chasing people off his property if they smoked, he must have been like grisly Adams and he like horses as John let him ride his one time and he had a ball. He owned property all over the place here in Republic county and in other counties, one time the guys wanted to go hunting on his property and he got to meet a star that used to play ball, as John told the story I could see the old man as the player signed a ball and gave him his autograph on a picture.

The man told them that he wantd three birds brought back to him after they were done and this they might have done along with their birds they got for them selves. John said they had fun on that day so long ago and then they left, I like to hear about the old stories from the people who lived so long ago not sure what year this took place but it was way before I moved here probably in the 70's or so which was about the time I was gettinng into trouble back in Nebraska, just a little child hooked on alcohol and drugs trying to find his way in this world. He has now passed away the old man, and in a way I wish I had met him the cantankerous old man, John had to drive a tractor out to his home stead and my it was brisk with the wind blowing in his face he then lost his hat and told his grandson to pick it up for him and put it in the truck. They he took off his hat and said it just about blew his hair off for which he didn't have any on the top so funny!. I have always liked John and Judy they are dear to my heart, and we get along just fine. They seam to hve a give and take love which has lasted the test of time along with 5 children which are living across the United States. Today is the 6th and it's that time to buy grocries for the month so we will head into town later this morning, harley also needs food the little guy has had to eat people food for the last couple of days but hey! He eats it well. He has been with me longer then any others and he is my buddy so spoiled I don't know what I would do without him, some of the stories people talk about you can tell they hold dear to their hearts and you can see the excitement when they tell them.

Judy told me about living on the farm before they had drinkable water and how they could tell a storm was coming by the color of the water dark orange ment a storm, and one time they had hail the size of soft balls knocking holes in the wooden shingels and ending up in the addick' it must have been hard living back in those days but they made it raising five children. She said you couldn't drink the water' it was only used for things like the toilet and doing dishes so they had to transport drinking water fromn town, back then Belleville wasn't built yet and when they needed things like lumber they had to travel 75 miles there and back on a lumber wagon drawn by horses my that would take two days one way if you were lucky and didn't run into rain. Then she told me about some people who had a farm out in the middle of no where and they couldn't make it there, so they sold the land and later learned that it was full of oil and the buyers became rich the oil wells are still pumping today so you know they are well off. They even built a school the people who bought the property and things are still going well for them today my land' they must be worth millions. From what I gathered the original owned wasn't upset that he sold because he said the land would of killed him, strange how things turn out. As I talk to some people I find that Courtland has been here for over 100 years and it could be closer to 125 but they weren't sure, the water system wasn't installed until the 70's but still they survived like Jessie James. Kansas was their home and they weren't going to leave it I think it has something to do with roots like the planting of a tree to stay in one place for ever, my roots are now planted here and I will see how tall the tree grows. For each year brings something new too life and you don't know what it is until it's at you're door step, a new life is possible here but you have to be strong and not let the wildness destroy you the doctors are few and far in between but in a pinch you can get to one. Like my brother Rod he has lived in small towns most of his life just off the beaten track of civilization away to protect what is his the ones he loves, something wonderful drew me to this place and maybe it's because I understand some things more then others. For truly I love the life and the people like John and Judy and there stories about the old times, to their kids they should be proud of their parents and this is something I'm sure they are. Growing up in the hard times and seeing the changes from bad to good, I bet John was a card when he was younger but also stern. Some say we are a like in some ways as we inspect things closely he tells me that he is glad that I work for the church and that makes me feel good inside. He also speaks his mind and that's always a good thing as we are all different special one of a kind brought together like brothers and sisters in the name of Jesus Christ' a family with many different parts and each part has a purpose. Judy was the first person that said the people loved me and on that day joy came to my heart the joy of being excepted after a life of being alone, life isn't easy but if you have friends then your world can open up to a new page each day, a new story to write about the life in Kansas a small little town just off the beaten path called Courtland' the buildings are stuck back in time to the time when life was hard but change is coming and in time the buildings will take on a new face of progress. For the old fire house still stands but is now vacant to a new place just across the street from the bank, and now a phone company stands where an empty lot once stood.

Progress not to fast but still changing with the time's, a town built in the 1800 and still standing through a century if you could write about the changes it would take another century but I think the town speakes for it's self by the people that reside here all warn with loving hearts, even the kids know me by name and wave as I drive by. They too cant see what the future holds but they will grow up with people loving and protecting them, anywhere else you wouldn't see the careing that people show for each other but in Courtland it's around every corner just waiting for acceptance. Yes I have felt it' more times then I care to count and they don't judge, maybe because they too have had some ruff times and know what it feels like to not be excepted. That feeling alone doesn't feel very good to someone that is or was lost in a world they didn't understand, my new home town goes out every Christmas to make sure everyone has a Christmas and people donate the funds so the kids can buy for their mother or father, sister or brother, this is a part of life here in Courtland' for no one should have to do without on that special day when our savior was born to take away our sins and give us a new life, it's not 5:00 Am. And the day is going to start so much to do but still I have fun doing it. There will be more stories about the lives of the people here, and maybe in some way a glimpse of their lives will live on.

I do know that writing about their ventures is a delight for me. And it lets me into the lives that they lived through the hard times, and also the good times. When their children were born into this christen community some meaning me. Cant see the forest from the trees but in the end it all works out as our lives come together, it's been a busy day getting groceries and all, but the day is coming to an end when I fall into that sleep which will bring me into tomorrow. It's funny sometimes how each day brings something new and I embrace it with all I'm worth, I got my coat from the thrift store and it was sitting right where I left it and I got to see a couple of people that I know like Dennis he is back to work after a long recovery from heart surgery but seams to be doing fine now. Friday me and Dennis talk from time to time as we had a close friend in common Walt' who has gone from cancer. I loved the song they played at his funeral I did it my way' I remember the stories Walt used to tell me and still they are in my mind rest in peace my friend. Through the years I have been having things done to my house but now it's up to me to finish the things that still need to be done maybe one day these things will come to pass, but it's now winter so those things are on hold for better weather. In Courtland you see the goodness of people and I noticed that pastor Kathy has Christmas decorations up some seam to celebrate different then I do, but there hasn't been a time that I havent been grateful for what I have in my new home in case something happens my insurance covers loss of payment on most of what I have meaning car and such. I wouldn't want to leve them holding the bag you might say without my debts being taken care of. I wont be able to send any gifts this year but it doesn't mean that I wont later when things pick up, times get hard but then a repeave seams to set in so we can move on and things can get better some know that I'm looking for work, but they have to know my situation befor I can start. My own work would be a life saver once it gets on the market but it's getting it there that will take a lot of time the opening up about my life where many cant talk about the subject, I never could understand why it's kept a secret in many peoples lives, maybe because they feel shame or it could be that they just don't want to talk about it it's hard to say whats in another persons mind but the stories need to be told about their journey in life and how they were able to over come them. It's another cold morning aand yesterday was no different as the wind blew at first I thought a storm was coming in but it seamed to change directions, I do know that tomorrow we are supposed to have snow if the front stays on it's course but like all things it can change in a heart beat and be warm instead of cold. Saturday the rains stopped yesterday but I did think we would have had snow by this morning and we didn't. but I do know that winter isn't far off as they are getting it in Minnesota at this time and up be South Dakota, on some days during winter I like to go outside when the cold is dry it doesn't seam to chill you to the bone like on most days. It can be a great time of year but I would never go hunting in it I like being warm to much, plus I don't like killing things especially the animals like deer and such. Many people love to go bird hunting during the season for pheasant but to me they are to beautiful with their long feathers a bright redish orange color. In Washington they have made Marijuana legal so now that fronteer has been lost although they have a lot of work a head of them to regulate it. Like they do alcohol, but still kids wont be able to leagely possess it, only adults over the age 21. One of my articals was picked up by the associated press and they say it cant be duplicated or re written why this has happened I don't have a clue.

It's the first time for this to take place but I think it will still reach people all around the world they are just letting people know that they must have bought the rights to it. This is what I think just the thoughts of a person trying to make a change, free speech is something we all have and we are protected by laws so we cant be harmed by those who don't like what we Wright. For writing has seamed to become my life, my thoughts and memories about what had taken place so long ago and it's like putting together a puzzle with a piece coming to me with each passing day. But the right pieces seam to be far and few in between leaving holes in my puzzle, I can hardly wait until I get them all and see what a beautiful picture it is. Or not' the things I write about seam to be locked in my memory for some reason waiting there to be brought out into the world for some reason, but why? Are they burried so deep and only show them selves once in a while. Even today after all these years change comes but what it brings with it is unknown, does our minds hold the key to us advancing and using more then we do at this time in our existence it seams odd that we only use 10% of what we have it would be like going to the store with a dime and expect something for $100.00 it just doesn't fit. Randy is up in the other room and I don't know why maybe he slept to long yesterday his med's make him up and then down I will never understand why. The prison system really did some damage and I don't know if it can be fixed, he seams to be adjusting to not being with the alcohol or drugs and I believe he will make it.

With absents grows strength and with each passing year he grows stronger to maybe one day make it on his own in this world. Not afraid of what he cant do but be able to do anything. Sunday morning' I don't really know why I started to put down days but it was brought up by someone working for a publisher. Is it important to do this? I'm not sure but it does help in someways by keeping me on track many writers do this I believe trying to catch that moment in time when things come together. I havent heard the birds or trains lately as they seam to come by the time I stop writing plus it's winter or almost winter, yesterday I went and cleaned for a time and then brought the papers home to fold them for our guests to only return them later when I was done and returned back home to rest until this morning. In my time I have spent most of my weeks doing little things like working at the thrift store and at the church, it seams to give me more to write about and I like the people. Yesterday when I went to work a lady left her lights on in her truck so I told her she better shut them off and she thanked me, it's not good to get stranded with a dead battery. The people seam content with their lives here and you can tell the farm people from the ones that live in town, most of the people in town are retired from farming but still you have the farm workers that live here also getting up early and heading out to their bosses house in the country. It becomes a part of their lives and they take good care of their workers. The other day I saw one of the farmers replacing a bathtub in one of the houses he rents to the Spanish people, they come down from Mexico and work in the fields for him and then leave to go back home during the winter. And I guess that gives their boss time to make the house liveable for them, I recall even back in the dust bole days the Mexicans would travel to the United States for work and they still do it today. Hoping to make a living for their families and giving them a better life in Mexico the exchange for a dollad is much higher then here at one time it was 100 to one but now days I'm not sure of what it is, but they say you can live well even on Socal Security in that country like a king they say. For a while I thought I had lost my fight about drug abuse but I haven't as there is still a law that companys have drug testing, so if they fail it then they loose their jobs to support their families. By passing the law and making it legal is just one hand in a poker game they havent won yet, and the game is far from over. Now it will be whats more important feeding your family or doing drugs. Which is a choice that will tell the story, the federal government still has it as illegal and those tried for it will still go to prison as far as they are concerned, but what will happen if it's made legal on the federal level then all those who were sent to prison will be set free and will be able to return home. Another situation like with alcohol and more of our people will die, it's like they are digging a hole that they wont be able to croll out of. But like with alcohol they wont help the ones that become addicted and they will have to fight their battle, on their own.

In all my years I never thought they would open that box but it's being done and then there is no turning back. I feel for the kids more then anything because their parents wont be able to take care of them and the court system will be really full. If you compare pot to alcohol kids will get into it and end up killing others another step in the wrong direction and they will have to live with it' I have heard that americans are destroying their immune system with all the cleaners they are using on their bodys, making it weak by not letting natural things come into it to help. I see this by people washing their hands up to five times a day and I brought it up to some people and asked how people survived 100 years ago when ths crap wasn't even thought of and they laughed, it just goes to show how powerful the mighty dollar has become. They think they are helping them selves when in reality they are destroying the most important thing to keep them alive very foolish. It's a good morning and I look forward to church this morning when we are all together to give praise to God the father and Jesus the son' bring us all joy in this day and bring us all peace for you are the only one who can give this to you're people. For the joy I feel today can't be measured by human standards so let it be what it may, in the town of Christmas you can see many things starting with the smiles on peoples faces, and this alone can bring joy to a heart that might be broken. I can hear the train going through town as it blows it's whissel but I could never understand why they do this because no one is up at this time of morning maybe they are spreading Christmas cheer but I doubt it as many get up set when they are awaken.

I'm just glad that I don't live closer to the tracks as it would shake the house apart Ha! I have many things to do so I will write later. It's the beginning of another week the 10th to be exact I slept pretty good last night but the morning came quick, it's pretty quiet and I cant hear anything out side. Last night they put on a Christmas show the kids that is but I was tired and had to retire for the night it was more for the kids families anyway to show what they are learning on Wednesday school. Their familys should be proud of their accomplishments, I don't see much of thee kids because when bible school is in I'm at the thrift shop dowing what ever there is to do but last Saturday we had good sales and they are talking about closeing until after the new year. If I remember right last year they were closed all winter because they couldn't get any volinteers but I told them that I would work just so I could get out of the house, it seams that each year they put up the nativity seen and the displays in the church and it looks beautiful. This year I have a statue of Jesus that sits in the foyer I had gotten it last year because it was beautiful, I went to the church after church to make sure things were ready for last night and it didn't take long too get the job done. I was supprised when w got a cold snap yesterday the temp must have dropped ten degrees in an hour and you could feel it to the bone just like if you were in a blizzard without the snow a sign that winter is here. This next year I will take on more in dowing things, and maybe build my strength even stronger then it is at the present in hope to make more money so we don't have to struggle as bad in the next year. I had plenty when we first moved here but now that is really cut in half almost and it's all I can do to make ends meet but I have faith that things will turn around and all will be ok' little brother is sleeping and hopefully he will sleep in until later so he doesn't doze off during the day. I have tried to get him to go to functions but he would rather just stay home, a mundane way to live but I have been there an when your feeling that way no one can break it but you. It took many years before I came out of my shell and in time he will find his way back into the world and like me I kicked my self in the butt for not doing it sooner. We are all different and unique, separated by our imagination and what we think about the world, I remember when he was joyest with not a care in the world but his stay away did something to him. Made him retreat back into him self like I did so long ago not wanting anything to do with the world, then He found me on that day and things seamed to change weather I wanted them to change or not. It seams when He gives you a gift you have to do something with it weather it's small or not but change comes sometimes even if you don't want it to, I change more each year and sometimes it's small but other times it can be big like the growing past the fear of going places. On our trip to Kearney I didn't feel that fear that I felt so long ago through the time I have been here it has subsided and my growth has come only by God's grace. It is His love for us that allows us to make strides in the things we do from creating things to making a home for our selves and others, a gift from the one on high Jesus christ his only son. I could see how He would want to be close to us helping in ways that others cant even fandom, so we can to one day make Him proud of us if we follow the path He sets for us as his children. Even when we fall short of our own goals He forgives us and lends a helping hand so we can one day find that journey we have been sent on.

Even when the people were sent into the desert He made a way for them, but that didn't stop the fear they had at first because it's a part of human nature. I am strong, I'm a master piece. Created by the one who created everything. He gave His approval of me before my birth and from what I have heard that was way before my coming into this world, I believe we all had His approval before we were sent to this place so we could work together and make this world a better place. Our labor is worth more then money that helping hand which helps those beautiful souls that might be lost, when I was sent back I didn't know what would become of my life but I did know something was going to happen that would change things. It's been a long road to where I am today and the remembering of things serve as a reminder of what can happen if you go down the wrong path, nothing happened over night except that I knew things had to change. I can't count the years that I was confined to my room afraid to go out into the world, even when it felt like it was going to be my last breath something kept me going and over the years the strength returned slowly. If you haven't been through this kind of thing then you can't know the struggles that I went through, but God seame to give me strength when I had none to give to take that next step. I recall when I first went out of town in Kearney fifty miles from home and the car broke down. I had to walk but with each step I wanted to give up, so tired. I ended up walking down the railroad tracks hoping the short cut would get me to the highway faster but I fell many times so I guess that wasn't a good idea, with each step I asked God for help and He gave it gladly but the fear was still there the fear that I wouldn't make it home.

It seams we have a survival mode inside of us and we will do all that's in our power to make it to where we need to be. My other brother was with me but he wasn't any help always looking over his sholder to see if he was being watched it was a time when the curse had a strong hold on him and I cant remember where the girl went, the car was left in a intersection by the court house as they left not to get into trouble. Then I finely made my way to the road and hitched hiked back to Kearney, after that episode I didn't go out again for about a year afraid of the out side world and that I would get caught up in it and get lost once again. In my home I felt safe and I knew no one could hurt me there but that was short lived when I went to make a phone call at 2:00 Am. I was talking on the phone when a police car came by and asked what I was doing and I replyed that I was talkig to a friend, they then wanted to search me because most people are in bed at that time of the morning so I let them search and then they were on their way. Again I didn't go out for quite sometime thinking I was watched by the law, because of the people I used to hang out with. Once they are drawn to you they don't want to look like fools and then one night they did look like a bunch of fools by coming to my house and accusing me of robbing agas station. My legs weren't even healed when they knocked on my door and said they found foot prints in the snow that lead to my back door, it was all I could do to walk at that time and they wanted to know where the gun was! I then told them I didn't know what they were talking about and they called me a lier, it was the first time I had been called those words and it hurt really bad inside. But these guys were on a miission and they didn't care about others feelings, the leader of the pack went on to tell me that he knew how hard it was to make things work not having money to pay bills and all I could say is really! Then I told them that they were on the wrong track, that I had been home all night and they better go and find the guy that did it. Then after a whild they brought a officer that knew me and we talked, he asked if I knew who had done the dirty deed and I told him no. by this time I was mad and I told him that they were letting the robber get away by wasting their time on me, finely they let me go and then they arrested the guy three days later. They never came and apologized to me and if I would have been a writer then I would have wrote a nasty letter about them, the strange thing was' that I had never been in trouble for such things as this, the only kind of trouble I had ever been in was drinking and driving nothing else. But they focused on me for some reason, maybe because my brothers had been into that kind of thing not robbing at gun point, but theft. And there reflection was cast on me, in a family you have three kinds of siblings the one who is reserved and baskfull and then the big mouth that is all talk. And then the one who walks in darkness with no regard for others or anyone. This person doesn't care who he takes from and you bettter hide anything of value, with him it doesn't matter if they steel from family because they feel that they or you wont do anything. And if you do' they wouldn't think twice of killing you or hurting you bad. Just that in a family can break them apart and make things to where you wouldn't care if you ever seen them again, so sad.

My brother Rod is a card' I remember when he fell in love with our other brothers wife, he had a nice Mustang and got mad one night and drove it up a tree because she didn't want to be with him any longer. Our other brother got sent to prison and she stayed with my brother and his wife, it seamed Rod was always trying to get someone elses women. Like he did with mine at the age of 16 what makes them do that? Trying to capture their youth again well it doesn't work.

Even though he messed around in his younger years he is still married to the same women since age 18 making their merriage the only one that lasted over 30 some years all the rest of us like me and little brother only got married once and that was at a young age him being 16 and my self being 18. But Randy's marriage lasted longer then mine, although Rosemary was thirteen and never finished school she would later go to cosmetology and then buy a hair salon where she still does her work today just with a different husband, they got along good at first but through the years it died along with their love, on her side anyway. The drugs became a wall between them and the alcohol of course it seamed to put little brother in a different world and once she started to learn that she could live without him she kicked him out and started life over. Which was hell on my mom because he ran there when ever he and others got into trouble, it seamed she got all the pressure, and it made her older before her time. Me on the other hand did the same but I was the child that didn't get into trouble like the child that hid the alcohol under her pillow and said I'm the good kid! To only later self destruct, I remember when they brought Randal home from the hospital their first born it looked like two kids playing with a doll so young but so happy and then later Routh came and they started to be a family. Irean had him brain washed because he didn't have any schooling and he had low self asteam.

And I think that's where the alcohol help in some strange way, but like with anything connected to alcohol it didn't last. After my marriage failed later my other brother would marry Diane and they had two kids Ricky and Jerry and being their mother was an alcoholic they to were cursed by addiction little Ricky anyway as Jerry went into the service and fought for his country. Those parts of the family were separated by miles as she then married again after Rick. I would see her later in life and she said she was trying to get a hold of me but I never did give her my number not wanting to go back in time. To me moving forward is the only way to not repeat bad things that might have happened in our lives, but still the memories are there of a love that once was. Enough of that. Back when I first started to talk with Margret it was like we had a connection and I knew somehow that I needed to get away from Kearney, it was like He was using her to have me make my move here. Then afterwards we didn't see each other any more like with my first wife she wanted to own me and that wasn't going to happen again in this life anyway, I have lived a somewhat lonely life but at least I'm happy for the most part. Not having to fight with someone about who is going to drive the car and if you don't have respect for someone then there is no use in trying to take it further especially if it's a new relationship so I stay alone in this world trying the bestway I know how to find that special someone who will complete me or maybe I am complete, and just need a partner someone to love and who will love me back. According to statistics there is five women for each man where did they come up with that one? I guess I'm the kind of person that cant just be with someone unless there is feelings there. No one night stands for me. Wednesday as me and Randy were talking yesterday something came to mind. People in the world of addiction sometimes get there by their spouse, they get married and then the guy starts to loose self asteam which causes him to try drugs and usually by this point they have to go on some kind of pubic assistance. Many a women have followed their husbans into this state of mind not knowing it until he leaves and then the women is stuck in the world of addiction with what ever amount of kids. But now they cant do without the drug they have choosen and not having any money only sets them further into that world by this time they are selling food stamps to fill that void of being high. Many of them have sex to pay for their highbut if they don't fit that bill then they will pay $200.00 in food stamps for just a gram of Methamphetamine, leaving their children with out food to eat. I have met many a women that have done this to just stay alive or though they thought until the kids are taken away and then they cry and say why me! It's a very sad sight to see when this happens so many broken hearts just because of the curse of drugs. After the children are put in foster care the parent only has so much time to get their life back on track and if it isn't done then they loose them for ever. In a system that doesn't care one way or the other, many of the kids have been lost iin the system and some even found dead.

To never be rejoined to their mothers or parents again, many a movies have been written about such things happening and some don't believe it can really happen but it does I have seen it first hand. The dealers have a way of making then think they are important and even have the women sell the stuff for them bringing the money back to them and then living with them, there is a word for these women but I don't use that language the sell them selfs into slavery to the dealers. Which in turn they treat them like crap beating on them when they come back short, the mind control that they have over them is a sight to see and their only escape is if the guy gets busted and even then' a lot of times the women will find a way to get them out to only later go to prison with their lives destroyed. I know one women who choose the dealer over her kids three beautiful kids were taken away, but the threat of sueing the state got them back after a year or so. People living in poverty fall the hardest; having nothing they tend to want to find that rainbo which usually doesn't come by selling or doing drugs it's an illusion something created in the mind to stop them from going nut's. they have never known God only the dark side of life, and only the side that is created in the mind all mixed up by the mind not working in the normal world. There has been many women that wanted to be with me in that world but for some reason I couldn't let it happen, something inside would tell me that it wasn't right so I couldn't act on it and still there I was lonely. I guess in my mind it was ok' to hurt your self, but it was not ok' to bring others down with you. As I see the pain some go through I wish sometimes that I had the power to take that pain away so they could be happy, but I have no supernatural powers to do this so I do what I can to help from a distence.

It's hump day and half the week is gone only a few more days until Christmas, it's the changing time of the year and then the new year will be here. And everyone will be another year older. Randy's birthday is in January on the 8th as a matter of face, and he will ring in the new year with just me by his side. As for looking to the future it's better left where it is and we will take one day at a time hoping things will look up or change for the better. I had to have the car fixed again as the thermostate went out and now I hope the fixing part of the car is over for a few years giving me a break from going into debt, at least it didn't break down on the road thank God. Antique road show is on finely so I will watch it for a while, many things come up that I would like to have and put in my home but the cost to get them is out of this world. 12/12/12 some say this day will have an impact on my life but to me I don't see what could possibly happen, they also say that it could be the end of the world when the Mayan calendar ends in nine days which also I don't see happening. Doomsday as some say' but I believe it's just the beginning of something wonderful happening, if we only look at the negative side of things then our world would be full of misfortune and there is enough of that today. It is written that the older we become the faster time moves and this is something I can feel as the months and years pass, I recall one women saying one day that I had lived here for several years when it has only been four at the most. Does some peoples time move faster then others? I believe so depending on their age, so strange' how a child can feel that the day is endless when to an adult it just flew by like the blink of an eye. The Mayan calendar only lasted 5,125 years in which now many are saying many things, a lot of people are in a panic building ark's with the beliefs that they will need it when the flood comes. As for the Mayan's them selves they don't believe in such crap, they seam to think it's a new beginning. A time to celebrate their survival after the destruction so long ago. Thursday and the train is running this morning as it blows it's horn there isn't anyone else up in these neck of the woods, not even the farmers they work so hard and need their sleep for the coming crop. I have oftend wondered how they get used to that life getting up at the crack of dawn but like any kind of life and work you just adjust to it. I know when I worked for Jack it became a part of me and I looked forward to the days of spending time in the tractor, during planting season it would rain and I would have to get out and break the clods off the disk so I could get going again, I used a big bar to do this and it worked well. In the mornings we would fire up the tractor and head to the fields having no light from natural sorces we would use the big lights on the top of the cab and they would light up half the field. I still remember the animals as their eyes glistened from the night or early morning and there was all kinds from skunks to racoons and even baggers, they were the mean ones attacking the tires of the ole 8650 John Deer and then going their own way. I did a lot of traveling from county to county but the work had to be done and for the most part it was fun, I oftend wonder how they are Jack and Luella! She was really into the church also like the women around here are and in someway it must have brought them peace.

When he had his accident all those years ago he changed and he knew God had something to do with it I can never thank them enough for their kindness back in those dark years, and if I would of stayed I probably would be working for him today, but God knew that change was coming in my life so I was sent away to try and figure out the things I needed to. Does He know what will happen in the future? I think so. But I will only know when it happens no foresight for me, not at this time. The train has gone and now it's quiet really quiet but when the sun comes up people will be getting off to work to start their day like they have for hundreds of years the way of farming has changed but the life remains the same from sun up to sun down they find something to do weather it's fixing fence or just checking on cattle to see if they are ready for market, the fields hold many things of nature and many don't see it because they have never been on a tractor especially city folks. They would be lost out in nature after living in the concreat slabs of the cities all piled together in one place and reaching as far as the eye could see, I have never been to a place like New York or even Dallas but I'm sure there are some good qualitys it's just that I have never wanted to go there didn't like the thought of seeing the homeless and the starving on the streets. Many have their own beliefs and some of them to me is nuts, like building an ark for a flood that will never come like the bridge that was built that went no where in Alaska. So many lives could have been saved by the money they wasted but no they had to have that bridge, why O'Lord does these things bother me? And why do I feel for those who suffer? Pandoras box has been opened and now the death tole is going to rise.

What would happen if those thoughts were taken away? The thought's of careing weather people suffer or not. The mind lets us care but we can seam to only do little about it, could it be that if more cared then the problem could be solved and if so then why isn't it done. As I look at my writings over the years they make me stand out, the one who tried to stop the destruction will it come to pass sometime in the future or will my efforts fall short for another 50 years when they see the destruction first hand? Some say I'm fighting a looseing battle but is it looseing when you keep that promise to God that you made so long ago? I know He can make the supernatural happen so I still feel there is that chance or a glimmer of hope that things will work out later in time. Time seams to be the corpret in this venture and only He knows when that will take place, my writing has become a way to express what's inside and bring out those things that might have been lost for ever. The memories and the stories of a time long gone from this world are kept alive when maybe they should have died long ago, but if that's the case then why would He put them into my mind? Maybe a way of repairing the damage that was once done. And if that's the case then when will it end? My journey has now taken me to a different place a place of peace where I live, I can hear Randy in the other room talking to someone who isn't there in a dream maybe where it's sunny and things are bright. Who really knows what dreams do? Could they open a door or shut a door better left alone for this is a question only He can answer, Friday and it's only 11 more days until Christmas. Little brother has been under the weather lately coughing during the night but he doesn't complain like me I guess in many ways, I havent been reading the inspireing books lately as I'm taking a break to maybe recharge my batteries or come at it from a different prespective but the message that they send are good ones. This time of year seams to go by pretty fast and before you know it the new year is here and within a couple of months the flowers start to grow. There is no train this morning but who knows it could show up later more towards morning when the sun starts to come up, as for the thrift store it' now closed for a couple of months or at least until after January and the people who need things can get a hold of Beverly just across the street. It seams strange to have light by a lamp instead of the one on the ceiling where it lights up the whole room but I will make do until I can get it going again, looking back now

I wished I would have gone to school for computers that way I could of made a living at that but you can't live on wishes and I believe all things turn out for the better good if that's the way it's supposed to be, as for the things I'm supposed to do I do them and things get better with each passing day. I have some old coin sets that I could give for Christmas but parents seam to get rid of them when they need money, I have given a few over the years and they are gone I guess what I'm trying to do is teach my grand babys about history but it never seams to get that far before they get sold for cash to pay bills or what ever they use it for. My time is coming down to the wire and only he knows how much time any of us will be here hanging in there by only our strength and love for him.

When our time comes we will think did I have any regreats and usually with most it's yes things left undone that we could of done instead of others, I need to be a public speaker so I can tell my story to the children so they can avoid the curse that will hit many of them. Dream makers and dream breakers as for the kids that have never touched the stuff they have a chance to open a great big world and become a part of it, and only their minds can stop them but when drugs are thrown into the mix their chance is very slim until they over come it. Like with me so much could have been done and no one will ever know if I could have been a teacher, is it too late? They say that God doesn't put something in your heart that you can't finish so yes there is still time to touch kids everywhere and in doing that you can help break the ties that might bind them kick drugs out of Kansas would be a great slogen and it would give kids a purpose and something to fight for that they can believe in. who knows maybe my writing has been to prepair me for this journey one that will be never ending, courage is something that's hard to master when you spent your life running from life but also it's something that can be turned around and make your life full over coming the odds of poverty and dispaire can bring you to a higher level then you have ever been before knowing kids will look up to you for something positive. My writing has reached the world in many ways but now it needs to be told in person, by the one who survived and over came those odds.

Children will embrace it knowing they are not alone in this world and that others have had the same situation in their lives the fighting of parents that leads to their break up but what they need to understand is that it's not their fault. And some of it can stend from when they weren't even born yet, their hearts are more softer then a parents. I remember when I was young a teacher came to our house and saw promise in me but at that time in life everything was out of control and I never did return back to school so that talent never got developed, so many kids today quit school by age 16 not wanting to go on because of this thing they call poverty made to work at a young age and loose the changce of becoming something bigger then them selves like the squirrel that settles for one nut to feed it's family when there is a hole tree of nuts just down the block. Sometimes panic sets in and we have to take what we really don't want, been there and done that. Many years ago I was told that being a writer was not something I couldn't accomplish but here it is all these years later and the story is still unfolding. I saw a new worker at panther paws yesterday and I was drawn to her. But what drew me to her was a missing tooth strange how some things can get your attention but she was also pretty at least in my eyes any way, I could tell that she was new because I know all the womens smiles and hers was different a little sweeter then the rest and who knows maybe we will become friends sometime in the future. I believe she lives in Scandia as most of the women workers do as far as I know or she could be from a farm taking on a job so the family can make ends meet, my imagination runs wild with many things but my true stories on addiction stay the same. All the destruction it causes and the lives it ruins. As I sit here a calmness comes over me, a calmness that only comes once in a while but it's excepted and I wish it came more oftend because with it comes peace. And then I pray' for all who is in my life from the old to the new and those who havent made it here yet, the new born child that is still in it's mother waiting for that time when it will make it's way into this world to bring with it change maybe another president or congressmen that will change the world or at least the nation. High hopes or far fetched dreams, the train is coming through at 4:55 this morning and the motor is chugging hard carrieing a heavy load. I can't see it but I bet black smoke is pouring out of it's stacks, and the wheels are a little uneven making a strange noise. Hansen Muller loads a lot of them with wheat and other crops as it runs down a spout to fill the cars hopper bottoms is what they are called and I remember them well from my youth especially cleaning them to get the rotten crap out of them so it didn't effect what they are putting into them and the smell is very rotten. I used to like loading them as it was very easy except for the dust that blew in your face that when you use a mask to keep it out of your lungs, there set up is much different then in Nebraska here they have silows and there the bins were big and round and made of steel. I think they could have the ability to build one like theres but not too much alfalfa in this part of the country, my land' they made the money out of that feed and it was shipped all around the world. When they closed we all were out of a job but not before we got our just do, the money didn't last long but we had fun with it while we had it. Little brother has been sturring around for a while now and he will be getting up before to long to start the day. I hope his day goes well better then yesterday, in the news today they had a shooting at another school right out of New York. The last I heard 28 were killed, Saturday morning and I was awaken by having no power that the only draw back to living out in the middle of God's land you never know when it's going to happen. We had rain yesterday and this morning and it could have been in part of why it happened but i would almost bet it was the peoples lights that they have in their yards rain and electricity doesn't mix.

From the black out I didn't get out of bed until 4:00 Am trying to keep warm as long as possible and then I lit the oil lamps so I could see, but as usual the lights came back on within a half hour from lighting them. I don't have any equilibrium when I'm in the dark as falling is a real possibility and it can scare the hell out of me another drawback to addiction and it leaves you with no control like your floating in dark space with nothing to hold on to. I guess that part never healed from the destruction so long ago, and there are other things which I cant do especially at night. As long as I have light then things are ok' but without it I'm lost like the child in the forest who has never been there before, having this really puts you in a place you don't want to be because all the insecuritys come back and that's what I'm trying to get over or change. As for the rain we have needed it for some time and now it's finely here, the farmers should be tickled. During winter we have at least one blackout but the electric company is usually on the ball to get it fixed as scoon as possible. The weight of the snow on the wires causes some of it but also tornados do a lot of damage when they go through here leaving us without power, Courtland has only had drinking water since the 70's but still before then people survived I have heard many storys about those times the color of the wated out of the wells which was only used for flushing the toilet or doing dishes. On another note maybe my car got washed last night and it's clean, or with the rain came dirt and it's filthy only know when the sun comes up. My heart goes out to the parents of the children that died yesterday such a shame that so many had to die over one person, I wonder what brought it on! You can never tell what pushes others buttons. Sunday they were saying on the news that the young man was mentally ill or bipolar and never treated for the problem, this kind of thing happens all the time in the U.S. and others suffer for it, yesterday Beverly and I packed about eight garbage bags to send to other places.

So they can use them, and help others in need who don't have much. Many are without' and it's nice to help out when you can, Randy has something on his mind but for the life of me I cant figure it out so he will have to see a doctor to find out what it is maybe depression or something else. An inbalance in his mind maybe that makes him want to sleep all the time but I know it's not good, I cant help but to feel sorry for the folks that lost their children and it is so sad that these kind of things happen some said the young man killed his mother first and then went to the school where he broke in and killed the principal along with other adults. This is something that might not ever get figured out being the young man is dead, so now they will have to pick up the pieces and go on in hope that it wont happen again. Maybe this kind of thing was kept from me in my younger years but now it's been let in and I wish it hadn't, I have only heard about such things in the last fifteen or so years after they took prayer out of the schools. Is there a connection? That is something I cant say for sure, at one point they said that his mother was strict and that could have caused the break leading into an exploshion in his mind. Like with kids that excell in school if they are pushed too hard they to can break later in life an it causes them to take up drugs and alcohol, so maybe they can forget no one really knows for sure. I wrote an article on it many years ago but like many things people excused it and moved on parents especially, the mind is a funny thing and if pushed to hard a break can take place sort of like brain washing and then all it needs is a fuse to egnite the break and then watch out they will destroy them selves or others as they are in that state of mind. I have wondered how I held it together all these years but with God there He takes that darkness away and replaces it with the light so we can go on and do great things which are inside of us, I cant hardly imagine the people back in christs time and how they managed to pull through some of what they went through but then again God was right beside them and they had a great leader. Only eight more days until Christmas, the time they believe christ was born and came to save the world from destruction. I find it strange how he didn't start until he was 30 years of age but I know that the father knew what he was doing, like with Melchisedek part of his life was left out also and it only told that he was the king of piece and a priest to the most high God maker of heaven and earth. But he was mentioned in the beginning of the bible where Jesus wasn't in GENESIS' where his life was first mentioned and then later as the book went on.

One of the writings was so poorly written that they had a hard time deciphering; it but they got it done. So that leads me to believe that all scribes weren't educated, imagine an old man in a cave writing what God told him to write! Sort of reminds me of my self with no education and having a hard time writing words sometimes but He has a way of bringing things out of people for his work. This must be where the supernatural comes in logic doesn't always apply in His realm He makes the impossible possible and we never see it because we are only human, in our world logic has to play a part but in His it doesn't. I am a masterpiece, created by the most high God. I am one of a kind, and it was said that I was good before my birth brought to this world to do good things. Praise be to the one on high, this Sunday was awesome as the Carlson's brought over a Christmas gift of a pork loin and boy was I surprised, but not shocked as they have a big heart. Things like this never happened in my family, but now I have a new one. It was such a delight to get the gift and she really meant it from the heart such a delight to know them, and the others in my family of new people.

Next Saturday I will help pastor Kathy take the Christmas baskets to the familys that deserve them so they will have a Merry Christmas, it will be the first year of me doing this and it will continue through the years such a delight to give, even more then receiving, and the feeling is out of his world. Monday morning' after the shooting at the school they had a bomb threat at a church in Newtown and I'm just glad that I don't live there, the things that are happening I will never understand but I do know that He is there for them in this time of loss and trouble to maybe take away the pain so many of them feel, some say many will blame Him for their loss but I know He didn't have anything to do with what happened tragedy hit's us all in one way or another but we live through it and move on to maybe be stronger or to fall victim to drugs and alcohol, as for me that isn't something I have to worry about because my demons are put to bed for a long time and now life goes on. In the years since my arrival I have seen many good things done here and I have been on the reciving end of that goodness by friends and others who have opened their hearts to me such a good feeling to be liked and wanted by so many. Jan supprised me by the gift and it wasn't expected that I would get one from anyone but some peoples hearts are bigger then others as I have seen this year, the joy of giving must really be in the hearts of the Carlsons and it's hard to tell who elese heart I have touched. One of the bible schools teachers said that they had left a mess after school but to me I don't really count that as a mess but jut a part of my job that I do to help make it nice for them so they can teach the little ones about the father, and now I will go on and keep doing my job through another year. Courtland is the first place where I have found peace and I will stay through the end of my days on this earth, a quiet little place where peace is found in my heart. Manythings will come up but through it all I will make it to bring in a new year of excitement and joy along with the other things us humans go through like fighting and argueing for those brief moments that will later lead to understanding, I sent Rosa-lee a Christmas card and also my children to wish them joy through Christmas season. They should of already gotten it and I hope it made their day, I'm staying here this season and not going out of town, my Christmas will be in the town that I love and as for the others well I hope they understand my not coming out there. At least for this year anyway, sometimes other get mad at you but you have to look through their anger and move on with your life, I have many thoughts on what's happening in the world but the world isn't my concern just my little town, if change can start in one place then it can spread but if it never starts then no change will take place like with a person, imagine being on a path of destruction and then being woke up by the father to tell you that it's time to move on to leave the old life behind you and start a new. This can be hard especially when you have lived only one way but the change is possible only through christ as it will be Him that changes you from the inside out like the tea pot that once was eugly and then was transformed into something beautiful and everyone wanted it but it wasn't for sale, everyone who gazed upon it wanted it for it's beauty but the tea pot couldn't see the beauty because it couldn't see it's self. When He transforms us it's always from the inside out where no one can see the transition, to friends you remain the same until the product is done and then they all want to be like you the beautiful tea pot. I know a strange way to put things but it's His way so others can see that change is possible. People are always watching what we do and if they see the goodness that resides inside of us, then they sometimes want to do the same sort of like that saying word of mouth sells more things then advertising.

Just a few more days until the birth of christ advent season where people read out of the bible and give thank's for the things God has given us, many people don't see what has been given and I think that an over sight on their part because all things are made possible through Him, us' we as people, are made in His image but also we have a gift of Him inside of us all allowing us to bring things into existence, no one person can do it by them selves and even with what He gave us it takes more then one. It's our dreams that are able to become reality, but how it's done I havent a clue. Still today I try and figure out how it's done and today I'm still stumped but I do know that all is possible through Him, as we learn to love and understand these things there must be a door that opens up to allow us to create something that's inside I wish I could see this thing which resides inside of us, this spirit that longs for things to happen. For surely it out lives these bodies to go on to another place which He has planned for us. That life ever lasting, the day is going well as we made a trip to town and then my daughter textme to let me know that it's J.C's birthday after Christmas I wish that one year I could get them everything they wanted and then I would be happy. As we went to the dollar store I saw Norman shopping for somethings and we said hi to each other, and that was followed by it sure was frosty out this morning. I used the back defroster on the car for the first time and it worked very good so happy that I didn't have to scrape the window like with my old car, those days were very cold ones standing out in the snow.

I'm hoping to get a Christmas bonus this year to help out with things but if it doesn't come that's ok'. Also I was supprised that I got one last year and it helped to catch up on things, it's the little things that my friends do which never seams to supprise me so different then where I came from where everyone is out for them selves and piss on the world. Things happen out of the blue around here and you can never tell what will take place next, next Tuesday is Christmas and most of my friends will spent the day with family as I will with Randy you see we only have each other in this world to make thing good and survive. Tuesday and it's only a week until Christmas, I slep in today but was restless most of the night with my arm hurting for God only knows what. It seams these bones are very hard to sleep on especially my arms, I think they call it arthritis brought on by the years of catching those bags of Alfalfa meal and pellets. Although the knowledge of doing such things still resides in my mind the ability of doing it again is gone, this is a sign that my youth is gone but my ability to do things less hard is still good and it's said that as long as you can do something with pride then your ok' with age comes becoming slower that's just the way life is so we adapt to the new things we can do and move on and with some it makes them feel useless for some reason but I know that there is plenty to do in this world. The other day a women asked if Randy and I were related and we told her yes she was wondering because we are always together, I told her that we are 18 months apart in age and she said that's mighty close. Some must feel that there is a connection between us always being together and there is, we are a like in many ways more so then I ever thought. We were never together in our younger years and Randy never had a role model except for someone who always got him in trouble, but I will leave his name out of this as he knows who he is. We are shaped in part by our saroundings and if they are not good then it tends to rub off on the person, but it can always be changed if the right person or persons come into your life. And God can make that happen if your exceptable to change, as for the change of going to prison it doesn't do a timid person any good if they have a alcohol or drug problem. A growing process needs to take place to where you can advance past the things that cause havic in your life, I can hear the train going through town off in the distance, you can also hear the diesl motors running while it sits still and now it's powering up and going on it's way. Starting out slow and then gaining momentum to get to where it's going to go, around here they don't have many accidents with trains but I was told how one time it hit a car out of Colorado passing through and it cut the guys head off not a pretty sight I bet. They didn't have arms that went across the tracks but now they do change brought on by tragity, they say that many accidents have happened on highway 36 but in my time here I havent seen any. The train is off and you can hear the wheels being out of round so many miles that are put on them running across the country and I bet they don't stop much except to pick up freight, the founder of the train would be proud of how his vision turned out and is still running today. Also the visionary of the oil pipe line would be proud with it's miles of pipe extending into Alaska these people were the fore fathers of this country helping it grow from where it was in the 1800's to where it is today, although their lives are gone their vision lives on so someone else can take over those people don't know we even exist but at one point they too were like us poor from poverty and then one day they got their break and created something great.

With some a business was left to them and then they took the chance to make it grow into an impire that would last through out their years. Not many get that chance but those who do take it to the limits and fight if they have to so they can build something great, but like Rome sometime in history they all fall off that mountain and crumbel to where there is nothing left. As I went to start the car it didn't seam as cold as other days and that means it might be a warm day, also the mill is running down the road it had been so quiet lately that I thought they were done for the year, but I guess not. I don't know if I will sing this year but the thought has crossed my mind maybe white Christmas would be a good one to sing.if I can get the words from the pastor, women don't have a problem singing but I think for men it's a macho things you know' they think it's not cool but O how wrong they would be to think that way it takes courage to stand before people and let them see you sing. Tomorrow we are going to get snow from what I hear and it's supposed to be quite a bit. Wednesday or hump day as it's called it's been a nice week so far and tomorrow should be even better, I can feel a change coming on as we get closer to winter but things have been on my mind more lately and I cant quite put my mind around it. I told Kathy I would sing the song white Christmas if she could get me the words for it and she said she could so we will see what happens down the road, some days I feel like singing and on others not so much. I guess that's just the way life works, I had an editoral in the news paper yesterday and to me it sounded good talking about pot and the out break of drugs that's going on in other states.

They have to know that it's gong to hurt a lot of people even children as second hand smoke is blown in children's faces like with cigarettes and how it's done today, but instead of it just being smoke it will be T.H.C.. Will all states adopt this curse? I do know it's still not legal on the federal government side of things and may never be legal, but the states have control of their own state and the government has no say if they prosicute the growers and dealers. Such a dilemma, O' well we will watch and see what will take place later down the road. On some sights if you use bad language they will take the foulness off of the sight so not to hurt others feelings and I find this to be important to people who write most days of their lives it's called a matter of opinion and we all have the right to voice ours but with discretion not to throw off the balance. When I write I use my words carefully not to offend the readers so they too can voice their opinion on certain situations, personal experience has taught me that only destruction comes out of the things they are trying to make legal and no matter how much they try to sugar coat it only destruction will follow. I admit I don't know it all but what I do know is that many kids will be hurt over this selling of marijuana, many countries have tried to make it legal but in the end they decided against it, many have used the turm that medical qualiutys out weighs the bad things that this will cause and to me they are just full of crap like they would do anything so they wouldn't have to hide to bring it across the border. But there are somethings that I agree on like the war on drugs which doesn't work very well when they take the money and use it for personal gain. Thursday morning and we got our first heavy snow through the night and the wind howeled like heck and it's still doing it. Now I will see how the car does in the stuff, later today when it warms up. It's going to test things as the day begins to unfold but at least we didn't have a black out with the power during the storm it droped snow from here to Nebraska' and I'm glad that I don t have to travel far for a while. Winter is finely here and the days could bring mighty cold winds again if they pick up, I told Randy that I would like to get a recker that way we could make some money. I couldn't believe how much they make when a storm hits two hundred and eighty dollars an hour just to pull someone out of a ditch or even more if they are really stuck, there are many ways to make money as long s you have the backing to purches what you need. I believe the farmers carry the weight of the bank and the community desides on things as a whole, I believe you should never get in over your head in debt but if you do then try your best to get out of it with dignity and go on with your life. As the bills pile up I have to get rid of some of the things I have they say everyone is I debt in the united states to the tune of at least ten thousand dollars as for me I'm not that far and I don't want to get that far but we still survive and go on with things the way they are. Back in the day I couldn't get any credit but now it's not a problem but managing it can get you in a bind if your not careful. I havent heard the train this morning but the day is young and no one is awake yet, not for an hour or so when they go off to work.

Things around here doesn't start poping until five or so and then you have those who work in Belleville that will have to dig them selves out before work or have their kids do it for them, that a good thing about kids they can do the grunt work for their parents and not mind it if they are the loving kind. Some might not even mind doing it' if they know saint Nick is coming with their most thought of gift. I can see the children in my mind opening their gifts with a big smile on their face on Christmas morning so excited when that day comes and I'm excited for them, it's too bad that one day they will break the spirit of Christmas like they have with so many other things and it makes me sad in my heart. The world is nothing like it used to be and it would be nice to travel back in time to when I used to open presents the joy I felt was out of this world and the world was right back then, at least in this childs eyes. The protection of our children is important not to let them see the things that goes on like war' I had never heard about it until I was in my twenty's and even then the impact wasn't bad until I got off the alcohol and drugs. When you are in that dark place you don't see the destruction war causees on the people who have to fight and then come back to a country that doesn't care and it's sad that 20% of the homeless are American Veterans that lost something in the war. The United States used chemicals war fair on their own people in other countries and then denied it for many years until it couldn't be ignored any longer and by then their lives were destroyed by not getting it treated, what kind of people do that to their own? I will tell you the ones that think money is more important then human life.

It's a shame that many of them had to turn to drugs and alcohol because the government didn't want to deal with the problem. Shame on you! Back to this first day of snow, I cant tell how much snow we got but I'm sure it's enough to get the road grader out to remove it from the streets. And then my car will get burried by the piles left by the side of the road no matter how I look at it I will have to work to get it free from the snow, I recall Norman diging me out many times and not charging me for it this showed the kindness in his heart and I'm glad that he is my friend' not because he done something for me mind you! But just because he has always been kind. A special spirit that you don't see very oftend, Doris is going through a ruff time and I pray that she will find peace which I think she has. She is also special, a calm soul. And if she likes you then in some way you you're self are special a glimps into your soul can change many things. Friday and they brought the Christmas baskets by after the snow as for me helping it wasn't possible because I cant get around to good with my legs being not to sturdy on the ice. So the grand daughter brought them I hate that my abilitys are limited by the damage but I will have to live with it, yesterday I got the car dougout and it worked just fine with no problems so it should be good to go during the winter. Through many days things start to change it seams to always be this way during Christmas maybe the change from one season as the snow will really pick up during the beginning of the new year, I'm in hope that I will finish some of the things I have started in the middle to the end of this year which has been good to me. Many years ago I would of never made it this far in learning new things but Courtland has changed that with the time I have on my hands and this winter I will have even more time to study, but all things don't stick in my mind like I would want them to. Just pits and pieces seam to stay the important parts I guess the ones that will bring change later on, I don't know why it is but through the years many things change my moods and well being even my out look on life but I seam to adjust to them and do just fine. I was called a fool by one of the people who are for the legalizing of pot but I wont take it to heart as many have been called the same thing it was about the smoke of pot getting into the lungs of a child but in my haste I worded it wrong, so now I will watch my words carefully. Some of the people are smart that use the stuff and they show it by mocking a person that shows a different opinion then them O well we live and learn in this world and we learn by mistakes we make along the way. Lord knows I have made my share of them but it's the learning that's important and my schooling hasn't allowed me the things I should have learned, the church was closed yesterday and I could tell that no one had been around there by the snow that was piled up by the back door so this morning I will go and dig it out it should be fun if it's not to cold out side. I have decided to not write about Marijuana for a time and see where it's taken, as for the people who find them selves in a fog they can find out what they need to by the internet. It seams I have been fighting this battle alone all these years so let someone else fight it for awhile.

I have to focus on my self for a time and I can only do one thing at a time, as this time of year brings doubt to my mind about certain things. And I have to work on them, in a way I'm stuck between two worlds but my focus is towards the better side of things. The good things that will bring me more piece then I have today it's like I go from one existence to another but never to the dark place where I once was where the really bad things happen, it's a quiet morning except for Randy coughing but soon he will be fast a sleep in a world that doesn't exist dreaming of things that he wont remember later. It's the beginning of another weekend an yesterday I read something that disturbed me. It was about a friend and I hope it isn't true but later I will find out our town is small and everything seams to come out at some point when it happens. I do know that some people are not what they seam kind on the out side but very different on the inside I have seen many people this way but it hasn't been around here just in the big cites where crime runs out of control. I know I said I wasn't going to get on the subject of pot for a time, but could people try to treat their children with this drug with out taking into account that it could hurt them? Many say it cures many things but does it really? Medical science doesn't have any proof that it cures anything but people are nieve and could take it upon them self to try and help their children that have become sick. Update on cure for school shootings by the N.R.A. Armed guards what a bunch of fools to even think that way, the problem is guns not more of them. It's the 21st of December and some feel the world will end on this day I have news for them it's not going to happen, anymore then Ventura is going to fall into the ocean.

That's Ventura Calif' they once said a bubble sit's off shore. And if it burst then the seaboard would take California, and sink it into the ocean. I was just a child when they told that story and what was said is that if it burst it would put all of California under the water that sits on it's shores now and a new beach front property would be Utah somewhere near the mountains. Us kids used to think it was an old wise tail but it's not and they have had many scientific studys on it, well it's Saturday and we are still here, it seams the world didn't end like so many believed. My thoughts on the subject is that change is coming a good change where things will get better not the end, but a new beginning and only time will tell what the change will be we will just have to wait and see. Later this morning I will go and make sure the church is ready for tomorrow, many people think that they need to be ready for something bad to happen but they have been doing that for quite some time even before my time on this earth and nothing has happened yet. Sometimes people let fear run their lives and that cant be a good thing but I my self have been there where frea came into my life but then left later and things still were ok' the mind is tricky and it can make you think some funny things, it's about the end to another week here in the heart land' and the mill is running down the road I heard it last night, as I was trying to go to sleep. I havent heard from any of the others from the church in the last week but we will get together tomorrow during church service and say our hellows. I havent got the time scedual for the Christmas celebrations at the church but I'm sure they will let me know when it is and then I can plan what ever, learning new things have become a part of me as I have learned that my life was no mistake. God used my life so many others could see that they weren't alone in this world, but we have to find our shape and our purpose. Other wise life will be a fighting battle and it wasn't meant to be, although I'm not sure how to go about teaching others in time it will come to me. Putting a square peg in a round hole doesn't work so we have to find the right fit, all the knowledge is there I just have to figure out how to present it with confidence, for that's my mission in this life he has given back to me. Sunday and only two days until Christmas. I'm going to practice a little on my song this morning with Kathy before she goes to Scandia to preach that way it will give me a better idea of how things will go, and I hope it goes well so God can enjoy the song. As for sleeping I was up at 1:00 Am and for the life of me I couldn't get back too sleep so this is going to make for a long day but hey you can only sleep so long right? As I read the news paper they are wanting to put police at every school across the United States to stop that kind of killing from ever happening again. My land' what is the world coming to? But I know the kids have to be protected and if that's what it takes then it will be on their sholders, more guns then less before to long it's going to be a battle field. I have had many opinions on things and have voiced my opinion on those things and in some areas change took place, I'm still reminded of the old women that said it does no good to voice your opinion but O how wrong she was, I never did see her again after I moved away but I'm sure she has gone to be with the lord she was mighty old back then maybe in her 80's or even older.

Many of the people I used to know have gone from this world even the young ones that only lived to be in their 30's or even younger taken by things like cancer or drug addiction even kids just brely in their teens have left this world because of alcohol or drugs such a great loss to their parents and them selves. I did learn that if someone is bent on leaving this world they will find a way no matter what it takes like Michal when he was only 24, he thought he wanted to be with his parents but did he really or was he looking for help the kind he couldn't get from people close to him. Before I was even born God knew I would go through the things I did and from what I read it was supposed to get my journey ready for helping others who have gone through the same thing, my mission in life is to save lives if they will listen. Taken from the gates of hell to come back and save lives what a legacy to leave behind a record of the good and bad things that have happened and how the father brought me through it all, making me the one who survived to tell the story of life and how you can survive in a world you don't understand at first. All problems that existed before my bithday on that year when I died were nothing because I didn't learn how to deal with them untill only after my 33 birthday and now I'm writing about my life what could be more important then to leave something behind to hopfully change things in others lives. My land' I didn't know I had this gift to write until I was in my 40's and O how he made it possible to teach me so many new things, the lost soul had found something he was good at and when I write I feel like I'm in my element my little part of the world where no one buds into my world.

Through the years I have found many things I'm good at and in time things will come together like it is written in my book of life. He wrote the book before my coming here and it cant be changed for anything, he even knows what I'm doing right now trying to capture what must be written, I have lived in many places but Courtland is the best by far no pressure is ever put on you except for what you put on your self life is supposed to be joyfull but we make mistakes and then have to correct them in many different ways and sometime that can bee the hardest thing to do, to say your sorry for what others had to go through even if they are gone from this world you have to make a mends in your mind and never go back wards in your journey back into something that wasn't good for you because that slope can be slippery and you could end up on your butt. Trying again to repair the damage that had taken place, all the twelve deciples had a problem that they carried with them one easy to anger the other very depressed but He used them to point out something. No matter what the problem God can help you with it, and can bring you from the pit even to a life that you will learn to enjoy. As for the problems that once plaged me they are faiding and are getting harder to remember as time passes like a shaddow that sinks out of sight to only show it's self once in a while so you can remember to stay on track. There are many things which come to me that I don't recall and it's strange sometimes when I try to put them together, a flash of a memory or just the sight of something I thought I had seen before. I remember after dad passed I thought I had seen him afterwards a man in a store and then he was gone, maybe to check on how I was doing or just seeing for him self that I was ok' the unknown is just that the unknown and I wonder what it would be like to communicate with them not this guy though. Our minds are limited by what we hear and see during our lives and in some cases we can imagine some strange things like my dad that time. Brought back by a memory of something that happened long ago but in the end you know it shouldn't be possible to see them because most people are programmed to not believe in such things. Today I got to sing in church and one women told me that it was really nice and she thanked me such a good feeling to know they enjoyed it, this is something I do once a year for Christmas and the rest of the time it's done in my home. Christmas Eve' and it's going to e a good day the trees are trimed for the children and their presents are hanging on each limb, we got them gloves this year just something to let them know that people care about them. I know it's hard to ge locked up when the Christmas season is here' been there and done that, I recall being put in the youth development center in Kearney Nebraska and it was a hard time in life not being around my parents. Although it gave me something it also took something away, there were kids from across the state and from every walk of life that found them selves in trouble with the law and was sent there to be rehabilitated so they could go back into society and try again to become a good person. My crime was shooting a sign be acccident but still I shouldn't of been in a park hunting squirrles, it was the first and last time I ever shot a gun. My friend told on me so he would get off the charges but today I don't hold it against him as life didn't treat him to good plus I was taught to forgive those who done me wrong, and you cant move forward until you have mastered this gift that God has given to us all. In singing yesterday I was really nervous and I almost triped when I came off stage but that goes with the being the center of attention and it will get better as the year passes.

Over coming your fears is a hard thing to do but He stands by us incase we fall and I noticed he didn't let me fall when I could have my God is always there for me even through the darkest times but I felt like I did a good job with the song not being prepaired for it. They will have a service to night at 11:00 Pm but it's not my time of the night to be up as usually I'm sleeping but we will see what happens when the time comes most of the people will be going out of town for Christmas, as for us we will stay home and it will be like the days before. Later this morning I will go and clean the church so it will be ready for to night it's always important to keep God's house clean as I surely wouldn't want him to come and see it dirty, you never know when the day will come right? As each year passes I seam to feel better about being apart of the community and if I can bring some joy to others and God then it's my pleasure to do it, as for being bashful it's still there but in time it will be a thing of the past and then my spirit will glide through this place I now call home. When they play the music it doesn't seam to be perfect but then either are we but with practice it could come together and be beautiful, all my friends clapped when I was done and that made me feel good inside who knows maybe one day I might get everything right and then they will really see the talent that I have it's still in the trial stages right now. But with each passing year it gets better and that's something to be proud of I know they knew I was nervous as I felt it deep inside when the sweat came.

All He expects us to do is to try our best and if we do that then things will be ok' even his developing of us takes time and it's something that cant be rushed, He will never give up on us so we should never give up on him to make us what we were created to be, even though we don't know what was witten in the book of life it's something good and before we leave this place we will see the finished product and we will be strong in what He creates a master piece formed by the hand of the all mighty God and it will be good. My land' the time seaams to fly as we are getting closer to the coming year, what will it hold for us? More destruction or a better life then the year before it who really knows. Like I said before the twelve deciples had many problems but as they stood strong by jesus they over came many of them, from depression to over coming anger and shyness of one or more of them. Moses had Aron to stand by him because he couldn't talk with out having a problem with it but in time that became a thing of the past, sometimes we need others to lend a helping hand when things are new to us because we havent developed that part of our lives. But with the Father and his son there are many things that can bring us to a new level, and create a new us you can have all the money you want and not be happy as I have seen so many times with rich people that have taken their own lives, they had everything but what was needed and that's peace within your self. People who need drugs to speak to others or carry on a profeshion don't really see the whole picture the shyness that is within us all can be over came with the help of the father but you have to have a mind set like when I sing you have to shut out the feeling of not being good enough, and focus on what you can do. It took years for me to do this and even then I didn't know if it was possible, but it was. We all have limits that we carry with us but to over come those limits is a great stride I can do things that others cant even think of doing because they have a block in their minds that wont let them go there, with age comes many things and one of them is to swallow your pride and move forward into that place which is unknown to you. Could I have done this at a younger age?

Probably not' but that isn't the point younger people look up to the elders and if you do things right then they havent made a mistake and you have helped them in what ever way. Public speeking is something that can help kids and the closer I get to being able to do that the stronger I too will become. As for having the answers to many things I don't know them all, but I can still learn as I move forward and master the thing I choose to take on. I like to think of my self as being modest' and I feel uncomfortable when praise or anything like that is shown because it was never shown before so that's something I will also have to work on in the future but for now things will be the same. Shyness isn't a bad thing but it can hold you back when you want to move forward so you need to find your way through that part of life and sadly it took over half my life to get just a little ways, when I'm passionate about something I don't want to stop talking about it.

Like with kids who feel out of place, they will try drugs to just fit in because they feel out of place and this is so sad when this happens. And before long they are lost in that world of darkness and it becomes their home like with the alcoholic who stays inside their homes all the time and goes out just long enough to get the booze they need. With many of them they have a spouce so they can bring in the money for the alcoholic to then teach their kids to be the same, it's something that's learned by kids because mom and dad has raised them up that way maybe not knowing that their kids will take on the life they will one day leave behind to become afraid of the world and loose in the long run. Christmas morning' and it's another cold morning. After cleaning the church yesterday I had to go and have Teabo's come and fix the furnace so they wouldn't be cold during service last night otherwise it would have been freezing in there and we cant have that. My letter was to spread the joy of Christmas to everyone on this special day that christ was born to maybe let the kids see that times were ruff back when some of us were children also and that things will get better, as for on this day a child was born one that would save the world later in his life. It's quiet this morning and nothing is sturring not even the mouse that visits once in a great while, we only have the snow that fell a couple of days ago but it's snow just the same so our white Christmas was given. It's a new time of year that only comes once in the 365 days but it's peaceful just like the people who live here, nothing of violence happens except for the family squabbles which sometimes gets out of hand but with some that's expected my self I never did like that kind of relationship maybe because it hurt others feelings and my own born to be sensitive to hurt.

And it's not nice' I don't know why I was created that way but I was, maybe so I could be different or to just understand the feelings of others. Life is like a roller coaster some days up' and then somedays down not knowing which day will be your good ones but through it all He is there right beside you to lend a helping hand. The joy that He brings with him is for us all not just one person, I see in some that they carry a peacefullness within them a joy almost knowing that He is there in times of trouble and that's a good thing but so many don't know that joy the joy of knowing that he will take care of things when times get too tough. This I believe is when a person can give their who being to God and Jesus and I hope to one day feel this but I have defences that take over sometimes and that's because of the life I once lead, refocusing your existence is hard but if you have faith then He will show you the way into a beautiful new existence one free from the ties that once binded you. People don't know what's inside of this soul they only know that He resides somewhere in this vessel teaching me new ways to bring out His goodness for His love towers over us all like a tent to keep us safe from harm. Many will be traveling on this day so I wish them a safe trip to make it home to their loved ones, soon the little ones will be sneeking out of bed to open their presents and I can see the excitement in their faces as they get the gift they wanted all year, but I can also see the little one who didn't get anything as the tears run down their face, but maybe my letter gave them a glimmer of hope and that enough for this guy on Christmas, just the knowing that it touched some people makes my writing more important then ever any thing that causes a good reaction is good. Peace to the world and all who reside in it, many times you can see or since when a child is withdrawn from others locked away in their own little world where they feel safe and breaking away from that is hard for them especially if they have lost someone close to them like a parent, to only be shipped off to someone they don't really know like a relative, and the damage can take a long time to heal if it ever heals at all. When kids have mental problems or any other problem they can be mislead to the world where they can hide and sadly the drug and alcohol world is a great place for such hiding, burried in the darkness of a world that doesn't help them at all. I learned something today that rabbits eat their own droppings because they cant digest it the first time around and some call them popsicles strang but it's true, I don't know why I put that in there but it's cute maybe learning about God's creachers is important. Kids that are taken out of their original home because of alcohol or drug abuse have a hard time trusting others and maybe it's because of the trama they suffer from the departing from their birth parents. But they never seam to be the same once it happens. Wednesday and Christmas is over I don't know why but it dosent have the family feeling like it did when you're a child when things would get exciting' when you woke up on Christmas morning maybe the thought of getting older makes you loose something in the years. The excitement I once felt when I was a child is gone but I know Christmas is more then getting giftss and things, it's the day christ was born and was brought to us through the father. Let us not forget Mary the one who carried him those nine months for her love for God was great, and her husbands love must have been also great.

Maybe I don't see the whole picture but I'm getting a glimps of how it must have been for them, I think the thirty years was a separation from his brothers and sisters to get him ready for what was going to happen next. For Jesus him self was God in body form I think he had to come here through Mary to be made human so he could understand what we felt. Just my opinion and we all have one, during the learning period God taught him what he needed to know to take on our sins upon him self so we could live. It's the middle of the week and the day is going to be a good one, I think Randy missed getting presents for others but things are tight right now maybe things will improve during this next year all we can do is weight and see. As for winter it's hitting all across the United States and even tornados are poping up in other states Texas and other places around there a mix of snow and here in the heartland but worst weather the further south you go as for our little town it's nice and safe and the worst thing would be to get snowed in with no heat. But that hasn't been a problem since my time here and life goes on, the thrift store is still closed but will open next month and if anyone needs something from there they can call Beverly she would be glad to open it for their needs such a nice women as they all are around here, my story was to help bring some healing to those who have lost someone during the last year as for me I think it helped in some small way. I know looseing pops was a heartache and still I miss him today but my feelings are kept secret only talking about them with Randy from time to time.

It seams He puts others in our lives to help deal with the loss of those who go before us that way we can become close. Still today I look on the internet for word from my father but there is none, could this be a sign that he doesn't know? For surely' if he knew my name then he woul of seen my articals through out the internet mybe he doesn't exist but why would she say so if it wasn't true that's not her personality. For some reason she wante me to know about him but why? I could have been content just thinking Herb was my dad it's all a mystery to me even 48 years later. I might have to come to turms that I might never find him and I know I will be able to go on I know who I am a child of God but why is some things complicated? Through the years I guess I had always wanted to find him but life can go on even with a hole inside you and in time it will be filled Hopely by God, my show is supposed to be on this morning so we will see at 4:00 this morning if it happens. My day is all planed out by the time most people get out of bed but change happen sometimes as the day goes on you can never fully tell what will happen, as for little brother he is sleeping well sawing logs as he is in that sleeping world. Supprise my arm isn't hurting this morning like yesterday and that is a very good thing although it pops every now and then. I never could figure out why it does that because it happens out of the blue just a constent ache that can hurt like hell, but these bones have been through a lot over the years and maybe they are mad at me for putting them through what I did. Next week will be January the start of a new year will I survive through the year it's very possible and I hope I'm here next Christmas the lord willing. Our bodies are resilient for what they go through always bouncing back from destruction. Second day after Christmas, yesterday I got the church cleaned and found one of our sisters purses so I called the husband and he came over and got it with a thanks you. I always like going to work as it lest me be closer to God in some way, I'm there more then I need be but it' always nice to make sure everything is in order plus it feels like my home for somee reason. Like my home here where He is when ever I need to talk to Him for surely God is good, as the year comes upon us many things will change and for many we don't have a clue what that will be. But we do know that we will become closer to Jesus as day turns into night and our calender keeps going, we were in the year when this one ends and we will be in the beginning of the new one and many joys and sorrows will come our way. Maybe not in the form of loss but hopefully in the form of joy, a time to clean our closets you might say and get rid of the garbage we have carried in the past. To bring in new things a better out look on life or just maybe bring in someone close to us a new soul to share life with, you never know what He has in store for us one thing I will give more effort to is reading the bible so I can understand more then I do on this day. The expansion of the mind is a good thing always keeping it informad about our past lets us in some way become better informed about what they went through, but my life here and now is also important and the miles I have traveled to get here. For each day is a gift and I notice that many don't realize this fact, I cant see getting up each day to just look forward to going back to bed it limits your ability to do things and when that happens then it's a waste of time.

In a while I will have to stip the floors so they will be ready for this new year but the tile is old and pulling up in the bathroom for the men, I might clean them too oftend because they were ok' before I started but also everything ages and they are no different it would be nice to have something with a pattern in it to make it look swanky, this next year I would like to paint the bell and the stand it sits on. I don't know if it has a purpose or not but it would look good silver and white with a gray platform, so many would admire it and it would really stand out like a marker. As the year comes upon us some will leave us but we will always remember them by their smiles and quarkey ways, the one thing that made them different from us will be the thing we will remember about them. Even with the hard times I seam to make it and enjoy life here for the most part but I have to ask His for more peace of mind, for the things I don't understand disturb me at times making me think that I'm less then I should be. But I know that in time more wisdom will be given to me as I go through this life, in this new year coming up I will finish my two books I have started and expand my knowledge about the christen life and fade away from the evil world as I know it. It seams that what I read for some reason is put into my life if only a little bit at a time, like change is taking place and that's what many say happens when you go from the old ways to the new. A rebirth of a soul can take a while but He seams to be able to do it without us really knowing it, I believe they call it a transformation like the butterfly going from a caterpillar to this beautiful insect that fludders around in the sky with such beautiful colors. We are like that at times turning into our selves, introverted is the word they use when a person retreats back into them selves so they are not attacked by their enemys, like the turtle who pops back in it's shell when something tries to eat them.

A protected space where no one else can go, I was like that most of my life but now I have my head out to check things out. I tried this once before but was sent back because of others that attacked me and it's hard to try it again but I did and so far things are ok' sometimes it's like they push you back there because they are afraid of you or don't understand what you're all about a threat you might say to their way of thinking far from me to criticize what they think or feel but the same respect should be shown to us all as we are all unique and special one of a kind. When He created us each one of us He broke the mold so no one could be like the other, variety is what He was creating but what He had in mind is unattainable to our simple minds. They say in the garden before he sined with Eve that he was without sin, and then sin was let in but to correct that problem He had to have someone without sin to correct it. So Jesus was born through a birth without sin because sex as we know it is sin, then when he was born a sign of his birth was given to the wisemen so they could witness this miracle that had taken place. Thus Jesus was born, we all have our own opinions on how things happened and we can share those if we havent read the bible all the way, this gives us a look into what we know by things which have come to us over the years. A test maybe to see how we process things. Could he of had two forms one before coming here which was a priest of the most high God or was Melchisedek a souls that resided here from the beginning, very confusing but the mind can make it's own rational thing out of anything. Jesus was made a priest after the order of Melchisedek meaning he was the top guy in the beginning of the bible and he had to of been created by God, but then like Jesus he disappeared for a long time with no record of anything sort of like the life of Jesus for all those years when He vanished, did he wonder in the wilderness or was he sent away to a school weight a minute how did schools start? Was He taught by God or humans this is a question I would like to know, as I know for a fact that God can teach us He is the only one who taught me. How can we explain a miracle? Most can't. but still they happen, in my passing I recall looking down and seeing the world and people squabbling over things that don't make since like it was a waste of time and they had better things they could be doing. Was this a sign that I shouldn't do the same thing? And if so, maybe that's why I'm still alone, because those things are absent from my life. The fighting and argueing that doesn't do anyone any good, and why am I drawn to helping others for surely it wasn't anything I used to do way back when. The transformation we go through is hard to see for us, but can others see this thing unfold? Does He give others a look into the changing of things like character? And if so then why don't we see it in ourselves? Could this be where the saying comes from I can't see the forest from the trees? Others can see it but for some reason we can't why is this could it be that we are blind to our own progress.

I find it hard to talk about such things and try to make since out of it but in the coming years these things might come to me, every new thing that is put into our minds is a seed and in time if things are right then that seed starts to grow so now that it's planted we will see what happens. Many words come to me from Him' and sometimes that surprise me because they seam to fit just right in some things that I write about, a helping hand you might say, from the one who loves me. It's been a great day and I even got the heater fixed on my car so we don't freeze all good things in good time. Friday today is my sons birthday and I bet he thinks I forgot about it, but I didn't. many think birthdays are something to not forget but mine has never been remembered by my kids, and I notice that it's the parents that make a big thing out of them and not the kids I never had anyone remember mine except for my family at church and they sing it which is awesome. Through the years that part has become something I don't forget and maybe it's because I have made it further then expected. My life has changed so much and it's scary sometimes but I know that my church family is also very important to me for without them I might be somewhere else like the people you see on television who sleep in a box. Methamphetamine is on the rise now in the big cities and I know there will be some kind of war over it, as kids keep getting hooked on it the body cant take that crap and it destroys many childrens lives and in the end they will suffer from this curse. The curse of addiction for which there are many forms.

People from around the globe will become hooked on the curse the ones with no since anyway Rosa-lee said she enjoyed my article in the paper about Marijuana and that brought back memories of a time when I needed a friend she seamed to always be there when I needed an ear to listen and that helped in a troubling time, as for the day it's going to be another nice one and I hope it gets warm again. Even 20 degrees feels like a heat wave at this time of year, it's still early and little brother was up when I got coffee unusual for him, but it does happen. As I look at some of the things I have written in the past I notice that He is mentioned in each one it's like a magnet His words' as I think about them each day. For things are changing and I can feel it in a strange kind of way something inside is changing course and it brings with it a kind of peace. My serving God is my way of feeling like my life has a purpose, a feeling inside that prevalent to me and it doesn't matter what others think. For the gift He gave me I give the gift of serving back to Him even though it can be strenuous at times, my journey will continue through the years of my life until I'm old and gray well the gray part is already here but you know what I mean. Saturday and the Methamphetamine problem is on the rise it's something that should be addressed so it can be taken care of, now they are bringing it into the cities and before you know it things will get really bad. You never know when the curse is going to hit a new place and now that they have opened that box I feel like it will spread like wild fire. Making Marijuana legal hs started something and like with the women it took very few to get it into a bill that States can pass Tuesday will be the first and many will somke their dope during this time but when something is made legal like pot there is always ramifications and the price I feel will be high. Sure they will try to regulate it like liquor but even with that they have never had any solid resoults of kids getting it, they will start out by saying you have to be 21 to possess it then they will later take it to court to have that age limit droped to 18 because if you can fight in a war then you should be able to smoke it, although it didn't work with alcohol it could very well be tried. I recall when I moved to Nebraska the age limit there was 18 years of age maybe because the problem wasn't felt as hard in small towns and the beer was only 3.2% which was very low for back then, my self I walked into a bar for the first time at the age of 15 years and no one questioned my age but boy that's when the trouble started. My mind wasnty fully developed or even close to being mature so with alcohol in the mix you do some foolish things, I was the one who thought they never got into trouble but then later I found out that even though you don't do things like steal just being around people that do can have the same effect. Guilt by association, and them being my brothers put into the mix by them bringing the crap around our home. And I know it had to of been really hard on our parents, kids can really mess things up when they get out of control and Rick was always going for what he thought was the free dollar. Then as he sat in prison he got bitter and when he would get back out the same thing would start again. Putting him right back in, the alcohol and drugs ruined his and others lives I would hate to imaging if drugs were legal back then for surely the gangsters would of killed him. Some grow up to think that the world owes them a living, and many think that way, but time is usually short for them as they make people mad at them.

I remember a guy that came to our house one time and for some reason he wanted to talk to someone I knew, it was the first time I thought someone was going to die. And now that I look at it from a different prespective it reminded me of a story in the bible of Sodom and gamora' the town which was evil, as the guy talked with this person he saw that he had no remorse for what he had done but then I stepped in and for some reason I explained how the person was not in their right mind and couldn't comprehend what he was saying. Then the guy asked if I understood what he was talking about and I said yes an then he left, it was a strange thing that had never happened before or since for surely if he would have been alone he would have been killed, these are things I don't like to talk about because they disturb me in many ways. So many close calls in a world he didn't understand and even today the damage is still there with this person but the alcohol and drugs are gone. I believe we are tested sometime to see if we have become more patient and in many ways I have but still that nitch hits me once in a while, but with what I have learned I seam to be able to stop it or hold it back until it passes and then it's gone. Yesterday was nice and I hope today is the same I find my self wondering a lot more about things, but I know in the end He is always beside me to guide me in most of the things I do. But stll mistakes are made to be corrected so we can move forward and try to find that peacefulness which resides in us all, will we ever see that greatness in this world? I sometime wonder' it's another day Sunday to be exact and it's cold once again.

Many things happen in our lves that we don't quite remember but by some Godley force we are brought together with them once again and with many of them they are written down. Our testimony is something that we are supposed to share with others to help them in some way, maybe they had something happen which they havent been able to talk about. Pastors and such are trained to help others with their problems so the person knows they are trained, but if you get a person that tells their life story then they will except most of what's told it's the honet part of life in which God has helped you through. Like with my demise so long ago, I never did think I would still be here thinking back to that time and remembering that it was all I could do to pull my self up in he walk way of my home each time took the breath out of me so hard at the time but today it would be nothing because I have gained so much strength. With each pull up I had God beside me telling me that I could do it and in time I believed it my self which helped in my recovery, before that I was called scooter as the only use I had of anything was my arms to pull me across the floor, and I'm glad that I had a good friend that helped me at times when I really needed him. I would scoot in the kitchen so he could wash my hair but standing up was very hard and he had to stand behind me so I wouldn't fall, if anyone saw me they would of thought I was close to death but through the careing of this fiend I was able to become strong again later in life. I believe that God didn't want my leving to become reality and He helped me in many ways, the reason for the mind to not remember was the damage that was done the doctor said when I talked my eyes were all over the place. Not making the connection that most people have it was like tying to do two things at once, but my eyes didn't correspond with my brain. Through it all my life has come very far and maybe that's in part by my not wanting to give up, I'm not like any one else and my story will be told so others might not give up on their lives also. It seams that drive to survive is within me but many things still come hard, a great lesson learned is that in life' we all want to live for ever. Yesterday is gone but today is a great day, we are allowed to share part of our life with others who also love God and in doing that we build a new family one that we never knew before but with their open hearts they except us with our faults. Our lives never turn out the way we except, because what our life is supposed to be only God knows He is the one who set in motion what will become of us. And this was done way before our birth in a place we call heaven, just like with Jesus his life was planed out. And it was set in stone about his comeing and his death to save this world from destruction, through the years each step has brought me closer to God in one way or another and for that I am very glad. The miracles that happened in my life were done so I would know that there is a God who takes care of his own, later I will go and open the church so we are all can be warm later, as for this day we will see what takes place. Again today I felt something changing but for the life of me I cant putmy finger on it. It was like I had known that Jesus was 33 when he died on the cross and the pastor just confermed it, why for so long did I think He was 30? Probably because that's what others tried to tell me.

It only makes since He was 12' when He went to His fathers house to listen to the teachers and learn the knowledge He needed to know. But now days that kind of teaching isn't around that I know of, what will it be like when He returns? Will there be a sing in the writings that are all around the world like the opening of a book a new book that will teach some what they need to know? The changes that take place in my life are strange and sometimes far from my understanding, but in time it will come to me when I need it most. Doris is very ill and hospice has started to visit her the cancer has made her real ill and the therapy hasn't done any good except to make her sicker then if she didn't take it. She was one of the people that showed me kindness when I came here and I will remembered her for a long time to come, I have been told that she is a women of God and I can see it each time we meet. There is a calmness about her that you don't see in many folks, but there are others that seam to have a certain peacefulness about their lives and maybe it's that they are at peace with the lord' some would say God works in us all differently and I believe He does because all of us are different in many ways and we don't all need the same thing. Through the time when things don't go right we seam to find our way to the place we need to be, I would like to see her again before her time is up and she goes to be with the father but with these things you have to be careful not to upset anyone. Upset the balance of things which are to come, the beginning of another week and I pray like I try to do each morning as life is given it is also taken away when our bodys give out but our soul lives on to travel to that place we call heaven such a comforting thought that we will still travel to one more distanation.

Could I have learned more if I would have been brought up knowing the father better? I think if you re brought up to love him and find that peace early on then your life can be more fullfiled but being I was older I choose the path I take now and I have to find my own way through this world. When Jesus was on the cross He was saying I love you this much with his arms spread out I have learned that our life story is what He wants us to let others see how he came into our lives and changed us as people. I have seen others who have changed their lives and for some reason they feel that many should feel the same way they do, but in this life none of us are the same. We all travel a different path and no one walks the same footprints it's just not logical, when Jesus left the boat that time he left his footprints in the sand for others to follow. Now weather they follow them is up to them, Randy is very sick this morning and I know it's that flue I just hope he doesn't give it to me because I can't afford to be sick at this time I prayed that He would not let me get it so I believe I'm covered. Illness isn't a thing that any of us care for and I pray for a good day without the sickness. In hope that I never get sick for the next few months anyway. It's New Years Eve and everyone will be celebrating to night I pray for their well being as a lot of them will be getting drunk, also thank you lord as the little ones will be in their beds away from seeing the foolishness that parents will go through to fit in or be a part of the crowd. Tuesday morning and the roads are blanketed with snow I'm hoping that I can get out to take the trash to the curb so they can pick it up. But we will see, here in a few hours. Most of the time the roads are clear but this is our first snow that we didn't expect or at leat I didn't expect and it can be a pain when you have to dig your self out with no help to speak of. I drove to the bar yesterday to get something and it was bad, but the good news is that I made it home without a problem and then the road grader came by and probably burried my car, it's now 2013 a new year' and the first day. And I'm sure many were out on the town in the big cities, as for here I don't know because I have never been to one of their parties, if they have one at all but I'm sure they do celebrate in some way. I have always seen that time of year from the dark side and have never paid attention to those who might not drink, it's been years since I paid any attention to the celebration of a new year. While on the computer the other day someone asked my daughter something about going out and she said never again not after what happened last time when she felt like she was going to die and spent a day in the hospital. It's sad that things like hat happen but it happened with my parents once and they ended up hiting a tree, people don't realize that others can be hurt when they do something like that or they just don't care. I shoveled off the walkway last night but I'm sure it's full again from the falling snow, one disadvantage from getting up early is no one will help dig you out because they are all still a sleep all warm in their beds. Living out in the country you better hope that you don't need any emergency care during a snow storm because you will have a hard time getting to the hospital and even if you somehow get there it will take hours.

I'm hoping for a nice day with no wind that way it wont be so bad when digging out the car, yesterday the cold was a dry cold and I could stay out in it for a few minutes, I don't like it when it cuts you to the bone because in just a few seconds can really get colder then heck. But I do have fun times out in the snow on a warm day and even play in it sometimes, Wednesday and yesterday wasn't bad as far as going out in the snow I started around five in the morning and was done by eleven or so taking the needed breaks inbetween to stay warm, also dug out the doorway at the church so I could bring the bag down here for the garbage truck to pick up with my trash. As for the car it did good in the snow better then I thought it would and I had no problems I'm just glad that they put new tires on the car before I bought it, it seam's I have the things I need to suvive here and the heat in the car is also now working fine. I did notice that it uses a little more fuel during winter but that's to be expected with warm-ups and all, but it was strange how I almost looked forward to going out side and diging snow. And later it will be back to work as usual doing what I do best cleaning, strange how I came here and ended up with that job but I know we all have to start somewhere in serving the lord and my job started when anothers stopped. Everything is ready when Sunday morning comes and the people don't complain, why should they I do a great job with what the lord has put in front of me. One day I will ask to paint inside the church to make some extra money so I will have some on hand for emergencies this just barely getting by is a pain in the butt with nothing to fall back on.

People know that the job situation around here isn't the greatest but I think I have proved my self to be worthy of a chance to help out in many ways. When dad died I thought I would have to move and then the church opened it's heart to keep me on, this I believe was the lords doing as pastor Kathy said they know how much I love God. My fear of singing has all but faded since I came here, and it's not very hard to do it these days especially when people come-up to you and say how much they liked it. Many people have a bucket list a writing down of things they want to do before they leave this world and singing can now be marked off of mine, as for the other things they will come to me later maybe in a dream or just pop into my mind like public speaking that would be a great accomplishment but I also know that this step will take time because I have to get it right in my mind. The thing I find most hard is that I could mess up, but I also know that He would step in and make sure I didn't fall on my face, limatations are set by our own mind and once we get past that first step then things can unfold. I remember when I first went to church the doubts I had that I wouldn't fit in were there just as plain as the nose on my face but then as time moved forward the doubts went away and were replaced by hope, it was like a journey into another world one where others would except the differences we all had. The most hardest thing was to break the barrier of self doubt and then to be able to move forward, not knowing if things would turn out the way you thought they should be but I think that where faith comes in the knowing that He is there the one you can't see. As for talking to Him. I have done that, but it's not like me talking to you it's more mental like a communication without words of mouth. Using only you're mind, even in the light there was no words only the mental communication but it was stronger there all the pain I felt back then was gone. To only return when I did it's hard to explain what happened back then but it made me not to want to leave, I guess in a way I knew that coming back was not going to be easy and I lived in fear for quite some time along with the pain that is still there. A reminder of what will happen if that road was taken again, today I wonder what relationship would be like after it's absents from my life. But if it would be like the last one then I'm better off without it, my expectations might be too high of waking up with someone who compleets your life, and then going through the day after a nice kiss good morning. In my being with other women I cant say for sure if it was love but then again it's been so long since that time, it could have been. To the young man that was lost. Trying to hold onto something that was attainable. I got a letter from someone today on my-space and his name was John I don't know for sure what it pertains to but I should find out when he writes me again, so many times I have been written to about deals of this or that but I never took them serious. This guy I don't know from the pope so we will see what takes place later this week, I sure could use some help at this time in my life but I would never do anything illegal. Thursday there is a place that might need some help so I will check on it later, you never know if it's a blessing when things like this come up but it's worth checking in to. The bad thing about living in a small town is that others have a hard time driving here to work, unless they live here because of the storms. we have to have dependable car no matter what so we can get around when need be, but this job would be just down the block right next to the church.

Will I be able to carry that big of a load I really can say at this time our church sold them the property so they could build the telephone company and it's no more then fifty feet away from where I work now. In my travels I have never found anything that has fallen into my lap you might say, and I wouldn't have to travel to work. Through my time in living here many more people have come to know me by my writings in the paper and they have to see that I'm a worthy person a person who does what he says he will do, for my word is my bond in this life and I have been able to keep it no matter what. Randy is getting better as the week goes by and I hope he is fully well by the end of this week so life can be good for him again, there is still so much I don't know about his condition but I have faith that things will turn around for him and that I don't get sick like he has been the last week. Payday is today and the bills will be going out this afternoon, then I can be grumpy about how we will make it through the month on a little to nothing that when the food comes in from the places that help people like me, and I'm glad that they do these things because you cant make it on your own on what you make. I guess we are meant to live with just getting by but it would be nice if a change would come, something to change everything so there wouldn't be so much stress in my life but that's for the ones who have become rich even though it doesn't bring happiness it does make life easier. I have finished my book that I was reading 'purpose driven' and it didn't take hat long to read the second time around and now I will go on to finish the book that Mark gave me the 'power of life bible' which should shed some more light on things I need to know.

It seams the only books I like are ones of inspration the ones that tell a story about life in general the lives of those who have gone before us. Like the brothers who sold their sibling into slavery Joseph was his name I believe, and although they were sorry for what they had done Joseph knew it was God's will that this thing happened to him. And he became a king of the land, trying to put things together that happened to him with my life isn't that hard, as the same thing happened so long ago but as time permitted they became a thing of the past. It's Friday and Randy was up before me I don't know why he is going through this stage but atleast he feels better then the last few days. In some ways It's like he is on another planet but he seams to be ok' with it sowing some things which need sowing, the mill is running down the street and the augers are going full force as you can hear them grind things or take the crops to where they need to be in the bin's I'm really not used to having him up this early but hey! I do the same thing each day out of habbit or training making me one person that is special. The two news papers have been on the ball publishing my work and I had complaments on what others have read even Valerie said I was doing a good job an she is one person that I know who smokes pot almost everyday saying it's a part of her . This is what happens when it's smoked from childhood, you get so attached to It that life or things are not the same without it. It has a calming effect to people who use it and without it they are a different person real bitchy for one thing and you can hardly be around them. They seam to reflect the way they feel onto others like with alcohol but only until they get what they need and then the world is hunky dorie, Randy said he feels great this morning and I'm glad that he is over the flue the wonders of antibiotics they seam to chase the bug away when it comes but I know that it will return again later this winter, it seams to come twice a year and then vanishes like the wind. As we were talking the other day he said again he couldn't live by him self because of his not being able to read, I already showed him that he can take his own med's but he has to do it at a certain time each day and not when he get's out of bed. The things he is taught now will last him for some time to come because in reality we never know how much time we really have, when I fist moved here I slept on the couch for a year or so and I remember the pain in my legs was out of this world, and I would pray to God, for him to take it away which He did' but times where tough back then not knowing anyone and afraid to ask for help but then the pastor took me to get a bed and after that things seamed to start looking up. I was afraid of my own shaddow back then but now I'm not afraid of anything. And the people who helped me became my friends and they are still my friends today. Nothing like the people I used to know who were drugged up all the time but good friends the kind you would take home to your mother, do we really fully understand life? I guess each person has their own idea of what life is all about, but in the end. We are many and do our best to live the way he wants us to live, my journey how ever long will allow me to do the things I never dreamed of before and my singing is a part of that dream.

And I have as big of an audience as I dare to have at each step, it's the way of a small town and part of why kids do so well in a small town setting. Each year I see kids growin up and taking on things like music, sharing what they learn, at the church. And they will grow into productive people later in life, I know that they told me six months was all I could expect if I would have stopped drinking, but even then I couldn't stop. Not until I took it all the way to deaths door, in the light is when things changed when I was told that my mission hadn't even started yet. It's hard to recall all of what was said to me, but I knew the power that it came from was much greater then I. I know the doctors were amazed when I returned but it had nothing to do with them bringing me back, I can't go there quite yet. Something inside stop's me from visiting that place. When I have lost family and friends in the past it was like an influx of feeling came over me and the tears couldn't help but fall, to then later turn into a feeling of hardness that would last for a long time and even exist today. It was like a wall went up to protect me from those feelings coming back, I don't know why but it's hard to write during the day when I'm distracted by the things that go on. Saturday and the mill is runing again but it's very loude for some reason it almost sound's like the train wheels of a train against the tracks and now it gone, so maybe it was cant tell without seeing out side. Yesterday Robert was at the Bank and said hi along with Mark he is the one I would really like to try and work for but again only time will tell if that will take place, the church is fine as I checked on it yesterday while I was out payinng bills, I have met many people who run up bills and then not pay for them and I cant see how they can do such a thing because my mind would haunt me for like ever.

My mind has been shaped to take care of such things even if I have to go with out in some things, yesterday was a very cold day and the ice hung off the car along with the trees being pure white from the frost on the branches, it was a beautiful sight with the country side all white as you drove down the highway. I really didn't want to go out because of the bone chilling cold but Randy needed something from the store that he thought he couldn't live with out, I do know that it will take time to get used to working for someone else other then the church but my duties will still be to the church first and then the others later after I'm done not wanting to break the vow I made when I started there. It's very confusing when the mind wants to take on new things but somehow I will work through it and feel good once again, the church has been my everything since I came here and I want to keep it that way. Farming is all that I can recall at this stage in life that I enjoyed to do but I like my job at the church also, I sort of feel like a kid in many ways but I know I'm not and I also don't know if I can handle the task of farming but we have to see if it's possible that just the person that resides in me. Next month they will open the thrift store and it will be back to work there also, I don't know why but time seams to be wanting me to do more and I could be misreading the signs but it all has to do with more then just making it here branching out into new areas and who knows what that can bring. Disappoint is something I don't want to do and also things could get worse if I really think about it and then I would really be in trouble. As time changes so do we as people and sometimes this is a good thing. Experiencing new things in our lives but you have to take care of things that you have given your word to, and then if you have some extra time you can take on other things which will rocket you to a new level, all through the time I worked for Jack I spent a lot of time out in the field away from people and closer to nature. it was an exciting experience seeing the animals in their natural surroundings, especially the badgers they are a sight in them selves protecting them selves from things that attack them even the tires of a tractor was a threat to them so they thought, but they were no match for the gain disk when it was droped on them. Many foxes ran through the fields or dogs' but they ran away from people not towards them, the cows were the funniest as they would run to the truck for their treats just a couple of words brought them running. Even the babys as they followed behind their mother, I guess it would be like the candy truck making it's rounds to bring them something that would bring them running and keep them in the fence. Many things to consider before I would walk back down that path, the limitations on my arms and back might stop me from doing some things. They had another shooting in another town just this week my land' what is the world coming to?. Gange violence has dictated how many of our young people live today and if given the chance they will destroy them along with them selves, these are people who don't have families and have turned to the streets making the gang their families and they live by robbing and selling drugs. On the street these people have to be stopped but how? So far they have been only in the mid to big cities where drugs run ramped and most are dead by their 18th birthday, or are put into prison where nothing is done to help them in anyway these are kids that feel lost and rejected by the world that abanded them and many of them come from foster homes.

Imaging that sent to a place where they say you can get help and then many of the girls are raped and thrown out like garbage, in ancient times kids weren't worth nothing thrown on a garbage heap until change came to their rescue. In todays society not many of the shows on television send a message but I have found that the old show of the rifel man teaches Mark many lessons about how to treat people in a good way no matter what. And it lets us also learn that things are not always what they might seam as many judge without knowing the whole story, but then are set straight later by facts. Our society is made up of many different kinds of people and the bad are just as prevalent in today's world as they were way back when, in my time I have learned new words but they don't come to me by learning them they just pop up from time to time out of no where and it leads me to believe that they were used before without my knowing it. Like they existed in another life one far from this one, the strangeness of things once forgotten by the mind to only return later what is the explanation for these thing? Does reincarnation exist? Or is it a myth, that was once thought of before our lives began seeing a place or things that trigger something inside a memory long forgotten or the face of someone that you sware you knew from a time passed, I have seen people that I know have left this world like my dad a long time afterwards but it's always just a glimpse! To maybe let you know that they are watching over you in some strange way.

As for others who have passed they never came back or atleast I have never seen them, Sunday morning and I couldn't sleep but it's quiet on this day with nothing running but the computer. I havent heard from anyone lately but Randy is doing fine since he got sick, it seams that flue is everywhere all across the United states my self I havent gotten it yet and I pray that I don't. I have always believed that getting the shots seames to triger it and the people get sicker not the soppiest like they clame, and then they have a hard time kicking it once a year I get under the weather and it lasts for about a week and then it's gone like it was never there but with Randy getting the shot he was sick for about two weeks and that one week to long for me anyway and then I can have a year that I don't get sick at all which really makes me happy, my life has been one of trials and then life goes back to normal or what I think is normal. But through it all I seam to come out ok' and then move forward. The big wigs in the town have run it for along time and then it gets passed down to the next generation being their kids but not until they have learned the business. It has to be hard to run a town but I think it's done in the same fashion as the country just on a smaller scale with a mayor and a trusty and then the others, like a big family in a way and God seams to come first in many of their lives. Many of the people I still don't know much about but when they feel comfortable around me they share a little bit of what life was all about in the beginning years back in the fiftys is when Norman and Doris lived in this house. So many people have lived here' and maybe got their start here struggling to get by like I do today a family thing this struggling to get by, it seams everyone goes through it but today they have a business and are fairing well except for Doris being sick with the cancer. I can't understand why this thing hits so many people around here, but it also hit's others far away. As they search for the cure itseams to get worse then better like the Aid's virous which is taking people every day as it runs through the country, if I only had the power to end such things I would do it. But He doesn't seam to give that much power to just one person in this world and the devil doesn't want it at all, he would rather see them suffer and then go down in the pit so much suffering in this place but also He has many new things coming into others lives. And who knows maybe a cure will come out of the goodness that God brings with him, it's strange how sometimes things are not what they seam to be. When a government wants to make quick money they seam to find a way and it's not always legal they have projects that they keep on the hush and they don't want the people to know about but it's the people who have to fund it. So many secrets kept from the people like selling drugs to fund something this is not anything unheard of because it's been put on the air more times then not. Marijuana is going to destroy a lot of this country and they will even transport it over seas to other countries, but no matter how much I bitch about it nothing will be done. They say it doesn't lead to other drugs which is bull crap, if it was to remain the way it came out of the ground then it wouldn't have gotten so powerful over the years.

Now that it's made legal we will watch what happens, they have a way of tracking these things. And I guarantee that more of our children will be stricked by this curse. And the jails will fill up with abusers of the drug, no way can they stop children from getting a hold of it any more then they can stop alcohol from reaching them. I recall one guy telling me that he isn't addicted to it yet he is for it to become legal and he is fighting for it, my opinion is that if you took him out of the reach of it he would go through withdraws like with alcohol. No one ever has a problem until it's to late after a person has dies or they die, this is the way of the beast like saying a tiger is harmless and then have it eat you. In that case absents doesn't make the heart grow fonder, the United States has never learned from any of the war's they have been in which leads some of us to believe they are not the brightest bulbe on the tree. Like in Iraq' they went in there to take control of the oil well's and weren't able to accomplish that task, many of the foolish things they do are over control or money. Like sending money they found back to the states bunkers full of money that had been stashed by the leader who later died. Although the money wasn't theirs they took it anyway and even service people were trying to get people over here to except shipments of the cash so they could live the good life when they returned. But I can't blame them as the government was doing the same thing and the service men and women just want something to fall beck on before they end up on the streets here in good ole America. Today little brother is still progressing to get back into feeling good and he said that this morning is the best he has felt in the last week or so thank God.

Monday according to some at church there has been a few people who have gotten sick in the last month or so from that flue but they seam to be doing ok' now after it left them, from what I gathered the flue seams to hit people with weak immune systems, and then you have others like me that it doesn't bother as much until that fine day when I seam to get sick once a year. Like it says in the bible we are all different but some are more prone to becoming ill, I know that I wasn't brought this far to end in such a way because when I get sick I really feel it maybe it's His way of letting us know that things can change in a heart beat. We had communion yesterday and everyone participated such a great things to have once a month this morning I will go and clean the church so it's clean for the week and then I only have to do it again on Thursday after Wednesday school has finished for the week I don't know why I'm in such a hurry about dowing other things but as they say an idle body doesn't move much and for some reason I like to stay busy it would be nice to save for something I have never had before but then again many new problems come with it when you venture out of your comfort zone, the house needs work and the only way you can fix things is by making more money to put away. Like with many others just getting by is a hard thing in it's self because it changes you knowing you have only so much to make it through the month and you have to stretch every penny to make it. I couldn't imaging living in Egypt during the old times out in the desert my land that had to of been hard making bricks out of straw and mud. But they seamed to make it out there with just a cloth covering them and wareing a wig but why the wig? Some say that it showed that you were wealthy maybe a king or someone close to them strange way of doing things. Do we need to connect with our roots? In some ways I think it's important but I don't think it defines who we are. In searching for my dad I get discouraged because I don't know how to go about it, the finding of the one who didn't want to be a part of my life or maybe he didn't know and would be just as puzzled as me if he found out. God could make it happen but since He hasn't then maybe He doesn't think it's important enough for me to go through it who really knows? But I do know that He is my father and maybe He is jelous of the thought of me taking the time away from Him, we are made beautifuly in the eyes of God. Imagine being made and then the mold thrown away because He didn't want anyone to even resemble any part of another, the power that He gives us should be enough but finding peace in having that power is hard to grasp when you have lived in the dark it's like going from one room to another and shutting the door, you have no concept of what's going on in the other room. Tuesday and I was sick yesterday. I knew it was coming but really didn't expect the same thing I had last year because it usually hits when I'm still mowing the lawn, it's a feeling like no other and it's a bad time to get that way especially during winter. The mill is running again and it's been running all night my sickness has stopped me from doing some things because of the confusion it's like you cant shut off your mind and that's scary. I don't know if I will go out this morning to take care of the trash because I don't want to get sicker.

My writing for the papers is done for a short time but once I'm back up to par then it will begin again you have to take care of your self during these times otherwise it could hit you worse then it is, during this time they don't like you to go to the hospital, because you could effect others so I will get some med's to take care of it by calling the doctor. And then getting plenty of rest. My land' it's like living out in the middle of no where, I was so used to being able to go to my doctor in Kearney and when I used to leave I usually felt fine but the good thing is that I will bounce back, as I see some kids now days the system has seemed to fail them coming from broken homes and put into a situation that's no better then the one they were in. but it's the lack of careing that effects them the most, coming from alcoholic homes is the hardest. That and parents that have mental problems which is reflected back on the children, even abuse from domestic violence is transferred to the kids as they learn from their parents. What they see is embedded in them but what's told to them is never given a chance to to sink in or take effect, if they are put into good homes they seam to reject it because of the home they were raised in. Left alone to fend for them selves or raise their brothers and sisters taking the place of their own parents because they have lost control of the family unit, I'm feeling a little better now after taking another antibiotic to fight off this flue. So who knows maybe later today it could be gone between that and praying I should be in good shape sometime in the future. Funny how this kind of thing can make you grateful for when you do feel good.

Hump day and I have been feeling poorly it seams that flue takes a lot out of you and it's nothing to mess with. Yesterday I went to the church and the pastor old me to go home until I get to feeling better it seams they understand the way a person gets when this crap hits them, my self I hope that it passes soon so I can get back to normal. The normal me is always up before the crack of dawn and I enjoy it very much the peacefullness that comes with the day so I can think and figure out how the day will present it's self. With this flue comes confusion and the loss of ability to think straight which is a bad thing nothing good here with this crap and it makes you want life to go back to normal we went to the dollar store yesterday and the blond was out sick with the same thing. Funny how you miss some people when you don't see them in a while. Like the dew on the lilly during spring, things are just not right, I thought the mill was running yesterday but come to find out it was a train sitting on the tracks and now I can hear the whissel off in the distance making it's way to town for another pick up those who lived close to the tracks must have their brains shaken; each morning as it passes by the rail road has been around since the beginning of the old west and really got popular when they had a fight with the oil companys to transport oil to placed the pipe lines didn't go, and then the oil companys stopped transporting oil that way because of them getting ripped off and then the fight between powers started. And it challenged the minds of some of the brightest people in the United States, strange how some things stick with us and others don't maybe because we know some things and it hit's the delete button when you duplacate something that's already in the mind. My life has many things to uncover and with a lot of them the search goes on to find that missing peace. The day is progressing and although we might think we know how it's going to turn out, in reality we don't. as sometimes we sit under a tree during summer the shade it's self is something that God provides for us to enjoy the day. As without it things would be much worse. I have always liked watching the birds as they sit on a lim and sing it sort of reminds me of my self as I grow and learn new songs, the songs them selves bring me joy as they are created in my mind before any music is brought to them. But I know the music that should be played while I sing strange how that comes to be even when I sing to harley the words come that I don't expect at the time words brought to life by a joy that resides in the heart, many times this can be interrupted by confusion and then forgotten for a short time to only come back later to bring it back to life by a melody that it fired up in the mind. January 8th Randy's birthday and he has hit the 53rd year mark, my how time goes by in this chapter of our lives over half a century has gone and now the other half has started, we don't look at life as a challenge but a gate way to a better place that will come one day weather we are ready for it or not. Just the thought of not being sick any longer can bring hope to those who have had to fight it most of their lives, and the releave of such things can bring with it a good feeling of over coming the odds. I have wondered many times if my world is separated from others separated by the the things that have happened through the younger years? Slowly the week is going by but still no relief in sight fur this flue, even though it's not as bad as it could be it's still a pain in the ass I took Randy to the doctor and he didn't do much but give him some over the counter caugh medicen to break up his caugh. I don't know why he is distancing him self from him but he is so things can change like I have said before and maybe he will have to find another doctor.

As there is only one more day in this week we will see how it goes with this flue my land' I never expected to feel like this but with faith and the helping hand of God I will get through it. I'm in hope that the rest of the week goes better then the first part, and then it will be much better then the first half or part. From what I understand Bob is going for his kemo therapy for cancer and if he doesn't make it that will be another one lost to the disease but his cancer could have been prevented if he would of stopped drinking it's called pushing the envelope and we have all done it me with death and now him with the cancer that could take his life maybe a wake up call to make him change his ways and get on the right track and stop dowing the things he hs been doing who really knows for sure' the liver can heal it's self but other orgens are not so lucky as they don't do the same thing. In the valley of death we see many things and the changing in life is one of them, you get a picture of how things would be if you get straight. I can tell that he will dream and they wont be all good ones as you look back over your life through those dreams and see where the changes need to be made. From the depts of your soul you will see where you need to start changing and then it's up to you if your going to change if not then you might end up somewhere else, a place you just might not like and it's frightneen in that place but the good news is that you can be the one to bring the change and then live a good life if that's what's in your future.

Life isn't always what you think it's going to be because it has many turns in it and something new can take a while to produce fruit and not many can say that. It's something that has happened in their lives as for my story I have traveled to many dark places and thought I would never get out of them, but none of them has been that going to hell and back like so many say. That is a farce' if you hear someone say they have never been drawn back into the demon then they are hiding something because nature wants us to see if we are missing something after the fall and in my case I found that the demon didn't have anything to offer except for the heartaches and the pain you go through when taking your life back and it's not worth going through again when you can stay on that path, fall but don't fall it's up to each individual if they want to travel that dark road and if they choose to go in and out of that dark place then one day they wont be able to come back out of it. Just my analogy on this kind of thing. Life in general is good but many things can mess with your mind like bills that you cant pay, that can be very depressing when you have never had to deal with them before and the devil is there on your front door step. To make it just as hard as possible for you, I have found out that it takes two people to survive in this world and if it's in a relationship then that could be better then just having someone live with you in a relationship you are working together but with someone living with you many times you have to deal with anger because there is never enough to make the bills go away and then you have to cut corners the ones you don't want to cut which can mess up things for you, although I took my little brother in' I find it hard to make ends meet because we both have a bad habbit or two like smoking, it seams to take a lot to pay for that one. Later I will talk to a friend about working for him and see where that will lead, for some reason I feel the need to get back out in the field to maybe give a little of my self to the farmer, we come upon many things that change the way we are and taking on different jobs could lead to us feeling fullfiled a lacking of something in our lives has to be found to fill that void which can exist in us for some reason. A drive that needs something to do so we can have a better life and not have to worry so much for worry can drive a person into a different realm that isn't good for the soul my existence depends on being able to pay my bills and I never thought my peace of mind would hinge on such a thing. T.G.I.F The weekend is about here and I'm feeling a little better then in the first part of the week I'm hoping it's about gone for this year and the road to recovery is happening. I was thinking about Bob and how he must feel going through those treatments in hope to beat the cancer, he has already lost a child and then two cousins to the same battle his child didn't have it but loosening her drove him into a deep depression and caused him to drink more like with my self when I lost my son so long ago it's not a good place to be. Although Roger Jr died before birth he was carried full turn right up to twelve hours before he was born, I don't like to talk about it and have avoided it for many years as for morning I did that part and moved on.

You never know when things are going to happen and you cant live your life scared of what you don't know so you go on and hope for the best, I was able to clean the church yesterday so it would be somewhat ready for Sunday but still have the restrooms to clean which only takes a short time, it seams I always have to have something to do to keep my mind off things and guide them towards the better things in life. Next month I will be back to work at the thrift store for a while until I can find something that pays, money or the lack of it is my enemy at this time but we always seam to pull through just by the skin of our teeth and that's no way to live always lacking in the needs of things. To me I should be able to save for that trip or fix the floor of my home so I don't one day fall through it but the chances of that happening are slim from what I have heard. As I continue my war on drugs many people want to down play my concers but it has little effect on me, I wrote another letter to my friend at the Kearney-hub about Marijuana and I hope it will open some peoples eyes to the fact that many children will be effected by it's being made legal the legal aspect isn't my point it's the effect second hand smoke will have on them, getting them high from even birth. And then them not knowing what reality is how could they know what it is? If they have been high from birth, making a drug legal because they want to get high legally carries many responsibilities which a high person cant handle, O they might be smart in the marketing place but the out come will be the same they have achers of marijuana just sitting waiting for production to the kids, and they cant use that excuse they can regulate it so they cant get their hands on it. Human life has little value these days as the mighty dollar trumps a human life.

What is a human life worth? According to some a prisnor in prison is worth 1% of their original value because they are locked up. But what about a person that lives to make the world a better place. How can you put a value on that person? Maybe by what they are trying to do but in God's eyes we are priceless the gift of life is the greatest gift. Saturday and they have a gathering at the church for someone who has passed it's at 1:00 this afternoon so I have to make sure things are ready cleaning wise also I took a birthday card to Norman for Doris and a song and letter he told me how music was her life and this was something I didn't know. But once he told me I felt that she would understand my song, I wish I could of gotten to know her personaly maybe she could of helped me with my music or maybe I could of learned to play the piano, so many things we miss when we don't try the new things that He gives us a song gone from sight or the not playing of that song because we are scared. That voice which tells us not to do it, shouldn't be listened to only the heart can bring music alive. As we talked he mentioned that they love me and that was a great feeling just the knowing that others do have love for you in their hearts. Even for a person that was once a stranger, I have a feeling love isn't given lightly here and when your excepted into this community then they treat you like family, some of the people are opinionated but that's expected in every place that you live the old women that is lonely trying to find a common bond to connect with others she might not know to well, Doris has been a good friend and I will remember her for years to come maybe one day as I sit on the back porch and sing a song, who can really say for sure. My friend Norman I will see him more through the years as we both grow older and maybe share a cup of coffee on some mornings but we will get closer as time allows it, it's hard to loose someone close to you as that void is opened up and has to be filled with something as for what his will be filled with only time it's self will tell that story. I hope he will live on for many years and be my friend but then again only time will tell that story, I never have asked how old some of them are maybe because it's none of my business their children are just a little younger then I, so I would be like their older friend one who has wisdome in the bad side of life the one who has traveled both the dark side and the goodness of God and believe me this side is much better away from the demons that can tear your world apart. Many of the young people are driven by the unknown the wanting to see or check out what they are missing in the world of drugs and alcohol and it's this curiosity that will get them in trouble, the first feeling of being high might be fun to some but with people who have health problems or mental problems the burdon will be worse. With many that are bipolar the Methamphetamine seams to make them feel more like a whole person but in reality it doesn't Meth cant change that two people exist in one body like with me and alcohol two people were there one created by God and the other which was created by the alcohol. They were separated by two things and the timed one was in the back ground watching as the other ran things but when I took my life back one of them had to go, and it started by destroying the one that was destroying me this vessel.

That God had created, my body was dieing and the only way to stop that was by stopping the one the alcohol had creater so the real me could live, in the light I was told that my journey hadn't started yet and I think He meant that I would know when one was gone the one who was destroying me. And then my journey would begin all through my life I never did get into much trouble but boy it was all around me at every turn it was just a reach away. But I was able to fight temtation and go the other way to only have it follow me in hope that I might let it in but I never did, all through my life I had a feeling that something was trying to destroy me but I was being protected by a force much stronger then it was. Like the devil and God were in a battle for my soul and so far God has won this fight, I believe there was such a battle in the bible and that person also didn't give in either. God knew this person and knew he had a pure heart and that's me, the only love I have for anyone is God the father because. He stood by me through thick and thin and wanted what's best for me even in the darkness I was His, I just had to find my way to that place where I belonged in his hands. Many kids think that if they quit school they can't return but that's so not the case! It just takes a little longer to get the job done, even having a baby at a young age can be corrected when it comes to getting a good education there are many programs that can take them to where they need to be. And they can still be a good mother. You hear that these things take place all the time by curious children wanting to know what love is like and then they get them selves into trouble and think it's the end of the world, when it's only a step backwards.

My life has been made up of set backs but still I moved forward to not let poverty or bad luck destroy me the human spirit is strong in this vessel, and I look forward to each day when I'm not weighed down by things of the mind. Sunday and it's chilly this morning yesterday didn't get up above 21 degrees so I spent most of the day inside my left lung hurts and I hope it will pass by later today, I don't really want to go and see the doctor because he doesn't seam to care about us like we are a burden to him. So I will see about another doctor when we go to Concorida. I don't know why but doctors that are in clinics seam to want to run you through there like cattle just to collect their fee from the government as some say we are the lower class of people that doesn't really matter, where do they come up with that? Maybe from the same place they came up with the slaves and peasants in the bible the ones who does all the work and is not noticed for what had taken place the builders of the great cities. You never hear about them but you do hear of the kings that put them into labor to do things they couldn't do them selves, I believe Moses was the son of a slave women and then hidden because they didn't want him to come to power later in years which he did anyway found floating in a basket and found by the kings daughter or sister and raised among them. It's strange how his life was supposed turn out and it came to be no matter who raised him another glimps that God's way will always be, no matter where we go He can see us and if we are supposed to make a difference then that will come to be no matter what others do in our lives He will somehow bring us to where we need to be for it says in the bible king's will become king's. And what ever we are supposed to be will come to pass even through hunger and famine we will end up in that place where our life story takes us, it says our book of life is already written. What I would give, to read it and see where this soul ends up later in life or am I writing my own book of life who really knows but Him. It is written that He changes us from the inside out so we don't really see the finished product until it's done like the tea pot that sat on the shelf all those years who thought he was eugly come to find out the maker made it more beautiful then it's eyes could even imagine and everyone wanted it but that wasn't meant to be. Through the years our tears fade away and we loose count of them but back in the far corners of our mind they are there, a reminder that sorrow and pain still does exist and can hit us in a moments time. Still today I'm not sure how I have come so far except that it must have been in the cards you might say, yesterday is gone but still we are here to carry on into this day and praise God for that. I was supprise when another letter was published yesterday by Mark at the Kearney hub, for my message is getting heard more these days as that was three in just a couple of months. Ans I asked if some thought one person could save the world or play a big part in it. My editorals go from the news paper to the web and are read around the Nation" and even around the world trying to bring an end to the loss of life but I also know that the user or dealer doesn't want to hear my message.

And if it interferes with things they might try to stop me or even kill me to stop the message but I cant let that stop the message that I was sent to send out, it wasn't no accident that I was sent back here and I believe my home was meant to be my office and the internet my audience. Through the sands of time my life has a purpose and that's saving lives as for these self made millionaire who make their living off the misery of kids they will be short lived, but still they will become millionair's all they are doing is taking out the middle man so drugs can flow freely through out the world and in doing that they kill more kids sort of like blood dimons you might say. My message has been on many networks and now we will see what takes place in the future, if it has any impact on others only time will tell if the seed takes root and the only one who can make it take root is the father. I feel a little better now thank God' the period of feeling like crap is one that I don't like but with prayer and certain med's it can be taken care of, this flue is a strange one it's like it hits you for a time and then leaves to only come back again later but my breathing is better and my lungs. No longer hurt, as bad as they did. Well the day is about to start so I will close for now. Monday and I slept most of yesterday after opening the chuch try to get this stuff out of me, according to the news many have died from this flue one minute they were fine and the next they went to be with their maker so I didn't want to effect any of the people at church. It's just the way I am thinking of others and they say all it takes is a caugh to spread it to another person, it's the beginning of another week and we will see how it goes later today. I do know that I have some things to do like vacuuming and such at the church and then it will be back home until this thing is gone. I have had Doris on my mind lately and I have been wondering how she is doing the subject is something that's hard to bring up to others because it's just hard for them to talk about and I don't like to pry into other peoples business. I could tell Norman was taking it better then I was told earlier and he said that Doris didn't have any of that why me she has excepted that it's time to join the father in heaven, I sure will miss her smile when I used to see her in the store she is a very strong lady of Christ. If I would of known she was into music I would have gone to her for help in putting the music to the words.

A chance missed by not learning about someone but her music will live on and other will know and learn about the good things she did, the song I sent over to her was a gift just a little something that might show her that there is a connection between her and other that love some of the same things she did. My music was meant for some thing and it can bring joy to some who understand it. Which I saw that many understand my songs even those who are younger then I, even children can grasp the words that are supposed to bring them joy and that's a hard thing to do these days with their minds on all the things they go through. A song that touches the heart of those who might not of ever got to hear it, if they didn't come to church. Giving your life to something like music becomes easy after you know that's what your life is for the combining of words to make other feel joy and happiness not sorrow but in the end that can also be made into something beautiful. Later this year I will write some more songs and hopefully they to will be written down for others to ejoy when I am gone from this place I now call home, a legacy what will mine be the writing I leave behind or the people I have helped over the years good question! But sadly we never get to see what that will be for it's only brought up after we pass from this world. What do I want done with my ashes? maybe leave them here to protect those who come after me. For truly this land is mine well it's belonge to God but you get the message, I pray that I live on for many more years and become even a greater writer then I am at this point. Many years have been spent on becoming better then I am now and like with all things in time we become better at the things we do, I don't hear the engines running this morning so it's quiet out side yesterday I didn't even get the paper because I didn't want to open the door letting in the cold but that's ok' I can pick it up this morning when it gets light out side. As for the not being able to walk in the dark it still exist so I don't wonder out much at night staying in the light of my home where I know I'm safe, maybe one day that blockage will leave but for now it still remains. The battle with addiction has kind of faided like a long lost memory but then sometimes something triggers it and I go back to writing about it I guess it will always be there just out of sight until someone needs help like the guy who changed his life because of what I wrote so long ago. In some cases all it takes is a trigger to open something up that they can relate to and then change is right there for them to follow through with a caring heart or someone to understand what they might be going through. In the darkness they don't see what's coming, no more then you can tell what day after tomorrow is going to be like but there is always hope that this time will turn out good for your life.

I have tried to answer some questions from readers but with their question comes their doubt and that can stop what is trying to take place, if they would only listen and take it to heart what I'm telling them then change could take place, but human nature wants them to argue the point. In all my years of telling parts of my stories I have avoided arguing because when that happens then nothing get's done. I feel like I'm on a different plain then they are because they are still going through the not believing stage that anything is wrong. Addiction becomes a part of their lives as they live in that dark place where they don't understand why it all happens to them, even the great foot ball player keeps everything in until that fine day when they loose it all. At first they don't see it coming but that doesn't stop it, that is just the way it works keeping the person blind to the fact that it will destroy them and then the fine day comes when they cant pick them selves up the pressures of life gets to us all and it doesn't matter if you are rich or poor. Like the plages of Egypt they didn't only destroy the strong but the weak also, along with the Kings and Queens. Addiction can take a life faster then you ever could believe. Just the wrong combination and a strong person will fall like he leaves off a tree in Fall. Perfectly healthy people have went out for one drink and fell over dead by others putting drugs in their drinks, and it happens every day with date rape drugs and others that they want to test and see what might happen.

Using people as crash car dummys is what they are doing and although it's not right they still practice it to find that right combination between this world and the next. Peace is something we all have been looking for and many think it can be found in war! But that's just an excuse to destroy others lives that don't think the same way we do is Americans free? When they are told how to think. In my books their not and some are programmed from birth like the computers are in todays world. Politicians are that way, because it runs in the families but even then they too can break like president Bush when he became addicted to alcohol from the pressures of his job, trying to find that balance that would let him go on and be somewhat sane but in the end he had to make a choice also! What was more important his family of the drug and from what has beengoing around it was the family that he choose, Or was it? Only he knows the true answer to that question and he isn't telling. An addict can manipulate those around them we see and hear about it every day. And for the most part they look normal because it's become a part of their everyday life and others havent seen them in any other state of mind, it's only when they slure their words that it's noticed I recall being able to drink a quort of whisky and still walk. But that doesn't last to long once your that far gone and it takes years to get that way. Today I'm still under the weather but I'm getting better and hopefully tomorrow will be even better, the slightest cold chills you to the bone and you shake uncontrollably not a good thing in my books but still you have to go across the river to get to the other side.I had to go and get med's for little brother so he wouldn't caugh so much and the med's did the trick so hopefully he will also be better tomorrow. As he talked to Stacy she said everyone has been sick down there and it was mostly the young and the old, more or less like it is here. We are having an artic front coming through and that doesn't help matters either, my self I like the dry cold if you have a choice? It's the end to another day good night. Tuesday , I feel very blessed because most of what I write s from memory and in the beginning I had no short turm memory. For some reason it was damaged in my dark days probably from the Meth I was taking, it's not uncommon to louse that part of the brain when you shove so many bad chemicals into it. But over time I believe it came back if just a part of it, O sure I have to write things down but I think most people have to do that look at Rosalee she had never done drugs and still she has to write things down she told me that it's just the way writers are. I remember looking her name up on the computer and I saw her book on there although she never made any royalitys off of it she made it onto the internet, and other can read her book on the hard times in the west growing up with almost nothing. She is one of the people who inspired me to write and to keep writing so my craft can be fine tuned, we still send each other Christmas cards during Christmas and I love to read what has been happening in her life alng with her kids which are now in their 40's and fifties. My shortterm memory must have came back during my writing years because I can now remember those little things better then before, the other day I had a dream and it's the first one that I enjoyed in many years it was so clear just like if I was living it. It was about me and mom and Oliver and we were living together like in the old days and I felt at peace in the dream like I belonged there and everything was right.

Really I didn't want it to end but then I woke up and I was back here at home, I felt a connection that I hadn't felt in quite some time like the picture was whole and complete. Maybe the dream was telling me something! I can hear the dove out in the tree this morning I remember when I used to hear them before I thought they were owls sitting in the tree waiting for a meal, but then someone told me that they were doves. Our town has many doves that live here and never leave. Like the other birds that fly south for the winter and I do my best to protect them by not running them over when I drive, you can see them each day as they eat the gravel in the road to digest their food but just the color of them is beautiful and I get a since that they have a spiritual connectiion with the town. Maybe it's from what I read in the bible as it talks about them quite offtent in that great book, it's like this place is their home and always has been maybe programmed into them from birth but they never leave and they have an abundance of food here where they wouldn't find anywhere else. After communion we don't throw the bread of life away we feed it to them and other birds so they can have a piece of Christ also and they survive as we do in a place He has created for us, it's another Tuesday so a week has passed since we got sick. Today I feel better then last week the only time I have to go out is to take the garbage out and then it's back inside so I can finish getting well, and then I should be fit as a fiddle I pray that the lord will help me get better and I ask this of Him each day or morning as I pray and sometimes it reminds me to pray.

It's the little things in life that sometimes brings us closer to God the healing of the flue or a cold but the connection is made when we pray, and I didn't know that just a year or so ago as I have just started praying not to long ago. But slowly a connection is made with Christ' and we talk more then we used to after praying I can feel a piece a calmness that comes over me and it makes for a great day especially when your other life was full of confusion, in my dream I felt that there was a message but it will take time to figure it out and I have time. I wonder if we find that peace we are looking for as we grow older? I do know that older people seam too be ok' with the slow movement that their bodies take on, adjustment as some would say. With age comes wisdom and it can be passed down to the younger generation if you can get them to listen that is the key to get them to listen. And stories can bring that to them if they are going through the same thing you did, kids think adults are made of iron but if you can show them that they too are vulnerable to things they are, then they should grasp what you are saying and try to learn from them so they can avoid the pit falls you went through. Love' the love of a town. Nothing in the world can compare to having people love you when it's been missing most of your life. They seam to be there for you even when you isolate your self from others and real love doesn't go away, many people who are addicted feel abanded and isolated for some reason as it was with me. But I felt like I was never a part of anything, separated by things out of our control like with me it was my brothers and sister I never felt like I was a part of them. Just a person left alone in the world to fend for my self and when you don't know the lord like I didn't back then it becomes very lonely. When I traveled into the light was the first time I felt a connection to something even though I couldn't see it the power was familiar like I had experienced it before, maybe at birth being I was being reborn but familiar just the same. I have always been a shy person and very easily could I drop a tear but through the years a wall came up to stop that from happening, a barrier that would stop my natural instencts from kicking in and that's not a good thing. The morning has started and we have blue skys I'm still hoping for warmer temps so I can wash my car but we will see how the day goes, it's now hump day the middle of the week and I'm hoping it's going to be a nice day. Yesterday wasn't bad but still the temps were below freezing only 20 some degrees as we went to the store I noticed a leack in the transmission but it didn't amount to much so I filled it other then that things have been a little better just have a caugh now and that should leave before to long, Randy slept most of yesterday so I hope he got enough sleep last night. Too stay awake today they have had somethings on the news about gun regelation and it bringing up some mad people with threats I don't know much about that side of things so I say nothing and let them battle out what they will do about the shootings of kids in schools. Some say to arm guards and have them in schools but if you ask me guns is what started the whole thing anyway. I wonder where it all went wrong schools used to educate kids for the world and now many of them don't even make it through school because of nut jobs or mentaly ill people thinking it's a shooting gallery. This kind of violence hasn't happened around here but you never really know when someone will loose their mind and do it again.

My self I have the patients that most people don't or at least I thought I did until yesterday when someone told me that I was a little impatiens, but that's just something that takes place once in a while when my short turm memory kicks in Ha! Sometimes it's like a flood of knowledge comes puring out and I can't control it but why that happens I don't have any idea, it's like something wants to get out and it comes out and I cant stop it. In the years since I have been here I have heard nothing about the kids from here being arrested for alcohol or drug abuse which is odd because I know it exists in almost every corner of the planet and now with pot being made legal the numbers will go up and then others will wish they would have took a closer look at things before attacking other things when writers get together and write about something they sometimes don't think and that puts them in a touchy place, it's the end to another day and I got the car washed along with getting Randy some smokes but I sure wish he would quit as he has burnt some spots in the carpet and that makes me angry which I don't like being. As it takes away from life if I lived by my self things would be pretty good and I would do it but money is a problem, maybe this next year I can make it happen who really knows for sure. It's funny how I go to bed at 5:00 at night but then I'm up before others even think about it making me the early bird of this town well I'm going to call it a night.

Thursday and I'm hoping for another nice day like yesterday my it was the warmest in a long time my sleeping habbits have been changing some and who knows maybe by the middle of summer I might sleep in until 8:00 in the morning, winter timeis hard on everyone and Randy has grown out of his pance getting bigger all the time. I hear him at night or during the night talking and it's strange that he talks to who or what ever more then he talks to me but my land he eats all the time. I think it might be time for a shrink to talk with him to find out whats going on in that mind, I'm not a doctor so I cant help him. January is over haif gone and by April it will be warm again if it's anything like last year and then the bodies will change with the weather for little bropothers sake I hope he gets smaller other wise he will sweat like all get out and that wont be good. He seams depressed for some reason and he doesn't talk about it but I have a feeling he ould with someone else like a theripest or a hear doctor, maybe I did the wrong thing by bringing him home but I couldn't leave him in that place for surely he would of died. How does one try to fix someone in his condition I show him all the love I know how but that doesn't seam to be working. My whats a person to do? Maybe have someone else take over and hope for the best. As for my self I'm not equipped to handle such things at this point, he can barely get off the couch because of his weight and then he almost falls over trying to get up. I see different behavior is different people but I do find that many give up on many things before they are completed, and that's no good. With Randy I finds that he doesn't like to be totally awake and there are many people that way as a matter of fact if they did awaken they wouldn't know what to do with the difference that life has to offer. Even I didn't want to be totally awake and that lead to some of the addiction problems, in my younger years just barly getting by without a life. An existence of a soul in limbo, not wanting to wake up from the sleep I was in. I recall many years ago wakeing up to just go back to sleep not wanting to know the world and all it's problems because I had enough of my own to deal with or not deal with. We can rationalize many things in life and at that time I just didn't wanted to be here no existence was better then what I had and when the day came when it happened I thought I was home free but that wasn't the case, or He wasn't going to let my life be a failure. For some reason I woke up and He told me that life could be beautiful, but I didn't see that for many years to come but progress was made with each step and I moved forward into that world I didn't quite understand as of then. In thr first few years I fought the alcohol but then something happened all the things I felt were changing and and it seamed that part was over and never did come back except for once when I went with a women who drank it was like I was seeing my self from long ago like I was put into the place that I had put others she would go to the bar every night after work and then come home half crocked which I didn't like but I put up with it for a while in hope that she might change and she didn't. so I sent her on her way, to maybe save my self I really cant say at this point. Through the years I learned that it would take time for me to get past the things others did with their lives and move on, in hope that I might survive and maybe one day write a book who really knew at that point in life because back then it wasn't on my mind like today 20 some years later my land' I couldn't put words together talking let along in writing.

I spent time living in my car because my brothers got us kicked out of our house and I was on the streets just me and Tiny Olivers dog until Oliver got out of the hospital from having heart surgery and then we got another place together his recovery was slow and long but I nursed him back to health and he did ok' for a long time while we shared our lives together like mom had asked me to do when she was dieing. Everything was fine until the others came back into our lives and then more trouble started with the bringing in of drugs and such and then one day I had it and threw them out needless to say they left but made it very hard on us by dropping by from time to time and wanting me to get high. I truly believe that if they would of stayed away things would have been better but they didn't, and that's when I started to ask God for help. Having little faith I didn't expect anything to happen but it did one Christmas I asked for a decent house and a car that wouldn't break down and by the next April we had it, and I felt blessed but seeing it happen was strange as people helped, it must have been his way of letting me know that he was there for me. In the house that Jerry had, it was unlivable but we had to take what was handy at the time and we lived there for about 8 years while he riped Oliver off for so much money buying things with his money and then saying it's his. I truly believe that he got rich off of doing that to him and others that were in dire straights. I tryied to get an atturney but none of them would take him to court saying he was a church going person and they didn't think he would do that. What a crock of crap I think most of his homes were condemned or torn down because they were so bad and then I had that one red taged and that's when the lord stepped in and we moved.

To the best house we ever had and I lived there for about 3 or 4 years and came to Kansas and to Courtland I was afraid at first because I knew that things wouldn't work out between me and the gal I moved to be with, at first I thought it was love but later found out that He had used her to bring me here maybe to find what I needed in my life a chance to get closer to Him and learn new things as I spend my last days here, many years ago someone asked why I didn't go public with my story and I replyed that I'm not out to make others money just my self so later I can help others that are in need. Because God knows there are many, what good would it do to make the rich richer when people go hungry here in the United States everyday they don't seam to get enough of the food grown right here where they were born, from dust I came and to dust I will return but while I'm here I have to try and make a difference to maybe leave something behind. A marker of my time here and then I will go quietly into the night with no regreats, through the gates that brought me here but still there is so much to do and I feel I have just tapped into the beginning of my journey the feeling of being able to sing is part of that journey. Saturday and I have found out some of why I get up so early or part of it, I don't seam to like to be around anyone on certain days for real! What's with that? The good and the bad thing or what? Through the years I have always liked being by my self to a certain extent and if your going to spend that much time with our self you better like who you have become, and I believe I have. But also with each time I write I give up a little part of me that part which used to be in my life maybe it's called letting go I really cant say at this point. Not everyone is going to connect with what I write but that's ok' but for those who do maybe they can find some help in the world of addiction that might hring them back from the brink of destruction and they can also know that even though it's a long haul in the end it was worth all the pain and suffering they have gone through. Trying to learn the things you should of learned as a child is harder then you think when half a centure has passed but also your not full of the things that could brain wash you, my dreams are more clear these days or at least the last one was and I hope they continue to be that way far into the future, as for my writing it will continue but I don't know for how long it's like this soul has a mission and when it's done then only God knows what will become of this body it's like it gets weaker all the time but that could just be my mind getting tired but who really knows for sure. My thoughts seam to be running at a slower pace on this day and I forget sometimes but hey! That's life right when I ask someone about last year they say they cant remember back that far, but to me sometimes it's like it was just yesterday maybe the mind trying to hold on to things to long cant really say for sure. Would I have wanted to go through loosing loved ones with my mind in that dark place well lets see 'no' but during the process it hurts like hell to only later weaken as time moves forward. Today I'm going to finish cleaning the church so it's ready for services tomorrow, when I was asked to stay last year it brought a good feeling into my life one that I have never felt before, for the first time in my life someone wanted me the person I have come to be and in time more changes will take place as God is working me from the inside out like the potter making me all I'm supposed to be and in the end I will be that tea pot sitting in the window that every one wants but cant have. Do we really see who we are? For only time will tell that story.

The bending of the rules; when we fall into that world of addiction we are bending the rules and shutting out the things we don't want to see or understand, but then at what point do we start to open our eyes after visiting that place where things are not the same as they are here going into that light to maybe not come back or maybe He thinks we need a wake up call to jolt us back to the real world but if that was the case why put so many things in out path to over come like when I was cripples, I can't count the tears I cried to be able to walk again. And the people who laughed made me want to give up, or did it trigger something inside of me survival mode maybe. And instead of giving up I just asked Him to forgive them because they didn't know what they were doing, what turned me from being bitter to really forgiving them? Did Jesus come up on the same situation in his time here? He must have. But still the memory is there why? I believe when you experience new things they seam to stay with you for a time and if you are making an transition from the old life to the new then the mind has to compensate in some way to make things make since for you a rational thery of things happening. Sunday and it was another cold one this morning yesterday it was in the 50's but like with most good things it was short lived by this morning.

But I'm liking this not getting much snow this year as it's all gone for the time being, and now if it stayed warm enough we can use some rain so the crops will take off like I jet. My personal feelings of things is that I wish we didn't get sick at all but with the weather changing all the time it cant be helped, no wonder the old folks stay in a lot as for me I like to venture out when I shouldn't but that's ok' it's just a part of my nature to be curious about things. As for getting out of debt I don't know if it can be done by just my disability check probably not, but my credit is good and I can survive in this place I now call my home. As for the outside world I don't have much contact anymore as each time I feel peaceful something wants to destroy it and it says that will happen in the bible misery seams to want company but it wont get it from me, I'm trying to find that balance that I felt at a very young age the balance of a child maybe when you were about 3 or 4 years old when you felt free from all the things which were bad. From the beginning I always felt like I was different separated by something I couldn't understand, and then before I could find out what it was my world changed. and in all the confusion I got lost like the mind went in another direction and He wasn't going to stop it, did He want me to experience those things and if so why? To maybe teach me how Jesus Christ suffered before He went to sit at His right hand on the thrown' I guess we can go through life remembering and not remembering things but what's the message really saying for even today I feel like I did when I was in school once in a while that those things didn't pertain to me for some reason. But then it's like I was brought back to the place that I left off my thoughts and memories are not all good but still I record them why does this happen? Why did he tell me to get that machine on that day and why did He teach me to write after it hadn't even been created yet? My writing that is. Although I didn't understand it I have been known for my writings, and my only teacher has been the father working through my mind to tell me something. I do know that many writers have had to have their minds slowed down to focus on things but with me that doesn't seam to be the case as my mind has traveled to many places, why bring someone a human that is through so much tragedy and then have them write about it? Is it to leave a record that others lives are not as messed up as they once thought. and that they can achieve anything they put their minds to. For each day is like going to school just as I get out of bed the only difference is that I do it right here at home, could you imagine how long this life would be if I lived to be 90 years old I would be the longest surviver of addiction on record that went to deaths door and back, as for my church it's like they are my protectors keeping me safe to see what He has instore for me to see how my life will pan out you might say. People changing their lives is a hard thing but it can be done if they want it bad enough, going from the darkness and checking out how they should of lived in the first place doesn't give them sight to what should have been but of what they wished it would have been. When I was in the accident in Colorado was the calmest I had ever felt when I should have been nerved up I wasn't. It was like I was giving control to God and He would do what was right, and we survived not going over that 300 foot clif.

Even people who lived up there said that He must have been watching over me especially when the back axel and tire came up and hit the hood of the truch just a foot or so from coming through the windshield. Why were these things shown to me after my demise? Before I never gave them another thought, I just went on with life. Do I see things different then most folks? I know most of the population would of chalked it up to luck but come on' not three close encounters. And each time He wraped His arms around me, and kept me safe. Monday and yesterday they were glad that I was back at church and so was I. They have gotten used to seeing me every Sunday as I don't usually miss a day unless I'm relly ill, I can always feel the love from them especially when I'm gone for a time. But I didn't skimp on still doing my job, through the years I have missed only the time you can count on one hand, if that. But through it all I still keep the bond between me and God, before I go back after being ill or sick there is something that said you wont be missed so I have chooose to ignore it and go on it was one of the spirits that lead me here the bad spirit that I learned to ignore long ago, and in doing that.

I have grown stronger through the years instead of weaker, I guess you could say that the church is my home away from home where I can be my self without any interfearence from others that might burst my bubble. It's my world, one chosen by my self and the father' I heard yesterday that Doris is still getting around with the help of family so I think she will be around for a time yet I would really like to see her and later I will ask Norman if it's ok'when the time is right.

Norman is still hoping for a miracle and I know that God grants them all the time or preforms them everyday, my land' I'm a walking miracle and I know his power. Spread through out the world by love, they have a thing now at church where you can sign a paper and help with the service to get familure with the Methodist way of doing things and in time I will attempt to try my hand at giving a message to bring my self and others closer to God the father and the son Jesus Christ. It will also take the help of the holy spirit to empower me as I move forward, could this be why iwas sent here? Well only He knows the answer to that question. But I do know this is the only place I have felt comfortable enough to try it my love for Jesus is that strong, in my life I have never liked moving backwards it just never made and since to me like back into a relationship that didn't work for they were lessons to be learned so you don't make the same mistake again a teaching part of things to show us what not to do again. My land' boy have I made some mistakes but as we move forward our past loves shouldn't be forgotten especially when it comes to our children for they were made from the same love that the father has for us, His love flows through us and into the children we bare and if we do our job right then they to will be protected by the hand of God' at times I think I have healing powers but as of yet I have only tried them on small things like pop's dog Tiny when I brought him back to life or I thought I did there he was laying dead on the floor and I massaged his heart and boom he came back.

Could it of been a miracle or did I just do the right thing at the moment? I do know that the electricity I felt is what started his heart again, or was it static shock from the carpet it's something only God knows the answer to. But he lived many months after that moment in time and it made Oliver very happy to have his buddy by him, I believe that our time here extended his life for a time. But some things can be only extended so long especially old age. I wonder if He gives these powers to some and not others to show that He is still working in our lives especially when we have doubts. It's going to be cold today much colder then last week but by the middle of the week it's supposed to get a little warmer and that would be ok' with me winter really isn't my cup of tea as I cant seam to stay warm but that comes with age and of course the abuse my body went through, I used to think that He would of repaired my body to profection but I think if He did that then no lesson would have been learned. The lesson of not destroying your self over foolish things, but the greatfullness is always there for what He has done in my life and it will always remain until I go to be with him one day. I believe He gives us gifts and when He does we are supposed to share the experiences with others to maybe gring them a little closer to Him, many times I could of left this place by my own hand and still He saw something worth saving "What does He see? A soul wanting to go on and learn, I still think there is something more that I haven't learned yet and maybe it's that peacefullness like when your in a garden and all the birds are singing and the squirrels playing with the rabbits just eating out of the garden tranquility is very real in the mind that is and it can take you to places that you never dreamed of or ben like a ride on a gondola through the streets of a city that is almost under water over seas but still that ride is in your mind.

I don't think my presents here is by accident maybe it's a training camp for me to learn more about my creater the one who made it possible for me to go on. For surely it wasn't something I wanted at first but through time things change even our way of thinking goes from bad to good if influenced by His hand and heart. There are some people who once knew you and what they saw is for ever in their mind which leaves them to miss the great things God can do in your life, by judging you they miss the miracles that God preforms in a persons life and that is their loss. They focus on the negative side of you and cant see the change which the Lord has created and that leaves them with no clue to who you have become and that's a shame for many times He brings change into this world, within His people to show that His power is still alive to day as it was yesterday and the years before we were even put here. People no matter how different give praise to God and it's the same God no matter what language they speak, as for those who have not believed they have made their own world without seeing his love and understanding and that's their choice given to them by the creator. He has always been and will always be, as for us we are only here for a short time to leave something behind to help others maybe get a head start on things they could avoid. It's another brisk morning as He has blessed us with another day, yesterday was a holiday so the mail and other government businesses were closed to celebrate Martin Louthor King day the first holiday named after a black man. We have come a long ways since those times when it was just one sided praies God for the change.

Even today they have movies about the old times when there were slaves and I never did understand how they could do that to a person. But it was done and now it's over, they call it progress and now we have a president that is of color doing a fair job but he seams like he isn't all black. Born off in the islands of some place in the United States if things are right with his birth certificate, when they held the elections for the second time I thought he might loose but he didn't and now he will be in the white house for another four years at least no War has started yet. I don't really remember the War in the 60's because I was so young but from what I heard in the 60's many of our loved ones died for nothing the Vietnam War' thousands shipped over there to die even when they knew we had lost that War' but that's not my focus on things pertaining to the past, of things like that. Even though it threw many familys into hardship when they lost family in another War that shouldn't of been. We face a greater 'War' here on the home front, as children die from addiction and there is no one to help or stop them. But through others going through it they can teach the children that it's not good to go there, I see the opportunity to move forward in starting to speaking in public through the church and I would really like to try my hand at it. So on ward Christen people for what you think you can't do, He will do for you. Many things change with each day and we don't always know what that might be I have been shocked by people who have seen things I have never seen, for some reason they can take a step backwards and look at someone and see many things changing that one like me might not see the growth of a Christen reborn and how their life changes like the channels on aa television set coming out of that dark place where they once lived and being brought into a place that they were meant to live if things would have been different. I wonder what it's like for a pastor or priest to see the change in someone that has given their life to Christ? Do they see it as a miracle or what? Maybe one day I will ask. How does one come to be born and then wake up so many years later? Into something they don't understand what happened to that precious time? The time when they didn't even know they were alive. Where is that world now? He does remember wakeing up, but to what' for the world is new but full of confusion. Where did he fit in feeling all alone like he is the only one walking around. And he asks where am I then a voice talks but it isn't a voice he has heard before it's more like a communication from something he doesn't know but then, he hears this something he cant explain, how can he tell others about this experience when he doesn't understand it him self. Humpday and I'm still not up to 100 % but that will come in time I hope it's soon, I wrote another letter to the Kearney-hub in Nebraska in hope to make people wake up about putting armed guards in schools but I don't know how it will turn out. When the spirit hits me I have to write to maybe change things so the world will be a better place, I didn't realize how stupid some people can be when it comes to saving lives but putting guns into schools isn't the solution. It will breed more trouble I sometimes wonder why I'm the way I am emotions really run high in this soul and at times it wants to cry out really cry out with the tears and the whole ball of wax, but something makes me write about it instead of cry maybe so others can see that I'm just like them I don't really know.

In my fight for life I find my self sometimes feeling alone in a world that will destroy it's self in time and the innocent will suffer right along with the others, and that shouldn't be. I don't know what the weather is going to be like today but I hope it's warm because I'm not, it's like my body is wareing out and I don't have any control over it. Or it's getting older one or the two, my life has been made up of climbing mountains and then falling down them again but in each instent I have made progress onto another plateau to only find out that I don't know what I'm there for. Then slowly things start to change and that place becomes the place I need to be for what ever reason a new start to something, like with the thing I have come accustom to. I know I'm still being changed and that He is at work inside of me, but what is He up to? They say everyone wants to know this question but never get an answer until his work is finished. I wish sometimes that I could go into a dream and come out with all the answers but I don't know if that is possible, even today' I don't have all the answers but I try as I search for them the meaning of our existence or mine. Why it was important for the things that happened to happen, if I read things right He knew that my life would be a living hell before I was brought here before I was put into my mother. And if I didn't know better I would think that He hated me, or did He ant me to see both sides of the coin you might say? I didn't suffer in the other world because I was num most of the time but in this one all I wan't to do is find something.

Maybe the part that happening to me today it's already another day and it's all I can do to wake up, it's like everything is in slow motion and I don't feel like myself strange how that happens sometimes but it does happen. Everything that is happening in the world can be explained by the bible and God but I find that a lot of people don't read His words and live by them so they don't have a clue of how to fix any thing, in many places they metal dectors which is something I didn't know about schools so me writing that letter probable didn't do much good at this time. The attempts we make to bring positive change doesn't always work but if you can hit a nerve with someone about something then they might have a reaction that can sprout something that you can build on. But I have found that no one likes to hear foul words for anyone a it shows ignorance with lies inside of them, they had Wednesday school yesterday so I will have some work this morning if it warms up a little. I'M NOT LIKE YOU' A soul searching in time, when I wake up all I want to do is cry. Half a century gone and still I don't know why, I had to go through so much pain to stay alive. When the pain comes I ask why' as for bad habbits I have one but the one could one day make me gone maybe back to that place I learned to love. The place where sorrow and pain are all gone and He is there to bring me home, where might this place be you ask? But all I can say is that you have to follow the light to find the path. The loss of life still burns in my soul but they were the lucky ones they got to go home, away from the place that brought them pain and I had to watch them suffer through their days. Remorse and love are so intertwined sometimes it makes you not to want to find it. How do you separate the two with one you die and the other lets you live through, through heartache and pain in a world where some don't have a brain. They will walk the streets and take from you and if it isn't enough they will kill you send you to that place where you to wont feel the pain. I'm sometimes happy, but most of the time sad. Because I know there is more to life then I had. Some see me in a different light smiling all the time to let them think things are right, but in my soul I know there has to be more. No more sorrow or pain where will I find it? Up above when He comes for me again, why have I written this on this day? Depression has found it's way, but fear not it will be gone again when I fight it off like the long lost wind that blows my way. Do I give in to the sorrow and pain or suffer through it for another day, death is final there is no give and take only the taking will take youto that place. Then one day when you think your gone you are pulled back by a power of love for He wants you to see that it wasn't the end, just a memory that scared you from within. Broken by the world before you are sent back broken but why? To repeat the circle one more time. They say He knows what He is doing but you have your doubts, and then you take a step forward to see that they weren't wrong. One day you find your self on the floor not able to get up because of the War' not the War of the world but the War that resides in you fighting the demons that are trying to destroy you. This War you keep to your self because no one understand the live you went through. One day He sends a friend to show you that it's the beginning and not the end. A Spanish boy with a heart so big and true and he helped you home when you didn't know what to do, he is now long gone back to Mexico where he calls home. His kind words will never be forgotten in this soul as they were like a light of hope. This is my story from long ago when life had no meaning and I wantd to let go, since that time I have come so far. could it of been that light I saw in the star.

A star from heaven that burnt so bright that I try to find it when things don't feel right, it gives me hope that He sees my road. The road I travel is unknown to me but I have faith that one day He will let me see, see the wonders that are in store for this soul that will one day go home. So many kids today take their lives and the parents try to understand it but without coming to turms for the loss of life, some can bring them peace but it's hard when you don't have all the answers. I believe it's not meant to hurt them but it cant help but to be felt, trying to understand why these things happen isn't attainable to the ones left behind but we can find comfort in knowing one day we will see them again. Friday morning my new song is a ruminate of amazing grace with my twist to addiction and how He lifted me of such a thing. I like to make things my own and the only way I can do that is by adding my own words the ones that helped to bring me thus far, in this world we are brought together by what we live through and many have traveled the path I have and in a way I speak for those who cant speak for them selves, so I tread lightly when I write trying to make since of whats going on in many others lives.

And I realize that many have gone through the gates of hell to get to where they are, I try to make it a happy song but at times that isn't possible. But if others can get together then maybe they too can bring some insight to the words of the song. Many of those who have fallen are very talented and some don't even know it because it been locked away in that place in their minds, and only when it's born again can they hope to bring it to life or back to life. Many people who went on to make a name for them selves havee fallen and didn't get back up, like Jemmy Hendrix a soul lost to addiction to never rise from the ashes that took him long before his time. Also the king of rock and roll Elvis Presley who fought his demons for many years and then dieing at the age of 42 years the same age of my father. All traped by the curse and couldn't get out did they make a pack with the devil or did they just give up on life it's self? They had the prestige and the money but even that wasn't enough to keep their souls going. I hope one day I will be remembered for the good songs I sing because they will belong to God the one that brought me out of bondage not the bondage of slavery but the bondage of addiction praise be to His name' it's not a bad morning so the day should go good as well although I got up early I feel fine, and I slept better then I have in weeks thank God and His son Jesus Christ. I can hear the train coming through town as it blows it's whistle, I like to hear the wheels as they ride on the steel of the tracks you can always tell when it coming or going depending on the weight of the train and you can even tell when a wheel is bad by the thump as it rolls along. Like my life really' with it's up's and downs but through it all we seam to make it to that place we need to be, I too have moved on and have taken down my momentous; of what I have written about over the years but fret not they are in a scrap book for safe keeping until later in life when the memories start to fade from old age, a good thing is that my grand children will have them when I'm gone from this world to maybe look at if they ever need to when the situation should arise with them or their children, I pray this never happens but we can never tell as I wont be here. The church being my home is a great place to try my music because I can be alone with my thoughts and a microphone, so I can hear my words much louder then I sound in person being very soft spoken makes it a little harder to be heard so it helps to make a friend to amplify things for me. I don't believe music has come from the church except for on Sundays so maybe I can change that in time while I practice my creation of song's. My words come easy as for the rest they also can come easy but they have to be made mine before I can sing them like a shoe that fits too tight you have to break them in and make them your own, in my story' my moms family missed the bigger picture. They saw their daughter give into temptation of the flesh but what they didn't see is the birth of one of God's children a person just like they were that needed their help so they turned their backs on her and I and sent us off hoping no one would notice that I was born of not the other kids father. And to me today that is ok' I can live with that, but they missed so much me growing into a man after being lost in a world for so many years. A man that learned to love the lord as many of them did, but in the bible it says to forgive and that's what I have done over the years so I could grow strong in my faith with our lord Jesus Christ' I remember grandma very religious but even she had a flaw. through the years I have learned that you solve problems not send them away or disgard them like they were nothing.

My mom was an inspration to me sitting up with me and singing at night when she felt all along but more then that she loved me. The best way she knew how, and we were close to each other more closer then all the rest of the kids combined. I don't know why it was this way but maybe looseing her chance with my father had something to do with it and I was that memory that almost was, where she lived wasn't very big a suburb of Duluth Minnesota but you can bet like here everyone knew each other. She once told me that a bare came to where we were living and she had to run to grab the kids after waxing the floors and she slid them across the kitchen floor to get away from it and lock the door so she could call their father, this was before my birth so they must have been getting along pretty good and then something happened to change the course of their lives and later I came into this world. Do we really ever know God's plan no I don't believe so for in a day things can change and the change can be beautiful or very eugly, but through it all He seams to have our back. If we fall He can lift us up like we do with our own children and go on with the day. Saturday and another weekend is here, they say it's supposed to be in the 50's and that is something I can live with the warm weather is a delight for me and it even lifts my spirits knowing I can go out side and get some fresh air. Not that I can't when it's cold, but you know what I mean.

I went and done a few things at the church yesterday and I enjoyed my self, the doing of things in stages really helps me in many ways as I don't get short tempered. Learning to not have that in my life is tricky but I know it can be done by replacing the bad things with the good, for many years I held on to some anger but was able to let it go after letting Randy know what he did to me so long ago when drugs was in his life his reply to what I told him was that he didn't remember it because of the drugs and then he cried and said he was sorry and I think we both felt better after letting it go so we can move on, it's one stage of healing that has to be done and he didn't even know he did it but it bothered me more then I thought. In time things will begin to heal as the lord brings new things into our lives, I find it strange how He can heal all things even the mind after it has been destroyed. He seams to reshape it with what it needs to move forward letting go of all the things that once cluttered up the mind, I slept good last night and didn't get up until 3:30 this morning what a delight to not have a fogged mind. I want to do some things to the house this next summer so my home will stand out, maybe put in a garden and have the water hooked up I used to love flowers especially Tulips that are a very strong flower sort of like me I guess Ha! Since I'm going to be here forever I have to make everything my own and make it a part of me. I have looked for someone on a dating sight but I don't have much confidence in that kind of thing so we will see what happens in the future, when a person reclaims their life they have to mend fences and I'm not talking about out in the field. The fences that were destroyed by the alcohol and drug addition, apologizing for the wrongs you have done to others especially family and friends I had to do that long ago and it helps you to mend along with them that you hurt. But don't expect it to happen over night because it won't, it took years to destroy the love you once had for someone and it might take years to mend those fences. But through time it will all happen if you are truly sorry for the things you did, in the dark world you are not you're self not the child that God gave His approvel to, before you were born. That person will come out later as you mend and start to rebuild your life at first you might not know the person that has been hiding in the back of your mind, that shy or bashfull person that didn't get to live in the out side world. He or She has been kept in the dark for so long that just the light will be like a miracle to them. And then the growing will start one step at a time, like a child learning how to walk for the first time and you can expect to fall from time to time as it's a part of growing. But the good news is that He will pick you up like a father would his own child and dust off your knees, His love and strength is much more powerful then ours and He will stand by you all the way. Drying you're eyes as you cry and telling you that it will be ok' for these are the things a father does for His child, and He will protect you no matter what comes against you. Death has come for me three times and each time Jesus was there to send it away, the miracles that have been in my life has been many. Since my computer took a dump about a week ago life has been different not getting up and writing each morning and it felt strange getting up and having to listen to the world not being shut out. As for things they are going good now and I got all the bills caught up and even got rid of a few of them but it did give me more time to read the good book and I have come far in my learning.

As Mark went on vacation I talked with Tanner and he asked if I might be interested in an open mick night if they start one and I told him I would, it would be great to get my music out there and see what others have to say about it. Another dream of mine to be full filled sometime in the future, and it's not something I will not let go of untill I do it. It's already the 9th of Febuary and there for a while I didn't know what to do it's very important to try and keep your self above water but I did make progress in that department now all I have to do is wait on the guy to fix the gutters on the house so no more water destroys the house. The people here are still helping in everyway they can but I need to stick to a budget so I can make it further down the road. I didn't feel the impact of dad leaving until this month and it was scary the thought of not having enough to live really does exist even here in the heart land' and in a minute you could loose everything if your not careful,I also found out that satin is still at work in my mind at times telling me thing that are not ture so I learn to shut him out. Through the years the lord has made a way fo me and I don't think he would let anything happen to his friend. But as the years pass I still learn more about him and I don't think I will ever know it all but I will continue to try and learn what I need to know through the books like the bible and other books that bring me joy, my land' I didn't know how much I would miss my computer until it was gone but now I can go on and write like the lord taught me.

It's been a nice day and now it's coming to an end, tomorrow is church and I know I will have fun talking with friends my pastor had me do something for her and I enjoy doing it when she ask's so much to be grateful for living here nothing compairs to my life here in Courtland and just when things I think couldn't get any strenuous I get a helping hand by people I know it is like the good book says it's better to give them to receive. In the days when I had nothing else to do I cought up on my reading trying to change things still in my life but I also found out that my qualitys are one in this universe being there is only one of me separated when I was born and the mold was broken by the father him self' through the years I find that if you keep things taken care of like your bills and such you can always get a hand to help in those times of need, as for a part time job I will still seek it to keep things going so things can stay the way they are and worry doesn't have to be down fall to my life I find that it really bothers me most trying to do your best and then have something screw things up. Many of the people admire me being able to over come the curse on my own, but with it brings many heartaches when your abilitys are limited by the damage the addiction has caused but God has brought me a long ways in my years of letting go of the curse. Some say it cant be done but from my experience that's false in the same way you loose a loved one the addiction can be lost by somehow putting it in the back of the mind where it will live like a bad memory to be washed away later after it's forgotten, we as people keep the thought alive by thinking about it and who really knows what brought on the destructive ways of not wanting to be awake the drugs and alcohol keep us in a kind of sleep not fully awake because many are scared of what the world is really like. Afraid of he unknown and what it has in store for us, it's frighting to think that I stayed a sleep for 30 some years before I finely woke up but maybe the accident has something to do with that happening being afraid that everything would be that way my land' I was only three years old when it happened, not a good was to see the world for the first time. If you ask me, my life has been one of trying to become alive and in many ways I have accomplished this but not in the big cities I'm just not a city person as far as I know and either is my little brother, he was telling me that my so called friends wanted him to move back to Kearney but he declined knowing they were just after his money it's strange how they wouldn't take him when he was in prison but now that the hard work is done they want him to leave me and go with them, but kindness trumps their greedy ways. In this world there are two kinds of people and they live for getting what they can out of others, and don't really care for what happens after they get it. Next year I will try and get my debts paid down more so I and Randy can do something together like brothers should do, maybe go fishing and catch some fish for the town so they can have a fish fry. Courtland has become a part of me in many ways and I will hope to get my life long dream done here and then people will see what God can do in a persons life, he took me from death it's self and yanked me out of t's jaws. And taught me how to live without being afraid of this world to be able to smile and just have a good time is precious to me anyway and living to look forward to tomorrow is priceless knowing he will be there even through the bad as well as the good times. My father knew me way before I was conceived and he knew my birth father so if he wanted me to meet him it would of happen, or still could happen in the years to come.

As I had my computer fixed it seams to work better then before thank God' even today I find that worry can make you old before your time, the feeling of hopelessness can really mess with your mind when you think you have done everything right and then it falls apart it's not a feeling I like being afraid that you will loose everything just from a lack of money. I have to secure a way that this wont happen ever but what's a guy to do? When you have tried everything. No worry now and maybe no wory ever when you put it in his hands, in my years since the addiction has left my life has been good limited by my own mind. The kids today are drawn into that destructive stage when they are pushed to hard or not loved enough by their parents but when you look at it it's them that take that step to try and find that balance in their lives which they never find in that world just out of their reach, trying to close out the world only destroys a connecion that we all need to make it in the world. One cant make it without friends and now that I have a family in Christ my family has grown and they don't get into my business looking on by a far and careing what happens to me. No one has ever done that before careing about the soul which resides in this body for they have to see something in me, maybe a glimmer of hope that change is possible Christens like to see people change from the world to becoming closer to Christ' this leaves the door of hope open and with hope anything is possible but it is given by the father and the son. Jesus is our hope that there will be better times in our future and he loves us all.

I cant count the times when prayer brought me through many ruff times when I wanted to give up, there has been a few people that have missed church in the last few months and although they are going through some ruff times it could be made easier if they would bring it to you father. Help them see' that through you things can be made easier if they put it in your hands, but I since them being afraid so they will have to make the choice one way or another. I think maybe I'm closer to god then most because of what he has done in my life, for surely I couldn't of done it on my own the healing and such was and is beyond human abilities. Even today I stumbel from time to time but I know that he is there to catch me when I fall and he makes everything make since, as our understanding of things may not be the same as his well really they are not! He doesn't live in this world or he says I am not of this world. When I looked down from where ever back then, it must have been a message but still I havent figured it out. It was like watching kids play with a bunch of toys strange but one day it will come to me, the message that is as hind sight is always 20/20. The day has gone fine but now the cold is moving in so I will stay inside for the rest of the day, being it's Sunday tomorrow will bring new things into the picture. Phillis was in church for the first time in weeks so she must be feeling better, it's such a delight to see her after being sick for so long and I pray that she will stay on the path to recovery. It's now the beginning of another week and I know my friends at Hord oil are still morning over the loss of their mother and Normans wife. I know how they feel as I went through the samething last year, and it's not a good feeling having that on your mind.I have had a lot of loss of life in my life but one thing is that the lord is always there for you, ready to take on what you cant handle or what you think you cant handle. My friend Norm must really feel it not saying that the kids don't but in time the good memories will out weigh the bad ones like they did with others that have been left behind, some say that God only cries for the living that it's the living that's left to carry on and this might be true but it doesn't stop the pain. And the feeling of loss can make some do some foolish things but hopefully that wont come to pass, this is a time when people need others to care about them and show that they care none of this trying to be strong when you don't feel like being strong a time to morn and a time to cry so the human spirit can move on and be happy once again. I feel their sorrow and pain as if it was yesterday but the lord brought healing unto me so I could survive through the ruff times, if I had to guess Leroy was the baby of the family and he might feel it more then the older ones but that isn't always the case depending on if there are wifes and children they can reflect their love on or towards. With me I was closer to my mom then anyone but that's just the way the other kids choose for it to be wanting their own families something that they built for them selves an extenton of them so the name could be carried on far into the future, when someone dies it effects us all when we love or care about someone and even though I didn't know it back then God is always there to pick up the pieces and put us back together again like the potter who made the tea pot we are the clay' in his hands, and at the end of life is when we will see how we turned out. Many have died this year already but most have been sick and some were ready to be with the father in heaven.

So their suffering ended and now what was taken from them here will be replaced with full sight and hearing and such. When I ascended' a lot that was hurting me had passed and it made me not want to come back and I know I would of fought harder to stay if I had known what I had faceing me when I returned, but now I believe that he had a bigger purpose for my existence something even bigger then I am my self. A purpose to spread the message that he is there for us all, to take on the burdens that will and can come into our lives. The fall of Rome you might say, if they could of seen what was comeing maybe they could of changed things from happening and the out come could have been different. Do we try and make thing's better or do we let them go on to a path of destruction if we have the power to help in some way? A very good question. Maybe the answer is in the writings of one who has gone through such a thing, many who become addicted at a young age are already lost searching for something but not all souls are looking for the same thing so it's hard to put your finger on the precise thing that made them that way. From a shy child to the man I am today is a big change, but I adjust and life is good when you have over come so many battles. For any of them could have taken my life over and over again and still he stood beside me through it all giving me a glimps of the good as time went on. In many ways I felt like a long lost service man just looking for that way to make it home from a War, and not knowing the out come of things when I get there love and peace be to the father, son, and holy ghost. Have my battles won me the war? Well only he knows the answer to that question.

But I do know that many will need help finding that path that will lead them home in the end, and home can be taken in different ways but to me it just means finding your true path in life. The one he meant for you to follow before you were conceived, that part is still something hard to wrap your mind around. The knowing that he knew us before we were even a glimmer in our parents eye, in my life I have traveled more then most as I have yet to find someone who has gone to the other side and given a second chance to balance the scales you might say. As living in the dark isn't living really when you are a sleep through such a big part of your life, it's the awakening that scares the hell out of you getting to know you self after a long sleep of 30 some years. But in the end you awaken and don't know what to do with this life you have been given, for the first time you get a glimps of what the real world is like and in many ways you don't like what you see but you move forward in hope that he has made a goood choice. Imagine going somewhere and being afraid of everything and then one night you re turned back from a destination because there was danger a head, you see the lights off in the distence and come to a slow croll and then stop an officer tells you that you have to go back in the direction you came but it being dark you are lost and you ask him for directions but he isn't from around there and doesn't know the country. I believe he was sent by my keeper to keep me safe and I was safe by not going that way, and I ended up on the highway that once almost took my life. My guardian angel as I call him saw the danger and interceded on my behalf to make sure I was safe from that harm, I had heard of such things happening but this was the first time it happened with me. And I know it was somehow a message from the father saying I will keep you safe, imagine it happening to you out in the middle of no where when your faith is being tested. Why did he send an officer? Authority seams to make us take a second look at things and when I turned around I saw a light of a house in the distence and turning into the drive way but had no response to my knock on the door so we left and found our own way back to the town we had come through earlier. That my friend was one strange occurrence and it helped to strength my faith in my creator, so many things with an answer but just out of my reach of understanding being I'm only human. At times' I feel like I have a power that was given to me when I went into the light a power that I don't fully understand yet, but when a disaster happens for some reason I stay calm maybe knowing somewhere deep inside that God wont let anything happen to this soul as he is my protector from the evil that exist in this world, did he know what would happen way before it did? This I believe is true as he is our keeper and our father. I was supprised when my contact connections was taken off my computer and it makes me mad to know I might not get them back, but I will see what I can figure out later in the day it being Monday it's just the start of he week so I will learn more about how things work on here. Always learning about things that pertain to the computer. Tuesday morning and the gutter guy is going to be here sometime today so I can have that fixed and then things should be back to the way it should have been in the first place when I moved in, the gutters are something you don't notice just looking at a house but I have known for a time that they needed fixing so what better time to have it done then now when you have the means to do it.

At least now the rain wont come pouring down the house and make things worse then they are, it kind of reminds me of back in the 1800 when the people had to have things like that done. But most of them had to do it them selves on a old wooden latter, as a matter of fact I diont think they had gutters in the 1800 the rain just ran off the roof. In many movies some would have a wooden barrel to catch the water to wash their hair which reminds me of a time when mom did the same thing with a bucket when we were camping, it wasn't the perfect life but it had it's fun times like going and catching crawdads after a rain in the creek those were the days until it became a way of life for us. But we were young and could handle it like all kids could when they are put in that predicament, everyday things change and you never know what you will write about until that day is here but we keep going until the time to stop is here and I can never tell when that time will be. I guess I miss out on many things but it's just the way things are traiding that old life for one without the drugs and alcohol, many times in the old life I would loose many days and even weeks by not knowing one day from the next and that's living only a half a life. One thing I don't want to do is loose my self in a make believe world like a lot of people do and then try to find your way out of it, so funny but it does happen.

In the days to come many new things will take place and that's what I like about this life nothing ever stays the same, this afternoon there is a funeral at the church so I have to have everything ready by 10:00 so they can have it not sure who died but they lived a long time I believe they were 92 and that's a full life. When we were in church the pastor was saying she wouldn't want to live that long but if you have all your scruples and a clear mind then it shouldn't be so bad as long as you can walk and get around, Herb has to be 80 something and he is doing good except for that time last year when he got sick when your that old getting sick takes a lot out of you. Well even at my age it does but not as bad. I cant hear the trains today like on most days so maybe they are passing us by today or else they will come through later and pick things up to be shipped out, many days are very exciting but then the others not so much, but the good out weighs the not so good. I was very delighted when the guy came and did the job with the gutters it looks so much better and now no more worring about the water over flowing where it doesn't belong, it's been a good day and I told him that I would call him if I need more work done because he did such a good job, his eyes poped open wide when I gave him the moneyand now he is off and on his way home from working. Well it's the end to another day and we will see what tomorrow brings. It's now hump day and almost half the week is gone, tomorrow I will get the oil changed in the car after going to Randy's parole appointment and then it will be back home to finish some things I have yet to do.

CHAPTER 14

We all have to find our way in this life and it can lead us down many roads then in time we figure out that we may have taken the wrong road so we correct it. And try going down another one like Dorothy in the wizard of ooze' but without the colored pictures because there is no color in the pictures I see. Randy is a great brother and I told him that we will make it through this together but right now I have to make this happen on my own. Because it's my vision and only I can bring it to pass at this time, starting out you have to make a box of how far you want to go and then fill that box so everything is solid, my box isn't filled yet so I will continue and make sure it's filled before I move forward. There are many people from many walks of life that would try something different and they can get that here in the Courtland area the labels are one of my concerns and I want them to read 'created in Courtland KS'. And then my name and so on and so forth this will also get the word out about this great place and the people will come even more then they do now during the festival which is every year, I want people to know that our dreams don't ever have to end after they take their lives back, that it's ok to keep dreaming even if you couldn't dream as a child. My dreams stopped when my brothers had their accident because I was afraid to go to that dark place and watch that film over and over again. A child's mind can scare the hell out of them and make them not want to go back into the place they don't understand anyway, the brass ring a time when He opens and shuts doors in your life behind one door you might find nothing if your not ready but if you are ready then anything is possible. That's the great thing about Him' with Him all is possible without Him nothing can come to pass by your own creation, O sure many have things handed down to them but it took a special person of faith to make it what it s today or before they left this world. God doesn't give things and take them away unless you are really bad and loose sight of where you were.

Before the blessings came to pass, if He thinks you deserve it then He will reward you with what you ask for. Many times I could of made it but nothing came to reality until I found where I needed to belong. You see I needed to be in that box I created until I could bloom and then in time I would be able to grow past my limitations, He says we are only limited by our own minds but He has the power to change us from the inside out as we go through life. He can let us see the things we need to see to bring things to pass, and it doesn't matter how old you are. Some get a vision like I did and just push it away and think it's a fluke but it's not a fluke it's a message. Tuesday morning and I need to make some more treats for the people as each day passes things are getting better you don't necessarily make a lot but it's getting established that matters at this point getting your name out there so they will know it's you taking this on. They seam to like the things I make so that tells me that I'm on the right track, Hoard Oil I where a lot of people come to get their cars fixed so they have the time to read the message. It's trash day so I have to go down to the church and get things done like vacuum and take out the garbage for the week, then tomorrow it's off to the thrift store for the afternoon and I'm hoping to have some new things come in. My life hasn't taken off you might say, but it's moving towards my dream the one that has come to me many times in the past few years, when I create I use my imagination like in writing I believe taking something that's true and bringing it to life. I haven't talked with anyone lately about my adventure and I don't want anything to interfere with this adventure.

As for my time it will now be spent creating maybe new things, the ladies want me to make some pickled deviled eggs so they can taste them and that I will do in the future I know if the guys like them then sales would be better in the future it's all about having passion for what you do and I seam to have plenty of that so far, right now I'm just trying new things I have always had a knack for something's but I know it's His hand that guides me and for that I'm grateful to you my father in heaven. When do we recognize that He is there with us in each step we make? When you recognize that He wants what best for us. We are made for greatness but it's our own mind that stops us sometimes because we don't seam to believe in our selves until later in life, many times I have said I was going to do this or that one day but never fully followed through with it so today with a new life I have a new venture. One that fits this middle aged man I don't have to move any faster then in any other day and the technical things come easy because I have thought this out many years ago when things weren't as vivid as they are today, I want to get a lot of stock before fun day that way I can sell some there. As for the shyness it seams to have left this guy because I can talk about this venture everyday with people who wonder how it came to be. My father in heaven gave me the ability to do this and as it says in the bible no man can stand in my way of something God puts forth, like with one door opening there is no man that can shut it 'only God' will my dream unfold fully 'yes' that is my dream and dreams are a part of us. They give us the ability to feel and they can also make us happy and if everything is done right then you succeed and can maybe pull your self out of this thing they call poverty, it's would be nice to not have to worry about things all the time to have that peace of mind to know that you will be alright. The wonders of this world is great. Today after work I'm going to have to make a run so I can get supplies that way I will always be stocked up and at this point it's the best thing to do because there is a three day setting period before they can go out. And you don't want to send them out any sooner as for the ones I just made I'm sure they have sealed and that's the most important part the sealing of things so nothing can hinder the process, I wish I could get better jars ones that are not so hard to seal but for now these will do. Little brother is amazed at how things are coming it's like he is seeing a miracle unfolding and he gets excited as I do when things are going right, the greatness of God can be felt in my heart and it will always be there as I move forward in time, if I just do the eggs it wouldn't cost as much and the return would be greater as for the sausage they cost up the butt so maybe I will just make a few of them and mostly the eggs my dreams were never unfolding in the other world and that had to do with being lost in a world that I didn't understand.

But now I'm awake and I see many things which could bring good to my life and to those I help on the way. Bring me greatness Jesus so I can help others with my gift as it's just not for me but those who touch my heart, many things are turning including the world and if they are all in sink then great things can happen for surely the heavens are on my side for once and this all gives power the power to make things happen bless me O Lord so I can feel the way I should have long ago I understand that I wasn't ready before but now I am guide me my father as you do so many and let me show others that dreams are attainable through you the one who made us who we are. You took us and blew your breath of life in us so we could do great things so let me continue to travel this path for a time anyway and thank you! Great father, son, and holy spirit. Three in one like the water that takes on three forms but still remains the one, let this flower bloom like the lily that stands strong and looks beautiful. O Lord you have seen to give me a chance and like before I wont let you down grace and peace to you this day and thanks for everything. I have started my batch for this morning and then it's off to the church to take care of my responcibilitys never loose sight of what came before because it's that which helped you, don't ever forget that. The day has went very well as I got the work done at the church and also stocked up on supplies, everything is still on course and things are moving forward I also paid on my bill at the station to knock it down and that felt good also. Everything is new in this life and I know if it wasn't for God this new life wouldn't be possible, the rebirth of my life has really just started all the new things which are coming in my direction give me hope that things will only get better.

When I first got here I felt the goodness which is in the people and that made it easier to become a part of this community funny before I was never a part of anything really, but now we pray together and talk together it's like with some of them I have known them all my life like a close family that cares about each other their pain and their sorrows are wiped away by goodness that God has placed here in Courtland. What brings such kindness love that's what and the ability to show it to those who need it at a certain time in their lives, when I wrote Phyllis' that Sunday she showed up in church and thanked me for the kind letter. I don't know how but I can feel things like that when someone needs an encouraging word to make that connection that someone is thinking about them. And being sick is no picnic especially when age isn't on your side. As we grow older our bodies seam to take longer to recover and that can get lonely, but I do know that she has children that care as she talks about them every so often. My buddy Harley is barking and I think it's because I have the door open for the first time this year cant help it as it's so nice out side over cast but nice, tomorrow it's back to the thrift store and who knows maybe I might have a couple of sales there also. It's coming to the end of the day so I will close for now later. Wednesday and things are wet last night a storm came through and scared Harley so he ran under my bed to hide thinking I would keep him safe, I don't know why he gets that way but he does. And when I got up' I threw him out to go and get into his bed I have to stop spoiling him by letting him get his own way it's another beautiful day that He has given us even if there is moisture on the ground. I got to see Roberts tractor and boy it's a nice one a new John Deer' and I'm sure it has all the bells and whistles like most of the new ones have, some say they even have a kind of GPS. Which lets you set I for turns and other things so you get the most bang for your buck when your in the field modern technology has come a long ways since my time in the tractors back in the 80's but still that kind of lessons are never forgotten sort of like riding a bike from what I'm told, when I helped Greg I didn't have and problem with the littler tractor he had it's the second to the biggest but it was from that time so long ago. Many farmers keep their equipment for a long time having it insured against breakage should something happen to it, I do know that a broken axel on a 8650 cost $ 20.000.00 to have fixed but they hardly break except for once in a while. As time moves forward I get to excited when making things and then the Lord tells me to slow down, my new adventure is supposed be something I enjoy and when I get in a hurry He tells me to stop for a while, the love He has for me is great and I can tell that He cares very much just by the messages He sends me. The greatness of the one on high is shown when He interferes and bring that peace back to me, for which I let slip away when I let things bother me, the thrift store opens at 2:00 today and I will open it or someone else depending on the time I get there. I have noticed that I have to give thing at least three or four days to start the action that takes place in my product otherwise I'm in a pickle Ha! My land' it takes a lot of work to do what I have taken on but I'm confident about my abilitys to see it through, like all things until you get to be good at it, it's hard but in time it will be like falling off a log and then things can increase but for now only the places I serve now will hold my product I'm not going to get other branches or stores.

In the future many things can happen but for now only my town will hold what I create, make it and they will come, this is an analogy. People go through life puttling their hands in many chimicals which make them not healthy, like the machanic who cleand parts for cars and many other things. Progress is something which can make you wealthy but it should be done in moderation so not to hurt your company and hurt it in the long run. In the news three women were found that were kidnapped over a three year period and they are alive they were kept in a house for over 10 years and their neighbors didn't even know they were there. Three brothers were arrested for the kidnapping they were of Mexican decent and one was a school bus driver until last year, who would of ever thought something like that could happen here? But I guess it does. The path I'm taking could make me known better by many that I havent met yet, in time I hope to become known as the one who created something not new but better taking the old and making it worth eating Lord knows their product isn't any good at least not in my eyes. I seamed to have always been in a hurry through life but now it's time to slow down and act my age He showed me that I can do it, and I should take that to heart moving to a slower pace while I still can. If something is reved up enough something will break and life is the same way and before you know it your old, in this business things don't happen fast so patients is needed and I believe patients is something gained by doing other things like working at the church and the thrift store a change out of the normal things we do. This is meant to be a side hobby and in time I will realize this it's something to do when you get board with your self.

Unlike some I can't just sit around too awfully long that causes a problem in it's self, the keeping of records is hard so maybe I wont keep them for now. Not until it goes to a greater level, Thursday theres always a wayto improve things you do. Yesterday I got the law mowed and the house trimmed around the base of it aand now it looks darn good, as for the dandelions they are everywhere but I cut them off very short in hope that they might die. Later I have to go down to the church and clean up being it was the last day of Wednesday school for the year summer is a time for the kids and they get to have their fun being out of school. The morning is nice and the rain has passed again. Last night I heard the thunder all through the night but my buddy didn't come to my door thank God, and that let me sleep better. Not having to be bothered by him allows me time to get my beauty sleep Ha! Saturday we are having a bake sale at the church and I have a few things down there so we will see how it goes, if I had to depend on sales at the thrift store I wouldn't make much so I'm glad that Norman has let me but things there. I havent went down there for a day or so and today would be a good day to go and see if they have sold any, they like doing this for me and I havent had any complaints it's sure nice to have friends. After the church is done then I will run down to get some gas because you never know when your going to have to go somewhere Mark called th other day to see how we were doing and I told him that we were fine his mother broke her pelves and has been laid up for a while she is 86 years old not a good time to break anything at that age because the bones are brittle but they say she is healing she just cant get out like she is used to. Even during the rain the temps were quite warm I do know the farmers cant get in the fields because they are soaked so they will have to wait for a windy hot day when it dries out, that's one thing about mother nature you cant control it. And if you don't have work to do inside then your stuck doing nothing especially if your used to being out side, I bet it would be hard going from being out side all the time to having to stay in your home or barn. Farming is a way of life for many doing many different things day after day to make sure that the crops get to the elStacytors, there are many stages to farming you have the family which is very important because if on gets sick then the others have to pitch in to take up the slack. And I think that part is what makes those families close that and church, I wish I would of come here many years before I did but still I'm glad that I made it. If the Lord has a place He wants you then that's where you will go even if you don't understand it at the time, everything is made clear through the Lord but it's done in His time not ours as we are never on the same page unless we listen very carefully to what he tells us. It's Him that makes us strong nothing else that I can tell, visions these are things that he gives us, the ability to see things in different lights like with some of the things I do for many of my ideas are given to me through Him he gives us power to attain wealth not others. For they are just a product or a way to get things out but we do need each other to help us with what we don't understand, like the women that said sometimes it's not what you know but who you know that can help you in times of need.

Does the things we are told as a child stay with us? Some do but sadly many of them don't because as we grow the mind changes even if we are in that dark place. Changes takes place any way they are just different I tried some Jars new jars and they are not worth a crap if they don't work right then you have to try something different maybe the women of the church can give me some pointers on that my usual jars do a good job but these new ones are different because they have such a small lid learn by doing is the way it's always been for this guy, the science of making things work is fascinating to me and in time I will get thehng of it. The guy that kidnapped those girl is facing more charges and murder is one of them according to the women he got one of them pregnet and then starved her for tow weeks and they punched her in the stomic so she would loose the child, this happened five times while they were in captivity killing five children all the charges havent been files so they have a very small window to get this done. I didn't know such evil existed but I guess it does, enough of that as I don't like togo there. It's another great morning and things are moving forward my day is going to be a good one as I move forward into doing more with this project I still have to get things done for fun day if I'm going to sell things there.but maybe I won't who really knows at this point when you try new things you have to learn as you go like with many experts, Friday and another weekend is upon us when people get out and have fun dowing all kinds of things but mostly they do the things they like to do I didn't know that some dig mushrooms which bring $ 100.00 a pound but you have to go places where you have to fight the ticks and other bugs not my kind of day as I don't like crawly things on me.

My forte is making things with my hands and see them enjoyed by others, which gives me joy. Just knowing I have this thing I can do lets me know that some of my mom still resides in me, from start to finish I have to watch closely how things go. It's been a nice day and things are going great tomorrow is work day for me I don't stop just because it's a weekend on any thing I do for one day is like the others just different things to do, my venture is still moving forward and things are going fine except for the getting the wrong jars and they didn't work so well had to throw some things away and I don't like it when that happens. But as it's said nothing ventured nothing gained it's all a work in progress and with each passing day things look up, keeping records is a little difficult but that too will come full circle in time. It's like I'm building everything from bottom to top so it will be like climbing those mountain's that I climbed so long ago, well it's coming to the end of the day and I did get the lawn mowed looks so nice peace and good night. Saturday and the plant has been running all night filling ben's, and I had good luck with making six jars yesterday and having them seal the right way, I have figured out that it takes over 100 hours to accomplish making the things I do but most of that time is just the jars sitting and taking in wht needs to be taken in to make it good beyond what the others do. As for sleeping it was hard but I finely got there after a while and then time must of flew because morning is already here, another day He has given us. Like with life we try new things and sometimes when we try the new things adjustments have to be made and then when the right ones are made we stick to them knowing they work sort of like riding a bike. It's bake sale day at the thrift store and I wonder how many of the ladies will bring their products in to be sold? This has taken place through the church for many years even before I was born not too long ago I think it's a way to show off their ability and feed those who have a sweet tooth God bless them all. Who would of thought

I too would be cooking at this age in my life? I do know I was taught by the best while she was here and when I run into a problem a spirit comes to help me figure it out, a great thing as far as I'm concerned. The other day I saw the women at panther paw's who is kind to us when we go there, it was kind of funny because I hadn't seen her there for a while as we were leaving I honked at her and she waved. I like to think that at time when people are down I bring them up just by a act of caring, I do know that at times I need the same thing and it helps when they show that act. Me and Ben were talking and it's good that he opens up I have seen many that get so down after looseing someone and many go into a depression which I don't see in him thank God' through the years we all loose someone but it's how we bounce back that's important how we handly things with that person gone. Like it says life has to go on and then we make a new way and try to make the best of it always thrive to do better then before that way things will fall into place.

It's been a awesome day as I made three sale this morning or should I say Leroy did? Anyway things couldn't be going better for the beginning of starting something new in my life. And I'm glad that I didn't try and make it bigger for the get go for that would of surely nade things harder then they are, the world is at my feet and this is something that has never happened before me the unknown person who struggled through life is finely getting his chance to become what ever he wants through the love and understanding of the father and son. At times I feel the holy ghost move through me and it can be overwhelming at times but I know all three are there with me in this new life I'm trying to make, as for doubts they come and go but for the most part I know He wouldn't of let me start if He didn't think I was able to make complete my journey. Now I can see the future through different eyes and feel it deep down in my soul, it's like the past is beginning to stay where it belongs and with each day something new arises. I also feel a great change coming and I have asked God to make it so and open that door which has been eluding me all my life, the change will come in every area of my life like finances, health and love, also the growth of my spirit will continue and my soul will keep on learning the ways which I need to know. In the past I have asked God to bring me wealth and other things, and now I can tell that He is doing this but it was in his time not mine, I promas lord' that I will work hard and give like I promised this is my word and my bond to you and them, the church. I have noticed that I sometimess get an over hipperness which causes me to let things out which should have been kept to my self but then I catch my self and try not to do it again.

This is all new to me so I pray that God will guide me and show me the things I need to know to succeed with my dream, I have called Courtland the town of dreams because that my feelings about this place never have I had things turn out the way they do here , it's like a part of heaven without actually having to die before you see it. A gift if you will' and it could have been for things I did which were right, in my life I have never let feelings of bad harm stay in my mind and many of the things that hurt others I try to repair because it's the right thing to do. God to me is like the potter that molds the clay and He only does whats right in His eyes and if we do our part then good things come to us, the darkness always didn't let me see the things which could of made things better. But now with God by my side He will show me the things I missed, I could never thank Him enough but I believe He sees whats inside of this heart the purity of love for others and and of course Him Jehovah' the first and the last. Well it's coming to the end of this great day and I thank Him for it, grace and peace to you . Sunday morning and I can hear the train off in the distance yesterday we saw one leaving and it had to of been over 100 cars pulled by three engines meaning it will go none stop to it's destanation which has to be a long ways away. I found more jars yesterday so I wont need any more for a time, the eggs I made last night came out good and they are ready to be put away. It's like the weekends lets me get busy so I don't fall behind and that's a good thing because during the week they seam to go pretty fast, as for my progress it's going good and it's like there is no turning back just forward is the direction this guy is taking into to a different stage of life. I now have 15 jars to fill and that will get done maybe today so I can fill the shelves, I believe each shelf can hold about close to two dozen jars making it 6 or 8 cases to fill my stock. Others have given me ideas about things but for now I will listen to my mind it's easier that way figuring out things on my own allows me to get things into prospective and when I get it all down then I can move forward with a solid foundation to make something great. I do know that my earlier life has allowed me to look at different things in a different light and in many ways it helps me to move forward, I can hear the augers going at the plant down the way letting me know that spring is finely here. I love spring it's a time when everything becomes new from the trees to the flowers and the grass they all seam to take on their own form letting the old go away and the new sprout like there's no tomorrow, what a great thing He does for us each year as He shows His love toward us. Although many bad things happen in the world our part of the world is not effected as bad as what's out there, as for crime it's minimal here in my town of dreams' and for that I'm glad not having to worry about such things allows us to grow in the places we need it without interference. As I move forward I can see the people from the past that gathered eggs so they could feed their families, it might not of been a big deal back then but it left a mark on this guy showing me that you can make things work even in the times when you don't think you can make it.

It's called a gift even though many don't share your vision it's your's to keep and it stays in the mind where no one else can touch it, locked away with no key. I do realize that one day it will have to be passed down and who knows maybe my children will carry it on but for now it's my dream and I'm going too live it to the fullest making adjustments where they need to be to make it the best it can be, my gift from God can't be stopped but by the one who gave it to me, man cant interfear with what He starts that's just the way of things a gift given cant be pulled it can just keep growing as long as you keep to your word, did I see this coming? I believe so but at first it came to me in parts a little here and a little there but it wasn't solid except for this time. I took a shot in the dark once in a while but the substence wasn't there not until I grew to over come some things and then the picture started to take form, like the picture in an artist mind not yet fully developed but the sight was there and he or she owned it. From one life to another is a long journey but when we make the right choices then our dreams can come true, I had always heard that dreams can come true and now mine is taking shape. I talked to Robert and he said he tried my product and liked it this is a good thing because he has many frinds that could eventuly like them also, then I left the church and went over to the other church where Norman's wife was being honored, the piano was beautiful and it should last a long time to help many people. I bet Norman and family was proud, some things are left here in memory of those who have passed and are still used today like the many benches which sit in front of businesses Pinkeys has one in front of their establishment where people gather on the warm days and enjoy a cup of coffee.

As time moves on we see many things, the moving on of a good friend which has passed and those who are left behind to go on with life as we know it. But in the end we all move forward and leaarn how to smile once again and some even learn to love once more before they leave this world. Life in general is funny sometims as we learn to meet new people and learn to laugh once again, when the sorrow leaves us. Some go through hell before they bring them selves to really care once again but I believe that's a process which many go through even my self. Douring the service I sang and it was good to not feel out of place as I consentrated on the songs. You don't want to let anyone see if your nervous but it does happen sometimes with new people around, as for me it wasn't there because I knew some of the friends there, and the women that made a place by her when I walk in. it's a different place then my church and I love mine with all my heart, today I'm going to clean and check things because they are having some kind of function on Wednesday' that gives me two days to get everything ready for that day and I won't let them down. I have to put one of my eggs through another bath or hear it up so it will seal but the rest of what I put together sealed just fine five out of six isn't bad and my shelfs are getting full, Doris did a lot for the church and I could tell that they all loved her, a soul that leaves that kind of mark is rare and her memory will be in the church for all time. How great thou are the ones who leave a love behind like she did, last week I saw Norman laugh for the first time and my heart was warmed. He sure is a great person, also Leroy laughed and joy fuilled the station. I think they were amazed at the ways I thought of selling the product by each piece and who knows it might take off somewhere down the line but for now everything is going good. My ideas are a little out of the scope of others but they work just the same many self made people have had ideas and brought them to life in this word but it's only the supernatural which allows it to become real. Meaning God' they call it a gift from heaven and it is a gift, brought through heaven to a deserving person or person's yesterday I brought some Hot one to the station so now they can try them many different people like many diferen't things and you have to appeal to them all and try to find that combanation which suites them all so they are happy. It's Tuesday and this morning the bug I got in my eye washed out dam I hate when they fly into your eyes as it hurts untill it comes out but I got the yard mowed anyway with one eye open. Strange how you can complete things when you put your mind to it, it's trash day and I hope the dogs didn't get into our garbage as it sat there over night Randy likes to take it out the day before so it's ready for today as for the heat it hasn't been to offely hot yet but they say it's supposed to get worse as the week goes on some days reaching into the high 90's and others having rain which is ok' with us here in the heart land. I havent heard from Dave lately but I believe he is doing alright I saw some sayings on his wall on face book about God and how He is taking care of him so there's not any worry about him at this point. I was supprised when he said he moved to Hastings's but in my heart I knew he would have to get out of Kearney too much trouble there for him.

During the nights I'm so tired that I fall a sleep quite fast and then before I know it the morning is here and then it's coffee time to try and wake up and get ready for the day, a good day is when everything goes according to plan, but you have to make allowances because you never know for sure how things will go and you have to take the good with the bad. That's just the way life is in this mixed up world, the good with the bad is something we all expect but through God He makes all things possible the changes we feel inside and the changes we make on the out side bring a balance of some sort making us better then we were before and this can only be done through Him the one who created us my father and yours in heaven. As the mind clears from the dust we see a better picture one that can make you better then before, I do know that everyone has their good and bad days it's just the way of life for us as people. But we hope for the best and in doing that things can be better the wakeing up and stretching to get the blood flowing it reminds me of when I was a child when we stretched to grow with each passing day. I can hear the augers turning down the road as the plant is running all night these days, but what for. I don't really know not going over there leaves a lot to the imagination and I can make up things that fit in my stories, I do know that a lot of trucks go through there especially during harvest and it would be a good place to put up a flyer so things can speed up my sales to another level, but I do know that it would mean more work for me.

It would be nice to do this only during harvest and that would give me time to stock up during winter making my days and week's ready for the next step. I really like doing the things I do and the accomplishments bring me fulfillment to this life, I guess you could say that it makes me feel like I'm doing something with the time I have here. Not that I wasn't doing something before, it's just different. We have many things we want to try in this life and I guess this is one of mine' the knowing that I could rise above where I came from and maybe accomplish something I put my mind to. It's no different then anyone else that learns a trade and puts it to use in this world to make a living, the goodness of the Lord will carry you through all your disappointments and make you stronger in the end. Not being afraid to dream because of something that happened in your younger life can allow you to move forward and hopefully wipe that bad memory away.and replace it with something new, as I walk through this time He helps me create the things I do as He is with me inside of this body that He created and if He is for me then who could be against me? I do know that I'm not going to talk about my venture with others until I have brought it full circle this will allow me to bring it to where it needs to be, and with His help things can go far. All I do' I do to help in some way to try and make a difference, I know I can't change the world but my world is here in my town of dreams and there is no limit to how far things can go. He created us for greatness and I hope to fulfill that vision He has for us, or in my life anyway. Many times I travel to different places but usually it's within my mind because I know that's the only way I can travel these days, by car you can't get there and by ship it's too far out of the way. We are allowed to travel through time in our minds to any place we would like to be and I travel to that place where we looked upon the world to see what ever we saw that day so long ago, I can't help but to believe there was a message in that time but still today I haven't figured out quite what the message was. If it's like the others it will show it's self in time, maybe he was saying that the world is my backyard and the possibilities are endless here. Who really knows but Him the one who gave me the vision of goodness, I can hear the birds singing this morning and that's a sign that we will have a good day so I should get to work, the day was awesome as I made a connection with the party line a station that's on the raido to advertise that I have my products at Hords oil aand the thrift store. It's the next step in my dream coming true and then later I will run adds in the news papers so it can reach near and far, when you start a business advertising is the best was to get the word out so they will come. Many people havent heard about my venture and this will open their eyes to the fact that they can get them and take them home, I have to make this work so I can finely move forward and hopefully see that other side of the coin I have only seen half of. We went to town to get my glasses fixed and I made an appointment for next Wednesday in the morning to get my eyes checked again after waiting five years, that way I will be set for a few more years. The day has been very hot so I mowed this morning to beat the heat nothing worse then having to sweat with bugs fllying in your eyes, it's now going on 4:30 so the day is about over but just beginning for those getting off of work.I can still remember going home from work to have supper and then watching television or going to the bar should the mood hit me. In all my time in growing up I never was a forward person a person that would hit on girls, I guess I was to bashfull in those days.

And in a way I'm still that way if I don't know a person, I took a pictue over to Ben that showed the mushrooms in my yard and like I expected they are not the good ones. Just my luck they will kill you if eaten, they say by the weekend we could get some rain and in a way hope we don't despite what the farmers want cant get everything we want all the time. Wednesday morning and I slept in a little, it's another beautiful day here in the heartland as the sun will be coming up in a couple of hours I just hope it isn't as hot as yesterday it was a great time to turn on the air-conditioning so we would stay cool and we did. I don't hear the plant running down the road this morning which is unusual but I do know that things have to be checked and rechecked to keep things going, I opened the window this morning to let in some fresh air as it seams to be hot in here for me anyway sweating isn't something you like to wake up doing, it must be an acquired taste. Many people don't have air-conditioning and it makes me wonder how they sleep when temperatures hit in the high 90's or even higher such a hard thing to do. I have some work that has to be done at church before I go to the thrift store so I will get an early start this morning and get it behind me that way everyone is happy, there are many things that we can do to help out with things around town as fun day will be here before you know it. My self I don't care to be out in the heat but what ever it takes to help out in some way I will do us old folks cant handle the heat very well listen to me I'm no old just middle aged, I hope we have a good turn out at the thrift store and many people come in to buy stuff we are getting new stock for this year and many people drop off things that are still good.

Like pance or blue jeans the Spanish people come to get clothes for work. You sure don't want to ware new clothes to mess up, many of the people buy them during the planting season.and some just come in to look at the things we have for crafts and other things which we have many things for those projects, even things like cameras although some are old they still work and you can get film for them. I always liked the old ones that develop right in front of your eyes, a great breakthrough back in the day. But now it's all different and they are not bulky as they can fit in the palm of your hand. And take a memory care which you can take 100's of pictures and have them developed in just a matter of minutes, can we all bring things to life I believe it's in us. Like creatiung something new it's all done by trial and mistakes we get one thing right and then move on to the next step and then when it's all done hopefully we have something new, sort of like with cars and how they bring out new models each year, they are tested and then they bring them to the public. Or market, we are made in His image giving us the ability to create and it doesn't come with a blue print as that's something we have to make just another step in building something good. But there are those who make things which shouldn't be made like weapons that kill others but that's just my opinion never did like killing in any fashion, and I will never will. My land' it's already 65 degrees out side and the sun isn't even up yet it's going to be a hot day but hopefully not as hot as yesterday, we as humans are funny strange because we never seam to be satisfied. In the Summer it's too hot, and in the winter it's too cold. But our complaints are just that complaints usually kept to our selves but voiced sometimes to deaf ears but that doesn't change the fact that we have them. I learned long ago that if you have a good idea you should keep it where it came from weather you recived it from God or who ever it should be kept safe or locked away so it can't be taken by others, in a perfect world you wouldn't have to do this but then we don't live in that perfect world only one where everyone want to get a head the one taking from the other isn't right if they careted it. Today I can hear the birds singing out side of my window such a beautiful sound they make and they have their babys right in my trees out side my window. Also in my gutters and where ever else they choose, but the doves stay' they are not like other birds when they make a place their home they stay even through the winter blessing us in some way with their presents. And I love watching them as they feel safe hopping down the road to pick up things in their mouths. The day was nice and I got the things done that I needed to, today I worked with Jane Erickson and she bought a couple of my jars of pickled eggs and sausage I know they will enjoy them as many people have since I began to make them again. I haven't had anyone not like them so that tells me that I'm on the right track, just having the ability to make them makes me feel like never before a since of accomplishment that can't be beat also I got the lawn mowed again to get rid of the dandelions they suree can be a pain in the but, butt hey it gives me my time with God. I don't know how the connnection between us is made except that I can go into a trance a place where we can only go.

This morning Norman came by in his truck and we talked for a few minutes he went to say thank you for coming to the church last Sunday and I told him that he was welcome, we talk more then before and we are becoming closer. I told him that I see great things coming to Courtland and he said he hopes so, I don't know how I see and feel these things but I do it's like it's a gift and I don't see anything bad happening for my town of dreams. It's coming to the end of another day so tomorrow will bring something new as it does everyday I still haven't told any of my family about my adventure, and I think I will keep it that way as my dreams are just that my dreams. Not to be shared by others just my self and my church, the things we aquire in life are for us as the one who made these things possible. And of course God knows as He is the one who allowed it to take place, it's now another day and it's that time of the morning when I'm left with all my thoughts. Today I have to make some more eggs so there will be plenty for the coming season when the guys are out in the field, this new thing is really going over good as I bring something new to my friends and others before you couldn't get them but to buy them one at a time and now they can have them when ever they want. To me it's a break through and I have to take that risk to bring something good to others that want them, everyone in life has to make a living and with me it isn't any different. It's a world full of adventure and I have to make my mark so others will know it's possible to use your mind to bring things full circle who knows maybe I'm supposed to do this kind of thing with my life seeing that other part is now gone.

I have seen many self made people and they talk about how they made it but they seam to always leave something out that part which sent them to being self made, and that's the helping hand of God. For only he can make the time right when everything can fit together, I was once told that nothing happens by accident either He is for you or He is not and in that case of Him being not then nothing would happen, this whole world was created for us His children and the good book says that He only wants whats best for us in this world. Later I will give birth to my idea and take it further but for now I don't want things to get out of hand as everything starts with a sturdy foundation and the foundation will be here in Courtland' where my church is without the guidance of God I wouldn't have brought this venture back to life it would of just stayed on a shelf waiting for me to do it, which the ability could have faded from this brilliant mind of mine. "Not" it's a gift and it was given by Him, the one on high our Lord and savior. For without Him we could do nothing it was Jesus that made things possible by his dieing on the cross, we as His sheep are dependent on him and if one strays then "He" will go after it to bring it back to where he belongs. I love that He cares so much but if I was the creator then I would watch over my creation also, being human we make our mistakes but if we ask for help God will surely lend that hand that we need. As we build something it gets to a certain stage and then we have to move it even further sort of like you do with a child, at first they stand and then after time they take their first step. This allows them to learn to walk and it's no different in life when my life had ended back so long ago I was brought to my knees not in a figure of speech but really brought to my knees and the learning process was hard for me, imagine having a mind that couldn't think right and having to scoot around on the floor just to do daily things not a pretty sight but I made it through this hard time and came out on the other end not whole mind you, but my spirit refused to leave this body and it has faught every step of the way. Many said it couldn't be done but they couldn't tell my mind that as it didn't understand defeat only little set backs which was over come in time, one thing I learned is that you cant tell God you cant do it because He can't be tricked. My land' He knows everything about us even though we don't fully understand Him but that's just our minds, it says He is in us so that allows us to create what ever we deside to do. There is a mystery to understanding our full potential the mystery of the unknown can make or break you, and some never see what they could be because they are frightened and I was no different. But at what point do you over come and move forward? My love for God cant be measured by any means as it comes before anything. All the days weeks months and years that I thought I was along He and only He stood by my side, people are like us with all the same faults and they go through some of the same things as we do. So when they haven't yet made it to where you are then they don't understand what your going through, many will never understand your life but the good news is that God does as He saw our lives before we were conceived and said it was good. None of us travel the same path and that's what makes things intrestion.

Like many who have been brought up in the church they learn a certain way that life is with Christen values, and then there is the person who goes through life not knowing these things. And they tend to get lost somewhere along the way, but even in this event the Lord never leaves them they have just been blinded by satin. Many can tell stories about how they dodged a bullet not getting hurt in a car accident but they didn't dodge anything, it was only by God's grace that they survived like the shepard who looks out for his flock He stopped the tragedy from becoming a disaster. And He went after that one sheep so he could live another day or many years to find his way. The day has been another good one and things are still moving forward, Leroy was telling me a story about a guy that found out he was selling pickeled eggs and he hadn't heard form him in a long time it seams he lives in a town called munden just a few miles from here, I could see the excitment in Leroys eyes when he told him the good news and then I told him to tell the guy that he cornered the market on the supply. I believe they are rivels of some sort and I know it made Leroy excited that he had someing that the other guy didn't, as for the business it's going great and I don't see it letting up anytime soon. All my dreams have come to me here and I will live them out for many years to come, like Leroy maybe as I know he loves it living here and I feel the same. Well another day has come to an end and now I will get the sleep I need for another good day tomorrow, the Lord has truly blessed me and I know that He knows my love is ever lasting. Now as time goes by the things I need to figure out will come to me and the Lord will be right by my side to teach me what I need to know, well good night.

Yesterday I made up six jars so I wouldn't run out and this morning I checked them and everything is great, there is one thing that I realize and that's to keep plenty on hand. I don't know if it is the radio but the messag is getting out and people are interested, it seams I have made a right choice by doing this and it makes me feel good to be able to supply this gift from the Father to the people and the good thing is that I don't have to do it in bars and liquor stores. Many years ago this dream came to me but the timing wasn't right and now it seams to be, it says that He wants to give you your heart's desire and this has always been mine. When I first moved here I asked for a sign that this is the place I was supposed to be and He showed me the stream and the lake in my back yard it wasn't as glamorous as the stream and lake in my dreams but it showed me my place. He does this sometimes to assure us that we are on te right track, in my dream the house was middle sized and the stream ran next to it, but here it runs down the walk in front of the house and the lake was on a piece of land in the back 40 even though things are different they are the same because they both exist in my world and when I'm not sure of something I ask Him to give me a sign that I would understaand and by God He does it, as for friends the ones I have are becoming closer to me and that makes this boy very happy. I now almost have enough to pay one of my bills and that's a good feeling, making things to last the winter is a good idea that way things are always on hand incase you don't have any food. Like making jelly as many people do and other things to last the winter months as for spending I'm very frugal when it comes to that and it helps when things are so tight. I understand how mom had to be that way especially with five little ones, she told me a story back when I was a child about how a bear almost got us kids when we were in Minnesota. She had just waxed the floor and we were out playing while it dried she had heard something and saw a bear, so she grabed us kids and flung us across the waxed floor and then ran into the house her self and called dad. She was so scared and then dad came home and got his gun but by then the bear was gone, I guess Duluth wasn't amuned to that sort of thing back in the 50's. I still remember grandmas house on Fairview road. Just on the out skirts of town in the sticks, they had lived there a long time as mom even grew up in that house. She had a stream on her property also and I remember the water bugs as I almost fell in one time and the apple trees she had a lot of them that she caned and made many things from apple jelly and apple sause, grandma as raised in the old ways close to God. I still somehow connect Oral Robert's to mom's side of the family and as for the other side I know they wer good people how do I know this? I'm a product of that clan and my heart is pure. When I get something in my mind it's hard for me to let go of it until I bring it full circle, this is something He designed in me before I was born and it stayed with me all through life. Sort of like a homing beacon that leades me to where I need to be at a certain time, as each day brings a new adventure I embrace it and try to bring it full circle my little way of dealing with life as I move forward.

And my home' what can I say it's my home and it will be passed down through the generations if the others have an adventure to follow of their own. It's a quiet place for which many things can happen even dreams can come true here as the Lord knows He made mine happen here in this town of dreams, like the wizard of ozz' a fairy tale place that is filled with dreams but you have to be able to see them before you can bring them into your life. I would almost bet that the Spanish people think this is a great place because of the jobs they have, in their country there are hardly any jobs and they sure don't pay like they do here. America the land of dreams where anything is possible, I have been searching for that dream for over 50 years and it's just now poking it's head at me so I can grab onto it. My job makes people smile' and the smile on Leroy's face was priceless the other day. And also Norman has smiled which is great for him a smile is worth a thousand words, if you can make someone smile do it as the joy is priceless. I still have to try and make some things for Funday but I'm sure that will take care of it's self, never rush things because it very well could back fire and no one want's that to happen. I have to visit with the guy from the bank and see when the eggs could be delivered if he still wants to do it that would make it easier then running to the store all the time, everything in moderation. As it's said, I'm going to bring a jar to my friend at the bank so he can get a taste of how special they are, they are' made by the hands that the Lord gave me and they will fill the belly of those who are hungry. I can start my day by eating just three of them and I'm set for hours of work, I wonder how others feel about the same thing.

I will even make some for church in the coming months but the timing has to be just right I know they would love them as so many others do. From start to finish I now travel this path for which He has given me and in the end I hope for a great ending, none if my siblings know about this all they know is that they want some when they visit and I send them home with a little. As for my jobs before this came into place they are the first thing that gets done, because I feel that they could have had something to do with this coming about. For the things I have asked for God has surely given but I also know that it takes hard work as everything that comes to you takes that, yesterday a customer came by to return a jar and he said how much he enjoyed them. Just that lets me know that I'm on my way to making people happy. This something I seam to do and it's a great feeling nothing better at this time, my pace works here in my town of dreams and the Lord knows this and brought me here accordingly. Somehow He knew I would prosper in my efforts to get a head as He saw things that I couldn't see at the time, and He brings me joy with each passing day the joy of being usefull with no regrets. The church will always come first in my life as it's through the goodness of that which I'm able to move forward, the replacing of the old with the new is something that has to be done so you can move forward in this life. If sware words once plaged you replace them with words of kindness it's like taking out the garbage you always come back with an empty can' to be filled up again, and the old is replaced by the new. You can start this by doing one thing at a time start with the words as with me I used to sware a lot but I replaced those words with ones of meaning to me, and then the foulmouth changed and the thoughts also changed it was invigorating to know that goodness could come from that step. The F word changed to my land' and so forth and so on, and before I knew it my way of thinkinbg also changed. This takes time but it works as you read the bible and study other books that inspire you, my change was a long time coming but He made a way for the change and today I'm a better person because of it. The weekend is here and I will see if the radio broadcast did any good at the thrift store, it ws hot yesterday and we turned on the air to cool it off it's sure nice to have such a thing that works fine and it should last many years as things grow. This morning I have to get some gas for the mower and I cant hardly believe the price over $4.00 a gallon it jumped over 60 cents in the last couple of weeks highway robery if you ask me, no wonder some folks are drilling for oil on their own property right here at home. That's something the government cant stop they call it back yard drilling I believe, but it cost so much to do it that most folks cant afford it twenty five to thirty thousand dollars a hole. But when they hit oil it pays for it's self over a year period and many of them become rich over night, as the time moves forward thing will start to grow and one day things will be really good. I have made the first step in going a head with my dream and I know in time it will unfold word of mouth travels fast around here especially when it's put on the radio and other places, before many couldn't get my product but I plan on making it a home name and then I will take it to the next level. When something new hit's the market it flies off the shelf and then you have a period where it lets off but just the farmers knowing they have access to it makes them want it more oftend.

If you think about it in the long run it can save them money by not having to go into town for things like supper they end up having it right there in the shed. As for me I can have three eggs for breakfast and then I'm good for half the day with all the nourishments one needs for that time. The guy that stopped by the other day really seamed to like them and he was the first to come to my house which is something I would rather not have happen, but he was plesent enough anyway. It's like the town knows that I have something here and I will never give out my secret it's mine given by a great person when I wa a child who would of thought that the vision would come true. I knew it would if the timing was right and only He knew when that would be, I have something else that I'm going to try again but it wont be until later when everything is underway. It's like they want me to succeed in my venture and that I will do. As for telling family about it this I wont do because it's my secret, and secrets are meant to be kept. By the person that has them, always do good deeds with what you have and it can come back on you in a good way. Saturday and rifleman is on this morning and I love the show as he teaches Mark the goodness and the bad part of growing up back in what I call the early days of the 1800's, all children should watch this show and how they lived back then. It's a little sticky this morning from the humidity but that will change as the day wares on, we havent gotten any rain lately but the grass is green very green for this time. And I hope it stayes that way far into the summer, I have to mow today and try to kill the dandelions which could be an everyday project as they havent died yet.

As I try to remember to pray in the mornings I give thanks to God for his goodness and although some days don't seam like they are good we should give thanks anyway because you know they could be a lot worse then they are. As for my self everyday is a good day and I know His love sarrounds me with each breath I take, this morning I'm going to the church to make sure everything is in order for tomorrow I just love when things are the way they should be. I guess I have a kind of style when it comes to cleaning everything in it's place and clean, such a delight to do these things for my brothers and sisters. As with most things when they first start your very excited and then after time they become a part of everyday life, this is what they call change and it will stay with you if everything is right. My thinking isn't what it usually is but I know that things can change in an instent when it comes to that, the weekend is about over and it's Sunday morning I cant get over someone paying with two dollar bills I know it had to take a long time to save them being their not made very much these days. Some go as far as 1976 which was just three years after I moved to Nebraska. As one guy put it they are addictive you just cant eat one, I like making them when things go right but if there is any trouble with them then it can be a bear but that's also something that can be over come with patients, I stocked up the supply on Saturday so now it's ready for he coming week. It's nice to see that I can do something good with these hands yesterday I mowed the lawn again and it looked nice but I'm still waiting for the dandielions to die off so I wont have to cut it so many time during one week. It's strange how we as people go through stages for instence at some periods I study the scripture and it can last a couple of months but then for some reason I have to take a break, but in that time it's like I'm applying what I have read or learned to the things I do. I havent seen Mark from the bank lately and it makes me wonder if he might be thinking about retireing, I do know that it isn't supposed to be for a few years until his son can run things he also is a great guy young but great just the same, during the next year or so it will tell if things willl go full bore and I hope it does this will allow me some better things down the road and if I do things right then the future is all mine and I can give like I have wanted to. It's the beginning that's hard getting things ready for what comes next and not really knowing what that might be, labels is one thing and on them our town in bold letters and then what they are, one lady came from out of town and got a sausage along with some clothes from the thrift store. She is a teacher that has retired so her talking to Cregs wife was easy for her, teachers seam to have some kind of connection and they understand each other as they talked about God and other things something special in them that lets them connect. My journey will take me to different avenues in my life and I will continue to learn the things I need to know He seams to know the things which will take me far and my new enterprise, as for my self He took away my doubts like He has so many times before and the fears have gone away. My venture will go far but for now it's kept a secret just known by my friends that live here in Cortland, I feel like I'm that special person my mom talked about when I was a little tike.

Although I didn't believe it back then now I'm starting to, for the Lord sure looks after me in His own way keeping me safe from harm and encouraging me to do good things. There isn't a day go by that someone doesn't wave or say hi to me, it's like I'm starting to fit in and the feeling is good. I'm sure by now that Mark has heard of my adventure it takes a mouth to say something but a blessed mind to take it to another level a mind created by the Father can do anything, I have to open the church ths morning and then I will see if the heat or the Air has to be turned on. Phillis is in the hospital she got sick a few days ago so they thought best that she go in and find out what's wrong, they are saying that she might not of had what they thought it was shingels but the prognosis isn't clear yet. They should know in a day or so, even thought doctors can fix somethings there are other things better left to the father like I have known on so many instances, the goodness of the Lord is always with us if we can adjust our thinking to that wave link and there are many that can't seam to do that and one thing that will keep you away from doing that is messing with our mind it's supposed to be clear to except this goodness and with many it's not because of the altering of things. Through life in the younger years we are not to mess with his creation meaning we should keep a clear mind but with all that goes on it's easy to break down and follow a path that we shouldn't be on , and then before you know it half your life is gone in just a blink of an eye. Sometimes I wish I wouldn't of blinked, but that's then and this is now and a whole new world has opened up one of goodness and if we play our cards right then it's the beginning.

For the sands of time that has already passed cant be gotton back but we can reset the hour glass and do better with what we have left, I learned long ago that what others think doesn't have anything to do with what you become, and some of us need a place like my town of dreams to make things happen for them selves. It gives them time that they might have lost if they would of stayed on that old path, as it says in the bible we all have greatness inside of us it's up to us to figure out what that greatness is, and then act on it. Give it birth you might say so it can grow up and thrive like the child that was brought up in the Christen home with values. In this life we will follow many pathes and if things are right then we will follow the right one the one He put us on, as for mistakes we will make many but we also have the power to correct those mistakes and make right what was wrong' you can call this a gift from the Father to us as we travel through this life and go to a better place. I believe this place is just a stepping stone for better things to come and our mind couldn't handle what comes next not at this point in life. Who knows we could end up using that other 90% of our minds when we get to where we are going the opening of the parts that has been closed through this time we have been here, with my self' it's like I have to take things to the limit before they will show them selves, you know stretch that cord as tight as it will go and then good things follow nothing comes easy for this guy and in a way maybe that's the way it should be. Because you don't loose sight of where you have been' when you think things are getting bad just turn back that clock and you can see where you have been and then you will be grateful for that little problem. Because it's usually not so big at that point compaired to what you have went through, I was supprised when I went to church as many told me about the editorial I had written in the Salina Journal and they liked it. My journey takes me to places that

I sometimes forget about but I have to admit that it was good, another gift that He has given me and I use it when He sends me a message. "This drug is a curse" was the main eye catcher and it went on to give this message. In the 1930s. They called it prohibition. As I read the comment in the paper on Marijuana, it didn't shock me that things are moving forward. But really, do you believe kids are going to listen to adults about smoking when you bring something twice as dangerous from an illegal market? Young people's minds are a great gift, and they shouldn't be encouraged to distort them.

The tax on marijuana on a state level should be as just as high as cigarettes. I see the ads on television and how they use vets whose legs are missing to try to stop kids from smoking. This trickery is just wrong, marijuana also causes cancer and emphysema, and you sure don't want to use it when you're pregnant. We know how the alcohol thing worked out with millions in treatment centers, which get closed at the drop of a hat.. Do you want your child going out with a friend who's getting high? Some adults don't set a good example, but they want their children to be different then they were. All children are a representation of their home life, and if it's messed up then they will show that. It can take years to show. Oh I can get angry sometimes and maybe say the wrong thing, but if the truth hurts then you know who you are. I get grief from some who support the legalizing of this curse , but that's to be expected. When your kids want a tast of what you're somking don't be shocked because you taught them how to be strong, right? Most of what I write comes from experience and the not wanting to see others have to go through what I did.

When it can be avoided, well another day has come to a close and I think we might get some rain again tonight they are having tornados in Oklahoma I just hope they don't head this way, as that's something we surely don't need right now grace and peace tomorrow is another day. Last night the power went off during a brief storm that went through so it knocked out everything for about an hour good thing I have a power serge device on my computer other wise it would of hurt it. There wasn't much rain with it only the thunder and lightening; it's now Monday and tomorrow I go back to the doctor to get things taken care of and I hope he listens to me, I'm still excited about my article and how I know it had to of touch many people. It's like He knows when my writings should be printed or published and when it will do the most good timing is very important in this business. On the 22nd the kids will be out of school for the summer and the pastors grand daughter is already home taking her break for the summer, she has a job so Kethy asked if I would let out Jack at noon on the days that she is at work and I told her I would she is leaving for a gathering of pastors somewhere but I don't have a clue where it is, she will be gone for about 4 days and then she will be back. I like taking Jack out he is a hoot and we get along just fine, I know many people will be able to relate to the story I wrote on Marijuana and I'm sure they wouldn't want their kids to go out with a friend that is high on the stuff it's a very dangerous drug and I don't know what the people are thinking when they want to make it legal. Like John was saying in church he has tried it but it wasn't for him one time he lost hours and that's scary, I know the effects first hand and my self I would never go back to it it's not meant to be the way it is with other chemicals sprayed on it.

Just a messed up situation all around, Mary my friend in church is in her 80's and she said she liked the way I put it out there. Change is difnitly coming and I can feel it in my bones, but it's a good change and I cant wait to see the out come. It was the first time so many people at church had said they liked my writing and wouldn't you know it they published it after I stopped the paper, I don't know why but my articals seam to come out in the Sunday paper and only on Sunday and I think it has to do with the way I write about God and how He has brought me through so much. I know I'm different but that's just the way I like it always set apart from others because they have yet to see the miraces of God in their own life. We are brought together by many forces but the force of God trumps them all, with His supernatural ways and I know he is working in my life today as he was when he saved me so long ago. Imagine being brought back to life after you destroyed your self, for surely God has a plan. One that is greater then all other things combined in my life as I move forward the changes will take place and I will embrace them with open arms as I have embraced God as my Father. It's been a long road to make it to where I am today and I know He stands by me in all the things I do, like our earthly father He sees the potential that is in us and if we make a mistake He is there to help in anyway He can , but He has an advantage he has all the tools which our earthly father only had the knowledge that was aquired during their lives. Like it says' He has the whole world in his hands, just because we can't see it doesn't mean it's not there as He can make things happen which is out of our understanding and in a way I don't think we are to understand them. They are just meant to be left alone so He can bring new things into our lives, we are allowed to walk in God's grace only by the grace of God the Father the Alpha and the Omega. For surely He sees the goodness which is in everyone of us and he brings that goodness out, I know He has to love us otherwise He wouldn't waste his time. Imagine being a father that could bring anything into existence and you have no worries about how you're child is going to grow up, that my friend is power, a power over everything. And we as people have sined many times in our lives and the sin is forgiven just by saying the words "I repent of my sins" and then the sins are washed away so we can start fresh and hopefully not repeat them again. But if we do then all we have to do is repent again until we finely get it right, sort of like falling off that mountain we don't give up we just start again knowing what made us fall. Trial and error' is what makes us better then before and while we do that He is working on the inside of us like the potter and the piece of clay once so eugly but now priceless by the hands of God.

Such a beautiful thought brought to you by God in the time most greatly needed when your spirit is down or you just need a boost to help you make it through the day or week these are things He does all the time but many don't see this gift because they have distorted reality, you cant see the natural if you're in another place it would be like trying to see heaven from hell it's just not going to happen. When I was in the first years of coming back I didn't see where I am today why? Because it wasn't in the picture at that time we only see in the now, nothing like God that created us as He sees our beginning and our end and if He didn't see this then we might not be. Who we are that special person that's different from others, my self I'm very glad that I'm not like my brothers but I love them just the same as much as a brother could love a brother. As I went to the store yesterday a friend told me to stop by the bank and pick up a couple of dozen s of eggs that he got for me off his farm, so today I will do that and get them pickled, after the doctors visit and little brother sees parole. It's a little after 4:00 right now and I slept pretty good waking up only a cuple of times during the night as the days go by my legs are giving me trouble but hopefully that willl get taken care of on this day so I can move forward as for the other things going on in my life things couldn't be better at the stage I'm in, taking thingss one step at a time and moving forward. Well it's garbage day Tuesday so I will go down to the church and take that out as for ours Randy took it out while I was gone yesterday so he wouldn't have to get up early his day doesn't go well if he gets up too early then his day just drags on and he is tired. I started to take my high blood pressure when I get up now and it seams to work better, before the timing wasn't right.plus I didn't like gettinnbg up at midnight.

Random thoughts sometimes has a message in them letting you know many things, but putting them together is something that's hard. Taking something and making since of it so others might here the message that's being sent out, my messages have a significance to them maybe by reaching into the mind of others as they go through some of what I went through. As for being a bright person that I am. Even with what I went through, still my mind is intact and it's also being challenged on a daily bases through the things that happen. I cant change what happened but I can make the best out of what He has given me, the knowledge I possess can't be bought like a car or anyother thing it stays in the mind to be released when needed. My personal vault you might say and no one has a key but me, with each passing day my intelligence grows and who knows where it will end up in the end? But I'm hoping that many more other people will be able to follow some of the ways I have pointed out to them. Nothing is written in stone except for the ten commandments and there is only one writter of that which is God him self, this day holds many new things in it because none of what happens will match what will come tomorrow. Wednesday morning and I have to check on things today down at Hord oil, it's been three days since my last visit so we will see what happens and see if the stock needs refilled. As for sleeping I did fine last night and am now refreshed yesterday the road trip was fine not using too much gas only about two and a half gallong so the car has to be getting about 28 miles to a gallon which is good for that vehical, as the movement goes forward I see many things taking place the creating of something that will last for some time is great, my friend down at the bank called me the pickled egg man telling one of the women there that I'm in the pickled egg business. A title finely after all these years and I will keep up with it for as long as God lets me do this thing I do many don't know about my business but the radio helps when they put it on in the mornings letting people know where they can get them and right now it's only at two places but it will expand in time to other places. When the word got out last week sales were good and I even brought some to my friend that gave me some eggs the size of a robbon egg all I can say is that the chickens must be little but that's ok' the guys down at the station even get excited when they sell some of them it's a new thing I have brought to Courtland as one day I will expand to where they can get them here in the heart land instead of having to order them from other states, it's a good feeling to take this to another level. Last night I opened a jar of them and they are great ready for sale, so now it's up to the people buying them. Really it's like planting a seed but I had many see that seed and tell others about it, in this place word of mouth travels far it's good advertising knowing the right people. I know my sister really liked them when she was here and one day I will send her some when I get going really good, I do know that like with all things it takes time to sell you're self and the product especially when you're first starting out. And then once it takes hold watch out if you do good then things will come to you, like the sales man that traveled across the nation to sell vacuums back in the old days would that analogy work today? That's a good question' but I don't believe so, as the price of gas is out of this world at $409 a gallon who could afford to travel. But I do know that there are many windows between here and other small towns, that I could put up flyers. Flyers they are a great thing, great advertising for the person that is just starting out, I do know I will have to make a trip to the lake to put some up and maybe find a buyer at a store there.

This will be a step I make when I have enough money for fuel, and then I will add that location to the advertising later down the line. One step at a time as I was taught by the Father when he helped me to walk, if you rush things then you open a door that you really don't want opened. Think each step through and then take it or if you are moved by the holy spirit then follow it these are steps that wont steer you wrong, "why" because God wants us to succeed in this life it's his gift to us when we work hard and make new what was once old. I one day see a big place that I will run where my product will go out to different places like so many before me I will have to make my own way up the ladder to success but people will want my product because it's reasonable and it cost far less then others that have come before me. My name will be spread from satisfied people all around Kansas, as that's my goal. It was a good day as I got my eyes checked and they ordered me somee new glasses now I will be able to see better when I read I also sold a jar of polish sausage and that paid for gas not much profit at this time but I know down the road that will come it just takes time, also we got some food from the government which wasn't much but it gives me something to give to the church when needed. It take us all to help others that have less then we do, Thursday and I didn't realize that memorial weekend is here and according to the triple A' most people will be driving this year instead of flying because of the hikes the air-lines have put on things like luggage and other out ragious things. My self I never did like flying and I wouldn't go there for any reason, the morning is nice so far but later thay are calling for rain this weekend and that will be a delight if that hole doesn't get any bigger in the back yard it just poped up from out of no where on the south side of the house.

As the weekend is about here many people will be gone on vacation and many of them will be at the lake driving their boats and having fun but we will be here at home, holding down the fort you might say just being grateful for the things we do have as the time moves on. The sales have slowed down for the time being but in time they might pick up again we will just have to see. It's like when it first started there was a flood of customers but now that they are full it has tapered off, it's not a big business but it's a little one and that's ok' for now. As the Marijuana topic comes up from time to time I have to attack it because I see the damage it will cause in our young peoples lives, as with alcohol and other drugs the child's life will be short lived by this curse. Others can't see it right now because they have no vision of the future, and the only way you can have vision is if you have lived the life of destruction, not only hours are lost but also days as you fall into the trap of addiction. Many will say there is medical reasons for using it but that's just a gimmick to make them think it does something when it doesn't, an addicted person will use everything under their power to make it easier to get. Like the pusher that sells the elegal drug to kids and then want to wash their hands of the whole thing once the kids are hooked, there is no honor between these people just the mighty dollar's that they have sunk into producing the drug. And if I have anything to say about it then it wont make it to Kansas. I get angry when they say it wont do any harm because I know they are not telling the truth, the two states that are making it legal doesn't produce the food we eat only places like Kansas and Nebraska grow the things we take to market, and of course there are others but it shouldn't be allowed inn these two states it would destroy the soil with all the crap they put on the plant. Imagine our kids taking in that crap and destroying their lives before it even gets started , not a pretty sight for truly careing parents to see. But for those who's lives have already been destroyed by the Marijuana it's a reason to keep doing it because they don't know life without it, they say I'm not addicted to it but that is only something that's in their minds, take it out of the picture and they wouldn't know how to handle life. No person in their right mind would hire a person that is on the stuff it would be like hireing a drunk and we all know how that would go. A women at the community center asked if I was the one who wrote the letter and I told her yes she said she liked reading it as it made a lot of since' she has known me for a few years and didn't know I did such writing, she also said she always wanted to write something but never got around to it. This is something only she can change if it's in her heart, I didn't expect to find out that so many read it but they did and to me it's a good thing. It lets me know that others care about my ability to write and it shows that I care about the youngsters; in our community and in other places to me they are our future for before you know it we will be all gone and they will be left to carryy on.

And if given the tools they too can try to stop the curse that wants to take over their lives , my land' I don't want to leave this world without trying to change things. The Lord gives us many talents and mine just happens to be writing it's a beautiful gift that he has given me and who knows where it will bring me later in life, someone has to speak out against the autrocities that are trying to make it's way into our society surely the meek wont do this, always afraid of what will happen should they speak out. For surely we have freedom of speech it's something God Him self gave to us all and our opinions differ but that's just life as he set it up my mission in life is to bring good change the kind that will last for some time when I'm not here any longer, like many before me they live on in the words they wrote and I hope my lessons also follow theirs. Even though we all have our limits God somehow guides us and gives us what we need to get the message out to those who need it, like the child who's dad or mother wants them to try the cures. This to me is unexceptable and they should be taught a lesson, I wish I had a machine that could show them the future should their lives take that dirt road that in it's self could scare them straight and if not then they would know where they are headed. Down a road of no return, which will lead to death. Lord forbid if they took that road because once you have traveled it it's hard to make your way back, funny I can write the words but as for knowing the simple things like editing I don't have a clue to how to do this but I feel someone does that will lend a helping hand later down the road, speaking out is something special and protecting the kids of this world is a great thing for the Lord knows' they cant speak when they are so young who gives them a voice I will.

The one who has followed that path which they also could end up following if they are not guided in the right direction, the world has so much to offer if they just stay off the drugs and not distort the reality they were born into. My editorial about dream makers and dream breakers didn't make it to the paper but maybe it was to childish in a way trying to think like a child but I am a child in many ways, it's something locked inside of us all mine just likes to come out and play from time to time. And letting people see it doesn't bother me any, when I see other short tempered I just shine it on and thank God that it isn't me having a bad day. And then I walk away if I cant brighten them up a little, like the lady at WalMart she was short tempered not wanting to do something as easy as changing a battery so I went away and told Randy my her day isn't going so well, but you never know what might of brought it on. So when we returned I helped her as good as I could making her day a little easier I hope' We don't travel much except for when we have to be somewhere important and then we don't stay long only long enough to get the deed done and then we are down the road. My life is like some would say going to school but I live it everyday of my life teaching my self the bible and other things that inspire me, but always the good things and not the bad changing if you will from one way to another hoping to find that place for which I need to be that place in the mind not distance like on a trip. You can do that anytime, for the goodness of the Lord follows us most everyday of our lives. And He is there even when we sleep changing things from the inside out. Today I put my add on television so that maybe it might bring up sales so we will see what happens in the next week or so I really don't know how this will work but sometimes you have to take a stab in the dark and see what falls out of it. Well it's the end of another day so until tomorrow good night. Friday memorial day weekend and everyone who is someone will be doing something, it's only 54 degrees out his morning but I have a feeling that it will get warmer as the day progresses. It's that time of year when you cant really tell if were going to have a spring or if it's going to go right into summer but were hoping for spring first the nice time of year when it stays cool for a couple of months anyway, last night I slept pretty good after talking to my daughter and giving her the good news about my business and she wished me well in my endeavor. The weekend should be intresting but I know some of my friends wont go to the lake, I couldn't believe when she told me that it cost 40 or 50 dollars to camp when you have to use their power for your camper that's as much as a motel for Pete sake' after mowing yesterday I filled in the sink hole with some bricks and sand but I don't know if that will do the job or not we will just have to wait and see, as we went and got some pop at the store in town we stopped by Scandia and our friend said to have a happy holiday. It seams that the people we know by passing must like us as they get friendlier as time passes, we are like two peas in a pod and when one isn't with the other they ask where the other is which feels good sometimes. Also I text Valerie and she is doing fine but she still feels the loss of those who have passed on and I know how she feels I don't believe you ever get over that one special love for a long time and if you go into another relationship it's not fair to the other person your with because your always thinking about the one that passed suddenly love is a hard thing for anyone to understand but it's something that should be in a persons life.

Even if they bicker from time to time, which they say is good for a person. I can recall not being in one for so long but then you wonder what you have missed and then the what if, and could of, come into play like with many things from our past but then you open your eyes and see the world as it is and then you thank Him for what He has given you. The gift of life, something so precious but confusing at the same time as you try to figure it all out which I don't think anyone really does it's the search that keeps us going like the one looking for that treasure that was burried a hondred years ago. It's the excitement of the hunt' that hyper feeling when you think you're getting close, kind of like when I think I see something I understand in the bible but then it wasn't what I thought it was so I go on searching in hope that it will come to me. I believe it's the same with a teacher when they think their student has finely caught on to something they never thought they would get, thrilling it is. To me anyway as I leaarn more and more with each passing day, my I feel great today and it really feels good to have a clear mind without the fog hanging over it. I havent talked to a lot of people lately just the ladies at the thrift store and they keep me posted about the going on's in the town, lord knows I don't mingel with many. Just the people that are in my circle the ones who are trying to help me, in many ways I think they want me to succeed and I hope I do but it's in God's hands as I have done what I believe I should have done, and now it's the waiting game as I hope people come from miles around.

I know that on fun day thousands will come through Courtland and many of them are bikers just business men out riding their bikes and traveling through the state, from what I have heard they have been doing this for any years and it wont stop anytime soon, one of the activities is when they go on the poker run from town to town and they give out a prise to the winner. Not sure what the prize is but it must be worth the run, then the kids have their time on the slip and slide and picking ducks for the duck race. O how I remember those days when they did it in Kearney, they would race them in the canal for big prises and money and of course braging rights that they won' it's mostly for kids so they can have fun during the hot season just cool fun from the heat. Saturday memorial day weekend I believe the add on television is doing some good although it takes a while for it to have an effect, during the weekend if someone needs anything they can come to me and I can hook them up this is still all new to me in many ways but it's still moving a head like I planed, pastor Kathy has gotten back from her trip and she looked tired it must have been a long drive for her but I do know she feels at home in her vehical so that's a good things, the thrift store isn't open today because of something that's going on an alumni I believe, but we will be open next Wednesday as usual. Still trying to get things going on my part. Yesterday I took a couple more jars down to the station and I brought one hot for ben I really like that young man he is such a polite kid, in this life many things are different as you look forward to getting up each day. Unlike in the old life when you just woke up to go back to sleep I now know all the things I could of done back then but didn't do them. My doctor is cool and he understands me much more then the other one did good thing I changed from one to the other, he was very supprised when I showed him my front page article in the Hub paper and I believe it helped him to understand me more then he did knowing where I came from and where I'm going from bondage to a life of freedom that I will bring upon my self. No one likes to be bound by the ties that bind them and I'm the same way like the slaves that freed them selves so long ago, to go and live a life without those shackles that limit what we an do in life. When I stocked up yesterday Norman said O you again, and I knew he was playing with me. We have been friends since I moved here and we will be friends for years to come I got him to laugh last week and I think it was the first time he has done that in quite some time such a kind man and I know the lord brought us close for a reason, as in many ways I'm like he is kind but shy in many ways like we are meant to be friends. I still cant get over him saying that he was glad that I'm me, that will stay with me for many years my friend and my buddy. Leroy is also kind taking on some of his father and his mother he is just a good person, and we are friends also.

First coming here I don't think Margret thought I would last but through the helping hand of friends I made and the lord I'm still here, and I will stay until my time is up on this earth my piece of heaven if you will where my dreams seam to come true. It's like the lord is looking out for me in many ways to make sure I have all that I need to travel through this life and to learn the things I need to learn, such a great God we have. It's a shame that many more don't know him in the way that others do His kindness and love for us and He wants us to spread the message to those who want to listen plant that seed which he will make take root. I told Norman that I see great things for Courtland' and they are yet to come, for God blesses those who follow him and many times they can't see it until they dig deeper into their faith and find out about the greatness of the lord. My self I had to feel it before I believed and God made that happen as I went through this life without others telling me that I couldn't do this or that, many will try to steel your joy and you cant let that happen and also they will try to steel your peace and that could be the reason why I moved away and came to this place I call my town of dreams, what has happened here with me is nothing short of a miracle as my days are beautiful and the nights are the time of rest. So I can go on to another beautiful day, I'm slowly getting the hole filled up in the back yard and maybe today the deed will be done but I have to only do so much at a time because of my limitations. In this world you have to make your own way and if you do things right then He will stand by you through it all and even lend a helping hand when you feel things are starting to slip, with me it wasn't hard to love God because I saw the goodness first hand. Even though we may not see it at the time we do see it in time.

When He shows us the path we were on and that cant happen until later in life when He allows us to be able to see that part of the picture with some they see only a fragment of whats going on and with others they might see them in bigger sections like a block, but the mind thrives to see the whole thing the beauty of the canvas when things are finished this is just the way we are as humans. Nothing can be shown before it's painted and we as the painter have to fill in the colors, and if it's all black then there is a problem or else you have one hell of a black ground ha! I have to say that many influenced me to stay here but my most important one was God for He moved people to help me when I needed it, but this I couldn't see coming until they offered it to me. Like the helping hand people and the church they wanted me to stay after pop's went to be with the lord' and truthfully I didn't know if I would be able to, it was like He steped in and lifted my burden so I could stand strong and go on with my learning. Just because others don't see what I'm teaching my self I'm being taught by the father and He is the only one who has to see where I'm going at this point, as for my love for Him' it can't be measured by anything on this earth because it's so different then the love you feel for another human. With a person you have to say it but with God you have to feel it deep down in the very being of your soul, when I was left alone to take care of pop's no one came around unless they wanted something. It was never to lend a helping hand or anything just to take and that wasn't a good thing to do but people will be people and if they are selfish then it's better to have them away then in your life. I have taken care of many that were sick in my family and if I had to do it all over again then I couldn't turn them down. What is one life if you can change even a few others? A special life that one would be' to bring change and help stop the suffering to even one is a great thing, we as people sometimes forget but many things stay within our minds so we can recall then later. Like the stories that are brought up by someone trying to make a change, if kids can see that even the older people have dreamd that can come true they too might try to bring their dreams to pass, for they have a better chance of making them come true then us the middle aged or elderly. They will be the ones who shape this world when we are no longer around and maybe that's why I'm so against the altering of their minds by drugs and alcohol for they will lead them no where, it's hard to believe that something so small as an ice-cream could stay in the mind of a person even after 40 some years but it does and the lesson learned from that one act will stay in that special place until your time is up here in this placce, will it carry on with you when you leave and go to that better place who really knows but God? But I do know that if you pass and come back it will be there. I don't know if the station is open this morning being a holiday so we will just have to see what takes place, last Saturday Norm brought over something for me because someone came in and he didn't want to leave it in the store that's a good thing about a town this small we are all neighbors and we can find each other at the drop of a hat if something important comes up.

The day has come to an end but I got a lot done like mowing the lawn and getting things ready for tomorrows service, I wonder how many will show up only time will tell. Also I went and got a few pop's to last the night as Randy wass running low and I just had to have one, the Oklahoma tragedy was bad but the people are strong and they will recover like they did in the last two that hit there over the last few years, it just goes to show that you cant tell what mother nature will do next. We have been blessed by not having such bad storms here lately and I hope they stay away, that's something we don't need here in out town of dreams or should I say my town of dreams? As I don't know if others have had them come true here in Courtland like I have, I don't know of many people personally that have started a business out of their home at least not like I have and not with the product I have chosen. Just doing it took a lot, but it was much easier to do it now then if I was in my earlier years. My concentration is much better now then it was back then, Randy must not feel too good as he has slept most of the day but I'm hoping he will feel better tomorrow as they say each day is a new beginning and hopefully he will feel better. I wrote something on face book hoping it would encourage others to help in the rebuilding of Moore Oklahoma' and I know people will do what they can do. As Americans we stick by each other and try to help when we can they have a long ways to go before they will have a home to live in, and if it's like Katrina many may have to go else where to find workfor a time anyway, I believe we have a common thread and that being God Him self who puts it in our hearts to help our brothers any sisters.

My land' they try to do the best they can but we all need a helping hand sometimes and when we draw together like one Nation, then there isn't anything we cant over come. The president is supposed to go to Moore sometime and see the dStacystation that has struck these people of God' and help in anyway the government can which should be a whole lot. We are supposed to be standing ready to help when a natural desaster happens and the government controls the funds which will help them rebuild, to make them stronger then before. I take back what I said about the jobs because if you look at it that's the place where jobs will be with the rebuilding of the town, what makes me angry is that their will be scammer;s that will take advantage of the old folks and others who might not be aware that they are out there so they should be careful when hiring people from out of state. This happened when Katrina hit and it happens when other disasterd strike folks, you hear about it all the time and it's sad but that doesn't change the fact that they are there like the wild dog that cant find food. You know we can never tell when something so bad will hit any part of our country and we should be ready when it happens instead of cutting funds from this to pay that, each time that is done something comes up to remind us of why that shouldn't be done. Like with the postal service they had plenty of funds until the government cut some of their funding for something else, changing with the times can be costly and it makes me wish that it could of stayed the way it was but I don't see that happening. I can hear the wind outside this morning and I hope it isn't blowing in a storm that's something we don't need right now especially with the tree in my yard that has died, it wouldn't take much to blow it down at this stage of the game and I don't have a chain saw to cut it up. Leroy could use the wood for his fire place as it's nice and dry and it wouldn't have to be seasoned meaning dried out , pastor Kathy will be at church and it will be good to have her back after her stay away from Courtland for a week, my hope was that she would get some rest but I could tell that she was tired when she picked up the mail when she returned. A pastor has a lot of responsibility, taking care of her flock and she does such a good job at it listening to all the problems of those who don't have anyone to listen to them, but she says she likes small towns because it's a family feeling and I'm getting to know that feeling as time goes by. Just yesterday as I was getting a pop at Hoards John drove by and yelled at me telling me to get away from the pop machine I had to laugh knowing he was kidding but it's just things like that which make you feel at home. And that feeling cant be matched by any means, I also got some more product ready as I was board durig the day and didn't have anything to do. Since my starting this venture things are getting even better as my time is not wasted by just sitting around, I cant imaging how many would get done if it was winter quite a bit really if you count the months that winter lasts, when you have something that can sell you got a gold mine but you have to have the people coming back and that's what I'm doing right now getting my clients you might say here in my townof dreams. The place where your deepest desires can be brought out to make something happen like the old and young women of the west that sold eggs to make it through the month it didn't seam very importand back then but it kept people alive to make it through another day.

My eggs would and could keep people alive and the same with the sausage along with tasting good it lasts for years, probably like alcohol it gets better with age but there is no alcohol effects, it's now 4:00 in the morning and soon the birds will be up singing such a delight to hear them each morning as they go to town on the music' another gift from God to us his people, they really flock around my house each spring the ones that travel south for the winter know where they were born and return there as for the doves they stay never wanting to leave for some reason they seam to feel right at home here in Courtland maybe thay are a gift also but those are just my thoughts, I see manythings others don't and that's because the world is in a hurry to go somewhere but where are they going ? I don't think anyone could tell me the answer to that one and maybe it's because they don't take the time to smell the roses or they don't know what one is, maybe one day I will plant some flowers and see how they would take I do know I can grow lillys as I have done it before. And O they were so pretty standing strong even through storms like we had back in Kearney when the neighbor got the roof blown off his garage, so much damage but they just stood there not bothered by the bad weather. That year even 100 year old trees were tore out of the ground but the lilly stood, what makes things so different? To where something new can weather the storm and the old tree couldn't. an act of God or did their time just run out after thousands of kids played on them, the park got hit the worst as those trees fell like dominos. It seams like disasters hit all the time but like in our community there are those who will lend a helping hand to clean up when the poor don't have the money to pay someone, I still have some of the pictures of what happened here a few years ago.

And the people all pitched in to lend a helping hand to make our town whole once again, thank God that the elStacytors didn't fall that year we would still be rebuilding that. But they stood strong like the people who live here, and strong is what they are. They have lived through many storms and seam to keep moving forward O ya age has gotten to some but there is a balance in the universe for when one leaves to be with the lord another child is born to take his or her place and the cycle continues for hundreds of years and the life line goes on far into the future. As I talk to people who have lived here for a life time they say there was a time when the town was booming with the kind of stores needed to keep the cash right here, but those days have moved on and now we have to travel to get the things we need to survive like grocries and other thing but the implament place still survives and the gas station where I bring my products. When I first got here you never heard of Courtland but today it's heard about in most of the editorals I write, how to me it's the good life and people are grateful when you say good things about your home and you're town for I'm proud of Courtland' the town with a big heart' never in the history of my life have I had people that cared about me so much. Here I was a stranger that walked into this town about 5 years ago not knowing anyone here but the shirt I wore told them that I was a christen, a believer of God. never so much has a shirt said so much, letting others know that you are a man of God' sent here for a reason a reason that hasn't been made clear yet but I know that will be a thing of the past once that window is opened. I have a a feeling that I have lived before and left something behind to find this time, I would chalk it up to a fluke but it comes back and it's been coming back for years. Maybe something burried back in the corner of my mind to be brought back to life when the time is right, who really knows what these messages mean? As for me, I just wait and if it's meant to be then it will show it's self without interfering with my everyday life. Even back then I was a creater of something maybe something that could help man kind can't really say for sure, Sunday norning is the best time of the week for me and maybe it has to do with the church. The gathering of people for one thing and that's to show their love for God, I still don't know the answer to why Melchisedek was brought into the picture but it has something to do with my life in some fashion maybe a distent relative or just something that drew me to the bible. Only He knows why He does the things He does the one and only God the creator of all things including heaven and earth, it was a great day in church as one of my friends bought me some jars for my project and pastor Kathy told me that jack was somewhere else while she was gone. The day is coming to an end and tomorrow is going to be the start of a new week although it's still a holiday memorial day, Saturday and Sunday was just an extended couple of days that were thrown in. also I got to see Roberts daughter as she drove down from Denver Colorado for the weekend to see her parents, she is so pretty but also so youthful maybe in her 20's I never did ask what she must be going to school for but I'm sure it's something important.

Memorial day and tomorrow we will be be back to our regular Tuesday trash day if you will and things will be great. Although it's memorial day I will still go to the church and get it ready for the week which shouldn't take long, this next Sunday they are taking up a collection for the people in Moore Oklahoma and then it will find it's way there. I believe all churches take up a collection for helping our brothers and sisters it's hard for us to asses the needs they have so the church will decide what goes to them this has been happening for hundreds of years, people reaching out to others in need after a distater happens it's how we roll' here in the United States, one helping the other sort of like seeing part of the bigger picture to where with others they only see their own lives especially if they are not working in the real world. In the world of darkness you only think of your self and don't really care about others suffering from disasters or any thing else for that matter, the people I know here are mostly church going people going through life helping those who need help how even small the help is it's the best we can do for them but it's not the amount of the gift it's the thought that brings joy to others. I wish many years ago I could of seen this part of life but like they say better late then never and God always gives us time to do what we have to do, it's the end of the month and things are still tight but I'm hoping that later it will lesson up a bit having hope is a great thing and no matter how tight it gets there is always a way to get by, with a dime here and a dime there just making it as we travel through this life He set in motion. I would like to build an empire one day but only time will tell if that can happen.

And it would take an act of God to bring it to pass, as only He knows when the time is ready as he adds a little here and a little there. If things are not right in your life that means they he isn't done with you yet, like making cookies the right ingredients are not in the recipe so give Him the time to put them in and things will be great. Our time frame isn't like his, like the potter who makes the beautiful pot if everything isn't just right all you have is a blob of clay, the story of the beautiful tea pot comes to mind when I think about how he shapes us. With time and the right ingredients He can make us stand out like never before, we are changed from what we used to be to something far beyond our beliefs it's the mind that he changes wiping all the bad things away and making it like they never happened. Bringing out a new person one that others have never seen before, and as for the old it's made new and this is done by study with me studying the bibly and other things that inspire me. Trying to find that part of me that had been missing all those years it's like going through history, a library if you will but it's in the mind and not in public records I believe all we need to know is kept inside of us locked away from the rest of the world. This is a look into my mind really a place that has kept things hid for more then a deckaid, God seams to bring out the good and leave the bad where it belongs for surely he doesn't want the ugly side of things coming out that would make the tea pot mighty undesirable, we are all a work in progress and he is the one who makes us who we are. The kind person that others want to be around this is a gift given by Him our lord and savior. When I showed my doctor the front page on my life I told him that I had made a promas to God that I wouldn't for get and write about my life so others can read my story and he said you have to keep that promas you know. For which I'm very aware of, not only that but they need to know that there is life after you have fallen from grace for the lord will pick you up and help you along the way, I'm not as good as I'm gonna get but I'm better then I used to be. Our fights might go on for a while but they will subside once He makes the adjustments that He knows has to be made, you can go from the gates of hell to a plain of existence that you have never known before a rebirth like you were born all over again. I cant say that everyone goes through the same steps but for me it was the whole ball of wax from crolling to standing to walking this was the way He choose to teach me and it worked. As for regreats yes there is some but for the most part he didn't leave me like so many others did abanded by those who said they cared but you have to also realize that others have a life to live so you have to suck it up and move on to another day, place, or time. How great it is that he brought me here to this one place where I could learn and be happy and then grow in spirit. This spirit inside of us cant be seen by us all we relate to is the body and the things it goes through for the spirit feels the things these bodys go through but for the most part they are strong it's just that we don't know how strong until it's tested. Many times you see how some treat their bodies as they try to destroy them by getting beat on, all in the name of money what a curse that one is.

If we are programmed then why does things change? We go from bad to good but this change doesn't come unless He wants to help us, we are made in His image or their's and we have the ability to attain Him within us making us good, that's all I have ever wanted but there is a block that he has to take away and when this is done then I will see things differently. I tried to sleep but couldn't we got some rain earlier but it subsided and now they are calling for more rain to night, tomorrow is the beginning of the week as far as I'm concerned as I never did care for holidays, as it's just another day in the heart land the one holiday I cared about at one time was Christmas and they ruined it with the people who didn't believe in God you know the kind I'm talking about the ones that have no hope in anything, I took Randy down to Panther Paws to get smokes and the women there asked do you need smokes Hun. And I replyed no it was the first time she called me Hun and it felt good, after the shower it got real hot out so I thought why not mow the lawn and I got that done. And now for a couple of days I wont have to mow, my yard looks really good when it's mowed so I try to keep it that way. As your home is your castle and you have to keep it looking good right? Now the sun is going down and I hope the weather doesn't get to bad, good thing I have a flash light in case we have a power outage. every time it happens it's a few hours until it's back up again and running, I would almost bet that mom would of loved living here because at times it's like camping with no lights. I sure miss those days as a child but I wouldn't traid these days for nothing, as each day is something new in my life and this time around God is a big part of my existence.

Does our loved ones see the way we have changed? I do know that the lord does as He is the one who changes us from the inside out as for the surface I don't think he pays much attention as it's superficial mostly seen by others, my life is on the right track at this time and I know that God had a lot to do with it happening. It's something ihave always wanted to have the ability to create something my self with out others being there to shoot down all my dreams. Although they are not big they are my own and they stay with me making them a part of me the creator, tomorrow the station opens and maybe then things will start to move a little faster I'm hoping that things will pick up that way I can get a little a head of the situation and move forward, Tuesday May 28th last niight we have a bad storm come through and the power went out for a while but they scoon got it back up, the stoorm spotters said there was rotation in the clouds just a mile and a half from Courtland but we didn't see any tornados just strong winds as the storm pushed through. One of the people from the news paper went next door while this was going on to get into the neighbors basement even I was a little scared while all this was going on as it was 80 degrees when it all started and then it droped into the 70's, I have only seen it get that way a few times since my moving here and it's never less frightening when the winds pickup that much. Ihave seen mother nature at it's worst and it's nothing to snease at, these towns have been here for many years and not one has taken any of them yet but there has been damage like when one took the warehouse down the road before I moved here and left only the toilet standing in the middle of it. I don't know if any shelters exist around here but it's doughtfull you are just on your own in situations like that, one day I would like to have a shelter built but for now it isn't in the cards only the thought of being safe exist. We have been through a few of the storms and each time we are still here so the lord has to be looking out for us here in Courtland' my town of dreams. I tried to wake Randy because the disaster whistle blew but I couldn't get him up for nothing sleeping to hard I guess but if one would of hit then he would have been a gonner sucked up into the sweet by and by with nothing left but maybe a bad memory, if that. I know my dead tree took a hit and today I will have to pick up the bark that has fallen from it and put it in the burn pile or should I say the crap pile where it will rott away and become ferderizer for the earth. I have some weed eating to do around the house and it has to be done within the next couple of days so things don't look to bad we are very blessed to be able to withstand the force of the weather but I know it's like the wind it comes and it goes leaving it's mark on what it has hit just glad to be here today praise God for who all blessings flow. As I pray for many of my friends including Stan in Oklahoma I know that God will take care of them he gives us that promise, we are all stronger then we even know a strength that is inside of us that only he knows the limits to. We are made in their image meaning the trinity set apart by what they have deemed not perfect but have the ability to become that way, could we ever be like Jesus was I don't think so as he was perfect before hecame to earth other wise he couldn't of taken the sins away that the first put on us so long ago when Eve ate from the tree. Harley had to come into my room while the storm scared him he was so afraid, my little buddy found comfort being with his master so cute.

As the day goes by it will be like any other day except for the picking up of the branches and the bark off the ground, and everything will be open today. I have noticed a change in Mark lately but I didn't know what was going on maybe it was a good thing they went on that trip before sickness struck, it just goes to show that you never know whats in the cards for any of us. You could be ok' one day and sick the next I'm just glad that everything is insured in case something happens, you don't have any thing written in stone on how long you will live but with God by our side we should live to be a ripe old age of at least 70 years my that would be a long time for this old boy. I got a message from Tonya thanking me for the message I sent her and the prayers for Stan those bowl blockages can be a bare as I know so well in my middle age, she means well but she talks too much for this old boy. But we are all different' as the father planed it that way no two the same yet we get along with that difference you being you and me being me with our minds so different, communication is important when it comes to family and even though our beliefs are the same but different we get along just fine, I believe they should take a trip down here to get some of my product it's no different then traveling to other places they go to and Stan comes to Kansas once in a while to sell cattle just a great trip for them all around. I miss them but I also know that you don't push people to visit the trip would be a mess if you did. Well the day is about to start I can hear the birds singing out side my window, last night they were quiet because of the storm and I even saw one bird hide under my tire well to get away from the storm.

Little did he know that the car would be the first thing to fly and he wouldn't of been safe so funny! A table for two me and you one day when He thinks we are ready to be joined together. I don't know you yet but when I do I will know that it's you, and the search will be no more just two souls going through life in love one part not wanting to exist without the other a connection that will last out the years. As for our lives they will be connected with something very strong like two peas in a pod rubbing up against each other and making love like there is no tomorrow, instead of it being an act it will be something that's wanted not tolerated by the two of us. A bond that can't be broken no matter how bad or good things get and the world will be at our door step to enjoy, no more sorrow or pain just nice days dancing in the rain, like the old movies we used to watch back in the 30's or 40's a time stopped in our minds. I will cherish you for the gift that God has given us and hold you when you cry so the tears will be washed away, our love will stand the test as we hold each other in the morning and listen to the birds sing our favorit tune knowing that God has a plan for that beautiful day, we will not fight because we know the sorrow it brings and we don't want that feeling in our lives. Only the joy which will come with the sun rises as it peack through the window, in this life we will share the things we will do you getting coffee on Monday and me on Tuesday and we will give thanks to the lord for the gifts he has given us that great feeling of love which wont bring any children but the act will be enough to fill our desires. Our love will stand the test of time as we hold each other with each passing day, a gift that God gives very few in this life. Together we will asend to the heavens when that time comes with no regreats, time to take out the trash so it's off to the church for a short time. We had a good day but to night they are calling for more storms I just hope it's not like last night, and we loose power again. As each day brings something new I found out that my reading glasses are ready but I'm not going to pick them up until tomorrow morning when it's cooler out side, we need a road trip anyway and it will be nice for that. Riding in the coolness of the day instead of in the heat, again the day is coming to a close or else it's over cast one of the two. Wednesday and the storm hit around the Salina area, while I was sleeping my daghter text me and said a tornado was spotted by there good thing we are 70 miles away from there to the north right on the border of Nebraska. I sent a letter through the mail to the Kearney-hub explaining my opinion on things and I know they will print it people want to know about the increase in the THC in marijuana like with other drugs having it in it's normal state wasn't enough for the growers they had to bring it to it's full potenchal using other chemicals so it's not as mother nature made it any longer. They used to use the excuse that it's natural and then there for should be made legal well that doesn't apply any longer when it's taken out of it's natural state. The ditch weed is harmless and it wont get you high because it's in it's natural state but if you put other chimicals on it then it's made into something else and becomes a carrier of the other drugs like Methamphetamine or even coke' what they are trying to do is sneak other drugs into society.

Thinking they are foolish and wont notice it, elephant tranquilizers was used in the 60's to boost the effects of Marijuana and when they found out that it would work they have been using other chimicals ever since and have been trying to put a label on it as medical Marijuana claming to treat what other drugs couldn't it's addictive and that's all there is to it. But I believe if they wouldn't of messed with in it's natural state then maybe it could have been used for things other then whats apparent. My land' they have messed with every drug out there and if they could they would make the United States a battle ground. Enough of that I don't like to get into politics never did like it, the thrift store is back open again today at two and I will open it if I'm there first but if not then Beverly will probable do it. This life to me is ideal no bull crap from others and I can live in peace without people wanting to pick my mind' just natural life without all them wanting to know things, people wanting to push for something usually has something to hide as for me I just write about the things I know and my life here has allowed me to do that. I was talking to Marks son and he told me about his step mother and how shee is supposed to have a full recovery I told him that I would pray for her and I will do that this morning for I believe that God hears my prayers the same as if He was here, I have made the connections I needed to make to get this business off the ground and now it's His turn to bring it to where it needs to be, if it wasn't for the lord I believe this wouldn't of got off the ground but He has always stood by me in the things I do as long as it's right.

The simple life is something I like very much no one bothering you and your allowed to live in peace, my thoughts have many interested in wanting to know more. And with more study I will come up with the answers but in my time not theirs, as they are all in a hury for some reason. Today I get my glasses and now I will be able to see better with out bifocals that seamed to always get in the way and they didn't help a bit finely a clear view of things without scratches on them it will be a delight, will have to take my change down to pay for them but hey it's worth it. The little things like having them is important to me as I don't need much, as I move forward things will pick up and they will get better. As for my writing it improves all the time as prefection sets in with each passing year, I talked to Norman yesterday about return customers and he said it would take time for things to catch on. I have always been an unpatient person so now that will have to set in slowing down, even further then I have thus far' many things have changed but still other things must change the battle in life has become a norm and now things are leveling out. My journey in life has taken on many forms during the last 20 some years but one day it will be made clear what my journey is the speaking out of others seams to be something I can do with my writing but boy it has taken many years. As for each day something new is brought to the table and I never know what it will be until the day has ended, it could be a smile or a wave or someone not agreeing with my out look of things you just never know. But in the end I sleep pretty well knowing I tried my best for that day, it's now Thursday and we closed the thrift shop because of the weather and no one else was there at 4:00 it got loude as we were getting ready to leave and then we lost power later here at the house for a short time, tornado alley as they call it was lit up from Iowa to Nebraske to Kansas all the way through to Texas and Oklahoma but after we got our little shot in the arm it seamed to leave here and I didn't hear anything the rest of the night thank God. I don't know what it will be like today but there is still a chance that more bad weather will come later today. This moornning it's quiet and for that I'm greatfull, something happens when the storms come through. Something in my soul gets out of wack I cant really put my hands on it but its strange, atleast it's nothing like the year when my trees became up rooted and I had to have them cut up, my land that was a process I hope isn't repeated. It took a long time to get things back in to the normal realm again of being cleaned up I was still weak back then and it took all that I had to clean it up took over a year of doing a little here and a little there but in the end I won out over it and time moved on, I know that old tree has to be removed but I cant afford it at this time. Maybe in the next few months it could happen for that's my goal to have it removed, I havent been down to the station lately except to get gas for the car but I'm hoping that within the next few days I will have had sold something. You can never tell about this market weather it will increase or decrease but I'm hoping for the best' we had a couple of people come in to the thrift shop and you could tell that they weren't from around here. And they looked around and then left the one women had tattoos all over her body and they were nice the guy was kind of like a biker guy ruff looking kind of like me but he said nothing well either did she for that matter.

You meet all kinds of people in a small town and you can never tell where they came from but it's nice to meet them anyway, on funday they come from all around even the little towns that are just down the road to people from Nebraska' and other States even Oklahoma. This year many will come and they will be welcomed with open arms as they spend theiir money here in Courtland, they will have a band and those who drink will go to the beer garden. It's all good and the kids will go swimming as the heat of the day rains upon them, the pool is the best fun for the kids during this time of the most hot days of summer they go there with their parents and just have a good ole time to beat the heat, the bible camp will be somewhere but I don't know for sure where it will be held, I still remember when they had it at the church that one year kids came from all around and they sat everything up on the church property. What a blast they had that year even though it wasn't at a lake or park well our town is like a village so maybe that helped, trying to guess at things is hard sometimes but for the most part most of it is in the mind you can about picture anything not knowing the facts about something, this morning I'm going down to the church to make sure they didn't make too big of a mess putting in the windows but I know there will be some and I have to keep my church clean' I feel like the care taker of God's house does that make since? Well really it doesn't matter what others think as long as I do my job.

Do any of us fully understand life? As for me I know I don't have the answers to many things but that doesn't stop me from trying to still learn. In a way I'm still trying to to find answers to many of the things that have happened in my life weather it makes since or not will come later when he shows me the bigger picture, as for now I take each day as it's given and hope that my understanding is enough for now anyway. I can still hear the thunder out side so maybe the storms are not over yet. After doing experiments with different size eggs I find that the small ones are not any good for this process and I won' use them again they seam to become too hard and end up like the golf balls that I tell people my are not like so they won't be used any more good thing I caught it before they went out. That would have been a disaster, it's small things like this that you have to check to keep everything above par the bigger the better as far as I'm concerned but not to big just grade A large will do the job. It's feels strange to not have Wednesday school having to go each time to clean up after them became something I have gotten used to, but it will return after school starts once again. Friday and I went to the church after they got done with the windows and my land you cant stay in there very long from the fumes that came with the caucking, it just about knocked me out. I'm hoping that it will pass as the crap drys I have never smelled any thing so strong and I know the older folks might get sick it just about made my head very dizzy, but I couldn't leave the windows open as the rain was starting and the wind blew like hell. My land what a sickneen smell worst then the gas I smelled as a child, I know that it must of gotten to the guys pitting in the windows strange how I didn't smell it the day before after they put in the ones in the eating room. When I went down there the wind was blowing like all get out so the windows had to be shut again, when they did ours there was never a smell and in the church they even unplugged the air freshiners because of the chance of a spart maybe today the smell will be gone who really knows until I get down there. I do have a lot of cleaning up after them but hey that's my job to wipe down everything and make sure iit's clean, I'm going to talk to Leroy and tell him that I got a case of eggs ready and about 9 sausage that way if anyone wants that large amount it's there ready to go but still I don't want to disapoint customes and that's why I take it slow at this point, through all the times that I have thought of this my main concerns is that I wont have enough to go around but then I have to look at the message for which the lord has given me that I can make it. And if He didn't think I could do this then he wouldn't of planted it in my heart, like he has done' it's not easy to make a going out of something especially when you havent done it before but with His strength and mine this will move forward and I might not be able to write as much, everything seams to be balanced and I want to keep it that way as he showed me this is supposed to be fun for me and not stress me out. Randy is up early this morning and I know he will be back in bed by noon trying to find the right combonation that will make his days go better, my rehab with him has taken strong steps as it seams that as long as the drugs and alcohol are not around then it doesn't inter his mind and that's a good thing. I have given him his space and now he looks at the world in a different light one free from the drugs and alcohol that almost destroyed him also.

He sees how I move forward without the stuff and he also sees the good things that are happening in my life since I took it back, to loose your life to Methamphetamine is a tragity but with strength you can over come most anything. It was the meth that made his body the way it is having to take all those pills to keep everything in wack because it threw his body off so much as with me so long ago but then one day I threw them all away and told God that if it was my time then it would happen, but I lived and here I am today still going strong. What happened is my life should of killed me but God had a different plan to reach out to others that might have been forgotten by society like I was, you should never feel alone in this world. As time moves forward all will become clear not for your whole life but for that time when you need God the most at the time when you feel like you could die he will step in and take control. I don't like when little brother gets up early because he wants to take his meds at the time of wakeing up and when you get off by three hours it throws off his time table and then it takes days to get it right again it's things like this which he doesn't look at, everyday at the same time and things will stay on course, managing this for him can be hell but he cant do it on his own I let him try one time and it was a disaster it took almost a week for him to get to feeling better the struggles of taking care of a brother but like pops I love him and will keep doing it. With Randy I only want what's best for him and at times he doesn't see it that way, my little brother. TGIF The beginning of another weekend and everyone will be glad for the time off from work a time to relax and have some fun.

As for me my work is never done or at least it seams that way but I do relax from time to time between my working and trying to make a go of my project. Only time will tell if things come full circle and I'm hoping it does but I cant drag my feet or things will pass like the wind. Saturday and it's just now 3:00 in the morning, yesterday I went and opened the church so it could air out and did some work that had to be done I left the window open over night so we wont have that smell in it and now today I will close them so the air can be turned on tomorrow, it gets muggy when it gets very hot and no one likes to sweat while in church. My mind seams to focus on certain things at one time so I run down and get them done so I can mark them off my list of things to do, my mind is a strange one only taking in what it can handle but it's solid on what it has learned through the years, it seams to know what it takes for things to become what they should be like the man that went through life not knowing what he had done in his early years of life he has been reborn into a great world where many know and like him. None of us really know their journey through this life as for training in schools they can become something other then their real journey the one that God puts them through, you might start out as a teacher but then find out later that you were meant to be a priest or a pastor spreading the word of God to others. One thing I know about pastors is that they have patients far more then a normal person lets say and the spirit dwells inside of them I know for certain that in certain situations I loose it or I'm calm very calm but that seams more in life or death situations, like going oer a clif when something happens. The journey I took with Rick that time left me beside my self as the wheel passed me up going down the mountain I feel if I would of let go of the wheel God would of drove me to a safe stop not wanting me yet at that time either. What a ride that was and even when it happened I couldn't see what was happening at the moment but I believe Mark knew as he was so afraid that it was our last day or night on earth. I believe I had to make it through that to find my way here to my town of dreams the place where I will live for ever, well not for ever because we go much further after we leave this place we call earth. For some reason we need to get intouch with our spirit and get to know it before we can move forward, as this body will grow old and die sometime and we wont have any use for it. I have felt my spirit when I passed so long ago as it looked down on the world to see things, but what was the message I was supposed to take back here with me? If I would have had a clear message then I could of already done it but like a puzzle the pieces keep being put together, one day it will come to me but for now I will keep searching the search is what life is all about like the tree that grew up to fast it has to be cut back so the roots can catch up with it too much at one time isn't good for you. The books I need to learn are right in front of me they are right here in my room but it's hard sometimes to study them, a little at a time goes much further then trying to shove everything in at once. God makes a way for us all even when we don't see it at the time we are brought together by the goodness of the lord to live in harmony. Sunday the 7th day of the week yesterday I saw Herb and he seams to be doing well these days, I really like him and I even go for a ride with him once in a while like last year.

The people like they wind in many ways but I have learned to except that. We all change now and then, the days have been cool here the last few days, because of the storms but I have a feeling that it's about to change once again to beling hot and then look out. because it can hit the tripple digits pretty fast. Right now the crop's are doing ok but when the heat gets to them it will make them hard to thrive like in the cooler weather, the last few years our crops have done pretty well more so then in the other parts of the country where the fields have turned brown by the heat. There is something here that allows this place to become more beautiful then the other parts of the country, call it God' hand that protects us as he does his children but we seam to have what we need to get by the bare truth of the matter is that I believe He has been with me even through those dark times in life. Looking after me as I went through those trying times when I didn't know what to do, at times I feel him so close that I could almost touch him but He keeps a distence to check on me. When will I be able to see the things that others do like pastor Kathy? Just her connection makes me want to feel that but I know it will take place in time as I keep seeking him. For me it's always been a feel and touch thing but with God you cant do either but you do feel something inside maybe a change that He is making to make you a better person, much better then you once was. Does these things matter enough to write them down? In my mind it does to show others that change is possible if and when you want it bad enough. Many go throught life wondering why they are even here, and if they are in a dark place they see no way out. It's hard to explain now that so much time has passed trying to put you're self back in those days of darkness when you got up just to get the next high. But that was life back then, and today my reason for getting up is to see the wonders that God has created.

It's like a mind change really replacing one bad habbit with one of good and it doesn't come all at once wanting to feel the goodness of God in most things you do can be habbit forming also. You want to feel that connection that makes you enjoy life to the fullest, a connection that takes all the worry away and replaces it with what ever God has planed. I me' as a person so wants to be that one who tried to change things so He will come into others lives like he has done mine, for the darkness has long since passed but I havent figured out why He chose me to try and change the ones that are still in the dark. In many ways I'm like a chid but I seam to always move forward not letting the things that have come to pass hold me back or am I by writing about it all the time. Many say they don't remember last year but this mind seams to recall most of it, am I holding on to things that should have been let go? I guess only he knows that for sure. My short turm memory has repaired it's self over the years, and that can be credited to the one who made me for it was Him that made whole what was once lost in my life. The people that wondered for 40 years has to of felt some of the things I feel sometimes, the feeling of not knowing how things would work out, but the ones that believed went on to claim the land that was promised to them. That land in a far away country, do we hold on to things that we shouldn't hold on to? Maybe but when you change that also changes in some people Monday the 3rd of June. It's still cool out and I believe it will stay that way until July or so and then look out it will get very hot out, one person toldme something that might become a problem but I will change that aspect of things to it fits better there are many things I don't know about yet so I will have to learn to deal with them as time passes words are very important when you advertise and you have to use them I the right format so it doesn't hurt you in the long run. Why people get into your face is beyond me but they do it anyway maybe jelous of what you can do that they cant, in all my years there has been something that stops me from moving forward and it's usually other people. The morning is cold but it will warm up as the day goes on making it a great day the first real spring we have had in quite some time without it going right into summer and being very hot. My concerns are valid so we will see what takes place later down the line, many want what's best for me but also you have the ones that don't want you to succeed. And Jesus said it would happen, they will persacute you as they did me but you have to stand strong in your beliefs and if you do that then you will move a head. Randy has been wakeing up early the last week or so to a new day and time but then it takes a lot out of him and he is a sleep by noon, but sometimes we all need a nap right? It's not like in our 20's when we had energy to burn now days we have to conserve every bit of it.

As the days start to turn to summer many will visit the pool as some did yesterday, I was seeing kids and mothers gathered around the pool but couldn't recall if they were swimming yet. Just a glance as I went and did some work at the church. Wednesday will be another day as we move forward into the week, but today we will pay bills and get all that taken care of that way I can relax and not have to worry for a while. With me I let things bother me too much and that robbs my peace of mind, have to quit doing that so my peace will return and I can go on feeling that which God has given. Through the years I have tried to make something happen in my life but something always stops me short of success why does that happen? My own limitations I guess not knowing the right channels to go through, as my mind is simple only being able to take in so much at a time. But you cant let others dictate What you can do and you can't do many will push your buttons out of being mad for some reason maybe their own failures of not being able to create out of their mind. But still why rain on someone elses parade when it makes them feel good to help others will my venture be pushed a side by one jelous person not if I can help it at times you need to fight back even if you like the person. The bills are not any higher this month but I know as the summer goes on they will increase, just a little mind you but they will get higher, and we have to meet that increase to survive in this place I love so much. Many have lived here before me and many will live here as I live here but for some reason many of them will move on as I remain. You cant let anything stand in your way of progress yesterday one of the ladies said how great my product is as she had tasted them and enjoyed them very much, I listen to things as that's what a writer do and you can take some things that people say and use them to your advantage like correcting things which will be corrected.

My friends wife is in rehab and I hope and pray that she will make a full recover she is such a nice women. Yesterday was the first time I saw him at the bank in quite a while, as the months pass I'm hopig she will come back down to the thrift shop I have missed them both. Mark seamed to be his ole self with a smile and he told me that we need to come to the park on Friday to get some food the bank is celebrating the 100 year anniversary my that's a long time. When I told Randy about it he didn't want to go at first but then I talked him into it with my charm, telling him that he has to get out sometime, and who knows maybe he might meet someone. You never can tell around here, it's going to be a great day as we move forward and what the temp will be is any-ones guess but I'm hoping for them to be in the 60's or 70's that way we wont have to turn on the air for a day or two keeping the bills down for a while any how, this time of year is great not too offely hot but also not too cold, just right for the season in the mornings you still have to use your sweater but not your jacket. Wednesday and I slept hard last night after my legs quit giving me trouble it only happens once in a while but when it does its like crazy legs with all the pain in the world. Not something others would like, also it's hard to wake up feeling like your in a trance and everything is in slow motion but this you will pass as I get my coffee. With each day that passes things get better though and I hope even better, I got the lawn mowed today along with changing the oil in the mower so now it's set for another year. Later I want to refinance my house so I can get some things up graded like carpet and a few other things plus get some things done on my car so that I wont have to worry about breaking down anytime soon or later for that matter, sometimes we need to make room so we can breath and enjoy things that we usually can't do something to realive the worry so we can enjoy life a little. The day was over cast, and the temp was just right as I went to work at the thrift store, but I had to take a short break to run Randy to town to get his med's but then it was back to work and it was fun. They are talking about another storm blowing in to night so we will probably get it and we can use the rain, as for the fields and the yards they are still green and I don't think it's that way all over. As for last year every state was burned up including ours but here in Courtland out little part of heaven stayed green for the longest time, it's now past 8:00 Pm the longest time I have stayed up in a couple of years but it does feel good because I know I should sleep in longer in the morning we will see. It was funny that I tried to get a pop from one of the machines and none of then would take my money, but that's the price you pay when you live in a small town the town closes up at 7:00 Pm except for the bar and I never go there to visit except to get smokes once in a while. The great life in a small town you just have to love it. Thursday morning and I slept great last night for the first time in a couple of days and didn't even get updduring the night, it was different to say the least. Today we will go to town and get some grocery's enough food to last the month, or persay part of the month because there is always something you forget. It's strange how you can go 14 miles and things are cheaper like with a furnace filter in Scandia 7 miles away one is $8.00 but you go to Belleville you can get them for $3.00 quite a savings don't you think? But the bad thing is that you have to watch your gas for the car because if it's too high then you don't save much good thing I get 20 some miles to a gallon right! My head is going to feel bold when she cuts my hair but at leasy it wont be in my eyes for a while.

Today I'm going to try my hot dogs and see how they go I have made them once before and Randy liked them after they say five or so months but this time I'm not going to let them sit so long maybe just a week or so and then they should be crisp like the polish sausage, who really knows how har I can take this to give people good food that will last a long time. They would be good even in a bomb shelter as long as It's not over three or so years, they have done many things with hot dogs over the last 100 years but no one has pickeled them except for me of course. If Randy says their good they must be he is my taster on new projects and things have worked fine, Imagine a child getting home after school and saying mom I want a pickeled hot dog just one would hold them over until dinner and I could even make them in single packages like they do with big pickles for some reason I have a vision for the future my future anyway and you can never know where it can take you. It takes courage to take that step into the unknown and find out if there is a future for something, with my mom it was making bread and rolls amoung other things and with me it's pickeling things something pickeled can last for ever according to some. And for sure they wont hurt anyone only holesome food to the every day person, the right ingreadients with certain things can last and last. I don't know how it would tast on the barby but I would like to think that it would give it a good flavor those and the sausage, it wouldn't work with the pickled eggs though they are in a class all their own. Today I have many things to do and working at the church is one of them have to keep things up there so we have a great clean place to go to service each Sunday, some say that the smell is still in the church so opening the windows should be done this morning to air it out a little more that caucking must be toxic and I cant have that with my brothers and sisters.

Making new things is my passion after God and it lets my mind think of new things no one else thinks of this is the difference between them and me I'm not afraid to take that chance as long as it's safe you could even drink my mixture straight and it would tast good so it's good for cucumbers also as Randy and I agree as long as they are crisp and right off the vine, you could probably do it with other salid things but I havent gotten that far yet. But I'm headed that way as I save the brine from the pickles eggs and sausage which is clean no wasting here it can all be used they give the cucumbers a nice crisp taste not just of vinigar but also the other things I put into it I believe it's the mixture that no one knows but me all things natural. The train is coming through town and it's loude blowing whistle has to wake people up but it doesn't bother me as I'm always awake before it even gets here, it's kind of quiet this morning don't hear a bent wheels just smooth rolling like a well oiled machine. The morning is cool and quiet and my efforts for change will not stop, some people even send my little notes that say I'm making a difference in Kansas that in it's self tells me that I'm on the right track to try and help and save lives. Many of the lives that others don't care about which is about 70% of the people, it was a great day as we got our hair cut and went to town and tomorrow the bank is having a 100 year celebration thanking their customers it should be a hoot to go to but I couldn't get Randy to go I guess he is still too shy yet. Maybe one day he will wake up but for now he is still a sleep in his own world, well it's coming to the end of another day so until morning. Friday very early and I was awaken by something not sure what it was but it did it's job, some time it can be a spirit and other times I really don't know what it is but it usually has something to do with writing it's always been my out let to things that I sometimes don't uderstand. Valerie called yesterday and said she was thiking about me and she wanted some pickled eggs as they were talking about them at the Ambry club and I was her topic for that day as she gets back on track, many people go to them and it helps them get off the drugs and that's a good thing for her as she is a bit of a talker. It's sort of like AA meetings the first step in many peoples lives to stay straight and God bless those places as many need them, as for me it took God to bring me through my battles but with him by my side I made it and it took good people to listen to my stories about how my life was almost taken because of it. She will have many changes in her life but as for me to understand them I may not be able to as I think she is a little beside her self at this time in her life, the years of abuse changes her in many ways from being hipper to being down when she doesn't have it but in time that will pass as long as she stays on track. I have known her for many years and really Marijuana has been her main problem along with the Methamphetamine having the two together gives her a high and a low together sort of the way Elvis lived his life uppers in the morning and downers at night to sleep.

The mixture of the two really throws off the body and it doesn't know which way to go after a while and then death sets in later like with Elvis he had many demons that he couldn't control like the loss of his twin brother I couldn't imagine how that was, it seams we all fight different things in our lives from demons that we create to ones that could really be there but stay behind the curtain not showing them selves but that is for another time, since many years have passed God has taken most of that away like with the bad habbits I used to have. It's like I'm in training still to be who I really am the child of the most high God and He is doing a great job with my life, from almost the gutter to where I am today is a big step in this world of mine breaking the ties that once binded me. We live in a different world today then it was back then and I don't see anyone that poses a threat to my different life I have started here, as for the church it's my home you could say and it's become a part of me in many ways from getting up in the morning and going down there to just visiting during the day. I find peace there as with no other place and I know every inch of it as my journey continues, I cant say what the future holds as I'm not a physic. Just someone going through life on his way to where ever God sends me or brings me, my world exist here where I am now and from what I feel this will be my home, many people will come and they will go but I will keep building my world here where I am loved by many. Some know my story but there are many that don't but one day I will let it all out holding a seminar on how to over come the addictions in our live, and my topic will be from death to christ the one who saved me.

There are many things that can happen in ones life and if you should fall into that trap of addiction you should always know something! and that is' that God is with you no matter how hard or how long it takes he is there right beside you even through that ocean of tears you will cry because of the pain you will endure. For our pain is nothing compaired to the pain Jesus suffered as they beat Him before he was put on the cross, oh' how he must have suffered so we could live. Usually what I learn in this life today I try to live because I know that with God it's never to late in someones life, when He can bring you back from death it's self that shows me how much he loves us. If you noticed I didn't say me because I'm not the only one he loves he loves you to and he will prove it by delivering you from the binds that tie your hands, my suggestion is to never give up even though our time is short here it's just a fraction of time we will spend in eternity. To me this is a place where we get ready to go and be in that place we will live for ever that place where devil doesn't exist, Jesus came to this world to save us and that he did but He also said he would return for us and I have to believe that He will. For to me God is all the goodness in the world and there is a lot of it. He gives us music in the mornings to set the pace for the day but it's what we do with it that which makes it good or bad, like with our choices if we make bad ones then we don't advance it's liike climbing that ladder if you miss a step you just might fall on you're rear. But then we get back up and climb it again, I cant count the times I have fallen back down but He has always been there to help me back up even if we don't see it at the time. Most of our changes come from within and they can't be seen by others until later when God has a finished product 'how great thou are! The one who showed me a different life and took my sins away but still we try to do our best in this world the hand of God is always upon us giving us that little tug trying to guide us in the right direction, Mark is going to see his wife Maggie this weekend and I told him to give her a hug for me it was just something the lord told me to say as he knows my heart and how pure it is. As to why mine is that way I havent a clue but I do know that I never have excited violence in my life of new or when I was in my right mind in the other world even, I guess I'm a product of a special kind as most people get angry and with me well I walk away not wanting to add to their misery. I got six jars done last night to add to my collection and now I may do six more today and keep stocking my shelfs until they are full that way I wont run out, keeping a good supply is very importand as I know so well I used to hate to go to the store and they were out of what I needed then you had to travel to another place and hope they had it. Life is good and if things stay in balance then you don't have much of a worry but keeping that balance isn't easy trying to do the right thing naturaly is hard because it takes time and practice forgetting things can rain on your world especially if others depend on you for something. Like your job or just you telling someone you will do something and then forget to do it, always try to keep you're word especially if it's important or even not important.

The picnic should be a blast they are having live music and plenty of food boy small town celebrations are great. In the days of old people came from all around to celebrations people opening their hearts to others and supplying a good meal, these kind of things I have never gone to before in the old life always being the one that felt out of place but now being invited by the one throwing the celebration is a great honor. Mark has helped me in many ways being the first to listen when I first moved here I remember telling him that it was too bad that people didn't forgive like God does and I think that touched something inside of him, his heart I believe as no one like to be remembered for their mistakes and that's what they really are and as we learn and grow in a different direction those things are changed by the power of God and the old is made new through love and understanding, as I talked to Valerie I told her she had to pick her self up and go on like it was a lesson and not to repeat it again and she said I know' if I have learned anything it's that you can do more good through love then you can with any kind of anger because anger breeds anger and love breeds love and understanding I have never seen much anger around here come to think about it maybe disappointment but never anger and not much yelling either it must be kept in the home away from public eyes which is good no one want to hear others privet problems between a man and a women, I have a friend that is mischief and he is in his 80's and people kid him about it it's kind of neat to see it in an adult that child which likes to show it's self once in a while like with me sometimes and they say once in a while that we are alike 'hey' like I said we all have a child wanting to get out so funny! He is my friend the child in me and him.

He laughs at me sometimes because when I first started church I wouldn't eat and now it doesn't bother me any more but he still kids with me about those kind of things, I have never had friends like the ones that are here and I would never leave them now that I have gotten to know them. My family in Christ is big, and I know they care about me very much and through the years that careing will turn to love because I'm so lovable just a good guy all around so I'm told! Boy the picnic was fun as they had all kinds of food and plenty to drink and the keyboard player was great live music while eating and getting to know my friends a little more. Saturday and I have some work today, Herb told me that he tried my pickeled eggs and he liked them and I told him my plan. Maggie has a set back but still she will make it I could tell how much Mark loves her a he told everyone about her condition and we will all pray for her speedy recovery. I never met a town so close as the people are here in Courtland and they all care about one another it's like a big family one being conncted to the other in some way, celebrations here are like ones I have never seen before and the ice cream was very good as for eating there was so many people I couldn't count them all and familys played Frisbee while they waited to eat, and there was a lot of women there many for which I have never seen before but then I stay with my church family most of the time. My one friend I gave a hug to well a couple of them really showing my love for them, I have to say that I'm grateful to God for bringing me here where I can have a big family like that one of my brothers and sisters. Why' do I say brothers and sisters because that's what we are one God to a whole bunch of us here in the bible belt or the heart land, to me they both mean the same the beatin heart of many brothers and sisters. As I saw the elderly people there are many. But also there are the young, the ones that will one day take over where their parents or grand parents will leave off later down the line of life. Mark to me is like an older brother just being in his 60 and I know how much he loves God as Maggie does also, Tanner is like his father even in voice and he would be like a brothers son in the family of love that lives here my land' it was peaceful there at the celebration and the weather was great not too hot or too cold just right to get out and get to know others. I wish Randy would of come but who knows maybe next time when he breaks out of his shell it's like he is afraid to be judged and that wouldn't happen here as I was told by Mark a long time ago. It takes a long time for the spirit to mend after a life like we have lived, but you do recover when you allow you're self to move past the scars that left their mark on you. And God heals all wounds with each passing day making you a new person even when you can't see Him at work our out side is important to us as people but to God it's whats inside as that's the only part that will out last these bodies. Our spirit and soul will go on but the body will return to where it came from back to dust, my self I have always believed that if life can be extended for someone when we leave this earth then it should be, by giving a part of your self to someone who hasn't really lived yet.

Like the child that doesn't have a kidney or the person with a bad heart it can be mended by the gift of life as being an orgen donor. For surely God would approve of this act of saving another befor we are dust once again. I have never understood anger by some but as it says in the good book we are all made different and maybe it's that way because no matter how different we are that change can come for the good, I was supprised when Herb told me that I could use the center to make my product and that's something I will consider when the business grows a little more. But for now it will be a home base business and I can handle everything until it starts to grow and I need more workers to put out more then I am now, it made me feel good that he offered me this option and I will keep it fresh in my mind. My land' kids need something to do during summer to make money so teens can find a job later when everything gets going and they wont have to leave home to do it, with me I have to create things out of love other wise it's just another project and then machines will take over and destroy that human connection that all my work takes many people have started their journeys in the same way as I, and one day it will be big a lot bigger then I' this is my vision for my future at this moment in time and I go into it with an open mind that God can change things at anytime. Who really knows this could be to build self strength within me and help me become stronger as time passes to build strength within your self you have to accomplish something on your own to create or build an important element that we need to feel like it says in the bible. We are like the creator but not the creator we need that connection and maybe it's because He lives in us, I may need to feel that something I have never felt before.

And then I will be able to move forward with confedence it's a great builder of self worth and can push you forward into a world you didn't feel in you're life of yesteryear's. The scars of your youth can be daunting, but He gives us the strength to rise above and over come all the bad things that have happened in those years, even though it takes a long time to find your self when you do then your life becomes what you make of it. No excuses' I was told that I was a dreamer most of my life and that's all they would be is dreams but I believe if you can dream it then you can bring it to life, but it can take some help and my friend will help with that. I had a vision this morning' and in the vision my pickeled Hot dogs were packaged in singel or double packages so people could grab one at lunch time or at breakfast and they were a hit around the world even in China and Hong Kong' my visions don't only show the present but into the future and it's the first time this has happened, what a great feeling. It's at the end of the day and I have read some of what was written to me by others and one person was saying that I'm riding a Jesus train in the hills of Kansas little does he know that there is no hills in Kansas, as for being closer to christ I like that better then living in the dark and not knowing where I'm going for they will be the ones who become lost. We got some rain today and in the morning I will go and get the church ready for service, it's easy for me being I get up so early and it wont take over an hour to get everything done, today I made some 'Big Dog' Hot dogs. So I will give them a few days and then try them to see how they turned out, if I'm right I might be able to put them on the barbecue with barbecue sauce. And if they are good then that will be a plus, Sunday morning and I ask you lord to heal Maggie as she goes through this battle she is going through and give her the strength she needs to gt well in Jesus name amen. when we sometimes face things we don't understand it good to ask God for help, as I have asked him many time to help me. And he does, when I couldn't get around I didn't know what I would do but a friend told me to pray maybe it was my spirit that needed the help the most but through it all I was able to over come my opticals and learn to walk once again in time. Nothing He does for us comes in our time only his as he knows when we need it the most the strength that is, it takes a long time to over come something especially when it comes to the body. With my self it took many years to bring back to life these legs so I could walk once more but I got there and today I get around pretty good for my self but there is limmations to how far I can go and make it back to where I started from. I recall pop's wanting to go somewhere and I would have to tell him that you have to make sure that you have the strength to get back and sometimes he would forget and have to call me to pick him up, it's an easy thing to forget when you focus on just doing it. One time I felt like my heart was going to pump out of my chest but I kept going and made it to where my home was at the time.

It was like he was there with me holding my hand so I wouldn't fall when I went over the over pass good thing the over pass had rails on it to hold on to, other wise I might of met that train I was watching as it was going east out of Kearney' little things seam to take on a new meaning when you over come them and move on with life. What was a struggle then seams to fade and go away but the battle you fought seams to stay in your mind' maybe as a reminder that all things are possible if you relly want and need it. My mom fought many battles also and over came them going from 140 pounds down to 80 but her spirit never seamed to give up and maybe that's the part that makes us strong, because really the spirit doesn't need the body to go on it seams to be a life force that even animals have. Like Harley he is so content just being by him self at times licking or washing him self, but the little fart hears a lot better then we do and I'm glad that it's his hearing and not mine. Wouldn't want to hear everything, even from a distance he hears other dogs and wants to go out and play with them. It's early and the day hasn't even started yet, the town doesn't start moving until around 6:00 but being Sunday many sleep in getting that rest they need to start the week over again and then pushing on, I havent heard the train in quite some time but then it will arrive sometime during this day to load and unload the train cars to be filled with wheat and corn, also milo, and soy beans. My land they sure are busy people that take care of that, but most of them are young and have many years a head of them. I kind of miss that but we got to except our selves as the years pass and we slow down.

In this life the new becomes old but time seams to go by so darn fast, as I recall a day being long as a child but not now a week is faster today then that day so long ago. Maybe it's showing us that time has control of it's self and we are just along for the ride so make the best use of your time and don't squander it away. Some are asking if there are bigger jars of pickled eggs so I have it in mind to get the biggger ones and try them out for a time, but boy that's a lot of work and doing it my self is really hard need someone to help maybe hire someone once things get going. From start to finish building an business isn't easy it's another thing I wish I had started at a younger age, but hey' if I have 20 years left it's enough time and the accomplishment will be in every news paper in the United States, I can see it now. Former addict builds own business and travels inspirational path, and then things would be heard. How I came to a little town and learned to make my dreams come true, after a life in the darkness. God gives us dreams for a reason and it's dreams that makes us who we are the children of God. It's the end of the day on this Sunday after-noon and I mowed the lawn again but not before I fixed the gas leak shure wouldn't want to get blown up. It's my favorite past time when there isn't anything else to do, my mind keeps trying to release many of the things that I try to figure out about matters that really don't matter at this time in my life. It's strange but in a way I feel that He has everything under control in the matters of my life and I feel that He is polishing me for the times a head, taking off the ruffness so I will be a polished and beautiful stone of some kind. It's the hard times that make us and how we handle them if you over think things then you will bring problems onto your self, sometimes you just have to let go and give them to God and let him handle. Also worring doesn't do any good although we are only human and it's a part of us as people of God. But once you find that peace then things go a lot better for us, you can worry until your blue in the face but it wont do you any good it will only drive you nuts. I feel something working inside of me some kind of change is coming but at this time I don't know what the out come will be, but if he is for me then things will move forward. I have a new careation but it has yet to be tested by one of us, maybe this coming week will bring out the success if it's going to happen. There are many ideas in my mind to help me rise above poverty and when they work then it's off to enjoying life a little more, I want to experience the things others have had. Am I wrong for wanting this as long as I work for it? Surely the lord' want me to experience that part of life also and then I can make a choice, many of the people in Jesus time had welth and many had it way beyond what they would ever use in their life time. I have lived poor all my life and it helped to build me as a person shape me as some would say like the tea pot that was just a piece of clay in the end it was beautiful, going to turn in for the night. Another day as it's early I'm going to try to let things happen in the natural here in the next few days and see what happens, what do I mean by the natural well if it's meant to be then it will happen. I put in long hours when I'm working on my hobby as I believe He wants me to put it, and if I move too fast then it stops being a hobby many times I have wanted to do this but didn't have the patients to short tempered brings many opticals and it also means your not ready yet. But now' doing it is like a science and I have most of it down except for the kinks that need to be worked out, and I can work them out on my own.

I was always good at science when I had the chance to go to school, which was when I had to do something while I was on the hill many years ago in my youth. It was like if I was made to do something, then I did it. But to do it on my own like today was something that wasn't going to happen, my life in those days was full of doubt not having any direction and made to have to do things was something I didn't like because usually I didn't enjoy it. But today the things I do are done with joy usually and I am always for the most part happy, I find that joy is more important then sorrow and it's easier to be positive then negative with joy you can give it to others and they take something from that but when your negative that also can be given and ruin anothers day which I don't like to do. Herb has been a banker for ever and I believe he belives in my hobby also, offering to let me use the kitchen at the building down town. He was telling me that they don't use it much an it's big enough to accommodate my needs and then some, so we will see what happens down the road. Life it's self is trial and error and the things we do are the same make an adjustment here and there to get things just right and then go on and hope for the best in the end, during my time I could make some meals that would knock the peoples socks off and make them want to come back for more like my beef roast and gravy such a good meal, and my chicken and gravy is also good. Who knows maybe this is a sign Herb wanted me to work down there for some reason and I know this by him asking me a long time ago, but it was never brought up again maybe because I never went down there and looked into it. Timing seams to be everything for some reason and it has to do with His timing and not mine, but if I'm not ready at that time then He takes the time to get me ready. I believe it's all in the plan His plan, and I'm just a tool that He will use.

Like the wrench to fix something that might be broken or to make something better then what it is at the present time, I except what he gives me and if I'm not perfect then it's up to him to make me the best I'm able to be. As for my life it's all in His hands and I tell Him how much I love him, this is something that comes up many times and I know He feels the same way about me and all of us in this world. I learned a long time ago that if you fall you need to do you're best to pick your self up and go on to make your self stronger. From barley being able to walk I came here and then I didn't know if I would make it then, but as He stood by me I got stronger. It was like a stage being set in my life and now I want to see the movie, from the darkness to the light or as some would put it from the pit to God's grace. I have made my way little by little a step at a time, and I know deep in my heart that He watched over me as I made those steps and in doing that He has brought me a long ways. I was even able to care for others on my journey and make their lives a little better like with mom and pop's and with Randy' I know that the kindness I have shown might not come back to me by other people but He has seen my heart and that's all that really matters in this journey. For time is just numbers on a clock that goes around and around, He sees the whole picture in our lives and as for us well we only see a day or so down the road. He knows what we need to become that person we were meant to be. All the glitches that will take place' and the correcting of them to get us back on track, I was listening to a news channel and they said that there has been a rise in children getting hooked on one of the most powerful drugs there is. And it has risen 80% in the last few years do to prescription drugs, this is a rise that you didn't see back in the 60's or at least I had never heard about it with children and little ones. My land some are starting at the age of 12 years and they see no end in sight. It can be treated but they need to go for treatment because it changes them and they are not the person they used to be, oh' how I know that life so well living in it for so many years. It's another day coming to a close so tomorrow I have some things to take care of and if everything goes right then it's on ward towards my goal, I don't get on face book much these days and when I do all you read about is others lives and their problems very sad sometimes. You hear about their highs and lows but mostly I like to spend my time dowing things in my community, many are supportive of my venture and even John noticed that I took his advice which must of shocked him. As I move further down the road with this I'm curious to see how everything works out from the planing to the finish, my friend Herb seams to be for me also and that says a lot. It's Tuesday and I wonder how Maggie is doing it's been a few days since Mark told us about her condition and I have prayed that she returns to us, many times we don't see the end in sight but He does as He can see around every corner that's in our path all the bumps and chuck holes which might make us think we have come to the end but they are just that, bumps which throw us off course for a short time.

As for us we will never see the whole picture but God does and He knows where we are going his grace will sustain us in all that we do. Each night before bed I tell Him that I love him and if I forget to say it He wakes me and that's a reminder that he is still here with me and then I tell him again or once more, it's been a way of life now living in this new world. Sometimes I feel his presents when I do something and I depend oon Him when and if things don't work out the way I think they should, it's Him that gives me what I need when I need it although it's through another person or he seams to let them know that it ok' when the struggles start it's him polishing me to make me better then before, that little extra something which many of us need to make life a little more interesting. When I try to push things too hard then he lets me know by making things even harder and He will say it's supposed to be fun, is it a wake up call to enjoy life and not worry so much? I have always struggled through the hard times and maybe that's what helped to shape me, going through those moments when I thought all was lost and then coming out on the other side better then before for surely I'm blessed by the one who said I was good before my birth. Many have a hard time visioning the trinity but I believe I understand it in a way that they might not but then that's just my opinion, like the water that runs down the brook and sustains life for the fish we eat. And the water that washes our clothes that is so hot you can't touch it, to the ice that makes our drinks cold and also freezes our food although they do many things they are still one form, like the father, son, and Holy spirit, one form but three.

I can hear the train coming through town this morning and I like that sound as it pushes across the country to destinations unknown to us. Many ride the rails from one place to another and with some it's a way of life sleeping in a box car's I couldn't see my self doing that but when life throws you a curve you can never know where you might end up. It's the middle of the week and today I go to work at the thrift store, it's taking longer then I expected to get bigger jars but They will come sometime in the next few days. And then I can move forward. giving them a choice of sizes might pick up sales a little bit and I can also go to bigger sized product as for the sausage they don't seam to sell as quick except for the Hot ones that Ben likes. He must feel like he is in seventh heaven being able to get what he wants just by being at work, now he is out except for what I have on hand but soon I will bring him some and then he will be set. If it wasn't for friends then this word of mouth wouldn't of been so popular, and I know how important it is many things are different here as I said before we are all like a big family. Many of the people at the celebration I hadent known but still they are family like the cousin you never met or the uncle that only came to see you once in a great while, all separated by their jobs and the things they do but are brothers and sisters just the same in the name of Christ Jesus. Some I may never know but the ones I do know are kind and careing and they really car not like the old of yesterday but of the new today, God is always the same but we as people change and maybe that's what He likes about us the change that He can make happen in us. Our out side isn't as important as our soul and spirit for they will go on, and the body well it will returnn to where it came from. I need to free up some money to get things going just a little faster and I will check on getting that done this week maybe someone will help and then it's forward onto betting back to making what I do best, the days are strange someday I can do things in a couple of hours but then some days it takes half a day depending on which things I deside to make. But I'm never idle once it starts and it makes the days go faster and before I know it the day is gone, and another has begun. Like the people who wondered in the wilderness I leave most things in His hands, our fathers hands. It's early and no one is awake but me and the animals the ones out side that is, like us many of them hunt at night like the birds that can see at night and chase rodents. Those little guys don't have a chance, when a hoot owl gets them. Many people work at night and if it wasn't for them we wouldn't have the trains going through at wee hours of the morning, and God bless the nurces that are at the hospitals during the night. It takes us all to make the world what it is and it's turning all the time, no sleep for the person trying to get a head. So they can relax later in life, I believe it would be nice to make things happen to where you wouldn't have to worry in your old age. But my world is different from those who just sit around my spirit seams to want to move forward with things and not stay idle, when you move all the time your doing what He wants you to, that and learning the new ways. Antique Road Show was a blast to watch this morning as they brought you into the past to see things worth over a million dollars, just a painting of a dam was worth that much money how exciting.

Today I have to have the television channel keep my add on so it doesn't expire and put it on the radio so more people can know about my project, although it's still morning the temp is already 78 degrees my land' it's going to be a hot one again should get my car washed while it's still somewhat cool out side. That way it will be clean for the next few days anyways, I'm amazed at how much things are worth from the past somethings I wouldn't pay anything for and others would pay thousands, now that's how different we are. Separated by different ideas my goal is to make a better life then I have now and in a few years this could come to pass if everything works out right in my ideas. A self made person can go far if the right breaks are there for him to use to move forward, the day was a hot one but we got through it and my work is done for the day. I set something in motion and now it's in His hands and later I will find out if it comes about, we didn't have any customers today except for two young kids my land' we usually have a few at least but that's the way it goes sometimes maybe Saturday will be better. It's 10:45 and I was awaken by not saying I love you before I went to bed it's strange how that happens sometimes but it does we all need to hear that in our lives even the lord. I Have noticed that you can get pickled eggs by ordering them off the internet but I know they don't have the taste mine has and that's what makes mine unique separated by my hands making them with love and their tasty, when this takes off then it will be a good thing as long as the lord is with me on this.

It's my first time in trying to do something like this so we will see what happened in the weeks and months to come, I have to believe that He is with me in doing this or maybe there is another thing I should be doing. I pray that he lets me know because I only have one shot at success, my writing could be a sign that it's time also Oh' what to do? I couldn't sleep after wakeing up earlier so I have to write, so that maybe my mind will get tired but you can never tell until it happens. I try to keep my promas to Him even when I don't feel like going on sometimes but He never gave up on me so I must push on towards that final day when things get finished my book has taken a long time many years of seeing things I would rather forget but I know in the end that He will be there by my side to help me through the hard times. I believe he will watch over my life and not let anything happen atleast until my journey is done. Through the years I have felt like I was in a vice not being able to move forward because of one thing or another but I did break away from my chains that once binded me and at least that was a good step in the right direction. I feel like I need to grow out of this stage of my life and advance to another level if there is another level or it could be old age ha! As we go through this life there are many stages that we go through, and it makes me wonder if we all go through the same ones? In the life of addiction you loose sight of the rational world and live in one you made for your self away from those people as we used to call them, the ones that were different from us the church people the ones that saw the world the way it really was. As we sank deeper and deeper into a world that didn't exist. Oh' we traveled the United States but we were never in our right mind as it was always clouded by the alcohol but it was acceptable by others because it was legal. That was something that should of never been but you cant cry over spilt milk, in those days I asked God many times to releave the suffering I was going through and I wouldn't do it again to only start it again the next time I felt ok' it wasn't until I read in the good book that we are shaped by our suffering as He changes us like the sand paper that takes off the roughness from the stone to make it smooth. And he gives us something to make us whole or what we believe is whole, His idea of us is to serve only Him and have no other. Now I might be over thinking things but He knows that I'm already His, from the depts of my soul to the spirit that will one day rise above this earth it's Friday and yesterday the women went through the church and cleaned out all the stuff that has been piling up for the last hald a century. I still want to put up my letter I wrote up on the bill board, many can relate to the subject because its about the father.and how he helped me in many ways, it's something I carry with me in my scrap book as a reminder of his love for us all. Many just read things once and then throw them away but the words do spark a feeling inside of them that they do know He is there in our time of need and in our time of despair. But what I don't get is the forgetting of things that he does for them, it's like it's here one minute and then gone thee next. Through my years it's like what he does for me stays in my mind and I think it's because he did so much in my life from healing me to bringing me back to this world to learn many new things. Through my time here I see the new things he brings to me but with them all there is no guarantee that we as people will not mess up and I pray that this doesn't happen. My love for God is far above anything else this world has to offer and I have to believe He knows this as I love you father, it's early but I'm going to try and go down to the church and hand my letter so others can read it.

My journey has put me in tight spots before but I over came them as I will over come anything that comes before me, I only see good things in my near future and I thank him for the goodness He has shown. As I travel down new pathes many things will brighten up my days and nights but I also know some will be filled with worry that will go away after a time and things will be bright once again. They will be made bright by the father as he wants me to have a good life here in my town of dreams. I never thought that there would be so many things that I could think of to do with my own mind but also I know that he has more to do with it then I, the making of new things which will bring me further in this life I want to live that life that's in front of me and enjoy the things which I can make, as I go down this road it will be trial and error and with his help I will make it through the hard times as well as the good. We have to be very diligent when we start something new, from learning about God to starting something new in this world. Could you imagine going from rags to riches? from addiction to being aware of ones self, that is a success story that many would like to read about. Because it would let them know that they to can have the American dream if they dare to dream it, we are limited by what we can bring to life and if we bring nothing then nothing is what we will have but if you can dream then things will unfold and become real in this world. I see a lot of people that could advance but they are at a stand still in life because they dare not to dream open that door and let his fullness be brought to you, this is my first step in doing this so later I will let you know the out come many times we get disappointed because things don't go the way we feel they should go but if you have faith then you could see a different result later on down the line.

It says my grace will sustain you it is suffient, I don't believe He would allow us to make a move if He isn't behine us that's the way I believe he works. As I grow is spirit the visions of doubt seams to fade a little bit and it lessonns each day as

I move forward, my friends are beside me as we go through this life and I know they are watching as my life unfolds what do they see? As I know their visions are different from mine, do they see who I really am? Or do they just see this person that has come to God in hope to change his life well that has changed his life. Sometimes I get brain farts, ideal that might help me get a head of things that are pressing but I have yet to work out all the kinks. I'm going to start a thing on a dating sight to see if I could meet someone, one women wrote me named Tami and she has a Ranch up in the hills of Kansas. Cant quite recall the name of the town but she is writing and that says something, my page on the sight tells about me and other things and my land' she is pretty with only one child a daughter. I have always liked country folks as they seam to be more down to earth more grounded you might say not like city folks which are usually uncertain about them selves always being in a hurry. City life to me is very ragged and I never did fit in with them it's the country life that I like dam I wish I had a horse. Another brain fart from somewhere I liked it when Stan took me riding a few years back, even my daughter got to ride with all the kids just riding in the yard was a blast for the little ones. One day my dreams will come full circle and I will have the things I want but it will take hard work on my part not just thought, it's June 14th and the month is about half over but all the bills are paid thank God for His grace. In my world you have to make your own way and all the hopes you have will be put to the test, as you try to move forward. Mistakes we all make them, but it's when we pick our selves up that we become more grown not only in spirit but in mind and body. As He makes us into what we are supposed to be, I see others with problems that I don't have and it makes me grateful for my time here I don't know if I could handle all their things which are on their plate. And I'm sure they would feel the same about my plate also, many cant do what I do and they will admit it when things stress me out my mind wonders to places that it doesn't belong but when you have faith then you can over come certain things my self I cant see things in the short turn, and maybe that from the brain damag but in the long turm things they are just fine. Like the child that cant see past the day as we get older we must get a little more distance of seeing the picture, I have come to believe that my mind is very different from other folks maybe I'm rewired different seeing things down the road instead of right now. I know Tanner didn't understand some of what I said and that because he is so young I missed those years and went right to where I am today must have been fun in those times.

But I don't recall them as that part of life was spent on trying to get healed, I have a big hole in some of my life so big that it cant be filled but I'm working on it slowely trying to bring things together and who knows what will happen when it comes full circle. Bam! Today I have to go and order some bigger canning Jars so I will have them for next week and then we will see what happens, maybe I will sell more or it could just be a shot in the dark you never know, but all thing are by trial and error when you make a mistake try to correct it. It's now the weekend and today is another work day, I will work at the thrift shop and see what we can bring in. from donations, it's going to be another hot day if it's anything like yesterday and who knows maybe it could be a record day. Never have had another sence that time when we brought in over $100.00 in two hours last summer. But it could come again you can never tell, it's hard to wake up this morning as my eyes don't focus very good but that will pass in time as the day wares on. When the things are just right then it's time to take advantage of the good luck as people here in this world call it His blessings are taken as good luck by those who don't know that it's Him doing things in their lives as it says in the book we as people call it luck, but in reality it's a blessing from God. If what they say is true then He knows the words I write each day about him, some stand out apart from those who just go through life with out saying or reading his name but with me I have to write for some reason to probable give thanks to the father for all he does in my life. As I wake each morning I know that it's only by his love that I'm here still today and that's something to celebrate having the ability to open your eyes with each passing day for truly He has been good to us all, each day brings something new and today isn't any different. As I was sleeping I got a call but wasn't awake to take it not sure who called but if it's important then they will call back I'm not awake at 8:45 in the nigh time, it just doesn't work for me as I get up so early to write about the things in my life.

God has been a big par of my life and it makes me glad that He took the time to help this old soul. Sometimes I have like visions that I left something behind and that I'm here to retrieve it but what could it be, something that is hidden from another life Oh! Who knows' as for sleeping I slept good with it being nice and cool in here and I don't believe I was awaken during the night. With most nights I wake up to sweating and that's something I don't like especially when I need the sleep, my friend left me some lids yesterday for my canning jars she is a sweet women and helps me out sometimes she has a heart as big as the world a great blessing to me during this time when things could go south, as for doubt's I have none for some reason it doesn't enter my mind except to write it. This is God's message I do believe to let me know that things are on track, as I awaken a little more my mind seams to clear giving me sight that isn't there when you first wake up. Later the birds will be singing' that great tune which will make my day complete I love listening to them in the morning it's like His wake up call but a little late for me but still I enjoy it as I walk out the door all those little creachers singing it goes to show that you don't have to be big to have a voice.and you shouldn't be afraid to use it, that call I had last night has me puzzled. As not too many people have my number and I shouldn't worry about it, my days are very important but keeping my life simple is more important as I go through this transition. My world is moving forward and all this is new to me but one step at a time as He told me when I was learning to walk again that's how we do it one step at a time and as we get stronger we move to a different area, my speech wasn't very good back then either but that too was repaired by His help. Through the light of day he brings me to different places to show me that not everyone is out to take advantage of what I have done, to try and make things work for the better my little letter should open some peoples eyes as it talks about God and how he has given great help in my life others don't see things like I do, but we are all different and our minds don't even work the same as some live in the moment and with me it's the future I worry about trying to have all the bases covered so no problem arises down the road, maybe this is how mom did it lord knows she had vision and a connection with me but why not with the other kids? Shouldn't think about that. Just embrace what we had the ability to read each others mind. Havent had that in a long time with anyone. I guess I don't let anyone get that close to me anymore, when she passed she told me to remember and I couldn't read her at that time but I did agree with her so she could go peacefully, like with telling her I would take care of pop's another promas kept even through the hard times when I wanted to give up. Maybe it was his love that kept me going pop's had a lot of that even though many couldn't see it, he was cantankerous but I understood him better then anyone and in the end I believe he believed in God.

Maybe he had always believed but he kept it to him self not wanting to be seam weak by other peoples standards as many know in those days you were brought up to be strong and not show your true feelings that is a misconception as Jesus was strong and still cried. I feel change coming on and I know it's his will that is bringing it, all through my life most things have been taken but now I feel like some is being given back even Tanner said is not a bad place to be. As time brings some things to a close God has the power to open new opportunities that will help me you just have to know when to move on it and blessings will come your way we call it luck but it's blessings given to the worthy, my promas was to never quit what He taught me and that's writing opening up my self so others may life after the change in their lives, my world is starting to change but I have a hard time with it not being there before I will have to learn like the child that had to be taught to walk. The aspects of the old will fade away and rebirth will take place if even for how ever long of a time I have I will embrace it God can give us plenty well really even more then just plenty for my world is going to change and I will see the new world that will be created, praise God through all blessings flow praise Him all creachers here below. The Alpha and the Omega the one true father the first and the last, he walks with me and He talks with me and He knows that I am His own, few words are spoken between me and the people but they seam to know my heart for some reason. Such a great thing God gives us to be able to change from the other side to this one. For every person has this chance before they meet their maker Oh sure his ways are different but also He allows us to make that connection so we wont give upon life which so many do.

It doesn't matter how far you have fallen He can still pick you up and help you adjust to new things what a great God we have. Never give up on life because it's the greatest thing that He gives us, many things I write are given from Him the father I guess in a way I'm a messanger that He is still in the heavens waiting for his people to get ready for what's to come his arrival. Could I have been put into that state to delay things to only be awaken in the time that I did so things could move forward for this power I believe He has the power to bring good out of bad or what we believe is a bad situation, the years that have passed were hard ones but I never gave up and I believe that was my spirit talking to God a devine connection to Him. I have heard many stories about who I am, some say I get my power and blessings from heaven and not the stars like most people do. Weather this is true or not I can feel the father getting closer to me and that peace is coming to me in a way that it will stay with me for the rest of my life. No more having to go through what had happened before this will be something of the past, I couldn't resist putting up my story showing I still believe God is the best father anywhere. Here he does so much but isn't really given credit for His work but with me He is always noticed! My God my Father. He created me and my mom was the vessel for which I was brought to this place, but it took a certain DNA To bring me here and that was given by Wes the earthly father I never knew but I thank him for being a part of the creation that made this wonderful person "ME" a light that still shines bright' we are shaped by our struggles and the out come of them but in the end we are made stronger then we were before. The body can be broken but the spirit can't as it thrives to stay alive, until that time comes when He wants to bring us home praise be with you father, some say an angel writes in His book and I know she or he must be busy in the wee hours of the morning with me. I will never falter in my beliefs there has been to many miracles in my life to ignore them, my God, my Father, my saviour. I'm going to try new things I havent done before for which I know will help me along the way as I move into a different direction, call it growing if you will but I will take these new stept to better things and make them easier. A guy came into the thrift store yesterday and needed to vent, he talked about his life and how alcohol almost destroyed him and he admited that he was no good to anyone back then. This is common with some folks after a life of addiction, when you're a talkative person you have to have someone to talk to so we listened and then he left, he bought some trinkets for his adopted kids as he plans on going and seeing them in the coming months he looked like he was trying to get his life back on track and I wish him the best, I could tell I have been in the same places sometime in my life when things didn't make much since and you didn't know what you were going to do. It was like another life time ago but the difference was that I worked everything out on my own with God by my side, he is also diebetic and cant eat the sweets I hope he doesn't have to take shots as I hear they are bad to. I was so blessed not to have those problems but still it took God to bring me through the tuff times, and he is here today when I still need help with some things my big dogs should go over once I make some more as Randy really likes them.

My world is different now and I hope things keep moving forward which I'm sure they will always trying new things to help pay the bills and so far it's been a success, like the guy that could be santa clause those times are behind me and I pray that they don't return. Well it's Sunday and I have to go down to thee church and get it ready for the service making sure that they air-conditioners are up and running so they can stay cool, my morning is going well and I was told not to be afraid of change as it should be embraced. change is good in this world when the change makes you better then before, and that is what I have done. The buying and selling of things seams to be in my blood maybe I was a sales person in another life who really knows. In the days of summer many thingss happen from the good thing to the not so good but through it all we seam to come out a head always hoping for that break that will make us a better life style. This is a hit or miss subject and I want it to be a success no matter what, my abilitys are great and who knows where it will lead in the future but for now hard work in a head of me and that's something I'm not afraid of, not in this life as it seams I have to move forward and grow in the spirit of God. Fathers day a great day to celebrate our father in heaveen the one who gave us so much, and I put up his letter that was published over many years ago it belongs in his church. Letting others see the love I have for Him for without him I probably wouldn't be writing this now he has given so much to me over the years and still does wonders in my life, as I'm still growing in many ways trying to learn new things as the world keeps turning. The world as I know it can be tricky and if you do the right things then he will bless you in many ways.

Does it take opticals to over come before we really open our eyes? With many it does but then we become strong once again and can do things we couldn't do before, and by the grace of God' we are given that second chance that chance to become more then we were before like the devine forces that guides us through this life. I can recall the world of cnfusion and I wouldn't want to go there again always worring about where things are going to come from like food and how the bills are going to be paid. That's a hard world and then in time it leaves and we become better then before, given a chance by people now the people you didn't think cared one way or another about you. All this is made possible by the grace of God not luck or changce your good deeds are becoming a part of you and your goodness is part of your character now, always look for the good. In the early days many of the doctors put me on many different drugs to keep things under control and I didn't like what they had done, I was always in a fog that I couldn't get out of then I found the right doctor and he finished brnging me back to reality. That world was one as bad as the one I had been in before with the alcohol, I didn't know what to do before I met Dr, Nelson and he took me off many of the drugs but still the heart pills remained among others so one day I told God that I was going to quit them all and if he wantd me then he would have to take me. To my joy and supprise he didn't take me but helped me through that period and that's how I'm still here today, my walking got worse after a while so they tried something different and that didn't work and they tried many pain medications like the ones they give cancer patients and that stuff didn't let me have control of my own mind so I couldn't have that. Finely they gave me a drug that I took for ten years until they took it off the market although it helped, and then they tried others but nothing worked and then they tried to put me back on the cancer drug and I wouldn't take it. Although I taught my self to walk there was always pain and I couldn't do much only being able to stand for a short time it was hard to get around as my mind couldn't seam to block out the pain and finely they found something that helped and today I still get around fairly good but through it all God had been with me and he is still here today. He has many plane for me and one is getting this business going and I'm trying to break away from the life that binded me, my friends think I awesome trying to do something that no one has done before around here. And they stand behind me in what I do such a great place the lord has sent me He must of known I would need their help in doing this, going on aventures is quite the thing trying new things and bringing a new product into this place. So one day I might be able to make a living at it, I don't want any thing to stand in my way in trying to full fill this dream and if He is for me then nothing can stop this from happening. He seams to know the things I need to move forward even if I don't and He lets me know that he is there every step of the way, I tried to pay a friend back but she wouldn't hear of it she called it a gift. And this just about brought tears to my eyes, just the knowing that there are people who care that much. Through the years the government has tried to mess things up for me and maybe my writings had something to do with it slaming them but they aired their mistakes on television so my little say shouldn't of ruffled their feathers.

I never could understand why the people don't have health care like so many other countrys have but then this is the United States and everyone is hungry for money, and the poor people suffer because of their greed' and end up in the grave way before their time to go there, the system is messed up. It's going to be a great day and it's another Monday the beginning of another week, I have many things to do and tomorrow I have to bring Randy to parole I sure will be glad when this is over but until then we will keep bringing him there and things will keep on track. I have to pick up supplies today if they came in and then it's back to work hoping to fill the shelfs in the kitchen not wanting to get too far a head of my self so I have to eat them for the next few months so funny! During the day I'm always trying to get around and do something cant seam to stay still for too long, it seams to be in my nature to keep busy and I have a flea market to go to next month and try to sell my creation, funny stuff but people make a living all the time doing things out of the ordinary. Through the sands of time many have brought things to flea markets to sell and I'm going to take advantage of this one and if there is any left then it off to fun-day. We are only limited by our minds and you would be amazed what our minds can do, scary sometimes when you think about it. Even though I droped the price a dollar at Norman's at the thrift store I didn't and some sold on Saturday strange how that works sometimes.

After I really get going then orders will come in but for now it's getting things out there and letting people know that I have them, a true test of a sales person another thing I never sseen coming maybe takeing something from the old and bringing it to something good does work. We are only limited by our minds some will see how easy it is to get them and then want them all the time' my self I didn't like eggs until I pickeled them and then it was like Katy shut the door, I have them every day at least once and I feel good all through the day. No worries about anything and the more I sell the more I can give to the kids that are trying to learn about God that is a win win situation, I recall going to flea markets many years ago and thousands of people do it. it's a good way to get to know people and make a little money at the same time. And you never know what you will find there, my product will be there for the first time although it been here for a little while but we will see what happens down the road it's a hit and miss product because it's an aquired thing and many people don't eat them all the time as for my self I still like them each day but Randy eats them more then most liking the availability of having them right here, home based businesses have been around for quite some time ever since the coming out of the computer but I expecct even before then many have tried many different ones from selling things to making things for the market. Tuesday morning and the train has already went through wakeing me up, so it does no good to try and go back to bed it's natural for me to be up way before everyone else in town it's something that was taught when my mind was being healed. Like after the fall of Rome it was rebuilt and now stayes on the path that God has brought it too weather the business work's I will know that I tried my best to dig my self out of poverty, and God will have given me that chance. We just need to sometimes prove to our selves that we have the courage to step out of our comfort zone to grow in ways that we have never tried but in the process we grow in many ways it gives us courage and fulfillment so that we may go on to better things or find out that we belong in something different. It's like the chances I missed are being given back to me but just at a later date in life, maybe to try and fill that void that has been in some of us while we were away in that other world which we don't want to return to. Failure is something that can happen to a lot of the people here in the real world but we learn to pick our selves up and go on with the knowledge of lessons learned and have no regreats of trying our hand at finding the good life, how do we find our nitch you might say? and a good message would be! that you shouldn't be afraid to try new things that you feel are right. We all have that one thing we are good at but it's up to us to bring it out, the search you might say so you can find that special project that will launch you to the top or get you started anyway. In life we will try the things which are in our hearts even if they have been absent for a long time when you were lost in that other world, what most addict's don't understand is that many other people wont give you the chance you need to build that place you want to be. But my chance was given through God and my friends here in my town of dreams, as for ever finding another place or people so kind as the ones here it probably wouldn't happen again.

My life my friends my town means the world to me as this is something I have never known before and it's the greatest connection I have found in the world, when you become displaced in the world it's becomes a part of your life, but that doesn't have to be the stopping point. We all have the power to better our selves and God gives us what we need to bring that about, if you fail or fall get back up and dust your self off and try again we will all make mistakes in life as that's part of lifes lessons but if you give up then you have learned nothing. God expects us to make them that's how we learn or at least I do, we are all a child of the most high God and He loves us but most people don't see this being blinded by the world order and the things in it, my land a lot of people cant even take the time to go to church and that's their choice but what they don't realize is that everything they have was made possible by God. Oh! Yes they work but what they have can be taken in a moment, just ask anyone who has been to the top of the ladder and then fallen off it. They will tell you how they had it so good and then everything came crashing down on them, they loose everything from getting into drugs because they did it to releave tension. That's all it takes is one time like with Methamphetamine the high is so tense that it makes you think your doing something when your really not it's all in the mind even these coke useres think they have it all under control that they will only use it for a little while but that little while doesn't exist. Because they were hooked from the start, you can try to fool your self but you cant fool family when your marriage starts to fall apart and your kids start to dislike you for what you have become.

The family unit can be the best part of life but you can loose it pretty darn fast once you start acting differently, going from the loving dad to someone they don't know at all. And then the pitty pot comes in on how they didn't mean for it to happen, chances given only destroys any love they may have had for you. My land CEO'S have fallen and then shot them selves because they lost the top of that mountain they climbed and I think it's sad when you put so much into something like that material. Wednesday and the guy is supposed to bring the truck by so I can see it, also the church front window needs cleaning and I will do that before work. I had a crazy dream about a tornado don't know why this happened but it did maybe a fluke of a dream but I was living in a trailor and it sucked out the walls then I woke up, very strange because nothing like that has ever happened before it was like the universe was trying to get me a message of some sort I joined a dating sight and found the women I had married in my 18th year of life and then went on to check out the others that were on there. Many years ago I told my self that I would never go backwards and make the same mistakes twice which I don't plan on doing, I was young back then and made many mistakes it was a time when I shouldn't of settled down but I thought I was in love and ready for a family. I had always liked her son Paul and he liked me and then things went south and the love I thought I felt was just the idea of wanting to be a fatther, then the restlessness settled in and I was on the move wanting to have a variety in life. She was faithful but I wasn't in my mind wanting to find something better that's just the way I was back in my youth when the most important part was the alcohol that I grew up on. I thought I had forgotten about those times but they came back when I saw her picture on the sight, as she too is looking for someone but it isn't going to be me. Later after we split up she got together with my brother years later and they had two children but their family unit was destroyed by the alcohol and drugs and then they too split up, and she went to Texas and married Harold Veach' a man from her younger years. They also had their problems with alcohol but managed to have a daughter in the process. When we were together the doctors said she couldn't have children but through some devine intervention she had three, but my brothers kids one of them anyway was into drugs and the other well lets just say he served his country and made something out of his life. He was so different from the other that he thought he had a different father, in familys there are usually two sides the meek and the one that getrs into trouble and my brothers sons was no different. One time Jerry I believe his name is asked if I was his father because he seamed to be like I used to be quiet and reserved and he never looked for the trouble that his brther got into. So many memories came back by seeing her that I wanted to forget but that's life something new always coming into the picture and then we learn to deal with them and go on. Those years are like flash backs as it was a time when I used Marijuana and got high all the time besides the alcohol when I didn't have one of them I had the other to fall back on like a security blanket. I didn't know anything about the coming down process when you stoped something and what it did to the body, because I was never without it I only found out when I passed away how bad it could get and that helped me to be able to leave it alone "NOT" Wanting to have to go through that horrible time again. I shocked everyone when I got out of the hospital and didn't touch it again but they stood by me not asking if I wanted it again.

And life went on, the years passed as I tried to come back but every step was hard from taking that first step after crolling to getting my mind to work once more. All the things doctors said couldn't be fixed was fixed by God my higher power. He showed me the love I needed to become strong once again and in time guided me to where I needed to be, as many things was taken away. He made manythings new to me showing me that it's never to late for change, it's amazing how when he did it he did it from the inside out and not the other way around changing me to maybe the person I should have been if the curse wouldn't of intered my life. Through Him I have had many miracles but at the time when they happened I didn't fully understand them because they happened very slighty, just a fraction at a time and sometimes I didn't notice them until they had happened. Like with the drug people who used to come over to my house after I stoped the curse, I didn't know how to stop them from showing up but He did and I asked him for help and He made them all go away and they never returned. Giving me the time I needed to get well and then it was Katy shut the door, it was hard to learn to live a sober life after all those years of being in the dark but I was able to do it with help the help of my father in Heaven. Even though there was doubt and fear that person which was hiding seamed to break to the surface, that bashfull guy that never got to grow up. The one who was pushed into the back corner of my mind. As for the out going false personality it was about at it's end of life destroyed by the curse.

I believe my life was spaired so I could try and help people who have fallen into that life of addiction and maybe in someway give them hope after the curse is destroyed, our spirit is stronger then you think but it must be invisible, a powerfull force of life that doesn't know the word of giving up. Although we cant see this force it's very strong and it will live on after these bodies are long gone to the place they came from, for years I struggled with being an organ doner but then I came to realize that my body could save someones life once I'm gone. This means to me' that part of me would live on through someone else that might have a lot to offer the world and what better gift then to let their life go on to make a difference, to the one who get this gift don't be sad be happy and make the best out of the gift. For it was touched by God so you could live and I hope you realize this, no it's not a fluke. He chose you for a reason so don't let him down go through the world and carry on good works as He would want you to. And if you feel something inside of you it's me tring to help in some way, everyone of us has a mission weather we follow it is up to us freedom of choice given by Him the one who created us. When you go through life you can see things and even feel that force that guides us through the times in our lives, many of the people we used to know are not in the place we have come to be, it's like they got stuck in that world we left behind and we have no intentions of visiting that place. Yesterday I made some hot links and some polish sausage so I will have to see how they go over when they have the River fest, it's a celebration of 145 years such a great thing to have once a year it's a Swedish thing and I believe it's when they founded the town back in the day, celebrations are fun and we do our part so that the kids can enjoy them selves ona special day. Then we have fun day here in Courtland and this year they will have a hot air balloon, my land' they are big but they should have fun. I want to help in the kids getting to have a good time so I will do a little something to help in that department we all try to do our part in many things here and I think that's what makes a community strong. Although some may not know it we are all brothers and sisters trying to make a difference in the lives of the young ones that live here I feel they have a chance of avoiding the curse Not' being under pure pressure in a town this size, or at least it isn't as bad as the big cities. We have to stand together in this life so we can do our part in making things better then they once was or preserving the goodness that resides here, I know from experience that it's once in a life time when you have so much caring in one place. As one women said some kids feel that others are nosey in a small town but to the older generation they call it love, the kids don't seam to get this until later in life when they have grown a little more and when they do see this some return to the farm and start to raise their own kids there. When you're my age you can tell how a child has grown up just by talking to them, the life on a farm is stable and they get most of the important things they need my land' it they want eggs for breakfest they can go out to the hen house and get them a store right in your back yard, I saw a girl yesterday and she was from a little town down the road a piece called Fomosa such a pretty women and I believe she is Spanish.

From what I gathered she takes care of her sister which is in a wheel chair for some reason, not wanting to pry into things when she left I told her to have a great day and she smiled. In small towns you don't have to be in a hurry to find someone it's like time is always there so you can feel good about what your going to do and if you don't feel like it's right, then the spirit guides you in a different direction. Today I want to do something special maybe give a gift of some sort to my favorit charity, the things we do depicts what the picture of our life will be or look like. My favorite thing' is to give back for what I have been given always keeping that good balance, my journey will last for a long time and I will keep learning about the right and wrong things to do but most important your word has to be kept even if it might take a little longer then you thought it would to come to your cences we as people forget things' and sometimes we have to be brought back to the important things we said we would do. If God cant trust you with little things then how can he trust you with the big things in heaven? Something that has stuck in my mind but is sometimes forgot so He lets us know or reminds us of this thing we call our word. In my life the travels have been many but none of them compairs to this place my town of dreams, at times when we forget maybe it's our own mind that wont let us move forward until things are made right. Before we can find that space which lets us feel at ease once again or peace. Our little person that resides in us brings things back to mind when we forget things and it talks to us, like a counscilor that tries to guide us in the right direction. So our life doesn't get out of sink, we all need some help from our brothers and sisters because life can be hard especially when changing.

God never said it would be easy to change like the moth or butterfly going from the caterpillar to something so beautiful. The metamorphoses' is a time that can be confusing not knowing what will happen next but if you try your best then God will bring about the change and it will be something beautiful, and I have seen some beautiful things here. These things I have seen with the butterflies that come here. Once just a worm and now they have taken to the sky and give us a beautiful sight as some even land on the porch from time to time, this could be something I'm going through taking on a new form of some sort a better form that will allow me to grow in the right way. I can feel when change is comeing but I never know exactly what the change is going to be, maybe it's supposed to be a secret until the unfolding or the change takes place. He never lets us know things before hand only when they are ready, as we tend to over think things. Funny how we do that' but we are only human with wordly thoughts and worries' grounded by being human, like a magnet to a piece of steel but if the polarity is reversed then the steel falls away like the butterfly that takes to flight after being grounded for so long. I don't have a clue of the life of a butterfly but they do go through some heavy changes in their time here, and then the process is repeated each year and it can happen not only in one place but all around the world. My land' being given these visions sometimes can rack your brain but that's how we learn. I have come to look at things in a different light what I used to call failures are now lessons or mistakes that can be corrected given the chance, like the math page you got wrong there is always a make up test to correct the mistakes. But you have to study hard before hand to plant that seed which will grow, my mind supprises me as it learns and grows in another direction. A direction that is just the opposite of what it used to be, once clouded by the fog that has since lifted to reveal a brighter and sunnier future. My land' it's going to be a good day. As I let Harley out this morning, I didn't know that the butterflies were back but there they were flying to the front porch light and I got a good feeling inside seeing them. For surely I didn't see them yesterday as I was out side. Strange how I talked about them and then they showed up maybe a sign that things will get better, as my thought's are more focused today I need to bend an ear and get some in put' from someone close to God. With many thing's that have happened in my life I couldn't talk to anyone because I didn't know the right way to ask questions I needed answered, you cant just go upto anyone and say I died a long time ago can I talk to you about it? They would turn away and run 'for Peat sake' but now a pastor. She can listen and give us guidance spiritual guidance. What seams complicated to us might not be to them, for they have many years of experience. Dealing with things we don't understand, I know a lady that works for the paper and she is so kind. we wave at each other as she sits on her porch on the not so hot nights, I take it that she must be in her 70's and still going strong we say hi when we see each other in the store. I would all most guess that she is a native here or from somewhere close by, it's firday and yesterday was a hot one but it wont compair to the days that are coming next month when it gets really hot in the thripple digits then you know that summer is here. I talked to the women that runs the library and she said that many people don't read as much as you would think.

As for my self' I only read once in a while when the spirit moves me. I have made up quite a few jars of pickeled eggs and some sausage in hope that they will move later on, in a way I'm depending on God to open the peoples hearts and make my venture a good one. With all the work I have done I'm hoping it pays off so I can recoupe some of what I put into them, when I talked to Leroy & Ben I asked if anyone had any complaints because they weren't moving very fast and they said no complaints from anyone so that's a sign that things are on track. The bikers will be making a biker run on River fest and maybe some of them will pick up on my product, and then they have the fun and games and the fle market. I find that many people like pickeled eggs but it's getting them that is hard because most people don't like to make them. But I do' with me it's like a science and most times everything just seams to flow right and with the strange times I get up the work can be done while it's still cool out. I let Harley out this morning and boy it's humid it almost feels like a sauna out side, dry and hot' I can tell that's it's not going to be a cool day so that's out of the question I hope this heat doesn't set the stage for the rest of this month. I kind of like the cool mornings when you can mow your lawn without sweating, Mark has come back from being with his wife and he said hi to me when I went into the bank it's nice to have him back, I have been praying for Maggie and I know God has to hear my prayers' I havent known her like I have Mark but we met one day iin the thrft store and I found her to be very nice she was looking for some sliver ware for the Art-Center and we found what she needed so that was a good day, many people find what they need there good clother and things for work like jeans and shirts.

In all my years I have finely found my place in this world where I can be me and not have to worry about what others think, I call it freedom to express who you are and you don't have to try and be something your not. A life that will let me grow in spirit and in confidence and I believe we all need to accomplish this in our lives it's what makes us stand out as we are the person God created us to be the out side world doesn't have any influence on our everyday lives as we live the way we would like to live, like the person that lives away from the order of society. We to live our own lives and enjoy the things we do, many might have thought that they wanted to live in the cities. But in time I feel they will return to the country life where things are simple as least for me anyway. A persons spirit can grow here like with the ivy that can grow up a tree that once lived but is now dead, like with life the old move on and the new starts. Even the mushrooms grow in it's place not leaving anything that doesn't replace life, such a great thing life replacing life and nothing goes to waste for the tree that once stood will warm the houses of those who get the wood. It's like a circle and everything goes through a stage before it's gone, like with our children we will grow old but they are here to replace us or should I say carry on? And the circle continues with their children and so on and so forth. My dream is coming into focus and I know He had to approved of this other wise it wouldn't be coming to pass, failure isn't an option' as I know He is always with me through the tuff times and through the good times. In time I would like to create a network of some sort to where if someone needs what I have they can just go to a store down the road and get it and so on and so forth, like a chain one hand helping the other when needed and it will lead to the beginning of things. He seams to give us the power to create and if we use it right then things will unfold and show it's hand, I am unique one of a kind and there is no one like me separated by a gift that only God gives. Tomorrow they are having a wedding so I will get the church cleaned Not' that it isn't clean already but to do a little extra this I will do today. We have many celebrations there and it's nice to have them, I used to be afraid of death but it has become a thing of the past because I know it's just another step in being closer to Jesus. Unbelievers don't know for sure where they are going but before the final judgment He will give them a second chance and then send them to where ever, do people really understand the magnitude of their own power when they make wrong choices? I don't think so. As in the family unit when one becomes an alcoholic it throws off the whole unit by behaviors that didn't exist before the negative forces are allowed to inter. In the world of darkenss you are not able to see the destruction because you are blind to seeing past the next drink or high, the openness that once existed is closed by the fog of not looking at things with a clear mind. Always wondering where the next drink is coming from closes the mind to things you once used to do out of love, and even the word love is far from your mind because the focus is on the dark side of things.

That once loved person becomes your enemy as you feel like you have to fight for that next drink and this is so sad, the once very loving person becomes in love with the curse and then they all feel the loss. The children blame them selves as they think they did something wrong when they did nothing, this can change the course of a childs life and make them feel inferior because they don't know what they did wrong. Usually with parents they don't see this as the child can hide it very well and then they can become alcoholics also because it's around them all the time. Like the child that hides alcohol in under their pillow and says they don have to worry about me I'm the good one, this sets the stage for a destructive life and the child doesn't have a chance. Been there and done that' but it took a greater power then I to bring me back the power of God is the stronges force there is and it can move us through dimensions to show us how powerful things can be, and He can change a life like he has done in mine. I met a women yesterday that loves pickeled eggs and then Randy said they are good with beer, she replied with she had her share of beers many years ago and I told her that I knew where she was coming from I had my share also it was a kind way to say that it isn't in our lives anymore. And she looked at me, I have to say that she was nice looking and very kind. I hope I see her in the future and we can exchange war stories, it helps sometimes to visit with someone who has gone through the same thing as I have. And it's especially nice if you can laugh about it sometimes, mistakes made, and mistakes corrected. Giving a new start to life but I wont talk about the women because I seam to read more into things then what might really be there it's the observing side of being a writer.

TGIF. Thank God it's Friday as some put it, another week has passed and the farm hands get a couple of days off to hoot and holler, to celebrate the working mans freedom from work. I remember when I looked forward to those two days but they flew by as fast as they came and that was a loss, clouded by the curse many times I didn't even know they had passed until I was awaken to go back to work. So instead of days of fun they were a blure wiped out by the drinking of the spirits' not a good thing. Today I wake up with a mind that is clear and I always remember what happened the day before, which allows me to build on some things and I like that. The humity is very high this morning and you can feel it when you walk out side, as the stickiness is apparent. But that's why we have Air-conditioning and other machines that will lower that effect and make it much nicer; the Air at the church will have to be on for the wedding. No one want to sweat through one of them so that will be taken care of, many times it's the beginning of two lives together but today! people usually live with one another for a time before making that leap of faith. And some even have children during the trial period. It's Saturday morning and I got a line on some equipment, they are having an auction in Concorida and I saw some things I need so things can grow like canters and pressure cookers a great investment for what I do and auctions are cheaper then thr stores. By going to this one I can get a little at a time and build what I need, plus you never know what else you might find so I see it as a win win situation. You never know when these things are going to pop up so you have to take advantage when you can, it's at a house so I take it that the people must of went bankrupt. These things happen when others get too far in debt and cant pay their bills, I was told that a negative energy has been trying to rain on my good fortune and I think little brother might have some negative energy being jelous but in the next two days that will change. God seams to always take care of me and I know this will pass, during the auction there will be other things that I might want to get but I have to be back by noon to work at the thrift store as it's an important part of thingts unfolding. I hope there isn't many people at this auction that way I can get the things for cheap and the cheaper the better in my world, I'm building for the future and in doing that I must get all the things I need to succeed which will make things easier. Later down the road I have a big thing which will take place and it has to do with something I'm working on, shareing your life experiences with the youth's of this place will let them know that it's ok' to dream. I slept pretty well last night and I expect to have a good day as I feel pretty good, I can always tell how my day is going to go by the first two or three hours of being up. And things feel good at this time, yesterday the news said that in a town in Nebraska the temp jumped by 20 degrees from 70 something to 90 something, this might not of been a big thing except for it happening at 3:00 in the morning which makes it very unusual almost unheard of. At least I have never heard of such a thing happening, not in all the years I have been alive or I just never heard it before.

Many thing become strange in this world compaired to the world that I used to live in, when you didn't notice anything that went on except for what happened in your own home. Now looking back I didn't get out much compaired to how things are today. Once a hermit' and now not so much, a great change for me and I like it. Many things have changed and I'm learning to grow with them, as for the church it's ready for the wedding but I know I will have to go and clean up after they are done. And that might take me into the night so everything is a go for tomorrow, it's going to be a busy day with the traveling and working but I hope I get my supplies which I will if the price is right. No one goes a to an auction to pay full price for things and that's why I'm going a dollar saved is a dollar earned, next you never know whats going to come to you, many thing don't come as expected you might think one thing and it shows up in a different form but it's the same thing you just have to figure it out and put it into pace. My bigger jars have sealed every time so far, and that's a great feeling knowing your doing things right. My visions came in three episodes first the thought of doing it, and then the test to see if it could be done, and then the final test putting it into action. I don't know why it happened this way but I believe it had to do with patients. In the beginning I didn't have any as I was still learning, I would do a little and then stop looseing intrest but change comes when you are having God work on your life. And that change comes from the inside, others don't see it until it's done and they miss the miracles that He put's you through. You experience a flood of movements that take place inside of you changing this and changing that until one day when He is finished Bam! Something beautiful happenes.

The person you used to be is no more, and like the flower that sprouts new life change has taken place. I believe He set this up so it can be done by just me because He knows I don't like to depend on anyone else, I find that many are not dependable and they let you down. I think I have done everything on my own and if something goes wrong then I can blame my self, my dreams are not others they belong to me and I have to make them happen. Then when things are on track I will be able to move forward, and then grow in due time. Once my stock is filled it will take little effort to keep it up, replacing what goes out with the new and keeping it on track will be quite easly done. But I could use a sales person somewhere down the line someone who could sell a ice blanket to the people up in the North Pole, this will be a very important job for someone the right person. I havent met many that can do that but I know there is someone out there, and advertising will play a big part in this effort, letting people know that I can deliver in just a short time. Kansas will be the first place to be able to get these things and then later it can move to other States I have seen this in my vision many years ago and I believe there is a reason that He hasn't let anyone move forward with my idea. You see it's mine' even though I have put it on the back burner sometimes trying to get my self ready for this leap of faith He knew it would happen and he kept it safe for me, many things have come and gone but my idea has stayed with me, and bringing it to life is very important to me. Doing something you have never done before is like giving new birth to something great, like with me he took out the old and replaced it with the new. Sort of like rebuilding a motor in a car by those actions the car is made new once again, so it can travel a long ways. Maybe even further then it did before, great analogy? Right ! But it's the best I can do for now and that's all he asks for. Taking things to a new level is exciting' and I pray that it all comes together for which I have no doubt, and if God is for you' then you have the best partner there is. Next Sunday is the fifth week and they will have a pot luck at church and have service in the over flow room where we have snacks on Sunday mornings, we have a great time on those days and we sing many songs. It's like a big family that gets together once in a while to share their joy, the joy of being God's children. Even some come from far away to be there for the celebration like with Robert and Jan Carolson children you never know how many there will be but we all have fun just the same. One day maybe Randy will join us but it wont be in the near future as he is still shy, I think I will invite Stan down and see if that sparks something in him and Tonya you can never tell if they might come, or not. The last time when pop's died they didn't come so you never know, it's going to be another hot day as I can already feel the humity in the house so I have to empty the machine and get it going again. The thing runs for about a day and a half before it has to be emptyed and then all is good for a while longer, Harley has been up since I got up wanting water so I took care of him and now he wants out. Now that I have done that he is set for the morning and he goes back to sleep under the bed, I have an idea of making pickled devil eggs for the fifth Sunday and that way people can try them that way. And get their own idea of my product, it could be what gets them going, many women don't want to go through the hassel of making them because they have to boil the eggs and cut them up but with my develed eggs you just take them out of the jar and mix the yokes with Miracle whip and mustard and a little paprika.

They should taste fine I will experiment with Randy and my self first and then go from there, I will pray that they will be good. I have many talents and I hope that they will bare fruit down the line, we never know what will go over until it's tried. I remember mom testing things on us kids many years ago when we were children and even into our adult hood and every time it was always good for us. My life is about to turn in a new direction and I can feel it but like with the other times it's still unknnown until it happens, the restaurant business would like it if my product turns out a great develed egg imaging from the bottle to the table with a great taste. Such a great vision a head of time, some used to call me a dreamer but a visionary would be a better word for it in such things as this. Always take your visions to the max otherwise you will never know how good or bad they might be and if they are bad then don't let others in on your secret until you profect it. I do know that many people have many different tastes and what might taste good to one might not taste good to another so the whole things is a hit and miss project just waiting to be tested, this morning I have to turn on the Air-Conditioning because I know it's going to be hot in the church. One thing you can always do is turn it down but to get it just right for everyone takes practice, and then it's in their hands weather to turn it down or up further it's different with older folks. The Connon camera I bought has many features and many lenses plus a big flash to give a better picture, I'm new to it right now but I will find it's secrets I think the big lense can take pictures of things like the moon and things far away. I have never seen such a lense and then you have the others that will work in other areas,

I always wante to take a picture of the birds in the fields when they are passing through and this should allow me to do this.

I have taken up some new hobbies since I moved here and now that will be another to add to my bucket list doing things you have never done before is what it's all about, as change comes in many forms and who knows what might come next? Catching the life of others as they live in this town I call my town of dreams, Monday and I missed the seeing th moon last night it was supposed to be bigger then usual a once in 14 months thing that happens some say. The dating sight I joined isn't something I'm interested in at this time so I will cancel it, and try to see what he has in store for me. I had never been much good at those kind of things and maybe there is a reason for it, my friend Mark O'Brien called me last night and asked for prayers his son got mixed up with something bad. The girlfriend of a drug dealer had gotten together with him and now threats are taking place you never know what people like that will do being all hopped up on drugs and the police wont help him either. The man already broke out the windows of his son's car and still nothing is done, the girl said he works for the police the drug dealer that is so they he informs on people that buy drugs so he can stay out of prison, it's like putting a bandaid on a gussing artery it will only hold for a moment or so. I had almost the same thing happen in my life many years ago and I asked God to intervean admitting to him that I was powerless to take care of the problem my self, and He heard me and made the problem go away I told Mark about this and I prayed that prayer I had forgotten so long ago asking God to intercept on his behalf and his kids. Not many know the supernatural power that can be used through God the Father but He is there to help in the time of need,and He can do things that we cant like sending someone off to where they cant hurt anyone any longer, my peace comes from Him and he knows that I need it to make it in this world. It feels good to not have to worry about those things in my life, I was telling Mark that the worst thing that happens here is that a cow gets out and the farmer has to go and get it and bring it home. Such a difference from that other life but most of this is because I chose to follow the one I love and respect and there is only one, the Alpha and the Omegs. Jesus was always present according to the good book because he is a part of God the trinity and he sure did a lot for us, I can't tell how hot the day will be but it will be apparent when the sun comes up, I believe they said in the 90's and that's hot enough to keep the Air-Conditioning going so we can stay cool through out the day. My beliefs are my own and they will stay that way through this life, I like the thought of being protected by the father so nothing can hurt or interupt my learning of things as I now it. I don't miss the confusion of that world I used to live in but I also know that other world can be brought into his one by people not in their right mind.

And that can lead to a real mess when two worlds collide one being negative and the other being positive it can be like shorting out a battery and then the explosion follows hurting many people. Many people and friends come to me when they are distraught, and that makes me feel good as they know I have an open mind to things that are going on. As for being a problem solver I have a hard time with that sometimes only working on my problems is hard enough, maybe I could drop a line to someone and open some minds in authority when we are told that citicens have equal right and protection under the law is that a true statement No' when drug dealers can threaten to blow someones house up and put it in a text message the law says they havent done anything wrong until they act on it. A little to late when they are all dead and then life goes on like nothng happens, since the beginning they have used people to turn on others so they can get the bigger fish and they give them protection no matter what they do and this is just wrong' and then later they go to prison anyway but this time for the deaths of insisent people on their hands. Tuesday morning and it's raining out side you can hear the thunder and see the lightin throught the windows but we have been lucky there hasn't been a loss of power, this all started yesterday when the rains came through but it will help the farmers not to have to irrigate so much as they have done in the past years. It's garbage day and we already got ours out for them to pick up, I just hope it doesn't blow away and end up across the street in the neighbors yard as it would make a big mess. Also I took a sign down to Hoards so things are on the up and up some people nit pick about things and we all know what can happen when others put their nose into others business.

Later when my cards get here I will go around and try to get more business from some bars even thought I don't care for them many people do go in there, and that would be good for business. Change comes when you least expect it and I'm hoping that going to bigger jars will do the trick, but it's just an experiment at this time. My days have been good so far except for the decrease in sales but I expected that to happen in such a small place as this when everyone gets their fill. The good thing is that no one complained about anything and that's a plus, there might have to be some travel involved but that wouldn't hurt anything as I like to travel from time to time and who knows maybe I might even make it to Oklahoma one of these days. It's been a while since I have visited family and friends, but getting things started here is the most importand at this time. When you sell something you have to make sure that you make a good product so the people will keep coming back, and I also realize that you can only eat so much of something. As for my self starting each day with a couple of them can make the day a good one getting all the nurishment you need to start that day and produce a good days work, plus you don't have to give them any special care they can just sit on the shelf and let nature take it's course. Now that the cycle has started it will be up to me to keep it going but I know that the lord wiill have to help me in this like he has in everything else. I used to wonder if he might not liike me depending on him so much but then later I found out that He wants to be a part of the things we do except for the bad things which no one like to be a part of. Norman built his business after purching the station in 1954' and it has stayed in the family ever since pride helped to build what is now known as a great business, my self I take most of my work to them and they always get it done to my satisfaction. I cant count the times when they helped me out with things I thought would be impossible to do but they came through with flying colors and made my cars hole once again. Today I'm going to call and have my oil changed in Concorida as they change it they also wash the car and it looks great every time another good place to go Womack Ford' and I get to look around at the used cars in hope to one day find some to sell it's a big world and there are many things you can do if you put your mind to it. The lightening & thunder has stopped for the time being but it will kick up again if the conditions are right, I like listening to it expecilly when it doesn't knock out the power I have gotten a power surge plug in for my computer and that should allow things not to get hurt should it happen again. My land' I have had this computer for over five years but it's a good one and keeps on running, except for the times when I have to take it in and have the bugs taken out. The days are longer as we just went into summer about a week ago but it's not as hot as last year yet and I think it's because we had a spring this year, last year it just went right into summer from winter and that's never any good but our part of the country faired pretty well, compared to the other places like Oklahoma and Nebraska' they got burnt up and the ground was very dry. everything had died while we stayed green some folks said it was like driving to an Oases when they passed through our little part of the world and that made us feel good, positive thinking can bring on many good things including a good crop in the midst of a bad year.

Should we try new things if it's put into our minds? Like when He brings something new to the table. I believe we all have a purpose and that it's in the search when we will find out what that purpose is, as for how long the search will take no one knows. I have met many folks that are still searching even into their 80's and they keep following the path which sent them down that path the search is what sometimes keep us going trying to find that place for which we belong, with many older folks the man and the women search together but then in life one might go away and be with the father, and it leaves the other alone but it doesn't stop the one who is still living from searching for that special something that's waiting for them. And in some cases it's the only thing that keeps them going, the hope of finding what's at the end of the rainbow. During the time when my heart was filled with doubt and fear I didn't wat to venture out at all but I did and things changed the fear turned to hope and the doubt turned to confidence. What allows us to over come such things? Is it that supernatural force that many talk about or is it the spirit that He created inside of us? That longing to live past the time we have here. Lord knows our spirits don't want to die and if they have their way they will live on, in that place He made for us. In the sweet by and by changing is important to us' when we have lived a life full of dispair, but that change has to be for the better. Wednesday and I was reading last night about the grace of God and how our voice hould be seasoned with it so not to offend or gossip about others, I also learned that gossiping is putting your self above others which isn't a good thing to do.

When we find or catch our selves in trouble it says that we can say grave grace and ask for help this lets the supernatural forces to come into our lives and help us, and we will see achange in things but not by our own doing but by Jesus Christ. Grace is given and cant be bought for any price this is His gift to us His children, I saw in the story where someone started something like I have many times but then they lost intrest this is becaue they or I had lost grace, but if you say grace to it then other forces come to your rescue meaning the Lord. Back in the day I had started this venture and then lost the ability of wanting to do it any more according to the story I had lost the wanting or grace He had given me and now sometime later I'm trying it start it up again but with more knowledge then I once had. So that feeling of completing it this time is stronger, it's God that puts things into our hearts and now he will compleet this building of something from time passed as I declair grace to it. In life just a few things have come to me this way and the first one I didn't get to complete because of things that where happining at the time. And back then I didn't know anything about His grace let along understand any of it so the opportunity sliped away and stayed gone after that as life went on, trying new things is what life is all about taking something that He puts into yourr heart is the way you start down that path. Many times we go through life and not even know what will become of things and that's when you leave things in His hands, it's not a time to be lazy but to work and depent on God to bring things through, it says that He knows your heart and he has a time when it will start and the time it will finish. Knowing every step you take, some say you make your own way in this life but I know that that I have felt his power many times when I was about to give up. Like when the miracles took place so long ago, during a time of despair. When others couldn't give me the answers I called on God for the answers and He always brought me through the times when I felt lost. Imagine a doctor saying you wont make it until morning and then by some miracle your still here the next day, this kind of thing went on for a long time years even and still I'm here writing this. He knows the beginning of the miracles and He knows when they will end, I'm taking a road trip to get my oil changes and my car washed although it takes them a while it's worth it because everything is new and clean, keeping the oil changed will give the car a much longer life and it hasn't even hit the half way mark yet the expected life of a motor is 300.000 miles and I want it to last that long giving me the time I need to get things going . Time is what w need to do things for which He puts into our hearts, it's hump day as they call it and half the week is already gone and it getting closer to the fifth Sunday which comes only once or twice a year. It's a time when we have pot luck and sing songs bringing joy to those who come to it just a good day all together. After the oil change we will head home and then I have to work at the thrift shop at 2:00 Pm. I'm going to bring a bigger pickled egg down to see if it will sell.

Beverly said someone wanted a bigger jar of them so now they will be there, you can never know what the nitch will be and it could be something as simple as that but we will see in the coming days. Thursaday and I'm still tired don't know how the day is going to go but little brother s moving in the other bedroom and the coffee isn't ready yet' my day doesn't start until my first cup of coffee. And then it's back to watching a movie when you can find something on, I don't do what I do for my self I do it for others and Lord knows the kids need it more then I do Studing to go to bible school really helps them learn about God. And the closeness they need to have with Him' it's just my opinion but I believe everyone needs to be close to the father so He can give them the blessings they need to go through life. Yesterday a family came into the store and they were fun to be around especially the little toe head blond boy that way as cute as a bugs ear, what ever that means Ha! I have to get tires on my car and have the boot checked that is supposley leaking also a bearing so nothing will happen when I start to to do a little traveling. My hobby is a good thing as that it helps others and from what I have read that's part of why we are here, to help others as we go through this life. I'm going to clean the floor at the church and then probable come home to stay out of the Heat, it's supposed to be in the tripple digits today and that's over 100 degrees my I'm glad that I can do things here at home when it gets this hot leaving the heat where it belongs out side. As for the future I don't know what it might hold but I do know that God will take care of me during my depressed times when things are really bad and for that I thank him.

In this life you never know what will pop up, I have come to the realization that it's not about the money but with the learning of the kids. Many people don't have the ability to send their kids to things like the pool and if I can help in anyway then I will do it, the little ones' isn't that what life is all about helping them to grow up in a good place like my town of dreams? And one day they will grow up to maybe come back to keep the spirit alive here in Courtland. The placce which took in a stranger that was once lost and gave him a home, my journey has many twists in it and this is just one of them doing something to help others which makes me feel good inside. The one girl said her husband has to have the sausage and when a man wants something then he should get it as he takes care of his family unit. When you start something and it's for a good reason then nothing else really matters, I have lived the life of not having enough and kids shouldn't have to live that way so I'm here to help in anyway I can. Lets say I'm a person who cares, so what' as long as it doesn't hurt anyone and it helps the kids that's all that really matters. Many people do the same thing and it makes this a better society one that some can be proud of , I don't see the world the way others do they work to make all they can to retire as they get used to the good life, but with me it's different. Something might start out one way but then along the way it changes and the focus goes to something different like with the kids, in the big city your not noiticed no matter how hard you try as people tend to try and out do others sort of like trying to keep up with the Jones but here in a place this small you can make a difference no matter how slight and the only thing you have to do is want to do it. Like with over coming things here you have the serenity you need to keep going. Did others try my stragity before me? This I couldn't tell you, but it gives me purpose in life to go on knowing I'm making some kind of difference in others lives the little ones that are important to my spirit for some reason. I have neve been able to understand why this is so important to me but it is, and that's all that matters at this point. In the days to come the temp will get hotter and it will give me a reason to stay where it's cool not liking that sweatness and sticky feeling, I'm in hope that things will go on like they are and things will unfold the way I have seen them. This morning Ben is supposed to get my car and put new tires on it and check a couple more things so it's safe for any trips I may take in the future, I never want to get stranded on the road when traveling because they will rip you off like there is no tomorrow. Plus it's always better to have a safe car, it's cloudy this morning but they are not calling for any rain so we will see what happens as they have been wrong many times about the weather. I have been playing with my computer trying to get to know it better and I have to say that I'm learning more each time, it's amazing how the mind can adapt to new things and mine is no different taking in things I havent even seen before. I put something on it that I shouldn't have and then was able to take it off after searching through some things like files, I have to say that it would probably take me years to figure it all out but at least I got a good start on it.

One of my friends came by the thrift store she is a women that works for the news paper, I don't know how she knew but she knew I was the one making this new product. She said she has a recipe also for pickled eggs so later I will ask her about it and maybe we can work something out, it's a great thing this pickeling eggs and it really doesn't take up much time just commitment to do it. This is a gift that the lord has given me way back but it took years before it came to be, it seams I wasn't ready before but now maybe I am. Firday and two more days until the fifth Sunday, the following week will be the 7th of July and our time change will take place when we start church at 9:15 and then it will go until winter, it's a little earlier then before but we will make it as we do each years. I try to encourage those who say it's to early but all you can do is tell them that they are missed and hope that they will come. As for the time change it really doesn't bother me as I'm up before the chickens anyway, it's sort of like my salvation to be there each Sunday unless I get ill or something. And then I wont go not wanting others to get sick by something I might get, so far I have only missed a couple of Sundays but I try to make it up by reading the good word when I'm home. I have a few study books on the christen life or Biblical Foundation Series, and right now I'm reading one called What is the Church? And it talks about many things including 'Finding our place in God's Family' Ben has ordered a wheel bearng fo my car and now in the next week it will be put on making it safe once again. As for the other things they are in good shape and wont have to be addressed until later toward's wintter.

It's good that my friends take care of my car needs that way I don't have to worry about them. I didn't expect to have to have this work done but it's always nice to catch it before anything bad happens especially out here in the country, a women came to the bank yesterday and saw my sign so she is going to tell her workers about it and I hope that will bring more people to buying them it all or most goes to a good cause and that makes me feel good, as I see things in the bigger picture sometimes it's a lot easier then the short virshion some see just in the day but with me it's more like a year, bigger numbers are easier to bring together. Next week is independence day the 4th of July' and then they have fun day after that, not sure which day it is but it's not too far from the fourth. And they will have a hot air balloon at the celebration. Depending on the tempature I will go and see the sights, the kids playing and having a good time and the adults of course. They have a run every year and many attend it but it has to be done in the mornings while it's somewhat cool out side, this lets most of them get out and have a good time while waiting for things to pop later in the day. I havent heard anything on Maggie lately but I pray that she is doing well' through all that she is going through. Bring her home safe Lord. Saturday and iwas exited when Ben came by yesterday to get my car and get the wheel bareing put in, that's something I have always liked about Normans station he takes care of the people around here. When something needs fixd he gets I done, the part only took over night to get here and I thought it would take longer. Ben has been working for the Hoard family for over a year and I have to say he has turned out to be a good machanic, I can tell he likes my car as the seat is always pushed back so he can low ride when he drives it my land' he is smaller then I am and I can hardly reach the gas peddle when it's returned. I can still remember when I used to do that in my younger years cranking up the stereo and going fo a nice ride, so now there is only one or two other things that need to be done but they can wait until later. In this part of the country you have to do things when you can afford them and hope that you get them done before something happens it's a way of life here in the hart land do good in everything you do and hope for the best when thigs can get better, my life has grown here in Courtland and I hope it grows even better then what it is today. As for my friends they are many much more then when I arrived and the numbers will keep growing as time goes by, even people I havent talked to before have come up to me and started to talk. Trust is a process, as the longer I live here the more they seam to be at ease around me and that is a good feeling also. In the beginning I only had my church family and now it's extended to out of the church but I'm careful about my contacts with those who still live in the world order, as I read more on the church I find that most christens have separated them selves from the world. And are not influenced by the ways of the big cities and the other things that accure in the devils realm. I couldn't imagine living in the big city and having to see people shot on a daily bases, as that's what the outside world has come to and it's going to hell in a hand basket. The peacefulness here has rubbed off on me and I want it to stay for as long as possible the only things people worry about here is just keeping our community safe from out siders, one time a strange car came through town and the police was called to chack out their intentions and what they were up to. Never heard anything after that, in the big cities they call it a gated community and I think they do the same things there as we do here protect the people of Courtland.

We do have a cop that lives here but I don't see him very oftend he must work at night in another town like Belleville but it makes the people feel safer that he is here. We can breathe easier and not have to worry about the place getting shot up, by people that don't care about others. When I came here people were stumped by my willingness to help others like with takking care of Walt but it seamed like the natural thing to do in my life, I have been doing it for so long it became a part of me like putting on your sox or even breathing that closeness has let me get closer to people and I would do it again in a heart beat. As the day goes on I will go down to the thrift store and work for a couple of hours, and then it will be back home to maybe clean the carpets so the stains are out of them. I couldn't believe that the price of carpet is so high and I will not pay the price they want it has over doubled in the last 7 years and that's just people ripping others off, they don't pay anything near that price for it. Shure glad that the women lives near by and she told me not to buy it in so many words my land the price was out of this world high-way robbery. If you ask me, the day is going to be a good one as it was pretty nice yesterday and now I have no worries about my car for the most part, it should be set to go a long ways before anymore repairs have to be done. Little brother was up early this morning along with Harley but they will both be back to sleep by noon when I go to work it's just the way things work around here. The Christen life is getting to know other Christens and the way they have the church set up they must expect many of them today.

I will go down at 5:00 or so and turn everything on like the Air-Conditioning nothing worse then being hot especially when cooking is involved, they ladies out did them selves as they always do on special days. I thought I would of slept in today but it wasn't in the cards not at this time. Jan was planting flowers like she does every year and it makes the church so beautiful I believe some have a green thunb and then others cant grow mush of anything as for the pot luck it will do really good and people will be able to see others that they havent seen in a while Sundays hold a special place in my heart as it was a time when I started to get to know the father more then before. And now even though it's only been 7 years I have learned more then I have ever known, the morning is humid and I will have to check the machine later to see if it's full and empty it. It's strange how I awaken with just my thoughts but it seams to set the stage for the day, yesterday while at work an old gentalmen came in from another town and got some of my eggs and sausage come to find out he was the brother to the women I was working with and we had a good time talking. Then he asked if he got a senior citizens discount on the stuff and I said yes, I think in some way it made him feel special and we closed the deal. It's strange how my ways are not the same as others as I see things differently from most folks what comes easily for them is hard for me and I have to barder with folks to make something happen and in most cases I'm pretty good at it, but still I'm new in this department just learning to read some folks by their actions. The women I work with is talkative and her brother is kind of quiet like me, but still very active I would say that he is in his 80's and still right there to complain about the system Welfair especially he doesn't like them for some reason saying they have to know all your business and he is right they seam to do that. Randy has gotten up by sleeping most of the day it doesn't leave much in you to sleep through the night in time he will awaken from that sleep but for now he sleeps for the most part, the addiction he went through took away a lot. As it tore up his body pretty bad having to take medication for just about everything, my hope for him is that one day God will heal him so we will see what happens in the future there could be another miracle in the family, he was telling me about his dream he had last night of buying a storage unit's and we made a killing at it paying only four hundred dollars for it and selling the contence for over thirty thousand. Now that's a dream I would like to see come true and you never know when such a thing could happen. Most people put things in storage because they want to keep them safe and then time passes and they cant pay the bill any longer, this opens a door to success sometimes for others and then they get the spoils of what they were keeping. Treasure stored away from long ago now becomes the bidders treasure and they can make a lot of money off of it, the old gentelman I talked with at the thrift store said family only comes by when they need or want something when their parents get old other then that they are never around leaving them lonely until thir last day comes. He had a chain around his neck that read God grand me the cerinity to change the things I can and the wisdom to know the difference.

This is a saying about getting your life together so I have to believe he went through some tuff times also in his life. The pot luck was great at church as we sat around and talked and ate some awesome food, and then I brought Randy some food home to eat and the first thing he ate was the ice-cream cake br DQ such a delight to find that he enjoyed it all. There was to many things to sample so his plate was pretty full and it lasted the day for him, they say they are having a cook off at fun day and Sam is thinking of intering the thing not sure what he would cook but it would be interesting to see who wins. As for my cooking skills I could probably inter but I don't know if I will, I believe the ladys should inter as they would do the best job seeing they have done it most of their lives. Monday and yesterday it was pretty nice out not to hot and not to cool just right for this time of year as they bring in the wheat, in the days a head I will find out what my bill is for the tires and the bearing being put on my car I'm hoping it isn't to offely bad but as with everything I have time to pay it in the future. My word has become my bond here and I plan on keeping it solid so my respect is kept in tact. At times when good fortune comes my way I pay the whole thing off allowing me to get everything settled, and then the circle continues, it's importand to support your community and keep the wheels turning so life can go on that way you can survive here in the heart land among the Christen faith. Today I will clean the Church and get everything ready for other things they might have going during the week, Tuesday and it's trash day don't really feel like writing not a wake yet but that will pass as the day goes on it's funny but at times everything seams to move in slow motion until the brain if fully awake. Many people must feel the same way in the beginning of the day dragging their butts around until they are fully awake, I know little brother goes throught it every day as he sits on the edge of his bed. Then other times I'm wide awake and even get up early without this like of like hang over.

Don't like this feeling and I can imagine how old people feel when they get this way in a nurceing home after visiting a few of them I wouldn't want to be there many of them sit in a chair like they are in a coma waiting to die from what ever ills them. Such a sad sight to see and I'm glad that Walt got to go and be with his daughter in his laast days. Even through the suffering he went through he kept his whits and had a clear mind until the cancer took him. He lived his life the way he wanted with no regreats and I have to believe he did believe in God to a certain point. I just wish I could of gotten to know him better and I would have if he would have had more time, the things that come to mind sometimes are different these days something from the past seams to find it's way through the clouds and pop up out of the blue but they are memories of time passed and in remembering them there are no regreats, just good memories from time long gone. When we knew someone special, as for the day it will be what it will be and we will take this gift He has bestoed on us. When we see something that we should do, it should be done with out complaint because it's a part of us to care for others like so many before us. God's way of seaparting us from others his children and it doesn't matter your age you can be 15 to 50 and your mission is the same to love God and his people. Wednesday the 3rd of July and after work we are off to Kearney for the fourth, it's been a while since we spent things time of year there and Mark has invited us to celebrate it with him and his family. Kearney is only about 119 miles so we should have no problem with any things on the way, it would be nice to see if we can get a vehical to sell back here at home so we can bring in more money. But we will have to see what takes place in that realm of things it's strange how we used to do it with other things but now everything is on the other realm of things and it feels good. If we can flip a car then our problems might be over for a time anyway and then get another truck to flip so we can build some capital, there is a good business in selling used cars if you can get your foot in the door and I might have an idea about that, as I still have friends in Kearney that might want to help if it can turn them a profet also it's a thing called honesty, but I know there is someone who has a vehical for sale there somewhere through a privet party that might be tight for money. We will go through a few towns on the way and that might be where we find one, you can never tell in this business or privet sale every one is allowed to sell about three cars a year in any state and if it's domne right you have no problem legaly it's a way to make a living in this economy and keep your head above water so you can stay alive. We will take harley with us and he will stay at my dougghters house.

Thank God for family when you need them also we will stop and see Leroy and see how he is doing his job has been the best thing for him over the last few years but we havent seen each other in some time this could be a bonding period for us if things go right and who knows maybe he might have a line on some vehicals that I can grab and take back home with me. Time has allowed me to be able to do these things but the bills are the most important getting everything paid before the trip and then I can sail into the wild blue younder with no worries. I have to make everything right before I leave so no one gets mad and that means working before I leave there are many farmer that have to have trucks to do field work and their workers need their own trucks to get out to the fields so 4 wheel drive trucks would be the best. We got up early this morning maybe from the excitement of going but early just the same and we cant wait to go, also there are many garage sales in Kearney so we might find something there also. Something to help make things interesting Mark knows Kearney better then anyone that I know so getting around shouldn't be a problem it's funny how I lived there for so many years but hardly ever went anywhere, being a shut in' isn't the greatest life but when your hooked on drugs all you think about is the next time you can get high. Mom never went anywhere for a lot of her life but that was her choice to stay home and take care of the family being a house wife was her greatest gift, even when we were grown we always knew that we had a place we could go to for refuge a place we could still call our home.

Life back then wasn't perfect but it was our life and I know she did all she could do for the situation she was in. life throws us all curves and sometimes we take the easy way out by not having to feel anything and that's when alcohol and drugs come in it shuts off the recepters to feeling pain and many other things that make us want to cry. Then one day the lord wakes us up and says hey you need to straighten your self up and then change starts one day you try life with out the things that let you hide for many years, I remember when I first stopped Methamphetamine, although it was still around I was able to say 'NO' But that didn't stop the others from trying to push it on me they would use any reason to get me going again. But I fought them and over came it, and then when they wouldn't stop coming around I asked God to step in and He made them all disapear to never be seen again. He seams to do things all the way and not half assed boom they were gone, I recall this one Mexican kid that came over one day and asked if I could buy some and quit later because he needed the money and I told him No' that it wasn't that easy well he told me good luch and he left. Later I heard he got into an accident and almost lost his life I wonder if that opened his eyes? Or if he kept on the same path only God knows the answer to that question. But I hope he woke up, Valerie wants to see me when I go so maybe I will text her so that can take place she could need some encouragement at this stage of her life and maybe I can supply it, a boost if you will as we all need that at one point or another and she wants some pickeled eggs. now that girl could sell some eggs she has a gift to gab, she could be my sales person just a thought. When I get back things will return back to normal and life will go on but maybe with a little twist if I find a vehical we will see. It's the 5th of July and our trip was a nice one but as usual we didn't stay long we got to see Shannon and the grand baby's and Mark and his family it seamed most of the people like Mark was sick and Even Stacy didn't want any company. After we got there Randy went to bed being wore out from the trip and he slept through the night until morning when he told me that he wanted to leave, it seams Kearney holds a lot of bad memories for him also and he wanted to come back to the town he has known for being peaceful, even to him there is something here that he has fallen in love with and I believe it's the quietness that exists here. While we were there I met with Valerie at the ambry club while she was in a AA Meeting and now I know she is on her way to being straight. We laughed and she cried a little not fully understanding why all the things have happened to her, so I held her and tried to make her feel better and I believe I did do some good in trying to help in some way. She said she wished I was still there and then she recanted by saying my leaving was the best thing I could of done, and this is something I know to be true. Kearney holds bad memories but we have to get past them and go on with life as we know it and sometimes change has to take place. For the ones that choose to stay, they too will heal but it will take longer for the scars to heal, Valerie was telling me that she has had a few relationships that failed and once ever had a married man as a live in companion but like the rest it didn't last. It's like she is trying to find that love she lost but it may never happen again as he died after her daughter pased away, with old friends it seams they loose the ones they loved the most by two's and then it's twice as hard to pick up the pieces but in time they will learn to live and love again and the heartaches will be a past memory. Mark called while we were on the road and said he felt bad because he was sick and not a good host and I told him it was nothing of the sort and I thanked him again for being my friend and letting us stay the niight.

You never know what to expect when you go somewhere but the trip was short and sweet, I could feel my heart racing as we got closer to the place we call home and Randy felt the same thing as we headed for the home stretch like the horse that lagged behind all through the race it was now time to kick it into high gear and bring it home. Before leaving I gave the grand kids a hug and we said our good by's also I gave Shannon a big hug and a kiss before departing on our way. I went by Leroys but he wasn't home so he missed our visit but there will be other times in the future, Shannon said he was hanging around little Bob again and that has never been a good thing as he can't seam to stay away from the dark side but we will see what happens in the time to come. As for being glad to be home this I am' my town of dreams where I can be me. I'm going to try my hand at leading the sermen on Sunday and see how that goes it will be my first time and I know the lord will be with me when I speek as he is with me in everything else, the serman is on how God saved us from the pit you could say it spoke to me in a way that no other has. He brought me from where I used to be to where I am today and for that I will always be grateful, my lord and my God on high. There was no violence while we were there and things were peaceful, April's husband had to work and he started a new job at Cash way Candy Co. when I got up that morning he was just getting off work he seams to love his job and that's a good thing, it's always good when you love your work that way youdont work a day of your life or so I'm told. I sent Maggie a letter telling her that I hope she gets well soon and that we all love her.

My out look on things has changed since I moved here I have went from a frightened and bashfull person to one that has broken the shell that this turtle used to live in. And things get better all the time could I one day become something different? This is possible through Christ, He can make things that you can't even imagine happen transforming a life from one thing to another isn't anything that He hasn't done before. All you have to do is look at the people in the bible for everyone of them had their own limitations that they over came,one studdered and one was bashful. Another had anger problems and another was full of doubt they all over came their handycap through the power of God so my quirks shouldn't be anything for God to help me with if he so choose' s to. In my time since change has taken place he has been there to lend me a helping hand but I also know that His ways are not the same as ours, he doesn't do things half way like we might do instead of putting a patch on things he makes them go away like with the people who used to steel my peace when I was trying to heal what a great God we have. My journey has taken me far but I also know that I have a long ways to go before He is done shaping me, what will I become could it be one of those things that you don't know the out come until it happens? This truly could be the case. Could this once lost soul find his way into serving the lord on a bigger level? For the child born into addiction could see a great change in the level of his life, going from that lost soul to preaching the word of God to others. We have all found our selves falling short of what we could be but with his help we can rise above what we are and become something more, it says that Jesus always was and I have to believe it's because God always was as one is a part of the other like the holy spirit is the spirit of God. The trinity' I wonder if God talks sometimes in the second and third person? As it says we created man in our image could it be that God was never alone with the trinity right there beside Him. But this is just the way my human mind thinks, we are all different with our own ways and no one thinks the same except for some that are close to loved ones. Still I havent found that connection I had with my mom in anyone else, no one has even come close except for Him but He isn't of this world. Saturday and things are back to normal with us being back home yesterday Norm drove by and waved as he was going up town to probably get his mail, this morning we will go and get groceries to last the month and then we will be set except for some odds and ends that we have to get. I believe we have to take our trips to town so we can be around others sometimes, other people we have met along the way. I met my friend and she still has a lot on her plate that she is dealing with so in time I can see that she has the ability to find that peace she is looking for 'my' I wish her the best in her search to find where she needs to be. Like with us all the years have caught up with her and I can see us being friends even when we are old any gray talking about the time I came to visit her at her AA Meeting, during my visit with her an old man had to share that he has had 30 years being sober and I told him that it was great. I have never been one to share my past with people who have only been sober for a few weeks or even months as they havent fallen yet and everyone falls at least once, if it's only to see what or if they are missing something.

Then the guilt sets in and they wonder why they did it. my stories go out to the public hoping that some of them that havent been in trouble can grasp what I'm saying and turn their life around, that's one thing about my situation I have not been ordered by any court to go to something that forces you to do something, for that doesn't work in many cases because later they will go back to the same old life and then the same thing starts over once again. In my town of dreams I'm excepted for who I am and the Lord blesses me with what I need, will I one day be that messanger that brings the word of Christ to others? This is a very possible situation once the Lord has perpaired me for this mission but the things inside of me have to be made right like talking in front of others with out doubt or fear, if and when I get past that then we will see what takes place. He works in my life different from others making the crooked straight and the straight to bend when it needs to, and all this takes time and that's something he has given me the time to be His messenger. Like many before me he healed them and brought them to where they needed to be as everything is possible through Him the master of all things. I know my salvation is in this place for which he sent me, my family is large and I have many that I talk with but even with that there are those who don't want to talk about certain things so on that note some things are left between me and God to work out and He helps me in most of what I do trying to understand the curse I was under. It is said and it is written that His grace is sufficient for us here on this planet.

I didn't want to bring things upon my self to fast and then take the chance to fail so I went slow in hope to figure things out as I went along, making things fit into that box I created for such a thing as this. Being able to separate the things from my life so it can stay on track, like with anything you have to have a personal life and keep other things separated from that. As I went to work it was nice to see friends again, my friends the ones that He has brought into my life, this place is magical and the world I left behind is just that a memory of something that used to be, it was like going through a curtain into a different place that once existed maybe a different dimension that existed at one time. But my reality is here where I belong, that or I'm living in a fantasy world who can really say but the one that brought me here, my place is here in this town of dreams and tomorrow I will read the serman for the first time in my life what a privaliege it will be to speak the words and then feel the things it will bring, the life I left behind is gone now and this new one is starting. I cant explaine some of whats happening but the change I talked about a while back is taking place, it's like my mind is changing and there is nothing I can do to stop it, not that I would want to if I could. God has a way of doing these things when He feels the time is right and this must be the time for change, even little brother feels the peace here and he couldn't wait to get home from the place that held bad memories for him. The uncertainty of what would happen there was very real for him and his peace was not with him in that place which put him away so long ago. My self' I couldn't fantom the idea of looseing so many years of my life by following someone into a bad situation, and then have them turn on you. Brothers are not supposed to be that way as the good book says to love your brother, as for what they did to me there is no anger or malice and my life goes on. For what I didn't have in that life has been given to me in this one the one that still learns and tries to follow the right path, when I read something out of the good book I try to apply it to my life and it isn't always easy but still I try to build my world with the Lord as close as possible so I can talk to Him about things that I can't talk to others about the deep things that are in my soul and spirit for these things are meant to be spoken to him the one who saved me so long ago. My job isn't to ask why but to try and follow the ways that He shows me, which is all together different from earthly things the things we attain here will not follow us into the after life for those things we won't need there, even these bodys will remain behind going back to dust but not until some of the parts can help someone else live. As God gave me life once again I too will give part of that to someone else kind of like the gift that keeps on giving wouldn't you say? The day is coming to an end so I will retire until morning. Sunday and it's hot out even this early, thank God for the things 'He' has given us to stay cool during this time of year and we sleep pretty well. I think more of the little things that others may take for granted like the things we need to survive on this planet non of the other things seam to matter as much as they once did, it's like a new beginning to things like a new season that can take you far into the future. The morning is quiet as the only thing you can hear is little brother talking to someone in his sleep, I have oftend wondered what goes on when things like that happen.

Is it the medication that puts him in that place or is it natural for him to talk to someone in a different place like that? Who could he be talking to that doesn't exist in the real world or do they exist. Maybe someone who teased him when he was in place no one but a doctor could find out for sure I guess, as for what they told me when he came home I have found out that it wasn't anything that love couldn't fix. You can be around a lot of people and still be lonely by keeping your self away from the bad people who are also in that place and I think he did that, being bashful about his weight really weighs on him but still he is that kid that I grew up with he is just a little bigger then before my brother and my friend. As I have watched others give the sermen I thought that it's time for me to try and see what I can do, the feeling is in my heart to do this and He says that we shouldn't ignore the heart just like he doesn't ignore His' my land' in all things there comes a winter and a season for those things that need to be done. The only thing I might not like about being a pastor is moving so much only spending a few years here an there and then it's off to another place but what if you didn't want to move on? The church has the say and you can do nothing about it this is something I wouldn't like but then God doesn't move someone until they are ready and his word is law in the church. We are somehow brought together through the spirit and if the people like you then you stay but they have had a lot of pastors come through my town of dreams not staying very long, I guess it takes a special kind of pastor to live in such a small town and I'm content here as I don't need the things the out side world has.

When you have had very little then very little is all you need to be content in a world so big, my world is what I make it and it seams like I teach my self by reading the studies that they teach in bible study or bible school different author but same meaning. The teachings of the word is given by God so we can live the life we should have in the beginning sort of like how the world should have been if things didn't fall apart in the garden of Eden when they didn't listen to Him, through the times when others were growing up they were learning about what I'm learning today so many of them have a very long head start on me but still I know that He is with me right by my side as I try my hand in new things the new beginning what will it bring with it? A new out look on life or a different view of how the world is supposed to be? Questions that only He can answer or someone that has gone through it. Pastor Kathy has livedd the life with God and she knows what needs to be done, it's says the elders of the church have to be sure that a person is ready before the person can get their blessing because if they are not ready then things can fall apart and they will fall like some of the Stacyngelists on television, they fell and only a couple have tried to redeam them selves very imbearising to them but more so to God. Jimmy Swagert tried to come back but wasn't able to not fully he even wrote a verision of the bible I believe, when you become a true believer of Christ God opens doors that would otherwise be shut and never is there to be a scandel that can stop people from following your teachings or God's teachings. It's all in the perseption of how He uses you there are three kinds of preachers a priest, a pastor, and a Stacyngelist, and then you have the pope but I never did understand them. My favorite Stacyngelist is Joel O'steen now he can fire you up and he speaks to everyone not leaving anyone out, and the lord has blessed him with so much. His dady got his calling at age 17 and he followed it, the lord does work in mysterious ways. I gave the call to worship and it was very plesent I didn't even get nervous, it was like everyone was for me to accomplish this thing I had never done before and I believe that's what Church families are for. To encourage us to move forward and break new ground in that place which we have never been before, there was no being afraid of not being able to do it as He stood by my side during that time. Even passtor Kathy helped in many ways and when the silent prayer came I was able to even do that, what a great feeling to come from where I came from and and be able to give a message with such meaning. I know that no one expected me to do such a thing as I'm still a quiet man but when I'm moved by the spirit I cant seam to turn it down because I know it's God speaking to me in a way that shuts out all doubt. My love for Him can't be measured by anything on this earth and I know that He loves me also it's like I'm doing the things that should have been done in my childhood years but as many say it's never too late to stand by the father or start a new venture in that direction, the change I was talking about has started.

And it feels good, in time there will be many more calls to worship and I hope to lead more of them it just goes to prove that we are limited by our own minds and if fear sets a plate at your table then you have a battle on your hands. Satin wasn't around when I desided to do this and God kept him away from me today is a new day and I go into it with clear thoughts as my time studing has really helped. It seams to let in the way of the others that had come before me and the changes I go through seam to come in stages not all at once this allows me to be ready for what ever comes next, the train has already gone through this morning and I could hear it as it blew it's whistle. Off to another part of the country I guess to pick up the products that are made my the good people that grow them, if I had to guess Nebraska is next on it's list the 'Corn Husker State. Where they grow what? Corn lol, as I start this next journey I really don't know what comes next but I do know that He will be there every step of the way to watch how things go and help me in areas that I need help in. It is written, that He sees everything to completion that He starts and with me it shouldn't be any different the teaching of one of His deciples is important to Him and I will go on learning even to the end of my days. Many times I have tried to figure him out but that just wastes time when you could be doing something else, I want to get some more of my product done. So I can be ready should someone want to buy them this is a great day to be alive as I move forward into the unknown I wonder what will happen next.

As I write about my life each day brings something different but I was intreaged by the meeting Valerie went to people talking about their problems like they were sitting at someones house. This is something that I don't like to do very oftend because of what others spread, one guy was talking about others that wasn't there and that is just wrong because they couldn't defend them selves on the subject. Many people think they know it all but in reality they know nothing gossip makes them feel important as they try and look down on others and it says in the bible that this shouldn't be done, in a way they take away from the truth of things because they don't know the whole story. Valerie has lived through a lot and I see her struggles she never got to work through the pain that has followed her through the last 5 years it's always easier to get high then to face something as I have learned through the years of my life. It's hard to change and it takes a long time to make your way through that maze or fog that followes you, but then one day you are given a step a baby step and if you move forward then it becomes a step in the right direction but if you don't take it then you are left standing in the dark, wondering what will happen next. Each day we are filled with emotions and feelings that can change in an instent and if we can catch those good ideas and send them to others you might change a life.

CHAPTER 15

Tuesday' and I woke up to a storm going through, I was wondering why Harley was frightened and now I know why he went under the bed. He has always been that way frightened of loud noises but for the life of me I don't know why, and I'm not going to worry about it. Through the years we have had many storms but the fire works on the 4th of July scares him the most, I went to bring some egg cartons to Norman yesterday and they brought out some jars that they had kept for me to refill. I'm hoping the storm will pass before I have to go out and take the Church trash to the street, it's strange in the morning how you can't see the sky but the storms let you know they are there by the noise and the lightening the flickering in the sky makes things bright even in the darkest situations letting you know that the storm is right out side. According to the weather station the storm reaches into Nebraska, just a few miles from here. At times I watch infomercials and I find that there are a lot of people selling crap to make money making clams that we have a government that deceives it's people which this doesn't surprise me one little bit, they take the peoples money that they are owed and put it in an account so they can draw on it later keeping them rich and used to the life style that they have by doing this. We us people here try to survive the best way we know how and they spend our money that we don't know about. You could have been left money from a relative and they would never let you know that it's there waiting for you. As one person found $ 98.000.00 that a aunt left her over 20 some years ago. It's hump day the middle of the week and I go to the thrift store at 2:00 this afternoon I'm going to bring some large jars down there as the last one is gone, people that go to the thrift shop don't necessarily go any where around the gas station they seam to be different in some way, the men go to the station more then the women and being at both places lets everyone have a taste of what they prefer.

Time is the main thing with these letting them be ready for consumption and having the person really like them is a must, I my self like the eggs very much and others they like other things if not for anything else but to taste something different. And then there are those who won't try something new because they are set in their old ways, variety is the spice of life so I'm told and if you don't try something new then you might be missing something wonderful, it's all in the taste of the person. But not many have tasted like mine a little different, I have to try new things my self before I will let them go out except for the hot things which the people at the station try and they always come back for more, Ben likes the hot sausage and the other kid likes the hot links. Being young their always up to try something new and then their friends try then or eat them all like the one kid said he went to bed and only two where left, this in it's self makes a person feel good because it gives him a sign that others are eating right. One day you will be able to get them in the package and they will go like hot cakes, kind of like a on the run lunch where they can take them with them to work. In the time of making them I will make them available in the gallons but I know that sometime down the line that will stop it's just a feeling at this time but I know it will come one of these days. I need to bring new thing out things that are healthy and then things will grow even further then where they are today, I have noticed that He stands by me during this time of uncertainty when the human mind isn't sure of it's self but then it becomes sure. Kind of like it flip flops but that's just the human mind and how it works the foundation is solid for there isn't any doubt there, it's just the ways they move that brings the doubt sometimes and in time that too will pass.

I don't know what the future will bring because no one knows that but I'm hopeful that everything will turn out alright as time goes by, it's the finding out that is exciting when the numbers drop and they need more stock this will tell if you will ever make it and if your blessed enough to make it. then things will be alright, in my beliefs it's God that allows such things to take place and if He starts something He doesn't do it half way He takes it to the finish line. A time set by Him from the beginning to the end and no man can stand in His way for it is written so it's the truth, many years ago I thought and believed that this could take place and even though it would start and then stop the memory didn't go away of one day making it. I can make all the things that the company's can and do it on a smaller scale and I know in time things will grow, if others stay away and out of my business. We learn by trying and if you cant even do that then you don't have a chance, God seams to bring things to pass and it's like he lends you a hand to get past the things you need to which is great, I text Valerie yesterday and she replied last night but I didn't understand what she wrote a sign that things might not be going very well, I tried to encourage her while I was there but she seams hell bent on doing things her way. Women are funny sometimes but they can survive using the thins God gave them, some can go through many relationships but that has never been my way of doing things. If you can find your way and learn to love your self then you can love others but if you get it wrong then you have made a mess of their lives and your's so what's the point. Do it right the first time than then maybe you will not mess up the other persons life. Thursday I find it strange how some people can't live without live without a companion and then you have others that can be content with the love of the father so they can get their lives straightened out, preference is what drives some of us looking for that one who we think will full fill our lives and then later find out that we have chosen the wrong person to only go back to being alone rather then have that person in our lives. That right there is hard knowing you didn't wait for a sign from Him and things fell apart, is it a lesson learned? Or is it a mistake that we have to live by and hope for the best the next time. We live by doing and correcting things in our lives that what we do as being human but the best thing you can do is to not do any harm to others and help those who need help, none of us have all the answer but the answers we do have could be the ones that others might need. We travel many paths in trying to find who we are and then one day it becomes clear after looking for something that had been right in front of us that we truly are the children of God, we may search many years for something and not know what it is and then one day we wake up and He shows us the way. For the things that have happened which I cant explain seams to become a part of our everyday lives and what happened in our younger lives doesn't seam as important.

Through Him we are given the chance to make things better then they were and the stories of Him taking care of us seam to come into focus, not doing anything to make things better is our own fault He seams to give us plenty of time to bring things into our lives like with doing something to make life easier, as I went to the country store and talked to them they will decide if my product can be sold there but labels are a must so they will know what's in them. I know a few people that might have the knowledge to get this done but it will take asking them and I have no problem with that at this time so we will see what becomes of this in the future' it's like I'm taking baby steps to get this done with no worries, for the time when I was frightened has seamed to go away and now only my self can stop things, this is his gift to me in a time of despair many make a living creating new things and in time that's what I will do but for now it only helps to make the days better we all are given the chance to become something different then what we were as young people through the years we are taught to handle our selves in different ways being role models for the young ones we used to be. And the change is great as long as we follow what's inside of us, they say the world is full of evil and good and I like to think that I'm good but we will see on judgment day if our understanding is what it should have been, there is a saying that some fly by the seat of their pence meaning they just get by but then you have those who excel far beyond where they thought they would be and these people are the ones

that are blessed.

Given a boost by the one who can give it and that's God him self. I don't know how He does it but He brings things to pass that we couldn't even think of like changing lives, but not so you can see it on the out side but inside where it matters. My land' so much has changed in the last few years that I cant keep up with it like with leading the call to worship He gave me the strength and held it there until I got through what a great gift this was. As I search the Web for a women I don't think that kind of connection will work as many of them are too far away, and of course my last encounter doing that ended in a not so good way, people can seam one way on a computer and then when you meet them it all goes to hell in a hand basket. Although I must have made an impression for Margret to call years later and say that she still loved me but I had to tell her that I'm not into dating at that time. Some can be persistent but for me once the connection has been broken then there is no going back, only forward into the future that would of other wise been not attainable if things would of worked out. In my life Sex doesn't play a big part unless I have feelings for someone and if they should break any trust then the whole thing is over call me a snob but sex should be kept between the two having it. Many put a great value on such things but for me it's something I can live without in other words take it or leave it no big thing to me at this point in my life. July is my time to be an usher in church I can remember a time when I was so nervous I thought I would throw up, but as with many things that have passed so has that feeling. I was like a little kid, That was just starting school but the church could see how I felt and the said nothing. Many things have changed and now I look forward to doing it when it's my time, I believe with the way things are my exceptence has come with open arms. As my brother's and sister's except me for who I am, the new comer to life some of the burden from them. Many of the old people can't do the things they used to do so it's up to the younger ones to step up to the plate and give them a helping hand, you can imagine the excitement I felt when I saw the children wanting to read the call to worship my land' it was exciting for me before there was no names and now there are a few. And if the numbers increase even more then this will be a great thing, even when we do something we are planting a seed and also with our words we can plant them but it's God that makes them grow. Little ones sometimes forget with all they have going on in their lives like playing and such, but if the chance to read will bring them closer to God then by all means they should take it and see where it leads them. God said come to me like a little child so if a child comes to Him then to me that's a great accomplishment, I remember being a child and being afraid of being in public let along talking to the big people because I thought they had the answers to everything which I later found not to be true later in life. God moves us all differently according to our limatations but when He feels we are ready He lets us know without any hesitation all other things are blocked out until we take that step and then we can get the ball rolling, and do that thing he has prepaired us for and the doubt disappears from our lives that once held us back. This is his grace working in our lives the grace of God that he gives to us all for the asking, I have never had things answered right away or given right away it's always in His time not mine but still the fact remains that it is given at some point bringing me closer to him.

Like when I moved here the Lord left no doubt in my mind to make the trip and He even used another to get me here and for that I'm grateful, as time moves forward more will come to Christ and I see it happening in the church I'm going to now and I hope it one day produces another pastor or preacher. That will be a testament to the power of the church, for one day all God's children will be there when the time comes and we are ready for His arrival. Two thousand years ago they said He would be coming soon and today they say the same thing but God's time isn't ours, and I believe a thousand years to him is nothing but a blink in His eye. So we cant put our time limit on Christ. 'No' one knows the time but the father not even the angels know when He will get here, so we wait for that special day when He brings His promas to pass. That promas that says one day we will be with him in His house of many rooms, planting a seed can happen without us even knowing it. It's done by good works or a word that sparks something in someone else that might of not thought anything about starting something new, if that makes any since. A good starting point is to try new things that you have never done before and believe me there are many that I have missed doing in my life but the good news is that it's never too late and it doesn't matter your age weather you are five or 55 years old you can do all things through Christ. Chances missed can come back to you again but it will be later in life, compare it to a base ball game and your up to bat. And you miss the ball by striking at it, you still have two more strikes to go and you might hit a home run that will launch you to another level. And that's your second chance at something new, and like with hard ship's. They are not the end but the beginning a stage of life to grow.

I'm not the same person I once was my whole life has changed, and it's like I'm being drawn into a new world one free from the bondage and ties that once binded me. It's hard to explain this transformation but it's taking place and it's just as sure as I'm writing this today, I have heard many stories about people like David in the bible but to have these things happen in your own life is very different and unexpected. Not being a king mind you but for the transformation from the old to the new, I know God hears about me as I write this sequence of advents that take place in my life and when needed He gives me what I need to keep moving forward. O I know that in many ways I am slow in understanding things but He has patients with me because he knows the way I have to learn, even during the reading I could tell how I was off in not giving it fast enough but that is me and what I take in seams to stay with me longer then others it's just the way I was made. When others are talking up a storm at church I'm taking in what they are saying sort of like I'm a recorder in a since, so different from others but the same in many ways. Today I'm going to wash the windows at the entry of the church so they will be ready for Sunday which is two days away, TGIF. As many would say the last day of the working week and the beginning of the weekend. Although to me one day is no different then the next except for Sunday, as my studies are constent with no certain time of day or night just when He feels I need to know more he will let me know that it's time, to broden my mind a little. It is written that we all have a piece of God in us and I believe this because it helps me when I need help and only God has been able to help me in certain things, for his grace is poured out on us each and every day that we need it. I want to take my reading at church a little further so one day it will be like a part of me you know without worry or being scared of messing up, practice makes perfect as it's written and one day who knows where this might take me. Saturday and it's back to work at the thrift store I hope we have a good day for the Church, I bought a computer from Janet and it has a bunch of problems wrong with it but in time I will get it solved. The guys came down to get it going for me and it didn't take them but a second to get things going, regreats yes now I do but that doesn't change anything I'm still stuck with it O well live and learn as the book says and I'm learning that you should be careful when buying things that are used. I stocked the station yesterday and got everything new once again, the sun seams to change the color of things when in direct sun light but when I brang them home I opened one of them and they were as good as ever. The only thing's I had to bring home was three eggs so I and little brother will take care of them by having them for breakfast, they are great for that the breakfast of champions. The paper comes every morning and like before there isn't much in it but still people get it to read the funny's and the few things that are going on.

I haven written much these days but I know that something will come up in the future to write about, next Saturday they will hold an auction in Concoida so maybe I might go and check it out to see if there is anything we can flip for a quick buck. I have went to the church and got things ready for the service tomorrow, and as for the loan. I seam to make enough to pay it each month, which is a bleessing in many ways. My laptop computer seams to still be my best buy of the century paying only eighty five dollare five years ago and it still runs like a new one only having to take it in a couple of times to have it worked on. I'm writing in the dining room this morning as the other computer takes up a lot of room in my bed room but I think I will put it away for a time until I change the fan on it so it doesn't make so much noise. I'm used to the peace and quiet during the mornings and with it running I wouldn't get much of that. The change in being in the dining room gives me a different prespective on things as little brothers room is just five feet from me and I hope he doesn't wake up until I wake him up at 6:00 like he asked me to, I would like to do many things around the house but the heat stops me from going out much man it's been hot the last few days. And I see no end in sight at this time, although we get a sprinkel of rain from time to time it doesn't do much for the crops when it's gone just as fast as it gets here. The streets can be flooded and within a couple of hours it's all dried up, but I'm glad that we have our home to live in and before you know it fall wiill be here and then it will cool off for the rest of the year. Only the summer is hot and as for spring well it makes up it's own mind weather it's going to be hot or not.

Many times we go from winter to summer but this year we had a little taste of spring and it was a blessing getting up in the cool of the morning' such a great feeling to listen to the birds and sit on the back porch drinking coffee. My mornings are filled with joy as the time moves forward and we see things in a different light, God has truly been good to us during our changing ways. I can recall when we couldn't get any credit from places but now it's like they all want to give it to you, so I have to be cautious and not bite off more then I can chew. That way the bills still get paid and we are good in things that are brought our way. One day I hope to win the lottery but that would be in His hands if it happens, it could happen! Anything is possible when God is for you, just don't expect it and you never know what might come your way. I would of never thought that life could be this way but it is and it all has to do with Him the one who made it possible the unexpected became possible through change, taking the old and replacing it with the new giving up the ghost you might say and letting in the light. Even at my age things change and what was important back in the day doesn't seam to be important any longer. For things are truly good at this point and time in my life, I believe some see just a little ways down the road but for me I see things in years not the little picture but the big one when it comes to finance. When my loan is half paid off my home will be done and then I can put that money to a different use giving me a break for a couple of years crunching numbers seams to be something I'm good at in the bigger picture seeing years down the road many can't see that far but in the end it will all work out for the better. When my short term memory was lost I didn't think I would ever get it back but through time and hard work it has returned and of course it took the power of God to heal what I had destroyed. Yes I take responsibility for what I destroyed but in doing that I also learned that God can heal anything, the mind is very tricky and only the creator of it can heal the things we will need to move on in life. And He does nothing half assed' He seams to eliminate the problem all together giving us a new start to things that have to do with our lives, as for the problems that once plagued me He has made new. What was old and wore out like this body that has been through so much, He rebuilt it and made it better then before all things changed through the power of prayer and of course through our talks when He guided me to where I needed to be. I talked about looking down from above and someone or something was with me and I now believe it was Christ, showing me what to look out for and the things I needed to avoid so I could make a difference in this place we call earth. The squabbles that so many go through that amount to nothing, a waste of breath you might say. For all that we do should have a meaning a purpose and if you try your best to make this happen then you should get a head, are we truly meant to live a life of wealth and means? And if so' then' I haven't come to that part of life yet when everything is wine and roses, in the good book it says that we are made strong by our struggles in life and that's how character is built and if that's the case then I must have a lot of character. Through the struggles we are made strong but I also know that He helps us along the way.

Even Jesus needed God's help and someone to talk to besides the people of this earth, could you imagine having people that sin and then being able to talk with one who has no sin? To me it would be like seeing both sides of the coin at once, no wonder Jesus choose to return to his Father but in doing that he made a way for us too also come to where he is. His death brought forth a great thing a chance for change that would change those who choose to follow him, that place I once almost made it too. I wonder where the souls went that was waiting? For surely they had a purpose in that place where I saw them. Where I felt that power that told me to go back, I know I didn't want to return as all the pain was lifted from me in that place even my body was gone at this point not feeling anything it was going through. And then like a dream I was returned and the pain returned with me, thinking back the pain was all I could think about at that time, until later when he told me that I would never walk again. I thought what a cheep trick and I didn't know what would happen next, I had a friend that was there from Mexico and he drove me around to the stores like a butler you might say and I still think about him today his name was Juan a Mexican boy visiting America and working to send money home to his parents and siblings so they could have a better life. Many come from other countries to find that dream of living without the struggles poverty, but do they find it when some are sold into slavery for sex and other things? At that point the dream become a night mare as they look high and low for their loved ones that are probably dead.

More people are sold into slavery every day by the rich that try to save a buck but in the end they usually end up in prison where they belong doing that kind of crap, believe it or not' we are all brothers and sisters in this place we call the world and it doesn't matter the color of your skin. The Mexican boy that helped me was a better person then many Americans I have met and it would be nice if I could see him again before I leave this earth, kindness comes in many forms and if you don't look for it then it can pass you by. Like the child that lost his life because he didn't see what destruction laid before him by doing drugs, that picture still haunts me knowing if I would of met him earlier maybe I could of changed things for him by letting him know what could take place before he took that Hit of Methamphetamine. But we can't live by what could have or should have happened we can only go on with our lives and hope it doesn't happen again, it was a another hot day but we managed to make it through the two hours we had to work and now I'm at home just taking it easy. As I found a good show to watch I'm amazed at how they come up with some of the movies they do, it's like the world is lead by what they watch on television so I'm glad that I don't watch it all the time, tomorrow I will try to lead the call to worship it's something that I think I might like to do one day in a bigger setting. Like what pastor Kathy does but not as much at this time, taking baby steps would allow me to grow further in my walk with God. I do know that I like doing this service and it gives me more education on the study of our Lord and savior widening my scope to things and see where it might lead, many couldn't or wouldn't do this but I am different from them that don't take the time to bring Him into their lives closer. To me' at times. He could be right next to me like I feel him sometimes but the absents of being able to see him make it hard for me to put the picture together, I know that if it wasn't for the home I live in I would of never been able to accomplish the things I have thus far in my existence. And with each passing day' I feel more at peace, the way I believe God meant for us to feel. Yes I have the everyday struggles that I had before but with a little more peace, I got bit by something and it bugs the hell out of me with all the itching that has come with it. I want to believe that it will pass and I hope it's just chiggers and not anything else worse then those I have put clear finger nail polish on them to cut off their ability to breath so if it works then by morning they should be gone, and I pray that they never come back they can make for a bad day. The movie I'm trying to watch is called the expendables and I have to say that it's a good one with many stars in it like Sellvester Stallone, it's about a country growing drugs to get rich and a fat cat from the United States has gone into business with an Army General that kills people who wont help them in growing the drug heroin or the poppy that makes it. You would think that people would learn by all the lives lost to the drug trade but they still destroy lives and go on with no remorse for those who have died because of them, and as long as people use it then it will be supplied but usually by the black market. It fits you know the black market and being lost in the darkness as the drugs take away from some being human, maybe one day it will be no more but for now it will stay and keep destroying lives.

Many children will never see the teen years dieing from drug overdoces because they felt they had to try and be the life of the party or fit in, it's something that never should have been tried by the timmid or interverted person. My town of dreams has none of the things my home town had in the drug traid and for that I'm very glad, it's something I wouldn't want to see happen to the children or young adults here. For Courtland is that town you only hear about once in a great while, the place that is left alone from the evil that rules the bigger part of the world. Unnoticed by the fat cats that seam to have control over the government the ones that are so rich that they could buy a country but choose to stay and destroy this one, I thank God for seeing that I needed to break away from the world order and live among my kind of people the ones that are different but the same as we all love God the father, son, and Holy ghost. I'm up later then usual as it's going on 8:00 Pm. Usually by now I'm in bed and fast a sleep but something has kept me up, maybe the prophesy that supposed to take place in my life most people are up until 10:00 each night but with me my days start mighty early even getting up before the chickens. I met one of Judy's children at work and she looks like her mother so that apple didn't fall far from he tree, I didn't see any of John in her but then again I didn't look for his traits in her they could be there somewhere. Sunday when I think about the elders I see the Army guy coming back from war to a great plaace and today some tell their stories about how they didn't like it in boot camp in Colorado, being up in the hills and all and he has a saying for it but something to do with witches and bitches but that has stuck with him even today it sure must have been hard.

When I was young I would hear things about people that went to war and how bad it was to be a soldger and then on the other hand the ladies would tell about their lost loves, the guys they were going to marry but they never came back. Through the years they fell in love again and had children but to listen to them the second love wasn't anything like the first, and I guess it never could be. The way the U.S Treated the people from other decents was not right being of Japanees origin and living here they were thrown into concentration camps just because they connections with family over there but you hear nothing of the germans when we destroyed Hitler and his Armys. I'm sure glad that I wasn't born yet at that time when things started to go to hell in a hand basket, back then it was the legalizing of alcohol and now over half a century later we are fighting to stop Marijuana from being made legal the drug like alcohol will destroy many more lives and children wont grow up to see theiir 20's and 30's such a waste of life if you ask me but they will do what they want to do. I wish they could see the destruction before it happens and then maybe they would take a second look at things but being human they can only see what they want to see. I slept with a sheet last night because my blanket wasn't dry yet and I like it when I have nothing heavy on me during the night it gives me room to move around without fighting the covers and waking up. My little problem isn't giving heck this morning so I will hope they will disapear by this after noon and never come back it's funny how something so small can make life so miserable but it can, these things can make for a bad day if you let it so I will try and take my mind somewhere else and focus on other things like giving the call to worship, it has to be hot this morning as the Air-conditioning is kicking on and off making it stay cool in this place I call home. My business cards are ready for me to pick up so I will get them when I take Randy to Concorida it will be like killing two birds with one stone and then it will be back home where we will stay cool the rest of the day and I will go to work for my self and see what develops, as I read my horoscope it said that I'm not to worry about others trying to steel what belongs to me meaning my project because whats easy to me would take them much longer to prefect, in other words it was given by God and no man can take it away. It's neat how He can give you something and others cant copy it because He wouldn't let them, to me that's God watching out for me and who better to watch your back then the creater of man? I know he sees all that I do and I know that it has been given his seal of approval and he is helping me to move forward for this is something only a loving God would do. As for people you have to watch out for them because some would try to steel your peace and you don't want that in this life as it's too hard to find that place when you have been lost. Kids sometimes give up on dreams because they don't come true fast enough and this I understand, none of my dreams came true until my later years when the war inside of me had been fought. The things I dreamed about as a child has finely came home so I can have a better life and when things work out then that life I once dreamed, will come to pass. I didn't make it to Scandia as the weather was to hot and others said that there was hardly any people there so maybe I'm supposed to just work here in my town of dreams for the time being, getting my friends and others to know they can depend on my stuff to be there when they want and need it.

Little brother was telling me that he feels better when he eats my product and that must be God at work there but still it's good and healthy food and I have had no complaints from anyone. Randy hasn't been sick at all since I started to make them and he eats them at least once a week the eggs even more oftend and I like them also when the mood hits me, when things are made with love it makes a big difference because it's made with the two hands that the lord has given us. And it may impart some of your spirit unto the ones that buy or eat it, my spirit is strong maybe even strong enough to share with others through the making of my product many stranger things have happened through the supernatural powers of the lord, and this would be one more He could add to His list. People read about these things but to see it happen would set the world on it's ear because lets face it the stories have been read but never seen or lived through today, a true miracle happpening would wake up some folks and I'm not talking about a preacher who clames to heal because that just doesn't fit. Many do such things to build am empire to only loose it later because they misused the power they were given by the church or by the father, and yet I have never seen one of them climb back out of the fall they took. Oral Roberts died with God in his heart and so have many more but still there are those who have fallen and I can't say what their fate was as only God knows that. Jimmy Swagert asked for forgiveness and he may have recived it but his minestry was never the same it fell like a ton of rocks to not be put back together again, when you say you will do God's work and then give your life to preaching the gospel you are held accountable to God and you don't want to try to deceive Him.

Could a person come from the place I came from and rise above all that has happened? Yes I have done it, pastor Kathy wasn't there at church today so I didn't get to do my thing with the call to worship so next week I will try again. I didn't know the women that preached today but she was from Republic county it was her first time at our church and the first time we met her, maybe one day pastor Kathy can go somewhere and I will be able to fill in for her should I find my way through giving a sermon. It's rained for part of the morning but now it's stopped so I should go to the church and make sure it's all locked up I will write some more tomorrow. Monday morning and we have to take a short trip to Concordia to pick up the cards I ordered, I now know why I didn't have a table top computer before they are to big and take up a lot of room for a bedroom the size of mine a laptop is alwas better because you can take then anywhere. Randy's parole officer has changes the date on when he sees him so it's today that we will travel instead of tomorrow, many things have changed and I really missed Kathy yesterday at the service. No one can preach like she does especially the women that took her place it was missing something I know passion' that's the word, I hope and pray that she stays here for a long time not wanting her to go for any reason she is family to me and those who also love her. I pray that the lord lets her stay here for many years to come my land she is retireing so it's not like she has a place to go and preach somewhere else as she has said this is her home. Maybe God sends us all to different placeas like he sent me here so long ago so I could learn at my own pace as I know it takes patients to teach me even when I'm being taught by God and my self, as for the things I don't understand even today I put them a side in hope that he will let me know when the time comes for me to understand the things I need to know. Even the best of prechers don't know all the answers so they let God guide them to where they need to be, he wont put too much on you so that you will fail it's always better to take baby steps then try to run all at once. Like with the baby bird after they get big enough the mother throws them out of the nest and they learn to fly but they have to get strong first and then the next stage cn continue it's like the circle of life there is a right time for everything to come into play, I smashed a spider this morning so today I will get my spray out and take care of them they are one thing I don't like and they can make you sick if the certain one bites you . Yesterday John invited the pastor to stay for coffee but I don't know if she did as I left right after the service, that's one of the things I don't like about the time change going from 10:45 to 9:15 you can't spend as much time before service just shooting the bull with friends but the good thing is that the time will change back during next winter or right in the middle or end of fall. change always take place no matter how slight for one time to the next we can see change and it's always coming, my studies are going fine but later this year I will have to get into a group so we can talk about what I or we have learned. Theology is something I might dabble in if the time presents it's self as for that field would be new to me, maybe it would shed some light on some things I don't have the answers to. When I was in school even as a child for some reason what they were teaching didn't seam important to me and maybe that's part of why I didn't stay besides the addictions that took up most of my time.

Today is the beginning of another week, and things will happen but as for knowing what those things will be I don't have a clue. In my time here I have had someone living with me and I believe this is a good thing I wouldn't know what to do if I didn't have another voice around to give me input, even if it was just to break bread and have coffee. I know that I have always needed to be needed by someone and I like taking care of my family they are not as critical as some would be if you were taking care of a stranger, although Walt was never a problem but a blessing in this life of mine. He knew that I would need help in making this town of dreams my home and he did all he could do to make it happen what a great guy and I miss him like I miss pop's. His old home is a reminder that he was here as I drive by it from time to time and the memory of pop's is right by the front step as I water the plant when it gets too hot out there, such plesent memories of lives long gone now but I will see them again when I take that final journey to heaven' it's that time of year when everyone is busy on the farm and the work has to be done they ladies are caning and the men are out in the field hard at it brining in the crops so they will be ready for market. The elStacytors are busy 24/7 as they load train cars and trucks to be shipped to the rest of the world, in my opinion they don't get enough credit for the things they do working on the farm is like second nature to the farmer getting up at the break of dawn and heading out after breakfast. They don't only grow our food but also take care of and grow the cattle that many of us eat, my land' farming has been their way of life for 100's of years in my younger day's I always wondered how pop's was able to get up so early and go to work sometimes hitch hiking 13 miles to work in another town, he was like a work horse always on the go to take care of the family he adopted.

I saw pastor Kathy yesterday and told her that she was missed at Church and she asked how the attendence was and I told her that not many came, just a hand full of those who weren't working the elders you might say but also there was the kids which bring a lot of joy to the Church when they come. The kids help out on the farm and they get along just fine with the people who take care of them just fine, the court system places them with the familys on the farm maybe so they can have that kind of up bringing and they come to Church to learn about God which is something new to them I'm sure. Ron I believe his name is was adopted as a child because his adopted mother couldn't have kids of her own, but still today he is there taking care of her as she once took care of him what a great man, and now that line of kindness is extended to these other children. Who knows maybe they will do the same one day and that line of kindness will continue, as I look at this place as my home others look at their homes the same way living here is just a great way of life, the Church is very important to me as my life takes shape and I want to learn more as time goes by maybe to be a leader in a youth group that would be awesome to teach them about the things I have learned since being born again in Christ' my out look on things have truly changed and the things that weren't important in my early years have come to be very important, my love for God surpasses all my expectations as I grow in spirit and learn more about the way of life that many have known since childhood. Except that I have an adult out look on things for which they seen things through the eyes of a child and then learned to grow from there, such a blessing to be brought up in a Christen sarroundings where they prayed before each meal. for truly the world has changed since then now everyone eats on the run thinking that the world will pass them by if they are not in a hurry, they don't hear the birds singing in the morning or see the squirrles playing as they chase each other across the yard or jump from tree to tree. I also like to watch the rabbits as they eat the clover in the front yard, it's just the way small town life is. They have day care for the children and the care givers have them walk each morning, it reminds me of a mother taking care of her children like the mother duck having her chicks follow her to the pond. I remember my mom doing the same thing back in my early years, taking us for a walk. Ever since I can remember I always felt the need to make an impression on others but now that I'm older that doesn't seam so important, but I do know that kids look up to their elders and we as adults should leave a good mark for them to follow. The love of God is for everyone yes everyone even us that might have gotten lost in life, He find a way to bring us back to His fold and then we go on.

It's never to late to learn, as long as the mind is still working good and we should fill it with the good things not the crap that once filled it. He makes a way to renew things that need to be changed for every bad habbit can be replaced with something positive from going to a bar to going to Church the first step, and then replacing the sware words with others that are good. I used to sware like a sailor but then one day I saw that these things needed to be changed, so I replaced them with other words although this was the first step in time change came to me and it was like those bad thoughts were gone. My land' Jesus died on the cross for us so we could live and he took our sins with him, he even defeated death by rising from the grave and assending into heaven. Such a great act of love He showed us on that day when it happened, it was a sight when Jesus called on his father for help when he needed it and God always answered him. The supernatural power of God was there every time even when he carried the cross to the place he would be nailed to, a person like us couldn't of done this because we are not as strong as he was. Some say we shouldn't cry but here we had the strongest of all and he shed tears many a times, and I know not anyone stronger then the one who created this place we call earth. People back then and even today can be mean, not having any respect or love for their brothers and sisters and if your in that dark place then it can be even worse as you don't see the world the way it is or should be. With me even though I was not evil I couldn't see past the next drink or high that was surroundings me, I locked out the rest of the world from my world and lived in a very small place which wasn't any bigger then my living room. This gave me control of that little space but even then I couldn't keep control of it as I would leave this world and then come back in. sort of like being in a coma but you couldn't hear the people around you, not a good thing to go through.

It's Tuesday and the trash has to be taken out so I will do that in about an hour I'm glad that we take ours out the day before my land we had enough of it. Every week something new comes into our lives and it can be small or it can be big you just can never tell, even the slightest thing like a new idea can bring change on a way to approach something in a new direction. It's like God is hard at work making us the best we can be and I really like it when something like that happens, we went into town for Randy's med's and got some chicken so I wouldn't have to cook. Such a great delight to not have to cook because I get my share of it most days, it's nice in the house today but out side is 88 degrees to hot for spending much time out there. Dam I for got something while we were in town altimers I guess Ha! Maybe next time I wont forget. Wednesday morning or hump day and it's pretty cool out this morning yesterday it ws in the 60's around this time but I know that the heat wave is headed this way. Harley is up but soon he will going back to bed I don't let him in my room any more as the bugs are out thick this time of year thicker then any other year as I got the hell bit out of me and that isn't plesent, next month I have my car to get registered and that is a chunk of change but I believe I willl be able to come up with it as I save every penny I can. This year on fun-day they are giving baloon rides for $ 10.00 per person, and I want to go up and maybe take some picctures I think that would be awesome if you could get the right ones showing the kids having a good time and the other things they do on fun day but usually the heat stops me from going not being able to stay out in it very long I would like to try out my camera and see how the pictures come out. I have two of them now but they are older ones that would have to be put on a memory card to get them on the computer if they even do that these days I know they have the advance ments in science to do it but we will have to see, Walmart has a good camera department and they can do just about anything with pictures my only concern would be the shutter speed and if it's working right so the only way to deturman if it's working right is to put it to the test of taking pictures and see what happens. Pawn shops have cameras that they sell pretty cheap so maybe a road trip is in our future to Downs or another town to check them out, the van I wanted to buy has it's problems but their not anything that cant be fixid by doing a vallve job on it and then it would be good to go and I believe it could be fliped for about four or five grand making back the money that came my way, it's just the asking if he would take less for it. Randy thinks it can be done but what he doesn't realize is that he is too big to do any of the work which would leave everything in my hands and it's been a long time since I have done such work. I do know that it would be great for taking field trips with the kids to places where they could go camping or just visit for a day, like to the water park. My land it should hold 7 or 8 kids plus it has a bed that folds down if they get tired on the way, but I don't think it's in the cards or not in the minds of those who would pay for it. Little brother is dreaming this morning and I oftend wondered what he dreams about is it the freedom that he feels or being locked away for so long the jury is out on that one.

The car hasn't leaked any oil lately so I'm hoping that the problem got solved and it will make it through next winter, but you never know what might pop up during this time of year but it's better to have it fixed during this time of year when it's warm out side. Harley just chassed something and I hope it wasn't a spider they seam to get in doring this time of year and I dislike them very much, they need to stay out side dam it. I need to have a lady come in and do the spring cleaning it needs a womens touch like back in the day, they seam to clean in places that I might not even think of and that would be a big help. There are some ladies from the church that do this so maybe I will talk to some of them and see if they can work their magic single people are never very observant when it comes to their own place but women see everything. As they like to change things and people. Every relationship I have been in they have always wanted to change me thinking they can save this soul but they never could for that job is for God and not the opiset sex, I have seen many women walk by my home either taking their kids for a ride or just power walking to stay in shape you can walk around the town in a hour or two and it's nice when they do it in two's having someone to talk to when you are stroling down the street, I havent seen any eugly ones that pass by only the good looking ones showing off their bodies and making their presents known I think some try to walk off the after effects of having children, trying to get back to the shape they were once in. although it's good to do that it doesn't happen very oftend because I only see then once or twice a year and that isn't a constent work out. Lol so funny as the times change so does the people one day they are happy and the next they are sad as with me I have the same days but not as much as I used to.

When you have God in your life the good days seam to out weigh the bad and it shows in the things you do, I like to smile when I feel the joy of God in me and others see this in you for some reason they can tell when He is working in our lives. It's like a glow that comes off of us as people that glow so many saw in Jesus before they took his life, but He had a mission before he came here he so loved the world that he came here to savce it. I remember my first prayer of Assurence 7-7-13 Deamons fall when Christens pray and witness together. Lives are healed when pretensions are cast aside. God extends mercy and peace to all who are sincerely penitent. Turn away from temptation, knowing that God will strengthen you in fulfilling the law of Christ. In the name of Jesus Christ, you are forgiven. This was the first of many that I will give over the years, but it is the start. Of heading towards another direction my life is surely changing and I like the way it's headed as long as I keep it up, when you are brought into a family you never want to see any of them leave and Janet will be missed as she tries to find her way. I don't know why but I can feel when things are not going good in someones life and at times they feel like they have to move on, and then later it happens they find out that it wasn't the place, because they feel the same way in the place that they went to or moved to. And when this happens it's telling you that you can't run from your self, then the rebuilding comes when you have to find the friends you will need to get through life. And you may choose the wrong ones if your not carefull, we seam to think that we know best but usually that's better left in God's hands. But we have to try our ways and if we fail then we give it to God or fall deeper into that place we don't want to be in, I don't know many peoples problems but I have learned that when things are too big for us to handle the only one to turn them over to is Christ' because people don't have the magic it takes to help when it's really needed, yes they can say the things you want to hear but to get the truth only He can guide you to where you need to be.I think in a way I might sound like a bible thumper but truly I'm not. I'm Just a person that has been touched by in some way by Him and my opinions are my own, in my world it doesn't do any good to not be who I am, that person that got lost so long ago is gone and the one that he created has come to the surface and in many ways he is still like a kid. I'm trying to find out who this person is so he can go on and live through some of what I have learned. I have to admit that at times I'm beside my self not knowing what to do next but then the answer comes to me later down the line and then I move on to see what He has in store for me, it's quiet this morning and I hear no one except for the snoring of my little brother but that's something I hear every morning sometimes it's bad and other times it not so bad depending on how he slept. In the beginning

I didn't know what to think because he talked to who ever, more then he talked to me. But then after a while it became something natural like hearing Harley wanting to go out side when I didn't want to get out of bed. It's the little things that I notice most of all and they let me know that I need to deal with those things in my life for I too have some of the same things that still need to be changed, I wouldn't know what to do if each morning was the same.

Like when I used to get up as a child and follow the same routeen after a while it became a part of my life back then like putting on your shoes and going through the day. Sometime I want change so bad that I expect it every day and when it doesn't come I get edgy not knowing what the day might bring. Even today I'm still learning like the kid in school not knowing what the asignement is going to be that the teacher has in mind, it's all a wonder to me until it happens the unknown being known and then learning more as time goes by. Material things are not very important to me but taking care of things like the bills and making sure they are paid so life can go on and we don't loose the things we have, my daughter I know is going to miss her mother when her time comes and I know that being there for her will be important. But through prayer I'm also hoping she gets a set of lungs, so she can be around for a time longer there has been to many passing in the last 5 years and really they need a break, with Debbie and her brother they went within a year of them selves and that caused a lot of heartache in that family especially with Shannon and their mother, Shannon is like her dad in many ways timmed nd bashfull but if you get her riled up look out because she can hold her own. My Son is the same way but it takes chemicals to bring his out, like with his father it gives him a false since of security and that's something we all have to work through in this life not being afraid to show those feelings. I looked at a van yesterday and it's nothing like I expected so we just drive by and came back home not wanting to sink tons of money into a project like that, it would only burry us deeper in debt and we cant have that.

With the things I wan't to do my goals are to try and get something to make money off of and today I'm going to pickel some more eggs as my supply is running low this will let me sit back for a short time until they are sold and then I will restock again but I don't want to get too far a head of my self as that can cause waste and that is never a good thing, our Spanish people came by at work yesterday and got some shirts they don't talk much as none of them speak English' they just smile a lot a bunch of great guys even if speech brings a boundry between us our actions are understood. Many cant afford the high dollar shirts at the stores so they come to us for what they need and they always leave happy knowing they got a good deal, on the computer I bought I think I will fix the fan motor and then sell it at the thrift store, it's too big for my room and I don't really like it being that big taking up so much room. And little brother doesn't know how to run one so giving it to him is out of the question. It's going on 4:00 Am. And the day is just starting but still the birds are not up yet to bring in the day, they don't start singng until around five when it gets light out side but then they sing like all get out' such beautiful music to bring in the day. And then you can hear it all through the day as well, just one of His gifts to us as we go through this life the gift that he gave them brings joy to us. Thinking back I can remember my mom singing like I do when I'm working in Church, maybe it's a way to make things better and take your mind off of our troubles, I still recall singing with her on the couch when Herb was gone. looking back it must of did something for her maybe make it to where it wasn't so lonely, I guess you can have children and still be lonely missing that connection between two adults but there has to be more, maybe we try to read more into something then there really is and that's what makes things complacted, always looking for that lost piece of information that may or may not exist who really knows for sure? I have always tried to search for what's missing and in reality maybe nothing is missing at all maybe life is what we make of it but if we make a mistake I do know that he will let us correct it. For the time we have has been written in the palm of his hand and only he knows when that time will come, our mission I this life has become much different then what I expected in the early years of my life things like death had never intered my mind but through the years I learned that there is a bigger picture here. Like with David the king' he didn't come into power until many years later and then it was by the king before him going nuts and thinking David was out to kill him, David couldn't take his life because he was part of the order and he had to wait until the king died. But even then David didn't hold up to God's rules like the king before him they both failed in a since but what the lord puts into motion no man can stop, even if it has a bad out come. I think we all fall short of His expectations but he still stands by us, maybe in hope that things will change or not.

Before he gives us something he knows if we will fail or not and if we fail he still lets us learn from that mistake. Many of the people in the bible had their faults and they were all different, one had an anger problem, while another was quick to judge, and even another stuttered, many had their own traits that set them apart from one another. And yet many of them lived over 100 years and some to 140 my land' no one lives that long today not even with science the way it is, but they say people are living longer because of it. Taking credit where it isn't due I believe, well the morning it about to start so my alone time is ending, little brother is up and I have taken out Harley. Through the day I will do many things but none is more importand then getting things done at the Church, it's my home away from home you might say that place where I can find peace when my soul and spirit is weary. Who would of ever thought that I would find my self here in my town of dreams? Surely this is my home. I'm amazed at how some will set them selves up for the end of the world, to me it's stupid but they will go as far as building a bunker that will house their familys in case the end comes. We all know that the end of times will come but the bible teaches that it's nothing to be afraid of for God will protect His own in those times, now atheist would be the ones that would believe in such things as having to protect them selves as they don't believe in the lord and that's their choice but in the end times they will see the fires of hell burning, some atheist have died seeing the hell that they would go and live out eternity in and many of them cried because they didn't think it existed.

My self I have never seen it and I don't think I would want to, I'm doing my egg thing today and it feels good to be able to work at your own speed without others bothering or hurring you. It's what makes life plesent and your helping others along the way, at times in life when we feel something is right it might not really be the best thing for us. I do know that by coming here I have aquired a new family something that had been missing through the years of my life, that deep connection which brrings love even further then we ever thought it could TGIF and it's time for the weekend they need sitters at the art building on the 27th so we will see if they have enough people to fill that slot. Or slots they have two of them one lasts an hour and the other three hours, I have done this before but remembering if it was on that day or not has eluded me Maggie used to take care of those things but with her being sick Peggy must be doing it I need to find out some things today so we will see what happens, when your excepted here you become part of a helping crew or at least that what I call it and you work with some great people and most are Christens even when they go to different churches. I believe there is four Churches here in Courtland but in reality we are all brothers and sisters brought together with one common goal and that's to love God the father, sometimes at night I also dream but with most of them I don't recall what they were and the ones I do remember are very strong it's like maybe some are to be remembered and the others well I cant really say it's like some may be important and others not so much. So far my little adventure has been kept just here where I'm protected sort of like the movie I watched a long time ago about guy that never aged, he had taken him self out of society or was never in it and he did all the right things working when needed and just doing things for people it was like the town had protected him from the out side world and he never had a reason to wonder. His words were that if you keep you're self bust the devil doesn't have time to come into your life. Being in his late 80's or 90's he didn't look over 50, was he cheating life? Or just living it by keeping him self away from the destruction that occurs whe others inter the realm of your existence. As for talking he didn't much unless he had something to say, I remember the girl that visited him she talked all the time and he didn't care for it using words that didn't make any since to him you know the words all shrinks use them' to try and get into your head and figure out what your all about. Shamefull words were used when they asked him if he had realtions with other people, it was funny when he told them that they should be ashamed and that they didn't grow up with manners. He was a man that didn't want anything to do with the out side world and that's kind of how I feel, at this point in my life. Many times small towns don't have much communication with the out side world except for what has to be done, a community that's a community in it's self and they get along just fine. O we get the mail and the news paper but other then that visits are made to see family about once a year or with some more oftend, as for being a part of this I love it and I wouldn't change it. It's a privilege to be a part of something so great, when I need to talk with God or sing him a song I just go to the Church and the music comes out my way of telling him thank you for what He has done in my life through the years I have always made it no matter how hard it becomes and I hope it will not stop securing my piece of heaven you might say right here on earth.

The day is going to be hot, just as hot as yesterday but we are blessed with what we have. Many have to live with drama in their lives as for me or us there isn't much of that to speek of and if it shows it's head we try to cut it off. I oftend wonder now how the others would feel about what has been accomplished with me and little brother, I do know that some would be proud going from that old life to this one. My self it's like the other didn't exist in some parts, today I'm trying something new searching the internet for investment cars and vehicles we have an up coming auction that will have a collector car in it and who knows maybe I can get it on the cheap and then turn it later. I have found that there are many ways to make money if you have the seed money but it's getting those funds that are hard I never new that you could find things at your finger tips on a computer and it's awesome that this can happen. After watching a movie on Brigg Young the leader of the morman Church I find that he never was a prophet just a man hungrey person that liked to think he was high on the totem pole in the religius realm, it's people like that which give a bad name to religion and ruin things for those who truly believe in God. Saturday and I have to go to town this morning to get Randy's stomach pills he has a really hard time without them and gets heart burn if he doesn't take them, I also have to work at noon sso going to the auction is out of the question matbe one day I will be able to take the day off but not now. In the winter would be a good time should we get a day that it's too cold to open the thrift store, I go through changes some times that I don't understand going from wanting to do everything to not doing much of anything, and then it changes again but to the other things. I can except and live with but I'm still looking for the middle ground to where everything is great all the time, and maybe it doesn't exist .

As for anger it doesn't come into my world very oftend and I don't know if that's good or bad, I have always been one that is hard to anger and evenn when it arises I have control over letting it out and the worst it's ever gotten is the yelling. It's my opinion that it can be controlled but only to a certain extent maybe I'm like those monks that live in solitude away from the outside world, so really there is no need to get angry. I recall when I made a pact with God about being celibate for 5 years although I kept the pact it has gone on for quite some time now and the one time that I finely ended it things didn't turn out very well, not finding what I thought I was looking for and then I turned back to God as things seamed more comfortable with Him, not having th pressure of a loud mouth and all the drama that went with it. I had never been much good with drama and Lord knows when you hook up with someone whos life is full of it you can loose that peace you have become acccustom to, so you back away and go back to that place where the peace returns. I couldn't imagine being in that place I visited today and my peace has returned to me she is out in the middle of no where and I didn't feel comfortable there, it's like they say God can use some people to bring you to where you need to be and he will even use emotions to get you there. Human emotions things like false love which was what it was at that time, getting us to where we need to be is important and that will allow us to grow in many ways like taking the insecuritys away the thing's you never got to develop when you were in that place of darkness. In that world you only exist a soul taking up space with no purpose but to wake up in the morning and pass out at night, in that space you start to learn that there has to be more to life then just a bottle more to life then just being prop that exists in a world with no purpose. For everyone that is on this planet we have something to do and sure as you get older you might not be able to do as much as you did as a young person but still you have to except that and do whats in your realm like the cowboy that used to ride the range, when age sets in you might be a teacher of what you used to do just because you get old doesn't mean that life is over and for some it's just begun. Teachers make so many thousand dollars a year and then when they retire that drops making things harder but usually they have a good retirement plan to hold them over until that time comes when they cant take care of them selves, o some get married but others become spinsters not wanting to or being able to deal with married life. So they live out their lives getting involved in things to take up their time, it says we grow from suffering and hard times and this could be true maybe it gets us ready for that after life when things change. Eternity is a long time but our time here is short and so much is expected of us especially being kind to other people, if everyone lived this way the world would be a better place. And we would see things differently throught the eyes of a careing and helpful person, I couldn't imaging being in the lions dean the out side world where people kill each other at the drop of a hat and even sell people into slavery and the sex trade. That world can stay where it is but still people try and change it and that's a good thing. My self I wouldn't know how to act in the big cities so I don't go there for he said that we should separate our selves from the world and that's what many of us do.

Breaking the mold, as I call it. The mold of having to need evil in our lives, peace is the way to molding our lives helping those who need help and making their world a little better. Many times we get caught up in anger and say things we don't really mean but as life goes on we make a mends for our short comings and then move on hoping that we havent broke something that cant be fixed, it was a nice day as we also got some rain I and Randy went to the auction and got drounded out and had to waid through some water, sure wish it would of came this way to Courtland but we did get a little and it's spitting some now. The day is about over so until later. Sunday morning and I got up at 4:00 slept in a little very unusual for me but it happened I had a dream about someone last night not to mention there name but it was different from the others that take place every now and again and then bam! I was awake, my project is still producing but things are at a slow pace. But the people know now where they can get them when the mood hits them I had always known that they would do something should I ever make them like before but I'm not going to push the project any harder then I have already. If I can break even by making the bank payments for the first five years then I'm happy and after that it will be mine to do other things with, a solid foundation is always needed before you can move forward. I love going to the place and they tell me that things are ok' and that they need more. The Church is ready for service this morning and things are going to be great since Kathy is back it's strange but I look forward to hearig her on Sunday morning and no one could take her place in my heart anyway when it comes to giving a good service, she was the one that welcomed me here on that day I stepped into the church almost 5 years ago.

And she has helped me through the tough times when I didn't think I could make it after pop's passed away, each time she has been there and they even gave me the job I hold dear to my heart today. Such great people we have here in the great town of Courtland' maybe one day it will grow once again and I would like to be a part of that maybe by opening a youth center that caters to the prevention of alcohol and drug abuse who knows. Little Bernt to me is the poster child to teaching others sign language and they are moving forward with that program. There are millions of kids that are born deaf and this could be the starting point for that so they don't feel left out in things like church and other things, just a great project all aroung so others can understand them. I sure there are many things going on that I don't hear about but that one started with a little boy born here in Courtland. They should call it the Brent foundation for the hearing inpaired and it would be born here in Courtland, to me I would be a good way to help. I have a feeling it's going to be a good day and I hope we got a lot of rain last night as I could hear the thunder before I went to bed, but that doesn't always mean that it will rain hard. My land' it's almost 5:00 Am so I will go and open the church. The service went well as we had back our pastor an morre people were there, even Jan's daughter was there they came down to visit for a week two of them what a blessing to her to have them home. One lives in Denver and I don't know where the other lives but they are home and maybe even for fun-day Jan is so happy and I'm glad for her and Robert, although the miles can sometimes keep people apart for a time it's always nice when they come back home even for just a visit. It's the beginning of a new week here in Courtland so many things will be happening but my focus is to make sure that I get my jobs done, we all play a role in this great place we call home and this week isn't any different as we wake up each morning and greet the day, what a great existence we have with our brothers and sisters this week many will be running or practing for the race the town has on Friday but they will do it in the morning when it's cool out side. The church is usually open for these races in case any one needs to use it for any reason so I will make sure that the doors are open, it's the 49th year of fun-day and already the tickets are sold out for the barbacue my land that's a lot of people eating but they will need a cool place to eat and that will be the art building where they have air-conditioning so they can enjoy their meal in the comforts of home. And have fun at the festivities, it a joyest time of year when most of the people get out once a year and enjoy them selves the young people anyway as for the old they had their time many years ago and now a new generation will step up to the plate and their offspring. The little ones that were born here and will go through school here learning all the things they need to have a successful life where ever they choose to go to collage, yes collage most of the farmers are well off here and it's something they all make sure happens with their kids.

Jan's kids used to run from the house next door over to this one so the wommen could baby sit for her and then when she got home they would run back and the day was ended. Such a lovely thought of that happening it reminds me of something mom would do back in the day when we lived in Los Angels and she had to work, the thoughts come back every now and again about my little boy days but then I have to turn them off and come back to reality, this time of life in the year of 2013 what a difference from 1962 when I thought things were much easier. But were they? Maybe I'm just seeing things through those eyes of a child. back then yes that's it! Today I have all the comforts of home and I wake up with a good out look on life but still something is missing maybe that one last part of life that so many have and it's called love a human connection that has Stacyded me for so long but I'm optimistic that it will come one day when he feels I'm ready. Tuesday and my coffee is ready for the morning as a matter of fact I'm having a shot now but it's still hard to wake up, trash day and I don't much feel llike going out but it's something that had to be done I don't like feeling under the weather but it happens some times and yet I still get my jobs done it's like nothing can hold me back from doing what I have to do. The slow-motion feeling I have today will pass as the days wares on and then I will be as spray as a chicken that wakes everyone up in the morning. Not my kind of morning when usually I feel good and have a great day so on this day things will be slow in getting around.

It's strange how some things change as the good feelings don't seam to stay over a period of a few weeks and then it's back to the time when I used to be able to barily walk, I notice a heavyness in my legs that cause me to kind of drag my feet and legs around not a good feeling when you have things to do, it kind of makes you think about those who are with no feeling at all some times when I'm standing is all I can do to stand still as my legs want to jump up and down so I can stan in one position, but as for my nerves that are steady and I don't shake in the hands just the legs and the feet maybe because they support the wholee body. In a few minites I have to go to the church and take out the garbage so we will see what happens then. I kind of feel like I'm in a stooper slow to react but it doesn't stop me from moving forward and writing and maybe that's a good thing. Wednesday and we are getting closer to fun-day the waking up gets harder each day as the body tries to adjust from the sleep to be coming fully awake, but hey that's just the way I am slow at the start but a go getter once fully awake. Through the days and years so many things change and sometimes I don't realise it until later when it's already happened the careing of others that I thought I didn't know somehow are made present by them saying hi as I walk down the street, Maggie sure has been missed in her time away her smile would brighten up even the darkest day's around here, I know what she is going through as I have been there before although not many know my story they don't know the hardship of teaching your self to walk again and having no one around to help except for your own strength and the help of God Him self this is when you start to believe deeply in the lord knowing only that he can help you rise above the things that this world can take from you. And then the day comes when you get those things back and it assures you that there is truly a god. I think my faith is what keeps me going the faith that I know there is an afterlife and how some of it will be, no more pain or sorrow just this wont just be given you have to work hard at it by completing your mission here on earth. O ya some take their own lives but still there is a place you will go, mental illness can break throught the gates if the person isn't in their right mind and there they will be made whole once again by the power of God but for those who kill and then are killed I cant say what will take place, they say there are many jobs in heaven some importand and then some not so importand but he makes the decision where we will play our part or be placed for his house has many rooms for his believers, the ones that truly love him the one that gave us life. Hump day as some call it and half the week is over I bet the boys are glad for the weekend to get here so I will have to work today and we will see what happens there, my land it's only going on 4:00 Am and I'm still tired sure hope I wake up soon. Finely I'm awake' and it only took four hours compaired to an hour on most days but that's life, I went to work and had fun laughing with the women I worked with she is funny. After work I came home and now I'm just about ready for bed as tomorrow comes early for me in this life.. It's almost two hours earlier then usual for me getting up but hey! I couldn't sleep I would like to talk about Methamphetamine for Dummies when you people try it your hooked. And there is no getting aroud it but to quit which most people can't it throws your life into a different world.

And you will think you are on top of the world but your not the uforia can make you not want to come back to this world, as your mind floats in another universe so you think. That world doesn't exist but in your mind and has nothing to do with this world we live in, and if you think others don't notice that you are different then your only fooling your self at this point. Staying up for days and then falling asleep for days on end only destroys your body as the drug eats at your spirit and soul. Then after years of the addiction you loose everything family doesn't matter not even your children and that's how some are lost to the foster care system and some are never seen again. They are taken away so they can have a chance to live without you destroying their lives as you have your own, these days most of the Meth comes from Mexico where they ship it by trucks and other means, but how much gets through only the cartel knows. It's Thursday morning and I couldn't sleep worth a crap maybe still haunted by the effects that the drus had on my life so long ago but today I put the time to good use by warning others about it's downfall and how it will make a slave out of you, no one sets out to get hooked on the stuff but it happens everyday as they flood the streets with the crap, I lived in that world for many years and they wouldn't think twice to snuff you out like putting out a candle. It's all about money the billions that they bring in each year off your habbit, and the longer you have the addiction the richer they get. Some of them have more money then banks and they hide it or wash it through banks to make sure it's clean, as for your life it's nothing to them you are just a number a dollar sign that makes them rich.

Children are exceptable to them because they usually live the longest and can bring in the most money from school's and other places as for the older folks they know their life wont last long, so they use them the best they can and then throw them away out in a field or a ditch somewhere and some even end up in abanded well;s out on farms that are not used any longer. Today my head hurts thinking back on these things but the story has to be told to save the children, so they can avoid the curse that will take their lives should they try or get hooked on the crap.

July 25th and they are pushing to get Marijuana made legal this should never take place because it's a gate way to Meth use, by mixing it with the Marijuana they are already doing it but some don't see it as some states are blinded by the money that it will bring in. as for you or I they don't give a shit about us as we are not on the scale of life the money scale that is. The after effects of Meth use is a life long battle and it's not an easy one as it destroys the body how I have ever lived this long is only by the grace of God my redeamer, maybe it was so I could tell you what to look for so you don't fall into it like I did. As I write this thousands of kids are becoming addicted to the curse and believe me there are many from alcohol to drugs they are both the same and one day you will realize this if it doesn't kill you first' even my writing at 3:00 Am is a after effect of the Meth use but the Lord showed me productive way to use this and that by writing this journal or book so you can have a chance to get away from the curse that will take you down to the lowest level of your life. My friend don't ever go there because you may not come back. The risk is too great to destroy you and your family if you have one, if you were to get to know me you wouldn't believe the kind of person I am. In real life I don't talk much and I'm very quiet but you cant tell it from the way I write, it just goes to show that you can't always judge a book by it's cover. My existence here in my town of dreams allows me to search the libery of my mind to find the things that might help others the most and that can be tireing sometimes especially at the wee hours of the morning, but I guess sleep will come when I'm dead. The Marijuana phase only lasted a few years until it wasn't enough and then it went on to other things which was just as bad if not worse, but the point here is that back then they didn't cut pot with all kinds of other drugs like they do today. Back then it took five hits to get you high and today just being in the same room you get high through the second hand smoke. Such a change from the1960 strange because I was born in 1958 so I wasn't very old when I started, in the beginning the alcohol did the job but that didn't last long. But still I always went back to it for that comfort of not dealing with the world running from life I guess it gave me a feeling of being a person instead of just a kid that was looked over by others and the alcohol and drugs gave me a since of being someone. With it my false went away the false of being shy turned into being brave and things I couldn't say to others sober I could when I drank or got high it was like it opened a door that had been shut and I like that about my self even though now I know it wasn't me. I was the little boy that got pushed to the back corners of my mind and hid there until the other was ready to die because of the damage he did to this body and soul, but during the fight they had the one who hid came out on top because he was stronger then the other.

Pushed away for over 30 years and forgotten until he rose up to drestroy the demon that had taken over his life. Murder wasn't in this child other wise he would of done it earlier so he waited until the demon was at it's weakest poing and he let him die, this was when the child asended to the higher plain of existence and was shown that life could be better. It was strange being without a body as he went through the light but he noticed that there was something greater then him there, a power that could recharge his soul and he came away with a different out look on life but being easy it wouldn't be. Thursday has been a good day but I had to help Valerie out which I know will come back to bite me in the ass, it's strange how I think I'm over her but still that connection keeps coming back one that won't go away. I told her that she owed me big time and that she will have to go to church with me when she visits to clean my house so funny but I won't hold my breath that she will make good on her word, tomorrow is Friday the beginning of fun-day and it runs through the weekend so I don't expect that too many people will make it to church like last year. Fun seams to be more important to some but as for my self it's just another day like Monday, I believe to me that the church is more important then having fun but that's my thoughts on the church and my father. The Alpha and the Omega, we had to go to WalMart so I could send her what she needed and then I bought a new coffee pot so I can give the old one to the thrift store, you would be amazed at the people looking for a coffee pot here in the sticks it's just shocking.

As the weekend approches on Saturday we have to go and pick up some food at the church it's going to be there this month instead of at the cafataria. I have made my quota for the loan this month so if everything keeps going that way I don't see and problem paying off the loan in the time allotted. Although my time is spent on different things I always find time to give thanks to God for what he has done in my life and for my friends that make some things possible. Friday and I got a call from Margreat last night and she was funny but also very high or drunk, and she told me how she loved me I know things work slow around here but my land it's been a few years since that brief encounter and she acted like it was yesterday. She said if she had a car she would of been right over and I told her Not a good idea, then she hung up and I thought that was it but she kept calling back so I had to shut off my phone. She told me that her kids were grown and now she was all alone and her world was falling apart, my self I didn't have much to say except to laugh a little with her as she said I was her angel back then and that she still loved me and I said it's too late for anything like that and she said God bless you. When you havent been around people who drink for a long time you really don't want to talk and repeat your self to many times so I ended the conversation and went back to sleep. Old flames are better forgotten in my books as I always seam to move forward not backwards learning from past mistakes is a great lesson as long as they are not repeated. I was humiliated when we were together by her and that's something I will never go through again, it's not a good feeling. To be treated less then someone else especially by one who says they love you such a disapointment on her part but also I told her that I didn't have any bad feelings towards her, which I don't but maybe I should treating me like she did. I have learned through life that holding ill feelings can also be bad for the recever no matter how much they were hurt, she went on to tell me that everyone of her friends were dieing or died and that too I could relate to but she is strong and will recover maybe one day we can talk when she isn't under the influence and be civil. As a person she is good in her own way but she isn't the women for me still torn by the two worlds that almost tore her apart so many years ago she has to make a stand and stick to it no matter what! Even when we feel weak from life. For life is a test to see if our faith is strong enough to stand the test of time and if it isn't then we fall apart like she has apparently, she delivers my news paper each morning so she must still be able to work a little. Looseing someone is hard on a person but through my life I have lost so many people that I try to stay away from funerals, when pop's went to be with the lord many of my friends sent gifts and for that I will be forever grateful. They new that I lost someone I loved dearly' and show their kindness like Christens do for one another and maybe that's part of why I stayed needing that comfort from my new family that I have grown to love so much. They have also allowed Randy to feel comfortable here and that's a great help as I need him as much as he needs me, it's giving us time to bond once again after so much brokeness between us for which a lot of it he doesn't remember.

As this is the first day of Funday many people will be coming to town and this weekend should be a weekend of joy for many the little kids will play games and get wet as the heat rises and some will even go up in the hot air balloon, the ones that are not afraid that is. The older ones anyway, I would like to take some pictures so I can make memories in my scrap book that's another thing no pictiure of memories from the past only a few of grandma and Herb and the one of mom and Oliver not much from a life time of living. But this year I will start new memories that will last the rest of my life, taking those steps to pass down some pictures of me and Randy and maybe some to the news paper of the celebration. Even the Kearney hub might print some of them you never know they have kept tabs on my success since I beat my addiction, God allows us to grow in a positive way but also it can happen in a negative way if you loose sight of where you have been and the lessons that your supposed to learn. As for slipping while you recover it happens but you have to pick your self back up and move on towards that goal you have set for your self, I guess I'm not a quitter when it comes to life. Although I have had my moments of weakness when I thought I wanted to give up, He has never left my side even through the hard times not once hasn't He answered me when I talked to him my father in heaven. Don't ever let others try and run your life because it's meant for you to make your own choices, and other people will screw up the things that are important to you. Let you're thoughts be your own created by the mind that he has given you as we are all different and no two are the same.

Coming here alone and scared has turned into a great life and today I share it with my brother I thought I had lost so long ago. It's a good time and I hope for many more years, as we grow old here in my town of dreams the place that opened it's arms to me. I don't ever think about leaving any more it's something that isn't in the cards and I know that He placed me here to stay with all my friends. Saturday morning yesterday a young man came by to work on the computer I bought a couple of weeks ago and he got it fixed, to be honest I didn't know weather it would get done but he was back in just a couple of hours and it ws done. He is a nice young man and I will use him again later if something should mess up, he showed me how to mail some of my chapters to should I need to later. it's offically fun-day and manyy people will be out running and the cars and tractors going down the main street of town,, it's a quiet morninng with nothing sturring anywhere except for the car or truck that went by a few mnutes ago. I'm sure that some people were up town last night but all in all this morning will be the starting point of the Celebration and even the kids will be out having fun with mom and dad near by as they play and get their chance to play the many different games those were the days when your young and don't have to worry about things like drugs and alcohol, as those things will come into the picture later in life when they are older, I wish I could see a world without those things but at this time in history it's just not possible as the war continues. Now days that have police officesr called the Meth busters and they go around and bust Methamphetamine labs and confiscate truck loads of the drug as they sent it across the borders from Mexico, like with Marijuana the drugs are getting more pure as they make it in mega labs in the hills of Mexico and then transport it to the United States' the more of it they bust and burn the more comes right back it's like a cancer never ending. For everyone they bust two trucks get through and if they want to fly it in, they can do that also by bribling customs officers giving them ten to twenty thousand dollares a shipment which is just a drop in the bucket to them to put it in a simple understanding way it would be like giving then a quorter out of a thousand dollars. That's how little it would hurt the dealers and it's happening right now this minute, somewhere here in the U.S. I don't recall it ever being this bad but it is and it's going to get worse before it gets better, just a bad situation all together. It's supposed to be nice today with the highs in the 70's or 80's, in all the years before it had been very hot so hot that I didn't even go out side or up town but many go each year no matter how hot it is and the kids well they can handle it being so young and having a pool to cool off in. I think the town getting that pool was the best thing that has been done for the children. They can have a great ole time when ever they want, the older people don't get out like they used to but they do drive around in heir cars and have a ball if it's not too hot. Ben was telling me that he won't be going this year for what ever reason but I didn't pry into why for those reasons are his own, in a way he is like the son I don't get to see very oftend and I really like him he is very smart when it comes to Mechanics. And he takes good care of my car when it needs it, later I will go down and open the Church so the runners can have a place to stop should they get tired or have to use the can' on face book my brothers X Wife contacted me and we have chatted a little it's been over 20 some years since she disappeared after her divorce from Rick and she said she had wondered what ever happened to us and now she knows. Life has also been good to her and for that I'm glad I recall her having a daughter and I think her name was becky, I vagely remember her but she would have to be in her late 30's or early 40's.

My time seams to just wiz by I know Alice has grand children she posted one of their pictures on face book the worlds biggest network and it was started in a garage I believe by two guys, amazing how some things start but it's the growing process that intreags me how one person will talk to another and then another. Venting is what a lot of people call it, showing how proud they are of their families like Stan & Tonya do every day it gives inspration to others to help in some way and that's a good thing usually, Sunday morning very early and there are lights on in town. With all the people that came for the celebration some are still out walking at this hour, and then they will be off to bed don't know who it was but they were headed west down the country road the house across th stret has it's lights on the one kitty corner from us where the Mexicans used to live and of course the neighbor across the street who is a trucker he must be used to getting up early always on the road like he is. I can see why some might still be awake as this celebration only comes once a year and they have to have as much fun as possible, it's a time to let off steam by some having a few drinks and I don't believe there is any fights around here. But I could be wrong have never been down town when the darkness has fallen, I would say that it's mostly for the young not saying that I'm old or anything. If this was Kearney you would hear the cops as they would break up fights and crap like that but here in Courtland it's quiet still this morning, when I went to take pictures yesterday I saw John and his daughter but he didn't see me as I was behind him, he had his lawn chair and was enjoying the paraide as many lined the main street. I didn't realize it but they could of use a few old cars in the celebration so maybe next year I might have one if things work out right.

Always did like the older cars as it's a blast from the past, Tom Garmen had his 1990 Mustang convertible my land that car is in good shape for it's age he must really take care of his things. And they had tractors from the past clear back into the 30' and 40's all restored, one little man drove a little cart that was made from wood and a battery that ran it he really looked like he was having fun with his cowboy chaps and hat on. As for the weather it was nice, almost cold out but I stayed around until I ran out of film and then it was back home and I started to make more product with no luck as the eggs were to old and I wasn't going to put them out as I only use fresh eggs. I know they must have had some bands that preformed but I didn't hear them like last year, last year they sounded like they were right next door as they were loud but also plesent everyone just out having fun. It's about the end of he month so today I should get my check from the church and put it away I want to keep things in sink' so I don't fall on hard times again at least not for a long time if ever. The thrift store was open yesterday and I hope they did well but we will see later in the week my old coffee pot is going down there and I don't think it will last long as some are wanting them like the women that said she wanted to start drinking coffee. As for the day it's going to be beautiful with the weather as cool as it is, and who knows maybe it might stay this way for a while or until the Indien Summer hits this part of the country. Going from nice to being hotter then hell but then fall will be upon us a time when we get ready for winter and get things bundled up so things go right for us, my lawn mower has lasted quite a while for being as old as it is and I think it will last another year or two but then I might haave to get a new one if it's in the cards we will just have to wait and see how things go, in this life as I have said before we make mistakes and I used to think that it was God punishing us but it's not. We learn by doing and when it's hard then we just adjust to a new way, trying to get a better picture of whats going on like with this project I have taken on many adjustments have to be made to get it just right and in time this will happen but for now we will see how it goes. I can hear the train chugging into town from off in the distence I canm tell that it must be about three miles out so it will be a while before it gets here, I love hearing it each morning as it lets me know that morning is not too far off. And the birds will be singing in about an hour, they set the tone for the day with the beautiful music they sing they have one purpose in life and that's to make beautiful music. God created them for our pleasure but so many don't see this being in the big cities with concreat replacing the country side, they get pushed away and if they didn't plant trees they wouldn't hear them at all. I love the country even though it can be hard to get around but we survive and have a good life a life better then what we had.

My town of dreams has provided us with what we need to live and at times I even get tickled when things go really well, one day I will have all that I desire and then things will be perfect. No more wanting just enjoying the peace that God has brought to my life, for I love Him so' Jusus you're the rock of the world the Son of the creator of all things although there are three it's but one. It says that you can ask for the Holy Spirit to come into you, but with it you have to learn what you can use and what you shouldn't use and this I have yet to understand but I do know that it's God which gives you this if He feels your ready. Seaprating the things you can use and the things you can't, I still have a lot to read on the subject but I know it will be Him that gives me understanding. As He rebuilds me from the inside out and to me that makes since because our spirit is inside and our bodies don't have anything to do with that kind of learning, God knew that I needed a new place so I could learn, a smaller place with less confusion so I could adjust and get on the right track even here I am separated from others not to fall away from what's been put into this mind of mine He sems to know me better then I know my self. And He should, as he knew me before I was even thought of when I wasn't even a thought in my parents mind. The understanding of how this could be has eluded me but maybe one day I will understand when He feels I'm ready to understand it. Like the person that can't see the forest from the trees I stand in amazement wondering what will take place next will I be able to see the beauty that's right in front of me? Or will it elude me? 'Not' He will open the gates so I can go through them and see the things I need to see.

My Lord and my God towers above this planet and sees the things I need to see to become more then I am, it's past noon and Church was fine. Monday morning and I found a leak in the closet where the heater and Air-Conditioning is, it has to of been leaking for a while but I put a bowl under the leak until Ican get it fixed never thought that would happen but I guess it comes withering an old house. Good hing I caught it before it could do a lot of damage, they sell a product which will seal it and iwill get some from the dollar store one can should be enough I just hope it didn't hurt and of the electronics in the heater. This rain has been going on for a few days now and I cant get up there until it quits sometime this week. It had to of started sometime within the last day because I didn't hear it or during the night and I sure didn't hear it yesterday morning when I was up. Hopefully not much damage was done it is running down the exhaust flue so that rubber in a can should stop it they use it on boats and gutters so I will give it a try it just has to work. We had the same kind of leak at the Church and they came and fixed it except it was in the kitchen there after they put on a new roof, you can never see these things coming before hand so you just have to catch it hopefully before and major damage is don't. Now that I have put something to catch the water the rest should dry out, I just hope it doesn't rain for the whole week. There is supposed to be a flue cover up there but I don't know if something happened to it or what we will see as the rain stops I sure hope the insolation isn't wet, other then that things are fine and I hope they stay that way I don't need any major repairs right now. Joshua gave me his card, so maybe I can call on him later this week and have him croll up there and check it out I'm sure he could use the money for something. One thing I always want to do is to keep things in good shape can't have my home falling apart for any reason. I have to live here the rest of my life, during the rainy season is when you find out about the little things that could turn into big problems if you let them go but a pound of prevention can usually fix most things. I do know that it will have to be done before the next rain or snow fall that way I will have no worries durinng winter, it's a quiet morning and that's how I can hear things as small as a drop of water. Thank God for silence, the streets are wet so I know it rained through the night it had to of rained a lot to bring this to my attention but Godseams to let me know when something is wrong He is always watching out for me. I know there are some things I have to do that I have put off so now it's time to do them before winter gets here, yes ole winter just a few months off and then it will be cold once again. don't care for that time of year either but it comes with the State we live in all States have their draw backs some too hot while others are to cold, but through it all we seam to survive and make it in this world. Everyone is sleeping as the night becomes day and I hope little brother gets the rest he needs to make it through the day so he doesn't sleep so much during the light hours. I cant believe how cold it's been at this time of year, last year at this time it was hotter then heck but now the grass is turning green once again from the flood of rain we have been getting, this should give the center pivots a break from having to work so hard. Just the other day we got an inch of rain and much more has fallen since that day so we should be good if it would only stop, I cant see outside so the amount I don't know about but we must of gotten a lot for the pipe to leak. Tuesday as the rain continued yesterday after a while the leak stopped but still I'm going to cover the area with the sealer, I was going to use or get it from the store but desided to wait until things dried out because it wouldn't do any good to put it over an area that's wet. I slept in this morning after getting up at midnight and thinking it was three O clock in the Am.

Even little brother was up before me and that's a first, it's garbage day so I have to go down to the church in a little while but I will bring it back here as there is so little and it isn't worth taking out the can down there. It's like we all pitch in and do different things we are a town with pride but not false pride, the pride of being proud of what we have here, and not too many other places can say that like in the big cities. I could never imagine having to get up in the morning or during the night to the sound of gun fire and people laying dead in the streets, it makes you wonder if change will ever come to those places. Many years ago they came out with a movie called the streets of LA and the whole place was a prison such a sad thing but it was in someones mind and created because they could see it happening, as for my town of dreams it will always be here a quiet place where none of that crap happens only the fight once and a while by young people as for the old they don't have any of that in them any longer calmed down by the triles of life and some like me have never been that way, the two separated by good and evil one not knowing why or how the other ever got that way. My town I hold dear to my heart and I know that others feel the same way as many of them have lived here their whole lives. Only to venture out once in a while to visit family that are long gone from here, maybe they felt they had to see the world but still many of the young people come back to try and raise their familys.

As the morning is upon us I had to reach out to my friend Stan so I can get some lables for my product, I feel this is something that has to be done before I move any further, so now I wait ontheir reply for help. My land it's already the 30th of the month so another one is under our belt moving futher towards winter, I like it when I can hear my friends going off to work but many of the farmers won't be able to get into the fields because of the rain we had. My land' I know they have to be flooded but the corn should do good if it's not too late. Just a couple of weeks ago it was dryer then hell but still our situation is usually better then the other parts of the country a place seaprated from the other towns where their crops fall to being used for feed. I remember when one State would have to help the other because they ran out of feed when the grass and other things burnt up, but this is natural for farmers to lend a hand to their brothers and sisters in time of need, we have to all pull together when things like this take place. Otherwise the system would fall apart and no one would make it, I call this hands across America' but I'm sure others have their own saying about such things. In the beginning if things would have been different the whole world would be pitching in to help one another but through violence and other acts many don't want to help and that is a shame. This week they are repairing the sidewalks in front of the Church and on main street hopefully this will let people park closer to the curb without tearing off their bumper. My self I don't park close to the curb because of that reason, and some old farts give me heck for it but Hey! You have to do what it takes to keep your car in one piece and I don't really care if they like it or not. On another note' I got the missing part to my exhaust on the heater vent well they are going to fix it anyway, I knew something was wrong when the water came in the furnace room. Also I got my lables ordered for my product and they should be here by the 6th of August, my land I didn't know how to do it but the people were great at Vista-print and helped me to get everything going. Another step towards moving forward and getting what I need also the kids are being helped through my efforts it isn't much at this time but it will grow as my project grows, every little bit help's when you do your best to do good. I took some more eggs and sausage down to Leroy's and now some more things should come my way in the coming weeks, I can't wait to see the lables when they get here they sure looked nice on the internet sight. I know now that the lord wants me to do these things on my own without others helping me to bring it together, these steps scared me before but now they are coming together and it's like growing up in a way, you know one step at a time. Life it's self is the same way we take baby steps and then move forward and hope for the best, well the day is coming to an end so later. Wednesday or hump day as I'm having the Lenox people put the flue cap on my house I hope it doesn't cost much but I'm sure they will be good to me it's the part that will cost a few dollaars and only about two minutes to put it on. Like I said you have to have everything fixed before winter and with me it's no exception, I'm still excited about the lables getting here and I can't wait to see my name in print like so many others who have come before me.

It's going to be the 1st tomorrow and then on Friday I will go and pay bills again to get them behind me for the coming month, it's something I look forward to when I know the money is there to pay them. It's like I move an inch at a time but still the direction is forward and my good name remains the same, I have learned so many things here and one of them is that no matter what others might say, you have to go through life with your head held high. Knowing you do your best in most things you do, I'm going to work on my project more so I can have things ready for when they go to market. My market the one I built in a thrift and gas station who would of ever thought that things would take off for me in a place other then a bar where this kind of product is sold to people who consume alcohol, but now your every day Joe can have them in their homes or in the field. Such a great feeling to create and then have people like them like they do, bachelors don't like to cook most of the time like the old gentlemen said to me at the thrift store. And his wife didn't cook much anymore do to their age I guess, my land' they had to of been in their 80's and from what I gathered the two had been together for about 20 years. It goes to show that it's never too late to aquire a partmer in life, I really liked him as he was whitty and still had a zest for life two old folks still together and by the traditional vows they had never married only but in their minds by living together for over 20years. I find that many people in these parts have kids before they marry and the reason for that I can't really say, but I do know that even if your not married there is a love there as it was with my kids mother.

And it extends into the children, my Son Leroy has never married and maybe it just hasn't been the right time who can really say for sure? But one day he might take the plunge, I know that even though my kids don't have my last name they are still my children maybe in the same way that we are God's children the last name doesn't matter, I don't recall Jesus having a last name either or God for that matter but still they are one with the holy spirit three in one' like the water we drink and the steam we use to cook and power things. Even to the south pole that stays frozen year around all created by one source. I'm taking the coffee pot down to the thrift store and then maybe later I will take the computer down so some one can use it in their life, many people want one but cant afford to buy a new one so this will give them their chance to have one at a reasonable price and they can get into contact with family if they so choose. You don't see them come up very oftend at least not around here, yesterday the workers hit a water line and we lost water for a time but it didn't take them long to get it up and working again thank God. Maybe I don't think like others but my life hasn't been like theirs either, for every thing I get I give credit to God for it because I know I couldn't do it on my own. Is that under-valuing your self? I don't believe so. As I got a hold of vista-print yesterday I didn't know if I could accomplish getting everything started but that voice inside told me that I could do it, I have always been the kind of person that had to be able to touch things before I would know they were real but that changed on this day. Going through life thinking that everyone was out to get me could have been a mistake something made up in my own mind as a defence to keep others at bay, not wanting to let anyone in and it has worked but at what price? Being defenceive can hurt more then it can help but we learn as we go through life and our mistakes become our lessons of what to do and what not to do. Through the sands of time we learn new things like to trust others, and for the most part that works but also there are those that will take from good hearted people and that's wrong. Like the guy at the store that said his girl-friend stole a lot of his things. When you open up your home to someone you hardly know you run a great risk of that happening, know the person before you open up your life to them because evil does exist that's just the way of the world. I still remember long ago when John told me that if there was ever anything I needed to just let him know and if he could help he would, to me those words were a shock because they were never said to me before, not by anyone. Especially someone that I had only known for a few years, this showed me that he trusted me and although I would never think of asking! this man put it out there and that made me feel good inside. It's like the things I missed that should have been said in my childhood are being said today, to maybe help me grow even further in my faith and in my hope that the world an change. I recall watching Star-Track the movie, and by then they didn't have problems with alcohol that movie must of gave me hope that one day this curse would be a thing of the past.

And I wish it could be so today a world free of the things that destroy lives, in the movie they were even advanced past the drugs that destroyed lives so maybe I hold on to that hope that one day it will be like it didn't exist. Fantasee well maybe but with people you never know we thrive to exist and there is no other like us, when our time comes for us to move on we still try and stay alive to our dieing breath and then the body dies and our spirit and soul move on. Many don't believe this but it's true as I felt my spirit in that place so long ago, a place that is nothing like this earth all your pain and sorrow is gone and it's replaced with joy and happiness until you are returned to this earthly body and then the suffering begins again. Could He of been showing me that enlightment does exist once we are rid of these bodies? I do know that I didn't want to return because I had seen and felt the things of this world, up there you only felt the joy and I wasn't even in heaven I don't think well I know? But why the souls from time past they were way before my time? Waiting for something. Could it of been His judgement or were they just waiting for a train ride? Too many unanswered questions and maybe they are meant to be just that, it's another beautiful day here in Courtland so far no rain but they are calling for it by tomorrow and this weekend, I slept pretty good last night getting up at 5:00 this morning and feeling content with the amount of sleep I got. I even feel better then when I get up early and that is strange not complaining but this doesn't happen very oftend, July is behind us and it the first day of August a new month when things will happen I don't really recall when fall gets here maybe in September or so there are many things that I don't pay close attention to but then with other things I seam to be what I would call up to date.

In this life we all come from somewhere weather it's our walk with God or weather we are traveling all alone, but then we seam to meet those people who help in many ways. I know that there are many who care where we are going, yesterday Rita has her great grand child at the thrift store with her and it was fun to watch them as the little one made friends with alittle boy who's mother was shopping. I tried to break the ice with the boys mother and got her to laugh which felt good laughter is always good for anyone, the coffee pot is now down there so it shouldn't last long we did pretty good business as we made a few dollars for the church and Beverly had made quite a bit before we even got there. I think she is a natural at that kind of thing being she has done it for a long time, my travel through this life has many opticals as change comes all the time, and each step takes a little longer. I have over come so many things but still there are some more but I'm better then I used to be, that wondering soul which didn't have any idea of where he was going , today I'm going to mow the lawn and get it trimed up. Since the rain it has grown quite a bit so it's time. Also I got the Air-Conditioning recharges in the car so it wont be so hot when we travel this will allow us to travel with out being miserable and lord knows how hot it gets in this part of the country, well another day has almost passed so maybe it's time. I have often wondered how it was made possible that I would come beck to the place it all started, the place where I almost lost my life. could we be brought to these places to be shown that our lives could of ended long ago? Or does He show us something else. Maybe how He spaired our lives so we could one day look back on it and say hey! He is great. Back in those days we or I couldn't see past the day or minute for that matter, as we were blind to what was going on. The alcohol would keep us a sleep and tranquil so we didn't really see the world like we do today for each day I now see, a week has gone by and with the minutes a day. So much changes as we get wiser and older as for the kids of today I can see some of their futures if they are addicted to alcohol or drugs, all that they will go through as they fight for their lives. My self I didn't want to wake up but the Lord had other things in mind with showing me that the world could be a place where living could be very good, and today the world is good it's funny how we leaarn and try new things even at my age, I'm doing things that I missed as a child and hoping that it might make me the person I was meant to be. His grace is there for the taking if only more would realize this aspect of things, you can't buy it as it's given freely from the one who created us His gift to us as we go through this life just as the forgivness of sin is also given if we ask but that doesn't mean we are to keep sinning even though He will forgive us over and over again, it's about time for bed so tomorrow I will write some more. O my land' it's raining like theres no tomorrow and the lake is taking form out in the back yard we usually don't get this kind of rain except for spring time the good news is that there isn't any leak's that I can tell so maybe they got that flue on the heater pipe fixed that goes to the roof. The business side if things is taking shape and I hope that the rain stops soon, it must of been raining all night for the back yard to have tha much water in it.

The lake is a reminder that I'm supposed to be here so it never bothers me when it shows it's self once in a while.

As for the day it's time to pay the bills that I didn't already pay and life goes on, I could see how some get all mixed up when it comes to keeping track of such things, but through the years I have learned very well how to do these things and it's like second nature to me. Before the women always did these kind of things but being single I had to learn them and for that I'm glad, it's like I don't like to depend on a women but it would be nice to let someone else have the worry. It would be a great tention reliver going through life with out having everything on my sholders but then I wouldn't be me the Roger that takes care of everything right! In a way I think it's good for a person to go through this kind of thing if they have the ability to do it as for little brother it's just not in the cards, I don't know what happened to him but reading is out of the question and the ssame for writing. I used to read to him and maybe I should start again in hope that those passage ways would open up but doctors say that he is just the way he is and nothing could change it, I guess they go by science and not the higher power. When I started long ago it was one step at a time and then most things came together after words' like putting together a puzzle so you could see the whole picture that he wanted you to see. The first time I saw somewhat of a miracle was when a young man was reading from the bible, he had let the lord into his life and the lord changed him. It could happen with Randy but he can't seam to take that first step yet! It's like he is afraid of something maybe getting to know others for all I know, but I never give up hope that one day he may learn.

We all learn in differen't ways and I trust God to guide him where ever he is taking him, last night he spilled his water while in bed and soaked his smokes. So now he has none, but I gave him some of mine. Why' because it says to share what you have with others and I try to do things for him, it's not something that happens all the time thank God' but we have to make it until the bar opens to get more. Since he came to live with me we have gotten along strange in a way because we didn't get to know each other until late in life, the triles we faced didn't let us be together as he had his life and I had mine but in his marriage he was brain washed. Not by the wife like you would think but by the step mother as she filled his head with all kinds of crap, saying he was wothless and without her he would have nothing, when you get married at 16 years of age you don't get to grow in the right way and with her adding her two cents it didn't help matters any well needless to say their marriage didn't last after she had two kids but by then he was already brain washed. I don't know how someone could do that to a person but they do it every day learning their weak points and then playing on them. Although us kids were all alcoholics she played on that also with us both as we were married to her two daughters, and in a way she still does the same thing as her kids still live with her my X wife included. I don't know how others live in the big city but I think it has to have something to do with the way we are wired if your not an out going person then this kind of life is for you, it's a place where you can figure out things on your own. And if you're high strung then you would probable want that kind of life with everything moving fast, especially a person that has missed so much in life you have to try and catch up with things. But the alcohol has made things slow when you become one at a young age my land' I had to of been about 8 years of age when it started so that's almost a life time being in the dark and then one day you are resqued and given a second chance more then one time, but at the time you cant see it blinded by the dark forces that want to end your life. One day you awaken and the world is moving to fast for you but you try and adjust and in time you do, then the one above brings you to where you need to be so you can grow and make friends. Almost gone from this world at one point you know He gave you a message and it's in the mind somewhere. Now all you have to do is figure it out so you learn from the people you meet' no one sees you the way you see you're self and this is a proven fact, the lake in the back yard has caused a sink hole and I hope it doesn't get any bigger, the mosquitoes are also out because of the water I was suprised when they said we got 4 inches of rain but that's about what it takes to fill my yard even the pear tree was under water and I have never seen that before. As I watched out my kitchen window you could see that the ditch was full to over flowing and had even brought twigs and other thing into the street so funny but the insects are not, their lives will be short lived once the water dries up but we did see some frogs hoping around and they are good for eating the bugs with those long tungs.

As I looked out the back door a dove was sleeping, and it's sibling was sitting on the power line maybe watching over it so nothing could get to it. They both seamed very young just old enough to fly for the first time and I'm sure mother was around somewhere, these are the things that other people in the city miss as they are not close to nature like we are here in the country. We see so many things here from the birth of a dove to a baby rabbit that takes off on it's own for the first time,and the squirrels they have their day also. Chasing each other across the yard to climb the trees and then jumping from limb to limb, no this isn't all we see but it's the births that I find exciting. As the birds live right out side my window and you can watch them bomb the bugs and eat them, wasps; are their most liked I guess as they have more meat to them. When I mow again in about two days I will have to watch for the limbs that have fallen out of the dead tree in the back yard they can be hard on a mower, as far as I'm concerned the rain can stop because my yard is green enough to last the rest of the year until the snow falls. I'm amazed at how the water is still standing in my yard like the lake that God showed me so long ago, does He show us signs to answer our questions when we have doubt about something? I believe He does. But it's up to us to put them together like the pieces to the puzzle of life, when in doubt ask, knock and the door will be opened, seek and you will find. All these things are in the good book and He tells us many things even though some don't listen.

They say out path is set before our birth. He has something He wants us to do and it will be done no matter how many wrong turns we take in life or how long it takes to get back on that right path, that He set before us well it's getting late so later. Saturday and things have been going fine we haven't had any more problems with the leak and it rained much more in the last coule of days then in the prior days when the leak started. so maybe it fixed it's self who can really say, but I haven't seen any of the Lenox people around so Monday I will tell then there is no need for their services. Unless they already fixed it I find it strange that it would start leaking but as I said with age comes brittle things especially shingles, going from the hot days of summer to the cold of winter. I was told that thr roof has a thirty year guarentee on the shingles but we all know how that goes nothing seams to last their expected length of time, so it wouldn't be a supprise if I might have to have it done. Would insurance cover it a good question that I should ask in the near future as I don't know much about those things, if it's anything like the car only if someone hit me or if they are uninsured then I'm in the dog house to get a replacement but we will see what it all covers by asking a good roof can save a life and so can a filled in sink hold. As I look at the hole I think there used to be a cellor there, and it's caving in. But why now instead of when I first moved in the change in weather I guess I don't recall having this much rain at this time of year before, my land' it was out of the usual norm for the end of summer or close to it. In September the kids go back to school, so the parents should be glad. It will give them a break from them being home every day so if you look at it the school is like a baby sitter in a way but they are learning at the same time. In our town many of the kids walk to school but also they have buses to get the ones that live out in the country I don't know the numbers but there are many that have their parents drive them. I see many of them bringing their kids to school each morning, the first step of the day as they wake up, I wish I could of grown up in Courtland I think it would have been great. The small country town it would have been hard to get used to but with everything time makes things all right, I recall when we first came here I was so scared not knowing anyone I felt alone even with pops by my side but we stuck it through and here I am today but pop's has been replaced with my little brother and the circle goes on. As more years pass we will grow stronger and do more things but I wish little brother would get out more he seams to think that he has to go somewhere out of town before he will go out side except for when we go to the bank of course. I can't see him even trying to go to church at this time but you never know what God might put into his head, I planted the seed long ago but still it hast taken root for some reason and he sees the things that take place in my life nothing short of a miracle is what it is. Even getting him out of that hell hole was God's doing but as of yet he doesn't see it or he does and feels pressured, lord knows I have felt that feeling before when scripture talks to me but that's what it's supposed to do and then you work through what it's speaking about. It was funny about one that she did about the pit it spoke to me and I responded by doing the call to worship little things like that bring more meaning then a person talking or yelling at me I don't know why but they do, just the words on a piece of paper speak louder then any person and maybe it's because it speaks to the soul and spirit.

In the coming months I will read more especially during winter when we are locked in the house for those three months or so with nothing else to do, mighty boreing during that time but we talk and keep each other company Sunday and yesterday was fine at work Beverly told me about her husband a little and how sick he was at the end my land' it was horrible how he suffered. With some people certain things hit them in their old age and the things I have never heard of before, such a tragedy when illness hits them before death many things go around in this world that they know little about and they have no cure for, Sunday my favorite time of the week when Church is going but we have to walk across a board to get to church being the sidewalk is under construction and the gutter of course making it so we have better run off when the rains hit. Still don't know if it will interfear with the highway 36 garage sale that's coming on September 21st through the 23rd, but I hope things go fine during that time. So the town can make some money it would be a good thing if we all made money to help out through the winter into the spring, money seams to make things easier as we go through life, it gives us what we need to help others and it helps us also in a way to bring a little joy to those who don't have as much as we have or some have shareing is a great thing when you have the means to do it and it brings joy to the spirit that dwells inside of us. If we see tragedy coming should we try to avoid it or let it happen this question I don't have the answer to but common since tells me that we should step a side and let it pass to where ever it's going.

As each morning when I pray the prayers are for others and seldom my self but at times I need the prayers just as bad as the others and they are given by the father, they come in the little things instead of the bigger ones and we have to figure them out if they are read right. I sent the first draft of my book to Mark at the Kearney hub, and asked him to give it a read so I will wait for a time before expecting an answer he is one busy man this I know. My story goes on as my life is still unfolding and it wont stop util I cant write anymore. I don't know what gives me the drive but it's there waiting to come out each morning something forgotten brought back to life maybe by a dream or something else, such a great life we have here as people help in any way they can. I thought I heard thunder just a little bit ago I'm hoping that we don't get any more rain as the day unfolds my hole in the back yard is too big as it is but we cant stop mother nature from doing her things I just hope it doesn't get out of control and take more buckets to fill it as for the sand it should of helped when I put it in there but a few shovels full doesn't amount to much and boy is that stuff heavy more heavier then dirt, but I have faith that it will be filled by Norman one of these days when it's dry out his tractor can hold quite a bit of dirt in the bucket. Well it's about time to watch the news. Monday andI have a few things to do today like stock some eggs down at hords the church alsohas to be cleaned after communion you wouldn't think but crums have to be vacuumed and the ehole church every Monday which takes all but an hour not much time is spent in the day to prepair for the days a head. To some it's no big deal that maybe a payment is late but to this guy it's a big deal, it's my responsibility to make sure that things are on course. O I have heard about people missing their mortgage payments for up to a year but that's something I never want to happen to me, but hard times fall on many of us in this life and it makes you feel trapt like you will never get out of it. many times mom couldn't pay the rent because of things that were out of her control but then later she would make them up by doing something for the land lord but I never knew what it was that she did , maybe do some painting for them on other houses or decorate like she did in the apartments when I was very young. There always seamed to be something that could be done to keep a house over our head. She always looked after her kids in that way as I believe all mothers do when the man is away but boy it makes it hard on a single mother. I can remember her crying many times as she didn't know what to do, if you haave enough to get by then you should be happy but then there is the next month and you can never know if security is going to be there. Back in those days rent was only a hundred and some dollars but when you didn't have a job it could feel like a million. Most people run through their money like water and don't worry about where it will come from as for me maybe that's something I have never been able to do, but at times it happens when the money is gone and you wonder where it all went not being able to afford even the slightest things you need one day I will make it to the top if God is willing to show me the way I have to trust that it's in my faith and my hope that one day it will all come together for the best. They say faith can move mountains but I just need it to help me in this endever and give me the strength I need to survive and climb one more mountain. It seams I have been climbing them for quite some time when do I get to level ground? So things can be on a level keel. My land' waking up took some time this morning but I made it, aand now the day starts.

When I moved in here the house seamed like a palace being much bigger then anything I had lived in before and now it seams so small with just five rooms including the kitchen and a bath, but it's mine and that's what matters later we can always build on to it if we want. It keeps us warm in the winter, and cool in the summer, and we don't have to starve because of a lack of food that's a good thing. A community pulls together to help those living amoung them so they can go on with life and make things better for them as for communitys in the big cities I don't have aa clue, I don't know why He put's us in certain places but he does to maybe grow in a certain way and be at home feeling that way adjusting to new things we have never experienced before, sometimes I can remember mom making bread and at times I can smell it out of no where in my home and this lets me know she is still around watching over me , also certain things pop used to do comes to mind that makes me laugh letting me know he is here also. The plant I planter for him blooms even when you would think it wouldn't because of the drought, these little things no matter how slight tells me that things will be ok' and that I shouldn't worry so much.. The morninng came early today as I couldn't sleep but it's also a reminder that I'm still here trying to make it the best I can no matter what. I havent heard from Margret lately since the night she called high or drunk but to me that's a good thing because people say things they don't really mean when they are that way and it shortly leaves their mind when they sober up. Such a delima when people are that way. I got the stickers for my product and now I can use them for that purpose should the lady lett me bring them doen to the store but I wont hold my breath just yet.

In the mornings Harley can be a pain as he always wants to go out side even before I'm awake so he has to wait until I have my coffee and then he is out the door, but he does more smelling around then any thing and then he is happy that no other dogs have taken his spots where he marked his territory, usually we have toast in the mornings when we are not out but today is grocery shopping day so we will stock up on what we need to get through thee month and that's almost everything. A friend went to germeny and he said he had fun but the check points were bad except for when he got to Kansas city but all the other placed were like on high elert, that in it's self would bother me being checked so many times. On another note the morning is fine but so humid do to the rain that we had. When I mowed the lawn yesterday I hit twigs that washed in the yard from the over flow of the drainage ditches, it seams when we get at least 4 inches of rain they over flow leaving a mess for me to clean up but hey! It doesn't hurt anything after the water receaded the mosquitoes left for a new place because I didn't get bit by one of them and to me that's always a good things. Even though we are out in the elements living in the country our homes protect us from the not so nice things, as for animals they are all around us but they much stay to then selve away from the human element knowing we are different from them, but the squirrles are another story and so are the rabbits they come close to the house knowing we don't mean them any harm. Little brother has been doing fine as long as he has his meds to keep him on track, it's strange how so many pills keep him normal but if that's what it takes then be it. This month I have to get the car taged and my land that cost a lot for only one year but it's a part of life here in the country, no wheels you go no where and then life would really be boreing and I don't think I would be able to stand it. It would be like being stranded in the middle of no where and that wouldn't be good. You have to always have your freedom no matter what, I don't travel around here at night because of the deer' they seam to like that darkness and run into cars and trucks just destroying them and if you only have one vehical then your left a foot. As I search the web many people use it for games something I have never gotten into but I know with some of them they can crash your computer and that's something I don't need right now. This game playing lets people interact with each other and that I also don't care for because you don't know where they are kind of like hide and seek in a way with phony names. My land it's only goinng on 2:45 in the morninng and I know I will probably be tired by the time I take the trash out at 6:00 but hey you can sleep when your dead right. If I remember right Hi 5 is a bar like game that I joined years ago I guess they never get rid of anything, we all change in time and those days disapear but on the computer they seam to last for ever. I started to take pictures of the town and the people I love and I wonder where it will end up in the end I find that I love doing this and I can give copys to my friends as gifts Norm already wantsa copy and later many more might want some. It will allow me to hone my hobby and see where it goes. Many others have made a living at this but I don't know if it will lead to that we will see what happened, other then that the day has been a great one with no calls from Margret to bother me.

We never know how or what God has instore for us so we try different things to see if we are good at it that's just the way life is here in a small town, and who knows what will happen in the near future maybe I can take pictures of some marriages that are preformed at the church. Well dinner was good as we had ribs in shake and bake' my first time doing that and we will do it again, just a great way to try something different in this world of change. It's now the next day and I'm going to try and get one of my films developed once we go to Concordia at WalMart it will be intresting to see if any of the pics came out and then I can go from there, Courtland should be seen in it's original state with all the shope that was once there and what has become since they closed many years ago. I have been told that once long ago it was a boom town not as in gold but in stroes almost two of everything including two grocery stores that have since closed way before I got here, many of the little towns have lost in size since back in the thirtys but who really knows what made them close? Competition with each other maybe or the cost of having things brought in on trucks. You would think that aplace lie the dollar store would be intrested in putting in a store here being there are so many small towns around us, and I have to believe that the town doesn't want to die at this stage of it. My Church has been here for 145 years since the day it was built or founded and it's a great place to raise kids because you don't have all the drugs that fill so many places today like the bigger cities and I'm not talking about the places like New York' because I have never been there but like in Ugean Oregon where you have to pick up needles in the parks that are left there by the drug useres.

Courtland is a place where family values still exist the core of the final frontier where people are friendly like back in the old days. Thursday August 8th yesterday I talked with one of the ladies I work with and I'm in hope that her husband might get rid of an old truck he has had sitting around for quite some time so Randy can have a project to get him self back on track to what he used to do before he lost it all the restoring of old vehicles, we have seen a few but they want too much money for them plus the selling of a four door car is much harder then a truck I believe, so we will see what happens down the road. The thing I started didn't last as long as I wished it would have but that's business it was like a phaze and now it's run it's course so I will try something new down here. I should talk to Dave Brown about the business he was going to start and see where he is on that it would be something new from the old bump and grind. Through life we try many things to find our nitch and I think I could sell things which is very unusual for me but hey we only go around once right? It's a quiet morning and I can't hear a thing except for the coffee pot which makes a noise once in a while, that and of course Randy snoring which doesn't bother me much anymore. The things we can get used to is a sign that maturity has taken place, we don't yell any longer about foolish things like before. The mornings are very still when harley isn't up trying to get me to take him out side so early little brother is coffing and it's from the smoking but there is nothing I can do about that maybe one day we both will stop only He knows for sure if he wants to keep breathing it's strange how we know things are bad for us but we keep doing it like smoking but we have always had one bad habbit in our lives and this one is the less of three evils, Valerie must still be in Jail for her pot smoking as she hasn't text me lately I hope it teaches her a lesson but you never know! She could get back out and do it again that's the problem with addiction to drugs the body craves them and has to have them sort of like food but you need that to live the withdraws are very real and it's not a nice thing to go through. It's very real the longing to have them again once you are free from the justest system, it's like that itch you can't scratch and it keeps coming back even if you have someone else scratch it. As for the smoking thing I have only been without it for a short time like when I was 16 years old, but still then I found a way to aquire it by going off the hill as I call it back in the 70's to visit mom for the weekend. And then it was back to the hill for another week if we could of only learned the value of things back then maybe life would be much better, but we are a product of our generation and smoking was very popular. As was drinking, I remember the country stars that visited my parents when they would have a party on Friday nights and they would sing all kinds of songs with the neighbors wanting to come over but many of them weren't allowed because the drunks would start fight and dad would have to throw them out. Even back then some men would beat their wifes even when they were showing that they were having a baby, I totally recall one man hitting his wife and dad had to stop it and the guy told dad that he was a golden glove boxer and that he was going to beat the hell out of him well that didn't happen as the guy flew over the fence.

Herb was like I am in a way quiet until riled, the guy left and I never heard or saw him again. If that was a sign of love then I didn't want anything to do with it. There was a lot to my parents marriage but with much of it us kids didn't see what was behind closed doors, we always thought it was a good marriage and that's what they wanted us to see a phony persona or a front' showing something that wasn't there by this time the love had gone out of the marriage and they wondered their separate ways mom would go out with her girl friend Owna Clifton and hook up, and dad well I never saw him with another women he was too much in love still with mom. They were married out of high school and dad loved her with all his heart! His love never died but hers did so that fence couldn't be mended. I recall dad following her around where ever she moved or went he just couldn't stand to be away from her but she found a new love and it lasted long after dad's death. Mom was very devoted to the person she choose it was nothing like the way things are today her love lasted a life time the second time around, I guess when you don't get it right the first time you get that second chance and that's all it took for her. I just wish my father could have been her second chance then I could of gotten to know him. But I can't cry over spilt milk my life goes on today and I'm still here. It's true what they say what doesn't kill you makes you stronger well it's the end of the day so I'm going to call it a night. It's Friday and another weekend is upon us yesterday was nice as the coolness was a very welcome but the news weather complained about that also it not beig hot enough, on one hand it's good but on the other it's not it seams they are never satisfied why is that? I know thy always have to have something to report about weather is bad or good.

Yesterday we went to the Antique mall in Scandia but never found anything we wanted so we came back home and did some things around here it's like treshure hunting when you go to places like that looking at the old stuff they have and picturing your self back in those days back in the 1800 when things were made strong and pretty. I really liked the red glass Nick knacks, they were made for people of statcher the people who used to own the big houses in the town. I have seen one of the houses and it looked grand with it's pillers standing strong on the porch you can tell it was made by someone who was well off when the town was young but now it sits all alone on a block that is surrounded by houses not made as well. There are many historical sights around here and they are not just in these two towns but in others like Jewell which isn't too far from here, the size of that town has even shrunk in the last 30 or so years but the old folks still make it their home not wanting to live anywhere else and who can blame them. If I had a choice I still wouldn't move for anything in a way it's like I was meant to stay in this part of the country and here I will stay, my friends are here the only ones that matter to me anyway as for the rest well life will go on for them and only in the end will we see what has become of those I used to know. One day I may find that thing I'm looking for but until that time I will enjoy the little things in life talking to my friends and and writing about my adventure that have brought me here to my town of dreams. I went to pay on my bill and Norman said he would have to wait until the guys got back because they wont teach him how to run the computer too old they tell him but I know he isn't to old, I have fallen in love with the people here and Normen is one of the people. Also his wife when she was here before her passing, and I know he missess her. I hope he will stay because his love is shown by his words, it's the little things that make the person not the whole thing but the small little things like the kind words when a person is feeling down or the hi when your day is going good. For the last few weeks things have been changing and I cant put my finger on whats talking place but I know it's good, as things seam to work them selves out for the better. I'm going to go down to the Church and see what I can do to clean things up after their meeting yesterdauy don't quite know what was going on but they have many things happening at this time of year and I believe we have chicken and biskets somewhere down the road. The change took a long time for me to adjust to my new life but it's still in progress as each year passes the change is small in many ways. I wish I had the power to heal Maggie but that's something left up to the lord I know that people can over medicate those who are sick and that can hurt them with Walter there was a few times when I thought he was gone but it was the medication putting him in another world. And it frightened me not knowing if he was alive or dead, then he would wake up and the concern was not what I thought. When you care for someone it's hard to watch as they slip away and it leaves a big hole inside of you that you might spend the rest of your life trying to fill once more, I know with my parents it took many years of destruction before I found my way out of the feeling of loss. But then life went on and I grew stronger, still today I remember the police pulling me off my mom after her death I had lost so much already and her passing broke the camels back you might say and I had been where she was going so I wanted to go with her.

And leave this place which had caused me so much pain, I knew at least there wouldn't be any more pain or sorrow there and we would be together. But God had different plans I was to carry on where she had left off and I did with taaking care of Oliver, for some reason that connection we had let me know that he would soon be ill and he became that way shortly after her death . Like with many of the doctors they said he would die but God did His magic and arranged for him to get what he needed to live, although very weak afterwards I nursed him back to health and I watched over him for many years to come. He had always been kind of slow but he knew I would take care of him, and I did. Just like I promised mom before she passed, their love was strong and lasted many years even until death. I like to think that all three of them are getting along in heaven with their hurts and anger behind them, living that life which should bring them joy. With doing things right we are given a break sometimes and it can come in many forms from that increase in your credit card to a break on something else in your life giving you a little more breathing room so you can pay the things you need to pay. I have liked the responsibility of being the care giver it seams to be something that's born into me the one who takes care of others like some of the people in the bible, even Mary took care of Jesus but yes I know she was his mother I wonder what kind of a child he was? For surely he had the favor of God being a part of him. They had to have that supernatural connection that some feel although I had it with mom it wasn't until death was close by that it really started to show it's self, the finishing of words that were spoken and the connection without words. It's Saturday morning and I didn't sleep but afew hours getting up and down quite a few times but thhe coffee is on and I looking forward to the day, Randy got ill las night for some reason and I think it had something to do with the breakfast mic muffens he bought and ate. It's the only thing that we both didn't eat only him, I had never liked that kind of crap at all not even fresh from Mickey D's. there are many things I wont eat that he does and low and behold he gets sick except for the time we thought we would try some new taco like things that also made us sick.

The things we try sometimes are not any good and there is a reason why they sat for so long in the freezer at the store, after we stopped eating them we felt better and then we knew it was that. Which made us sick, many things that are frozen at the store have been thawed before and then refrozen which can always make you sick, I try to watch the things I eat and even sometimes I will eat just a little and then wait to see if there is a reaction to it. Like with meat' if it's not red then I wont buy it, even though they have the old stuff on sale sometimes. Price cut for quick sale, or should be frozen right away if not used, this is a sure sign that I don't want it and I don't buy it. Yesterday I was talking with Ben' and he was saying that he feels in the near future the only way you will be able to buy something is if you have avredit card , and this I believe as we the United States leans towards the plastic market to get our food and other things we need. He also believes that WalMart will own most of the gas stations before too long and this is something else I can vision sometime down the road. Change is coming and there is no getting around it, although I feel change sometimes and think it's in my life it could that kind of change which is coming. I had a dream the other night and for the life of me I cant recall all the aspects of the dream but it was different from the usual in this one I had somewhat control over things but then it went away like many visions before it, does dreams speak to us? Is it our other side of the brain trying to communicate with that part which is awake? They say at night the other side comes alive the side that sleeps during the day, and visa versa always learning new things and dealing with the old while the other side is resting. Many times you will hear the saying I will get plenty of rest when I die, this to me is people that push really hard to solve things like puzzles or the mysteries of life and problems but in the end they solve nothing, we as humans have to sleep but in the world today they have machines that don't need this human quality. They can go on for days on end and never need rest until they break down and need fixing so maybe that's their rest lol. Who can really say for sure? My reading on biblical things seam to help me sleep if I read a little before turning in could this plant a seed for some dreams? I suppose it could and then maybe that's why I don't recall the full dream, because I havent read the full thing.

Like the women said in the movie it's the search that keeps us going. Yes some people are searchers and others are on a mission that they can't figure out, I'm sure this keeps the mind active instead of letting it fall a sleep into that black space or is it black? It could be just as light there as it is here on earth, I glad it's Saturday because Rifle Man is on, and each weekend he traches his son about life back in the old days as I call the 1800's it's not just a show or movie but a learning experience for Mark his son. All the right and wrongs of life back in those day's my land' I have so much to do today and it seams like I always do just a little and then fall away from it and I don't know why this happens. Sunday and yesterday went fine as I worked with the librarian at the thrift store. It's always fun to talk with her we talk about many things including the kids and how they learn she is a teacher of sort, reading to the children and watching their faces as they get what's being said in the stories manythings she wants to do like getting movies that they can check out and take home to watch it's only a matter of time before it becomes reality and I see her getting the grant, Sunday Mornings are my best time of the week, when I spend time with the people of the church and we have coffee and such afterwards I like to talk with John and Judy and the others to see who things have been going in their lives. So I can write about the adventures some of them take Maggie has not been doing too well and I'm going to tell Mark if there is anyway I can do to help to let me know, the story of my my life has been something I have held on to and I'm being moved to finely show it to Mark so he may understand that I have been where Maggie is today walking the roap of life and death.

I found that it's God that helps us in our darkest hour and death has nothing when it comes to Jesus as he defeated it and rose from the dead to be with his father and with us, he is the one who brings our messages to God so he can grant them. And we all have to go though Jesus christ to be heard, lord grant me the power to help Maggie as I did the others like mom and Oliver and now her if you will allow it to happen let people see the miracles that you can bring today as they did in Jesus time so more people will come to you. Give me the power to heal lord now is the time for that to happen if you so choose to bring it, so I can do my job when I told the librarian that I had been in a wheel chair for 10 years she didn't relly know what to say but I knew she could understand the magnatude of loosing the ability to walk and then getting it back that in it's self is a miracle. It's been a long road but I made it back from that place , I havent seen Maggie yet but I would like to so I can see if the signs are there the signs of fighting for her life if she still cant walk then she has a long road to go down. Not saying her condition is the same but she might have to scoot before she can stand to build her upper strength and then go from there, I was like a limp rag before I started. No control of anything but through time things started to become stronger and it kept building from there, many people don't know how to deal with such things but to me it's just something some of us go through and other may never know what to say when you tell them about the story yesterday she was at a loss of words and maybe it was because that kind of thing had never come up before. Only when a person has walked in your shoes can they begin to understand the life you have lead, the life of going from the weakest point ever to once again being strong or even stronger then you once was. Monday and I know why I don't want to tell everyone about my life it's because most people will put a lable on you once the story is out and I think it could do more damage then leaving things the way they are, but you never know what might happen in the future maybe when I'm old it wont really matter. There is one good thing and that I have the writings to back it up which it always a good thing the news paper did a story on me many years ago and it reached many that would of other wise not of started to take their lives back, and It set me on a new course to try and bring more people to trying it. Trying to take that long journey which would eventuly free them from the curse that had a hold on them, in this world you have to make your own way and if you don't do it then your stuck on a place where you don't really want to be. My journey thus far has brought me many things and in the future many more things will come my way but I have yet to see those things and who knows maybe one day my good fortune will change things for others letting them know that there is a way out from the darkness. Many years ago I was frightened to do many thing s but today I take those chances in hope that I will have back up in the word of Christ. It's like something is being set free that was once locked up and it lets me explore new avenues like getting this van that I hope to make a little money on , when you put work into something usually you don't get all your money back out of it but I'm hoping that my luck will change that for me.

    Flipping cars or vehicals can bring you extra money if it's done right so I will try my hand at that for a while I hope to bring something about. Investing is what I call it investing in something other then your self like this van we can do many things with it, use it for camping or to go fishing on the cool days, bringing about a change that can in rich our lives and going and doing things can do that. Back in the old days having a van let you explore new and intresting things but you have to always have to have a plan in case things fall apart, my life has been one of caution and now I'm going to stepout of my comfort zone and see what takes place as my jourey continues, many people go all out to try and find their nitch but mine might be right here with the fixing of this van he priced it so someone would be able to fix it and still have fun with it and this might let me do this. My car has to be registered this month so I will het that done and not have to worry about it for another year, the rain is coming down this morning so our little world will get a little greener here in Courtland I always love the rain but with my heater leaking I don't want much of it to fall right now until it's fixed it's been almost a week since they ordered the part and they still havent fixed it but I realize that it takes time for such things too take place. The gift of something can sometimes bring you to a new level and bring back abilitys that you have forgotten like machanics it's been a long time but still the ability is still there because you learned it long ago some things stay with you and they have to be brought back to life. I did what I was feeling yesterday and let Mark read the message that was written about me in 2007 it's been over 6 years since that front page article and I have kept it locked away all that time he is my friend and so is Maggie and I told hm if I could help in anyway to just let me know, something I don't do for just anyone.

It's Tuesday and it's trash day so later I will go and get it taken out slept in a little this morning but it felt good although I'm not awake as of yet, need more coffee to get there and it will happen in an hour or two the wakeing up part of life is very different from the old days back then you had no idea of what time of day you would get up and sometimes it wouldn't be until noon. Such a difference from those times in life when you were young to now when your middle aged. My triles have brought me far and landed me in my town of dreams, the night didn't bring any rain so my little bucket should bee almost empty except for what we got night before last, I wish they would seal that pipe and get those things taken care of but I will have to go down there once again to remind them that it has to be done or else I will have to do it my self and that might not be a good thing as unstedy as I am, but He seams to make a way for us even in the darkest moments. Mark has always been good to me and at times it does my heart good to share my story with someone, maybe it will give them a better understanding of me in many ways like the lady that was lost for words we had to hange the subject. Because she didn't know what to say, very common for me to see these things happenn in my life as many havent gone through what I have it's like I'm looking for an answer but no answer comes not even after this many years. Still separated by the thing that others don't go through I may have to just keep things to my self, and go on with life. Through the years of growing up you don't get the picture not the one your supposed to see as your life is blackened by not being in this world all the time the addiction had control through the younger years and nothing was clear until I destroyed the curse, for all I know the family could have been cursed back four generations but it says that we as people can destroy the curse with us. And not let it go on any longer but the stopping of it has been hard or it was back then and today I'm free from those binds, to wake up each morning and more or less have a normal life. Many parents think they didn't do a good job in raising their children but that doesn't really come into play as no matter how good you are, you cant stop the curse only the person can for which has it. In many familys only one or two might fall into the curse and it puzzles some folks because they didn't have a problem with it this is the curse skipping a generation. If back in the 1700's your family member was cursed and then nothing in the 1800's it's just skipping around and might not show it's self until the 1900's once it's been activated only you the person that gets it can stop it and we all have that power even if we don't think we do the grace of God makes us strong in a way that we can't fandom or understand because we believe we are not very strong. But in reality we are stronger then even we think.

Many people that don't believe in God think it's them that makes things happen and I believe they are wrong, it's only by His goodness that we move forward and accomplish the things we do. My self I couldn't picture a world without God in it, a place where no forgiveness is shown a place where you are condemned for the things that might have happened in your life that may have been wrong. With God all is forgiven if you ask and then you can go on with your day with out feeling bad or frightened about anything, when I enter the Church my spirit takes flight and does the things which may have not been possible any other place and it's because I feel His presents when I'm in the holy place yes it's a holy place to me where you can shut out the out side world and be alone with God. From what I have read in the history of God and Jesus we are the Church us the children of God and He holds us near to him, O we go through many things in life and make mistakes but in the end He gives us that chance to redeem our self of the wrong things we have done. Wednesday and I slept in again it started to rain yesterday but it didn't last that long thank God today I'm going to go down and get the part for my flue and I don't care how far I have to go to get it but you would think they would have it at one of the hardware stores so we will see after I check with the Taboos. I know the rain has to be doing some damage coming through like it does. Many things can go wrong if your not careful, Harley is dreaming this morning as I can hear his little noises he makes when he is in that place he is so funny. I sometimes wonder what he dreams about in his little world it seams all together different from him being awake it's sort of like a bird churp when he makes those noises. Yesterday morning I got out and mowed the lawn getting it ready for the next rain my lawn is important to me and I have to keep it trimed so things don't look like crap just they way I like to do things here in my town of dreams.

I can never know what the future might hold as he only gives me sight of cetain things and sometimes the way I look at things can be wrong, it just depends on the sight or vision I get it's the way things are in my world my new world the one that will last for ever more. When I get the van going I will talk to a friend about selling it down at his place but for now it will remain here until things are done with it, my land it's beautiful it just needs a little loving care that I can give it when the time is right Randy said it was a good buy but he knows little since things happened to him. It's like he forgot most of what he learned so long ago and I'm the same way, it's like the mind changes as you get older and your focus goes to different things bringing you to a new place in life as for little brother I don't know where his mind is at this time maybe stuck in those dreams he has almost every night or morning. My knifes got here but they weren't what I expected but stll have a little wiggle room to make a few bucks if things go right, it seams like life is about the mighty dollar and if you are broke then confusion sets In about things that can make life very trying I got what I needed toget for the van and I's on it's way not we have to hope their garentee holds out. Science has come a long ways so I'm not supprised that they created something to stop a leack without tearing things apart they say it will last the life of the thing you use it in meaning any motor if we were back in he 60's it wouldn't of been available but if it would have been then dad would have had less work to do on many of his motors. After wards I will take it for a drive and see how it acts it's supposed to do wonders and I hope it does Thursday and I got my credit card to help with bills it willl be something that I use sparingly to maybe pay off one of my others and have it for the things of importance, credit is the only way the world is going to work in the near future or sometime down the road. Half the month is gone and I already have the payment I need for next month just a great way to have things going for now anyway also I have to get some more things to pickle and that will keep going for now until when ever I deside to advance things. The market for things can very one week maybe it will be good and then the next it will slack off but so far I have made what I needed to get by in this life, I watched little house on the praiery last night and o how I love that movie. They worked hard back then and had a home to show for it and some ground sort of like I do today to survive in this world but also life was good for them as they had a family to help each other. In this day and age we do the best we can and hope for the best buying some things to sell to make ends meet I know that there are thinng I can do to balance things out to live the life I have come to be acustom to just breaking even will pass as the years go by and I become well known for my hard labor, it's all in the managing of things weather you will make a go of anything even this to me is new but I can see a rainbow down the road even if it's a ways down there. This morning I'm going down to the Church to make sure things are set for our service this Sunday so I will have some work cut out for me little brother has been dreaming lately more then usual and I told him that he might be experiencing the lord talking to him seeing he doesn't listen when he is awake and maybe he will except that in his mind when the dreams are good ones. I do know that He talks to us in many ways to maybe get something across so we can change our ways and come to be closer to him.

It's a great morning and they got my cap on my heater vent finely so no more rain should make it's way into the heater room. This will give me more peace not having to worry about such things, and I can put that at the back of my mind, worry seams to be something that has a hold on me sometimes but if I can stay a head of the game then things should work out fine. I bet everyone goes through this kind of thing, I'm not ready to be awak yet so I will go back to trying to wake up. At least it's Friday and the end of the week is here and my pipe got fixed so no more rain will come through now all I have too do is get the van sold to reecoupe my investment and a little more on tope of that like the car sales man do on a everyday bases it sould be a vehical that someone could live in if they were homeless and feel proud because it is very good looking and the motor is great with no misses, only 90.000 miles on it so it could have a long life a head of it, many people around here like to go fishing and it would be great for that or up by other lakes that are around the country. I know my parents would of gave their right arm to have one like this so we wouldn't of had to camp out side so much. In California it would go for thousands just because of the way it's made it's unique compaired to others that I have seen and that's what makes it worth money. Fixing one step at a time will be my goal and then we will see what goes on from there my little bus as we will call it if you really look at it this could be the first ride bus to the store for people who are shut ins but that's just a thought and it would get the people out that are never leaving their homes. I have made the first step in seeing if anything might materilize out of this so we will see what happens so many possibilitys in this world of ours to do good things.

Today I'm going to get the tags on my car and I hope things go all right that way I'm set for another year and there will be no worry there. We have many important things that we have to take care of just to survive in this world but we seam to get them done so life can go on my joyest days are when I get things done that need to be done and my down times are when things fall apart like in the movies with the raddle and roll of life. As I talked to Margret she was without a car so I take it that she lost her truck and her car such a bad break for her as she goes through more hard times but in time she should find her way, I could tell that she was searching for something many years ago but must not have found it but that's no reason to give up hope on anything try and keep trying so we can rise above what life throws at us it's never easy going from one life to another but when we make it that is a time for celebration even today I'm just learning about the computer age and believe me it isn't easy trying to get all those things into your mind is hard but I seam to be able to do it just a little at a time. Saturday and the startingonthe van has begun from whay I gathered a tune up was done last year so I moving beyond that point and studding on te the leack so that can be behind me this is going to be trial and error on my part dut I think I have the know who to get it done it's simple semantics, but you cant afford to have others do it because the cost would enormous. Not all I have to do is put in a thermastate to regulate the heat and get some oder eaters for the smell of of the carpet whick fabreeze should cover back in the old days the Mexicans would use such vehicals to transport familys over here to America but now days they are used for camping as they were meant to do in the beginning, my self I would like to keep it if the price of up keep wasn't very high and I could get the short fixed that's in it so many delimas to consider when you don't know enough about somethings but still we learn by what we do in this world and if we learn then that's ok' so many projects are going on at this time and I have to keep then going to learn more new things who knows what this might bring out of it, but I do know that it takes money to make money that's just the way the world is in this place at this time. If you cant sell something here ship it to another place and let them do what ever they want to do with it. My time has to be spent doing for the community and maybe a break every now and then will let me pittle with something like this who really knows? My land it's early and I'm not used to being up at this time but when your awaken then you have to follow what comes next no matter what it is maybe put on some eggs for next week so other can have some to take home with them after the garage sale and bake sale you can never tell whaat some want to eat. I only have two bolts to take off and then I can replace the part and see where it goes from there, by the looks of the stuff is shouldn't plug anything up so no worries there. My car had more build up in it this this van did and my car is 23 years newer amazing how that workd some times you think you can make something old new and many times it works just a few miles meant that things are in good shape.

This could be my new adventure and take my patients to a new level when I get it mastered in time, I can hear little brother getting up so it wont be long now he has his lights on and now he is up later I'm going to put on some something for greakfast and see how the day goes my nerves are calm today so maybe the eggs will peel better, I'm not like most people who get up early when I get up it's usually for the day unlett I get real tired and take a nap but everyone does that right? Everyone my age and older that is. Through the struggles of life we do what we can do to make things better for our selves and if we get pissed off about something it always passes as time goes by. don't even look at it like your beling punished but look at it like your learning something maybe new in a way Sunday disturbing news my nieces son dies and my son is going to treatment because he is about to loose it mentaly, tey are taking him to a good place called Richard youngs there in Kearney where he can get the help he needs for a while I know of this place very well as I have been there manyyyears ago and they do great work at detoxing people, although I thought the curse would end with me my child has the same curse and now it's time for him to break away from it. This curse will destroy any one in it's path like it trid to destroy me so many years ago, Leroy is like me in many ways timmid and afraid of life without being screwed up but maybe now that will change. He took his nefues death hard and it will stay with him for quite some time but it's now time for him to think of him self, I had taken him to places to get help before but he ended up going back home to the same old situationm.

It's hard when you try and everything fails but there is always a light at the end of the tunnel is you just look for it and God will give you a helping hand if you truly want it don't worry my son I willl be on my way next week, I have my doubts about teling Randy because he is timmid like me and he is not as strong as I am mentaly, so many in our family circle have dies in the last year and a half and they have all died in Kearney I wont let my son be the next one.maybe bring him home I really cant say at this point. We all go through loss in this world but it's a part of life and I know that God will comfort them while they go through this time. Tammy must really be hurting lousing two sons in such a short time and that's not counting their grandma and grandpa such a sad sight to see your grandbabys leave before you their loss effects everyone not only their familys but those connected with it. There is a kind of loss that takes a while to move passed Jerrod and her other son will always be in her heart and be missed. I don't really know how to act in these situations as I know death takes a long time to heal but loosing one so young will take ever longer we as parents are not supposed to out life our kids so I'm told, but it happens and then we carry the burdon of remembering the tragic way they went it could almost make a person want to hide from the world, why would God bring someone through such a thing like addiction and let their kid's pass away to me it doesn't make since. The rise of one to the fall of two sometimes it makes you question why' don't get me wrong it doesn't change my faith but it makes me ask questions. Monday morning' yesterday we got he van running right and boy it sounds good now all we have to do is change the screen in the transmission and put in new fluid. Years ago they used to do what I'm going to do to it and everything would work fine but now most places like to do it by machine which to me takes away from the fun of being a machanic. I didn't think I had it in me to go back to this kind of thing but I have to admit that it was fun in a way, fixing up things and hoping for the best result when your finished. My daughter really liked the van and she really liked the pictures I sent her, after this project we will try to start another but we will have to see how things go it was like dad was with us in doing this telling up what to do and we came through with flying colors it's like the bible says you never know how things are going to turn out until the product is finished I have to do some work at the church this morning but then it's off to Concorida to see Randys parole officer and then to WalMart to get a few things to finish the project. It's always good to take your time in doing things so nothing gets messed up and hen your set. It's early this morning and usualy I'm a sleep but something nside work me up maybe bordom or just the excitement of finely being on my way to learning all over again what it takes to try something new again not new to the mind but to the hands my temper was short when I started this journey but now it's calmed down since I see progress.

Dad used to say to walk away when things got to tuff and that's what I did when I got angry just cool off is what he used to tell me and it will all make since when you come back to it good advice but still it puts me out of my comfort zone. It's a far cry from writing and doing that kind of work, but who knows maybe in time I can do both and later that could lead to another job somewhere down the line. The miracles of the mind it doesn't let you forget what you learned for the good even in that dark place we once lived, as for angels I do believe they do exist and I see dad as he guides me through certain things telling me to step back and take another look, if things go right then we should be finished with the van today if we can get a jack from my friends at Hoard oil a loner you might say to replace a few parts so it's road ready. Driving it with the way the transmission is would only destroy it further but I believe it could be a quick fix. For the last few years I have barly scraped by but I did survive and now I wasn't to move up to something more another hobby to bring in some money, the vehical has to be safe an that's all that matters please lord stand by me and help me through this undertaking make everything solid Amen. I know if I slept more I wouldn't get so up tight about things but a lepard cant change it's spots at this time maybe later my routeen will change but for now things will go the way they are I as shocked when got done with the van yesterday and the feeling was great now all I have to do is sell it and recoupe my investment so I can go on to other things. The one guy might even buy it him self if I can talk good enough as for the way it drives it's great and there is nothing wrong with the trans.

It was so clean that you could eat off the inside of it and the motor runs like a top now all I have to do it clean it up a little before taking it down there.. It would be great for the average ccamper that like too go fishing and needs a place to sleep when they get tired like I do sometimes. As for the air it is supposed to work but I have never tried it, while under it I saw wraped pipes that went to the back blower that cools the back side of the van so I know everything is there, as for the little things they have to be done by the person that buys it you know to make it their own but the beauty of the thing is the best not a scratch on It that I can tell and the under carage is very cllean with no rust from winters past, my self I would love to keep it but I don't have the means to registe two vehicals and I have other adventures in mind to bring about other things to do. This has been an experience doing thee work on this but it will be a while before I do it again to much of a change for this middle aged man, it's like God had rewired me fo something differen and yet I'm not sure what it is yet. Does he have a way of doing that for some people yes! For this I know for sure the knowledge is still there but the will is hard to find to travel back to that place you wanted to leave behind although I had good times working on machanics there were memories that I would rather forget plus being in tight corners make me feel uncomfortable especially when it can fall on you that would be a lot of weight on this old body. It's Tuesday and it's trash day Randy already got ours out but now I have to take it out for the church and then I'm done for another week or until bible school starts again the little tikes do a lot of activities that make a mess but no worry Mr. Roger is there to clean it all up so things are kept just right. My love for this town has grown beyond my belief and the things I do really do make a difference or at least that's what I'm told, it's a delight to be who I am today even if I'm still alone for the time being but it's by choice and not andthing else. I could of went back to Margret but I have a thing I live by and that's to never go back wards in time for anyone not even sex or a relationship why are some of us that way? God only knows. It's like I'm an explorer always chacking into new things like hobbies, as for little brother he cant do anything any more being so big he cant even fit under a van his talent he once had is gone but his companion ship is very vital even if I yell at him sometimes. The van has cruse control and tilt steering so anyone could drive it, even a kid but that's not advised. Through the years I have always wanted something like this but I cant afford to keep it. My job iis to find them and fix them up if I get this sold it should rebuild my credit cards back to their glory and keep me in good standings with the bank so everything goes fine. My payment for next month is sitting in a box ready for the bank. This lets me put it there and forget about it so it's not gotten into , I find that the security of your home is the best place as long as you don't let in thiefs. I have trusted before to only get ripped off by the ones I didn't really know and boy that can put you back a long ways especially if your trying to pay bills, with little brother I didn't know what to expect because he had taken from others in his past life but he supprised me and has taken nothing when it comes to my personal things. If he needs something then he will tell me and I try to work out a way to help him if I can, as for needing something he doesn't want for anything and I maake sure of that he is my blood and my brother as for him still being lost he is in a way but I know that one day God will open his eyes and let hm see the wonders that he has in store for him.

The things I learn about God I learn on my own and by the church and their gracious ways always there to help when they can in times of trouble. I had a good day taking the van for a ride and finding out that I didn't get the bottom radiator hose on tight, but got it fixed now and things are going fine. You sure can tell the difference between driving a van then a car so much different, next thing I have to do is sell it to recoupe my investment and pay some bills again.

Wednesday morning and I sent some picyures to Tonya so she can puyt them on face book for me thank God for family I know she will get the job done. It was a restless night but finely I got back to sleep, Randy beat me up his morning and is doing laundry he also couldn't sleep, now I play the waiting game with the van to see how many bites I get on it . The train is running through this morning and I just love the sound of the engines as they pass through our fair little town. Today is the twins funeral and we couldn't go it was really hard on Randy and he called Cinda to tell her how sorry he was about the death of the child, through the years my Church family has stood by me in every way not denying anything I would need even sending me on vacation when I couldn't afford to go and see my children. I pray that th lord looks after and keeps them safe all through their lives so nothing bad ever happens I know my heart would break if anything happened to any of them, God has always stood by me even through the toughest times. It's another beautiful morning in the heartland as I wake up to feeling great, little brother said someone stopped to look at the Van yesterday and took down the number so I expect they will call if they are interested. Many of my friends from other States have commented on the van saying it's worth more then I'm asking so my price should be met one of these days I have had it up only one day and the comments are very good.

I know many will try and jew me down but I feel I should stick to my price as it's well worth it, the van hasn't even been somked in like most vehicals these days. God is smiling on me and I pray that it continues through my time, you just don't see vans like that any more especially with the upper windows making it stand out like it does my friend Charles said it's worth 6 or 8 thousand but I have set my price and it will stay there for now anyway. To me this is a once in a life time opportunity to run across something this rare my self I have never seen a van like it and you can even play cards in it when the table is put in it's being seen across face book, where ever it reaches. And I know it's across the whole United States and maybe even the U.K. today I'm going to clean it and get the mustiness out of it from sitting so long it's a survivor classic that can live on for a long time. Thank you father for showing me that some hard work will pay off if you put your heart and soul in it, this is something I would like to continue to do for years to come besides my other projects. I'm now out of eggs so I'm making some more and in time I'm going to need to get some sausage so my stock is back up to where it needs to be. My spirit runs high on this day and I'm hoping things turn out really great even with my side line. Sometimes I get over excited but then after a while things go back to normal it's just the beast of my nature, some do things that are bad but with me it's just the opposite I do good things and sometimes it's like getting something new for the first time. You know? The feeling you got when your parents bought you a used bike. It might have been old to who ever owned it before but to you it was like Christmas' all through life everything was second hand but to us it was like new and we took good care of it like my first car I wish I still had it my land it would be worth a mint in the world today, a low rider Thunderbird made when they really made cars out of steel and not plastic. This morning I'm going to go down to the Church and check on things to make sure all is ready for this Sunday our day to be together as brothers and sisters. We are very close my Christen family more close then my real family, and it's because we all live here and are not separated by miles that make us loose touch with each other. It's TGIF as some say the end of the working week and the beginning of the weekend, next month the highway 36 garage sale begins and thousands of people will travel to it and I think that's when I will have good odds on selling the van if not before, they have an stabilizer you can buy for when you change the oil In a vehicle and I'm going to get some for it. As I have no idea of when it was changed last I want it to be ready for someone to just drive off with it once it's bought. I have always been a stickler for doing things right and this is no exception with this vehicle so a trip to town will be needed this morning and I will get what I need, I notice that I'm not the only one who talks to God about different things like problems that I see in the world and here at home. Craig's wife does the same thing and the lord answer's her when she has her conversations with Him.

As we talk when we work together it's nice that we can communicate with each other sometimes laughing and just having a good ole time, as I went to the bank yesterday I saw Mark and he asked if I was starting a car lot and I told him yes. We talked and he asked about the van so told him about it the things we used to do that were legal back in the day have come around and now I would like to get into selling once again you can make some money and hopefully have a less stressful life while doing it. Although I'm not fully into the working on them again I believe in time that things will change like with changing the oil and working on the engines once more, it was a gift back then and since It was a gift it can be given back or ignited to bring favor to me. Randy really used to do it but with his weight and health he cant do much except to be here for support and give me some pointers on some things. I wrote a letter to Nebraska so he could get his good time back and I will send it off this morning hoping for a reply by next week, if he gets it back then they should let him off parole and we wont have to make those trips down there to Concordia unless we just drive down for something like car parts or groceries. You know the usual, this month we both have a doctors appointment on the 29th and I like it when we get in at the same time it saves on Gas going back and forth, he is sleeping right now and I hope he stays a sleep for a few hours yet that way I can get my alone time that I haven't had in quite a while.

Our love for each other has grown in the last two years and it's beginning to feel like we were never apart. Like the years had never separated us, it's funny how he has grown on me but I believe that was God's purpose for bringing him back into my life, He knew we both needed someone besides the others that are now in our live and we needed to build that brethrens feelings back into our lives. I know as well as I'm sitting here that brothers are supposed to be close, you hear of Cane and Able but our friendship is nothing like theirs ours is made out of love and it draws us closer to each other. We help each other when we can and really I don't see it as a burden when he needs something, although the well has to be filled back up when it runs low talking about financial things. Although I have taken on something new to do part time my values are still in place the helping and giving of my time to help others. It's just the right thing to do in this world of ours and it brings people closer so they can get to know each other, as time passes I feel closer to Jesus then ever before and I believe that's the way it's supposed to be. It said somewhere that He isn't interested in our past just our future and that brings me comfort to know that He loves us that much, my faith is built on what he has done in my life because I can't explain it away like the non believers can and do. Saturday' yesterday I got two of the rims painted on the van and boy it looks good now all I have to do is the other side and I'm done with the wheels, it's strange really hat the ambition has returned even after all these years next Friday we have a doctors appointment and then we are set or a few more months or until spring. My mind thought this was September so I had to get it straightened out funny how that happens sometimes when the body has been busy, but still the things that I do take more time then they used to the movement of this frame needs a little lube job so it can move more easily and I get my ambition from the lord. All I do is with his help for He is my rock and my salvation in this place I call home, this morning I have to work at the Church and then down to the thrift store for a couple of hours but after that I have the day to finish the job I started. I was very surprised when the mayor drove by and said what a nice job I was doing on the van wheels, it's little thing like this that make me want to do a great job just the kind words of a friend can empower you beyond belief and give you that drive you need to make something look great. On the other hand it's about that time to wash it but that will come when the work is done and the thing looks beautiful all things in good time as we say here in my town of dreams. I have always wanted to do something like this and now it's also coming to pass we will see what takes place before winter hits, sale or no sale either way I have a great vehicle one that will get pretty good gas mileage. Through time many things come our way and we are allowed to test our abilities once again, I thought doing mechanics had left my blood but it seams to still remain. And the old feelings I used to get with my father come back the excitement of turning a wrench and seeing the end results something good coming out of something broken. Like with my life so long ago, it was broken and now it has been fixed by the father in heaven when your car or truck is broke you g to a mechanic. And when your life is broken, you go to and ask God for help to fix it. My self I want to see some very good things happen and if it's fixing broken things then that's what it will be.

I also got a vacuum from the thrift store in Belleville that is great for the van, it's small with a beater bar and does a great job. I can also use it in my car as well a lot better then the old thing I used to use that could hardly pick up anything, it's like a blast from the past working on things and in time I will get used to it. My Ranchero was the love of my life when it came to driving a fast car but also there was others that were beautiful like my GTO I had when I was a kid all the bells and whistles you would want in a car but then boredom came into the picture and I sold it. If we could of seen what we see today we would of kept the old cars as to days cars are made out of plastic and Tin' nothing like before. I think I will drive the van on the concreat slab to finish my project less bugs there and the chiggers wont get you, my life has taken many different turns from being lost in this world to finding my way through the addictiions that once took my life. Who would of ever thought that He would rebuild me and leave some of the good things stll there? Like the ability to still work on car and the other things I do, my land' what a great God we have. Many years ago I was in sales but it wasn't the kind of sales you wold think, so I turned it around and Bam! I find that really I can sell anything once I put my mind to it. It's all in getting past the shyness or bashfullness or just getting to know people, to find out what makes them think the way they do. The Church has helped me a lot in that department moving past what held you back in your younger years, teaching you the things you didn't get to learn when you were a kid. Today I'm a brand new person because of the Church made new through the power pof God.

I will get some other cars down the road and fix them up to resell, those and other vehicels which willl be worth my while I love doing it and it will stay with me for a time anyway. Tomorrow is the 25th and I might read the call to worship giving pastor Kathy a break we will see what happens, although my bashfullness is better then before, it's making great strides in becoming something of the past. But I do find that with my new hobby time is less then before, because I have to split it up between different places. The Church, the thrift store, and of course my things I do around the yard and in the driveway. But I'm kept busy through it all and I love what I do, as for writing it's become a part of my life no different then getting out of bed each morning and I always thank God for what He has brought my way. The lonely travelor has found his way home and he found it in the town of his dreams, what a blessing to live in a place that loves so much. Maggie must be doing fine as I haven't heard and bad news yet her road will be a long one but if I know God He will brng her through and make her better then before. Stronger in mind spirit and soul a piller of strength that will live for many more years to come, in all my experiences I have found that He always takes things to the finish. I have never seen Him only do part of something like in the stoy of the guy trying to get his ife back, the pushers kept coming but God was stronger and had them put away so they couldn't do any harm to the god soul trying to find his way home. As for the pushers stories of how they ended up where ever, I couldn't say for only they know their own story. Bu I bet it scared the hell out of them, Sunday and yesterday was very hot after gtting the tires finished I had to come in so I could cool down before going to they thrift store. The lady I worked with had to of been in her 80's and she was very nice, she even bought a jar of my eggs. She told me that she had never tried them in her life but she woud give it a try and I could imaging her liking them. Even the old are trying something new what a great thing to have happen, I know she goes to our church but I don't see her there very oftend or else I just don't look to see her either way she is real nice. The van needs a few things but I think I will let who ever buys it do the work they are little things and don't cost much to fix if you do the work your self, it's a used vhicle so you got to expect to do some things to it it's a survivor vehicle one that has been in a barn for many years so time has caused it to need a few things and most people like to fix up things them selves, like I like to do from time to time it's the heat that really gets to me and I work out enough as it is. Through time we will come across many cars and things that can make a way to survive in this world, but also we have to keep things paid and on the home front so nothing interferes with my good standing at the bank. My ventures will bring many things and I hope that I can and will see them when they show them selves. I miss many things by not getting out very oftend but working on the vehicals get me past that point as things improve by doing and not staying in the house all the time. As for making a future out of working on cars I believe I could because I can get the parts pretty reasonable through the internet and it only takes a couple of days toget them.

It seams being in a small town can have It's advantages you have your peace of mind and you can do things at your own speed like in the shows of mayberry RFD with Don Knots working at the station sometimes it's just the perfect place to be when you don't want to be have anything to do with the out side world. Andy Griffen was also in the show that lasted many years until he went to another show and became a lawyer, from the beginning I never did feel like I fitted in when it came to the big city but I stayed many times for one reason or another but now I'm home where I belong and here I will stay and make a life for my self and little brother the joy of being who you are in it's self is priceless no one to bother you as you do your thing and you live just far away enough to where they don't come and see you very offend. Each of us living in our own world and having our own families, but still nothing can take the place of your children. Maybe one day I can afford to have repairs done and I can get some new carpet that would be great, it's very early and little brother is still a sleep I hope he sleeps in so that maybe he can help me today. The quietness is shaddered by the noise of the dehumidifier, the machine that was once quiet as the morning has gotten old and the parts are getting wore out. Sort of like life with the elderly what used to work alrighht gets brittle and we still go on as if nothing has changed, it's Normans birhday sometime this week or next and I saw him in Church yesterday. You could imagne what a blessing it was to have him there then I went and got gas for the car and he was working on the lawn mower getting the blades sharpened, I told him that it was Sunday and he told me that he was a work a holmic. You have to find something to do with your time after looseng someone you loved so much and think it's his way of dealing with that loss.

Lord knows we all deal with that kind of thing in different ways I my self dealt with pops by doing somewhat the same thing at the Church. My place of refuge is there when I feel down and blue it's a great place to talk to the lord when you want to figure out things like what to do next, I sometimes find my self in a dark place where I feel alone not knowing what to do next but at least it's not that dark place where I lived a long time ago that dungen that kept me locked away from the real world. I cant tell what the future will hold but things should be good later down the road anxiety, sometimes gets to me when something new comes my way and then it takes a while for it to pass. Some use medication for it but I choose to ride it out knowing that he will bring something new the next day something different then the day or two before it's now Monday and little brother is dreaming but what about I don't really know and when he wakes up he usually don't remember what it was either, I know he wants to work on cars but I don't see it in him as he is too big to even work on them and he has no energy to go out in the heat. Well either do I have the fortitude to do much in the heat, when things go right then all is well but when things don't go right then it seams everything falls a part. This vehical is my life line right now and it has to sell before I can move forward, Randy was telling me about his dream of Oliver and Ted Clinebell pulling a shopping cart full of aluminum cans and they looked wore out. That was something pop's did when he couldn't find work and he made a good living at it but boy it was smelly and he would have to get into the shower when he got home which for some reason he hated. I have been a person that has to be able to touch something before I will be able to believe that it' real except for the things with God, never being able to touch him hasn't stoped my believing that he does exist. And I know why' it's the things He has done in my life helping me turn things around wouldn't of been possible without him, I heard one women say that others think Christens are weak because they have to believe in something other then them selves but O how wrong they would be it's him satin that puts those words in their mouths and he is trying to destroy all belief in God the father. This what I call a war' has been going on long before my time on this earth and it will probably continue long after I'm gone to my home in heaven, it's another quiet morning as the van will be in the news paper starting today even the picture will stand out when other see it I'm hoping they will come running to get it so I can move on to getting something else to traide it's the little things that make life intresting having something others might want to take on as a project so they can make things better then they once was, if I had the resources I my self would like to build it for the future make something so nice that other would want it but then knowing how things are in his world it would just add worry to someone steeling it. And I don't need that inmy life right now, as I was talking to the young man that now works on my computer he asked what I wrote about and I explained what happened so long ago and brought him to some of my sights and he was interested in seeing more so I told him to go to my sights and read what this old man has done with his life.

To me it's better to try and change lives then to do nothing. Try and bring people to their sinces in this world so they can live a longer life instead of it being cut short because of something that man made like drugs and alcohol. I know there are some that disagree with what I do and really I don't care because they are the ones that are trying to destroy our childrens lives and ours. Living through what I have is very rare going up to deaths door and then having God pull you back because you haven't really seen or learned about the world and how good it could be, narrow minded thinking in that dark place is really all you have besides the demons in your own mind telling you what you should do. In other words when you are not close to God the demons pray on you because you havn't seen the light of the father, but once the light has been lit you feel change and if it comes to fast then you wind up just confused so you take a step back or He adjust things so they happen a lot slower so the mind can adjust from that life to the next or this one where everything is different. You wake up to the same morning instead of one filled with things that shouldn't be my change came after I went into the light but many people don't ever get that far. They just die off like the plants, which comeback every year but they are different in some way stronger in many ways as they keep coming back like an exercise when you use your God given talent, nothing about me is the same as it once was everything has changed the world isn't altered by the perseption or seing things through a mind that was once destroyed. But it remembers the things it went through to get here today.

I had never seen a place like Courtland' before O yes little town but nothing like this place I call my home, for it's one of a kind a town set apart from the others and it survives just fine on it's own out here in God's country I believe in a way He has blessed Courtland for a good reason, but what that reason is I cant quite put my finger on. Maybe long ago there was one deserving of he blesssing that lived here who could really say? But I do know that this is where I will stay until he changes things 'not me' but Him the one who created me. I talked to Mark and told him that I lowered the price of the van and he told me not to get taken so I felt that he had my best intrest in heart, my personality wont let me be bold like I should be and that's not something to let get in the way of business. You are out there to make a living but then so is th rest of the world and they will take you for what they can, so stick to your guns when it comes to getting a head other wise people will run all over you like the Elephant which runs to water after being away from it for a time. I just found out that my good friend Norman Hoard had a slight stroke tonight I will pray for him to get better, he has been a good friend and I pray that he recover from this ordeal. He hasn't been his self since his wifes passing but that to be expected with the loss of a loved one, I hope he lives a long time because I know some that have been without a loved one gives up because they don't see life without them. Help him lord and bring him back I sure would miss him in my world, we all loose someone at one point or another but we have to go on give him the strength lord and rebuild what ever is wrong with him and let him know that he is loved by all here in Courtland. He is a piller in the community and has done much for many including me, father give him the gift of getting better and if I can help him in anyway let that happen also. For my care giving skills are excellent as you know, since I have known him he has been a quite man but O so giving helping the Church and all. That's something you don't see in bigger towns because people don't get close in those places. Wednesday morning and I can hear the train coming through it seams like it's a long ways out but it will be here in no time. I wonder if they heard the same train whistle back in the old days like in the 30's and such the morning is quiet as little brother is sleeping I hope Norm had a restful night he is going to have to slow down because of him age and boy he wont like that like with pop's he never did want to stop working until a stroke hit him, but when you get older that's just a part of life.your body slows down so you have to match the pace and find something else you can do or else risk the having another heart-attack As I went down to the station Ben told me that Norm should be home today so I'm hoping for the best and that he gets home, they have said or told him that he should take it easier but he is set in his ways starting the station at 19 years old. My land' that is young but he had the drive and love from his wife to bring him through everything, Norm has to be in his late 70's or early 80's as John is 84 and still going strong, it's like they have a code to live as long as they can here with God by their side. He is so great the lord our God He seams to bring us through most of our troubles and we become better for it, our triles is what test us and makes us stronger as we go through this life. Our up and downs in this world bring us to a place of peace once we get things figured out but what might be peace one day might not be it for the next the ever changing world is a place where we all change even if we don't see it at the time.

The words of God go through my mind sometimes even when I don't expect them to. I will find my self in the relm of the words of the bible sometimes and it can even be in he words of a song, something trying to come out as my life lives on but I have to let it do it on it's own and not rush it. It's like a changing from the inside, and no one else is doing this but Jesus the lord of my life. What else does he have in store for me what will tomorrow bring? Thursday morning and we go to Concordia this morning yesterday I had one guy stop by and another call it's the beginning of labor day weekend and many want to go camping which would be an exelent time to sell the van it would be great for camping. Monday is a holiday so I will have to get things done that need being done and then Tuesday is the second of the month for which things will really have to be getting under way, I don't think much of the months anymore not like I used to when my mind ran every day like a ten day clock it has seamed to slow down for some reason maybe it's getting what it needs to move forward so it can handle the things it needs to. My journey has taken me places I never thought I would go and you don't have to travel in a car to get there when before I used to feel negative energy I would move away from it and now it's like it doesn't exist for some reason could I of brought the negative energy into my life? Well I don't believe so because I only felt it around prople that could do me harm and when I couldn't handle it then I turned it over to God for his intervening and he would take care of it. What a great God we have, in this world you have to survive the best way you know how and flipping cars seams to be a trait that I could get into never knew I had that kind of talking in me but it's there somewhere waiting to get out.

I believe we all need time to grow and if we miss that or part of that in our younger years then if we are blessed later he will allow time to make up for that loss and bring us to a new place, as for my self I'm still growing in ways that I don't even undertand and I don't know if I will fully understand it. Through the grace of God he allows us to grow in many ways but with him he changes us from the inside out and we need to allow him to do this, not through obligation but through his love for us. Friday morning and it's the beginning of the weekend for some the lake will be the perfect place to be, and for others home. We went to Concordia yesterday and now we don't have to go back for three more months the controlling of things get a little better each day as I move towards the goal of breaking away from the ties that bind. the ties that many see but not as much as me being in country surely helps to make things better then they would be anywhere else especially in the big towns that seam miless from here, I'm hoping that things will take a turn for the better if the guy come up from the other part of the state and buys the vehical I have as requested I sent him pictures but never heard back from him so things are up in the air about that right now, I heard some sawing last night as someone was making something out side and I think it came from down the street maybe a add on to a porch or something like that they are always working on something in my town of dreams even the side walks are getting done down town and the water goes off from time to time letting us know they have hit a water pipe and service will be delayed for an hour or two but like always it goes back on. My neighbor is getting ready for some traveling as they have brought back the streamliner that they lived in while their house was being built, my that house has come a long ways in just a year and a half fully built with all the the things you would need to have a nice home here in Courtland. The lady that passed not too long ago has someone living in her old home, I hear different things about the rent price on the place but $450.00 a month seams to be the price. To me the house seams to be newer then mine but it was built by hand from what some have told me, some say her husband built it out of scraps he had found somewhere which made him pretty handy while he was alive. It seams we all have our good and bad side, some better with their hands and others better with words as some would tell but in the end we are all remembered for the things we do and weather they are good or bad depends on us as people. When I first came here many people wanted to make changes in their lives and by me being here they were able to make those changes like with the women who used to care for the inside work at the church she wanted to find another job and was able to once she retired and then I replaced her but only at the job she plays the piano and orgen on Sunday mornings when she is moved to and Judy plays the other times making sure there is always some one for the music. The community that cares is what Courtland is through the sands of time it has stood and will continue to be here long after I and many more are gone, then the children will grow and take over where we leave off. The kids are growing faster each year as it seams all thing grow faster now as I watch the seasons go by, before too long fall will be upon us with winter to follow that. The train is going through town as I can hear the whistle off in the distence and I love that sound as it reminds me of the people who used to ride the rails when you would see them on television.

All of them in their dirty clother as the dust from the tracks blows through the box cars, I can still see a vivid image of the cattle as they too road the rails back when the train first started. Many times the trains had shut down but they were always back up and running again smothered by the oil industry back in the 1800's they over came the hard shiips that the Vanderbelts threw at them and went on to make the rails stronger then ever sort of like the United States when they are at war with other countrys always trying to prove them selves stronger so they can be number one in the world. The two companys sometimes worked together when it would benifit them but that was for only a short time during the 1800's and then they went their separate ways, they say this is what made America strong like it is today and maybe so but it was at the expence of the people. For without them there wouldn't be any rails or oil industry it was their blood sweat and tears that made the United States what it is today, Saturday morning and an gentleman from some other town is coming over it seams he want's to look at the van. He ws telling me that he is going to need a van to put a lift on because he is becoming less able to get around then before, although it would be great for that he will still need to come up with something other then an old truck to get this van from meit's like bardering one person having what the other needs so you have to figure out a good salution to make things worrk right, the thrift store is closed today due to construction on the streets so it might be open next Wednesday which is fine with me it was Beverly that called me to give me the news so now it's been a week since my last working day there. Tomorrow is communion day for the church so I have to have everything ready this morning so all I have to do is take it into the sanctuary, tomorrow morning.

I have been doing thing to the van and yesterday morning we took it for a ride to Beleville and boy it ran great with no problems this is what I like when things go right it had a little bit of speed to it also as it didn't like to drive below 65 and 70 miles an hour those where it's good speeds, and I believe it would of liked it if I would of drove even faster. All the things work fine on it and he will be getting a good buy to convert it to a crippled persons van I do know those lifts cost a lot of money and to have them installed well I have no idea. To me it hit my heart when he said that but you cant let emotions come into play when business is at hand. We all have to live and we do it the best way we know how so we can go on with life as we know it, I have a sneakiest feeling I might know this old gentalmen but we will see when he gets here this morning. If it is him. I already like him, and that can pull on my heart strings being a softy like I am but the good lord tells us to love thy neighbor and he is right in all things he tells me so we will see how much love this old guy has if things go right then we will both be happy and things will go on from there. Through this life we or I will meet many people, some good and some bad but it's up to us to separate, the two. And only hold the good friends near and dear to us, this will be my first experience in this field so we will see how it goes from here. Through this next winter I will do my best to survive in making my oblagions, to my people that have put their trust in me although I have never been late on things I would like to keep it that way holding my head up high as I walk down the street and feeling that pride which comes with being a good person. I remember when I had nothing and it was all I could do to get food to survive the month but through the years change has come to this newly born Christen and as the years pass things seam to be getting better, moderation is the key to surviving in the world for me anyway. And I seam to do a pretty good job at it. who knows maybe one day I might be in a place where I don't have to worry as much as I do today this would truly be a blessing should this take place. I remember back when I was a child dad would take in side jobs so he could have a little extra money to buy the thing he wouldn't usually be able to buy if he didn't do them, and life was good back then he had his own garage off the house that he would do his work in there. I will never forget when he bought mom her car she just had to have because of the color and the raidio worked, they didn't even get it home before is took a turn for the worst but dad rebuilt the motor and had it running like a top it was so fast that it lifted up the front end and it frightened her so bad that she wouldn't drive it so they gave it to Rod for his 16th birthday and he raced everyone in town. It only had a two speed power glide transmission and the motor was too much for it and he caught it on fire one night racing, it was a good thing the milk man came by other wise it would have been a total loss but dad got it up and going again and then sold it too much of a car for a kid that young.

I don't know why or how I remember some things but they have been in the back of my mind since childhood, maybe it is a way to hold on to the good memories. Herb was a good man and did his best but somethings are short lived when the curse inters your life, what was once the priority in your life becomes second only to the curse it gets a hold of you and doesn't like to let go. Even family comes second but once the day is taken care of then the rest comes into play, the one that is cursed can become that loving person you once knew. But then when the time comes to make sure you have what you need your focus goes to that until it's secured for a time, the curse usually takes the person and destroys them as they stop doing the things that made you love them at one time. If science was as it is today they probably could of helped dad but back then they didn't even know what it was, Parkens made him shake so much that he couldn't do his job putting all those little parts into a transmission had to be done just right other wise nothing would work. He could accomplish more on a weekend having a beer then he could do all week if he didn't have it and some bosses understood his condition but when it would get out of hand then he had to find another one which happened quite a few times leaving us without a home or having to move to another place but I always loved this man who cared for me like I was his own when he didn't really have too but it was his choice to do so. Mom always knew I wasn't his but I wonder if he always knew? Not sure about that one it didn't get brought up much. But I know now that our moving from Minnesota was brought on by it her family was a stickler about gossip and with her brother being a pastor it wouldn't sit well with the church back in those days the 50's was another time when you just didn't do somethings, I don't think mixed races even happened back then but I could be wrong. I know the rich exploited the colored people back in the 1800's but I didn't keep up with how those things changed.

Today is very common to have a different colored partner but back then I'm not sure so I wont go any further with that. My opinion is that we are all brothers and sisters in Christ and the color of our skin shouldn't matter, I don't believe He sees colors not in the since that we do. Black brown red or white we are all brothers and sisters with a heart and a soul, and some of us can do somethings better then others and some not so much the creator of our existence doesn't interfear with our squabbles as the ant is to us we are probably to them. I can remember when I first found out that the people are the church I got excited not knowing this and it made a difference in my life as to how I looked at things. The place I clean is just a building but it has importance and has to be kept clean so I do my job with grace, many people use it to learn about our creator and I love it when children learn something new and want to share it. One of the children is learning the piano and who knows maybe she may one day take over for the elders that play now but that's something only time will tell. At her age you never know what will happen in the years to come because things can change in a second like with my life things are at a point now that the past is fading away and it's getting hard to recall the dark days of my life. Good riddens to those times as they move further and further away from me, I wonder sometimes why we remember those times and all I can come up with is that they are supposed to be lessons learnd and they are not to be repeated like an old girl friend if the situation wasn't good then you surely don't want to go back in time to that time and relive it all over again there would be no rime or reason to it plus it wouldn't make any since, with all or most of the women in my life they would like to give it another try but my mind can't see that happening because they were not so good of a relationship and some I don't even remember because of the curse, just blotches in a life long gone. Some where short only lasting a year or so but still I can count them on one hand. And maybe it was supposed to be that way so I could have this time to learn about God my true father, earlier I saw a flicker of lighteen, and now it's raining out so I will go down to the church later and get my work done when I can see better I don't do so good in the dark with judgment, it's been that way ever since that day so long ago but it's getting better as time passes. Never figured out what caused it but I'm grateful for the imporvments in the other areas in my life, we all get gifts but for some they don't see them until later in life like with me sometimes it can be a long time before I see things the way they really are. Today I had a visit from the old gentelmen but I wasn't going to just give my van away like he wanted, and then Mark came by to look at the van because he might have a buyer for it. Come to find out a lady at the bank's parents used to own it and must know it pretty well, I told my friend that he could buy it for a certain price below what I was asking for in the paper but hey he is my friend and has done a lot for me over the years so I return some of the grace.

Today it's supposed to be 101 degrees out side and they can keep it there as for us we will spend the day inside where we can control the tempature and not sweat. Some people came by today and wanted to clea my carpets Kerby was the name and the sold them in these small, I told them hat I couldn't afford to buy one asi know the price is really out there wanting hundreds of dollars for one of them and it seamed no matter how hard I tried to tell her no she kept insisting on it making me feel uncomfortable by me saying no. I really didn't want to oblagate my self to something that cost so much and then she left but not as happy as she could have been if I had bought it, part of me said yes but then the other side said no like one side fighting with the other and I don't like that feeling. She went on to ask what I did for a living and I told her that I was a writer trying to help kids that have fallen into alcohol and drug addiction which she had fallen into it her self earlier in her life, it never amazes me how the young can relate to that subject fighting it at one point or another.in their lives but with most of them it has only lasted a few years as they grow. Not lasting anywhere as long as my fight did, theirs seams to last only a couple of years when mine lasted well past a decked and almost two of them, I know many would read my book once it's out there but it's that final step that frightens me. Who knows maybe in time the good lord will help me past that stage of the opera, I could see that she could relate to me maybe even more then I understood. I do know that the story has to be told in the near future or by next summer when winter has passes during winter would give me the time

I need to rise above most of the problems I still face and then it's Kady shut the door as I start to move forward.

When I go up early I could still smell the freshness from the carpet being cleaned and it makes me wonder if I should of gotten it to keep it this way. The mornings have been hot and muggy with the humidity being up there to almost a 100 percent. I believe yesterday it was 97 percent and it's hard to breath in that kind mugginess. I seam to thrive to keep busy with the things I do and today I'm hoping that Mark will come by and give me some good news about the guys wanting to buy the van, it would be a blessing if it got sold so things can move to the next step in my project, I can hear thunder off in the distence and wouldn't you know it I washed the van last night it seams to always rain after I wash something like my car or anything else that's left out side, I really wish it wouldn't rain but I cant stop mother nature and she seams to know when we need rain. This morning is the earliest I have gotten up in quite sometime thinking the clock says one thing when in reality it says another, we have communion to day so I have to be at the church a little early to get it all set up. And turn on the Air-conditioning so it isn't so hot in the church, the good news is that it's supposed to cool down come Monday and then maybe fall will be here. A time of cool nights and mornings then getting hot during the day a great time when the leaves fall from the trees and change color and they turn to molch as we go into winter and he snow starts to fall on the ground. I know winter is going to be hard as we go from the heat of summer to turning on the gas to keep us all warm, one bill goes down when the other goes up sort of like a traid off that keeps the wheels turning during the year. I'm glad that Randy went back to bed as I don't like to listen to others so early in the day. It's just now quorter after 2:00 in the Am and I like this quiet time when I can gather my thoughts for the day trying to figure out how things will go as time marches on. To me' being a salesman can be trying as people tryu and jew you down from the price you want for something I guess it's in our nature to get the best deal we can and save what we can to make it through the times a head, as for me the good years are still a head of me the ones that will make a difference in my life and others. It would be great to inspire someone to change their lives being that piller that made it through the darkness and into the light, what a great feeling that would be in my life to have others look up to you for the hills you have fallen off of but got right back on and climbed that mountain that almost took you down to the pits that could of ended your future from happening. To me my opinion' is that God is stronger then the counter half meaning satin or the devil can't hold a candle to him the creator of all things.. I wonder sometimes if the heylow aroung Jesus head is something that others saw or was it a mark that God put upon him to let other know that he was His son, the one true king that saved us on that day 2000 years ago. We as people couldn't imagine the torement he went through on that day they hung him from the cross, but in my songs I like to think that it's as pertinent to today as it was back then.

Our lord died on the cross so we could live and be here today,, did or does he know something we don't? This could very well be as they say he knows everything even the hairs that will fall from our heads as we grow older. I don't believe I love anything more then the one who brought me back to life and the strange thing is that you would think I would be angry because I didn't get to stay where I was in the world of peace and tranquility for the time I spent there was priceless and I would welcome it again when he feels it's my time. Imagine being with the king of kings for ever no more suffering, sorrow, or pain and no confusion of any kind in that perfect setting we call heaven. I just checked my email and I have a follower on twitter it's always nice to see whats on a young persons mind especially in their teens when impression is almost everything, if you weigh your words you can bring together something great. I can put my self at that age and at the time I was in trouble trying to get my life on track but the main coulpret was still the alcohol clouding my mind with non beliefs, and then staying in that place of wondering if ii should go this way or that way finely after many years of falling I got tired of not seeing the bottom and pulled my self up by my boot straps to walk once more. Was it the will of God that brought me back or was it my own doing? I believe it wouldn't of been possible for me to do it on my own because so much damage had been done, he was the only one who gave me hope and faith that another day would arise and bring with it something beautiful like life it's self. The day will be here before too long in about three hours and then I will go and do my job of setting up things and cooling off the church, if they didn't have Air then we would cook like the bacon on the stove and no one wants that.

In the days before our existence many things happened and they traveled the world without all the technology we have at our finger tips. All these things were done by using wood and other things to keep a boat together, my' how they must have had faith to travel from one coast to another not knowing if they would make it or not. In a way it would be like me walking from one coast to another and I know that can't be done. But just the image I can relate to for their faith must have been very strong. It is said that our history is wrong as people visited the home land before Columbus discovered America and it was religious people wanting a place where they could worship God in their own way, it was a strange time back then but if we would of been there I think we would understand it more then what some read in books. For if the knowledge is wrong then history is wrong. Monday and it's laborday Communion went well yesterday and we had many children there, they had to set up another table in the back of the overflow room so everyone would have a place to sit I like it when that many people come and it shows that the lord is still there for us all. Strange how things change in this world compaired to the other one that seams to be faiding from my life, the kids helped with the candles and I think pastor Kathy likes that. Next Wednesday it's bible school for the kids again and I will spend more time cleaning because lets face it kids don't pick up after them selves and it's been that way since like for ever. The mayor came by on Saturday to look at the van and I think he liked what he saw but cant be sure as he is a quite person like my self. You can be that way and still go through life with many friends I know he feels comfortable around me as he road his gulf cart into my yard to look at the inside, by that time I had cleaned the spots which were on the carpet and they were gone like they had never been there. Now I have only a little more to do and it will be ready for the next family to enjoy they sell kitss for those kind of vans that make them look even better then it does now I noticed that the under carage would look cool if it was painted black a shiny black to set it off, back in the day I would of gave my right arm to have something that looked so nice, and I would have been the talk of the block everyone likes to stand out from the rest of the people letting their friends see their reflection or persona of how they live some would say that your car is a reflection of the person who owns it. And if it's kept up then so are you, I see people all the time with their food thrown all over their car which lets you know that they are messy in their home as well as their car. Little messy then their house needs picking up from time to time but a jungle messy then their home is trashed, like the lady who lives alone and hoards all the things they feel will bring them comfort. Break up's can cause people to feel depressed and go into a shell the same kind of shell I lived most of my life in and many don't come out, not wanting to experience this feeling again they bury them selves in clutter using it as a security blanket but all it does is cause more depression as they go deeper into that world of being alone. My self' being alone gives me more time to get to know God' now that might sound strange but it's O so true, because your not involved in the drama that takes up a lot of peoples lives, they go through argueing and fighting when I'm reading something new about our creator. Weigh the two' and I'm sure you would rather read then fight about something stupid. When things throw you into a depression then something is wrong something is not healthy in your life and it has to be fixed.

That's when a shrink comes in and boy that cost more money then most of the people I know make to justb survive, so now you have no money to eat and that brings on another problem especially if you have kid's. many would say to keep your self busy but that just masks the problem that will come up again when you loose your job and then where would you be? I have to make things work in my life so I can go on and become more self supportive, because lets face it no one is going to take care of you in this life. I spent almost 30 years taking care of my family which by the way are gone now and I still do it today to a certain extent, I recall the women that asked who will take care of me when the time comes and my reply was probably no one, and she came back with something that supprised me she said that the lord would take care of me as long as I believe. And now thinking on it. He probably will bring something into my life to help me through that part of my journey, my journey' I have traveled down many paths but they all lead in this direction to bring me to my town of dreams. There is so much I would like to do but right now the timing is off by a little bit, so I will be patient until that time is just right when things unfold in my favor. I have plenty to look forward to in the coming years and if my business takes off then my worries will be a thing of the past like the life I left behind. A new flower blooming for the first time you don't know if it will drop seeds to grow again but there is a good chance that they could, this is life taking the chance that all things will come to be and it helps if the lord is on you're side prayse be to Him! I can still smell the freshness of the carpet being cleaned and I hope it lasts a long time should Harley not piss all over the place. Randy is making biscuits this morning as we ran out of bread but these should be good not having them in a year or so something different from the every day toast.

I had to move the van yesterday because it's close to fall and the sap out of the trees was dripping on it, can't have that! I cant get over how good the van looks and I have some ideas of how to make it look even better should I get it done, it stands out like a new penny all bright and shiny you can tell others kept it garaged most of it's life and that's a good thing not being out in the elements of the snow and rain. Tomorrow is hump day and today the trash has to be taken out, I got some paint for the van's under side to give it that nice and clean look so maybe they can se how good of care it has gotten over the years it's the 3rd of September now and things will start to cool off so the air-conditioning shouldn't have to be used as much giving us a break from the heat, you can tell that fall is just aroung the corner as the sap from the trees seams to fall off the branche of the trees and get on the ground or what ever is sitting under them so I have to be careful with where I park the van not to get it all over the place my land you can hardly get it off once it's on there. Also tomorrow bible schoool starts so my work will increase at the church but through the years it has become just another thing to do plus I like doing it, as I took Sam's dog out last week he paid me for doing it even though I didn't ask and tried to tell him he didn't have to do that. But he insisted that I take it some talk about others but in the end their love for one another seams to trump and gossip that might occure, last week the thrift store was closed do to construction on the streets so I hope that they are past that point this week so we can open again and make some money. It's little things like that which interfear with business but at the end of the day it's all good, just another delay in the cycle of life that will be caught up later it's the cycle of life that brings not expected things and we just have to deal with them as they come. The other day I came home to find three jars on my doorstep so I took it that Norman must have been up and about, the rest that he got must of charges his batteries so now he will be back to his normal self but I hope he slows down a bit so he can stay out of that hospital. I have never liked those places and either did mom she would rather stay at home and suffer then to go to those places, as we both say people die there and it's not a good place to die. The recall of her passing was a bad time for me as the police tried to pry me from her gurney and all I wanted to do is go with her, I felt lost at the time but still her passing didn't throw me back into alcohol I just felt lost and even more so when pop's went to be with the lord but time seams to heal most wounds and we go on with life as we know it but to where? We really don't know until we get there or get through the mourning of loss. Now is a time when change comes as the fall approches people will be getting ready for winter, staying in because it's cold out side or just playing because it feels like the right thing to do playing out side that is.

The time when Mark told me too get into the house still has a grip on my mind, it was a nice day except for the snow falling and I had to clean off my car. The temp was way down there and he didn't want me to get sick I guess, but I did go back in the house where it was nice and warm and I didn't get sick that day. My neck is bothering me this morning it seams I slept on it wrong night before last, yesterday we think we saw Denny Eggie as he gave us the thumbs up when we were at the station in Belleville I didn't reconise him but Randy said something. That this man gave us the thumbs up and that could only be Denny he hadn't seen my car before so I took it that he liked it. Denny is a car guy and he has family around these parts he has many tropheys for winning races in different parts of the country and I believe he has won some from here also, the sarrounding areas I mean like in Belleville and other race tracks that fill Kansas, maybe he came back here to get away from the memory of looseing his grandson you can never tell really. His hair was as white as snow being all gray from age and hard work all his life, Randy was the one closes to him both being in cars and such and the lack of education didn't seam to bring any bariers between them talking shopand all. As the years pass we will see him again and I will try to remember him next time clearier so I can say hi' the memory is very odd you would think I would of recalled him but I didn't, anyway. It's bill day the third of the month so now I will get everything behind me for this month and see where I stand in that area I already sent out the payment for one bill, and now the rest come to be wiped out so my worries wont go into the full length of the month. My self I worry too much wanting things to be just right so worry doesn't come into the picture if I could achive that then life would be perfect.

For me anyway as for making it and being rich I guess I have both but not as some see it. Rich yes in friends and that's more important then any other material thing in this world, it's night time and Charles showed up at my door around 8:00 Pm. It was very unexpected when I heard Harley barking because he has neve done tha before not that constent so I got out of bed and let them in, I have to say he hasn't changed much in the 30 some years since our last visit. They were telling me that it's their weding anniversary so on the spure of the moment they took off and are now headed to Nebraska so they could visit other realitives and a few graves that they havent seen in quite a while it's funny that they should take this time to visit as it was very unexpected to me. He was telling me that he asked some guys at the station down the street if they knew where I lived and they gave them directions, not used to these kind of visits that take place in the spur of the moment but it is nice to see him and his wife after all these years. It just goes to show that you never know who might show up. Like my self Charles gets up early but really it's a time when we can remember back to a time when life wasn't so complicated, just kids running around and getting into trouble. Now the years have changed us, and the years have caught up with us. Although we are older Charles still talks like there is no tomorrow maybe looking for something, a connection to the past that wasn't resolved in our younger years. Or he is just having fun while he is still here traveling around seeing parts of his life that he misses while he was away, during the time that he is here I will show him around and see what he thinks of our big city my town of dreams' the place where I will grow old and one day meet my creator, the world has changed In the last 40 years. As the day goes on this should get intresting almost every word is about things that have to do with the creator, he has a lot of anger built up inside and he doesn't seam to want to or cant let go of the hurt that he has. When it comes to anger I seam to not have that inside but on special situations it does flare up but though the life of being a Christen, he has a way of getting on a person. I think he is very mixed up about things and maybe one day he will figure it out, I used to think I was mixed up about things but there are others that are more mixed up then I. I missed work on Accident today which is unusual for me I guess it was charles coming but how can that be when they left at 7:00 his morning and I wasn't supposed to be at work until two in the afternoon it seams I do forget sometimes and I don't know why one of my friends from church came by and brought some tomoatoes for us and we were glad to get them nd I thanked him as he left, my friends are good friends here and they look out for me especially when they have garden stull that is too much for them to eat. As for looking for work I'malways looking for something to ocupie my time but this missing work has to stop, I think I have missed about three days all together this year and was late about two days but it's never on purpose just a slip of the mind for getting they have my phone number so if it's real busy they could of called Charles learned something while he was here to maybe not worry so much about others that don't see things his way.

I learned in this life that not everyone will see things the way we might, so you have to let them be them selves and learn in their own way. Everyone is different that just the way we were created and you can't please everyone some might seam closer to God but in time we all will see the things he wants us to see and that will bring us as close. I did learn something thou and that's I'm very calm around people who are hiper so who knows maybe I would be a good teacher for helping with the kids. We will see somewhere down the road, I recall one person saying that it would be good to have a male teacher in Wednesday school one to help out with the kids and maybe show them authority, you know the male dominace plus you learn at the same time as the kids do. Could I get back my youth? Well no' but I could gather the knowledge I didn't get back then, that missed opportunity. And make it a thing in the present to me kids are neat watching them learn about different things. I don't know when I will see Charley again but I wish him and his wife well in the search for what he needs, altimers hit his father and he forgot the ones he loved and maybe some of that is in Charley I could see that he had a hard time dealing with some things, that diease takes from people but then later it is given back when we go to be with the lord. What a great thing this giving back of things we have lost in this life, my pickled eggs havent been selling lately and I think it's because others have taken it upon them selves to start making them for their own familys or them selves either way they had a good run but don't get me wrong I never give up on anything, maybe it's time to see the lady down the road. And sell them there if she would allow me to, I now have the lables she had been talking about so maybe it's a possibility.

Randy got up just long enough to take a wiz and then it was back to bed so he could get the rest he needs to start the day. My self I have to clean the church after the kids from yesterday it's no telling how much of a mess they made but I always get it done cleaning is something I'm pretty good at and lord knows I have been doing it for years it's become a part of me in this new world I have created for my self and little brother shares in my accomplishments. I did find out that my letters still get to Mark at the Kearney hub paper as a couple of weeks ago I had one of my articles published I didn't know if they desided to not write them or not but like always it came out right at the time I needed to know that I still am making a difference. Firday and I got a visit from Norm last night saying he might have a buyer for the van but he needed to know some more about it so I'm supposed to go down there this morning and give them to him at the station. It would finely be great to have it sold and then I will get another vehical to fix up and maybe that will help in many ways keeping things going for years to come. In the realm of surviving you have to do what you can do and have a happy home even if it's just you and your brother, I havent heard from Charley since he departed day before yesterday but I'm sure that he will contact me when he gets back to the home stead in Arkansas through face book. I didn't realize how bad his arm was until saw it for my self and boy it's really messed up he can't even drive a car but he has moma to do that for him and she is a sweet women hardly says a word unless Charles gets out of hand or too loud he is a very excitable person like he was when he was young the only differenct is that he is older now, he told me that he thinks of our childhood when we talk on face book he sees me as that 14 year old and then he comes back to reality and realizes that it's 40 years later I wonder if he will inharet his fathers disease of for getting things they say it runs in the blood passed down from father to child of mother to child I guess only time will tell if he will aquire this from him. What I saw in him was might not of been anger but regreat that he couldn't see his parents before they left this world, and it's something we all go through when we can't be there in the final minutes of them leaving this world, I know as close as I and mom were I too wasn't there in the final minutes and it made me feel bad inside but then time passed and I did the things she wanted me to do so I have no regreats. Charles liked mom and Olivers picture on the wall in my room and he said it brought back memories of the old days like it does with me sometimes when I'm ffeeling blue the happy times when life was simple, although I went through many things living in that dark place there was a glimmer of light at certain times which I couldn't see until now strange how things don't become clear until later in life and by then those times have already passed. My world today is so much different and the change has made me a better person not being able to do wrong in any situation if I see it, and then you have some things you can't see because you don't know anything about the situation and that bring you to another place high in the mountain my mountain where you can figure out things, life in general is learning and with learning you sometimes make mistakes.

TGIF It's the beginning of the weekend a time when a lot of people will celebrate not having to work by going out and getting drunk and although I know that kind of life I found out that it surly wasn't for me the hang overs were something that wasn't plesent begging God to make it go away as you sat over the toilet swearing to never do it again. Although the promas came to pass it took many years to keep them almost death but they were kept once my life got better, and today things are pretty fine as my word is my bond and I keep it when I don't forget things. I hope that the day goes well today as we go grocery shopping for the food we need to get through the month and then maybe that will set the stage for the rest of the month smooth sailing as they say, if I was to gotten everything right on things then the month goes well but if you try and not succeed then something hasn't come full circle.. Keep your heart pure and then things should work out.

You don't go out to do wrong that just isn't cool or polite. Tomorrow I work again at the thrift store and I hope no one is angry but I seam to get angey at my self more then they get angry with me. Strange how that works I demand more of my self then others demand out of me maybe because I know my potenchal and how far I should be able to go and other don't really know anyone, not fully even lovers don't know everything about each other and that's what makes life intresting findinng out those things as you get to know each other and walk through life. I met Leroys brother yesterday and they are so different like night and day in personality, this brother makes his living by getting cars cheap and selling them like I do very out spoken in many areas but still I like him. In every family you have the one that shy or bashbull and then the other who is out going and this is Leroys brother he jokes around and trys to make the best of things and that in life is a quality that not found very often. He has his brother check out the van and he told me that it's worthonly in the teens but to me it's worth more then he will offer, I understand that in this business you have to get the best deal.

So he is going to sleep on it and let me know sometime in the future, it's only been a week since it was on the market and others might come and see it sometime down the road I don't know if I should let it go for that low of a price but we will see. It would have to be in my numbers now not his. It's Saturday morning and I have the Church to get ready for tomorrow services like wash the windows and mop the floor so they are nice and clean, I believe my job is always going to be there or at least as long as I'm here which will be for ever. I have to make sure I get to work this morning so that's my top priority in getting things done today all else is second fiddle to my scedual as for the van it can sit for a while and I will have no regreats it's part of the game to barder back and forth and see who wins in the end, I cant believe how hot it was yesterday and humid as well but we made it through the day with flying colors staying inside most of the time except for when I mowed the lawn and moved the van from one side of the yard to the other other then that it just sits there waiting for someone to come along and give it a new home. That's the difference between some folks they seam to have all the money and I have just enough to get by it's not fair boo who! We havent heard from the parole board about little brother getting his good time back but we might hear something next week if everything comes together that would make him happy and maybe he would cheer up. He has traveled a long road since he got released and he has done good minding his peas and ques not to get into trouble, I havent talked with Charles since he got home but I hope heis doing fine, I really liked talking to him and getting parts of his life since we were separated in our younger years so much has happened in 40 years and it doesn't seam like that long ago, not 40 years. But it has been that long life fills us with many different things in our journey from the good things to the bad but we always hope for the best at the end of the tunnel, things going from good to bad and then bad to good. My greatest time has been here in my town of dreams where I feel like I fit in no phony fasod has to be put up here just be your self and you can make it all the way with out making enemies. My land it's only quorter to four and I'm already tired again maybe one day I will be able to sleep in but for now things will remain the same getting up and writing about life as I know it I can't write about what I don't really know but the things I do know are embedded in my mind like a chissel has put them there inbeded them in my mind for some time to come, during the day things seam to go well and there isn't any problems with family or friends and I like that about living here no one to try and change things change you as a person that is left in God's hands to do His work from the inside out but you have to be willing to listen and look for the signs that he puts in front of you, to me nothing is clear at first it seams to take sometime for it to sink in especially with my mind.

But at the end of the day he seams to get the message to me and I follow it to the best of my ability as for the cuss words that used to be there I believe most of them are gone but still I'm only human and slip once in a while to only catch my self later down the line as for God he will always stay in my life the one who saved me so long ago. It's been a great Saturday but I found out some things about a person and I'm so glad that I'm nothing like him, for his words were twisted to meet his agenda and I'm glad that I didn't fall for his game. As for my van the price will stay where it is and he will never get his hands on it through trickery I guess I'm used to being around people who shoot straight from the hip and are honest, deceiving people hasn't been something I have been around that much and when it happens to me I get a little angry. As for the thrift store it wasn't open today when I went down there, so back home I came out of the heat that feels like it's 100 degrees humid as hell compared to other days of cool weather. It's Sunday morning and I slept pretty well it's days like this which I like the most a quite Sunday morning with no noise at all except when little brother or harley gets up or a car goes down the road probably some young kid heading home after a night out with friends. My brothers kid wrote me and asked if I had a good visit with Charles or if he drove me nuts and I told him it was a good visit, for some reason some must think he is off a little bit and for that reason I say nothing about certain things no need to add to things that are not good, my brothers side has always thought or had the right kind of life to them anyway but I couldn't see my self walking in their shoes it's just that our worlds are different from one another's. The difference between Charles is that he is vocal about things he is not sure of, it's like he throw's it out there to try and test people and many don't feel comfortable being put in that situation' not even my self when I have to ignore somethings.

Through the years I have always kept most of what I feel to my self not wanting to rock the boat you might say and when he asked me questions I would tell him that he shouldn't let them steel his peace, that is something given by God for the person. In a way he reminds me of a bible thumper not meanting it in a bad way but as someone who needs to hear his own voice and needs to be right about his beliefs it seams to me that it's the only thing he holds on to. For change has come to him surely from when we were children, this morning I have too open the Church and get things ready for later this morning, as for the quiet sometimes it can be nerve racking but we go on with life as we know it. He once asked if I wanted to live with them and I had to tell him no as ineed that quiet time to depress sometimes from others coming into my life now since he left it will take a while for things to get back to normal for he to gets up at the same time as I do and if I had to be around that all the time then I would go nuts as Rod's son asked our worlds are created for us to live in and we shape them so we can go on with our lives, and not someone else's. All things take time as we go through this world and we have to except that time is or isn't always on our side and one day can be great and another not so much. I haven't talked with anyone from Church lately as last Sunday seams so far gone from the page today, but we all live our lives and hope for the best through Jesus Christ. The changes come how ever so slight and we move on in this world hoping to find what we need to keep going, as for my friends they are still there off in the back ground in case I even need them and they are good friends the ones you would take home with you. Monday and it's quite again this morning except for Harley coing over to me to let him out yesterday I watched a couple of movies after church and boy they were good ones that I had never seen before about love mostly and I could relate to them I wish sometimes I could find that special someone and make a happy home, yesterday Norman came to church and it was good to see him after his hospital stay I can tell that maybe he will slow down for a time now and take some time for him self. In familys there are two different kind of children the ones that are quiet and the ones that are not the interverted like my self and the out going like my brothers, and their views will very in some areas it's the quiet ones that get to stay with the parents the longest because they feel a need to take care of them as it was with me and my parents. Our bond stood the test of time as we went through life and even today I take care of Randy in this life the one that became O so different from the one I used to live I don't know how I did it back then but I did and it had to of been by the grace of God that I was able to, today it isn't so hard as it was back then wakeing up with a clear mind and not having that dark cloud hanging over me. I think of mom now and again but the pain that once existed has gone from this life and only the love exists I used to think about the bad times but that too has changed to the good, living this long is new to me as I never thought it would come to pass as the doctors thought I guess I really did too but there is a force beyond our understanding when I got into that wreck so long ago it was like my body and mind went to a different place, one of peace. And I wasn't frightened but everything came out alright in the end and we went on with our lives.

It seams when I come close to a disaster that peace hits me like I'm moving into another dimention and I wish I felt that way all the time but it only happens when I'm close to death why is that? Who really knows but the one who created me for this world, I have spent many years trying to find the answers to my questions but they never come just glimpses of things that maybe I should put together. As for life I have to say it's been good after the other life I lead so long ago, that one' I wouldn't wish on anyone but the good news is that it can be changed to a better life of existence with no curse walking beside you only God the creator of the universe. Many don't follow the lord but with me He has proven his love and understanding when you think everything is going to fall apart he seams to step into my life to brinng things to where they need to be. Everyone who has intered my home thinks it looks nice but after years of living here I don't see it like I used to it's what the pastor calls the new wareing off and I guess that would be so after so many years my people or friends are always welcome in my home as many of them havent ever seen the inside. But Jan has and of course Craig when I used to work for him in the beginning, Jan is a person that's very emotional careing about other like she does and Robert is a very kind soul also the two fit like a glove being married for many years their children are in their thirtys or late 20's making them a little older then I and they love God very much, like many do. It's being raised up in a Christen home that shaped their lives and it's a good way to be raised getting to know the lord from childhood and knowing that he is there in times of trouble. For those who don't believe I feel sorry for as they will never know the love that the lord has for them and the kindness that he shows to his people, religion has been around long before I came to this earth and it will continue long after I'm gone from this beautiful place.

As for my beliefs they will stay with me for eternity and I will carry them into the next life the one that should have been in the first place. Then I will get to see what Eve and her partner left behind when they ate from the tree of knowledge, they had to leave pairadice and set out on their own I can only imagine how they must of felt when God turned away from them and let them fend for them selves, to me God is everything that is good in the world and he has a reason for the things he does like bringing me back but still today I havent found out why this took place. I think I need more knowledge the kind that comes with age and it's not learned for hind sight is always 20/20 we can see the past but not the future if only we could switch them around for a time anyway. Funny but I know this cant take place at the present time, I wish I could of stayed in church as a child but we are brought up by our surroundings and what ever they are we will become if our parents loose that connection then we as children will loose ours especially if we are very young. Like the Calf that follows it's mother and learns the things she teaches them, when we are born we cant just break off from our parents and go our separate ways we wouldn't survive in this world with out that connection because it just couldn't happen. Our fathers teach us the manely things and the mother teaches the things we need to survive should we be a batchlor in this life making them both very important like two halfs of a coin if you don't have both half's then the coin is not worth anything. In my life I have had to use both of what I was taught on my mothers side especially cooking for others as they got ill made me better then I would have been should I have lived alone and I like cooking to a certain extent but it would be nice to have someone to share this task with, this morning I have some work to do but as usual it shouldn't take long. Just vacuuming and dusting to make sure the church is clean for the week I don't like people coming in to a dirty place Imagine that a dirty church never happen not on my watch. Little brother is up for the day now all he has to do is stay awake if that's possible this new thyroid medication has done something to him and he sleeps a lot wish they could get it right so he could adjust to it. We went to town and ran into a guy that is homeless it seams he lost a child not to long ago and now finds his family out on the streets, this kind of thing is what I'm talking about when I say I don't have it as bad as others. I told him that I didn't know of and one to help and then it hit me to go back and give him our pastors number so maybe she can help them, I know what it's like to be out there with no one that cares but his story touched my heart and I had to try. I had seen Kathy help other so you might say I left it in her hands and God's.

She will know what to do because she has the resources, I couldn't imagine looseing a child and then loose your home a little bit afterwards. As we talked he told me that he does tatoos and that if I ever needed any work done on mine then he would do it for me, he went on too tell me about getting out of prison and although it's nothing to brag about he felt that he should tell me about it. My self it doesn't matter if a person has made mistakes as long as they learned by them and of course he has done his time, in my heart I hope that Kathy can help them as to me it's the Godly thing to do. While going back to give him her number God spoke to me telling me it was the right thing to do. I can still remember the guy she helped a couple years back that was from Minnesota passing through and she helped him the best wayshe knew how seeing these people remind me of where I once was all lost and confused in this world but then someone came to my resque and then was fine after years of getting back on track, I could just about see tears in this young mans eyes but he wouldn't let them come made hard by the place he had been. Maybe once a long time ago those tears could of come but prison makes a person hard beyond what they would have had to of been if they would of never had to of gone there. It took almost a year before Randy came around and we started to get along as his out look on life was much different then mine, I had always tried to look at the brightest side of things and there wasn't any bright side to him being locked up. I can't even imagine how he felt when they told him that he was going home after all that time maybe a sigh of relief came to him I don't really know, on the day when I went to get him I wanted to cry because of the weight he had put on he reminded me of the marshmellow man in ghost busters.

But I didn't let my feelings show either being strong for both off us as we got out of that town called Lincoln Nebraska' to never return once we were on our way. He was amazed at the sights as we drove south out of Nebraska and came into Kansas I was very confused when the parole thing came to be, having to travel to Salina for the first time was not a good thing as I didn't know my way around. But we made it and then I couldn't wait to get back home to my town of dreams where I felt safe. Safe from the violence that takes place out in the outside world, in the time I have let him stay here I was going to get him his own place but he wouldn't have it frightened by not knowing the out side world for so long so God put it in my heart to let him stay and slowly things changed. For the better I might add, as for the guy and his wife I don't know what happened to them yesterday but I hope they found a place in this God for given place not meant on a sarcastic note just God's countys. I didn't know the older gentalmen that was writing something down but maybe he to was a messanger from God sent to help in some way really you can never tell who He will send until they are there standing in front of you. I had always heard that Kansas was the bible belt and it's shown in the way they help people like the travlor from Minnesota who daughter was hooked on Methamphetamines I gave him some tips on getting her help sure would like to know what the out come was. But I know it's hard to help those close to you because you have a place for them in your heart and that can stop you from doing your best you have to let go and hope that others can reach them in time, the first step is the hardest admitting you have the problem and then once you do that things start to unfold but it isn't uncommon to fall back into it to see if you are missing anything and usually they find that they weren't missing anything. Tuesday and the train is coming through also the mill down the road is running spreading the chaft from the crops through the air my car is covered with the crap but still life goes on and we do the best we know how, through the sand's of time we meet others that have fallen on hard times much worse then the times we have faced in our time here but I have to believe that they too will recover and go on with life as they know it, for each one of us make our own world that protective place for our selves and family like the bubble that houses love it flows freely within that space and all in it can feel that love. Courtland is like that a protected place where love can shine through. My town of dreams where things come to pass, I'm amazed at how close the people are here but it isn't something that happens over night you have to earn their trust over a period of time and it's going on five years since my life started here, the trust must never be broken otherwise you would find your self out in the cold sort of speak. Maybe like the Amish we are a community that would rather live in love then what the out side world has to offer, for every day you hear about the killing of people on the streets through the news and the news papers if I had my way those things wouldn't happen but it's not my world I only own a pin head of the existence of this planet a dot on the map showing where I belong, not many have that in the world today but it all starts somewhere and expands from there.

As I take out the trash this morning I also have to clean the windows at the church but I won't do that until later when the sun comes up, you can't even tell that I cleaned them just the other day kids putting their hands all over them but it's cleanable and then I can hope it last a while before doing it again. As for the vacuuming it's done until Thursday when I see how much of a mess they make at Wednesday school it's a job never ending as long as we have children there will be a mess to clean up so my job should last my life time anyway and then another will take over once I'm wore out. That's just the way it works in this world but thank God that I'm not replaced by a machine like they do in many places. It's now Wednesday and yesterday I put an add in the Kearney hub so now maybe I will get some bites on the van from there, my number is a local number for folks in Kearney but I did put that it's in Kansas where the van is also they are putting it in the red book which comes out of Kearney the picture should sell the van once it's up and running. Now all I have to do is play the waiting game to see if things unfold. Things haven't been good for Maggie but I don't know the whole story of the progress yet, it seams no matter how far you think you are from things like death your friends seam to go one way or another I don't know if the thrift store will be open today but I will check to see anyway, for the last couple of weeks it's been closed because of the work they are doing hump day is what they now call Wednesday well really it's been called that for quite ssome time now and they even have a camel on television making jokes about it.

The day is going to be another hot one but still I have to get the windows done later this morning as it's the start of Wednesday school I thought it was last week but they said in church that it's this week. I havent heard anything about the guy that was at the dollar store weather he got the help he needed but all I can do is hope for the best for him and his family and know that God somehow reached him to let him know that he is there. The economy is tight right now and not many people are looking for new vehicals but I know that who ever get this one will get a good deal even if they have to trave a few miles everything on it works even the lights when the door is open lighting up the back so some socker mom can take their children to school ot if it's a camper just wanting to go to the lake for the weekend, this area is new to me so I have to play it by ear on how to go about it, the days are brought together by changes and who knows maybe this will be a change for me. To me change comes either swiftly or very slow depending how He wants things to go but I always have hope that things will be the way he wants them to be. Kansas is an electronic state when it comes to titles for vehicals but if nolean is held against it then you can have the open title to sell it to other people no matter what state they live in. Thursday and I will check and see how thee kids did yesterday at the church, it's not always the same there. One time it might be a total mess and then other times not so much, because they know that if they help to pick up things I don't have to do as much but still it's my job and I do it well. Before the months seamed to fly by but now for some reason they have slowed down or I don't pay as close attention to them as before, strange how that works sometimes but still we make it through each month with no problem except for the usual things that bother people. I don't know when the thriift store will open again but I'm sure they will let me know when it's my time to work. I feel that when they do open we should have a flood of people that havent been able to get in there for sometime. The Mexicans havent been in since the closeing and they will need shirts and pance as their jobs are very demanding and their clothes ware out fast. They work for the people that have the store on highway 36 and the mellons are of many kinds some I havent even seen before they look like must millons and some with warts on them for which I don't know their names goards I guess, last night an old lady called to find out about the van wanting something for a women with three children. It seams the women takes care of her husband in an old folks home and she must want to do something nice for her as her car is old with no air and it gets hotter then hell out during summer, I told her that the air would have to be charged but I didn't think she was listening to me part of getting old I guess she said she would call back sometine to see if it worked. From what I can tell there must not be too many vehicles out there that would suit her purpose I know three kids can me hectic when driving around having to have them in seatbelts, I will go a little further and see if the air works as I don't know the system that well I have never turned on the air in the back to see if it blows cool air but I will try it this afternoon after work at the church. I do know you don't want to have any work done around here as the price of labor is high maybe it would be cheaper in the big city or if the lady knew someone that does that kind of work.

A truck just went by and I love that about Courtland you don't have that busy trafic like in the bigger towns when a car or truck goes by every two minutes, just a peaceful place when everyone looks out for their brothers and sisters, I got up a little late this morning as I had a hard time going back to sleep after the call it seams some even the elderly stay up longer then I do. Maybe trying to hold on to life as long as they can I do know she has to be old having a husband in a nursing home it seams when things get too hard for the wife that's the last resort before they go and be with the lord, and any help is greatly appreciated when they take care of them. There seams to always be a certain person that connects with the elderly and they are the one that are special, they have a certain soul that others don't have the careing side of them is greater then their own needs even with children. I call them the special ones that take care of everyone but them selves or put them selves last in this world, harley has gotton up so now I will take him out side don't like him going in the house and he will if I don't let him out also little brother is up for the day so now my day will begin it's going to be an intresting one seeing what the lord brings to the table. It's strange how things that bothered you last year doesn't today, as a fact most of it isn't remembered, the little things you did as you move forward into a new year they are somehow forgotten to maybe come back later who really knows only the lord knows what we need to travel through this world. O we think we know but really we don't except for the everyday things like food and drink to stay alive on this planet, looking for love has Stacyded me in my time here and I chalk it up to maybe not being ready for that step.

When I have taken things into my own hands befor they always fell apart so now I will give Him the rains and see where he takes me. For surely He couldn't do any worse of a job and maybe even a better one then I have or I'm looking for something that doesn't exist the kind of love that the old folks have the love that will last out the ages, so maybe when I'm old and sick she could take care of me. I think true love has missed me as it's been so long that I now cant remember it, is this truly the way the lord meant for it to be? He knows I want it but it's never been given like most of my life I have to fight tooth and nail for everything I get. But that's something I don't think you should have to fight for, it's something that should be made by a connection. I do know that women my age don't appeal to me for some reason I always look for the younger ones but then I would have to deal with the maturity of them being younger and most are always in a hurry thinking life will pass them by when it won't with my patients I can put up with many things in life but I still wish I had more it's like a calmness comes over me when kids are around and maybe that because I can see things they can't. Like the way their life is headed and weather they will fall or go on to bigger and better things, being older you have lived what they are going to live later down the road and you can guide them but always guide them in the right direction towards the Lord I wish I would have had that direction in childhood but I believe He had better plans for me by having me go through the things I went through to maybe show them that my direction wasn't the right one or was it? I cant say for sure only He knows the answer to that question and He isn't shareing it with me not yet anyway. This morning I got the church cleaned and then got a call from Jan Carolsen asking if I would work on Friday and Saturday of the 20 and the 21st and of course I said yes, also she asked if I was working this Saturday and I said yes if they were going to be there we all pull together in this town of dreams that's my anoligy of it not so many others have the same feelings I have but like they say we are all different and no two are the same. Well the day is comning to an end for me anyway going to bed at five or six at night so I can get up early to have my alone time away from everything my peace of mind , all together different from most folks for they couldn't get up that early and who would want to but me the writer of the morning? The transformation from the old life to this one is very surrel so until Friday morning good night. TGIF A new day to look forward to yesterday they had a meeting at the church so I was glad that I went early yesterday to clean things up, our garage sale is going to be a good one and I work from eleven till one on those two days. I never did hear back from the old women so I can mark that one off. I still have a few weeks of it runing in the paper and then on the 20th it comes out in the red book, I still want to see if I can put the van down at thee insurance company so maybe it would sell there you might say I'm trying to cover my bases like a good sales man would. It's next week that we have the garage sale so I hope we make a lot of money for the church to keep helping other as they need it.

My self I have never fully understood the workings of that part of the church and I have a feeling it would be hard for me to grasp, even if I could put the van in front of the church more people would be able to look at it and then it might sell better. Last year people came from all around even the little towns from around the Courtland area and as we know the more people the better chance of selling it, it would be nice to one day to open a car dealer ship and make a good living at it. As for those who are not serious about buying I wish they would stay away it's better to have interested people then those who just want to drive it around, I never knew that selling things would be so hard but the president has the country fighting to just stay alive. Once the country was booming and now it's all you can do to feed your family good thing he will be out of office in acouple of years then maybe things will get better we hope! My land it's supposed to be not so hot today with temps in the 80's or low 90's a far cry from the triple digits we have been having so I believe fall is about here when we will be able to wake up to cool mornings and not run the Air-Conditioning as much as we did during Summer one bill will go down and another will go up as we use the heat once again. I have to say that the year has been a good one with no miss haps or anyone getting sick for truly the lord hass watched out for us there. I try to understand why people look at the out side of people and then I realize that only love lets you look past the beauty that on the outside, take my daughter for instence her husband isn't the good looking man he used to be when they were kids but still through it all she still loves him even though he is much bigger then he used to be. I believe love lets you see past the superficial out side of beauty and into what inside, but it takes love for this to happen the getting to know a person from what you see inside of them. But if the love isn't there then you may never see that inter beauty it stays hidden from the other person, superficial looks are not that important but they do bring a connection or draw you to the other person at first.

Then after years of being together they seam to not matter as much as they did in the beginning, like with all things age brings a lack of the beauty that they once saw in the beginning and life goes on between the two of you as you grow older together. A love that test the sands of time can bring a togetherness that will last through the ages, and some get so close that they can read each others minds or finish scenteces strange but o so true, the months that once flew by have changed to weeks but even they have slowed down to every two or three days. It's Friday the 13th of September and I'm supposed to have a good day according to my physic charts but I belivev more in God then it those people they seam to always want money out of you to read what the stars have in store for us. This I should be abe to get from the father and not have to communicate with them, so many have told me different stories and one is that I draw my strength from heaven and not the stars by passing the way others get their readings. For surely it wasn't the start that saved me so long ago but the hand of God the father that plucked me out of the pit and brought me back to this place we call earth, although I wanted to stay in the other demention he wanted me to learn all the things I missed as a child. The learning to trust other and to be a part of something bigger then my self, will I learn all that I need too know ? I guess only he has that answer but I have to say that I'm on the right track. Today I have a few thing to do and one is to wash the windows coming into the Church and sweep the carpet in the walk way Saturday and it's a little nippy out side before to long we might have to turn on the heat to take the chill off this morning it's only supposed to be in the 50's and that quite a change from the 70's that it has been. As for summer it's over. And now the colder weather will be coming our way mild at first but then colder then hell, I really don't care for winter but when you live here it's to be expected so you better get ready for it most of our day during winter are spent inside staying warm like they did back in the 1800 except we have an advantage gas heat which they didn't have back then. My it must of been hard going out and getting wood to heat your place but for thhe ones that were better off they coal and oil to burn although my house was built in 1919 it didn't see those hard times except for maybe when they couldn't pay the electric or gas bill there are many that cant do that even today so they move away and start over somewhere else hoping to have it easier, if you cant pay your bills then you wont be able to make it here not in this little town and I know other towns are much worse off then here as the price of things keep rising my land they even tax food here to where Nebraska never did. It just goes to show that each state is different and they have their own ways of doing things, my storie is about my life after addiction and how you can make it if you really try but most of what's needed is money to pay bills so you can stay where you want to be. I have tried to find a women on line but it seams sinceless to try and connect with someone so far away also I have found that some people know me by my limp just a scare from a life passed sort of a reminder that things can go south in a hurry if your not careful. I checked out my credit score and found out that it's fair to good just a few more steps and it will be in the black you might say.

The world sees us by numbers and the higher the number the better your credit is, as for my self I don't see things that way I only see the good things in life and hope for the best in everything I do. Such a different way then others think as we move forward into another part of the year, I'm hoping to a change in this life and from what I see it might be coming. Later I will watch rifleman and see how they tamed the west farming was a big part of things and it's still the same today just different. Alcoholics are taken advantage of when they are under the bottle others use them and will even pay them with booze not wanting to have them get sober from the old days even they take advantage blaming them for all their problems. Being at your lowest point in ife lets you see sometimes how they take advantage of the fact that they have fallen that far like being put into a box with a label. Sunday and yesterday I worked with one of the ladies from church she is the one who takes care of my pay checks and we talked about many things but it was fun talking to her and then before we knew it the two hours was gone. And we headed home for the day, also we went and got pizza for supper and had to stop at the dollar store to get pop and smokes like we really need them right the whole day was intresting but still getting back home was the greatest feeling the knowing that you are where you need to be. This morning I have to go and clean the toilets after putting in some cleaner yesterday so they could soak, my move ments are not very good right now still kind of a sleep from a cold pill I took last night and I wont take another one that's for sure making me feel rum dumb and that's not good when I first get up it's like I'm waking from another world and it takes time to come out of that world I would almost give anything to go back to sleep but that cant happen as it takes me too long to wake back up just now my eyes are starting to become open and if it wasn't for the coffee I don't know that they would.

I may be strange to some people but it's just the way I am , talking about God in the many ways I do but my approach is different from others, just the other day a lady came through from a another state and said she wouldn't mind living here. Many people will flock from the big cities to get away from the bad things that go on there this writer even sent a resamay to the paper in hope for maybe getting a job in our small town. If most people are smart they will set up a job before moving here that way they coud have security and not end up in a place like assisted living, Courtland needs to grow but there isn't enough houses for some that might want to come back growth is important in any town if they are going to survive and the houses are very few to pick from O you have the elderly that will one day end up in long turm care and then their homes will be for sale but that could be a long ways away as no one wants to leave the home they had built for them selves. Monday and it the beginning of a new week and I wonder what will happen the garage sale is this Friday and Saturday and maybe I can sell some thingss there and then of course we have the biscuits and gravey supper with all the trimings, not sure where they will have it this year but it will be either at the Church or school and there wouldn't be any other better place to have it. I'm hoping it will be at the church after services I havent been at the station lately because the gas pumps havent been working right yesterday I had to drive eight miles to get gas for the lawn mower and I shouldn't have to do that the pumps are old well one anyway and they will have to get a new one someday when they get tired of fixing it. At work on Saturday the lady I worked with told me that they don't even have hard paythed roads to her town of formoso a town not to far from here and if they get a flash flood sometimes that cant get in or out of town it seams some of the towns are falling apart from age as the buildings are now gone some stood a 100 years but weather and miss management has left them in reunions. These days it's harder to wake up as my body is showing it's age but still I move forward and I will do so until I cant walk again, I believe I have always knows it wouldn't last for ever but it's coming faster then I thought so I try and put it out of my mind and let it be what can a person say as long as they gave it their best, my hands and mind still work fairly good so I will ware them out in time leaving nothing left and then what will be will be only God knows whats in store for me I was amazed at how cold it got yesterday never getting over the hight 50's and the rain fell most of the day, such a great time to catch a cold but that Goodness I didn't get one it's the change in the seasons that bring on these things and it 's only around fall.

Tuesday and it's hard to wake up I saw Mark yesterday and forgot to aske if I could pit the van at his pops insurance company so I will have to do that in the next couple of days before the garage sale in town don't really know what he will say but it's worth a shot. Yesterday on border wars they busted a simi full od drugs amounting to over one and a half million dollars another one off the streets spreading that poisen to the children of the United States and it was all in Marijuana being shipped from Mexico one of the drug capitals of the world. It's only 3:15 Am and I'm still having a hard time motivating with a chill in the air so I know it's cold out side should turn on the heat for a while to warm things upand I did don't like the cold like I did when I was young back then it was easy but now not so much now days with this old body, Mark at the hub said to keep the letters coming so one of these days I will write another one and tell a little bit about the story of how I quit. It's done I wrote the story and now I will wait for a reply from Mark or see it in the paper. Wednesday knowing when to stop fooling around on the computer with women yesterday I ws talking to a few women and it was like it became addiictive I wish my stories could go so well and easy, at first it made me feel like a kid again but then it set in that it's other peoples lives that I'm giving hope to hope for love hope for romance but in my world it doesn't exist. One nice women from the Phillipines really likes me but how can this be when miles of ocean separate us? I guess my words give her hope that love still exists and she will do almost anything to find it, I really didn't know the poer of my words until then. She was telling me she is a made and that she is poor so I tol her that we are all poor but rich in love, now how do you break off that connection just erase them like they were never there or do you go on with the game as I put it what a delima first no women and now too many you can talk until your blue in the face but it doesn't sseam to matter to them the lonely ones that don't have anyone but their computers. I never knew I could reach across the ocean and talk to someone who is as lonely as I am.

But there out there trying to find that true love so they canm be happy, to what extent will they go to bring that special gift of love to them selves? Is it a drrive for sex or just someone to talk to who really knows but this could corrupt my mind if I let it. With me I have to watch my words because they can cut like a knife and you don't want to hurt anyone. It's hump day and they are having a garage sale in Belleville at the storage sheds so maye we might check them out and see what they have well we went and things were too high so we came back home but on the way we stopped ay Panther paws. And they said we could park the van up there for a couple of days tosee if it sells so we will try that and see what happens. It's Thursday sso we need to get some things ready for the garage sale on Friday and Saturday, Kansas is the only place that I have seen such a big one like this so maybe things will go better in the selling of the van. As for my time trying to meet women on the computer it was a bust wasting my time and screwing up my computer so now that's not an option any longer I will just stay to my self for the time being and hope someone from around here will come along I have never been a people person not like others they can go on and talk like it's nothing but ny thoughts come into play before I speek, not wanting to say the wrong thing . I have others wanting to chat witth me on the net but I don't want to take that change of my computer crashing like it did before what's a person to do life along isn't bad but I feel that I am missing something important in life that connection between two adults yes sex and all that goes with it, this kind of thing is just human nature and it's not to be fought. Other wise you rob your self of something. Friday the 20th bearley by an hour and I hope for a good weekend if thigs go right, the mornings are the hardest for me trying to get my mind worling from being in a dark cloud sleeping all night. Yesterday I got a new razor from a garage sale and it only cost five bucks just like brand new little brotheer got one a while back and it was the same thing for $30.00 so it was a great savings on my part. I'm sure there are many more deals out there but things will have to wait until I sell the van so I can have some money. I can never tell when something is going to happen but I do ask for God's help in a lot of things like with the van. I have seen other vans around and they cant compare to the beauty of this one all looking like crap and falling apart, GMC Has always made a good product and they should last the test of time so I hope that He answers mmy prayers and it sells. It would be great for a young family with about five kids if it sells then I will be back on my feet once again foor a time anyway, I have to work at the church around 11:00 this morning until 1:00 and then I'm free for the day until the garage sale is over tomorrow afternoon, it's strange writing about your life because so many things happen that might not be important at the time but put together with other things that happen and you have a story a story about someones life.

As each day brings us to a new chapter of life we see the many things that happen your selves and others trying to make it in a world so life can be good but sometimes it's hard and others not so hard hoping for that break that will let you live in peace and harmony. It says in the good book that God wont bring you to a place where he won't sustain you and I have to believe that, but the road can be a bumpy one if your not careful and at times you can fall on your face. As He said my grace is ssuffient for you and this I have to believe, I had to tare down the old walls that were built when I was in that dark place and I have done that for the most part and not I have to erect something new maybe like putting out a welcome mat in front of my door saying all welcome in this house. Later I will see if anything needs done at the church before anyone gets there that way it will all be ready for the day, getting things ready will be the hardest part. It's going on 3:00 in the morning and still I'm barely awake it's going to be a long day for this old fart, as for others they are still a sleep all snuggled in their beds and they don't know what's happening right now. The internet thing seams to be a phase that I go through once every few years trying to find something close to love but it never happens it's like it walks right by me, but then maybe it's not time yet. Why things happen the way they do I don't have a clue but I have to trust that God knows what he is doing as sometimes my doing is blured by things of this world and I get confused. Living this life is a learning process with it's up's and downs and many times my downs out weigh my up's if you know what I mean but then no one ever said life would be easy.

How did my parents do it? For surely their whole life wasn't struggling or if it was I didn't see it in the younger years, of course a child wouldn't with such a simple mind of wanting to play all the time parents protect their children from such things as the destruction of this world but does it help when they do finely see whats happening? It's like the mind gets bombarded by everything rushing in at once and I could never separate the two. On Friday I got a call from someone passing through that could be intrestd in the van but for the life of me I don't know where 613 area code is he ssdounded excited and said he would call back, on there travels of garage saleing people come from as far as florida and California and I know they could get good money for it there and surfer would love to have it or a Mexican, parking it on the hill must have been a good deal. As with most things I asked for God's assistence last night to get it sold and now maybe it will happen. I'm finding new ways of making a living although I'm a little slow at it but still things will look up in time, I know not many of those vans are left in the united states so I should get what I want I have two things going for me these days and I hope they both take off on the road to success so my life can be whole with things I would like to do. It's funny in a way one person making a living off another like the old man in the scooter so much talent but yet age and bad health got to him and he had to let it all go, I saw things he made that just boggled the mind working tractors made of wood and he wanted a good price for them $100.00 not to big a price to pay for someones talent to bad he couldn't of taught one of his kids the traid or maybe they just didn't have the passion for it. The sands of time make us all old so we better enjoy life while we can he seamed to be in his late 70's or maybe even early 80's and he said life is cruel but what he meant by that I cant really say but he did say they put him away for a couple of years. It's Saturday morning and I couldn't sleep maybe by all the excitement or just being restless who can say at this pointmy day are strange any how. For each one is different and I never know whats going to happen next, but through the sands of time I know I will survive for a time yet any how. As for my kids I love them dearly but I cant burden them with my problems they have their own lives to live O they might get mad at me sometimes but that's something they will over come as the years pass and I'm gone from this world you see they don't see the world the way I do and for that I'm glad but also it's been a long day traveling to se the sights bbut now th day has come to an end, I was a sleep an someone called about the van from North Platt waking me up and not getting back to sleep is almost impossible so I moved my computer into my room that way I can really be along don't know if I put the coffee on but I sure hope so that way I don't have to do it in the morning. A couple of ladies came by the church this afternoon and wantwed my card so they can get a holdof me later for my product and I hope they call God sure works in strange ways when I'm in my own element I feel safest withnoone around but my friends.

I know it's the lables thaat drew the ladies to my product as hey read all about them and now I'm hoping for the best as I waight for their reply, never would of guessed they were from Nebraska but they were just a few miles down the road about 70 miles to be exact, who knows what will become out of this. Thank you father for their visit good night if I can get back to sleep. Sunday and the morning seams sstrange not being out of my room yet and that way my peace has returned, I didn't expect a call yesterday ior last night but I took it in hope that someone would connect with the van. Our garage sale endsed yesterday and I don't know the numbers of the cash it brought in but that's ok they know, my self I made a few bucks on my product and now the word is gettinng out even in Nebraska. The difference is that my goods tast good and the others well they tast like crap, I wish I wouldn't of got a hold of those people on the internet as theey never leave me alone these days the young ones want to taalk all the time and I'm just not a talker when it comes to personal things but I did find one women from across the sea that really seams to like me and we talk from time to time I cant spell her name but it's something like neaih 46 years of age with two girls that look like they are about grown should check on her it's probable afternoon there well that's done so now the day can go on smoothly getting the business cards was oone of the best things I had done thus far and although I havent given many out it still gets me out there.

Sunday you would think you could rest but with me it just doesn't happen being up early really takes a toal on a person being awake 18 hours a day only leaving 6 hours to sleep if that no wonder I have bags under my eyes all the time pushing my self too hard but who knows in the long run it might pay off no one has made a living without hard work and my life isn't any dfferent but hey you only live once right? The sound of silenceis priceless except for the things that race through your mind that you really don't understand it's the corner stone of life to make a living and build that impire that you want to have but mine would be different then most not infused by drugs and crap like that just harrd work'if you had the capital you could build this company very big but jous one person couldn't do it. Three maybe but not one, loosing intrest is my biggest problem not having the patientss to keep at it for very long and I have to say that's my fault and I have no excuses except that I'm me and maybe that's a part of my make up who really knows but God He created this person this one of a kind what ever I supposed to be. In an hour I have to check on things at the church so this will be the last page in this chapter it's already one page over the limit I set. Life is funny in many ways and you never know who you might meet weather a stranger or some ass hole that just doesn't talk any since or at least you cant understand where they are coming from, two different worlds two different people both on different journeys going somewhere in this life grace and peace be with you father on this day show me what I'm supposed to do' yesterday as I watched the people from aroung the country come through our little town many of them loaded up their trucks and trailers full of stuff and now today they are gone back to where they live it was like a flock of geeas traceling south for the winter and they wont be back

CHAPTER 16

Until next year. September 23rd and the van is gone to Wisconsin where it will make it's new home didn't quite get what i8 wanted but it was close enough. The guys were very polite as one was taking his kid to collage out west and I told them that I hoped they had a safe trip' it seams you meet all kinds of people in this world and they had a good personality. At5 first I thought they were from Nebraska but they weren't and now the search goes on for another vehicle to flip. They were real happy with what they got so I'm happy also it built things back up to where they needed to be. My next adventure will be to travel and try to sell some of my product around here sort of like having two hobbies, I know my friends worry about me not being in good health but I will keep pushing forward until that day comes. To me in this life you have to make your own way and if you cant do it them you just might not make it, in a way it's like I'm chasing a dream and once I have it I won't let go living poor all your life you never get to see the better things in life well now it's my turn today I will make a few phone calls and have it taken out of the news paper's and off the television that way I can use them again in the future. Right now God has answered my prayers and it will be up to me to keep things going as long as this body holds out. God is good to those when they do good things with their lives I would never change a thing about coming here to God's country. As long as you can sustain your self then you have it made in the land of the free, I gave randy a little money so he will be kept happy and really it wasn't any sweat off of me. My land it's only 2:39 in the morning and I have to try and get my meds filled today so I don't have to suffer and longer.

When your body has been through what mine has you can hope for that miracle of walking without pain but that one that might not ever come so we do our best to survive in a world that will one day take us but I hope it isn't for a long time. I'm grateful for the time he has let me learn about the many things that I would of other wised missed should I have stayed there with him so long ago, I guess we are supposed to suffer sometimes so we will know the good times when they come. My days will be full but my main jobs will be with the church it sustains me when things are difficult to me the vehicles made in the 80's and back are the best made so I wont be buying anything new that's for sure, but they also have to be in good shape to make the buyer happy do want anyone unhappy as I wouldn't want to be that way. To me the road to life is what you put into it and if you do a good job then things work out it all falls apart through the sands of time people have been making money and now it just might be my turn, buy cheap and sell high after a little work is done on them and if you can give them a good deal to keep them coming back. These mornings I don't have the power I used to have because of the pain but still I push on and if I break then t will be a time to rest a while. This time in the morning is great for me, a time when I can put my thoughts together and see how the day goes no people clouding up your mind with their morning pull shit and how bad they have it for one day I will tower above many and help them in the process it's the little people that need the help not the fat cats that have lived their lives in luxury and have now fallen off that mountain they stood on long ago.

In Jesus time he helped those with less then others and I shell do the same God willing' I never could understand the United States they used to tell people to give up your poor hurting and your crippled but now days they want to take that away, a word given a word broken given by one and broke by another this is what some call change throwing everything our fore fathers wrote into a way of life. They took God and prayer out of the schools and replaced it will guns and disturbed kids one hell of a change and it's not for the better back when I was a child you never heard of guns in schools or around them. Meth is a life stealer it destroys the soul and spirit and it will never let you go, but there is always hope for those who try to take their lives back, and for those who cant do it then they will spend many if not all their lives lost in the place they choose . There is no easy way to put it about messing with things like Meth and even Marijuana and other drugs they cause you to loose part of your self. But now growing up and starting at a young age you never know who you are really the soul never develops like it would with a normal child or the spirit for that matter. It's like you go through life not knowing the ability you really have and it cant be shaped the way He intended, not until that part of your life is changed and brought back to the way He meant for you to learn., some days you could find your self feeling sharper then the average bear and then other days it's all you can do to bring your self out of the cave you built for your self, like with the bear winters are spent a sleep in an illusion of how things should be and after years of doing that you never want to leave that cave or your home. You become someone your not a mirror image of a human being. O you walk and talk but it's not the same and most of your memories are those of a child because your mind never did get to catch up with your body. When these things take the place being normal your not, normal rational reasoning is something that never develops until later if you decide to change that part that was damaged, and a lack of schooling could really hurt the out look on your life. Sure I tried to go to school but the attention span wasn't there cut short by the damage that was done and patients was replaced by quick anger when you couldn't figure something out so you would quit and give up not wanting to deal with things like anger. To me I didn't like to be angry because it took so much away and it's something that lets others see a part of you that really doesn't exist or you don't want it to exist, because it feels bad. I wanted to be not what I was but something better, and that wasn't allowed to happen until I grew up after my death, but even then patients came slow and you earned them they weren't given like grace is. When I went to work for the Church my patients had started but I had to work along so I could work on my self with God's help, it was only through His help that I over came many things and learned at my own speed. Recalling first and second grade I must of has ADHD Because I couldn't sit still long and my mind wouldn't do what I tried to get it to do, so I would just right down anything so I would be done when the other kids were. Although I knew it would give me a failing grade it didn't really matter because it stopped the other kids from making fun of me by being slow.

Regrets yes I have them but I survived even with that handy-cap and went on to learn things less then I was capable of. Through the sands of time many chances were there but I couldn't quite grab hold of them lacking self confidence in my self.

Although many times I came close to death it wasn't God's plan for me to stop at that particular time in life, and when my body shut down it wasn't his plan to let it end there either. Will time come to a close for me? For this I'm sure but it wont be until He feels I'm ready, I have no say in the matter and He has many more things for me to do yet. Although my job is not as hard as it once was when I was younger it's still important as I have the ability now that I never had back then and that was something God has done in my life from mussels to mind one shrinks while the other grows a creating process that allows what was once lost to bloom like the flower that once was a seed, patients is something that develops even a seed needs to grow and without water it dies and never comes back. But catch it before it's death and give it living water then it comes back more beautiful then the mind can imagine, as for mistakes we will all make them but it's the learning that brings us back to life, a dream set into motion can live but along the way we learn by what we do wrong and what we do right. And if it's meant to be then God will blow in our direction giving us what we need to make things happen. Wednesday and it's hump day, it's another quiet morning without the birds even singing yet. Last night I watched a show called fishes it's a show about some people falling in love over the internet and yes I know sounds impossible but it happens one guy had beetling with a girl for 7 years since the age of 12 years old and finely wanted to meet her, but things weren't what they seamed as she went through some hard times but he had always been there for her emotionally.

The two guys that bring people together found out their stories and they met for the first time although the guy got hurt a little they stayed friends and their lives went on hoping that one day they might find them selves together. She had problems with life and her friend helped emotionally always being there for her even after she hurt him, the thing they call love can happen over the net by the words we choose to use when we connect with others, and I can relate to how they must have felt as I once felt the same way about Margret when we first met many years ago. As many say love is blind so I guess your appearance doesn't matter at the time when two hearts meet through words, anyway we had met after a while but it didn't work out being so different from each other but the giddy feeling felt great while it lasted. But then it died almost as fast as it appeared. Not knowing someone in person you miss the things that probably will annoy you later down the road of life, like he thought she was thin but in real life she was a little heavy which seamed to not matter much to him but it shows that the mind doesn't always see some things that are right in front of our face. As the internet still is growing some put on pictures of people they are not, and that really hurts some relationships thinking you fell in love with one person and it wasn't them at all. It happens every day as some are not proud of how they look and think the other wouldn't like them if they weren't good looking or pretty, after Margret I swore to never find another that way but I'm now talking with Kerrie T and she seams like a nice women. She has a child of around 9 years of age John or Jake not sure which is his name but maybe one day I will talk with him also to see how he has grown up, with manners and such. Kerrie seams to love the lord so that's something we have in common, and she seams to care about me in her own way as we are all different. I can tell she could be a jealous as many are, and the age difference I don't know about but we will wait and see what happens later. She wants to talk or chat at lunch time to maybe find out more about me so we will see how that goes when the time comes, I have seen others from around here have girlfriends or wife's that are different from them meaning they might be mail order brides or girl friends so it's something that happens. I can hear the train coming into town as the whistle blows from far away, they had the tracks closed for a couple of days a week ago but it's now open once again to let the cargo come through. It's getting close as I hear the wheels on the tracks and the big motors running like all get out, Randy was up early again this morning but now I can hear him snoreing once again trying to get more sleep before the day starts. I can tell that Kerrie is very young as she acts like a 29 year old women very excitable at that age and they want what they want, not being able to see any of the future because they are so full of life. I Wish I had the vigger a young person has but also I wouldn't want that at my age being laid back has let me get used to being my self, I know the energy difference would be kind of hard to deal with as women like to always be doing something and this life is for the laid back person like my self. But you never know what God has in mind for two people, maybe He will send me someone to watch out for and take care of me when I'm old and gray.

24 years difference we would be in different places and time in our lives, maybe she is looking for stability that an older man can give her a person that wouldn't wonder like the young ones do. Always looking for that better women or so they think' as I to was once that way thinking the grass is greener on the other side of the fence. And finding out that it was the same or even worse then what I had, so then you have to sleep in the bed you made for your self and a lot of times you don't like where you ended up. Life is new to me living it the right way for the first time without the baggage that comes with a women, but then sometimes the women can help you grow in areas that have been neglected for many years. Letting my self be open to this kind of thing could change me in many ways and help me to learn to love once more and that's something I have been asking for, but how do I know it's the right one? I just asked Him to give me a sign so we will wait and see what happens. In the past when I asked for a sign he gave it gladly letting me see that He is still right by my side but it never happens right away it always takes time unless He feels something is wrong and it can hurt me, for which at that time He will step in and take over to destroy or teach the other person a lesson. With me I get angry when I'm pushed into a corner and that's something I don't like. But also I don't like hurting other peoples feelings either but sometimes it has to be done if they don't listen to the words I have to say. Thursday and the train came through last night as I was getting into bed even after a nice day the town is peaceful as it usually is and this morning is the same so peaceful. Later I will go and clean the church so everything is ready for Sunday when we have service in the over flow room where we meet and have snacks, it's too bad that I couldn't get

Randy to come to church but like it says you don't want to push to hard and scare them off.

My land' he has to see the good things that are happening in our lives and he has to know that the things come from God, I'm hoping in time he will see the good things He brings to us even more. They are things that can't be explained away by our mortal ways, the train is coming through again so it wont be long until many of my friends wake up and get ready to start the day. It's the only time when the noise is louder but once it's gone then things turn back to being peaceful, I finely got a text from Tara but still I have no idea of where it might lead we will just have to wait and see. Gorge had another heart attach but they caught it in time two of them in less then two years, they said they messed up when he had the first one. In my book he should of never went back to drinking but to tell someone that is like talking to a wall as in many ways he is like his father stubborn and full of thinking he knows best about his health which he doesn't. that's two knocks on his door will he open it or just go on the way he is? And find him self at that door all alone one of these times, I pray for my friends and the others that are fighting health problems hoping that He will heal them while they still have sometime here on this planet. I didn't sleep very good last night but I was able to fall back to sleep pretty easy after focusing on It, my supplies are somewhat full right now so I can take some time to do other thing like mow my lawn sometime this morning. I think I only have about two more times to cut it before the fall will be at it's end, and then winter will set in an we will spend a lot of time inside away from the cold that will freeze everything. I made a couple of dollars as I went and got a pop at the station yesterday I like buying them there as it gives me change to fill my Budweiser bottle and it's big could hold many pounds of my favorite things. I can hear Randy in the other room as he talks in his sleep strange how he does that but it's a part of his life and I have learned to except It. I have many things to do but I will do them at my own speed so not to ware me out before the day ends, I bought a Mr. Eraser so I can get the marks off the floor at the church, those black souls really make a mess and this weekend many more people will be in church singing and eating just enjoying them selves as the pastor gives her sermon to us the people. Tara what a nice name this women has and I hope we can become friends first and then maybe something more later as we explore each other in writing back and forth to see if we match I won't expect too much out of this at first but I will hope that maybe we can make a connection and be good friends. I have always wanted someone a little younger so I can watch their energy at their age and see how different it is from mine, I'm laid back and younger people are not maybe the combination will be a good thing you can't really tell until you connect physically. So we will see what happens down the road her picture is very nice and she looks serious about what she writes about, wanting a man that is close to God and answers to Him instead of man.

The month is about over and then October will come in with a force all the trees will turn red and amber as the leaves fall to the ground and turn into fertilizer for the grass. That must be what keeps my lawn so nice that and mowing it, showing others that I'm proud of me place here in my town of dreams. Sometimes

I get stuck on what to say to a women but if it's right then the words should fall like the leaves off the trees, I know that I sweep Margret off her feet back in the day just with the words God gave me will it happen again? That's a thought, but I will hope for a better ending this time I hope she has a good heart one that can sustain me the way I need to be a partner to go through life with holding hands and maybe kissing a little here and a little there. As for Children I don't know about that if she has them then that's fine but to start a family at my age would be hard, my land' by the time they are ready for school I would be in my late 60's or early 70's but many have had children late in life some even in their 80's how did they do it? Maybe have a maid to help out! that's funny. They did have them though in their house holds and one even had a child for one of them. As I tried to get to know Tara I suddenly changed my mind as it's not proper to ask others for money before they even meet you, but I should of expected it with the way the world is today. So that's another person I will chalk off of getting to know her world is way to different from mine. I got a call from a publishing Co. And they want to publish my book and I'm going a head with it because it's God's plan that I do, I never realized that this could be my dream starting to unfold as I have held on to it for far too long. It's my testimony given by God so the rest of the world can read about my life, the good times and the bad but through it all I am still here fighting for what I feel is right.

All the pain and sorrow has diminished as the years have passed but still some of the memories are there. Not as strong as they used to be but like the death of a loved one they are stored somewhere in my mind, for God Him self showed me that life was worth living and I live today through His love and understanding. Friday as I slept I had dreams but for the life of me I couldn't put them together, as I have read many things about our father in heaven I was stuck on something that kept running through my mind and that is that God won't put you where he can't sustain you, sort of like his grace I guess as he says that His grace is sufficient for us His people. It's early but it's the same, another day that he has given us. The guy I talked to yesterday really wants to put my book together so the world can read it getting it on the new reading devices would be another step forward and I would own the rights to it all, and then maybe I could pull my self out of poverty. Although I have had a taste of having enough I cant let it destroy the person I am the one who came from that dark place so many years ago. The one who choose to follow our Lord the best way I know how, the changes in my life are many and each change is different in a way from just little things to the things that sustain me in this life. Moving forward is scary but I feel He is with me in this step that I take by allowing me to feel many things like excitement and being over whelmed, I will know later if things are going to pan out as I take a step at a time into this new world even the guy said I already have followers as my internet people have reached many thousands, this alone will open up many people to follow my life of miracles. Being afraid is normal when you let you're self go into new territory, and it will take time for me to adjust to people knowing who I am. Personally I like my peace and I will have it here in my town of dreams where I now live no people will enter my life without my approval first as I have seen many writers seclude them selves because of the publicity my seclusion has been of my own doing not wanting to have people ask to many questions about my way of living as I feel it's none of their business what is happening to me today except for what I have to say each day in my writings I guess you could call it a journal of how things have changed through the years, from the darkest moments to the brightest of days when I feel Jesus walking right beside me. Still today I have no anger in me for what took place from the crying on some days to the moments when I felt blessed to be able to over come the curse of addiction, my land' the learning experience was a great step towards becoming a new me, the one I didn't know and that I had to release from the bondages that kept him in the back corners of my mind. That shy child that never got to grow up as the other ran things, we all must have a double inside of us and mine had to be given a chance to live as he quit growing when the other came out at childhood. Imagine living in the shadow's and not realizing you were even there until you had to fight to stay alive, they could of both died that day but the child was stronger then the one that almost killed them both. Each month I look forward to breaking bread with my family as it's a reminder of what He did for us so long ago the giving of life so we could live and the instructions of how we can live a great life. I have been communicating with a women from Mexico City and although she doesn't know much English we understand each other through tag's that are on the sight, she is or seams to be a wonderful women.

The others are just out to get what they can get and to me it's something I don't care for, Silvia seams to be a quiet person like my self and we send little messages back and forth. I don't feel pressure when we communicate and that a good thing for me, she also believes in God our Lord. I can tell she has traveled to many places seeing her pictures of different counrties and they are beautiful, places I have never been or will I probably ever see but who knows maybe in the future. I was shocked when I got a call from someone the other day and it almost sounded like they were from another country but our connection was bad and we got cut off strange, I havent heard the train this morning so it's probably late and I have to go to work for a bit 5:00 Am comes faster then before for some strange reason and now everyone is up. O wait' the train was late but I can hear it coming about 10 miles off so it will be here in a while, today we go and look at a van to see what it sells for at the auction who knows what will happen as the day moves forward. Well I looked at the van and it's not worth much so I might have to let someone else get it if the price is too high, as I think about my testimonial I'm getting that feeling that everyone would know who I am as for my personal life I wouldn't have one any longer but I know that the story has to get out there like many have said. But I don't listen to people only Him the one that brought me this far, as like the storm that shot through last night Harley barked like all get out' and then the screen door flew open and I had to shut it. Don't know how many times it will take that much abuse but it still stands like the strong peace of metal it is, my land the wind must have been blowing 50 miles an hour. And I'm sure there are some limbs down in the yard we will only see when it gets light out.

I had gotten up about five times during the night and each time I was able to go back to sleep thank God' many writers have written fairly good books that didn't make them any money until their third book and I feel I have three of them in this series of stories. So be next year things should be on track breaking out is a good word for my experiences. Breaking the ties that once banded me from seeing the real world and how it truly is, the storm last night didn't knock out the power and for that I'm glad they raise hell with the electronics in the house and now it's all calm as it moved off to another part of the State or maybe even into Nebraska' spent most of my life there except for the stints in other States which added up to about five years or so. In all the other places I have traveled none of them came close to Courtland as the alcohol had it's hooks in me back then, here in my town of dreams my life is one of being straight without being a sleep alcohol changes us all the quiet person becomes something their not, and the angry people become more angry because of the way their life is. I have never had much of a problem at being angry and maybe that's what helped me to change, anger just adds to the other problems we have and when it can't be controlled is when others get hurt. Anger management is something many people have to get help with as it stands in the way of progress. And it will stop you from moving forward, most of what I had was self inflicted only hurting my self instead of others. So I took all my problems to the lord in hope that He could show me the way turning four letter words into things that could help and not destroy, my direction now is to just keep moving forward and find that special snitch which will bring me even further into the place that I want to be as my life goes on the walk I will take will be closer to God as we have been separated through my early years imagine getting a feeling for him in your younger years and then it's all pulled away and in time you being only human begin to forget. And then that parking lot you used to play in at the Church is replaced by other things. To me it was almost like he had walked away from me but now I know he didn't it was us walking away from him, but the change in the situation was very different going from that to the alcohol it was like I went to sleep changing me the person to someone else. The child had to grow up too fast and didn't get to be a child and maybe that's why I sometimes feel like a child today, especially during winter when I want to play in the snow such a charge sometimes but still I do it by my self. Out there throwing snow balls in the yard and having a good ole time, even the squirrels and rabbits come out to play once in a while such a sight to see God's little pets doing their thing. Last week I saw a squirrel digging up his nuts for some reason, maybe getting his house stocked up for the Winter months who can really say. My yard is full of wall-nuts and I see them taking them somewhere it's so cute to watch as three of four of them run around and climb the trees. Like us in many ways they too have to be ready for when the food runs out as the ground turns to solid ice.

Winters are hard sometimes' but for the last couple of years they have been mild with little snow cold as heck but not as much snow and now they say we are supposed to have a bad one because of the locus that came this year. I never could figure out how they connect these things but they do, and like the weather man they are not always right. We go through this life sometimes messed up but with the help from God we can get back on track, even if we don't know what on track means. Starting over in a new life is hard when you have only known one way to live. Taking all that you thought was right and finding out that it was all wrong you become like a baby learning to crawl, and then learning to pull your self up so you can stand in hope that one day you might walk. Having these things, and then having them taken away is very hard especially when your told that you will never get them back in other words they take your hope away and throw you out in the world and expect you to not make it, I was told many times that I couldn't do something and that just drove me to try harder to prove them wrong sort of like I call it tamatoo and you call it tomato but the fight begins and if I have my way I will win. Missed moments I have had many of them like the moment that your voice was just right but you were in the wrong place for others to notice. Or the moment when the world seamed just right but you had no one to share it with, to me if you could catch those moments then life would be just the way it should be. But seldom we find things the way they should be or the way we would like them to be.

The perfect life when things just fall into place, when I sing at the church my soul is released and it can feel a freedom like no other, no boundries to hold it back as I sing to the one that's most important in my life the one who is all things, even the keeper of my heart and soul. As my spirit takes off sometimes it climbs to the highest point that a spirit can climb or fly, for this feeling I know quite well as I flew when I was in that place so long ago. No body was needed in that place where the spirit dwells but you could see the human form as you watch the other souls waiting just waiting to take that train to where ever. The things that hold us here are released like the catapiller that sheds it's body for a set of wings to sour above the land, they go from something that's ugly to a beautiful insect. Some years you can see the catapiller as it crossed the highway to get to another field but why they do this is beyond me, maybe like us it's just a part of nature to follow a certain path to get to the final destination. I know on numerous times thousands of them were crushed by cars and trucks going by, imagine seeing these little worm like creachers taking a strole across the highway all fuzzy and furry. We didn't loose any crops to them but I think they are born in the fields or pastures around the fields, here in Kansas is the only pace I have ever seen them. Kind of reminded me of tamato worms but they had a horn on them back when I was a child. The day is coming to an end and I didn't get what I wanted at the auction but I did get a few bells like mom used to collect and we had fun gong should do it more offtend just to get to know people, I met a couple of people there and they were nice. One letting me sit by her as most of the seats were filled up, it was the kind of thing I could do every week as I didn't spend much. I wondert if some have made a living from going to these places? I do know it's fun and exciting my land' the toys were flying out of there especially John Deer toys by the box fulls something to think about as we move into the future. The lady told me that she could tell that I wasn't from there and I told her I came from Courtland, there are many things that I missed while growing up but maybe I can find my way to those things as time allows it to happen. I got up at four something this morning and that's ok a little extra sleep never hurt anyone, my land' Randy even beat me in getting up and that's unusual for him on most mornings. I can hear some dogs barking down the street so someone is up very early being Sunday everything has to be set for this fifth Sunday as we sing in the over flow room and have some chow or as some call it brunch, to me the opening of the church on Sunday is important because we have some that have to come through the back door as life has left them disabled like my self but worse off I can still move around and it's hard for some of them. Pastor Kathy is the best pastor I have ever known and she cares for her sheep like the shepard that she is supposed to be, she has been by my side through it all and I'm sure there has been others that could tell a story or two about her kindness. Like the guy that works for the store in Belleville, I don't know why his story has stuck with me but I know that Kathy helped him in some way. It's like she says you have to watch for the ones that might do you wrong and with this guy it was a women that took all that he had.

So like many he had to start over, I don't know why some are that way maybe having to steel to make it through life because they are too lazy to work them selves, women are hard for me to understand as I go through ths life so I feel it's better to leave them alone. Not wanting the drama that comes with a women or wanting it but not having enough trust to bring a relationship into my home, if I let just anyone into my home then no one is special and I like special people the ones that you can trust' the ones you can leave in your house and go to the store. But no one has gained that kind of trust yet except for my little brother, once lead by the wrong people and now has changed to follow the right ones a big change but it took a great lesson before he turned to the honest side of life mistakes made and lessons learned as we go through this life of honesty. To me being honest can be hard sometimes but we seam to come to that fork in the road and make the right disions and it all comes from within by God changing us as people, the other day I saw a girl that use to work at the dollar store and she was here in Courtland at the station just down the road. I hadn't seen her since she quit her job but for some reason she is here, and I think she has the house just a block over the house where the old women passed away after 90 some years. They were asking four fifty a month for the home and I know it was rented just a few weeks a go or it could have been a few months time seams to fly by sometimes with me not knowing why but it does. As we embark on another chapter of my life we will see many more changes take place, as for today it's going to be a great day as my mind wakes up to do the things I need to do the people around here inspire me to keep going.

Even though they cant see it our lives are supposed to be linkd in one fashion or another, it looks like Maggie might not get any better but how can they tell whats on God's mind? I have heard the samething about me but still here I am reluctant to believe that any doctor knows for sure what will take place Miracles happen all the time and at first I didn't think I would be here over 20 years later but only He deturmans that not us His children. Many wrote me off a long time ago and when that brain mantality is set then it's hard to change that in some folks, I have never visited one of the sick and maybe in a way I'm supposed to mayby to show them that all is possible with God. Maggie is only in her 60's and that's far to young but if it's God's plan then he will bring her home where she can celebrate her life and the good things she has done. Funny thing the lord he never forgets but we as people do and some of the things we do forget is the goodness that others have done I recall the first day that I met her in the thrift store, she was quiet but felt the need to let me know who she was. And from that day forward I would always wave at her in passing my lord' I will miss her should that time come, they told me to get ready also but that was something I couldn't except in my spirit and it helped to make me stronger in the long run. Through the years they them selves didn't seam to be like years but just time going by faster then before sometimes a year was like a month and a month like a day and I can't explain why that happened but it did. As for the life of old it seams to fade away like those memories of a lost loved one or spouse, in time they become not as painful but the momories stay with us through out our lives, the good time and the bad but through time only the good remain. Like that smile or something else they did to make a day a little brighter, and we can't ever forget the meals weather good or bad but in my life no one could match my mothers cooking and she passed it on to me. I guess she thought I would be a single peson and needed to know how to cook. Many things have been passed down through the years and taking care of family seamed to be one of them, my relationship with my little brother is like a motherly thing making sure he takes his med's when the time comes. As lord knows he needs help in ddoing that, I tried to get him to keep track but it didn't work he got the scedual all messed up and went into another place his mind can't go there so mine has to do it for him and he is doing well today it's been three of them that have had to have that done but it's ok' with me I have that instinct to be a care giver as I spent most of my life doing it. Imagine changing your own life and careing for someone else at the same time it kind of gives you someone to talk to while traveling from the old world to this one where today I'm happy. Many lessons have been learned through the years and one of them is to always do your best to help when you can for this God's wish for his people to love and care for each other, to maybe try and fix that curse that was put on us all so long ago. It's Monday and the beginning of a new week Normen's son had a child the other day 9 pounds and some ounces my that's a big baby but you could see how proud he was as we asked the childs name he said he heard the size and the name sliped his mind.

New life begins and the old end it's just the way of the world making things new as we move into the future for one day I will be gone and the grand babys will take over. I just hope the world isn't so messed up that they can't fix it. Now the government is shutting down and many will suffer because they can't do their jobs right, the world is in a mess because of them. They spend the peoples money and have wasted so much on things that should of never been put into play, starting wars that should of never been started. One day they will destroy them selves by (GREED) and then wonder why it happene stupid people is why it's goinjg to happen . I see things different from others they see whats in front of them and I see it from a distence far away from Washington DC' as for my self I wouldn't live there for nothing. It's bad enough seeing the destruction from a distence let along seeing it first hand, they try and say that they learn from their mistakes but they never have they do something wrong and then hope that it will go away like a cold or a head ache. No one speaks their mind anymore wait they have never spoke their mind. They just sit back and hope that things will change and that process has never worked, what I don't understand is how come we have people with all this education and they don't use it to change bad things into something good, o you hear about some but (GREED) is the motivator even with saving lives everyone has to have their cut and by the time it gets to the one in need it's all gone or they get a couple of dollars out of millions.

Not a way to run things in my thoughts they use segments of things to generate a fortune and they keep it for them selves, that's part of why poverty has never gotten changed they use it as an excuse that it has to be there. It was there in the beginning so we have to keep it, what a crock of shit pardon the French but it's better then my English. Now they say they need to cut everything to the disabled and elderly what another crock of shit the government needs to quit spending our money like it's water off a ducks back that will make those who are poor better off. I never have liked politics and probably never will, it's Tuesday morning and it's trash day we got the can out yesterday but didn't put out the bags until this morning, as I know the dogs would tear them up during the night and scatter the stuff all over the place. The mornings have been cool and then a little hotter during the day but nothing like the hot days of summer when you would wke up to 70 ande 80 degree weather, as we drove into town yesterday to get Randy's thyroid checked I noticd that the leaves are turning red on the bushes that are on the hill side such a beautiful sight and it lets us know that winter isn't far down the road when the weather will turn mighty cold. After I get things done at the church I will return home and then pay some bills as it's the 1st of the month, some bills I pay early and others you don't dare pay to early as it will mess things up with my system and up until now I have had a good one. The many things that I do to keep me busy is just enough to get by in another two months I will have property tax to pay and that takes a chunk out of the budget that I have set up. I took the big coins I got over to Mark and left them with Peggie to put on his desk so he can figure out where they came from that should be a hoot, I have always liked doing little things for my friends but not many get these gifts for if I got them for everyone then none would be special, sort of like letting people into your home if you let anyone come in then no one is special. I havent seen Richard since Kearney and he quit calling once Randy came to live with me but that's his loss. I know his daughter is doing fine as she is on face book from time to time running for worthy causes like cancer and such, also she has turned out a lot different then she would have should she had known about Rick earlier in her life. Being her uncle I try to say hi from time to time, but they have their own lives to live her and her husband and child. She turned out very beautiful for being Rick's child. In this life we sow our oats you might say and sometimes something comes from that and he got a beautiful child he sould feel blessed. The kids around here run and they have the whole town to run in that in it's self is something great, it's quiet this morning and I haven't heard the train yet. but it's coming' as it does each day at different times you never know the time for sure as it changes with the things that are happening in the world I don't know if they shut down the government this morning or yesterday but they have threatened to do this and it hurts many starving people in the world but I guess to them the poor don't count. Like the slaves in Africa the government doesn't care about them either, the cause of addiction to these things that will kill you is brought on many different ways but mostly by kids seeing it while they grow up. As for a home free of these things most people don't seam to have a need or want for them but the ones that get caught up in it find them selves unable to get away from it as it gets it's hands around them and wont let go. I recall many times wanting to stop but the timtation was too strong when you felt bad all you had ot do is grab for it and what ever was wrong was gone.

Like many before me the thought never got passed the mind, actions is what it takes to over come this curse and of course having the power of God on you're side made a world of difference, as you try to fight off the demons. I always liked having Him in my corner and I know if he wasn't there then I wouldn't be here today sort of like the world if He didn't create it then we wouldn't be here. So many try and disprove the existence of God but every time they try they are the ones that fall short of proveing it. Some tried to prove we came from apes and that fell short, then they tried to prove we came from fish or something out of the Ocean another failure and then those who say space people create us also falls short. These are people who want to prove them selves because they are lost in this world, O not by drugs but in life in general they have to prove that they are better then anyone or anything. And as long as they try to disprove God they will fall short everytime my land' His power towers above all else man isn't smart enough to figure out God's plan for this world, and they waste so much of their short time here not being happy one failure after another but in their mind they are right so there is no changing it. We are vessels for life and when the time is right our father plants the seed that grows in the women to create us, the off spring of our brothers and sisters before us. Trying to draw a line between God and us isn't hard, for He is the love we all feel and He resides in all of us many people go through life hating the world even after they over come their demons and I could never understand this thing they call hate' it takes more energy to hate then to love for love flows freely and hate you really have to work at.

My self I could never understand drama but then I don't have the mind of a women. Many of them must stay awake at night to think of some of the things they do and that's not putting them down, they are just made that way as their mind is always running. Mine would get tired just after a day they want to look pretty well they look pretty, some of them. And others not so much, beauty is in the eye of the beholder and if a magnet draws them to a women then it doesn't really matter whats on the outside. They get skinny and they get fat but through it all the beauty is in the man that loves them, most people fall in love with the spirit and soul but there are those like my self that like pretty things at first and then it grows as time passes and pretty doesn't matter much any longer. You don't get better looking with age it doesn't happen. It's Hump day' or Wednesday whichever, yesterday I ran into some spiders that are making their rounds and I don't believe they are just visiting me as Normen told me they are at his house also I have never seen them so much before and they are making their spider webs in the trees and around the house very strange to me we have always had them but not as big some being the size of quorters and they even get on my car. Should we get a good rain that should wash them down the street and whipe them out or if we get a good freeze that would also work many times they make holes in the groung but this year I havent see to many of them doing that. The political people are fighting so I'm trying to stay away from that, my land they must not have a happy life at all always fussing and fighting between them selves. And now they have closed the parks so no one can get to them to have fun or go camping. We seam to connect with others as we move forward in this life and some are very religious and others not so much, Charles is a funny guy and we get along just fine who would of thought after not seeing each other for 40 years that things would be so good. He had invited me to come down and see him and I hope that one day this will be possible, to see the back hills of Arkansas and go fishing for a morning or a day. I never did ask if he owned his home or not but that doesn't really matter I know that he has been there for so long that grew roots in that land there, I wonder if they too have garage sales in their part of the country as each state is different in some ways. They are still working on the road or down town so I wonder if the thrift store will open today it's been closed for a few weeks now and I'm ready to get back to work idle hands get stale. I have a notion to go and see Sam and see how he is doing haven't talked with him for sometime now and he hasn't said much in Church, I had always thought that he might be a hiper person and it just goes to show how wrong our perseption can be about people we meet out side of the church. He is very calm in many aspects and he does such a good job at watching over his parents for truly his love for them is great! I want to do something for his kindness but it hasn't come to me yet of what to do but I know it will sometime in the future. The mornings are cold and the days are still warm but I know we will wake up to snow on the ground in the coming months, it would be a good time to get a new pair of shoes so I can have them broke in by the time snow fall. that way I wont be falling on my butt sliping and sliding on the ice. As for the town it seams to grow a little at atime maybe by one person every two years but still it's growth in the right direction and it brings people together christen people.

My experience here has allowed me to grow in many directions being able to get along with both the ones that don't go to church and those who do and they both are kind in their own way. I seam to be able to separate the people who say a lot and say nothing, you know them as bull shitters and as for me I guess it's the same way, like a politicion. Thursday morning and I don't feel to good I have pain like no tomorrow in my lower extremitys or my down there stull I don't like to talk about I fell like I'm all plugged up maybe it's time for a salid to see if it might work, we have rain this morning as we can hear it outside with the thunder sometimes. I don't feel bad persay but the pain can drive you nuts the rain is coming down like there is no tomorrow sort of like it did during the flood that lasted 40 days and nights, but the good thing is that my Air and heater isn't leaking like it once did, no more trouble there thank God and of course the guy that put it up there as the day progresses I will go and get the bills paid and then Go to work at the church yesterday was bible school so I know there is a mess and I have the honor of cleaning after they learn about the Lord. I find my self distracted sometimes by the internet but the distraction is short lived as I get tired of talking to some people that I meet on there, Charles seams to be the only one that communicates about God but I find some of what he talks about amusing. As I'm still learning new things each day, I don't know truly how long I could be around him but I feel a calmness about our talks when we do speek about our father in heaven. For a person to remember what you were like as a child and then to see you 40 years later and notice the change towards God is remarkable.

It shows that change is possible even after that long of a time, the calmness which resides in you is shared by many even the ones you have only known for a short while. And they too can see the change in you during those few years or so, it's like growing up at first your scared but then overtime you grow on them as they grow on you. And the bridge is crossd when you meet in the middle of that bridge hands are stretched out in love to greet one another, for the love I feel for my brothers and sisters is genuine not fake and they too feel the same way. I can tell if someone is having a good day as they will wave in passing and I love to be able to do that but then with others they kind of shrug off your wave if their day isn't going too well but hey that's ok' we all have days that we don't want to bond with folks in any manner so we go on our way and hope they have a better day later. As for the absents of love between a women and a man I believe if you are still learning about the new life you have, it's not that important to be distracted by others as you ar still on your journey. With my self I have been alone for so long it's second nature to me to be that way, do I miss a lot of what life has to offer maybe but I'm content where I am at this moment in time even in the bible it says that some are meant to be alone and they are the ones that can have more time to study God's word and become closer to him in their walk through this life. If I have questions that I don't understand I take it to my pastor and hopefully she can answer them, if not. I study until I find what I'm looking for and then try to put the pieces together like the puzzle a chilld puts together, when it's finished I feel the excitement they also feel and no I cant explain it not at this time. It's strange how on some days we can write with a clear mind and others not so much, I got the church cleaned this morning and then came home not feeling very well so I'm hoping that tomorrow will be a better day as for now the day has come to an end so I will close for the time being. Firday October 4th well I feel a lot better this morningso I shoul have a good day, the guy that died on the next block had a truck and I was going to try and get it but my land I would have to sink a lot of money into it and at this stage of things that isn't possible so I will pass it up for now. It's not like it's going anywhere soon I ordered thee paper towels for the bathrooms at the church so they might get here by the time we run out or before that way we always have them. Little things you notice when you're a janitor is funny sometimes like the women are more aware of the germs then men and they go through more paper towels then men. This morning my mind isn't working too well as I cant see things the way I used to it's like I'm shut in a box and my thoughts cant expand out of that box like something frozen in time with no way to see into the future or the past for that matter, but the other day I saw Margret at panther paws with her son and she was loud maybe trying to get my attention but I turned and left and we drove home with our smokes she never has really bothered me but she does call from time to time maybe just to get under my skin.

But I pay no mind to her when she does that out here you have to have someone to talk to and friends are hard to find, I told her that I don't hate her it's just that we didn't click in our ways of living . She did tell me one time that I would fit in here in Courtland but I thought at the time she was being a brat she sees the world differently then I so our views are very oppiset from each other here in Courtland we hear things about others and I heard that she went back to drinking which is the worst thing someone can do it means that they have given up on them selves and that's something you just don't do, as for Valerie she has found love again and now it persueing that avenue so after helping her out again I have separated my self from her and we no longer talk maybe I'm angry that she took advantage of our friendship but if that's the case it too will pass like with all things through time something was and now is not. Margret once told me that she was not long for this world and yet she is still here it just goes to show that nothing is written in stone unless the lord puts it there. Even my days or years are not known by me only he knows when that time will come and he doesn't share it with us, my day is going too be a good one as I'm not sure what will happen but I do know that I need some things down at the station and maybe take some things away for each day brings something new to the table and we deside what we will do in that day. I know that somethings need refilled at the church so I will do that on this day and get things ready for Sunday it's communion this week so I have to get that ready by Saturday setting thing out so they thaw and setting up the table for which it will stand or sit on.

Working at the church has become like tieing my shoes a part of each day is set a side for me to go down there if for nothing else but to sing to the lord, and then it's back to what ever I was doing before hand I don't think the thrift store will be open until all the work is done and it's behind us no one wants anyone to be hurt during this process of the town getting a make over. A great town Courtland is' my town of dreams and it doesn't matter that I might be the only one who sees this. There could be many reasons that I see it that way growing up not having anything, and then finding my way here to have my own place although things change my gratefullness will not it will be until my time is no more. And I hope that many years pass before that day comes or at least until I get everything paid off, it would be nice to have a rental here that way I could make a little and put it away for that raining day when I need it. I have talked to many about this thing called the outsiders, and they said it just a thing that some feel and many others that weren't born here feel it stronger then I do. I feel like this is the place I was supposed to be at, and my not being born here makes it even more special. As I grow and love the place even more then those who take advantage the Lord puts us in places where we might let others see his power and that it's just as strong today as it was back in the day 2000 years ago when he died for our sins imagine the trinity three in one which means that God him self came to earth now he wouldn't of done that if he didn't love us. Because we have sinful ways but he is able to forgive and let us start a new, like the child that falls sin forgive sin forgive until they are strong enough to stand on their own two feet. Yes good people die but they celebrate in heaven while we morn just the opiset of what we do here and if they could tell you something they would say don't cry for me, God takes care of his own weather we are here or there in the sweet by and by He is my rock and takes good care of me. He has given me tasks to accomplish and although they might not be very big He says if I cant trust you with small ones then how can I trust you with the big ones you will have when you come to heaven, laying out the importance of our work here on earth. I was never forced to come to love Him it just came naturly through what I have lived through and giving my life to him was pretty easy even though I have never seen him even in the light only his power was there and it was greater then anything I had felt before. I cant imagine the surge of power when he returns but it will be greater then anything this world has ever felt, they say the skys will open and this I believe for what I felt when I was there was like a motor just ideling and it was stronger then anything. Athiest will be lost when the day comes as they do everything to disprove the existence of he lord thinking they are the ones with the answers when they don't know nothing first they tried to prove we came from apes and now that this has fallen short they say we came from the Ocean or from Aliens. There is one answer and it's so simple but they choose to believe so many other things instead of the real answer for this is their loss to get to know him and regreat will follow when the time comes so I'm told. Saturday and we didn't get the storm that was traveling through Nebraska and Kansas the news said high winds and tornadoes which we didn't want any part of anyways. During the night I didn't hear a thing but we had our flashlights ready just in case because when the lights go out you don't see a thing nothing at all.

It's communion tomorrow so things have to be set out and I will do that today, yesterday I had to make sure that we had what we needed and today it will be set up. The thrift store is closed still so I wont have to work this afternoon but we got a lead on a truck in another town it needs some work but I think we can handle it it will just need a shifter put on the floor and it will be good to go, it's great having a hobby so you can keep your self busy at times not wanting to get board around here. Through the times when you can't do anything it's always nice to maybe turn a wrench, and I have kept all my tools through out the years. Little brother is yelling at our other brother in his sleep and I have heard this many times but this is the first time I have ever heard his name being mentioned and it mkes me wonder what had taken place back then. My other brother was never afraid of the law but Randy is a different story like me in many ways I never wanted to be around them the law that is especially after being accused of something I didn't do so long ago, but in time they caught the guy and never did say they were sorry for putting me through the crap they did on that day was the first time I was called a lier in my life and it make me not care for them too much. All through life we make our own path and mine never wanted anything to do with the law, and for the most part I havn't had any dealings with them. In my time here in Kansas I haven't even been pulled over for a driving infraction as I'm a very good driver and only travel when things need to be done like shopping to the doctor and going to WalMart for which I go once a month to see if there is anything we might need or a toy I might want to get but mostly we are frugal and live the best way we know how.

I have always tried to be an honest person trying my best to keep things in balance like it says aand sometimes I give more then I have to but all in all I do my best. As for friends I have all I need and they range from kids to the adults which have a heart of gold when your in a pinch, I recall one time when I was on drugs eating at Mickey dees and I hadn't eaten in a while just the food hitting my stomic made me fall out of the car, it was the worst I had ever felt and it ws then that I knew something had to change but I was so high I couldn't figure it out at the time. Then later it hit me that my life wasn't going anywhere it was like being locked in a box the same routeen everyday getting up in the mornings and getting hight and then falling a sleep to wake up the next day and doing it again, it was like playing the same chord over and over again and I knew it had to change. Then one day I said the hell with it and went what some call cold turkey I was still on many medications given by the doctor and I quit them all heart medication and all, I was tired of the old life and wanted something new something to look forward to a brighter tomorrow perhaps and then after going through many of the withdraws I set my self a goal and it came to me. I knew I would need help with this change of life so I spoke to God again and he told me that things will be ok' I don't pretend to say that the demons didn't come back because they did but with God's help in time they left and never came back. I wanted something different and the Lord knew that I would have to move on in time but the timing had to be just right, and that timing wasn't in my time but his little baby steps were taken because as you all know the human part of me wanted it right now and that just doesn't happen in God's realm. The days lear to months and the months into years but eventualy everything came to pass, all the things I had ever wanted was given to me when I excepted God into my life and those dark days seamed to disapear like a bad memory not saying that things were easy because they were not. I struggled with many things trying to change this life from changing the way I talked, to how I held my self when I walked. And these things don't happen over night I used to sware like a sailor but in time that changed the words they went from the f word to something else more plesentand the lord gave me the replacement words from 'my land' to many others that would replace the filthiness of the devil, and things moved forward from there giving me a new out look on life as I knew it. Change is hard and it doesn't happen over night it can take years before you notice the change and with me it took that long, to my self I think I'm slow never being tested before but I find something trivial and maybe my mind just doesn't want to deal with it as it's too confusing. Many things I think I'm not meant to get being created for only one purpose. But through the years when I get stuck I call on my friends and usually they can shed some light on the subject, and usually it isn't as bad as I thought they make a phone call and it's straightened out.

I still feel as if there is some brain damage from the past but I'm hoping it too will be healed in the time I have left. As my beliefs are that all things are possible through Christ, I have traveled the path of nothingness to having a home and what I need to eat and I believe He had a lot to do with it. Taking a lost soul and bringing it back to life so it can finish it's journey, but what is that journey? For truly he isn't letting out any of the secrets and it would be nice if he did or would it? With somethings they just have to be lived in other words the cards have to be played before you know who wins the game. I wish it was easier but it's not! Today we went to check out the truck in the other town and foud it to be a piece of crap so we didn't get it, you would be amazed at the price people want for junk these days but that's something I don't need is junk my thoughts are if you cant flip it for more then you paid for it then don't get it. But we did get some good food while we were there and it was a nice ride down there, we have to make our own intertainment around here so we do what we got to do in that realm. When mom got sick she was transported to Nebraska by my brother and it was a good thing that she was, as it saved her life at the time but even after her recovery she never was the same and maybe she too sustained brain damage but she never gave up until later in life maybe tired of trying to go on. It was in those days when we grew close much closer then with the other kids as they didn't want to have to take care of her, but there is usually one like my self in every family the one who is close to their parents more then the rest. Lets face it some who get married at an early age also cling to the family they created and that was the case with Rod and Susie my sister getting married at 16 years of age and Rod at 17, they felt the need to break away from the family and they did making their own lives and children to boot. With susie she just fell in love but for Rod he just wanted to get away.

And he settled in Nebraska making Marry his wife later having mom move there to the place he called the good life which it was for many ears. I didn't hear about what Herb did until later in life but it never came to pass so I wont say it, looseing the only one you have ever loved had to be hard on him and in the end he gave up on life all together. the funeral was a good one with him having all military rights and they paid for his stone back in Kearney but still life went on as usual and we grew deeper into the addictions that destroyed me at age 32, my whole life was surrounded around booze and we had plenty of it as we grew up it was never out of anyones sight always at their house. So when we wouldn't have the money to get it we would just visit mom and the day would be fine she liked for us to visit as she was always lonely each day cleaning the house when she had her halth, and then later she would take in some homeless people down on their luck and help them to start over again. With the women they had to keep the house clean and hold onto a job if there was any to be gotten, and the guys they too had to have a job to make up the rent and other bills. I don't know how she did it but she managed to run a tight ship and if she didn't like a person then they weren't staying in her home and believe me she didn't care for some of them so out the door they went kicking screeming and some crying but out just the same. She liked her flowers and had us plant them each year so she could watch them grow, and the yard had to be cut and cleaned once a week which was done by the men that stayed. It was like she cared for the people and soon they started to call her mom her first call at being others mom was back in California when a gang adopted her the Ave Rats as they wer called back them and they watch out for her and her family even pops had a tatoo that said protected by the Ave. they weren't what you would call gangsters they were kids from broken homes and they found a love at mom's house that they didn't get at home where it should of came from. They never did crowed her they just needed a little love sometimes and mom's heart was as big as a gold nugget, late things would change and we moved away but for what has Stacyded me maybethe Aveanue was growing to fast I really cant say but we did find our selves in Nebraske a few years later and dad followed to only die a few months later anxiety soon took him over after not getting a job that he applied for and whouldnt you know it the owner of the shop stopped by two days after his funeral to offer him the job he wanted a little too late, if only he came a week earlier things would of changed him but he was at his whits end. I don't like funerals but I will pay my respects when it's someone I know someone that helped to make my journey here a good one, it says that God doesn't bring us people but he does place them in a certain place so others can see things that might have Stacyded them through the years and this in it's self can bring a change of some sort. It's Sunday morning and my land it's cold out side meaning winter isn't far off just down the road maybe and things will change from hot to cold and icy the plants will start dieing off to shrubble to leave their seeds behind for the next season and then in spring new growth will arise some good and some bad like the weeds and dandylions.

But during winter we will be snug in our homes keeping warm by the fire and reading a good book hopefully the bible or some other inspirational book that shows the goodness of our father, it's strange how change comes sometimes unexpected and out of no where but it does come, I wonder how Maggie is doing? Although they say she wont get better I have that glimmer of hope that she will and recover like I did so long ago that would be two miracles of great importance here in Courtland so let this happen dear Lord the creator of all things bring Maggie back to her family if that is your will. I have always thought of shutins as people who don't want to get out in the world but that might not be the case they could be stopped by not having any wheels to drive I do know thet the guy at the other station brings things to some of them so they can eat but I wonder why they get that way? Not knowing the while story I wont say anything. Mom was that way until she choose to change it and being lonely can bring some of that on not having anyone around because the kids have moved away to try their luck at the big city life. It's a preference of where you want to live, but I like the small towns as some remind me of the old days back in the 1800 when I wasn't even thought of. What draws us to these different times in history? Maybe we were around back then and forgot something when we died in another life and have come back to get it I recall something like that in my memory banks but it's very vage like it's was put away there before this bodies time. Could that be possible? No not in this life, or could it? As the leaves fall everyday now it won't be long before they are all on the ground turing into food for the grass that will last out the winter.

Although my visions are still small one day they will grow like the seed planted for the flowers, everything starts out small even us when we are born but before that God heald us in his hand and planted us in our mother saying it was good. Many believe this but if it's true then did he plant the evil seed also? The ones that will cause all the havic in the world. Maybe to prove that change is possible in this time and space it's Monday and the plant is running down the road trying to get the harest in I suspect. It hasn't run this hard in months but now is the time when the bins are full and they run iton the ground and cover it with tarps for the winter months, and then slowly they use it up first before whats in the tanks. Many years ago when I worked at Western Alfalfa, we did mostly the same thing but with alfalfa creating new products like the pellets but it must have been too hard for them to make a success out of it as the bins would catch fire there at the first and then w would have to put them out with resparators on. All this was done by the flunkies the ones that loaded the trucks and ran the mill part of the company, I can see how my body is messed up but back them you had to have a job to feed your family and that was the only job around in that area. We made good pay checks but the money didn't last long when you spend your weekends dinking and what ever else came up, the poor man truing to make a living but drinking them selves to death at the same time, I held many other jobs but they didn't last long making earth stoves for a company in Arizona just welding things together so people could stay warm during the winter months, and then the family unit would want to move so we did and everything would fall apart again starting over in a new place was hard and maybe that's part of why I don't want to move any more, that and I love my friends here in my town of dreams. What will the future hold well I'm trying something new and that's not to look to far into the future and maybe that might help make things go a little slower yesterday in church the pastor asked if I felt any better and I replyed yes and hat the prayers helped. When I really feel bad the church prays for me and I know the lord has to feel that love that they have for me if it wasn't for them I wouldn't have many things but through the years they have learned to trust me and that's the greatest feeling ever. Through the life that is now gone brighter days are a head and the love they haver for me towers above almost anything, I still have trust issues but I hope to work them out in the near future rising above them also in hope to be a better person. It's Halloween this month and I got the kids a bunch of candy to fill their bags, it's the only time when I can spoil them each year. We are tight nit here in Courtland and although I don't have any children here they become part of that and I like to spoil kids because I know that they have to go home and usually dad gets his pick out of what they have at least my dad did that when we were kids so long ago. It's strange how some things stay with you like a name or a person you thought you had forgotten but when brought up you seam to grab onto something that jars your memory, like when little brother brought up something the other day from our childhood I cant quite remember what it nwas but the memory came to me once it was approached.

As the holidays are approaching we will have many things to do and this year they are having a dinner at the seanior center on thanksgiving, such a great thought that Sam had for those who don't have family around here and we could bring meals to those who are shut in's if it's approved by the pastor such a delight to have someone who cares that much, if I'm not wrong this will be the first year that they try this and I would like to be a part of that. It's always good to give for the feeling is not like any other the joy you feel when someone smiles is greater then anything else, we got grocries yesterday so we are set in that department for some time now. Restocking everything we could think of and then some our sppetites change from month to month and you never know what you will want but we eat good and that's what matters the most, funny how things change before food wasn't important except to grab a bite every now and then while you were loaded but now it's the most important thing to keep us in good health so we can live as long as we can the prespective is so different. I have good frinds that leave things at my door like the things grown in the garden and although many time I'm over stocked with these gifts I eat what I can an then things go on until the next year when they fill me up again such caring people and I love them all, there are two farmers that bring me things and it just started this last year. The helping hands neighbors also bring some food to make sure we don't starve in this world of plenty, it's the government that cut aid to people struggling and I don't believe they really care or else they wouldn't do this.

Shutting down the government because they disagree with each other about things such a waste. Tuesday and the plant is still going, someone brought something and put it on my doo step I have a sneeking feeling it was either Norman or Jan Carlson my friends that something I can use with a clear and good feeling those words friends. It's trash day and I have some things to do today my little project that I do each week, when I first came here I was lost not only being in a new place but learning all the things I would need to know as time passed and my friends were there to help in anyway they could, I went to Jan one day and she helped me to figure out some things as I didn't know much about the problem I was having at the time so we got it taken care of and then things went on but it was nice to have someone that knew about these things. She told me once that it isn't always what you know but who you know that helps you out sometimes, it's another cold morning and it wont get warm until later in the day so we have to ware coats to stay warm. As for the leaves on the trees they are falling but not at a fast pace just some here and there I hoping that the tree doesn't fall waiting on them to cut it down it seams we all forget things during the week days or any days for that matter you just cant remember everything so we have to be reminded once in a while, as for little brother he will not be able to take care of things once I'm gone so I will have to have that set up before any thing happens should it ever come to pass in the future. Some timess I feel good but other times not so much but I will hold on until everything is taken care of I guess we all have these thoughts but when the time comes will be up to the lord, Maggie has been on my mind in the last couple of days and I pray for strength for them all. To carry them through this time of loss should it take place, I have been where she is and my fight was a long one as even today it hard to do somethings being dragged down isn't something anyone wants to go through but if He has a plan for you to do more then He wont take you I'm living proof of that, as for each step I took many of them have been wiped from my mind as they were very pain full and maybe I don't want to recall them because of that fact. The getting up when it was all you could do to stand and move around I cant count the tears that I cried as God has a way of taking those memories away so you don't have to relive them again. No one wants to go through something like that twice as once is enough at least for this guy, I hope for the best each day and usually they come but I do know that one day my time will be over. It would be nice to be burried here where I found my dream in the people and God and each day my strength grows stronger but I know He only wants to have a relationhip with each and everyone of us as we travel through this life. We have many religons iin this world and each one believes their way is the right way but is there really a right and wrong way to give thanks to the lord? Many would have you think so the conflect has been going on since the beginning of time but all I know is that my God loves us all and he is the same God as everyone else's. As I talked with a women today about a job working from home I told her about my storie and how things were not yet where they should be and she thanked me for my testimony and said God was going to bless me, she went on to say my cedi score was in good standings and it wouldn't cost me any money out of pocket. Just knowing this brightened up my day to know that my effort havent gone unnoticed.

She went on to say that would be blessed and I could tell she was a religious women just by the way she spoke, I got a call from a guy that has a van for sale and he droped the price and was wondering if I was still interested this could be a great deal if I get it for the right price so I can sell it and make a profit. He lives in another part of the state so travel is in the fortcast to get it. Should he sell it to me, he has to ask his wife and them will call me later, he didn't say no so it could go wither way. It's been a nice Tuesday and it got warm in the 80's just right for this time of year but you can tell that a change is coming, it's strange how I can feel it sometimes but it happens more then a few times a year and really I cant tell if the change is in me or my sarrounding's. I'm hoping for great things to happen and if my feelings are right they will take place also I feel God doing things in my life and things are going to turnaround for this guy something to launch me towards success to make life better. Since my turnaround in life I havent really loved any one but the lord it's a special thing we have a connection that cant be broken by anyone, he has seen me at my worst but also trying my best in trying to make things work, trying to figure out my place in this world now for some they might think this is strange but to me it's all new like a brand new toy. A fresh start in the world after a life time of not being noticed by, all that I am belongs to Him nothing I do has a reservation when it comes to the lord. Sam asked me to watch his dog this weekend so that's something I will do for him so his father will have a chance to hear again, you might ask what one has to do with the other well they need someone to let the dog out so they can take his father to get his hearing inplant.

I have always liked Sam we talk in church and we get along just fine having God first in our lives you would be amazed at the things we talk about and the lord always seams to be in our conversations at one point or another, here in my town of dreams He is always first and when friends ask if I would do something He gives me a signal weather to say yes or not but usually the asnwer is yes. My friends are close to God the way I am He seam's to be in everything I do and usually what I take on comes out good with His help because I can do nothing without Him there to guide me, my father the one who created us all and gave us what we need.

Well the day is coming to an end so until later. Wednesday and it's cold out as each morning gets a little colder we snuggle up with just a sheet but during the day we have to ware a coat to stay warm but just until about noon and then the temp goes up, you can tell that the body goes through some changes during this period so the blood can thicked for winter like many of the animals they too go through this change but my little buddy sheds year around I don't know what's up with that. But harie dogs only shed once a year the big ones like saintbanards and the ones that save lives up in the mountains, I call them the snow dogs like the ones that pull a sled up in Alaska. Strange how Harley couldn't survive up there but they can and maybe it's because harley is an animal that has lived no where but in the house never tested out in the elements to see how it would be to be able to live on his own, my little buddy will live out his life with me keeping me company. It's going on his 5th birthday and the vet told me that they live about 12 years which I don't think that nuber is right Tiny lived to be over 15 years of age keeping Oliver company and I know the little dog held on as long as he could but it didn't stop pop's heart from breaking when the time came and I had a heck of a time comforting him during that time in his life. I hadn't thought of this before but now that I think about it Tiny should be with pop's in heaven also, and their joy returned to them. I have wondered from time to time what would have been if I would of stayed that feeling of no pain or sorrow and feeling joy would it have stayed with me? For this I have no answer to. But I couldn't of fought to stay when He wanted me to come back even I knew that you don't go against God in any fashion although I didn't know much about him at that time in life he made me a believer that he does exist buy the things he did in my life. We all have a connection to him it's just that some don't use it and never learned how to communicate with him in that supernatural realm that he lives in, it would be awesome to have some of he power that the lord has and if I had some of it I would do good things with it like bringing people together that were once separated by religion or the lack of. My walk with Jesus has brought me far much further then I could of done on my own, and today I stand in front of the world a changed man one that went from one life to another. A positive change for me and a great step for the world of addiction for my life has lead me to a new world one of hope and happiness where I can grow and be a part of this place they call earth, I have kept my life much in the closet you might say not letting anyone in. that way the world couldn't be so cruel to me and stop my move forward, if you have to defend your self all the time then you cant grow in spirit.

This will cause you not to be able to move forward because all your time is spent answering questions and I don't like that, for my life is my own and I own it not a bunch of other people. My walk is slow and eventually I will make it to where I'm going. Many people are hounding me to release my life's progress but I will take it as slow as I want to because anything rushed never gets done right, I still remember being in grammer school and they would give you only so long for a test and when the time was up I would be no where near done, so the next time I rushed because I didn't want to be called stupid by the other kids pressure isn't a good thing with kids especially if they need some help but even then I was too proud to ask and they pushed me through like I didn't exist and the memories are still there even after 50 years. Hump day the middle of the week, I talked to Charles this morning on Skype he never seams to amaze me with his funny ways always saying his friends should fine God. In this life there are many who are different and surely he is one of a kind with his anoligy of things much different then most peoples but still his love for God stands out and you can tell how much he loves the lord, his wife couldn't sleep last night so she was up when we talked I have had that same thing but usually could fall a sleep after a while it's not a good feeling having to stay up all night. In the younger years I had it quite oftend but it was brought on by the bad habbits I had which in her case it's nothing like that.

We seam to go through many changes in our lives some good and some bad but usually the good prStacyils after a time, I tried to wake up Randy a bit a go but he doesn't seam to want to wake up so I will let him sleep until when ever. Tomorrow I start to take care of Sam's dog so I have to be there by noon tolet her out she is a good dog and minds me well with little effort, I seam to attract people who trust me and too me this is a good thing tjis afternoon Jan called to let me know that there wouldn't be any thrift store work so now it's Thursday and I have the church to cleaan, there are 31 souls learning about God and that's a good number for a town this small and I love it when they all come out of the church to go home it's like a bunch of kids getting out of school and their mothers and fathers are there to greet them. Now my job will be to get everything back in order for the service on Sunday, I take my job seriously as it's something that has to be done each week. People depend on me in the same way they they depend on some one to work at any job Christmas is coming and the ladies will be putting up the decarations so I will have to make sure that things are cleaned up afterwards which takes about three trips to the church a week just another part of my job that I love so well. The mill is still running down the road and it's going on a week of solid noise from that place, as time goes by we get used to the different noises at certain times of the year they come and they go but I like it most when the season is over and the quiet returns.who want to hear a machine running 24/7 it can even keep you awake if your restless my legs get heavy sometimes and they feel like lead as I drag them around which is something I don't like but through it all I seam to make it and I'm reminded of that turn I took so long ago down the wrong path, and I wouldn't wish it on anyone not even my enemys for which I have none that I know of. It's a different time of year a time when everyone pulls together and makes the town beautiful we even got new street lights down town and they look sharp. New things are coming to Courtland and we will great them with open arms, I'm hoping that later we will be able to use the hoist at the old station for which they park the street sweeper at right now. This in it's self would allow us to get more vehicals and put our finishing touches on them so they will sell and make a profit there are many ways to become self employed but you have to find that nitch that we all have inside of us that one good thing your good at so that way you wont fall on your face, I got up late this morning so I must of needed my sleep to me 4:00 Am. Is early but to others it's not an option to be up so early as they have hard days a head of them, working in the fields has changed since the old days today they have tractors that will turn around on a dime without you touching the steering wheel all you have to do is punch in a number and your set. More or less your just there for the ride unless something happens that has to be fixed the tractor has come a long ways but still they cant do the work of the human being in fixing things. As they cant think they only run by programs that we put into them. Yesterday it was in the 80's and I'm hoping it isn't as hot today maybe in the 70's would be nice with just a cool breeze blowing but I know that I have to get the rest of the lawn mowed on the south side of the house don't like doing it in the wind as the bugs blow into your hair and face if I do it in the morning then the coolness keeps the dirt down and also the bugs, I have a feeling it's going to be a nice day.

Although we havent had the thrift store open I know we can make things up as we go into the Christmas season we have many things we put away until it gets close to Christmas and then we take them out and put them up for sale, I never did hear back from the ladies which came through when we had the garage sale so I take it that they done need any help in or with what ever they were going to do. It sliped my mind that they might be calling so some of my phone calls could have been them and I just didn't answer the phone there was a number that came through last night so I should check it's call back number and give it a ring it's different then the others that are telemarketers but I have a feeling that's what it is and I was right a high pitched sound that about hurt your ears. Last night we got some rain I can always tell when the ground is wet out on the road a reflection of the moon shines on it, and boy is it pretty the morning is slow in coming as I'm still tired but once the coffee kicks in things will speed up. Maggie died on the 9th of October she will be greatly missed she never did recover from her illness and now she will be laid to rest this Monday, it's Saturday morning ad I could hear the augers running most of the night I went and took Sam's dog out and it looked like she had pups but I'm not sure when the day begins I will check and see if they got the road done up town so maybe I can go to work today.

The weather has been nice here in Courtland and they are getting a lot done now that the harvest and new planting has begun don't know when it will be finished but it shouldn't take too long as some of them work around the clock so they can get paid for their crops, the guys have come back to finish the house next door but still they have a long ways to go before it's completed. In this part of the country you have to have central heat & air other wise you just live a miserable existence and I know this because I have lived it here once with just window air, it doesn't cut it in the heat that comes in the summer or the old furnace that doesn't keep you warm during winter. Everything has to be up dated as time goes on and if your smart then you will be able to make the payments, by having someone live with you or working harder. If we lived in the city we would be hardly making it but here in the country we do fine and have no problems to speek of I'm moving towards a different direcion one that would allow me to get a head a little more but like with everything it takes time days fly by and the progress is slow but it's moving in the right direction to hopefully be debt free one day, but for now the pendalem just moves back and forth and I greet most days with a smile and don't focus on my past as it can get you down some times. As we loose our loved ones we have to keep living and put some things behind us as with the addictions that once plaged us they too become a thing of the past as life changes and with God's help they get washed away like the rivers that go out into the ocean in other words giving our lives to the father lets us walk away from the tragitys that tied us down fore so long. Many are so caught up in the moment that they cant see these things that are tearing apart their families, they can't see what will come next all the heartache and pain that they will cause but there is hope for those who live through it, a brighter tomorrow and better things for their kids and family anything is possible through God the father. As I test these dating sights I find that many of the women are just out to make a connection and then let it go later sort of an amusement for them it's not a good idea to go there. My self I loose intrest in them fast for some reason but there are certain ones that I wouldn't mind seeing in person, the ones that hang in there and send little messages flerting with me, when love has been absent from your life you don't know how to take things sometimes and that can leave something missing with some things other things get lost like the feeling for someone you might be interested in. Sunday morning and I couldn't sleep so here I am awake and dressed at 2:25 Am with the only sound of the plant down the road. I guess I didn't leave any room for others in my life but I'm working on it trying to change I also realize that by having my book printed it will leave me open to questions by others and that's something I never considered in the beginning, but in life we have to take some chances to break away from the shell we have made for our selves in hope that other things might make it's way into our lives I had always been a loner but for some reason I feel the need to change that in my life my need for happiness in the department of love. As I watch some of the movies like the one on Jesus I couldn't help but feel that he was alone in many ways being so different from others.

I have a bad feeling that holding things in can really hurt you in many ways because you don't express your natural feelings that He has given us, and in thus. You may stop growing in that certain direction like with being shy or bashfull, I don't know what brings us to these places but we sometimes end up there and alone many people go there but I have no idea of how llong they stay there. Isolation can sometimes give you time to think on many things but if you over think things then you might make things worse, do I feel the pain of others and take it upon my self to feel this? This could very well be but you have to learn when to let go and move on like the others do that were close to the person that has passed. My journey has taken me to some places that I wouldn't have gone to if I would of stayed in the other world drounded by the curse that almost took my life. The distance we put between us and others is of our own doing and sometimes it can hurt us more then it will help, but we go on in hope that change will come one day that maybe He will bring that right person into our lives the one we couldn't seam to catch. I know that's putting a lot into something I can't see but I have to believe that one day God will bring this to pass, I believe this is what they call faith in the one who created us. Many people feel these feelings but they are never spoken as they keep them to them selves burried in their minds for ever and these are the ones who might not be able to write or put down what they think or believe I was told that not many people can type, and this I believe. As we are all taught in our own way how to deal with things it's just something that God thought I needed to make it through this life and it has helped a lot of people like my little brother.

My ability to type got him out of prison and brought him home and then you have all the other things I have done over the years that have taken on a new noticeability that there is life after addiction He seams to know what we need to make it in this world but with some of it I still don't understand. My feelings are not always the feelings of others or maybe they are and they never express them in writing or in person afraid of what others will say about them. Should we be afraid of something that might not exist? Or should we throw it out there and see where it lands my self I had always had a hard time trusting others and it's still prevalent today as I talk about things some don't understand it's like I'm from another planet or do they understand and are afraid of it. My views are my own but everyone wants to know, it's now Sunday night and I was awaken for some reason maybe to write more but in a way I get tired and want to sleep it's like I get an epiphany but ii don't understand it. Monday morning and whistle of the train is blowing constently it the first time it hs ever woke me up from a somber sleep, I have tried to figure out some things in my mind and have come up with that some people around here are like me in the timmed fashion. Some shy while others are out going depending on their age and what they have learned in life but usually the younger generation is the most out going brought up in a new age when things come to them fairly simply kind are not spanked like in the old days when they got into trouble and maybe that's what makes them so different but still the same.. Yesterday after church I went to lock things up and there was a bunch of peoplr there in new silver cars which I didn't reconise so I left and came back home until this morning when I will go and clean the church, I still hvent heard about my order yet of paper towels but they should be in this week sometime so I can stock the bathrooms and have them all set up. I remember when I moved here I thought things would work out with the women I had met but now I'm kind of glad that He brought me here through the works of something that would change I guess it was His way of getting me here to this place I now call home. If we would of stayed together disaster would of set in as we were too different people traveling the same uncertain path at the time, later I would hear that she was having troubles and they were the kind that I had already been through so it was good that we parted and went our own separate ways. Although my mind can travel back in time this body won't let it's self go there, mistakes made are just that mistakes and they shouldn't be repeated if at all possible the bad ones that is. But as for finding something your looking for never give up on that because I believe if your meant to find love it will come to you once you go after it. It's easy to put on a mask as some call it so some cant see who you really are like on the internet when some pertray they are someone their not. As for my attention spand it isn't as long as it should be so I have to take breaks from my writing, in the beginning I never knew I would still be at it all these years later but for some reason He doesn't want me to stop so I go on in hope that the story will come out the way I want it to. Like I said the train woke me up this morning at two Am and I'm not quite used to being up that early but I will take a nap later to make up for it as my body has energy to burn for some reason, I have climbed the mountains He has put in front of me and although I have fallen down a few times it never stopped me from making that climb bruised knees and all.

Now I embark on another journey one that will take me to where I need to be maybe into the arms of a beautiful women that loves God as I do. My land' the rain is coming down and it's falling hard you know it is when you hear it on the roof of the house I just hope it's a passing storm, the ash fault sure is shining like it does when we have an ice storm during winter but you cant go out in that. Now the thunder is sounding off like a big ole cannon and then it's quiet all of a sudden and Harley is scratching at the door wanting dad to protect him ya right like anything is going to get him right? Can a dog since something we can't being in tune with things he comes to me like he has a hair ball in his throat but once rubbed he settles down and goes under the bed to rest once again, the strange love of a pet. But from the beginning to the end he is there for me to comfort me and I him, it's like he know something that I or we don't and he tries to tell me what's going on as for him going out side there is no way as he is afraid to get wet. Many people go through life without knowing the father but with some He sets His sights on them and doesn't let up for this is what's happening in my life and it's been going on for years, with some rehab is nessary but with my self God steped into the picture the day I went into the light and He has been with me ever since I can be doing something and He will step in and tell me to do something else and if I don't listen then things can get bad many times we don't understand what he wants but in time he always makes it clear through ways of persuasion the marking of something new or taking something old and bringing it into the world today. I like that He followes me keeping me from the things that took me that day forthis journey has been a long one but I couldn't of had a better partner then God, through the storms of my life He has always been there.

Even though sometimes I couldn't see him for truly He is the greatest power there is with just a wave of his hand he can cure a person of what's destroying them. But that doesn't mean it's going to be easy for you it will be in the fight of your life as you go through things you never knew possible even now I feel him here with me as I put down these words and he has a message he will never put you where his grace won't sustain you and he will never give you a mountain you cant climb. In the beginning I had to crawl up the mountains that was set before me and although it took longer I always seamed to make it to the top with a little help. Tuesday morning and on Friday I have to go to the other side of the state to Hutchinson so we can look at a van, it's supposed to be in real good shape so the trip just might pay off by getting it and bringing it back here and reselling it. Although it's a ford they do hold their value to some folks especially the folks that know a head of time that they will one day not beable to walk, they seam to give them time toget them set up for a wheel chair lift or anything else they might need. I try and use caution when buying something as many like the old ones have the old air-conditioning units but ths one would have the newer one in it allowing it to be charged for half the price of thee old, dad used to say that checking things out is only half the job. The guys wife is on dialiaces for something so I'm talking it that they need the money for that the love of a wife is more important then money to some. It's trash day but the church doesn't have much so I will bring it home and put it with mine in front of the house, in th days that follow I will try and get some thing done that I have been putting off for a while and then things will be back on track. Our journeys in life are as important as our walks with Christ, we do many things to try and make things better for our selves but we must never loose sight of the love we have or the promises we make to others in doing this things stay in balance and life can be good but I can't help but feel we are here for a certain purpose maybe to help other along the way and bring them to a place of peace if that's possible. I know that once my book is out there the flood gates will open with people wanting to know how I have made it thus far but my faith in God has brought me here and many won't be able to connect with that because they too havent found that place where they feel they need him. My daughter has been up set lately because her mom isn't doing well and calls her names thus causing her to cut her self my land I don't understand how a person could be so hatefull. I recall many times her mom saying she wished she was dead in her younger years and that's part of why I didn't stay with her it even got so bad that I would get up at one or two in the morning and leave so I wouldn't be there when she woke up thus going to mom's so I could be or have a good day. Mom was a very happy person but she let others get her down and I'm sorry that happened to her even though I had nothing to do with it but we grow and hopefully learn from the mistakes, here I have regreats for something I didn't even do how wrong is that? Maybe one day I will forget about it.

I wouldn't have gotten as far as I have if I would of stayed in Kearney but I felt that I needed to get out of there to make a new start and that I have done through the help of friends and others that have come to love me, as for my journey it still goes on and you never know when it will end but when the time comes I will be ready to join other that have gone before me. I spent most of my life being scared of things I shouldn't have been scared of, but with God's help I'm still moving forward in hope to find that certain thing I'm looking for. Wednesday and yesterday I put up a new flyer at the station because the sun had faided the other one so now I can let this one last through the winter, day after tomorrow I go and look at the van to see if I want it or not and if so I will bring it home with me. It seams like I know when God is about to bless me and just enough to help me get by through my life nothing used to go right for me but since I moved here to my town of dreams things seam to be happening in a super naural way and I don't question why it happens I just go with the flow, also I feel many changes are going to take place but I can't quite put my finger on it although it could be something great through my days I have been experiencing something new a feeling of being free for some reason free from the burdens that have haunted me for some time now. When you don't feel right it sometimes gives you a lot to think about and in the end you hope that you made the right move. Reservations we all have them but you cant let that feeling run your life other wise you will miss out on some good things like having something of your own one day, in a way it's like I'm being showed that I can do all things through God and he will protect me alone the way.

The way I feel right now it's like the world is opening up to me and like the farmer that puts his last dime to grow a crop I put my last into things I feel that will grow and bring something new having hope and faith that He will make things grow for me. I guess it's called taking chances but I wasn't always this way in my younger years I played everything safe and stretched every dime to just survive, but something is new right now and it's happening right before my eyes. Call it favor with God or what ever but it's happening it's going to be another cold morning and it's not supposed to get above 50 degrees but by Friday it should be nice and warm so I can travel, the lord will not take you where his grace can't sustain you for his grace is sufficient for us all. My strength comes from God and has always came from him it was just that I didn't know it in my younger years, it was him that brought me to where I am today and I know this just as well as I'm sittiing here right now. He wanted me to live so I could see that good people existed as before I trusted no one, we have to learn many things before we leave this earth and right now I'm learning to trust other as I travel this path he has put me on. Having fear can defeat you before you even get started if you let that fear control who you are but once you push past that point then you can over come most anything, in my life it's been one step at a time over coming each thing that didn't grow when I was a child. Thursday yesterday we took a trip to Concorida and on the way home I almost hit a couple of donkeys on highway 81 just north of town. I wasn't paying much attention to the road but thank God little brother was and I hit the breaks just leaving them enough time to get by me, you hear of this happening but you never think it might be you that gets hit and then out of the blue you know that God was watching over us. Even Randy who has been skeptical of how much God is working in my life seen his wonders on that trip then there was the old man that was hitch hiking, we seen him going into Concorida making his way north and when we got to Belleville he was hitching a ride west on highway 36 for which we were headed so something inside told meto pick him up and I did. We went on to have a chat or talk and I told him my story about how I had died and the good lord brought me back because my journey hadn't even started yet, as we talked I asked where he was headed and he said denver Colorado so I brought him as far as our turn and he said' I didn't even get my sign out before you picked me up and I pay ten cents a mile. I told him to keep his money and he said no that he liked to pay his way, then he asked if he could take our picture and of course we said yes and he asked our names so we told him Roger & Randy Mattson he said he likes to document the kind people that he crosses paths with and truly we were two of them. It was a feeling like no other when he left we both felt charged like a power was given to us and we turned and we parted ways, he was a well dressed older gentalmen and told us about times when he declined a ride from some that were drinking and one person was very unpleasant that was a passenger in one of his rides. Many things have happened to me since I moved here that are out of the ordinary and this was one of them. Like the stranger, I had met many years ago that came into the church on his way back to Minnesota. We had found our way in the same year that I had passed being in 1992 and had both been sober since, my only explanation for these things is that God is still watching over me and he wants me to know it.

As we parted leaving the guy at the cross roads we told him God bless and that he would be watching over him in his travels, and he replyed god bless also he took our picture and at first I was laughing then I smiled and he asked if I could laugh when he took the picture. So I did out of kindness and we parted, I know the lord will look after him in his travels and I wish him a safe journey. Today I start to take out Sam's dog while he is gone with his parents to get his dad's hearing inplant, it's something he asks of me from time to time but I don't mind doing it for him I really like him and his parents they are good Chrisstens and attend my church. The accident that could have been assured me that Randy and I belong together one looking out for the other as we go through this life, if he wouldn't of been in the car I surely would of hit the donking and I could of met the lord sooner then I thought. From now on we will ware our set belts and pay more attention to the road instead of looking around when I shouldn't, a message from the lord that things could turn eugly in a moments notice but we are safe and that's all that matters. Tomorrow we take that trip to see about the van and I will drive safer this time, do we really know when the lord will come back maybe not but this happened for a reason, my faith has been restored even stronger then ever now that at times we are visited by people or things we don't fully understand. This is the second time a stranger has visited me could it be a sign of good things to come? I sure hope so, because I know he only comes when he is truly needed. In my time in he last few years I have been visited twice could it be something supernatural or was it just two men passing through I guess only God knows the answer to that question. But I might tell of this one day when I tell my story about my journey, as for meeting these two people I feel blessed to have visited with them.

Also a man called about the van I used to have and we talked. I told him that it sold to a guy in Wisconsin that came and picked it up, but I might have another one this weekend. He went on to say that he really liked GMC'S or Chevys but he would keep my number in case he didn't find another one, this leaves a door open to where he might settle for a Ford should it turn out to be something I would get. Right now I'm going by a feeling a supernatural feeling that I should go and see it and I only get these feeling when something might turn out in a good way, for truly I feel the lord looking out for me in many areas of my life and it will always be this way as I learn more and more about him and our savior Jesus Christ' this morning I will go and clean the Church as Wednesday bible school is over for the week. The two dollars that the old gentalmen gave me has been put away to record this adventure that took place on the 16th of October in the year of our lord 2013. What will today hold? I cant really say at this point but I will let it be what it will be and have a good day I saw the old man before the donkies and a desaster was taken away and then later saw him again and gave him a ride so I have to believe that we were meant to cross pathes for how ever short of a time. Friday morning and little brother beat me up this morning so he must be excited that we are going on this trip, the guy called last night to see if I was still coming and I told him yes that I would be there by around noon. This is the time when you use caution because you have to check everything out not to get a lemon and then end up with a head ache. So far my luch has been holding on ventures like this but you just never know, if nothing else we will have traveled to another part of he state to get to know it a little better. As I commented on Tonya's picture of a T bone steak she had put on face book, she told me to come down and it was mine for which I told her that I would be there in 20 minutes and put a 'lol' next to it meaning laugh out loud. Where she lives from my place is about 300 and some miles and I know she wants to see her uncle Roger, it's been almost three years since our last visit and we will have to get together one again before my time for travel Is over. This could make or break me but I'm hoping for the better side of things at this point if like a crap shoot really but still the idea of making some extra to last the winter feels good. While driving I have to make sure we ware our seat belts so we don't end up hitting anything or anyone, I was amazed at how when I saw the old man the accident for some reason was not to happen and then I ended up picking him up on my way home. It's not everyday that something like that happens but his kindness still has left a mark on me for some reason, by some supernatural force we were to meet on our different journeys in life and he knows our names.

Many different things can and does happen in this life for instence the travler I met at the church just a few years back, I could tell that he had a messaqge and I believe it was that the lord can put others together even when they are hundreds of miles away. The car is fueled up and the travel plans are made now all we have to do is wait for the sun to come up so I can see good, I'm going to get something to help me write a little faster and I wont have to do it the old fashion way. It's called the dragon and it remembers everything and corrects missed spelled words and the other thing just by talking to it, things made easier by someone who had a great idea all you have to do is talk to your computer and it puts it down this will allow me to release more of whats inside even the words that I dismiss because I cant make the connection for some reason many law inforcement officers use this method as the describe cases of unlawfulness. I know it will take time to master this new method so I might have to posepone my release for a time but in the end I feel it will be worth it to get things right. I don't know why I always strive for perfection because as He knows we are far from that being perfect, but many use this method in their jobs and other things and do just fine some even good writers as they make a living at what they love. The travlor was headed to the mile high city where pastor Kathys son lives, and I hope he is there by now and home with his wife. I dought I will ever see him again but it was nice to meet such a man in this day and age a trusting man just traveling the side highways of America.

Harley hasn't gotten up yet but I'm sure it wont be long before he wants out, yesterday I made a bunch of pickled eggs and sausage enough to last about a week or so and then I will have to make some more. I'm only limited by he way I tend to move forward as we are not meant to waste food for any reason at church we even feed the birds whats left over after communion. Waste not want not. The trip was a wast of time and we hit a snow storm on the way back, my land It had to of been the first storm of he year and you could hardly see 5 feet in front of your face but the car handeled fine and we made it ok' the van had been abuse with one window shot out by a BB Gun and the front end being wrecked it would of cost too much money to fix it. The storm was strange as it would rain and then snow but some was sticking to the fields, and we saw onecar with the whole front end gone like it had hit a deer. I have to say that the good lord was watching out for us on this trip and we made it home safe, traveling like that wares out a person especially when you have to stand in the rain while talking to the guy. I told him no sale and he said he was sorry that we had to travel so far, but we got to see another part of the state anyways so now we know how to get there not that we will be going back any time soon. He did give us a lead on another vehical but the guy is from Arkansas or lives there now, we are just glad that we made it home with no miss happens. My little buddy Harly was excited to see us and he showed his love when we walked in the door all excited that we made it home, Sam's little dog was also excited to see me so I took her out and then rubbed her and said see you in the morning. I don't mind doing this for Sam as he is a good person and we get along just fine, I hope things went well for his father and I hope he got his implant so he can hear. Sunday and it a little chilly out side as we go into winter I cant help but feel it's not far off. The snowstorm we hit made the papers and now everyone knows about about it happening. As for the day yesterday it was a good one I went over to Sam's and took out the dog so she shouldn't have crapped in the house, Sam was supposed to get back last night so now my little chore is done until the next time. We felt the cold from the storm but didn't get any white stuff thank God, the funeral yesterday was of an old friend a women that I believe visited the thrift store from time to time and even worked there volunteering I reconised her picture from somewhere and tried to put two and two together so my recall may be wrong but I believe it's her, the lady that said God would take care of my in my old age. I don't know how things will be in the future but I hope for the best always for my frinds and family, the train is moving through town this morning but it's not as noisey as the times before just pullling the loads of grain to maybe get them ready for hauling. They will travel to the stock yards of New York and also to other big cities like Huston Texas, among other towns like Omaha so the harvest can be transported to other countries. Here they say we have the starving but they keep sending our crops and food to other countries why? On the Courtland channel they advertise about the thanks giving dinner so in November that's one meal that the less fortunate will get to have. It's the first time they have tried this but I know it will be a success, it has taken on form in every other town that I have lived in. In Kearney they feed thousands every year at thank's giving and they also do it for Christmas I believe, it's a way to help and bring joy to others during this time of year. The old people get lonely and this could bring them together if for nothing else to visit for that day.

During my brief talk with the women on the computer I found that many of them are just on there to get money from people, but I shouldn't of got so mad when I said no. they give you every reason under the book and rationalize that you owe them in some way maybe for the chat who knows so I have to be cautious about who I talk with, if I was a millionair then I could help but I'm not and that's just the way it is now I don't get as many emails as before because of the words I used in my profile line. I was just littng the scammers know that they need not bother with me and that's being honest, Monday and it's going to be a nice day so I can do somethings I have been meaning to and it's also quiet with nothing going out side no trains or the mill running so I'm taking that as harvest is done. Down the highway about 5 miles they are stacking the corn on the ground and then they will cover it with a tarp that's heated so it will keep through out the winter strange how they do something's these days but it seams to work. I believe they put it there for the ethonal plant that's just down the road from the barnyard as they keep cattle there that are going to market, and boy what a smell you just about have to plug your nose when diving by or else puke. Just another place in the heart land, I wrote a short story about me and pop's and sent it to the news paper so they could put it in there it tells about how he helped one of the western singers many years ago when he was in his younger years. Through time and space we learn what to do and what not to do in this world and I just wanted to give him his space on a writing seeing he never did have an eduction just a good ole boy trying to make it in this world, Johnney Cash was his idle back then and he was happy to help build his first place.

As we move forward in time things change and the hurt we once felt by loss seams to take a back seat in our minds making room for th new things that will come our way. Some say our loved ones never leave us they just go to another plain of existence and they watch out for us it's just that we cant see them any longer, can some people with a gift communicate with them I believe it's possible just as possible as that same person can tell if you're an old soul or not. To me an old soul is someone who has lived before like the little girl I saw one time on a show called the medium, I think she can talk to spirits when they approach her thus giving her sight into a living persons life. From what I have seen she can know things that cant be explained because the living person hasn't ever told anyone about their deep dark secret, and yet she brings these things up letting the living know that their loved ones are truly talking with her. And the way she explains their death is only known by the person she is reading. There is another medium and his name is John Edwarda I believe and he also has this gift, we are all here on a mission but for many of us we don't see what it is blinded by the things that are going on in this world we cant focus to bring the message through like they can, and sometimes we need to hear from our loved ones weather it's good or bad. The most important things is that from what I saw there has never been a bad message just comformation that they are ok' and that thy love us, what happened at their time of death was destiny and their time was over on this earth and usually nothing could have been done to save them they just went home to be with the father and now they are at peace, Norm came to church yesterday and it was good to see him getting out among the people he has known most of his life they sat and talked and then it was time for me to go home. Where I spent the day and rested, it's now Tuesday and boy I'm hoping it isn't a cool as it was in the mornings just last week, I had my article published in the Salina Journal and it sounded good so I put it in my scrap book for safe keeping. It has taken many years but it seams when ever I write something it's published giving me a look at where things are at that moment in time. I know for a fact that many are hungry for putting an end to their addictions thus bringing them selves out of the dark and into the light, many will complete this action and others won't, as they give up on life in general. Depression can cause many to drink but what they don't realize is that alcohol is a depressent and will drive them further into that world, and many play hell trying to get out of it looking for that quick fix you might say but the sad thing is that there isn't a quick fix. Only when they realize this can they move forward and walk away from that world, while under the influence the world out side doesn't exist as the mind shuts off and doesn't even know whats going on. Black out's is what many call them brought on by the alcohol or drugs taking over the mind and sometimes a person even looses days as I have done on many benders. Not even knowing you are a live, one time I can recall waking up in jail and not knowing how I got there. Thus having a black out which many people have when their life isn't there own.

Some will ask how a chimical can do such a thing and I believe it's in the transition from going to being sober to one of intoxication, the feeling is out of this world to someone who hasn't been there before and it's very addictive. We all have two people inside of us the one we are and the one we want to be, and if you don't like who you are then the alcohol and drugs bring the other out , if in the natural you are bashfull or shy the chemicals allows you to change this and it's gradual with each drink or how high you get. The further you get away from your natural self the more you become bold instead of being shy you are out going and everything changes, but you loose something in doing this that connection you might have had with God can seam furthr away and the longer it last the further you move away from it. Until it's not there any longer in doing this we loose sight of the one who created us, but he never looses sight of us as we travel the wrong. As He knows that one day we will come back to him funny how he knows us better then we know our selves and He should being the creator and all, as we walk our own path we experience many thing that others don't. Like from going from one world to another and back letting us see what other don't and in doing this we might be able to help those that have become lost, either in that world or even between the two worlds. If this can be done then your life has meaning, some say we leave a foot print like the foot print that was left in the sand so many years ago. To maybe help others as we go through this life, I have been told that many creative writers fail do to not having enough faith in them selves although this may be true I believe as long as you don't give up there is always hope for those who write about life. I do know that the stories are never ending once you start for even every day life has a story of some sort.

My journey will not end until I take my last breath and the good lord brings me home, so many times I get exited for no reason at all and it's at that moment that I wish I could bottle it. For surely it would sell to those who never feel the joy that God can bring into your heart, I just wish it could happen more then it does that way everyday would befilled with the joy of Christ. Wednsday and he train is coming through this morning I havent heard it in quite some time and maybe it's because harvest is about over, the thrift store opens today after being close for th funeral last Saturday. Randy is doing fine and so am I as we go into winter but I can feel a change coming on from the weather change I get a lot colder very easly so I will have to bundle up more now that it's coming, as for the warm weather it's gone for the year and we have to get ready for the cold and snowy weather. Not that it's a bad thing it's just takes a little getting used to as the body's temp goes up and down , the milow is being put out on the ground on a concrete slab to keep it warm for the winter the last to be harvested and the first to go out once spring planting starts. Our community is a growing one as the fix the streets and put up new street lights this will really help in the coming years as I feel my town of dreams will grow and not die. They have many incentives for the kids around here to go to collage and then return to help in the community, one young person is going to be in agriculture so she can come back and practice her learning among the people who love her I believe they have a program that helps them with school giving them what they need to move forward in life. As for the ones that leave and don't come back well I don't know much about them, and what they have found in the outside world but young people in their 20's have returned and that tells me that something is being done right. I talked with one young person and she said she went to beauty school but then wanted to return because that world is much too different then where she grew up, Thursday and today I will go back to work it was fun at the thrift store yesterday as one of my friends came in and brought in a couple of cameras, she seams to be soft spoken as a few other ladys are around here. I slept in this morning so I believ my body needed itand I woke up feeling pretty spry, this is the time of year when my mind wonders from one place to another and I havent a clue of why it does that eaccept for it might be getting ready for winter the changes are really hard when they come and sometimes I mess up when things don't go right, they had Wednesday school yesterday so today is clean up time for me getting everything ready for Sunday as it approches, we did a little sales yesterday and that will help with the mission work that's coming up I cant wait to see Sam's dad to see how he hears after his surgery I hope now he will be able to take in most of what's taught in church on Sundays. Like Oliver was people who cant hear very well seam to make their own world in that narrow place in their mind I guess it's like living in a box that no one else understands because the world of hearing is shut out to them they don't hear you so they start to live in their own world the sound of the birds seam to disapear as the condition gets worse with pop's he wanted to go and take rides to see other parts of the country this brought him great joy, maybe in a way it replaced not being able to hear using his sight instead of his ears.

They say when you go deaf your other sinces kick in and this could have been the case with Oliver trying to survive after all that had happened to him through life. He did give a good fight before he went to be with the lord but death was coming and I think he knew in some way, today I wrote my first letter here to the Courtland Journal it been almost 5 years in the making so I will see how things go. Every time I write to a new news paper it's a different experience. TGIF it's Firday the ending of the week but the beginning of the weekend I will go and check on things down at Norms and seehow he is doing I like to keep in touch with my friends especially the ones here in my own town many things happen in a wheeks time around here and this week I didn't have to watch Sam's dog maybe finely going to the doctor is over for his father and now he will hear again an inplant like that has worked on a child but I'm not sure about an adult but the way things are any more, anything is possible. His dad used to drive and when they told him that he couldn't any longer it hurt him as that was something he always liked to do, going for rides like Oliver used to do it took almost 20 years before pop's excepted that he couldn't drive safely and even then he was never the same having that taken away from him, I guess in a way it was like looseing his freedom or right of passage to do what he wanted. Good thing they don't have car's in heaven ha! I have never excepted fully my writing skills or else it has become so natural to me that it's no different then putting on my shoes, like my every day routeen of doing things it's the first thing I do in the morning . Randy is moving around in his room so I take it that he is awake but for how long is anyone guess.

We seam to still get along fine and I don't see it changing anytime soon, my land' he has come a long ways in the year or so since he came to live with me and I'm so proud of his accomplishments not going back to the alcohol or drugs like so many others do I believe if you take the timtation away then there is no reason to go back to it you are given a clean slate to start a new yes a new life without it around as a reminder of how things used to be. He too has come from the same back ground as I and this is proof that we can over come all things if we put our mind to it, unlike me he has chosen to walk his path alone except for the help that I give him and the encouragement that has brought him a long ways. I have no doubt that if he would have been around our brother he would of ended up back in the place that I finelt resqued him from the lord moves in mysterious ways in his life and mine. We were finely brought back together by the force that is good and not the other that helped to send him where he was, I don't believe prison works for everyone it can take a meek man and turn him hard to where he hates the world and then usually it's all down hill from there but Randy was saved by the grace of God and given a second chance like my self but still he hasn't woken up yet to see that others care for him. Like the people in Jesus time that were saved from the king what should of taken 11 yers took 40 but you know there was a lot going on as people started to change and for those who didn't realize the lord had them covered it took them more time. I never did hear what happened to them all but many became a part of the bible, I don't know what will happen today but I do know that there is something I need to do, will it come to me later for this I'm sure of as I venture out to do different things. Finely they got the roads finished so now the thrift store will be open on it's regular days and now maybe the customers will start coming again we have already seen the Mexicans come back and buy thing so maybe the others will start to flow in, I havent seen my friends that came to buy pickled eggs but in time they will show up I hope. When I told them that they were habbit forming I wasn't kidding and they came back during the state garage sale so I had to go home and bring some to the church, it's a great hobby to have as many like them and it helps to pay the bills. Saturday morning and it's cold out

I dislike that feeling so things are going to change in keeping the house warmer my day is going to be fun as they have the bake sale at the thrift store I start at 12:00 noon and usually most of it is gone by the time I get there but I'm hopping that my things sell you can never wish too much in this world for good things to happen, I told Norman hi yesterday and he replyed back in kind. As he was about to change a tire on a cattle tariler Good thing they had a spair on the tung of the trailer my normal things sell great but as for the special asked for things if no one picks them up then they sit there and that kind of makes me upset. So I will stick to the original making of things and not make anything special for folks especially the young people, that forget sometimes or they just change their minds and then I'm stuck with getting rid of them through the trash. I was taught to never waste food but when you over stock then you have no choice, if I had my way I would only make them for the folks around here but others come from near and wide and sometimes want to try them and then usually they come back.

I havent seen much of Phillis lately I sure hope she is doing well she has been ill off and on for the last year and I know how being sick can put a damper on things, my self I havent been sick but a couple of times and even then it's too much. Mark is doing as well as can be expected and his spirit is back as we laught when I went into thebank the other day. Peggie is getting married today and I wish her well in her walk with her husband they have been together for a long time so it's natural that this step takes place my friend for which there are many called me sweety the other day and that made me feel good maybe one of these days I will ask her for coffee and see what she says you never know until you try and that's a fact, some are taken away so someone new can take their place if that's in God's plan and you never know when or who that might be I don't know if my letter will get published but I'm hoping for the best and then that will be three news papers publishing my stories. Could it be in the timing this I believe it could be as I'm cautious about things and it allows me to move forward, not flooding everything at one time allowing others to see that they are not alone in this world trying to get their lives back we all have our demons and they give a good fight but they can be over come with the help of the lord, for He allows us to start a new once we make that giant step and reclaim what it ours. I have come so far from the beginning those times when I didn't know weather I would be here the next day to it being 20 years later He seams to guide my steps and like the lamb I follow the one who has kept me from harm as his love is wraped around me like a blanket. Each day I'm drawn to witing like the fly is drawn to the light that keeps it warm, my first thought of the day is to write as I drag my self out of the bed.

And maybe that's part of what keeps me going the knowing that one day my words will be heard around the world where the people can read about my travels and how I over came the opticals that almost destroyed me. As for talking about my ventures sometimes it's easy but then at other times it's so hard, not always remembering what had happened when I want to put it down on paper, a slip of the things I want to write Stacyde me at times but in the end I hope to be able to answer some of the folks questions about how I was able to over come the curse that almost took my life. As for being out going I don't think I will ever be that way but what I have learned is that God has a way to bring the good things out of a person Sunday and I talked with Chuck yesterday on Skipe it's amazing how electronics allows you to see and hear other people many states a away but it does. He gets up about the same time as I do but talking at that time wouldn't be a good idea as I have to let my brain wake up, I asked if owned his land and he said yes that the 250 archers was split between his wife and her brothers so they live fairly close to each other and split the taxes so it's easier on theem all I couldn't imagine what the taxes would be on that much land but his parsel is about 50 archers. He said it's tember land and they have all kinds of wild life there even black bares which have come to the house once in a while, that to me would be scary but he has a gun to chase them off when they get too close. He loves his home the way I love mine and will probably be there until his time comes to be with the lord, we greew up together as children and his parents kind of took me in during my wild days when I was living in the darkness of the curse and they were good people. His father Wayne had a shop and I would work down there once in a while while Chuch went to school although that part of my life is still vage Chuck was telling me that we used to go fishing together but that too has never made it back to my mind, I wonder why somethings never come back like our fishing trips as children maybe because I was in that dark place and didn't want to remember. Millie was a breat women Chucks mom and she was very kind to me they played music together and Chuck was the only one who took after his mother and father they would play in bars and at the VFW Club and church socials well maybe not at the bars came quite remember that part for sure but they loved music I used to sing with a band when I was young but I never stayed with them still being shy and had to have the alcohol to make me brave enough to go on stage O if I would of stuck it out then I might have gotten over the fear but I never gave it a chance, it seams I was always running from something back in those days and maybe it was growing up that I was afraid of. The fear of getting old must of held me back in many things but now that I'm older those things seam trivial compaired to my life now as everything that was once new has also grown older and are still with me in many ways.

As we mature our hang up's also mature and they don't seam as bad now as compaired to the old days looking through the eyes of an elder gives you a better out look on things, when I drank all the time I thought I would end up shaking like Herb did, but that wasn't the case. As the years passed and the curse was lifted also was the shaking and in time it left and never came back, another blessing that was given to me by the Father. As for some they continue to shake through their older years and I know that has to be hard Randy has that problem but nothing is ever said about it because he is aware of it and it could send him into his shell deeper like the turtle that hides from his enemies. It's a great morning and they say it's supposed to be In the 60's a good time to wash the car if it doesn't rain, I would like to open a car lot and sell things from my home this would allow me to move forward and make a good living but it would be with older cars when they made them to stand the test of time not the ones today made out of plastic and tin, I have never had the breaks that I have today when I was young but I sure wish I had some of the cars I used to have, many times you come across things you least expect and sometimes that gives you a lift or a break. I know there are many cars just sitting around that people don't drive any longer and if we had a wrecker we could haul them away for them, making a good living at it so many opertunitys if you just get the right break and they come to you if the good Lord finds you worthy of such a thing.

What will happen in the years to come now that the addiction has passed and I'm doing my best to follow God's plan for my life. Do I just ride it out? And not worry. For that would be the perfect anoligy of things but I don't think I'm there yet, I need a partner someone that I can get close to that will help me follow my dream and maybe a lover would be the right person a women to support my ideas and work with me instead of against me. That would be a change, seeing in the past I had to carry the ball all the time. If things were just right then that life of worry would be a thought or a memory. Hellen is her name I believe the women that called me sweety last week she is a great soul and she talks to me each time she comes down to the thrift store and sometimes I want to believe she comes down there just to see me. I know it must be lonely for her since her husband died last year so maybe I will ask her out for coffee the next time I see her, that would give me some insight into getting to know her and it would let me see if we might get along, I'm very cautious about people coming into my life because I know eventuly they might end up in my life and I'm not sure about making that step or taking it. When we bought the television for Randy the women knew me and I didn't have a clue of who she was, but they treated me with kindness so what they have heard about me must have been good other wise they wouldn't of been kind. The guy went out of his way to make sure we were happy with what we bought and even made two trips to our house to exchange the televisions that didn't work, now that's honesty and I'm glad that we have such honesty people in our community. People come into our lives and they go but the ones around here are here to stay making this there home for a life time and it's good to have them for friends as they can help make things better with just a hi or a smile or even a wave as you drive down the street like the farmers do as they head out to their fields, it's hard to become part of a community but once they know your honest that opens a door to trust and you don't want to break that trust for any reason. I recall a counslor at the school telling Margret that you have to use caution meeting someone on the internet and you don't want to move them in your home, I believe she would change her tune if she knew that I was the one that didn't want to move into her home. An uneasy feeling tells you that it isn't the right thing to do so we parted and today I'm well known as a good person making it on my own in my town of dreams. Monday and the end of the month is about here yesterday church went find but there wasn't as many people as I thought there would be anyway the message she gave ws clear, Sam asked if I still wanted to help with thanks giving dinner and I told him to just give me a call it will be a great thing this dinner and who knows maybe next year more will come to it as this is the beginning of something new and great. As the day becomes light outside we will have some things to dolike clean the church but one good thing is that it didn't get too dirty with our friends just being a few, John didn't show up and either did his wife so I'm believe they went out of town for a few days. My friend John is a person of habbit going out to the farm each morning to check on his cattle and make sure things are alright. My self I don't know where any of the farms are except for a few that are way out there that I visited many years ago when we took the back roads to the lake and it only being one time I could never find my way back there for anything, Harley is up this morning so I had to take him out yesterday he was sick for some reason and I don't know why but today he is better running around as usual and being happy also the mill is running down the way trying to get all the crops done for the year and then it will be closed for a time until the wheat crop grows through the winter and becomes the first crop of 2014 when spring gets here.

When they are not putting up crops they are putting fertalizer on the fields with a machine I call the grasshopper, it's so big that you could just about drive a small car under it between the wheels my self I had never seen a machine like it until I moved here they didn't have any in Nebraska that looked like it does. The wonders of machanics doesn't supprise me in this day and age of things an I'm sure many more new things will come up in thwe future, one man wrote a story about the prison system and how it cost so much to take care of them and the children are educated for half the price that keeps them housed, he wanted to know if anyone else thought it was wrong that this was taking place so I will write about it later it seams I build my own audience when it comes to addiction and they reply to the news papers and in other ways the good thing about the news papers is that they cant give out your address or phone number which allows me my peace of mind because really I know many would hound me if given the chance, if they were like I was I always wanted to know how things were done in something I didn't understand. Friday will be the first and then we will get our checks so the bills can be paid, a great start to the month of November just a month before Christmas and I will give something to the kids so they can buy for their parents a small gift that says that they love them. And that they are grateful for them, my friend that takes care of foster kids hasn't came to church and it has to do with them going back to their mother. I can only imaging how hard it must be on her and her husband to have the kids move in and then after loving them they leave, but she surely has to know that she helped in their bringing up so maybe it will have a lasting effect on them and one day they may see them again. Back in the day mom did the same thing but with adults, giving them a place to get a new start many of them being alcoholics and drug addicts some turned their lives around but also there was those who never did change.

And they were the ones that ended up in prison and other places, you can only do so much for a person and then it's up to them to take over and become what they will be. I got a call from a publishing Co. and they want to publish my work but in a way I'm scared, maybe it's success that scares me or something else that I cant see yet. The women said she wants to help make my dream come true my dream about people reading and learning from my life, in a way I know it's wrong to keep it all to my self but how do I get over this feeling? I guess just go for it and see what takes place. It's scary treading in new waters that you have never swam in before but it can make my dreams come true should it be a success.

Tuesday morning I got up late from not being able to sleep last night until 10:00 Pm. It was a restless night but eventuly I got to that place I like to be, it seams when I don't tell Him that I love Him my nights are restless and I struggle with things like falling a sleep but then sleep comes and I wake up a new man. The train is going through and the whistle is loud but this time it's headed out of town so I missed it's arrival' which had to of been a coouple of hours a go. I have to take the trash out here at the house and down at the church so we are set for another week of not having to worry about things like that, when addiction is in your life you loose sight of the things that are good and you do many things to stay in that addictin cycle. As with me I never did get into trouble like the others that I knew and I a cridit it to being much like my mom who stayed home most of the time, not wanting much to do with the out side world. This allowed her to choose her friends and not let anyone in that she didn't like or care for, people who fall into addiction are not always there by their own choosing when something tragic happens somehow they find their way to the stuff and the way it is they find comfort in not feeling those bad feelings that consumed them and that's the point of addiction it lets you forget the bad things that have happened in your life and many don't want to remember things like the loss of a child or loved one. It brings them to a state of numbness where many stay and many never come out of that state because it's hard to face the hurt and rise above it. You could compare it to giving up in a since not wanting to live any longer with out that person or giving up on the feeling of love it's self, and in a way I did the same thing but I'm getting better as time moves forward. The hardest part is to admit that the problem exists and many wont or cant do that so they stay on the same path until they except this fact but once realization set in and they except that their spirit needs set free, then change can find it's way into their lives and still the hardness isn't easy but in time they can grab hold of what important and go on. My land' with me it's been so many years that much of what I did has only been captured of the pages of my life living from day to day and hoping that I aquire what I need to go on. Looking back is the only way I can recall somethings but then with others I don't recall them at all. As for having a women in my life the search goes on and who knows maybe she will walk into my life sometime in the future, lord knows I have the patients it takes to find the right one as many years have passed since that time.

Like with the old life it has to pass before you can feel comfortable to bring someone new into your life and I have been waiting for many years. Like the tree that looses it's leaves to only come back the next year stronger then ever I too will find the right women for me, a women that is on the same level maturity wise as for the younger ones I don't think it would be a good fit. There is a reason why they were born in another century but many find comfort in the younger ones the older person is kind of laid back while the younger one is out trying to find them selves this gives the younger one security because the older one wont wonder having already been through that in their lives when they were young. When people are going through alcohol andd drug addiction they really don't know how to make that connection if they havent already been married once or twice but there is a reason why it didn't work. From personal experience being seaprated causes a rift between two lovers as for the one who is going through this phase the chimicals are their main focus not wanting anything to get in the way of them getting their high and then the family comes second which it should be the other way around in my battle my having fun was more important then anyone else and that makes a person selfish, not careing what the other was feeling. It's hump day and half the week is gone already headed into another month of thanks giving when people will share a meal down at the seanior center with others that have a hard time douring the seasional months. This year comes a change by having this meal the first of many to come I hope, young and old are welcome to attend as we say a prayer before the meal and give thanks to God for the bounty.

Now we have the streets done and they sent me a letter saying that we cant use ice melt on the side walks or anywhere that the repairs were made, I still havent gotten my check for this month so I will have to check on it something is wrong because usually it's there on the 28th and I cant get a hold of the person that makes out the checks I wonder if she is sick, through the years we have had many different functions during this time of year and I will be a part of it and help out as much as I can with my little part it takes many people to be able to pull this off and everyone pitches in so it's like a family thing with the people of Courtland all joined together through Christ. When Christmas gets here we will have the celebration as many do with lights lighting up the main street for we now have pretty street lights a lot better then the old ones that stood for many years like they say out with the old and in with the new, making everything perfect for the season. My worries are not many when things go right but when you hit a snag then things can fall apart like when you forget something or have to adjust to something new in your life but all in all my life has been good here thus far, this morning I will go and do a little extra cleamning at the church getting things ready for the season. It still crosses my mind sometimes when I think about how they took prayer out of the schools this wasn't a good move on the governments part, because now it's replaced with Gun's being brought into our childrens lives for which many children would of never seen a gun if this tragedy would of never happened and they call it a persons right to bare arms. What a crock of crap, I notice that my consentration isn't very long just talking with the women on the phone kind of sucked the life out of me trying to put together the things she was saying this is due to the damage that was caused so long ago. It's like my head wants to blow off so I have to take a break and regroup my self for a time, many people have been following me through the years and I didn't even know it until the one lady told me so, I do know that one person has kept every article on alcohol that I have written beck in Kearney but I don't know their reason for doing this it never dawned on me to ask her why she does it but I like to think I have a fan base out there among the people. I have tried so hard to change things but there is still resistence from those who are not ready for change and we are given the right to choose by God and that cant be revoked by any man, if I had a magic wond I would wave it and make the problem go away but in doing that no one would learn anything. It's in the steps we take that makes us who we are and we have to learn from our mistakes as we go through life other wise it's useless and the mistakes would be repeated. We got some rain last night so the moisture should help the crops take root and become strong to stand the test of winter, making for a good harvest next spring the train is coming through town so it will pick up it's load and be on it's way to other parts of the country.

To do the same thing there are many small towns like our's that ship by rail and then it ends up on a boat to other countries where they use it to grow their own crops. They say China is the biggest population in the world and you can see it with the people packed in the streets, I couldn't imagine being in that big of a city where you bump into others just by walking down the street and the places they live in is no bigger then a walking space with a bed. It's Halloween and to night the kids will be out getting candy I like to spoil them by giving more then most people plus their candy is something I cant eat being hard and all so I make sure that they take most of it. The kids look cute in their costumes and the shy ones is the ones that get the most from this once shy guy, I know the feeling of being that way and still today I recall when my neighbor bought me some ice-cream when mom & dad didn't have enough money for all of us kids but it made me feel much better when Anna bought it for me. When I didn't get my check on time my friend offered to loan me some money so I excepted her offer but then gave it back within a couple of hours my friends will do most anything for me, as we move into the new year I will keep writing in hope to still get the message out to those having a hard time with addiction they must have faith in them selves before they can move forward and learn to live without it in this mixed up world, like with me it was easy to fall into that trap when the alcohol was around all the time. When people got sad, it seamed to make them happy but you cant build on a chemical not something that can be taken by the tip of a hand it's just not that easy. Hard work is what it takes to over come yourr problems and then once they are behind you the world seams to change, and good things can come your way. This is what He did for me on my journey to a sober life because he knows how hard it can be to recover from such a tragic addiction He has always been with me even when others walked away and left my life.

And it was like life would go on not only for them but for me also giving me new adventure for which I could use in my every day life. You might say that I clinged to God for strength and the will to go on and He gave it to me even through my darkest hours He held me up and told me that I could do it, I believe this book is my catalist my venting place where I can not only help others but also help my self and it's become a big part of my life even today as the years pass by maybe this is why I start each day by writing my storie or adding to it. The lord knows that I can make a difference in the world of addiction because I have been there and fallen down so many times that I cant count them but till getting up and moving forward into a world that I'm still learning about, maybe I'm like the child I once was except I'm learning now instead of in my childhood maybe making things easier for me in some way. Because I know I didn't have the patients back when I was a child, today when things get ruff I go to the church and talk to God or else I sing to him in hope that He will give me the answer that I need and then I can go on with my life, like this morning I will go and sing and clean up at the same time making sure that his house is ready for Sunday. We all have a mission in life and mine is to do the things I'm doing now but still I feel many things need to be done like this book for instence to inspire others that addiction doesn't have to be the end of this life but the beginning of something new and exciting from the teachings of God to the inspirational stories I have read about others that have had near death experiences and lived to tell about it. Although none of them were like mine still they felt the same thing the peace that comes with traveling to another place of peace. None of what happened here was important there, as it was like I was living in that moment and time didn't exist in the spiritual world but O how I felt the power the same power that sent me back here, as for what each day brings only God knows that and when it comes I just ride it out and hope that things get better along the way. Our struggles are what makes us strong so my strength should really be up there because I go through it each day, hoping that one day I will find that peace that comes with each passing day, in my life I seldom get angry but that could be because I'm a person that doesn't go out into the drama that others face everyday of their lives. And yes I have to be pushed sometimes and that confusing to me when I don't really know what to do, torn between what to do and what not to do for surely if I make the wrong move then things can fall apart but if the right move is made then I could be set for life because my story will live on through others and then maybe one day they too can tell their story and I could be in it the one that gave them hope for a brighter tomorrow, although I sometimes find it hard to express my self I do it better through my writing because you don't have a bunch of people throwing questions at you. This is too confusing to me Roger Mattson' as today I'm still learning my communication skills but they are getting better as time passes. My friends help in this process as they know me better then anyone my church friends that is, as for others they know only what they have heard but I do know many of them know that once I was crippled by the curse that almost took me in my younger years.

Places which used to not be nice to me have changed and now are very kind maybe because they heard part of my story but the rest has to be told and it's only a matter of money that stops me. Will my friends see that this has to be done so I can close another chapter of my life and start a new, according to my consultant I should have a good run having almost three books written so far. It will be broken up into three books being it's so long and then my story can go on and live as long as I do the roilitys should be out of this world or around it, seeing it will be published in other countries. This is a problem around the globe not just in the United States, Randy woke up with a Charley horse and I thought he was havng a seizure so I went in and rubbed his leg so it would go away it seams I'm needed not only in writing but also taking care of him. I told him that he needs more exercise and he does as he gets heavier as each year passes just sitting in his room not the kind of life I would want to live but I have lived there in my days of addiction never leaving my room just getting up and staying high, it was during this time that I knew my life had to change and with God's help I did change throwing everything away and starting down a new path. One that would set me free from the curse that kept me there in that bed, I couldn't walk to good in those days but slowly things changed for the better after I threw the curse away. Going cold turkey was hard but being poor you had to do your best with what you had and that was the only way for me, I told God that it was time to live or die which ever he wanted to give me and He gave me life.

A chance to live on and tell others about my journey and how I made it through the troublesome times and the struggles that came with it, O the opting out was there but this soul wouldn't take it as that would have been the easy way out just giving up and dieing for dieing that way takes no effort but to live now that takes strength and only He could give me this strength that comes from within side of me. Will this year be the new beginning of another chapter of my life? Or will I keep writing with no return? For another year only the day will answer that question, while being cautious about things I look to my friends for advice so not to fall into a trap that will hurt me in anyway. Friday and I had Mark check out iuniverse and they have bad reviews from some folks writing two books and getting nothing in return, I know that my book is more important then to have to go through something like that and I'm not going to Waste all these years and get riped off. I just cant let that happen my work is too important to me any way so I will wait for the other publisher to get a hold of me and then move forward, hoping that things will take shape as we move into the end of the year. My journey has brought me thus far and I cant take any chances with it falling into the wrong hands and sitting on a shelf for many years my land' I can let it do that here on my computer and keep adding to it. With this other company everything is split half and half so they will try as hard as I do to get things going, idle hands move nothing this would be a great time to get my Dragon system going so all I have to do is talk and it will be put down, like talking on the phone really but the words will be recorded on to my words App, this will all be knew to me as I move forward into another stage of writing and who knows maybe it will be faster in this new realm of publishing but my journey continues into this new year of 2014 where more things will change. I havent talked to Chuck lately and I believe I should chat with him today so I can get my morning serman, there isn't a time when he doesn't get me in a good mood when things seam down and this is good for me, we talk about the old days when we were kids and some of the silly things we did such a good friend and I'm glad that we connected after all these years. It's hard to believe it's been over 40 years but the friendship has lasted and it still goes on to this day, I don't know when I will see him again but I'm sure he will pop up next summer when I least expect it. Many now know some of my writing and how I got this far working hard in the wee hours of the morning but it's my way of living in this world of His, my way of dealing with life as I move forward. I have come to thee realization that I will have to read more as they set up a web sight forr me and that will take a lot of concentration which thus far mine has been short only being able to read so much at a time before my head hurts but that will change as I move forward and make my mind stronger like with writing it doesn't just happen it takes years of pushing forward and using the parts that haven't been exercised in many years. I know that the person on the other end tried to push her company on me and that's something I don't like so I am walking away from them and trying a new avenue one that will give me resoults.

It was a little cold this morning but last night we had a few kids stop by for Halloween and they looked so cute in their outfits, even Tanner brought his kids by and they all got some candy some were wanting more and of course I gave it to them but still I have so much left that I will take it to the church so they can eat it in Wednesday school, in a way it's like I'm seeing the things I didn't get to do when I was a child and it makes me feel good that they have this time in their lives to be a child. But how soon they forget in the coming years they wont remember this year or at least some of them won't. I know that my memorie of those days doesn't exise except for the times when we had candy fights living in a tent but it was fun, being a little boy hiding candy in my sneakers and in my sleeping bag, it was like I never ran out of candy and the others would want me to share so I did. I can still picture mom sweeping the camp ground keeping it nice any clean as she did with all her homes when we had one, a real stickler for things being clean she always had it set up like a home and it was her home when things got ruff but the love was always there too even though the curse had made it's mark on the family, lord knows we couldn't always sit at the camp so we would venture out and go to the corner market for beef jearkey which us kids loved. I remember Mary a girl I had met while at the lake and we had fun that summer going swimming and fishing, her parents were set pretty good having a pickup and camper that they slept in but she took to my parents fairly well as her mom and dad met mine and approved of her friendship with me.

The summer went by fast as they had to leave and go back to L.A. so her father could go back to work. I never did see her again even though we were still there the next year some times people are taken out of your life because they can't go where you are going and He can do that with out us even knowing about it, like with many that are now gone from the pages of my life Valeire is one such person that wasn't ment to be here I had seen her with other men while we were friends and really the way she treated them was not right in my books so why would I want that? They got along like me and my kids mother and that wasn't a good match. Twial is still going strong and my land' she has to be close to 90 years by now. I remember all the hell she went through with her children but her love for them was always strong and still is today I havent seen her in quite some time since the 4th of July about 4 years ago. It's Saturday and the hrift store is open today so this morning I will go and fold pamplets at the church and mop the floors then around 10:00 I will go and get some things from town that I need, part of my everyday life here in the heart land that I love so much even my friend that reads my cards of destiny says I will come into something big and it involves my banker how does she know these things? But I feel something happening in the realm of my future as I talked to Mark the other day about such a thing, for I will surely need help in this undertaking I'm going on it's like my world is making a turn and it's for the better not the worst. If all things come into play then my dreams will come true and I will be able to answer the questions that so many might have for me. But in the beginning it might be hard having lived my life away from the noisey world out side, through many triles I have come and still I have them today but with a little more understanding then I had back in the dark days, if I have learned anything it's that we need to believe in our self and for me I believe God has a reason for bringing me thus far to help those who might be on the edge of no return. I think in a way I have always wanted to work from the comforts of my home so I can be more in tune with my self. There is no place lie home to me, what will happpen from this point on only God knows but I feel good things coming the breaking out of the shell I have lived in for so many years. Many don't share their experiences with others but my feelings on that matter is that if you can help someone from taking their own life then you should do your part to help bring them out of that and go on with life, as life is precious to God and should be to us the ones that he gave life to. Many cant use a computer so the books will help them and for the others well I will do some public talking that might shed some light on how they can get their lives back, and that will help also, my life has been about writing even though I couldn't do it back in the day when my world was turned up side down. Today I start on a new adventure one that might free me from this shell that I have put my self in, like the baby chick that breaks through the egg when it's born to see a world that they have never seen before it's the baby steps that brings us to walking and then running and then nature takes over as we learn to grow.

It doesn't matter if you get a late start in life as long as you learn to grow and in the end He will be pleased with what you have done. With me I had to let God into my life so I could feel the changes as they took place, the not being able to see Him' doesn't really matter, when you feel his power and notice things changing. Many time your own mind will fight you and that's when you have to take another look at things maybe what you think is happening isn't really happening at all, yes today I fight the demons but I have one advantage usually I'm able to push them away and ask God for a sign to let me know that things are going to be ok' I love my God the one who created me mom and dad were just a vessel a means to a beginning and then He takes back over and shapes us to what we will be, like the tea pot that was so eugly in the beginning but then turned out to be priceless in the end. This is what God wants to do with our lives make us as beautiful as possible something that everyone wants to be a part of, will we have all the answers no but we will be able to help others that are lost in that darkness and cant see a way out. As the time draws closer I get a little excited about the journey I'm going to start and I know that He is with me as we walk side by side as for the words I will need I trust that he will give them to me when I start to talk to people and help them see that they are very important to Him, in this world of His. We are here only for a short time so we must do our best to make a difference and help others along the way, as for having all the answers I don't have them but what I have learned can help those who cant see a way out and might do something foolish give me the power lord to bring them what they need in that time of despaire.

My journey He talked about so long ago could be just starting so I will take it one day at a time and see what transpires. Will He bring me to where I need to be? For this I have no doubt if it's His will, for I will do this for the glory of God and if he is with you then who could be against the creator off man. Sunday morning and it's another good day haard to wake up be still I havent had my coffee yet it's like I'm always drawn to thesse pages before my day starts maybe to keep my mind in shape or as sharp as it can be. I remember as a young person not wanting a relationsship until I could give the other person what they needed and I was never allowed to let that transpire because they didn't want that. But for me it was very importand for some reason maybe to bring that fairy tale life into existence who can really tell at this stage of life? Some things are planted so deep into my mind that it's hard to bring them out, so I wait until He helps me bring them out in hope that they will bring something to pass, so many don't know Him and that's a shame although we may not be able to see him his power is there when we need Him.the power which shows it's self when we least expect it. As for my self I couldn't imagine life without him because I know He is there when I need Him most the times when I couldn't get out f the house and the times when I prayed for his mercy to heal this body, I am one that never gives up no matter how hard things get and yet when a day ends I always see the next day with Him walking by me. Who could ask for more? He knows what we can do and what we cant and he never leaves us along giving us a little more strength with each passing day to push towards that final goal that we want to achieve. So many have made it to the top and yet they have fallen from the mountain to parish into the world of addiction and then die, but usually they have had the curse forr many year they were good at hiding it from the people like with many rock stars that have taken their own lives because they couldn't see a way out. Many of them take a break for a year or so but the end result is always the same especially when they loose a loved one like Mindy did a year or so back when she took her own life after her boy friend took his I havent been in that world but also ii dontt believe I would want to although they had the money and fame it's that which brought them their down fall, many go through the addiction prosess and some survive but not many. My journey is to do the things I want to do without that burden hanging over my head, and feeling the peace that He can bring into our lives as we move forward into the unknown none of us know what tomorrow brings but when it gets here we should make the best of it in doing what comes to us. Although we sometimes have doubts those can be washed away with just a thought from God guiding us in the direction he wants us and we don't know where that might lead from one day to the next I have seen him guide me to places I would of never thought of and yet there I was in a new place with a new beginning. I was told that He brings us to where we need to be to maybe show others that he is there for them no matter what they have done in the past it can be washed away and a new life started, my business is to make sure that they get the message and that way they can choose what direction they want to take weather it's to the light or to the dark side of things.

No child has to go through the path I took many years ago addiction wasn't as bad in the 1800 lets say, at least in small communitys where their wasn't any alcohol or drug stores but then in the 30's it made it's day view by the government letting it be sold through out the United states and the death rate climbed and people were dieing off. In the 21 century they will make Marijuana legal as they did with alcohol and bad things are going to happen. It's Monday and again I'm not quite a awake I have been having a hard time getting used to this time change getting an hours sleep more then usual but in time I will come around with this new thing on my plate it will take sometime before I can put it into the back of my mind and go on writing as usual, when I get writers block I try and change the subject in hope that He will bring something new to the table maybe a memory that I have forgotten about many years ago and usually he shows me something but at times it might only be a flicker of the whole picture and then the rest comes later I recall while camping we used to take bottles of spinyada wine to the down pour of the lake and just sit there for hours drinking it. This was normal for us back as a child when it was around all the time and even the girls would join in by this time it was a normal thing to me as I hid from my problems off not feeling in adiquet getting up each day to the same ole thing. Although some would of loved that kind of life I didn't not having many friends and as I grew the friends were less and less because of the gypsey life we lead, three weeks here and three weeks there never having a solid foundation to grow up in.

Most of the time the nights were cold and the mornings colder but like troopers we stuch it out getting up in the mornings and going fishing and then it was like our troubles would go away for a short time, to only return later sometime we would travel to town for our favorit treat of beef jerky. At the corner market just down the hill from where we camped about 5 miles, it's strange how I can remember those days better then the ones later in life. For the later years are like a hit and miss because of the alcohol living in the other demention just next to this one, our father taught us what he knew about his craft of being a machanic but still there was so much more to life then that. Later we would move into a house in Oak View and that when I remember things starting to happen although it was a dump dad would work on the land lords things for the rent but then mom wasn't happy there it was a small community and the base ball field was just next door to our home and we had all the noise from there, kids hitting the balls into the window's and breaking them out made mom nuts so we moved to another place that was a little quieter and then things were better for a time until we had to move again. I had a cousin that got killed on Maricopa highway going to the wheel a bar up in the mountains on his way downhe took a sharp curve to fast and went over the highway patrole came and got my mom and dad to see if it was him and it was I don't remember much after that he was a twin to his sister and was in the armed forces stationed in California Craig was nice to us kids and I remember him being around once in a while with his girlfriend Glina boy was she beautiful. I cant imagine how his family felt when they lost him being I was so young it seams things like that didn't last long with children reflection of the past might not be as accurate as we remember them but I do know that I missed him being around as he liked kids. Most of what I write I from memory and that my views on things that took place in my life, when things started going south with my parents it didn't take but a few years before they split and then Oliver came into our lives, at first the other kids were mad about mom being with him but it didn't matter to her and really it didn't matter tome either because I liked him. He had always worked hard and made a stable home for mom and us kids, he always took good care of her and I believe that why she asked me to look out and make sure he had a home when she left this world she knew he was getting up there in age and wanted him to not have to live on his own again, so as the years passed we stayed together until he passed. I didn't know what I would do once he passed so I talked with God about Randy and he told me it was time to bring him home and that took almost a year to do with writing letters to certain people and then one day I got a letter saying they now realize that someone cares for him and they let him come home when I picked him up I wanted to cry because of the way he had changed and it wasn't for the better he was over 100 pounds heaver and didn't look good but off we went and I got him home to only almost loose him again when his gullbladder went to heck, but the good lord stood by me and brought him through the surgery in the hospital down the road they tried to do something with him but he almost died there so they shipped him to Salina where he got better care during that time I prayed like never before and the good lord heard my prayers he was scared because he didn't know where he was.

They had rushed him by the emergency unit over 70 miles and during this time prayers were comeing at him from everywhere in my little town the pastor prayed with me as we asked the lord to watch out for him and those prayers were answered by him getting better, we have doctors around here or not too far away but it's not like in the big cities where you can get to one on a moments notice it's work in progress as one day they might have what we need closer to the folks. So now I take care of Randy as it seams to be my mission on this earth to take care of others like with Herb then mom and then Oliver now it my brothers. As he leades me I will go and do whats asked of me, we all have a mission in this life and mine is what it is. I just hope people can take something from this and apply it to their lives as we don't know when it might be too late to reverse the damage we bring to our selves. The train is blowing it's horn this morning it's such a peaceful time of the day when everyone is still a sleep but! Not me I'm always awake or try to be trying to put together what will take place later in the day. I do know the trash man will be here later so I have to get that taken out, always on Tuesdays and then the rest of the day is my own. It's now Thursday and I had a dream about the old days whe things weren't good I found my self back in Kearney waiting to get high on Meth and in the dream I even tried it, idont know why this came up but maybe it was because of having to read about it again in these writings who really knows the answer to why this took place but it felt real even after all these years. Maybe the mind wont let you forget even if it's in a dream but I do know that is a place I wouldn't want to visit again, could the subcongence be telling me something? That maybe it could happen again if I'm not careful.

I know I don't deal well with stress and maybe that could of brought it on maybe a flash back in a dream was telling me that I have come so far, so many thing's about the mind that I don't understand but maybe one day it will makee it's self clear. It's going tobe another great day as I clean up at the church after bible school yesterday, in the other world you don't walk away from it and then go back as that can get you killed so it's better to stay away from it all together. Even when you have been set free from the curse some of it could return later and at the time you don't know how to take the message, it could be that the mind is getting rid of all the bad things that happened. Through it all we find our way to freedom and can go through life like it was only for a season that we were in that dark place, a tempary situation that has passed turning another page in life. We may all get messages from up above but we have to learn to interpet them. Friday and last night was a peaceful one but the morning is cold, many things are happening in the news we have the health care system that is bad at the present and we have what they call an out break of kids using perscription drugs which has been going on for years they just didn't want to hear about it until they could capitalize on it. They say that it kills more people then all other drugs combined but they also say that about smoking now days as they try and get Marijuana legalized so more of our kids can get hooked on it, it all has to do with money and places that are trying to help kids but also destory them at the same time doesn't make any since to me. When will it all stop? The government never wanted to let people know many of the things today back when it could of saved more peoples lives why now? They are trying to confuse the public about these things so the pot can be brought in it's a thing called confuse and concer in other words they want th money that Marijuana can generate through taxess like they did with alcohol, many times I get so discusted trying to change thing but I cant fight the capital with all there money I'm only one person trying to make a change so our kids can live longer and have a happier life, yes some say I'm nuts while others think I'm funny trying to stop it. I'm just a vessel sent from God to try anyway, through the years that I have been writing some things have changed like laws but it's not enough more has to be done in order to stop this from happening. Through my time on this earth I have stayed away from the public other wise my story would of never been heard it would have been burried a long time ago but I have to keep the message going so they will know that they too can be set free of the curse that will destroy them and it will do it's attended job as long as people can make money off of it. Through the change in transportation with the ships and air-plains they can fill our country with the drugs they sell on the streets and they will kill anyone that stands in their way it's just what money does to some people the more they have the more they want and then they end up not careing what happens in the after math, I have asked God why should I care? And His reply is, you are made that way and I know that I am.

My fight has just begun and it will only get harder as things are shuved into my face like with dead lines or more of what I feel but Courtland lets me contact my inter self and you cant put a price on that the peacefulness let me do the things I need to do. I can hear the whisle of the train as its coming into town so more box cars will be unloaded to be filled with grain to send to other countries and the cycle continues, now days I do a lot of thinking of how to make the change happen but like I said I'm only one man with the lord behind me and that' something many don't have. Sunday morning and things are ready for the day I have been talking with a women from the provence of where the huracane hit the other day and I seam to really like her, for some reason we connected and I told her how to read about my story on the internet and she did so now I don't know whats going to happen next but she said she would get the word out to her friends out there in

Milan. You see the problem isn't just in the United States but around the world with every nationality and many other coltures it's early and I will try to connect to her later when I'm done here as the day went on we talked and she inspired me by reading my poetry that is on the web she also said that God had given me a beautiful gift of writing and this I believe with all my heart. As the sands of time are running I want to know my full potencial for which I haven't gotten there yet for God knew I couldn't handle it all at once how great thou are the one who brought that good memory back.

It's strange how it only appears when I start to feel the felings of love once again, what is it that brings things out only at a certain time in my life? For God has the answer and in time He will let me know, we are both alone and maybe the lord wants to change that as she has a motherly quality to her even though she is younger then I. But not too young, in her late 30's going to be 40 on January 28th. I can tell she has feelings for me but I'm not rushing into anything, as I couldn't sleep I had to get up and write maybe it's my way of trying to figure out where I'm going. Not in traveling mind you but in the universe, I know I have many works of art inside of me and they are in writing showing others this gift has eluded me until now and maybe it's time to wake it up once again. So it can come full circle, waking up the mind isn't easy because each time I had to feel love before the poetry could come out like the flower that blooms in spring. The more I talk with Eliza the more I want to be with her and maybe it's that feeling that brings the goodness out of me who knows one day I might be written up with the worlds poets in the data base that houses them all the great ones. My poetry comes from life and whats happening at the time but it needs a trigger to get it going and that trigger is love or the start of it, I have always loved kids and hers has been brought up to show respect for their elders which is a good thing my poam has been recorded in a song and still today I have it the master and the copies which will be brought out of the closet. It's like I have to promote my own writings and I believe He has a reason for that happening could my time be coming into a season for truly this could be, but I need to capture the trigger that will start it all again the feeling of love. When I'm inspired by caring and being cared for nothing can stop me. It's Monday and this next Sunday we have a chicken and biskits supper at the school, this is something we have once a year to raise money for the church so we can help more people. I know emergency relief will be needed in the Philipins after the hurricane hit this past week, we always help when the church is called upon by our brothers and sisters no matter where they are. It always feels good to me to help when it's needed, later I will go and clean so my job will be done for the next few days and then I can concentrate on my writing for a little while maybe get these few pages done. With me things can happen on the spur of the moment and ideas can come when I'm no where near my computer thus leaving me open to forgetting what came to me, maybe I need a recorder to catch those moments so they are not lost for ever or they could come back later at another date one doesn't really know for sure. On my adventures I have traveled far but none of the places I went can compare to my town of dreams, O it might sound silly to call it that but these feelings and thoughts are mine given to me by the one who made me. I'm not supposed to be like others and this I have excepted when He sent me back, lord knows many others could never understand how my mind works because I don't understand it sometimes either. It's Tuesday and on Sunday we will have a community celebration and then of course thanksgiving and Christmas. The town is having thanksgiving at the senior center so I'm excited how the turn out will be, I hope many come and eat with us at this time. That way I will get to know more people from around the communit, I remember going to Saint Louis as a child on vacation with Tom Clifton and his mother. It was the first time I almost lost my life by taking some medication I shouldn't have, they rushed me to the hospital where I had my stomic pumped but by the time I got there it had all ready went through my system. The doctor said he had done all he could do and now it was up to me weather I would pull through or not, and I pilled through but didn't wake up for four days and then I didn't know where I was.

Come to find out I was on a farm in the middle of no where, I remember before it happened I was eating at a restarunt and then my face fell into my food. I had mashed patotes and corn in my hair and on my face and that was the last thing I remembered before my ride in the Ambulance, later after it was all over and we were ready to go home Tim's mom called my parents to say we were leaving and that we would be home in a couple of days, it was a memorable vacation but I never wanted to go on another one. I was an alcoholic in those young years and being without it during the trip make me want to try something else to maybe replace the feeling that alcohol gave me which that drug didn't come close to, replacing one thing and hoping you would get the same reaction doesn't ever work. I never did try that again until I was well into my 20's mixing them all together hoping to find that untamite high which would allow me to face life the way it was. Many times we would mix things together and sometimes things worked out fine, like alcohol and codean one would let you do twice as much of the other. It's like that saying about alcohol one is too little and a thousand is never enough, and O how true that is, when my life was changed I had to learn that you can never go back to that place not even for a viisit. I never did go back but one time when I had an argument with a women I had dated for a few weeks in the early days, and it was at that time when I realized that I was still too weak to have someone that drank in my life. So we parted and she went on her way although she said she loved me I couldn't take the stress, she worked at a bar and came home late every night and she would be tipsy.

The difference between us was very great and I just couldn't be around it, she was one of the women that we took in because she didn't have a home or place to live. She saw her children that had been taken away from her once a week and she had to travel to a small town out side of the city they were cute kids and wanted to come home with her but couldn't because of the courts so that lead me to believe that she had a troublesome past but I didn't pry into her business because I know we all have things in life we have to work out. Blond hair and blue eyes was her standing out quality's, and I can say it would of worked if the alcohol and drugs weren't in the picture. We visited her kids when she felt like it but most of the time they were there in the town not far away, after our break up I don't know what happened to her but I heard that she found another guy and got into some trouble which landed him in prison and her in jail for sometime. It seams that's the nature of the beast when those two chemicals are put into someones life and usually they fall hard, I have always had a hard time staying focused on one thing thus causing me to make some mistakes but I'm still learning as each day goes by, with all that's going on through the season we are kept pretty busy and everyone pitches in so it isn't so hard on others we all have a job to do and it doesn't matter how little the job is or how small. For all the little things add up to one big one like the chicken and biskets supper they have every year. It's hard to believe it's been five years but it has and unlike some the police has never visited my house. After mom's passing in Kearney I thought it was all over having to live in my car on the streets while pop's was getting his new heart valve, it showed me that things can fall apart in a moments notice but then everything came together as God watched over me. Like the song me and boo me and Tiny traveled and parked on different streets having the cops called on us from time to time. But they understood what I was going through during that time, one thing I don't ever want to be is homeless and here in my town of dreams I'm not yesterday was Wednesday school so I have some work today. As I gave Silvia a look at my poem and she sent me a comment saying something like this, if I could give you a gift, it would be for you to see how special you are as you are truly a special person. From those words I take it that other see something I don't, I wonder why we don't see our selves as others see us maybe we would be that friend that stays in that friends zone you know the good person that everyone likes but wouldn't go out with. Back in the day I was quite a catch, but my world was not ready for something solid. Half the time I didn't know many things and I could count my girlfriends on one hand and still today it's the same way, I don't know why but many of the women don't appeal to me and the younger ones are taken. It's like I'm at that age where I'm too old or too young for the others , some in their late 30's seam to find me attractive but I don't know about them it's like we are on a different wave link they are raising children and I'm done with that stage of life could I adjust yes I believe I could but like with all things it would take time. The one women I talk to is the only one my age and she lives in Mexico, a sweet soul and a careing soul. When we met on the internet she was somewhat shy if my radar is working right, but then we sent each other Tag's saying different things like good morning and I hope you have a great day. Later I would learn that she could write in English so maybe the other way was easier for her.

She has been to many places in different countries by the pictures she has on her sight places I would only dream about going if I had the means. What does a person carry with them as they go through this life? For me kind words seams to be my baggage, as I was at work yesterday I found an old typewiter and it was electric boy I could make those keys sing but it was missing something an automatic return and a self spacer. These are things I need to be able to write well and of course a correction ribbon to correct mistakes, this morning I'm going to copy my poem so I can put it on my sight on face-book and maybe even inter it in a poem compatition you never know when you might have something that others only dream about, the content has to do with my life at a time when I felt the pain of others but since I moved here I realize that that pain I felt ws myy own, maybe it's like not seeing the forest from the trees as some can't see inside them selves and I'm no exception. We have the community get together this Sunday and people from all around will be coming even those that live in the littler towns that are not too far from here, every year the school or the church is filled up with those who have a heart with many some family members are still doing their thing in the field so they will get them some to go meals and bring them to them Courtland has the best chicken and biskets in the world and it shows by the number of people that show up each year, amazing grace is what it is as everyone pulls together to bring this too a success. Then we have the celebration of the church standing after 125 years and then Thanksgiving at the seniour center, I have to fill out a form for a Christmas basket that they give out to us who have little.

The joy out weighs the troubling times by far and God's people are brought together to enjoy this time when we are all brothers and sisters. The breaking out of a persons shell is hard when it didn't get done as a child because through the years the shell gets harder and it takes twice as much effort, but when people love you that shell can be broken because there not there to judge you but too help you get past that stage. And it can be a joy no like a bat beating it's self against a wall. Just yesterday the pastor brought our friendly neighbors package by as we got home from town and she asked my little brother if he was keeping me in line and he said yes, many new things will come our way in this next year but the sad thing is that I don't know what will take place. Weather the changes will be good or not, so I pray that only good things will come. Things that will allow me to possibly help others. I could do so much more if I had the means but it's aquireing those means that's hard, maybe in the future things will turn around and I hope they do. My inschurence company asked if I was going to the celibration at the aart center and I told her that I was, it's next Sunday and this sundy is the biskets and gravy. Tomorrow is Saturday and so I have to work for a couple of hours getting things put away and sold is my greatest job that I like, many people I have never seen before come in and then they are not strangers any longer. To me Friday is a kick back day as I havve nothing to do except what I deside to do and I never know what that might be my adventure has died off and now I'm having to bring some things back home but what I'm going to do with them is beyond me maybe start something new winter is a slow time of year so we have to do the best we can with what we have, making it through winter is hard for everyone even some that have lived here all their lives but we make it and sometimes we even enjoy a good road trip to places like Concordia. Tomorrow is the day of chicken and biskets so people are going to be busy getting everything ready my land they had enough food at the church for an Army so they will be bringing it to the school sometime in the next day then it will be school as usual on Monday, mostly the kids help out with the clean up as for them calling me to work at it they didn't but that's ok' I have enough to keep me busy. But I did enjoy serving a few years back, little brother has never been to one of our meals and hope that one day he will. Saturday and it's another cold morning last night the train went through and blew it's whistle right at the same time that pickers blew theirs on television, theres was old and came from an old steam engine and this guy had it on his wall at a place they were picking. I have seen many new cars on the streets these days and they look like theycame from outer space with their black bodies and tinted windows, the thrift store opens at 10:00 and I have to be at work by noon I don't know why but there is a change in the air and I cant tell if it's good or bad. I do know that I have to get my taxes paid and I will try and do it this next coming week so that's behind me nothing worse then getting behind on bills I wish they would all go away so my stress factor isn't so high that way I could relax and have no worries. I have taken on reading another book but this time I will read it a little slower and try to get the meaning of what it's trying to say.

One thing I did find out is that if your always in a hurry your probable doing to much we have a purpose in this life and although I'm still looking for mine many times we can miss it by not paying attention to the signs the ones that He can sometimes give us on our way through this life Sunday and it's a little cold out this morning yesterday we did good at the thrift store as old customers came in from other towns, one lady bought her daughter a coat who is homeless in Oregon. She cant figure out why she is homeless because she has two houses left to her some time ago, it's the nature of the beast when thing come into your life you never expected. I have a thought on the matter but I wont go into it not knowing the situation many people have everything and then one day it's gone like the wind that blew through a certain place in the past, we seam to think that a living can be made in a certain way and then it's lost to never come back again. I know how it feels to be homeless as I was that way once and I wouldn't want to be that way again living out of your car with an animal although I loved Tiny it was hard as no one had a place for me during that time. Kearney was still growing but hadn't gotten a homeless shelter yet and today they have a few of them helping those who don't have a home, sort of like mom did back in the day when some had to live on the streets. The passing of time has made things new once again in and I like where it has brought me in the book it says He sends us to where we need to be and this I believe because I'm here in my town of dreams where I have learned a lot young people that are addicted cant hold a job as the addiction comes first in their lives they work for a while but then the demon shows it's self once again and they fall from where they are and go back into it I call this the nature of the beast and that's what it exists for to break you down.

Back in my younger days I too was at it's mercy because it made you feel like you could take on the world but little did I know that it was all in my mind, nothing was in reality not one thing back in those days because without it the after math would set in the shaking and the hallucinating of things that weren't there Herb went through those things also and it wasn't until then that I knew what he was going through. Mine started at a young age bairly in my teens and it got worse as time and years went by asking God to help me through it as I traveled down that path abd He did help me until it was time to change so many broken promises at the time, but in the end I ended up keeping them and it brought me to where I am today. As I see it my journey is still going and there is no end in sight, although

I'm older my ambishions are still there to one day break free from poverty and have a good life to where I can help others that have gone down the path I have seen. Letting others see your life might bring them to the realization that change is possible in all of us from the gates of hell to the light of the father, the thing we go through are meant to be as our mission was put forth before our birth the Lord needed the right DNA to bring us to this place we call earth home or what ever, we are a part of the greater plan and he made everything for us the ones that he loves. It is written that some are meant to be alone but why this is I don't have a clue, one would tell you that it gives more time to get to know God because you don't have the distractions of others and great things are planed for your life but we as humans don't see this at the time as our visions are narrow and can't see into the future. As children we lived in the moment and as we grew that moment went into days, and looking at that can be scary as many thing go through your mind like what if's and what will be these are things we don't really want to think about as it makes us unsure of things. The wind is blowing this morning very hard as I can hear it through the trees maybe blowing in a storm that could drop some snow I sure hope not, the church is always open unless we get really bad weather and then we don't open it not wanting anyone hurt. The glory of God is in this place and I have a feeling it's always been here, when I was in the other places during my growing up years I never had a problem with leaving those places as a matter of fact I welcomed leaving them but that would never happen here. It's like something you have looked for all your life and finely found it, the place where he will lead you to your destiny. Many think they have the answers these physics but they don't know nothing about what He will do Monday morning and Harley was up before I was wanting to go out side funny thing though he never stays out long not wanting to be out in the cold for very long. Last night we had baritoes and boy were they good.

Little brother doesn't seam to want to meet other people other wise I would of taken him to the dinner at the school, he is very touchy about his weight and thinks people are looking at him when they are not really they have more to do then that. In many ways he is like pop's not wanting to go out but maybe that will change one day when he gets his confidence back. This next Sunday we are having the celebration of the churches 125 year of being built and it will take place st the Art center where seating will be limited to just members and staff, we also got a letter from Westly university congradulation for being here so long and I know it will get hung up on the wall in the church as an accomplishment to the people. The people are many that are members but some live so far in the country it's hard to make it there as I don't know many of their circumstances, through the years that I have been here many changes have taken place and many young people have come and gone working here in this small town. Ben has learned a lot from the Hord's in working on cars and stuff and he is a good machanic always there like the Hords to fix the things that need to be fixed Judy told me a story about how Norm went out to their field to fix two flats when they hit something that's just the way people are around here always lending a helping hand when it's needed it's another great day as I get ready for the morning but nothing gets done until I get my coffee, they reported that tornados hit Illinois and many other states destroying a lot of homes and other things. It's the worst disaster that has hit this late in the season in over 100 years and then you have that typhoon that hit our brothers and sisters over seas killing thousands of people just last week and making many of them homeless I have a friend that lives there and she said it was a mess, for us over here we send aid and help the best way we know how in hope that they will recover.

I couldn't imagine having to go through that and maybe that's part of why I live in so far out in the country away from the ocean many years ago there was a story going around that if the bubble burst in Oxnard all of the Caliifornia coast would go in the ocean, but I don't know if that was a myth or a fact just something I heard as a child while growing up. In the day when I was very young all the the kids wanted to come over because they thought our parents were cool letting us drink and smoke but if they would of only known what would take place later in our lives they too would of never wanted to touch it. I never did fit in when it came to school thinking I wasn't smart enough to make it so later I would give up and quit but now I know that was the worst thing I could have done. Your not supposed to be smart when your young that's why your in school to learn to be smart and then it goes on from there, As your gift grown after school but I had it all mixed up you never learn everything because your not meant to know everything. From what I have read our mission is given by God and then we follow that path he sets us on, all other things are just a way to make a living in this life but our true path is to the one He made for us before our birth. It says he wrote our lives out in the book of life before we were given to our parents the date we were born and the date we would leave here and be with Him in the kingdom of God. I never could understand why He didn't give us a sign or tell us what we were to do while we were here, but maybe it would of interfered with free will if we knew thus not having it to make our own mistakes. And that would go against what He gave us, in this life we will make many mistakes and we have to learn by them helping us to grow in the manner set forth in the bible. I was just talking to Eliza and she is going to send me a Christmas present boy that made me feel good it will be the first one I have gotten since like for ever. She is special in my mind and I hope that one day we might meet to ge together not only as friends but as a couple, what a great ending that would be to finely find what has been missing out of my life a bond. As for her children they have to be good kids coming from one so special but I wont jump the gun at this point and say anything else. I'm hoping that I might be able to move forward with my book but only time will tell at this point, the train is coming through as the whistle blows off in the distence and now the big motors are sounding very loud the closer they get to town. The wheels are steel on steel and you can tell if they are out of round as they will limp like a horse that has a bad leg only making contact at certain times. My little buddy Harley is resting on my bed dam' I said I wouldn't let him do that anymore but my heart is big especially when he has been sick yesterday, he only gets that way once in a while so for that I'm glad.

Never want anything to happen to him my little buddy my friend, it's trash day so I have some things I have to do good buy for now peace. Hump day and it's cold out side many times I look at things maybe in a different view, sometimes I sleep good and other times not so much the change in the weather can sometimes make it to where your not able to sleep very well being cold you have to bundle up so the cold doesn't get you I remember mom always having to have the window proped open even during winter so she would have a breeze coming in of some kind to keep her from being hot just the opiset of what I am.

So funny sometimes even though we had our boughts with the curse we loved each other and the longer the other kids didn't come around the closer we grew. Back in those days we only each other I guess you could say that me her and pops were the only ones left and I felt abanded when they also left leaving me alone with just my typewriter and the memories that we shared, when mom went to be with the lord I wanted to go with her so I climbed on the gurney with her and it took six cops to get me off of there telling me I would be ok' I recall she was still warm and there was no way I wanted to be here any more without her she had been my life taking care of her during the years that she had been ill. But really it was more then that as I saw the pain she went through and Oliver too for that matter, my self I don't believe the others cared as they had a rezentment to Oliver for taking the place of Herb. And my sister blamed mom for her fathers death but why she did that is beyond me, maybe it had something to do with her being daddies girl as she was spoiled as a child always getting her own way. As for the boys we didn't expect anything when dad would take mom and Sue out on the weekend and buy them what they wanted sister got and had every record that the new singers put out but like most material things they faded away. Sue got married for the first time at 16 years old but being so young it didn't last and they broke up after David went in the service, I don't recall much about him except that they must have been in love to take that step my the problems we go through as young kids.

I don't recall much of my child hood as I spent most of my time drinking maybe not wanting to be awake so I stayed a sleep during those years but the fun times I remember like selling advacdoes to the people in our neighborhood, and the sarrounding areas the Mexicans really liked them and we got them out of our own back yard. Unlike today they were big almost as big as a soft ball so we sold them for 25 cents a piece and had a good thing going until we moved and then that was over, I recall one time that a kid was picking on my little brother and the kid got mad and threw a sprinklet at Randy and stuck it in his head boy the crap hit the fan that day as they rushed him to the hospital. My self I didn't know if he would live or die being only about five years old but later he was home and resting with stitches in his head, it seams we all got married too young little brother at sisteen and sister at the same age they never got to grow up and it showed later in life when things fell apart they became lost without the other half and little brother fell a apart going deeper into that dark place and getting into trouble by following some people he shouldn't have. I guess not having the other half of their lives they took up with others that made them feel excepted and that's when people doing drugs step in and made him feel part of their family. People in that dark place connect like normal people do but it's all together different while Christen people connect with God they have another task at hand surviving in the world of darkness, and it's very dark there not knowing from one day to the next if you will be around. Some well with many of the dealers or pushers would go to someone's house if they didn't pay what they owed on time and threaten to kill their families, one of my friends had wanted to try and get rich off of selling the stuff and when he fell short of the payment they threatened to take his cars and if that didn't work they would do the same thing about their families and they always lived in fear of what was going to happen next. Well needless to say he got out of that situation and never went back to it a lession learned the hard way, no good comes out of destroying others lives. I always made it a practice not to remember names because that could get you killed and even today I don't recall many of my friends names but that not by choice just a defence system that was built into me many years ago. I wish I could get a teen center built here so the kids would have a place to go, a teen Christen center where they have a pool table and pin ball machines. With a pop machine, and books they can read to help them on their path. Believe it or not these things can help a person grow in many ways, Christen books to help them learn about God and Jesus the opening of a door that could lead into the realm of goodness. If I would have had the solid foundation of the Christen life I wouldn't be writing this today so I have to believe that He had this purpose in mind when I went through the things I went through, He delivered me to this time and place for a greater purpose and taking care of my little brother must have been part of that. I have spent many years working and taking care of my family not my family persay with a partner but my family in blood, which has left me without the loving of a partner the physical love that has been missing for so long. My land' it's hard to believe it's been almost 20 years since I told God that wouldn't take a partner for five years even though I tried to find one on my own it didn't work lasting only a short time, it's like I loose intrest in them or I havent found the right one that can sustain me in happiness.

At first it's great but then over time no matter how short I fall away from them it's like I loose intrest or they change one or the other. The newness wares off and it makes me not want to look for it again until something stures inside of me, like a longing to be loved again. The short times seam to last for a few years and then I'm looking for it again, maybe in hope that the next it will be forever. Always trying to find that special one that is like me or can become a part of me so we can love and go through life together. Although none of us are the same He says that there is someone for all of us but I haven't found mine yet, that special soul that longs to be loved as I do. The one that will become my other half and we can be happy together. I do know that when she comes my little brother will find it hard to deal with because it's only been us for so long he will panic and wonder how he will make it but he will as life goes on. There has to be a time when I'm supposed to be happy as for now the ride is being ridden but change will come sometime in the future I look towards God for the answers sometimes and usually He will answer me when I'm in the thick of things of things my self I'm not sure what will take place in the next few weeks but I hope and pray that things come full circle, the plant is running this morning as I listen to the augers sing the tune of getting things ready for the winter and then they will be silent for a few months until sprinng. I believe it's the plant running or it could be the wind they seam to make the same noise a howeling sound like the wind makes when it's blowing through a canyon in the western days when you watch the movies.

It sounds like it's howeling through the trees they were calling for snow and rain last night and weather it made it here is beyond me not looking out side yet too dark, little brother is up so he couldn't sleep either these things happen sometimes from time to time as for work yesterday it went well making a little head way in our two hours it was fun. As for the milll running I was wrong it's just the strong wind from the storm Marijuana is becoming a big topic and many wont stand for it to be in their community as it destroys the brain and turns it into an egg. Those using it fall from reality and end up in a world where nothing makes since. We cant let them bring this stuff into our childrens lives to destroy them before the brain is even developed. It would be a disaster. I liked a segment about Marijuana and how it shouldn't be made legal and it goes as far back ad the old testment, those using the stuff say it doesn't hurt anything but in reality it maked you odd that person that stands out away from the normal people my land' no one wants to hire a fool that destroys their own life let along that destroys others we are to live our lives as we are visitors from another country although life here seams long to us, it's but a few minutes to the lord and we should ask Him to show us it through His eyes and it says this He will do. Many of the users of pot say it will be regulated by the people who run our country and I say they don't want that burdom on them as I never would but they don't live in this world not really they go in and out of reality and think it's hunky dorie, destroying many kids lives. If I had a wish, it would be that none of our kids would have to go through the curse of addiction they would be brought up in Christen homes with God as there main focus to help them realize that they have a loving path to follow one free of the curse that could destroy them. In my life although I went through those things it was for a reason that only God knows maybe to bring about a change in the world so they wouldn't have to go through it, my self I think it would have been awesome if I would of never known about the stuff that way I could of played in the fields of green grass and just been a child with no worries but to go to school and learn the things children learn. Today I got something in my message box on myspace but I'm not quite what it means yet so I will wait for a reply from the people who sent It, if it's what I think it is then my world could change beyond my beliefs. They are calling for rain and sleet through the day and who knows what it will bring with it, I got my work done for the day so now I can stay in out of the cold my land it's freezing to the bone and I hate that kind of cold when you can't seam to get warm no matter how much you bundle up. As for the guys at the station I know they too will stay warm with the heating system they have there, Marijuana is trying to push forward but I hope it makes no progress in becoming legal as it would destroy many lives. The good book says we are to love the lord with all our hearts souls and minds with people who distort the mind they cant accomplish his part of giving them selves to God. In todays society kids and adults alike will sell them selves for the next high or fix even for booze at times, many times the down fall is brought on by looseing a loved one or family member it's always been easier to fall into the darkness then to pull your self out of the pit and go on with life.

Children are sold for their parents habbit to be filled and although some don't want to believe this the fact is that it happens every minute of every day, then comes the time when the parents loose their kids and they cry about it and wonder why it happened to them . When they should be wondering how they let it go that far, my self I don't like to talk bad about anyone but there are those that are a peace of crap to be setting their children up for the fall that will take place later in life. And with many they would give up their kids for that next high as that is their first mission to feel that needel iside their arm. Kids are traided for the drugs so the deailer can have sex with them it's all part of the game they play with others lives. All through my writing I have kept a polite approach to helping others but there comes a time when the public should hear the truth, the abuse has to go on for years sometimes before the authorities even hear about it and then by that time the damage has been done. The kids or young adults have taken on their parents addictions and later in life they will put their own kids through it to destroy them also later, do parents know what they are doing when this happens 'yes' they have to know. But they have lost the family values that they might of once had through difficulties in life, no excuse for any of it as I know so well because I have been there and done that. We are given a second chance through Jesus Christ our saviour to try and make life better or turn it around but if the person doesn't want this then the help is hopeless, it would be like beating a dead horse for when there would be no use.

The world is full of addicts that don't care about anyone not even them selves. In the beginning of my journey I tried to be friendly with the friend I used to have but it didn't work, so I moved to a place where I could find my own peace. You can't have those people around you when your trying to change your life because no matter how hard you try they pull you down with them, and you have to face it they are going no where and they don't want you to go anywhere either. As misery loves company, many times I didn't think I would make it but God showed me that I was special. Not like other people try to do but in a different way the connection isn't like anything in this world and it never will be, I cant explain it in words but it comes from the inside out in the place where He works on us to mold us into what we should have been in the first place. I know that I'm not where I want to be but I'm better then I once was with still a battle or two that I have to fight, one of these days things will come easier to me once I have been made into what He wants for my life. Some say people change because they have to and with me it really wasn't that way as I wanted to change to go on another adventure that would bring me to a different place in my life one free of what held me back before, the not going to school might have been a blessing or a curse which one I haven't figured out yet. It was like I had always had my own mind and I stuck to what I believed. Not wanting it changed for some reason, in the old days parents let their children drink John was only in his teens when it started with him and then in his 30's he passed from mouth cancer some say it was awefull the way he died having all the surgeries that took his looks away once a good looking guy he was then turned into something different. He didn't live long after it started to spread and they buried him within a year, I couldn't imaging the pain he went through but it had to of been bed. I never heard what happened to his wife as she disappeared after his death to never be seen again, she was good for him for some reason maybe it was love or maybe something else one will never know for sure. Through the sands of time we meet different people and many we like and then we have the others who we really know nothing about, the ones that sit back on the side lines and just stay out of the picture. I talked with Eliza this morning and she was feeling a little down but I seamed to lift her spirits with just a few words of kindness, she has high chelestrol and was worried but I told her that I had the same thing and she needs to cut back on being sad only happiness can cure that as long as she stops being stressed, I know how hard it can be to raise two children by ones self and I hope that one day she can come here and be with me. It would be nice to have someone who would spend the rest of their life with me and help out where help needs to be. I havent came right out and said it yet but I think I'm fallling for her or her spirit which resides in the tent. She believes in God as I do and who knows maybe I will be able to bring her over here one day to start a new chapter in both of our lives she seams to be a quiet soul except for when we talk together. Not asking anything from me like so many others have in the past and she is even sending me a T-shirt through Fed-x she seams to have a giving soul not wanting anything for her self, that's the kind of women I would like to spoil because she would be happy with just the little things.

I would like to try and have a family one more time and I think my kids would welcome who ever I chose to be a part of that. I just want to be complete and have the other half ofme by my side. The kids would like the schools that are here and they could grow to know this country, this would be the final step to being happy should the lord find me worthy of this next step. We all hear about the fairy tail ending and I would like to have that but I also know it seldom comes out that way, only God could bring her to me. It's TGIF Friday for those who don't get it. As the weekend is upon us we have many things we have to do our service for Sunday will take place later in the day with the 125 anniversary of our church being celebrated, many will come but we only have room for so many in the Art center then we will have service afterwards in the church it will be a full day for some and just a delight for others as we eat together and give thanks for the years that we the people have existed and the people before us who gave so much to bring this day here today, all my friends will be there and I hope I have clean cloths cant forget to wash them. It's going to be another beautiful day, but I hope it's without the cold and rain so I can go out and get some things done tomorrow I will go back to work at the thrift store and I hope we bring in more money then on Wednesday. I find my self wanting to get on the computer more these days in hope to talk with Eliza, it like I miss talking with her could this be the start of something that could last? I sure hope so, it's like I have known her most of my life the way we talk together and I love it.

She could be the one even though she is far away and to have her next to me would be great, she is nothing like the women here in the United States although there is nothing wrong with them or anything I just think she would fit me perfect as I scence she is shy like me and she wouldn't wonder like so many do here. Back in the old days they had mail order brides and I have met one who was in her 80's, she told me that she came from New York when she was young and she never left after she was married. That wass before I moved here so I don't even know if she is still alive, many things can happen in five years and I cant count the old people who have passed since my arrival. Life is full of supprises and we never know when change will take place or weather the change will be good or bad it's all in the cards and the way you play your hand. I have seen things go from good to bad in a heart beat and visa virsa it just how things go sometimes in life. But we have to take the good with the bad, it's another cold November morning usually we have snow by now but it hasn't made it's way here yet. And I have a feeling that when it does it will be a big storm they say it's supposed to be bad this year but I'm hoping it's not as I don't like diging our afterwards with a shuvel, one of these days I will have to get a new one because the old one is about 10 years old and ready to break the ageing of the wood in this changing weather makes things rot pretty fast I'm hoping that things will go back to normal later as we get deeper into the end of this year, all the holidays are keeping us busy and tomorrow we have our celebration at noon a time to give thanks for the church we attend each week my land' I cant even fantom 125 years but I do know that some of our people have been here around for a portion of that time at leasy 50 of those years and it's great that they have loved God for all that time. My self it's only been a fraction of that time since God found me on that day and even today I still have him in my life how great is that? I try and do my best to keep my part of things going as we all have a job to do in the church and working at the thrift store is just another thing I like doing. The train is coming through as I write this to pick up or drop off some box cars, it is written that God molds us so we can fit in at the place which we live making us a part of a community and I feel this when it happens this morning I will go down and make sure the church it ready for tomorrow, the lunch will be at noon and then a service afterwards around 2:00 in the afternoon maybe this will help in some way, to bring more people to our house of worship all these things are new to me as I march forward in the name of Christ learning as I go the things I never got to learn before. Sometimes we doubt our selves and when that happens we need to look to God for the answers and this I do and He answeres me not through words but through signs and feelings this lets me know that it's ok' to move forward, I am but a vessel in this world of His and everything I have is his it's just borrowed while I'm here and then when I pass it returns to Him for someone else to use. Even my home is his borrowed for the short time that I'm here and someone else will take my place when that time comes someone who will want to learn about the lord as I like to.

I don't have the answers for all things but I do know that when I'm stressed I take it to the lord and He lets me know what to do. An old friend of mine asked if he could be put on my friends list on face book and I excepted. I had thought he had died long ago but he had been away for a time and man he looks good after his time away I don't know where he is living but if I had to guess it's back in Kearney not a good place for him as that's where he got into trouble before it's like getting into a car wreck and then getting back in the same car and doing it over again. From what I have learned we are ambasitors for God not meant to get to attached to things in this world because this world isn't our home, it never has been or will it ever be. God said I am not of this world and either are you this world is not your home so don't get too attached to the things in it. For all the things in this world will pass away and believe this has to do with the new coming of Christ, all that my parents had has pased away and the things we have will also pass away, I have always liked the thought of Going to heaven and maybe that's why I follow the words of the bible. Although I don't fully understand the bible it's clear about that part, our home is a better place and that's why we go through disapointments here so we may know the better things that await us life here is a test according to some "Those in frequent contact with the things of this world should make good use of them without becoming attached to them, for this world and all it contains will pass away." Compaired to other centuries, life has never been easier for much of the western world. We are constantly entertained, amused, and catered to. With all the fascinating attractions, mesmerizing media, and enjoyable experiences available today, it's easy to forget that the pursuit of happpiness is not what life is all about..Only when we remember that life is a test, a trust, and a temporary assignment will the appeal of things lose their grip on our lives. We are getting ready for something more better. "The things we see now are here today, and gone tomorrow. But the things we can't see now will last forever. Th fact that earth is not our home explains why, as we follow Jesus, we experience difficulty, sorrow, and rejection in this world. It also explains why some of God's promises seem unfulfilled.

To me this is not the end of the story, because life will go on after these bodys die off and we are released to go to that better place. It's Sunday the day of the celebration the birth of our church 125 years ago and from what I gathered many will attend. It's a great day to remember the birth of something so great as brothers and sisters come together, they will give thanks to God for these years and we will then move on to the now for which this brings together people who may have not attended the church in a long time. This should be a new learning experience for me, in my life I never could be with someone that I had just met for without feelings nothing exist a good thing to follow with all the HIV That's going around absents is always better when nothing is solid. My story is one of good and bad choices that I have made,so many things could of turned out different if I had made more wrong choices. I couldn't imagine how life would of turned out if I would have been careless about sex. Many of the people I have known through the years have died by not being careful but out of respect I won't use their names even though they are gone. Could things of been different if I would of went to high school out side of the place I was living at the time very much so. I guess counting your lovers on one hand is a plus for me, in this world we will find friends and maybe even some we might become closer to but caution is always the best deal. Monday and I got a comment from Eliza asking God to watch over me such a great gesture from a pretty lady we had our celebration on Sunday and Sam brought over some food and asked if I ordered Chinese there were people from Nebraska and all over the church was full beyond compasety the meal he brought over was roast beef and all the fixing, Wednesday I have to help in getting everything ready for thanksgiving setting up and stuff and then the ladies come in and put up the decorations. It's going to be a great thanksgiving as long ass the weather holds, we have told everyone about it so by word of mouth it should begreat, one guy came up to me in church and asked who I was and I told him that my name is Roger Mattson and I shook his hand he said he used to live here about 50 years ago annd I told him that it was nice that he came to visit. It was nice that they all came to visit my land' there must have been 100 people there to celebrate with us on the 125 anniversary of Methodisum, the man that came was the one who sees over all the churchess here in Kansas and Nebraska my he has a great job and he can be funny, that's what it takes to reach some people and one day if the lord willing I would like to try my hand at it spreading the word of God that's our mission on this earth because in the end we are going to need what we are taught for the next and final stage of our lives.

God the one so grand that he gave his son so we could live from what I understand this isn't our home we are to pass from this place like mom and pop's did to live for ever in a place we cant even fantom in this world. Many are afraid of death bu from the glimp's I got there is nothing to be afraid of only peace and harmony, it's a little colder this morning but I hope the tempature goes up as the day wares on making it a nice day for all of us. The peacefulness is very inviting this morning as I can't hear nothing but a few dogs barking down the road, it's this time of the day when things seam so peaceful and in a way I think God knew what I would need to be at peace here in the heart land , I still recall the accident that must have brought me here all those years ago even then I must not of listened to what was happening because all those years later it was that which brought me back here. I have to say that yesterday I felt more alive then ever with all my Christen brothers and sisters around me for they had learned something at the church I go to now pastor Kathy said that the bishop was her mentor through the time she has been a pastor and he had helped her a lot my she is a great pastor, so full of love and understanding and she truly cares for her flock that she has been in charge of The good book says that we are to bring more people to christ and this gives Him glory to his name.

Only when we bring more people to christ will our job be somewhat done then you have to hold them close to your heart. Many pastor have come here and many have left but Kathy loves everyone for who they are and that makes a big difference, no matter if your cripples or whole the out come is the same God loves us all. Many times I forget this when personal problems hit me and when I should take my problems to God I take it to someone else for a helping hand. Who knows maybe one day I will get it perfect but for now it's a learning thing with me the learning of right and wrong things to do when you feel there is no way out. It's Tuesday and it's cold out side the other states are getting a bunch of snow as for us not yet have we gotten a big amount and I hope we don't for a while maybe Christmas would be a good time but not until then God seams to let us dig a hole that can worry us sometimes but through it all a lesson is learned that could make us better, and choose our battles more wisely through the time that I have been making things the market goes up and down, and who knows where it might end up by the time I get things straightened out. Little brother caughs a lot during the night and I wish he would quit smoking but that like telling someone to quit breathing after a life time of doing it. Through the winter it get's mighty cold here with ice hanging off the houses and the trees letting us know that winter is finely here, the town goes to sleep you might say as many stay in their homes but the dogs are out scavenging for food which sometimes I feed them by putting things out on the back porch. All God's creachers have to eat no matter what . Like with all things there is a reason for them being here on earth the birds sing and even the ants have their jobs of being ant's for which I'm glad they don't get into my house very oftend they are a pest, I don't really know what He has instore for me next but I'm sure it's something good as I move forward in this journey. The breaking of bread is the day I really like and we do it once a month at the beginning of the month it's a time when people who love God come together and take the juice of the vine, I have a lot to do this morning as I take out the trash and get things back to normal so everything will be clean once again. When the seed's of addiction is planted early the child they grow not knowing their full potenchal as the curse turns them away for learning the new things in life, but there is hope no matter how long it's been. For me it took many years of trying to find out who I was and still I'm trying to do that you have to give your self to something bigger then you are. It's another cold morning here in Courtland but a person can only rest so much then they have to get out and do something thank God I'm going to help with things at the center today and tomorrow that way maybe I can keep busy with things and my mind off of the other things that bother me I don't know why but something is happening but I can't put my finger on it the down fall of something maybe or the beginning of something great we all must have premenitions but to be able to inturpet them is some else. When things come to me I don't know the way to bring them about. Many years ago I tried to break free from the curse and it wouldn't let me but then after many time's of trying it came to be that it would leave but why did it? This had to be a force of God or else I was that strong and didn't know it. As for having help from others that didn't come until later when my writings started to get out to the public, on the 1st I will see if everything goes the way I hoped and if not then I will have to figure out something else.

I always try to do my best with getting everything paid on time but hard times might be on their way as things might take a turn towards the depression days for me any way. I liked it better when things weren't so pressing as I was used to being without but now that I had a taste of the other side of the coin it's hard to turn back but life is full of struggles and we have to work through them. I keep my tax stubs by my computer so as to remind me that they have to be paid to keep the house, many of my friends have gone through the ruff times and came out on the other side so I willl too. When we set our minds to something we should do it with out reservation and then hope for the best out come. Thanksgiving day it's cold out side and later I have to go and serve the people who are coming to the center for thanksgiving I asked my friend how many reservations they had and they replyed about ten but that doesn't mean that that's the only number of people that will show up, there will be more many more I hope we don't want anyone to go hungry in my town of dreams but in reality some might be too shy to come in, so if they like we can deliver if at all possible. It's a time for giving and helping others a time for peace in the world today, we still havent gotten any snow but the rest of the country is being snowed in by the blizard I sure hope they make it to where they are going during this giving time of year, my days are filled with doing things but yesterday I missed working at the thrift store I don't know why it happened but it did not paying enough attenchion to the time I guess.

Next month is Chrristmas and it's just around the corner, three days start the count down and I don't know what I will be doing during that month some of the older people are set in their ways but I know change will be coming in the future as the people start to move from the bigger cities into the country where they can at least find a home to live in. if the town would build a low income place many more would come but even here the housing is hard to find, some places are empty by the old folks dieing but that seams to be the only time something becomes available and maybe that's why they are fixing up the house next door. To sell it to a family that has kids, bringing up the count of young people here to Courtland. One never knows the reason for people doing the things they do, I'm just grateful that my home is secure for now anyway we can never know what the future holds in this world today. Like a book that was made into a movie long ago it will be the strength of the people weather my town of dreams grow, for one book brought people out of curiosity to a place to see what one writer saw. Can we ever know exactly why things happen the way they do? Maybe God has a hand in all of it. Weather something fails or is given rebirty to, like with my self I feel rebirth is always better then failing. A fresh new start to something that could of died, all that I am was born here in my mind and it's only fitting that my dream doesn't die like so many other things in this world. I hope to one day have another love but I know it will take making a good living first so the kids will be provided for, some things cant be written yet because they haven't happened so until I know for sure we leave it at that. I find that there are many lonely women out there just as there are men, you have to find the one that touches your heart before you move forward. And try to fill that void and then you don't really know if it will work out once you really get together in person. So many things to consider when finding the right person for your self Elzia sounds right for me, she is so kind and would make a good wife should that happen. Yesterday was thanksgiving and we had a fun at the center with all our good friends young and old, one thing a young man said stuck in my mind and that was that happiness is a mind set. He brought his wife and children to enjoy the celebration and me and Robert and Kathy made up the plates for them we had to of had 40 or so people who showed up and we hope for many more next year one of the servers ws the retired principle of the school from many years ago, it was the first time I had ever been a part of such a great thing and I could feel God's presents there in the center, many of the people I knew from chuch but there was others that I had met for the first time. For the first time I felt like I was part of a family a bigger picture of things that are great, like Elzia said it's the little things you do that touches others hearts and leaves a mark. Sam Brown and Kathey Aeillo made the arangements for the event to happen and many donated some of the food for the feast and for that we were all grateful, life in my town of dreams is becoming more real then ever now and at this point I plan on staying for what ever time God gives me here, John was a card as usual and had us laughing it was such a good time. For maybe one day the stories you here about hunger will be no more in the richest Nation in the world, why it's that way is beyond me at this point but I know in my town of dreams there should be no one going hungry.. Saturday morning and I can hear an air-compressor running somewhere but the only one I know of is down at the station and that's two blocks down the road or it could be on the train that's going therough town, a lot of noise for this time of morning being it's only 2:00 in the Am. I cant get the celebration out of my mind and how well it went for the first one we were all like family with our differences there was nothing but joy. We are all made different but yet still the same in many aspects.

Our town knows each other and not one person was rude obnoxious during this time and we all helped to clean up before we left, Phillis is having her birthday there today so I hope she has a great one. Her illness has kept her from coming to church sometimes but that can't be helped as it would only make her sicker to be out in the cold air during winter, and I hope she is around for many more years to come. All my friends are dear to me as I have learned to love each and everyone of them. Although we were brought together in their later years in life we have become like family and who knows maybe I was brought here to write about there lives so they wont be forgotten. I haven't seen Norman lately' I sure hope he is still doing fine and is not sick, his heartatache sure caught some by surprise. But they say he has always been a hard worker making a way for his family through out the years, he hasn't been the same since his wifes passing a love that grew through out the years to be taken away after a life time. He needs something to remind him that with all of us we are only here for a little while and then we will spend eternity in heaven with our loved ones to be parted no more. God's promas to us as we follow Him. Elzia wrote me to let me know that her and the kids are at the zoo having a good time watching the bird show with her friend she is such a good mother.

I can't know what it's like to live where she lives different coltures and stuff I have never been out of the United States. But maybe one day I can see other parts of the world, you never know what He has in store for us as we make a path through this world. I do know she has a phone as she send a message from the zoo so maybe one day we can talk. As for today I need to check the church to make sure it's ready for tomorrow and I will do that later when it warms up also I have to work at the thrift store if they are open. Sunday and the thrift store wasn't open this weekend and the church isn't ready to be cleaned as they are still working down there getting things ready for Christmas, I went and sat out the things for communion and the ladies were busy as heck so there might be a little I will have to do this morning but communion is most important right now my land' it's another cold morning here in the heart land and yesterday it was up in the 50's the seasons change and things come and go but my town of dreams will always be here at least through my life time the black burns was saying that plots at the cemetery were only about $17.00 in the old days and they bought a few of them I could imagine the price of them now probable in the thousands, my friend Mark called when I was a sleep so I returned his call yesterday, he was telling me about how he might go out to take care of his sisters home in some other state, which would be good for him or he might go to Colorado to a cemenary to learn more about the word of God which would also be good but through his words I could tell that he missed me being around. As it says as one door opens one is shut so we can move on with our lives, through the ruff and tuff times we are given a chance to correct some things in our lives so we can go on to better things like doing the good work of the lord. I don't really know what the future holds for me as of yet but I do know that my writing is a big part of it, it could be that it helped me to make it through the tuff times so I wouldn't go back to the way life was so long ago. And if it has done that for me then maybe others can learn from it also never give up on your self you have the power to over come anything given the right situation and break's we never will know when our ship will come in untill it shows up on your door step and then I have a feeling that all will be ok. I saw Norman yesterday as he was going to get his mail so I take it that he is doing alright he sure is a good friends as is all the people here in my town of dreams. I have seen many things in my life both good and bad but the good out weighs the bad by far, the addiction is far behind me now and has been for quite some time and it's like I would like to one day write about better days in my life. Actor Paul Walker diesin a car crash this weekend he was known for playing the cop on the Fast and the Fearious I seams he was in a car and hit a tree and then a street light it just goes to show that we never know when pur time will come he was only 40 years old RIP. 40 years old isn't old really I can remember not seeing that far into the future almost ending up where he went at the age of 32 years it's strange how they couldn't garentee me until morning and now here I am today 23 years later. Truly a blessing from God that I'm here, it could of happened a few times but it didn't the first time here in Kansas so long ago and then in Colorado. I believe He tries to let us see that we are blessed.

But with us being only human many don't want to see these things when their lives are spared by the creator who made us. I know that back in those days I didn't see it either as life was all jumbled up with the everyday things that went on, just making it through a day was hell especially when your addicted to alcohol and drugs it took all you had and then some not until I took my life back did I start to see the blessings of God and he showed me that life didn't have to be that hard struggling to make it through a day let along a year. Back then I couldn't see what I see today or as far, although I can't do the things I used to, maybe it's for the best always trying to please everyone but my self and hold onto someone that I really didn't want to be with. It wasn't until my later years that I found out that I'm much better at being alone then to be with someone I didn't really care for towards the end so much time wasted when I could of found something different. If we added up the time wasted on this earth how much of that time would be mine? Years I suppect but now being 55 I should have a few more years left the lord works in mysterious ways to bring about events that can bring us to different places. Two worlds exist here on earth one set in the darkness of the devil and the other living in the light of goodness to help others as we go through this life he has given back to me so long ago, where the mind is clear as for the days of giving up on life they too have been a thing of the past for quite some time so I move forward in hope for a better life. Don't get me wrong I just want things to be better then they were back in the dark ages of my past, as for my time here I don't even know.

How long my clock is set for, it plainly says that he set a time for our birth and a time for us to go and be with him we know the first our time of birth. But the time of our death is still in his hands, unknown to us until the time comes three times he could of taken me but each time it wasn't my time. That's riding on the edge of life but still it wasn't my time, it's that time of year when pop's comes to mind when we used to have Christmas together although we didn't have much we shared what we had with each other. Making that time special, he was special to me being my dad for so many years. As for the others they wouldn't even consider taking him in let along careing for him, but we made it through the good and the bad times to finely make it here to Courtland where he rest in peace. Now days Christmas doesn't seam as exciting as it used to be but I do have the church and my friends, speaking of church I didn't make it today feeling poorly for some reason with my eyes swelled shut. But now things seam to be going back to normal or what I know is normal to me anyway, I know they will all wonder what happened because I never miss church strange how we change one thing for another when you take one bad thing out of your life, something good has to replace it and I replaced those bad things with the lord the one that created me. Monday and it's 22 days until Christmas each day will bring something new as we move forward towards 2014, I wonder what's in store for us as I learn more about the lord will times get better for the homeless and starving or will they just stay the same we will see. As I watched a show on the homeless many of them live in Alaska where the temps are freezing, as I watched one state trooper stop to check on one old man laying in the streets because they seam to go to sleep on the streets there and then freeze to death in their sleep. The guy was so drunk that he couldn't stand so they took him to jail so he could sleep it off for 12 hours, as he was being put in the troopers car his wife came running and she said she would take care of him. But they couldn't let her do that either, as she was drunk but could walk they told her that they can't let one person a little less drunk take care of the other. Alcohol seams to be a bad thing there with the people and some towns don't allow it at all, and if you get caught with it you go right to jail along with the drugs dealers and users. It's a never ending cycle it seams especially up there where it's so cold, this reminds me of Jerry Allen my uncle when he would take trunks of wiskey back with him on the plane working on the pipe line. Some would rather drink then have a home or a place to stay warm that's just the nature of the beast when it gets it's hooks into you. Jerry has been dead for many years but he was a good man at heart caring for those close to him, his heart was wide for many but the booze and Marijuana killed him. We kids thought he hung the moon because he would take us camping and let us do our own thing, when it came to alcohol and things. He was an Iron worker building big buildings by hanging from the steel beams of a building, my self I could never of had that much nerve but he did it. He worked hard and he lived hard until that night when they hauled him off for the last time to the hospital, after he was buried they sold the house an we went on a road trip and never did stay in one place too long.

Little brother married his only daughter which was very young at the time and they had tow beautiful children later in years they split up and got divorced. And the cycle of life keep going they now have their own kids which makes little brother a grand father, as far as I know he has never seen his grand children but I hope one day this will happen. I know from experience that regreat is hard, but it says in the good book to never stop moving forward and maybe in that time the past will be washed away. So a new life can start. With me it took many years of working on my self breaking that shell I lived in for so many years sort of like peeling an orange really and not knowing what's inside once it's peeled, very scary back then but I like to think I turned out ok' but it took more then just my will power it took a hand from God to show me the way. Sometimes it would come in a dream and other times when I was wide awake like an epiphany you might say, when I would ask why he would give me a little piece of the vision showing me why things happened the way they did. And then one day it was clear I was supposed to go through those things so I could write about them first hand, my life story that could help to change others lives. My spirit must be an old one because sometimes I feel like I don't fit in this world, maybe brought here for a certain purpose one that will be made more clear later. The things I have seen in this world with poverty and the other saddens me but like I have said before I'm only one person.

Will the world change or will it destroy it's self I surely hope it isn't the ladder, so much good could be done if given the right opportunity. As for the homeless there are shelters but like one man said I wasn't always this way I was once a teacher, but then one day I lost it all. This is something you hear about all the time I can't help but remember the old gentelman that was hitch hiking and how he took our picture I wonder where he is now? In Denver maybe as that's where he was going to be with his wife. He was kind and careing and we had a good talk, he knows our names as we said good by just down on the highway from here when we parted ways we told him God bless and have a safe trip and he gave me two dollare for the ride strange but cool. Who could he have been? Like the stranger that came to the church a few years ago out of no where that was from Minnesota the same place I was born and we stoped the destruction of our lives in the same year many things have happened that I can't explain, maybe spirits sent to check on me I can't really know for sure. It's been a good day and tomorrow should be even better, I met a women at the water company and she told me that I smelled good which made me feel real good she is a pretty women and I'm going to see if I can get to know her. I was about to go to bed so I told God good night as he has been good to me for so long and he has gotten use to me telling Him good night. And when I forget to tell him this he seams to wake me up before my time to get up, as a reminder that I had forgotten to tell him. Everything I hoped for has come together so forward is the only direction I can move and pray that the full circle comes together like a ring that bonds a marrige, well now I'm getting tired so until later. December 3rd 2013, the year is coming to a close as we get closer to Christmas and this year I have gotten what I asked for a chance to move forward in my life but something strange happened last night as I had a dream that my brother I havent seen since I moved from Kearney was trying to kill me somewhere on a farm. I don't know why this dream took place but some say there is a message in dreams maybe a warning from God that something could happen I'm not quite sure why I happened to have it last night but it could be a caution signe for something. With me dreams are usually not bad but I didn't like that one, with the day not started yet I can't say what might take place today. My friend wasn't in at the bank but his son took care of me so I could get things going and not have to worry about things for a while, it seams my honesty speaks for it's self when it comes to being trusted by others. When I see and hear about some being dishonest that song has never played in my mind, I guess doing good pays off in the long run of things. Later this morning we will go down and get the bills paid so that's behind us for the month and then we will do what ever comes to mind like vaccume and clean the carpets and then the kitchen so everything is ready for the holiday season, I also have to have a friend come over and set up my computer with this new soft ware that way I can go on with my writing. He is a good kid and he is breaking out in his own business something we all have taken steps into so that maybe one day we can have a way to not have so much stressing our lives. Yesterday I changed the oil in the car so now it's set for 7500 more miles, and it will save money in the long run not having to have it done again until next spring. We had a beautiful day yesterday as the temp was in the low 60's but the weather is supposed to change by the weekend with chances of snow not something I look forward to, having to take Randy to Concorida on the 10th but in years passed we have always made the trip with no problem.

On the 8th the kids from Wednesday school are putting on a program and I so want to go, they are learning so much about the lord and it shows like when they learned sign language to communicate with Brent and then on the 125 year celebration for the church they did a little play sining the lords prayer. This is a big thing for children as for us old folk it's a lot harder, I believe it's easier to learn as achild like the rose that blooms they are still growing but then when you get to be full grown it's harder because the rose is fully open and only closes at night, like when we go to sleep. I love the kids as they get smarter each year and even learn my name, sometimes when I drive by the school they wave and yell hi Roger a message that they see many thing so we adults have to make a good impression. The one child is learning to play piano and she has become good over the last year or so, it shows the learning process at it's finest. Kids are great, when I have paid the bills what ever is left usually kust lasts the month but we survive and that's all that matters maybe God willing we wont have to worry so much by this time next year and things will be a little easier. I talk to God more then most folks but He is a big part of my life and he is my buddy as I walk through this life He is always there when I need a hand no matter if it's talking or just having His company when I'm confused about something. I tell him good morning and good night especially good night or else he will wake me up until I do say it, that might seam strange to some but not me. As I have been doing it for a long time, I asked him to bring me a good women this year so we will see what happens this is the first year I have asked for such a thing. Well ! All things are possible through God and this I know because the bible tells me so.

The ladies got the church decorated and boy it looks beautiful they always make it beautiful each year and put in a great deal of time into it it's like their passion and we are all grateful for their hard work. I'm told that some believe I'm a gift from God and I believe I am also, I came here a stranger but that soon changd as we learned to love each other there is no better feeling then to be loved to me anyway. Even though it was hard in the beginning I stayed, and I'm now happy happier then I have been in years and it gets better all the time I believe all kids should grow up in a community just like my town of dreams. For the love and the grace of God is truly here in this little town in the heart land and with every beat of that heart the town grows stronger, one day I would like to be like a secret helper and help those who have life hard you know the ones that can't afford to have enough food or need other things. For this I would love to do God willing to have enough to share to give to others and make their lives a little happier, the gift of giving I will do when things give me the chance to accomplish this. It's always better to see a smile on a childs face then to see the sadness from not having enough, who knows maybe through this book I can do these things. God knows there is a reason he has lead me down this road and brought me to this time and place, as for my self I only need enough to stay a float so I can make this happen. I can't say why I feel this way but the feeling I have comes from the heart and the wanting to change things. It says many things we are supposed to do in the bible but I think many fall short of that goal, a guy named John Piper notes, God is most glorified in us when we are most satisfied in him. We bring glory to God by loving others believers and we become a part of Gods family when we are reborn again,, at that stage things are made new as that's my belief. When it happened and I came out of the coma, I knew something had happened. That a change had taken place but back then I couldn't put it all together and I don't believe I was supposed to at that time as my mind wasn't up to par or normal, still damaged by the things I went through it ws all I could do at that point to make it through a day. And when the bad news kept coming it made mme wonder why I would be put through such a trying time, but I fought to the best of my ability to go on and slowly progress came. My mind didn't uderstand much of what was happening at that time as doctors said the brain damage couldn't be fixed or in other words it couldn't be reversed. I don't believe we think about God to much at that point with all the things I had on my plate and even trying to remember it all today is almost impossible because the brain was damaged but I slowly built up my strength and went on with life, I remember one time talking to my doctor Dr. JD

Nelson and I told him that I didn't know why I was even allowed to live because I thought at that time I really didn't wan't to be here. And him being a brother in Christ he told me that God had a greater perpose for my life and in time I would find out what it was, at that time it seamed to me that I was always waiting for something to happen, it was the beginning of my journey and I hadn't a clue what would take place.

I felt pain very deeply inside and I didn't like that pain wising sometimes that my legs wouldn't of gained feeling at times it felt like a bad tooth ache and I cried almost every day. On some days I cried until I fell a sleep and then when I would awake the pain returned, like a little child that had broken their leg all I wanted was for it to go away and it never did so I believe my mind got used to the pain shuting it out by some miracle, when I came home I knew something miraculis had happened and I never did go back to the alcohol knowing somewhere in my mind that I had been given something but what it was I had no clue not until years later. At that time I had no understanding of what was to come because God doesn't share the future with us only the present time we are in and my understanding of the world was nill nothing because my world was the dark side that world where many folks live each day and they don't even know they are there. As my life was different I didn't know anything but I did come back through the light with those two words that I knew nothing about (Melchisedek) and (Epiphany) which in time drew me to finding out what they meant, so I asked some folks if they knew and they had not a clue except for one man Fran but this was after I had found out the meaning of them. I guess you could say I pulled a history question on them and it was devious, but out of the members in bible school Fran knew that Melchisedek was God's priest but he didn't know the story so I told the class. He was born like unto the son of God, without mother, without father, or without decent. He was ever present nither having the beginning of days, not the end of life.a priest continuly. I believe he was around in the beginning as he is mentioned in GENESIS as the King of Salem who brought forth bread and wine to Abram and blessed him, for which Abram gave a tenth of all to him.

This is the first book of the bible and then later he is mentioned a few books later and then it's like he disappeared, then later Jesus was made a priest after the order of Melchisedek a priest for ever more. It says that Jesus was ever present and being a part of the trinity this would be so, and it makes me wonder if Jesus was Melchisedek before he came to earth and was reborn into Mary. It's like this story leaves you up in the air because it has no ending but then it really doesn't need one because if you are meant to know the whole story then God will bring it to light making the impossible possible, nothing is beyond God having us understand something if were meant to understand it. It's Wednesday' and the wind is blowing out side as you can hear it through the trees, it reminds me of the time when I lived in Flag Staff Arizona at kbob national forest. Before each storm the wind would blow hard and bend the trees letting us know that a storm is on it's way, so we would hurry and get grocries to last through the storm so we didn't starve. It was a old house trailor and very cold because the walls were so thin, you could almost feel the weather inside but it was shelter from the storm and that's all we needed at the time. It was during his dark time when I got the call that my mother was dieing so needless to say I left my wife and went back to Nebraska so I could see her and then spent the next deckaid nurceing her back to health. Some have wondered how they could bring glory to God?

The son told the father, "I brought glory to you here on earth by doing everything you told me to do" Jesus honered God by fulfilling his purpose on earth. We honor God the same way. When anything in creation fullfills it's purpose, it brings glory to God. Birds bring glory to God by flying, cherping, singing and doing other things like bird like activitys that God intended. Even the lowly ant brings Him glory when it fullfills the purpose it was created for. God made ants to be ants, and he made you to be you. Some saint said, "The glory of God is a human being fully alive!" There are many ways to bring glory to God, but they can be sumed up in His five purposes for your life. We bring God glory by worshiping him. Worship is our first responsibility to God. We wprship him by enjoying him, " In commanding us to glorify him, God is inviting us to enjoy him." God wants our worship to be motivated by love, thanksgiving, and delight, not duty. We bring glory to God by becoming like Christ. Once we are born into God's family, he wants us to grow to spiritual maturity. What does that look like? Spiritual maturity is becoming like Jesus in the way we think, feel, and act. The more we develop Christlike character, the more we will bring glory to God. The bible says, As the spirit of the lord works within us, we become more and more like him and reflect his glory even more. God gave me a new life and a new nature when I accepted Christ. Now, for the rest of my life on earth, he wants to continue the process of changing my character. The Bible says, "May you always be filled with the fruit of your salvation, those good things that are produced in your life by Jesus Christ- for this will bring much glory and prase to God. Thursday I don't know all the answers but I do know e loves us all through his being ther for us. I give glory to him by singing something I couldn't do in the beginning because my mind wasn't working the way it should have been, but through his careing he healed those things.

I like it when I get communion ready for everyone and in a way that says a lot about how I feel. He has become a part of my everyday life just by making sure I get up each day. I don't know if they had Wednesday school yesterday but I will check later this morning, my purpose here is to do the things I do here in Courtland for everything that's created has a purpose and when that purpose is fulfilled that also brings glory to him. Even Harley has a purpose being a dog and he shows me love everyday that's his purpose to be him self in this world, my little buddy. They are calling for snow over the next few days but I hope it doesn't get too bad yesterday it was icey so we had to be careful going to town the ice was built up on the windows and it took some time to get it thawed. This next Sunday the kids will put on a Christmas show and I so enjoy watching them it's like I fill up with pride for some reason and I think it's because I'm proud of them. As I go through this life I would love to be like Christ, he was very humble and kind and this is the way we are to become. I do my best to be humble and I'm kind to those I know my brothers and sisters, many people like Martin King said I had a dream.

A visionary about things to come and the changes he talked about came to pass later after he was killed, God gave him those dreams but it was up to him to say what they were like with everything created it has to be fulfilled before it brings glory to God. When I learn something new like the way Jesus lived I try to addapt that into my life and although it takes time I'm humbled when I meet someone as I'm a product of his good ness something he created out of nothing like many thing on this earth.

Sam asked if I would take out his dog today and tomorrow and I told him that I would, he is a good friend and so is his parents. They believe and love the lord as many of us do that go to our church, but I have found out that there are others that are true believers we just go to different churches. There is three other churches here in my town of dreams, one about six miles out side the town and the rest are here in the town we are all connected by one thing and that is the love we all share for God. The preference of the church we go to is totally our own but like it says that is just a building it's the souls that make the church my soul your soul and anyone elses that wants to love the lord, Jesus had two brothers, but you don't hear about them in the teachings not very often, for the lord gave them to Mary' and her husband. A gift from the one on high as of yet I don't know anything about them but maybe later I will learn more. It's another cold morning as winter has set in for the season, a cold time when I should study more to keep learning. We bring many things with us when we move somewhere but in the end we take nothing with us because we wont need anything when we go to our final home. And what was taken from us here will be returned when we get home as for me many things have been given back here. The ability to walk and the healing of the mind, and body, to a certain extent. All gifts so I can become better then I oncee was, these things are needed to lead a somewhat stable life on this planet and so far I'm doing fine. My story is winding down as I move towards the end but I do know that others will come other with more joy in them happy times that I will share with others as my life continues, what will the next year bring? I suppect a little of everything but through it all my love will never change for the one who gave me that second chance. In the beginning I was like the baby being born clueless of what would take place in the imediate future or distant, for that matter. Like the letter you might get in the mail you never know whats inside until you open it, and read the pages could be something good or a bad news letter you never know until you take that step of faith. I believe we all need something to believe in otherwise whats the point? I like to think my steps are guided by the one who made me over or fine tuned me for this second chapter that will be great, love makes the world go around and I can tell that He is pure love as he created all that we know. The Alpha and the Omega the first and the last, as for my hobbies they will take time as everything does that's good, you can't see whats down the block until you put one foot in front of the other and go down there, the steps in life. Have you ever seen a whipper will? Created by God for us to enjoy their beauty and listen to their songs? We are the same way when we are given an ability and then put it to good use. We glorify God by being a part the church and doing good things for others, it says that others see when the spirit is in us thus giving them the fire to want to be the best they can be.

Long ago I had a hard time making that real in my mind, but then as time passed I began to see. A friend said that if she could give me a gift it would be the gift to see what other see when they look at me, such a heart felt feeling that gave me. But it also made me wonder what others saw, what is it that I don't see? And will I one day see this thing they see? Today I don't see the broken part of what used to be only the love I have for thee, like the child that starts to grow little by little progress is made and strength is built. As for my strength it comes from God for without him I have none of my own, I could of very well gave up back in the day when I felt so alone but I wasn't alone. Something drove me to go on and it's still driving me today. A strength that at one point I didn't know I had, a driving force. Something invisible that resides within this body as for the body it's self it's just a tent, a tempery home so we can live in this place they call earth. As I look at things from a sciencetific point of view I surely should of never survived, but if I look at it through the supernatural then it's probably something that He can do at will. I'm very delighted today as I got a call from my publisher and things are moving forward, in a way I'm still beside my self not having moved in this direction befor but I'm optimistic that things are going to unfold the way he means for them to. As for me writing to the news papers that! Will continue probably until the end of my days, you might say it's my way of helping while things unfold. I know that God wouldn't have me write all these years for it to wind up being a mistake because he doesn't make mistakes, somewhere in the story there is something for others to figure out and it will take a bright mind.

As we first start down the path of addiction the person doesn't realize how much of a mess they have made out of their lives. At first it's fun, and then when the fun runs out it becomes a substence, you can't live without. It Impacts every area of their lives and the things that used to be important seam to take a back seat to the curse, and they loose everything. Soon love doesn't exist except for the love they have for the addiction and then the children suffer for their wasted life, it's hard for some to believe these things but as a person that has lived through it I know it's a fact. My Christen brothers and sisters many of them have never seen this mess at work, they have been kept from it through their belief in God and having a good place to live like my town of dreams. I got the church cleaned this afternoon but I had to wait until it got a little warmer out as the cold would bite right through your pance, I also took Sam's dog out for him so he should be happy when he gets home tomorrow night. My spirit is on high as I feel new things coming my way and I know that my hard work will pay off in the end as I move forward, well time to call it a night. Morning comes fast for me as I get up before anyone, today even the dogs are still asleep out on the town usually I can hear them when I get up barking at everything that moves even the squirrels run from them not wanting to get eaten, nature at it's best is here and we feed the animals from time to time knowing many of them don't have enough food. I know that He would feed them if he was here as God takes care of his own creation it's TGIF Friday the end of the week and Christmas is only 19 day's away they had to cancel the childrens Christmas play because they weren't ready so it's going to happen sometime before Christmas we just don't know when. Yesterday was a cold day and I bet it didn't get above 30 degrees if that, but I was able to venture out and do the things I needed to get done. Sam's dog was happy to see me when I let her out, making these strange noises like she was going to pea her self, as for my daughter I text her yesterday to see how she was doing and she told me that I must know when she is down in the dumps. I told her I had the same connection with grandma Carol, it's like I know when something is wrong come to find out she had been having trouble with her X ole man. And her mother is back in the hospital for the 10th time, I don't know if they will get her a new seyt of lungs but I do know if they are they better hurry as hers is failing. Shannon told me that all they can do is make her comfortable for now and hope she gets a little stronger, she is too weak at this point for them to do anything. I do know that I will have to comfort my daughter should that time come. She is so fragual for some reason maybe her being around that crap has made her weak everyone always throwing their problems on her thinking she has all the answers, for some that's too much to bare. Having the weight of others on your sholders when it's all you can do to handly your own problems a lot of people don't care if you are having a hard time and they take advantage, thinking she can fix them you don't have to be an addict to live in the darkness they can draw you in by coming around you. And sometimes you have to turn them away, and get new friends.

I have seen it all and been to places that would frighten the life out of some, like the dream I had at the beginning of the week about my older brother trying to kill me. But I was protected and I could tell that I was for some strange reason. Like the many times I almost died a calmness came over me and it was like God had closed his hand of protection around me, when I feel threatened sometimes I can just look into a persons eyes and they will turn around and walk away, wondering why they wanted to hurt me in the first place. I have always had this what ever it is and it has served me through my life only having about two fights in the years that I have been on this earth, and when they happened the curse was inside of me always drinking or being drunk when it took place. As for fighting when I have been straight it has never happened because you use common since when you are in the real worl, speaking of the real world that was an adjustmant that took many years but if you stay true to your self then you will make it. I wish I could of saved Mark back in my youth, he comes to mind from time to time dieing at the age of 24 years. He told me that he never quite fit in being raised by alcoholic parents and then having them die from it, I recall before he died he told me that he wanted to go and be with them as he felt he had no one here. My parents raised him most of the time but it wasn't the same as having your own parents Jerry was gone most of the time working, and Leida just stayed home drinking her self to death. Not the perfect setting for Mark but mom did the best she could with him, one morning we woke up and he was gone.

I had known him since he was five years old so he spent about 15 years with us before his passing he was my little buddy you might say, a drinking partner and believe me that world isn't kind to it's victims'. Many people are clueless that they have a problem having never addressed it before, they go through life thinking it's normal to be a drunk because their parents were the same way and probably there parents before them. Having no information about the curse or not eve realizing that it is a curse can make life less then what it's supposed to be, I recall the mornings getting out of bed with a hang over and I thought it was normal dragging your self to make coffee. Who knows how many years was wasted in just those few hours to waking up, then you had to preform your job but by this stage it's as natural as the drink you had an hour earlier. Working for Western Alfalfda in Nebraska the guys would go out and drink their lunch and have a hambugar, many of them drank because it was part of their up bringing and it was the same with me. Randy thought his life was over when they sent him to prison, a place he didn't belong they should of sent him to a treatment center so he could learn about the things that got him in trouble. Wrong choices can destroy a life also as he knows all so well now, before pop's died the lord came to me sort of like a heads up that something was going to happen. And He told me to bring Randy home it was a hard thing to do after what him and our other brother did to me but the lord told me to forgive them so after sometiime I did. I wrote to the parole board and told them that I would take him into my home if they would let him come to Kansas and after some time they wrote back saying they didn't think he had any family that cared about him and that they would release him to my home. To be honest I was scared because of what they did so taking him was a big chance for me, then one day while driving a song came on and it was called brotherly love and that put the last stitch in the shirt. I knew by the sign's that God would help me in this endevor so I moved forward but all the while I asked pop's if he thought it would be ok' and I think he knew that he was going to be with the lord and didn't want me to be alone. It took about eight months to get a release date and when the day came I drove to get him getting lost at least five times, when I got to the prison we had to wait for the final step's to be taken and then I saw him for the first time in six years and I wanted to cry. He wasn't the same person having gained over 100 pounds because of the damage that the Methamphime had done to him, I couldn't show my emotions so I acted like nothing had changed. We hugged each other and left the place that either saved him or destroyed him, I could see the tears in his eyes as he was so happy to finely be free and we got out of the big city to never return. After getting home he thanked me for what I had done for him and I told him that's what brothers are for, at first it was hard because he snored and believe me he could wake up the neighbore for a block, before this all took place a friend told me that they had seen him and he looked close to death. I would like to take credit for getting him out but really it was God's doing giving me the little messages on how to accomplish this task, and I just followed his directions. Forgiveness is powerful even when you have doubts about it. After a time pop's passed away and then it was just me and Randy.

I thought it would be smooth sailing but by far it wasn't, I almost lost him and called on God for assistence again pastor Kathy came to help me as she did with the funeral of pop's. This time it wasn't a funeral but the rebirth of my brother, they had to transport him from Belleville to Salina because they almost lost him there. Her called me and said they were trying to kill him but they were doing their best to find out what was wrong and save him, they had to take out his gullbladder and within a week he was back home. As in everything God has stood by me and him even though he sometimes cant see it, you might say he is just starting to realize that God is a part of his life now. And if not for the lord he wouldn't be here today, as time passed I started to notice things and that he wasn't the same person that went into prison. One day I was watching a movie and it brought tears to my eyes then I went into his room and he was crying also, thinking it was a by chance happening I dismissed it but then a few days later the same thing. That's when I knew we were more a like then I ever thought possible and it might have something to do with us being born only 18 months apart. Me in 1958 and him in 1960 on January' he has over come the earge of wanting to go back to the old life the one that almost destroyed him also. Today we both are set free from the curse but even with it gone we know we can never visit that dark place again. The destroyer of life for some is the bottle and with others the substence that remains illegal. Just because they made alcohol legal doesn't mean that it's not a drug, but many will argue the point. The ones that are lost in that world of no return, peace be with them.

As we keep moving forward the old is washed away and who knows where we would be if we didn't have today? Now my little brother will have to learn to take the next step in the adjustment of living that life he was meant to live. And who knows maybe one day he will find his happiness that he has been searching for. The window of opportunity is always right in front of us, but we have to be able to see it before we can walk through that door. Today I only have the family that's here and that's enough for me, they never bother me as I learn to grow in the light of things to come. The day is very cold out and the temp is six below zero it could freeze a person if they were out in it for very long, so I try to not go out if I don't have to that way I don't get sick and have to stay in bed. We went to get groceries so now we don't have to go to town for a while hoping by next Tuesday that it will be warm out, as each day passes each day I give thanks for the home we have. It keeps us warm during winter and cool during summer just a blessing all around when you think of others who have to sleep in cardbord boxes and eat out of the garbage cans, it's the weekend and there ar things to do, Sam should be home by now so I don't have to go over there today. Also we got the bullitin from the church that comes out each month and mine and others pictures are in it, although they look good I wish they ould of been in color to show us better. My camera could take some good pictures should I decide to up dated, it but for now the pickins are slim as we try and make it through winter always make sure you have enough to make it through the hard times of winter, that way spring will take care of it's self hopefully. We go through many different things each year but in the end we make it alright moving into another year, I believe Jan Carolsen was the one who took the pictures after most of uus ate. That thanksgiving was great and I didn't feel out of place like I used to when I was in that other world, since little brother came to live with me I have found that in many ways we are the same not wanting to leave this place I call my town of dreams, when he first got out I took him to that place he got into trouble meaning Nebraska and the magic started as he wasn't there for a couple of hours and wanted to leave this showed me that he was ready to move on and leave that life behind that life of destruction that almost killed him. We travel through many doors in this life but once one is shut then another opens we hope always hope for the best when this happens and usually that's what we get, many things come to me that have never visited before like the strange dreams that come and go Randy tells me that he dreams all the time and he has done this since childhood, as for me these dreams are far and few inbetween only remembering a few that have stuck with me through out the years. The one I had the other day and the one as a child almost drounding in the swimming pool but even then I started to breath under water when that one happened very strange for this guy.

In the good book it says that the old will dream dreams and the middle aged will have visions and this I believe that's when you know the end of days is near, but how long the end of days is I don't have a clue. It could of started after I was born or it could have been under way already before my birth, one never truly knows these things. The station closes on Saturdays now that it's winter and maybe Norman will get the rest he needs I guess when you have worked hard all your life it becomes a part of that cycle that drive which will shape you as a person, I love that family very much and all that works there down at the station. If I need something all I have to do is ask Norm or Leroy and they will help me it's like we are brothers and we are in Christ. Many times I didn't know what I would do when my car broke down and they rescued me by getting things fixed so I could make sure pop's got to the doctor. Pop's always liked the rides to Grand Island looking at the country side and wishiing we owned a part of the country, well today we do own a little part of Kansas but it's ours for the short time we live here, we never truly own anything here we only posses it for our stay. He plainly says that this is not our home, our home is in the after life. I have many thoughts on why I was sent back but I believe I hadn't learned the things I needed to learn. My views on this life was very dark when my pasing came shadowed by darkness only giving me one view of the world and he couldn't let that be. As there is always two sides to a coin, the things I see today are much different from the darkness that I lived in, only seeing the world through distorted eyes didn't let me see the good that was taking place right under my nose.

My world wasn't meant to be so clouded but through the dark forces that was all I saw, death at every turn and heartache followed very closely.. But today he has shed some light on my world letting me see the goodness of others, trust was a big issue with me as I never saw the other side of that coin only the darkness of those living in the dark. The only light I ever saw was the goodness of my mom when she would help others that were alone in the world, some sleeping on the curb because they had no where to go you could Say that she put out her hand and brought them in to give them what they needed no matter what it was a hot meal or a place to stay either for a night or a week. But they had to help! And that was a must she didn't care if they spent the whole day looking for a job as long as they tried she would be there sort of like a mother Tara you might say, just a good person through and through even though she was fighting her own demons. We all have them in one form or another through the hard times she learned that helping was always better them turning them away, many loved her for what she had done and then some took advantage this was unexceptable to her, and she would catch it throwing the users back out into the world she tried to save them from. I never could understand why some where that way but like she told me one day you cant save or help them all there is to many of them, and she was right maybe that's part of why I help through the news papers not having to see their dispair as that would probable throw me off track of my job or journey. I can't let them get close to me getting personaly involved would only take from my message and they need to know the whole story, I was glad that mom had went to bible school during her high school years as it taught her kindness towards other when she needed it most. And although the addiction had a hold of her life she was very caring and did the best she could. Today Randy is doing fine and we are content in the little town that we adupted or it adopted us. The rebuilding of things like main street will ashure that things will be here for another 75 or so years, long after we have left this place and gone home to that eternal life in the heavens. For one day I will be fishing on the banks of Jorden with Harley in my lap, that's a thought don't you think? To make God smile is the glory of my life and I know that things done half way doesn't make him smile, so I try my best to complete the things I start. The church has to be made ready for whats coming this month so the day will start with scrubbing the floors and then what ever comes next, it's the little things that I notice when cleaning that sets our church apart, without my glasses I cant see much but with them I don't miss anything on the floors giving it that extra touch that it needs. In our walk with God we have a goal and that goalis to be more like Christ, now what does that mean? We do our best to be humble and reframe from the things that left us in the dark. This is my opinion but we are to be the best we can be I know in the beginning my life wasn't what it should have been, as I was lost in that other world. I don't really care what others say about the changing process because I know it takes a lot of effort and time, some would have you believe it can be done in a week month or even a year but that's not the case. With many it took half a life time to get lost and it will take the other half to bring things right, I know that God knew that I would live the first years of my life wondering in a world I didn't understand thus leaving the other half with just enough time to come full circle.

But many never find what they are looking for O we think we know all the answers but in reality we really dot have a clue, to find enlightment is hard and one persons enlightment is never he same as another persons sort of like a dog chassing it's tail they never catch it. My thoughts of what enlightment is may very well differ them other peoples and we all have our opinion on this matter, even the followers of Christ didn't find this until they left this world. Some others would say that it's not having a care in the world but this too would also be wrong as if we didn't have a care then we couldn't grow, some of the things I have seen in people are things I couldn't even think of doing like taking from others that have worked so hard to aquire them, maybe I was born at the wrong time or have come back for something that I left here long ago that thought has always been in my mind since childhood. An old soul, in search of something I had lost over 100 years ago could it be possible for a soul to come back if it was embedded in it's spirit? All good questions but finding the answer will be almost impossible without help. There are a few people that think I'm a vessel from God sent back to change something, but if I am. What am I supposed to change? Maybe in time things will open another door to show me but for now I don't know, as the year is coming to an end next year will bring something new to the table maybe success! maybe failure, one never knows for sure.

When each day brings you delight you have found that needel in the hay stack that one thing that stands out from all other things in the world, as the hay is the cludder of all the things that are common. Like the tea-pot that sat on the shelf for 100 years, life was breathed back into it and then everyone wanted the beauty that wasn't for sale. No person has the same things as others do separated by a quirk or something out standing as for me I don't see things in the same way as my brothers and sisters do and I can feel it while I'm in another world they are not, making hard it for communication at times. Sunday and we got our first snow fall during the night about three inches I suspect this is comeing atabout the right time but I hope we don't get anymore having to travel on Tuesday. Finely it's time to let things rest so I will end this chapter of my life and start on something new. I'm not sure where the shovel is to dig my self out but it has to be here somewhere now I just wait for the first light to venture out side, the snow makes it look like almost day but still the darkness is out there and I don't do night since I lost my equillibrum all those years ago. Another part of learnig not to venture out into that dark place, well it's almost 4:00 in the mornig and it doesn't get light until six or so as for the heat it's stayed warm during the night and I rested just fine it was like I had a dream during the night something warning me to take another direction but I don't have a clue what it was all about a tingling all over my body that I had never felt before. Later I will go and open the church and make sure the heat is set just right so my brothers and sisters are warm during service. This is the end of things but not the end of my writing grace and peace be with you all.

Living in God's grace (4) There's a saying that goes like this your talent is a gift from God and what you do with that talent is your gift to him. A friend gave me this same because I believe it's true God gives us all talents whether we use them is up to us, that's one so convinced this talent he gave me for writing is a gift to me. And by completing it is my gift to him for he taught me to write no one else, as I go through the rest of my life sure I will write more pleasant things other than death and alcohol addiction but for now this is my venture to help other people that's the most important thing I can do right now to try and save lives. It gives my life purpose and makes me feel good at the same time well today is February 6 and it's 3 AM. I slept for about five hours and was wide awake this happens from time to time it's like he is telling me that's all the sleep I need. When people get hooked on methamphetamine they seem to forget a lot I can remember one time when this guy came to my house and thought he had lost something, and he tore up my bedroom looking for it. Then come to find out he left it at another person's house as hell bad methamphetamine can destroy the mind well anyway I had to throw them out of my it reminds me of when those two people got caught in a snowstorm they said they were on methamphetamine and were delusional in other words their minds or working right.

Between the Meth and the cold the temperature in their bodies had reached 108° thus making them delusional they had no idea of where they were or how they got there for that matter at one point they were even talking to cattle thinking that they were people this is caused by the body shut down because it can't keep itself warm. That had to be a horrific night for those two young people and later their parents would bury them because of the use of methamphetamine now when a drug can do that to a person it should be one of the last things you would ever want to take, but still people do it. "Why" because people lose hope and faith in themselves and when that happens they don't really care if they live a. And doing drugs helps them to forget the bad things in lives. It reminds me of when I used to go to work I would work all day and at the end of the day I would go to the bar and buy a case of beer and go home I didn't realize it things in but I was unhappy with the situation I was in I didn't really get along with the girlfriend I was living with we were always fighting and the alcohol made that go away for a while anyway but then I sobered up and the problem was still there. By not eliminating the problem altogether it just went on day after day week after week year after year there were many warning signs but I had that feeling that no one else would want me.

This too is a problem so common between spouses I knew something was wrong but I wasn't smart enough to get away from and in doing this it caused more problems than ever. When I watch he segments on television about drugs sometimes I get angry because many times they are missing the point, just like with this marijuana situation the people that are hooked on it are trying so hard to get a bill passed that would allow to be brought into the homes of children this is definitely not a good move by the full's who play the full's game. When are people going to wake up and relies that no good will come out of addiction just like the one lady that got per are taken out of school and be one of these fools that gets drugs into the houses of our loving children if I had all the money I spent on alcohol and drugs I would've been a millionaire buy now. Child's mind is still developing and it can only go so far when they are under the influence of drugs thus causing their learning potential to be limited by the surroundings so much of the arguments could be avoided if I would just listen to the voice inside of me because it's never wrong God gives them to us but most people don't even know they're there whenever you hear that voice inside you know don't do that you better listen to it because it's a warning mechanism to help guide you in the right direction if you ignore it then more than likely you would get into trouble. Is just like if a person drinks then they want to drive a car and they know they shouldn't that's the warning, I'm talking about that little voice that resides deep inside of you the one that keep you out of jail and keeps you out of trouble. For the most part I usually listen to mine and that's how I kept myself out of prison when all the others were taken there when you take a person out of the home the financial situation drops greatly and this hurts the family unit. Have you heard that same? You don't know what you have until it's gone. How true that is, there's a song that really relates to my life not the bad parts of my life but to how I have changed it, and it's called some people change it's a beautiful song put out by Kenny Cheney, music helps me a lot because when I'm down and blue I can listen to it and it picks me up. And what God raises my spirits I like to sing because it brings me such joy it's like it brings out the inner beauty and I can sing with the best of them of course at home because I am still shy, I need to find out how to get over that. Well my little brother is finding his way he sent me a picture of the Virgin Mary and it says are mother walked through my house today and took all my troubles away. I'm sending her to you to take your troubles away I love the thought behind it and I will keep it hung on my wall. Even John in the Bible was put into prison so all things are possible with God there been a lot of people saved in prison and to me it doesn't matter where you are God will find you. Right now I'm down because it seems like the bills are piling up with no end in sight I don't know what I will do it seems like everything's comes crashing down all at once the pressure is intense and I don't know if I can handle it only time will tell. But I'm sure when this book goes to the publisher it will take care of that, I find my life interesting and I'm sure other people will too. too many people have seen and gone through what I have and it makes for good reading. Right now times are hard but with my faith and trust in God I have no doubt things will get better. It usually when things get the hardest that he pulls us through the dark things that are going on in our life, as for the government they don't have a clue about the addiction problem that's happening here in the United States they always have to look at numbers and numbers just don't cut it when it comes to this cursed they can try to rationalize it all they want but they will never get nowhere until they have someone in the That has experienced these things in life. I feel he is testing my faith to see how strong it is and he will find out that I will never give up I endure things most people can't even imagine and I'm still here. My heart is filled with joy today because my step dad is the happiest I have seen him in years it seems things are looking up for him and I'm glad. The guy that was his payee with his Social Security and the veterans checks had been robbing him blind on the years.

Although this man controlled his checks he was not paying the bills and he even went as far as to pay Oliver for working for him with his own money this is what I mean by crooked people. He is a crook, one time when I was I was out of money I got a loan from him for $100 and he charged me $100 interest but I was naïve back then and didn't do anything about it I will not let him steal from my father he is done it for far too long and now he's even say in the rent wasn't paid which is kind of funny because he's a stupid landlord I don't know how the American live with themselves he was he only soul that had control over $966 a month there's no way he owes that man money. Today is another beautiful day. 2:30 AM I couldn't sleep again as he pulled me up. You know it's a shame when people are allowed to do things to this man, Oliver as a good heart and will do anything for a person I told him a long time ago that his boss was evil and to watch out for him self but he didn't listen and this just goes to show I was right my predictions are seldom wrong. It took time but this gift I have is usually right now we would go to battle and win, once the devil gets his hands on you he doesn't like to let go but with God by my side I can't lose slavery went out under two years ago. I will leave it situation in God's hand he will do with right Oliver never used to have much faith but over the years his faith is grown strong as he watches the changes in me and he knows God has had a hand in it.

My spirit is one of rebirth like the bird that died so long ago I believe they call it the Phoenix and from what I understand it went down in flames and was raised again from the ashes. Like I've said before if you can learn to live with yourself than you on the right. God gives us all and enters strength that usually doesn't come into play until our lives are totally out of control and even then most don't know how to tap Into it, I affirm that only God can grant you the power to use it for it only comes out when you think all hope is gone and, I talked about a friend that's in treatment and he stopped by yesterday to see me in Oliver and he thanked me for the letter I wrote to him. He said he let his counselor read it and he told him that it was a spiritual letter when he goes back he is going to write a story about it. I'm just glad I could help a friend I know he will find his way, I have found that some people don't understand my deep felt feelings and I also find that I understand why, it's because they have never went through what I have. How can you expect a person to fully understand your most inner feelings or self it's impossible because you are the only one that has experienced it, what I write about comes from within not from what's around me and as time goes on I'm sure shallow people will understand me less but that's their problem not mine for only God can give a person the power to look into another person and be able to see what's really there. I sometimes feel if I could find someone that felt the same way as I do they could help me understand "why" he has chosen me to be this way it's not that I'm not grateful it's just that there's a lot I still don't understand and can't comprehend, like I've said before I'm eager to learn but at times I'm impatient about things and that confuses me and causes my head to hurt. I know God has my best interest at heart but that doesn't change the fact that it times I'm confused and I don't like that feeling. I know for a lot of people things are black and white but not for me maybe I give myself headaches by thinking too much who knows but I'm sure God will guide me for he brought me this far and I'm sure he wont abandon me. I can't help but feel that Oliver's boss is cooking the books but I'm sure the government will find the discrepancies I know he has been stealing from all over for years lining his pockets as a say.

I know God won't for sake us and everything will be all right, I feel my writing of words will be what I leave behind for people to learn from it will give some hope for a brighter tomorrow as addiction doesn't have to be the end of things it can be the beginning of a new life for a lot of people I've found that people turn to alcohol and drugs because they lose hope and that's something they have to get back and this book may be able to help them in some way, you would be amazed at how much hope this book can give a person just look at how far it has brought me, I can honestly say that if it wasn't for this book I probably wouldn't have gotten this far it is help me in many different ways spiritually and other ways to. It is help me to get in touch with myself my true self the one that was hiding all those years the one I brought back to life by getting rid of the other one. You see I don't believe to spirit can occupy one body at least that's my theory and I believe when a person decides to take back their own life their true self will show itself, but it will be weak like a baby and it has to be nurtured like a child does until it can grow and reach maturity of the young adults. Than it takes over the body and destroys the evil one that has been destroying the persons life, alcohol and drugs are part of the devil side of a person.

All they do is take from a person being they never had to life is a most blessed gift that God gives us besides knowledge and it's when you combine the two that you find your true path in life. Most can't do it or even Phantom's how to accomplish this task it is only done when you have God's blessing in this I feel I have otherwise I would've never been sent back here it's only by his grace that I'm on this path I'm on. For he is my inspiration and my strength I don't expect things to be easy but he will show me the way he has never left me wandering without a purpose so I will again put things in his hands and let him guide me. Well this day is coming to a close I will write some more tomorrow. Good morning it's a beautiful Sunday and I feel pretty good this morning I was thinking about why some people turn to substance abuse and I think there's all kinds of reasons and some of them are, not liking new job, arguing, stress, being brought up in and around it, low self-esteem, all these things can be taken to the maximum level which causes a person to break down and lose control which is never a good thing and also using the substances is never a good thing to try and get over a problem. Many times if a person is too kind others will take that as a sign of weakness and abuse it they should never be allowed to happen when a person shows kindness that is taken his weakness it gives a stronger person the advantage." Why" because even if a person is just being kind a stronger person can think they have an upper hand on them. When this happens I separate myself from not allowing it to become part of a problem that I don't want anything to do. Oliver told me this morning that he got up early again and he happened to mention that it's a habit that he's had all his life and through the years I have seen this with him being a hard-working man you have to get up early, as we talk sometimes and he tries to understand addiction he asked me if I could put it into words and I told you know that happened you have of getting up early? Imagine being hundred times stronger but with alcohol involved it's like the mind and the body is driven to get its hands on those things. And the sweet old fart said yes I understand, and you only have one more habit to break and that smoking. Then I kind of humorously said yes I have to get rid of that also but for now I have to have at least one bad habit until the time is right to quit and smoking is less harmful to me at this point. God will let me know when the time is right he hasn't let me down yet, and as time passes I'm sure I will quit sometime in the future but for now it will remain, that reminds me of the same my mom used to say. Take my out all but leave my smokes alone, I know when the time comes it will be hard to quit but I found out that nothing is easy in this life. God put all kinds of hurdles in our path for us to overcome and as I march on, I will clear this one also. There's a lot of things God does in my life that I don't understand but I also know he won't put a mountain in front of me that I can't climb. There are so many cruel people in the world and some I can understand but there are many that I do, as a to have traveled to those dark places that they really don't want to be in flash I got a letter from the Buffalo County substance abuse committee inviting me to one of their meetings it's an abuse prevention program that helps others with addiction and they would be a great place to partner up with to help more people Mark said he would give me a ride so I won't have to take a taxi there. I think that was nice of him, I wrote a man I used to know that I haven't seen in 20 years he doesn't know it but he is made a great difference in my life when I was very young, I never got a hold him before because I heard that he was dead now I year that he got shot but he made it and I wrote him. It seems he is a counselor where a friend of mine is going to treatment in Omaha, when my friend mentioned his name I was shocked and I told him that I knew him and I also told him to tell him hi for me. This man made a great impression on me for me to remember him always years.

He was a nice man but he was also Stern well enough of that, when I go to this substance abuse committee it's to see how their taking care of the problem here home. We have to put a stop to this destruction of life but it seems to me that they are working more on the prevention of things instead of those who are already addicted I feel helping the ones that are already having problems with it is so important but so is the prevention aspect of it. There's too many people out there that need help right now and they should be ignored as prevention is a good thing but you can't shut the door on the people that have already been infected when I wrote that article on teen drinking a friend told me to watch out but I have never had any repercussions from trying to help others and also I have to take it from the source and he is a person that is addicted to quite a bit of things. Many people don't like to hear about their problems or the truth they don't like to think they may be the reason for a disaster in their lives no one does for that matter I don't really know how people take me when I tell them about my life but then again I can't worry about that I can't worry about what might happen when it may never come to that all I can try to do is make a difference so no one else has to go through what I went through. I believe there is a purpose for my life and that purpose is to try and make a difference in this world.

My voice is just that my voice and my opinion is just that my opinion and some people don't like it one of voices but that's their problem not mine I find that people don't like to admit when they are wrong. And they are afraid of the truth especially if it concerns them why this is I'm not sure but it's been happening for generations and I'm afraid it will never change because people, most of them anyway don't like change they would rather go on the way things are which would be wrong. We are intervening in new era and when that happens things have to change whether people like it or not as time goes on they will adjust. It isn't something that's going to be easy but it has to be done I feel some drastic changes are going to take place what they are going to be I don't quite know yet but I will find out he lets me know the things I need to know when the time is right. It's amazing how much patience you can accumulate over the years young people don't seem to have much patience but that has to be expected with all the testosterone in their bodies it seems it decreases as you get into your 40s but then again that just might be me. I don't know any other people that live the way I do in isolation it's a hard way live but I find most people that are married fight a lot and that's something I don't want them in life, maybe and I'm looking for the right person for me I know my soul mate is out there and one day I will find her that my search will be over. I'm not the kind of person that can just sleep with anyone I have to have feelings for a woman I'm going to be with that's just the way God designed me if there's no feelings than there's no relationship and I think that's for the best with all the diseases that are going around I'm content being alone for right now it gives me time for myself to search my soul and make sure of what I want in this life. I'm just hoping it won't be my downfall because you can get used to being alone and knowing your own moods, but adjusting to someone else's is a different story. I often think how many other people in the world are like me. I don't know of any I get along with some people but that doesn't mean I could live with them I feel I'm set in my ways at this age, and I don't know if I could change. I've seen people and relationships and most don't last that's why we have so many children without fathers today, I admit I was one of them father's. But when you can't get along with the mother there's no other way to go it's less destructive to leave than to stay because grown up in a family that fights all time can destroy the child's life they get to think it's normal for parents to fight and it is to a certain degree but it's not something I like to do. I find that many women like to be in abusive relationships or what they call being with the bad boy. When a woman leaves that kind of relationship and find someone that's loving and caring they tend to destroy that one and go back to the other four I guess in a way you could say this is an addiction in itself and they have been doing it for thousands of years. It kind of goes back to the animal instinct if you keep the lion in a cage for years and then one day try to set them free by opening the door, that lion will not leave that cage because it is walk back and forth and it for many years and his spirit has been broken like the lion when a woman has been in an abusive relationship they tend to stick to that kind of behavior in a man so they will tend to go back to the same situation if they find a loving person they don't know how to handle it and have to go back to the old ways.

I went to the hospital the other day with a friend and her step dad had to have a biopsy on his brain and they told him that they found out it was malignant they giving 3 to 6 months to live he's an older gentleman, I think that's what I want to do volunteer to visit with the terminally ill. Maybe I can help in some way I know it would make me feel better than I do. I have to find a purpose for the rest of my life and I feel that will bring me closer to God I feel I'm to alone, so I will try and make some new friends. For some reason I feel comfortable at the hospital so I'll do some volunteer work up there they say some patients don't have any family and I feel in the to go and visit with some of them sure I don't know them but that won't stop me. Some things happen for a reason and I feel me going up to the hospital was a sign. There was a man up there that looked really worried about his wife from what I understand she was going into surgery and he was real worry so I introduced myself and told him not to worry God was with him and his wife and it seemed to help, they seem like a nice man but he had a heavy heart I tried to comfort him but I'm not sure if it worked or not. God I hope it did, as we walk through this life some of us don't get scared until something tragic happens and usually we're not prepared for the worst but talking with God can help us get prepared for what's to come. Myself I'm not afraid of what's going to happen to me when my time comes for me to pass over into another life I will be scary because I know God is with me.

Just as he is with me now and every day from here to eternity I know he will guide me to the place I need to be. Once I save up for a car I will be able to start going to the hospital and see the ill patients, I think this will be a good thing for them and me because when I'm there I feel calm, well today is another good day and I found a house in a paper for rent I'm going to check on it today and see if it's better than this fire trap, I do know the rent is cheaper and that's a good thing when you don't have much money rich people don't know how easy they have when it comes to something like that people living in poverty have to watch every penny they spend otherwise they will cease to exist but I guess when you're born into it can't be helped especially if your whole life has been rough but there's always that slight chance that one day you will be able to overcome those things in life that have held you back but it always seems someone is trying to stop you from getting ahead in life and that's not right, because it seems some people at least certain want like to make themselves rich off of the less fortunate and I consider them to be scavengers they make the living off of other people's misery and it has to be stop somewhere. But it is up to God to punish them on judgment day if it has caused the death of both of people's. Well it's Tuesday, February 15 I'm going to see the doctor for a checkup and have him order an MRI to see if my lungs are messed up from the asbestos and mold that's in this house it seems to get worse as time goes on. Tomorrow I have an appointment with this woman at social services to get food stamps and see if they can help with the deposit on this other house. If they can't or won't help I don't know what we will do they are supposed to help people in trouble but that's something I'm going to find a, I know my doctor will fax over whatever they need he knows my situation and how hard it is on my health. I feel compelled to have this house condemned so no one else will have to suffer from the disease as it carries no one should have to live like this and I will make sure they never have to. I have a hard time swallowing my pride to ask for help but I will get over that hurdle I have never had to ask for help before, I realize things get hard at times but we somehow get through it with the help of others because sometimes things in life just get out of control. But God will forgive as long as you learn from your mistakes it's when you don't mind that we get into trouble as we go through this life sometimes we make mistakes but that is just normal as a child we make a lot of them but that's a part of growing up and as we get older were supposed to make less of them so they say, but experience has taught me that life is trial and error when you make a mistake you do your best to correct it and put it behind you because you can't live in that moment or time that it happened that's how we learn from our mistakes as a child we crawl until we feel secure enough to advance to walk a little but not without help from someone or something to secure ourselves like holding onto a chair are grabbing onto your mother's stress it's a security that helps us move forward to advance in a positive way without it. It would be much harder to achieve this goal, even today in God's eyes I'm still at child that was holding onto its mother stress God takes care of us like our mother did at one time.

I can help but feel we are bound to go to a higher plane of existence and this place is just a learning center for us a place where we learn from our mistakes and not repeat them if at all possible. Like I have said before God loves us all in if we didn't make mistakes than we would be human some people make it harder than it really is I know this for a fact I was one of those people and was flying by the evil ways. But he rescued me from a life of self destruction that's not something you want to go through it's a learning process of what not to do in life and that's why am writing this book to show people that they don't have to go through what I did. And if they happen to have already started down that path it can show them away to turn things around and get back on right path there's a lot of people that get lost in have a hard time finding their way back and that's when they need help. We is people should be able to guide them back on track but it's good to know that if we can't do it God will, take over and guide them. Experience has taught me that sometimes no matter what we do some are beyond our reach and when this happens God has to take over for a while anyway until he gets them back on track. You would be amazed at what God can do when these things happen to me the alcohol and drugs I was unreachable by human standards it took God to set me straight I feel it took me to that place to let me feel how it will be when I one day come back to and there was nothing to be afraid of he showed me things I had never seen like all those souls in waiting. They seemed a piece with themselves as they should be, I set myself apart from the rest of the world for one reason to be at Harmony with myself to feel comfortable being me and this I have accomplished but still I think some people have a hard time understanding my compassion for doing things I guess at times I like to jump in with both feet and that can be dangerous you're supposed to test the waters before you go in.

Well I got my results back from the doctor and they are fine so that eliminates that problem I'm glad I don't have a tumor on or lung disease those were the only things I was worried about, that saying they say that goes like this you don't know what you have until you lost it, is so true. They are saying that at the beginning of the war it would cost $1-$200 billion what a joke it's already cost 400 billion with no end in sight I can't help but get upset at the stupidity of the government by starting this war in the first place but everyone has a different opinion about what should've been done so this opinion is just mind we will be able to go get another place to live thanks to the help of a nice lady and social services it seems on things get the roughest somehow I light shows through it's like God is telling me not to give up and I won't because he is beside me even when things seem hopeless. Somehow we seem to make it and to me that's a good thing they say God looks after his own people and this I believe to be true, because he has never forsaken me when I have felt like giving up his always been there for me and for this ungrateful this lady that helped me at the social services I'm going to write her a thank you letter. My doctor started me on some antidepressant I'm not sure how they will mess with my mind that I'm hoping they won't you see him the real emotional person and sometimes my emotions run away with me in other words my emotions take over sometimes. And these pills are supposed put the serotonin levels back to normal I guess it's a chemical imbalance or something like. I hope it works you see my mind has a tendency to wander sometimes and my emotions can sometimes take over and run me instead of me them I guess it happens to us all at one time or another in our lives. But I don't like it when it happens, I have a feeling things are going to turn around for us for once it's all confusing right now but it will clear up after a while. Getting this pickup will help get us moved so we don't have to depend on other people for help, I've never found a person you can totally depend on I guess it just doesn't happen in real life family included as we go on into the future I feel things will change for the better without this landlord hanging over our heads anymore all is done is train all for dry of money and I feel he will pay when the day comes for us all to be judged by God looking back I think my parents realized that the time that they were destroying our lives I can imagine what my life would've been like if alcohol wasn't in our lives but that's something I can't change it's neither here or there it's sort of like that saying been there did that. Well it's Sunday and another day is past the weather doesn't know what it wants to do one day it's raining and the other snow but I feel winter is over finally we don't have much of a winner this year it's like the seasons are changing the winners are more warmer than years past.

While this month is been hard the money is running sure and I'm just about out of quarters it helps to save but it wasn't quite enough I don't know what we would do when it runs out "God help us" I can't give up I have come to for to give up now. But I guess what will be will be it's more or less in God's hands now, through all the trouble sometimes I went through I never saw this coming but I guess we don't see any of them coming. As the next week passes I will be able to tell better if we will make it through this month I feel so alone in this fight for survival and that saying comes into play you don't know what you have until it's gone, my life is been nothing but ups and downs like a rough ride on and see and I can't help but wonder when the ocean will be calm again. I know God to bring me back here to go this way this would be humiliating well Hall I can do is hold on for the rough ride because I feel it's going to be bumpy. I've asked for all the help I can get but everything takes time that something I'm running out of I don't know how long the body can go without food but all over has to be said three times a day he's a big man, I have party cut myself down to one meal a day and that isn't a me a really maybe a hot dog or two but I believe the Lord will see us through I have that much faith Oliver's runs a little short so I will carry him most of the way because my faith will not weather in the worst of storms that's one thing God is made rock solid with a little help from me his seems when everything looks it's worse God pulls me through.

I guess it's my charm ha! At times when I've felt like giving up he is told me to stay strong because your faith will pull you through as long as you have faith in yourself and God nothing can harm you and this I believe is true because he has kept me safe all these years, as this bad time passes in my life I hope to see much brighter tomorrows in the future hear something I don't understand, I don't have a penny to money and here's a credit card place off for me credit card that's in the last thing I need in my life right now more bills I can hardly take care of the ones we have is in life grand? It sure can be though life throws you curves but that's the way life is. I even had to go down and get a homeless prevention package to help with the deposit on a home so we can get out of this dump that's how bad it's getting I find myself getting depressed more often than usual but I guess that can be expected the way things are going lately I can't help but feel at times society is trying to squeeze me out up the pitcher the state makes it to where I can hardly get by in life this book will be my only chance of getting out of poverty if it doesn't work I don't know what I would do. So many trials so many hurdles, when will it stop Lord? You put these things in front of me for reason, help me father to understand these things you put in front of me please give me a clue to what they mean for your the only one that knows their meaning. I wait patiently for your reply but not patiently things are closing in so please answer me father right now I feel sad seems all over getting ready to leave me like mom did and I don't know what to do without him I love him so much but there's nothing I can do about it he starting to cry today and said he wants tiny to be buried with him I can sense when things like this is going to happen and it saddens me deeply please father help me through this crappy time I don't know what to do father. It's like I'm being bombarded from all directions I'm confused and scared, guide me father lead me through this trying time for I am blind in this world of yours take my hand and guide me through this ordeal I'm going through father you are the only one that can help this I ask in your son's name amen. Well it's coming to the end of another day so I will write more tomorrow good night, well it's Wednesday and I slept good again last night, Oliver's going to takes scrap metal down Anderson's wrecking to sell. I told him to take the radiator I haven't the garage with him he should get about $15 out of it should help with getting some food I'm sure glad the bills are paid otherwise we would really be in trouble but that is the case times are hard right now and boy are we feeling it I never know what tomorrow will bring from one day to the next but I'm optimistic that the next one will bring something a little better than the one before. We should be grateful for every day we have on this earth even in bad times because that's what makes us strong in spirit so many don't realize how good they got it until it's all gone. Sometimes a person has to swallow the pride to be able to make it in this world but that doesn't hurt anything because it usually false pride anyway the same kind that doesn't let you admit when you are wrong when you know you are.

That kind of pride isn't needed in this life as far as I'm concerned. Well I'm counting the days to see if we make it eight more to go or should I say 10 until a third of the month if we make it tell them we will be okay but it's really going to put my faith to the test but I'm sure it will stand the test of time. For he is great and will forsake me, I'm his creation and he loves me he won't let me falter and with her away. He is the first and the last and that's all I need to know because he gave life back to me no one else and I don't think he would want it to end like this because it would make any sense it wouldn't have any purpose so I will just hold on as tight as I can and see where he takes me that's about all I can do at this point but I'm optimistic things will work out for the best I called the real estate people to see if that house is still available I left a message for to call me back well she called and they rented the house. So we will have to look for another one oh well there should be more in the paper I will look in it tonight. Well another day is coming to a close so I will write some more tomorrow. Well last night I talked to a lady that has a three-bedroom trailer for rent in elk Creek for $325 a month it sounds like it would be nice and quiet and that's what I need to keep writing I'm supposed to call him tomorrow to see the place if I can get a ride maybe Mark give me a ride up there if he is feeling up to it I think I like it there it's a nice little town with friendly people and I know a few people there it won't be like going into a place where there all strangers as a matter of fact my doctor has his office there and that's a good thing.

As time draws near the more I get confused because I have no vehicle to move with, I feel helpless to do anything because my movement is limited it's like I can hardly breathe. I'm not used to feeling helpless and it wears on my nerves but I'm sure that will pass as things get better and my life finally settled down, it's been a turmoil for so long not knowing what's going to happen from one day to the next now maybe things will start to fall into place. Well here's another day gone by I will write some more tomorrow. Well a friend of mine got a hold of me his name is Tom and he's going to give me a ride to check out the trailer I go to church with him when he can pick me up and he is a good friend so we will see what happens once I meet with this person. Lately the days pass so fast I can hardly keep up with them it seems the older you get the faster time speeds up I don't know if that's normal are not but it is for me, Oliver went to work for a friend of his boy was he happy. He's the kind of person that asked to keep busy otherwise he'll get cramped up and hurt all the time I can see sometimes in his eyes that if he can keep busy he will give up on living and he doesn't want that not yet anyway he also feels he has to have a purpose in life and he loves to do odd jobs for people and makes them feel like he is still useful. I love him dearly because he is a good man and he has helped me so very much as much his eyes helped him you see years ago they wanted to put them in a home and I wouldn't let them because I feel once a person goes into one of those places is just a matter of time and he wasn't ready to go yet. That was years ago and he is still here with me but if he can keep busy I feel he will pass away and I would lose a good friend, so I will stick by him until it's time besides I gave my word and that's the only thing you can truly call your own you're only as good as your word. Most people don't understand him like I do he still has dreams and that is one thing no one can take away from, he dreams about winning publishers clearinghouse he said that dream for 10 years so I don't interfere with it I just tell him maybe one day it will happen I encourage him to hold on to his dreams because without them life will cease to exist. Sometimes we sit around and talk about the old days and he will chuckle and say I wish I knew back then what I know today I could've been a millionaire and we laugh and say yes isn't it funny how hindsight is 20/20 but we can't live in our past. I figure Oliver could a saved a lot of money if that landlord wouldn't of been paying him out of his own checks I don't want to talk about this guy very much because to me he's a scum of the earth pardon my French slavery was supposed of went out in the 1800s but this was beyond slavery robbing a person to have them work for you and then pay them with money they already had this gives bank robbery an equal opponent. Well today is Saturday and it's cold out today it seems this winner is like a yo-yo it can't make up its mind whether it wants to be warm or cold but it won't be long before stays warm out.

And the rains will come, I like the rain the way it makes everything grow. It's like a new birth you can watch it progress as things grow stronger and blue into beautiful flowers and what ever else it brings each year. I find it amazing how God made most living things to hibernate during the winter and come back to life during the spring and grow during the summer it's a vicious lifecycle that no one can stop but him, bears even do it, but I guess we all have to rest sometime in our lives we as people just rest more often I often wonder how it would be if we rested like they do say three months out of the year I bet people would be wound up like an eight-day clock I guess that would be so good there's enough confusion in this world the way it is. Have you ever watched the tree as it blooms? I think that's so beautiful it reminds me of a child coming out of the womb for the first time it opens its eyes to see for the first time the people who will raise it and in that second it knows its mother as it suckles on her breast and gets nourishment to grow just like the flower it's in those first hours that the child knows its mother and feels the connection between itself and her. Then as time passes the mother shapes that child's world and becomes like a God to that child. The child relies on its mother for everything nourishment, changing his diapers, teaching it to lock, talk, love-hate, all the things that makes it a good person but it could do without the hate. The mother teaches it the way God intended us to learn from him but so many don't learn his ways for one reason or another whether it's their upbringing or hatred has been let loose in her life. Since I have come back here I don't like what I see violence hatred and greed.

All the things that are going to destroy this world you see most people are selfish and greedy and that will be their downfall it is in only American's but everybody on this planet, they don't care who they have to kill to accomplish their goal and that's sad. No compassion for life or other people maybe one day it will change but I doubt it the people of this world are set in their ways they have become accustomed to war and destroying everything that is beautiful in this world just look at all the innocent lies that have been taken for no good reason. Sometimes when I'm asleep I dream that one day this world will find peace but I'm afraid it won't happen. When most of the people are gone generations lost to self-destruction all because they waited too long to find peace right now I feel helpless to do anything about it because I'm just one person in a world of billions and I'm not heard by anyone except for the words I write in his book and sometimes have published in the newspaper, the Lord said they will listen in the day of thy power but when that will be I'm not quite sure, for only he knows when that will be not me. Right now getting tired of saying so much and not hearing anything in return all of these words mean nothing unless others hear them, well I went with Mark and looked at a house and I think we will get it if Oliver agrees to it which I think you will once I explain everything to in we won't be pain anymore money so that will be a good thing but at least we will be out of this place this cage that has bound us for the last eight years .Well today is Monday and Mark is supposed to come over this morning so we can get some things done. Oliver wants to go over and see the house before we go any further with renting it, which he has a right to seeing where he is going to live. I think it's a quiet place to live as our neighbor is 89 years old so she won't bother us, and I like her but she can't get around to good and she is almost blind kind of like Oliver in a lot of ways. I feel sorry for the elderly folks of this world but they feel they have done their part and I hope they go to heaven. In part they are luckier than us they have lived their lives and are now to go do a better place than here if you think about it where they are going is a lot nicer and they won't have to feel pain anymore I believe when they get to where they are going wherever is not working will start working again because with God all things are possible and what's not whole will be made whole some people think life ends in a slow ride in a Hearst but there's more to life than just what we see this I believe to be true I believe this world is just a stepping stone to a whole new world that we know nothing about but I believe it's a much better place than here, we are all promised eternal life once we are reborn and change our wicked ways even up to the end people will be given a second chance to accept God as her Lord and Savior even to their dying breath should they not except then what happens will happens.

I believe in the end we all have to be accountable to the Lord for the things we have done wrong and although he will forgive us our shortcomings if it is not asked for that it will not be given many don't understand that we belong to God he made us for his purpose. It says in the Bible that the meek will inherit the earth and for the rich it will be like threading the head of a camel through the eye of the needle. Some people think given 10% of their income to the church will buy their way and the heaven and this is something that can be done no one can buy their way into his for we came into this world naked and we will go out the same way with nothing even the homes we think we own are not ours they belong to God he just lets us borrow it why we're here for however long even these bodies are not ours they belong to the creator the one that made them and as for our cars and other things we think we own we don't own them either they are on loan from the great Jehovah Gyro he was the first and he will be last the alpha and the Omega even as we live out our lives here we will not know the full purpose until that final day when he finds us worthy of being with him. Trying to buy your way into heaven doesn't guarantee that the pearly gates will be opened, like that saying, you would have better luck threading a camel through the head of the needle than for a rich man to enter the gates of heaven maybe that's because most rich people think they can take it with them well they can't.

Well today is the second of the month and I haven't found another house yet but I am optimistic something will become available if not we will have no choice but to stay here until May, then school will be out and there will be more houses available to rent this is a college town and once they're gone for the summer there'll be a lot of houses available. Thank God for summer, it's like getting a reprieve from the student's because most of them go home for the summer. God must've heard my prayers I'm finally having things look up for me I feel God is heard my words. We sent the rent over to the slumlord and I sent a letter with it telling him what we needed to be fixed and he said he would send a plumber over in a couple of days, I received a call from my sister and that surprised me we haven't talked in years and I had been angry at her for something she did to my mother but I guess it's time to forgive things that happened in the past God forgive me. So I think it's time to forgive her so now I will have no anger toward her God will give me the power to let it go. I think having resentment toward her has stopped me from growing as far as I should've grown, it's been told you have to be able to forgive all trespassers that have trespassed against you so with that done maybe now I can move ahead with my life. God works in mysterious ways he won't let a person in fans until they have solved all their past problems and the problem I had with my sister was eating at me even though I really didn't realize it on the outside, when he give you a second chance in life you need to wipe the old slate clean and start a new, I feel that's why he give second chances to get rid of the old baggage that is been weighing heavy on your mind heart and spirit. I have learned that when you love someone whether it's your brother or your sister you should never let anger take hold of your life because when it does the cloud your judgment and can make you make mistakes you will regret later in life. When I was younger my family didn't want anything to do with me really but since I have changed my life away from the bad elements they can easily take hold of a person it seemed take care more about me and me about them family is supposed to be close and with the help of God maybe it will be again. As time goes on I hope we will get closer, but only time will tell that by her calling me it shows me that she wants to at least try to mend the fence that has been broken or torn down over the years and maybe makes new ones. Father you sure work in strange ways but I like it, and I love you for it one day we will all have to get together and have a family reunion. And I pray it doesn't end in a disaster but only time will tell if it will ever happen, I have to say I never expected to hear from her so her call was a surprise she even asked if I knew who was calling and I told her well it sounds like my sister. I asked her out she liked Oklahoma? And she said it was all right but it wasn't where she wanted to be, but time would tell where she would end up. I wish her nothing but the best in all her endeavors, it seems we all get lost at one time or another in our lives but when you finally find yourself back on the right path it really makes you feel good about yourself.

Then the past seems to fade away but not until you face it I look around and all I see is his love embracing me, for I be lost if not for the grace of God well today is Monday and the guy is supposed to get a hold of me about a truck because if we're going to move further down the line we're going to need one if there's one thing I have learned it's that you can't depend on other people to do things for you or help you when you need it the most. It's like that saying God helps those who help themselves, and this truck will help me do that. I've never been one that likes to depend on the other people even in a relationship because for one reason or another it never works, but I've always been able to depend on myself and I think it's because I know what I need. I have also found out that I don't think I could live with anyone else because I'm too set in my ways over the years of being alone, I know what I want and I think it could cause some problems in a relationship, most people don't see the world like I do they don't see the destruction that's going on a Jew see what's up from the in their everyday lives and that might be fine for them but it's not for me. I don't know what happened to me when I came back but I'm different than I was before and I like it you have to be comfortable with yourself and that I am. In my younger years I wasn't comfortable with myself for some reason and that's in part why I turned to the alcohol and drugs it seems people accepted me more easily when I was high whether that was true or not I can't really say.

People seem to accept a person more when they have money or they have something they want and that's two of the worst reasons to accept anybody as we all know exception is a big part of life if people don't accept you it makes life a lot harder but you can't survive with the friendship of just a few people they say you really only have to have one true friend in life and back in the day mine was my mother we laugh together and cried when our friends faster way. I didn't realize it back then that they were going to a better place than this world it wasn't until I pass that I knew there was a better place, all your worries, all you problems, seem to disappear and the pain I felt was gone. That's why a believe this world takes from you, and what it takes you get back when you Passover all you problems disappear like they were never there but making the transition to coming back was hard I personally didn't want to come back it was God's choice to send me back and I knew there was a reason for him to do so. So much of a reason it was imperative that I come back why these things happen in my life only God knows but he must have a good reason for it otherwise he would do it, I sometimes think back to when my mom died and I can still feel that heart wrenching pain when she left, it's like it never goes away but it does become bearable over time that's a pain I wouldn't wish on anyone because it makes you feel like you going to die. When I ascended it didn't hurt anywhere near as much as my mother dying and Eielson wondered why I didn't feel that pain when Herb died, I guess the longer you are with someone the more it hurts. But over the years my heart has become harder than I would like it to be, I play it safe with my feeling because I can't stand pain. Don't get me wrong, I can stand physical pain just not the pain comes from the heart it hurts too much and it causes me to lose out on a lot of opportunities for to be with someone. I guess I need to let my guard down a little to see what happened. Sometimes in life you have to take a chance so I think I will do that when the time presents itself again, I have written a letter to unsolved mysteries in hope they can help me find my birth father Wesley Leroy Hanks in doing this I hope to find out if he is alive or dead either way I hope to find closure to that part of my life so I can move forward but I have hope that he is still alive or that I have some brothers and sisters out there somewhere well it's another fine morning 10 March and putting the letter in the mail today I have no idea how long it will take before I hear back from them but I am optimistic they will either write or call in the weeks and months ahead. I feel real grateful to a friend of mine for suggesting this idea to me otherwise I might not of ever came up with doing such a thing. She said they like to solve mysteries so this should give a big one, I can remember my brother's father taking me to work with him and I really enjoyed it that's where I learned to work on cars, he was a doctor of motors through RE arbor Ford in West Covina California I have never known a man that is a better mechanic he could rebuild the motor within 24 hours and he was also a transmission specialist. He knew every aspect of: and I'm grateful for all that he taught me.

I have never had to take the car to a mechanics shop before because of the knowledge he gave me and it was fun, I was watching the story on the TV called in the womb and I find it amazing how life starts a child in the womb look so beautiful and I find it amazing how the child can hear music and grow to love it while it's still in his mother. I find it interesting how protected they are when they are in the mother and how they don't have a worry in the world. Seeing them grow in that fluid is really different, I have learned that although I can see in some respects I'm blind by shutting myself off from the rest of the world. I have closed off a lot of my feelings it's like I'm shutting the door a little at a time in hope that someone will push it open but I'm afraid, it won't happen. But you never know what can happen, today is March 15 and I'm still looking for a new place to live I wrote a letter to the landlord of the this house with no satisfaction so he leaves me no choice but to move I think it's for the best in my I sometimes remember my parents moving all of the time and it makes me wonder how they did it. Myself I don't like to move, maybe that's why I stay in one place so long I don't like the feeling of being unstable. I had it too much in my childhood and it scares me still today, I was told that writing a book will help you face your fears but I don't know about that I do know it brings things back you would rather forget about but as some say you must face the unpleasant as well as the pleasant and I would agree with that if there were more pleasant times but in my case there is. If I could find my father he could shed some light onto what happened why he never came back for me.

That leaves a lot of questions opened in my mind and they need to be answered somehow, deep inside I have the feeling I might have siblings out there somewhere and I would like to meet it would be exciting to meet another part of my family another part of my father to see if they are anything like me to see if their hearts are as full of love as mine is. I know he has to be good man because he is a part of me and I'm a part of him, I just don't understand why he abandoned me for so long. On my mother's defense I can see her not wanting to destroy the family unit but it happened anyway our family was torn apart by the disaster that happened in the 60s that in alcohol destroyed everything I had my and I never wanted to repeat itself again in my lifetime anyway. God is shown me mercy and for that I'm grateful but I can't help but feel I have other family out there somewhere and I need to find them it's like a missing part of the puzzle you can't quite get the whole picture until all the pieces are there, sure I could go through life not knowing what happened but why? I feel I have a right to do what happened to my family on the Hanks side. Mom never said if he had a brother or sister so that's unknown to me. I feel now I should ask more questions about my father but I guess it's a little too late, I hope when solve mysteries can look into for me I think that would be so cool they like to take things that are unsolvable and sold them I feel they could get more done than me they have the power of the media behind them, if my father did die there should be a record of what happened with the was killed in the war or whatever and if I'm his only surviving relative well then I should be able to get his service records from the government. And they should compensate me for my father's death I realize that might be putting the cart before the horse so I need to back down a little it takes a person with more means than me to find my father's on counting on a source that I know nothing about, I'm relying on their reputation to do the work it seems that anything that gets on television has a power to get results whether it's from the government or media I have to face it TV gets better results than anything else. Probably because millions of people watch it every day I no one unsolved mysteries gets results, but well it's coming to the end of another day so I will close for now. A new day, I got my truck today and boy it feels good to have something to drive it's been a long's time since I've driven is kind of hard to drive a four-speed with my legs is weak as they are but they should get stronger as time passes it will be like therapy for them the more I work them the stronger they will get, and I like driving so the two go hand in hand. I'm not able to work them like a normal person constantly I have to give them a break every now because my legs don't work like a normal persons does. With me it takes a lot of concentration with every step, I'm hoping this time goes on it will become a natural thing to work the clutch and brake pedal but it will take time. How much time I don't really know but I'm sure I will master it, there's so much we take for granted the little things like walking.

Most people don't have to think to walk but in my world I have to use my brain for everything I do to move my fingers and my toes even my eyes takes constant concentration. Most people do these things automatically but with me it's not automatic and I have learned to accept this in my life, I guess that's why get so mad at times when I see people abusing what God is give. Call me cynical but that's the way I feel I'm grateful for everything he has given me, but at times I get angry that he sent me back to this place I didn't want to come back but I did, because he thought it would be best for me. Who am I to question God's motives for he is he only one that can see the whole picture not me, I'm hoping things will become clearer the older I get has for now I can't see that far down the road so I feel like I am walking with blinders on in hope that he will take them off one day. Even though I have some site I'm blind and this I accept because he guides me in my endeavors so I put my life in God's hand in hope that he will one day find me work to join him in heaven. For I adopted him as my father seems I don't have I can find in this world anyway, I'm in hope that the people I've wrote will be able to help me find my birth father. It's always been a mystery to me that he never came back to see me after he left in 1958 I can't figure out why a person would do that to their son, that is what makes me think something happened to him.

And they don't want to acknowledge it why else would they not give me information about him there can't be too many master sergeants that were in or around Duluth Minnesota in 1958 or 57 especially a Wesley Leroy Hanks I haven't checked Arlington Cemetery yet, who knows he might be on the wall of unknown soldiers but I do know he was a soldier fighting for his country so there has to be a record of him being in the service. They told me that I needed to know his Social Security number and that is something I have never had and it's beyond me on how to get it, I hear after 20 years his service record should be public. I was watching a commercial with Larry the cable Guy on it and he has to lady if she ever farted and cracked her back? I like that guy he brings a little down-home comedy into people's lives. Well it's Monday, March 2nd yesterday we were hit with a winter storm that seems to want to hang in there yesterday morning I swear 7 inches of snow off of my truck and when I got up this morning I had to do it again as there was another seven or 8 inches we must've gotten 14 or 15 inches in the last two days that's the most know we have gotten in the last year. But that's a way it goes our last snow of the year is usually the worst, I don't really know what the temp is yet but you can bet it's cold probably around 18°.I can see why some people become ill with temperature shooting up in the 50s and 60s and then dropping down to around 2° I'm just glad I don't gets sick too often seem to know matter how bad things get things could be worse than they are. That's why I'm glad God stays by my side. Songs out that I really like and one is by sugar land and the other by Brooks & Dunn one is called make me believe and the other is called believe two great songs that will one day pop the charts I believe these kinds of songs will one day bring people together in spirit a unity of our brothers and sisters. When music and touch the heart and spirit of others it as the power to bring them together as I like to call it as a family, the words of people can destroy or heal the human spirit depending on the way they are used then again it depends on the person or persons putting it out there of how much healing or damage it will do I find it ironic how people are so wrapped up in themselves that they don't care about other people, a lot of them say they care for when it comes right down to it they don't. Thinking of country stars Carrie Underwood holds the number one spot with Jesus take the wheel this is a beautiful song that will launch her career she is so beautiful and are heart speaks to you in her songs. There are other singers that are good but these three will have number one hits if they haven't already, well today is another day I can't help but think of my father and makes me sad that I have been held to find him. But that will pass as time goes on, it's still something that has to be solved before my life is through on this earth. Some people don't realize that a lot of us people like me don't want anything to do with their wars and disagreement I was born to love and live in peace not to have anything to do with the destruction of anything positive. What goes on in this world doesn't have anything to do with me, if people choose to destroy everything that is good then they can do it by themselves I won't have anything to do with destroying anything on this earth.

Well another day is come to an end and tomorrow's just around the corner, the weather is something else I woke up last night and it was freezing in here so I had to turn on my electric blanket I only use it when it gets really cold out because we have to conserve on energy well enough about that problem my son stopped by last night to see if I needed to go only where but as usual we didn't, it was nice to see him and to know that he was thinking about me I have found out over the years that most people don't do anything without wanting something in return except for me of course when I do something for a friend comes from the heart or else I just don't do it. I don't expect anything in exchange because what comes from the heart is a gift from you to that person and should be treated as such, in today's society everything is made by the almighty dollar they use it in everything they do nothing is done without a price. Even charity has a price but they won't admit it, why because it's supposed to be charity and charity supposed to be free like the rich giving to the poor, they set up foundations in a loved one's name that is passed on and collect money to fill up the foundation and then use it for themselves and it never reaches the ones that needed it. They should've had these people exposed I feel it's a shame that the peoples who name the foundation is in that it passed would probably turn over your grace if they knew what their living relatives for doing in their so-called memory these people should be stopped they give charity a bad name. But most of them don't care otherwise they would do it they feel they have to have a way to Stacyde taxes they don't think of the people that are starving to death right here in our own backyard or the people that are sleeping in the streets.

They don't see the little children wondering where their next meal is coming from or if they will die during the night. They stings are issues that need to be addressed before anything else but most of the people don't really care about others. And that's the plain truth. The world is full of phony people that have to put on the phony front to make themselves feel and look better than they really are, I feel pity for those people because they are not satisfied are comfortable with themselves. They have to go through life pretending not facing reality and this is one action that can cause people to turn to alcohol and drug addiction take a look at the underachievers more than likely their parents tried to show other people down her throat like a brother or sister. And they were use words like why couldn't you be like so-and-so there a doctor or lawyer in a parent doing these things to a child they don't realize that they are destroying that person self-esteem are they do realize it and don't really care, sure alcohol and drugs gives you a feeling that there is a chance that this feeling only lasts a long only while the person is under the influence it makes some people stable until it's too late and it is taken over the whole life. Then it destroys everything that is meant anything to you in your life. From family to all you have touched there is no good that comes out of drugs and alcohol they turned most people into something not, they give a person a sense of false self worth. What do I mean by false? Not real it doesn't exist anywhere but in my, you might say your mind plays tricks on. Because it's fooling you no one else your mind and be a best friend or your worst enemy it depends on how you treat it, if you fill it with poison then it's going to deteriorate you feed your mind and control it it's up to you what goes in it still after all these years of taking my life back there are things that entered my mind that should've never been because in the end what you thought was pertinent at the time wasn't at all. There are many warning signs about a person if people just look for but most people don't they just passing by not caring one way or the other at the times when the body is being abused so is mine by altering its state, look at our world it's just now starting to rebel against all the destruction they did in the beginning of the 19th century and beyond. You hear of hurricanes happening biblical proportions, the hurricanes are much worse today than at any time in the past and the tsunamis he never heard of before or at least I hadn't. For every action has a reaction and whether it's good or bad a lot of times depends on us and the things we do, destruction breeds destruction and the same with positive things good deeds will produce better people and that's what we really need in this world.

For people to join together for a good cause and then stick by it until the end. Once something is put into motion it can be stopped like with the wars we go through now we have all these crippled soldiers at a company back home and over half of them will live on the street because of families can't deal with the destruction that has happened from mental illness to just caring for the person that is lost a limb. As I go into 2006 I feel there's going to be changes, so dramatic that only God can explain then or the Bible. More hurricanes even greater than the ones we had last year along with more earthquakes and volcanoes erupting it's going to be beginning of the most disasters times in human history, and man can't blame anyone but themselves for the destruction that's going to occur. "Why" because they brought it on themselves. All the killing that's going on in the Middle East is uncalled for, and the president head is bigger than his body he thinks he's invincible and that's when people get dangers. When they think they can't do no wrong and they're above anyone else when you put those two elements together it's like putting fire to the dynamite and we all know what happens when those two things are brought together. Nothing but destruction, visions I get as I call them come to me in dreams or when I'm in a tranquil state like falling asleep or waking up. When I wake up in the morning sometimes I can go back into that state of mind and pick up where I left off when I woke up, but mind you this don't happen too often most of the time I can't remember what happened until something triggers something in my mind something familiar with the dream.

Have you ever had something happen to you that was familiar like you have had the same thing happened before in another life and sort of like déjà vu, they have sophisticated words for some of the things that have happened to me but I don't recall what you are so I use words I know to best the scribe it. Plus most of the people I know don't understand what those words mean anyway, this book is written so anyone should be able to read it as God intended. For he is of one that put me on this path to write about my life, I sometimes wish I could've started it earlier in life but if I would've it would've ended up a different story than what it is today. I wouldn't of got to experience all that I have life, experience has taught me that when God want you to do something there's nothing you can do to change his mind. He loves us all but very few show their gratefulness for the things he does for us, most people are too wrapped up in themselves to even consider other things so many people die for no good reason. War destroys more lives than anything else, that in starvation and they haven't put out an effort to stop either of shares they say they have but their politicians and I haven't met one of those people that I would trust. Today is Friday the 24th yesterday for slumlord stop by to tell Oliver that we haven't paid the light bill and we better get it transferred into Oliver's name, how stupid can a person be he knows he destroyed Oliver's credit any can't get it in his name without a deposit as for the deposit that was posted been made the landlord put it in his pocket it seems he knows he has us over a barrel and he is squeezing us as hard as he can, so I called and PPD and they told me the bill is a do yet that we should get it on Monday or Tuesday so that was another one of his lies. Great example to set for a Christian man, I know he is mad because Oliver had his money put back into his name it seemed ever since he became Oliver's payee he has been ripping them off for years. It seems no matter how hard Oliver tries he hasn't been able to save any money because a slumlord would never give him any of his check and when Oliver Would asking for some money he would tell them that he spent it on bills which was a lie well enough about that person all it does when I talk about him it make me sad .Well today is Sunday the Lord's day and he is brought another person into my life and for that I'm grateful we have Bible to study together every Thursday at 2 o'clock is a nice young man and he is teaching me a lot about our father for these things I need to know and as my knowledge of God grows I'm sure we will become closer he makes it so much easier to learn about the Gospel, when I was going to church everything move too quickly and I wasn't learning much and there was a lot I didn't understand this young man makes learning easier for some reason I can relate to what he is saying and that brings me joy. The learning process is supposed to be pleasant not mind-boggling, he has invited me to his church and I'm thinking about going to see how they worship the Lord well another day is come to an end. Today is Monday and my friend is supposed to stop by to take me down to the authorities meaning the police station to let them know what the slumlord is doing with Oliver and hopefully they will bring a close to this chapter in our lives, the only concern I have is my friend showing up but I think he will. I feel God put us on this path so I will see it through, well another day is come to an end. Oliver says the police department are probably in cahoots with the slumlord see and he deliver subpoenas for them and the courts Oliver feels that the landlord is untouchable because of the things he does for the court system.

I prayed last night for God's guidance and I know he heard me so I will see where it leads me in this problem. God is never let me down before if it's meant to be it will be people should he able to destroy other people's lives like that it just isn't right I know if I would've done something like that they would've put me away. Some people are above the law I know that isn't right but that's just the way it is it's like they say money talks shit walks, I was told one time that if you have enough money lawyers can get you off with murder and that is a quote from a lawyer that used to be high up in the court system. As long as you have means you are above prosecution in this country today. I'm going to call Dave the building inspector to come over and check out this house so he can see what's going on here. Well today is 28 March and the building inspector came over at 10 o'clock this morning and inspected the house and took pictures like I said earlier the house is a disaster waiting to happen he took pictures of the foundation that's ready to collapse it is bowed inward putting pressure on the water pipes,, later this week is going to have another expert come over and look at it. Last night I got down on my knees and prayed to my father for guidance because I really didn't know what to do or how to do it but he assured me things would be okay, for he has never left me scared before I think my faith is what has brought me through everything I have gone through. My faith in myself and in God has been the best thing that it's ever happened to me, I get my patients from Oliver this is something you learn it isn't something that can be given to you.

I feel it something you earn by learning to understand other people like I said earlier Oliver's 85% deaf and when I talk with him it's different than when I talk with other people probably because I have to focus on what he is saying there are times when I have to repeat myself three or four times like yesterday we had to go and get copies of Oliver's electric bill for the last six or so years and the lady asked to see his identification well him deaf I had to raise my voice a little bit so he could hear me and once he grasp what I was saying he got out his ID I had to apologize to lady and explained that he was half deaf then she showed me the papers and I told her I had to get out my glasses because I was blind. And she said well this is a challenge I'm dealing with one that is deaf and another that is blind and we sat there laughing I have to admit it was funny the kind made my day and that made me feel good, I miss laughing years ago I laughed quite often if not with other people that with myself on the kind of person that can come up with some funny stuff if it hits me at the right time. I feel our father can sometimes stop us from getting to down on ourselves and others, today is March 30 and I'm in hope that the bank papers arrived today so I can get them to Jan the one investigating offers case. I never had much faith in the police station before and I think it was because I was falsely accused of something I didn't do years ago, but God told me to forgive them and I did so that's in the past and that's something none of us can change. The only thing we can try to change his today and the future, for yesterday is gone and can't be recovered, a thing that once was and will never be again for doesn't exist anymore. Our time on this earth is recorded only by God for he gave us life no one else, everything we do good and bad is recorded in heaven or wherever he keeps those records. If he wasn't such a forgiving God or spirit none of us would make to everlasting life for he is the one and only the alpha and the Omega. Some want to embrace it and others don't for their own reasons whatever they are, the building inspector came over and put a letter on the house saying it's going to be torn down because it's a fire hazard and the foundation is unstable he also said we could get the landlord for not providing a livable house in other words he was running us a place that was unlivable for the last eight or so years. There's a lot about the law I don't understand but I wish I did know more about it. But the police know all that and it's their job to protect us all, well now for some good news we found the house for sure now I went and signed the lease papers yesterday and the landlord gave me the keys to the house so we will start moving in today if the weather lets us.

I feel God is smiling on us as we make this move for he knows how hard it's been for us not only health wise but mentally so many times he tests us in our faith to see how strong we are and I feel he is testing me many times to see if my faith remains strong to overcome the adversities of trials in my life. Here something funny, yesterday my brakes went out on the truck so I went got to do backbreaking and the master cylinder for it, well little did I know I was so out of shape the old brakes came off okay but I hardly had the strength to put them back on and I got real flustered and wanted to give up so I asked for some help from our father's and days usual he came through. But the funny thing is I still have no brakes so I have to do a little more work to them. So I had to quit for the night and get some rest haven't done this kind of work and 14 years so I guess I lost touch with how to do it so today I will get out my mechanics book and do some reading on the brake system. Anyway there are some people that have helped me in this well another day has arrived to April 2nd last night and stayed at our new house the Lord it was peaceful and I slept better than I have in long time. Yesterday me and the boy Leroy finished putting the brakes on my truck and I have to say we did an excellent job the brakes never worked better thank God for that one finally my life is looking better and it makes me feel real good.

Well today I went and got some more of our belongings and tomorrow we will get the rest, I do find myself getting tired much easier these days though we have made a lot of progress in our endeavors. The Lord has granted me his help in everything I do lately have been that of grateful, these last two weeks have been heaven sent I find when I get tired my mind starts to wander so I have to back up and regroup. I find it so great how much God loves us for without him I would know what to do, thank you father from the bottom of my heart. I find that I have to do something's at my pace and it's better that I'm left alone when I'm doing it because other people just confusing me when they are around because usually there in a big hurry and I'm not, life is too short not to enjoy what you are doing. My daughter came by and saw the house today and she really liked it and so did the grandchildren I went to the store with her so I could sit with the kids in the Van while she went into the store to get some groceries, her older daughter asked me if I could grow some corn in our garden and I told her yes we can then she started asking me about of the things that can grow like tomatoes squash and other kinds of vegetables and I told her she can grow them all. Gotcher is blessed her with intelligence she is as smart as a whip and so are the other children I'm glad my children have raised theirs right, they will go far in life and have a better chance at accomplishing what they want to do in the future. I can tell they love the grandpa when my daughter dropped me off from getting groceries I gave her and the kids a big kiss goodbye and little Eric my grandson puckered up his lip because he wanted to kiss to, so I gave them all the kids and told them I love them I find myself getting emotional when it comes to my loved ones but I guess that's normal when you love someone the way I love them all, there isn't anything in the world that would do for them because their my very own. No one can take that from me except God and of course I'm sure he isn't ready to do that for many years yet. Well it's another day that is come to an end with God willing I'll write Some more tomorrow. Well it's another beautiful day and I slept fairly good last night but it seems all over isn't getting all the sleep he needs and I think it's because he doesn't have the bed yet so tonight I will give him mine he's a lot older and needs to get as much rest as possible, to make his day complete. Otherwise he is moody and that causes me to have a short temper, I wrote Alain a thank you letter today for all she has done for us I haven't met anyone quite like her before she is one of those people that there are very few of. Today the clutch of my truck us started to go out for needs adjusted so tomorrow I will try to adjusted I hope it's that easy, well today is 5 April seven days until my birthday and I will be 48 years old not bad for a guy that passed away at 32 years old with God's help I have the odds and overcome the adversity that life is thrown me I find myself lucky that I have happened to make it this far and I keep my faith in God and myself. I found out that if you don't have faith in life you will never overcome addiction because it takes a higher power than what's on this earth to get you through it. Well Oliver one over to the old house to get some of this things and the landlord called the cops on the because he said Oliver was trespassing he is a slick person he does things no normal person would do like park down the road and spy on people, I can remember a few years ago we wanted to move and the landlord said if we did he wouldn't pay the bills at our new house in a way holding all our hostage because he wanted all the his money.

We know now we should not let him be Oliver's payee but the past is in the past and it can't be changed all we can do is change today and future I have to put this in God's hands because I know he will do the right thing when it comes to people like this guy I've also put it in the hands of the police because I feel the need to trust them again for so long I didn't trust them because I was falsely accused of doing something I didn't do. But that was also in the past and can't be changed, God is give me the ability to forgive and this I have been able to do. With itself, I can't stand the whole reason towards other people because his scars the soul and spirit and I don't need that in my life at this time or any other time either I have met a few people through this ordeal and have found out that they are not all like the landlord, I will keep writing my book as long as God keeps guided me towards the right direction to do it. Today 6th of April and I'm in hope that the papers will come in from Wells Fargo Bank they will show the pattern of what's been going on with Oliver's finances. I believe God has his own way of making things right that have been wronged and the people that do others wrong are held accountable for their actions, I seen so many things in this life and most of it is been bad but with the guidance of God things will be made right.

Today I will go over and check the mail to see if the deposit money has come in and I hope it has selected it to the landlord. He has been real patient through all of this, Oliver was edging the sidewalk and he said that the old landlord came by and honked I guess in a way he wanted all over to the back to work for but Oliver was smart enough to say no after being assaulted by this man caused all over the cut his pants and his fingers. I told him to stay away from him because the laws taking care of things now he needs to let them do their job is, but it's hard for him to grasp that the cops are actually doing something about the abuse. The old landlord had him thinking the law wouldn't do anything to him so I had to convincing that he isn't above the law. But still it is an old man and it's hard for him to believe because the guy has brainwashing over the years, challenging that he was called and showing him a badge. I believe no one should be above the law and if they are something is wrong a lawyer once told me if you had enough money he could get you off with murder, but I hope the court system is in that way the officer assured me that he isn't above the law and justice will be done but we have to have all the evidence in before they can go ahead and take the next step. I believe justice will be done I have to believe or else I will lose my trust in it and that wouldn't be a good thing. The laws are put in effect to protect the people of the United States so things like this won't happen, and if they do happen they can be corrected. I can't imagine what the world would be like if everyone was above the law, I don't think it would last long we would destroy each other and to me that isn't a good thing. I have a feeling that Dave will support us when we taking to court for running us a house that is unlivable I wrote a thank you letter and sent it to the Kearney hub in hopes they will print it to let people know that helped us know how grateful we are for their kindness God inspired me to write it so it should be printable. Today is 7th of April, and I'm going to try and get some more things hung on the wall today, things are finally coming together we have a nice home that is disaster free and we don't have to worry about getting sick anymore. At least now I can look forward to getting up in the morning and feeling good about where I am, I truly believe God is watching over us as we move forward in this life he has a great love for us and for that I'm grateful for without a him none of this would be possible. I have found out something though my joints and bones are not as limber as they once were, we had to leave some things behind because they were infected with Bad water so we don't have any beds yet and the floors ours hard as a rock but that will get solved before too long were going to look at some beds today at garage sale and hopefully we will get them if they're not too high on the prices. When we moved, it got me overwhelmed and I'm just getting back to normal but it feels good to have a decent home after so many years in that other house I felt trapped like an animal in a cage not being able to advance in life and that can destroy the human spirit if it goes on long enough. The spirit has to be free and be able to soar to ultimate heights it's what keeps us alive inside, as I think back I'm glad I wrote those articles in newspapers because they will still be there when I am gone from this world and if my grandchildren choose to read them they can identity time in their lives. And hopefully they'll read this book as they grow I hope they can learn from this book the do's and don'ts of life, when I wrote that letter thanking the people the editor of the paper called me to ask if I brought the letter down and I told him yes so they are going to print it I think that's really nice of them.

When I feel something in my heart I have to express it in one form or another but usually it comes out in my writing I call it a gift bestowed on me by God there is no greater explanation for what I feel when I write. When words can make you cry I automatically know they will reach into other people's hearts and make some of them to the same well my songs by Brooks & Dunn has still stayed at number one on the charts, and for good reason. When a song touches spiritual levels it becomes a great inspiration to people and this song does that wholeheartedly. Well another day is come to a close so I'll write some more tomorrow. Well it's Saturday the beginning of another day I slept good last night I said earlier that the thank you letter was going to be published in the paper as of yet it hasn't come out but I do believe it will be in today's paper so we will see if it is. I find that when you submit something to the Kearney hub that comes from the heart usually they find it worthy of printing, although I have submitted some things that haven't been printed I found out that they only print so many things from one person in a 30 day period then you have to wait for a while it's just the way their policy is and I respect that they are nice people and care about the readers there is another song that has come out by Gary Allen it's called life isn't always beautiful this singer does this song a lot of justice and it explains how life can sometimes not be so perfect.

As I walked through this life I can't help but think God intended these things to happen to me so I could meet and understand that all people are not bad. Most of the people I have met in my life I didn't trust for one reason or another and now new people are coming into my life these people seem to be kinder and more caring the kind of people you would enjoy knowing, but this will take some adjustment to get used to it because I haven't totally been able to trust anyone in a long time. But as time goes on I'm sure that will be a thing of the past just like my past life, some people think they can't change but they're wrong we all have the ability to change for the better that is one gift God has given to us all, I find some people are afraid of change because they don't know what the future holds for them and I feel that's where the leap of faith comes in. If a person doesn't take a chance every now and then they will never know what they're capable of, accomplishing for example my writing I never thought I had enough experience to write but God showed me that I had a talent that is rare. After I started to write I never stopped, a talent is something God gives to you and what you do with that talent is your gift to God. A friend gave me a saying that I think it was to encourage me to keep writing and it has worked I love writing more than anything else, God gives us all a way to express ourselves with some it's their work and with others it's music or helping others he gives us all the gifts to help us through life but some like me it takes quite a while to find them, but I believe it's better late than never to find yourself and what your purpose is supposed to be in life I feel at home writing because it's something I'm good at, if you met me you would never guess I was in one that wrote this book in person I'm somewhat shy why do I say that? Probably because I don't say much I usually keep my feelings to myself and express them in writing that way I can think them out before I say them a lot of people don't think before they talk and sometimes that can get you into trouble. Person is responsible for their own actions whether they are good or bad and I like to do the right thing when I talk or act but it doesn't always work out right because emotions can get in the way along with anger but if you have enough time to think things through usually you can do the right thing. While today is Sunday the Lord's day arrest, I've a few things I have to do today and one thing is getting Mark's car fixed or in so he can go to the hospital in Omaha next week for his tests. He isn't mechanically inclined so I will do it for him God knows he is helped us enough times and I still believe in that same do on the others as you would have them do unto you, Mark is a real smart person and I love them dearly so his safety is important to me and I don't want him dead up stranded on the side of the road somewhere.

I woke up this morning and tiny was barking I found this unusual because it never barks in the morning, and I found him in his in Oliver's bed Oliver's room with the door shut so I let them out and he was happy we seem to get closer than before maybe it's because I don't yell at him is much as I did, I have noticed less stress since we left that hellhole. Even tiny acts less stressed being in our new home right now he is laying about 5 feet away from me trying to go back to sleep, I have also found out I have inherited some of my mom's good qualities and one of them being I don't like a unclean house choose to wash and wax or floors by hand and I find myself doing the same thing. My floors shine like class and a person could eat off of them if they had to, they say cleanse leanness is next to godliness those were my moms words to me so many years ago and they seem to have stuck with me but they didn't come to light until recently when things started to change for the better. Even when I cook it's like she is next to me guiding me in my every move for reminding me that I know how to do what I'm doing a kind of reassurance that I have the knowledge to do it, because she is the one that taught me to cook and let me tell you I make the best gravy in the world chicken gravy anyway I guess she knew I be a bachelor in my middle years anyway and I would have to survive somehow.

Oliver likes my cooking so well he won't let anyone else cook, a friend of mine came over to our other house and tried to cook for us but he didn't like it and she is a line cook at a restaurant and the funny thing about it was he told her so. I tried to tell him to shut up because I knew he was hurting her feelings but I couldn't get through to him he is one stubborn man and has to speak his mind. At 78 years old he has a right to be the way years God knows I can't amble change is a special person God is brought into my life for reason and who in my to question God's reason for doing something? I believe I'm just the messenger a tool God uses to reach as people otherwise how else could you explain my writing this book? For a taught me all I know about writing don't get me wrong I will need his help to get this ready for print, but he gave me enough experience to write it no one else and I feel if I wasn't any good at it the newspapers would print my stories I keep everything that is published the mind hanging on the wall as a reminder of how far I've come I feel this accomplishment is a greatest one, and I've only been doing it for a few years. Some people think that their opinion doesn't carry any weight so they don't even try to voice it, I was talking with an elderly lady one day in an office and we were talking about different things but mostly about things people do wrong and how they should be changed and she said it would do any good to voice what you thought. This I don't agree with but I do think the words have to be said in a certain way so they be effective and people will listen to them, if everyone thinks that the thoughts don't matter than nothing will get done and things will never change. This one that I talked to was 85 years old and it made me wonder why she would give up on changing things, how does a person know if it would change things if they don't even try? Experience has taught me that nothing is impossible with God by your side for he sees all things that have passed and that are to come. And he wouldn't have me waste my time on something that was a positive I feel everyone's opinion matters but if they don't voice it then a very well can't be heard, a lot of people in think this world is gone to hell in a hand basket and soda like to a certain extent but if we give up on trying to change it then we are helping destroyed and are just as guilty as the others. It's only hopeless when people stop trying if everyone stops trying life would have any reason to exist and every thing would come to a standstill, no matter what your beliefs are if you believe in it supported or fight for it. It's your right is a person and a child of God. Well another day is come to a close so I'll write some more tomorrow I'm getting tired and my mind keeps wandering you all have a good night God bless. Well it's Monday and another week to look forward to I'm in hope that the bank papers will get here this week I know they should because it's going on three weeks and that said it would only take two. I hope there were word is good because we really need those papers to get things going, but I will continue to leave it in God's hands there is nothing as powerful as he that made everything on this earth. For he has the power to make things right when they are wrong he can make people see the truth when we can, for he is our father and us his children. There's a lot of things we miss that our parents don't and I feel it to same way with Jesus. For he is our overseer the one that can watch over us all like little children in a playground if we do wrong he lets us know about it and it it's the same when we are being good, I feel this world it's a place that will shape us as individuals to go on that journey to the afterlife. The life that is never-ending, eternal in a life that will never end with no more suffering no more pain, no more heartache, no more disease. Just tranquility and harmony peace and love a place where our. Spirits can soar forever and ever without ridicule shame or doubt, for with him all things are possible. But we have to prepare ourselves because he won't put up with our insecurities and jealousy lack of love, faith, and bickering because these are things that people create not God, excuse me love and faith he did create.

All the things of this earthly world will be left here when we leave this place my belief is that God doesn't see color race or creed to him we are all one race not black and white, yellow or brown, for those are things that people set apart not God. God meant for us all to live in harmony not to bicker among ourselves and maybe one day we will learn this but until then we will waste energy doing the same old thing. I find it interesting how so many times I was going to close this book but God had different plans I guess because I'm still writing it and I will continue to write it until he says to stop or it's time, I never know what I'm going to write from one dated the next four I leave that in his hands to guide me in everything I do. Even though I don't fully understand why he sent me back here, I feel it was to learn something I didn't learn before and in time I'm sure he will make it clear what that is. I feel sorry for Oliver he is in so much pain over being assaulted by the landlord I have applied hot and cold patches on the shoulder but it doesn't seem to do any good and he won't go to the doctor because he says he can afford it. It's an unjust thing the landlord did assaulting him like that, I'm not a violent person even though I feel like knocking him around the backyard for what he did to Oliver, but that would not accomplish anything' it would just make me as guilty as he is. He will answer for his crimes against humanity God will see the that, no person has a right to assault someone that hasn't assaulted them especially a 78-year-old man. His bones are brittle at that age and they feel the pain more easily than young people.

And should be treated with respect, I'm amazed at how old people are treated today, they have lived their lives and should be able to do the things they want to do with the rest of their lives. Oliver's the kind of person that can't sit still very long and I think the reason is because he had to work so hard in life. He is one of the most honest people I know, I can remember one time he forgot to pay for something at the store and we got home the first thing he said was don't use that creamer until I take it back and pay for it so I gave him a ride back to the store so he could pay for, now in my life I haven't known too many people that would do that most of the people I have known over the years would've just forgot about it. I find that some people are just downright mean to others and why this is maybe because they don't like themselves, I feel that if a person is not happy they throw off a reflection of themselves and other people pick up on it. We have the power that surrounds us and whether it's good or bad depends on the person but I find that I can pick up on this power and it tells me whether to get close or stay away. We are just starting to get settled down in our new house and it feels good not to have all those worries hanging over us anymore, it's like a path has been cleared for us to move forward instead of standing still the spirit has to be able to soar to whatever level God intended and negative energy stops that from happening. When you are surrounded by negative energy it's hard to break away but with God's help it's possible I'm sure glad he's on my side for without him I would know what to do. I can't help but feel one chapter in my life is coming to a close and another is about to begin, but what it hasn't store for me I will find out as time passes but I'm sure it won't be as negative as the last one, although it's had some positive affects on my life also. I also find my children and grandchildren are opening up to me more than they used to and this I find to be a good thing, they seem to be moving closer to be and I like that feeling. It does my heart good and now I'm not afraid to let them in, I have no doubt we will become a lot closer as time moves on for I love them with all my heart. God gave him to me for a reason, maybe to help me grow in a positive way and learn some patients. I know that's part of why he sent Oliver into my life, I find that patience is something you earned as you get older I don't really know how it works but it does and it makes you a better person as you learn it, there's so many things your body goes through when it gets less and less dependent on chemicals over the years I have noticed a lot of changes and I have to say they are for the better.

Well I just got done putting the vacuum advance on my truck and I must say it looks good so far I have to the help of Oliver to tighten up the power steering pump, once he gets back from the store like a said before things are looking up and be in a mechanic helps a lot not having to pay someone to fix things for you without the vacuum advance hooked up use a lot more gas and at the price aghast today you have to conserve as much as you can. It's really a good motor and should last a long time as little as I use it but it was a lifesaver when we had to move that was the main reason I got it. Because I have found out that in life you can expect other people to be available right when you want them to be, heck they have their own lives to live. Without being harassed by everybody that needs a ride this way I can depend on myself. And no other people,, well I went to get some gas at the station and the news people were there and they asked my opinion on the gas prices if I thought they would go down and I told them no they asked if it would cause me to travel less and I told them yes it would so I might be on the TV news sometime this week or month. My letter finally came out in the newspaper thanking the people that helped us in getting out of that death trap I thought it would take some time to get it done and I'm glad it did my spirit is running high today thanks to those things happening, and I called the bank and they told me the paper should be here tomorrow so things are looking up for us in that department.

Well for the first time in my life I was on television last night on the news and I have to say I look pretty good for my age and it made me feel good, I had always wondered what I would look like on TV and I look like a country boy and I couldn't get over how clear the pitcher was. Well that was last night and my thank you letter came out yesterday that was 11 April and today is the 12th my birthday, I believe God is sending me a message that everything is going to be better for me and Oliver. The bank papers are supposed to be here today so we can get this taken care of and I believe once it's behind us we will be able to move on with our lives. But this injustice has to be taken care of so no one else gets taken advantage of by that person, last night Oliver was in so much pain that I had to use a back massager on his shoulders he shouldn't have to go through that. Just because a certain person can't manage his anger, but I feel justice will prStacyil when we bring them in front of a judge people after realize you can't beat on someone just because they won't let you keep exploiting them. This person knew what he was doing when he took advantage of Oliver and myself, he wouldn't let us move it was like we were In a prison. Oliver was unable to move because this person had control of his money and wouldn't let him. Sure I could Oliver at that house but it's not in this human soul to keep his word to a dying woman, I made a promise I would take care of him until it was his time to go be with the Lord and to me as a person you are only as good as you word because if you word is no good then you are nothing I just hope when the day comes and I'm the way Oliver is someone will take care of me. But that won't be for long time yet today I turn 48 years old and I'm glad I made it this far Herb the only father I had ever known died at the age of only 42 years I remember wonder what he was thinking a lot of the time for he was a quiet person when he didn't drink of course some people are but I still would've liked to know. I realize now he had a lot of problems but it would've been nice to see him play with his grandchildren I'm sure he would've been proud of them just as I am, your children and your grandchildren our next extension of you that will live on long after you are gone and hopefully should the situation arise they will learn from your mistakes. So they won't have to go through the same things in their lives, I hold my children and grandchildren close to my heart because I love them so much. I want them to know the love I feel for them and I tell them all at times how much I love them, because it is something that is precious in life. Wouldn't you know it yesterday I washed my truck and it rained it's kind of funny though because I can see the black clouds forming in the north and I knew it was going to rain and kept Washing my truck oh well at least it's clean. I got Mark's car fixed today so he is happy, I didn't realize it until last night but Kenyon called me and invited me to go with them to church. He says they were having a celebration it was a day Jesus was born but at the time I didn't put two and two together because yesterday was also my birthday on the same day, now I don't know how often a person has a birthday on the same day as Jesus but it made me feel good. When I got done with Mark's car I went in and went to bed for a while because I was so tired then it didn't dawn on me that we celebrate our birthdays together. It wasn't until I had what I call a vision last night that I realized then, we or I should a gone to church with him Kenyon is a real nice young man and he is smart and I think he was trying to tell me something when he called but I didn't put the two together.

My relationship with God started when I wasn't on this earth, it started when I went into the light when he sent me back with those two words. Although it took years to figure them out the things I learned in between that time was very helpful in changing my life, when I was in the hospital someone visited me and gave me a thing a booklet and also with that booklet a white stone with a name written on it that what no one knows but me I had forgot about that white stone for long time and now I don't know where I put it. Well I went to the doctor the other day and he said I had high cholesterol and how can this be when I ate like a bird? Maybe that's a problem, I don't eat enough and I don't get the nourishment I need. Well I will try and do what he said to do and see if that makes a difference, I know I have to do something different if I want to be around another 50 years and I do. Well it's a fifth of May and I'm going to try and get a hold of a lawyer to see if we have a case against the landlord, I feel the faster we move on this the better that way you won't have time to try and cover things up because he is a smart person but I hope justice will be on our side. The officer that investigated the case said something that got me to thinking and that's why the landlord would have all of his money put into a company account something doesn't smell right here maybe a phony corporation.

Well today is 6th of May, and two of my grandchildren are going to be baptized day and my daughter asked if I wanted to go and of course I said yes so we have to be there at 1 o'clock this afternoon. I feel this is a good thing she is finally doing, I know it should've been done right after the birth but better late than never. I'm in hope that this will bring them closer to God as it is intended to do because you can't walk too close to our father and if they started a young age they will have more time to accomplish this gift God gives to us all. It's just that some people live their whole lives and never accomplish this goal has for me it took too long or maybe not, it is written that God plans every step we make so he must've known the way my life would turn out. As we go through life many lessons are learned and if we listen to him we will drop closer to him sometime during our life span. For God is the only one that sees a whole picture so he must've known I would go to that part of life and in the end come out a better person, but today I'm on the right track or path and one day my life will come full circle. Yesterday I went out and mow the lawn as I was told to get more exercise from my doctor I've known for some time I wasn't getting enough exercise so I figured it was about time to get into better health so I can be here for my grandchildren I look forward to seeing them when they grow up and become gentlemen and women. They love me a lot and I them so I feel I owe it to them to be around as long as I can, I know God is looking out for me but I also have to look out for myself as well. When I get up in the morning I always turn on CMT because music soothes my soul and it makes for a better day when I get a good nights sleep. When I sleep good it amazes me how good I feel the next day calm and content not on edge like I do when I don't get a good night sleep I like it when I'm not so bitchy to people it feels much better. I have to admit there's still a lot of things I don't understand but I do know when I come up with creative ideas it's usually the Lord that gives them to me or guides me in the right direction to find them and I consider this a gift. As I keep learning, things come more easily to me at times my mind is like a sponge and absorbs a lot of knowledge that gets sorted out later. But I have found out that I don't forget things like I thought I did they just get put into another part of the brain until they are needed later, at times I find things pop into my mind that I thought I had forgotten but didn't like all the memories of my past life I thought they were wiped clean but they weren't something was just blocking them from coming to the surface. They say you can't overcome a problem until you find out what caused it and I know why I turned to chemicals at the age of 11 years old, I was afraid of not being accepted and alcohol numbed that feeling so I wouldn't have to deal with the and as they say alcohol stops the production process in other words it stops the brain from growing and absorbing knowledge.

It seems to limit the brings growth or slows it down. But once you quit using the chemicals it starts up again and you have to learn things all over, as with me I took it too far and had to learn everything over again and believe me it wasn't easy. Now I will keep learning until the day I pass over once more and this time I believe will be my last, because I believe I was sent back to retrieve this information and as time goes on things change our thoughts are actions our lives, and whether it's for the better is up to us. Life changes us all and that's what God intended it to do I believe when we change the world around us changes and that's how the world advances in technology different mind can create different things and so on and so forth. Just because a person is smart doesn't mean they can't fall vicTom to alcohol or drugs some of the smartest people have fallen vicTom to this plague that is destroying our children and our young adults and even us grown adults some adults live their whole lives being alcoholics or drug addicts all because they followed in the parents footsteps I've always been a true believer that children learn by example and when you're born into an alcoholic home that doesn't diminish the drive a child has to be like their parents even though it's not good for them that's why parents should lead by example not allowing their children to consume alcohol at a young age.

When children are born into alcoholic home there's an 85% chance they themselves will carry this cursed or gene in the blood it's like, a crack baby born into an addictive world to have to go through with draws once it comes into this world for that child the chance of becoming addicted are a lot higher. Having the curse and you can pop up at any time and it could be like me early in age but then again it might not hit until later in years say from your 20s to your 50s. Or it could even skip a generation and affect your kids, they don't know why this happened but it does and the outcome is usually not good. Although my children see me near-death and I explained to them that they should never fall into this the gene was passed on my son had the same problems as I did but somehow it skipped my daughter and I thank God for that that it's get my daughter that is for my son he might have to learn like I did the hard way, although my addiction started in my childhood in my heart I feel kind of responsible that it was in my son's genes but I know he will make it as I did one day he will open his eyes and find the thing he's been looking for he, doesn't realize it yet but he is looking for the same thing I was a closer understanding to life a closer walk with Jesus. I fought it every day of my life until I decided it wasn't going to run my life anymore, and for some people that have never had an addiction there's no way they can understand it a book can't teach you about what the body goes through for this is just not possible. Psychologists go to school for years to understand how the mind works so they can help those who are mentally challenged. But to experience the degeneration and the regeneration of the body cells is another thing altogether, everyone's mind works different for those who are slow they may not be able to comprehend words but they somehow have the ability like my little brother to read a blueprint like it's nothing something that some can't do others can and they can do it with less. Not being able to read doesn't always mean that the person is stupid their mind is just wired a little different, it's canny how my little brother can't read words but he can follow blueprint with no problem and I'm just the opposite strange how things work out in life. When he was on the boys training school he was able to get out in three month, as for me it took 18 months but back then being very young and influence by chemicals I had anger issues I had to work out. So many people ridicule others because of their upbringing and was some it wasn't their fault if the people put more time into helping these people the world would be better off. It's just like these people that want credit for trying to help the starving people of the United States they don't deserve credit not tell this problem is dissolved, people let been taking credit for solving this problem for the last 80 years and it isn't any better today than it was 80 years ago so there isn't any progress being made just the rich getting richer and the starving dying on the street along with the homeless people.

There's no sense in that, we are the richest nation on the planet and yet we don't have enough homes for everyone (why) I will tell you, most people don't care if these brothers and sisters live or die. It's sad I know but it's true all their worried about is where they can stash the money well they can take it with them God won't allow it. There's a saying, you would have that are luck trying to thread the head of a camel through the eye of a needle than for rich man to get into heaven, for these things I believe to be true God doesn't want to treasure made by the blood of innocent people. So for you greedy people out there think about that one you can't take any of the with you, we came into this world but naked and we will leaves the same way. I know we won't need such foolish things in paradise for all we will ever need will already be there, I believe God will provide for his people as he wanted to do in the beginning. Adam and Eve, had it made until they messed it up they wouldn't of wanted for anything being in God's grace but they listen to Satan and look what that got them. Nothing but hell and as time passed the Lord started to trust some of the people, we are getting better but we have a long ways to go why do you think we have to die before we go to heaven or hell? I believe he judges us by what we do with our life doing good towards others in time should become a natural thing like it was with Jesus he never felt obligated to perform the miracles that he did it was like a natural thing following his feelings and that's what we need to do but us being human we got a long ways to go.

As with me there are many things I would like to do to help those who are suffering through addiction, but everything has a beginning and as with everything on earth some of us are not equipped to provide the financial part of things so we keep learning and hoping that the Lord will show us away to bring our dreams about. They say if you believe in something long enough and hard enough it can be brought to pass or brought into reality and this is something I do all the time they be in a way I'm hoping that others will see my good works and maybe help out in this worthy cause to save the lives of the ones that call themselves the lost souls. They say that suffering is a part of life and suffering somehow makes us stronger so I believe, it helps us to grow in our walk with Jesus. What this world takes away from us we will get back up there whether it's caused by car wreck or just natural he won't take anyone before their time for this I know for a fact he sent me back here didn't he? Our lives are predestined laid out before our birth and if that part of our lives isn't fulfilled before something happens to us than we are sent back to fulfill it. Then once that's done we can move on to that better life, without all the childish games people play. I believe we are all on a mission to do good in the world to leave a legacy of good works, so others may learn from like we did. I believe we are put here to accept others and help them in their time of need and if everyone did this then there would be any starvation or homeless, all around the world the same problems exist. It would be nice if we could leave something behind that can solve the problems of others just by reading a book, and for those that go through those problems that can't read there is audio. Well today is Monday, 8th of May and I didn't sleep as well last night as I did the night before I was awakened at 3 AM this morning and I don't know why, but I have had a lot on my mind since yesterday and it makes for a restless night. I wish I could shut off my mind at night but as we all know that is impossible, I have often wondered why the mind keeps running even when the body is tired is too bad the two could shut down at the same time it makes for a good nights sleep so the body could wake refreshed and the mind rejuvenated to start a new day. I don't like to wake up with the cloudy mind everything seems to get scrambled but at times I get a good nights sleep and that makes for a wonderful day, I have been looking at pictures of my children and I find it amazing how more beautiful they get with age. My granddaughters are eight and four and the eight year old has really grown up for her age when she gets into junior high school she's going to have to fight the boys off with a stick, I don't remember any of my schoolmates looking that good my generation must've fell from the ugly tree at least what I remember of it all I know is that their daddy has his work cut out for him and he better be ready for those days. Because they are going to come up fast, as with everything when it gets to a certain stage it takes off and grows like a weed and I'm glad their mother and father are proud of them all. I'm in hope that my grandchildren will get to read this book so they may avoid some of the things that messed up my life, I think I will go to Sally's and get some picture frames for their pictures it seems I never have enough of them my daughter gets their pictures taken every chance she gets. I guess it's a way of keeping record of their growth a way to reflect on the past in a positive way.

Well today is May 13th and I'm going to my grandson's birthday party on this day at 2:00 AM, this should be fun I wrote an article for the paper the other day it was my opinion on alcohol and it's called alcohol changes lives; ask me about it and it goes something like this. According to the Kearney of article, the consumption of alcohol by youths is down. It came down faster than expected. I feel this is just the tip of the iceberg. If people keep stressing to youths to be themselves without the use of alcohol, the numbers will improve even more. All children have a spark of divinity. At the most things, it's hard to ignite that spark, but with support from the elders in their lives, it can be done. I feel that spark is what people have been trying to ignite for a long time. It's a creativeness within all of us, something buried so deep that some lose interest before they can find. Some feel alcohol brings this out, but it doesn't. It only makes a person go further away from it. Alcohol only clouds a person's judgment. It doesn't bring out the creativeness we all have inside of us. It stops them from growing in the same way alcohol stops the development process in the brain. As long as a child uses alcohol they will never know their full potential because it stops the create a process from reaching its potential. I know this will for a fact. I drank most of my life, and it got me nowhere fast. Finally, I quit 14 years ago. Now I wish I had it never used it. I can't even imagine how far I would've gone without the use of the. Who knows, I could've been a teacher by now, but alcohol took all that away from me. It gives you a false reading of everything. Once it gets a hold of you, it doesn't like to let go because it's always been easier to grab a drink than to face your own problems.

That, my friends, is a fact. When things get too tough in life, most people like to take the easy way out by avoiding their problems. It starts out with one problem, but then it grows like a cancer. Soon it can't be stopped without help. By then most don't think they need help. That's why they say before you can get help you have to come to terms with the problem and admit you have on. That's something most alcoholics can't do because they are blind to the fact that alcohol controls their lives. It doesn't only affect adults. Children suffer because of it. Some children think see in their parents drink all the time is normal. It's not. I saw it, and I'm telling you it's not normal for a parent to drink: time. I know this might make some people mad, but it's true. If our children are to have normal lives, they should know some of the facts so they can choose which way they want to go. The world has endless opportunities for those who use their brain in a positive way. I believe it's never too late for your brain to develop again, even after years of abuse. It's a gift God gave us all, so don't you think we should put it to good use? God didn't make any of us the same. We are unique. That's what makes us all special. This letter was published on May 11th 2006 in Kearny Nebraska by the Kearny hub newspaper. It's dedicated to all those people that have a problem but can't admit it, maybe as time goes on they will be able to see how much it hurts our children, and put a stop to it. I have seen the pain this problem causes and I wouldn't wish it on anyone, but I also realize some will never admit they need help. And to those people you have to come to terms with it sometime or you will lose all you have in life and mess up your children's lives to. I went to my grandson's birthday party and boy the all the children had fun but I noticed some parents didn't have much patience with their children, and others had all the patients in the world strange the way people very in their understanding of children some of the children were happy and content while others cried and were getting upset, it was like you could tell which ones were going to have trouble in life in which ones weren't. Little Eric has a new name for his grandpa and it's Papa, it made me feel good when he called me that. He got 12 outfits for his birthday so he should have enough close for a while but all he was really interested in was the candy, I feel my three grandchildren will make it all right in life. Because they are loved and well-adjusted, and they were brought up right. I love them all dearly. You could tell everyone was nervous probably because we don't get together very often but that should change as the years go by, I have a strong feeling that I'm coming to the end of the things as they are. But I feel there will be others as my life goes forward into the future. I have a gift to see things different than others do, I can tell they are all wrapped up in the now. How do I put this they are not able to separate the rat race from their lives and concentrate on what's important. I do know. I'm different from them in many ways and I like it that way. I like to watch people and their reactions to different things because there's are not the same as mine like I said in that letter God didn't make any of us the same.

We are all different and unique. I'm in hope that my writing will change some people's outlook on the lives of their children but only time will be able to tell, that if the consumption of alcohol by use continues to go down than I can feel I did a little to help the cause. But it will take a lot more people helping than just me, words carry a lot of power and if they are used right and can touched the hearts of people I find that the heart speaks louder to people than just words do. You have to be able to trigger something in the heart before people will listen to your words. I have found out that compassion triggers a reaction in people and this is a good thing because without compassion there is no reaction and if you can't get people to react to your words then it's all for nothing. I really feel this book can help a lot of people so I will look forward to the day it's published, I firmly believe God put me on this path and what God puts into motion no man can stop. I can't even count the hours put into this book but that doesn't really matter it's what's in the heart that counts and if you can reach a person's heart and things can change hopefully for the better, this book is written by me but inspired by God for he taught me all I know. Without his help this would never have come to light this book shows some of the power God has, when I write sometimes I go into a place where I can be reached by other people but when I do this it takes a lot out of me. It's like another dimension somewhere I can be alone away from the negative energy and the confusion of this world a place of peace, hopefully one day I won't have to go there but until that time I will keep making my world a private one with the exception of family.

Grown-ups pushed that ability into the back of their minds. And for some they can never recover it again for one reason or another, the only reason I was able to recover mind is that I had to let that 11-year-old boy out to take over this body and eliminate the one that destroyed it in the first place. People that think they know me, don't know me at all it's the other person they knew not me the person I am today. The other person is long gone and will never return that's another blessing God gave me. To wipe the slate clean, and give me another chance to live with him teaching me without the distractions of the outside world. I have a long ways to go yet but I know he will be right beside me, for he will never for sake me like people do. I have learned a valuable lesson from people never depend on them only yourself. Because if you depend on them you will cause problems for yourself and you don't need that in your life because it can set off a chain reaction of all kinds of problems that you don't need in your life. As a person starts to depend on themselves most problems would disappear and life itself becomes much easier, less stress means better health. And when you make a decision to do something to it. Don't procrastinate about it just charge it head-on with a positive outlook, there's nothing you can't do if you put your mind to it. If a person goes through life doubting themselves than they will never get anywhere, it takes a positive attitude to try and overcome your faults in life. When someone pushes you down! Get back up and kick ass in a positive way. But don't criticize them rise above that and move on with your life, I will tell you a little story. The mother of my children read one of my articles in the newspaper one day and she asked me why she never saw this side of me. And I had to tell her that the person she knew was dead he didn't exist anymore and she asked how could this be?. So I told her I kill him and she said that was impossible and I told her no it was the fact, and she said but your year and I said no that person is gone all you see is the body another part of the mind took over after I destroyed the Roger you knew after all the years of abuse the child within came to light the child that was pushed away in the far corners of my mind. The one that never got to live his dreams, the one that was cut out in his prime of life never able to mature or grow like a child should be able to. You can't take a child's youth away and not expected to rebel later in life whether it comes back better than it was or worse that part of the mind has to be allowed to grow no matter what but with some they die before they can accomplish this. I was blessed can't gave me a second chance to tell my story of life and how it can change if you believe in yourself and him, for he top me no one else

He gave me the power and my words to make a grown man or woman cry, things that are so deep you wouldn't think it was possible to reach those depths. I have written things that have made me cry and I never thought that was possible, my one friend called me a publishing fool and he said he feels like I'm going to move on with my life and forget about him. I don't think I could ever forget about him or his family, because it times I thought I was going nuts and he encouraged me to keep writing he said you're not going nuts. It's God opening your mind to new things that you never thought possible and it will take some time to adjust and get them working. So I believe it's like my legs it's a miracle only God can give, I have found that most people don't believe in miracles well all I can say to them is it's your loss because they do come to light when the time is right. I've seen them with my own eyes and more than once I feel sorry for people that don't believe in God and what usually causes this is a tragedy that has taken place in their lives like losing a child or someone you love or that is close to you. They couldn't understand why those losses took place so they lash out and as usual they blame God, because he isn't here to defend himself not that he would have to. He gives life to us all but do you hear of someone thanking him for this kindness not too often (why)? Because it's something people expect from him and when they don't get it they cursed him how unjust is that? If people would show more gratitude for what he gives us then things could be better if he so chooses for them to be. But know they have to play the blame game, and blame all their problems on him when they can't figure them out. And most of the time the answer is right in front of their faces, people cause their own problems and when they come to terms with that fact they will be better off. All I know is, life is what you make it. Whether it's good or bad is entirely up to each person, but people need to quit blaming God for their misfortunes. I don't really know maybe that's the only way they can make it through a day is by blaming someone or something for their problems. Because it's hard to solve problems it takes a lot of work you have to go back in time in your mind to accomplish this task, all the way back to when the problem started.

As for me I had to go back to the age of 10 or 11 when the drinking started but I had to eliminate that person that took over my life and release the child that was pushed back into the back corners of my mind. When I first started this journey I didn't know he was still alive but with God's help I found in and boy was he scared he was so timid and fragile but in time he showed himself and that was when the work started. He knew that the person who took over his body was weak and dying soul together we took his body back and started to rebuild the but we had to finish getting rid of that person that took this child's life away from it so we waited until we got weak then we pushed him over the edge and in doing that we killed him. And once we did that that little boy that was afraid of rejection came the light them with help from God he started to learn about all the things he had missed in all those years, and boy was he eager to learn. The Lord taught him things that most people know nothing about. He was like a sponge sucking everything in but he had a problem fear! And rejection what the world except him this time? But he was soon to find out that things had changed and the tables were reversed would he accept the world? The way it is and this he had a hard time doing with all the destruction starvation and homeless people so he had God teach him how he could try and change things and that's how this book came to be. A depiction of many different areas in life. You will never find a book like this one anywhere in the world because it tells how the spirit can and will help you through the hardships of life, each day brings something new to this world maybe not in material form but in spiritual form. But a person has to be exceptive to it and most can't do that because of all the garbage that's floating around in this world. When a person let's things interfere with speaking to the spirit than they don't know what's going on in the places that's important, we are all spirit, were just put here to learn before we move on to that greater place but what we learn here is really important (why)? Well I haven't figured that one out yet but I will in time. All I know is that it's important to our development there's something here on earth that are spirits need to move on whether that thing is faith or something else I will find it out. My world is different from yours I can't and won't let destruction into my life I don't want to be a part of it, the things people do to each other is in Pauling to me and I don't want any part of it. But I do see why God lets the world keep the following because it's on the right track, I see good things in people and it can be passed down through generations and maybe one day they would get the picture but for now that corruption will continue until people opened there eyes and realize that war and destruction isn't the answer.

People make life hard no one else they bring destruction and sorrow to themselves but that doesn't mean I have to be a part of it, maybe that's a lesson God's trying to teach me. That we can make a choice to be a part of the destruction or take ourselves away from it, I think that's why he gave us freedom of choice so we may one day learn from our mistakes and not repeat them like so many do. Mistakes are a natural part of growing up, but if we don't learn from them then we are wasting precious time. It says that God is patient and will wait until we are ready, he loves us all but there's some people that don't learn. It wasn't until quite a few years ago that I realized that the mind is something a person should waste. Sometimes my spirit gets wound up like an eight day clock and I start writing his message and I can't stop until it thinks I am done, but like I said when I think I'm done doesn't mean that I am done. He might have other things he wants to get out then he will take over and then I have no control over him he does what he wants, and I'm just his tool as we all are just one of the people he uses to spread his words. And get it out to his people. I prefer to write the things he tells me and that makes it better for me to concentrate on things that are important, well I just got a call from Evelyn she is a person I help. She is 84 years old and can't get around to well so I help her with things around her yard, she is a sweet woman and just need to little help now and then so I help her. Well yesterday I helped Evelyn plants and flowers and that made her really happy I'm glad I could make her smile a little, it only took couple of hours but I enjoyed giving a helping hand she is in his youngish he used to be and people that are getting on in age sometimes me someone should talk to because it can sure get lonely sometimes.

Today and going to mow the lawn before it gets too long we like to keep it short it looks better that way, well I was reading the newspaper last night and a good friend of mine passed away and it saddens my heart. She had been battling drug addiction for a long time but it seems it got the best of her she was only 44 years old and a mother of three, I know her family will miss her dearly her children are lovely children and I feel for them. It just goes to show some people don't win the battle it triumphs over them and that's why I stress the importance of getting help when a person has a problem like this, some can learn to deal with it and some can't. Today I had a friend asked me if I could help him if he had a hard time getting off chemicals and of course I said yes, people that haven't had a problem with drugs or alcohol don't know what the body goes through all the changes and they're not pleasant either. For a person to be able to fight this addiction they have to be strong mentally because getting off of it is only the beginning your mind will play tricks on you to try and convince you to go back to it, and you have to be able to fight this temptation and believe me it will take all of your strength to do this. If a person thinks it's a walk in the park, then they are in for a big surprise because it's not. It will take everything you have and then some it will tear down every fiber of your being, if it wasn't for writing this book I don't think I could've made it with out the help of other drugs. But my faith in myself and God brought me through it, I truly believe God has a reason for me to go through this in I think that reason was so I could tell people how I got through it. I will tell you now I don't think God did it to punish me it was something I had to learn in life. I don't know any drawn out words to explain it just simple ones and I think they do the job just fine most people can understand what I am saying in this book it doesn't tear down anyone whether you have an education or not I have written this book so everyone can understand it so it can help more people. This is my way of turning a negative aspect into something positive, God gave my body the ability to heal itself and he can do the same for you but a person has to believe in themselves there isn't anything you can't do if you put your mind to it. Like I tell the children in my articles we all have a spark of divinity within us but alcohol and drugs stops the process from developing it's only when we stop the use of it at our minds start to develop again. I believe this with all my heart otherwise how could you explain this book? God gave me this gift no one else and he wants me to pass it on to you so maybe it won't be so hard for you as it was for me I'm not able to explain how or why I was able to do it all but I did. A lot of people give up too easily on things and that's what makes them fail, when a person gives up on themselves too soon they are not trying hard enough. My favorite saying is God won't put a mountain in front of you that you can't climb and I don't think they were talking about only physical strength everyone has strengthened the minds.

As well it's physical strength, I know this for a fact because my legs are not the strongest. But they give me by, a person has to want to get the life back more than anything else in this world and some choose not to go down that path because it's too hard to do, so they keep on the road of destruction and wish they would've stopped but wishing will never get you anywhere in life. I don't claim to have all the answers but I do have a few of them, enough to get a person started on the right path and once they're on it well it's up to them, they have to wanted it. I believe, now this is just my opinion. Using one drug to get off of another isn't solving anything because you just didn't depended on that one, so what the hell is a person doing? Trading one addiction for another it just prolongs the addiction longer than need be. And why prolong suffering? Because you will suffer some getting off of it, that's unavoidable. It's a price everyone has to pay. But it will pass before you know it, then things will get easier your mind will take you to places you never knew existed. I know, I have been there and it isn't something you can explain away. I don't have a name for it, for it is unexplainable it's something you have to experience before you will be able to come full circle. I have lost track of all the changes your body goes through some pleasant and some not so pleasant. At times your spirit will soar to heights you never knew was possible, at least mine did and it was the greatest feeling I ever felt ones that only God could give to the spirit.

I think it was his way up telling me everything would be all right that the hard part was over. After that everything started to level out and the fight was over, then I started to rebuild everything and my mind started to work like a trip hammer all sorts of things ideas came to mind and he stood by me all the way he didn't abandon me like people to when you're going through this process you will find out who your friends are and only your true friends will stand by you and support you. The others will fade away like a ship in the night never to be seen again, but this is a good thing for you because you don't have to worry about them coming back. If it wasn't for music and writing this book I could've surely went nuts, but it's good to know I have friends that will stand by me through thick and thin. During this time I have lost a couple of friends, you see, stopping the destruction of alcohol and drugs can also take its toll on the body if you are not in very good health. The longer you use these chemicals the less chance that you can recover, I'm not going to try and paint a pretty picture of recovery but I will tell you that after 25 years of abuse I recovered and I'm feeling great these days, the ability to help others get off of chemicals gives you a great feeling of accomplishment. That is my gift to them because I know how it feels to go through it alone and it can be very lonely with no one to support your decision, but it's something I had to do on my own (why?)? Because I wanted my life back that bad. And I was even willing to die for if need be, I had already passed once and I knew God didn't send me back here to die again that soon because I knew he had a reason for my living again. To be reborn is exciting want to get over the dStacystation like I did. For some reason I didn't have much faith back then and I think the reason was because I was crippled, but that was soon to change when I opened the door to acceptance and as time passed my faith grew stronger and stronger then after a while nothing could shake my faith. I noticed some people think a person has to go to church or they don't have faith this I find not to be so faith comes from within and God give you faith, whether it's by things he does in your life or in other ways but it changes your life forever and think start to get better. To me it let your spirit soar to new heights even further than before, but I think if you were to lose faith things would start to fall apart and that's why mine is, how do I put this? etched in stone there's nothing that could make me lose faith. Probably because of what he's done for me it's something no man on earth could do and no energy could accomplish. It's' something that can't really be explained in mortal words you have to experience it before you could understand it something so powerful nothing in this world could compare. While yesterday I had a friend come over and I haven't seen her in a while but it was good to see that smile on her face and she is still going good she was another person I helped. It seems like the word gets around when you help people. Some people think alcohol is bad for them but that's just the way alcohol works most people don't even realize they have a problem with it.

Until it's too late and it has done the damage, what do I mean by damage? Well the destruction of the nervous system among other things like blackouts. Domestic violence, destroying their children's lives by allowing them to see this kind of behavior and they always hurt the one day love the most. Why? Because they are the closest thing to them with alcoholics the destruction isn't right away it has sort of what I call a waiting period usually a few months or even years and the sad thing about this chemical is it makes you feel un-destructible, like you can do anything. This is the false reading it gives to people whatever another person has done they can and will try to do it better without thinking they will try things they have never tried before and this is where false creativeness comes in. As I said earlier by this time the brain isn't firing on all its cylinders and can be very dangerous by this time the brings getting false reading and this caused from alcohol and drugs. Alcohol and drugs are the same thing though they call him something different methamphetamine, cocaine, speed balls, they all destroy the development process in the brain. And you can see this as the person goes through what doctors call the DTs and it's not a pretty sight they shake can get six so bad at they call on God, please God help me get over this one and I will never drink again to only run out and get another bottle or beer, by this time the mind is even trying to trick God but that can be done because he knows all things but what I'm saying here is alcohol can't can venture mind that you don't have a problem when you do.

I can remember my dad and myself saying I just need one drink to get over this angle but one isn't enough I there is 1000 by this time your life is almost over because you have to destroyed most of your internal organs kidneys, liver, heart, pancreas, among other things like your brain, and nervous system. And most of these things can be fixed and the sad thing is your mind will trick you into believing there's nothing wrong until they plant you and the ground, then it's too late to do anything about it. Everything you love is gone along with your heart and soul, most people let this happen because they can't face their problems since a child my life around I haven't come across the problem that's worth dying for. Sure alcohol drugs makes you feel good for a while but then it takes over and it isn't so fun anymore and usually people have to lose everything before they wake up if they wake up at all. They have AA to help people and it can work to a certain extent, but sometime in life you have to take control of your own life and move on. I have found with a lot of people it's easier to talk about it with other people but with me being the kind of person I am I find it easier to write about it, it's a gift I have received from God to help me through this rough time in life. I believe I brought this problem on myself and I'm the one that has to fix it so I can go on with life the way God intended, a person can't go through life with clouded judgment it only takes away from what the world is really supposed to be like. Satan rules this world at the present, but one day God will take back what is his and there will be no more war, starvation, and homelessness. For he will rule this world not people, only God will have complete control over this place we now live. As time goes on and the time gets nearer to when he will take back this world the violence will increase and more will die but in the end God will rule than the past will be written so it's never repeat it again. But that's then and this is now, what I'm trying to tell people is that it's never too late to go from the life and destruction to a life of helping people that have had the same problems as you, we all make mistakes in life that's how we learn but to keep repeating the same problems over and over again doesn't teach you anything it causes you to get stuck in one place for too long of a period. Sort of like playing a record that skips you don't get to hear the whole song, and that my friends can be annoying. Have you ever heard a song over and over in your mind and can't get it out well imagine one doing that but you only hear half of the song it would make you wonder where the other half was wouldn't it? And you don't need that playing in your mind it would be like being in a race and taking two steps than stopping it could be very confusing. I went to the store today and this friend I know told me I better take care of myself she heard about my cholesterol and she wants me to be around for long time. It's friends like that that makes it all worthwhile it gives a person a sense of belonging which we all need.

Without it we feel useless, this is the kind of friend I'm talking about when I'm talking about a true friend. Which most people don't have enough of, they say you can never have enough friends but I prefer just a few that I can really trust. I have found that a lot of people that act like your friend really are just Fair-weather friends, when things get hard in life they take off like a bullet. Never to be seen again, well today is May 20th and I don't know what the Lord has in store for me today or any day for that matter for each day is different in new some good some bad but in the end I always know that it was a learning process for that day. Tomorrow, I told a friend not go to church with him to trying get a feel for it as with a lot of things I have to feel comfortable with the place. I find that most churches have their own Bible written the way they feel about God it's like religion is at war' each side having their own opinion of what life is really about and I don't really want to get caught up in that kind of war, I know God is good and I know he loves us all and wants only the best for us all. But why do people have to think their religion is the best one don't we all have the same God? I always thought so, as time goes on I will visit more the strictures and find the answer to these questions I have. (Why) is religions a competition and why do some religions feel there's is better than others? For I believe we are given the freedom of choice but does that give us the right to compete for God to love.

God loves us all the same even the lost souls who are searching for that something they can't seem to find. It took the United States 150 years to gain its independent from what I understand and here in this war they are trying to shove our way a life on to another nation that has slipped the way they do for thousands of years, I guess I'm angry with the government and other main bodies because they are always trying to change other nations and yet they do it at the cost of ignoring their own people we are not any better off than them the only difference is they kill each other, but are we doing the same thing when we start our people to death? If other countries saw that the American people didn't have starvation then they might want to think twice on the American life. But until we stop starvation in the USA I don't see this happening because we are not giving them a solution to the problem we are making ours worse by giving all the American money away, the American people have to work hard for what they have but the United States government just gives it away. Mostly for the mistakes they have made either by destroying another's country or killing innocent people, when a country allows people into the country and can't feed their own people there's something wrong and as long as this goes on than the problem will still exist. And as long as the president allows this problem to go on the more American citizens will die. It says in the good book that one day we will stand before judgment and we will be asked just to question one what did you do with the life I gave you, as for the other question I'm not quite sure what it is, so I will wait until I know. The president took on the responsibility of every American citizen in the United States so he should do something about the starving and the homeless here. I noticed he had to put in his two cents into the Terri Schiavo case where he didn't belong, him and his brother but they lost as usual. Those are things a government needs to stay away from because they have no right interfering in such things, well to get off that subject. I woke up this morning and Oliver and tiny were fast asleep in Oliver's recliner, I still don't know why he gets up so early in the morning all he does is eat and fall back to sleep for hours on end. Maybe that's what happens when you get that old, I really don't know. But if that's the way it is and that's a way it will be. I have learned a lot from him through the years and I will keep the promise I made so many years ago, he sure loves that dog of his they both sleep in a chair and tiny sleeps right on his lap. There like two peas in a pod and Oliver worries more about the dog then he does about himself but they look good together, if anything happen to either of them I'm sure the other would die of a broken heart. When Oliver is gone to the store tiny just sits in the middle of the living room waiting for him, if that isn't love I don't know what is, tiny knows when it's time for bed at night and he runs to get into bed with Oliver and the bed is about 3 feet off the floor. I can sometimes hear tiny fall out of the bed at night because it makes a loud thump, but Oliver picking back up and shoves him under the covers they are so funny together.

I feel sorry for tiny in many ways the poor dogs expected life in years was only about 12 and here he is still around after 15 years. I believe it's the love that they have for each other that keeps tiny going and that's a rare commodity, I feel sorry for tiny because he has arthritis so bad and that times he can hardly walk. By this time in Tony's life Oliver has to carry him to bed as I believe his life is coming to an end there were a few times when I thought we lost the as he laid on the floor lifeless and then I went over and put my hands on him and prayed and boom he got up like there was nothing wrong strange how that works. It's a good thing tiny is in a St. Bernard Oliver would never be allowed to carry them up the stairs, I have to say he acts more lively in this new house than he did in the other no more steps to climb. As time passes I know things will get worse for the two of them but all I can do is love them until the time comes from the Lord to take them home with him, Oliver told me one time that he thought he would go to hell because of the way he lived and I told him I didn't think so. That he had done a lot of good in his life more good than bad, I truly believe he will go to heaven when the time comes our God is a just God and can see the good even if there was some bad. I don't pretend to know how God thinks but I do believe the good outweighs the bad here on this planet, even though at times I get angry at things that are going on. I don't believe in killing and never will but I can't change other people's minds, some more set on destruction so they choose to die for their country which is their right.

If they choose to do so but preserving life is more important to me. As the churches say Satan rules this world at the present but one day he will not, and he will be cast into the fiery to burn forever and that Jesus will for 1000 years I honestly don't know if I will see it in my lifetime but if I do I will praise the Lord our God forever. He gave me life where there was none and though I was crippled I walk, for these are things that only God can do, miracles I believe them because I'm one of them who else could do these things? No one else but god has the power over life and death not even Satan. He can only take he can't give life when the world is rid of him then God will raise the dead once again and reward them for their services to him and finally there will be peace in this world. I realize now that there won't be peace until his coming, and the path of revelations has to run its course before this can happen so be it. I will watch for the signs as the years pass but I won't get involved in the destruction that will take place in this world. I will watch and record what happened as I was told to do, right now I'm not involved in what the world does to it's self and I feel better that way. I will observe the things that goes on until it's my time to go from this world, I think I was put here in this town for reason. What other reason would there be for me to be here? I have left before but always came back and never felt the need to leave again, in a way I feel like my roots are here and here's where I'll stay unless Lord sent to me in another direction than I would leave but not until then. I have found that God uses us for many different reasons and we don't always know what they are going to be but with his guidance they usually end up pretty good. At times I wish I could see things the way he does so I could get a perspective of things that are to come. But only he is able to do that we are not worthy of this gift though at times I feel he gives some of us a glimpse of the future to help us understand things a little better but it usually isn't much, just a glimpse from time to time. I got up this morning and was concerned because all of our hadn't been up yet and it's 6:30 AM, I know the other day I told him that he should sleep in more often but I didn't expect him to take me seriously, I just checked on him, and he seems to be breathing that is the only way I know how to check on him. Who knows maybe he is trying to break his old habits of getting up at 4:30 AM I will find out in a little while. I just when in the woke them up to check on him and he is fine, it kind of puts a scare into me because he is never done this before. After he became fully awake he seems to be more spunky this morning than ever before so I guess it's a good thing for him. My friend Mark goes and experiments with different doctors and when he called last night and told me his Dr. lost his license and it kind of shocked me. Then he proceeded to tell me that his other doctor doesn't know how he is still life, he told him that he was in stage four liver failure and needs a liver transplant. The Dr. is supposed to call him later to let him know what's going on. I prayed to the Lord for him as I do for all the sick that are suffering, I feel the Lord is kept them alive this long so there must be a reason for it.

Today's the 24th of May and it looks like it's going to be a nice day mid to upper 80s I don't really have anything planned for today so we will see what the day brings. I might help Mark if he needs it, well today is over boy that was quick. I spent the day helping my son change motors in his pickup and let me tell you every muscle in my body hurts but that's what happens when you haven't did mechanic work for a number of years, you don't realize really how many muscles you have until they heard but it's good for me. It will help lower my cholesterol as I was told I need more exercise and a change of diet God as it is I eat like a bird, I even started to eat wheat bread yuck. But I want to be around for a while so I have to take care of myself you know what I mean, I really had fun showing my son what to do and he caught on fast, he gets that from my side of the family. It's just that I got away from that kind of work for so long it takes a while to get back into it. Me and my son are pretty close and I enjoyed doing things with you can tell we're cut from the same cloth I can see things in him that used to be in me and some of the things I like but others I don't. But none of us are the same and I'm grateful that he is my son sure he has some little things he needs to change but doesn't everyone? As we go through life we learn many lessons but to be able to is a hard thing to do many people I have come across seem to either not want to solve their problems or they don't know how to solve. And others just don't give a shit. They feel at home blaming others for their problems and it's so easy to do, is starts out with one problem but then it grows like the cancer that take so many lines.

Since beginning of time it's always been easier to grab for the chemicals instead of solving the problems in life, for surely it was never the taste of alcohol that drew me to it as I never liked the taste so it must've been the feeling that it gifts that took old me. Many think those two things will make it better and it does for a while but then it sets off a chain reaction that eventually destroys a person's life. With 80% of those addicted the addiction does it's job very well as it kills many in its path. The reason most people feel they don't have a problem with it is because they are able to go to work and complete their jobs each day, little do they know that in time the job just like their family will play second fiddle to the addiction one day leaving them alone without family or job. Why was I put on this path point these things out? For the longer the problem of addiction goes unsolved the harder it will be to get your life back. I recall many unpleasant times from being a child staggering down the street to being an adult falling in the gutter for those moments in time seem to stay somewhere inside until they are dealt, you can run from life all you want but eventually those life altering things will catch up with you and then you have to travel to the time when it all started. Maybe this is what they mean when they say we travel back down the road we leave behind but in the mental sense not the physical which by the way takes a lot of time. There is no one that has automatic recall of that time in their lives because it's been buried so deep under all the other crap that is plagued you through the years it's only one that crap gets cleared away that the door to that problem opens. So many people don't realize that if you want the cancer to stop it has to be cut out and even after that it takes treatment before it can be cured, but most would rather go through life blind and not even acknowledge that they have a problem and this is where you get most your alcoholics and drug addicts they are too scared of their problems they are rendered helpless to the idea that they can fix them. Because as they say there isn't a problem that can't be solved. Sometimes it can take quite a while but is something that can be overcome For this I know, because I have had every problem there is for a person in my position and caliber of life. Believe me there are others that have a lot more than the in this world. But people that let these things build up have a real problem because they don't want to deal with, and then tell they do this will continue all through their lives. Only when they get a handle on their lives will they be able to solve the problems, life is hard there's no doubt about it. But it can be made easier if a person learns to deal with the problems as they arise. They would get so cluttered up and people would fall behind, if they just learned to solve the one in the time. I heard the saying is a child and my mom used to use it you should never go to bed angry because it's better to resolve the problem on that day than to carry it into the next lesson makes for a better night sleep, this is a good thing to do because that way you don't have extra baggage carried over into something that's supposed to be beautiful the following day.

Some people have problems with letting go of things like problems or material things, sort of reminds me of the hoarder when they finally have to turn loose of their possessions it's almost like with every piece that leaves a part of them leave with it. When the problem of addiction arises many will start out too straight now through lives. But then something happened along the way and they fall back into their old ways, thus making the recovery twice as hard as it used to be. With every step on this journey nothing has been easy when it comes to taking your life back as temptation is around every corner and in the beginning, it's very overpowering giving it more strength than you have. I recall spending many months away from people in hope to regain my life I once had, the tears came and they went but in the end I was able to do what I didn't believe I could do this was at a period when I had no faith or hope. You would think I would be doomed from that point on but as time passed the Lord gave me these things I need the faith to believe in myself and the hope that he would make these things possible. As for every step of the recovery there are some things that I have forgotten but the pain, sorrow, and fear. If I would of had people around me during this time I would've never been to recover.

There's one thing we all must admit, and that is this world is balanced with good and evil and we don't need the evil. As time goes on and you improve in your undertaking it will become clear which is which and you all know what to avoid and what can help you. This book was written to help people and try to set them on the right path all the things in this book I have lived, and a lot of them are hard to relive but I had to do so I could turn something negative into something positive that's really what this book is all about turning the tide, taking something negative and turning it into a positive force. If you can accomplish this in your life time then you can be proud. A lot of people let those negative forces get a hold of them and that's it they don't even try to fight it because it totally consumes them and only when they realize this can they developed the willpower to fight back and win if they want it bad enough. But I have found that a lot of people would rather stay consume by it because they say it's too hard to fight back and for those people I feel sorry because they have given up on life. Life is a constant battle between good and evil and when you let evil win life must not have any meaning for that person, nothing is easy in life and the sooner people realize this the better off they will be. Writing this book was an easy job but I felt it was something I had to do with my life to turn the forces and have a positive outlook on things to come, because I couldn't do that before living with the boundaries of negativity can and will destroy your life unless you rise above the challenge life has thrown at you. And believe me they can throw a lot of things your way during a lifetime, but the good news is you can handle them if you learn to and also want to. You see the people I have helped with addiction they needed support but more than that after I told them my story of how I was sent back some of them didn't understand why which is another thing that had me puzzled for a while. So then I would go on to tell them it wasn't my time yet to go and if they tried anything foolish and it was there time to go, God would send them back also. And that there wasn't a guarantee how they would be sent back, I guess just the thought of them come back cripple or mentally challenged change their way of thinking along was carrying the hell out of them. They then looked at me for inspiration when they see how good I am doing for some reason they want a part of that and that itself inspires them and gives them strength to stay strong, they know it's not easy but what in life worthwhile is easy? And to be able to gain control of your life again is a greatest accomplishment you will ever achieve. I have seen many people that have a passion for life but for some reason it's short-lived like with after addiction, they seem to lose hope and find themselves sleeping on the time hoping that things will change in your sleep. And this is something that will never occur it's sort of like they have given up and don't have that zest for life, it seems no matter how hard I try that is something I can't wrap my head around. In the beginning they are so grateful but as time moves on they seem to fall back into the darkness for some reason and this is not a good thing, it gets to where they even don't want to get out of bed and this is just a life wasted because the laziness I've seen many people die in their beds and family included and this is a hard thing for me to see.

With these people depression seems to set in and they don't a lot of deal with so what's a person to do? I can't let this kind of thing impact my life because I have fought too hard to live once again so maybe in time for all things considered they might have to move on because if you let it being around that kind of thing can rub off if you not careful. Here they said for years in prison and when they first get out there happy but then that happiness fades and it's like they are back in prison, this is a mindset created by them as they have given up. It's a shame to have someone else fight so hard for you and then you destroy that by things that could've been changed for the better, but weren't. With many it's like they go in and out of depression and you never know how they are going to act from one day to the next, for it surely isn't anything you would want others to see so you hide it away from the eyes of those that don't come around too often. As with most things having a relapse isn't unheard of but you have to stay strong and try to avoid the problem, but if it happens stop it and go on it's a part of the process that many go through. With many it's like they are testing themselves to see if they still wanted it or not and most find out that they don't want. Let's call it curiosity but this usually happens about a year after not doing it, and they find out that they're better off without it. Strength is the key in this process and understanding from those around you if you can get loved ones to support you the better off you will be there's something about feeling love for others and help you rise above the addiction had with me that love connection was with God in Oliver. I'm sure it wasn't easy for Oliver having to put up with my shortcomings but like the Lord he hung in there. When you first get off of it you are like a baby far venerable to the slightest hint of doing it if someone comes to your house with it for one, their are not your friend. And you need to tell him to leave otherwise you will fall vicTom to it again there's a saying it's called the serenity prayer. God grant me the serenity to accept the things I can't change. And the courage to change the things I can, and the wisdom to know the difference. These are words to live by you see I was fortunate the cravings were taken away from me and it makes it a lot easier to write about it.

In creating these pages I had to relive all the aspects of my life over again it wasn't easy to do because some things I would've rather forgotten but in doing so it is made me even stronger than before and this is a good thing for me. Well today is Friday, 26 May and I think we will go on foot across on mom's grave, I haven't been there in quite a while so I think it's time. Life isn't always beautiful sometimes it's just not fair but in the end it will be a beautiful ride it took troubles and make a stronger and our experiences that make us wiser. To be able to leave the past behind is something that every person will be able to do once they start on to the road recovery, and it's an exhilarating feeling one that you will only experience at a certain part in your life while you are taking that life back although it to feeling like no other the emotions that it brings with it are overpowering and if I could put them into a bottle they would sell like nothing but these are feelings and emotions only God can give so when you receive them cherish them. This is Memorial weekend a day to give thanks to the soldiers that gave their lives for us all, and I pray for a weekend without casualties of people that are still alive. We still have trouble with our youths drinking, the other day I read in the newspaper that three miners were cited for MIP here in Kearney, it just goes to show we have a lot of hard work ahead of us. Some youths think it's cute to drink and I can't stress how wrong they are what starts out as cute usually ends up in a catastrophe, if not right away later down the line. Children don't realize what they are dealing with a force beyond their comprehension that renders them helpless against it, most of them don't have the strength to fight it. And it preys on the young people because they are naïve and want to gets a hold of them it doesn't like to let go, most of the children that get caught up in the web of destruction can get out it's sort of like the spider and the fly once alcohol and drugs gets a hold of a child it drains them of life the same way the spider gets its nourishment from the fly. And as long as children keep letting this happen the spider will keep draining their life force from them, you can compare the spider and the fly with the forces of good and evil because evil is the strongest force there is in a lot of people and it has the power to turn a good person bad if they are not strong enough to fight it. And it's been this way for hundreds of years I just think no one has presented it in the form that I have, plus it to the only way I can explain the good and bad elements in this world the forces of good and evil are unbalanced because Satan rules this world at the present so it's harder for a good person to stay that way without fighting the bad elements.

When a person is young they are impressionable and can be led astray, and evil can make things seem to be positive when there negative that's how much of an upper hand Satan has over most of the people in this world he uses the illusion to try and control the people and he likes to start when they are young. As with most things, young people don't have the experience to avoid the negative forces in this world and the negative forces know this and take advantage of it. Whether it's alcohol, drugs, or something else worse. I know this for a fact I have fought these negative elements all my life and for the first half of my life they won. I didn't know how to fight them off until the Lord guided me in the right direction this negative force is ruthless and it will destroy your life if you let it and it has many different ways to do it. Not only by alcohol and drugs but by other things like turning a once good person into a thief among other things it uses everything in its power to turn a good person bad, maybe that's why impart it's hard to be a good Christian these days it's a constant battle between good and evil. But if you don't fight the evil then you will fall vicTom to it like I said before young children and adults are there pray they live off the life force of our children and young adults and that's just the beginning because once they are hooked they destroy those lives unless they can somehow be stopped which is the only way I know how to do that is to cut off the spider's head and gain control over your life again

Once you can do that there are places that can help you, you're not alone in this world even if you think you are. There are places that can help you with your problems, you don't have to fight them by yourself there are millions of people that have a hard time dealing with their problems that's why they have AA and NA among other so you can get help and have someone to talk to about your problems to try and get to the heart of the matter to try and find out what caused you to turn to those things in the first place but it will take some time because most people can't remember the things that push them to use these things. With some it's been many years since I came face-to-face with that problem that push them over the edge and they might be reluctant to face it again because I know what it did to them way back when, today is Sunday the 28th and a friend came over this morning to visit and she spent most of the day here. Earlier we walked to the store and it was nice to walk and talk to each other I have always had feelings for her but I haven't let them develop because I know she isn't ready for something solid like a relationship yet she is still trying to find herself and one day she will.

But I won't be the one standing in her way of progress, I think we are all trying to find ourselves for one reason or another. It's something we all have to do some time in our lives, she has some issues but then don't we all. She called me out the back door to see some snakes that were on the back porch so I can't them and put them in the neighbors yard across the street, it's strange to see three of them together I really don't care for them and I hope they won't become a problem. I had some snakes and I was young one time I brought one into a bar wrapped around my neck and needless to say they threw me out, so I had to drink alone that night you do some foolish things when you drink things that you would not normally do. I can still recall my first girlfriend I was so shy I had to drink a few beers before I could get up the nerve to ask her to be my girlfriend. Courage in a bottle, that was something I should've been able to do without the use of alcohol. You see it's little things like this that can send you down the wrong path it worked that time so whenever I change girlfriends I went to the alcohol for support, like I said in my article it gives you a false reading of everything it acts like a friend but it's not because you become dependent on it for courage something you should be able to tap into without the use of alcohol it's little things like this that can ruin your life. It starts out as something small but then accelerates like a cancer does like me being shy that's something you should be able to overcome in a short period, but by using alcohol to covered up you really don't get over it. It just gets put on the back burner so it can bother you later. These kind's of things are avoidable if you just don't use alcohol, it's little things that get out a hand and become bigger problem and the sooner people start to deal with those little problems and get them out of the way the better off they will be, you can't let those little problems hang around until later because later never comes and they just start piling up until there are so many that you lose track of the one that caused you the problem in the first place.

Then from then on they keep piling up until you don't exist anymore you just become a big problem everyone wants to get rid of, by then no one wants to help you and you don't know how to dig yourself out of the mess and it's at times in your life that you find everything hopeless, abandoned, so lost and distraught that you want to give up on everything and disappear. But within that little timeframe something happens, call it God's grace or whatever but it opens your eyes to show you a direction to take so you don't have to give up on life. As a matter of fact it gives you strength to carry on with your life to turn it into a new adventure in a positive direction to try and help those less fortunate than you were, you see a lot of people have to reach this plateau before they can excel upward. They call this hitting rock-bottom for some like me it took death something so tragic that it rattles your whole being, Well today is Monday Memorial Day I will be glad when things change from the way they are and I can feel change coming it's hard to explain but I can feel something is going to take a drastic change I don't know why get the feeling but they haven't been wrong yet, I've decided to put my own clutch in now all I have to do is see how much it costs for the clutch. I'm in hope that I won't need a pressure plate or throw out bearing as that would really run into some money and I don't have that much to spend on it, I have to get by as cheap as possible that seems to be the story of my life and I can't help but to get angry sometimes. It's like my whole life is been this way sometimes I don't mind it but other times it really makes me angry. As a nothing ever seems to go my way but I should be used to that by now, strange how I have all these dreams and still it's a struggle to make it from one day to the next one day all of this will change and the world will be full of what I need and it will feel good not to want for anything just once in my life, I realize after go through these kinds of things to learn certain lessons in life but I wish I would've learned them sooner that way this would be much easier than it is.

I feel God is letting me rediscover some of my talents so it will be easier for me (you know) like mechanics otherwise having a place to do the work will run you broke, if a part cost 50 or $60 you can bet it will cost you three or 400 to have it put in like with that vacuum advance and that distributor if I would have a place do it they would charge me $150 but the way I am I keep parts off a bold Ford fan's and interchange them with pickups and it didn't cost me anything to change it I had to do some drilling but I got it done and it runs good now, I have also Other parts that will work on my pickup like starters carburetors alternators, things that would cost quite a bit to get I feel it's always better to be safe than sorry the price they want for things these days are out of this world but something to have gone down in price like a master cylinder they used to cost 45 or $50 in the 60s and 70s and today they have a lifetime guarantee for 14 bucks. Now I don't know what you think about that but to be that is good thing. I'm hoping the price of the clutches have gone down the same way so I will keep my fingers crossed you never know about these things as time passes I will become more familiar with the things I used to know. I'm having to learn everything over again as I had to do with my walking so I will take it easy and slower this time because this knowledge should be cherished and preserved I don't claim to know how things work in a person's genes but I do know that if the father has mechanical skills they can be passed down from generation to generation but why this is I have no idea but it's strange and I would be scared to try and figure it out. There are so many things that I have been able to figure out yet in life and maybe him not supposed to figure them out but that doesn't change the fact that they interest me and make me curious. The other day my son and I were working on his truck and he got disgusted working on something but his anger showed itself and I was compelled to show him that it didn't half to get him mad that it's better to take a step backwards and look at the situation for the proper solution and when I fixed the problem he just smiled and I told him that God wanted us to work on this together so we could help each other in different situations and maybe he could get control of his anger. And me' maybe give me more patients in different situations by working together we could at least try and gain control over these two things, well today is the 30th and Evelyn wants me to come over at 10 o'clock and help her with some things around her yard like cut out the dead parts of her rosebushes and open a window or two. I like helping the elderly because they really appreciated it. On supposed to start working for Elizabeth later this month and I'm hoping to have my truck fixed by then so we will see what happens.

I slept good last night and it feels good to wake up refreshed so I am ready to tackle the day head on. Besides doing knows things for Evelyn I don't know what else the day has in store for me but whatever it is I will accept it. My son should be over today to finish his pickup and that will get that project done, so I can start on another one my pickup. I will try and attempt to put the clutch in myself and see how that goes, I know I have the knowledge it's just putting it to use that scares me because I have never done it before but like they say no pain no gain I'm confident I can do it but it's a unknown that scares me what other problems are going to arise when I get into it I hope none but you never know, I still haven't driven it since I adjusted the clutch maybe I better do that this morning. Well I went out and tried to drag pickup and it worked fine so I'm good to go to help Evelyn 10 o'clock if it doesn't rain hopefully the clouds will burned off God willing, I feel this is going to be a good day but why feel this way I don't know it's just a feeling I have and usually they are not wrong. We'll see when I get back from Evelyn, I pray everything goes right. I hope my son can get the parts he needs at the junkyard today so he can get his truck back on the road. He was telling me that his girlfriend said he should've had it running by now but what she doesn't realize is that you have to have all the parts before you can complete something. She don't have many patients either this younger generation I don't know about them, maybe they can be taught only time will tell I have studied my son's generation and I have found that they want things to happen right away

For everything that pops into place like a puzzle and life isn't that way they are in too much of a hurry for things to happen and some of the pieces come up missing the pieces that tells us what life is all about. Myself I don't like to get caught up in the confusion that's why stay away from most people I don't like the negative energy they put out it interrupts my positive flow of energy. Now this might sound strange to some people but when I'm around people with negative energy it drains me and I haven't figured out why it does that yet you know how they say good conquers over evil well I'm looking at that theory but to be it seems that the negative forces in this world are stronger than the positive ones, maybe that's because Satan rules here in this world at the present. And wherever he is there's always something negative going on, all I know is that some people have a more powerful negative force than others like the lady I met at the vacuum cleaner place. Venus called this morning from the library and told me to tell her boyfriend pick her up there because she wasn't going to walk in the rain I couldn't pick her up because I don't have reverse in my truck. I will sure be glad when I get it fixed I don't like it when I can't go where I want to but you have to take the good with the bad that's just the way life is and as with everything there's a good side to everything. Well it doesn't look like I'm going to be able to help Evelyn today it's raining cats and dogs outside and it doesn't look like it's going to let up for a while so I'm stuck inside for today anyway, maybe tomorrow will be a better day for doing yard work if it clears up you never know what Nebraska weathers going to do its unpredictable. Well another day is past and another is coming in the horizon I like to watch the sunrise it so pretty, I don't think it's got arraigned today it's pretty clear out but the rain we got yesterday was needed for the farmers I think it's neat how the worms come out when it rains, and how they end up in the gutters just to dry out afterwards. I am told the worms allowed the ground to soak up the water by drilling those holes in and it helps to saturate the ground with water. Yesterday would be in my summer working on his truck my grandson was sitting by the toolbox playing with the tools, and Leroy asked him if he wanted to be a mechanic or work on cars when he got older and he said yes. You can tell he likes it he gets so engrossed with and playing with them. That boy would make a good mechanic with the right training, I can't get over how he looks like I did when I was young the blonde hair soul blonde even it almost looks white. My nickname was snowball and it was fitting considering I look so much different than my brothers and sister, and the other grand son will look the same way when he gets a little older I can tell they came from my gene pool they look so much like I did when I was at their age. I really need to take some pictures of them for my photo album I never had their many pictures of me taken and I don't know why that is.

I do remember one of the when I was about five years old and my hair was still white. I wish I went to It maybe my brother in Oklahoma has one of us all, I think I will call him find out if he has any of them he would have them if anyone would. At times I find myself going back to those days my life and feeling those happy feelings when I didn't have a care in the world, before things interfered with my growing up. When your child you don't have all the worries you get when you're an adult I love to be in a child protected by my parents they didn't let the negative forces in this world coming to ours we were protected, then alcohol came into my life and I didn't get to grow the right way to learn how to deal with problems as they raised. All alcohol does is teach you how to avoid problems not how to work on them that chemical seems to cover up problems and once it starts it's hard to stop it because you have grown up your whole life avoiding them. When you have ever had a problem in the past you just grab for another drink and it would go away so you thought anyway it just doesn't go away it just gets put on the back burner you might say until later, so it can blow up in your face. Some people think alcohol gets rid problems well let me tell you it doesn't it causes them, and they usually end up bigger than they were before because of neglect.

Let's look at one, let's say you have to get up early in the morning so you can go for your answers for a test but you have a hangover well instead of just getting the like you would normally do, the alcohol from the night before is telling you don't worry we got a covered and you fall back to sleep before you know it, it's 11 o'clock in the morning and you have missed the test so what happens? You know you're in trouble and instead of going and facing the teacher you get a drink to help numb the feeling of shame. Many people think this kind of thing doesn't happen but it happened more than people realize and a lot of times the parents never see it, or if they do they just shrug it off. Well on another note I just got done with my son's truck now he has something to drive. I think doing this together with him brought us a little closer and that taught us both something, what may seem the obvious isn't always what it seems. Me and another mechanic that had been doing this for years diagnosed the problem wrong, we thought it was a blown piston and come to find out it was a bad modulator on the transmission allowing transmission fluid to bypass the modulator it had a ruptured diaphragm that caused this problem so all in all we got wrong. Oh well it happened sometimes no one is perfect at least it's running now and a good lesson was learned don't always go for the easiest problem to be so. Because it might not be the right one, in the morning I have to take Oliver to catch the shuttle to Grand Island for his quarterly checkup at the VA and then pick him up after he is done at the Holiday Inn here in Kearny and bring him home he seems to like going there as he brings home bird houses and wallet kits. He can put them together when he gets bored these are things the Veterans Administration does to help soldiers. Today while working with my son I gave thanks to God forgive me a chance to be able to show him how much I love and he thanked me for my help, and I said you bet that it was fun doing something together and we should do things together more often and I think he liked that idea. That's a second time we have done something together in the last few months, he sure is close to my grandson and believe me he is a handful. He needs discipline before it's too late and I've told my son this but whether you do something about it is up to him all I can do is voice my opinion and he has to take it from there. I feel God was with me in working on that motor even when I felt like getting angry I didn't, I just talk to God about it and everything worked out for the best. He could've made it a lot harder than it was if he wanted to, the Lord knows that patient isn't my strong suit in life but I'm working on it the best I know how and eventually it will come to me. I still have a lot to learn and it will take some time I really don't know if we ever learn all we are supposed to be for our time is up on earth but I guess we come close on some things and not so close on others. I'm still trying to figure out things what goes here and what goes there, I don't know if I will ever figure out all there is to know about life but I will try. I can remember back when I was a child my mother used yell at my dad because the car wouldn't run at times, then she would go on to say, it's just like a mechanics car to never run. But they can fix everyone else's and that really made her angry because to her she should of had the best running car on the planet.

I remember one time my mom bought a car because she liked the color of it and the radio worked, she didn't think about how it ran anyway my dad no more than God at home and it blew up. So he told her that he would have to rebuild the motor so they got it into the garage and started to tear down And this he did while he wasn't working but he got a good discount on parts so it cost to provide $180 to rebuild it and when they got it done my mom would drive it around the block and then never again because of car was too fast, when she stepped on the foot feed the front end lifted off the ground and it scared the hell out of her. When she got back she handed him the keys and told him to give it to their oldest son which was my brother Rod and him being only 16 years old he ran the hell out of racing everything he could, there was one time when he was racing in new Mustang and the motor was too strong for the transmission so transmission fluid. Blew over the motor and it caught on fire luckily for him a milkman was coming by and they poured milk on the fire to put it out it was equipped with a 390 engine with a two speed power-glide transmission which was too small for the motor is back in those days nobody wanted to speed power-glide and here today everybody wants them and they even use them at the racetrack.

Well today is June 1st the beginning of a new month, I have to take all of her to catch a shuttle to the hospital at 7:30 well it's hurricane season again and I bet we will get our share of them but not us here in Nebraska on top and about the United States as a whole all the coastal seaboard I predict we will have quite a few hurricanes is year stronger than the ones that ravished the coast in the last year, causing more destruction than ever before and it will because by people not listening to God he will send out a lot of messages for people to listen to but whether they will listen is another story. People are blind to some of the messages because they choose to ignore them, even when it's as plain as the nose on their face. I feel this is his way of talking to us as he tries to guide us in the right direction and I feel it's his way of telling us that things have to change and with some they will not accept this for one reason or another, because they don't believe. They don't think they can be forgiven for what they have done in life but they need to understand God forgives us every day of our lives because we are not perfect and never will be that's why it's good to have God on our side he is able to forgive all our sins because we are his people and he is our Lord Jesus Christ. People should be grateful that he can forgive us so easily of our indiscretions all through life we make mistakes and some learn from them and some don't, and with many they wait until it's too late and by then they are either in jail or prison but all isn't lost there. John the Baptist had to go to prison to find his way that shows me that it doesn't matter where you are when you accept Christ into your life, it's never too late to change your life even though some will try and stop you from accomplishing this endeavor. Well a friend of mine came by today his name is Craig him and his girlfriend are trying to get off methamphetamine they have been clean for a couple weeks, I wish them nothing but the best and trying to fight this plague that has ruined so many lives he said he is going through drug Court but I'm afraid that isn't enough to make a person quit using drugs, they have to want it more than life itself. They have to want to be free of the burden of drugs and want back what drugs has taken from them whether it's family or something else. Any person that gets addicted to drugs or alcohol loses something and with most they can't get it that back no matter how hard they try. The reason for this is that some don't find their way back from the darkness that alcohol and drugs lead to as it starts to rule their life instead of ruling it themselves, and as long as they let this happen they will continue to be lost. For these things are sad but true only when a person can take responsibility for their actions can they be set free, but not until then. Well today is Saturday, 3rd of June, and we had a few thunderstorms last night yesterday me and Mark went to pay bills and I told him to stop by Bob's Apco to get some pop so we did and when he was taking me home he went to stop at a stop sign and spills his pop all over the floor for, I couldn't help but laugh but boy did he get upset and then he said oh well it'll soak in. I couldn't help but feel sorry for him because I know he will have to clean it up later, I slept good last night and feel good this morning. I went to Evelyn's yesterday and did some work for her, it seems she had a flood inside of one of her walls so I had to move some things for her so they would dry out she's the kind of person that keeps everything and I notice that a lot of older people do that may be in a way they are trying to hold onto their past as I know things were hard during the depression.

Back in the day when they bought their furniture it was made to last, not like today's furniture made out of pressed sawdust. They knew how to make things back in the 30s and 40s if you buy solid wood today it cost you an arm and leg and most people can afford to buy that good stuff, well I will posit for now so I can make out a list for shopping. Well I went shopping yesterday and it didn't take long to spend $120 but that was mostly and meat, I figure I can get the rest at the dollar store. I used to go shopping with my mom on occasions and she showed me how to shop that woman can make a dollar go a long ways but she didn't live in today's world where the prices have gone through the roof when she was alive I can remember her going shopping for a family of five spending $25 to $50 a week but she knew how to make things stretch by making many different kinds of meals, she could make one chicken feed seven people by making things like chicken and rice and boy was that good stuff I think I could remember how to make it if I put my mind to it so maybe I will try and make some next week. I sure miss her meals and her stuff bell peppers, and was that good. I still know how to make them though, for some reason I haven't been able to let go of her memory and at time's it bring tears to my eyes. But I guess that's normal, because you shouldn't forget your loved ones. I truly believe I will see them again in the afterlife, she will be smiling when I see her again and also my other friends that went to be with the Lord.

I find that it's lonely without a companion in life but I also believe someone will come along in time for me to live what's left of my life a happy person, God wants my life to be the way it is for now and for some reason I agree with him even though I don't know why. I see couples all the time together some fight like cats and dog's but I guess they like it that way, myself I want to find someone that I can be happy with I've had enough fighting in my life and now I just want to be happy and maybe build up a nest egg for the future so I won't have to worry about things when I get old. I know in the future that things are going to get harder before they can get better that's just the way life is, life gets hard and then it gets harder until it wants to ease up on you. But you never know when that will be, today is Sunday and I slept in late until 7:30 AM and it felt good as it makes for a clear head to start out the day to damn going to clean the house so I won't have to do it tomorrow. Then hope that Elizabeth will call so I can start helping her with things that way I might be over get my truck fixed somewhere down the line, she said she had quite a bit of work to be done so I will keep hoping for things to turn out for the best. I think I'll call her tomorrow and see what's going on, well it's Monday and it's raining pretty good outside so I don't think I will be going anywhere today I love it when it rains it makes everything smell so fresh. I can remember one time when I was a child my mom used to put out big pans to catch it, and I asked her what she did that for which he told me that she uses it to rent to her hair as it made her hair softer. I guess she liked to play around like that and sometimes she and my sister would run around in it & have fun, when we were camping it rained always and I always like to stay in a tent as a little boy I didn't like the rain for some reason it scared me when the thunder and lightning would hit I how is thought the lightning was going to hit us I really can't remember my dad getting scared, I guess he was used to it. Boy those were the days I love going camping even though we didn't have a home to live in, we made the campground our home mom would make sure that it was always clean I even caught her sweeping the ground like it was the floor of the house and she always had flowers on the table with a tablecloth it looks pretty and we were never a shame to bring our new friends over to our camp. And we always had fun fishing in those days so long gone I still like to take back to those times and remember how much fun we used to have our lives weren't all that bad our parents loved us the best way they do how I remember when I was about four or five the ice cream man came by and the other kids got ice cream and I didn't and I ran across the street to a little German ladies house and she asked me what was wrong and I told her, that the other kids got ice cream and I didn't get any.

So she said wait here snowball and I will be right that, in this beautiful lady walked to the store and bought me a box ice cream and handed it to me. She said that she would keep it in the freezer and I could get someone ever I wanted to well by this time the other kids has eaten and all their ice cream and here I was out in the yard eating mind the other kids got jealous because their ice cream is gone and mine was brand-new specially my older brother and sister got jealous and asked me for one and I told them no because they didn't give me any of theirs then they started to cry and I asked him how it felt to be left out of something and they said they didn't like. So I went over to my local friends house and asked her if I could get three more for my brothers and sister? And she told me yes that they were mine to do whatever I wanted to do with them so I got three more and to them to my brothers and sister, but then I told them that when they got ice cream again they had to give me some and they agreed so I gave it to them and the crying stopped it made me feel good to do that and I still remember that feeling today 50 years later. After that every time they got ice cream I got one and I went back over to the ladies house and thanked her for her kindness. That's all I can really remember about that lovely lady she made a difference in my life and for that I will always be grateful I think the name was Olga. As the years passed I got to know a few more other people of interest but it never lasted long because we moved so much, but I did learn a lesson from all that all of this when people are cruel to you don't stoop to their level rise above it and show your true self because really we are all here to learn different lessons and you shouldn't let other people's problems become your own.

Because as we all know we all have enough of our own problems to last a lifetime, I just went and ran an ad for a friend in the newspaper to sell some things for and his girlfriend to help them pay their bills they are having a hard time since he was arrested for being in the wrong place at the wrong time it was nice that he reached out to be he knows I don't have anything to do with legal things. He needed someone to talk to he had been clean for a few years now but he relapsed and got into trouble, I wish more people would listen to me about doing jokes because when they don't they end up in jail. Then they call me and tell me how they wish they would've listened to me but the world is full of would of and should of his, it comes down to. Most people don't have enough faith in themselves to be able to take on the task of getting their life straightened out don't get me wrong I don't mind helping people if they're going to help themselves but I guess it makes me angry when my work ends up in vain and they end up in prison or jail. Mark came over at midnight last night it seems his 16-year-old daughter was putting on fake nails and that glue made him sick and he could hardly breathe so he stayed the night here to give his lungs a rest. He has COPD and emphysema is a lungs are not that good so he can't be around those kind of chemicals. Another friend took a trip to Kansas and rolled her car Cornfield, she said it through her dog clean out of the car it was a good thing the dog was in a pet carrier otherwise it would've probably died but the good side of this thing was that she wasn't too bad, she was at work yesterday but she still has to go to the doctor to get checked she had a few bruises. Hopefully she will be all right, well I just got done cleaning the house and I can see how women think they are underpaid for housework it's hard work cleaning the floors and watching them and keeping things clean is one hell of a job especially making meals. You have to think of something do every day it's a good thing I only have Oliver to cook for but I make good meals because he eats like a horse and we don't let anything go to waste, because I believe in the saying waste not want not so I fixed him a lot the leftovers. It's hard to cook for just two people I'm like my mom and away she could always make meals out of almost nothing and they would taste great I sure miss her cooking. But she time he good when it comes to making meals, I still haven't made her chicken and rice dish yet but I will Oliver used to love it but I have to get some bell peppers onions and celery. Maybe I will make it tomorrow who knows it all depends on how the day goes, well I went and bought me an exercise bike seems I can't ride on it seems when I lost the use of my legs I also forgot how to write a bike so I will learn how to all over again it should be a challenge like everything else in my life it seems my whole life is been a challenge but then again what is life? If there isn't any challenges. For these things I find interesting I tried writing it earlier and it seems it will do the trick, I also notice that it builds up the arms as well as something else I meant hope that writing is like will lower my cholesterol and help my legs in the process more are less like killing two birds with one stone. While this could be the fixer of all the things that are wrong with me if I don't have a heart attack before I get it done, for some reason I'm in a good mood today can you tell? Hell life can change so fast sometimes one minute your blue and the next year happy as hell for no apparent reason I guess for being alive sometimes I enjoy being a smartass even if it only makes me laugh I can amuse myself sometimes and laugh for hours and it feels good even if it's only me laughing. Well I'm thinking about finding something to do with my spare time because sometimes I feel like I'm going to go nuts from just being around here, I get bored easily and need to do something. I'm going to take back an application this afternoon and see if I can maybe get a job for a while and see how that works out it's been a while since I've written my brother he doesn't even know my address yet so I think I better drop him a line or letter now I will pick this up later. Well it's another day and I got that letters and off to my brother.

At times I don't know what to say to him except that I love and I find it hard to write to someone in prison but I expect it's harder for him not being able to write, I really don't know why he can't write but some say is a blockage that stops us from happening and he's not alone many other people have the same thing. Myself I had to learn on my own of course with God's help but he didn't mind he helps those who help themselves, I wonder what today will bring I never know from one day next so each day brings something new to the table. Oliver is sleeping in his chair I really don't know why he gets up so early but if it is just a habit then you may do this for the rest of his life since he is stopped working he really don't know what to do with the self and I know this has to be hard on him. Tom picks him up every Sunday so he doesn't get too stiff but his coordination is off and he has fallen twice in the last week but I'm glad he hasn't broken anything I think is going back into his childhood but that's okay he's kind of funny at times and we laugh about it sometimes, my granddaughter was put in the hospital the other day for some kind of infection that she is home now and that is a good thing. Kids have so much energy I wish I had half of it my land I would probably never sleep. Craig came by with his girlfriend and the judge told him he had to move to one of the counties that have drug court so he will have to move to Kearney are some where.

I've seen people come and I have seen people go because of the curse of addiction and I have lost many friends because of in the end with most of them there lies were cut short because they couldn't resist that temptation of the drugs. I have lost as many as three friends in one year and it so like it's coming down to me being the only one left some were young and that others old. Some of the people into future will make it and some won't it depends on them and the strength they have, as for God he will continue and he won't let you down if you don't let yourself down but I have found that you have to turn your life over to him, to me it to you only way to achieve freedom from the burdens life has thrown at you. But I truly believe there isn't anything life you can't overcome with the help of our higher power, for me it was God for others who knows what they're higher power is. Without God none of this book would be possible for he guided me to the adversities of addiction and made me twice as strong as I was before now I have to look towards the future and leave the past behind me, I have learned many things in his life what to do, what not to do. We all travel different paths and although we are the same in many ways we are different in the way we learn and understand things that life brings to our attention. Well it's August 17 and I'm back I thought I was done writing but I find that I'm not doing the last time I wrote a lot of things have happened for one I've finally got a car that I can depend on, I find it funny how things come together and I feel my writing should be neglected. I have had a call from the editor of the paper and he encouraged me to keep writing because I'm making a difference in others' lives with my wisdom of things that are happening in the world today. And the other day I got to meet him for the first time he said he had to meet this person that can write like I can. I guess you can only send a letter once a month and he said I was sending them in once every three days, but I can't help myself I feel there's so much to do to open peoples eyes to the destruction about all drugs I need to try and change the mindset of our youths so they don't think they have to drink every time they go out in many ways it's a television station that fill their heads with crap about alcohol and other things they don't show the lasting effect of addiction just the party and part that they believe is fun.

The whole movement of addiction is based on the amount of money they can bring in as for them truly caring about the people they don't. I tried to make a difference alcoholics have a tendency to forget because of the alcohol abuse but if you can keep something fresh in my by writing it and it has a chance to sink in no matter how slight the chance is. For so long I felt like I was fighting an uphill battle but now others have joined in for my fight for life, as for satin he doesn't want anybody to recover and he won't lift a hand to help anyone. More and more people are trying to get involved with changing things for the better but they don't use my methods because a lot of them haven't lived the life of destruction that I have and they don't have the insight that I have. The other day I met the editor of the newspaper and he shook my hand and we introduced ourselves, I felt that he is a person that cares for our children and young adults. But there's so much more work to be done on this matter and these words you are reading are my own experiences so they come from the heart and from the pain I felt over the years, I want our children to know that they are not alone in this fight to get their lives back and I can't stress how important it is for a child to have a normal life so they can excel in everything they do. The mind is something that should be wasted because it has so many possibilities, so before you ruin your life think of these words before you do something stupid with your life like drinking alcohol or indulging in the drugs. I would like to take the time to put my last published article on these pages so they don't get lost, so here it goes it's called parents can break alcohol abuse cycle . Many times when a child becomes an alcoholic or drug addict it starts at home so parent should be good listeners during the last cruise night we had 14 youths were cited for possession of alcohol why had these numbers grown? It seems on summer rolls around and the heat rises, a lot of people think that drinking will cool them off.

But it actually doesn't, alcohol dehydrates the body in Zaragoza same way that methamphetamine raises the body's temperature to hundred and 8° this is an healthy. When the body is dehydrated the brain shrinks because it doesn't get the fluid that it needs. That's why some drinkers get hangovers and others get sick. During summer, drinkers and more likely to pass out while driving. Have you ever had a few drinks and a bar during summer then go outside into the heat? It takes a few minutes but the alcohol it you like a ton of bricks and this I know from personal experience it takes a few minutes for it to fully hit you but when it does it can drop you to you knees and. And can cause a loss of life if you then get behind the wheel, people's demeanor changes when they have alcohol in them, and alcohol won't let them admit it. It's not until the cops throw them in jail and they show up in court when they're sorry. Youths' alcohol use will increase during the summer because it's available to them, either to their parents or from a close friend. This is a problem and it must be stopped. Some parents only show concern when someone is struck down, but any parent who allows a child to consume alcohol is asking for trouble. Being a parent, I have already affected my children by what I did when I was young, and I regretted it, but I thank God my daughter wasn't affected by this cursed. Yes it's a curse, because alcohol problems are usually handed down through generations. The curse can be stopped if you care enough about the people it has affected. But if it's not stopped, it will carry on and cause more destruction. Parents, you are the ones who shape your children's future. This isn't a losing battle as long as parents care for and love their children. It's these letters at keep me going because I know I'm making a difference in someone's life and I think that's what God intended me to do. Well here are a couple more letters can listen to the paper later seeing they will only print one every 30 days but it makes me feel good to know that I'm an exceptional writer so here's another one. As parents we don't always do everything right when it comes our children, but as time goes on we get a chance to fix those things and sometimes it's hard to do for one reason or another. But if we don't at least try to correct them and that doesn't say much for us, as a child I can remember after becoming an alcoholic asking my parents for alcohol and they never turned me down. Why because of guilt and at times when they would say no I made them feel so guilty that they felt they had to give it to me. I realize now that it was wrong but back then I didn't know any better. Even in today's society when it comes to things like marijuana the parents use the excuse well I can't condemn them for using it because I did it one time this is a lazy way of not helping children or maybe they still use it hiding it in the closet you might say like some cave people do today about what they are. Children live in the moment not for tomorrow and that's all it takes to destroy child's life.

We may start out thinking they look cute when they're half crocked, but it destroys their self-worth being a child of alcoholic parents when I didn't drink I didn't feel accepted baby because I was a shy child until I got alcohol in my system, that's why say it gives you a false reading of everything because it takes away the person you were born to be. And when a person is allowed to grow that person gets pushed back into the far corners of your mind, meanwhile the one you created runs your life the one that has to be intoxicated all the time and sooner or later that one is going to self destruct. Mine did, then if you don't want to die you are somehow able to bring the real you out of hiding which isn't an easy thing to do. But in time it can be done, but now that 11-year-old child is scared because he didn't feel accepted all those years ago and he doesn't know if he will be accepted now today. This is just a glimpse of what happens when a child or young adult becomes addicted to alcohol and becomes an alcoholic it's a scary place to be. I myself, would want anyone to have to go through what I went through there many signs that let's a parent know that they are about to lose her child but with many of them they choose to ignore it like it wasn't taking place. Even today I'm still teaching that shy person how to make right what was once wrong, and as time goes on he will keep learning the values of life. As I look back I realize I can't change anything in my past but I can try and change things today and in the future, we all have to learn from our mistakes.

It's when we don't learn from them, when everything seems lost. A lot of parents don't see this but some are enablers wanting to have someone to drink with when they have lost everything they had. When the young adult can't get alcohol they turned to their parents, because it has always worked in the past. A parent that drinks knows how it feels to not be able to stop that craving for alcohol or drugs so they will do almost anything to help that child get it. There's a fine line here because the parent feels like they're helping and they're doing just the opposite they are allowing that child to use them as a scapegoat because the mind of an alcoholic child or young adult really knows how to get to their parents than from then on it's all a mind game to them. Who want to exploit it, children can really make a parent feel guilty about certain things but they parent has to take a stand to be able to change things they have to put away the guilt and start being a parent. For those parents that let's say experimented when they were young, should feel guilty because that was in the past and you can't change that but they can't change the future their children's future and that's what at stake here it makes me feel good to know that what I'm doing right now is changing lives and I think that is what I was meant to do while I'm here in this lifetime. What makes it easy for me is a relationship I have with my children they love me and I love them, there isn't anything I wouldn't do for them within reason and I never interfere with their lives because they have to find their own way in life. And I will not destroy that, I have help them accomplish some things that otherwise would do been possible but all that does is make our love stronger. I just hope that when the time comes to depart from this world that they won't take it too hard because to me that will be a time of celebration because I will be safe with God. All that I have all that I own the lungs to God as it is just borrowed while I'm here on this earth. Well today is the Lord's day arrest and ensures peaceful I love days like this when I can sit on the front porch and smell the fresh air after a nice ring, and watch the squirrels play as they jump from tree to tree to the house roof and chase each other, I sometimes wonder what they are talking about when they make those noises as one chases the other they seem so happy. I sometimes wish life could be more that way instead of all the wars and starvation, in the beginning I know God didn't mean for the world to be this way and I know that one day it will be the way he meant for it to be we just have to be patient until that time comes, and one day we will see the glorious world he intended us to live in and all that is been wrong will be made right all the love I feel for him can't be described as mere words it's a deeper feeling one so deep that maybe only he can feel it. Maybe one day this world will find peace but until then the destruction will carry on. I hope one day I will see it but I have my doubts maybe my grandchildren will see if the Lord willing.

As the years pass I know the Lord will take me to where I need the to someplace where I will be needed and that I can learn more about him, there's been many miracles in my life and being sent back it's just one. From what I understand many people don't remember the miracles that happen in life and they just fade away like an unfulfilled dream the ones that you don't remember, but for some reason he wanted me to see the miracles that had happened in my life as I feel a force drawing me some more but where that destination is I don't quite know you as each day passes I can feel my mind healing itself make things new once again after the lifelong battle with addiction. At this time in my life I forget a lot of things and I believe that's due to the short term memory loss caused by the alcohol. Abuse, all alcoholics go through the stages of not remembering and that's how some of them find themselves in jail with no memory of how they got there. Myself I said this happened to me once or twice and it's a scary feeling not knowing how you got somewhere losing all touch with reality and not knowing if you hurt anybody in but I was lucky the hurting someone there came to pass. I had three miracles happen in three states one in Colorado and one in Kansas, and Nebraska for these are things that I had forgotten from my being destroyed but later they would return to me after the mind started to heal itself.

It's strange how I was a laborer all my life and then I was thrown into writing when that part of my life was over it just goes to show that you never know what God has in store for you. He is the one that determines if you complete your journey in this life and for surely if it's not your time to go then it will not take place, even though my coming back has always been hard for me to understand I know there's a greater purpose for my life here on her some say it's all in the cosmos that we are part of a greater design one bigger than any one person or being. As each year passes I draw closer to God and hope that one day and he let me fully understand all the saints that I've gone through, was it to save the children was that my mission? To try and change the minds of many so they may see that alcohol and drug abuse it's no good, like the 16-year-old child who lost his life before he started like the many millionaires have also lost their lives trying to fight the battle of addiction. All these people put up a good fight but In the end they lost his seemed that curiosity got the best of them was some of them even have in many years of sobriety, it says in a good book that we are put here to make a different than I hope in some small way that I have made a difference for those who are fighting this cursed of addiction my messages are clear when they are published in the paper and I pray that many take it to heart so their children won't have to fight this war to live.

Although the third miracle was the biggest the other two were just as pertinent maybe in a way it was his way of showing that I have a lot to do here, from what I have gathered we are put here for God's use for his amusement and also for him to love I guess in a way we are his masterpiece like the little teapot had sat on the shelf for so many years looking ugly then one day the master recasts the teapot and reshaped it giving it a different look and a different meaning for some. When I had the accident in Colorado me and Mark surely thought we were going to die but then it's a last will and like time stood still and we came to a stop just a few feet from going over the cliff, the Lord spared us that day and we should of been grateful but with the alcohol ruining our lives all that that happened became like a fluke and soon the miracle became just luck. From that day forward I always check my cars out before going on the trip, then we had the accident in Kansas back in the 1980s to where this time my brothers that were hit by the car were looking inside and see me as I was pinned understand it was kind of a weird time because he gave me a glimpse in part of what I saw as a child when they were hit by that car on that Sunday morning if you take everything that is happened in my family's lives you would see that it was full of miracles from mom and dad surviving the car wreck that almost killed them to dad's surviving again after he went over a cliff I don't know why I am able to see the states now but I am. They say hindsight is 2020 but if you forget that hindsight then it's 0/0 only God can give you site of your past life no one else and if it's pertinent to your life today then maybe in someone it will help you on your journey, Through this life. As one old lady said our journey is in the search but if you search for things in yourself and you missing the picture, all we are and all we become is for greater purpose for God's purpose to somehow bring us to where we need to be at a certain place and time.

The addiction cycle can end up being one page in a book or it can become a whole book it all depends on what you make it. It says in the good book that where we live is not by any accident it's by God putting us where we need to be at that time. So as for now my journey is not over, I have always felt somewhere deep inside and I am an old soul sent back to retrieve something I left long ago that will make life good. I don't know why I have this memory but it is there and maybe one day it will come to be, for the people I have met since my recovery from addiction have been good to me all of them in their own way helping me to survive this world. I can't help but feel then I have one more stop to make in this life a place where I will see my dreams come. Full circle. At this time I feel to spirit moving inside me one that says to move away and one that say's not to go so I will take these two spirit with me wherever I go, I have met someone on the Internet her name is Margaret and we are starting a relationship I will go down and visit her in Kansas to check out and see how the situation is. She is asked me to move there so I'm thinking on it at this time, I have talked to Oliver about it and he says yes let's go so later I will go down and check it out. The Lord seems to move me in mysterious ways and maybe this is a place he wants me to go so I can learn more about. I can't help but feel there some kind of connection to this place and I need to find out what it is' it's called Cortland Kansas a small town in the middle of nowhere where I can write and study on the word of the Lord. Maybe it'll let me make that connection I need so deeply inside a bringing together of God and one of his children being me. Ever since the accident with my brothers I have felt lost in a world I don't understand, she seemed like a nice but then things could be different in person you can't truly tell how a person is until you meet them so we will see what the future will hold. I've always lived in small towns so this one being a little smaller should make much of a difference it will be the adjustment that will be hard first.

God brings many different things into our lives and he has the power to teach us what we are supposed to do. From what I feel inside he has spend a lot of time on me trying to get everything back to the way it should of been, I do know that he loves me otherwise he would waste his time on me. We all have the path that we follow and when we have a hard time following that path he can guide us to where we need to be, my love for him can be measured by anything on this earth I spent over 15 years been celibate holding on to the hope that he would help me walk again and see the world through a new set of eyes. The celibate thing what's a promise made to him that was to last five years but it ended up being over 15 years, why would someone go that long without sex? Well in the beginning it wasn't easy but then as time passed it seems less important than the other things that were going on. Although times have been hard we seem to have made thus far holding on to hold that the Lord would fulfill his words, it says don't might take care of the birds and rabbits than why would I not take care of you. This is a promising he made long ago before I was even though of and many people have hung on to this hope or proms' feel drawn to search for a new place to live and who knows maybe this place will be the place that the Lord is drawn me to I seem to have an urge to go down the and maybe see if that will be my next destination. Although I know in small towns there's a lot of gossip I can keep myself from becoming a part of that, and maybe do some good there in helping other people. All through life I had always known that there are better things for me as for moving to a big city that will never happen not with all the corruption and violence that goes on there and I don't want to be just another homeless person with no place to go. In small towns they accept your they don't and I'm in hope that I will be accepted I have assured that says the Methodist Church on it and I will wear that like a badge of honor when I started the church there this will let them know that I'm a child of the most hi God the alpha and the Omega the first and the last father we will ever need although it took a long time to reconnect with God I feel I have finally done it. Although my journey didn't start here on earth it did start in life when I was sent back, this set off a chain reaction that seems to keep John me closer and closer to my father. Jesus died at the age of 32 and was risen in three days I died at the age of 32 and was risen in minutes is are some kind of Celeste real connection here well I guess only God knows he answer to that question .Later' me and Jesus would celebrate her birthday's on the same day Easter Sunday, 12th of April and later again years down the road.

Do we as human beings search for something that connects us to the characters in the Bible? I believe with some of us we do, in hope that maybe we could follow their ways and somehow turn out okay. Melchizedek and epiphany were two of the words that are brought back with me, although these were to had no meaning to me at the time later they would become very pertinent to my search and finding my way. God somehow put them in my mind for some reason, maybe to somehow lead me to the Bible so I could read on the many subjects that it holds. As it stands now, the things that I read I try to live by as I go through the good book. So it's to me like a learning manual that teaches us how we should live as, for me it's better to read just versus and try to adapt them into my life but to read the whole Bible through wouldn't work for me as I would probably forget the versus as fast as they were read. I have heard many people say that they have read the whole Bible but when it comes down to those words being locked in of the mind it doesn't happen for us easily as the words are read with some they are forgotten and if you can't take something good from something you read then maybe they're missing the point. All the prophets in the Bible made it there by making a difference and if you don't understand something then you surely can't make a different words can be good or they can be bad and I like to only attain the good to maybe get enough out of it to encourage others that God is away.

For Jesus is a shepherd and we are the sheet and if one of us get lost he will leave the others to find the one now to me that is totally awesome. To know that the Lord would lead to the many for the few making everyone of them special in his eyes, when I arrived in that small town there will be resistance as that is human nature but with my sincerity and honesty I hope to make a difference and maybe make that town my laugh. As we move into the future and we get older we are somehow able to see into the future a little more but a lot more than when we were children, for my love of God will bring me far and I'm in hope that one day all the hardships will be gone. My faith in God cannot be shaken as he is brought me too far for that to happen I have never loved anyone as much as I love our Lord Jesus Christ we have so much in common and that is love. Through the twist and turns of life I find comfort in knowing that he is here next to me when I have doubts we talk and he takes those doubts way. When I'm frightened he seems to make my fears vanish, I never really know from one day to the next what is going to a happen in my life whether I'll get good news or bad news. I believe I will call Cortland my last stop in this journey a life, and who knows maybe great things will come of this as we move forward into the coming years for each days from this day forward my love for grow stronger and stronger for our Lord Jesus Christ. In the many years since my resurrection he has guided me like he has always done except now I'm more aware of the world I live in, I have traveled through the gates of hell and return to go on and lead a better life. A life free from the addiction and bonds that once held me, my Lord and Savior is my rock he guides me to lay down in green pastures. I once was lost but now I'm found through the love and understanding of our Lord Jesus Christ' he died for our sins in a world of despair and corruption although he never did anything wrong he was judge by people and sent to death to die on the cross. Before his arrival God knew that he would have to tie in and Jesus knew also giving his life so we could live how hard that must of been on his mother to see him carry the cross to his death, a mother's heart broken and shattered. I believe she knew that he would also die for I'm sure the Angels told her before that time came to prepare her for the miracle that would take place. I don't believe any of those brothers for siblings seeing him as the Messiah but that's only natural in a family help human beings, just like I could never see one of my siblings being the Messiah which goes to show human beings are limited to foresight. As for my true mission here on her in time I will learn to understand but the scary thing is that I might be searching for it the rest of my life.

The Cross

Words & Music by Roger Mattson

The Cross

come, Thy will be done on earth as it is in heav-en. Give us this day our daily

bread, and make sure the chil-dren are fed. It's not their fault that the world is

this way. They're made from love, this is true the same way God cre-a-ted

you. Bless them as they go through life to day. They get

mad as you can see; that's just the way it's meant to be. They will

grow and that will fade a - way. You died on the cross, this is

true so we could live and love You. It's a shame that more don't see it this

way.

The Light on the Water

Words & Music by Roger Mattson

There's a light on the wa-ter____ that most don't see. There's a light on the wa-ter____ that guides me to Thee. There's a light on the wa-ter____ that leads to sal-va-tion____ you see. Fa - ther, please____ don' leave me.____ And at the edge of the wa-ter____ there are foot-prints____ in the sand that leads Him to save____ His fel-low____ man. We all know it's no sec-ret____ what God____ can do, for He cre-a-ted ev-'ry-thing____ in-clud-ing me____ and you. And I can see____ where the

Lord is lead-ing me._____ And I do know____ one day____ in heav-en I'll

stay. For ev-'ry riv-er____ we see flows right out to the sea. This is His heart tell-ing

me____ That's just the way it's___ meant to be._____ And when my time is through, that won't

stop Him from lov-ing you._____ Yes, He loves us all, you see.____ That's just the

way it's meant to be.____ Lah dee dah dee dee dee His love is end-less____ you see.____

___ That's just the way it's____ meant to be._____